C000241876

The
Pub
Guide

CREDITS

This 9th edition published 2005 © Automobile Association Developments Limited 2005. Automobile Association Developments Limited retains the copyright in the current edition © 2005 and in all subsequent editions, reprints and amendments to editions. The information contained in this directory is sourced entirely from the AA's information resources. All rights reserved. No part of this publication may be reproduced, stored in a retrieval system, or transmitted in any form or by any means - electronic, photocopying, recording or otherwise - unless the written permission of the publishers has been obtained beforehand. This book may not be sold, resold, hired out or otherwise disposed of by way of trade in any form of binding or cover other than that in which it is published, without the prior consent of all relevant Publishers. The contents of this book are believed correct at the time of printing. Nevertheless, the Publisher cannot be held responsible for any errors or omissions, or for changes in the details given in this guide, or for the consequences of any reliance on the information provided by the same. This does not affect your statutory rights. Assessments of AA inspected establishments are based on the experience of the Hotel and Restaurant Inspectors on the occasion(s) of their visit(s) and therefore descriptions given in this guide necessarily contain an element of subjective opinion which may not reflect or dictate a reader's own opinion on another occasion. See page 5-6 for a clear explanation of how, based on our Inspectors' inspection experiences, establishments are graded. If the meal or meals experienced by an Inspector or Inspectors during an inspection fall between award levels the restaurant concerned may be awarded the lower of any award levels considered applicable.

The AA strives to ensure accuracy of the information in this guide at the time of printing. Due to the constantly evolving nature of the subject matter the information is subject to change. The AA will gratefully receive any advice from our readers of any necessary updated information. Please contact

Advertisement Sales: advertisingsales@theaa.com

Editorial Department: lifestyleguides@theaa.com

Front cover photos sourced from AA World Travel Library/Clive Sawyer left, The Swan, Kent middle and www.seafish.org right. Prelim photos from AA World Travel Library/Clive Sawyer. Photographs in the gazetteer provided by the establishments.

Typeset/Repro: Servis Filmsetting Ltd, Manchester.

Printed and bound by Oriental Press, Dubai

Editor: Denise Laing

Pub descriptions have been contributed by the following team of writers: Phil Bryant, Nick Channer, David Foster, Alice Gardner, Julia Hynard, Denise Laing, Olivia Laing.

Published by AA Publishing, a trading name of Automobile Association Developments Limited, whose registered office is Fanum House, Basing View, Basingstoke RG21 4EA. Registered number 1878835.

A CIP catalogue for this book is available from the British Library.

ISBN-10: 0-7495-4622-0

ISBN-13: 978-0-7495-4622-9

A02436

Maps prepared by the Cartography Department of The Automobile Association. Maps © Automobile Association Developments Limited 2005.

Ordnance Survey® *This product includes mapping data licensed from Ordnance Survey® with the permission of the Controller of Her Majesty's Stationery Office. © Crown copyright 2005. All rights reserved. Licence number 399221.*

CONTENTS

06
Smoking in Pubs- Time to stub it out?

13
AA Seafood Pub of the Year

Welcome to the Guide

We aim to bring you the country's best pubs, selected for their atmosphere, great food and good beer. Ours is the only major pub guide to feature colour photographs, and to highlight the 'Pick of the Pubs', uncovering Britain's finest hostelries. Updated every year, this year you will find lots of old favourites as well as plenty of new destinations, for eating and drinking and great places to stay across Britain.

Who's in the Guide?

We make our selection by seeking out pubs that are worth making a detour for - 'destination' pubs - with publicans exhibiting real enthusiasm for their trade and offering a good selection of well-kept drinks and decent food. Pubs make no payment for their inclusion in our guide. They are included entirely at our discretion.

Tempting Food

We are looking for menus that show a commitment to home cooking, making good use of local produce wherever possible, and offering an appetising range of freshly-prepared dishes. Pubs presenting well-executed traditional dishes like ploughman's or pies, or those offering innovative bar or restaurant food, are all in the running. In keeping with recent trends in pub food, we are keen to include those where particular emphasis is placed on imaginative modern dishes and those specialising in fresh fish. Occasionally we include pubs that serve no food, or just snacks, but are very special in other ways.

THAT SPECIAL PLACE

We look for pubs that offer something special: pubs where the time-honoured values of a convivial environment for conversation while supping or eating have not been forgotten. They may be attractive, interesting, unusual or in a good location. Some may be very much a local pub or they may draw customers from further afield, while others may be included because they are in an exceptional place. Interesting towns and villages, eccentric or historic buildings, and rare settings can all be found within this guide.

Pick of the Pubs & Full Page Entries

Some of the pubs included in the guide are particularly special, and we have highlighted these as Pick of the Pubs. For 2006 around 687 pubs have been selected by the personal knowledge of our editorial team, our AA inspectors, and suggestions from our readers. These pubs have a coloured panel and a more detailed description. From these, over 100 have chosen to enhance their entry in the 2006 Guide with two photographs as part of a full-page entry.

Beer Festivals

For 2006 we have included a list of beer festivals held in pubs listed in this guide, as so many of our readers are enthusiastic about them. This enthusiasm is shared by publicans and micro-brewers, with increasing numbers running their own festivals. The list is on pages 17 so you can plan your visits to the pubs mentioned.

AA Classifications and Awards

Where the following ratings appear next to an entry in the guide, the establishment has been inspected under nationally recognised Classification schemes. These ratings ensure that your accommodation meets the AA's highest standards of cleanliness with the emphasis on professionalism, proper booking procedures and a prompt and efficient service.

AA Star Classification

★ If you stay in a one-star hotel you should expect a relatively informal yet competent style of service and an adequate range of facilities, including a television in the lounge or bedroom and a reasonable choice of hot and cold dishes. The majority of bedrooms are en suite with a bath or shower room always available.

★ ★ A two-star hotel is run by smartly and professionally presented management and offers at least one restaurant or dining room for breakfast and dinner.

★ ★ ★ A three-star hotel includes direct dial telephones, a wide selection of drinks in the bar and last orders for dinner no earlier than 8pm.

★ ★ ★ ★ A four-star hotel is characterised by uniformed, well-trained staff with additional services, a night porter and a serious approach to cuisine.

★ ★ ★ ★ ★ Finally, and most luxurious of all, is the five-star hotel offering many extra facilities, attentive staff, top quality rooms and a full concierge service. A wide selection of drink, including cocktails, is available in the bar and the impressive menu reflects and complements the hotel's own style of cooking.

★ AA Top Hotels

The AA's Top Hotels in Britain and Ireland are identified by red stars. These stand out as the very best and range from large luxury desti-nation hotels to snug country inns. For further details see the AA's website at www.theAA.com

◆ AA Diamond Awards

The AA's Diamond Awards cover bed and breakfast establishments only, reflecting guest accommodation at five grades of quality, with one diamond indicating the simplest and five diamonds the upper end of the scale. The criteria for eligibility is guest care and quality rather than the choice of extra facilities. Establishments are vetted by a team of qualified inspectors to ensure that the accommodation, food and hospitality meet the AA's own exacting standards. Guests should receive a prompt professional check in and check out, comfortable accommodation equipped to modern standards, regularly changed bedding and towels, a sufficient hot water supply at all times, good well-prepared meals and a full English or continental breakfast.

Restaurants with Rooms

A Restaurant with Rooms is usually a local (or national) destination for eating out which also offers accommodation. No star or diamond rating is shown in the guide but bedrooms reflect at least the level of quality associated with a two star hotel. A red symbol indicates a restaurant with rooms that is amongst the AA's Top Hotels in Britain and Ireland.

◆ Red diamonds indicate the very best places in the 3, 4 & 5 Diamond rating.

AA Rosette Awards

Out of the thousands of restaurants in the British Isles, the AA identifies, with its Rosette Awards, some 1800 as the best. The following is an outline of what to expect from restaurants with AA Rosette Awards. For a more detailed explanation of Rosette criteria please see www.theAA.com

@ Excellent local restaurants serving food prepared with care, understanding and skill, using good quality ingredients.

@@ The best local restaurants, which aim for and achieve higher standards, better consistency and where a greater precision is apparent in the cooking. There will be obvious attention to the selection of quality ingredients.

@@@ Outstanding restaurants that demand recognition well beyond their local area.

@@@@ Amongst the very best restaurants in the British Isles, where the cooking demands national recognition.

@@@@@ The finest restaurants in the British Isles, where the cooking stands comparison with the best in the world.

Smoking in Pubs – Time to Stub it Out?

By Julia Hynard

TIME WAS WHEN A DRINK AND A CIGARETTE AT MY LOCAL WAS THE ULTIMATE IN RELAXATION: A CHANCE TO KICK BACK AND PUT MY RESPECTABLE WORKADAY SELF ON HOLD. MIND YOU, THIS WAS A TIME WHEN I WAS SMOKING ALL DAY IN THE OFFICE, A PILE OF BUTTS GROWING IN MY ASHTRAY AS I WRESTLED WITH THE DEMANDS OF THE DAY – AN INCONCEIVABLE IDEA IN THE THIRD MILLENIUM. MY 15-YEAR SMOKING CAREER ENDED WITH THE CONCEPTION OF MY FIRST CHILD 18 YEARS AGO, AND NOW WHEN I VISIT A PUB WITH FAMILY OR FRIENDS IT'S THE PALL OF SMOKE IN THE BAR OR THE STENCH OF MY MORNING-AFTER CLOTHES THAT IRRITATES IN MORE WAYS THAN ONE.

The tolerance zone for smoking has decreased remarkably in the last decade with smoking bans at work, in shopping centres, places of entertainment and on public transport. The common sight of shivering shop and office workers out in the street, fag cupped in hand, harks back to the first experimental puff behind the bike shed. The expulsion of smokers into the streets underlines the very naughtiness of the behaviour, a naughtiness that in itself can be quite seductive. Beyond the privacy of one's own home, the pub seemed the last bastion for the unreconstructed smoker to take his (or increasingly her) ease. The pub is traditionally The Last Bastion – for male only company, and for child-free company. But how, now, do we feel about the smoking?

In the most recent survey of Smoking-related Behaviour and Attitudes published by the Department of Health and produced by the Office of National Statistics, respondents were asked to give their views on smoking restrictions in pubs. Over half thought that pubs should be mainly non-smoking with smoking allowed in designated areas, but only 20% of those questioned favoured an outright smoking ban. Consultation by the Scottish Executive, though, found that eight out of ten respondents said that smoking should be banned in public places such as pubs and bars in Scotland. FOREST, the Freedom Organisation for the Right to Enjoy Smoking Tobacco, accepts the

need for some restrictions on smoking but is looking for a compromise which can accommodate smokers without inconveniencing non-smokers. They would welcome the introduction of more smoke-free areas/designated smoking areas, and encourage the installation of better ventilation and modern air cleaning systems. In its campaign, FOREST refers to an independent survey carried out by BMRB International for the Tobacco Manufacturers' Association, which found that less than 17% of all adults agree that smoking should be banned in pubs, clubs and bars, while 86% feel that the smoking situation in pubs, clubs and bars has improved in recent years. Most people (75%), however, still feel that more improvements are needed. For example, 24% felt that a requirement for good ventilation would be an attractive option. The survey found greater support for smoking restrictions in restaurants, with 32% opting for a complete ban and 14% for where food is served.

The patron of FOREST, TV chef and restaurateur Anthony Worrall Thompson says, *"Why should the anti-smoking lobby dictate our lifestyle at the expense of our well known culture of tolerance?"* and: *"Legislation is not an option. Britain must not become a nanny state."*

Nevertheless, smoking bans have happened in New York, Norway and Ireland, and look set to happen here soon. The Scottish Executive has declared its intention and the Government has pledged to 'legislate to

ensure that all enclosed public places and workplaces other than licensed premises will be smoke-free. The legislation will ensure that all restaurants will be smoke-free, all pubs and bars preparing and serving food will be smoke-free; and other pubs and bars will be free to choose whether to allow smoking or be smoke-free. In membership clubs the members will be free to choose whether to allow smoking or to be smoke-free. However, whatever the general status, to protect employees, smoking in the bar area will be prohibited everywhere.'

The campaigning organisation ASH (Action on Smoking and Health) opposes the Government's idea of exempting pubs that do not serve food. The Government estimates the number of pubs in this group as between 10% and 30% of the total (there are around 55,000 pubs in England and Wales). However, a British Medical Association survey of 29 councils shows that 13 had more than 30% of their pubs in the no-food group, and in Leeds the figure was 88%. The implication is that such pubs are concentrated in poorer communities and that 'allowing them to be exempted from a smoke-free law will simply undermine Government efforts to reduce health inequalities.'

Ireland introduced its workplace smoking ban in March 2004, along with a fine of ¤3,000 for publicans permitting their customers to breach it and a telephone hotline to allow the public to report breaches. How has this affected the pub trade there? Well, a report from the Irish Central Statistics Office, produced seven months after the ban was introduced, found that bar sales were down 2.8%. Mind you, the decrease the previous year had been 7.1%. According to a survey by the Irish Brewers Association, there was a drop of 6% in beer sales from April to September following the ban, compared with sales for the same period in the previous year. A number of British pub chains are considering a smoking ban and have been running trials in selected pubs. J D Wetherspoon has gone further with a commitment, made in January 2005, to ban smoking in all 650 of its pubs, though it seems unlikely that they will meet their target of May 2006. Reports from their first 11 show a dip in bar sales but a rise in food sales, much as they had expected. Ahead of all compulsion to do so, 62 pubs in this Guide that we know of have already banned smoking on their premises. We were interested to know why and how they were faring, so we took a look at a representative selection from around the regions.

Kilberry Inn, Kilberry, Argyll & Bute

The Kilberry Inn has been no-smoking for around four or five years, a policy inherited by new owners, David Wilson and his partner. They are happy to maintain the smoking ban which seems appropriate to a food-driven pub. David is emphatically in favour of the proposed new anti-smoking legislation: 'It's been proved that it's bad for you; it's bad for the staff and it's bad for other customers. This is for the well-being of everybody.'

Horse Shoe Inn, Pickering, North Yorkshire

The Horse Shoe Inn was taken over as a family-run concern 16 months ago, and the four new owners agreed unanimously on a no-smoking policy, in part because cancer has affected their own lives. One of the owners, Paul Tatham, explained that it was an easier policy to implement as newcomers to the inn, particularly as the Horse Shoe is very food ori-entated and has letting rooms. He reckons that about 90% of customers accept the decision, 5% smoke outside and the rest don't want to know, but new customers have been attracted specifically because it is a completely smoke-free inn. Paul feels that a big player like J D Weatherspoon committing to the no-smoking rule has helped the idea to be accepted, and that the proposed legislation has 'got to happen'.

The Black Friar, London EC4

The smoking ban at the Black Friar began as a three-month trial by the company in November 2004. The fact that it is still in place speaks to its success. When I spoke to David Tate on a Friday afternoon at 4.30 the place was packed with thirsty workers ready for a smoke-free pint.

Wasdale Head Inn, Wasdale Head, Cumbria

The inn is 90% no-smoking, but there is one area in the bar, around the fire, where smoking is permitted and is used mainly by younger people.

The Bell, Alderminster, Warwickshire

For seven years The Bell has been no-smoking throughout apart from a tiny entrance bar. Owner Vanessa Brewer says it's the mess and smell associated with smoking that brought her to this decision, particularly when people were stubbing out on her beautiful flagstone floor. She is not, however, in favour of a general smoking ban for pubs, her view is that if people are prepared to run a pub where smoking is permitted then they should be allowed to.

The Ship Inn, Noss Mayo, Devon

Zoe Bailey, one of the team at The Ship Inn, explained that they had gone no-smoking in January 2005. Previously they'd had a no-smoking policy upstairs only. She said it was really nice for the staff, because working behind a bar with smoke blowing into your face is not a pleasant experience.

Kinmel Arms, St George, Conwy

When I spoke to owner Lynn Cunnah-Watson, she and her husband were just a couple of weeks away from implementing a no-smoking policy throughout the building. They had given customers 12 months' notice to get used to the idea, and installed a bespoke sail-like cover over a heated area in the garden, where customers will be still be able to light up. Lynn had been following the changes in Ireland with interest and felt it would work for them as relatively few of their customers smoke. She said that of course people can harm themselves by eating too much or drinking too much, but when people smoke it affects everyone's health. The pub has a staff of 20, and Lynn says she feels responsible for them and doesn't want them coming to her in 10 years' time saying that they have lung cancer.

The pubs mentioned in this feature all appear in the 2006 *Pub Guide*. Don't forget, however, that establishments may change hands during the currency of the guide, resulting in a change in smoking policy.

These Pubs are completely Non-Smoking

BERKSHIRE
LAMBOURN
The Hare Restaurant
@ The Hare & Hounds

BUCKINGHAMSHIRE
GREAT MISSENDEN
The Rising Sun
HADDENHAM
The Green Dragon
SPEEN
King William IV
SKIRMETT
The Frog

CAMBRIDGESHIRE
CAMBRIDGE
Free Press
Cambridge Blue

CUMBRIA
WASDALE HEAD
Wasdale Head Inn
LOWESWATER
Kirkstile Inn
YANWATH
The Yanwath Gate Inn
BOUTH
The White Hart Inn

DERBYSHIRE
BIRCHOVER
The Druid Inn
ROWSLEY
The Grouse & Claret
BEELEY
The Devonshire Arms
FROGGATT
The Chequers Inn

DEVON
BIGBURY-ON-SEA
Pilchard Inn
NOSS MAYO
The Ship Inn

DORSET
GODMANSTONE
Smiths Arms

ESSEX
MANNINGTREE
The Mistley Thorn
EARLS COLNE
The Carved Angel

GLOUCESTERSHIRE
ASHLEWORTH
The Queens Arms
ASHLEWORTH
Boat Inn

HAMPSHIRE
CADNAM
The White Hart
EVERSLEY
The Golden Pot
WICKHAM
Greens Restaurant & Pub

HEREFORDSHIRE
HEREFORD
The Ancient Camp Inn

KENT
WROTHAM
The Green Man
WESTERHAM
The Fox & Hounds
CANTERBURY
The Old Coach House
The White Horse Inn

LANCASHIRE
WHALLEY
The Three Fishes

LONDON POSTAL DISTRICTS
LONDON EC4
The Black Friar

NORTHAMPTONSHIRE
FOTHERINGHAY
The Falcon Inn

NOTTINGHAMSHIRE
NOTTINGHAM
Cock & Hoop

OXFORDSHIRE
STOKE ROW
Crooked Billet
NORTH MORETON
The Bear
WYTHAM
White Hart
WOODSTOCK
Kings Head Inn

RUTLAND
BARROWDEN
Exeter Arms

SHROPSHIRE
MUNSLOW
The Crown Country Inn

SOMERSET
HASELBURY PLUCKNETT
The White Horse at Haselbury
LOVINGTON
The Pilgrims

SUFFOLK
LAVENHAM
Angel Hotel

CHILLESFORD
The Froize Inn
NAYLAND
Anchor Inn

EAST SUSSEX
HARTFIELD
The Hatch Inn

WEST SUSSEX
CHILGROVE
The White Horse

WARWICKSHIRE
WITHYBROOK
The Pheasant
ALDERMINSTER
The Bell
LOWSONFORD
Fleur de Lys
ILMINGTON
The Howard Arms

NORTH YORKSHIRE
WHITBY
The Magpie Cafe
SAWLEY
The Sawley Arms
PICKERING
Horseshoe Inn
MIDDLETON (NEAR PICKERING)
The Middleton Arms

JERSEY
GOREY
Castle Green Gastropub

ARGYLL & BUTE
KILBERRY
Kilberry Inn
CRINAN
Crinan Hotel

FIFE
MARKINCH
Town House Hotel

PERTH & KINROSS
KILLIECRANKIE
Killiecrankie House Hotel

CONWY
ST GEORGE
The Kinmel Arms

DENBIGHSHIRE
ST ASAPH
The Plough Inn

GWYNEDD
BLAENAU FFESTINIOG
The Miners Arms

AA Pub of the Year

for England, Scotland and Wales. Selected with the help of our AA inspectors, we have chosen three worthy winners for this prestigious award. The winners stand out for being great all-round pubs or inns, combining a great pub atmosphere, a warm welcome from friendly efficient hosts and staff with excellent food, well-kept beers and comfortable accommodation. We expect enthusiasm and a high standard of management from hands-on owners.

Pub of the year for England

The Red Lion, Stathern p300

A rejuvenated inn with a traditional feel, and unspoilt countryside all around. There are plenty of places for relaxing, including a stone-floored bar, a lounge with a comfy sofa, magazines and newspapers, an informal dining area, and an elegant dining room. Expect classic pub food and innovative country cooking.

Pub of the year for Scotland

The Black Bull, Lauder p620

A cosy old coaching inn with loads of character, recently brought back to life from a semi-derelict state by enthusiastic owners. Three dining areas see to the food side of things, and the Harness Bar serves Broughton Ales amongst a host of other drinks.

Pub of the year for Wales

The White Swan, Llanfrynach p648

A white-painted inn in the heart of the Brecon Beacons National Park. Polished floors, exposed oak beams and a vast inglenook fireplace are the reason that the building simply oozes charm. This upmarket 'local' is particularly popular with walkers and cyclists.

Fish is the dish

Seafood is one of the healthiest and most delicious foods that you can choose when eating out. With thousands of tantalising dishes to choose from, ranging from Champagne and oysters to melt in the mouth kippers with garlic butter, there is literally a dish for every occasion.

There are around 100 exciting varieties of seafood available to buy in the UK, so there is plenty of opportunity to be more adventurous and try a wider range of seafood.

Why not try beer battered New Zealand hoki and chunky chips or succulent langoustines next time you eat out at a pub?

Sea Fish Industry Authority,
18 Logie Mill, Logie Green Road, Edinburgh EH7 4HG
Tel: 0131 558 3331 Fax: 0131 558 1442
E-mail: marketing@seafish.co.uk Website: www.seafish.org

AA Seafood Pub of the Year

The Sea Fish Industry Authority (Seafish) exists to promote the use of seafood throughout the UK. With around 100 varieties of seafood available to buy in the UK, seafood is a healthy option that offers a great diversity of flavours and textures. For the 2006 guide we have sought out some of the pubs that make the most of seafood on their menus and produce the finest fish and shellfish in the country.

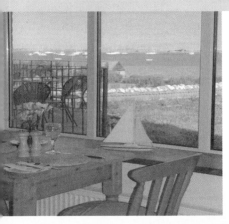

Winner for England
The White Horse, Brancaster, Norfolk (see p337)

A stylish dining pub with fantastic views over the tidal marshes. Scrubbed pine tables, high-backed settles, an open log fire in winter and cream walls contribute to the bright, welcoming atmosphere. Fresh seafood is what all the fuss is about here.

Winner for Scotland
The Old Inn, Gairloch, Highlands (see p608/9)

A restored 18th-century inn set in the Flowerdale valley, looking out across Gairloch Harbour. The attractive white building has been carefully restored, and the views could scarcely be more glorious, with the isles of Rona, Raasay, Skye and even the Outer Hebrides visible from across the harbour. Loch Ewe scallops, Gairloch lobsters, Minch langoustines, brown crab, mussels and fresh fish are regularly landed, and it's not surprising that seafood is the house speciality,

Winner for Wales
The West Arms Hotel, Llanarmon Dyffryn Ceiriog, Wrexham (see p659)

A 16th-century former drovers' inn in the Berwyn foothills. Still a locals' bar, but also well known for its quality food, including an interesting range of fish and seafood. Warmth and character ooze from its undulating slate floors, ancient timberwork and vast inglenook fireplaces.

Best use of seafood

The following restaurants have received a symbol for Best Use of Seafood sponsored by Seafish

ENGLAND

Bedfordshire

BEDFORD
Knife & Cleaver Inn
BLETSOE
The Falcon
OLD WARDEN
Hare and Hounds

Berkshire

COOKHAM DEAN
Chequers Inn Brasserie
HUNGERFORD
The Swan Inn

Buckinghamshire

BLETCHLEY
Crooked Billet
CHALFONT ST PETER
The Greyhound Inn
CUDDINGTON
The Crown
GREAT MISSENDEN
The Rising Sun
GREAT MISSENDEN
The Polecat Inn

Cambridgeshire

ELY
The Anchor Inn
FEN DITTON
Ancient Shepherds

Cheshire

ASTON
The Bhurtpore Inn
CHOLMONDELEY
The Cholmondeley Arms
KNUTSFORD
The Dog Inn
PRESTBURY
Legh Arms & Black Boy Restaurant
SWETTENHAM
The Swettenham Arms

Cornwall & Isles of Scilly

CONSTANTINE
Trengilly Wartha Inn
CRACKINGTON HAVEN
Coombe Barton Inn
KINGSAND
The Halfway House Inn
MARAZION
Godolphin Arms
MYLOR BRIDGE
The Pandora Inn
ST MAWES
The Victory Inn
TREBURLEY
The Springer Spaniel

ZENNOR
The Gurnards Head Hotel

Cumbria

AMBLESIDE
Drunken Duck Inn
APPLEBY-IN-WESTMORLAND
Tufton Arms Hotel
CARTMEL
The Cavendish Arms
HAWKSHEAD
Queens Head Hotel
KESWICK
The Horse & Farrier Inn
RAVENSTONEDALE
Black Swan Hotel

Derbyshire

BAKEWELL
The Monsal Head Hotel
BIRCHOVER
The Druid Inn
HATHERSAGE
The Plough Inn
HOLLINGTON
The Red Lion Inn

Devon

BRANSCOMBE
The Masons Arms
COLEFORD
The New Inn
DREWSTEIGNTON
The Drewe Arms
HORNS CROSS
The Hoops Inn and Country Hotel
LEWDOWN
The Harris Arms
ROCKBEARE
Jack in the Green Inn
SALCOMBE
The Victoria Inn
SLAPTON
The Tower Inn
STOCKLAND
The Kings Arms Inn
STRETE
Kings Arms
TORCROSS
Start Bay Inn
TOTNES
The Durant Arms
UMBERLEIGH
The Rising Sun Inn
WOODBURY SALTERTON
The Digger's Rest

Dorset

BURTON BRADSTOCK
The Anchor Inn

EAST MORDEN
The Cock & Bottle
EVERSHOT
The Acorn Inn
IWERNE COURTNEY OR SHROTON
The Cricketers

Essex

ARKESDEN
Axe & Compasses
BRAINTREE
The Green Dragon at Young's End
MANNINGTREE
The Mistley Thorn

Gloucestershire

AMPNEY CRUCIS
The Crown of Crucis
ARLINGHAM
The Old Passage Inn
ASHLEWORTH
The Queens Arms
COWLEY
The Green Dragon Inn
DIDMARTON
The Kings Arms
TETBURY
Gumstool Inn
TODENHAM
The Farriers Arms

Hampshire

BROOK
The Bell Inn
CADNAM
The White Hart
CHALTON
The Red Lion
EAST TYTHERLEY
Star Inn
OVINGTON
The Bush
ROCKBOURNE
The Rose & Thistle
SPARSHOLT
The Plough Inn

Herefordshire

ASTON CREWS
The Penny Farthing Inn
KIMBOLTON
Stockton Cross Inn
LEDBURY
The Feathers Hotel
ROSS-ON-WYE
The Moody Cow
WEOBLEY
The Salutation Inn
HUNSDON
The Fox and Hounds

Isle Of Wight

FRESHWATER
The Red Lion

Kent

CANTERBURY
The White Horse Inn
GOUDHURST
The Star & Eagle Hotel
GOUDHURST
Green Cross Inn
HAWKHURST
The Great House
IVY HATCH
The Plough
PENSHURST
The Bottle House Inn
ROYAL TUNBRIDGE WELLS
The Beacon
WHITSTABLE
The Sportsman

Lancashire

BISPHAM GREEN
The Eagle & Child
BLACKBURN
Millstone Hotel
CLITHEROE
The Assheton Arms
FORTON
The Bay Horse Inn
WRIGHTINGTON
The Mulberry Tree

Leicestershire

STATHERN
Red Lion Inn

Lincolnshire

BARNOLDBY LE BECK
The Ship Inn
STAMFORD
The George of Stamford

London Postal Districts

LONDON E14
The Grapes
LONDON SE10
North Pole Bar & Restaurant
LONDON SW3
The Admiral Codrington
LONDON W2
The Cow

Norfolk

BLAKENEY
White Horse Hotel
BRANCASTER STAITHE
The White Horse
BURNHAM MARKET
The Hoste Arms
BURNHAM THORPE
The Lord Nelson
CLEY NEXT THE SEA
The George Hotel
COLTISHALL
Kings Head
HOLKHAM
Victoria at Holkham
RINGSTEAD
Gin Trap Inn
SNETTISHAM
The Rose & Crown
STOW BARDOLPH
The Hare Arms
THOMPSON
Chequers Inn
THORNHAM
Lifeboat Inn
TITCHWELL
Titchwell Manor Hotel
WARHAM ALL SAINTS
Three Horseshoes

Northamptonshire

BULWICK
The Queen's Head
MARSTON TRUSSELL
The Sun Inn
WADENHOE
The King's Head

Northumberland

CARTERWAY HEADS
The Manor House Inn
WARENFORD
Warenford Lodge

Nottinghamshire

COLSTON BASSETT
The Martins Arms Inn
ELKESLEY
Robin Hood Inn

Oxfordshire

BRIGHTWELL BALDWIN
The Lord Nelson Inn
CHINNOR
Sir Charles Napier
CHURCH ENSTONE
The Crown Inn
CLIFTON
Duke of Cumberland's Head
FARINGDON
The Trout at Tadpole Bridge
STADHAMPTON
The Crazy Bear Hotel
STOKE ROW
Crooked Billet
SUTTON COURTENAY
The Fish

Rutland

CLIPSHAM
The Olive Branch
LYDDINGTON
Old White Hart
WING
Kings Arms

Shropshire

BURLTON
The Burlton Inn

CLEOBURY MORTIMER
The Crown Inn
LUDLOW
Unicorn Inn
The Roebuck Inn
NORTON
The Hundred House Hotel

Somerset

APPLEY
The Globe Inn
COMBE HAY
The Wheatsheaf Inn
EXFORD
The Crown Hotel
FROME
The Horse & Groom
HINTON ST GEORGE
The Lord Poulett Arms
LOVINGTON
The Pilgrims
MONTACUTE
The Phelips Arms
SHEPTON MALLET
The Waggon and Horses
STANTON WICK
The Carpenters Arms
STAPLE FITZPAINE
The Greyhound Inn
WEST HUNTSPILL
Crossways Inn

Suffolk

BARNBY
The Swan Inn
BROCKLEY GREEN
The Plough Inn
DUNWICH
The Ship Inn
ICKLINGHAM
The Red Lion
LIDGATE
The Star Inn
MONKS ELEIGH
The Swan Inn
POLSTEAD
The Cock Inn
SNAPE
The Crown Inn
WALBERSWICK
Bell Inn

Surrey

OCKLEY
Bryce's at The Old School House
WEST END
The Inn @ West End

East Sussex

ALCISTON
Rose Cottage Inn
DANEHILL
The Coach and Horses
FLETCHING
The Griffin Inn

15

ICKLESHAM
The Queen's Head
MAYFIELD
The Middle House
OLD HEATHFIELD
Star Inn
RYE
The Ypres Castle Inn
SHORTBRIDGE
The Peacock Inn
WADHURST
The Best Beech Inn

West Sussex

CHARLTON
The Fox Goes Free
FERNHURST
The King's Arms
HENLEY
The Duke of Cumberland Arms

Warwickshire

FARNBOROUGH
The Inn at Farnborough

West Yorkshire

SHELLEY
The Three Acres Inn

WILTSHIRE

BRADFORD-ON-AVON
The Tollgate Inn
BRADFORD-ON-AVON
The Kings Arms
BRINKWORTH
The Three Crowns
CORTON
The Dove Inn
LOWER CHICKSGROVE
Compasses Inn
ROWDE
The George and Dragon

Worcestershire

MALVERN
The Red Lion
OMBERSLEY
Crown & Sandys Arms
TENBURY WELLS
Peacock Inn
TENBURY WELLS
The Fountain Hotel

South Yorkshire

CADEBY
Cadeby Inn

North Yorkshire

ASENBY
Crab & Lobster
AYSGARTH
The George & Dragon Inn
BOROUGHBRIDGE
The Black Bull Inn
BREARTON
Malt Shovel Inn

EAST WITTON
The Blue Lion
HAROME
The Star Inn
MOULTON
Black Bull Inn
NORTH RIGTON
The Square and Compass
OSMOTHERLEY
The Golden Lion
PATELEY BRIDGE
The Sportsmans Arms Hotel
ROSEDALE ABBEY
The Milburn Arms Hotel
THIRSK
The Carpenters Arms
WASS
Wombwell Arms
WEST TANFIELD
The Bruce Arms
WEST WITTON
The Wensleydale Heifer Inn
YORK
Lysander Arms

SCOTLAND

Argyll & Bute

ARDUAINE
Loch Melfort Hotel
CLACHAN-SEIL
Tigh an Truish Inn
LOCHGILPHEAD
Cairnbaan Hotel & Restaurant
PORT APPIN
Pierhouse Hotel & Restaurant
TAYVALLICH
Tayvallich Inn

Dumfries & Galloway

PORTPATRICK
Crown Hotel

Fife

KIRKCALDY
The Old Rectory Inn

Highland

CAWDOR
Cawdor Tavern
FORT WILLIAM
Moorings Hotel
GAIRLOCH
The Old Inn
GLENELG
Glenelg Inn
PLOCKTON
The Plockton Hotel
Plockton Inn & Seafood Restaurant
SHIELDAIG
Shieldaig Bar

Perth & Kinross

GLENDEVON
The Tormaukin Country Inn and
Restaurant

KILLIECRANKIE
Killiecrankie House Hotel

Scottish Borders

SWINTON
The Wheatsheaf at Swinton

WALES

Carmarthenshire

PONT-AR-GOTHI
The Salutation Inn

Conwy

COLWYN BAY
Pen-y-Bryn
CONWY
The Groes Inn
LLANDUDNO JUNCTION
The Queens Head

Flintshire

NORTHOP
Stables Bar Restaurant

Gwynedd

ABERDYFI
Penhelig Arms Hotel & Restaurant

Isle of Anglesey

RED WHARF BAY
The Ship Inn

Monmouthshire

ABERGAVENNY
Clytha Arms
LLANVAIR DISCOED
The Woodland Restaurant & Bar
TRELLECK
The Lion Inn

Pembrokeshire

LAMPHEY
The Dial Inn
STACKPOLE
The Stackpole Inn

Powys

BRECON
The Usk Inn
NEW RADNOR
Red Lion Inn

Vale of Glamorgan

ST HILARY
The Bush Inn

Beer Festivals

We list here a selection of pubs that appear in this guide, that hold usually annual beer festivals. For up-to-date information, please check directly with the pub. We would love to hear from our readers about their favourite beer festivals. E-mail us at lifestyleguides@theAA.com so that we can list your preferred venue in the 2007 Pub Guide.

Bhurtpore Inn, Aston, Cheshire. 01270 780917. July

The Burnmoor Inn, Boot, Cumbria. 019467 23224. and Brook House Inn, Boot, Cumbria. 019467 23160. Joint beer festival held over three days in June. More than 70 real ales to sample, along with a barbecue, fish supper and black pudding bonanza.

Eagle & Child, Staveley, Cumbria. 01539 821320.

The Queens Head Inn, Tirril, Cumbria. 01768 863219. The reopened Tirril Brewery's output, along with other locally brewed beers, can be tasted at the annual beer and sausage festival held in August.

Wasdale Head Inn, Wasdale Head, Cumbria. 019467 26229. Its location may be remote, tucked away at the end of a closed valley, but that doesn't stop large numbers descending on this old drovers' inn twice a year

The Royal Hotel, Hayfield, Derbys. 01663 741721. A full entertainment programme and 50 cask ales is the reward for anyone visiting the beer festival here in the second week of October.

Mildmay Colours Inn, Plymouth, Devon. 01752 830248. Barrel-rolling contests are all part of the fun at the August Bank Holiday weekend .

Greyhound, Corfe Castle, Dorset. 01929 480205. The summer beer festival involves around 50 real ales and ciders, a hog roast, a barbecue and a seafood buffet.

The Bankes Arms Hotel, Studland, Dorset. 01929 450225. The large hotel garden is the showcase for Morris dancing, stone carving, and a great selection of around 60 real ales.

The Hoop, Stock, Essex. 01277 841137. The late Spring bank holiday is at the centre of 10 days of celebrations here, with 120 ales and ciders.

The Sun Inn, Feering, Essex. 01376 570442.

Red Shoot Inn, Linwood, Hants. 01425 475792. Festivals held twice a year in April and October. A Wadworth pub that is allowed to brew two of its own beers.

The White Horse, Petersfield. 01420 588387. 3-day festival in mid- June

The Old Oak Inn, Lyndhurst, Hants. 02380 282350.

Cartwheel Inn, Whitsbury, Hants. 01725 518362. The August beer festival here includes Morris dancers, a spit-roasted pig, a barbecues and around 30 real ales.

Tichborne Arms, Tichborne, Hants. 01962 733760.

The Wellington, Wellington, Herefordshire. 01432 830367

Swan in the Rushes, Loughborough, Leicestershire. 01509 217014. 2 annual festivals

The Victoria, Lincoln. 01522 536048. 2 festivals

Junction Tavern, London NW5. August BH. 020 7 485 9400

Hill House, Happisburgh, Norfolk. 01692 650004. Summer solstice

Stuart House, Kings Lynn, Norfolk. End July town festival at hotel. 01553 772169

Angel Inn, Larling, Norfolk. 01953 717963. August.

The Railway Tavern, Reedham, Norfolk. 01493 700340. Beer festivals held twice a year in two 10-day celebrations in April and September. Local bands play, and on Sundays there are family days with a bouncy castle and a barbecue. 75 real ales from all over the country can be tasted.

The Old Coach House, Ashby St Ledgers, Northants. 01788 890349.

Home Sweet Home, Roke, Oxfordshire. 01491 838249.

Grainstore Brewery, Oakham, Rutland. 01572 770065.

Sun Inn, Craven Arms, Shropshire. 01584 861239. Easter & August BH

Mill at Rode, Rode, Somerset. 01373 831100.

Jervis Arms, Onecote, Staffs. 01538 304206.

Queen's Head, Brandeston, Suffolk. 01728 685307.

The King's Arms, Fernhurst, Surrey. 01428 652005.

The Surrey Oaks, Newdigate, Surrey. 01306 631200. The late Spring bank holiday is the time for visiting this pub, and sampling around 20 real ales and ciders.

Kings Arms, Fernhurst, West Sussex. 01428 652005. Has 3 days over late August BH.

The Owl, Little Cheverell, Wiltshire. 01380 812263. Festival been held for around 12 years during June. Bouncy castle and occasional entertainer for children, with a band or singer in the evening for adults.

Smoking Dog, Malmesbury, Wiltshire. 01666 825823. Last weekend in May.

The Bell, Pensax, Worcs. 01299 896677.

Waterfront Inn, Doncaster, South Yorkshire. 01427 891223. May festival.

How to use the Guide

Sample Entry

1 ——NICEPLACE   Map 01 TG22 —— 2

4 ——**The Fox Inn** NEW ◎♦♦♦ 🏠 ♀ —————— 3

   Sand-next-the-Sea SD23 1NL
5 —— ☎ 01114 71144444 📄 01114 71133333 **email:** foxypub.co.uk
   web: www.thenicepub.co.uk
   Dir: From A4 to Hambleton, then R on to B161 to Wartham.
   Timeless 14th-century village pub within easy reach of the
   coast. Unspoilt bars, real ale from the cask, and hearty
   English cooking using fresh local ingredients. Typical
   dishes include game pie, cheese baked crab, ham and
   lentil soup, chicken and rabbit pie and, for pudding,
   golden syrup sponge. B&B in adjoining cottage.
6 ——**OPEN:** 11.30-2.30, 6-11, closed 25 Dec **BAR MEALS:** Lunch —— 7
   served all week 12-2,Dinner served Fri & Sat 6.30-8.30. Av main
8 ——course £6.80. **RESTAURANT:** Dinner Thu-Sat 7-10.30
9 ——◎: Brewery Name ◀: Greene King IPA, Woodfordes Wherry, —— 10
   guest beers. **10 FACILITIES:** Children's licence; family area;. —— 11
12— Garden, outdoor eating.
   NOTES: Parking 10 No credit cards.
   ROOMS: 5 bedrooms 1 en suite. From s £24 d £42 ◎ Indicates —— 13
   no-smoking pub.

1 GUIDE ORDER Pubs are listed alphabetically by name
(ignoring The) under their village or town. Towns and villages are
listed alphabetically within their county (a county map appears at
the back of the guide). The guide has entries for England, Channel
Islands, Isle of Man, Scotland and Wales in that order.

Some village pubs prefer to be initially located under the nearest
town, in which case the village name is included in the address
and directions.

Pick of the Pubs Around 100 of the best pubs in Britain have
been selected by the editor and inspectors and highlighted. They
have longer, more detailed descriptions and a tinted background.
Over 100 have a full page entry and two photographs.

2 MAP REFERENCE The map reference number denotes the
map page number in the atlas section at the back of the book and
(except for London maps) the National Grid reference. London
references help locate their position on the Central London and
Greater London maps.

3 SYMBOLS See Symbols in the column on pages 5 and 6.

4 ADDRESS AND POSTCODE This gives the street name
plus the postcode. If necessary the name of the village is included
(see 1 above). This may be up to five miles from the named
Location.

☎ Telephone number 📄 Fax number

email and websites: Wherever possible we have included an email
address and a website.

5 DIRECTIONS Directions are given only when they have been
supplied by the proprietor.

6 OPEN indicates the hours and dates when the establishment
is open and closed.

7 BAR MEALS indicates the times and
days when proprietors tell us bar food can
be ordered and the average price of a main
course as supplied by the proprietor. Please
be aware that last orders could vary by up
to 30 minutes.

8 RESTAURANT indicates the times and
days when proprietors tell us food can be
ordered from the restaurant. The average
cost of a 3-course à la carte meal and a
3- or 4-course fixed-price menu are shown
as supplied by the proprietor. Last orders
may be approximately 30 minutes before
the times stated.

9 ◎ BREWERY NAME indicates that the
pub is independently owned and run. The
name of the Brewery is the one to which the
pub is tied or the Company who owns it.

10 ◀ The beer tankard symbol indicates the
principal beers sold by the pub. Up to five
cask or hand-pulled beers served by each
pub are listed. Many pubs have a much
greater selection, with several guest beers
each week.

♀ The wine glass symbol followed by a
number indicates the number of wines sold
by the glass.

11 FACILITIES This section includes
information on children (i.e. if a pub
welcomes children, has a children's licence
etc), and gardens (e.g. outdoor eating,
barbecue area). We also indicate where
dogs are welcome.

12 NOTES Information on parking and
credit cards.

Credit Cards Not Taken As so many establishments take one or more of the major
credit cards only those taking no cards are
indicated.

13 ROOMS Only accommodation that has
been inspected by The AA, RAC, VisitBritain,
VisitScotland or the Welsh Tourist Board is
included. AA Stars and Diamonds are shown at
the beginning of an entry. Small Stars or
Diamonds appearing under ROOMS indicates
that the accommodation has been inspected by
one of the other organisations.

The number of bedrooms and the number of en
suite bedrooms are listed. Accommodation
prices indicate the minimum single and double
room prices per night. Breakfast is generally
included in the price, but guests should check
when making a reservation.

Key to Symbols

@ **Rosettes**
The AA's food award. Explanation on p6

★ **Stars**
The Rating for Hotel accommodation.
Explanation on page 5

ᵖᵖ **Restaurants with Rooms.**
Category of inspected accommodation
(see page 5)

♦ **Diamonds.** The Rating for Bed &
Breakfast accommodation. Explanation
on page 5

🐟 In conjunction with the Seafish Industry
Authority, we include a symbol to
indi cate that a pub serves a minimum
of four main course dishes with sea fish
as the main ingredient.

♀ Indicates the number of wines available
by the glass

🍺 Denotes the principle beers sold.

NEW Pubs appearing in the guide for the first
time in 2006

Website Addresses

Web Site addresses are included where they
have been supplied and specified by the
respective establishment. Such Web Sites are
not under the control of The Automobile
Association Developments Limited and as such
The Automobile Association Developments
Limited has no control over them and will not
accept any responsibility or liability in respect
of any and all matters whatsoever relating to
such Web Sites including access, content,
material and functionality. By including the
addresses of third party Web Sites the AA does
not intend to solicit business or offer any
security to any person in any country, directly
or indirectly.

TELL US WHAT YOU THINK

We welcome your feedback
about the pubs included and
about the guide itself. We
are also delighted to receive
suggestions about good pubs
you have visited and loved.
Reader Report forms appear
at the very back of the book,
so please write in or e-mail
us at
lifestyleguides@theAA.com
to help us improve future
editions. The pubs also
feature on the AA
website,www.theAA.com,
along with our inspected
restaurants, hotels and bed
& breakfast accommodation.

WALKS FOR 2006

As a popular feature of the guide we
have again included 25 Pub Walks to
try. Not too challenging - between 3
and 6 miles in length - perfect for
building up a healthy appetite or
working off a filling meal. Walk directions
and details are supplied by the pubs
featured in these pages. There is a
complete list of all the walks on page
660 in the index section at the back of
the book.

How do I find my perfect place?

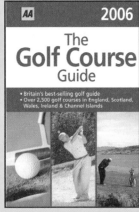

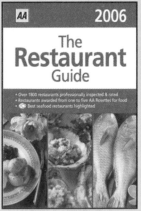

England

Pub of the Year for England

The Red Lion

Stathern

(see p300)

England

ENGLAND
BEDFORDSHIRE

BEDFORD   Map 12 TL04

Pick of the Pubs

Knife & Cleaver Inn NEW ♦♦♦♦ @ ⌲ ♀
The Grove, Houghton Conquest MK45 3LA
☎ 01234 740387 ▤ 01234 740900
e-mail: info@knifeandcleaver.com
web: www.knifeandcleaver.com
Dir: Just off A6, 5m from Bedford
This friendly 17th-century free house stands opposite the
medieval church of All Saints, Bedfordshire's largest
parish church. The inn has many historic associations,
including the Jacobean oak panelling in the lounge bar,
which came from nearby Houghton House. This was
formerly the home of the Conquest family, who gave their
name to the village. Light meals and hand-drawn ales are
served in the bar, where leather sofas and winter log fires
bring a welcome comfort. The non-smoking conservatory
restaurant specialises in fresh seafood, as well as a varied
choice of meat and vegetarian dishes. In summer, meals
are also served in the attractive cottage-style garden.
Start, perhaps, with a water melon and feta salad; main
course selections include steamed mussels with rosemary,
redcurrant and red wine sauce; and daube of beef shin
with black olive rosti. Home-made desserts like mango
tart with lime curd round off your meal.
OPEN: 12-2.30 (Sat 12-2 7-11 Closed: 27-30 Dec, Sun eve)
BAR MEALS: L served Mon-Fri 12-2.30 D served Mon-Fri 7-9.30
Sat 12-2 Av main course £6.95 **RESTAURANT:** L served
Sun-Fri 12-2.30 D served Mon-Sat 7-9.30 Av 3 course à la carte
£28 Av 3 course fixed price £14.95 ⬚: Free House ◖: Fullers
London Pride, Interbrew Bass. ♀: 29 **FACILITIES:** Garden:
Orchard garden, terrace, fountain Dogs allowed Water, Food
NOTES: Parking 30 **ROOMS:** 9 bedrooms en suite
1 family room s£49 d£53 No children overnight

The Three Tuns
57 Main Rd, Biddenham MK40 4BD ☎ 01234 354847
e-mail: thethreetuns@btinternet.com
A thatched village pub with a large garden, play area and
dovecote. It has a friendly atmosphere, and is popular for its
wide-ranging bar menu. Choose from sandwiches and snacks
or popular main courses like burgers, seafood platter, and
steaks with fries. There's also a range of home-made dishes
such as the steak and kidney pie, curry of the day, seafood
platter, steak in red wine, and peppered pork. Children's
meals are also available.
OPEN: 11-2.30 6-11 (Sun 12-3, 7-10.30) **BAR MEALS:** L served all
week 12-2 D served Mon-Sat 6-9 Av main course £7.50
RESTAURANT: L served all week 12-2 D served Mon-Sat 6-9
⬚: Greene King ◖: Greene King IPA, Abbot Ale.
FACILITIES: Garden: Large decking area/lawn with heaters Dogs
allowed Water **NOTES:** Parking 30

◖ Principal Beers for sale

BLETSOE   Map 11 TL05

Pick of the Pubs

The Falcon ⌲ ♀
Rushden Rd MK44 1QN ☎ 01234 781222 ▤ 01234 781222
e-mail: info@thefalconbletsoe.co.uk

A 400-year-old coaching inn set in the rolling hills of
north Bedfordshire, the Falcon has a large frontage onto
the A6 affording the easiest of access. To the rear of the
pub, mature grounds sweep down to the Great River
Ouse, and there is a popular riverside beer garden. As
you might expect at such a venerable hostelry, there is at
least one resident ghost and a secret tunnel leading to
nearby Bletsoe Castle. Lots of oak beams complement the
dark wood panelling in the dining room, and real log fires
welcome customers from far and wide. Specialities are
the Falcon's famous steaks served with pepper, stilton or
diane sauce, and fish dishes such as pan-fried sea bass
with coriander and lime oil coulis. Lunchtime options
extend to snacks (home-made soup, sandwiches and
salad bowls) as well as cod and chips or oven roasted
tarragon chicken breast.
OPEN: 12-3 6-11 **BAR MEALS:** L served all week 12-2.15
D served all week 6-9.15 Av main course £9.50
RESTAURANT: L served all week 12-2.15 D served all week
6.30-9.15 Av 3 course à la carte £17 ◖: Charles Wells
Bombadier, Charles Wells Eagle. ♀: 7 **FACILITIES:** Garden:
Lawned garden with mature trees, by river **NOTES:** Parking 35

BROOM   Map 12 TL14

The Cock
23 High St SG18 9NA ☎ 01767 314411 ▤ 01767 314284
Dir: Off B658 SW of Biggleswade
Unspoilt to this day with its intimate quarry-tiled rooms with
latched doors and panelled walls, this 17th-century
establishment is known as 'The Pub with no Bar'. Real ales
are served straight from casks racked by the cellar steps. A
straightforward pub grub menu includes jumbo cod, roast
chicken, gammon steak, breaded lobster, and breast of Cajun
chicken. There is a camping and caravan site at the rear of
the pub.
OPEN: 12-3 6-11 (Sat 12-4, Sun 12-4) **BAR MEALS:** L served all
week 12-2.30 D served Mon-Sat 7-9 **RESTAURANT:** L served all
week 12-2.30 D served Mon-Sat 7-9.30 ⬚: Greene King ◖: Greene
King Abbot Ale, IPA & Ruddles County. **FACILITIES:** Garden: 12
tables on patio, lawn area Dogs allowed **NOTES:** Parking 30

EATON BRAY   Map 11 SP92

The White Horse ♀
Market Square LU6 2DG ☎ 01525 220231 ▤ 01525 222485
Dir: Take A5 N of Dunstable then A5050, 1m turn left & follow signs

Old world pub with beams and brasses run by David and
Janet Sparrow for the past 17 years. During this time it has
built up a good reputation for its home-cooked food. Choose
from Village Fayre dishes (braised lamb shank), or Chef's
Specials (sea bass fillets in parsley and lemon butter). Special
events throughout the year include Burns' Night, Malaysian
Festival and Italian Week. The large secluded garden includes
a children's play area.
OPEN: 11.30-3 6.30-11 (Sun 12-3, 7-10.30) **BAR MEALS:** L served
all week 12-2.15 D served all week 7-9.30 Sun 7-9 Av main course
£9.50 **RESTAURANT:** L served all week 12-2.15 D served all week
7.30-9.30 Sun 9 Av 3 course à la carte £22.50 ⊕: Punch Taverns
◀: Greene King IPA, Shepherd Neame Spitfire, Tetley's. ♀: 8
FACILITIES: Garden: Large secluded garden at rear, with play area
NOTES: Parking 40

KEYSOE   Map 12 TL06

The Chequers
Pertenhall Rd, Brook End MK44 2HR
☎ 01234 708678 ▤ 01234 708678
e-mail: Chequers.keysoe@tesco.net
Dir: On B660 N of Bedford
In a quiet village, a 15th-century inn characterised by original
beams and an open stone fireplace. Take a ridge-top walk for
fine views of Graffham Water in anticipation of a warm
welcome, good real ale and some fine pub food. Food served
in the bar includes chicken curry, fried scampi, steak in a
grain mustard cream sauce, chicken breast stuffed with Stilton
in a chive sauce, or salads, sandwiches and ploughman's.
Good wine list. A play area in the garden, overlooked by a
rear terrace, is an added summer attraction.
OPEN: 11.30-2.30 6.30-11 **BAR MEALS:** L served Wed-Mon 12-2
D served Wed-Mon 7-9.45 ⊕: Free House ◀: Hook Norton Best,
Fuller's London Pride. **FACILITIES:** Children's facs Patio & grassed
area fenced off from car park **NOTES:** Parking 50 No credit cards

LINSLADE   Map 11 SP92

The Globe Inn ♀
Globe Ln, Old Linslade LU7 2TA
☎ 01525 373338 ▤ 01525 850551
Dir: A5 S to Dunstable, follow signs to Leighton Buzzard (A4146)
First licensed in 1830 as a beer shop to serve passing trade on
the Grand Union Canal, the Globe was originally a farmhouse
and stables. Close by is the site of the famous 1963 Great
Train Robbery. Pub favourites on the menu range from pork
Stroganoff and vegetable moussaka to triple tail scampi, and

continued

sausage and tomato casserole. Home-baked jacket potatoes,
salads and butties are also popular perennials.

The Globe Inn

OPEN: 11-11 (Jan-Feb 12-3, 6-11, Summer 11-11) (Sun 12-10.30)
BAR MEALS: L served all week 12-9 D served all week 12-9
Av main course £7 **RESTAURANT:** L served all week 12-3 D served
all week 6-9 Sun 12-9 Av 3 course à la carte £20 ⊕: Greene King
◀: Greene King Abbott Ale, Old Speckled Hen, IPA & Ruddles County
Ale, Hook Norton. ♀: 16 **FACILITIES:** Large garden seats approx
200 Dogs allowed Water **NOTES:** Parking 150

MILTON BRYAN   Map 11 SP93

The Red Lion ♀
Toddington Rd, South End MK17 9HS ☎ 01525 210044
e-mail: paul@redlion-miltonbryan.co.uk

Set in a pretty village near Woburn Abbey, this attractive
brick-built pub is festooned with dazzling hanging baskets in
the summer months. Comfortable, neatly maintained interior,
with beams, rugs on wooden floors, and well-kept ales. Wide-
ranging menu offering roast rump of lamb with potato purée,
wilted spinach and ratatouille sauce; supreme of chicken
stuffed with ricotta cheese, basil and parma ham on wild
rocket and roasted cherry tomato; and baked Cornish cod.
OPEN: 11.30-3 6-11 (Winter closed Sun & Mon evening Closed: Dec
25-26) **BAR MEALS:** L served all week 12-2.30 D served all week
7-9.30 Av main course £8.50 ⊕: Free House ◀: Greene King IPA
& Old Speckled Hen, Abbot Ale, plus guest beers. ♀: 7
FACILITIES: Garden **NOTES:** Parking 40

NORTHILL   Map 12 TL14

The Crown ♀
2 Ickwell Rd SG18 9AA ☎ 01767 627337 ▤ 01767 627279
Dir: Telephone for directions
This delightful 16th-century pub, in its three-acre garden, lies
between Northill church and the village duck pond. This is a
popular area with walkers, and the Shuttleworth Collection of
vintage aircraft at the Old Warden Air Museum is just down

continued

England

NORTHILL continued

the road. Freshly prepared meals include lasagne, cottage pie, and salmon supreme, as well as main course salads and chargrilled steaks.
OPEN: 11.30-3 (Summer all day Sat-Sun 6-11.30 Closed: 25 Dec)
BAR MEALS: L served all week 12-2.30 D served Mon-Sat 7-9.30
Av main course £8.20 **RESTAURANT:** L served all week 12-2.30
D served all week 7-9.30 Av 3 course à la carte £22 ⊕: Greene King
⊄: Greene King IPA, Abbot Ale, plus guest ales. ⏟: 7
FACILITIES: Garden: Very large safe garden Dogs allowed Water
NOTES: Parking 30

ODELL   Map 11 SP95

The Bell ⏟
Horsefair Ln MK43 7AU ☎ 01234 720254
Dir: Telephone for directions
A Grade II listed 16th-century thatched pub operated by the
same management for nearly twenty years. Within, it contains
five small interlinked eating areas all served from a single
long bar, while outside is a patio and aviary next to a
spacious garden that leads down to the River Ouse. It
maintains a high standard of fresh home-made dishes
complemented by fine real ales and a good selection of
wines. A sample from the menu includes omelette with two
fillings, garlicky chicken Kiev, breaded cod fillet and chips,
braised lamb shanks, tandoori chicken, or steak and kidney
pie. Other options include the specials board, sandwiches,
and jacket potatoes.
OPEN: 11-3 6-11 (Sun 12-2.30, 7-10.30) **BAR MEALS:** L served all
week 12-2 D served Mon-Sat 6.30-9 Av main course £8
RESTAURANT: 12-2 6.30-9 ⊕: Greene King ⊄: Greene King IPA,
Abbot Ale & Ruddles County & seasonal beers. ⏟: 6
FACILITIES: Garden: Large garden with patio for 40
NOTES: Parking 14

OLD WARDEN   Map 12 TL14

Pick of the Pubs

Hare and Hounds 🐾 ⏟
SG18 9HQ ☎ 01767 627225 ▤ 01767 627209
Two log fires and four separate eating areas suggest that
this lovely old pub takes the comfort and well-being of its
customers very seriously. Set in a tranquil and
picturesque location just off the A1, and handy for the
Shuttleworth Collection of old aircraft and cars, it has
been renovated recently to provide a warm and
welcoming place with its natural charm kept intact. Food
is a great strength, and the owners are happy to pass on
details of their suppliers. Fresh fish including monkfish,
sea bass, mussels and scallops are popular in summer,
while traditional roasts are also regulars on the menu.
Starters include deep-fried tiger prawns with orange, chilli
and cardamom sauce; baked camembert with cranberry
sauce and walnut bread; and smoked haddock risotto.
Main course samples include haddock in a beer batter
and chips; salmon fillet saffron risotto; and cod in Thai
spiced broth.
OPEN: 12-3 6-11 **BAR MEALS:** L served Tue-Sun 12-2
D served Tue-Sat 6.30-9.30 **RESTAURANT:** L served Tue-Sun
12-2 D served Tue-Sat 6.30-9.30 Av 3 course à la carte £20
⊕: Charles Wells ⊄: Wells Borndardier Premium & Eagle IPA,
Adnams. ⏟: 8 **FACILITIES:** Garden: Lawns
NOTES: Parking 35

RADWELL   Map 11 TL05

The Swan Inn ⏟
Felmersham Rd MK43 7HS ☎ 01234 781351 ▤ 01234 782352
e-mail: stewart.mcgregor@virgin.net
web: www.theswanradwell.co.uk
Dir: Off A6 N of Bedford

Dating back over 300 years, this stone and thatch built inn is
located in a country setting by the River Ouse, which offers
some of the best fishing in the south of England. It's a good
location for walkers, and there's a large garden at the rear
ideal for families. Traditional favourites include lamb and mint
sausage and mash or steak and ale pie, while among the
specialities are homemade pasta with lobster, prawns and
crab, and oriental vegetable strudel.
OPEN: 11-11 (Sun 12-5) Closed: Mon **BAR MEALS:** L served
12-2.30 D served 6.30-9.30 Sun 12-3 Av main course £8.95
RESTAURANT: L served 12-2.30 D served 6.30-9.30 Sun 12-3
Av 3 course à la carte £14.95 ⊕: Charles Wells ⊄: Wells Eagle &
Bombardier. ⏟: 7 **FACILITIES:** Child facs Garden: Large garden
looking onto countryside Dogs allowed **NOTES:** Parking 25

SHEFFORD   Map 12 TL13

The Black Horse ⏟
Ireland SG17 5QL ☎ 01462 811398 ▤ 01462 817238
e-mail: countrytaverns@aol.com
Dir: Telephone for directions

Set in a beautiful garden of an acre and surrounded by fields
and woodland, this pretty inn is covered in flowers in
summer, and brightly lit inside. Old beams prop up the
ceilings and the large brick fireplace, and engender a cosy
atmosphere helped by well-spaced tables separated off into
cosy sitting areas. The memorable food attracts a devoted
following, and an extensive wine list ensures that there is
something to match every dish. Lunchtime sees a selection of
imaginative light meals like risotto with herb marinated
mushrooms and parmesan, salmon and scallop terrine, and
chef's choice of sausages with red wine and shallot jus. In the

continued

evening the tempo increases, with escalope of veal on apple and black pudding mash, braised blade of Scottish beef in mushroom stock, and griddled whole plaice with prawns in a lobster velouté. Puddings are another high point: Grand Marnier soufflé, and poached pear in red wine and cloves are just two examples.
OPEN: 11.30-3 6-11 (Sun 12-6 Closed: 25-26 Dec, 1 Jan)
BAR MEALS: L served Mon-Sun 12-2.30 D served Mon-Sat 6.30-10 Sun 12-5 Av main course £11.50 **RESTAURANT:** L served Mon-Sun 12-2.30 D served Mon-Sat 6.30-10 Sun 12-5 Av 3 course à la carte £17.50 **◄:** Green King IPA, London Pride. ♀: 10 **FACILITIES:** Child facs Garden: Landscaped 1 acre garden, seating available Dogs allowed Water **NOTES:** Parking 30

SILSOE   Map 12 TL03

The Old George Hotel
High St MK45 4EP ☎ 01525 860218 ▤ 01525 860218
The former ale house, in the heart of the village, for the workers of the Wrest estate. Many original features survive to lend atmosphere to the locals' bar and spacious dining room. Nearby places of interest include Woburn Abbey and Wrest Park itself. Conventional bar meals use breads, meat and vegetables from local sources, but meals in the dining room are more adventurous: fruits de mer platters, pheasant jardinière and beef Wellington. Jazz nights and an organist every Sunday.
OPEN: 11-11 **BAR MEALS:** L served all week 12-2.30 D served Mon-Sat 7-9.30 Av main course £6 **RESTAURANT:** L served all week 12-2.30 D served Mon-Sat 7-9.30 Av 3 course à la carte £20 Av 5 course fixed price £11.95 ☺: Greene King **◄:** Greene King & IPA. **FACILITIES:** Garden: Food served outdoors Dogs allowed by prior arrangement **NOTES:** Parking 40

SOUTHILL   Map 12 TL14

The White Horse ♀
High St SG18 9LD ☎ 01462 813364
e-mail: jack@ravenathexton.f9.co.uk

A village pub retaining traditional values, yet happily accommodating the needs of non-smokers, children and those who like sitting outside on cool days (the patio has heaters). Locally renowned for its chargrilled steaks from the Duke of Buccleuch's Scottish estate. Other main courses include Cajun chicken, chargrilled pork loin steaks, Whitby Bay scampi, and stuffed breaded plaice. Greene King beers, with London Pride up from Chiswick. Old Warden Park and its Shuttleworth Collection of old planes is nearby.
OPEN: 11-3 6-11 (Sun 12-10.30, all day BH's)
BAR MEALS: L served all week 12-2 D served all week 6-9 Sun lunch 12-9, Wed-Sat dinner 6-10 Av main course £7.50 **◄:** Greene King IPA, London Pride, Speckled Hen, Flowers. ♀: 22
FACILITIES: Garden: Large grassed area with trees & seating Dogs allowed in garden, water **NOTES:** Parking 60

STANBRIDGE   Map 11 SP92

Pick of the Pubs

The Five Bells ♀
Station Rd, Stanbridge LU7 9JF
☎ 01525 210224 ▤ 01525 211164
e-mail: fivebells@traditionalfreehouses.com
Dir: Off A505 E of Leighton Buzzard
A stylish and relaxing setting for a drink or a meal is offered by this white-painted 400-year-old village inn, which has been delightfully renovated and revived. The bar features lots of bare wood as well as comfortable armchairs and polished, rug-strewn floors. The modern decor extends to the bright, airy 75-cover dining room. There's also a spacious garden with patio and lawns. Hosts Emma Moffitt and Andrew Mackenzie offer bar meals, set menus and a carte choice for diners. The bar menu typically includes dishes such as smoked chicken, sun-dried tomato and pine nut salad; battered fish, chips and mushy peas; baked courgettes stuffed with goat's cheese and mint with a mixed salad; rib-eye steak with fries; and chicken, ham, leek and mushroom pie. From the pudding menu, look out for chocolate and orange torte and raspberry crème brûlée.
OPEN: 12-3 5-11 **BAR MEALS:** L served all week 12-2.30 D served all week 7-9 **RESTAURANT:** L served all week 12-2.30 D served all week 7-9 ☺: **◄:** Interbrew Bass, Wadworth 6X, Hook Norton Best Bitter, Well's Bombardier. ♀: 8
FACILITIES: Garden: Large, traditional garden. Patio area
NOTES: Parking 100

SUTTON   Map 12 TL24

John O'Gaunt Inn NEW
30 High St SG19 2NE ☎ 01767 260377
Dir: Between Biggleswade and Potton, off the B1040.
The landlords at this traditional inn located in a picturesque village have been in charge for almost 30 years. No piped music, fruit machines or cigarette dispensers, though a lot goes on here - everything from summertime Morris Men dancing and skittles to meetings and conferences. Shepherds pie, steak and kidney pudding, tuna pasta crumble and beef casserole with herb dumplings feature on the varied menu.
OPEN: 12-3 7-11 **BAR MEALS:** L served all week 12-2 D served Mon-Sat 7-9 Av main course £6.90 **◄:** Greene King IPA, Abbot Ale, Moreland Original, guest ale. **FACILITIES:** Garden: Large enclosed garden with seating Dogs allowed Water **NOTES:** Parking 16 No credit cards

TILSWORTH   Map 11 SP92

The Anchor Inn ♀
1 Dunstable Rd LU7 9PU ☎ 01525 210289 ▤ 01525 211578
e-mail: tonyanchorinn@aol.com
The only pub in a Saxon village, the Anchor dates from 1878. The restaurant is a recent addition to the side of the pub, and the whole building has recently been refurbished. The licensees pride themselves on their fresh food and well-kept ales. Hand-cut steaks are particularly popular (they buy the meat at Smithfield, butcher it and hang it themselves). An acre of garden includes patio seating, an adventure playground and a barbecue.

continued

England

TILSWORTH continued

OPEN: 12-11 **BAR MEALS:** L served all week 12-2.30 6-10 Sun 12-4 Av main course £9 **RESTAURANT:** L served all week 12-2.30 6-10 Sun 12-4 Av 3 course à la carte £25 ☺: Greene King ◀: Green King IPA, Abbot Ale, Wadworth 6X. ♀: 8 **FACILITIES:** Child facs Garden: 1acre+ of garden, seats, BBQ, patio Dogs allowed Garden **NOTES:** Parking 30

TURVEY
Map 11 SP95

The Three Cranes ♀
High St Loop MK43 8EP ☎ 01234 881305 📠 01234 881305
Dir: Through Olney, R at rdbt onto A428, then right towards Bedford

Ivy-clad, stone-built inn dating from the 17th century, in a pretty village setting next to the church. A typical menu offers oven baked salmon fillet, steak and ale pie, spicy Cajun chicken breast, lasagne, whole baked seabass, and a choice of steaks. Sandwiches, ploughman's, jacket potatoes, and salad bowls also available. Refer to blackboard for today's specials.
OPEN: 11.30-11 (Mon-Thu closed 3-5.30 Open all day in summer) **BAR MEALS:** L served all week 12-2.30 D served all week 6.30-9 Av main course £8.95 **RESTAURANT:** L served all week 12-2.30 D served all week 6.30-9 ☺: Greene King ◀: Greene King IPA, Abbot Ale plus 3 Guest ales. **FACILITIES:** Garden: Food served outside **NOTES:** Parking 12

BERKSHIRE

ALDERMASTON
Map 05 SU56

The Hinds Head ◆◆◆◆
Wasing Ln RG7 4LX ☎ 0118 9712194 📠 0118 9714511
e-mail: hindshead@accommodating-inns.co.uk
Dir: A4 towards Newbury, on A340 towards Basingstoke, 2m to village
With its distinctive clock and belltower, this 17th-century inn still has the village lock-up which was last used in 1865. The old brewery (last used in 1921) was recently refurbished to provide a new restaurant. Sample menu offers lasagne, HSB sausages and mash, battered cod, lamb shank with seasoned mash, salmon with Hollandaise sauce, porcini mushroom ravioli, and sirloin steak.
OPEN: 11.30-2.30 (Sat 6-11, Sun 12-3, 7-10.30 5-11) **BAR MEALS:** L served all week 12-2 D served all week 6.30-9 Sun 12-2, 7-9 **RESTAURANT:** L served all week 12-2 D served all week 6.30-9.30 ☺: Gales ◀: Gales Best, HSB. **FACILITIES:** Garden: Walled garden **NOTES:** Parking 50 **ROOMS:** 16 bedrooms en suite s£67.50 d£80 No children overnight

ALDWORTH
Map 05 SU57

Pick of the Pubs

The Bell Inn
RG8 9SE ☎ 01635 578272
Dir: Just off B4009 (Newbury-Streatley rd)
One might be surprised to discover that an establishment offering no meals at all can hold its own in a world of smart dining pubs and modish gastropubs. Well, be surprised. The Bell not only survives, it positively prospers and, to be fair, it does serve some food, if only hot, crusty, generously filled rolls. And since it is one of the few truly unspoiled country pubs left, and serves cracking pints of Arkell's, West Berkshire and guest real ales, this alimentary limitation has been no disadvantage. The Bell is old, very old, beginning life in 1340 as a five-bay cruck-built manor hall. It has reputedly been in the same family for 200 years: ask Mr Macaulay, the landlord - he's been here for thirty of them, and he has no plans to change it from the time warp it is. A 300-year-old, one-handed clock still stands in the taproom, and the rack for the spit-irons and clockwork roasting jack are still over the fireplace. Taller customers may bump their heads at the glass-panelled bar hatch.
OPEN: 11-3 6-11 (Closed: 25 Dec) **BAR MEALS:** L served Tue-Sun 11-2.50 D served Tue-Sun 6-10.50 ☺: Free House ◀: Arkell's Kingsdown, 3B, West Berkshire Old Tyler & Maggs Magnificent Mild, Guest Beer. **FACILITIES:** Garden: Peaceful, old fashioned Dogs allowed on leads **NOTES:** Parking 12 No credit cards

ASCOT
Map 06 SU96

The Thatched Tavern ♀
Cheapside Rd SL5 7QG ☎ 01344 620874 📠 01344 623043
e-mail: thethatchedtaverns@4cinns.co.uk
Dir: Follow signs for Ascot Racecourse, through Ascot. 1st left (Cheapside) then 1.5m to pub on the left
Just a mile from the racecourse, a 17th-century building of original beams, flagstone floors and very low ceilings. In summer the sheltered garden makes a fine spot to enjoy real ales and varied choice of food. In the same safe hands for over ten years, the kitchen produces a range of traditional English food and international dishes. A sample menu offers corn-fed chicken supreme, pork and leek sausages and mash, pan-fried calves' liver, rack of lamb with prune and apricot farce, or baked mushroom and herb pancakes.
OPEN: 12-3 5.30-11 (Fri-Sun Open all day) **BAR MEALS:** L served all week 12-2.30 D served all week 7-10 Sun 12-3, 7-9 Av main course £15 **RESTAURANT:** L served all week 12-3 D served all week 7-10 Sun 12-3, 7-9 Av 3 course à la carte £25 ☺: ◀: Fuller's London Pride, Scottish Courage, IPA. ♀: 8 **FACILITIES:** Garden: Food served outside, patio Dogs allowed Water **NOTES:** Parking 30

Do you have a favourite pub that we have overlooked? Please use the Reader's Report form at the back of this guide to tell us all about it

PUB WALK

The Swan
Hungerford - Berkshire

THE SWAN,
Craven Road, Lower Green, Inkpen
RG17 9DX
☎ 01488 668326
Directions: South down Hungerford High
Street, Left on common, pub 3 miles.
*Heavily-beamed 17th-century inn close
to the Wayfarers Walk, a wonderful
area to explore on foot. The much
extended interior has homely open
fires and photographic prints. Owned
by local organic beef farmers, who
cook with organic supplies*
Open: 12-2.30 7-11 (Sat-Sun winter
12-3, 5-11) Open all day wknds summer
Closed: 25-26 Dec
Bar Meals: L served all week 12-2
D served all week 7-9.30 Sat 12-2.30,
Sun 12-3 Av main course £8.50
Restaurant Meals: L served Wed-Sun
12-2.30 D served Wed-Sat 7-9.30 Sunday,
lunch only, 12-3 Av 3 course à la carte £26
Dogs allowed. Garden and parking
available.
(for full entry see page 31)

Distance: 2 miles (3.2km)
Map: OS Landranger 158
Terrain: Downland, farmland and light
woodland close to the Hampshire border.
Paths: Quiet roads, field paths,
sheltered drove tracks
Gradient: Gentle climbing

*Walk submitted by Nick Channer &
checked by The Swan*

A pleasant, easy walk exploring the dramatic landscape of Berkshire's remote south-west corner.

Turn left out of the Swan car park, pass a seat on the green and keep right at the junction. Pass a turning on the left for Combe Gibbet and Upper Inkpen and turn left at the 30-mile speed limit sign to join a footpath.

Cross a stile and follow the fence to the next stile which lies hidden beneath trees in the field corner. Emerge from the undergrowth and you'll see Inkpen church ahead. Make for the gate across the field, join the road opposite Church Farm House, turn left for a few paces and then right to visit the church. Parts of St Michael of All Angels date from the mid-13th century and the lychgate was built in memory of a former rector here. The church remains in view for much of this gentle ramble, nestling comfortably at the foot of the hills.

Return to Church Farm House and walk down the lane to the next junction. Turn left towards Shalbourne and Ham and follow the road out of the village. At the speed sign, look over to the left for a very good view of the church. Pass a path on the left and make for Drove Cottage. Turn right here and follow the track. Turn right further on and pass a galvanised gate on the left.

The path becomes enclosed by trees and bushes now and begins to climb steadily. Continue between thick vegetation and through delightful tunnels of trees before the path descends gently to a junction. Turn right and follow a sheltered path, looking for a waymarked turning on the left. Take the path and follow it to a stile on the right. Cross it to a small field and follow the boundary to the road. Turn right and return to the Swan.

England

ASHMORE GREEN
Map 05 SU56

The Sun in the Wood ⚲
Stoney Ln RG18 9HF ☎ 01635 42377 📠 01635 528392
e-mail: suninthewood@aol.com
*Dir: A34 Robin Hood rndbt, left to Shaw, at mini rndbt right then 7th left
into Stoney Lane, 1.5m, pub on left*

Standing in the shadow of tall trees, this popular, extensively
refurbished pub occupies a delightful woodland setting and
yet is only a stone's throw from the centre of Newbury. Stone
floors, plenty of wood panelling and various prints by Renoir
and Monet add to the appeal. The extensive choice of food
includes fillet steak Rossini, pan-fried calves' liver, and sea
bass fillets. Freshly baked baguettes are available in the bar
from Tuesday to Saturday.
OPEN: 12-2.30 6-11 **BAR MEALS:** L served Tues-Sun 12-2
D served Tues-Sat 6-9.30 **RESTAURANT:** L served Tues-Sun 12-2
D served Tues-Sat 6.30-9.30 Av 3 course à la carte £12 🍴: Wadworth
🍺: Wadworth 6X & Henrys Original IPA, Badger Tanglefoot. ⚲: 15
FACILITIES: Child facs Garden: Lovely country garden among
national woodland **NOTES:** Parking 60

BINFIELD
Map 05 SU87

Stag & Hounds ⚲
Forest Rd RH42 4HA ☎ 01344 483553
Historic old pub, with a collection of sporting prints and a
restaurant. Low beams, log fires, front terrace and a legend
about Elizabeth I and some Morris dancers. There's a large
enclosed garden, and decent bar food, with Friday night being
fish night.
OPEN: 11.30-11 **BAR MEALS:** L served all week 12-3 D served all
week 6-10 Av main course £7.50 🍴: Eldridge Pope 🍺: Courage
Best, Bombadier. ⚲: 8 **FACILITIES:** Garden: Large enclosed, 40
tables Dogs allowed Water **NOTES:** Parking 90

BOXFORD
Map 05 SU47

The Bell at Boxford ⌂ ⚲
Lambourn Rd RG20 8DD ☎ 01488 608721 📠 01488 608749
e-mail: paul@bellatboxford.com
Dir: A338 toward Wantage, right onto B4000, take 3rd left to Boxford

Mock Tudor country pub at the heart of the glorious
Lambourn Valley, noted for its pretty villages and sweeping
Downland scenery. Cosy log fires add to the appeal in winter,
and the patio is popular throughout the year with its array of
flowers and outdoor heating, hog roasts, barbecues and
parties. Starters range from baked goats' cheese to Oriental
tiger prawns, while main courses might include herb-roasted
salmon, lamb chump, and wild mushroom Stroganoff.
OPEN: 11-3 6-11 (Sat 6.30-11, Sun 7-10.30) **BAR MEALS:** L served
all week 12-2 D served all week 7-10 Av main course £12.95
RESTAURANT: L served all week 12-2 D served all week 7-10
continued

Av 3 course à la carte £22 🍴: Free House 🍺: Interbrew Bass,
Scottish Courage Courage Best, Wadworth 6X, Henrys IPA. ⚲: 60
FACILITIES: Garden: Heated terraces, holds approx 80 people Dogs
allowed **NOTES:** Parking 36 **ROOMS:** 10 bedrooms en suite
1 family room s£50 d£70 (♦♦♦)
See advertisement under NEWBURY

BURCHETT'S GREEN
Map 05 SU88

The Crown ⌂ ⚲
SL6 6QZ ☎ 01628 822844
Dir: From M4 take A404(M), then 3rd exit

Overlooking the village green and set amid a large rose
garden, this popular local has a welcoming interior with
striking whitewashed walls and low-beamed ceilings. The
head chef, Michael Field, uses local and organic produce
whenever available, resulting in fresh, unfussy dishes. Main
courses include braised lamb shank with roasted root
vegetables; smoked haddock fillet with a lemon and
parmesan risotto; and locally made sausages with onion
gravy and mashed potato.
OPEN: 12-3 6-11 **BAR MEALS:** L served all week 12-2 D served all
week 6.30-9.30 **RESTAURANT:** L served all week 12-2 D served all
week 6.30-9.30 🍴: Greene King 🍺: Greene King IPA, Ruddles Best.
⚲: 8 **FACILITIES:** Garden: Large rose garden overlooking village
green Dogs allowed DogRun **NOTES:** Parking 30

CHADDLEWORTH
Map 05 SU47

The Ibex ⚲
Main St RG20 7ER ☎ 01488 638311 📠 01488 639458
*Dir: A338 towards Wantage, through Great Shefford then R, then 2nd left,
pub is on right in village*

Originally two cottages forming part of a 17th-century farm,
this Grade II listed building was later used as a bakery and
then an off-licence before eventually becoming a pub. In
more recent years it was run by ex-jockey Colin Brown who
partnered the legendary Desert Orchid for many years, and
kept the cosy lounge bar with low ceilings and bench seats.
Popular bar menu includes chicken and leek pie; beef and ale
casserole; liver and onions; and seafood bake.
OPEN: 11-11 (Sun 12-11) **BAR MEALS:** L served all week 12-3
D served all week 6-10 Av main course £9.50
RESTAURANT: L served all week 12-3 D served all week 6-10
Av 3 course à la carte £12.50 Av 3 course fixed price £19.95
🍴: Greene King 🍺: Greene King, Ruddles Best, IPA Smooth, HSB.
⚲: 7 **FACILITIES:** Garden: Dogs allowed **NOTES:** Parking 40

CHIEVELEY **Map 05 SU47**

The Crab at Chieveley
North Heath, Wantage Rd RG20 8UE
☎ 01635 247550 📠 01635 247440
e-mail: info@crabatchieveley.com
Dir: Off B4494 N of Newbury

Attractive thatched dining pub surrounded by outstanding open countryside. More than 360 years ago, during the Civil War, Cromwell spent the night of 27 October 1644 at this inn before doing battle nearby. Fish and seafood are the speciality here, with an extensive choice of dishes and a variety of blackboard specials. Typical examples include grilled Dover sole, crab and lobster salad, Thai sea bass, and turbot hollandaise. Alternatively, try crispy roast duckling or prime Angus rib steak.
OPEN: 11-11 (Sun 12-10.30) **BAR MEALS:** L served all week 12-2.30 D served all week 6-10 **RESTAURANT:** L served all week 12-2.30 D served all week 6-10 ⊕: Free House ⬛: Fullers London Pride, Boddingtons, West Berkshire, Black Sheep. ♀: 14
FACILITIES: Child facs Garden: Seating and terrace with BBQ & marquee Dogs allowed **NOTES:** Parking 80
ROOMS: 10 bedrooms en suite 2 family rooms s£100 d£120

COOKHAM **Map 06 SU88**

Pick of the Pubs

Bel and The Dragon ♀
High St SL6 9SQ ☎ 01628 521263 📠 01628 851008
e-mail: cookham@belandthedragon.co.uk
Dir: Telephone for directions
The Cookham Bel and the Dragon (one of three establishments sharing the same name and philosophy) is situated on Cookham's picturesque high street. One of the oldest licensed houses in England, it's built of wattle and daub with a trendy rustic interior featuring wooden tables, bold coloured walls, a real fire and stripped floors. There's a strong emphasis on food here, with a lengthy menu featuring many dishes that can be ordered as starters or main courses. Begin with the likes of lamb shish kebab with smoked chilli jam, roasted pepper and lemongrass soup or crayfish, shrimp, mango and papaya tian. Follow with slow roasted lamb shank on a herb mashed potato with rosemary and citrus jus; Thai marinated duck breast with sautéed sweet peppers and chilli jus; or chargrilled rib-eye with blue cheese and peppercorn sauce.
OPEN: 11.30-11 (Sun 12-10.30, 25-26 Dec Closed in the evening) **BAR MEALS:** L served all week 12-2.30 D served all week 7-10 **RESTAURANT:** L served all week 12-2.30 D served all week 7-10 ⊕: Free House ⬛: Brakspear, Marstons Pedigree. ♀: 10 **FACILITIES:** Garden: Pond, terrace & garden Dogs allowed

COOKHAM DEAN **Map 05 SU88**

Pick of the Pubs

Chequers Inn Brasserie ♀
Dean Ln SL6 9BQ ☎ 01628 481234 📠 01628 481237
e-mail: info@chequers-inn.com
Dir: From A4094 in Cookham High St take right fork after rail bridge into Dean Lane. Pub in 1m M4 junct 8/9 4m

A historic pub with oak beams and open fire, tucked away between Marlow and Maidenhead in one of the prettiest villages in the Thames Valley. Kenneth Grahame, who wrote *The Wind in the Willows*, spent his childhood in these parts. Striking Victorian and Edwardian villas around the green set the tone, whilst the surrounding wooded hills and dales have earned Cookham Dean a reputation as a centre for wonderful walks. Today, the Chequers offers carefully-chosen wines and a good selection of ales to go with a menu that is varied and dedicated to the use of fresh, excellent produce. Sample the likes of chicken liver and foie gras parfait; seared scallops, asparagus and chorizo; roast rump of lamb with orange and red wine jus; and baked fillet of cod, pea risotto and herb butter. Morlands Original, Ruddles Country Ale, and Scrumpy Jack cider will competently see to the drinks side of things.
OPEN: 12-3.30 5.30-11 **BAR MEALS:** L served all week 12-2.30 D served all week 6-9.30 Fri-Sat 6-10 Av main course £10.95 ⊕: Free House ⬛: Morlands Original, Ruddles County, Guiness. ♀: 10 **FACILITIES:** Garden: Small lawned area with benches and parasols **NOTES:** Parking 35

CRAZIES HILL **Map 05 SU78**

Pick of the Pubs

The Horns ♀
RG10 8LY ☎ 0118 9401416 📠 0118 9404849
Dir: Off A321 NE of Wargrave
Set beside a narrow lane in a small hamlet, this whitewashed timbered cottage started life in Tudor times as a hunting lodge to which a barn (now the dining area) was added some 200 years ago. Sympathetically refurbished by Brakspear's Brewery, it remains a delightful country pub that has three interconnecting rooms complete with old pine tables, exposed beams, open fires, rugby memorabilia, and a peaceful atmosphere free of music and electronic games. Dishes listed on the daily-changing blackboard menus may include sweet pepper, tomato and asparagus pasta bake, chargrilled sirloin slices in mushroom and red wine gravy, or pork and honey sausages with spring onion mashed

continued

England

CRAZIES HILL continued

potato and onion gravy. Fresh filled baguettes and home-made desserts are also available.
OPEN: 11.30-2.30 6-11 (Sun 12-6, 7-10.30 Closed: 25-26 Dec)
BAR MEALS: L served all week 12-2 D served Mon-Sat 7-9.30
RESTAURANT: L served all week 12-2 D served Mon-Sat 7-9.30
🍺: Brakspear 🍺: Brakspear Bitter. **FACILITIES:** Garden: Dogs allowed in garden only, please ask staff **NOTES:** Parking 45

CURRIDGE Map 05 SU47

The Bunk Inn
RG18 9DS ☎ 01635 200400 📠 01635 200336
e-mail: alison@thebunkinn@btconnect.com
web: www.thebunkinn.co.uk
Dir: M4 junct 13, A34 N towards Oxford. Take 1st slip rd then right for 1m. right at T-junct, 1st right signed Curridge.

Not so long ago local builders used to bunk off to this now smart, considerably extended inn with beams, brasses, log fire and attractive bar. Starters such as parsnip soup with hazelnut pesto, and ham hock and caper terrine with apple chutney offer appeal, followed by rack of venison with wild mushrooms; and fillet steak stuffed with dolcelatte and wrapped in pancetta. Nine blackboard specials daily, and gourmet cheeses.
OPEN: 11-11 **BAR MEALS:** L served all week 12-2.30 D served all week 6-9.30 **RESTAURANT:** L served all week 12-2.30 D served all week 6-9.30 🍺: Free House 🍺: Arkells 3B, Wadworth 6X, Fuller's London Pride, plus guest ale. 🍷: 9 **FACILITIES:** Child facs Garden: Dogs allowed **NOTES:** Parking 38 **ROOMS:** 8 bedrooms en suite 1 family room s£65 d£80 (♦♦♦♦)

See advert on this page

EAST GARSTON Map 05 SU37

The Queens Arms 🍷
Newbury Rd RG17 7ET ☎ 01488 648757 📠 01488 648642
e-mail: queensarms@barbox.net
A charming 19th-century village inn enjoying a close association with the racing world of the Lambourn Valley. Jockeys, trainers and punters fill its bar and restaurant on Newbury race days, and the food lives up to expectations. A large terrace and garden are ideal for summer, complete with BBQ area, and an adventure playground appeals to children.
OPEN: 11-11 (Closed on 25 Dec at 2pm) **BAR MEALS:** L served all week 11 D served all week 10 Av main course £8.50 **RESTAURANT:** L served all week 11-11 D served all week 7-11 Av 3 course à la carte £15 🍺: Free House 🍺: Fuller's London Pride, Wadworths 6X. 🍷: 12 **FACILITIES:** Garden: Large garden, terrace, BBQ area Dogs allowed **NOTES:** Parking 40

EAST ILSLEY Map 05 SU48

The Swan
RG20 7LF ☎ 01635 281238 📠 01635 281791
e-mail: theswan@east-isley.demon.co.uk
Dir: 5m N of J13 on A34. 18m S of Oxford on A34
16th-century coaching inn nestling in a peaceful downland village close to the long-distance Ridgeway trail. Enclosed terraced gardens ideal for a drink or lunch. Traditional pub fare includes a selection of pies and cod and chips.
OPEN: 11-11 (Sun 12-10.30 Closed: Dec 25 Rest: Dec 26, Jan 1 closed evenings) **BAR MEALS:** L served all week 12-2 D served all week 6-10 🍺: Greene King 🍺: Greene King, Abbot Ale & IPA.
FACILITIES: Garden: Dogs allowed **NOTES:** Parking 40

HARE HATCH Map 05 SU87

The Queen Victoria 🍷
The Holt RG10 9TA ☎ 0118 940 2477 📠 0118 940 2477
e-mail: kempjo@aol.com
Dir: On A4 between Reading & Maidenhead
A country cottage-style pub dating back over 300 years, handily placed between Reading and Maidenhead. It offers excellent draught beers and an interesting choice of wines. The menu mainly features satisfying and traditional pub grub, but there is also a more adventurous specials board which usually includes a vegetarian option. The location of the Queen Victoria on the edge of the Chilterns means that there are some good countryside walks nearby.
OPEN: 11-3 6-11 (Sun 12-10.30 Closed: Dec 25-26)
BAR MEALS: L served all week 12-2.30 D served all week 6-10 Sun 12-9.30 Av main course £6.95 **RESTAURANT:** L served all week

continued

12-2.30 D served all week 6-10 Sun 12-9.30 🍽: Brakspear
🍺: Brakspear Bitter & Special. ♀: 11 **FACILITIES:** Garden: Dogs
allowed Water **NOTES:** Parking 20

HUNGERFORD   Map 05 SU36

Pick of the Pubs

The Crown & Garter ◆◆◆◆ ♀
Inkpen Common RG17 9QR ☎ 01488 668325
e-mail: gill.hern@btopenworld.com
web: www.crownandgarter.com
Dir: From M4 junct 13, follow signs for A4 to Hungerford. Once on A4
turn left to Kintbury and Inkpen. At village store turn left onto Inkpen
Road, follow road to Inkpen.

A 17th-century pub reputedly visited by James I on his
way to see his mistress. Nearby is Coombe Gibbet, where
two lovers were hanged for killing the woman's husband;
their bodies were laid out in the pub after they had been
taken down. There have been four gibbets: the original
rotted away, the replacement was struck by lightning, the
third lasted a hundred years or so until felled by a gale in
1949, and finally there's the one you see today. Eat in the
bar or the restaurant, choosing from a menu offering
traditional English food, such as chargrilled steaks; and
more modern creations such as pan-fried venison with
dauphinoise thyme potatoes, spiced red cabbage, swede
purée and chocolate game jus; and a half dozen Thai
curries of varying intensities. The enclosed beer garden is
perfect for downing a pint of West Berkshire Brewery's Mr
Chubb's Lunchtime Bitter.
OPEN: 12-3 5.30-11 (Sun 7-10.30) **BAR MEALS:** L served
Wed-Sun 12-2 D served all week 6.30-9.30 Sun lunch 12-2.30 Sun
dinner 7-9.30 Av main course £13 **RESTAURANT:** L served
Wed-Sun 12-2 D served all week 6.30-9.30 Sun lunch 12-2.30 Sun
dinner 7-9.30 Av 3 course à la carte £25 🍺: Mr Chubbs, Good
Old Boy, Murphys, Boddingtons. ♀: 6 **FACILITIES:** Child facs
Garden: Fenced garden with play area Dogs allowed
NOTES: Parking 30 **ROOMS:** 8 bedrooms en suite s£55 d£80

 Pubs offering a good choice of fish on
their menu

Room prices show the minimum double and single
rates charged. Room rates in hotels and B&Bs
often vary depending on the facilities, so be sure to
check prices with the establishment before booking

Pick of the Pubs

The Swan Inn ◆◆◆◆ 🐟
Craven Rd, Lower Green, Inkpen RG17 9DX
☎ 01488 668326 📠 01488 668306
e-mail: enquiries@theswaninn-organics.co.uk
web: www.theswaninn-organics.co.uk
Dir: S down Hungerford High Street (A338), under rail bridge, turn
left to Hungerford Common. Turn right signed Inkpen 3m.

The Swan lies just below Combe Gibbet and Walbury Hill,
the highest points in this part of southern England. Inside,
exposed heavy beams, open fires and old photographic
prints help to retain the much-extended pub's original
character. Unusual stained-glass door panels are worth
studying while sampling a pint of Butts Jester Bitter from
Hungerford. Local organic beef farmers Bernard and
Mary Harris own the Swan, and almost everything on the
menus makes use of fresh organic, GMO-free produce.
Attached to the pub is their farm shop where home-cured
bacon, gammon, beef and a range of country sausages
(they're members of the British Sausage Appreciation
Society) make a visit doubly worthwhile. The pub has one
menu for the bar, and another serving the restaurant, on
which Moroccan couscous and roasted peppers; roasted
cod loin Portuguese style; and steaks may feature. Home-
made desserts are a specialty.
OPEN: 12-2.30 7-11 (Sat-Sun winter 12-3, 5-11) Open all day
wknds summer Closed: 25-26 Dec **BAR MEALS:** L served all
week 12-2 D served all week 7-9.30 Sat 12-2.30, Sun 12-3
Av main course £8.50 **RESTAURANT:** L served Wed-Sun
12-2.30 D served Wed-Sat 7-9.30 Sunday, lunch only, 12-3
Av 3 course à la carte £26 🍺: Free House 🍺: Butts Traditional,
Butts Jester Bitter, Maggs Magnificent Mild, guest ales.
FACILITIES: Garden and terraces with seating and tables Dogs
allowed Water outside **NOTES:** Parking 50
ROOMS: 10 bedrooms en suite 2 family rooms s£50 d£75
See Pub Walk on page 27

England

HURST   Map 05 SU77

The Green Man ♀
Hinton Rd RG10 0BP ☎ 0118 934 2599 ▦ 0118 934 2939
e-mail: info@thegreenman.uk.com
Dir: *Off the A321 next to Hurst Cricket Club*

Once part of Windsor Great Park, this building dates from 1646. Low ceilings and log fires make for a cosy interior, where good beers and some value-for-money wines can be enjoyed. Food choices are varied and include light bites, salads and more elaborate specials such as roast monkfish cooked in Vermouth crème fraîche; or Caribbean coconut chicken curry. Look out for regular themed menus. The garden has a heated patio and a popular children's play area.
OPEN: 11-3 5.30-11 (Sun 12-3, 7-10.30 Sun 6-10.30 May-Sep)
BAR MEALS: L served all week 12-2.30 D served all week 6.30-9.30 Sun 12-3, 7-9.30 Av main course £7.95 **RESTAURANT:** L served all week 12-2.30 D served all week 6.30-9.30 Av 3 course à la carte £15
🍺: Brakspear ◀: Brakspear Bitter, Special & Seasonal Ales. ♀: 7
FACILITIES: Children's licence Garden: Large garden with heated patio area **NOTES:** Parking 40

KINTBURY   Map 05 SU36

Pick of the Pubs

The Dundas Arms ♀
53 Station Rd RG17 9UT ☎ 01488 658263 ▦ 01488 658568
e-mail: info@dundasarms.co.uk web: www.dundasarms.co.uk
Dir: *M4 junct 13 take A34 to Newbury, then A4 to Hungerford, left to Kintbury. Pub 1m. By canal & rail station*

In the early 1800s, Admiral Dundas, who lived in Kintbury, gave his coat of arms to this pub, changing its name from The Red Lion to The Dundas Arms. Today it is a well-established village local (the landlord has been here for 37 years, and his parents ran it before him) and a country pub/restaurant of distinction. Standing beside the Kennet and Avon Canal, it was derelict for about 40

years before being restored to become one of the South's most popular leisure waterways. Enjoy it by taking a walk along the towpath, or sit at one of the outdoor tables. Dishes on offer might include hot spicy chicken breast salad with guacamole; pan-fried pigeon breasts on celeriac purée with pepper and redcurrant sauce; roast duck breast with cider and apple sauce; or spinach and red pepper lasagne. Lighter alternatives roam around coarse chicken liver pâté; and grilled goat's cheese on Italian bread with sweet tomato purée. The pub has a good choice of real ales, and an extensive wine list.
OPEN: 11-2.30 6-11 (Closed Sun evening 25 & 31 Dec)
BAR MEALS: L served Mon-Sat 12-2 D served Tue-Sat 7-9 Av main course £10 **RESTAURANT:** D served Tue-Sat 7-9 Av 3 course à la carte £25 🍺: Free House ◀: Butts Barbus Barbus, West Berkshire Good Old Boy, Adnams, Best Bitter. ♀: 6
FACILITIES: Garden: Riverside patio **NOTES:** Parking 70
ROOMS: 5 bedrooms en suite s£75 d£85 (♦♦♦)

KNOWL HILL   Map 05 SU87

Pick of the Pubs

Bird In Hand Country Inn ★★★ ♀
Bath Rd RG10 9UP ☎ 01628 826622
& 822781 ▦ 01628 826748 e-mail: sthebirdinhand@aol.com
web: www.birdinhand.co.uk
Dir: *On A4, 5m W of Maidenhead, 7m E of Reading*

In the late 1700s, legend has it that George III sought out the hospitality of this inn when his horse threw a shoe whilst hunting. Such was his gratitude that he granted a royal charter to the landlord. A royal welcome is still the promise of the Bird in Hand, which has remained in the same family for three generations. Dating back to the 14th century, its features include a main bar whose oak panelling came from a Scottish castle. Bar snacks are available, whilst a more serious restaurant menu offers an appealing mix of modern and classic dishes. You could start with carpaccio of fresh tuna with braised fennel, and move onto fillet of sea bass on celeriac mash with chinon lobster sauce. If you're staying the night, keep an ear out for the phantom coach and horses that can be heard at night in the inn's oldest part.
OPEN: 11-3 6-11 (Sun 12-4, 7-10:30) **BAR MEALS:** L served all week 12-2.30 D served all week 6.30-10 Sun 7-9.30 Av main course £7.95 **RESTAURANT:** L served all week 12-2.30 D served all week 7-10 Sun 7-9.15 Av 3 course à la carte £25 Av 3 course fixed price £18.95 🍺: Free House ◀: Brakspear Bitter, Hogsback TEA. ♀: 12 **FACILITIES:** Garden: Garden next to patio with fountain Dogs allowed **NOTES:** Parking 86
ROOMS: 15 bedrooms en suite 1 family room s£90 d£100

continued

LAMBOURN — Map 05 SU37

The Hare Restaurant @ The Hare & Hounds ◉
Ermin St RG17 7SD ☎ 01488 71386 🖥 01488 72329
e-mail: cuisine@theharerestaurant.co.uk
Dir: On B4000 at Lambourn Woodlands. From motorway: M4 Junct 14

With the help of ex-Mayfair chef Tristan Mason, this 16th-century coaching inn in the beautiful Lambourn Valley has long been a favourite with the horseracing fraternity. Customers come here for the innovative dishes made from local, seasonal produce. Try red mullet with squid, roasted vegetables and candied lemon dressing; puréed saffron tapioca with langoustine bisque; or duck with hot apple jelly, fluffy oat cakes and date chutney.
OPEN: 12-3.30 6-11 (Closed Sun evenings 1 wk Dec, last 2 wks Jan)
BAR MEALS: 12-2 7-9.30 **RESTAURANT:** L served Tue-Sun 12-2.30 D served Tue-Sat 7-9.30 Sat Dinner 7-9.30, Sun Lunch 12-2.30 Av 3 course à la carte £35 Av 3 course fixed price £15 ⊕: Free House ◖: Wadsworth 6X, Fuller's London Pride, Guinness, Heineken.
FACILITIES: Garden: Food served outdoors Dogs allowed Water
NOTES: Parking 35 ⊕

LITTLEWICK GREEN — Map 05 SU87

The Cricketers ♀
Coronation Rd SL6 3RA ☎ 01628 822888 🖥 01628 822888
Dir: 5m W of Maidenhead on A4 toward Reading. From M4 junct 8/9 take A404(M) to A4 junct

Standing in the shadow of a lovely walnut tree and overlooking the vast village cricket ground spread out opposite, this late 19th-century inn has an intriguing clocking-in clock inside, possibly once owned by the Great Western Railway. The village has been a location for the *Midsomer Murders* TV series, and was once the home of composer Ivor Novello. A simple menu offers the likes of game casserole, moules marinières, mushroom Stroganoff, and lamb shanks.
OPEN: 12-3 5-11 (Sat 12-11, Sun 12-10.30) **BAR MEALS:** L served all week 12-2 D served Mon-Sat 7-9 Av main course £6.95 ⊕: Hall & Woodhouse ◖: King & Barnes Sussex Bitter, Badger Best Bitter, Tanglefoot. ♀: 7 **FACILITIES:** Dogs allowed **NOTES:** Parking 15

 Brewery/Company

Disabled people and those with Assist Dogs have new rights of access to pubs, restaurants and hotels under the Disability Discrimination Act of 1 October 2004. For more information see the website at www.drc gb.org/open4all/rights/2004.asp

MAIDENHEAD — Map 06 SU88

The Belgian Arms
Holyport SL6 2JR ☎ 01628 634468 🖥 01628 777952
e-mail: enquiries@thamessideevents.com
Dir: In Holyport village, 2m from Maidenhead, off Ascot road

Originally known as The Eagle, the Prussian eagle inn sign attracted unwelcome attention during the First World War. As a result, the name was changed to reflect an area where the fiercest fighting was taking place. Things are more peaceful now, and details of local walks are listed outside the pub. The attractive menu includes snacks and light lunches, as well as hot dishes like sausages, mash and onion gravy, and spicy beanburger and chips.
OPEN: 11-3 5.30-11 (Sun 12-3, 7-10.30 Dec 25 Closed eve)
BAR MEALS: L served all week 12-2 D served Mon-Sat 6.30-9.30 Av main course £7.50 ⊕: Brakspear ◖: Brakspear Best, Brakspear Special. **FACILITIES:** Garden: Large lawned area, overlooks village pond Dogs allowed **NOTES:** Parking 45

MARSH BENHAM — Map 05 SU46

Pick of the Pubs

The Red House ◉ ♀
RG20 8LY ☎ 01635 582017 🖥 01635 581621
Dir: 5m from Hungerford, 3m from Newbury & 400yds off the A4

Formerly known as The Water Rat, this handsome brick-and-thatch pub not far from the River Kennet is deep in *Wind in the Willows* country. However, with its name change came a new and contemporary style of inn-keeping. An interesting à la carte (modern British with a French accent) or a set-price bistro menu are offered. Served in starter or main dish sizes is a wild mushroom tart with poached egg and hollandaise sauce, and from a choice of eight main courses, the carte has pan-fried fillet of sea bass with a fennel and tomato compote, spicy black eye beans; pan-fried medallions of venison on braised red cabbage, rosti, ginger bread and quince sauce; and roasted Barbary duck breast with petits pois, chestnuts, morels and boudin blanc. Classic desserts include pear belle Helene, and warm bread and butter pudding. The suntrap patio is an ideal spot in which to down a pint of ale or enjoy a meal in fine weather.
OPEN: 11.30-3 6-11 **BAR MEALS:** L served Mon-Sun 12-2.15 D served Mon-Sat 7-10 Av main course £14.50
RESTAURANT: L served Mon-Sun 12-2.15 D served Fri-Sat 7-10 Mon-Thur 7-9.30 Av 3 course à la carte £19 Av 2 course fixed price £13.95 ⊕: Free House ◖: Fuller's London Pride, Stella Artois, Carlsberg, Murphys. ♀: 9 **FACILITIES:** Garden: Terrace, lawn **NOTES:** Parking 40

England

NEWBURY   Map 05 SU46

Pick of the Pubs

The Yew Tree Inn ♀
Hollington Cross, Andover Rd, Highclere RG20 9SE
☎ 01635 253360 📠 01635 255035
e-mail: gareth.mcainsh@theyewtree.net
Dir: A34 toward Southampton, 2nd exit bypass Highclere, onto A343 at rdbt, thru village, pub on right

A 17th-century oak framed inn set in rolling countryside, with scrubbed pine tables, low beams and an inglenook fireplace in the main bar. A rambling series of rooms includes the restaurant area, where log fires and candlelit tables create an inviting atmosphere. The imaginative menus, completely overhauled by celebrated chef Marco Pierre White, are available throughout the inn, along with a range of fine wines and traditional beers. Fish specials include Brixham mussels with saffron cream, noodles and **OPEN:** 10-12 **BAR MEALS:** L served all week 12-3 D served all week 6-10 Sun 12-4, 7-9 **RESTAURANT:** L served all week 12-3 D served all week 6.30-10 Sun 12-3, 7-9 🍽: Free House 🍺: Guest beers, London Pride. ♀: 8 **FACILITIES:** Children's licence Garden: Front patio/terrace, food served outdoors Dogs allowed **NOTES:** Parking 40

PALEY STREET   Map 05 SU87

The Royal Oak NEW 🏵 ♀
SL6 3JN ☎ 01628 620541 e-mail: parkinson2002uk@yahoo.co.uk
Dir: From Maidenhead take A330 towards Ascot for 2m, turn left onto B3024 signed White Waltham, 2nd pub on left
Owned by TV personality Michael Parkinson and his son Nick, the pub offers restaurant food at good value prices. Regular jazz nights feature artists such as Jamie Cullen, Clare Teal, Lucie Silvas and Peter Concotti, and the walls are adorned with TV and sporting memorabilia. There's a fixed-price lunch menu, and a carte offering the likes of mussel and saffron risotto, and roast chump of lamb with Provençale vegetables and rosemary oil.
OPEN: 11-3 6-11 (Closed Sun nights) **BAR MEALS:** L served all week 11-2.30 D served Mon-Sat 6-10 Sun 11-4 Av main course £12 **RESTAURANT:** L served all week D served Mon-Sat Av 3 course à la carte £25 Av 3 course fixed price £19.50 🍺: Fullers London Pride. ♀: 10 **FACILITIES:** Children's licence Garden: Mediterranean courtyard area **NOTES:** Parking 50

> Pubs with Red Diamonds are the top
> ♦ places in the AA's three, four and five
> diamond ratings

The Bell at Boxford
Lambourn Rd, RG20 8DD Tel/Fax: 01488 608721/608749
email: paul@bellatboxford.com   www.bellatboxford.com

The Bell is a traditional 'Inn of distinction' that is personally run by Paul and Helen Lavis, who have been your hosts for the past 20 years. Their trademark is a relaxing informal approach that offers the highest of standards to make your visit an enjoyable experience.

The Good Pub's **Wine Pub of the Year**, besides offering an extensive wine list, boasts 10 modern bedrooms; a cosy bar with log fires and Real Ales and an à la carte restaurant providing a relaxing environment for all your needs.

The Bell's food boasts both Bar and Bistro menus. Changing daily, the blackboard menus reflect the best the Market can offer. An extensive bar menu featuring home made pies and pastas and we are known for our excellent 100% pure beef burgers.

The Bell has 10 en-suite bedrooms all with TV, radio, telephone, hairdryer, trouser press and tea & coffee making facilities. A Wi-Fi Hot Spot throughout totally complimentary.

4 miles from Newbury, Hungerford and Lambourn located on the Lambourn Road in the peace and quiet of the Countryside. Ideally situated for Newbury Businesses and the Racecourse along with the beautiful Lambourn Valley.

See entry under BOXFORD

PEASEMORE   Map 05 SU47

Fox & Hounds
RG20 7JN ☎ 01635 248252
Dir: 3 miles from Jct 13 M4, A34 to Oxford
Next to the village cricket ground, these old buildings were converted into a pub some 100 years ago. The pub stands at the edge of a pretty village dotted with thatched cottages enjoying stunning views over the Berkshire Downs. The main bar has comfy leather sofas and a double aspect log burner. Popular home-made food includes pastas, fish, beef, a variety of pies including Guinness and mushroom pie, liver and bacon, steak and kidney pudding, traditional lasagne, and a vegetarian selection.
BAR MEALS: L served 12-2 Sat-Sun D served 6-9 Tue-Sun Av main course £7.25 🍺: West Berkshire Good Old Boy, Mr Chubbs Lunchtime Bitter. **FACILITIES:** Children's licence Garden: Food served outside Dogs allowed **NOTES:** Parking 40

READING   Map 05 SU77

The Flowing Spring ♀
Henley Rd, Playhatch RG4 9RB ☎ 0118 969 3207
e-mail: flowingspring@aol.com
A lovely country pub overlooking the Thames flood plain at the point where the Chiltern Hills strike out north east towards Bedfordshire. The proprietor likes his establishment to be known as "a pub that serves good food, rather than a restaurant that serves lousy beer". Representative dishes on the combined bar/restaurant menu include home-made curries, shoulder of lamb, and rib-eye steaks. It's a Fullers pub, so Chiswick, London Pride and ESB are all well kept on tap.

continued

OPEN: 11.30-11 **BAR MEALS:** L served 12-2.30 Mon-Sun D served 6.30-9.30 Wed-Sat ◖: London Pride, ESB, Chiswick. ♀: 7 **FACILITIES:** Child facs Garden: Large garden bounded by streams Dogs allowed **NOTES:** Parking 40

The Shoulder of Mutton
Playhatch RG4 9QU ☎ 0118 947 3908
e-mail: grwillows@hotmail.com
Dir: From Reading follow signs to Caversham, then join the A4155 to Henley. At rdbt turn left to Binfied Heath, pub on left

Renowned locally for good food and a beautiful Victorian walled garden with conservatory and terrace, this renovated pub with its low beamed ceilings and large open fireplace remains full of character. An imaginative menu includes the interestingly-named Pretty in Poussin (tamarind glazed baked poussin, coconut couscous) and Anchors Away (salmon and asparagus wrapped in proscutto ham). Popular seafood nights are a feature, but will need to be booked.
OPEN: 12-3 6-11 (Sun-Mon 7-11, Sat 6.30-11 Closed: 26-27 Dec, 1-2 Jan) **BAR MEALS:** L served all week 12-2 D served all week Av main course £6 **RESTAURANT:** L served all week 12-2 D served all week 6.30-9 Sun 7-9 Av 3 course à la carte £20 Av fixed price £20 ▤: Greene King ◖: Greene King IPA & Ruddles County.
FACILITIES: Garden: Spacious Victorian walled garden, conservatory **NOTES:** Parking 40

Sweeney & Todd
10 Castle St RG1 7RD ☎ 0118 9586466
Town centre pie shop with well-stocked bar. The selection of pies is excellent, as are the pies themselves. A great stop after a hard day's shopping.
OPEN: 11-11 **BAR MEALS:** L served all week 12-10.30 D served all week Av main course £8 ◖: Wadworth 6X, Adnams Best, Badger Tanglefoot, plus guest ales. **NOTES:** No credit cards

SONNING   Map 05 SU77

Bull Inn ♦♦♦♦ ⌂ ♀
High St RG4 6UP ☎ 01189 693901 ▤ 01189 691057
e-mail: bullinn@accommodatinginn.co.uk
web: www.accommodating-inns.co.uk/bullinn.html
Dir: Telephone for directions
In *Three Men in a Boat*, published in 1889, Jerome K. Jerome called the 16th-century Bull 'a veritable picture of an old country inn'. Were he to return, he'd find little changed. The inn beside the church, with its beams, tiled floors and winter log fires, is still splendid. The extensive menu is bang up to date, with Thai green chicken curry; goat's cheese and red pepper cannelloni; brie and cranberry parcel; tuna pasta bake; and vegetarian, vegan, gluten-free and dairy-free options.

continued

Bull Inn

OPEN: 11-3 5.30-11 (Sat-Sun all day) **BAR MEALS:** L served all week 12-2 D served all week 6.30-9 All day Sat-Sun Av main course £10.25 **RESTAURANT:** L served all week 12-2 D served all week 6.30-9.30 ▤: Gales ◖: Gale's HSB, Best, Butser Bitter. **FACILITIES:** Children's licence Garden: Patio area Dogs allowed Dog Bowls **NOTES:** Parking 20 **ROOMS:** 7 bedrooms 6 en suite 1 family room s£95 d£95

STANFORD DINGLEY   Map 05 SU57

The Bull Inn ♀
RG7 6LS ☎ 0118 9744409 ▤ 0118 974 5249
e-mail: admin@thebullstanforddingley.co.uk
Dir: A4/A340 to Pangbourne. 1st left to Bradfield. Through Bradfield, 0.3m left into Back Lane. At end left, pub 0.25m on left

A 15th-century free house, with a modern dining room overlooking the grounds and classic car memorabilia in the saloon bar. The original building has a wealth of timbers and the remains of a wattle and daub wall. Bar snack, carte, Sunday lunch and children's menus offer a good choice: maybe home-made soup, steak, wild mushroom risotto, or seared turbot on spinach. Folk and blues nights and classic bike and car rallies are regular events.
OPEN: 12-3 6-11 (Sun 7-10.30) **BAR MEALS:** L served all week 12-2.30 D served all week 6.30-9.30 Sun 7-9.30 Av main course £9.50 **RESTAURANT:** L served Sun 12.30-2.30 D served Wed-Sat 6.30-9.30 Av 3 course à la carte £19.50 ▤: Free House ◖: West Berkshire Brewery Ales, Brakspear Bitter. ♀: 7 **FACILITIES:** Garden: Large secure area, plenty of tables Dogs allowed Water **NOTES:** Parking 50

The Old Boot Inn ⌂ ♀
RG7 6LT ☎ 01189 744292 ▤ 01189 744292
Dir: M4 junct 12, A4/A340 to Pangbourne. 1st left to Bradfield. Through Bradfield, follow Stanford Dingley signs
Set in the glorious Pang Valley, in a village of Outstanding Natural Beauty, the original 18th-century Old Boot has been extended to include a popular, non-smoking conservatory.

continued

STANFORD DINGLEY continued

Fresh seafood choices are announced daily, and include the likes of seabass, cod, scallops, haddock and swordfish.
OPEN: 11-3 6-11 (Sun 12-3, 7-10.30) **BAR MEALS:** L served all week 12-2.15 D served all week 7-9.30 Sun 12-2.30, 7-9.30
RESTAURANT: L served all week 12-2.15 D served all week 7-9.30
Av 3 course à la carte £22.50 🍽: Free House 🍺: Brakspear Bitter, Interbrew Bass, West Berkshire Dr Hexters, Archers Best. ⬜: 8
FACILITIES: Garden: 0.5 acre overlooking farmland Dogs allowed
NOTES: Parking 40 **ROOMS:** 6 bedrooms en suite 1 family room s£65 d£80 (♦♦♦♦)

SWALLOWFIELD   Map 05 SU76

Pick of the Pubs

The George & Dragon ⬜
Church Rd RG7 1TJ ☎ 0118 9884 432 📠 0118 9886474
Don't judge a pub by its façade, at least not this one. It may look unassuming, but it has a smart, cosy interior with stripped low beams, terracotta-painted walls, log fires and rug-strewn floors, and it has earned quite a reputation for its food. Dining takes precedence over drinking, and booking for lunch or dinner would be prudent. Main courses include Caribbean jerk chicken with jollof rice and mojo salsa; fillet of sea bass with creamed spinach and aubergine ragoût; and wild mushroom and asparagus tagliatelle with gorgonzola cream. A typical specials board could offer a starter of smoked quail filled with winter fruits and nuts on poached apricots, followed by grilled cod with a smoked haddock, mussel and clam broth with champ mash.
OPEN: 12-11 (Sun 12-10.30) Closed: 26 Dec Closed eve 25 Dec, 1 Jan **BAR MEALS:** L served all week 12-2.30 D served all week 7-10 Sun 12-3, 7-9 Av main course £10.95
RESTAURANT: L served all week 12-2.30 D served all week 7-10 🍽: Free House 🍺: Fullers London Pride, Wadworth 6X plus guest ale. ⬜: 6 **FACILITIES:** Garden: Dogs allowed only in bar **NOTES:** Parking 50

THATCHAM   Map 05 SU56

The Bladebone Inn
Chapel Row, Bucklebury RG7 6PD ☎ 0118 9712326
e-mail: jeanclaude@thebladebone.net
Dir: 5m from Newbury and the A4, 2m from the A4 at Thatcham
Over the entrance of this historic inn hangs a bladebone which, according to local legend, came from a mammoth that once stalked the Downs. It is more likely that it was used to indicate that whale oil was sold here for use in oil-burning lamps and probably of 17th-century origin. More a dining venue nowadays than a village local, it offers a traditional English menu alongside a Mediteranean mezze that must be booked in advance.
OPEN: 12-3 6.30-11 **BAR MEALS:** L served Tue-Sun 12-3 D served Tue-Sat 6-10 Av main course £10.95 **RESTAURANT:** L served Tue-Sun 12-3 D served Tue-Sat 6-10 Av 3 course à la carte £20
🍽: Whitbread 🍺: Fuller's London Pride, Good Old Boy.
FACILITIES: Garden: Large garden with seats and tables Dogs allowed in bar and garden only **NOTES:** Parking 20

⬜ 7   Number of wines by the glass

THEALE   Map 05 SU67

Thatchers Arms ⬜
North St RG7 5EX ☎ 0118 930 2070 📠 0118 930 2070
Dir: Telephone for directions

A warm, friendly country pub in a rural area, The Thatchers Arms is surrounded by many footpaths and lanes for walkers. Although in a small hamlet, the pub is only a five minute drive from the M4. There are good garden facilities and a separate patio area. The menu features a range of steaks, and a variety of fish and seafood dishes. Many family facilities are available, and senior citizens day is on Wednesday.
OPEN: 12-2.30 5.30-11 (Sat 12-3, 6-11, Sun 12-3, 7-10.30)
BAR MEALS: L served all week 12-2 D served all week 7-9.30
Av main course £10 **RESTAURANT:** L served all week 12-2 D served all week 7-9.30 🍽: 🍺: Fuller's London Pride, Spitfire, Green King IPA, John Smiths Smooth. ⬜: 8 **FACILITIES:** Garden: Dogs allowed Water **NOTES:** Parking 15

TWYFORD   Map 05 SU77

The Land's End Pub & Restaurant NEW 🐟 ⬜
Lands End Ln, Charvil RG10 0UE
☎ 0118 934 0700 📠 0118 903 4017
Dir: From Reading on A4 to Twyford, turn right onto Old Bath Rd. Turn right at 1st rdbt onto Park Ln, pub 0.5m along
A family pub on the River Loddon, right by a ford. There's a spacious beer garden, patio and barbecue outside, and low ceilings, old beams and open fires within. The main menu changes weekly, with brie and red onion risotto, and breast of chicken with black pudding stuffing typical. With fresh fish coming in daily, there's always the possibility of fillet of gurnard braised in red wine and garlic; or medallions of monkfish with pink peppercorn sauce.
OPEN: 12-3 6-11 (All day Sat-Sun) **BAR MEALS:** L served Tues-Sun 12-2 D served Tue-Sat 6.30-9 Av main course £8.50
RESTAURANT: L served Tues-Sun 12-2 D served Tues-Sat 6.30-9 Av 3 course à la carte £17.50 🍽: 🍺: Brakspear 🍺: Brakspear, guest beers. ⬜: 14 **FACILITIES:** Child facs Garden: Large patio & gardens leading to river Dogs allowed Bowls **NOTES:** Parking 80

WALTHAM ST LAWRENCE   Map 05 SU87

The Bell
The Street RG10 0JJ ☎ 0118 9341788
Dir: On B3024 E of Twyford From A4 turn at Hare Hatch.
Since 1608, when it was left to the village in trust, the rent from this 14th-century inn has been donated to local charities. The same menu operates throughout, offering a variety of meat pies and puddings, chilli, enchiladas, lamb and pork shanks, chicken tikka, and fresh fish on Fridays. The landlords are twin

continued

England

brothers, Scott and Ian Ganson. The area is convenient for many public footpaths and is ideal for gentle walking.
OPEN: 11.30-3 5-11 (Sun 12-7) **BAR MEALS:** L served all week 12-2 Sun 12-3 D served Mon-Sat 7-9.30 Av main course £10 **RESTAURANT:** L served all week 12-2 D served 7-9.30 Mon-Sat Sun 12-3 Av fixed price £10 🍴: Free House 🍺: Waltham St Lawrence No.1 Ale plus 4 Guests. **FACILITIES:** Garden: Large patio with tables, large garden Dogs allowed Water bowls provided, dogs on leads **NOTES:** Parking 5

WARGRAVE
Map 05 SU77

St George and Dragon NEW ♀
High St RG10 8HY ☎ 0118 940 5021
Dir: (3.5m from Henley in A321)
A friendly Thames-side pub, in one of the river's most scenic locations. Heaters on the outdoor decking make it possible to enjoy the view all year round, while inside are open kitchens, stone-fired ovens and log-burning fires. The menu offers the familiar - pizza, pasta and steaks - and the not so familiar, such as duck confit with pak choi, egg noodles, black bean and chilli sauce; and swordfish with Tuscan bean cassoulet and chorizo.
OPEN: 12-11 **BAR MEALS:** L served Mon-Sat 12-2 Sun 12-3.30 D served Mon-Sat 6-9.30 Sun 6.30-9 **RESTAURANT:** L served Mon-Sat 12-2.30 Sun 12-3.30 D served Mon-Sat 6-9.30 Sun 6.30-9 Av 3 course à la carte £20 Av 3 course fixed price £14.95 🍺: London Pride, Bass. ♀: 9 **FACILITIES:** Children's licence Garden: Large decking area wih mooring for boats **NOTES:** Parking 50

WINKFIELD
Map 06 SU97

Rose & Crown
Woodside, Windsor Forest SL4 2DP
☎ 01344 882051 ▤ 01344 885346
e-mail: info@roseandcrownascot.com
Dir: M3 junct 3 from Ascot racecourse on A332 take 2nd exit from Heatherwood Hosp rdbt, then 2nd left

A 200-year-old traditional pub complete with old beams and low ceilings. Hidden down a country lane, it has a peaceful garden overlooking open fields where you can see horses and llamas at pasture. The tastefully-refurbished bar and restaurant provide comfortable seating in which to enjoy real ales, good wines and food prepared with care and cooked in a confident and robust style. New owners David and Peter Hancock in May 2005.
OPEN: 11-11 (Sun 12-7) **BAR MEALS:** L served all week 12-2.30 D served Tue-Sat 7-9.30 Av main course £7.95 **RESTAURANT:** L served all week 12-2.30 D served Tue-Sat 7-9.30 🍴: Greene King 🍺: Greene King Abbot Ale, Morland Original-IPA. **FACILITIES:** Garden: Next to large field Dogs welcome in garden **NOTES:** Parking 24

WINTERBOURNE
Map 05 SU47

Pick of the Pubs

The Winterbourne Arms ♀
RG20 8BB ☎ 01635 248200 ▤ 01635 248824
Dir: From M4 S on A34, 1st slip road
A large, black and white freehouse set in the beautiful village of Winterbourne, ten minutes' drive north of Newbury. It must look very different from the bakery it was 300 years ago, but you can still see where the old bread oven was before the building became the village local. A cosy atmosphere is created inside by subtle wall lighting and traditional features - inglenook fireplace, exposed stone walls, beams and interesting bric-à-brac. Meals offered include Sunday brunch (noon to 7pm), which ranges from late breakfast dishes to roast beef with all the trimmings. There is also a carte for lunch and dinner plus a daily blackboard menu with fish and game in season. Typical main courses are burger with pickles and relish at lunchtime, and braised lamb shank, celeriac mash and port and redcurrant sauce at dinner. In summer you can sit in the garden and admire the rural views.
OPEN: 12-3 6-11 **BAR MEALS:** L served Tue-Sat 12-2.30 Sun 12-5 D served Tue-Sat 6-9.30 Sun lunch 12-5 Av main course £10.50 **RESTAURANT:** L served Tue-Sun 12-2.30 D served Tue-Sat 6-9.30 Sun lunch 12-5 Av 3 course à la carte £20 🍴: Free House 🍺: West Berkshire Good Old Boy, 6X, Old Speckled Hen, Guiness. ♀: 12 **FACILITIES:** Garden: Garden in front of pub with tables Dogs allowed **NOTES:** Parking 40

WOOLHAMPTON
Map 05 SU56

The Angel 🏅🏅 ♀
Bath Rd RG7 5RT ☎ 0118 9713307 e-mail: mail@a4angel.com
web: www.A4angel.com

An impressive Virginia creeper-covered building, dating from around 1752, with a large front terrace. Many original features remain, like the splendid Regency board room with chandeliers. In an atmosphere that is both informal and relaxing, a wine list with more than 20 selections by the glass augments dishes like cream of home-smoked haddock with poached oysters, supreme of corn-fed chicken with rosti, roast parsnip dumpling and mushroom sauce, and steamed timbale of lemon sole and lobster with caviar.
OPEN: 12-3 6-11 **BAR MEALS:** L served all week 12-2.30 D served all week 6-9.30 Av main course £10 **RESTAURANT:** L served all week 12-2.30 D served all week 6-10 Av 3 course à la carte £25 🍴: Free House 🍺: Interbrew Flowers Original & Boddingtons. ♀: 20 **FACILITIES:** Children's licence Garden: Japanese water garden **NOTES:** Parking 40

England

WORLD'S END
Map 05 SU47

The Langley Hall Inn 🐟 🍷
RG20 8SA ☎ 01635 248332 📠 01635 248571
Dir: N towards Oxford on A34. Take Chieveley & Beedon sliproad, left then immediately right onto Oxford Rd. Langley Hall is 1.5m on left
Friendly, family-run bar/restaurant with a reputation for freshly prepared food, real ales and a good selection of wines. Fresh fish dishes vary according to the daily catch - maybe pan-fried crevettes, grilled Dover sole, quick fried squid, or steamed sea bass. Other favourites are braised lamb, beef stir-fry, and Thai chicken curry. Outside there is a large patio and garden, completely enclosed for the safety of children and dogs, plus a petanque court.
OPEN: 11-3 5.30-12 (Fri-Sat 11-12, Sun 11-7 Closed: 26 Dec, 1 Jan)
BAR MEALS: L served Mon-Sun 12-2.30 D served Mon-Sat 6.30-10 Sun 12.30-4 Av main course £12 **RESTAURANT:** L served Mon-Sun 12-2.30 D served Mon-Sat 6.30-10 Sun 12-4 Av 3 course à la carte £23
🍺: Enterprise Inns ◀: West Berkshire Brewery - Good Old Boy, Mr Chubbs, Lunchtime Bitter, Youngs. 🍷: 9 **FACILITIES:** Garden: Enclosed patio & garden; petanque during summer Dogs allowed Bar only **NOTES:** Parking 25 **ROOMS:** 3 bedrooms en suite s£50 d£70 (♦♦♦♦) No children overnight

YATTENDON
Map 05 SU57

Pick of the Pubs

The Royal Oak Hotel ★★ 🏵🏵
The Square RG18 0UG ☎ 01635 201325 📠 01635 201926
e-mail: oakyattendon@aol.com
Dir: From M4 J12, A4 to Newbury, R at 2nd rdbt to Pangbourne then 1st L. From J13, A34 N 1st L, R at T-junct. L then 2nd R to Yattendon
A 16th-century timber-framed coaching inn on the village square, this quintessentially English country inn has been re-faced in the red brick that you will see today. The Oak - as it was formerly known - has played host to such luminaries as King Charles I and Oliver Cromwell, but today it's rarely interrupted by anything more than the clip-clop of passing horse-riders. The village bar remains popular, though the culinary emphasis is based on a brasserie-style menu and an extensive wine list. Starters like cream of celeriac and fennel soup or Cornish mussels are the precursor to main dishes such as pan-fried fillet of beef with green pak choi; poached halibut bouillabaisse with potato aïoli; or roasted vegetable strudel with lemon spinach. Round off your meal with appetising desserts like apple and rhubarb compote or pistachio soufflé.
OPEN: 11-3 6-11 **BAR MEALS:** L served all week 12-2.30 D served all week 7-10 **RESTAURANT:** L served Mon-Sat 12-2.30 D served Mon-Sat 7-9.30 🍺: ◀: 6X, West Berks Good Old Boy. **FACILITIES:** Garden: Traditional garden **NOTES:** Parking 15 **ROOMS:** 5 bedrooms en suite s£95 d£110 No children overnight

We only include details of accommodation that has been inspected by the AA (big Stars or Diamonds at the top of an entry), or the RAC, VisitBritain, VisitScotland or WTB (small Stars or Diamonds at the end of an entry)

BRISTOL

BRISTOL
Map 04 ST57

Brewery Tap
Upper Maudlin St BS1 5BD ☎ 0117 921 3668 📠 0117 925 8235
e-mail: brewerytap@smiles.co.uk
Dir: Telephone for directions

Pub adjacent to Smiles Brewery so all the ales are freshly brewed next door. It's a traditional English pub with an emphasis on real beer, though lagers, Guinness, cider, wines and spirits are also served. A menu of pub favourites is offered, including various hot and cold sandwiches and a steak and Smiles pie, all home made. New owners 2005.
OPEN: 11-11 (Sun 12-6 Closed: 25-26 Dec, 1 Jan)
BAR MEALS: L served Mon-Sun 11.30-3 Av main course £5.50
🍺: Smiles ◀: Smiles, Best, Original, Heritage. **FACILITIES:** Dogs allowed

Highbury Vaults
164 St Michaels Hill, Cotham BS2 8DE ☎ 0117 9733203
e-mail: highburyvaults@youngs.co.uk
Dir: Take main road to Cotham from inner ring dual carriageway
Once a turnpike station, this 1840s pub retains a Victorian atmosphere and seating in its many nooks and crannies. In days when hangings took place on nearby St Michael's Hill, many victims partook of their last meal in the vaults. Today, it's a business crowd by day and students at night feasting on chilli, meat and vegetable curries, casseroles, pasta dishes, and jacket potatoes. No fried foods. Young's beers, no music or fruit machines and a heated garden terrace in which to chill out.
OPEN: 12-11 (Sun 12-10.30) **BAR MEALS:** L served all week 12-3 D served Mon-Fri 5.30-8.30 Av main course £4 🍺: Young & Co ◀: Smiles Best & Heritage, Brains SA, Young's Special & Bitter. **FACILITIES:** Garden: Heated patio, seating for 100 people

continued

PUB WALK
Royal Standard of England
Beaconsfield - Buckinghamshire

ROYAL STANDARD OF ENGLAND,
Brindle Lane, Forty Green, HP9 1XT
☎ 01494 673382
Directions: A40 to Beaconsfield. Right at church rdbt onto B474 towards Penn. Left onto Forty Green Road, then 1mile. *Historic inn dating from the 9th century and named by decree of Charles II after it had served as Royalist headquarters during the Civil War. Wealth of interesting original features, good choice of ales and a wide-ranging menu.*
Open: 11–3 5.30–11 (Sun 12–3, 7–10.30)
Bar Meals: L served all week 12–2.15 D served all week 6.30–9.15 Av main course £10
Children welcome. Dogs allowed. Garden and parking available.
(for full entry see page 40)

A peaceful and varied walk, linking two pretty villages with Civil War history and surrounded by delightful Chiltern views.

Leave the pub car park (please ask permission before parking) and turn left down the lane. In 100 yards (91m), turn right over the stile and follow the path through a former orchard, heading diagonally right downhill to a stile by an electric pylon. Continue downhill along the right-hand field edge, and enjoy the view.

Climb a stile and follow the path through mixed woodland to another stile and sloping field. Head across this field, where the path leads to a track, and turn right towards the farm. Cross a stile and walk to the lane outside the farmhouse. Turn right, pass barns on your left, then climb the stile immediately beyond them.

Cross the field to the stile in the opposite corner and proceed ahead through the coniferous wood. Keep ahead at a fork to a stile. At the next stile turn sharp left and shortly cross another stile on the left. Turn sharp right alongside the tall hedge to reach a wide fenced track with a farm ahead. Turn right, then where the track curves left, keep ahead and bear half-left across the field to a stile and track. Walk up the track to a lane and turn right.

At Gnome's Cottage, on the right in 150 yards (136m), turn right then left at fork, passing between hedges to a stile. Cross the field to the stile opposite, turn right, then right again to follow a bridleway downhill between trees. Turn sharply left downhill on reaching the metalled lane, then turn right along a narrow road.

In 100 yards (91m), take the footpath left up to a barn and turn right through Corkers Wood. Exit via a stile on the right and follow the right-hand hedge down through the field to Brindle Lane, the pub, and a well-deserved rest.

Distance: 3.5 miles (5.6km)
Map: OS Landranger 175
Terrain: Farmland, patches of woodland
Paths: Field and woodland paths, bridleways
Gradient: Undulating; three short medium climbs

Walk submitted and checked by The Royal Standard of England

England

BUCKINGHAMSHIRE

AMERSHAM
Map 06 SU99

The Hit or Miss ♀
Penn St Village HP7 0PX ☎ 01494 713109 📠 01494 718010
e-mail: enquiries@hitormissinn.co.uk
Dir: Off A404 (Amersham-Wycombe rd)
This 18th-century cottage has been in business as a pub since
1798 and was named the 2004/5 Chilterns Pub of the Year.
You'll find it in lovely countryside between Amersham and
Beaconsfield, overlooking the cricket pitch where the pub's
namesake team plays. There are plenty of local scenic walks
to help build up an appetite for dishes such as harissa
marinated chicken; Barbary duck with fresh mango; or baked
potatoes and sandwiches with various fillings.
OPEN: 11-11 (Sun 12-10.30) **BAR MEALS:** L served all week
12-2.30 D served all week 6.45-9.30 Sun 12-8
RESTAURANT: L served all week 12-2.30 D served all week
6.45-9.30 Sun 12-8 Av 3 course à la carte £20 🍽: Hall & Woodhouse
🍺: Badger Best, Tanglefoot, Sussex. ♀: 14 **FACILITIES:** Child facs
Garden and patio area with picnic tables Dogs allowed on hard floor
only; water bowls **NOTES:** Parking 40

The Kings Arms ♀
30 The High St, Old Amersham HP7 0DJ
☎ 01494 726333 📠 01494 433480
e-mail: info@kingsarmsamersham.co.uk
web: www.kingsarmsamersham.co.uk
Historic atmosphere fills the bars of this 15th-century, black
and white timbered inn. There are always four real ales on
offer, two drawn directly from the cask behind the counter.
The bar snack menu lists sandwiches, pies, pasta and chicken
tikka, while the restaurant offers a carte and fixed-price menu.
A sample from the restaurant menu offers mousseline of
salmon with a crab sauce, duck breast with honey and
peppercorns, sea bass with saffron and orange, and braised
lamb with flageolet beans. The façade of the pub was used in
the film *Four Weddings and A Funeral*.
OPEN: 11-11 (Sun 12-10.30) **BAR MEALS:** L served all week 12-3
Av main course £6 **RESTAURANT:** L served Tue-Sun 12-2 D served
Tue-Sat 7-9.30 🍽: Free House 🍺: Rebellion IPA, Burton Ale, Guest
Beers. ♀: 9 **FACILITIES:** Children's licence Garden
NOTES: Parking 25

BEACONSFIELD
Map 06 SU99

Pick of the Pubs

The Royal Standard of England
Brindle Ln, Forty Green HP9 1XT
☎ 01494 673382 📠 01494 523332
*Dir: A40 to Beaconsfield. R at church rdbt onto B474 towards Penn. L
onto Forty Green Rd, then 1m*
Dating from the 12th century, this welcoming country inn
has striking stained glass windows, beams, flagstone
floors, and a large inglenook fireplace. Situated in a part
of the world renowned for Civil War battles and
skirmishes, the inn became a Royalist headquarters, and
it was this that led to its splendid and impressive name.
The inn is a perfect base for walking and even better for
recuperating after a long hike, cooling your blisters and
refuelling with such dishes as braised venison steak with
caramelised pears, slow-cooked lamb marinated in mint
and honey, sea bass fillet with tarragon and tomato
velouté, or the pub's renowned beef and Owd Roger ale

pie. The specials board might include green spring
vegetable frittata or duck breast with ginger citrus sauce -
good sandwiches too and desserts like knickerbocker
glory are well worth making room for. A range of real
ales includes Marston's powerful Owd Roger - not
suitable for drivers!
OPEN: 11-3 5.30-11 (Sun 12-3, 7-10.30)
BAR MEALS: L served all week 12-2.15 D served all week
6.30-9.15 Av main course £10 🍽: Free House 🍺: Marston's
Pedigree, Brakspear Bitter, Fuller's London Pride, Greene King.
FACILITIES: Children's licence Garden: Paved seating area with
floral borders Dogs allowed Water **NOTES:** Parking 90
See Pub Walk on page 39

BLEDLOW
Map 05 SP70

The Lions of Bledlow ♀
Church End HP27 9PE ☎ 01844 343345 📠 01844 343345
*Dir: M40 junct 6 take B4009 to Princes Risborough, through Chinnor into
Bledlow*

A traditional free house overlooking the Vale of Aylesbury.
With its rambling low-beamed bar and log fire, this unspoiled
country inn has frequently been used as a location for the ITV
series *Midsomer Murders*. In summer, the spacious rear
garden overflows onto the village green. The printed menu
varies from a simple ploughman's, to home-made pies or
cheese and pepper lasagne with garlic bread. Look out for
daily-changing specials and vegetarian dishes.
OPEN: 11.30-3 6-11 (Open all day Sat-Sun May-Sep Sun 12-3,
7-10.30) **BAR MEALS:** L served all week 12-2.30 D served all week
7-9.30 Sun 7-9 Av main course £7.50 **RESTAURANT:** L served all
week 12-2.30 D served all week 7-9.30 Sun 7-9 Av 3 course à la carte
£17.50 🍽: Free House 🍺: Wadworth 6X, Scottish Courage Courage
Best, Marston's Pedigree, Brakspear Bitter. ♀: 8
FACILITIES: Garden: Lawns, patio, village green at front Dogs
allowed Water, Biscuits, Toys **NOTES:** Parking 60

BLETCHLEY
Map 11 SP83

Pick of the Pubs

Crooked Billet 🏠 🛏 ♀
2 Westbrook End, Newton Longville MK17 0DF
☎ 01908 373936 📠 01908 631979
e-mail: john@thebillet.co.uk
See Pick of the Pubs on opposite page

◆ Diamond rating for inspected guest
accommodation

continued

Crooked Billet

The Crooked Billet is a 16th-century former coaching inn with a thatched roof, original oak beams and open log fires. Once surrounded by open countryside, the sprawl from Milton Keynes has now caught up with it. Don't let this deter you - there is a large garden - but the real attraction here is the food and wine. The inn is owned and run by a husband-and-wife team, and both have impeccable pedigrees.

Emma Gilchrist was head chef at Nicole Farhi in London's Bond Street, while husband John, who's responsible for The Crooked Billet's astonishing 300-bin wine list (all available by the glass), introduced a list more than three times that length when he was the award-winning sommelier at top Mayfair hotel, Brown's. Emma's monthly-changing menus are based on the finest ingredients, local where possible, and the suppliers - even the apiarist - are acknowledged in the menu. The menu itself is worthy of considered appraisal. It runs the range between a lobster club sandwich as a bar snack, and a detailed 8-course tasting menu. In between,

starters may include ham hock, foie gras and sweet sherry mosaic; or pan-fried mackerel fillet with pickled cucumber and courgette. You might move on to roast chicken breast, pea and bacon potato cake and crispy chicken livers; or chargrilled sword fish, chilli and coriander braised rice, with black mouli salad. Desserts can be sophisticated, like dark chocolate and raspberry terrine with pistachio ice cream; or simply a bowl of fresh cherries with a glass of Armagnac. The cheese board has won multiple awards and, unsurprisingly, the perfect wine can be chosen for each course. The proviso, of course, is that booking is vital.

OPEN: 12-2.30 5.30-11 (Sun 12-4, 7-10.30) Closed: 1st 2 weeks Jan, 25-26 Dec
BAR MEALS: L served Tue-Sun 12-2 D served Mon-Sat
RESTAURANT: L served Sun only 12.30-3 D served Tues-Sat 7-10 (Sun 12.30-3) Av 3 course à la carte £22
🍺: Greene King
: Old Speckled Hen, Badger Tanglefoot, Hobgoblin, Ruddles County. ♀: 300
FACILITIES: Large open garden, 14 tables **NOTES:** Parking 25

◎ ▷ ♀   Map 11 SP83
2 Westbrook End, Newton Longville MK17 0DF
☎ 01908 373936
🖹 01908 631979
✉ john@thebillet.co.uk
Dir: From M1 junct 13 follow signs for Milton Keynes, then Buckingham. After 6m, L to Newton Longville. Pub on R as you enter village.

England

The Peacock ♀

HP14 3LU ☎ 01494 881417 e-mail: andy.callen@dine-on-line.com
Dir: Located on B482 Manlow to Stokenchurch road. 2m from j 5 of M40.

The oldest part of this pub dates from 1620, featuring original
beams and a fireplace dating from the early 1800s. It is
situated on top of the Chiltern Hills overlooking the common.
At lunch alongside a bar snack selection of baguettes, ciabatta
and ploughman's, the menu offers pies, steaks, and giant
Yorkshire puddings with different fillings. At dinner you could
expect beef goulash, lamb shank in red wine, or vegetable
lasagne. Children are particularly welcome as there are two
specially designated areas just for them.
OPEN: 11.30-3 5.30-11 (Sat 11.30-11, Sun 12-10.30 Winter closed
Sun eve and Mon) **BAR MEALS:** L served all week 11.30-2.30
D served Mon-Sun 6.30-9.30 Sun 12-3 Av main course £11
RESTAURANT: L served Mon-Sat 12-3 11.30-2.30 (Sun roast and
rolls) D served Mon-Sun 6.30-9.30 Av 3 course à la carte £18.50
🍺: Punch Taverns 🍻: Brakspear Bitter, Sheppard Neame Spitfire.
♀: 8 **FACILITIES:** Children's licence Garden: Food served outside
NOTES: Parking 30

The Royal Oak ♀

Frieth Rd SL7 2JF ☎ 01628 488611 ▤ 01628 478680
e-mail: info@royaloakmarlow.co.uk

Less than a mile up the road from Marlow, this whitewashed
old village pub also has easy access from both the M4 and
M40. The sprawling gardens with their fragrant herbs and
sunny terrace set the tone for a warm and relaxed welcome in
the bar. Here you'll find local ales from the Rebellion Brewery
in Marlow Bottom. There's a wood-burning stove in the snug,
and a cheery dining room with rich fabrics and glowing dark
floorboards. Seasonal local produce features extensively in
the kitchen, where the staff are just as happy rustling up a
'small plate' as preparing some serious gastronomic treat.
Expect pan-fried calves' liver with roast onion mash and sage

continued

gravy; wild mushroom polenta cake with wilted spinach, pea
and parmesan sauce; and baked whiting on parsley,
cauliflower and potato gratin. Finish off with a sticky pudding,
or British cheeses with fig chutney.
OPEN: 11-11 (Sun 12-10.30 Closed: 25-26 Dec)
BAR MEALS: L served Mon-Sat 12-2.30 Sun D served all week 7-10
12-3 Av main course £12 **RESTAURANT:** L served all week 12-2.30
D served all week 7-10 Av 3 course à la carte £22.50 🍻: London
Pride, Brakspears, Rebellion. ♀: 15 **FACILITIES:** Garden: Terrace
with large tables and canopies Dogs allowed Water bowls
NOTES: Parking 42

The Pheasant Inn ♀

Windmill St HP18 9TG ☎ 01844 237104
e-mail: mrcarr@btinternet.com
Set on the edge of Brill Common, the large garden and
veranda at this 17th-century beamed inn make the most of its
fine hilltop position, with impressive views over seven
counties and the windmill and common. There are winter
fires, and the popular blackboard menu offers fresh salmon,
plus local steaks and pheasant in season. Roald Dahl and JRR
Tolkien were both frequent visitors to the pub. Annual Brill
Music Festival first Saturday each July.
OPEN: 11-11 (Sun 12-10.30 Closed: Dec 25-26)
BAR MEALS: L served 12-2 Mon-Fri Sat, Sun 12-2.30 D served Mon-
Fri 7-9 Sat 7-9.30) Av main course £9.95 **RESTAURANT:** L served
12-2 Mon-Fri Sat, Sun 12-2.30 D served Mon-Fri 7-9 Sat 7-9.30)
Av 3 course à la carte £18 🍺: Free House 🍻: Hook Norton, Spitfire,
Boddingtons, Adnams. ♀: 8 **FACILITIES:** Garden: Beautiful views,
seats 80 Dogs allowed **NOTES:** Parking 25

The Old Thatched Inn ♀

Adstock MK18 2JN ☎ 01296 712584 ▤ 01296 715375
e-mail: manager@theddthatched.co.uk
Licensed since 1702, this thatched and beamed 17th-century
inn has come through a refurbishment with its traditional
beams and inglenook fireplace intact. A modern conservatory
and the timbered lounge provide a choice of eating place
where the menu plus specials and light bites is offered. Pork
and sage sausages; Imam Bayildi aubergine with apricot,
onions and pine nuts; fresh oven-baked cod; Caribbean
chicken; steak and kidney pudding; and rod caught rainbow
trout are all part of an interesting menu. Desserts include
blood orange mousse torte and apple and rhubarb crumble.
OPEN: 12-3 6-11 (open all day bank holidays & weekends)
BAR MEALS: L served Mon-Fri 12-2.35 (Sat 12-9.30, Sun 12-9)
D served all week 6-9.30 **RESTAURANT:** L served all week 12-2.30
D served all week 6-9.30 Av 3 course à la carte £25 🍻: Hook Norton
Best, Sharps Doom Bar, Tom Wood, Deuchars. ♀: 8
FACILITIES: Child facs Garden: Floral terrace with tables, lawned
area Dogs allowed Water provided **NOTES:** Parking 20

The Wheatsheaf ◠ ♀

Main St, Maids Moreton MK18 1QR
☎ 01280 815433 ▤ 01280 814631
Dir: From M1 junct 13 take A421 to Buckingham, then take A413
Old world village pub serving real ales, quality bar snacks and
an à la carte menu in the spacious conservatory overlooking
the secluded beer garden. Options include chicken breast in a
cream and stilton sauce; duck breast with Madeira sauce; and
stilton and broccoli pasta. Fish specialities include breaded
Whitby fish and chips, and salmon steak in a lemon and lime
sauce. Children's play equipment is a recent addition.

continued

OPEN: 12-3 6-11 (Sun 7-10.30) **BAR MEALS:** L served Mon-Sat 12-2.15 D served Mon-Sat 7-9.30 Av main course £7
RESTAURANT: L served Mon-Sat 12-2.15 D served Mon-Sat 7-9.30 Av 3 course à la carte £20 ☺: Free House ◀: Hook Norton, Black Sheep, John Smiths, Side Pocket For A Toad. ♀: 30
FACILITIES: Child facs Garden: Large secluded garden, chairs on lawn/patio Dogs allowed Water **NOTES:** Parking 15

CHALFONT ST GILES   Map 06 SU99

Pick of the Pubs

Ivy House ♀
London Rd HP8 4RS ☎ 01494 872184 ▤ 01494 872870
e-mail: enquiries@theivyhouse-bucks.co.uk
web: www.theivyhouse-bucks.co.uk
See Pick of the Pubs on page 44

The White Hart ♀
Three Households HP8 4LP ☎ 01494 872441 ▤ 01494 876375
e-mail: enquiries@thewhitehartstgiles.co.uk
Dir: *Off A413 (Denham/Amersham)*

Oak and brown leather furniture and a refurbished bar characterise the quiet, relaxed atmosphere of this prettily-located 100-year-old inn, giving it a welcoming, contemporary feel. The menu offers the likes of loin of pork en croute, carpet bag fillet steak, supreme of chicken, lamb shank, and calves' liver. Fish dishes include baked sea bass with vegetables and Thai fish sauce, and seared blue-fin tuna.
OPEN: 11.30-2.30 5.30-11 All day Sun, BHs **BAR MEALS:** L served all week 12-2 D served all week 6.30-9.30 (Sun all day)
RESTAURANT: L served all week 12-2 D served all week 6.30-9.30 (Sun all day) Av 3 course à la carte £20 ☺: Greene King ◀: Greene King Morland Original, IPA & Old Speckled Hen, Abbot Ale, Rev. James. ♀: 12 **FACILITIES:** Garden: Patio and garden Dogs allowed Water **NOTES:** Parking 50 **ROOMS:** 11 bedrooms en suite 1 family room s£77.50 d£97.50 (♦♦♦♦) No children overnight

CHALFONT ST PETER   Map 06 TQ09

Pick of the Pubs

The Greyhound Inn NEW ♀
SL9 9RA ☎ 01753 883404 ▤ 01753 891627
e-mail: reception@thegreyhoundinn.net
Dir: *M40 junct 1/M25 junct 16, follow signs for Gerrards Cross, then Chalfont St Peter*
The 14th-century Greyhound has a macabre place in English history. Not only are its grounds believed to be where the last man hanged for stealing sheep was executed, but a former patron was Sir George Jeffreys, known as the Hanging Judge for his harsh sentencing policy during the Monmouth Rebellion. While still a local magistrate he held court in a room above the restaurant, mention of which brings us neatly to the food here. The cooking style is essentially classic British with a modern twist, producing starters such as moules marinière, shallots, parsley, white wine and cream; chargrilled chicken Caesar salad; and avocado, orange and prawn salad with Marie Rose sauce. From a balanced list of main courses choose from deep-fried haddock in beer batter; whole baked sea bass; pan-fried calves liver; home-made shepherd's pie; and leg of duck confit, among many others.
OPEN: 11-11 Closed: 1 Jan **BAR MEALS:** L served all week 12-3 D served all week 6-9 Av main course £10
RESTAURANT: L served all week 12-3 D served all week 6-9 Av 3 course à la carte £22.50 ☺: Enterprise Inns ◀: London Pride. ♀: 12 **FACILITIES:** Children's licence Garden: Outside terrace with tables, chairs & umbrellas Dogs allowed **NOTES:** Parking 25

 Pubs offering a good choice of fish on their menu

We endeavour to be as accurate as possible but changes to times and other information can occur after the guide has gone to press

---

Restaurant and Bar Meal times indicate the times when food is available. Last orders may be approximately 30 minutes before the times stated

---

Not all of the pubs in the guide are open all week or all day. It's always best to check before you travel

---

Most of the pubs in this guide book pride themselves on the quality of their food. This may take a little time to prepare

---

Website addresses are included where available. The AA cannot be held responsible for the content of any of these websites

---

Pick of the Pubs have that extra special quality that makes them stand out from the crowd. Their entries are highlighted, and may be a full page

Pick of the Pubs

Ivy House

A beautiful, family run, 18th-century brick and flint inn in the middle of the Chilterns, going from strength to strength, both in cuisine and accommodation, under the watchful eye of Jane and Anthony Mears.

In the nine years since this capable couple took over, their pursuit of top quality food and drink has been a surefire route to success for The Ivy House, while the recent addition of five luxury en suite bedrooms can only increase its reputation. In fact, with this move, it has effectively become a real inn again. Inside the pub itself, beams, open fires, books, brass and armchairs create a warm, relaxing atmosphere, as such features almost invariably do. The kitchen is Jane's domain, where she presides over starters such as goats' cheese, chorizo crisps, artichoke and rocket salad; and steaming platter of giant Mediterranean prawns in their shells, served with a basil oil and sweet chilli sauce,

and mains like pan-fried ostrich fillet with a mango and orange sauce; spicy four bean hotpot; hot Cajun spiced salad; and pan-fried sea bass fillets. From the specials menus come the likes of slow-roasted lamb shanks; chargrilled Gressingham duck breast with a rich plum and port sauce; fresh salmon and basil fishcakes; and pan-fried marlin fillets on a bed of chilli salsa. For dessert, why not try hot chocolate sponge pudding with melting chocolate fudge sauce, or Bailey's dark chocolate truffle torte laced with Baileys and double cream? Being an independent free house, there's a good range of real ales like Hook Norton Old Hooky, and a superb collection of fine wines.

OPEN: 12-3.30 6-11 (Sat 12-11, Sun 12-10.30)

BAR MEALS: L served all week 12-2.30 D served all week 6.30-9.30 (Sat 12-9.30, Sun 12-9) Av main course £10.95

RESTAURANT: L served all week 12-2.30 D served all week 6.30-9.30 (Sat 12-9.30, Sun 12-9) Av 3 course à la carte £20 ☺: Free House 🍺: Fuller's London Pride, Brakspear Bitter, Wadworth 6X, Hook Norton Old Hooky. ♀: 22

FACILITIES: Child facs Courtyard & garden with outstanding views Dogs allowed (not in restaurant) Special dietary needs catered for

NOTES: Parking 45

ROOMS: 5 bedrooms en suite s£75 d£95 (♦♦♦♦)

♀   Map 06 SU99
London Rd HP8 4RS
☎ 01494 872184
🖹 01494 872870
📧 enquiries@theivyhouse-bucks.co.uk
🌐 www.theivyhouse-bucks.co.uk
Dir: On A413 2m S of Amersham & 1.5m N of Chalfont St Giles

England

CHENIES   Map 06 TQ09

Pick of the Pubs

The Red Lion ♀
WD3 6ED ☎ 01923 282722 📠 01923 283797
Dir: Between Rickmansworth & Amersham on A404, follow signs for
Chenies & Latimer

In a lovely village in the River Chess valley, a free house
where a packed menu offers hot and cold French sticks,
baps and snacks, starters and main meals. Most of the
starters can also be served as mains, among them
antipasto with tomato and onion salad, and chicken and
liver paté with bread. Other main dishes include curried
sausage and herb meatballs; balti potatoes with spinach
and feta; Barnsley chop with red wine gravy; beef goulash
with sour cream; rump and rib steaks; and lightly seared
fresh tuna loin. A perennial favourite is lamb pie - the
'internationally acclaimed, aesthetically and palatably
pleasing' lamb pie, that is - which heads a list of home-
made pastry-filled items including mahi mahi chilli pie.
Fresh salads are available on request. Hot bacon and
Milky Bar in a bap deserves investigation.
OPEN: 11-2.30 5.30-11 (Closed: 25 Dec)
BAR MEALS: L served all week 12-2 D served all week 7-10
🍴: Free House 🍺: Wadworth 6X, Rebellion's, Lion's Pride, Vale
Best. ♀: 10 **FACILITIES:** Garden: Benches beside main bar
Dogs allowed Water **NOTES:** Parking 14

CHESHAM   Map 06 SP90

The Black Horse Inn ♀
Chesham Vale HP5 3NS ☎ 01494 784656
Dir: A41 from Berkhamstead, A416 through Ashley Green, 0.75m before
Chesham R to Vale Rd, btm of Mashleigh Hill follow rd for 1m, inn on L
Set in some beautiful valley countryside, this 500-year-old
pub is ideal for enjoying a cosy, traditional environment
without electronic games or music. During the winter there
are roaring log fires to take the chill off those who may spot
one of the resident ghosts. An ever-changing bar menu
includes an extensive range of snacks, while the main menu
may feature steak and Stallion Ale pie, trout and almonds,
various home-made pies, steaks and gammons, stuffed plaice,
or salmon supreme.
OPEN: 11-3 5.30-11 (Sun 12-3, 7-10.30) **BAR MEALS:** L served all
week 12-2.30 D served all week 6.30-9.30 Sun 7-9 Av main course
£8.95 **RESTAURANT:** L served all week 12-2.30 D served all week
6.30-9.30 Sun 7-9 🍺: Adnams Bitter, London Pride, Speckled Hen.
♀: 12 **FACILITIES:** Garden: Food served outdoors, patio, pond
Dogs allowed **NOTES:** Parking 80

The Swan ♀
Ley Hill HP5 1UT ☎ 01494 783075 📠 01494 783582
e-mail: swan@swanleyhill.com
Dir: E of Chesham by golf course
Once three cottages, the first built around 1520, qualifying as
Buckinghamshire's oldest pub. Condemned prisoners,
heading for nearby gallows, would drink 'a last and final ale'
here. During the Second World War, Clark Gable, James
Stewart and Glen Miller frequently drank here after cycling
(cycling?) from Bovingdon airbase. Menus change several
times monthly, and a blackboard features daily specials.
Steamed fillet of salmon with lobster sauce is typical.
OPEN: 12-3 5.30-11 (Sun 12-4, 7-10.30) **BAR MEALS:** L served
Mon-Sat 12-2.15 Sun 12-2.30, D served Tues-Sat D all wk summer
RESTAURANT: L served Mon-Sat 12-2 Sun 12-2.30, D served
Tues-Sat 7-9, D all wk summer 🍴: 🍺: Adnams Bitter, Fuller's
London Pride, Timothy Taylor Landlord, Marston's Pedigree. ♀: 8
FACILITIES: Garden: Large garden, patio, benches Dogs allowed
Water

CHICHELEY   Map 11 SP94

The Chester Arms ♀
MK16 9JE ☎ 01234 391214 📠 01234 391214
e-mail: foodjunkies@btopenworld.com
Dir: On A422, 2m NE of Newport Pagnell. 4m from M1 J14

A philosophy of buying well and keeping things simple pays
dividends at this comfortable roadside pub near Chicheley
Hall. Bar lunches and Greene King ales are always available,
and in fine weather meals are served in the pub garden.
Home-made soup or mixed seafood salad support main
courses like chargrilled lamb chops; whole sea bass; or
chicken chasseur.
OPEN: 11-3 6-11 **BAR MEALS:** L served Tues-Sun 12-2 D served
Tues-Sat 6.30-9.30 Closed Sun eve Av main course £11
RESTAURANT: L served Tues-Sun 12-2 D served Tues-Sat 6.30-9.30
Av 3 course à la carte £22 🍴: Greene King 🍺: Greene King IPA &
Ruddles County. ♀: 8 **FACILITIES:** Garden **NOTES:** Parking 25

 Brewery/Company

Disabled people and those with Assist Dogs have
new rights of access to pubs, restaurants and hotels
under the Disability Discrimination Act of
1 October 2004. For more information see the
website at www.drc gb.org/open4all/rights/2004.asp

CHOLESBURY   Map 06 SP90

The Full Moon
Hawridge Common HP5 2UH ☎ 01494 758959 ▤ 01494 758797
Dir: At Tring on A41 take turn for Wiggington & Cholesbury. On Cholesbury Common in front of windmill
A windmill behind the pub sets the scene for this 16th-century coaching inn, beautifully situated on the borders of Cholesbury Common and Hawridge Common. Inside, you'll find beamed ceilings, flagstone floors and winter fires. Six cask ales and an international wine list support the extensive menu, with organic meat and poultry supplied by Eastwoods of Berkhamstead. A range of fish dishes might include plaice, cod and pancetta fishcakes or sea bass stuffed with crabmeat, spring onion and ginger, plus daily chef's specials. Look out for beef braised in Guinness, or pheasant casserole.

OPEN: 12-3 5.30-11 (Sat open all day, Sun 12-10.30 Closed: 25 Dec) **BAR MEALS:** L served all week 12-2 D served Mon-Sat 6.30-9 Av main course £11 **RESTAURANT:** L served all week 12-2 D served Mon-Sat 6.30-9 Av 3 course à la carte £22.50 ⊕: Enterprise Inns ◗: Interbrew Bass & Adnams , Fuller's London Pride, Brakspear Special, 2 Guest Ales. ♀: 7 **FACILITIES:** Country pub garden, canopy, heat lamps Dogs allowed Water **NOTES:** Parking 28

CUDDINGTON   Map 05 SP71

Pick of the Pubs

The Crown ♀
Spurt St HP18 0BB ☎ 01844 292222
e-mail: david@anniebaileys.com
See Pick of the Pubs on opposite page

DENHAM   Map 06 TQ08

The Falcon Inn NEW ♦♦♦♦ ♀
Village Rd UB9 5BE ☎ 01895 832125 ▤ 01895 835811
e-mail: falcon.inn@btconnect.com
Dir: 0.75m junct 1 M40 exit and follow signs A40 Gerrards 100yds from exit turn right into Old Mill Road. Pass church on right. Enter village, pub is opposite village green.
The Falcon Inn, dating back to the 16th century and situated opposite the village green, is very popular with walkers and locals. Specialising in real ales, it is also known for its award-winning fresh food. The area around the pub is known for its exceptional walks – there's an outstanding country park which links up with the spectacular Colne Valley.
OPEN: 12-3 5-11 (Sat 11-11, Sun 12-10.30) **BAR MEALS:** L served all week 12-2.30 D served all week 12-2.30 Sun 12-3 Av main course £9 **RESTAURANT:** L served all week 12-2.30 D served 6 days 6.30-9.30 Sun 12-3, 6.30-9 Av 3 course à la carte £22 ◗: Guiness,
continued

Timothy Taylor Landlord, Bombardier, Brakspear. ♀: 9
FACILITIES: Garden: Bright sunny area seats 50
ROOMS: 3 bedrooms en suite s£75 d£95 No children overnight

Pick of the Pubs

The Swan Inn ♀
Village Rd UB9 5BH ☎ 01895 832085 ▤ 01895 835516
e-mail: info@swaninndenham.co.uk
Dir: From A412 follow signs for Denham.

Despite good motorway access and a location just minutes from the London suburbs, this double-fronted Georgian inn feels peaceful and secluded. Set in the pretty, unspoiled village of Denham, the wisteria-clad building is everyone's idea of the ideal country pub. A log fire burns in the cold winter months, whilst the private dining room is equally suitable for intimate dinners or business meetings. Hidden away out the back you'll find a sunny, secluded terrace and large gardens. Wadworth 6X, Morrells Oxford Blue and Courage Best are mainstays of the thriving bar trade, and the modern British menu has attracted a new following. The kitchen caters for all tastes, from a quick weekday sandwich to more serious meals. Try Welsh rarebit with smoked haddock and turnip gratin; duck on truffle mash with fig jus; or mozzarella, roast sweet pepper and field mushroom pastry.
OPEN: 11-11 (Sun 12-10.30 Closed: 25-26 Dec)
BAR MEALS: L served all week 12-2.30 D served all week 7-10 Av main course £11.75 **RESTAURANT:** L served all week 12-2.30 D served all week 7-10 Av 3 course à la carte £22.50 ◗: Wadworth 6X, Courage Best, Morrells Oxford Blue. ♀: 15 **FACILITIES:** Garden: Terrace on 2 levels, large lawned area Dogs allowed Water **NOTES:** Parking 12

DINTON   Map 05 SP71

Seven Stars ♀
Stars Ln HP17 8UL ☎ 01296 748241 ▤ 01296 748241
e-mail: secretpub.company@virgin.net
Dir: Telephone for directions
A picturesque country pub in the charming village of Dinton close to Aylesbury Ring. Dating from around 1640, with inglenook fireplaces, wooden settles and a cosy old snug to prove it. Sandwiches, light bites, grills, burgers, and specials are served in the bar, while the restaurant menu runs to favourites like liver and bacon, and steak and kidney pudding, with tuna Mexicana among several fish options.
OPEN: 12-3 6-11 (Sun 12-3, 7-10.30) **BAR MEALS:** L served week 12-2.30 D served all week 6.30-8.45 Av main course £7.50 **RESTAURANT:** L served all week 12-2.30 D served all week 6.30-8.45 Av 3 course fixed price £12.50 ⊕: ◗: London Pride, Worthington 1774. ♀: 6 **FACILITIES:** Garden: Lawn with small patio Dogs allowed in the garden only. Water provided **NOTES:** Parking 20

The Crown

Having successfully run Annie Bailey's bar-cum-brasserie in Cuddington for a number of years, the Berrys turned their attention to improving the Crown, a delightful Grade II listed pub nearby. Customers will find plenty of character inside, with a popular locals' bar and several low-beamed dining areas filled with charming prints and the glow of evening candlelight.

A choice of beers on tap, an extensive wine list and an eclectic menu add to the enjoyment of a visit here. A short menu lists various snacks, salads (hot duck and bacon, Mediterranean vegetable and goats' cheese), and sandwiches (steak, or prawn and crab). For a starter you might choose seared scallops with chilli jam and crème fraîche, winter broth with leeks and pearl barley, caramelised onion, leek and cheese tartlet, and white crab meat with prawns on mixed leaf with Marie Rose dressing. Main dishes may feature smoked haddock on bubble and squeak with cheddar crumb topping; beef and mushroom casserole; breast of chicken with almonds, wild rice and Amaretto glaze; rib-eye steak; finely sliced calves' liver and bacon with caramelised onions; and chargrilled Mediterranean vegetables with grilled goats' cheese. Don't forget desserts like treacle sponge pudding, chocolate fudge brownies with vanilla ice cream, raspberry and vanilla cheesecake, and tarte au citron with crème fraîche and raspberry coulis, if you can find space! Beers like Fullers London Pride and Adnams will help to wash it all down.

OPEN: 12-3 6-11 (All day Sun)
BAR MEALS: L served all week
12-2.30 D served all week 6.30-10
(Sun 12-8) Av main course £10.50
RESTAURANT: L served all week
12-2.30 D served all week 6.30-10
(Sun 12-8) Av 3 course à la carte £20
Av 3 course fixed price £20
🍺: Fullers 🍺: Fullers London Pride,
Adnams. ♎: 9
FACILITIES: Garden: Small patio area
NOTES: Parking 12

🐟 ♎   Map 05 SP71
Spurt St HP18 0BB
☎ 01844 292222
✉ david@anniebaileys.com
Dir: Off A418 between Aylesbury
and Thame

England

DORNEY
Map 06 SU97

The Palmer Arms NEW ♀
Village Rd SL4 6QW ☎ 01628 666612 📠 01628 661116
e-mail: info@thepalmerarms.com
Dir: *From A4 take B3026, over M4 to Dorney*
The Palmer Arms, dating from the 15th century, is well-located in the beautiful conservation village of Dorney. Its owners are passionate about providing high standards of food and service, and like to think of their cooking as 'English with a twist'. Seasonal game dishes are always available. It is open every day for lunch, afternoon tea, dinner and all-day coffee.
OPEN: 11-11 (Sun 12-10.30) **BAR MEALS:** L served Mon-Sat 12-2.30 Sun12-3 D served Mon-Sat Av main course £15
RESTAURANT: L served Mon-Sat 12-2.30 Sun 12-3 D served Mon-Sat 6-9.30 Av 3 course à la carte £28 Av 3 course fixed price £13
🍴: Free House 🍺: Greene King Abbot Ale, Old Speckled Hen, IPA,Guiness. ♀: 14 **FACILITIES:** Garden: Landscaped gardens with water features **NOTES:** Parking 50

FARNHAM COMMON
Map 06 SU98

The Foresters ♀
The Broadway SL2 3QQ ☎ 01753 643340 📠 01753 647524
e-mail: barforesters@aol.com

There's a real buzz at the Foresters - formerly the Foresters Arms, which was built in the 1930s to replace a Victorian building. Located close to Burnham Beeches, a large woodland area famous for its coppiced trees, it offers a combination of good drinking and a busy restaurant renowned for the quality of its food. The daily menu might include pan-roasted duck breast with carrot and parsnip rosti; leek, sweetcorn and ricotta roulade with tomato grilled aubergine; and fresh haddock and chips.
OPEN: 11-11 Mon-Sat (12-10.30 Sun) **BAR MEALS:** L served Mon-Sat 12-2.30 D served Mon-Sat 6.30-10 Food all day Sun Av main course £12 **RESTAURANT:** L served Mon-Sat 12-2.30 D served Mon-Sat 6.30-10 Sun food 12-9 🍴: Simply Pubs 🍺: Fullers London Pride, Draught Bass, Youngs Special Bitter, Carling. ♀: 9
FACILITIES: Decking area, beer garden Dogs allowed Water provided

FINGEST
Map 05 SU79

The Chequers Inn ♀
RG9 6QD ☎ 01491 638335
e-mail: christian@chequersinn.wanadoo.co.uk
Dir: *From M40 left towards Ibstone, left at T junc at end of rd, stay left, pub on right*

Set deep in the Chiltern Hills, opposite a splendid Norman church, the Chequers is a 15th-century redbrick pub with log fires in the winter, and a delightful sun-trap garden with rural views for summer imbibing.
OPEN: 12-3 6-11 (open all day in summer and wknds)
BAR MEALS: L served all week 12-2 D served Tues-Sat 6-9 Av main course £7.95 **RESTAURANT:** L served all week 12-2 D served all week 6-9 🍴: Brakspear 🍺: Brakspear Bitter, Ordinary Old Mild & Special. **FACILITIES:** Garden: Beer garden, food served outdoors Dogs allowed in the garden only **NOTES:** Parking 60

FORD
Map 05 SP70

Pick of the Pubs

The Dinton Hermit
Water Ln HP17 8XH ☎ 01296 747473 📠 01296 748819
e-mail: dintonhermit@btconnect.com
Dir: *Off A418 between Aylesbury & Thame*

A pub for nearly 400 years, the Dinton Hermit remained much as it was until 2002 when the current owner undertook a major makeover to turn it into a country hotel, with bar facilities, a restaurant and accommodation. The name comes from local character John Bigg (1626-1696) who became a hermit after objecting to his boss's involvement in beheading Charles I. Today the pub offers a good range of beers - Adnams, Vale Brewery Wychert Ale, London Pride and Batemans - in both of the beamed and warmly decorated bars. Contemporary British cooking using locally sourced fresh produce might deliver crispy duck

continued

salad with warm plum and star anise dressing, followed by roast sea bass with coriander, garlic and soy. Finish with a home-made pudding or British farmhouse cheeses. In fine weather sit outside on the terrace and lawns and enjoy the country views.
OPEN: 12-11 Closed: 1 Jan **BAR MEALS:** L served Mon-Sat 12-2 Sun 12-3.30 D served all week 7-9.30 Av main course £15 **RESTAURANT:** L served Mon-Sat 12-2 Sun 12-3 D served Mon-Sat 7-9.30 Av 3 course à la carte £25 ⊕: Free House ◀: Adnams Bitter, Vale Brewery Wychert Ale, London Pride, Batemans XB. **FACILITIES:** Garden: Large garden with patio area and seating **NOTES:** Parking 40

FRIETH   Map 05 SU79

The Prince Albert
RG9 6PY ☎ 01494 881683 📠 01494 881683
e-mail: lacysti@aol.com
Dir: 4m N of Marlow, Bucks. Follow Frieth road from Marlow. Straight across at X-rds on the Fingest road. The Albert is 200yds on the left.
Set in the Chiltern valley near Hambledon and Marlow, this traditional family-run pub offers fresh home-cooked food and a wine list from around the world. There is no music, no cigarette machine, and no TV; just a friendly reception and warm open fires. Soups, filled baguettes, stews, chillis, curries and pies are all made in-house with traceable local ingredients. The situation is a good one for walkers.
OPEN: 11.30-11 **BAR MEALS:** L served Mon-Sat 12-9 Sun 12-5.30 D served 12-9 Av main course £6.25 **RESTAURANT:** L served 12-9 Sun 12-5.30 D served Wed-Sun 12-9 Av 3 course à la carte £12.95 ⊕: Brakspear ◀: Brakspear Bitter, Special. **FACILITIES:** Garden: Large garden, seats approx 50 Dogs allowed **NOTES:** Parking 20

The Yew Tree
RG9 6PJ ☎ 01494 882330 e-mail: yewtree2003@aol.com
Dir: From M40 towards Stokenchurch, thru Cadmore End, Lane End R to Frieth
A huge yew tree spirals majestically outside this 16th-century red-brick pub in this truly rural Chilterns village. Renovated to upgrade the interiors, the Yew Tree has an exceptional lounge bar where weary walkers relax over a well-earned drink and carefully prepared food. A good selection of dishes includes poached halibut with wilted spinach, salsify, pea purée and red wine sauce; and rib-eye steak with all the trimmings. Outside, the well-kept gardens offer seating and home to three llamas.
OPEN: 12-3 6-11 (Sun 12-5) **BAR MEALS:** L served all week 12-2.30 D served all week 6.30-10 (Sun 12-5) **RESTAURANT:** L served all week 12-2.30 D served all week 6-10 ⊕: Free House ◀: Adnams Bitter, Fullers London Pride, Rebellion. **FACILITIES:** Garden: Well kept garden with seating; llamas kept Dogs allowed **NOTES:** Parking 60

GREAT HAMPDEN   Map 05 SP80

The Hampden Arms
HP16 9RQ ☎ 01494 488255 📠 01494 488094
e-mail: louise@thehamptonarms.fsnet.co.uk
Dir: From M40 take A4010, right before Princes Risborough. Great Hampden signed
Whether you're celebrating a special occasion or just want a quiet pint of real ale, you'll find a warm and friendly welcome at this mock Tudor pub restaurant in the heart of the beautifully wooded Hampden Estate. The menu features such dishes as game pie set on a rich port sauce; baked halibut steak with a watercress, mussel and cream sauce;

continued

and roasted vegetables set on a rocket and parmesan salad. Lighter snacks are available, and there is a good choice of hot puddings.
OPEN: 12-3 6-11 (Sun 7-10.30) **BAR MEALS:** L served Mon-Sat 12-2 Sun 12-3 D served Mon-Thurs 6.30-9 Fri & Sat 6.30-9.30, Sun 7-9 Av main course £10.95 **RESTAURANT:** L served Mon-Sat 12-2 Sun 12-3 D served Mon-Sat 6.30-9 Sun 7-9 Av 3 course à la carte £20 ⊕: Free House ◀: Adnams Bitter, Hook Norton, Boddingtons.
FACILITIES: Garden: Large wooden area **NOTES:** Parking 30

GREAT MISSENDEN   Map 06 SP80

The George Inn
94 High St HP16 0BG ☎ 01494 862084 📠 01494 865622
Dir: Off A413 between Aylesbury & Amersham

Established as a coaching inn in 1483, the George has always had strong ties with nearby Missenden Abbey. The small, cosy bars boast a wealth of old beams and fireplaces. The restaurant offers a relaxed non-smoking environment for lunchtime sandwiches, baguettes and jacket potatoes, as well as hot dishes like home-made steak and kidney pie; seasonal game; or tomato and mozzarella tortellini.
OPEN: 11-11 (Sun 12-3, 7-10.30) **BAR MEALS:** L served all week 12-2.30 D served Mon-Sat 6.30-9.30 Av main course £7.50 **RESTAURANT:** L served all week 12-2.30 D served Mon-Sat 6.30-9.30 Av 3 course à la carte £15 ⊕: Inn Partnership ◀: Adnams Bitter, Adnams Broadside, Interbrew Flowers Original. **FACILITIES:** Child facs Beer garden & patio Dogs allowed Water **NOTES:** Parking 25 ⊛

Pick of the Pubs

The Polecat Inn 🌿 ♀
170 Wycombe Rd, Prestwood HP16 0HJ
☎ 01494 862253 📠 01494 868393
e-mail: polecatinn@btinternet.com
Dir: On the A4128 between Great Missenden and High Wycombe
Small, low-beamed rooms radiate from the central bar of this charming 17th-century free house in the Chilterns. The owner, John Gamble, bought the Polecat fifteen years ago when it was closed and in a somewhat dilapidated state of repair. He renovated and extended the building to create an attractive inn retaining many of its original features. A colourful three-acre garden with tables for alfresco summer eating is another of the Polecat's popular attractions. Local ingredients and herbs from the garden are the foundation of the wide-ranging menu and daily blackboard specials, with food freshly prepared in-house. In addition to various snacks, sandwiches and jacket potatoes, there's also a full menu at midday and in the evenings. Expect braised shoulder of lamb with tomato, rosemary and olives; cold poached salmon salad with lemon and dill

continued

England

mayonnaise and new potatoes; and pineapple tarte Tatin or bread and butter pudding.
OPEN: 11.30-2.30 6-11 (Sun 12-3) Closed: Dec 25-26, Jan 1
BAR MEALS: L served all week 12-2 D served Mon-Sat 6.30-9
Av main course £9 ⊕: Free House ◖: Marston's Pedigree, Old Speckled Hen, Interbrew Flowers IPA, Morland. ♀: 16
FACILITIES: Garden: Dogs allowed **NOTES:** Parking 40 No credit cards

Pick of the Pubs

The Rising Sun 🐟
Little Hampden HP16 9PS ☎ 01494 488393
& 488360 ▤ 01494 488788
e-mail: sunrising@rising-sun.demon.co.uk
web: www.rising-sun.demon.co.uk
Dir: From A413, N of Gt Missenden, take Rignall Rd on left (signed Princes Risborough). 2.5m turn right signed 'Little Hampden only'

Beautifully situated 250-year-old inn tucked away in the Chiltern Hills surrounded by beech woods and glorious scenery, close to the Ridgeway. A network of footpaths begins just outside the front door, so it's a perfect base for country walks. Reached down a single track, no-through-road, the pub seems to be miles from anywhere, yet London is only 40 minutes by train from nearby Great Missenden. The proprietor prides himself on a well-run, clean and welcoming establishment, strictly non-smoking throughout. An interesting menu offers starters which can double as snacks, and an extensive à la carte selection for lunch and dinner. A good choice of seafood includes baked red snapper Catalan style, with tomatoes, anchovies, olives and capers; other main course options are steaks, a speciality curry, and roast hickory smoked chicken with barbecue sauce.
OPEN: 11.30-3 6.30-10 (Sun 12-3 only Open BH lunchtime)
BAR MEALS: L served Tue-Sun 12-2 D served Tue-Sat 7-9
Av main course £9.95 **RESTAURANT:** L served Tue-Sun 12-2
D served Tue-Sat 7-9 Av 3 course à la carte £23 ⊕: Free House
◖: Adnams, Brakspear Bitter, Spitfire, Youngs Special.
FACILITIES: Garden: Fence enclosed garden with seating area Dogs allowed Water and food if necessary **NOTES:** Parking 20

⊛ The Rosette is the AA award for food.
Look out for it next to a pub's name

Pick of the Pubs

The Green Dragon ⊛⊛ ♀
8 Churchway HP17 8AA ☎ 01844 291403 ▤ 299532
e-mail: paul@eatatthedragon.co.uk
web: www.eatatthedragon.co.uk
See Pick of the Pubs on opposite page

Pick of the Pubs

The Stag & Huntsman Inn
RG9 6RP ☎ 01491 571227 ▤ 01491 413810
e-mail: andy@stagandhuntsman.com
Dir: 5m from Henley-on-Thames on A4155 toward Marlow, left at Mill End towards Hambleden
Warm and welcoming 400-year-old brick and flint pub in a quintessentially English village frequently used as a film and television location. *101 Dalmatians*, *Midsomer Murders*, *A Band of Brothers* and the children's classic movie *Chitty Chitty Bang Bang* have all been filmed here, so it's not surprising many tourists love it. After an exhilarating ramble in the hills, relax in the cosy snug, or choose the public bar for a traditional game of darts or dominoes. Alternatively, savour the bustling atmosphere of the L-shaped, half-panelled lounge, with its low ceilings, open fire, and upholstered seating. There's also a dining room, where you can sample Huntsman steak, marinated chargrilled chicken, fresh salmon fishcakes, beer-battered haddock, or a giant Yorkshire pudding filled with the stew of the day.
OPEN: 11-2.30 6-11 (Sun 12-3, 7-10.30, Sat 11-3, 6-11 Closed: Dec 25, 26 Dec & 1 Jan evening) **BAR MEALS:** L served all week 12-2 D served Mon-Sat 7-9.30 **RESTAURANT:** 12-2 7-9.30
⊕: Free House ◖: Rebellion IPA, Wadworth 6X, guest ales.
FACILITIES: Large, landscaped garden, BBQ Dogs allowed Water **NOTES:** Parking 60

Crooked Billet
Ham Green HP18 0QJ ☎ 01296 770239 ▤ 01296 770094
e-mail: info@crookedbillet.com
Dir: On A41 between Aylesbury & Bicester
Located in peaceful Buckinghamshire countryside, this 200-year-old pub is believed to be haunted by Fair Rosamund, a girlfriend of Charles I. Extensive and tempting menus include both à la carte and fixed price choices. Starters may include risotto of sea scallops with wild mushrooms, and leek and egg baked pots. Among the main courses can be found pan-fried monkfish or duck breast, fillet of lamb, or wild venison, all with unusual but delectable-sounding accompaniments. Sandwiches made from home-made bread are a lighter option.
OPEN: 11-11 **BAR MEALS:** L served Mon-Sat 12-6 D served Mon-Sat 6-9 Sun 12-8 **RESTAURANT:** L served Mon-Sat 12-6 D served Mon-Sat 6-9 Sun 12-8 ⊕: ◖: Hook Norton, Worthington 1744, London Pride. **FACILITIES:** Child facs Garden: Large seated area surrounded by woodland **NOTES:** Parking 50

Pick of the Pubs

HADDENHAM – BUCKINGHAMSHIRE

The Green Dragon

The Green Dragon is attractively located in the old part of Haddenham, close to the village green and 12th-century church. The pub dates back to 1650 and was once a manorial court, as the last man to be executed in Buckinghamshire discovered to his cost. Over the last five years pub co-owner and chef Paul Berry has built up a formidable reputation for his food, and the place gets very busy so booking is strongly advised.

Local produce from local suppliers is to the fore, and fresh fish arrives post haste from Devon. A carte menu is available at lunch and dinner, offering a comprehensive range of dishes with starters that can double as light bites for a speedy lunch. Avocado and crab tian with a lemon confit ginger and lime dressing; salmon and crab fishcake with a lemon and basil roullie; and smoked salmon and crayfish salad might be followed by braised shank of lamb on a simple mash; steak and kidney suet pudding with Wychert ale; and sautéed calves' liver and bacon on spring onion mash. For a mid-week evening meal, the 'Simply Dinner' menu on Tuesday and Thursday night offers particularly good value at £11.95 for two courses - a starter and main course or main course and pudding. Here you will find avocado and pancetta Caesar's salad; breast of guinea fowl on roasted root vegetables and black pudding; and caramelized rice pudding among the choices. Haddenhams' own Vale Brewery supplies Notley and Wychert real ales, and there is a wine list of some 50 wines including eight available by the glass. There are two grassed areas with garden furniture where you can sit outside in summer.

OPEN: 11.30-2 6.30-11 Closed: 25 Dec & 1 Jan
BAR MEALS: L served all week 12-2 D served all week 7-9.30 (Sun 12-3) Av main course £11
RESTAURANT: L served all week 12-2 D served all week 7-9.30 (Sun 12-4) Av 3 course à la carte £24 Av 2 course fixed price £11.95
⊕: Enterprise Inns
◖: Vale Notley Ale, Deuchers IPA, Wadsworth 6X. ♀: 12
FACILITIES: Garden: Two areas of grass with garden table
NOTES: Parking 18 ⊗

◎◎ ♀　　　　Map 05 SP70
8 Churchway HP17 8AA
☎ 01844 291403
🖹 01844 299532
🄴 paul@eatatthedragon.co.uk
🆆 www.eatatthedragon.co.uk
Dir: From M40 A329 to Thame, then A418, 1st right after entering Haddenham

England

LONG CRENDON   Map 05 SP60

Pick of the Pubs

The Angel Inn ◉ ♀
47 Bicester Rd HP18 9EE ☎ 01844 208268 🗎 01844 202497
e-mail: angelrestaurant@aol.com
Dir: A418 to Thame, B4011 to left Crendon, Inn on B4011

Gastro-pub status is conceded to this 16th-century coaching inn, which dishes up great food in the air-conditioned conservatory or out on the patio or sun terrace. Wattle and daub walls and inglenook fireplaces testify to the inn's age, and there's plenty of character too in the assorted scrubbed pine and sturdy oak tables set on light wooden floors. Real ales are served, along with cocktails, champagne and wine by the glass, but food is the focus. Fish is the speciality, listed on the daily blackboard menu - maybe grilled fillet of natural smoked haddock on leek and mustard mash with poached egg, or trio of king prawns, salmon and monkfish with asparagus and baby leeks. Options from the regular carte range from baguettes and open sandwiches to roast guinea fowl on a hot wild mushroom, leek and asparagus salad with crispy polenta and tarragon cream. A short fixed price lunch is also available, priced for two or three courses.
OPEN: 12-3 7-10 (Sun closed eve) **BAR MEALS:** L served all week 12-3 D served Mon-Sat 7-9.30 **RESTAURANT:** L served all week 12-2.30 D served Mon-Sat 7-9.30 ◉: Free House ◪: Oxford Blue, IPA, Brakes Beer. ♀: 11 **FACILITIES:** Garden: Patio, terrace at rear of pub Dogs allowed Water
NOTES: Parking 25

Pick of the Pubs

Mole & Chicken ♀
Easington Ter HP18 9EY ☎ 01844 208387 🗎 01844 208250
e-mail: shanepellis@hotmail.com
Dir: Off B4011 N of Thame
Built in 1831 in the Chiltern Hills, this village inn was known as The Rising Sun for some years before gaining its peculiar name. Now a fashionable Buckinghamshire dining pub, the oak-beamed bar has cosy fireplaces, rag-washed walls and flagstone floors. The terraced garden has views across three counties. Menus appear on boards over the fireplace's oak lintel and include the house speciality of fishcakes with mild curry sauce, skewers of chicken satay, or shell-on prawns nicknamed Horses Douvay. Main courses comprise marinated and slow roast rack of pork ribs; roasted pig cheeks on leek and potato mash with a red wine, plum and shallot sauce; penne pasta tossed in sun-dried tomato pesto; and roast lamb

continued

shoulder with honey and rosemary sauce. Local pheasant with shallots, red wine, bacon and sage is definitely one to look out for.

Mole & Chicken

OPEN: 12-3.30 6-11.30 (Sun 12-9 Closed: 25 Dec)
BAR MEALS: L served all week 12-2 D served all week 7-9 Sun 12-9 Av main course £12 **RESTAURANT:** L served all week 12-2 D served all week 7-9 ◉: Free House ◪: Ruddles Best, Greene King IPA, London Pride & Old Speckled Hen. ♀: 8
FACILITIES: Garden: Good view of rural landscape
NOTES: Parking 40

MARLOW   Map 05 SU88

The Kings Head ⬡ ♀
Church Rd, Little Marlow SL7 3RZ
☎ 01628 484407 🗎 01628 484407
Dir: M40 junct 4 take A4040 S, then A4155
This flower-adorned pub, only 10 minutes from the Thames Footpath, dates back to 1654. It has a cosy, open-plan interior with original beams and open fires. From sandwiches and jacket potatoes, the menu extends to the likes of sea bass with ginger, sherry and spring onions; lamb shank with rich minty gravy, mash and fresh vegetables; pheasant casserole; tuna and mozzarella fish-cakes; and stir-fry duck with plum sauce.
OPEN: 11-3 5-11 (Sat-Sun 11-11) **BAR MEALS:** L served Mon-Sat 12-2.15 Sunday 12-8 D served Mon-Sat 6.30-9.30
RESTAURANT: L served all week 12-2.15 D served all week 6.30-9.30 Sunday 12-8 ◉: Enterprise Inns ◪: Brakspear Bitter, Fuller's London Pride, Rebellion IPA, Timothy Taylor Landlord.
FACILITIES: Garden: Safely behind pub, lots of tables & chairs
NOTES: Parking 50

MOULSOE   Map 11 SP94

The Carrington Arms ⬡ ♀
Cranfield Rd MK16 0HB ☎ 01908 218050 🗎 01908 217850
e-mail: thecarringtonarms@4cinns.co.uk
Dir: M1 junct 14 A509 to Newport Pagnell, 100yds turn right, signed Moulsoe, Cranfield. Pub on right
This grade II listed building is surrounded by farm land in a conservation area. For those who prefer to enjoy cooking as a spectator sport, this should fit the bill. Customers can 'create' their own menu from the meat and seafood counter, which the chef then cooks in full view of his expectant diners. Aberdeen beef, monkfish, tiger prawns, oysters and even

continued

> ♀ 7   Number of wines by the glass

Canadian lobster from the tank are all on offer, along with ostrich, and steak and oyster pie.

The Carrington Arms

OPEN: 12-3 5.30-11 (Sun 12-3, 7-10.30) **BAR MEALS:** L served all week 12-2.30 D served Mon-Sat 6.30-10 Sun 7-9.30
RESTAURANT: L served all week 12-2.30 D served Mon-Sat 6.30-10 Sun 7-9.30 ☻: Free House ◀: Morland Old Speckled Hen, Green King IPA & Guest Ales. ♀: 14 **FACILITIES:** Garden: Patio & lawned area Dogs allowed in the garden only **NOTES:** Parking 100
See advert on this page

OVING   Map 11 SP72

The Black Boy ♀
Church Ln HP22 4HN ☎ 01296 641258 🖹 01296 641271
e-mail: theblackboyoving@aol.com
There are 30 tables in the huge garden of this old pub. On the same land, long before the green-fingered brigade got to work, Cromwell and his soldiers camped here before sacking nearby Bolebec Castle during the Civil War. Prisoners were put in the pub's cellars, and one unfortunate who died in custody now haunts the building. Don't let that deter you from enjoying a range of Aberdeen Angus steaks; pheasant; chicken ballotine; venison sausages; sea bream or perch.
OPEN: 12-3 6-11 **BAR MEALS:** L served Tues-Sat 12-2 Sun 12-2.30 D served Tues-Sat 6.30-9 Av main course £11.75
RESTAURANT: L served Tues-Sat Sun 12-2.30 12-2 D served Tues-Sat 6.30-9 Av 3 course à la carte £20 ◀: Spitfire, Youngs Bitter, Batemans Bitter, Adnams Bitter. ♀: 10 **FACILITIES:** Garden: Large garden with pergolas & views of Aylesbury Dogs allowed Water **NOTES:** Parking 20

RADNAGE   Map 05 SU79

The Three Horseshoes Inn NEW ♀
Horseshoe Rd, Bennett End HP14 4EB ☎ 01494 483273
Dating from 1745, this delightful little inn is tucked away down a leafy lane. The owner gave up a lucrative City career and returned to her roots to refurbish the pub frequented by her father. Stone floors, original beams, a bread oven and an open fire are among the features. Expect field mushrooms with mozzarella, and cottage pie at lunchtime, and fillet of beef Stroganoff, pan-fried pork fillet, and baked whole sea bass in the evening.
OPEN: 12-11 **BAR MEALS:** L served Mon-Sat 12-2.30 Sun 12-4 D served Sun 7-9.30 Av main course £8 **RESTAURANT:** L served Mon-Sat 12-2.30 Sun 12-4 D served all week 7-9.30 ◀: Adnamss, Brakspears, Guest beers. ♀: 6 **FACILITIES:** Garden: Overlooking pond **NOTES:** Parking 30

Tel: 01908 218050 Fax: 01908 217850
email: thecarringtonarms@4cinns.co.uk

Carrington Arms
Cranfield Rd, Moulsoe, MK16 0HB

If you like to see your food being cooked, interact with our chefs and choose as much or as little as you like – the 19th Century pub's unique dining experience allows you to do all of the above.

Daily our fresh meat and seafood counter is stocked with prime Scottish Estate beef, fresh fish, tiger prawns, oysters and live lobster. It's then cooked on the open grill in the restaurant.

With an extensive wine list, guest ales and 8 en-suite letting rooms you won't want to leave the picturesque Pub and village.

SKIRMETT   Map 05 SU79

The Frog ♀
RG9 6TG ☎ 01491 638996 🖹 01491 638045
Dir: Turn off A4155 at Mill End, pub 3m on
From its pretty, clay-tiled dormer windows to its overflowing flower tubs, this eye-catching whitewashed free house exudes warmth and tranquillity. Set deep in one of the loveliest valleys in the Chiltern Hills, The Frog lies close to the heart of *Vicar of Dibley* country. There are attractive rural views from the delightful, tree-shaded garden, and you may be tempted to enjoy one of the recommended local walks. Once inside, this family-run pub does not disappoint though in wintertime you may have to queue for a place on the unusual wooden bench that encircles the fireplace. In the non-smoking restaurant, the wide ranging international menu is changed monthly, and daily specials are featured on the blackboard. Fresh ingredients and confident cooking produce home-made soups, Irish fry-up, and braised lamb shank. There's always a good selection of fish, too; expect haddock in beer batter, red mullet, sea bass, or bream.
OPEN: 11.30-3 6.30-11 (Oct-May Closed Sun night)
BAR MEALS: L served all week 12-2.30 D served all week 6.30-9.30 Av main course £8.50 **RESTAURANT:** L served all week 12-2.30 D served all week 6.30-9.30 Av 3 course à la carte £17.95 ☻: Free House ◀: Adnams Best, Hook Norton, Rebellion, Fullers London Pride. **FACILITIES:** Garden: beer garden, patio, outdoor eating Dogs allowed **NOTES:** Parking 15 ⊗

England

SPEEN
Map 05 SU89

King William IV
Hampden Rd HP27 0RU ☎ 01494 488329 📠 01494 488301
Dir: *Through Hughenden Valley, off A4128 N of High Wycombe*
Nestling in the Chiltern Hills, this 17th-century, family run pub and restaurant boasts log fires in winter and a popular terrace and garden ideal for summer drinking. Choose from an interesting range of blackboard specials that might include Thai green chicken curry, grilled red snapper and trio of Welsh lamb cutlets.
OPEN: 12-3 6-11 (Sun 12-4) (Sun closed evenings)
BAR MEALS: L served Tues-Sun 12-2.30 D served Tues-Sat 7-10 Av main course £8 **RESTAURANT:** L served Tue-Sun 12-2 D served Tue-Sat 7-10 Av 3 course à la carte £20 ◐: Free House
◖: Batemans, Hook Norton, Fullers London Pride, Tetley.
FACILITIES: Garden: lawned area with cast iron feature, patio Dogs allowed **NOTES:** Parking 50 ⊛

STOKE MANDEVILLE
Map 05 SP81

The Wool Pack NEW ♀
Risborough Rd HP22 5UP ☎ 01296 615970 📠 01296 615971
Dir: *(3m from Aylesbury)*
Beneath the thatch and low beams you'll find a stylish interior featuring open kitchens, stone-fired ovens and log burning fires. The atmosphere is relaxed, friendly and informal - and, in summer, the beautifully landscaped decking is just the place for alfresco dining. A simple, up-to-the-minute menu features lots of comfort appeal, with homely things like pizzas, steaks and pasta as well as contemporary, global touches such as spit chicken, Belgian fries and aioli.
OPEN: 12-11 **BAR MEALS:** L served Mon-Sat 12-2.30 Sun 12-8 D served all week 6-9.30 Av main course £13.95
RESTAURANT: L served Mon-Sat 12-2.30 Sun 12-8 D served all week 6-9.30 Av 3 course à la carte £22.50 ◖: Greene King IPA, London Pride. ♀: 10 **FACILITIES:** Garden **NOTES:** Parking 100

TURVILLE
Map 05 SU79

Pick of the Pubs

The Bull & Butcher ♀
RG9 6QU ☎ 01491 638283 📠 01491 638836
e-mail: info@thebullandbutcher.com
Dir: *M40 j 5 follow Ibstone signs. Right at T-junct. Pub 0.25m on left*
Even if you've never been to Turville or this delightful black-and-white-timbered 16th-century pub, you may well recognise them immediately you arrive here. The village has earned itself celebrity status over the years as a popular location for numerous film and television productions, most notably *Midsomer Murders* and *The Vicar of Dibley*. Several of these classics have been immortalised in the pub menu too, for example there is Dibley Pudding and Midsomer Burger. Movies shot in the area include *Chitty Chitty Bang Bang* and the lesser-known *Went the Day Well*, filmed in Turville at the height of the Second World War. After an exhilarating walk in the glorious Chilterns, relax in the pub's recently refurbished bar, surrounded by original floor tiles and natural oak beams. An appetising menu ranges from smoked fish platter and venison and vegetable casserole, to oven-roasted rump of lamb, and chicken, mushroom and tarragon pie.
OPEN: 12-11 (Sun and BH 12-10.30) **BAR MEALS:** L served 12-2.30 Mon-Sat D served all week 7-9.45 Sun and BH 12-4 Av main course £12.95 **RESTAURANT:** L served 12-2.30

Mon-Sat D served all week 7-9.45 Sun and BH 12-4 Av 3 course à la carte £24 ◐: Brakspear ◖: Brakspear Bitter, Brakspear Special, Hook Norton Mild and Brewers selections. ♀: 14
FACILITIES: Garden: BBQ, outdoor eating, fenced garden Dogs allowed **NOTES:** Parking 20

WENDOVER
Map 05 SP80

Red Lion Hotel ♀
High St HP22 6DU ☎ 01296 622266 📠 01296 625077
e-mail: redlionhotel@wizardinns.co.uk
A 17th-century coaching inn located in the heart of the Chilterns, popular with regulars and providing a welcome break for cyclists and walkers. One menu is served throughout offering the likes of grilled fillet of sea bass with lime, ginger and coriander marinade on linguine pasta, seared barracuda supreme, or slow cooked shoulder of lamb with cheddar mash and redcurrant, rosemary and red wine gravy.
OPEN: 10-11 (Sun 10-10.30) **BAR MEALS:** L served all week 12-9.30 D served all week Av main course £7.50 **RESTAURANT:** L served all week 12-2 D served all week 5-9.30 Av 3 course à la carte £19
◐: ◖: Courage Spitfire, Red Lion, plus guest ales.
FACILITIES: Garden: Food served outside **NOTES:** Parking 60

WEST WYCOMBE
Map 05 SU89

Pick of the Pubs

The George and Dragon Hotel ♀
High St HP14 3AB ☎ 01494 464414 📠 01494 462432
e-mail: enq@george-and-dragon.co.uk
web: www.george-and-dragon.co.uk
Dir: *On A40, close to M40*

Built on the site of a 14th-century hostelry, this 18th-century former coaching inn in a National Trust village has welcomed generations of visitors. Indeed, some from a bygone era are rumoured still to haunt its corridors - notably Sukie, a beautiful servant girl with ideas above her station, who met her fate at the hands of three spurned locals. The hotel is reached through a cobbled archway and comprises a delightful jumble of whitewashed, timber-framed buildings. The range of real ales is excellent, and the eclectic menu draws influences from all over the globe. Varied and freshly-prepared dishes include spinach timbale; sea bass with rösti; mushroom Stroganoff; lamb tagine; tandoori chicken; and a range of grills. A lengthy dessert list covers all the classics. Visitors to the area will enjoy exploring West Wycombe Caves, and the stately houses at Cliveden and Hughenden Manor. New licensee Sue Ranes, and new owners Enterprise Inns.

continued

continued

OPEN: 11-2.30 (Sat 11-3, 5.30-11) 5.30-11 (Sun 12-3, 6-10.30)
BAR MEALS: L served all week 12-2 D served all week 6-9.30
⏱: Enterprise Inns 🍺: Scottish Courage Courage Best, Wells
Bombardier Premium, Greene King Abbot Ale, Adnams
Broadside. ⚲: 12 **FACILITIES:** Child facs Garden: Large
garden adjacent to car park Dogs allowed Water
NOTES: Parking 35

WHEELEREND COMMON   Map 05 SU89

The Chequers 🐟 ⚲
Bullocks Farm Ln HP14 3NH ☎ 01494 883070
e-mail: thechequers.inn@virgin.net
Dir: 4m N of Marlow
A 17th-century inn located on Wheeler End Common, with
two beer gardens and well-kept landscaped grounds. The
Chequers is known locally for its real ale and freshly
produced food, served in attractive surroundings with low
beams and log fires. The regularly changing menu features
local game and seasonal fish and meat dishes, such as Thai
fish cakes, roast monkfish tail, roast breast of West Wycombe
pheasant and chequered venison.
OPEN: 12-3 5.30-11 (Fri-Sun all day) **BAR MEALS:** L served Mon-
Sat 12-2.30 Sun 12-4 D served Mon-Sat 7-10
RESTAURANT: L served all week 12-2.30 Sun 12-4 D served all week
7-10 ⏱: Fullers 🍺: Fuller's ESB, London Pride, Jack Frost &
Summer Ale, Guest ale. ⚲: 7 **FACILITIES:** Garden: Beer garden,
benches Dogs allowed Water & biscuits **NOTES:** Parking 18

WHITCHURCH   Map 11 SP82

The White Horse Inn ⚲
60 High St HP22 4JS ☎ 01296 641377 🖷 01296 640454
e-mail: whitchurchhorse@aol.com
Dir: A413 4 M N of Aylesbury
In a picturesque village setting, this 16th-century inn boasts an
open fire and a resident ghost. The kitchen uses best local
produce and has a good local reputation. Choose from more
than twenty steak dishes (all Aberdeen Angus), or maybe sea
bass or grilled mackerel.
OPEN: Tues-Sun 12-3 6-11 (Sun 12-4.30) **BAR MEALS:** L served
Tues-Sun 12-2 D served Mon-Sat 7-9 Av main course £7.50
RESTAURANT: L served Tues-Sun 12-2 D served Mon-Sat 7-9
Av 3 course à la carte £15 ⏱: Punch Taverns 🍺: Brakspear Bitter,
Young's Bitter, Batemans Bitter, Adnams Bitter. **FACILITIES:** Garden:
Patio, food served outside Dogs allowed Water **NOTES:** Parking 20

WHITELEAF   Map 05 SP80

Red Lion
Upper Icknield Way HP27 0LL ☎ 01844 344476 🖷 01844 273124
e-mail: tim_hibbert@hotmail.co.uk
Dir: A4010 thru Princes Risbro', then right into The Holloway, at T-junct
turn right, pub on left
Family-owned 17th-century inn in the heart of the Chilterns,
surrounded by National Trust land and situated close to the
Ridgeway national trail. Plenty of good local walks with
wonderful views. A cosy fire in winter and a secluded summer
beer garden add to the appeal. Hearty pub fare includes
prawn marie-rose, rib-eye steak, sausage and mash,
vegetarian lasagne, haddock and chips, warm baguettes and
jacket potatoes.

continued

Red Lion

OPEN: 12-3 5-11 (All day Wkds) **BAR MEALS:** L served all week
12-2 D served Mon-Sat 7-9 Av main course £7.95
RESTAURANT: L served all week 12-2 D served Mon-Sat 7-9
Av 3 course à la carte £12.50 ⏱: Free House 🍺: Brakspear Bitter,
Rebellion, Guinness. **FACILITIES:** Garden: Grass area, benches,
tables, beautiful views Dogs allowed Water provided
NOTES: Parking 10

WOOBURN COMMON   Map 06 SU98

Pick of the Pubs

Chequers Inn ★★ ⊛ ⚲
Kiln Ln HP10 0JQ ☎ 01628 529575 🖷 01628 850124
e-mail: info@chequers-inn.com
web: www.thechequersatwooburncommon.co.uk
Dir: M40 junct 2 through Beaconsfield towards High Wycombe. 1m
left into Broad Ln. Inn 2.5m

Steeped in history, this 17th-century inn is a splendidly
snug spot on a cold winter's night. On a summer's day it's
bright and sunny, and through the leaded windows of the
bedrooms the open countryside looks beautiful. The bar
has a wonderful open fireplace blackened by countless
blazing logs, and quiet corners in which to retreat. Award-
winning classic French and English cuisine makes use of
fresh, usually local, ingredients. For those in a hurry a 45-
minute, three course menu may offer paté, red onion
confit and toast; ratatouille risotto with pesto and
parmesan; and vacherin of fruits with raspberry coulis. In
the palm-decorated restaurant, feast on seared scallops
with spinach, frog leg and bacon tartlet with garlic and
parsley sauce; fillet of roast beef with roast and puréed
parsnips, spinach and green peppercorn sauce; and
marshmallow parfait with berry compote. Outside is a
large garden area with tables and chairs, and a barbecue
in summer.
OPEN: All day **BAR MEALS:** L served all week 12-2.30
D served all week 6.30-9.30 Av main course £8.95

continued

England

WOOBURN COMMON continued

RESTAURANT: L served all week 12-2.30 D served all week 7-9.30 Av 3 course à la carte £25 Av 2 course fixed price £13.95 ⊕: Free House ☕: Ruddles, IPA, Abbot, guest bitter. ♀: 12 **FACILITIES:** Children's licence Large garden with tables & chairs; BBQ in summer Dogs allowed in the garden only **NOTES:** Parking 60 **ROOMS:** 17 bedrooms en suite 1 family room s£72.50 d£77.50

CAMBRIDGESHIRE

BARRINGTON
Map 12 TL34

The Royal Oak ♀
West Green CB2 5RZ ☎ 01223 870791 ▤ 01223 870791
Dir: From Barton off M11 S of Cambridge
One of the oldest thatched pubs in England is this rambling, timbered 13th-century building overlooking what is (coincidentally) the largest village green in England. Yet it is only six miles from Cambridge, three miles from the M11 and a mile from Shepreth Station. A wide range of fish dishes includes scallops, trout, scampi, tuna, swordfish, tiger prawns, squid and other seasonal offerings. Also a carvery on Sunday. **OPEN:** 12-2.30 6-11 (Sun 12-10.30) **BAR MEALS:** L served Mon-Sat 12-2.30 Sun 12-3.30, D served Sun-Thurs 6.30-9 Fri&Sat 6.30-9.30 Av main course £7.50 **RESTAURANT:** L served Mon-Sat 12-2.30 D served Sun-Thurs 6.30-9 Fri&Sat 6.30-9.30 Av 3 course à la carte £22.50 ⊕: Old English Inns ☕: IPA Potton Brewery, Adnams, Everards, Elgoods. ♀: 6 **FACILITIES:** Child facs Garden: village green **NOTES:** Parking 50

BROUGHTON
Map 12 TL27

The Crown NEW ♀
Bridge Rd PE28 3AY ☎ 01487 824428 ▤ 01487 824912
e-mail: simon@thecrownbroughton.co.uk
Dir: Just off A141 between Huntingdon and Warboys, next to church in centre of village
A village consortium bought the pub to save it from closing, painted the walls mustard, tiled the floor and brought in some scrubbed pine tables. Chef/proprietor Simon Cadge now offers a regularly changing menu, supplemented by daily specials and ciabattas at lunchtime. Applying throughout the open-plan bar and dining area, this might typically include Barnsley chop with boulangère potatoes and spinach; and roast red mullet with chicory and artichoke risotto. **OPEN:** 12-3 6-11 (Open all day Sat-Sun Closed: 1-11 Jan) **BAR MEALS:** L served Wed-Sat 12-2 Sun 12-3 D served Wed-Sat 6.30-9 Sun 12-3 Av main course £11 **RESTAURANT:** L served Wed-Sat 12-2 Sun 12-3 D served Wed-Sat 6.30-9 Sun 7-9 Av 3 course à la carte £20 Av 3 course fixed price £13.50 ☕: Adnams Broadside, Elgoods Black Dog, Greene King IPA, City of Cambridge Hobson Choice. ♀: 8 **FACILITIES:** Children's licence Garden: Large open plan garden with patio area Dogs allowed **NOTES:** Parking 25

BYTHORN
Map 12 TL07

Pick of the Pubs

The White Hart
PE28 0QN ☎ 01832 710226 ▤ 01832 710226
e-mail: bennetts.fsnet.co.uk
Dir: 0.5m off A14 (Kettering/Huntingdon rd)

In a peaceful, by-passed village just of the A1/M1 link, the White Hart plays host to the chef/patron's eponymous bistro and restaurant, Bennett's. Though the local pub trade is not ignored, it is in a succession of dining areas that one can expect to find the crowds, drawn by bar meals as well as bistro and restaurant menus that have inspired a good following. In the bistro you might find spicy Thai chicken; wild boar sausages and mash; braised lamb shank; moules mariniere, and escalar in a prawn sauce. From the seasonal restaurant menu the dishes on offer might include pan-fried calves' liver with red onion chutney; duck magret with orange and apple pasta; saddle of venison with Madeira and parsnip purée; and a selection of steaks. Three-course, fixed-price Sunday lunches make the White Hart a favourite with weekend visitors too. **OPEN:** 11-11 (Sun 11-2.30) Closed: 26 Dec, 1 Jan **BAR MEALS:** L served Tue-Sat 11-2 D served Tue-Fri 7-9.30 Sat 7-10 Av main course £8.50 **RESTAURANT:** L served Tue-Sat 12-2 Sun 12-2.30 D served Tue-Sat 7-9.30 ⊕: Free House ☕: Greene King IPA & Abbott Ale. **FACILITIES:** Garden: Dogs allowed in the garden only **NOTES:** Parking 50

CAMBRIDGE
Map 12 TL45

The Anchor ♀
Silver St CB3 9EL ☎ 01223 353554 ▤ 01223 327275
Situated at the end of the medieval lane that borders Queens' College in the heart of the University city, this attractive waterside pub appeals to students and visitors alike. Hard by the bridge over the River Cam, in fine weather the riverside patio is an ideal spot for enjoying one of a range of good ales including guest beers while watching the activities on the water. The more adventurous can hire a punt for a leisurely trip to Grantchester (of Rupert Brooke and Jeffrey Archer fame), and on return sample a choice of hearty meals that includes lasagne, home-made pie, and roast beef. **OPEN:** 11-11 **BAR MEALS:** L served all week 12-3 D served all week Av main course £5.50 ⊕: Whitbread ☕: Flowers Original, Bass, Wadworth 6X, Pedigree. ♀: 12 **FACILITIES:** Children's licence Riverside Patio Dogs allowed

---

Room prices show the minimum double and single rates charged. Room rates in hotels and B&Bs often vary depending on the facilities, so be sure to check prices with the establishment before booking

---

 Principal Beers for sale

Cambridge Blue
85 Gwydir St CB1 2LG ☎ 01223 361382 ▒ 01223 505110
e-mail: c.lloyd13@ntlworld.com
Dir: Town centre
There's a University Boat Race theme to this friendly non-smoking pub. Here you can see the bow of the 1984 boat that hit a barge and sank, as well as pictures and other rowing memorabilia. The garden has a children's Wendy-house and rabbit enclosure. Real ales from small local breweries accompany daily blackboard specials, whilst home-made soup, vegetable chilli and granary bread, and filled jacket potatoes are always on the menu.
OPEN: 12-2.30 5.30-11 (Sat & Sun 12-3, Sun 6-10.30) Dec 25-26 Half day **BAR MEALS:** L served all week 12-2.30 D served all week 6-9.30 ⊜: Free House ◄: Woodforde's Wherry, Hobson's Choice, Adnams, Elgoods Black Dog Mild. **FACILITIES:** Garden: Grass, wooden picnic tables on paving slabs Dogs allowed on lead Water ⊛

Free Press ⌣
Prospect Row CB1 1DU ☎ 01223 368337
e-mail: freepresspub@hotmail.com
Students, academics, locals and visitors rub shoulders in this atmospheric and picturesque back-street pub near the city centre. Non-smoking for over a decade, it has open fires and a beautiful walled garden - but no music, mobile phones or gaming machines. Punters are attracted by first-rate real ales and nourishing home-made food such as chilli with garlic bread; goat's cheese salad; filled toasted ciabattas; venison sausages; and salmon filled with couscous and vegetables.
OPEN: 12-2.30 6-11 Closed: 25-26 Dec, 1 Jan
BAR MEALS: L served all week 12-2 D served Mon-Sat 6-9
⊜: Greene King ◄: Greene King IPA, Abbot Ale, Dark Mild plus Guest ales. ⌣: 10 **FACILITIES:** Garden: Small walled courtyard garden Dogs allowed after food service ⊛

DUXFORD
Map 12 TL44

The John Barleycorn
3 Moorfield Rd CB2 4PP ☎ 01223 832699 ▒ 01223 832699
Dir: Turn off A505 into Duxford
Traditional thatched and beamed English country pub situated close to Cambridge. Originally built as a coaching house in 1660, it was renamed once or twice, until 1858 when the current name was attached. The same menu is served throughout and ranges from a cheese sandwich to tournedos Rossini. Typical dishes are large leg of lamb in mint gravy and chicken breast with garlic and herbs.
OPEN: 11-11 (Sun 12-10.30) **BAR MEALS:** L served all week 12-5 D served all week 5-10 Av main course £8 **RESTAURANT:** L served all week 12-5 D served all week 5-10 Av 3 course à la carte £17.50 ⊜: Greene King ◄: Greene King IPA, Abbot Ale, Old Speckled Hen, Ruddles Best & County. **FACILITIES:** Garden: Large patio area **NOTES:** Parking 40

ELSWORTH
Map 12 TL36

The George & Dragon ⌣
41 Boxworth Rd CB3 8JQ ☎ 01954 267236 ▒ 01954 267080
Dir: SE of A14 between Cambridge & Huntingdon
Set in a pretty village just outside Cambridge, this pub offers a wide range of satisfying food to locals and visitors alike. Expect Mediterranean king prawns; prime Scottish steaks; and fresh cod, haddock or plaice from Lowestoft. For a lighter meal, ploughman's lunches and sandwiches are available: try rump steak in a focaccia sandwich roll. Monday night special menus - pheasant suppers, roast duck feasts and more - offer good value set price meals.

continued

OPEN: 11-3 6-11 (Sun 12-3, 6.30-10.30) **BAR MEALS:** L served all week 12-2 D served Mon-Sat 6.30-9 **RESTAURANT:** L served Mon-Sat 12-2 Sun 12-2.30, D served Mon-Sat 6.30-9.30 Sun 6-9 Av 3 course à la carte £19 ⊜: Free House ◄: Greene King IPA, Ruddles County, Greene King Old Speckled Hen. ⌣: 8
FACILITIES: Garden: Patio area and garden with fountain **NOTES:** Parking 50

ELTISLEY
Map 12 TL25

The Leeds Arms
The Green PE19 6TG ☎ 01480 880283 ▒ 01480 880379
Dir: On A428 between Cambridge & St Neots
Built towards the end of the 18th century and named after a local landowner, the Leeds Arms has been under the same management for 26 years. It is a free house and motel, located opposite the village green, where the cricket team plays in season. Food is offered both in the restaurant and from an extensive bar menu of hot and cold snacks. Steaks are a speciality.
OPEN: 11.30-2.30 6.30-11 (Sun 12-2.30, 7-10.30) Closed: Xmas/New Year week **BAR MEALS:** L served all week 12-2 D served all week 7-9.45 Av main course £8.50 **RESTAURANT:** L served all week 12-2 D served Mon-Sat 7-9.45 Sun 7-9 ⊜: Free House ◄: Greene King IPA, Adnams Broadside, Scottish Courage John Smith's Smooth.
FACILITIES: Garden: Patio, tables, grass area **NOTES:** Parking 30

ELTON
Map 12 TL09

Pick of the Pubs

The Black Horse ⌣
14 Overend PE8 6RU ☎ 01832 280240 ▒ 01832 280875
Dir: Off A605 (Peterborough to Northampton rd)

Although the Black Horse is within easy lunching distance of the Peterborough business park, this is a genuine village inn. Its warm country atmosphere is somewhat at odds with parts of its history: Harry Kirk, the landlord here in the 1950s, was an assistant to Tom and Albert Pierrepoint, Britain's most famous hangmen; Harry's son is now said to haunt the bar. It was also once the village jail, and the building later became a morgue. But today's clientele is very much alive, and its current landlord is having to expand the car park to meet growing demand. The real ales include Everards Tiger and seasonal Nethergate brews, while superb food features bar snacks (lunchtime only) and full à la carte in the restaurant. During the summer a tapas menu is available if ever the kitchen is closed, and there's a traditional set Sunday lunch menu. The delightful one-acre rear garden overlooks Elton's famous church and rolling open countryside.

continued

England

ELTON continued

OPEN: 12 -11 **BAR MEALS:** L served all week 12-2.30
D served Mon-Sat 6-9 Av main course £10.95
RESTAURANT: L served all week 12-2.30 D served Mon-Sat 6-9
☺: Free House ◀: Bass, Everards Tiger, Nethergate, Archers.
♀: 14 **FACILITIES:** Garden: Large garden patio area
overlooking church Dogs allowed in the garden only. Water
provided **NOTES:** Parking 30

ELY   Map 12 TL58

Pick of the Pubs

The Anchor Inn ♦♦♦♦ ◉ ▷◁ ♀
Sutton Gault CB6 2BD ☎ 01353 778537 🖹 01353 776180
e-mail: anchorinnsg@aol.com
web: www.anchor-inn-restaurant.co.uk
Dir: From A14, B1050 to Earith, B1381 to Sutton. Sutton Gault on left
The Anchor was built in 1650 to accommodate Scottish
prisoners of war conscripted by Cromwell to dig drains
for the fens. It has been an inn ever since, now fully
modernised with two spacious en suite bedrooms. The
crime and disease-ridden fens of the 15th century have
themselves blossomed into a fine agricultural landscape.
Nevertheless, the old free house retains much of its
original character, with scrubbed pine tables, gently
undulating floors, gas lighting and log fires. Daily
deliveries of quality produce are reflected in the menus
and, in summer, meals can be enjoyed on the terrace
overlooking the New Bedford River. The same menu is
served throughout, supplemented by daily specials,
including seafood dishes such as baked cod on pease
pudding with creamy mustard sauce. Other options range
through potato gnocchi with roast butternut squash,
rocket and mascarpone; and chargrilled venison haunch
on parsnip purée, braised red cabbage and chocolate jus.
OPEN: 12-3 7-11 (Sat 6.30-11) Closed: Dec 26
BAR MEALS: L served all week 12-2 D served Sun-Fri 7-9 Sat
6.30-9.30 Av main course £12 **RESTAURANT:** L served all
week 12-2 D served Sun-Fri 7-9 Sat 6.30-9.30 Av 3 course à la
carte £25 Av 3 course fixed price £14.50 ☺: Free House
◀: City of Cambridge Hobson's Choice, Boathouse Bitter. ♀: 8
FACILITIES: Child facs Garden: Terrace overlooking the river
NOTES: Parking 16 **ROOMS:** 2 bedrooms en suite
1 family room s£50 d£79.50

FEN DITTON   Map 12 TL46

Pick of the Pubs

Ancient Shepherds ▷◁ ♀
High St CB5 8ST ☎ 01223 293280 🖹 01223 293280
Dir: From A14 take B1047 signed Cambridge/Airport
Named after the ancient order of Shepherders who used
to meet here, this heavily-beamed pub and restaurant
was built originally as three cottages in 1540. The two
bars, a lounge and a dining room all boast inglenook
fireplaces. Located three miles from Cambridge in the
riverside village of Fen Ditton, it provides a welcome
escape for those who like to enjoy their refreshments
without the addition of music, darts or pool. Among the
fish dishes on the menu are fillet of sea bass on a bed of
creamed leaks and home-made fishcakes. Meat eaters are

equally well catered for with, among other items, half a
casseroled guinea fowl in Burgundy with roast vegetables,
Barnsley lamb chops, and pork loin steaks in cream and
mustard sauce to choose from.
OPEN: 12-3 6-11 (Fri-Sat 12-3, 6.30-11, Sun 12-5) Closed: 25-26
Dec **BAR MEALS:** L served all week 12-2 D served Mon-Sat
Av main course £12.50 **RESTAURANT:** L served all week 12-2
D served Mon-Sat 6.30-9 Av 3 course à la carte £22.50
☺: Pubmaster ◀: Adnams Bitter, Greene King IPA. ♀: 8
FACILITIES: Garden: Lawned shady garden, garden furniture
Dogs allowed Water, Fireplace **NOTES:** Parking 18

FENSTANTON   Map 12 TL36

King William IV ♀
High St PE28 9JF ☎ 01480 462467 🖹 01480 468526
e-mail: kingwilliam@thefen.fsnet.co.uk
Dir: Off A14 between Cambridge & Huntingdon (J27)
This rambling old inn stands adjacent to the clock tower in the
heart of the village. Originally three 17th-century cottages, the
building now boasts low beams, a lively bar and the aptly-
named Garden Room. The varied lunchtime, evening and à la
carte menus range from bar snacks and traditional Sunday
roasts to imaginative contemporary dishes. Expect venison
steak on sautéed potatoes; mushroom Tatin with bean
cassoulet; and roasted cod, houmous and pea guacamole.
OPEN: 11-11 (Sun 12-10.30) **BAR MEALS:** L served all week
12-2.15 Sun 12-3.30 D served Mon-Sat 6.30-9.45 Av main course
£5.80 **RESTAURANT:** L served all week 12-2 Sun 12-3.30 D served
Mon-Sat 7-9.45 Av 3 course à la carte £21 ☺: Greene King
◀: Greene King Abbot Ale & IPA, Guest Ales. ♀: 9
FACILITIES: Child facs Patio area Dogs allowed Water
NOTES: Parking 14

FORDHAM   Map 12 TL67

White Pheasant ▷◁ ♀
CB7 5LQ ☎ 01638 720414
e-mail: whitepheasant@whitepheasant.com
Dir: From Newmarket, A142 to Ely, approx 5 miles to Fordham Village. On
left as you enter Fordham
Named after a protected white pheasant killed by a previous
landlord, this white-painted, 17th-century free house is set in
a Fenland village between Newmarket and Ely. Rug-strewn
wooden floors, tartan fabrics, soft lighting and scrubbed,
candlelit tables characterise the interior. Food ranges from
sandwiches and salads to a restaurant carte. Samples from
the specials board may include pan-fried Atlantic halibut with
Thai curried mussels, pan-fried Orkney king scallops with
beetroot tartar, or beef stroganoff with wild rice.
OPEN: 12-3 6-11 (Sun 7-10.30) Closed: 25-30, 1 Jan
BAR MEALS: L served all week 12-2.30 D served all week Av main
course £7.50 **RESTAURANT:** L served all week 12-2.30 D served all
week 6-9.30 Sun 7-9 Av 3 course à la carte £25 ☺: Free House
◀: Woodforde's Nelson's Revenge, Norfolk Nog, Admirals Reserve,
Wherry. ♀: 14 **FACILITIES:** Child facs Garden: Pleasant area, child
friendly Dogs allowed Water bowls **NOTES:** Parking 30

Website addresses are included where available.
The AA cannot be held responsible for the
content of any of these websites

---

continued

England

FOWLMERE   Map 12 TL44

Pick of the Pubs

The Chequers ♀

High St SG8 7SR ☎ 01763 208369 ▤ 01763 208944
Dir: From M11 onto A505, 2nd right to Fowlmere
There's a strong sense of history at this bustling free
house. William Thrist renovated the building in 1675, and
you can still see his initials over the main door. Samuel
Pepys stayed here in 1660 and, in its time, the inn has
also served as a chapel of rest. But the pub's sign reflects
the more recent past, with blue and red chequers
honouring the British and American squadrons that were
based at Fowlmere during World War II. Today the
Chequers is known for its imaginative cooking served
formally in the smart, galleried restaurant or in the more
relaxed surroundings of the bar or attractive garden. The
extensive seasonal menu includes grilled Dover sole;
poached duck breast in sea salt and ginger; and Italian
aubergine parmigiana with potato and mixed leaf salad.
Leave room for pan-fried russet apples with sugar and
Calvados; or hot date sponge with sticky toffee sauce.
OPEN: 12-2.30 6-11.30 Closed: 25 Dec **BAR MEALS:** L served all
week 12-2 D served Mon-Sat 7-10 Sun 12-2
RESTAURANT: L served all week 12-2 D served Mon-Sat 7-10 Sun
7-9.30 ⊜: Free House ◖: Black Sheep Special, Fuller's ESB, Hook
Norton Old Hooky, Oakhams JHB. ♀: 10 **FACILITIES:** Garden:
Grass, borders, flowers & plants **NOTES:** Parking 30

GODMANCHESTER   Map 12 TL27

The Black Bull Coaching Inn ◆◆◆◆ ♀

32 Post St PE29 2AQ ☎ 01480 453310 ▤ 01480 435623
Dir: Off A1198 S of Huntington
Five minutes' walk from the Great Ouse River, this 17th-century
inn sports beams and a large inglenook fireplace. Examples of
fish main courses include sea bass, baked sardines, monkfish
and poached salmon. Steak and ale pie and chips, braised
knuckle of lamb, tournedos Rossini and baked leek and stilton
crêpes provide a meat and vegetarian balance.
OPEN: 12-11 **BAR MEALS:** L served all week 12-2.30 D served all
week 6-9 Av main course £10 **RESTAURANT:** L served all week
12-2.30 D served all week 6-9.30 ◖: Black Bull, Old Speckled Hen,
Hobsons Choice, Bombadier. **FACILITIES:** Garden: Patio area Dogs
allowed in the garden only **NOTES:** Parking 30
ROOMS: 8 bedrooms en suite s£69 d£70 No children overnight

GOREFIELD   Map 12 TF41

Woodmans Cottage

90 High Rd PE13 4NB ☎ 01945 870669 ▤ 01945 870631
e-mail: magtuck@aol.com
Dir: 3m NW of Wisbech
Popular pub run by a hard-working brother and sister team.
Their efforts have paid off, and Woodmans Cottage remains a
successful local with well-kept beers and a good choice of
locally-sourced food. Established favourites include seafood
platter, Chinese rack of ribs, lamb and mushroom with red
wine, minty lamb shank, nut roast, the mega mix grill, and
Cajun chicken. There is also an award-winning sweet trolley.
OPEN: 11-2.30 7-11 Closed: 25 Dec **BAR MEALS:** L served all
week 12-2 D served all week 7-10 Av main course £7.50
RESTAURANT: L served all week 12-2 D served all week 7-10
Av 3 course à la carte £22.50 ⊜: Free House ◖: Greene King IPA &
Abbot Ale, Interbrew Worthington Bitter. **FACILITIES:** Child facs
Garden: walled patio area **NOTES:** Parking 40

GRANTCHESTER   Map 12 TL45

The Green Man ♀

High St, Grantchester CB3 9NF ☎ 01223 841178 ▤ 01223 847940
A delightful old pub retaining many original features,
including low ceiling beams (beware!). In winter roaring log
fires burn in the re-opened fireplaces, and in summer
customers can sit out in the restored gardens. Real ales,
lagers and fresh coffees are served, plus a list of wines
available by the glass. The menu is augmented by frequently
changing blackboard specials. Bubble and squeak, home-
made curry, Thai fishcakes, and lamb in Dijon mustard are
typical of the range. The village cemetery contains a WWI
memorial that includes poet Rupert Brooke.
OPEN: 11.30-3 5.30-11 (Sun 12-3, Summer all day)
BAR MEALS: L served all week 12-2.30 D served all week 6-9 Food
all day in summer Av main course £8 ⊜: Punch Taverns
◖: Adnams Bitter, Broadside, Greene King IPA.
FACILITIES: Garden: Patio, food served outside **NOTES:** Parking 10

GREAT CHISHILL   Map 12 TL43

The Pheasant ▷◁ ♀

24 Heydon Rd SG8 8SR ☎ 01763 838535
Dir: Off B1039 between Royston & Saffron Walden
Stunning views and roaring log fires characterise this traditional
village free house, where Nethergates' and Greene King ales
easily outsell lager. There are no gaming machines or piped
music to disturb the friendly, sociable bar; and, in summer,
bird song holds sway in the idyllic pub garden. Freshly-made
sandwiches come complete with chips and salad garnish, whilst
home-made dishes like rabbit casserole, poached haddock, or
wild mushroom lasagne cater for larger appetites.
OPEN: 12-3 6-11 (Sat 12-12, Sun 12-10.30) **BAR MEALS:** L served
all week 12-2 D served all week 6-9.30 Av main course £10
RESTAURANT: L served all week 12-2 D served all week 6-9.30
Av 3 course à la carte £20 ⊜: Old English Inns ◖: Nethergates IPA
& Umbel Ale, Greene King IPA. **FACILITIES:** Garden: English country
garden, mature trees Dogs allowed **NOTES:** Parking 20

HEMINGFORD GREY   Map 12 TL27

The Cock Pub and Restaurant NEW ♀

47 High St PE28 9BJ
Dir: 2m S of Huntingdon and 1m E of A14
There's been a spring in the step of this village pub since
Oliver Thain and Richard Bradley arrived some five years ago.
Transforming it into an award-winning dining pub, they've
retained traditional values, with well kept real ales, log fires
blazing when the weather demands, and a welcome for
walkers and dogs. In the wooden-floored restaurant fresh fish
including pan-fried halibut fillets, and chef's various home-
made sausages, may prove irresistible.
OPEN: 11.30-3 6-11.30 **RESTAURANT:** L served all week 12-2.30
D served Mon-Sat 6.45-9.30 Sun 6.30-8.30 Av 3 course à la carte
£22.95 Av 3 course fixed price £17.95 ◖: Woodfordes Wherry,
Elgoods Black Dog Mild, Golden Jackal, Wolf Brewery. ♀: 11
FACILITIES: Children's licence Spacious garden patio area with
seating Dogs allowed **NOTES:** Parking 30

HEYDON   Map 12 TL43

The King William IV ♀

SG8 8PN ☎ 01763 838773 ▤ 01763 837179
Dir: A505
A 16th-century countryside inn with an old world interior. It
has beams and an inglenook fireplace, and is full of antiques

continued

England

HEYDON continued

and farming implements, with unusual oak tables suspended from the ceiling by chains. A good range of freshly prepared food is available with a particular emphasis on vegetarian dishes. On the menu there may be grilled swordfish steak with avocado and mango salad, confit leg of duck marinated in Rioja and oriental spices or spinach and spring onion cakes with Dijon mustard cream sauce.
OPEN: 12-2.30 6.30-11 Closed: 25-26 Dec Jan 1
BAR MEALS: L served all week 12-2 D served all week 6.30-10 Av main course £9.50 ☺: Free House ☜: IPA Greene King, Adnams, Abbot Ale, Fullers London Pride. **FACILITIES:** Garden: Food served outside Dogs allowed in the garden only
NOTES: Parking 50

HILDERSHAM   Map 12 TL54

The Pear Tree
CB1 6BU ☎ 01223 891680 ▤ 01223 891970
e-mail: di_jamieson@yahoo.co.uk
Dir: Just off A1307
Overlooking the village green, this small pub retains its traditional atmosphere with oak beams and a stone floor. Popular with walkers and locals alike, it has a widespread, well-deserved reputation for food. Daily specials might include Cumberland sausage, oven-baked whole fresh trout, almond and asparagus terrine, and chicken breast fillet. To follow, expect treacle tart, fruit crumble, Bakewell tart, and bread and butter pudding.
OPEN: 11.45-2 6.30-11 (Sun 12-2, 7-10.30) **BAR MEALS:** L served all week 12-2 D served all week 6.30-9.30 Av main course £6.95 ☺: Greene King ☜: Greene King IPA & Abbot Ale.
FACILITIES: Country garden, flowerbeds and lawn
NOTES: Parking 6

HILTON   Map 12 TL26

The Prince of Wales ♦♦♦♦ ♈
Potton Rd PE28 9NG ☎ 01480 830257 ▤ 01480 830257
e-mail: Princeofwales.hilton@talk21.com
Dir: On B1040 between A14 and A428 S of St Ives
The Prince of Wales is a traditional, 1830s-built, two-bar village inn with four comfortable bedrooms. Food options range from bar snacks to full meals, among which are grills, fish, curries brought in from a local Indian restaurant, and daily specials, such as lamb hotpot. Home-made puddings include crème brûlée and sherry trifle. The village's 400-year-old grass maze was where locals used to escape the devil.
OPEN: 11-2.30 6-11 (Sat 12-3, 7-11 Sun 12-3, 7-10.30) Winter Closed Lunch Mon-Thurs **BAR MEALS:** L served Fri-Sun 12-2 D served all week 7-9 Av main course £7.50 ☺: Free House ☜: Adnams, Timothy Taylor Landlord, Smoothflow, Worthingtons. ♈: 9
FACILITIES: Children's licence Garden: Patio with tables and chairs
NOTES: Parking 9 **ROOMS:** 4 bedrooms en suite s£50 d£70 No children overnight

HINXTON   Map 12 TL44

The Red Lion
High St CB10 1QY ☎ 01799 530601 ▤ 01799 531201
e-mail: info@redlionhinxton.co.uk
Dir: 1m from M11 junct 9. 2m from M11 junct 10
16th-century, Grade II listed inn at the centre of the conservation village of Hinxton, with a sympathetically designed extension from the mid-1990s. The bar and informal dining area are in the original building, while the more formal

continued

restaurant area is in the extension. Fresh local produce forms the basis of the menus, which cover poached haddock fillet, confit of duck leg on champ potato, and steak and ale pie in the restaurant; jacket potatoes, oven-baked baguettes or sandwiches in the bar.
OPEN: 11-3 6-11 (Sun 12-4.30, 7-10.30) **BAR MEALS:** L served Mon-Sat 12-2 Sun 12-2.30 D served Sun-Thurs 6.45-9 Fri-Sat 6.45-9.30 Av main course £9 **RESTAURANT:** L served Mon-Sat 12-2 Sun 12-2.30 D served Sun-Thurs 6.45-9 Fri-Sat 6.45-9.30 Av 3 course à la carte £19 ☺: Free House ☜: Adnams, Greene King IPA, Woodforde's Wherry, plus guest ales including Nethergates & Ridleys.
FACILITIES: Garden: Terrace with seating, lawns with benches
NOTES: Parking 40

HOLYWELL   Map 12 TL37

The Old Ferryboat Inn ♈
PE27 4TG ☎ 01480 463227 ▤ 01480 463245
e-mail: 8638@greeneking.co.uk
Dir: A14 then right onto A1096 then A1123 right to Holywell
Renowned as England's oldest inn, built some time in the 11th century, but with a hostelry history that goes back to the 6th, the Old Ferryboat has immaculately maintained thatch, white stone walls, and cosy interior. A pleasant atmosphere - despite the resident ghost of a lovelorn teenager - in which to enjoy hot chicken curry, roast rack of lamb, steak and ale pie, fish and chips, and Greene King ales.
OPEN: 11.30-11 **BAR MEALS:** L served all week 12-2.30 D served Mon-Sat 6-9.30 Sun 12-8.30 Av main course £8.95 ☺: Greene King ☜: Greene King Abbot Ale/IPA, Old Speckled Hen. ♈: 6
FACILITIES: Child facs Garden: Food served outside. River views Dogs allowed in the garden only. Water **NOTES:** Parking 100

HUNTINGDON   Map 12 TL27

Pick of the Pubs

The Old Bridge Hotel ★★★ ⊛⊛ ♈
1 High St PE29 3TQ ☎ 01480 424300 ▤ 01480 411017
e-mail: oldbridge@huntsbridge.co.uk
web: www.huntsbridge.com
Dir: Signed from A1 & A14
Owned by the Huntsbridge partnership of chefs, who manage four dining pubs in and around Huntingdon, Oliver Cromwell's home town. Ivy covers every square centimetre of the handsome 18th-century façade, windows and porch excepted, of course. Décor throughout acknowledges its original character, from the panelled dining room and main lounge with their fine fabrics, quality prints and comfortable chairs, to the 24 individually styled bedrooms. Walls in the more informal Terrace dining area are all hand-painted, one particular work having taken over four months to complete. Starters might include tuna carpaccio; and home-made black pudding with mashed potato, caramelised pear and red wine sauce. To follow, daily fresh fish from Cornwall; roast Bleesdale pheasant breast with braised red cabbage; and lightly seared salmon with saffron and coriander salsa. Lighter dishes include seranno ham with piquillo peppers; Cotswold pork sausages with mashed potato; and deep-fried fish and chips with pease pudding. Everything is home made.
OPEN: 11-11 (Sun 12-10.30) **BAR MEALS:** L served all week 12-2.30 D served all week 6.30-10.30 **RESTAURANT:** L served all week 12-2.30 D served all week 6.30-10.30 Av 3 course à la carte £25 Av 2 course fixed price £12.50 ☺: ☜: Adnams Best, Hobsons Choice, Bateman XXXB. ♈: 15 **FACILITIES:** Child facs Garden: Drinks served only **NOTES:** Parking 60
ROOMS: 24 bedrooms en suite 1 family room s£95 d£125

England

The Three Horseshoes NEW ♦♦♦ ♀
Moat Ln, Abbots Ripton PE28 2PA
☎ 01487 773440 ▤ 01487 773440 e-mail: abbotsripton@aol.com
After a six-year redevelopment programme, the picturesque
Three Horseshoes has reopened under new management.
The thatched and colour-washed free house retains many
original features, and now boasts five elegant en-suite
bedrooms. You'll find hand pumped Adnams real ales and
traditional snacks in the bar, and a 54-seater non-smoking
restaurant offering fine dining in a relaxed, contemporary
atmosphere. Expect seared swordfish with crushed new
potatoes; duckling with stir-fry noodles and vegetables; and
cherry tomato risotto.
OPEN: 11.30-3 6-11 **BAR MEALS:** L served Tues-Sat 12-2 Sun
12-2.30 D served Tues-Sat 6.30-9.30 Av main course £8
RESTAURANT: L served Tues-Sat 12-2 D served Tues-Sat 6.30-9.30
Av 3 course à la carte £25 Av 3 course fixed price £15 ◀: Adnams
Bitter, Adnams Broadside. ♀: 12 **FACILITIES:** Garden: Large garden
at rear, pond and seats at front **NOTES:** Parking 100
ROOMS: 5 bedrooms en suite 1 family room s£55 d£70

KEYSTON   Map 11 TL07

Pick of the Pubs

The Pheasant Inn ⊛ ♀
Village Loop Rd PE28 0RE ☎ 01832 710241 ▤ 01832 710340
e-mail: pheasant.keyson@btopenworld.com
web: www.huntsbridge.com
Dir: Signed from A14, W of Huntingdon

The Pheasant is a 15th-century, thatched free house in a
sleepy farming village, and belongs to a small group of
chef-managed dining pubs in the
Huntingdon/Peterborough area. The large bar is a
traditional and unspoilt mixture of oak beams, big open
fires and simple wooden furniture, while the three distinct
dining areas are comfortable, intimate and relaxed. The
food is Anglo-Italian, veering towards simple rather than
fussy, with monthly changing menus making good use of
seasonal ingredients in both traditional and modern ways.
Typical are pappardelle pasta with pesto, toasted pine
nuts and parmesan; breast of Goosnargh duck with truffle
honey, turnip gratin, savoy cabbage, stuffed with confit
duck and vanilla sauce; and pistachio, pear and almond
pudding, with pistachio ice cream and cardamom and
orange syrup. Three Suffolk real ales and a widely
acclaimed wine list.
OPEN: 12-2 6-11 (Sun eve, 7-8.45) **BAR MEALS:** L served all
week 12-2 D served all week 6.30-9.30 **RESTAURANT:** L served
all week 12-2 D served all week 6.30-9.30 Av 3 course à la carte
£25 ⊜: Huntsbridge ◀: Adnams, Village Bike Potton Brewery,
Augustinian Nethergate Brewery. ♀: 26 **FACILITIES:** Child facs
Tables outside front of pub **NOTES:** Parking 40

KIMBOLTON   Map 12 TL16

The New Sun Inn ♀
20-22 High St PE28 0HA ☎ 01480 860052 ▤ 01480 869353
e-mail: newsuninn@btinternet.com
Dir: A1 N, B645 for 7m, A1 S B661 for 7m, A14 B660 for 5m
An impressive array of flowers greets visitors to this 16th-
century inn near Kimbolton Castle. As well as being a real ale
pub, it offers a good choice of wines by the glass. Dishes from
the restaurant menu include king prawns in hot garlic and
ginger oil, or whole baked camembert to start, then venison
sausages with grain mustard mash or home-made steak and
kidney pudding as mains. Lighter meals, such as jacket
potatoes or sandwiches are also available.
OPEN: 11-2.30 6-11 (All day Sun) **BAR MEALS:** L served all week
12-2.15 D served Tue-Sat 7-9.30 **RESTAURANT:** L served Tue-Sun
12-2 D served Tue-Sat 7-9.30 ⊜: Charles Wells ◀: Wells
Bombardier & Eagle IPA, Greene King Old Speckled Hen. ♀: 12
FACILITIES: Garden: Patio Dogs allowed

MADINGLEY   Map 12 TL36

Pick of the Pubs

The Three Horseshoes ⊛ ♀
High St CB3 8AB ☎ 01954 210221 ▤ 01954 212043
e-mail: thethreehorseshoes@huntsbridge.co.uk
web: www.huntsbridge.com
Dir: M11 junct 13. 1.5m from A14

The Three Horseshoes is a picturesque thatched inn with a
bustling bar and a pretty conservatory-restaurant. Outside,
the garden extends towards the local cricket pitch and,
inside, apart from locals, there's a mixed crowd of
business people and visitors from nearby Cambridge. It's
best to ring and book at weekends. Owner/chef Richard
Stokes is a local from the Fens. He offers imaginative
dishes with lots of flavour and a certain amount of Italian
flair. Starters include pea and mint soup, and carpaccio of
beef with rocket and horseradish crème fraîche. The
Italian influence extends to the wine list and to main
courses like double-baked spinach & ricotta torte,
chargrilled Cumbrian rump steak with grilled Italian
vegetable salad, or pizzetta of red onions, plum tomatoes
and smoked mozzarella. Puddings could include cherries
marinated in Valpolicella and vanilla or malt milk ice
cream.
OPEN: 11.30-3.30 6-11 (Sun eve 6-8.30 except Oct-Apr)
BAR MEALS: L served all week 12-2 D served Mon-Sat
6.30-9.30 Av main course £12 **RESTAURANT:** L served all
week 12-2 D served Mon-Sat 6.30-9.30 ⊜: Huntsbridge Inns
◀: Adnams Bitter, Hook Norton Old Hooky, Smile's Best, Guest
Beers. ♀: 20 **FACILITIES:** Garden: Large garden, seating for 50
NOTES: Parking 70

England

MILTON
Map 12 TL46

Waggon & Horses
39 High St CB4 6DF ☎ 01223 860313
e-mail: winningtons.waggon@ntlworld.com
Dir: A14/A10 junct. Past Tesco, through village, approx 1m set back on left
Imposing mock-Tudor roadhouse set back from the village street, noted for its unusual large collection of hats inside as well as a good selection of draught beers. Expect home-made chilli and curry among a long list of main courses that might include traditional Cornish pasty, haddock and chips, nut roast, and Cajun bean stew. For something lighter there is a range of doorstep sandwiches, jacket potatoes and baguettes.
OPEN: 12-2.30 5-11 (Sat-Sun 12-3 Sat 6-11, Sun 7-10.30)
BAR MEALS: L served all week 12-2 D served all week 7-9 Av main course £5 **RESTAURANT:** L served all week 12-2 D served all week 7-9 **◖:** Elgoods Cambridge Bitter, Elgoods Black Dog Mild, Elgoods Pageant, Elgoods Seasonal Ales. **FACILITIES:** Large garden with swings, slide, pétanque, benches Dogs allowed on a lead
NOTES: Parking 8

NEWTON
Map 12 TL44

The Queen's Head ♑
CB2 5PG ☎ 01223 870436
Dir: 6m S of Cambridge on B1368, 1.5m off A10 at Harston
This quintessentially English pub, dating back to 1680 (though the cellar is much older), has been run by the same family since 1962. No fruit machines or piped music interrupt the lively conversation in the two small bars. Hot lunches are limited to home-made soup, Aga-baked potatoes with cheese and butter, and toast with beef dripping, plus a dozen varieties of cut-to-order sandwiches. Evening meals consist of soup and cold platters. Ales dispensed direct from the barrel.
OPEN: 11.30-2.30 6-11 (Sun 12-2.30, 7-10.30) Closed: 25 Dec
BAR MEALS: L served all week 11.30-2.15 D served all week 7-9.30 Sun 7-9.30 Av main course £3 **◉:** Free House **◖:** Adnams Southwold, Broadside, Fisherman, Bitter & Regatta. **♑:** 8
FACILITIES: Food/drink served on village green Dogs allowed Water **NOTES:** Parking 15

PETERBOROUGH
Map 12 TL19

The Brewery Tap
80 Westgate PE1 2AA ☎ 01733 358500 ▤ 01733 310022
e-mail: brewerytap@hotmail.com
Dir: Opposite to Peterborough bus station
Visitors to this unusual American-style pub can view the operations of the large Oakham micro-brewery through a glass wall. The vast space of the pub was once a labour exchange. There is always a minimum of ten real ales available at any time. The Tap has a capacity of over 500, specialises in real Thai food, and runs a night-club.
OPEN: 12-11 (Fri-Sat 12-1.30am, Sun 12-10.30) Closed: Dec 25-26, Jan 1 **BAR MEALS:** L served all week 12-2.30 D served all week 6-9.30 (Open all day Fri-Sat 12-1.30am) Av main course £6
RESTAURANT: L served all week 12-2.30 D served all week 6-9.30 (Fri-Sat 12-1.30am) Av 3 course à la carte £15 Av fixed price £10.15 **◉:** Free House **◖:** Oakham, Jeffery Hudson Bitter, Bishops Farewell & White Dwarf, Interbrew Bass. **FACILITIES:** Dogs allowed Water

All AA rated accommodation can also be found on the AA's internet site
www.theAA.com

Charters Bar & East Restaurant
Town Bridge PE1 1FP ☎ 01733 315700 315702 For Bookings ▤ 01733 315700
e-mail: manager@charters-bar.fsnet.co.uk
Dir: A1/A47 Wisbech, 2m for city centre & town bridge (River Nene). Barge is moored at Town Bridge
Charters is a 176ft long barge which was sailed over from Holland in 1991 and moored right in the heart of the city, on the River Nene. The East part of the name applies to the upper deck, which is an oriental restaurant with dishes from Vietnam, Japan, Thailand, Malaysia and elsewhere. Twelve hand pumps dispense a continually changing repertoire of real ales, and a good selection of foreign beers is always available. Friday and Saturday nights are a treat for blues lovers, with a late night live blues club.
OPEN: 12-11.30 Mon-Thu (12-late Fri-Sat) Closed: 25-26 Dec, 1 Jan
BAR MEALS: L served all week 12-2.30 **RESTAURANT:** L served all week 12-2.30 D served all week 6-10.30 Sun 6-10 Av 3 course à la carte £17 **◉:** Free House **◖:** Oakham JHB, Oakham White Dwarf & Bishops Farewell, Hop Back Summer Lightning, Interbrew Draught Bass. **FACILITIES:** Garden: Large beer garden on riverside Dogs allowed **NOTES:** Parking 15

SPALDWICK
Map 12 TL17

The George Inn NEW ▷ ♑
High St PE28 0TD ☎ 01480 890293 ▤ 01480 896847
Dir: 6m W of Huntingdon on A14, j 18 towards Spaldwick/Stow Longa
Originally a large private residence, the George was opened as an inn in 1679 by Frances and Robert King. The master bedroom still features preserved Heurician wall paintings, while original beams and fireplaces remain intact. Traditional British and Mediterranean influenced dishes from an extensive menu include roast lamb chump with panhegerty potatoes; and chargrilled yellow fin tuna loin with Parmesan crackling drizzled with pesto. A good choice of wines is available by the glass.
OPEN: 11-11 Sun 12-10.30 **BAR MEALS:** L served Mon-Sat 12-2.30 Sun 12-2.30 D served Mon-Sat 6-9.30 Sun 6-9
RESTAURANT: L served Mon-Sat 12-2.30 Sun 12-2.30 D served Mon-Sat 6-9.30 Sun 6-9 Av 3 course à la carte £20 **◖:** Adnams Broadside, London Pride, Old Peculiar. **♑:** 20
FACILITIES: Children's licence Garden: Small beer gardens to front and rear **NOTES:** Parking 25

STILTON
Map 12 TL18

Pick of the Pubs

The Bell Inn ★★★ ◉
Great North Rd PE7 3RA ☎ 01733 241066 ▤ 01733 245173
e-mail: reception@thebellstilton.co.uk
web: www.thebellstilton.co.uk
Dir: From A1 follow signs for Stilton, hotel is situated on the main road in the centre of the village.
Dating back to 1500, though it might be even older, the Bell is known as the birthplace of Stilton. Located just off the A1, it is also associated with famous highwaymen, most notably Dick Turpin who sought shelter here while being pursued by the law. Significant restoration work took place in 1990, with plans astonishingly similar to those drawn up in 1736. In more recent times Clark Gable and Joe Louis visited the Bell when they were with the American Air Force stationed nearby. Beamed ceilings, a stone floor and open fires imbue the Village bar with great character, enhanced by

continued

real ales and an extensive menu. Expect roast Norfolk turkey, braised lamb rump, and roasted cod fillet in the bar and bistro, while the restaurant offers the likes of rolled fillet of rainbow trout, chargrilled fillet of beef, and seared long stem artichokes among other choices.

The Bell Inn

OPEN: 12-2.30 6-11 (Sun 12-3, 7-10.30) Closed: Dec 25 **BAR MEALS:** L served Mon-Sat 12-2 Sun 12-2.30 D served Mon-Sat 6.30-9.30 Sun 7-9 Av main course £8 **RESTAURANT:** L served Sun-Fri 12-2 D served all week 7-9.30 Av 3 course à la carte £10.50 Av 3 course fixed price £25.05 🍴: Free House 🍺: Greene King Abbot Ale, Oakham JHB, Interbrew Boddingtons, Fullers London Pride. **FACILITIES:** Garden: Stone courtyard, food served outside **NOTES:** Parking 30 **ROOMS:** 23 bedrooms en suite 2 family rooms s£75.50 d£99.50 No children overnight

STRETHAM   Map 12 TL57

The Lazy Otter 🍴 ♀
Cambridge Rd CB6 3LU ☎ 01353 649780 🖹 01353 649314 *Dir:* Telephone for directions
With its large beer garden and riverside restaurant overlooking the marina, the Lazy Otter lies just off the A10 between Ely and Cambridge. The pub's location beside the Great Ouse river makes it popular in summer. Typical dishes include jumbo cod, lemon sole topped with crab meat, or fisherman's medley, as well as a selection of steaks and grills. **OPEN:** 11-11 **BAR MEALS:** L served Mon-Sat 12-2.30 Sun 12-4 D served all week 6-9.30 Av main course £7.50 **RESTAURANT:** L served Mon-Sat 12-2.30 Sun 12-4 D served all week 6-9.30 Av 3 course à la carte £15 🍺: Marston's Pedigree, Wadsworth 6X, Interbrew Flowers IPA, Scottish Courage John Smith's & Courage Best. ♀: 8 **FACILITIES:** Child facs Garden: Large beer garden along river front **NOTES:** Parking 50

THRIPLOW   Map 12 TL44

The Green Man
Lower St SG8 7RJ ☎ 01763 208855
e-mail: greenmanthriplow@ntlworld.com
Dir: 1m W of junct 10 on M11
A rejuvenated early 19th-century pub standing at the heart of a quaint rural village famous for its annual daffodil weekend and pig race. It offers fixed-price menus and guest ales that change regularly. Typical evening dishes include braised shoulder of lamb and foie gras, and roast duck breast, while the lunchtime choice might include goats' cheese and roast pepper cannelloni. Picnic tables in the large landscaped garden for al fresco meals.

continued

The Green Man
OPEN: 12-2.30 6-11 **BAR MEALS:** L served Tue-Sat 12-2.30 Sun 12-3 D served Tue-Sat 7-9.30 **RESTAURANT:** Lunch served 12-2.30 D served Tue-Sat 7-9.30 🍴: Free House 🍺: Eccleshall Slaters Original, Hop Back Summer Lightning, Batemans XXXB, Milton Klas Act. **FACILITIES:** Garden: Patio **NOTES:** Parking 12

CHESHIRE

ALDFORD   Map 15 SJ45

Pick of the Pubs

The Grosvenor Arms ♀
Chester Rd CH3 6HJ ☎ 01244 620228 🖹 01244 620247
e-mail: grosvenor.arms@brunningandprice.co.uk
Dir: On B5130 S of Chester
A rather austere Victorian building, the pub was the venue for meetings of the Royal Lord Belgrave Lodge of Oddfellows in the 1860s, when it was the Talbot Inn. Nobody knows when or why the name changed, but in its more recent history it was shut up, musty and unloved, until rescued by the current owners in 1992. These days the pub has a spacious, open-plan interior including an airy conservatory, a panelled, book-filled library, and a suntrap terrace. Decent wines (including 16 by the glass) accompany the bistro-style food, and there's a huge selection of malts, bourbons and real ales. The menu ranges from sandwiches and starters of black pudding and kidney skewer or pan-fried squid, to mains like steaks; and butternut squash and lemongrass risotto; or grilled whole sea bass with Savoy cabbage and crispy fried potato. Children welcome until 6pm, but no prams or pushchairs. **OPEN:** 11-11 (Sun 12-10.30) **BAR MEALS:** L served all week 12-10 D served all week 12-10 Sun 12-9 🍴: Free House 🍺: Interbrew Flowers IPA, Westwood-Eastgate, Robinson's Best, Caledonian Deuchars IPA. ♀: 16 **FACILITIES:** Garden: Large terrace, ample seating, walled garden Dogs allowed Water bowls **NOTES:** Parking 150

ASTON   Map 15 SJ64

Pick of the Pubs

The Bhurtpore Inn 🍴 ♀
Wrenbury Rd CW5 8DQ ☎ 01270 780917
e-mail: simonbhurtpore@yahoo.co.uk
See Pick of the Pubs on page 64

The Bhurtpore Inn

An intriguing name for a pub usually means a colourful history – and so it does here. The Bhurtpore takes its unusual name from a city in northern India where a local landowner, Lord Combermere, was involved in a fierce battle in 1825.

The present owners' family had run the pub back in the 19th century, and in 1991 they reclaimed their piece of history by buying it back and turning it into a lively and comfortable village free house. The pub now offers freshly prepared food, together with an exceptional range of Highland malts and real ales from small independent craft brewers. Five imported draught beers are supported by over 150 bottled beers, including one of the largest ranges of Belgian ales in Britain. Expect no less from the award winning food. Starters could include black pudding slices in a coarse grain mustard and apple sauce; baked potato shells with bacon and melted cheese; and smoked chicken, bacon and parmesan flakes on mixed salad. Mains might be along the lines of lamb shoulder braised in a mint and sherry gravy; grilled duck breast in a damson and Belgian ale sauce; pork fillet slices in an apple and cider sauce; sea bass fillets sautéed with spring onion, ginger and coriander on a lime and coconut sauce; cod fillet baked with mozzarella and cherry tomatoes and basil; chicken breast in a stilton and smoked bacon sauce; a selection of curries and balties including chicken, lamb, vegetarian and sometimes beef or pork are also available.

OPEN: 12-2.30 6.30-11 (Sun 12-10.30) Closed: Dec 25-26, 1 Jan
BAR MEALS: L served all week 12-2 D served all week 6.45-9.30 (Sun 12-9) Av main course £9
RESTAURANT: L served all week 12-2 D served all week 6.45-9.30 (Sun 12-9) Av 3 course à la carte £16.50
🍺: Free House
🍻: Salopian Golden Thread, Abbeydale Absolution, Weetwood Oasthouse Gold, Copper Dragon Golden Pippin. ♀: 9
FACILITIES: Garden: Lawned area behind pub with countryside views Dogs allowed Water
NOTES: Parking 40

Map 15 SJ64
Wrenbury Rd CW5 8DQ
☎ 01270 780917
✉ simonbhurtpore@yahoo.co.uk
Dir: Between Nantwich & Whitchurch just off the A530

England

AUDLEM
Map 15 SJ64

The Shroppie Fly
The Wharf CW3 0DX ☎ 01270 811772 🖹 01270 811334
e-mail: grmagnum@aol.com
Dir: Jct 16 M6, A500, then A529
Originally built as a canal warehouse for the Shropshire Union Canal, this interesting building was converted to a pub in 1974. The name comes from the salvaged horse-drawn barge that now serves as the bar and is a major feature. The main menu includes broccoli and cream cheese bake, mixed grill, Goan chicken curry, spinach and ricotta cannelloni, and a selection of sandwiches and ploughman's. There is a separate specials board offering some 20 or 30 extra dishes.
OPEN: 11-11 (Sun 12-10.30) **BAR MEALS:** L served all week 12-2.30 D served all week 6-9 Av main course £6 🍴: Interbrew Boddingtons Bitter, Flowers Original, Old Speckled Hen.
FACILITIES: Garden: Food served outdoors Dogs allowed
NOTES: Parking 60

BARTHOMLEY
Map 15 SJ75

The White Lion Inn
CW2 5PG ☎ 01270 882242 🖹 01270 873348
Dating from 1614, this half-timbered and thatched inn with character bars is in a lovely rural setting, and has associations with the English Civil War. It offers bar food including exotic open sandwiches (hot sirloin and stilton; blue stilton and redcurrant sauce) and ploughman's. More substantial dishes include chicken fajitas; fresh salmon with a choice of sauce; and local roast ham and pineapple. Strictly no chips!
OPEN: 11.30-11 (Thurs 5-11, Sun 12-10.30) **BAR MEALS:** L served Fri-Wed 12-2 (Sun 12-2.30) Av main course £5 🍴: Burtonwood 🍴: Burtonwood Bitter, Top Hat & Guest ales, Marstons Pedigree.
FACILITIES: Garden: Paved courtyard with tables Dogs allowed on leads, not in bar during lunch **NOTES:** Parking 20

BOLLINGTON
Map 16 SJ97

The Church House Inn 🏩 ☿
Church St SK10 5PY ☎ 01625 574014
Dir: From A34 take A538 towards Macclesfield. Through Prestbury, then follow Bollington signs
There's a homely feel to this stone-built village free house with its beams, log fires and agricultural decorations. The pub also features a small enclosed beer garden. The varied menu ranges from lunchtime baguettes, burgers and jacket potatoes to main dishes like Barnsley lamb chop with red wine and cranberry sauce; and salmon fillet with cream and dill sauce. Vegetarian options feature on the daily specials board.
OPEN: 12-3 5.30-11 (Fri-Sun open all day) **BAR MEALS:** L served all week 12-2 D served all week 6.30-9.30 Av main course £6.50
RESTAURANT: L served all week 12-2.30 D served all week 6-9.30 (Fri-Sun open all day) Av 3 course à la carte £12.50 🍴: Free House 🍴: Greene King IPA, Timothy Taylor Landlord, Stella, Interbrew Boddington's. ☿: 12 **FACILITIES:** Child facs Children's licence Garden: 4 tables, enclosed on 2 sides **NOTES:** Parking 4

> Not all of the pubs in the guide are open all week or all day. It's always best to check before you travel

BROXTON
Map 15 SJ45

The Copper Mine
Nantwich Rd CH3 9JH ☎ 01829 782293
Dir: A41 from Chester, L at rdbt onto A534, pub 0.5m on R
Convenient for Cheshire Ice Cream Farm, the 14th-century Beeston Castle, and the Candle Factory at Cheshire Workshops, this pub has a conservatory with fine views of the surrounding countryside. Favourite dishes include halibut with mustard rarebit, sea bass with smoked oysters, crispy roasted duck with orange liqueur sauce, and a whole rack of honey-glazed pork ribs. Patio and lawn with mature trees.
OPEN: 12-3 6-11 (Sun 12-10.30) **BAR MEALS:** L served Tues-Sun 12-2.30 D served Tues-Sun 6.30-9.30 Av main course £6.95
RESTAURANT: L served Tues-Sun 12-2.30 D served Tues-Sun 6.30-9.30 Av 3 course à la carte £13 🍴: Free House 🍴: Worthington Cream Flow, Pedigree & Banks Real Ale.
FACILITIES: Child facs Garden: Large patio area with flower gardens & lawns **NOTES:** Parking 80

BUNBURY
Map 15 SJ55

Pick of the Pubs

The Dysart Arms ☿
Bowes Gate Rd CW6 9PH ☎ 01829 260183 🖹 01829 261286
e-mail: dysart.arms@brunningandprice.co.uk
Dir: Between A49 & A51, by Shropshire Union Canal, opposite church
Named after local landowners the Earls of Dysart, this Grade II-listed pub dates back to the mid-18th century, when it was built as a farmhouse. At some point in the 19th century it then started selling ales, taking over as village pub. The interior is full of antique furniture, old prints, scattered bookshelves and open fires, all in airy rooms set around a central bar. Home-grown herbs are used in an enticing menu served throughout the pub. Begin with grilled goat's cheese on garlic foccacia and grape chutney; or parma ham and fresh fig salad with toasted pine nuts. Follow with something from the wide range of main courses like fillets of trout on sauté potatoes; Moroccan style lamb stew; pasta linguine with roast butternut squash and shitake mushrooms; grilled chicken and pepper kebabs with turmeric rice; and Mediterranean vegetable casserole. To finish in style try apple and almond tart with raspberry coulis; walnut and date sponge; or chocolate Amaretti truffle torte.
OPEN: 11.30-11 (Sun 12-10.30) **BAR MEALS:** L served all week 12 D served Mon-Fri 6-9.30 Sat 12-9.30, Sun 12-9 Av main course £10.95 🍴: Free House 🍴: Phoenix Struggling Monkey, Weetwood Eastgate, Thwaites Bitter, Caledonian Deuchars IPA.
☿: 14 **FACILITIES:** Garden: Great views of church & hills Dogs allowed in bar only; water **NOTES:** Parking 30

BURWARDSLEY
Map 15 SJ55

Pick of the Pubs

The Pheasant Inn ☿
CH3 9PF ☎ 01829 770434 🖹 01829 771097
e-mail: info@thepheasantinn.co.uk
web: www.thepheasantinn.co.uk
See Pick of the Pubs on page 66

Pick of the Pubs

The Pheasant Inn

A delightful 300-year-old, half-timbered, former farmhouse in beautiful rural surroundings, from whose terrace you can gaze back across the broad expanse of the Cheshire plains, and pick out local landmarks.

During the winter it's probably best to stay inside for cosy meals and drinks at one of the tables standing on polished wooden floorboards, or just grouped around one of the brick pillars, warmed by open fires - reputedly it has the largest log fire in the county. There's also a stone-flagged conservatory and flower-filled courtyard. From the new owner's menu you could begin with sizzling monkfish and tiger prawns in sweet chilli jam with toasted pesto dipping bread; or tender chicken satay. Main courses include chilli (or three-bean for vegetarians) with tortilla chips, jalapeno peppers, glazed with cheese and sour cream; chicken Caesar salad with poached egg; pan-fried fillet of beef with sauté potatoes, green beans and cherry tomatoes in red wine sauce; classic bangers and mash with onion gravy; and salmon and prawn fishcakes with lemon mayonnaise and tomato and spring onion salad. For dessert, try warmed waffle with honeycomb ice cream and chocolate sauce, or syrup pudding with creamy custard. From the light bites section of the menu you can order Morecambe Bay shrimps sautéed in garlic butter on Cheshire cheese rarebit; Bury black pudding and new potato salad with poached egg and mustard seed dressing; and crispy duck with hoi sin sauce in a tomato wrap. The wine list has bins from Alsace to Valdepeñas, with several reds and whites by the glass. Beers include Weetwood Old Dog from Tarporley.

OPEN: 11-11
BAR MEALS: L served all week
D served all week Av main course £9
RESTAURANT: L served all week
D served all week
⊕: Free House
▤: Weetwood Old Dog, Eastgate, Best, Hoegarden and guest Bitter.
♀: 8
FACILITIES: Child facs Children's licence Garden: Ten tables, views of the Cheshire Plains
NOTES: Parking 40

★★ ⊛ ♀   Map 15 SJ55
CH3 9PF
☎ 01829 770434
▤ 01829 771097
ⓔ info@thepheasantinn.co.uk
ⓦ www.thepheasantinn.co.uk
Dir: From Chester A41 to Whitchurch, after 4m left to Burwardsley. Follow signs 'Cheshire Workshops'

CHESTER Map 15 SJ46

Albion Inn
Park St CH1 1RN ☎ 01244 340345
e-mail: mike@albioninn.freeserve.co.uk
web: www.albioninnchester.co.uk
Dir: *In Chester City centre adjacent to Citywalls and Newgate overlooking the River Dee*
The home fires still burn on winter nights at this living memorial to the 1914-18 war. It is a traditional Victorian street corner pub, with a splendid cast-iron fireplace, enamelled advertisements and World War I memorabilia adding to the period atmosphere. Trench rations range from the 'Great British Buttie' to lamb's liver, smoked bacon and onions in rich cider gravy, or Staffordshire oatcakes with a cheese and broccoli filling. Home-made puddings are offered from the specials board. The new pub cat is called Kitchener!
OPEN: 11.30-3 5-11 (Sat 11.30-3 6-11, Sun 12-2.30 7-10.30) Closed: 26 Dec-2 Jan **BAR MEALS:** L served all week 12-2 D served all week 5-8 (Under review call to confirm) Av main course £7.25 ⊕: Punch Taverns ◖: Timothy Taylor Landlord, Jennings Cumberland, Banks Mild, Westons Old Rose Cider. **FACILITIES:** Dogs allowed Water/cold sausage **NOTES:** No credit cards

Old Harkers Arms ♀
1 Russell St CH1 5AL ☎ 01244 344525 ▤ 01244 344812
e-mail: harkers.arms@brunningandprice.co.uk
Dir: *Follow steps down from City Road on to canal path*
One of Chester's more unusual pubs: a Victorian former warehouse on the canal. The new owner describes his pub as "a typical London-style boozer - in Chester". It's light and relaxing, with comfy leather seating, high windows, lofty ceilings and a bar created from salvaged doors. A range of guest beers is offered in addition to the regulars, as well as over 150 whiskies. Food is available all day.
OPEN: 11.30-11 Closed: Dec 25 **BAR MEALS:** L served all week 11.30 D served all week Sat-Sun 12-9.30 Av main course £7.95 ⊕: ◖: Cains IPA, Weetwood Best, Oakham JHB, Pheonix IPA. ♀: 12

CHOLMONDELEY Map 15 SJ55

Pick of the Pubs

The Cholmondeley Arms ♦♦♦ ⌐◇ ♀
SY14 8HN ☎ 01829 720300 ▤ 01829 720123
e-mail: guy@cholmondeleyarms.co.uk
See Pick of the Pubs on page 68

CHURCH MINSHULL Map 15 SJ66

The Badger Inn ♀
Over Rd CW5 6DY ☎ 01270 522607 ▤ 01270 522607
Originally known as the Brookes Arms, this 15th-century inn later changed its name to the Badger Inn and became a coach stop on the route between Nantwich and Middlewich. The badger was part of the Brookes' family crest and has been used as the inn sign for many years. The menu here concentrates on steak dishes, as well as grills and curries. Baguettes, bar snacks, burgers and breakfast also available.
OPEN: 12-11 **BAR MEALS:** L served all week 12-9
RESTAURANT: L served all week 12-9 Av 3 course à la carte £18 ◖: Mansfield Bitters. ♀: 8 **FACILITIES:** Garden: Beer garden with benches, umbrellas Dogs allowed Water bowls provided **NOTES:** Parking 30

CONGLETON Map 16 SJ86

The Plough ⌐◇ ♀
Macclesfield Rd, Eaton CW12 2NH
☎ 01260 280207 ▤ 01260 298458
e-mail: theploughinn@hotmail.co.uk
Dir: *On A536 (Congleton to Macclesfield road)*

Like a giant jigsaw puzzle, an ancient Welsh barn was transported here in hundreds of pieces to become a marvellously atmospheric restaurant adjoining this Elizabethan inn. From the specials menu come poached fresh salmon and prawn salad; chicken Madras with rice; and lamb Henry with mash. The carte offers lightly grilled turbot with lemon butter, and fillet steak cooked at the table. Apple crumble and custard is a typical dessert.
OPEN: 11-11 (Sun 12-10.30) Closed: Dec 25 Dec 26 Open evening only **BAR MEALS:** L served all week 12-2.30 D served Mon-Sat 5.30-9.30 Sun 12-8.30 Av main course £8.95
RESTAURANT: L served all week 12-2.30 D served Mon-Sat 6-9.30 Sun 12-8.30 ⊕: Free House ◖: Boddingtons, Hydes, Moore Houses, Storm Brew. ♀: 8 **FACILITIES:** Garden: Secret garden **NOTES:** Parking 58

HANDLEY Map 15 SJ45

The Calveley Arms ♀
Whitchurch Rd CH3 9DT ☎ 01829 770619 ▤ 01829 770619
Dir: *5m S of Chester, signed from A41*
First licensed in 1636, this coaching inn has plenty of old world charm, with beamed ceilings, open fires, and a choice of classic pub games including cribbage, dominoes and boules. The wide ranging menu includes speciality salads (try salmon Caesar or Cheshire cheese) and mains sandwiches. Fresh fish and game feature on the main menu and specials board, with options such as Creole crab cakes; Breton chicken; and whole baked trout St Clements.
OPEN: 12-3 6-11 (Sun eve 7-10.30) Closed: 25 Dec (eve)
BAR MEALS: L served all week 12-2.15 D served all week 6-9.30
RESTAURANT: Lunch served Mon-Sat 12-2.15 Sun 12-2.30 D served Mon-Sat 6-9.30 Sun 7-9.30 ⊕: Enterprise Inns ◖: Interbrew Boddingtons Bitter & Bass, Castle Eden Ale, Wadworth 6X, Marston's Pedigree. **FACILITIES:** Garden: Seating and tables, boules court Dogs allowed Water **NOTES:** Parking 20

Do you have a favourite pub that we have overlooked? Please use the Reader's Report form at the back of this guide to tell us all about it

Pick of the Pubs

CHOLMONDELEY – CHESHIRE

The Cholmondeley Arms

Still recognisable as the village school it used to be until it closed in 1982, The Cholmondeley Arms took on its new persona six years later when the current owners, with the help of Lord and Lady Cholmondeley, who live in the nearby castle, converted it into an elegant country pub.

The development cheered up the locals no end as, almost 100 years earlier, an earlier Marquess of Cholmondeley, a passionate teetotaller, had closed all the licensed premises on the 25,000-acre estate. Since reopening it has won many regional and even national awards in recognition of the way (and here we quote the owners) "this quintessential English pub" is run. It's the kind of place one could eat in several times a week without getting bored, and without breaking the bank. All food is freshly prepared, wherever possible using local produce. From its always-available set menu come fish, chips and mushy peas; steaks; stuffed pancakes; and, at lunchtimes only, devilled kidneys on toast. Among

the house specials are starters of home-made soups; hot baked prawns in sour cream and garlic; and chicken liver and Grand Marnier pâté with Cumberland jelly; while usually appearing in the main courses section are grilled fillet of sea bass with butter and herbs; quenelles of salmon with lobster mornay sauce; hot Madras beef curry with rice and chutney; and four seasons salad, prawns, egg, crispy bacon and croutons. Home-made puddings are a speciality: chocolate roulade, black cherry pavlova, hot fudge bananas, ice creams and sorbets. Children are made especially welcome. Across the original playground is the secluded School House, providing guest accommodation in fully equipped en suite bedrooms.

OPEN: 11-3 7-11 Closed: 25 Dec
BAR MEALS: L served all week
12-2.30 D served all week 7-10
Av main course £9
RESTAURANT: L served all week
12-2.30 D served all week 7-10
Av 3 course à la carte £20
🍽: Free House
🍺: Marston's Pedigree, Adnams Bitter, Banks's, Everards Tiger Best.
♀: 7
FACILITIES: Child facs Garden: Large lawns Dogs allowed
NOTES: Parking 60
ROOMS: 6 bedrooms en suite
1 family room s£50 d£65

♦♦♦ 🐟 ♀   Map 15 SJ55
SY14 8HN
☎ 01829 720300
📠 01829 720123
📧 guy@cholmondeleyarms.co.uk
Dir: On A49, between Whitchurch & Tarporley

England

KNUTSFORD
Map 15 SJ77

Pick of the Pubs

The Dog Inn ◆◆◆◆
Well Bank Ln, Over Peover WA16 8UP
☎ 01625 861421 📠 01625 864800
e-mail: info@doginn-overpeover.co.uk
Dir: S from Knutsford take A50. Turn onto Stocks lane at 'The Whipping Stocks' pub and continue for 2m
The Dog Inn in Over Peover (pronounced Peever) was originally a row of cottages, built in 1804 as a grocer's shop and later a shoemaker's and a small farmstead. It was not until 1860 that it became a beer house. The traditional timbered building is located in the heart of the Cheshire countryside between Knutsford and Holmes Chapel, and in summer it is bedecked with dazzling flowerbeds, tubs and hanging baskets. A wide use of fresh local produce - and guest ales from local micro-breweries - attracts a faithful following for its interesting cooking. The menu offers chef's specials, and main dishes like gourmet sausage of the day; chilli con carne; steak and kidney pie; and curry of the day. There's also an à la carte menu for more substantial meals, where you can choose between haddock and prawn au gratin; salmon fillet; battered cod; smoked salmon and prawn pancake; and sea bass with fennel and lemon butter sauce.
OPEN: 11.30-3 4.30-11 (Sun 11-11) **BAR MEALS:** L served all week 12-2.30 D served Mon-Sat 6-9 Sun 12-8.30 Av main course £10.95 **RESTAURANT:** L served all week 12-2.30 D served Mon-Sat 6-9 Sun 12-8.30 🍺: Free House 🍸: Hydes Traditional Bitter, Weetwood Best, Skipton Brewery, Moorhouses.
FACILITIES: Garden: Large patio, food served outside Dogs allowed **NOTES:** Parking 100 **ROOMS:** 6 bedrooms en suite s£55 d£75 No children overnight

LANGLEY
Map 16 SJ97

Leathers Smithy
Clarke Ln SK11 0NE ☎ 01260 252313 📠 01260 252313
e-mail: leatherssmithy@supanet.com

Splendidly located pub overlooking the Ridgegate Reservoir and Macclesfield Forest with a country park at the rear, offering what the landlord describes as 'the most beautiful views in Cheshire'. The name commemorates William Leather, a 19th century licensee, and the building's previous role as a village forge. Food options range from light bites and salads to chicken Caribbean, penne Italian, plaice in breadcrumbs, Smithy pork fillet, and Leathers farmhouse grill.
OPEN: 12-3 7-11 **BAR MEALS:** L served all week 12-2 D served all week 7-10 **RESTAURANT:** L served all week 12-2 D served all week 7-10 🍸: Theakstons Best, Bombadier, Old Speckled Hen & Guest cask ale. **FACILITIES:** Garden: Dogs allowed in the garden only **NOTES:** Parking 25

LOWER WHITLEY
Map 15 SJ67

Chetwode Arms 🍷
St Lane WA4 4EN ☎ 01925 730203 e-mail: gfidler6@aol.co.uk
Dir: Chetwode Arms on A49 2m S of junct 10 M56, 6m S of Warrington
A 400-year-old former coaching inn, situated in a small country village. It has one of the best crown green bowling greens in the country, and is the focal point of the village - a best-kept village award winner. Freshly cooked food is prepared from produce supplied by small local businesses, and is offered alongside a comprehensive wine list and a selection of lagers and real ales. Typical menu includes medley of butcher's sausage, Chetwode chicken curry, fish casserole, and pork and sage burger.
OPEN: 12-11 **BAR MEALS:** L served all week 12-3 D served all week 6-9 **RESTAURANT:** L served all week 12-3 D served all week 6-9 🍺: Inn Partnership 🍸: Greenalls Bitter, Cains Bitter, Marston's Pedigree. 🍷: 12 **FACILITIES:** Garden: Patio overlooking bowling green Dogs allowed **NOTES:** Parking 60

MACCLESFIELD
Map 16 SJ97

The Windmill Inn 🍷
Holehouse Ln, Whitely Green, Adlington SK10 5SJ
☎ 01625 574222 e-mail: thewindmill@dsl.pipex.com
Dir: 100yds from Macclesfield Canal
The Windmill, which has recently changed hands, is a beamed former farmhouse set in lovely Cheshire countryside. It is located close to the Macclesfield Canal and some fantastic walks, including the Middlewood Way. The lunch choice extends from a snack to a three-course meal, and in the evening you might choose market fresh fish or pot roast saddle of rabbit, with side orders of chunky chips, roast Mediterranean vegetables or courgette fritters.
OPEN: 12-3 5-11 (Summer and weekend all day)
BAR MEALS: L served all week 12-2.30 D served Mon-Fri 6-9 Sat-Sun 12-9.30 Av main course £12.95 **RESTAURANT:** L served all week 12-2.30 D served Mon-Fri 6-9 Sat-Sun 12-9.30 Av 3 course à la carte £25 🍺: 🍸: Timothy Taylor Landlord, Black Sheep, Old Speckled Hen. **FACILITIES:** Child facs Garden: Dogs allowed Water **NOTES:** Parking 60

MARBURY
Map 15 SJ54

The Swan Inn 🍷
SY13 4LS ☎ 01948 662220 📠 01948 663715
A country inn with a friendly atmosphere and a reputation locally for good food. Sitting amidst Tudor houses overlooking a small mere, it boasts a large rural beer garden, and plenty of good walks, as well as cycle and bridle paths. Snacks or full meals are served, including giant hot dog and chips, roast rack of lamb, beer-battered salmon, prawns and cod with chips, monkfish with oriental stir-fry, and sea bass with mushroom risotto. Recent change of ownership.
OPEN: 11-2.30 7-11 (Open all day wknds) Closed: Dec 25 **BAR MEALS:** L served Tue-Sun 12-2.30 D served Tue-Sun 7-9.30 Av main course £7 **RESTAURANT:** L served Tue-Sun 12-2.30 D served Tue-Sun 7-9 Av 3 course à la carte £16.99 🍸: Tetley Smooth, Adnams, Flowers IPA. **FACILITIES:** Garden: Food served outside. Beer garden Dogs allowed Water provided **NOTES:** Parking 40

 Pubs with this logo do not allow smoking anywhere on their premises

MOULDSWORTH — Map 15 SJ57

The Goshawk ♀
Station Rd CH3 8AJ ☎ 01928 740900 ▤ 01928 740965
Two miles from Delamere forest, this relaxed country pub has recently been refurbished with both the décor and the food coming under serious review. The menu now reflects an English/French bistro style - confit duck leg or king prawns with monkfish being typical starters, and guinea fowl breast with diane sauce, or pot roast pork representative of the mains. Fish is ubiquitous too, with eight dishes available from bouillabaisse to lobster thermidor. The decked area at the back overlooks a crown bowling green.
OPEN: 12-11 Closed: Xmas & New Years day
BAR MEALS: L served all week all day D served all week Sun to 9 Av main course £10 **RESTAURANT:** L served all week D served all week Av 3 course à la carte £17 **◀:** Timothy Taylors Landlord, Bombadier, Greene King IPA, Black Sheep. **♀:** 14
FACILITIES: Garden: decking overlooking crown bowling green
NOTES: Parking 50

NANTWICH — Map 15 SJ65

The Thatch Inn 🐟 ♀
Wrexham Rd, Faddiley CW5 8JE
☎ 01270 524223 ▤ 01270 524674 e-mail: thethatchinn@aol.com
Dir: Follow signs for Wrexham from Nantwich, inn is 4m from Nantwich

The black-and-white Thatch Inn is believed to be the oldest as well as one of the prettiest pubs in south Cheshire. It has a three quarter acre garden, and inside you'll find oak beams, and open fires in winter. The menu is divided between options from the grill; traditional favourites (pies, roasts and casseroles); tastes from afar (nachos, lasagne, curry); and fish, summer salads, light bites and a children's menu. Speciality coffees are a feature.
OPEN: 11-11 Sun 12-10.30 **BAR MEALS:** L served Mon-Sat 11-9.30 Sun 12-9.30 D Mon-Sat 11-9.30 Sun 12-9.30 Av main course £7.95 **RESTAURANT:** L served all week 12-9.30 D served all week 12-9.30 **⊕:** Free House **◀:** Marston Pedigree, Timothy Taylor Landlord, Wheetwoods, Archers. **♀:** 24 **FACILITIES:** Child facs Landscaped garden with seating Dogs allowed Water **NOTES:** Parking 60

PENKETH — Map 15 SJ58

The Ferry Tavern ♀
Station Rd WA5 2UJ ☎ 01925 791117 ▤ 01925 791116
e-mail: ferrytavern@aol.com
Dir: A57, A562, Fiddler's Ferry signed
Set on its own island between the Mersey and the St Helen's canal, this 12th-century ale house has been an inn since 1762, and welcomes walkers and cyclists from the trans-Pennine Way. Beneath the low beams in the stone-flagged bar you'll
continued

find a range of unusual guest beers and over 300 different whiskies, including 60 Irish. No food available.

The Ferry Tavern

OPEN: 12-3 5.30-11 Sat 12-11, Sun 12-10.30 **⊕:** Free House **◀:** Scottish Courage Courage Directors, Interbrew Boddingtons Bitter & Old Speckled Hen. **♀:** 10 **FACILITIES:** Garden: Dogs allowed Water, Toys **NOTES:** Parking 46

PLUMLEY — Map 15 SJ77

The Golden Pheasant Hotel ♀
Plumley Moor Rd WA16 9RX ☎ 01565 722261 ▤ 01565 722125
Dir: From M6 junct 19, take A556 signed Chester. 2m turn left at signs for Plumley/Peover. Through Plumley, after 1m pub opposite rail station.
In the heart of rural Cheshire, the hotel has a large restaurant, bar area, public bar, children's play area and bowling green. The menu offers substantial choice, from bar snacks such as nachos or panninis, to a more elaborate restaurant menu, including pork medallions in apricot and tarragon reduction. Real ales are pulled from the attractive handpumps installed by J.W. Lees, one of the country's few remaining independent family breweries with its own cooperage.
OPEN: 11-11 (Sun 12-10.30) **BAR MEALS:** L served all week 12-2.30 D served Mon-Fri 6-9.30 Sat 12-9.30, Sun 12-8.30 Av main course £6.95 **RESTAURANT:** L served all week 12-2.30 D served Mon-Fri 6-9.30 Sat 12-9.30, Sun 12-8.30 Av 3 course à la carte £20 Av 2 course fixed price £12.95 **⊕:** J W Lees **◀:** J W Lees Bitter, GB Mild & Moonraker. **♀:** 15 **FACILITIES:** Child facs Children's licence Garden: Seating front and back of pub Dogs allowed Water **NOTES:** Parking 80

The Smoker 🐟 ♀
WA16 0TY ☎ 01565 722338 ▤ 01565 722093
e-mail: smoker@plumley.fsword.co.uk
Dir: From M6 junct 19 take A556 W. Pub is 1.75m on left
A 400-year-old thatched coaching inn named after a horse rather than the tobacco consumption of its regulars. The Smoker was an 18th-century white charger, bred for racing by the Prince Regent. The inn's wood-panelled interior provides a traditional atmosphere, with beams, log fires and horse brasses. A good choice of food is offered from a full menu of starters, light bites, main courses and blackboard specials, with options from bruschetta to Kashmiri lamb.
OPEN: 11-3 6-11 (all day Sun) **BAR MEALS:** L served all week 11.30-2.30 D served Mon-Sat 6.30-9.30 Sun 12-9 Av main course £8.25 **RESTAURANT:** L served all week 11.30-2.30 D served Mon-Sat 6.30-9.30 Sun 12-9 Av 3 course à la carte £15 **⊕:** **◀:** Robinson's Best & Hatters Mild,Double Hop, Old Stockport. **♀:** 10 **FACILITIES:** Child facs Garden: Large lawned area, 15 large dining benches **NOTES:** Parking 100

PRESTBURY   Map 16 SJ87   SWETTENHAM   Map 15 SJ86

Pick of the Pubs

The Legh Arms & Black Boy Restaurant ♉
SK10 4DG ☎ 01625 829130 ▤ 01625 827833
Dir: *From M6 through Knutsford to Macclesfield, turn to Prestbury at Broken Cross. Pub in village centre*

The Legh Arms is of Tudor origin and was originally a black and white building made from wattle and daub. However, it was considerably rebuilt in 1602 and added to in 1627. Its most famous guest was Bonnie Prince Charlie who stayed here en route to Derby during the ill-fated 1745 rebellion. Today it is a very smart country pub with a large suntrap garden, with the original well still in place. In the restaurant, seated beneath the inn's original oak beams, guests can choose from an extensive menu which often features herbs from the inn's own garden. For more informal eating, the bar menu features a range of light bites and sandwiches. Starters could include omelette Arnold Bennet with lobster; Japanese sushi; or the Legh Arms fish broth and grilled pear with parma ham and mozzarella salad. Among the mains might be roast local pheasant, lobster Thermidor, or the Legh Arms beef Wellington, and there's a separate vegetarian range.
OPEN: 12-11 **BAR MEALS:** L served all week 12-2 D served Mon-Sat 7-10 Sun 12-10 Av main course £7.50
RESTAURANT: L served all week 12-2 D served all week 7-10 Please phone for details Av 3 course à la carte £27.50 Av 3 course fixed price £14.95 🍺: Frederic Robinson 🍺: Robinsons Bitter, Hatters Mild. ♉: 8 **FACILITIES:** Large suntrap garden with well **NOTES:** Parking 40

SHOCKLACH   Map 15 SJ44

Bull Inn Country Bistro NEW
Worthenbury Rd SY14 7BL ☎ 01829 250239 & 771084
e-mail: jaw@fsbdial.co.uk
Built in 1850, this welcoming pub has maintained many original features, including exposed beams and a cosy log fire. The menus are extensive, with plenty of variations on the house specialities of pies, grills and fish: beef and ale pie perhaps; or a poached fillet of sea bass. Other options include pan-fried pork fillet with black pudding; and broccoli and vegetable pancake. There is also a children's menu.
OPEN: 12-3 6.30-11 **BAR MEALS:** L served Wed-Sun 12-2.30 D served Tues-Sun 6.30-9 **RESTAURANT:** L served Wed-Sat 12-2.30 Sun 12-2.30 D served Tues-Sun 6.30-9 Sun 7-9 🍺: Mansfield Cask, Pedigree, Guinness. **FACILITIES:** Children's licence
NOTES: Parking 30

Pick of the Pubs

The Swettenham Arms ♉
Swettenham Ln CW12 2LF ☎ 01477 571284 ▤ 01477 571284
e-mail: info@swettenhamarms.co.uk
web: www.swettenhamarms.co.uk
Dir: *M6 junct 18 to Holmes Chapel, then A535 towards Jodrell Bank. In 3m right (Forty Acre Lane) to Swettenham*

A charming, 16th-century free house, originally a nunnery and once linked to the 700-year-old church by a tunnel where bodies were stored before burial. Perhaps that's why ghost stories abound, although there's nothing chilling about the large open fireplaces warming the beamed interior. There can be few, if any, mainstream tastes not catered for on the extensive menu, ranging through starters of garlic mushrooms, black pudding roulade, and game terrine, to main courses such as roast leg of local lamb with garlic and rosemary; sirloin steak au poivre; roast half duck with red plum sauce; prawn-filled baked salmon in filo pastry; roast monkfish tail; and vegetable strudel. There are plenty of lighter meals, children's meals and sandwiches too. A lavender and sunflower meadow, created by owners Frances and Jim Cunningham, adjoins the Quinta Arboretum and Nature Reserve, the lifelong project of Jodrell Bank radio astronomer, Sir Bernard Lovell.
OPEN: 12-3 6.30-11 (open all day Sun)
BAR MEALS: L served all week 12-2.30 D served Mon-Sat 7-9.30 Sun 12-9.30 **RESTAURANT:** L served all week 12-2.30 D served all week 7-9.30 Av 3 course à la carte £25 🍺: Free House 🍺: Jennings Bitter, Carlsberg-Tetley Tetley Bitter, Beartown, Hydes & Guest Beers. ♉: 8 **FACILITIES:** Garden: Arboretum and nature reserve, meadow **NOTES:** Parking 150

TARPORLEY   Map 15 SJ56

Alvanley Arms Hotel ♦♦♦♦ ♉
Forest Rd, Cotebrook CW6 9DS
☎ 01829 760200 ▤ 01829 760696
web: www.thealvanleyarms.co.uk
Dir: *On the A49, 1.5m N of Tarporley*
This 400-year-old coaching inn has a strong shire horse theme, with displays of rosettes, pictures, harnesses and horseshoes. Next door is the Cotebrook Shire Horse Centre, owned by the same family. Alongside the cask conditioned ales are freshly prepared dishes based on ingredients from local family businesses. Vegetarians are well catered for, and there's a choice from the general or chef's special menu, from

continued

England

TARPORLEY continued

shoulder of lamb to medallions of monkfish, plus tempting home-made puddings.

The Alvanley Arms

OPEN: 12-3 5.30-11 (Open all day Sun) **BAR MEALS:** L served all week 12-2 D served Mon-Sat 6-9 Sun 12-9 **RESTAURANT:** L served all week 12-2 D served Mon-Sat 6-9 Sun 12-9 ☺: ◖: Robinsons Best & Guest Beers. ♀: 8 **FACILITIES:** Large beer garden, overlooks lake **NOTES:** Parking 75 **ROOMS:** 7 bedrooms en suite s£35 d£75 No children overnight

The Boot Inn ░◇ ♀

Boothsdale, Willington CW6 0NH ☎ 01829 751375
Dir: Off the A54 Kelsall by-pass or off the A51 Chester-Nantwich, follow signs to Willington

Originally a small beer house, now expanded along a charming row of red brick and sandstone cottages, where quarry-tiled floors, old beams and open fires give the interior a character of its own. The pub offers well-kept ales and freshly prepared food. Specials might include braised shoulder of local lamb with root vegetables and red wine; or bass fillets deep-fried in sesame batter, served with a chilli and tomato salsa. There is an excellent range of snacks and vegetarian dishes. **OPEN:** 11-3 6-11 (All day Sat-Sun & BHs) Closed: Dec 25 **BAR MEALS:** L served all week 11-2.30 D served all week 6-9.30 (Sat-Sun & BHs food all day) Av main course £8.50 **RESTAURANT:** L served all week 11-2.30 D served all week 6-9.30 Av 3 course à la carte £25 ☺: Punch Taverns ◖: Weetwood, Timothy Taylor Landlord, Bass, Cains. ♀: 8 **FACILITIES:** Garden: Small, natural suntrap Dogs allowed Water **NOTES:** Parking 60

> Restaurant and Bar Meal times indicate the times
> when food is available. Last orders may be
> approximately 30 minutes before the times stated

The Fox & Barrel ♀

Forest Rd, Cotebrook CW6 9DZ
☎ 01829 760529 📠 01829 760529
e-mail: info@thefoxandbarrel.com web: www.thefoxandbarrel.com
Dir: On the A49 just outside Tarporley, very close to Oulton Park Race Circuit

A landlord here once gave shelter to a fox being pursued by hounds, hiding it in the pub cellar until the pack and huntsmen had gone. He set the fox free the following day, though it isn't clear if the animal was sober! Inside this award-winning pub are wooden floors, old tables and odd chairs and a cosy open fire. Popular favourites on the menu include rump of lamb on a grain mustard mash with bean casserole, Scottish salmon fillet, pan-fried Barbary duck with roasted fruit red wine jus, or broccoli and blue cheese tartlet. Bar snacks, sandwiches and baguettes also available. **OPEN:** 12-3 5.30-11 Closed: 25 Dec **BAR MEALS:** L served all week 12-2.30 D served Mon-Sat 6.30-9.30 Sun 12-10.30 **RESTAURANT:** L served all week 12-2.30 D served Mon-Sat 6.30-9.30 Sun 12-3 6-9 ☺: Pubmaster ◖: Scottish Courage John Smith's, Marston's Pedigree, Draught Bass, Jennings Cumberland Ale. ♀: 15 **FACILITIES:** Garden: Patio, picnic tables **NOTES:** Parking 40

TUSHINGHAM CUM GRINDLEY   Map 15 SJ54

Blue Bell Inn

SY13 4QS ☎ 01948 662172 📠 01948 662172
Dir: On the A41 N of Whitchurch
In what must be a unique tale from the annals of pub-haunting, this 17th-century black and white magpie building that oozes character with its abundance of beams, open fires and horse brasses was once haunted by the spirit of a duck. Believe that or not, the Blue Bell remains a charming characterful pub with well-kept ales. The menu is based on traditional English fare, with specials prepared daily. **OPEN:** 12-3 6-11 (Sun 12-3, 7-11) 25 Dec Closed eve **BAR MEALS:** L served Tues-Sun 12-2 D served Tues-Sun 6-9 Av main course £6.50 **RESTAURANT:** L served Tues-Sun 12-3 D served Tues-Sun 7-9 ☺: Free House ◖: Hanby Ales, Ansells Mild, Pardoes Old Swan, Cheddar Valley Cider. **FACILITIES:** Garden: Picnic benches Dogs allowed Water **NOTES:** Parking 20

WARMINGHAM   Map 15 SJ76

The Bears Paw Hotel ◆◆◆◆ ░◇

School Ln CW11 3QN ☎ 01270 526317
& 526342 📠 01270 526465 e-mail: enquiries@thebearspaw.co.uk
Dir: From M6 junct 18 take A54 then A533 towards Sandbach. Follow signs for village
Delightful country house hotel conveniently situated within easy reach of many Cheshire towns and some of the county's prettiest countryside. Wide-ranging menus offer an extensive selection of starters, including chicken liver paté, smoked

continued

haddock fish cake, and bacon and black pudding salad, followed by breast of chicken stuffed with spinach and brie, and red mullet on a crab mash. Beef lasagne, cod supreme and Cumberland sausage are other options.
OPEN: 5-11 (Sun 12-10.30 Sat 12-11) **BAR MEALS:** L served Sat-Sun 12-6 D served Sun-Thurs 6-9 Fri-Sat 6-9.30 Av main course £10 **RESTAURANT:** L served weekends 12-6 D served Sun-Thurs 6-9 Fri-Sat 6-9.30 Av 3 course à la carte £20 Av 4 course fixed price £14.95 ⊕: Free House ◀: Tetley Cask, Hoegaarden, guest ales.
FACILITIES: Beer garden at front and rear **NOTES:** Parking 100 **ROOMS:** 12 bedrooms en suite 1 family room s£60 d£70 No children overnight

---

WARRINGTON   Map 15 SJ68

Ring O Bells 🍴 ♀
Old Chester Rd, Daresbury WA4 4AJ
☎ 01925 740256 🖷 01925 740972
Alice in Wonderland author Lewis Carroll was born in Daresbury, his father having been the village curate. Formerly a grand old farmhouse, it became a pub in 1872 and now draws in the crowds with its sandstone buildings and beautiful terraced garden. Seasonal, fresh produce is used in roast duck with morello cherry sauce; grilled seabass; and beef and Theakston ale pie. Daytime snacks include ploughman's, jacket potatoes, and focaccia sandwiches.
OPEN: 11-11 (Sun 12-10.30) Closed: 25 Dec Eve
BAR MEALS: L served all week 12-10 D served Mon-Sat 12-9.30 **RESTAURANT:** L served all week 12-10 D served Mon-Sat 12-10 Sun 12-9.30 ⊕: ◀: Bombadier, Scottish Courage Theakstons, Courage Directors & John Smiths, Guest Ales. ♀: 24
FACILITIES: Garden: Terraced garden, seating for 130 people
NOTES: Parking 100

WINCLE   Map 16 SJ96

The Ship Inn ♀
SK11 0QE ☎ 01260 227217 e-mail: Shipinnwincle@aol.com
Dir: Leave A54 at Fourways Motel x-rds, towards Danebridge, Inn 0.5m before bridge on left

Reputedly the oldest inn in Cheshire, the Ship is a 16th-century red-sandstone pub with connections to the Shackleton expedition to the Antarctic - the sign features a picture of the Nimrod, Shackleton's ship - and is close to some of the finest walking country in the north-west of England. An interesting choice of real ales is complemented by a frequently changing blackboard menu. Typical examples from the printed menu include Timothy's Thai curry, goats cheese and braised leeks filo parcel, oven roasted whole chicken breast, and grilled Danebridge trout. Sandwiches and lighter meals available.
OPEN: 12-3 7-11 Sat 12-11, Sun 12-10.30 **BAR MEALS:** L served Tue-Sat 12-2 D served Tue-Sun 7-9 Sun 5.30-8 Av main course £9

continued

RESTAURANT: L served Tue-Sat 12-2 D served Tue-Sun 7-9 Sun 5.30-8 Av 3 course à la carte £20 ⊕: Free House ◀: Wye Valley, Timothy Taylor Landlord, York, Beertown. ♀: 9
FACILITIES: Garden: Lawned terrace Dogs allowed
NOTES: Parking 15

WRENBURY   Map 15 SJ54

The Dusty Miller ♀
CW5 8HG ☎ 01270 780537

A black and white lift bridge, designed by Thomas Telford, completes the picture postcard setting for this beautifully converted 16th-century mill building beside the Shropshire Union Canal. The menu, which tends to rely on ingredients sourced from the north-west, might offer Maynards oak-smoked horseshoe gammon steak with free-range eggs; Cumbrian mixed grill; slow-roast duck breast; and jugged beef.
OPEN: 11.30-3 6.30-11 **BAR MEALS:** L served Tues-Sat 12-2 Sun 12-2.30 D served all week 6.30-9.30 Sun 7-9 Av main course £10.25
RESTAURANT: L served all week 12-2 D served all week 6.30-9.30 Av 3 course à la carte £18 ⊕: ◀: Robinsons Best Bitter, Double Hop, Old Tom, Hatters Mild & Hartleys XB. ♀: 12
FACILITIES: Garden: Canalside garden accessed via footbridge Dogs allowed Water, Kennel **NOTES:** Parking 60

WYBUNBURY   Map 15 SJ64

The Swan 🍴 ♀
Main Rd CW5 7NA ☎ 01270 841280 🖷 01270 841200
e-mail: bistrobonsamis@btconnect.com
Dir: M6 junct 16 towards Chester & Nantwich. Left at lights in Wybunbury
The Swan, registered as an alehouse in 1580, is situated next to the church in the village centre. All the food is freshly prepared on the premises and includes prime steaks, braised lamb shank, and beef and Jennings Ale pie. A good range of fish dishes includes posh fish pie, peppered salmon on Greek salad, smoked haddock rarebit, famous fishcakes, and beer-battered fish and chips with mushy peas. The menu also features hot sandwiches, ploughman's, and sandwiches.
OPEN: 12-11 (Mon 5-11) **BAR MEALS:** L served Tue-Sun 12-2 D served all week 6.30-9.30 Sun & BHs 12-8 Av main course £8.95
RESTAURANT: L served Tue-Sat D served all week ⊕: Jennings ◀: Jennings Bitter, Cumberland Ale, Guest beers. ♀: 9
FACILITIES: Garden **NOTES:** Parking 40

> Pick of the Pubs have that extra special quality that makes them stand out from the crowd. Their entries are highlighted, and may be a full page

PUB WALK
The Halzephron Inn
Gunwalloe - Cornwall

THE HALZEPHRON INN,
Gunwalloe TR12 7QB
☎ 01326 240406
Directions: 3m S of Helston on A3083,
R to Gunwalloe, then through village.
Inn on L overlooking Mount's Bay
*Spectacularly-located freehouse
dating back 500 years (though it was
dry for 50 years until 1956), and with
a smuggling history. Real ales, and a
twice-daily menu based on local
produce.*
Open: 11–2.30 6.30–11 (Summer
evening 6–11) Closed: 25 Dec
Bar Meals: L served all week 12–2
D served all week 7–9 Summer
6.30–9.30 Av main course £12.50
Restaurant Meals: L served all week
12–2 D served all week 7–9 Summer
6.30–9.30 Av 3 course à la carte £20
Children welcome (toys & blackboard).
Garden, terrace, courtyard, raised area.
(for full entry see page 78)

Distance: 3 miles (4.8km)
Map: OS Landranger 103
Terrain: Paths, tracks and roads
Paths: Coastal - cliff paths and tarmac
road
Gradient: Steep cliff path and stretch
of moderately steep road

*Walk submitted and checked by A.M.Q.
Thomas, The Halzephron Inn, Gunwalloe*

One of Cornwall's loveliest and most spectacular coastal walks offers stunning views of Mount's Bay with its stretches of beautiful sandy beaches.

From the pub car park, cross the road and go down the lane towards a cove. From here there are many glorious views, along the shingle beach to Mousehole and Land's End. Turn left along the track, then head up steeply towards Halzephron Cliff. Follow the path round to the right and along the impressive cliffs - scene of many famous shipwrecks over the centuries. Look out along here for kittiwakes, cormorants, gulls and lapwings.

Continue round to Gwinian Head and at this point you begin to drop down gently to Dollar Cove, named after a Spanish galleon wrecked on the cliffs below in 1785 with a cargo of 2 1/2 tons of gold coins. Gold doubloons and other coins have been found on the beach. While here, have a look at the beautiful 13th-century church of St Winwaloe. The decorated panels inside were originally part of a 16th-century rood screen made from a ship, the St Anthony, wrecked in 1526 en route to Portugal from Flanders. The golden sands of Church Cove with Mullion golf links behind them and Poldhu cliffs across the bay - setting for Marconi's wireless station - create a spectacular scene.

Take the road up the hill, following it between traditional Cornish hedges filled with wild flowers and birds, and make for a magnificent view across Mount's Bay at the top. After the view has been suitably appreciated, head down the hill and back to the inn.

England

BLISLAND
Map 02 SX17

The Blisland Inn NEW
☎ 01208 850739
Dir: 5m from Bodmin, between Bodmin and Launceston. 2.5 m off A30 signed Blisland. On the village Green.
An award-winning inn in a very picturesque village on the edge of Bodmin Moor. The superb parish church was a favourite of John Betjeman who wrote about it extensively. Most of the traditional pub fare is home cooked, including a variety of puddings. Leek and mushroom bake is a perennial favourite, while lasagne, sausage and mash, and traditional farmhouse ham, egg and chips are also popular.
OPEN: 11.30-11 Sun 12-10.30 **BAR MEALS:** L served Mon-Sat 12-2.15 Sun 12-2 D served Mon-Sat 12-9.30 Sun dinner 7-9 Av main course £6.95 **RESTAURANT:** L served Mon-Sat 12-2.15 6.30-9.30 Fixed price menu only Sun lunch Av 3 course à la carte £15 Av 3 course fixed price £5.95 🍺: A number of guest ales..
FACILITIES: Child facs Garden: Picnic tables and chairs at front of the pub Dogs allowed Water, chews, loan lead

BODINNICK
Map 02 SX15

Old Ferry Inn
PL23 1LX ☎ 01726 870237 🖷 01726 870116
e-mail: royce972@aol.com
Dir: A38 towards Dobwalls, take a left onto A390. At East Taphouse turn left onto B3359. Continue for 5m to Bodinnick

Situated 50 yards from the scenic River Fowey and adjacent to the former home of Daphne Du Maurier, this friendly, family-run free house is perfectly situated for walking, sailing or touring. The Eden Project and Heligan Gardens, among other top attractions, are nearby. Bar meals range from battered cod to home-made chilli chicken, while evening specials might include a medley of fresh fish and chargrilled sirloin steak.
OPEN: 11-11 (Sun 12-10.30) (Nov-Feb, 11.30-2.30, 6.30-10.30) Closed: 25 Dec **BAR MEALS:** L served all week 12-3 D served all week 6-9 Nov-Feb 12-2, 6.30-8.30 Av main course £7.95
RESTAURANT: L served Sun 12-2.30 D served all week 7-9 (7-8.30 winter) Av 3 course à la carte £20 🍺: Sharp's Bitter.
FACILITIES: Garden: Patio overlooking River Fowey Dogs allowed **NOTES:** Parking 10 **ROOMS:** 12 bedrooms 8 en suite 1 family room s£70 d£70 (♦♦♦♦) No children overnight

 Pubs offering a good choice of fish on their menu

BOLVENTOR
Map 02 SX17

Jamaica Inn ♀
PL15 7TS ☎ 01566 86250 🖷 01566 86177
e-mail: enquiry@jamaicainn.co.uk
With its cobbled courtyard, beamed ceilings and roaring log fires, this mid 18th-century former coaching inn set high on Bodmin Moor is steeped in atmosphere. Daphne du Maurier set her famous novel of smuggling and intrigue here, and the Smugglers Museum houses an extensive collection of smuggling artefacts. Expect a warm welcome and a range of home-cooked food from bar snacks to steak, fish, and vegetarian meals, plus a selection of real ales.
OPEN: 9-11 **BAR MEALS:** L served all week 12-2.30 D served all week 2.45-9 **RESTAURANT:** L served all week 2.30-9 D served all week 2.45-9 🍺: 4x, Doombar. ♀: 8 **FACILITIES:** Children's licence Garden: Lawn area with tables **NOTES:** Parking 6 **ROOMS:** 6 bedrooms en suite (♦♦♦)

BOSCASTLE
Map 02 SX09

The Wellington Hotel ★★
The Harbour PL35 0AQ ☎ 01840 250202 🖷 01840 250621
e-mail: info@boscastle-wellington.com
web: www.boscastle-wellington.com
Dir: In Boscastle, follow signs to harbour, turn into Old Road, hotel ahead.

Listed 16th-century coaching inn with an interesting history, including being at the centre of the 2004 Boscastle floods, and a reputation for being haunted. Located at the end of a glorious, deeply wooded valley, the inn was renamed in 1852 following the death of the Duke of Wellington. Beamed ceilings and real log fires in winter help to create a cosy and intimate atmosphere. Dishes in the Long Bar range from honey-roast ham and sirloin steak to traditional battered cod and various omelettes.
OPEN: 11-3 5-11 (May-Sept open all day) **BAR MEALS:** L served all week 12-2.30 D served all week 6-10 Sun 12-9 Av main course £6 **RESTAURANT:** D served all week 7-9.30 Av 3 course à la carte £25 🏠: Free House 🍺: St Austell HSD, Skinners, Spriccan Ale, Wooden Hand Brewery. **FACILITIES:** Child facs Garden: National Trust walks, natural spring Dogs allowed Water bowls **NOTES:** Parking 20 **ROOMS:** 15 bedrooms en suite 2 family rooms s£38 d£74 (★★)

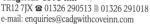

CADGWITH
Map 02 SW71

Cadgwith Cove Inn
TR12 7JX ☎ 01326 290513 ⓘ 01326 291018
e-mail: enquiries@cadgwithcoveinn.com
Dir: 10m from Helston on the main Lizard road

Set right on the Lizard Coastal Path overlooking a lovely cove on the peninsula, this inn is an ideal meeting place for walkers. Meals can be served in the garden, and the large patio has sea views. As the focal point of the farming and fishing community, seafood is a speciality, with popular choices like Cadgwith fish casserole; crab; gurnard; and seasonal lobster. Folk night Tuesday, Cornish singing Friday.
OPEN: 12-3 7-11 (Jul-Aug & Sat-Sun open all day)
BAR MEALS: L served all week 12-2 D served all week 6-9 Jan/Feb Av main course £8 **RESTAURANT:** L served all week 12-2 D served all week 6-9 Av 3 course à la carte £15 🍴: Inn Partnership 🍺: Interbrew Flowers IPA, Sharp's, Abbot Ale, Regular Guest Ales.
FACILITIES: Garden: Large patio with sea view Dogs allowed · Biscuits **NOTES:** Parking 4

CALLINGTON
Map 03 SX36

The Coachmakers Arms
6 Newport Square PL17 7AS ☎ 01579 382567 ⓘ 01579 384679
Dir: Between Plymouth and Launceston on A388

Traditional stone-built pub on the A388 between Plymouth and Launceston. Clocks, plates, pictures of local scenes, old cars and antique trade advertisements contribute to the atmosphere, as do the fish tank and aviary. There's plenty of choice on the menu, from chargrilled steaks, steak and kidney pie or hot-pot, to oven-baked plaice, vegetable balti or salads. Regulars range from the local football team to the pensioners dining club. On Wednesday there's a charity quiz night, and Thursday is steak night.
OPEN: 11-11 (Sun 12-10.30) **BAR MEALS:** L served all week 12-2 D served all week 7-9.30 Av main course £4.95
RESTAURANT: L served all week 12-2 D served all week 7-9.30 Av 3 course à la carte £15 🍴: Enterprise Inns 🍺: Doombar, Worthing Best Bitter, Abbot Ale, Tetley. **FACILITIES:** Dogs allowed Water **NOTES:** Parking 10

CONSTANTINE
Map 02 SW72

Pick of the Pubs

Trengilly Wartha Inn ★★ ◎ ⌂ ♀
Nancenoy TR11 5RP ☎ 01326 340332 ⓘ 01326 340332
e-mail: reception@trengilly.co.uk
Dir: SW of Falmouth

Two families moved down from London in 1988 to run this remote country inn, and have built up a great reputation and won many awards while retaining their laid-back style. The Cornish name means 'settlement above the trees', and indeed the inn and its six acres of gardens and meadows lie in the peaceful wooded valley of Polpenwith Creek, an offshoot of the Helford River. The river yields the oysters that appear on the menu during the season, while the sea and surrounding farmland supply much else. A great choice of fish dishes might include sea bass on a cauliflower and Cornish blue cheese risotto; roast monkfish with chorizo and butterbean stew; and grilled John Dory with saffron corn pancake. Alternatives are local venison sausages, shank of English lamb, or a vegetarian mushroom sampler. The inn lies just off the coastal path in amazing countryside crisscrossed with ancient footpaths.
OPEN: 11-3 6.30-11 25 Dec No food **BAR MEALS:** L served all week 12-2.15 D served all week 6.30-9.30 (Sun 12-2, 7-9.30) Av main course £12 **RESTAURANT:** L served none D served all week 7.30-9.30 Av 3 course fixed price £26 🍴: Free House 🍺: Sharps Cornish Coaster, Skinners, Lizard Ales, Cotleigh brewery. ♀: 17 **FACILITIES:** Garden: Walled garden, benches, pergola, terrace Dogs allowed Water bowls **NOTES:** Parking 40 **ROOMS:** 8 bedrooms en suite 2 family rooms s£49 d£78

CRACKINGTON HAVEN
Map 02 SX19

Pick of the Pubs

Coombe Barton Inn ♦♦♦ ⌂ ♀
EX23 0JG ☎ 01840 230345 ⓘ 01840 230788
e-mail: info@coombebarton.co.uk
Dir: S from Bude on A39, turn off at Wainhouse Corner, then down lane to beach

Originally built for the 'Captain' of the local slate quarry, the Coombe Barton (it means 'valley farm' in Cornish) is over 200 years old and sits in a small cove surrounded by spectacular rock formations. Local seafood is a feature of the menu and includes sea bass, lemon sole, plaice, salmon steaks, and halibut. The kitchen is also known for its vegetarian specials, steaks and Sunday carvery. Bedrooms are comfortable and one suite is suitable for families.

continued

OPEN: 11-11 (Winter weekdays closed 3-6)
BAR MEALS: L served all week 11-2.30 D served all week
6.30-9.30 Sun lunch 12-2.30, dinner 7-9.30 Av main course £8.50
RESTAURANT: L served all week 11-2.30 D served all week 6-10
🍴: Free House 🍺: St Austell Tribute & Hick's special Draught,
Sharp's Doom Bar Bitter, Figgy's Brew (Skinners), Safe Haven
(Sharp's). ♀: 7 **FACILITIES:** Garden: Patio Dogs allowed
Water **NOTES:** Parking 25 **ROOMS:** 6 bedrooms 4 en suite
1 family room s£35 d£60

CUBERT   Map 02 SW75

The Smuggler's Den Inn 🔍 ♀

Trebellan TR8 5PY ☎ 01637 830209 🖷 01637 830580
e-mail: hankers@aol.com web: www.thesmugglersden.co.uk
Dir: From Newquay take A3075 to Cubert crossroads, then right, then left
signed Trebellan, 0.5m

Thatched 16th-century pub two miles from the coast in an
attractive valley setting. Interior features include a long bar,
inglenook wood-burner and barrel seats, and facilities extend
to a family room and beer garden. Well-kept real ales tapped
from the cask are served alongside a range of snacks and
meals. Fresh fish and seafood are always available - moules
marinière and Smugglers fish pie. Other options are local
sausages with horseradish mash or a vegetarian cassoulet.
OPEN: 11-3 6-11 (Winter 12-2) Mon, Wed Closed Lunch Winter
BAR MEALS: L served all week 12-2 D served all week 6-9.30
Av main course £10 **RESTAURANT:** L served all week 12-2 D served
all week 6-9.30 🍴: Free House 🍺: Skinner's Smugglers Ale, Betty
Stogs Bitter, Sharp's Doom Bar, Trebellan Tipple. ♀: 8
FACILITIES: Child facs Garden: Large fenced beer garden, tables &
chairs Dogs allowed Water **NOTES:** Parking 50 **ROOMS:**

DULOE   Map 02 SX25

Ye Olde Plough House Inn 🔍 ♀

PL14 4PN ☎ 01503 262050 🖷 01503 264089
e-mail: alison@ploughhouse.freeserve.co.uk
Dir: A38 to Dobwalls, take turning signed Looe
Set in a lovely village handy for the Cornish coast and
countryside, this welcoming 18th-century free house features
slate floors, wood-burning stoves, settles and old pews. The
lunch menu includes pub favourites like pasties, baguettes,
and home-made soup, whilst freshly prepared dinner dishes
include roast shoulder of lamb, and Mediterranean vegetable
lasagne. Lemon sole with asparagus and vermouth sauce is a
typical choice from the daily fish specials board.
OPEN: 12-2.30 6.30-11 (Sun 7-10.30) Closed: Dec 25-26
BAR MEALS: L served all week 12-2 D served all week 6.30-9.30
RESTAURANT: L served all week 12-2 D served all week 6.30-9.30
🍴: Free House 🍺: Sharp's Doom Bar, Interbrew Bass, Worthington.
♀: 9 **FACILITIES:** Garden: Fenced grassed area, 6 tables Dogs
allowed Water if requested **NOTES:** Parking 20

DUNMERE   Map 02 SX06

The Borough Arms

PL31 2RD ☎ 01208 73118 🖷 01208 76788
e-mail: Borougharms@aol.com
Dir: From A30 take A389 to Wadebridge, pub approx 1m from Bodmin

Popular with walkers, cyclists, anglers, families and local
businesses, this large pub is situated directly on the Camel
trail. Traditional pub fare includes a light menu of sandwiches,
ploughman's and jacket potatoes; typical pub dishes like
grills, a daily curry, lasagne, and jumbo cod, plus daily
specials and a fill-your-own-plate carvery.
OPEN: 11-11 (Sun 12-10.30) **BAR MEALS:** L served all week
12-2.15 D served all week 6.30-9.15 Sun 12-2.30, 6.30-9.30 (carvery)
RESTAURANT: L served all week 12-2.15 D served all week 6.30-9.15
Sun 12-2.30, 6.30-9.30 (carvery) 🍴: Scottish & Newcastle
🍺: Sharp's Bitter, Skinner's, John Smith's Smooth.
FACILITIES: Child facs Large garden with kids play area Dogs
allowed Water **NOTES:** Parking 150

FEOCK   Map 02 SW83

The Punch Bowl & Ladle 🔍 ♀

Penelewey TR3 6QY ☎ 01872 862237 🖷 01872 870401
Dir: Off A38 Falmouth Road
A traditional thatched roadside inn handy for Truro and
Trelissik gardens. It was originally three farm cottages, was
once used as a custom house, and there is even a resident
ghost! The cosy bar offers real ales from St Austell brewery,
and in warmer weather you can enjoy a drink in the walled
garden. The owners offer daily fish and seafood specials using
local mussels, salmon, crab, scallops and sea bass. Other
dishes include lamb shank and ploughman's.
OPEN: 11.30-11 (Sun 12-10.30) **BAR MEALS:** L served all week
12-2.30 D served all week 6-9.15 Av main course £7.95
RESTAURANT: L served all week 12-2.30 D served all week 6-9.15
Av 3 course à la carte £18 🍺: IPA Tribute, HSD. ♀: 8
FACILITIES: Garden: lovely views Dogs allowed Water bowls
NOTES: Parking 60

FOWEY   Map 02 SX15

The Ship Inn ♀

Trafalgar Square PL23 1AZ ☎ 01726 834931 🖷 01726 834931
Dir: From A30 take B3269 & A390
Built in 1570, the Ship is the oldest pub in Fowey. Ideally
placed for two of Cornwall's most popular attractions, the
Eden Project and the Lost Gardens of Heligan. Striking features
inside include a stained glass window in the restaurant. Real
fires and ales and a long tradition of genuine hospitality add
to the charm of the place. The menu includes dishes such as
fisherman's pie, beer battered cod, local sausages and mash,
vegetarian spring rolls and Ship Inn chicken.
continued

England

FOWEY continued

OPEN: 11-11 (Winter times vary please telephone)
BAR MEALS: L served all week 12-2.30 D served all week 6-9
Av main course £6.95 **RESTAURANT:** L served all week 12-2
D served all week 6-8.30 🍽: St Austell Brewery 🍺: St Austell
Tinners Ale, Tribute & HSD. **FACILITIES:** Dogs Water, biscuits

GOLDSITHNEY   Map 02 SW53

The Trevelyan Arms ◆◆◆◆
Fore St TR20 9JU ☎ 01736 710453
e-mail: georgecusick@hotmail.com
Dir: 5 miles from Penzance. A394 signed to Goldsithney

The former manor house for Lord Trevelyan, this 17th-century
property stands at the centre of the picturesque village just a
mile from the sea. It has also been a coaching inn and a
bank/post office in its time, but these days is very much the
traditional family-run Cornish pub, recently refurbished. Food
is fresh and locally sourced, offering good value for money.
Typical dishes are rib-eye steaks, home-made lasagne and
chicken curry.
OPEN: 12-11 **BAR MEALS:** L served all week 12-2 D served all
week 6-9 L Sun 12-2.30 Av main course £6.50
RESTAURANT: L served all week 12-2 D served all week 6-9
Av 2 course fixed price £10 🍺: Morland Speckled Hen, Sharps
Doombar, Flowers IPA, Guiness. **FACILITIES:** Child facs Front patio
Dogs allowed water **NOTES:** Parking 5 **ROOMS:** 2 bedrooms
en suite s£25 d£50 No children overnight

GUNNISLAKE   Map 03 SX47

The Rising Sun Inn
Calstock Rd PL18 9BX ☎ 01822 832201
Dir: From Tavistock take A390 to Gunnislake, pub is through village and
0.25m on left. left at traffic lights and 0.25m on right.
A traditional two-roomed picture postcard pub set in award
winning terraced gardens overlooking the beautiful Tamar
Valley. Great walks start and finish at the Rising Sun, which is
understandably popular with hikers and cyclists, locals and
visitors. The menu, available in the bar and restaurant, takes
in fresh fish (sea bass, John Dory), Thai pork curry, home-
baked gammon, chicken enchilada, and stuffed roast pepper.
OPEN: 12-2.30 5-11 **BAR MEALS:** L served Mon-Sun 12-2
D served Mon-Sun 6-9 Av main course £6.95
RESTAURANT: L served Mon-Sun 12-2 D served Mon-Sat 6-9
(Closed Sun eve) Av 3 course à la carte £14 🍽: Free House
🍺: Interbrew Bass, Sharp's Cornish Coaster, Skinner's Betty Stogs
Bitter, Timothy Taylor Landlord. **FACILITIES:** Garden: Large terraced
garden, views of Tamar Valley Dogs allowed (Not in restaurant)
NOTES: Parking 14

GUNWALLOE   Map 02 SW62

Pick of the Pubs

The Halzephron Inn ♀
TR12 7QB ☎ 01326 240406 📠 01326 241442
e-mail: halzephroninn@gunwalloe1.fsnet.co.uk
Dir: 3m S of Helston on A3083, right to Gunwalloe. Through village,
inn on left
The rugged coastline on this part of the Lizard Peninsula
is known as the Cliffs of Hell, or in Old Cornish, Als
Yfferin. Until the early 20th century it was called The Ship,
taking on its unusual new name in 1958 when, after some
50 'dry' years, it regained its licence. It was undoubtedly
once the haunt of smugglers - who else would have used
the hidden passage in the bar? Today's contraband-free
visitors will find a warm welcome, a good choice of real
ales, and a large selection of malt whiskies, as well as
delicious food prepared from fresh local produce. Lunch
and evening specials in the bar area and bistro-style
restaurant include beef stroganoff with a timbale of rice;
game sausage on blue cheese mash with red wine and
onion gravy; and roasted brill on savoy cabbage with
bacon and beurre rouge sauce.
OPEN: 11-2.30 6.30-11 (Summer evening 6-11) Closed: 25 Dec
BAR MEALS: L served all week 12-2 D served all week 7-9
Summer 6.30-9.30 Av main course £12.50
RESTAURANT: L served all week 12-2 D served all week 7-9
Summer 6.30-9.30 Av 3 course à la carte £20 🍽: Free House
🍺: Sharp's Own, Doom Bar & Special, St Austell Tribute, Organic
Halzephron Gold. ♀: 6 **FACILITIES:** Garden: Lawns, courtyard,
terrace with sea views Dogs allowed Dog bowls
NOTES: Parking 14

See Pub Walk on page 74

GWEEK   Map 02 SW72

The Gweek Inn
TR12 6TU ☎ 01326 221502 📠 01326 221502
e-mail: info@gweekinn.co.uk
Dir: 2m E of Helston near Seal Sanctuary
A traditional family-run village pub, whose location at the
mouth of the pretty Helford River makes booking a table a
wise precaution. A reputation for odd goings-on was recently
given further credence by a Paranormal Society investigation.
It also has a reputation for value-for-money food, typically
southern fried chicken, jacket potatoes, steak, kidney and ale
pie, traditional roasts, and children's meals. The chalkboard
lists locally caught seafood.
OPEN: 12-2.30 6.30-11 (Sun Eve 7-10.30) **BAR MEALS:** L served
all week 12-2 D served all week 6.30-9 (Sun 7-9) Av main course
£7.50 **RESTAURANT:** L served all week 12-2 D served all week
6.30-9 (Sun 7-9) 🍽: Punch Taverns 🍺: Interbrew Flowers IPA, Old
Speckled Hen, Sharps Doom Bar, 3 guest beers. **FACILITIES:** Child
facs Garden: BBQ, food served outdoors Dogs allowed on lead
NOTES: Parking 70

England

HAYLE | Map 02 SW53

The Watermill 🐟 ▷

Old Coach Rd, Lelant Downs TR27 6LQ ☎ 01736 757912
e-mail: watermill@btconnect.com
Dir: From the A30 take the A3074 towards St Ives take left turns at the next two mini rdbts

The old watermill here was in use until the 1970s. Today the building is a family-friendly free house offering fine Cornish ales and an excellent selection of meals. Bar meals include local speciality sausage and mash; steaks; and tomato and courgette lasagne. Upstairs at the Watermill is a separate restaurant with dishes such as roasted chicken breast with a tarragon and yoghurt marinade. Local fish (grilled sole; paella with local seafood and chicken) available.

OPEN: 11-11 **BAR MEALS:** L served all week 12-2.30 D served all week 6.30-9.30 Av main course £6.95 **RESTAURANT:** L served all week 6.30-9.30 Av 3 course à la carte £17.50
🍴: Free House ◀: Sharp's Doombar Bitter, Dreckley Ring 'o' Bells, Skinners Betty Stogs. **FACILITIES:** Child facs Garden: Acre, stream, pergola, ample seating, lawn Dogs allowed Water
NOTES: Parking 35

HELFORD | Map 02 SW72

Pick of the Pubs

Shipwright Arms

TR12 6JX ☎ 01326 231235
Dir: A390 through Truro, A394 to Helston, before Goonhilly Down L for Helford/Manaccan

Superbly situated on the banks of the Helford River in an idyllic village, this small thatched pub is especially popular in summer when customers relax on the three delightful terraces, complete with palm trees and glorious flowers, which lead down to the water's edge. Summer buffet offers crab and lobster subject to availability, alongside various ploughman's lunches, salads, home-made pies, marinated lamb fillet, steaks and a wide range of international dishes. Barbecues in summer on the terrace.
OPEN: 11-2.30 6-11 Winter closed Sun & Mon nights
BAR MEALS: L served all week 12-2 D served all week 7-9 Summer hrs in bar & restaurant Av main course £8.75
RESTAURANT: L served Sun 12-2 D served Tue-Sat 7-9 Winter hrs in bar & restaurant 🍴: Free House ◀: Castle Eden, Greene King IPA, Sharps Doombar. **FACILITIES:** Garden: Terraced patio leading to river/sea Dogs allowed on leads

◆ Diamond rating for inspected guest accommodation

HELFORD PASSAGE | Map 02 SW72

Ferryboat Inn ♀

TR11 5LB ☎ 01326 250625 🖷 01326 250916
e-mail: ronald.brown7@btopenworld.co.uk
Dir: From A39 at Falmouth, towards River Helford

Beautifully positioned on the north bank of the Helford River, this 300-year-old pub overlooks a safe beach and stands bang on the Cornish coastal path. Enjoy the views from the nautical-themed main bar, whose French windows open onto a spacious terrace. Well-kept St Austell ales are backed by a good range of wines, available by the glass. Food includes chicken salad, ploughman's, daily-changing fish specials and Ferryboat ocean pie.

OPEN: 11-11 (Sun 12-10.30) **BAR MEALS:** L served all week 12-2.30 D served all week 6.30-9 Av main course £6.25
RESTAURANT: L served all week 12-2.30 D served all week 6.30-9 Av 3 course à la carte £10.95 🍴: St Austell Brewery ◀: St Austell HSD, Tribute. ♀: 8 **FACILITIES:** Child facs Garden: Patio, food served outdoors Dogs allowed **NOTES:** Parking 80

HELSTON | Map 02 SW62

Blue Anchor Inn

50 Coinagehall St TR13 8EX ☎ 01326 562821 🖷 01326 565765
Dir: A30 to Penzance, then Helston signposted

One of the oldest pubs in Britain to brew its own beer, this unpretentious, thatched pub dates from the 15th century when it was a monks' rest home. The inn has also been the haunt of Victorian tin miners, who collected their wages here. Sample excellent 'Spingo' ales in the low-ceilinged bars, tour the brewery, and tuck into stew and dumplings, fish pie, beef in Spingo, lamb hotpot, or a crusty filled roll.
OPEN: 10.30-11 **BAR MEALS:** L served all week 12-4 Av main course £4.95 🍴: Free House ◀: Blue Anchor Middle, Best, Special & Extra Special, Braggit. **FACILITIES:** Garden: Food served outside. Secluded, sunny garden Dogs allowed Water provided **NOTES:** No credit cards

KINGSAND | Map 03 SX45

Pick of the Pubs

The Halfway House Inn ▷ ♀

Fore St PL10 1NA ☎ 01752 822279 🖷 01752 823146
e-mail: info@halfwayinn.biz web: www.halfwayinn.biz
Dir: From either Torpoint Ferry or Tamar Bridge follow signs to Mount Edgcombe

Tucked among the narrow lanes and colour-washed houses of this quaint fishing village is the family-run Halfway House Inn, set right on the coastal path. Named because it used to represent the border between Devon

continued

England

KINGSAND continued

and Cornwall, it now signifies the dividing line between the conservation villages of Kingsand and Cawsand. The inn has been licensed since 1850, and has a pleasant stone-walled bar with low-beamed ceilings and a large central fireplace. Locally caught seafood is a feature of the small restaurant, and menus might feature assorted smoked fish platter, roast garlic monkfish, and scallops and seafood paella. Alternatives may include pork tenderloin with apricot compote on couscous; steak and kidney pudding; spinach and ricotta salad; and various steaks. For the casual lunchtime visitor a good selection of baguettes, baked potatoes, and ploughman's.
OPEN: 12-3 7-11 (summer open all day)
BAR MEALS: L served all week 12-2.30 D served all week 7-9.30 Winter 12-2, 7-9 Av main course £10
RESTAURANT: L served all week 12-2 D served all week 7-9 12-2, 7-9 Av 3 course à la carte £18 ⊕: Free House ◑: Sharp's Doom Bar Bitter, Sharps Own, Marstons Pedigree, Courage Best. ♀: 10 **FACILITIES:** Child facs Dogs allowed Water, Dog chews

---

LAMORNA Map 02 SW42

Lamorna Wink
TR19 6XH ☎ 01736 731566
Dir: *4m along B3315 towards Lands End, then 0.5m to turning on left*
This oddly-named pub was one of the original Kiddleywinks, a product of the 1830 Beer Act that enabled any householder to buy a liquor licence. Popular with walkers and not far from the Merry Maidens standing stones, the Wink provides a selection of local beers and a simple menu that includes sandwiches, jacket potatoes and fresh local crab. The management have been at the Wink for over thirty years, and prides itself on using as much local produce as possible.
OPEN: 11-11 (Winter 11-4, 6-11) **BAR MEALS:** L served all week 11-3 D served all week 6-9 ⊕: Free House ◑: Sharp's Doom Bar, Skinners, Cornish Knocker Ale. **FACILITIES:** Garden: Dogs allowed in garden only **NOTES:** Parking 40 No credit cards

---

LANLIVERY Map 02 SX05

The Crown Inn ♦♦♦ 🐟 ♀
PL30 5BT ☎ 01208 872707 📠 01208 871208
e-mail: thecrown@wagtailinns.com
web: www.wagtailinns.com/index_files/crownhome.htm
Dir: *From Bodmin take A30 S, follow signs Lanhydrock signs, left at mini-rdbt, in 0.3m take A390, Lanlivery 2nd right*

Dating from the 12th century, this charming, historic pub has been serving travellers for the last eight hundred years. It is set next to the church of St Brevita, on the Saint's Way, a
continued

thirty mile track that runs from Padstow to Fowey past an assortment of holy wells, standing stones and chapels. Inside, there's a traditional rustic atmosphere, with low beamed ceilings, thick stone walls and open fires. In summer months, the pretty garden is an ideal spot to while away an afternoon over a Pimms and a lingering lunch. The kitchen takes pride in the use of local Cornish produce, including cheeses, steak and plenty of fish fresh from nearby Fowey. Steak and Glory pie makes use of the pub's own Glory ale; whilst a hearty ratatouille celebrates three local cheeses. The specials board offers seafood, depending on the morning catch.
OPEN: 11-3 6-11 (open all day during summer season)
BAR MEALS: L served all week 12-2.15 D served all week 7-9.15 Summer 12-9.30 Av main course £8.95 **RESTAURANT:** L served all week 12-2.15 D served all week 7-9.15 Summer 12-9.30 ⊕: ◑: Sharp's Doom Bar, Crown Inn Glory, Coaster, Eden Ale. ♀: 7 **FACILITIES:** Garden: Cottage style, wrought iron furniture Dogs allowed Water, treats **NOTES:** Parking 40
ROOMS: 4 bedrooms en suite s£55 d£80 No children overnight

LOSTWITHIEL Map 02 SX15

Pick of the Pubs

Royal Oak Inn ♀
Duke St PL22 0AQ ☎ 01208 872552 📠 01208 872552
Dir: *A30 from Exeter to Bodmin then onto Lostwithiel. Or A38 from Plymouth towards Bodmin then left onto A390 to Lostwithiel*
Smugglers reputedly used the tunnel believed to connect the cellars of this 13th-century free house to the dungeons of Restormel Castle, a short way up the River Fowey. The friendly saloon bar, warmed on cold days by an open log fire, is the place to mix with the locals, while offering a full à la carte service is the quieter lounge bar. Steaks, including a 16oz T-bone, are served with either a chasseur or pepper sauce. The specials menu offers Barbary duck; Mrs Hine's (the landlady) steak and kidney pies and curries; garlic king prawns; and sea bream with citrus sauce. There are sweets specials too, such as treacle sponge and custard; and strawberry and redcurrant cheesecake. Lunchtime snacks include a range of sandwiches, ploughman's and fried chicken and fish dishes.
OPEN: 11-11 (Sun 12-10.30) **BAR MEALS:** L served all week 12-2 D served all week 6.30-9.15 **RESTAURANT:** L served all week 12-2 D served all week 6.30-9.15 ⊕: Free House ◑: Interbrew Bass, Fuller's London Pride, Marston's Pedigree, Sharp's Own. **FACILITIES:** Garden: Patio with palm trees & tables Dogs allowed **NOTES:** Parking 15
ROOMS: 6 bedrooms en suite (★★)

Ship Inn ♦♦♦♦ ♀
Lerryn PL22 0PT ☎ 01208 872374 📠 01208 872614
e-mail: shiplerryn@aol.com
Dir: *3m S of A390 at Lostwithiel*
The Ship dates from the 16th century and is the sole pub in the idyllic riverside village of Lerryn. The River Lerryn joins the Fowey River a mile or so further down stream, and the wooded banks inspired Kenneth Graham to write *The Wind in the Willows*. It's still a great area for walkers. Typical dishes include local plaice cooked with cheddar and cider; vegetarian tagliatelle; venison, pheasant and rabbit pie; and for dessert: Cornish nog.
continued

Ship Inn

OPEN: 11-11 (Sun 12-3, 6-10.30) **BAR MEALS:** L served all week 12-3 D served all week 6.30-9.30 Av main course £10 **RESTAURANT:** L served all week 12-3 D served all week 6.30-9.30 Av 3 course à la carte £16 ⊕: Free House ◀: Interbrew Bass, Sharp's, Skinner's. ♀: 9 **FACILITIES:** Child facs Garden: Dogs allowed **NOTES:** Parking 36 **ROOMS:** 5 bedrooms en suite 1 family room s£60 d£80

LUDGVAN   Map 02 SW53

The Old Inn ♀
Lower Quarters TR20 8EG ☎ 01736 740419 ▤ 01736 740419 e-mail: samuel.page@tesco.net
A pub for just 100 years, although the building is three times as old. The number of main courses in the atmospheric restaurant is limited, but they are chosen with care and may include roast monkfish with crispy parma ham; pan-fried chicken breast with Calvados, cream and caramelised apples; puff pastry with sweet red peppers, poached egg and hollandaise sauce; and Cornish venison pie with red wine, marjoram and orange sauce.
OPEN: 12-2.30 5.30-11 **BAR MEALS:** L served Tue-Sun 12-2 D served Tue-Sun 7-9 Av main course £6.95 **RESTAURANT:** L served Tue-Sun 12-2 D served Tue-Sat 7-9 Av 3 course à la carte £10 ◀: Tinners, Guinness. ♀: 8 **FACILITIES:** Garden: Dogs allowed dog bowls and chews **NOTES:** Parking 25

White Hart
Churchtown TR20 8EY ☎ 01736 740574
Dir: From A30 take B3309 at Crowlas
Built somewhere between 1280 and 1320, the White Hart retains the peaceful atmosphere of a bygone era and offers splendid views across St Michael's Mount and Bay. Fresh fish is a feature from Thursday to Saturday, and other popular dishes include toad-in-the-hole, steak and kidney pie and home-made lasagne (including a vegetarian version). The bar offers a good choice of malts and Irish whiskies.
OPEN: 11-2.30 6-11 **BAR MEALS:** L served Tue-Sun (all Etr-Oct) 12-2 D served Tue-Sun (all summer) 7-9 **RESTAURANT:** L served Tue-Sun (all Etr-Oct) 12-2 D served Tue-Sun (all summer) 7-9 ⊕: Inn Partnership ◀: Marston's, Sharps, Interbrew Flowers & Bass. **FACILITIES:** Garden: Dogs allowed **NOTES:** Parking 12 No credit cards

MALPAS   Map 02 SW84

The Heron Inn
Trenhaile Ter TR1 1SL ☎ 01872 272773 ▤ 01872 272773
Set in an area of outstanding natural beauty, this Cornish inn overlooks the river Fal: you might spot herons from the riverside patio. Choose from a range of seafood dishes and specials to enjoy as you birdwatch: fresh Cornish crab, cod

mornay, smoked haddock and more. Real ales to wash it down include Dotchy and I.P.A.
OPEN: 11-3 6-11 **BAR MEALS:** L served all week 12-2 D served all week 6-9 Av main course £6.95 **RESTAURANT:** 12-2 7-9 ◀: HSD, Tribute, IPA, Dotchy. **FACILITIES:** Children's licence Dogs allowed water **NOTES:** Parking 13

MANACCAN   Map 02 SW72

The New Inn ♀
TR12 6HA ☎ 01326 231323 e-mail: penny@macace.net
Dir: (7m from Helston)

Thatched village pub, deep in Daphne du Maurier country, dating back to Cromwellian times, although obviously Cromwell forbade his men from drinking here. Attractions include the homely bars and a large, natural garden full of flowers. At lunchtime you might try a locally made pasty or moules marinière, and in the evening perhaps sea bass and chive fishcakes with tomato coulis and sautéed vegetables, or slow-roasted lamb shank, red wine and redcurrant gravy.
OPEN: 12-3 (Sat-Sun all day in summer) 6-11 **BAR MEALS:** L served all week 12-2.30 D served all week 6-9.30 (Sun 12-2, 7-9) Av main course £8 ⊕: Pubmaster ◀: Flowers IPA, Sharps Doom Bar. ♀: 10 **FACILITIES:** Child facs Garden: Large, natural, lots of flowers Dogs very welcome, Water **NOTES:** Parking 20

MARAZION   Map 02 SW53

Pick of the Pubs

Godolphin Arms ★★
TR17 0EN ☎ 01736 710202 ▤ 01736 710171
e-mail: enquiries@godolphinarms.co.uk
web: www.godolphinarms.co.uk
Dir: From A30 just outside Penzance follow signs for Marazion. Godolphin arms is 1st large building on left as you enter Marazion.
Located right at the water's edge opposite St Michael's Mount, the Godolphin Arms affords superb views across the bay. It's so close that the sea splashes at the windows in the winter, and you can watch the movement of seals, dolphins, ferries, and fishing boats returning to Newlyn with their daily catch. From the traditional bar and beer terrace to the more homely restaurant and most of the bedrooms, the Mount is clearly visible. The Godolphin is a family run affair, with the emphasis on a friendly welcome and good service. Seafood figures prominently in the restaurant - the specials blackboard lists the daily choice which might include whole Megrim sole, or local seabass with a Newlyn crab and prawn sauce; and seafood tagliatelle. Alternatives include West Country lamb shank; and pork fillet with apple and cider jus. The

continued

continued

England

MARAZION continued

bar menu offers a choice of sandwiches, salads, and a pared down list of main courses.
OPEN: 10.30-11 (Sun 12-10.30) **BAR MEALS:** L served all week 12-2 D served all week 6.30-9 Summer all day Av main course £7 **RESTAURANT:** L served all week 12-2 D served all week 6.30-9 Av fixed price £15 **🏠:** Free House **🍺:** Sharp's Eden Ale, Skinner's Spriggan Ale, Sharps Special, Skinners Knocker. **FACILITIES:** Garden: Terrace overlooks waters edge, seating Dogs allowed Water bowls **NOTES:** Parking 48 **ROOMS:** 10 bedrooms en suite 2 family rooms s£45 d£70 No children overnight

MEVAGISSEY Map 02 SX04

The Rising Sun Inn ♦♦♦ 🏠 ♈

Portmellon Cove PL26 6PL ☎ 01726 843235 📠 01726 843235
e-mail: cliffnsheila@tiscali.co.uk
web: www.risingsunportmellon.co.uk

Superbly situated next to the beach in a beautiful cove and overlooking the sea, this 17th-century Grade II listed building is partly built of shipwreck timbers. Cosy beamed bar with snug and a cellar bar serving real ales and continental beers. The kitchen offers a host of local seafood dishes, plus roasted red pepper and stilton lasagne or local free-range chicken. After 6pm, children over 13 only are welcomed.
OPEN: 11-3 6-11 (BHs, Jun-Sep 11-11) Closed: 1 Nov-28 Feb **BAR MEALS:** L served all week 12.30-3 Av main course £6.95 **RESTAURANT:** L served all week 12.30-3 D served all week 6-9 Av 3 course à la carte £23 **🏠:** Free House **🍺:** Adnams Bitter, Fuller's London Pride, Timothy Taylor Landlord, Skinners. **♈:** 12 **FACILITIES:** Dogs allowed Water, beach **NOTES:** Parking 60 **ROOMS:** 7 bedrooms en suite s£42.50 d£55 No children overnight

The Ship Inn ♦♦♦ ♈

Fore St PL26 6UQ ☎ 01726 843324 📠 01726 844368
With Mevagissey's picturesque working fishing harbour mere yards away, you can understand why there's a separate fish and seafood menu. Beer-battered cod, oven-baked mackerel with cracked black pepper, Cajun salmon fillets, and half pints of prawns are served all day, alongside home-made steak and ale pie, trio of speciality sausages, home-cured honey roast lamb, and home-made lasagne. Doorstep sandwiches at lunchtime are served on thick crusty white or brown bread.
OPEN: 11-11 (Sun 12-10.30) **BAR MEALS:** L served all week 12-3 D served all week 6-9 Summer dinner 12-9 **🏠:** St Austell Brewery **🍺:** St Austell Ales. **♈:** 8 **FACILITIES:** Dogs allowed **ROOMS:** 5 bedrooms en suite 2 family rooms s£35 d£50

MITCHELL Map 02 SW85

Pick of the Pubs

The Plume of Feathers NEW

TR8 5AX
Since its establishment in the 16th century, the Plume of Feathers has accommodated various historical figures - John Wesley preached his Methodist views from the pillared entrance, and Sir Walter Raleigh used to live locally. The present owners took over the pub three years ago and have turned it into a successful destination pub restaurant; the imaginative kitchen is gaining an excellent reputation for its food, based on a fusion of modern European and classical British dishes, with an emphasis on fresh fish and the best Cornish ingredients. There is always a daytime specials board, which changes at 6pm to include an extensive choice of 'on the night' creations. Dinner could start with pan-fried Cornish scallops and Oriental sauce; and fishcake deep fried in Panko breadcrumbs with salsa rossa. Mains choices include honey-glazed lamb shank with cippoline onions; Saltmarsh lamb marinated in Moroccan flavours with houmous; roasted whole sea bass with crushed herb potatoes; and pan-fried cod with chorizo mash.
OPEN: 10.30-11 **BAR MEALS:** L served all week 12-3 D served all week 6-10 Av main course £12.50 **RESTAURANT:** L served all week 12-3 D served all week 6-10 Av 3 course à la carte £20 **🍺:** Doom Bar, John Smiths Smooth. **FACILITIES:** Child facs Garden with exotic trees & bushes, seating **NOTES:** Parking 50

MITHIAN Map 02 SW75

Miners Arms

TR5 0QF ☎ 01872 552375 📠 01872 552375
Dir: From A30 take B3277 to St Agnes. Take 1st right to Mithian

16th century character pub with slate floors, wall paintings, a cobbled courtyard, exposed beams and ornate plasterwork ceilings that were made for a visit by Edward VII in 1896. Claiming to be the second oldest pub in Cornwall, this was previously used as a courtroom and a pay house for local miners. Recent change of hands.
OPEN: 12-11 (Closed Mon lunch Oct-Feb) **BAR MEALS:** L served all week 12-2.30 D served all week 6-9.30 **RESTAURANT:** 12-2.30 6-9.30 **🏠:** Pubmaster **🍺:** Sharp's Doom Bar, Guinness, Old Speckled Hen. **FACILITIES:** Enclosed garden seats 40, courtyard seats 20 Dogs allowed Water provided **NOTES:** Parking 40

 Pubs offering a good choice of fish on their menu

England

MORWENSTOW
Map 02 SS21

The Bush Inn
EX23 9SR ☎ 01288 331242
Dir: Telephone for directions
Originally built as a chapel in 950 for pilgrims from Wales en route to Spain, The Bush is reputedly one of Britain's oldest pubs. Set in an isolated cliff-top hamlet close to bracing coastal path walks, it only became a pub some 700 years later. The unspoilt traditional interior, with stone-flagged floors and old stone fireplaces, has a Celtic piscina carved from serpentine and set into a wall behind the bar. Hearty traditional food includes generously filled sandwiches, ploughmans, soup and stew.
OPEN: 12-3 7-11 (closed Mon) **BAR MEALS:** 12-2 ⊕: Free House ⬤: St Austell HSD. **NOTES:** Parking 30 No credit cards

MOUSEHOLE
Map 02 SW42

Pick of the Pubs

The Old Coastguard Hotel ★★ ⊛ 🐟 ⊈
The Parade TR19 6PR ☎ 01736 731222 🖷 01736 731720
e-mail: bookings@oldcoastguardhotel.co.uk
web: www.oldcoastguardhotel.co.uk
Dir: A30 to Penzance, take coast road through Newlyn to Mousehole, pub is 1st building on left

Formerly a HM Coastguard look-out station, the hotel is perched high above the lovely old fishing village of Mousehole, with fabulous views across Mounts Bay. Now in sole charge, Bill Treloar has brought in light, airy décor with smart but informal service to match. The kitchen is committed to creating innovative dishes, with great use being made of the nearby Newlyn fish markets, with dishes like mixed grill of fish with lemon crushed potatoes, buttered spinach and a caper and olive tapenade. There is also a good balance of meat and vegetarian dishes; perhaps herb crusted local lamb with pesto, or filo pastry basket of roasted vegetables with Cornish blue cheese and roast garlic dressing. In summer you can enjoy the large garden and terrace with sea views.
OPEN: 12-11 (Closed: 25 Dec) **BAR MEALS:** L served all week 12-3 D served all week 6-10 Av main course £15
RESTAURANT: L served all week 12-3 D served all week 6-10 Av 3 course à la carte £25 ⊕: Free House ⬤: Sharp's Doom Bar, Interbrew Bass. ⊈: 7 **FACILITIES:** Child facs Garden: Large garden, full sea views **NOTES:** Parking 15
ROOMS: 21 bedrooms en suite 3 family rooms s£38 d£80

 The Rosette is the AA award for food.
Look out for it next to a pub's name

Ship Inn ♦♦♦♦ 🐟
TR19 6QX ☎ 01736 731234 🖷 01736 732259
e-mail: ship.mousehole@freeserve.co.uk
Beautifully located on the harbour, this old-world inn lies at the hub of the community, attracting many of the village's more colourful characters and seadogs. Seafood landed at nearby Newlyn figures prominently, with dishes such as cod in crispy beer batter, home-made fish pie, whole Dover sole, fresh Newlyn crab and fillets of sea bass stuffed with crab and wine cream sauce. Other options feature game pie, locally-made burgers, casseroles and doorstep sandwiches.
OPEN: 11-11 (Sun 12-10.30) **BAR MEALS:** L served all week 12-2.30 D served all week 6-9 ⊕: St Austell Brewery ⬤: St Austell's HSD & Tinners Ale, Tribute, IPA. **FACILITIES:** Dogs allowed
ROOMS: 8 bedrooms en suite s£40 d£65

MYLOR BRIDGE
Map 02 SW83

Pick of the Pubs

Pandora Inn 🐟 ⊈
Restronguet Creek TR11 5ST
☎ 01326 372678 🖷 01326 378958
Dir: From Truro/Falmouth follow A39, pub is well signed
Visiting yachts are welcome to tie up outside this thatched and white-painted pub, which is one of Cornwall's best-known waterside inns. The building dates back to the 13th century, and was renamed in memory of the 'Pandora', sent to Tahiti to capture the 'Bounty' mutineers. Sadly, the ship was wrecked in 1791; the captain was court-martialled on his return, and retired to Cornwall where he is believed to have bought this inn. Now, solid fuel stoves and open log fires drive out the winter cold, and in summer you can relax on the attractive riverside patio. Lunchtime brings sandwiches, jacket potatoes and cheese or seafood platters. You'll also find plenty of good home cooking: Pandora favourites like seared Bodmin Moor beef with chargrilled aubergine and spinach gateau; and grilled local sea bass on tomato and shallot confit are served in the non-smoking restaurant.
OPEN: 11-11 (Sun 11-10.30) **BAR MEALS:** L served all week 12-3 D served all week 6.30-9 Fri/Sat dinner to 9.30 Av main course £10 **RESTAURANT:** L served all week 12-3 D served all week 7-9 Fri/Sat 7-9.30 Av 3 course à la carte £24 Av 2 course fixed price £18 ⊕: St Austell Brewery ⬤: St Austell Tinners Ale, HSD, Bass, Tribute. ⊈: 9 **FACILITIES:** Garden: Seated waterside terrace extending into river Dogs allowed Water **NOTES:** Parking 30

PELYNT
Map 02 SX25

Jubilee Inn
PL13 2JZ ☎ 01503 220312 🖷 01503 220920
e-mail: rickard@jubileeinn.freeserve.co.uk
Dir: Take A390 signposted St Austell at village of East Taphouse, turn L onto B3359 signposted Looe & Polperro. Jubilee Inn on left on leaving Pelynt
The name commemorates Queen Victoria's Golden Jubilee in 1887, although the inn actually dates from the 16th century and was formerly known as The Axe. The interior has a homely, welcoming feel, with its oak-beamed ceilings, blazing winter fires, and Staffordshire figurines of the queen and her consort. Local seafood features, along with home-made ribs, curries and pies.
OPEN: 12-3 6-11 **BAR MEALS:** L served all week 12-2.30 D served all week 6-9.30 **RESTAURANT:** L served all week 12-2.30 D served all week 7-9.30 ⊕: Free House ⬤: Interbrew Bass, Sharp's Doom Bar, Skinner's Betty Stogs Bitter. **FACILITIES:** Garden: Dogs allowed **NOTES:** Parking 70 **ROOMS:** 11 bedrooms en suite (★★)

England

PENZANCE
Map 02 SW43

Dolphin Tavern
Quay St TR18 4BD ☎ 01736 364106 ▤ 01736 364194
A 600-year-old harbourside pub overlooking Mounts Bay and
St Michael's Mount. In this building, apparently, Sir Walter
Raleigh first smoked tobacco on English soil and, the
following century, Judge Jeffreys held court. Haunted by not
one but several ghosts. An old sea salt gazes out from menus
offering West Country ham, eggs and chips; home-made steak
and kidney pie; grilled local Megrim sole; and Newlyn crab
salad. All-day bites and children's meals are also available.
OPEN: 11-11 **BAR MEALS:** L served all week 11-2.30 D served all
week 6-9 Sun 12-9, Summer 11-9.30 Av main course £8 ●: St
Austell Brewery ◀: St Austell HSD, Tinners Tribute, Cornish Cream.
FACILITIES: Garden: Pavement patio area Dogs allowed Water

The Turks Head Inn ♀
Chapel St TR18 4AF ☎ 01736 363093 ▤ 01736 360215
e-mail: turkshead@gibbards9476.fsworld.co.uk
Dating from around 1233, making it Penzance's oldest pub, it
was the first in the country to be given the Turks Head name.
Sadly, a Spanish raiding party destroyed much of the original
building in the 16th century, but an old smugglers' tunnel
leading directly to the harbour and priest holes still exist.
Typically available are mussels, sea bass, John Dory, lemon
sole, tandoori monkfish, pan-fried venison, chicken stir-fry,
pork tenderloin, steaks, mixed grill and salads. A sunny
flower-filled garden lies at the rear.
OPEN: 11-3 5.30-11 (Sun 12-3, 5.30-10.30) Closed: Dec 25
BAR MEALS: L served all week 11-2.30 D served all week 6-10 Sun
12-2.30, 6-10 Av main course £8 **RESTAURANT:** L served all week
11-2.30 D served all week 6-10 ●: Punch Taverns ◀: Young's
Special, Greene King IPA, Sharp's Doom Bar Bitter, Guest Ale. ♀: 14
FACILITIES: Child facs Walled garden Dogs allowed

PERRANUTHNOE
Map 02 SW52

The Victoria Inn ♦♦♦ ♀
TR20 9NP ☎ 01736 710309 ▤ 01736 719284
web: www.victoriainn-penzance.co.uk
Dir: Off the A394 Penzance to Helston road, signed Perranuthoe

This 12th-century inn is reputed to be the oldest in Cornwall.
The original part was built by the stonemasons who built the
village church, to provide themselves with accommodation. It
is beautifully situated close to a sandy beach, and the coastal
footpath and makes a pleasant stopover, with its
Mediterranean-style patio, good food and en suite
accommodation. There is a daily selection of fresh fish, steaks,
game and a good choice for vegetarians.
OPEN: 11.30-2.30 6.30-11 (July & Aug open at 6pm)
BAR MEALS: L served all week 12-2 D served all week 6.30-9 Sun
7-9 **RESTAURANT:** L served all week 12-2 D served all week 6.30-9
continued

The Victoria Inn
Churchtown, Perranuthnoe
Cornwall TR20 9NP
Tel: 01736 710309   Fax: 01736 719284
www.victoriainn-penzance.co.uk

This 12th century Inn, reputedly the oldest hostelry
in Cornwall, nestles in the centre of the idyllic village
of Perranuthnoe, a short walk from the pretty beach
and coastal footpath. With its sheltered
Mediterranean style patio, comfortable bar and good
food it makes a pleasant stop-over for a relaxed lunch
or evening meal. Expect to find daily fresh fish and
home cooked meals, including a good vegetarian
selection together with well kept beers. Three pretty
en-suite bedrooms complete the picture.

Sun 7-9 Av 3 course à la carte £18 ●: ◀: Bass, Doom Bar, Abbot
Ale. ♀: 8 **FACILITIES:** Child facs Garden: Paved Mediterranean
style Dogs allowed in bar only; Water provided **NOTES:** Parking 10
ROOMS: 3 bedrooms en suite s£35 d£60 No children overnight
See advert on this page

POLKERRIS
Map 02 SX05

The Rashleigh Inn ♀
PL24 2TL ☎ 01726 813991 ▤ 01726 815619
e-mail: jonspode@aol.com
Dir: Off A3082 outside Fowey

A 300-year-old stone built pub that literally stands on a beach
in a small, safe cove. The main bar used to be a boathouse
and coastguard station. Panoramic views can be enjoyed from
the multi-level sun terrace. Real ale selections vary according
to season, and there is a good choice of malt whiskies. The
pub's location ensures a great catch of fresh fish and seafood
every day, and these are usually featured on the specials
continued

board. The bar menu offers sandwiches and ploughman's along with fish pie and steak pie.
OPEN: 11-11 (Sun 12-10.30) **BAR MEALS:** L served all week 12-2 D served all week 6-9 snacks 3-5 everyday Av main course £7.50
RESTAURANT: L served all week 12-2 D served all week 6-9 Av 3 course à la carte £23 ⊜: Free House ◖: Sharp's Doom Bar, Cotleigh Tawny , Blue Anchor Spingo, Timothy Taylor Landlord. ♀: 8
FACILITIES: Garden: Multi-level terrace, overlooks Polkerris etc Dogs allowed Water bowls on terrace **NOTES:** Parking 22

POLPERRO
Map 02 SX25

Old Mill House Inn
Mill Hill PL13 2RP ☎ 01503 272362 ⊠ 01503 272058
e-mail: enquiries@oldmillhouseinn.co.uk
Dir: Telephone for directions
In the heart of historic Polperro, this 16th-century inn has been extensively refurbished. Here you can sample well-kept local ales and 'scrumpy' cider beside a log fire in the bar, or sit out over lunch in the riverside garden during fine weather. Local ingredients, with an emphasis on freshly caught fish, are the foundation of dishes on the restaurant menu. Traditional roasts are served on Sundays.
OPEN: 11-11 (Winter open at 12) **BAR MEALS:** L served Tue-Sun 12-2.30 Sun carvery 12-3 **RESTAURANT:** D served Tue-Sat 7-9.30 Av 3 course à la carte £15 ◖: Sharps Old Mill Ale, Carling, Skinners, Erdinger Weiss Beer. **FACILITIES:** Garden: By river, benches, grassed Dogs allowed Water & Bonio **NOTES:** Parking 6

PORT GAVERNE
Map 02 SX08

Pick of the Pubs

Port Gaverne Hotel ★ ★ ♀
PL29 3SQ ☎ 01208 880244 ⊠ 01208 880151
Dir: Signed from B3314, S of Delabole via B3267 on E of Port Isaac

Just up the road from the sea and a beautiful little cove, this delightful 17th-century inn is a magnet for locals and holidaymakers alike. It is a meandering building with plenty of period detail, evocative of its long association with both fishing and smuggling. Bread is home made, and locally supplied produce is to the fore, particularly fresh fish. The bar menu offers chicken liver and brandy pate, creamy vegetable risotto, and half pint of prawns along with sandwiches and ploughman's. At dinner you might try smoked haddock au gratin; grilled Dover sole with herb butter; whole baked bass with lemon grass, garlic and ginger; sautéed supreme of guinea fowl with a lemon, cream, mustard and cayenne sauce. Walkers from the Heritage Coast Path can pause for a pint in the small beer garden, or at a table in front of the hotel.

continued

OPEN: 11-11 **BAR MEALS:** L served all week 12-2.30 D served all week 6.30-9.30 Av main course £7.50
RESTAURANT: D served all week 7-9.30 Av 3 course fixed price £25 ⊜: Free House ◖: Sharp's Doom Bar, Bass, St Austell Tribute. ♀: 9 **FACILITIES:** Garden: Paved area with heat and light Dogs allowed Water provided **NOTES:** Parking 15
ROOMS: 15 bedrooms en suite 2 family rooms s£50 d£80

PORTHLEVEN
Map 02 SW62

The Ship Inn ⌖
TR13 9JS ☎ 01326 564204
Built into steep cliffs and approached by a flight of stone steps, this 17th-century smuggling inn has wonderful views over the harbour, especially at night by floodlight. Inside is a knocked-through bar with log fires, and a family room converted from an old smithy. Real ales are properly served alongside dishes of smoked fish platter, crab thermidor, chargrilled lamb steak, and chicken tikka masala. The snack range also features fresh Cornish crab.
BAR MEALS: L served all week 12-2 D served all week 7-9 ⊜: Free House ◖: Scottish Courage Courage Best, Sharp's Doom Bar, Old Speckled Hen. **FACILITIES:** Garden: Terraced. Overlooks the harbour Dogs allowed Water

---

PORTREATH
Map 02 SW64

Basset Arms ⌖ ♀
Tregea Ter TR16 4NG ☎ 01209 842077 ⊠ 01209 843936
e-mail: bas.bookings@ccinns.com
Dir: From Redruth take B3300 to Portreath
Typical Cornish stone cottage, built as a pub in the early 19th century to serve the harbour workers, with plenty of tin mining and shipwreck memorabilia adorning the low-beamed interior. As you'd expect, seafood dominates the menu. Look out for grilled seabass fillet, tuna steak with sweet chili sauce, turbot stuffed with prawns and mushrooms, large grilled fillet of plaice Veronique, and whole trout with almonds.
OPEN: 11.30-2 6-11 (all day in summer) **BAR MEALS:** L served all week 12-2 D served all week 6-9 **RESTAURANT:** L served all week 12-2 D served all week 6-9 ⊜: Free House ◖: Sharps Doom Bar, Worthington 6X, Abbot Ale. **FACILITIES:** Child facs Garden: paved seating area, barbecue Dogs allowed on leads only **NOTES:** Parking 25

RUAN LANIHORNE
Map 02 SW84

The Kings Head ⌖
TR2 5NX ☎ 01872 501263
Dir: 3m from Tregony Bridge on A3078
With its pretty sun-trap sunken garden overlooking the tidal River Fal, this popular Victorian summer pub enjoys a rural location in the heart of the Roseland Peninsula. New owners offer locally sourced produce, from mature cheddar sandwiches to fresh local mussels and Cornish steaks. Lunch menu includes baguettes and ploughmans; for dinner try spinach and Parmesan risotto or zipperback prawn stir-fry. Excellent puddings, complemented by organic Jersey clotted cream, and west country cheeses.
OPEN: 12-2.30 6-11 (closed Mon Oct-Apr) **BAR MEALS:** L served all week 12-2 D served all week 6.30-9.15 Av main course £10.50
RESTAURANT: L served all week 12.30-2 D served all week 6.30-9 Av 3 course à la carte £18 ⊜: Free House ◖: Skinners Kings Ruan, Cornish Knocker, Betty Stoggs. **FACILITIES:** Garden: Sunken beer garden, terrace with seating Dogs allowed **NOTES:** Parking 12

England

ST AGNES   Map 03 SW75

Driftwood Spars Hotel ♦♦♦♦ ⌂ ♀
Trevaunance Cove TR5 0RT ☎ 01872 552428 ⓕ 01872 553701
e-mail: driftwoodsparshotel@hotmail.co.uk
Dir: A30 onto B3285, through St Agnes, down steep hill, left at Peterville
Inn, onto road signed Trevaunance Cove

Flowering baskets introduce a dash of colour here, enhancing
the pristine white walls of this 300-year-old pub, previously a
tin miner's store, a chandlery and a sail loft. An old
smugglers' tunnel completes the picture, while stunning views
and roaring log fires add to the appeal. Try rack of barbecue
ribs, chilli beef, breaded scampi, or roast vegetable lasagne.
The pub's own free-range eggs are used, and there's an
appetising Cornish cheeseboard.
OPEN: 11-11 (Fri-Sat 11-12, Sun 12-10.30) Rest: 25 Dec Open 2
hours **BAR MEALS:** L served all week 12-2.30 D served all week
6.30-9.30 open all day Aug Av main course £8
RESTAURANT: L served all week 12-2.30 D served all week
6.30-9.30 ⓖ: Free House ⓫: Carlsberg-Tetley Bitter, Sharp's Own,
St Austell HSD, Cuckoo Ale. ♀: 15 **FACILITIES:** Garden: Dogs
allowed **NOTES:** Parking 80 **ROOMS:** 15 bedrooms en suite
5 family rooms s£40 d£90

ST AGNES (ISLES OF SCILLY)   Map 02 SV80

Turks Head
TR22 0PL ☎ 01720 422434 ⓕ 01720 423331
e-mail: drat@turkshead.fslife.co.uk
Dir: By boat or helicopter to St Mary's and boat on to St Agnes

Britain's most southwesterly inn is named after the 16th-
century Turkish pirates who arrived from the Barbary Coast.
Noted for its atmosphere and superb location overlooking
the island quay, this former coastguard boathouse is now
packed with fascinating model ships and maritime
photographs. Lunchtime brings soup, salads and open rolls,
plus daily blackboard specials. In the evening, a rib-eye
steak or home-made cheese and asparagus quiche might
precede sticky toffee pudding with clotted cream.

continued

OPEN: 11-11 **BAR MEALS:** L served all week 12-2.30 D served all
week 6.30-9.30 ⓖ: Free House ⓫: St Austell Dartmoor Best &,
Carlsberg-Tetley Ind Coope Burton Ale, Ales of Scilly, Scuppered.
FACILITIES: Garden: Patio overlooking sea & enclosed garden Dogs
allowed

ST BREWARD   Map 02 SX07

The Old Inn ⌂ ♀
Church Town, Bodmin Moor PL30 4PP
☎ 01208 850711 ⓕ 01208 851671
e-mail: darren@theoldinn.fsnet.co.uk
Dir: A30 to Bodmin/Launceston. Continue for 16m just after Temple turn
right and follow signs to St Breward. B3266 Bodmin to Camelford road
take turning to St Breward as indicated on brown signs.
The Old Inn is located high up on Bodmin Moor in a village
surrounded by spectacular scenery. It was constructed in the
11th century by monks who built the parish church next door,
and retains its slate floors, wooden beams and log fires. Real
ales and home-made dishes are served in the bar and
restaurant, including fish, steaks, roasts, venison, and
Moorland Grill. Wedding receptions and other functions can
also be catered for.
OPEN: 11-3 6-11 (Open all day Fri-Sun) **BAR MEALS:** L served all
week 11-2 D served all week 6-9 Sun lunch 12-2, dinner 6-9 Av main
course £7.95 **RESTAURANT:** L served all week 11-2 D served all
week 6-9 Sun lunch 12-2, dinner 6-9 Av 3 course à la carte £25
ⓖ: Free House ⓫: Bass, Sharp's Doom Bar Bitter, Sharps Special,
Guest Ales. ♀: 24 **FACILITIES:** Child facs Garden: Garden &
decking area Dogs allowed Water **NOTES:** Parking 35

ST DOMINICK   Map 03 SX46

Who'd Have Thought It Inn ⌂ ♀
St Dominic PL12 6TG ☎ 01579 350214 ⓕ 01579 351651
e-mail: thewhod@vku.co.uk
Dir: Take A388 from Saltash towards Callington. After 3m take signs for St.
Dominick. At T-junct in St Dominick turn right, pub 500yds on right.
Set between St Dominic and Bohetheric, this country pub has
fabulous views over the Tamar Valley, best appreciated from the
conservatory. There are two bars, the Silage and the Straw (the
former with darts, TV and a jukebox), and slightly more formal
lounges. Food is freshly prepared from fine West Country
produce, including locally landed fish, such as cod in beer batter
or fillet of sea bass with honey, ginger and lemon grass glaze.
OPEN: 11.30-2.30 6-11 **BAR MEALS:** L served all week 12-2.30
D served all week 6.30-9.30 Av main course £8
RESTAURANT: L served all week 12-2 D served all week 6-9.30
Av 3 course à la carte £15.50 ⓖ: Free House ⓫: Bass, Betty Stoggs,
London Pride, Doom Bar. ♀: 10 **FACILITIES:** Small garden with
spectacular views Dogs allowed Water provided **NOTES:** Parking 50

ST EWE   Map 02 SW94

The Crown Inn
PL26 6EY ☎ 01726 843322 ⓕ 01726 844720
e-mail: linda@thecrowninn737.fsnet.co.uk
Dir: From St Austell take B3273. At Tregiskey x-rds turn right. St Ewe signed
on right
Hanging baskets add plenty of brightness and colour to this
delightful 16th-century inn, just a mile from the famous 'Lost
gardens of Heligan.' The owner helped restore the gardens
over a period of ten years. Well-kept St Austell ales
complement an extensive menu and daily specials. Expect cod
in beer batter, local steaks, rack of lamb, and liver and bacon
among other favourites.

continued

The Crown Inn

OPEN: 12-3 5-11 **BAR MEALS:** L served all week 12-2 D served all week 6-9 **RESTAURANT:** L served all week 12-2 D served all week 6-9 🍴: St Austell Brewery 🍺: Tribute, Hicks Special, Tinners, plus guest ale. **FACILITIES:** Garden: Two marquees, heated fenced, well lit Dogs allowed Water **NOTES:** Parking 60

ST IVES   Map 02 SW54

Pick of the Pubs

The Sloop Inn ♦♦♦♦ ♀
The Wharf TR26 1LP ☎ 01736 796584 📠 01736 793322
e-mail: sloop@btinternet.com web: www.sloop-inn.co.uk
Dir: On harbour front

Believed to date from around 1312, the famous Sloop is one of Cornwall's oldest inns. With its low, open-beamed ceilings and slate floors it still feels venerable, despite the changes that must have taken place during almost seven centuries. The public bar, with its unusual long tables and benches, is a favourite with fishermen and painters. In here and in the lounge bar are drawings by Hyman Segal (died 2004) who won a scholarship to St Martin's School of Art aged 12, while downstairs is a permanent exhibition of works by artists associated with the St Ives School. It has a reputation for good food, especially the locally caught fish and shellfish such as moules marinière, Newlyn cod and smoky bacon fishcakes, and St Ives Bay mackerel fillets. Other possibilities are freshly baked baguettes, steaks, pasta, and home-made lamb and mint pie, bangers and mash, and spinach, red onion and brie pancakes from the specials board.
OPEN: 10.30-11 (Sun 12-10.30) **BAR MEALS:** L served all week 12-3 D served all week 5-8.45 Av main course £6 🍴: Unique Pub Co 🍺: Scottish Courage John Smiths, Sharp's Doom Bar, Greene King Old Speckled Hen & Morland, Interbrew Draught Bass. ♀: 12 **FACILITIES:** Garden: Cobbled forecourt overlooking harbour **ROOMS:** 16 bedrooms 13 en suite 4 family rooms d£60

ST JUST (NEAR LAND'S END)   Map 02 SW33

Pick of the Pubs

Star Inn
TR19 7LL ☎ 01736 788767
Dir: Telephone for directions
Plenty of tin mining and fishing stories are told at this traditional Cornish pub, located in the town of St Just, near Lands End. It dates back a few centuries, and was reputedly built to house workmen constructing the 15th-century church. John Wesley is believed to have been among the Star's more illustrious guests over the years, but these days the pub is most likely to be recognised for having featured in several television and film productions. A choice of local beers is served alongside some good bar food. Dishes on offer include home-made pies (beef, and chicken and ham), soups, pasties and - in season - crab dishes, notably crab Averock: white crab meat with a cream and mustard sauce. Monday night is folk night, and there's live music on Thursdays and Saturdays, too, in a whole range of styles.
OPEN: 11-11 (Sun 12-10.30) **BAR MEALS:** L served all week 12-2 D served all week 5-8 Av main course £6 🍴: St Austell Brewery 🍺: St Austell HSD, Tinners Ale, Tribute, Dartmoor. **FACILITIES:** Garden: Appletree, roses, pine & palm, patio heaters Dogs allowed on a lead only **NOTES:** No credit cards

ST KEVERNE   Map 02 SW72

The White Hart
The Square TR12 6ND ☎ 01326 280325 📠 01326 280325
e-mail: whitehart@easynet.co.uk
Opposite the 15th-century church, the White Hart is known for the ghost of a former landlady, Lettie, who knocks things off the shelves if customers get too rowdy! The lunchtime bar menu offers ploughman's and huntsman's platters, various sandwiches, baguettes and jacket potatoes. Also a good choice of dishes for children. More extensive bistro menu - also served in the evening - includes much locally-caught fish, including whole hot baked crab, John Dory with herb crust on parmesan mash, and seared sea bass.
OPEN: 11-2.30 6-11 (July-Aug all day wkds)
BAR MEALS: L served all week 12-2 D served all week 6.30-9.30 Av main course £9 **RESTAURANT:** D served Wed-Sun 7-9.30 🍴: Pubmaster 🍺: Interbrew Flowers Original, Greene King Old Speckled Hen, Sharp's Doom Bar. **FACILITIES:** Garden: Terace & bench seating. Herb garden Dogs allowed Water, Bonios **NOTES:** Parking 15

ST KEW   Map 02 SX07

St Kew Inn
PL30 3HB ☎ 01208 841259 e-mail: des@stkewinn.fsnet.co.uk
Dir: Village signed 3m NE of Wadebridge on A39
Attractive stone-built 15th-century inn near the parish church in a secluded valley. Retains much of its original character, notably its large kitchen range and slate floors. One menu is offered throughout, with dishes ranging from fish pie, and beef in Guinness with herb dumplings, to specialities such as speciality steaks. Fresh fish comes straight from Padstow.
OPEN: 11-2.30 6-11 (Sun 12-3, 7-10.30, all day Jun-Aug)
BAR MEALS: L served all week 12-2 D served all week 7-9.30 Av main course £8.50 **RESTAURANT:** L served all week 12-2 D served all week 7-9.30 Av 3 course à la carte £18 🍴: St Austell Brewery 🍺: St Austell HSD, Tinners Ale & Tribute. **FACILITIES:** Garden **NOTES:** Parking 80

England

ST MAWES   Map 02 SW83

Pick of the Pubs

The Rising Sun ★★ ⊚ ♀
The Square TR2 5DJ ☎ 01326 270233 ▤ 01209 270198
e-mail: info@risingsunstmawes.co.uk
Step outside this splendidly situated pub and the scene
that greets you never fails to impress. This is the
picturesque harbour of St Mawes, Cornwall's yachting
mecca on the Roseland Peninsula and a popular but
dignified resort enjoying a mild climate. The larger Lizard
Peninsula shelters the town from the vagaries of the
Atlantic, which means that on fine days the terrace is the
ideal place for a drink, and for watching the yachting
world sail by. The pub's reputation for fine food owes
much to Ann Long, a renowned master chef, whose
ultimate objective is to seek ways of ringing the changes
and doing things differently. One of her typical bar menus
might propose ratatouille au gratin, or Mediterranean
salad with chorizo, goats' cheese, salami, peppers and
olives. To follow there could be Bakewell tart, sticky toffee
pudding or fruit crumble. Imaginative lunchtime
sandwiches are also served.
OPEN: 11-11 (Sun 12-10.30) **BAR MEALS:** L served all week
12-2.30 D served all week 6.30-9 **RESTAURANT:** L served Sun
12-2 D served all week 7-9.30 ⊜: St Austell Brewery ◖: Hicks
Special Draught, St Austell Tinners Ale. ♀: 11
FACILITIES: Garden: Paved terrace overlooking harbour Dogs
allowed Water **NOTES:** Parking 6 **ROOMS:** 8 bedrooms
en suite 1 family room

Pick of the Pubs

The Victory Inn ▷
Victory Hill TR2 5PQ ☎ 01326 270324 ▤ 01326 270238
e-mail: info@roseland-inn.co.uk
Dir: Take A3078 to St Mawes up the Victory Steps by the Habour

Close to St Mawes Harbour on the Roseland Peninsula is
this friendly fishermen's local, named after Nelson's
flagship. These days it doubles as a modern dining pub,
offering the freshest of local seafood, and harbour views.
The blackboard specials change daily according to the
catch, with dishes such as pan-fried monkfish with ginger
and mango salad, or sea bass with spring onions, sweet
potato mash and basil sauce. There's also a choice of pub
grub dishes - fresh mussels with fries, pasty and gravy,
sausage and mash - while lunchtime snacks include white
Cornish crab sandwiches. In addition to the range of real
ales, there's a decent selection of wines by the glass, plus
speciality spirits - malt whiskies, Cognac and Calvados.

OPEN: 11-11 (Sun 12-10.30) **BAR MEALS:** L served all week
12-2.15 D served all week 6.30-9 Av main course £7
RESTAURANT: L served Mon-Sun 12-2.15 D served Mon-Sun
6.30-9 ◖: Sharps, Bass, Ringwood, IPA. **FACILITIES:** Child
facs Food served outside, overlooking St Mawes Dogs allowed
Biscuits, water and toys

ST MAWGAN   Map 02 SW86

The Falcon Inn ♦♦♦♦ ♀
TR8 4EP ☎ 01637 860225 ▤ 01637 860884
e-mail: enquiries@thefalconinn-newquay.co.uk
web: www.thefalconinn-newquay.co.uk
Dir: From A30 8m W of Bodmin, follow signs to Newquay/St Mawgan
Airport. After 2m turn right into village, pub at bottom of hill

Under new ownership after 15 years, this 18th-century pub
lies in the sheltered Vale of Lanherne. Its large, well-tended
garden has attractive terraces, wisteria-covered walls and a
beautiful magnolia tree which flowers twice a year. Fresh local
scallops are served in chilli and lime butter, and hake caught
offshore comes in a caper and white wine sauce. A speciality
is the Falcon Feast, a 12-oz sirloin steak with all the trimmings.
OPEN: 11-3 6-11 **BAR MEALS:** L served all week 12-2 D served all
week 6.30-9.30 Av main course £10 **RESTAURANT:** L served all
week 12-2 D served all week 6.30-9.30 ⊜: St Austell Brewery ◖: St
Austell HSD, Tinners Ale & Tribute. ♀: 7 **FACILITIES:** Child facs
Garden: Large garden, sheltered, safe Dogs allowed Water
NOTES: Parking 25 **ROOMS:** 3 bedrooms 2 en suite s£26 d£74

ST MERRYN   Map 02 SW87

The Farmers Arms
PL28 8NP ☎ 01841 520303 ▤ 01841 520643
Dir: B3275 between Padstow and Newquay
A lively and vibrant community pub dating from the 17th
century. Nearby is the fishing port of Padstow and the 'seven
bays for seven days', and some of Britain's most beautiful
beaches. Excellent golf courses and stunning coastal walks are
also close by. One menu is available throughout, offering such
dishes as beef in ale pie, lasagne, ham, egg and chips and
rack of ribs in barbecue sauce.
OPEN: 11-11 (Apr-Oct 11-3, 5-11) **BAR MEALS:** L served all week
12-2 D served all week 6.30-9 (Food all day Whitsun-Sept) Av main
course £7 **RESTAURANT:** L served all week 12-2.30 D served all
week 6-9.30 Av 3 course à la carte £9 ⊜: St Austell Brewery ◖: St
Austell HSD, Tinners Ale, Tribute, plus Guest Ales. **FACILITIES:** Dogs
allowed Water **NOTES:** Parking 80

> ★ Star rating for inspected hotel
>   accommodation

continued

ST NEOT
Map 02 SX16

The London Inn ◆◆◆◆ ⏲
PL14 6NG ☎ 01579 320263 ▤ 01579 321642
e-mail: lon.manager@ccinns.com

Dating back to the 18th century, this pub was the first coaching inn on the route from Penzance to London. The bar and dining areas have a good deal of charm and character, with old beamed ceilings and polished flagstone floors. Seafood platter, salmon and halibut are among the fish dishes, while other main courses include lamb shank in a spiced port sauce. Lighter fare ranges from ciabatta bread with a variety of fillings, including roast beef, chicken, bacon and cheese, to a choice of ploughman's lunches.
OPEN: 12-3 6.30-11 (Sat 12-11, Sun 12-10.30)
BAR MEALS: L served all week 12-2 D served all week 7-9 Av main course £6 **RESTAURANT:** L served all week 12-2 D served all week 7-9 🍺: Doombar, Courage Best, John Smiths + guest ales. ⏲: 16
NOTES: Parking 15 **ROOMS:** 3 bedrooms en suite s£40 d£55

SALTASH
Map 03 SX45

The Crooked Inn ◆◆◆◆ 🐟
Stoketon Cottage, Trematon PL12 4RZ
☎ 01752 848177 ▤ 01752 843203 e-mail: info@crooked-inn.co.uk

The inn was originally two cottages, accommodating the cooks and gardeners of Stoketon Manor (see the remains across the courtyard). It has been run by the same family for 20 years and welcomes both children and animals. The conservatory and children's play area are great attractions in summer. An extensive menu includes a varied vegetarian selection and a list of specials, such as spicy bean hotpot, beef fajitas, and scallops with ham and cream sauce.
OPEN: 11-11 (BHs 11-10.30) (Sun 11-10.30) Closed: 25 Dec 26 Dec 12-3 **BAR MEALS:** L served all week 12-2.30 D served all week 6-9.30 Av main course £6.50 **RESTAURANT:** L served all week 12-2.30 D served all week 6-9.30 Av 3 course à la carte £12.75
🍺: Free House 🍺: Hicks Special Draught, Sharp's Own Ale,
continued

Skinner's Cornish Knocker Ale. **FACILITIES:** Child facs Garden: 10 acres, enclosed courtyard, seating,decking Dogs allowed
NOTES: Parking 60 **ROOMS:** 18 bedrooms 15 en suite 15 family rooms s£45 d£70

The Weary Friar Inn ◆◆◆◆
Pillaton PL12 6QS ☎ 01579 350238 ▤ 01579 350238
Dir: 2m W of A388 between Callington & Saltash

This whitewashed 12th-century inn with oak-beamed ceilings, an abundance of brass, and blazing fires lies next to the Church of St Adolphus, tucked away in a small Cornish village. A typical selection from the menu includes venison pie, spit roasted chicken, fillet steak with wild mushroom sauce, spinach and mushroom bake, and Cornish crab cakes. Salads, sandwiches, afternoon cream teas and ploughman's are also available. Curry and other themed nights are popular.
OPEN: 11.30-3 6.30-11 (Sun 12-10.30) **BAR MEALS:** L served all week 12 D served all week 9.30 Sun dinner 12-9 Av main course £8.95 **RESTAURANT:** L served all week 12 D served all week 11 Av 3 course à la carte £15 🍺: Free House 🍺: St Austell Tribute, Tinners, Interbrew Bass, Fullers London PrideSharp's Doom Bar.
FACILITIES: Garden: sun trap, seating, illuminated fountain Dogs allowed Dog bowl **NOTES:** Parking 30 **ROOMS:** 12 bedrooms en suite s£45 d£60

SEATON
Map 03 SX35

Smugglers Inn ◆◆◆◆
Tregunnick Ln PL11 3JD ☎ 01503 250646 ▤ 01503 250646
There's a warm and friendly atmosphere in this 17th-century free house, which stands in an idyllic spot opposite the beach. Local real ales are served in the comfortable bar, where you'll find darts and traditional pub games as well as Sky Sports. The extensive bar menu includes pan-fried chicken breast, roast lamb chops, and baked duck breast, supported by a regular Sunday carvery.
BAR MEALS: L served all week 12-2.30 D served all week 6-9.30 **RESTAURANT:** L served all week 12-2.30 (Varies to season) D served all week 7-9.30 🍺: Free House 🍺: Real ales from local brewery.
FACILITIES: Garden: Patio area Dogs allowed Water
NOTES: Parking 10 **ROOMS:** 5 bedrooms en suite 2 family rooms

SENNEN
Map 02 SW32

The Old Success Inn ★★ 🐟
Sennen Cove TR19 7DG ☎ 01736 871232 ▤ 01736 871457
e-mail: oldsuccess@sennencove.fsbusiness.co.uk
Once the haunt of smugglers and now a focal point for the Sennen Lifeboat crew, this 17th-century inn enjoys a glorious location overlooking Cape Cornwall. Its name comes from the days when fishermen gathered here to count their catch and share out their 'successes'. Fresh local seafood is to the fore,
continued

England

SENNEN continued

and favourites include cod in Doom Bar batter, steaks, chilli, and vegetable lasagne. Live music every Saturday night in the bar.

The Old Success Inn

OPEN: 11-11 **BAR MEALS:** L served all week 12-2.30 D served all week 6.15-9.30 **RESTAURANT:** L served Sun 12-2.15 D served all week 7-9.30 Av 3 course à la carte £18.50 Av 3 course fixed price £17 ⊞: Free House ⚫: Doom Bar, Sharps Special, Skinners.
FACILITIES: Garden: Beer terrace, stunning views of Whitesand Bay Dogs allowed **NOTES:** Parking 16 **ROOMS:** 12 bedrooms en suite 2 family rooms s£31 d£80

TINTAGEL   Map 02 SX08

The Port William ◆◆◆◆ ♀
Trebarwith Strand PL34 0HB ☎ 01840 770230 ⓑ 01840 770936
e-mail: theportwilliam@btinternet.com
web: www.theportwilliam.com
Dir: *Off B3263 between Camelford & Tintagel, signed The Port William*

Occupying one of the best locations in Cornwall, this former harbourmaster's house lies directly on the coastal path, 50 yards from the sea. There is an entrance to a smugglers' tunnel at the rear of the ladies' toilet! Focus on the daily-changing specials board for such dishes as artichoke and roast pepper salad, grilled sardines, warm smoked trout platter, and spinach ricotta tortelloni.
OPEN: 11-11 (Sun 12-10.30) 12 opening in winter
BAR MEALS: L served all week 12-2.30 D served all week 6.30-9.30
Av main course £8.50 **RESTAURANT:** L served all week 12-2.30
D served all week 6-9.30 Av 3 course à la carte £15 ⊞: Free House
⚫: St Austell Tinners Ale & Hicks, Interbrew Bass. ♀: 8
FACILITIES: Garden: Patio overlooking sea, food served outside
Dogs allowed Water **NOTES:** Parking 75 **ROOMS:** 8 bedrooms
en suite s£42.50 d£60

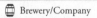
Brewery/Company

Tintagel Arms Hotel
Fore St PL34 0DB ☎ 01840 770780
Dir: *Hotel opposite Lloyds Bank*
This 250-year-old stone-built inn, with its quaint beamed bedrooms and Cornish slate roof, is located in one of Britain's most famous villages, close to the remains of the legendary castle associated with King Arthur. The menu in Zorba's Taverna obviously has a Greek influence, with the expected moussaka, kebabs, stuffed vine leaves and Greek salad. Fresh fish dishes might include swordfish, tuna, cod, salmon and bass, and there is a choice for vegetarians.
OPEN: 6-11 (Sun 6-10.30) Closed: Nov-Jan **BAR MEALS:** D served all week 6-9.30 Av main course £6 **RESTAURANT:** D served all week 6-9.30 Av 3 course à la carte £12.50 ⊞: Free House
⚫: Interbrew Bass, Sharp's Doom Bar. **NOTES:** Parking 7

TORPOINT   Map 03 SX45

Pick of the Pubs

The Edgcumbe Arms ◆◆◆◆ ♀
Cremyll PL10 1HX ☎ 01752 822294 ⓑ 01752 822014
e-mail: edgcumbearms1@btopenworld.com
Dir: *Please phone for directions*
The inn dates from the 15th century and is located right on the Tamar estuary, next to the National Trust Park, close to the foot ferry from Plymouth. Views from the bow window seats and waterside terrace are glorious, taking in Drakes Island, the Royal William Yard and the marina. Real ales from St Austell and quality home-cooked food are served in a series of rooms, which are full of character with American oak panelling and stone flagged floors. Fresh local seafood and Cornish beef steaks are a feature of the menus alongside a daily curry and steak and ale pie. A good choice of bar snacks is also offered. The inn has a function room with sea views, and a courtyard garden; it also holds a civil wedding license. A bridal suite is included in the range of pretty bedrooms.
OPEN: 11-11 (Sun 12-10.30) **BAR MEALS:** L served all week 12-2.30 D served all week 6-9 **RESTAURANT:** L served all week 12-2.30 D served all week 7-9 ⊞: St Austell Brewery ⚫: St Austell HSD, Tribute HS, IPA, Cornish Cream. ♀: 10
FACILITIES: Garden: Large picnic area with tables Dogs allowed Water and treats **NOTES:** Parking 12
ROOMS: 6 bedrooms en suite 2 family rooms

TREBARWITH   Map 02 SX08

The Mill House Inn NEW
PL34 0HD ☎ 01840 770200 ⓑ 01840 770647
e-mail: management@themillhouseinn.co.uk
Dir: *From Tintagel take B3263 S, turn right after Trewarmett to Trebarwith Starnd, pub is 0.5m down valley on right*
A private dwelling until 1945, the 18th-century Mill House was indeed originally a mill. Halfway down a valley in delightful woodland, the slate-floored bar with wooden tables, chapel chairs and log fire has a strong family-friendly feel. In the dining room over the old millstream, maybe choose battered cod, chips and peas; pan-fried fillet of Port Isaac halibut, king prawns, mussels with chilli and coriander dressing; or Michaelstow lamb noisettes with rosemary and tomato sauce.
OPEN: 12-3 6-11 (Open all day in high season) Closed: 25 Dec
BAR MEALS: L served all week 12-2.30 D served all week 7-9 Sun 12-4. Not Sun-Mon eve in winter Av main course £7
RESTAURANT: L served all week 12-2.30 D served all week 7-9 Sun

continued

12-4. Not Sun-Mon eve in winter Av 3 course à la carte £25 🍷: Free House 🍺: Sharps Doom Bar, Sharps Special, Red Stripe. **FACILITIES:** Child facs Children's licence Garden: Tiered front terrace Dogs allowed **NOTES:** Parking 60

TREBURLEY
Map 03 SX37

Pick of the Pubs

The Springer Spaniel 🏆
PL15 9NS ☎ 01579 370424 🖷 01579 370113
e-mail: thespringer@wagtailinns.com

See Pick of the Pubs on page 92

TREGADILLETT
Map 03 SX28

Eliot Arms (Square & Compass) 🏆
PL15 7EU ☎ 01566 772051 e-mail: eli.bookings@ccinns.com
Dir: From Launceston take A30 towards Bodmin. Then follow brown signs to Tregadillet.

This old coaching inn is built from Cornish stone and boasts a huge collection of clocks, Masonic regalia and horse brasses. It was believed to have been a Masonic lodge for Napoleonic prisoners, and even has its own friendly ghost! Customers can enjoy real fires in winter and lovely hanging baskets in summer. Fish features strongly, with delicacies such as moules marinière and grilled sardines. Other options include Cajun-style chicken, and home-made vegetable curry.
OPEN: 11.30-3 6-11 (Sat-Sun all day) **BAR MEALS:** L served all week 12-2 D served all week 7-9 **RESTAURANT:** L served all week 12-2 D served all week 7-9 🍷: Free House 🍺: Doom Bar, Scottish Courage Courage Best, Speckled Hen. 🍷: 16 **FACILITIES:** Seating areas around pub Dogs allowed **NOTES:** Parking 20

🍺 Principal Beers for sale

TRESCO
Map 02 SV81

Pick of the Pubs

The New Inn ★★ 🏆
New Grimsby TR24 0QQ ☎ 01720 422844 🖷 01720 423200
e-mail: newinn@tresco.co.uk
web: www.tresco.co.uk/holidays/new_inn.asp
Dir: By New Grimsby Quay

The only pub in Tresco, the New Inn is on most visitor's itinerary, and in the evenings becomes the island's social centre. It is open all year and is handy for New Grimsby Harbour, Tresco Stores, the Island Hotel and Abbey Garden. Maritime artefacts abound: walls are panelled with exotic woods jettisoned by a freighter, the mahogany bar top is from a French wreck, and the pub's signboard was salvaged from The Award, wrecked in 1861. Lunchtime favourites include burgers, sausages, sandwiches and salads. At dinner you might find oriental chicken linguini; slow roasted belly pork; or ricotta, butternut squash and pinenut risotto. Alternatives are seafood from the specials board or the daily curry. Some of the ales come from Britain's most south-westerly brewery, Ales of Scilly on St Mary's, and there are eight wines available by the glass. Many of the 16 double rooms have ocean views.
OPEN: 11-11 **BAR MEALS:** L served all week 12-2 D served all week 6-9 limited menu available all day Apr-Sept Av main course £8.95 **RESTAURANT:** D served all week 7-9 Av 3 course fixed price £29 🍷: Free House 🍺: Skinner's Betty Stogs Bitter, Tresco Tipple, Ales of Scilly Maiden Voyage, St Austell IPA. 🍷: 8 **FACILITIES:** Child facs Garden: Patio area with sub-tropical plants **ROOMS:** 16 bedrooms en suite d£170

TRURO
Map 02 SW84

Old Ale House 🏆
7 Quay St TR1 2HD ☎ 01872 271122 🖷 01872 271817
Dir: A30, Truro City centre
Olde-worlde establishment with a large selection of real ales on display, as well as more than twenty flavours of fruit wine. Lots of attractions, including live music and various quiz and games nights. Food includes 'huge hands of hot bread', oven-baked jacket potatoes, ploughman's lunches and daily specials. Vegetable stir fry, five spice chicken and sizzling beef feature among the sizzling skillets.
OPEN: 11-11 (Sun 12-10.30) Closed: Dec 25
BAR MEALS: L served all week 12-3 D served Mon-Fri 7-9 Av main course £5 **RESTAURANT:** L served all week D served Mon-Fri 🍷: Enterprise Inns 🍺: Skinners Kiddlywink, Shepherd Neame Spitfire, Scottish Courage Bass, Greene King Abbot Ale.

Pick of the Pubs
TREBURLEY – CORNWALL

The Springer Spaniel

When the menu of a pub tells you that availability of fish depends upon the current market and game on the success of the shoots you know that the least you can expect from the food is freshness. This unassuming-looking roadside hostelry may not look very different from many other pubs, but it's a different story inside.

It dates from the 18th century, and the old creeper-covered walls conceal a cosy bar with two high-backed wooden settles, farmhouse-style chairs, and a wood-burning stove to keep out the chill on cooler days. The atmosphere is friendly, and conversation flows naturally, making it easy for the visitor to glean interesting facts about Cornish rural life from the locals. If you're looking for noisy electronic games or intrusive music, you'll have to go elsewhere. It was once part of a farm, and remains homely and welcoming, though these days it is the terrific food that provides the biggest draw. Blackboards in the bar list the lighter snack options - freshly filled sandwiches and rolls, decent soups and daily specials - as well as the more serious choices that are also served in the separate beamed

dining room where the setting is slightly more formal. Dishes vary according to the seasons, and include imaginatively conceived and attractively presented game - throughout the year when in season. Starters might include mushroom pot; and chargrilled local scallops with a sweet chilli sauce, while mains vary between local wild boar sausages, mash and gravy; stilton beef; Trelawney cheese and vegetable pie, and the ever-popular home-made crab Cornish pasty. Desserts might be dark chocolate tart; home-made gingerbread with toffee sauce; or bread and butter pudding. Children's meals are also available. Well-kept ales include Sharps Doom Bar, Cornish Coaster and Springer Ale, and there's an interesting wine list and 15-year-old malt whiskies to complement the menu.

OPEN: 11-3 6-11
BAR MEALS: L served all week 12-2 D served all week 6.30-9 Av main course £8.95
RESTAURANT: L served all week 12-2 D served all week 6.30-9 Av 3 course à la carte £20
🍺: Free House
🍺: Sharp's Doom Bar, Eden Ale, Springer Ale, Cornish Coaster. ♀: 7
FACILITIES: Garden: Landscaped with seating, heated umbrella Dogs allowed Water & Biscuits
NOTES: Parking 30

    🐾 ♀   Map 03 SX37
PL15 9NS
☎ 01579 370424
🖷 01579 370113
✉ thespringer@wagtailinns.com
Dir: On the A388 halfway between Launceston & Callington

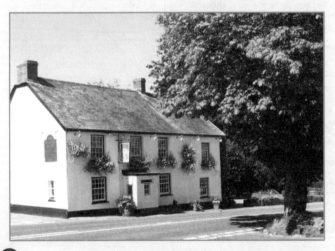

TRURO continued

The Wig & Pen Inn
Frances St TR1 3DP ☎ 01872 273028 🗎 01872 277351
Dir: City centre nr Law Courts, 10 mins from railway station
A listed city centre pub originally known as the Star, that
became the Wig & Pen when the county court moved to
Truro. There is a ghost called Claire who lives in the cellar, but
she is friendly! The choice of food includes such home-made
dishes as steak and ale pie, curry, casseroles, steaks and
vegetarian dishes, and a range of fish options such as sea
bass, John Dory, mullet or monkfish.
OPEN: 11-11 (Sun 12-10.30) **BAR MEALS:** L served all week
12-2.30 D served all week 6-9 Av main course £5
RESTAURANT: D served Summer all day, winter Thurs-Sat 6-9.45
Av 3 course à la carte £25 Av 3 course fixed price £25 ⊕: St Austell
Brewery ◀: St Austell Dartmoor & HSD plus guest ales.
FACILITIES: Garden: Patio area with pot plants Dogs allowed in non
eating area

VERYAN   Map 02 SW93

The New Inn ♦♦♦♦ ♀
TR2 5QA ☎ 01872 501362 🗎 01872 501078
e-mail: jack@newinn-veryan.fsnet.co.uk
Dir: Off A3078 towards Portloe

Based in a pair of 16th-century cottages, this unspoilt pub is
set in the pretty Cornish village of Veryan, close to safe sandy
beaches and interesting walks. It has a single bar, open fires
and a beamed ceiling, and the emphasis is on good ales and
home cooking. Simple, satisfying dishes abound with seafood
featuring heavily - from prawn cocktail or deep-fried whitebait
to sea bass fillet with pesto and pine nuts. Meat-lovers might
enjoy a Greek-style slow-roast lamb shank, ideally eaten in
the garden on a warm summer evening.
OPEN: 12-3 6-11 (Winter 12-2.30) **BAR MEALS:** L served all week
12-2 D served Mon-Sat 7-9 ⊕: St Austell Brewery ◀: St Austell
HSD, Dartmoor Ale & Tribute. ♀: 8 **FACILITIES:** Children's licence
Garden: Secluded garden, large tables, patio **ROOMS:** 3 bedrooms
2 en suite No children overnight

WADEBRIDGE   Map 02 SW97

The Quarryman Inn
Edmonton PL27 7JA ☎ 01208 816444 🗎 01208 815674
Dir: Off A39 opp Royal Cornwall Showground
Friendly 18th-century inn that evolved from a courtyard of
quarrymen's cottages. Handy for the Royal Cornwall
Showground and the Camel Trail. Among the features at this
unusual pub are several bow windows, one of which includes
a delightful stained-glass quarryman panel. Expect prime
sizzling steaks, whole sea bass stuffed with bacon and bay
leaves, fish pie, and oven-roasted lamb shank on the menu.
continued

The Quarryman Inn
OPEN: 12-11 (Sun 12-10.30) **BAR MEALS:** L served all week
12-2.30 D served all week 6-9 Av main course £11.50
RESTAURANT: L served all week 12-2.30 D served all week 6-9
Av 3 course à la carte £20 ⊕: Free House ◀: Sharps, Skinners,
Timothy Taylor Landlord, Various Guest Ales. **FACILITIES:** Garden:
Slate courtyard at rear of pub Dogs allowed Water provided
NOTES: Parking 100

Swan Hotel ♦♦♦ ♀
9 Molesworth St PL27 7DD ☎ 01208 812526 🗎 01208 812526
Dir: In centre of Wadebridge on corner of Molesworth St and The Platt
A town centre hotel that is family friendly, and serves St Austell
Hicks and Tinners as well as guest ales from the tap. Typical
pub food includes scampi, beer-battered cod, crab, salmon en
croute with dill cream sauce, and prawn salad. There is
outdoor seating on a patio area. Recent change of hands.
OPEN: 9-11 **BAR MEALS:** L served all week 12-9 D served all week
6.30-9 Av main course £6.50 ⊕: St Austell Brewery ◀: St Austell
Hicks, Tinners & Tribute, Guest Ale. ♀: 13 **FACILITIES:** Child facs
Children's licence Garden: Beer garden with parasols and seating
Dogs allowed in the garden only **ROOMS:** 6 bedrooms en suite
2 family rooms s£40 d£60

ZENNOR   Map 02 SW43

Pick of the Pubs

The Gurnards Head Hotel ♀
Treen, Zennor TR26 3DE ☎ 01736 796928 🗎 01736 795313
e-mail: gur.bookings@ccinns.com
Dir: 5m from Penzance. 5m from St. Ives on B3306.

An imposing colour-washed building that dominates the
coastal landscape above Gurnard's Head, this traditional
Cornish pub (stone-flagged bar, open fires) is just the
place to get stranded on a wind-swept winter's night.
Here you can see Cornwall at its most brutal, but on
warmer days there are some great walks along the
continued

England

ZENNOR continued

coastal path or the rugged Penwith Moors, strewn with wild flowers and studded with ancient Celtic remains. The menu is based on wholesome local produce, so as you'd expect there's plenty of seafood. Look out for twice baked leek and goat's cheese soufflé; pork and leek sausages; The Gurnards Head mixed grill; filo wrapped prawns; Greek meze; whole sea bream; pan-fried shark steak; Moroccan spiced lamb tangine; and Thai style fish cakes. Live music and storytelling evenings are regular events. **OPEN:** 12-3 6-11 (Sun eve 7-10.30) **BAR MEALS:** L served all week 12-2 D served all week 6-9 Av main course £9 **RESTAURANT:** L served all week 12-2 D served all week 6-9 ᐅ: Free House ⬤: Gales HSB, Skinners Ales, Guest Ales incl. Butcome Smiles. ♀: 18 **FACILITIES:** Garden: Large patio & lawn area with sea views Dogs allowed Water and biscuits **NOTES:** Parking 60

CUMBRIA

AMBLESIDE   Map 18 NY30

Pick of the Pubs

Drunken Duck Inn ♦♦♦♦ ⊚ ▷ ♀
Barngates LA22 0NG ☎ 015394 36347 📠 015394 36781
e-mail: info@drunkenduckinn.co.uk
web: www.drunkenduckinn.co.uk
See Pick of the Pubs on opposite page

APPLEBY-IN-WESTMORLAND   Map 18 NY62

Pick of the Pubs

The Royal Oak Inn ♀
Bongate CA16 6UN ☎ 017683 51463 📠 017683 52300
e-mail: royaloakinn@mortalmaninns.fsnet.co.uk
The Royal Oak has a long and venerable history with parts of the building dating back to 1100 and the rest to the 17th century, when it began life as a coaching inn. Today, sympathetically modernised and offering good food and ale, it proves popular with locals and tourists alike. The pub is especially popular as a touring base for both the Yorkshire Dales and the Lake District as it is situated conveniently between the two. Its well-maintained character interior comprises a classic tap-room with blackened beams, oak panelling and an open fire; a comfortable beamed lounge with a real fire and plenty of reading material; and two dining rooms. Ingredients for the wholesome food are sourced locally wherever possible, and the menus change on a daily or monthly basis. Cumberland sausages, chicken carbonara, mussels, stuffed trout, pork medallions in Madeira and mushroom Stroganoff are typical choices, along with various steaks from Cumbrian fell-bred animals and home-smoked produce. A good choice of real ales includes a number from local brewers, augmented by some 50 malt whiskies. **OPEN:** 11-11 12-10.30 (Sun 12-10.30) **BAR MEALS:** L served all week 12-2.30 D served all week 6-9 Av main course £8 **RESTAURANT:** L served Mon-Sun 12-2.30 D served Mon-Sun 6-9 Av 3 course à la carte £13 ᐅ: Free House ⬤: Black Sheep, John Smiths, & Guest Ales. ♀: 8 **FACILITIES:** Dogs allowed Water **NOTES:** Parking 8

Pick of the Pubs

Tufton Arms Hotel ▷ ♀
Market Square CA16 6XA ☎ 017683 51593 📠 017683 52761
e-mail: info@tuftonarmshotel.co.uk
web: www.tuftonarmshotel.co.uk
See Pick of the Pubs on page 96

ARMATHWAITE   Map 18 NY54

The Dukes Head Hotel ♀
Front St CA4 9PB ☎ 016974 72226
e-mail: info@dukeshead.hotel.co.uk
Dir: From A6 follow Armathwaite signs
This has been a pub since the building of the Settle to Carlisle railway, and for the past 15 years the Lynch family have welcomed walkers, climbers, anglers, and all who appreciate comfort and courtesy. The wide-ranging menu offers such delights as butter bean and black olive paté; home-made pheasant and venison broth with port and barley wine; skewered monkfish, bacon and fennel with rice; local steaks; and roast duckling with apple sauce. **OPEN:** 12-3 5.30-11 **BAR MEALS:** L served all week 12-1.45 D served all week 6.15-9 Av main course £9.20 **RESTAURANT:** L served all week 12-1.45 D served all week 6.15-9 Av 3 course à la carte £15.50 ᐅ: Pubmaster ⬤: Jennings Cumberland Ale, Carlsberg-Tetley Tetley's Bitter, Black Sheep Bitter. ♀: 6 **FACILITIES:** Garden: Lawned area surrounded by trees Dogs allowed Back bar only, Water **NOTES:** Parking 26

BARBON   Map 18 SD68

The Barbon Inn
LA6 2LJ ☎ 015242 76233 📠 051242 76233
e-mail: barboninn@aol.com
Dir: 3.5m N of Kirkby Lonsdale on A683

A 17th-century coaching inn with oak beams and open fires, situated in a quiet village between the lakes and dales. Popular bar meals are smoked salmon baguette and Morecambe Bay shrimps; more substantial dishes include Lakeland lamb casserole, roast breast of duck, and halibut steak. **OPEN:** 12-3 6.30-11 (Sun 6.30-10.30) **BAR MEALS:** L served all week 12-2 D served all week 6.30-9 Av main course £7.50 **RESTAURANT:** L served Sun D served all week 7-9 ᐅ: Free House ⬤: Theakston. **FACILITIES:** Garden: beer garden, outdoor eating Dogs allowed **NOTES:** Parking 6

Pubs with Red Diamonds are the top
♦ places in the AA's three, four and five
diamond ratings

Pick of the Pubs

Drunken Duck Inn

Set amidst the fells and surrounded by sixty quite stunning private acres, the Drunken Duck epitomises the Lakeland inn. The curious name is attributed to the hastiness of a previous landlady who, finding her ducks lifeless on the ground, began to pluck them for the pot. Far from dead, they were in fact completely smashed, a damaged beer barrel having leaked its contents into their feeding ditch.

Don't fear: she knitted them jerseys to cover the bald patches, and their descendants are probably still waddling the locale. The inn has its own Barngates Brewery, supplying itself and 40 other outlets with brews named Cracker, Tag Lag and Chesters Strong & Ugly, after much-loved dogs. The interior is a successful mix of traditional and contemporary, with oak flooring, leather chairs and a striking bar made from local slate. The food side of things ranges from properly home-made sandwiches available at the bar to an elegant candlelit dinner in the restaurant. A real virtue is the dedicated, intelligent use of local produce. Even the hand-churned butter is given its source, all meat comes from nearby farmers, and the cheese list relies entirely on traditional artisanship. Inventive dishes really do justice to these ingredients. You could start with tempura battered okra with lime and cardamon marmalade; or Cartmel Valley smoked salmon on Nicoise salad. Next, sample noisettes of Herdwick shearling (Beatrix Potter's favourite breed) with beetroot and mustard purée; pan-fried wild halibut with girolles mushroom, spinach tartlet and potted Flookburgh shrimps; or brill roast with pancetta, with blood orange hollandaise. An excellent wine list rounds things off. Stylish accommodation is provided in five superior de luxe rooms, with two suites across the courtyard affording splendid views of the Langdale Pikes.

OPEN: 11.30-11
BAR MEALS: L served all week 12-2.30 D served all week 6-9 Av main course £14.50
RESTAURANT: L served all week 12-2.30 D served all week 6-9
⊕: Free House
🍺: Barngates Cracker Ale, Chesters Strong & Ugly, Tag Lag, Catnap & 1 Guest Beer. ♀: 20
FACILITIES: Children's licence Garden: Private gardens, leading to fells Dogs allowed Water
NOTES: Parking 40
ROOMS: 16 bedrooms en suite d£95

◆◆◆◆ ◎ 🐟 ♀
Map 18 NY30
Barngates LA22 0NG
☎ 015394 36347
📄 015394 36781
📧 info@drunkenduckinn.co.uk
🌐 www.drunkenduckinn.co.uk
Dir: From Kendal on A591 to Ambleside, then follow Hawkshead sign. In 2.5m inn sign on right. 1m up hill

Pick of the Pubs

APPLEBY-IN-WESTMORLAND – CUMBRIA

Tufton Arms Hotel

Set in the heart of a valley so beautiful and unspoilt that the only name for it is Eden, this 16th-century family-run coaching inn is renowned for its hospitality. It is a landmark in the centre of the medieval market town of Appleby-in-Westmorland, where it attracts visitors who come to enjoy the many countryside pursuits available locally, including pony-trekking, golf, fell walking, and fly fishing.

The less energetic will also find much to engage them, including discovering the charms of this former county town of Westmorland, and touring the Lake District or Yorkshire Dales National Parks, both within easy reach. The Milsom family, the present proprietors, have lovingly restored the Tufton Arms to its former Victorian splendour with rich drapes, period paintings and elegant furniture. The stylish conservatory restaurant overlooks a cobbled mews courtyard; light and airy in the daytime, this room takes on an attractive glow in the evening when the curtains are closed and the lighting is soft and romantic. The preparation and cooking of superb quality food has led to accolades for chef David Milsom and his team, whose wide selection of delicious dishes are made from the finest and freshest local ingredients. The resulting cuisine is an appealing blend of the classical and the modern, with fresh local meat, game, fish and seafood appearing on the menu. Dishes like fillets of sea bass on spinach with a smoked salmon butter sauce; medallions of monkfish wrapped in parma ham with a tomato-basil sauce; nicoise salad with pan-fried fillet of sea bass; and pan-fried cod steak topped with Welsh rarebit on roasted vegetables will meet with approval. The bar offers sandwiches and tasty light meals like rice and pasta dishes, omelettes, and Mrs Ewbank's beefburger.

OPEN: 11-11 Closed: 25-26 Dec
BAR MEALS: L served all week 12-2 D served all week 6.30-9
RESTAURANT: L served all week 12-2 D served all week 6.30-9
⊕: Free House
◀: Tufton Arms Ale, Coors Worthington Bitter, Interbrew Flowers & Boddingtons, Tennants. ♀: 15
FACILITIES: Dogs allowed
NOTES: Parking 15

🐟 ♀   Map 18 NY62
Market Square CA16 6XA
☎ 017683 51593
🖷 017683 52761
℮ info@tuftonarmshotel.co.uk
ⓦ www.tuftonarmshotel.co.uk
Dir: In centre of Appleby-in-Westmorland

BASSENTHWAITE — Map 18 NY23

Pick of the Pubs

The Pheasant ★★★ 🏵 ♀
CA13 9YE ☎ 017687 76234 📠 017687 76002
e-mail: info@the-pheasant.co.uk
web: www.the-pheasant.co.uk
Dir: A66 to Cockermouth, 8m N of Keswick on left

A former coaching inn, the Pheasant dates back 500 years and is set in its own attractive gardens and woodland close to Bassenthwaite Lake. Huntsman John Peel was a regular and the Cumbrian painter Edward Thompson bartered for beer in the pub - two of his originals hang in the bar. The interior is beautifully decorated, with period furnishings set against polished parquet flooring, fresh floral arrangements and blazing log fires. The mellow bar is richly inviting with panelled walls and oak settles, and offers a selection of 50 malt whiskies and 12 wines by the glass. Light lunches are served in the lounge or bar, and there's a more formal lunch and dinner menu in the beamed dining room. Local specialities include Thornby Moor Dairy cheeses, potted Silloth shrimps, smoked rainbow trout, and roast rack of Lakeland lamb.
OPEN: 11.30-2.30 5.30-10.30 Sun 12-2.30 Sun 6-10.30 Closed: Dec 25 **BAR MEALS:** L served all week 12-2 Av main course £8.50 **RESTAURANT:** L served all week 12.30-2 D served all week 7-9 🍴: Free House 🍺: Theakston Best, Interbrew Bass, Jennings Cumberland Ale. ♀: 12 **FACILITIES:** Garden: Garden seating 25 Dogs allowed Kennels **NOTES:** Parking 50
ROOMS: 15 bedrooms en suite s£80 d£140 No children overnight

BEETHAM — Map 18 SD47

Pick of the Pubs

The Wheatsheaf at Beetham ♦♦♦♦ ♀
LA7 7AL ☎ 015395 62123 📠 015395 64840
e-mail: wheatsheaf@beetham.plus.com
Dir: On A6 5m N of junct 35
Despite its upmarket designation, the Wheatsheaf is still a place where you can just pop in for a pint or two of Jennings Cumberland ale. This family owned and run free house offers a tranquil retreat of uncomplicated charm. The 16th-century former coaching inn stands beside the church in the attractive village of Beetham, tucked away off the main A6 one mile south of Milnthorpe. The owners have created a smart, well-furnished non-smoking dining room, where candlelight burns in the evenings. Throughout the inn you'll find personal touches like fresh flowers and table decorations, as well as local and

national newspapers and magazines. Six delightful en suite bedrooms provide uncluttered homeliness, and the traditional bar with its real fire offers an abundance of local character. A commitment to purchasing fresh local produce underpins the home cooking. Lunchtime bar meals include ciabatta sandwiches like Wheatsheaf Club; egg mayonnaise with crispy bacon; or smoked salmon with dill. Bigger appetites might begin with filo parcels of melting cheese served with a tomato, coriander and garlic salsa; seared scallops set on confit new potato and drizzled with a ginger and honey soy reduction; or avocado, crab and salmon fish cakes enhanced with Thai spices. For the main course, expect choices like slowly braised lamb shank on creamy mash with a redcurrant and red wine reduction; Wheatsheaf sausages with Cumberland gravy; or pan-seared Gressingham duck marinated in honey, coriander and cumin. Fish lovers are well catered for, with options like sea bass; salmon; monkfish or red snapper. Or, for something really special, opt for fillets of lemon sole wrapped around a prawn and salmon farcie with a mint pea purée and glazed with a seafood bisque.

The Wheatsheaf at Beetham

OPEN: 11.30-3 5.30-11 (Sun 12-3) Closed: Dec 25 **BAR MEALS:** L served all week 12-2 D served all week 6-9 Av main course £14.95 **RESTAURANT:** L served all week 12-2 D served all week 6-9 🍴: Free House 🍺: Jennings Cumberland Ale & Bitter, Guest Ales. ♀: 8 **FACILITIES:** Garden: small outside seating area Dogs allowed Water **NOTES:** Parking 40 **ROOMS:** 6 bedrooms en suite 1 family room s£55 d£80 No children overnight

BLENCOGO — Map 18 NY14

The New Inn 🐟 ♀
CA7 0BZ ☎ 016973 61091 📠 016973 61091
Dir: From Carlisle, take A596 towards Wigton, then B5302 towards Silloth. After 4m Blencogo signed on left
A late Victorian sandstone pub in a farming hamlet with superb views of the north Cumbrian fells and Solway Plain. The menu here might offer chargrilled chicken breast topped with ham and cheese, and served with mushroom, cream and brandy sauce; chargrilled lamb fillet with mustard and herb crust, served on pecorino and spring onion mash; roast Norfolk duckling with peach brandy sauce; or grilled plaice fillet with lemon shrimp butter. A selection of malt whiskies is kept.
OPEN: 12-3 7-11 (Sun 12-3, 6.30-10.30) Closed: 1st 2 weeks in March **BAR MEALS:** L served Sun 12-2 D served Wed-Sun 7-9 Av main course £12 **RESTAURANT:** L served Sun 12-2 D served Wed-Sun 7-9 Av 3 course à la carte £20 🍴: Free House 🍺: Yates, Carlisle State Bitter, Hesketh New Market, Black Sheep. ♀: 10 **FACILITIES:** Child facs Garden **NOTES:** Parking 50

continued

BOOT   Map 18 NY10

Pick of the Pubs

The Boot Inn formerly The Burnmoor Inn ♀
CA19 1TG ☎ 019467 23224 ▤ 019467 23337
e-mail: enquiries@bootinn.co.uk web: www.bootinn.co.uk

The whole family is welcome at this traditional 16th-century free house nestling at the foot of Scafell Pike - and that includes the dog! In cooler weather a log fire burns in the beamed bar and, naturally enough, the pub attracts many hill walkers. Quality and style are the keynotes here, and the nine comfortably furnished bedrooms all have en suite facilities. The restaurant dates back to 1578, but there's also a new conservatory and dining area with spectacular all-year-round views of the western fells. Real ales feature strongly, and the Burnmoor has joined with other local pubs to run beer festivals in June and November.
OPEN: 11-11 **BAR MEALS:** L served all week 11-5 D served all week 6-9 Sun 11-5, 6-8.30 Av main course £7.50
RESTAURANT: L served all week 11-5 D served all week 6-9 Sun 11-5, 6-8.30 Av 3 course à la carte £18.50 ⊕: Free House
◖: Jennings Cumberland, Jennings Bitter, Roosters Brewery, Black Sheep. ♀: 8 **FACILITIES:** Child facs Children's licence Garden: Part paved part grassed, seating 40 people Dogs allowed Dog blankets, water **NOTES:** Parking 30
ROOMS: 9 bedrooms en suite 2 family rooms s£32 d£64
(♦♦♦)

Brook House Inn 🗠 ♀
CA19 1TG ☎ 019467 23288 ▤ 019467 23160
e-mail: stay@brookhouseinn.co.uk

Family-run inn located in the heart of Eskdale with glorious views and fabulous walking country all around. The owners take great pride in the quality of their food, beer and accommodation, and they make all their own bread, marmalade, jams, desserts and sauces. Fresh, seasonal

continued

produce goes into the dishes - local where possible. Dishes include Moroccan vegetable and bean casserole; local Cumberland sausages with chive mash; and king prawn curry.
OPEN: 11-11 Closed: 25 Dec **BAR MEALS:** L served all week 12-5.30 D served all week 5.30-8.30 **RESTAURANT:** L served all week 12-4.30 D served all week 6-8.30 ◖: Theakstons Best, Timothy Taylors Landlord + up to 4 guest ales. ♀: 8 **FACILITIES:** Child facs Children's licence Garden: Terrace with seating; views across valley **NOTES:** Parking 25 **ROOMS:** 7 bedrooms en suite s£45 d£65
(♦♦♦♦)

BOUTH   Map 18 SD38

The White Hart Inn ♀
LA12 8JB ☎ 01229 861229 ▤ 01229 861229
e-mail: nigelwhitehart@aol.com
web: bed-and-breakfast-cumbria.co.uk

The Bouth of today reposes quietly in the Lake District National Park, although once it had an occasionally noisy gunpowder factory. When this closed in 1928 villagers turned to woodland industries and farm labouring instead, and some of their tools now adorn this 17th-century coaching inn. Ever-changing specials are available, served in the upstairs restaurant that looks out over woods, fields and fells, or the horseshoe-shaped bar offering six real ales, including Cumbrian brews.
OPEN: 12-2 6-11 No food Mon-Tue lunch time except BH
BAR MEALS: L served Wed-Sun 12-2 D served Mon-Sun 6-8.45
RESTAURANT: 12-2 D served Wed-Sun 6-8.45 ⊕: Free House
◖: Black Sheep Best, Jennings Cumberland Ale, Tetley, Yates Bitter.
♀: 7 **FACILITIES:** Child facs Children's licence Garden: West facing terrace **NOTES:** Parking 30 ⊛

BOWLAND BRIDGE   Map 18 S048

Pick of the Pubs

Hare & Hounds Country Inn ♀
Bowland Bridge LA11 6NN
☎ 015395 68333 ▤ 015395 68777
See Pick of the Pubs on opposite page

> We endeavour to be as accurate as possible but changes to times and other information can occur after the guide has gone to press

> Room prices show the minimum double and single rates charged. Room rates in hotels and B&Bs often vary depending on the facilities, so be sure to check prices with the establishment before booking

Pick of the Pubs

BOWLAND BRIDGE – CUMBRIA

Hare & Hounds Country Inn

Wonderfully located below Cartmel Fell in tiny Bowland Bridge, this 17th-century coaching inn has the beautiful Winster Valley almost to itself. The licensees are no strangers to the area – they previously ran this pub from 1979 to 1981.

Flagstone floors, exposed oak beams, ancient pews warmed by open fires, and cosy niches combine to create a traditional country pub atmosphere. The bar menu has the usual ploughman's, baguettes with various fillings, salads and hot plates, such as minute steak, fries and salad; Cumberland sausage and thyme mash; and vegetarian lasagne. The seasonal main menu offers hot goat's cheese and beetroot filo parcels with a bacon and frisée salad; button mushrooms, grilled with Welsh rarebit and smoked bacon toppings; or fresh mussels

marinière as possible starters. Main courses include roast duck with honey, ginger and bitter orange sauce; breast of chicken wrapped in pancetta with wild mushroom and madeira sauce; rigatoni pasta bake with wild mushrooms and sunblush tomatoes; and grilled fillets of sea bass with dill mash and thermidor sauce. Children will enjoy the safe garden play area with swings, while the grown-ups soak up the views. The Hare and Hounds is on the edge of the Lake District National Park, and is only ten minutes from Lake Windermere.

OPEN: 11-11 (Sun 12-10.30)
BAR MEALS: L served all week 12-2.30 D served all week 6-9 Av main course £7.50
RESTAURANT: L served all week 12-2.30 D served all week 6-9 Av 3 course à la carte £15
🛢: Free House
🍺: Black Sheep, Jennings, Boddingtons. ♀: 10
FACILITIES: Child facs Garden: Orchard and hard area with tables Dogs allowed Water
NOTES: Parking 80

♀   Map 18 SD47
Bowland Bridge LA11 6NN
☎ 015395 68333
📄 015395 68777
Dir: M6 onto A591, left after 3m onto A590, right after 3m onto A5074, after 4m sharp left & next left after 1m

England

BRAITHWAITE
Map 18 NY22

Coledale Inn
CA12 5TN ☎ 017687 78272 ▦ 017687 78272
e-mail: info@coledale-inn.co.uk
Dir: From M6 junct 50 take A66 towards Cockermouth for 18 miles. Turn to Braithwaite then on towards Whinlatter Pass, follow sign on left, over bridge leading to hotel
Built as a woollen mill in about 1824, this traditional pub was converted for pencil making before becoming an inn. Peacefully set above Braithwaite village, it is full of attractive Victorian prints, furnishings and antiques, with a fine cellar that includes cask-conditioned local ales. Its terrace and garden are very popular with walkers. Expect prawn salad, roast shoulder of lamb, beef in beer, and various fresh fish dishes.
OPEN: 11-11 **BAR MEALS:** L served all week 12-2 D served all week 6-9 Av main course £8.45 **RESTAURANT:** L served all week 12-2 D served all week 6-9 Av 3 course à la carte £13.95 ⊕: Free House ◖: Yates, Theakstons, Jennings Best, John Smiths.
FACILITIES: Child facs Garden: Lawn with benches Dogs allowed Water **NOTES:** Parking 20 **ROOMS:** 16 bedrooms en suite s£28 d£66 (♦♦♦)

BRAMPTON
Map 21 NY56

Blacksmiths Arms ♦♦♦♦ 🔲 🍴 ♈
Talkin Village CA8 1LE ☎ 016977 3452 ▦ 016977 3396
e-mail: blacksmithsarmstalkin@yahoo.co.uk
web: www.blacksmithstalkin.co.uk
Dir: From M6 take A69 E, after 7m straightover rdbt, follow signs to Talkin Tarn then Talkin Village

Dating from 1700, this attractive village inn was originally the local smithy. The property was added to so that refreshments could be served while horses were being shod, and the building was further extended in the mid 1800s. The well-balanced menu is supplemented by daily-changing blackboard specials. Menu options range from fresh haddock fillet in beer batter; King Arthur's chicken in asparagus and white wine sauce; and Barnsley double lamb chop.
OPEN: 12-3 6-11 (Sun 12-3, 6-10.30) **BAR MEALS:** L served all week 12-2 D served all week 6-9 Av main course £7.50 **RESTAURANT:** L served all week 12-2 D served all week 6.30-9 Av 3 course à la carte £13 ⊕: Free House ◖: Black Sheep Best, Coniston Bluebird, Hawkshead, Scottish Courage John Smith's. ♈: 20 **FACILITIES:** Garden: Tables during summer months, lawn & paving **NOTES:** Parking 20 **ROOMS:** 8 bedrooms en suite 2 family rooms s£35 d£50

 Pubs with this logo do not allow smoking anywhere on their premises

BROUGHTON-IN-FURNESS
Map 18 SD28

Blacksmiths Arms
Broughton Mills LA20 6AX ☎ 01229 716824
e-mail: blacksmithsarms@aol.com
Dir: A593 from Barrow-in-Furness towards Coniston, after 1.5m take left signed Broughton Mills, pub 1m on left
The Blacksmiths Arms, set in a secluded Lakeland valley, dates back to 1577 and was originally a farmhouse. The interior is beautifully preserved, with the original farmhouse range, oak-panelled corridor, worn slate floors and low beams. The chef proprietor uses local suppliers, and beer from local micro-breweries can be enjoyed with a meal or on its own. Dishes might include Morecambe Bay potted shrimps; deep-fried brie with vodka and redcurrant sauce; breast of chicken stuffed with mozzarella and sun-dried tomatoes; and seared tuna steak.
OPEN: 12-11 (Sat-Sun 12-11 Oct-May 12-2.30, 5-11) Closed: Dec 25 Rest: (Winter Closed Mon Lunchtime) **BAR MEALS:** L served Tue-Sun 12-2 D served Mon-Sun 6-9 Av main course £8.75 **RESTAURANT:** L served Tue-Sun 12-2 D served Mon-Sun 6-9 Av 3 course à la carte £17 ⊕: Free House ◖: Jennings Cumberland Ale, Dent Aviator, Barngates Tag Lag, Moorhouses Pride of Pendle. **FACILITIES:** Child facs Garden: Patio area tables and chairs Dogs allowed **NOTES:** Parking 30

BUTTERMERE
Map 18 NY11

Bridge Hotel ★★★ ♈
CA13 9UZ ☎ 017687 70252 ▦ 017687 70215
e-mail: enquiries@bridge-hotel.com web: www.bridge-hotel.com
Dir: Take B5289 from Keswick
Spend a weekend at this 18th-century former coaching inn and enjoy its stunning location. Main courses from the restaurant include sliced duck breast served with a confit of leg with a honey and orange glaze; and poached plaice roulade. The bar menu offers Cumberland hotpot, Cumberland sausage and a good range of vegetarian choices. For smaller appetites there's a good selection of salads, sandwiches and toasties.
OPEN: 10.30-11 (open all day in summer) **BAR MEALS:** L served all week 12-6 D served all week 6-9.30 Av main course £5.95 **RESTAURANT:** D served all week 7-8.30 ⊕: Free House ◖: Theakston's Old Peculiar, Black Sheep Best, Buttermere Bitter. ♈: 6 **FACILITIES:** Children's licence Garden: Dogs allowed **NOTES:** Parking 60 **ROOMS:** 21 bedrooms en suite s£49 d£98

CALDBECK
Map 18 NY34

Oddfellows Arms
CA7 8EA ☎ 016974 78227 ▦ 016974 78056
Situated in a scenic conservation village in the northern fells, this 17th-century former coaching inn is in a stunning location and is popular with walkers on the Cumbrian Way and coast-to-coast cyclists. Lunchtime snacks and a specials board supplement the regular menu, and favourite fare includes roast duck, steak and ale pie, lamb Jennings, pork and cider casserole, poached salmon, double Barnsley chop, and Cumberland sausage. Sandwiches, jacket potatoes, and salads are also available.
OPEN: 12-3 6-11 (Fri-Sun all day All day & all week in Summer) **BAR MEALS:** L served all week 12-2 D served all week 6-8.30 **RESTAURANT:** L served all week 12-2 D served all week 6.30-8.30 ⊕: Jennings ◖: Jennings Bitter, Cumberland Ale. **FACILITIES:** Garden: Beer garden Dogs allowed Water **NOTES:** Parking 10

England

CARTMEL Map 18 SD37

Pick of the Pubs

The Cavendish 🍽
LA11 6QA ☎ 015395 36240 🖷 015395 35082
Dir: M6 junct 36 take A590 follow signs for Barrow-in-Furness.
Cartmel signed. In village take 1st right
This 450 year-old coaching inn is Cartmel's oldest
hostelry. Families and dogs are welcome; the pub's oak
beams, log fires and uneven floors create a traditional,
cosy atmosphere, and outside there's a tree-lined garden
overlooking a stream. Lunchtime sandwiches are served
on locally-baked bread with a portion of chips, whilst
evening diners in the non-smoking restaurant might
expect seared tuna loin; herb-crusted lamb rump on
celeriac mash; or sweet and sour vegetables with rice.
OPEN: 11.30-11 (Sun 12-10.30) **BAR MEALS:** L served all week
12-2 D served all week 6-9 Sun 12-6 Av main course £7.95
RESTAURANT: L served all week 12-2 D served all week 6-9
🍴: Free House 🍺: John Smiths, Cumberland, Bombadier,
Theakstons. **FACILITIES:** Child facs Garden: Tree lined adjoining
garden overlooking stream Dogs allowed **NOTES:** Parking 25

COCKERMOUTH Map 18 NY13

The Trout Hotel ★★★ 🏵 ♀
Crown St CA13 0EJ ☎ 01900 823591 🖷 01900 827514
e-mail: enquiries@trouthotel.co.uk web: www.trouthotel.co.uk
Dating from about 1670 and once a private house, the Trout
became a hotel in 1934. The hand-carved oak staircase and
marble fireplace are among the many striking features. The
menu boasts a wide range of starters, old favourites and snacks.
Try king scallops with wild mushrooms and balsamic glaze;
gnocchi on wilted spinach with dolcelatte and mascarpone
sauce; or fish pie. Finish with soufflé omelette with strawberry
filling; home-made ice-cream; or trio of crème brûlée.
OPEN: 11-11 **BAR MEALS:** L served all week 9.30-9.30 D served
all week Av main course £7.95 **RESTAURANT:** L served Sat & Sun
12-2 D served all week 7-9.30 Av 3 course à la carte £35 Av 4 course
fixed price £14.95 🍴: Free House 🍺: Jennings Cumberland Ale,
Theakston Bitter, John Smiths, Marston's Pedigree. ♀: 24
FACILITIES: Child facs Garden: Riverside garden, food served
outside **NOTES:** Parking 50 **ROOMS:** 43 bedrooms en suite
1 family room s£60 d£90

CONISTON Map 18 SD39

Black Bull Inn & Hotel 🍽 ♀
1 Yewdale Rd LA21 8DU ☎ 015394 41335 🖷 015394 41168
e-mail: i.s.bradley@btinternet.com
Dir: 23m from Kendal via Windermere and Ambleside from M6 junct 36
onto A590
Built at the time of the Spanish Armada, this old coaching inn
has a lovely village setting in the shadow of the Old Man.
Award-winning real ales are brewed on the premises, and
excellent food is served in both the bar and restaurant. Fish
dishes include smoked trout, peppered mackerel and fresh
battered haddock; meat courses range from straightforward
Cumberland sausages to the more complex pheasant and
chicken breast stuffed with haggis and black pudding.
OPEN: 11-11 (Sun 12-10.30) Closed: 25 Dec
BAR MEALS: L served all week 12-9.30 D served all week 12-9.30
Av main course £8 **RESTAURANT:** L served all week D served all
week 6-9 🍴: Free House 🍺: Coniston Bluebird, Old Man Ale,
Opium, Blacksmith & XB. ♀: 10 **FACILITIES:** Child facs Children's
licence Garden: Riverside patio outside Dogs allowed Dog beds and
meals **NOTES:** Parking 12

Sun Hotel & 16th Century Inn ♀
LA21 8HQ ☎ 015394 41248 🖷 015394 41219
e-mail: thesun@hotelconiston.com
Dir: From M6 junct 36, take the A591, beyond Kendal and Windermere, then the
A598 from Ambleside to Coniston. Pub is signed from the bridge in the village.
A 16th-century inn with a 10-room hotel attached, this was
Donald Campbell's base during his final water speed record
attempt. The bar has stone floors, exposed beams and a
range of real ales. The menu offers such delights as seafood
paella; pan-roasted pheasant with baby spinach ragout; and
Hungarian goulash with dumplings. Outside is a large quiet
garden with benches, and the conservatory offers exceptional
views that can be enjoyed whatever the weather.
OPEN: 11-11 (Sun 12-10.30) **BAR MEALS:** L served all week
12-2.30 D served all week 6-9 Av main course £12
RESTAURANT: L served all week 12-2.30 D served all week 6-9
Av 3 course à la carte £21.50 🍺: Coniston Bluebird, Black Cat, Yates,
Black Sheep Special. ♀: 7 **FACILITIES:** Children's licence Garden:
Large garden with benches, trees Dogs allowed Water in the bar
NOTES: Parking 20 **ROOMS:** 10 bedrooms 9 en suite
3 family rooms s£40 d£90 (★★) No children overnight

CROOK Map 18 SD49

The Sun Inn ♀
LA8 8LA ☎ 01539 821351 🖷 01539 821351
Dir: Off the B5284
A warmly welcoming inn dating from 1711, The Sun is steeped
in tradition with winter fires and a summer terrace
overlooking rolling countryside. The best local ingredients are
used to create a variety of dishes, such as venison steak with
wild mushroom sauce, game casserole, and fell-bred steaks.
The bar snack and regular menus are supplemented by daily
specials, and fresh fish is also featured.
OPEN: 12-2.30 6-11 (Sat 12-11, Sun 12-10.30)
BAR MEALS: L served all week 12-2.15 D served all week 6-8.45
RESTAURANT: L served all week 12-2.30 D served all week 6-9
Av 3 course à la carte £19 🍴: Free House 🍺: Theakston, Scottish
Courage John Smith's, Courage Directors, Wells Bombardier. ♀: 14
FACILITIES: Garden: Terrace Dogs allowed **NOTES:** Parking 20

CROSTHWAITE Map 18 SD49

The Punch Bowl Inn ♀
LA8 8HR ☎ 015395 68237 🖷 015395 68875
e-mail: enquiries@punchbowl.fsnet.co.uk
Dir: From M6 J36 take A590 towards Barrow, then A5074 & follow signs
for Crosthwaite. Pub next to church on L
Steven Doherty, previously head chef to Albert Roux at Le
Gavroche in London's Mayfair, came to this 17th-century Lakeland
pub in 1996. Since then his pub-restaurant has won countless
awards and has become a highly popular venue. With its warm and
friendly atmosphere, the bar appeals to walkers and casual visitors
who can relax amongst original beams, low ceilings and open fires.
Steven's exciting cooking skills produce starters such as crab and
prawn pancakes, or chicken liver parfait with toasted pine kernels
and a damson, sultana and balsamic glaze served with toasted
raisin and walnut bread. Mains might be boned and rolled saddle
of rabbit with a grain mustard mash, or roasted chump of
Cumbrian fell-bred lamb sliced on a horseradish mash with a salad
of mixed beans in a mint dressing. All perhaps followed by a honey
and Drambuie crème brûlée, or a soft chocolate and ginger tart.
OPEN: 11-11 (Sun 12-10.30) Closed: 2wk Nov, 2wk Dec
BAR MEALS: L served Mon-Sun 12-2 D served Mon-Sun 6-9
Av main course £12.95 **RESTAURANT:** L served Tues-Sun 12-2
D served Tues-Sat 6-9 🍴: Free House 🍺: Black Sheep Best,
Barngates Cracker Ale, Greene King Old Speckled Hen. ♀: 21
FACILITIES: Garden: Patio, terrace garden Dogs allowed Water
Bowls, only guide dogs inside **NOTES:** Parking 60

England

ELTERWATER   Map 18 NY30

Pick of the Pubs

The Britannia Inn
LA22 9HP ☎ 015394 37210 ▤ 015394 37311
e-mail: info@britinn.co.uk
Dir: A593 from Ambleside, then B5343 to Elterwater
Built about 500 years ago, this is the quintessential
Lakeland inn. Set in the centre of the picturesque village of
Elterwater, it overlooks the village green beneath the
dramatic fells of the Langdale valley. The Britannia really
comes to life in summer when colourful hanging baskets
dazzle the eye and the garden fills up with customers (and
occasionally Morris dancers). In colder weather, the thick
stone walls, log fires and beamed ceilings come into their
own, and at any time the inn offers a welcome escape
from hectic life with a big selection of real ales and a wide
choice of fresh home-cooked food. There is something on
the menu to please everyone from popular favourites to
the more unusual with an emphasis on local produce and
Lakeland specialities. These may include Waberthwaite
Cumberland sausage, roast leg of Lakeland lamb, breast of
Lakeland cornfed chicken, and fisherman's pie.
OPEN: 11-11 **BAR MEALS:** L served all week 12-2 D served all
week 6.30-9.30 Av main course £9 **RESTAURANT:** L served all
week 12-2 D served all week 6.30-9.30 Snacks available 2-5.30pm
🍴: Free House ◖: Jennings Bitter, Coniston Bluebird, Timothy
Taylor Landlord. **FACILITIES:** Children's licence Patio Dogs
allowed Water **NOTES:** Parking 10

ENNERDALE BRIDGE   Map 18 NY01

Pick of the Pubs

The Shepherd's Arms Hotel NEW
LA23 3AR ☎ 01946 861249 ▤ 01946 862472
e-mail: enquiries@shepherdsarmshotel.co.uk
Dir: 4m E from A5086, in centre of Ennerdale Bridge village

Located in the village of Ennerdale Bridge on one of the
most beautiful stretches of Alfred Wainwright's Coast to
Coast footpath, this relaxed and informal free house is very
popular with walkers. Jennings Bitter and Yates Fever Pitch
are amongst the variety of real ales on offer; during the
autumn and winter months two welcoming open fires bring
warmth to chilled parts, and the bar is a venue for local
musicians. A varied menu is served in the bar and non-
smoking dining room, together with a selection of fine wines
to complement your meal. Specialities include home-made
vegetarian, fish and local game dishes. Dinner might begin
with chicken liver and brandy paté, moving on to spinach

and Wensleydale tart or local lamb chops with mint sauce.
After finishing, perhaps, with rum and raisin pudding, diners
can relax by the fire in the comfortable lounge.
OPEN: 11-2.30 5.30-11 Apr-Oct open all day
BAR MEALS: L served all week 12.15-1.45 D served all week
6.15-8.45 Av main course £7.95 **RESTAURANT:** L served all
week 12.15-1.45 D served all week 6.15-8.45 Av 3 course à la carte
£15 Av 3 course fixed price £18.95 ◖: Jennings Bitter, Timothy
Taylor Landlord, Coniston Bluebird, Yates Fever Pitch.
FACILITIES: Child facs Children's licence Garden: Patio area
with tables, chairs, umbrellas Dogs allowed **NOTES:** Parking 8

ESKDALE GREEN   Map 18 NY10

Pick of the Pubs

Bower House Inn ★★
CA19 1TD ☎ 019467 23244 ▤ 019467 23308
e-mail: info@bowerhouseinn.freeserve.co.uk
web: www.bowerhouseinn.co.uk
Dir: 4m off A595, 0.5m W of Eskdale Green

Alongside the village cricket field, this fine 17th-century
stone-built former farmhouse overlooks Muncaster Fell in
a most scenic and unspoilt part of Cumbria. The Bower
House's traditional appeal is irresistible: oak beamed bar
and alcoves welcome locals and visitors alike, and a
charming candlelit restaurant offers a varied selection of
hearty, imaginative dishes. Cider and onion soup; smoked
Herdwick lamb with minted apple chutney; pan-fried
calamari rings in a spicy oriental sauce; grilled goat's
cheese with hazelnut dressing; roast haunch of venison
with red wine and juniper berry; escalope of veal with
ham and Gruyere; chicken breast with apple and tarragon
sauce; baked halibut in red pesto crust; Aberdeen Angus
sirloin steak with choice of sauces, are among the
favourites. Twenty eight en suite rooms make the Bower
House an ideal holiday retreat throughout the year.
OPEN: 11-2.30 6-11 **BAR MEALS:** L served all week
12.30-2.30 D served all week 6-9 Av main course £8.50
RESTAURANT: D served all week 7-9 Av 3 course à la carte £20
Av 4 course fixed price £25 🍴: Free House ◖: Theakston
Bitter, Jennings Bitter, Greene King Old Speckled Hen, Dent Ales.
FACILITIES: Garden: Garden with lawns and good views Dogs
allowed in the garden only **NOTES:** Parking 50
ROOMS: 28 bedrooms en suite 2 family rooms s£45 d£37 No
children overnight

🍷 7   Number of wines by the glass

continued

England

King George IV Inn
CA19 1TS ☎ 019467 23262 📠 019467 23334
e-mail: info@kinggeorge-eskdale.co.uk
Dir: A590 to Greenodd, A5092 to Broughton-in-Furness then over Ulpha Fell towards Eskdale
What we see today is a 17th-century coaching inn, although Roman origins are likely. It lies in one of Lakeland's finest hidden valleys, close to the narrow gauge Ravenglass & Eskdale steam railway, known affectionately as La'al Ratty. Inside are open fires, oak beams, low ceilings, flagged floors and antiques. Dishes include home made steak and Old Peculier pie, curry, pan-fried liver and onions, ostrich fillet, and salmon in Martini, orange and ginger sauce. Vegetarian and small meals, pizzas and sandwiches.
OPEN: 11-11 **BAR MEALS:** L served all week 12-8.30 D served all week 12-8.30 **RESTAURANT:** L served all week 12-2 D served all week 6-9 ⊕: Free House ◀: Coniston Bluebird, Black Sheep Special, changing cask ales. **FACILITIES:** Garden: Beautiful views, ample tables Dogs allowed **NOTES:** Parking 5

GARRIGILL   Map 18 NY74

The George & Dragon Inn
CA9 3DS ☎ 01434 381293 📠 01434 382839
e-mail: info@garrigill-pub.co.uk
Once serving the local zinc and lead mining communities, this 17th-century coaching inn is popular with walkers who enjoy log fires that stave off that brisk North Pennine weather. Look on the menu to find local Cumberland sausage, steak and ale pie, gammon steak, battered cod or Whitby scampi. There are plenty of Yorkshire puddings, jacket potatoes or sandwiches for a lighter meal.
OPEN: 12-2 7-10.30 (Sat 12-11) (Sun 12-4) Winter closed lunch Mon-Thu 7-11 **BAR MEALS:** L served all week 12-1.30 D served all week 7-8.30 **RESTAURANT:** L served all week 12-1.30 D served all week 7-8.30 ⊕: Free House ◀: Black Sheep Bitter, Bitburger, guest ales. **FACILITIES:** Children's licence Tables on village green Dogs allowed Water, Biscuits, Toys, Leads

---

GRASMERE   Map 18 NY30

The Travellers Rest Inn ♀
Keswick Rd LA22 9RR ☎ 015394 35604 📠 017687 72309
e-mail: stay@lakedistrictinns.co.uk
Dir: From M6 take A591 to Grasmere, pub 0.5m N of Grasmere
Originally three miners' cottages, the inn dates back over 500 years and has been owned and run by the same family for the past 13. It's full of character inside and surrounded by beautiful scenery outside, with stunning views from the beer garden. A good range of beers and an extensive menu of traditional home-cooked fare is offered, ranging from sandwiches and cold platters to mixed Cumberland chargrill, and Borrowdale trout stuffed with prawns.
OPEN: 12-11 (Sun 12-10.30) **BAR MEALS:** L served all week 12-3 D served all week 6-9.30 (Mar-Oct, 12-9.30) Av main course £8 **RESTAURANT:** L served all week 12-3 D served all week 6-9.30 (Mar-Oct, 12-9.30) Av 3 course à la carte £16
BREWERY/COMPANY: Free House ◀: Jennings Bitter, Cumberland Ale, & Sneck Lifter, Jennings Cocker Hoop. ♀: 10
FACILITIES: Garden: beer garden, stunning views, picnic tables Dogs allowed Water bowls provided **NOTES:** Parking 60

Pubs with Red Diamonds are the top
◆ places in the AA's three, four and five
diamond ratings

GREAT LANGDALE   Map 18 NY20

The New Dungeon Ghyll Hotel ♀
LA22 9JY ☎ 015394 37213 📠 015394 37666
e-mail: enquiries@dungeon-ghyll.com
Dir: From M6 into Kendal then A591 into Ambleside onto A593 to B5343, hotel 6m on right
Traditional Cumberland stone hotel dating back to medieval times, and full of character and charm. The hotel stands in its own lawned grounds in a spectacular position beneath the Langdale Pikes and Pavey Ark. Local specialities, expertly cooked, are served in the smart dining room. A sample dinner menu offers pan-fried venison in port wine, steak on haggis mash, chargrilled salmon fillet on asparagus spears, roasted vegetable risotto, whole baked rainbow trout, and crispy local lamb with mint and rosemary.
OPEN: 11-11 (Sun 11-10.30) **BAR MEALS:** L served all week D served all week **RESTAURANT:** D served all week 7-8.30 ⊕: Free House ◀: Scottish Courage Courage Directors, Greene King Ruddles Best, Thwaites Bitter, Lancaster Bomber. ♀: 7
FACILITIES: Garden: Constructed from local slate, views of valley Dogs allowed **NOTES:** Parking 30

GREAT SALKELD   Map 18 NY53

Pick of the Pubs

The Highland Drove Inn and Kyloes Restaurant NEW ♀
CA11 9NA ☎ 01768 898349 📠 01768 898708
e-mail: highlanddroveinn@btinternet.com

Travel through the gorgeous Eden valley, along flower-decked winding lanes, past dramatic fells and prehistoric stone circles, and you'll soon come across this traditional white stone droving inn. A father and son team are at the helm of the three hundred-year-old establishment - and they're in the process of giving it some tasteful refurbishment. It's very much a village inn, with locals mixing merrily with tourists, fishermen and walkers. Enjoy cask conditioned ales or tuck in to the high quality food. The kitchen makes excellent use of local game, fish and meat: seared Nile perch fillet on stir-fried vegetables; pan-fried pheasant breast with confit leg and glazed chestnuts; or twice-baked sugar ham with black pudding and parsley sauce. The area has many attractions, including nearby Hadrian's Wall.
OPEN: 12-3 6-11 Closed Mon lunch (Sat 12-11)
BAR MEALS: L served Tues-Sun 12-2 D served all week 6.30-9
RESTAURANT: L served Tues-Sun 12-2 D served all week 6.30-9 Av 3 course à la carte £18.50 Av 3 course fixed price £13.50
◀: Theakston Black Bull, John Smiths Cask, John Smiths Smooth, Youngers Scotch Bitter. ♀: 14 **FACILITIES:** Children's licence Garden: 'Flintstones' bedrock, with waterfall, pond Dogs allowed **NOTES:** Parking 6

England

HAVERTHWAITE
Map 18 SD38

Rusland Pool Hotel Restaurant & Bar ♀
LA12 8AA ☎ 01229 861384 📠 01229 861425
e-mail: enquires@ruslandpool.co.uk
Dir: M6 junct 36, A590 towards Barrow-in-Furness for 17m. Hotel on R
Previously known as the Dicksons Arms, the Rusland Pool has
been a pub, a cafe, a restaurant and private cottages. Close
by is Lakeland, offering some of England's finest scenery,
perfect for touring by car and exploring on foot. Only a
stone's throw from this traditional coaching inn is magnificent
Morecambe Bay with its winding channels of water and vast
expanses of sand. The menu includes chef's specials which
might feature local mallard breast, lemon sole, Lakeland
Herdwick lamb Henry, and asparagus and pine nut risotto.
OPEN: 11-11 **BAR MEALS:** L served all week 12-9 D served all week
Av main course £8.95 **RESTAURANT:** L served all week 12-9 D served
all week 🍽: Free House 🍺: Tetleys, Boddingtons. **FACILITIES:** Child
facs Children's licence Garden: Terraced area overlooking Woodland
Dogs allowed Water on request **NOTES:** Parking 35

HAWKSHEAD
Map 18 SD39

Kings Arms Hotel ♦♦♦
The Square LA22 0NZ ☎ 015394 36372 📠 015394 36006
e-mail: info@kingsarmshawkshead.co.uk
web: www.kingsarmshawkshead.co.uk
Dir: A591 to Ambleside, then take B5286 to Hawkshead, pub in village green

Charming 16th-century pub overlooking a village square that
William Wordsworth, John Ruskin and Beatrix Potter would
have known. Oak beams and an open fire help to give the
inn's interior plenty of charm and atmosphere. Main courses
are likely to feature beef goulash, stilton and broccoli quiche,
steak and ale pie, mixed game and redcurrant sausage, lemon
pepper turkey steak, and tempura battered hake. Good range
of snacks, toasties and ciabattas.
OPEN: 11-11 (Sun 12-10.30) 25 Dec Closed eve
BAR MEALS: L served all week 12-2.30 D served all week 6-9.30
Av main course £6.50 **RESTAURANT:** L served all week 12-2.30
D served all week 6-9.30 🍽: Free House 🍺: Carlsberg-Tetley Bitter,
Black Sheep Best, Yates, Hawkshead Bitter. **FACILITIES:** Child facs
Children's licence Garden: Walled area, picnic tables Dogs allowed
Water **ROOMS:** 9 bedrooms 8 en suite 3 family rooms s£35 d£60

Pick of the Pubs

Queens Head Hotel ★★ 🏅 🏷 ♀
Main St LA22 0NS ☎ 015394 36271 📠 015394 36722
e-mail: enquiries@queensheadhotel.co.uk
Dir: M6 junct 36, A590 to Newby Bridge. 1st right, 8m to Hawkshead
A timbered Elizabethan pub in the centre of historic
Hawkshead, which was already very old when William
Wordsworth attended the local grammar school and Beatrix

continued

Potter created Peter Rabbit. (The Beatix Potter Gallery and
Grizedale Forest tracks are close by.) One of the curios on
show in the bare-beamed interior is the 20-inch Girt Clog,
worn in the 1820s by a mole catcher with elephantiasis. The
surrounding lakes and fells provide many of the ingredients
used in the meals, including Esthwaite Water trout,
Graythwaite estate pheasant, and Ms Potter's beloved
Herdwick sheep. The same menu is offered throughout,
with sandwiches, salads, light bites, grills and main meals at
lunchtime. An equally extensive evening selection might
offer spinach soufflé with mixed leaves and basil oil; slow
roasted lamb King Henry with rosemary sauce; or baked
cod with tomato fondue and herb crumb.

Queens Head Hotel

OPEN: 11-11 (Sun 12-10.30) **BAR MEALS:** L served all week
12-2.30 D served all week 6.15-9.30 Sun 12-5 Av main course £7.50
RESTAURANT: L served all week 12-2.30 D served all week
6.15-9.30 Sun 12-5 Av 3 course à la carte £25 🍽: Frederic Robinson
🍺: Robinsons Unicorn, Hartleys Cumbria Way, Double Hop. ♀: 11
FACILITIES: Child facs Children's licence Garden: Small gravel area
with tables Dogs allowed Fresh water outside **NOTES:** Parking 14
ROOMS: 14 bedrooms 11 en suite 2 family rooms s£60 d£84

The Sun Inn
Main St LA22 0NT ☎ 015394 36236 📠 015394 36155
e-mail: thesuninn@hawkshead98.freeserve.co.uk
*Dir: N on M6 junct 36, take A591 to Ambleside, then B5286 to
Hawkshead. S on M6 junct 40, take A66 to Keswick, A591 to Ambleside,
then B5286 to Hawkshead.*

The Sun is a listed 17th-century coaching inn at the heart of
the village where Wordsworth went to school. Inside are two
resident ghosts - a giggling girl and a drunken landlord - and
outside a paved terrace with seating for 32. Traditional local
food is served - lamb chops on black pudding mash in the bar
and sea bass on leek and potato mash in the restaurant; look
out too for bangers and mash with Cumberland sausage.
OPEN: 11-11 (Sun 12-10.30) **BAR MEALS:** L served all week
12-2.30 D served all week 6.15-9.30 food all day Sat-Sun Av main
course £7 **RESTAURANT:** D served all week 6.30-9.30 🍽: Free

continued

England

House 🍺: Barn Gates Cracker, Jennings, Hesket & Newmarket plus two guest ales. **FACILITIES:** Children's licence Garden: beer garden, paved terrace, seating Dogs allowed

HESKET NEWMARKET   Map 18 NY33

The Old Crown NEW
CA7 8JG ☎ 016974 78288 e-mail: louhogg@onetel.com
Dir: From M6 take B5305, left after 6m toward Hesket Newmarket
Regulars here can sleep soundly, knowing that their favourite pint will always be waiting for them, because both the pub and its associated micro-brewery are owned by co-operatives of local people and other supporters. There are ten Indian curries to choose from, including chicken muglai, lamb Madras, mixed vegetable and pork chasnidahl; also Cumberland sausage, egg and chips; cod and prawn crumble; and 'Doris's steak and ale pie.
OPEN: 12-3 5.30-11 Closed Mon-Tues afternoon
BAR MEALS: L served Wed-Sun 12-2 D served Wed-Sun Av main course £5 **RESTAURANT:** L served Wed-Sun 12-2 D served Wed-Sat 6.30-8.30 Av fixed price £7.50 🍴: Free House 🍺: Doris, Skiddan, Blencathra, Helvellyn Gold. **FACILITIES:** Child facs Garden: Dogs allowed

HEVERSHAM   Map 18 SD48

Blue Bell Hotel
Princes Way LA7 7EE ☎ 015395 62018 📠 015395 62455
e-mail: stay@bluebellhotel.co.uk
Dir: On A6 between Kendal & Milnthorpe
Originally a vicarage for the old village, this hotel dates back as far as 1460. Heversham is an ideal base for touring the scenic Lake District and Yorkshire Dales, but pleasant country scenery can also be viewed from the hotel's well-equipped bedrooms. The charming lounge bar, with its old beams, is the perfect place to relax with a drink or enjoy one of the meals available on the menu, including potted shrimps, sirloin steak, Cumbrian game pie and Isle of Man crab.
OPEN: 11-11 **BAR MEALS:** L served all week 11-9 D served all week 6-9 (Sun 11-8) Av main course £7.95 **RESTAURANT:** L served all week 11-9 D served all week 7-9 (Sun 11-8) Av 3 course à la carte £17 🍴: Samuel Smith 🍺: Samuel Smith Old Brewery Bitter.
FACILITIES: Child facs Garden: Quiet garden, decoratively furnished Dogs allowed **NOTES:** Parking 100 **ROOMS:** 21 bedrooms en suite 4 family rooms s£39 d£79 (★★)

KENDAL   Map 18 SD59

Gateway Inn
Crook Rd LA8 8LX ☎ 01539 720605 & 724187 📠 01539 720581
Dir: From M6 junct 36 take A590/A591, follow signs for Windermere, pub on left after 9m

Located within the Lake District National Park, this Victorian country inn offers delightful views, attractive gardens and welcoming log fires. A good range of appetising dishes

continued

includes chicken casserole with red wine and herb dumplings, grilled fillets of sea bass with ratatouille and mussels, and roasted butternut squash filled with leeks and stilton. Traditional English favourites of liver and onions or rabbit pie are also a feature.
OPEN: 11-11 (All day wknds) Closed: Dec 26
BAR MEALS: L served all week 12 D served all week 9 Av main course £9 🍴: Thwaites 🍺: Thwaites Bitter, Thwaites Smooth.
FACILITIES: Garden: Terrace, food served outside Dogs allowed Water, dog food **NOTES:** Parking 50

The Gilpin Bridge Inn ♦♦♦ 🐟
Bridge End, Levens LA8 8EP ☎ 015395 52206 📠 015395 52444
e-mail: info@gilpinbridgeinn.co.uk
Dir: Telephone for directions
Good food is the chief attraction at this popular pub which takes its name from a Norman knight who resided here after fighting the crusades. An extensive menu and a selection of daily specials are available in the lounge or restaurant, ranging from Bo-peep pie - tender pieces of lamb braised in a root vegetable and rosemary sauce under a golden pastry cover - to grilled lamb cutlets, bubbling hot lasagne, and halibut steak.
OPEN: 11.30-2.30 5.30-11 (Open all day Summer, BH's)
BAR MEALS: L served all week 11.30-2 D served all week 5.30-9 (Sun 12-9) Av main course £6.50 **RESTAURANT:** L served all week 11.30-2 D served all week 5.30-9 Sun 12-9 Av 3 course à la carte £12.50 🍴: 🍺: Robinsons Best Bitter, Old Stockport Hartleys XB, Unicorn, Cumbria Way. **FACILITIES:** Child facs Children's licence Garden: Patio area adjacent to pub Dogs allowed **NOTES:** Parking 60 **ROOMS:** 10 bedrooms en suite 2 family rooms s£45 d£55

KESWICK   Map 18 NY22

The Farmers NEW
Portinscale CA12 5RN
Dir: M6 junct 40, follow A66, turn off 0.25m after B5289 junct, into village of Portinscale
The pub's long history includes a spell as a 'jerry', or unlicensed house, but now it is one of Keswick's foremost food-led pubs, offering seasonally changing menus. Typical starters are gravlax with horseradish and mustard dressing; and deep-fried smoked duck with hoi-sin hash browns. Then slow-braised lamb shank in red wine, herbs and garlic; and mild potato curry, smoked haddock and poached egg to follow. Breads, soups, sauces and desserts are prepared freshly on site.
OPEN: 12-11 **BAR MEALS:** L served all week 12-2 D served all week 6-9 **RESTAURANT:** L served all week 12-2 D served all week 6-9 Av 3 course à la carte £18.50 🍺: Jennings Bitter, Jennings Cumberland Ale, Jennings Cumberland Cream. **FACILITIES:** Child facs Children's licence Garden: Raised gravel beer garden overlooking fells Dogs allowed Water

Pick of the Pubs

The Horse & Farrier Inn 🐟 ♀
Threlkeld Village CA12 4SQ ☎ 017687 79688 📠 017687 79823
e-mail: info@horseandfarrier.com
Dir: 4m E of Keswick on A66 12m W of Penrith junc 40 M6 follow A66
This old stone inn has been part of the picturesque village of Threlkeld, lying below Clough Head and Blencathra Mountain, for over 300 years. There's a welcoming atmosphere in the traditional-style bars, decorated with hunting prints and warmed by crackling log fires when you need to dry or thaw out. Cumbrian brewer Jennings supplies the real ales, and an extensive wine list draws on major world sources. Good food, chosen from various menus, is

continued

England

served in the intimate, non-smoking restaurant and bar. At lunchtimes there are always sandwiches, including Greenland prawn, while main courses generally include favourites such as griddled Cumberland sausage with chive mash; poached smoked haddock fillet; and spinach and ricotta cannelloni. At dinner, look out for steamed sea bass with pancetta and sage risotto; pan-roasted duck breast with saffron egg noodles; and vegetarian specials.

The Horse & Farrier Inn

OPEN: 11-11 (Sun 12-10.30) **BAR MEALS:** L served all week 12-2 D served all week 6-9 **RESTAURANT:** L served all week 12-2 D served all week 6-9 🍴: Jennings 🍺: Jennings Bitter, Cocker Hoop, Sneck Lifter, Cumberland Ale & Guest Ale. 🍷: 13 **FACILITIES:** Child facs Children's licence Garden: Long garden with views of Blencathra Mountain Dogs allowed **NOTES:** Parking 60

Pick of the Pubs

The Kings Head 🍷
Thirlspot CA12 4TN ☎ 017687 72393 📠 017687 72309
e-mail: stay@lakedistrictinns.co.uk
web: www.lakedistrictinns.co.uk
Dir: From M6 take A66 to Keswick then A591, pub 4m S of Keswick
Look around and take in the stunning scenery around three of Lakeland's major peaks - Helvellyn, Blencathra and Skiddaw. With sweeping pasture and arable land all around at lower levels, the view surrounding this 17th-century former coaching inn is truly sublime. This could be the ideal pub to take as the permitted luxury on *Desert Island Discs*. On warm days and in summer, the garden is the best place to enjoy a meal or drink. Inside, old beams and inglenook fireplaces are traditional features of the bar, while a separate games room offers pool, snooker and darts. Popular real ales include beers from Theakstons, the Jennings brewery in nearby Cockermouth, and there is a fine selection of wines and malt whiskies. An extensive menu of good value bar and restaurant food, including daily specials, is served, with baked tranche of salmon, beef stroganoff and vegetarian options, on offer. In the elegant restaurant try choosing from the fixed-price menu: freshly made traditional English dishes and local specialities include Jennings steak and ale pie, Waberthwaite Cumberland sausage with mash, fillet steak, confit duck, and scampi. Otherwise there may be dishes like steamed pork belly, braised minted joint of lamb, or baked fillet of Whitby cod wrapped in prosciutto. Complete the meal with traditional apple and pear crumble with creamy vanilla custard sauce, or a choice of local cheeses. There are also facilities for banquets and wedding receptions of up to 100 guests, and seventeen comfortable bedrooms with a delightful resident's lounge.
OPEN: 12-11 (12-10.30 Sundays) **BAR MEALS:** L served all week 12-3 D served all week 6-9.30 Av main course £8.95

RESTAURANT: L served all week 12-3 D served all week 7-9 Av 3 course à la carte £25 Av 4 course fixed price £20 🍴: Free House 🍺: Scottish Courage Theakston Best Bitter & Old Peculier, Jennings Bitter, Bluebird Bitter, Greene King Abbot Ale. 🍷: 10 **FACILITIES:** Garden: Delightful, spectacular views of fells Dogs allowed Water **NOTES:** Parking 60
ROOMS: 17 bedrooms en suite s£20 d£59 (★★★)

The Swinside Inn ◆◆◆
Newlands Valley CA12 5UE ☎ 017687 78253
e-mail: info@theswinsideinn.com web: www.theswinsideinn.com
Situated in the quiet Newlands valley, the Swinside Inn is a listed building dating back to about 1642. From the pub there are superb views of Causey Pike and Cat Bells - among other landmarks. Nearby is the market town of Keswick, a good base for visiting the area's many attractions. Inside are two bars, traditional open fires and oak-beamed ceilings. Extensive bar menu may offer lamb Henry, Cumberland sausage, Swinside chicken, and fresh, grilled Borrowdale trout.
OPEN: 11-11 (Sun 12-10.30) **BAR MEALS:** L served all week 12-2 D served all week 6-8.45 **RESTAURANT:** L served all week 12-2 D served all week 6-8.45 🍴: Scottish & Newcastle 🍺: Jennings Cumberland Ale, Scottish Courage John Smith's & Courage Directors, John Smiths Smooth & Theakstons Best Bitter. **FACILITIES:** Garden: Dogs allowed **NOTES:** Parking 30 **ROOMS:** 6 bedrooms en suite 2 family rooms

Pick of the Pubs

Pheasant Inn 🍷
Casterton LA6 2RX ☎ 015242 71230 📠 015242 73877
e-mail: pheasantinn@fsbdial.co.uk
web: www.pheasantinn.co.uk
See Pick of the Pubs on opposite page

Pick of the Pubs

Snooty Fox Tavern 🍷
Main St LA6 2AH ☎ 015242 71308 📠 015242 72642
e-mail: info@snootyfox84.freeserve.co.uk
Dir: M6 junct 36 take A65, tavern 6m
One of the Mortal Man's group of traditional country inns, the Snooty Fox is a listed Jacobean coaching inn at the centre of Kirkby Lonsdale, the 'capital' of the scenic Lune Valley. Inside are roaring fires in rambling bars full of eye-catching artefacts, while adjacent to a quaint cobbled courtyard is the pub's own herb garden, which signals its commitment to fresh, locally sourced produce. Oven roasted snails, stuffed baby squid, and smoked chicken breast wonton might appear among a choice of 10 starters. A similar range of main courses could include fillet steak foie gras finished with port and game reduction, or marinated pork fillet on coriander and port-glazed shallots. Classy seafood dishes are a feature of the daily specials, such as pan-fried dive caught scallops with herb fondue. The surroundings are comfortably convivial and well-appointed en suite bedrooms promise a good night's sleep.
OPEN: 11-11 (Sun 12-10.30) **BAR MEALS:** L served all week 12-2.30 D served all week 6.30-9.30 (Sun 12-6) Av main course £6 **RESTAURANT:** L served all week 12-2.30 D served all week 6.30-9.30 (Sun 6.30-9) Av 3 course à la carte £20 🍴: Free House 🍺: Timothy Taylor Landlord, Theakstons, Black Sheep. 🍷: 8 **FACILITIES:** Garden: Beer Garden Dogs allowed Water **NOTES:** Parking 9 **ROOMS:** 9 bedrooms en suite 1 family room s£37 d£57 (◆◆◆) No children overnight

Pick of the Pubs
KIRKBY LONSDALE – CUMBRIA

Pheasant Inn

Definitely a pub worth turning off the M6 for, the Pheasant, in the delightful hamlet of Casterton, is a whitewashed 18th-century inn run by the Dixon family. All around are the fells of the beautiful Lune Valley, the market town of Kirkby Lonsdale is only a mile away, and within easy reach are the English Lakes, Yorkshire Dales and Forest of Bowland.

In the welcoming oak-beamed bar you'll find a choice of real ales, including Cumbrian brew Aviator from nearby Dent, and wines by the glass. Dinner is served daily (lunch is on Sundays only) in the oak-panelled restaurant where the menu (also doing duty in the bar) offers mostly traditional English fare freshly prepared from local ingredients. Start with deep-fried breaded mushrooms with tartare sauce, smoked mackerel mousse with toasted home-made bread, or fresh fruit sorbet. Typical main courses are roast crispy duckling with sage and onion stuffing and apple sauce; breaded scampi; tournedos rossini with madeira sauce; halibut steak cooked in dairy butter; seafood mixed grill;

and, for vegetarians, cannelloni stuffed with finely chopped button mushrooms, asparagus spears and parsley cream sauce. The specials menu changes daily, so more temptation will be put your way. To follow, there's a profusion of freshly prepared sweets and puddings. In fine weather you can sit outside on the patio or lawn, from where there are beautiful views of the fells. For guests who want to stay and explore the area, accommodation is available in 11 individually furnished en suite bedrooms, all with colour televisions, direct-dial telephones and tea-making equipment. There are also excellent 18-hole and nine-hole golf courses not far away.

OPEN: 12-3 6-11 (Sun 12-3, 6-10.30)
BAR MEALS: L served all week 12-2
D served all week 6.30-9
RESTAURANT: L served Sun 12-2
D served all week 6.30-9
🍺: Free House
🍺: Scottish Courage Theakston Best & Cool Cask, Black Sheep Best, Marston's Pedigree, Dent Aviator.
🍷: 7
FACILITIES: Garden: Lawn, tables, beautiful views. Patio area
NOTES: Parking 40
ROOMS: 10 bedrooms en suite
(★★) No children overnight

🍷   Map 18 SD67
Casterton LA6 2RX
☎ 015242 71230
📄 015242 74267
📧 pheasantinn@fsbdial.co.uk
🌐 www.pheasantinn.co.uk
Dir: From M6 junct 36, A65 for 7m, left onto A683 at Devils Bridge, 1m to Casterton. Village centre

England

The Sun Inn

Market St LA6 2AU ☎ 015242 71965 📠 015242 72489
e-mail: sunhotel@totalise.co.uk
Dir: From M6 junct 36 take A65
A popular 15th-century pub, renovated in the 17th century, and rumoured to have a resident ghost, the Sun Inn has two open log fires to add to the atmosphere. During excavations to the yard in the 1960s, a tunnel was found that connects the pub with the church. Recent change of ownership.
OPEN: 11-11 (Sun 12-10.30) **BAR MEALS:** L served all week 12.30-2.30 D served all week 6-9 Av main course £8.95
RESTAURANT: L all week 12-2.30 D all week 6-9 Av 3 course à la carte £19 Av 3 course fixed price £8.95 ⊕: Free House

The Whoop Hall ★★ ⊛ ♀

Skipton Rd LA6 2HP ☎ 015242 73632 📠 015242 72154
e-mail: info@whoophall.co.uk
Dir: From M6 take A65. Pub 1m SE of Kirkby Lonsdale
16th-century converted coaching inn, once the kennels for local foxhounds. In an imaginatively converted barn you can relax and enjoy Yorkshire ales and a good range of dishes based on local produce. Oven baked fillet of sea bass with tagliatelle verdi and tiger prawns, and stir-fried honey roast duck with vegetables and water chestnuts are among the popular favourites. The bar offers traditional hand-pulled ales and roaring log fires, and there's a terrace and children's area.
OPEN: 7-11 **BAR MEALS:** L served all week 12-6 D served all week 6-10 Av main course £5 **RESTAURANT:** L served all week 12-2.30 D served all week 5-10 Av 3 course à la carte £15 Av 3 course fixed price £17 ⊕: Free House ◀: Black Sheep, Greene King IPA, Tetley Smooth, Caffreys. ♀: 14 **FACILITIES:** Children's licence Garden: Terrace & lawn areas with good views Dogs allowed Water provided **NOTES:** Parking 120 **ROOMS:** 25 bedrooms en suite s£67.50 d£85

The Bay Horse

Winton CA17 4HS ☎ 017683 71451
e-mail: wintonpubks@whsmithnet.co.uk
Dir: Junct 38 M6, A685 To Brough via Kirkby Stephen, 2 miles N

Standing in a moorland hamlet off the A685, the Bay Horse has low beams and an open coal fire in the winter. A modern dining room is also popular for functions. Expect several vegetarian choices, plus perhaps pork in a green peppercorn sauce.
OPEN: 12-2.30 6.30-11 **BAR MEALS:** L served Wed-Mon 12-2 D served all week 6.30-9 Av main course £7.50 ◀: Black Sheep, Theakstons plus Guest ales. **FACILITIES:** Garden: Food served outside. Views of North Pennines Dogs allowed **NOTES:** Parking 4

Pick of the Pubs

Three Shires Inn ★★

LA22 9NZ ☎ 015394 37215 📠 015394 37127
e-mail: enquiries@threeshiresinn.co.uk
web: www.threeshiresinn.co.uk
Dir: Turn off A593, 2.3m from Ambleside at 2nd junct signed for The Langdales. 1st left 0.5m, hotel 1m up lane

This 19th-century hotel stands in the beautiful valley of Little Langdale. The traditional Cumbrian slate and stone building was erected in the 1880s, when it provided a much-needed resting place and watering hole for travellers on the journey over the high passes of Hardknott and Wrynose. Inside is the expected traditional charm: bare beams and brickwork in the bar, and floral country-house décor in other rooms. Comforts include excellent real ales (Jennings' Best, Cumberland and Coniston Old Man from nearby breweries), and a good selection of malt whiskies. Food is also a strength: in the bar you'll find 'Simply soup and a sandwich', home-made beef and ale pie, fish cakes, and ploughman's. The dinner menu shifts up a gear to specials like crab tortellini, smoked pheasant, rich game pie, and marinated lamb rump. Children are catered for with the usual favourites; dogs are welcome in the bar but not in the hotel.
OPEN: 11-11 (Sun 12-10.30) (Dec-Jan 12-3, 8-10.30) Closed: Dec 25 **BAR MEALS:** L served all week 12-2 D served all week 6-8.45 **RESTAURANT:** L served none D served all week 6.30-8 ⊕: Free House ◀: Jennings Best & Cumberland, Coniston Old Man, Hawkshead Bitter. **FACILITIES:** Children's licence Garden: Terrace and gardens next to stream **NOTES:** Parking 20 **ROOMS:** 10 bedrooms en suite 1 family room

Pick of the Pubs

Kirkstile Inn ♦♦♦♦

CA13 0RU ☎ 01900 85219 📠 01900 85239
e-mail: info@kirkstile.com web: www.kirkstile.com
Dir: Telephone for directions
For some four hundred years, the Kirkstile Inn has nestled between Loweswater and Crummock Water amidst the stunning scenery of the Cumbrian fells. The Kirkstile is ideal for walking, climbing, boating and fishing, or just relaxing over a jar of local real ale; it makes its own ale in a 36-gallon plant called the Loweswater Brewery. The menu offers the likes of Lakeland steak and mushroom pie; Kirkstile pasty; and wild mushroom and feta cheese

continued

lasagne. A tempting choice of puddings includes hot sticky toffee pudding; and Cumberland rum Nicky. Accommodation is provided in 11 attractively appointed bedrooms, nine with en suite facilities. No wonder current owners Helen and Roger Humphreys call it the stress free zone, and it's now completely non-smoking.

Kirkstile Inn

OPEN: 11-11 Closed: 25 Dec **BAR MEALS:** L served all week 12-2 D served all week 6-9 Av main course £7.50
RESTAURANT: D served all week 6-9 Av 3 course à la carte £15 ▣: Free House ◖: Jennings Bitter, Coniston Bluebird, Yates Bitter, Melbreak. **FACILITIES:** Child facs Children's licence Garden: Located away from road with river running by Dogs allowed Water **NOTES:** Parking 40 **ROOMS:** 11 bedrooms 9 en suite 2 family rooms s£45 d£76 ⊗

MELMERBY   Map 18 NY63

The Shepherds Inn ♀
CA10 1HF ☎ 01768 881217
e-mail: theshepherdsinn@btopenworld.com
Dir: On A686 NE of Penrith
Well-known in the North Pennines, this unpretentious sandstone pub looks across the village green towards remote moorland country, close to miles of spectacular walks. Renowned for its extensive choice of country cheeses, including Lanark Blue, Westmorland Smoked and Allerdale Goat. Diners are drawn from far and wide to sample the lunchtime snack menu (baked potatoes, sandwiches and home-made scones) or specials such as rogan gosh, Cumberland sausage hotpot or prime Cumberland grilled steaks. An interesting mix of well-kept real ales.
OPEN: 11-3 6-11 (Sun 12-3, 7-10.30) Closed: 25 Dec
BAR MEALS: L served all week 11.30-2 D served all week 6-9 Av main course £8.50 **RESTAURANT:** L served all week 11.30-2 D served all week 6-9 ▣: Enterprise Inns ◖: Jennings Cumberland Ale, Black Sheep Best, Boddingtons Cask, J S Magnet. ♀: 8 **FACILITIES:** Children's licence Dogs allowed **NOTES:** Parking 20

MUNGRISDALE   Map 18 NY33

The Mill Inn ♦♦♦ ♀
CA11 0XR ☎ 017687 79632 ▤ 017687 79981
e-mail: margaret@the-millinn.co.uk
Dir: From Penrith A66 to Keswick, after 10m R to Mungrisdale, pub 2m on L
Set in a peaceful village, this 16th-century coaching inn is handy for spectacular fell walks. Charles Dickens and John Peel once stayed here. The inn has an annual pie festival which raises money for charity with its huge selection of pies. At lunchtime, hungry walkers could tuck into local Cumberland sausages or home-made fishcakes. Evening

continued

specials include tempting pies with fillings like local lamb and apricot; steak with roasted onions; and spiced chicken.

The Mill Inn

OPEN: 12-11 (Sun 12-10.30) **BAR MEALS:** L served all week 12-2.30 D served all week 6-8.30 Av main course £9
RESTAURANT: L served all week 12-2.30 D served all week 6-8.30 Av 3 course à la carte £18.50 ▣: Free House ◖: Jennings Bitter & Cumberland plus guest ale. ♀: 6 **FACILITIES:** Children's licence Garden: Landscaped, seats 30, overlooking river Dogs allowed (£5 to use bedrooms) **NOTES:** Parking 40 **ROOMS:** 6 bedrooms 5 en suite 1 family room s£40 d£60

NEAR SAWREY   Map 18 SD39

Tower Bank Arms ◁▷ ♀
LA22 0LF ☎ 015394 36334
e-mail: sales@towerbankarms.fsnet.co.uk
Dir: On B5285 SW of Windermere
Next door to Hill Top, Beatrix Potter's former home, this 17th-century country inn was immortalised in *The Tales of Jemima Puddleduck*. It's an ideal base for exploring the Lake District. The celebrity wall displays portraits of famous people, many of them patrons of the inn. A choice of cold and hot dishes ranges from salads, potted shrimps and cheese flan to game pie, Cumberland sausage and Barnsley chop.
OPEN: 11-3 6-11 (Summer 6-10.30 Sun, Mon-Fri 5.30-11) Closed: 25 Dec eve **BAR MEALS:** L served all week 12-2 D served all week 6.30-9 Av main course £7.50 **RESTAURANT:** L served all week 12-2 D served all week 6.30-9 ▣: Free House ◖: Theakston Best & Old Peculier, Wells Bombardier, Barngates Tag Lag. ♀: 7 **FACILITIES:** Children's licence Garden: 5 tables, 30 seats Dogs allowed **NOTES:** Parking 8

NETHER WASDALE   Map 18 NY10

The Screes Inn
CA20 1ET ☎ 019467 26262 ▤ 019467 26262
e-mail: info@thescreesinnwasdale.com
Dir: Travel to Gosforth on A595. Continue through Gosforth for 3m, then turn right signed Nether Wasdale. The Screes Inn is in the village on the left.
Nestling in the scenic Wasdale valley and close to Wastwater, this welcoming 300-year-old inn with its cosy log fire, choice of real ales and large selection of malt whiskies makes an excellent base for walking, mountain biking, or diving. The menu offers marinated organic lamb with mint gravy; chick pea and potato curry; and home-made steak and kidney pie. There is a children's menu, and a good choice of sandwiches at lunchtime.
OPEN: 12-11 Closed: Dec 25, Jan 1 **BAR MEALS:** L served all week 12-3 D served all week 6-9 Av main course £7.50
RESTAURANT: L served all week 12-3 D served all week 6-9 ▣: Free House ◖: Black Sheep Best, Yates Bitter, Coniston Bluebird, Derwent. **FACILITIES:** Child facs Children's licence Garden: Seating area to front & side of pub, BBQ area Dogs allowed Water **NOTES:** Parking 30

OUTGATE   Map 18 SD39

Outgate Inn
LA22 0NQ ☎ 015394 36413
Dir: From M6 junct 36, by-passing Kendal, A591 towards Ambleside. At
Clappersgate take B593 to Hawkshead then Outgate
A 16th-century Lakeland inn only a mile down the road from
where Wordsworth went to school. Without doubt he was
inspired by the glorious walks and magnificent scenery
surrounding this former tollhouse, which retains many
original features. Winter fires and weekly jazz evenings help
create an inviting atmosphere. An extensive and varied menu
offers Lancashire hot pot, macaroni cheese, Thai green
chicken curry, and pan-fried escalope of corn-fed chicken.
OPEN: 11-3 6-11 (Sat 11-11 Sun 12-10.30) **BAR MEALS:** L served
all week 12-2 D served all week 6.30-9 (Sun 12-9)
RESTAURANT: L served all week 12-2 D served all week 6.30-9 (Sun
12-9) ⊕: Hartleys ⏺: Robinsons Best, Cumbria Way, Fredericks &
Hartleys XB. **FACILITIES:** Children's licence Garden: Beer garden at
the rear Dogs allowed Water **NOTES:** Parking 30

RAVENSTONEDALE   Map 18 NY70

Pick of the Pubs

Black Swan Hotel 🐟 ♀
CA17 4NG ☎ 015396 23204 📠 015396 23604
e-mail: reservations@blackswanhotel.com
web: www.blackswanhotel.com
Dir: M6 junct 38 take A685 E towards Brough

Ravenstonedale is a peaceful, unspoilt village in the upper
Eden valley in Cumbria, lying between the Lake District and
Yorkshire Dales National Parks. The hotel is a grand, solid-
looking, Lakeland stone affair built around 1899. It offers an
à la carte menu complemented by daily specials, and an
extensive bar menu. Typical dishes include steak and ale
pie, minted lamb, venison pie, and sirloin steak, with as
much of the produce as possible coming from
Westmorland, the original county which was merged with
Cumberland to form Cumbria. Wednesdays are fish specials
days, although there is always a good selection of fish on
other days, with fresh battered haddock, grilled plaice fillet,
baked cod steaks on avacado and prawns, or fisherman's
pie usually available. Traditionally made local cheeses grace
the desserts menu. Local beers include Tirril, brewed at
Brougham Hall. The pub's sheltered garden leads across a
bridge over a beck to a natural riverside glade.
OPEN: 9-11 (Sun 12-10.30) **BAR MEALS:** L served all week
12-2 D served all week 6-9 snack menu all day
RESTAURANT: L served all week 12-2 D served all week 7-9
⊕: Free House ⏺: Black Sheep, Scottish Courage John Smith's,
Dent, Derwent. ♀: 8 **FACILITIES:** Child facs Children's licence
Garden: River & garden Dogs allowed **NOTES:** Parking 40

Pick of the Pubs

The Fat Lamb Country Inn ★★
Crossbank CA17 4LL ☎ 015396 23242 📠 015396 23285
e-mail: fatlamb@cumbria.com
See Pick of the Pubs on opposite page

Pick of the Pubs

Kings Head Hotel ♦♦♦ ♀
CA17 4NH ☎ 015396 23284
e-mail: enquiries@kings-head.net web: www.kings-head.net
Dir: Ravenstonedale is less that 10 mins (7 m) from junct 38 Tebay
on A685 & 6m from Kirkby Stephen

With a history dating from the 17th century, in its time
this building has served as an inn, a court and jail,
cottages, a temperance hotel and latterly licensed
premises again. Though recently refurbished after severe
flooding, the Kings Head retains its old world charm and
traditional values, with cask ales, 45 malt whiskies, home-
cooked local produce and real log fires. The menu
includes among its starters, a half rack of ribs, soup of the
day and moules marinière, while the main course can be
selected from dishes such as Cumberland sausage with
apple sauce, chicken fillet poached in white wine, cream
and mushroom sauce, or chilli con carne. There are
interesting specials, a salad bar, and a chargrill. The
accommodation comprises 3 rooms, 2 of which are en
suite. Keep an eye out for one of three friendly ghosts.
OPEN: 11-3 6-11 (Fri-Sat Open all day Spring & Summer)
BAR MEALS: L served all week 12-2 D served all week 6-9
Av main course £7.95 **RESTAURANT:** L served all week 12-2
D served all week 6-9 ⊕: Free House ⏺: Black Sheep, Dent,
Carlsberg-Tetley Tetley's Imperial, Over 100 Guest Ales. ♀: 6
FACILITIES: Children's licence Garden: By river, offset from
building, tree canopy Dogs allowed Water, food bowls
NOTES: Parking 10 **ROOMS:** 3 bedrooms 2 en suite
1 family room s£35 d£50

Do you have a favourite pub that we have overlooked?
Please use the Reader's Report form at the back of
this guide to tell us all about it

Website addresses are included where available.
The AA cannot be held responsible for the
content of any of these websites

England

Pick of the Pubs

RAVENSTONEDALE – CUMBRIA

The Fat Lamb Country Inn

Dating from the 1600s, this is a sprawling country inn with solid grey stone walls and its own nature reserve. The Fat Lamb is set in magnificent countryside between two of the country's most beautiful national parks - the Lake District and the Yorkshire Dales. Don't be surprised to see horses waiting in the car park along with the cars, as this traditional inn hosts pony trekkers holidaying in the area.

Over the 27 years he has run the inn, Paul Bonsall has created his vision of the perfect place to escape, whether to drink, eat, stay, or all three, undisturbed by pool, video games and juke box. His chefs use local ingredients whenever possible to produce dishes with styles ranging from traditional farmhouse to the best of modern cooking from around the world. Faced with bar snack, carte or fixed price dinner menu, all possibilities are tempting. From the bar come home-made lasagne, mixed sausage platter, and chilli bean pot. The carte offers starters of smoked local trout with red onion relish, and savoury filled pancakes, followed by sautéed chicken with coriander, apple and cider sauce; duck ragout with pears and ginger; seared supreme of salmon with roast vegetables; rack of lamb with a mint and honey jus; and rich casserole of beef in Guinness. From the set menu expect the likes of macaroni and tomato bake, and oven roast ham with parsley sauce. The informal garden doubles as a pleasant eating area, and the private nature reserve, set just behind the pub, offers 15 acres of peace and beauty.

OPEN: 11-2 6-11
BAR MEALS: L served all week 12-2
D served all week 6-9
RESTAURANT: L served all week
12-2 D served all week 6-9
🛢: Free House
🍺: Cask Condition Tetley's Bitter.
FACILITIES: Child facs Garden:
Open grassed area surrounded by
shrubs Dogs allowed
NOTES: Parking 60
ROOMS: 12 bedrooms en suite
4 family rooms s£50 d£80

★★   Map 18 NY70
Crossbank CA17 4LL
☎ 015396 23242
🖷 015396 23285
📧 fatlamb@cumbria.com
Dir: On A683 between Sedbergh
& Kirkby Stephen

SEATHWAITE   Map 18 SD29

The Newfield Inn ♀
LA20 6ED ☎ 01229 716208
e-mail: paul@seathwaite.freeserve.co.uk
Dir: A590 toward Barrow, then right onto A5092, becomes A595, follow
for 1m, right at Duddon Bridge, 6m to Seathwaite

There are stunning views of the fells from the garden of this
early 17th-century free house, located in Wordsworth's
favourite Duddon Valley. The building, which has been a farm
and a post office in its past, boasts a real fire, oak beams and
a wonderful slate floor. The menu encompasses home-made
dishes like tomato and basil pasta; salmon fillet with lime
butter; and Cumberland sausage and chips. There's an ever-
changing specials board, too.

OPEN: 11-11 25-26 Dec limited hours **BAR MEALS:** L served all
week 12-9 D served all week 12-9 Av main course £7
RESTAURANT: L served all week 12-9 D served all week 12-9
Av 3 course à la carte £14 ⊕: Free House ◖: Scottish Courage
Theakston Old Peculier, Jennings Cumberland Ale, Caledonian
Deuchars IPA. ♀: 6 **FACILITIES:** Child facs Garden: Sheltered,
seating for 40, stunning views Dogs allowed Water
NOTES: Parking 30

SEDBERGH   Map 18 SD69

The Dalesman Country Inn ♀
Main St LA10 5BN ☎ 015396 21183 ▤ 015396 21311
e-mail: info@thedalesman.co.uk
Dir: junct 37 on M6, follow signs to Sedbergh, 1st pub in town on left

A 16th-century coaching inn, renowned for its floral displays
and handy for walks along the River Dee or up on Howgill
Fells. The lunchtime menu concentrates on the likes of home-
made pies, hot sandwiches, and fresh fish in crispy beer
batter. The more ambitious evening choice extends to seared
chicken fillet with caramelised shallots and spinach, seared
lamb's liver with black pudding, grilled haddock with saffron
potatoes, and game casserole with a puff pastry lid. There is a
patio and garden, and a good wine selection.
OPEN: 11-11 (Sun 12-10.30) **BAR MEALS:** L served all week
12-2.30 D served all week 6-9.30 Sun 12-8 Av main course £8
RESTAURANT: L served all week 12-2.30 D served all week 6-9.30
Sun 12-8 ⊕: Free House ◖: Carlsberg-Tetley, Scottish Courage
Theakston Best Bitter, Black Sheep. ♀: 9 **FACILITIES:** Children's
licence Garden: Wooden benches & tables at pubs front
NOTES: Parking 8

Restaurant and Bar Meal times indicate the times
when food is available. Last orders may be
approximately 30 minutes before the times stated

SHAP   Map 18 NY51

Greyhound Hotel ♀
Main St CA10 3PW ☎ 01931 716474 ▤ 01931 716305
e-mail: postmaster@greyhoundshap.demon.co.uk
Dir: Telephone for directions

Built as a coaching inn in 1684, the Greyhound is a welcoming
sight for travellers after crossing Shap Fell. It offers a choice of
up to eight real ales and a good selection of wines. From the
evening menu expect vegetable and mascarpone lasagne;
lamb Henry in wine, redcurrant and onion gravy; and home-
made steak and ale pie. All meats are locally sourced. Good
choice of children's dishes; snack menu at lunchtime.
OPEN: 11-11 (Sun 12-10.30) **BAR MEALS:** L served all week 12-2
D served all week 6-9 Av main course £8.50
RESTAURANT: L served all week 12-2 D served all week 6-9
Av 3 course à la carte £16 ⊕: Free House ◖: Carlsberg-Tetley
Bitter, Young's Bitter, Greene King Old Speckled Hen, Jennings Bitter
plus Guest Ales. ♀: 10 **FACILITIES:** Children's licence Garden:
Food served outside, patio Dogs allowed **NOTES:** Parking 30

TEBAY   Map 18 NY60

The Cross Keys Inn ♦♦♦
CA10 3UY ☎ 015396 24240 ▤ 015396 24240
e-mail: www.stay@crosskeys-tebay.co.uk
web: www.crosskeys-tebay.co.uk
Dir: Just off M6 junct 38. Along A685 to Kendal

A little gem of a free house, allegedly haunted by the ghost of
Mary Baynes, the Tebay Witch, still looking for her black cat
which was savagely disposed of by a former landlord. An
extensive lunch and evening menu - available in both the
restaurant and bar - offers steak and mushroom pie,
Cumberland sausage, Catalan chicken, chicken and ham
pudding, smoky bacon pasta, smoked haddock and spinach
bake, and salmon and broccoli mornay. Black Sheep Best
Bitter on tap.
OPEN: 12-3 6-11 (Open all day Fri-Sun) **BAR MEALS:** L served all
week 12-2.30 D served all week 6-9 **RESTAURANT:** L served all

continued

week 12-2.30 D served all week 6-9 ☺: Free House ◧: Black Sheep
Cask, Carlsberg-Tetley Tetley's Cask, Smooth & Imperial.
FACILITIES: Child facs Children's licence Garden: Large patio area,
large lawned area Dogs allowed **NOTES:** Parking 50
ROOMS: 9 bedrooms 6 en suite s£30 d£40

TIRRIL   Map 18 NY52

Pick of the Pubs

Queens Head Inn ♦♦♦♦ ♀
CA10 2JF ☎ 01768 863219 ▤ 01768 863243
e-mail: bookings@queensheadinn.co.uk
*Dir: A66 towards Penrith then A6 S toward Shap. In Eamont Bridge
take R just after Crown Hotel. Tirril 1m on B5320.*

A privately owned, traditional free house dating from
1719, chock-full of beams, flagstones and memorabilia.
One of the four open fireplaces still has the original hooks
used for smoking meats. Look in the bar for the
Wordsworth Indenture, signed by William, the great poet
himself, his brother, Christopher, and local wheelwright
John Bewsher, to whom the Wordsworths sold the pub in
1836. Obviously a marketing man, Bewsher shrewdly
changed the inn's name from The Board in time for
Queen Victoria's coronation in 1837, and today's house
best bitter is named after him. Fare includes brie tartlet
and pasta dishes to start, followed by steamed suet
pudding with steak and Tirril's ale filling, escalopes of
venison, chicken rogan josh, steaks, shoulder of lamb and
wholetail scampi. Fresh fish, vegetarian meals and
specials appear on the blackboard. Ale and banger
enthusiasts shouldn't miss the annual Cumbrian Beer and
Sausage Festival in mid-August.
OPEN: 12-3 6-11 (Fri-Sun all day All day all wk Apr-Oct) Dec 25
closed evening **BAR MEALS:** L served all week 12-2 D served
all week 6-9.30 Sun 12-2, 7-9 Av main course £9
RESTAURANT: L served all week 12-2 D served all week 6-9.30
Sun 12-2, 7-9 Av 3 course à la carte £19 ☺: Free House
◧: Tirril Bewshers Best, Thomas Slee's Academy Ale & Charles
Gough's Old Faithful, Brougham Ale & Cumbrian guest ales.
♀: 10 **FACILITIES:** Children's licence Small garden, adjacent to
car park and lounge Dogs allowed Water **NOTES:** Parking 60
ROOMS: 7 bedrooms en suite

We only include details of accommodation that
has been inspected by the AA (big Stars or
Diamonds at the top of an entry), or the
RAC, VisitBritain, VisitScotland or WTB
(small Stars or Diamonds at the end of an entry)

TROUTBECK   Map 18 NY40

Pick of the Pubs

Queens Head Hotel ♦♦♦♦ ♀
Townhead LA23 1PW ☎ 015394 32174 ▤ 015394 31938
e-mail: enquiries@queensheadhotel.com
web: www.queensheadhotel.com
*Dir: M6 junct 36, A590/591, W towards Windermere, right at mini-
rdbt onto A592 signed Penrith/Ullswater. Pub 2m on right*

The Queens Head has stayed true to its roots as a thriving
17th-century coaching inn in the Troutbeck Valley.
Accommodation is offered in comfortable en suite
bedrooms, but even those just calling in for sustenance
will appreciate the dramatic views across the Garburn
Pass. The rambling bars are full of character, with open
fires and ancient carved settles. Accomplished cooking is
the watchword here, with an imaginative range of dishes
served in both bar and restaurant. The lunch menu offers
hearty fare, such as pan-fried lamb's liver on champ; or
fettuccine tossed with wild mushrooms, topped with a
poached egg. All weigh in at around the £6 mark. The
evening menu continues in the same vein, and there's a
fixed price menu - also with choices at each course. Even
the children's choice maintains standards, and there's a
lovingly composed cheese menu provided you've got an
inch of space.
OPEN: 11-11 (Sun 12-10.30) Closed: 25 Dec
BAR MEALS: L served all week 12-2 D served all week 6.30-9
Av main course £11.95 **RESTAURANT:** L served all week 12-2
D served all week 6.30-9 Av 3 course à la carte £25 Av 4 course
fixed price £15.50 ☺: Free House ◧: Interbrew Boddingtons
Bitter, Coniston Bluebird, Old Man Bitter, Jennings Cumberland
Ale. **FACILITIES:** Children's licence **NOTES:** Parking 100
ROOMS: 14 bedrooms en suite s£67.50 d£100

ULVERSTON   Map 18 SD27

The Devonshire Arms NEW
Victoria Rd LA12 0DH ☎ 01229 582537
& 480287 ▤ 01229 480287
Located on the outskirts of the bustling market town of
Ulverston, this popular pub is home to a wide range of cask
beers and guest ales, as well as two dart teams. The menu
focuses on classic pub grub, with plenty in the way of light
bites: baguettes, burgers, jackets and the like, as well as some
more filling mains. These range from home-made mince and
onion pie to vegetable korma curry.
OPEN: 11-2.30 5.30-11 (Open all day Sat-Sun Autumn-Winter 6-11)
BAR MEALS: L served Thurs-Tues 12-2 D served Thurs-Tues 6-8.30
Sun 12-2, 6-8.30 Av main course £6.50 ◧: Boddingtons Bitter,
Tetley Smooth. **FACILITIES:** Child facs Children's licence
NOTES: Parking 6

Pick of the Pubs

Farmers Arms ♀
Market Place LA12 7BA ☎ 01229 584469 ▤ 01229 582188
e-mail: roger@farmersulufreeserve.com
A warm welcome is extended to locals and visitors alike at this lively 16th-century inn located at the centre of the attractive, historic market town. A bustling market on the cobbled streets attracts shoppers on Thursdays and Saturdays and is overlooked by the pub's sunny patio from which patrons can enjoy a drink or a summer meal while watching the changing scene. The town is host to many festivals so there is always something of interest. Inside the visitor will find a comfortable and relaxing beamed front bar with an open fire in winter. Landlord Roger Chattaway takes pride in serving quality food; his Sunday lunches are famous, and at other times the varied and tempting specials menu lists roast Barbary duck, moules marinière, chargrilled large king prawns with garlic and chillies, and stir-fried marinated chicken in a sesame Cantonese sauce. The lunchtime choice includes hot and cold sandwiches, baguettes or ciabatta, and various salads.
OPEN: 10-11 **BAR MEALS:** L served all week 11-3 D served all week 5.30-8.30 Av main course £6.95 **RESTAURANT:** L served all week D served all week ⊕: Free House ◀: Hawkshead Best Bitter, Hoegarden, John Smiths. ♀: 12 **FACILITIES:** Children's licence Garden: Sunny patio garden,outdoor heaters and canopy Dogs allowed outside

Royal Oak
Spark Bridge LA12 8BS ☎ 01229 861006
e-mail: info@royaloaksparkbridge.co.uk
Dir: From Ulverston take A590 N. Village off A5092

Set in a small village, this large, 18th-century pub offers a varied menu. Dishes include breaded sole filled with crab and prawn sauce, fillet steak stuffed with stilton cheese and wrapped in bacon served on a port wine sauce, steak and mushroom pie, Cumberland sausage and chips, roasted sea bass served on creamy mashed potatoes, chicken and ham pie, or seared scallops on salad. Try the enormous Royal Grill (steak, sausage, pork loin, black pudding, gammon and eggs). New landlord 2004.
OPEN: 12-3 6-11 (Sun 12-10.30) **BAR MEALS:** L served all week 12-3 D served all week 6-9 (Sun food all day) No lunch Mon-Tue out of season Av main course £8.50 ⊕: Enterprise Inns ◀: Tetley, Jennings Cumberland, Black Sheep and Guest Ales.
FACILITIES: Garden: Food served outside Dogs allowed Water
NOTES: Parking 30

Wasdale Head Inn ◁▷ ♀
CA20 1EX ☎ 019467 26229 ▤ 019467 26334
e-mail: wasdaleheadinn@msn.com
Dir: From A595 follow Wasdale signs. Inn at head of valley
Dramatically situated at the foot of England's highest mountains and beside her deepest lake, this inn is a perfect base for walking and climbing. Oak-panelled walls are hung with photographs reflecting a passion for climbing. Exclusive real ales are brewed on the premises and celebrated by two annual beer festivals. Menus suit outdoor appetites: red snapper on king prawn and roquette salad; and roast chicken with parsnips and shallots.
OPEN: 11-11 (Sun 12-10.30) Winter close at 10
BAR MEALS: L served all week 11-9 D served all week 11-9 Winter 12-8 Av main course £7.50 **RESTAURANT:** L served D served most evenings 7-8 Av 4 course fixed price £25 ⊕: Free House ◀: Great Gable, Wasdale Ale, Burnmoor, Yewbarrow. ♀: 15
FACILITIES: Garden: View of mountains, food served outside Dogs allowed Water **NOTES:** Parking 50 **ROOMS:** 15 bedrooms en suite 1 family room s£49 d£98 (♦♦♦♦) No children overnight ⊗

Pick of the Pubs

Brackenrigg Inn ♦♦♦♦ ♀
CA11 0LP ☎ 017684 86206 ▤ 017684 86945
e-mail: enquiries@brackenrigginn.co.uk
web: www.brackenrigginn.co.uk
Dir: From M6 junct 40 take the A66 (signed Keswick). Then take A592 signed Ullswater. Located 6m from M6 and Penrith
The Brackenrigg is a white-painted roadside hostelry that makes the most of its elevated position with sweeping views across Lake Ullswater and the surrounding fells, including Helvellyn in the distance. The inn dates from the 18th century and has a traditional bar with an open fire, where there's a good choice of real beers and wines by the glass. Very much a food-led pub, it relies on fresh produce, much of it local, to enthuse visitors from near and farther away. The bar menu is supported by a changing specials list, but otherwise offers the likes of lamb Henry, pasta bake, fish and chips with lemon and dill-scented beer batter, and Cumberland sausage (made in the village) with apple mash, mushy peas and onion gravy. Theakston's Best, Black Sheep Special, and Coniston Bluebird are among the real ales served. There is plenty to do nearby.
OPEN: 12-11 (Sun 12-10.30) Nov-Mar closed btwn 3-5pm (Mon-Fri) **BAR MEALS:** L served all week 12-2.30 D served all week D served all week Av main course £8.95 **RESTAURANT:** L served all week 12-2.30 D served all week 6.30-9 Av 3 course à la carte £24.95 ⊕: Free House ◀: Theakstons Best, Jennings Cumberland, Black Sheep Special, Coniston Bluebird. ♀: 12
FACILITIES: Children's licence Garden: Garden has views of Ullswater & the valley Dogs allowed Water provided
NOTES: Parking 40 **ROOMS:** 17 bedrooms en suite 8 family rooms s£33 d£56

We endeavour to be as accurate as possible but changes to times and other information can occur after the guide has gone to press

WINDERMERE — Map 18 SD49

Eagle & Child Inn ◆◆◆ ♀

Kendal Rd, Staveley LA8 9LP ☎ 01539 821320
e-mail: info@eaglechildinn.co.uk web: www.eaglechildinn.co.uk
Dir: *Follow M6 to junct 36 then A590 towards Kendal join A591 towards Windermere. Staveley approx 2m*

Several pubs in Britain share this name, usually taken from family crests incorporating a legend of a baby found in an eagle's nest. The pub's attractive riverside gardens are delightful and all around is excellent walking, cycling and fishing country. Meat and fresh bread come from the village, game from nearby. On the menu might be fresh local trout; pan-fried duck breast; gammon with pineapple; and beef and Black Sheep ale pie. Well-kept local beers - Coniston Bluebird, perhaps.
OPEN: 11-11 Dec 25 restauraunt closed **BAR MEALS:** L served Mon-Fri 12-2.30 D served Mon-Fri 6-9 Av main course £7.95
RESTAURANT: L served Mon-Fri 12-2.30 D served Mon-Fri 6-9
◀: Black Sheep Best Bitter, Coniston Bluebird Bitter, Dent Ales, Yates Bitter. ♀: 8 **FACILITIES:** Child facs Garden: Riverside location, secluded rear terrace Dogs allowed **NOTES:** Parking 16
ROOMS: 5 bedrooms en suite 1 family room s£40 d£60

New Hall Inn

Lowside, Bowness LA23 3DH ☎ 015394 43488
Dir: *Telephone for directions*
A listed building dating from 1612, the pub retains many original features, including oak beams, flagstone floors and open fires. It was originally a coaching inn, and one of its best-known visitors was Charles Dickens. The smaller bar was once a blacksmith's, where beer was passed through the hole in the wall. Along with baked potatoes, sandwiches and ploughman's, the menu offers fisherman's pie; and mussels.
OPEN: 11-11 (Sun 12-10.30 Closed: 25 Dec)
BAR MEALS: L served all week 12-2.30 D served Mon-Sat 6-8.30 Sat 12-7 Av main course £7.25 ☺: ◀: Hartleys XB, Robinsons Unicorn, Double Hop. **FACILITIES:** Children's licence Garden: Patio Garden

Pick of the Pubs

The Watermill Inn ♀

Ings LA8 9PY ☎ 01539 821309 ▤ 01539 822309
e-mail: all@watermillinn.co.uk
Once a timber mill crafting shuttles and bobbins for the Lancashire cotton industry, this inn is very popular with walkers, not least because of its impressive selection of real ales - up to 16 on offer at any one time. To accompany them, the menu has many daily specials, with popular choices being venison sausage, beef and ale pie, Wrynose mixed grill, Cumberland sausage, and Watermill chicken.

OPEN: 12-11 (Sun 12-10.30) Closed: 25 Dec
BAR MEALS: L served all week 12-4.30 D served all week 5-9 Av main course £8.25 ☺: Free House ◀: Coniston Blue Bird, Black Sheep Special, Jennings Cumberland Ale, Hawkshead Bitter.
FACILITIES: Children's licence Garden: Paved area Dogs allowed Biscuits & water provided

WORKINGTON — Map 18 NY02

The Old Ginn House

Great Clifton CA14 1TS ☎ 01900 64616 ▤ 01900 873384
e-mail: enquiries@oldginnhouse.co.uk
Dir: *3 miles from Workington, 4 miles from Cockermouth, just off the A66*
In the 17th century wool was treated by 'ginning', a process carried out in today's unusual rounded Ginn Room bar. The character of the old buildings, around an attractive courtyard, remains uncompromised by carefully integrated modern facilities. An extensive menu of mostly traditional pub dishes does duty at both lunchtime and in the evenings, with Cumberland sausage and fried egg; roast half chicken with stuffing; beef stroganoff and rice; and penne pasta carbonara.
OPEN: 12-11 Closed: 24-26 Dec, 1 Jan **BAR MEALS:** L served all week 12-1.45 D served all week 6-9.30 Av main course £6.95
RESTAURANT: L served all week 12-1.45 D served all week 6-9.30 Av 3 course à la carte £15 ◀: Jennings Bitter, John Smiths Bitter, Murphys. **FACILITIES:** Child facs Children's licence Garden: Courtyard **NOTES:** Parking 40 **ROOMS:** 19 bedrooms en suite 4 family rooms s£45 d£60 (◆◆◆◆)

YANWATH — Map 18 NY52

Pick of the Pubs

The Yanwath Gate Inn ♀

CA10 2LF ☎ 01768 862386 ▤ 01768 899892
e-mail: enquiries@yanwathgate.com

The Yanwath Gate Inn has been offering hospitality in the North Lakes since 1683. Nowadays, however, the busy kitchen is the driving force as new owner Matt Edwards and his team of chefs dish up traditional and modern cuisine utilising an abundance of quality fresh local ingredients. This is a place where you can enjoy a pint of Hesket Newmarket, Tirril or Jennings beer (only Cumbrian ales sold) while you choose something from the appetising menu. Fish is delivered fresh every morning and bread is baked on site. Start proceedings off with tian of black pudding and haggis topped with a poached egg and Cumbrian ham, before roast fillet of beef with chilli roast potatoes and wild mushroom fricassee. Each dish is cooked and prepared to order, and the regularly changing menus make full use of plentiful

continued

continued

England

YANWATH continued

local produce. A cosy reading area in the bar ensures a relaxed mood for diners wishing to eat either there by the log fire, or to take a table in one of the two restaurants. **OPEN:** 11-11 **BAR MEALS:** L served all week 12-2.30 D served all week 6-9.30 Av main course £13.50 **RESTAURANT:** L served all week 12-2.30 D served all week 6-9.30 Av 3 course à la carte £30 ☺: Free House ◀: Jennings Cumberland Ale, Jennings Smoothy, Guiness, Hesket Brewery. ♀: 9
FACILITIES: Children's licence Garden: Secluded terrace, lawns, landscaped garden Dogs allowed **NOTES:** Parking 40 ⊕

DERBYSHIRE

ALFRETON   Map 16 SK45

White Horse Inn ♀
Badger Ln, Woolley Moor DE55 6FG
☎ 01246 590319 ▯ 01246 590319
e-mail: info@the-whitehorse-inn.co.uk
Dir: From A632 (Matlock/Chesterfield rd) take B6036. Pub 1m after Ashover. From A61 take B6036 to Woolley Moor

Situated on an old toll road, close to Ogston Reservoir, this 18th-century inn has outstanding views over the Amber Valley. The bar food menu offers such dishes as Thai fish cakes, braised belly pork and black pudding, or chicken stroganoff - as well as an extensive range of sandwiches. From the main menu, expect Moroccan chicken tagine; winter game casserole; or sweet pepper, mushroom and mozzarella bruschetta. There is a good choice of real ales, and an extensive wine list. **OPEN:** 12-3 6-11 (Sun 12-10.30, all day summer wknds) **BAR MEALS:** L served Tue-Sun 12-2 D served Tues-Sun 6-9 no food Sun eve Av main course £7.50 **RESTAURANT:** L served all week 12-2 D served Tues-Sat 6-9 Sun 12-4 ☺: Free House ◀: Jennings Cumberland, Adnams Broadside, Blacksheep, 1744. ♀: 8
FACILITIES: Child facs Children's licence Garden: Large patio with picnic benches Dogs allowed Water **NOTES:** Parking 50

◆ Diamond rating for inspected guest accommodation

Disabled people and those with Assist Dogs have new rights of access to pubs, restaurants and hotels under the Disability Discrimination Act of 1 October 2004. For more information see the website at www.drc gb.org/open4all/rights/2004.asp

---

ASHBOURNE   Map 10 SK14

Barley Mow Inn
Kirk Ireton DE6 3JP ☎ 01335 370306
On the edge of the Peak District National Park, this imposing 17th-century inn has remained largely unchanged over the years. Close to Carsington Water, ideal for sailing, fishing and bird watching. There are also good walking opportunities on nearby marked paths. Ales from the cask and traditional cider; fresh granary rolls at lunchtime and evening meals for residents only.
OPEN: 12-2 7-11 (Sun, 7-10.30) Closed: Dec 25 & Dec 31
BAR MEALS: 12-2 ☺: Free House ◀: Hook Norton, Burton Bridge, Whim Hartington, Archers. **FACILITIES:** Garden: Dogs allowed **NOTES:** No credit cards

Dog & Partridge Country Inn ★★ ⌣ ♀
Swinscoe DE6 2HS ☎ 01335 343183 ▯ 01335 342742
e-mail: dogpart@fsbdial.co.uk web: www.dogandpartridge.co.uk
Dir: Telephone for directions
This pub has a particular claim to fame: it was extended in 1966 to accommodate the Brazilian World Cup football team, who practised in a nearby field. Its extensive menus offer such dishes as halibut in Pernod, and ostrich steak in a whisky and cream sauce, alongside all the traditional favourites. Vegetarians are well catered for, and a local speciality is a Staffordshire oatcake with a choice of fillings accompanied by red cabbage, beetroot and salad.
OPEN: 11-11 **BAR MEALS:** L served all week 11-11 D served all week **RESTAURANT:** L served all week 11-11 D served all week ☺: Free House ◀: Greene King Old Speckled Hen & Ruddles County, Hartington Best, Wells Bombardier, Scottish Courage Courage Directors. **FACILITIES:** Child facs Garden: Good patio area with lovely views Dogs allowed **NOTES:** Parking 50
ROOMS: 29 bedrooms en suite 16 family rooms

BAKEWELL   Map 16 SK26

Pick of the Pubs

The Lathkil Hotel
Over Haddon DE45 1JE ☎ 01629 812501 ▯ 01629 812501
e-mail: info@lathkil.co.uk
Dir: 2m SW of Bakewell
Lead discovered by the Romans in the hills and dales of the Peak District was still being mined until 1860, which explains why the hotel used to be called The Miners Arms. You can eat delicious home-cooked food at lunchtimes and evenings while enjoying (at least in daylight hours) the glorious views along Lathkil Vale. In summer, take your pick from hot and cold buffets. More extensive choices offered at dinner might include plaice with prawns and capers; baked sea bass with tarragon and lemon; steak, kidney and oyster pie; garlic and honey pork; and fillet steak garni. Vegetarians should find something appealing among mushroom and spinach slice with cranberry sauce; brie, courgette and almond crumble; or lemon and thyme rice with rocket. Local Hartington Bitter and other cask-conditioned beers served.
OPEN: 11.30-3 7-11 (all day Sat-Sun) **BAR MEALS:** L served all week 12-2 Av main course £8 **RESTAURANT:** D served all week 7-9 (Bookings only on Sun) Av 3 course à la carte £18.50 ☺: ◀: Whim Hartington, Timothy Taylor Landlord, Wells Bombardier, Marston's Pedigree. **FACILITIES:** Garden: beer garden, outdoor eating & grassed area Dogs allowed Water **NOTES:** Parking 28

Pick of the Pubs

BAMFORD – DERBYSHIRE

Yorkshire Bridge Inn

In the heart of the Peak District, the inn, which dates from 1826, takes its name from an old packhorse bridge, the only crossing point over the River Derwent on the road between Yorkshire and Cheshire. Close by are the Howden, Derwent and Ladybower reservoirs, which caused much controversy when they were being created in the first quarter of the last century, but are now beautiful attractions in their own right.

In 1943 the RAF practised on them before the Dambusters, as they were christened, made their dramatic bombing raids on the Ruhr dams in Germany. In winter the bars, with their plentiful beams and attractive chintz curtains, are welcoming and cosy, while in warmer weather you can sit outside in the courtyard or beer garden. For all-year-round dining the Conservatory, with large, spacious windows enjoying excellent views of the hills, is popular. Sandwiches and filled jacket potatoes are prepared at lunchtime only, but available all day are grills, salad platters, and a range of hot dishes including

chicken tandoori sizzler; home-made steak and kidney pie; giant prawn cocktail; breaded fried scampi; pot-roasted lamb; and lasagne verde. Blackboards list the day's home-made soup, fresh fish, vegetarian dishes, and speciality sausages. For dessert you may be offered ice creams, home-made apple and toffee crumble, chilled lemon soufflé, or a chef's special. Apart from the reservoirs, there are plenty of other places to visit in the area - Chatsworth House, Haddon Hall, Peveril Castle and the Blue John Caves, for example - so if an overnight stay is in order, accommodation is available in 14 en suite bedrooms, including one with a four-poster.

OPEN: 11-11
BAR MEALS: L served all week 12-2 D served all week 6-9
RESTAURANT: L served all week 12-2 D served all week 6-9.30
⊖: Free House
🍺: Blacksheep, Old Peculier, Stones Bitter, Worthington Creamflow.
FACILITIES: Child facs Garden: Walled courtyard, numerous seating areas Dogs allowed
NOTES: Parking 40
ROOMS: 14 bedrooms en suite 3 family rooms

★★   Map 16 SK28
Ashopton Rd S33 0AZ
☎ 01433 651361
📄 01433 651361
📧 mr@ybridge.force9.co.uk
🌐 www.yorkshire-bridge.co.uk
Dir: A57 from M1, left onto A6013, pub 1m on right

BAKEWELL continued

Pick of the Pubs

The Monsal Head Hotel ★★ ⏾ ♀
Monsal Head DE45 1NL ☎ 01629 640250 📠 01629 640815
e-mail: Christine@monsalhead.com
web: www.monsalhead.com
*Dir: A6 from Bakewell towards Buxton. 1.5m to Ashford. Follow
Monsal Head signs, B6465 for 1m*

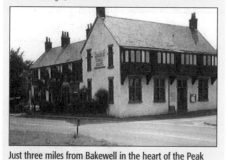

Just three miles from Bakewell in the heart of the Peak
District National Park, the hotel offers superb views over
the hills and dales. The complex is ideally located for
walkers and includes a delightful real ale pub converted
from former stables, with flagstone floors and a
welcoming fire in winter. The range of cask ales includes
Timothy Taylor Landlord and Abbeydale Moonshine, as
well as lagers, wheat beers and wines by the glass. One
menu serves the bar and non-smoking restaurant,
providing a flexible choice of nibbles, as well as small
plates such as marinated salmon or oven-baked goats'
cheese. Larger appetites are catered for with options like
pork loin cutlet served with apple mash and black
pudding; and chicken breast with stilton and smoked
bacon in a white wine, onion and chive sauce. There's
also a light snack menu and daily blackboard specials.
OPEN: 11.30-11 (Sun 12-10.30) Closed: 25 Dec
BAR MEALS: L served all week 12-9.30 D served all week
Sunday 12-9 **RESTAURANT:** L served all week 12-9.30
D served all week 7-9.30 Sunday 12-9 ⊕: Free House
⬢: Scottish Courage Theakston Old Peculier, Timothy Taylor
Landlord, Whim Hartington IPA, Abbeydale Moonshine. ♀: 15
FACILITIES: Garden: Dogs allowed **NOTES:** Parking 20
ROOMS: 7 bedrooms en suite 1 family room s£45 d£50

BAMFORD   Map 16 SK28

Pick of the Pubs

Yorkshire Bridge Inn ★★
Ashopton Rd S33 0AZ ☎ 01433 651361 📠 01433 651361
e-mail: mr@ybridge.force9.co.uk
web: www.yorkshire-bridge.co.uk
See Pick of the Pubs on page 117

Pick of the Pubs have that extra special quality
that makes them stand out from the crowd.
Their entries are highlighted, and may be a
full page

BARLOW   Map 16 SK37

The Tickled Trout
33 Valley Rd S18 7SL ☎ 0114 2890893
A few miles outside Chesterfield, this quaint country pub is
located at the gateway to the superb Peak District, renowned
for its walking and splendid scenery. Within the pleasant, cosy
atmosphere you can sample the inn's straightforward menu:
among the fishy choices are fresh local trout with almond
butter, beer-battered cod, and grilled monkfish with a tomato
and basil sauce. The specials board should fill out the choices
for those not inclined towards seafood.
OPEN: 12-11 **BAR MEALS:** L served all week 12-2.30 D served all
week 6.30-9 Sun 12-3 Av main course £6.50
RESTAURANT: L served all week 12-2.30 D served all week 6.30-9
⊕: Free House ⬢: Marstons Pedigree, Mansfield Smooth, Batemans
XXXB, Marstons Finest Creamy. **FACILITIES:** Child facs Garden:
Patio with bench style tables beer garden Dogs allowed
NOTES: Parking 20

BEELEY   Map 16 SK26

Pick of the Pubs

The Devonshire Arms ♀
The Square DE4 2NR ☎ 01629 733259 📠 01629 733259
e-mail: jagrosvenor@devonshirearmsbeeley.co.uk
See Pick of the Pubs on opposite page

BELPER   Map 11 SK34

Pick of the Pubs

The Bluebell Inn and Restaurant NEW ♀
Farnah Green DE56 2UP ☎ 01773 826495 📠 01773 829102
e-mail: bluebell.inn@btinternet.com
Dir: Situated in Farnah Green, 0.5m off A517
The Amber valley contains such diversely beautiful
countryside that it has been classified a world heritage
site. This recently refurbished 18th-century coaching inn
nestles right at the heart of it, affording some wonderful
walks and, for the less energetic, far-reaching views. The
bar maintains a traditional, low-beamed feel, while the
restaurant is sleekly modern, with polished oak tables and
high-backed leather chairs giving a feel of relaxed
elegance. Smart dishes match the surrounds: fresh
linguini with crab, chilli and chives as a starter; pan fried
sea bass fillets on sweet potato purée with broad beans
and lemon butter; or breast of Gressingham duck with
marmalade glazed cocotte potatoes, pancetta wrapped
shallots and Grand Marnier flavoured jus as a main.
Everything is cooked in house, and the well-balanced
wine list will appeal to a variety of palates.
OPEN: 11.30-3 6-11 **BAR MEALS:** L served Tues-Sun 12-2
D served Tues-Sat 6.30-9 Av main course £8
RESTAURANT: L served Tues-Sun 12-2 D served Tues-Sat
6.30-9 Av 3 course fixed price £23 ⬢: John Smiths Keg,
Guinness, rotating cask ales. ♀: 7 **FACILITIES:** Garden: Large
patio area with seating **NOTES:** Parking 45

Not all of the pubs in the guide are open all
week or all day. It's always best to check before
you travel

Pick of the Pubs

BEELEY – DERBYSHIRE

The Devonshire Arms

This civilised dining pub nestles in a picturesque village at the gateway to Chatsworth House, one of Britain's most palatial stately homes. Beeley's twisting lanes lie within the Peak District National Park, and the village itself is a designated conservation area. The Devonshire Arms has a long history, having been built as three honey-coloured stone cottages in 1726 and converted into a popular coaching inn in 1747.

John Grosvenor, the present owner, keeps a list of all the innkeepers since that date. In July 1872 a tremendous thunderstorm made the road here quite impassable. History was repeated in August 1997, and a marked beam in the bar records the water level of the second flood. Charles Dickens was a frequent visitor, and it's rumoured that King Edward VII often met here with his mistress, Alice Keppel. Today, you'll be greeted by oak beams, stone flagged floors and winter fires. Families, walkers and cyclists are always welcome, and motorists will appreciate the large car park. Meals are freshly cooked to order, and the extensive menu is also served on the patio in warm weather. Come for home-made soup and a sandwich if you must - but starters like grilled goat's cheese with mixed leaves and tomatoes; or melon with summer fruits, herald a fine selection of main courses. Choose from traditional haggis and neeps; Barnsley chop with mint jelly; or roasted vegetable lasagne. The weekend begins on Friday evenings with an extensive choice of fish - deep-fried cod in beer batter; trout with spinach and almond stuffing; and seafood platter are typical - and continues with a leisurely Victorian breakfast menu between 10 and 12 on Sunday mornings.

OPEN: 11-11 (Sun 12-10.30 Closed: 25 Dec)
BAR MEALS: Food served all week 12-9.30 Av main course £9
RESTAURANT: Food served all week 12-9.30
🍴: The Oak Group
🍺: Black Sheep Best & Special, Theakston Old Peculier & XB, Interbrew Bass, Marstons Pedigree.
⌾: 6
FACILITIES: Garden: Dogs allowed Water **NOTES:** Parking 60 ⊗

⌾ Map 16 SK26
The Square DE4 2NR
☎ 01629 733259
🖹 01629 733259
📧 jagrosvenor@devonshirearms beeley.co.uk
Dir: From A6 onto B6012 at Rowsley

England

BIRCHOVER   Map 16 SK26

Pick of the Pubs

The Druid Inn 🔶 ℥
Main St DE4 2BL ☎ 01629 650302 ▯ 01629 650559
e-mail: mail@druidinnbirchover.co.uk
Dir: *From A6 between Matlock & Bakewell take B5056, signed
Ashbourne. Take 2nd left to Birchover*
The ivy-covered free house was built in 1846 and
extended in the early years of the 20th century. After a
devastating fire on New Year's Day 2002 the inn is now
back to normal. New owner Richard Smith, who also has
Sheffield's Thyme Restaurant, offers Druid Bitter and a
regular guest ale. He aims to develop The Druid into a
good quality Derbyshire inn, serving proper food, good
wines and real beer.
OPEN: 11-11 **BAR MEALS:** L served all week 11-2 D served all
week 6-10 (Sun 11-4) **RESTAURANT:** L served all week 11-2
D served all week 6-10 Sun 11-4 Av 3 course à la carte £22
⊟: Free House ◖: Druid Bitter & guest ale. ℥: 12
FACILITIES: Garden: Terraced area **NOTES:** Parking 36 ⊛

BIRCH VALE   Map 16 SK08

Pick of the Pubs

The Waltzing Weasel Inn
New Mills Rd SK22 1BT ☎ 01663 743402 ▯ 01663 743402
e-mail: w-weasel@zen.co.uk web: www.w-weasel.co.uk
See Pick of the Pubs on opposite page

BRADWELL   Map 16 SK18

The Bowling Green Inn ♦♦♦♦ ℥
Smalldale S33 9JQ ☎ 01433 620450 ▯ 01433 620280
Dir: *Off A6187 onto B6049 towards Bradwell. Near bowling green*

This 16th-century coaching inn enjoys stunning views over
beautiful countryside. The new owners are proud to provide
traditional country cooking washed down with weekly-
changing guest ales. The good-value menu, supplemented by
daily specials, includes asparagus risotto; Derbyshire lamb
chops; home-baked ham; and a good selection of
sandwiches. Tempting home-made puddings are on offer: try
banana pancakes with toffee sauce. There's a children's menu
and large beer garden with secure play-area.
OPEN: 12-11 (Sun 12-10.30) **BAR MEALS:** L served all week 12-2
D served all week 7-9 Sun 12-3, 5-8 Av main course £6.95
RESTAURANT: L served all week 12-2 D served all week 7-9 Sun
12-3, 5-8 Av 3 course à la carte £15 ⊟: Free House ◖: Stones,
Timothy Taylor, Tetleys, Kelham Gold. ℥: 8 **FACILITIES:** Child facs
continued

Children's licence Garden: large patio area, spectacular views
NOTES: Parking 80 **ROOMS:** 6 bedrooms en suite 2 family rooms
s£35 d£55

BRASSINGTON   Map 16 SK25

Ye Olde Gate Inne
Well St DE4 4HJ ☎ 01629 540448 ▯ 01629 540448
e-mail: theoldgateinn@supanet.com
Dir: *3m NW of Carsington Water*
The inn was built in 1616 of local stone and salvaged Armada
timbers, and has one or two supernatural residents. There is a
huge inglenook fireplace with a range, and a smaller one in
the snug. Connections are claimed with Bonnie Prince
Charlie's rebellion. The inn is written daily on blackboards
and features a wealth of local produce. Among the choices
are braised beef in ale with dumplings, lamb steak brushed
with rosemary and redcurrant, and Cajun chicken. Fish and
game and a choice of baguettes at lunchtime.
OPEN: 12-2.30 6-11 May close on Mon Sat 12-3, 6-11 Sun
12-3,7-10.30, **BAR MEALS:** L served Tue-Sun 12-1.45 D served
Tue-Sat 7-8.45 Sun 12-2 Av main course £6.50 ⊟: W'hampton &
Dudley ◖: Marstons Pedigree, Hobgoblin. **FACILITIES:** Quaint
garden Food served outside. Dogs allowed Water provided
NOTES: Parking 20

BUXTON   Map 16 SK07

Bull I' th' Thorn 🔶
Flagg SK17 9QQ ☎ 01298 83348
Dir: *Telephone for directions*
Hospitality has been offered to travellers at the Bull i' th' Horn
since 1472. Standing high and solitary on the main A515, it
was for centuries a prominent coaching inn on the Derby-
Manchester route in the heart of the Dales. The oak Tudor
panelling and flagstone floors provide the setting for coffee,
bar snacks, lunches, restaurant meals and functions. Food and
drink can also be enjoyed in the large walled garden.
OPEN: 9.30 **BAR MEALS:** L served all week 12-2.30 D served all
week 6-8.45 All day Sat-Sun Av main course £7
RESTAURANT: L served all week D served all week Av 3 course à la
carte £15 ◖: Robinsons Best Bitter. **FACILITIES:** Garden: Large
open plan walled garden Dogs allowed Water **NOTES:** Parking 70

CASTLETON   Map 16 SK18

The Castle ℥
Castle St S33 8WG ☎ 01433 620578 ▯ 622902
Dir: *Exit the M1 for Chesterfield and follow signs for Chatsworth House.
After reaching Chatsworth House follow signs for Castleton. The Castle is
in the centre of the village*
The Castle in the heart of the Peak District has been a
coaching inn since Charles II's reign. The four resident ghosts
may go back that far too! Open fires ensure that entering on a
chilly day after some brisk fell-walking is like getting into a
bed that's had the electric blanket on. As for eating, you could
start with black pudding and bacon salad, or salmon and
broccoli fishcakes, and proceed to minted lamb cutlets or
chilled Cajun salmon steak salad.
OPEN: 12-11 (Sun 12-10.30) **RESTAURANT:** L served all week
from 12 D served all week until 10 ⊟: Vintage Inns ◖: Tetley Bitter,
Cask Bass, John Smiths, Black Sheep & Guest Ales. ℥: 18
FACILITIES: Garden: Patio and outdoor furniture, great views
NOTES: Parking 18

 Brewery/Company

The Waltzing Weasel Inn

If pub names intrigue you, then you'd better ask the new owners about the logic behind this one because we don't know! This country inn set amid the Peak District hills is loved by outdoor enthusiasts and business people alike, although the latter will have to remember to turn off their mobile phones in keeping with the house policy that prohibits music and gaming machines.

There is plenty to do within reach – shooting, fishing, riding and golfing, and visiting Haddon Hall, The Chestnut Centre, Castleton, Bakewell, and Buxton with its splendid opera house are all on the agenda for the tourist. Country antiques are a tasteful feature of the bar, while from the garden and mullion-windowed restaurant there are dramatic views of Kinder Scout. The chefs provide fine, honest food using local produce wherever possible. Bar menu regulars include sardine tapenade; stir-fried vegetable crêpe; sautéed red onion, garlic and roasted sweet peppers on a basil pastry crust; hot smoked Loch Fyne salmon; seafood tart; Peak Pie (comprising meat, game, mushrooms and red wine topped with puff pastry); Moroccan vegetable casserole; roast leg of Kinder lamb; tarte Provencale (a baked layered mixture of aubergine, peppers and tomato topped with cheese, olives, and herbs); and Fantasia Italiana, a confection of delights that varies daily and can even be made to suit vegetarians. On Sundays only, traditional roast beef with Yorkshire pudding is a popular institution. Live jazz is played regularly.

OPEN: 12-11 (Sun 12-10.30)
BAR MEALS: L served all week 12-2 D served all week 7-9.30 Sun 7-9 Av main course £12
RESTAURANT: L served all week 12-2 D served all week 7-9 Av 3 course fixed price £27.50
⊕: Free House
🍺: Marston's Best & Pedigree, Timothy Taylor Landlord, Greene King IPA.
FACILITIES: Garden: Large patio, lawn shrubbery Dogs allowed Water & Toys **NOTES:** Parking 42

Map 16 SK08
New Mills Rd SK22 1BT
☎ 01663 743402
📄 01663 743402
📧 w-weasel@zen.co.uk
🌐 www.w-weasel.co.uk
Dir: W from M1 at Chesterfield

CASTLETON continued

The Olde Nag's Head
Cross St S33 8WH ☎ 01433 620248 🗎 01433 621501
Dir: A57 from Sheffield to Bamford, through Hope Valley, turn right
Grey-stone 17th-century coaching inn in the heart of the Peak District National Park, close to Chatsworth House, Haddon Hall and miles of wonderful walks. Reasonably-priced breakfast, lunch and evening menus include dishes such as fresh cod and chips; lamb shank with rosemary and redcurrant jus; and brie and broccoli pithiver. The evening can then be happily spent with a pint of real ale or a malt whiskey in front of the open fire.
OPEN: 9-11 **BAR MEALS:** L served all week 9-9 D served all week Carvery 12-9 **RESTAURANT:** L served all week 12-6 D served all week 6-9 Carvery 12-9 Av 3 course à la carte £24 **⬧:** Timothy Taylor Landlord, Black Sheep, Worthingtons, Edale. **FACILITIES:** Child facs Dogs allowed **NOTES:** Parking 15

The Peaks Inn ◆◆◆◆ ♀
How Ln S33 8WJ ☎ 01433 620247 🗎 01433 623590
e-mail: info@peaks-inn.co.uk web: www.peaks-inn.co.uk
In the heart of the Peak District National Park and overlooked by the Norman Peveril Castle from which Castleton gets its name, this smart but cosy inn has been completely refurbished. A typical menu features bangers and mash, scampi, mushroom pasta, 16oz rump steak, and steak and ale pie. Try one of the Peak burgers for a really satisfying experience. The beautifully furnished bedrooms have oak beamed ceilings and en suite bathrooms.
OPEN: 11-11 **BAR MEALS:** L served all week 12 D served all week 9 Av main course £5.95 **⬧:** Black Sheep, London Pride, Tetley Smooth, plus guests. **♀:** 9 **FACILITIES:** Garden: Patio area with tables, benches, flowers Dogs allowed **NOTES:** Parking 40
ROOMS: 4 bedrooms en suite d£80

DERBY   Map 11 SK33

The Alexandra Hotel
203 Siddals Rd DE1 2QE ☎ 01332 293993
Two-roomed hotel filled with railway memorabilia. Noted for its real ale (11 hand pumps and 450 different brews on tap each year), range of malt whiskies, and friendly atmosphere. A typical menu offers chilli con carne, liver and bacon, home-baked ham with free range egg and chips, filled Yorkshire puddings, ploughman's lunches, omelettes and freshly-made filled hot and cold cobs.
OPEN: 11-11 (Sun 12-3, 7-10.30) Closed: Dec 25
BAR MEALS: L served Sun 12-2.30 Av main course £3.75
⬧: Tynemill Ltd **⬧:** Castle Rock, Nottingham Gold, Belvoir Star Bitter, York Yorkshire Terrier. **FACILITIES:** Dogs allowed
NOTES: Parking 12 No credit cards

DOE LEA   Map 16 SK46

Hardwick Inn 🏠 ♀
Hardwick Park S44 5QJ ☎ 01246 850245 🗎 01246 856365
e-mail: Batty@hardwickinn.co.uk web: www.hardwickinn.co.uk
Dir: M1 junct 29 take A6175. 0.5m L (signed Stainsby/Hardwick Hall). After Stainsby, 2m L at staggered junct. Follow brown tourist signs
Dating back to the 15th century and built of locally quarried sandstone, the Hardwick Inn is pleasantly situated on the south gate of the National Trust's Hardwick Hall. The pub has been in the same family since 1928 and retains its historic atmosphere; in winter, open coal fires warm the interior. All meals are freshly prepared, with menu choices like grilled sea

continued

bream and prawns; vegetable wholemeal crumble; and game and ale casserole.

Hardwick Inn

OPEN: 11.30-11 **BAR MEALS:** L served all week 11.30-9.30 D served all week Mon 11.30-9 Av main course £6.75
RESTAURANT: L served Tues- Sun 12-2 D served Tues-Sat 7-9 Sun 12-2 Av 3 course à la carte £16.95 Av 3 course fixed price £13.50
⬧: Free House **⬧:** Scottish Courage Theakston Old Peculier & XB, Greene King Old Speckled Hen & Ruddles County, Marston's Pedigree. **♀:** 24 **FACILITIES:** Child facs Children's licence Garden: Large garden, pond & picnic table, extensive lawns

EYAM   Map 16 SK27

Miners Arms ◆◆◆◆ ♀
Water Ln S32 5RG ☎ 01433 630853 🗎 01433 639050
Dir: Off B6521, 5m N of Bakewell
This welcoming 17th-century inn and restaurant in the famous plague village of Eyam gets its name from the local lead mines of Roman times. Choices from the seasonally changing menu might include rack of lamb with roast vegetables and rosemary cream sauce; or seared tuna steak with swede pûrée and a carrot and coriander jus. Standards such as sausage and mash with onion gravy and fish and chips are also served. Lighter bites include an interesting range of hot sandwiches on ciabatta bread.
OPEN: 12-11 **BAR MEALS:** L served all week 12-3 D served Mon-Sat 5.30-9 Av main course £9 **RESTAURANT:** L served Sun 12-3 D served Tue-Sat 6-9 Av 3 course à la carte £20 **⬧:** Free House **⬧:** Interbrew Bass, Stones Bitter, Coors Worthington's Creamflow. **♀:** 7 **FACILITIES:** Garden: 12 outdoor benches front & back Dogs allowed Water, food for overnight dogs **NOTES:** Parking 50
ROOMS: 7 bedrooms en suite 2 family rooms s£30 d£60 No children overnight

FENNY BENTLEY   Map 16 SK14

Pick of the Pubs

The Bentley Brook Inn NEW ★★
DE6 1LF ☎ 01335 350278 🗎 01335 350422
e-mail: all@bentleybrookinn.co.uk
This fine old building was originally a medieval farmhouse, dating from the early 19th century. Within its eight acres is a beautiful meadow with many species of rare wild flowers, and for trout fishermen there are 270 yards of the well-stocked Bentley Brook, to which the inn has full fishing rights. Beer connoisseurs will enjoy the range of pure real ales brewed in the traditional way by Leatherbritches, the Bentley Brook's on-site brewery. The kitchen uses local produce wherever possible, and makes all its own sausages, black pudding, dry cured bacon,

continued

England

oatcakes, and bread rolls. Jams, pickles, preserves, fudge, shortbread, Christmas puddings and Christmas cakes are hand made to traditional recipes in small batches at the inn, and sold in the kitchen shop. The menus serve a wide range of soups, appetisers and light bites, sandwiches and baguettes, grills, jacket potatoes, fish, vegetarian, and mains like roast rack of lamb; veal chop; and Dover sole.

The Bentley Brook Inn

OPEN: 11-12 **BAR MEALS:** L served all week 12-9 D served all week 12-9 Sun 12-8 **RESTAURANT:** L served all week 12-2.30 D served all week 7-9 Av 3 course à la carte £25.85 Av 3 course fixed price £21.45 ●: Leatherbritches Bespoke, Leatherbritches Hairy Helmet, Goldings, Marstons Pedigree. **FACILITIES:** Child facs Large terrace and lawn, fully fenced Dogs allowed **NOTES:** Parking 100 **ROOMS:** 10 bedrooms 9 en suite s£52.50 d£76

The Coach and Horses Inn ♀
DE6 1LB ☎ 01335 350246 ▤ 01335 350178
e-mail: coachnhorses@aol.com

Beautifully located on the edge of the Peak District National Park, this family-run 17th-century coaching inn is handy for Dovedale and the Tissington Trail. The cosy interior features stripped wood furniture, low beams and memorabilia. The pub is locally renowned for its well-kept ales and good home cooking: daily-changing menus could include lamb chump steak with mint gravy, salmon fillet with asparagus, roast butternut squash with chili bean and vegetable casserole, or rabbit, black pudding and smoked bacon pie. **OPEN:** 11-11 **BAR MEALS:** L served all week 12 D served all week 9 Av main course £7.95 **RESTAURANT:** L served all week 12 D served all week 9 ●: Free House ●: Marston's Pedigree, Timothy Taylor Landlord, Black Sheep Best, Harrington Bitter. ♀: 6 **FACILITIES:** Garden: Gravelled area seats 36, water feature **NOTES:** Parking 24

The Bulls Head Inn ♦♦♦♦ ♤ ♀
S32 5QR ☎ 01433 630873 ▤ 01433 631738
e-mail: wilbnd@aol.com
Dir: Just off A623, N of Stoney Middleton

Family-owned inn set in a conservation village in the heart of the Peak District National Park. It has flagstone floors, roaring fires and an inglenook fireplace in the oak-panelled dining room, and is a welcoming venue for walkers and their dogs. Dishes like minted lamb casserole, and plaice with mushroom sauce from the regular menu are supplemented by specials such as roast sea bass with fennel, and wild boar steak with orange game sauce. **OPEN:** 12-3 6.30-11 (Open all day Sun) **BAR MEALS:** L served Tue-Sun 12-2 D served Tue-Sun 6.30-9 Sun 12-2, 5-8 Av main course £7.50 **RESTAURANT:** L served Tue-Sun 12-2 D served Tue-Sun 6.30-9 Sunday 12-2, 5-8 Av 3 course à la carte £18 ●: Free House ●: Black Sheep Best, Marston's Pedigree, Tetley Bitter, Fuller's London Pride. ♀: 8 **FACILITIES:** Dogs allowed Water **NOTES:** Parking 20 **ROOMS:** 3 bedrooms en suite 1 family room s£45 d£65

Pick of the Pubs

The Chequers Inn ♦♦♦♦ ◉ ♀
Froggatt Edge S32 3ZJ ☎ 01433 630231 ▤ 01433 631072
e-mail: info@chequers-froggatt.com
Dir: On the A625 in Froggatt, near Calver
Some pubs look so inviting it's hard to pass them by. This traditional 16th-century country pub nestling in the Hope Valley is one of them. And it really does 'nestle' - below beautiful Froggatt Edge, with its westward panorama of the Peak District National Park, reached by a steep, wild woodland footpath from the elevated secret garden. Reminders of former times include a horse-mounting block, and the old stables housing logs for the crackling winter fires. The smart interior has rag-washed yellow walls, bare board floors, Windsor chairs and bookcases. One of the five cosy, en suite bedrooms has a four-poster bed. The menu is essentially European and British, and holds an AA rosette for its quality. You can expect to see seared scallops with toasted pinenuts, crispy pancetta and basil pesto; chicken and mushroom roulade with sage and bacon sauce; pan-fried calves' liver with celeriac purée and red pepper sauce; and fillet of pork wrapped in basil and parma ham with apple jus. Blackboard items change daily. **OPEN:** 12-2 6-9.30 (Open all day Sat & Sun) Closed: 25 Dec **BAR MEALS:** L served all week 12-2 D served all week 6-9.30 Sun to 9 Av main course £12.95 ●: Free House ●: Charles

continued

England

FROGGATT continued

Wells Bombardier Premium Bitter, Greene King IPA. ♀: 8
FACILITIES: Garden: Secret woodland garden, views over Hope Valley **NOTES:** Parking 45 **ROOMS:** 5 bedrooms en suite s£65 d£65 No children overnight ☺

GREAT HUCKLOW
Map 16 SK17

The Queen Anne ♦♦♦ ♀
Great Hucklow, nr Tideswell SK17 8RF ☎ 01298 871246
e-mail: mal@thequeen.net
Dir: A623 turn off at Anchor pub toward Bradwell, 2nd R to Great Hucklow
A warm welcome awaits at this traditional country free house with its log fires, good food, and an ever-changing range of cask ales. The inn dates from 1621, and a licence has been held for 300 years. Comfortable en suite bedrooms make an ideal base for exploring the spectacular Peak District National Park. Bar food ranges from freshly-made sandwiches to grills, and includes favourites like steak and ale pie, beef stew and Yorkshire pudding, and chicken jalfrezi.
OPEN: 12-2.30 6-11 (Sun 7-10.30, Mon New Year & Easter)
BAR MEALS: L served Mon-Sun 12-2 D served Mon-Sun 6.30-8.30 (Tue L between New Year & Easter) ☺: Free House ◖: Marstons Bitter, Shaws, Storm Brewery, Kelham Island. ♀: 10
FACILITIES: Garden: Lawn overlooking the hills Dogs allowed
NOTES: Parking 30 **ROOMS:** 2 bedrooms en suite d£60

GRINDLEFORD
Map 16 SK27

Pick of the Pubs

The Maynard Arms ★★★
Main Rd S32 2HE ☎ 01433 630321 🖷 01433 630445
e-mail: info@maynardarms.co.uk
web: www.maynardarms.co.uk
Dir: From M1 take A619 into Chesterfield, then onto Baslow. A623 to Calver, right into Grindleford
This fine stone-built inn stands grandly in immaculately kept grounds overlooking the Derwent Valley, in the heart of the Peak District National Park. You may eat in either the Longshore Bar or in the Padley Restaurant, with its large windows facing the gardens. Choose the bar and the menu could well offer seared breast of chicken with mushroom risotto and balsamic oil; Moroccan-spiced braised lamb with couscous; or grilled sea bass on champ with tomato and olive salsa. Opt for the restaurant and discover other possibilities, such as eggs Benedict with chive oil, or smoked haddock fishcake as starters; main courses of fillet of beef with fondant potato, wild mushrooms and caramelised red wine onion; pan-fried calve's liver with olive oil mash, onion fritters and grilled pancetta; and pan-seared red mullet with shellfish paella and lobster oil. For dessert, try sticky toffee parkin pudding with stem ginger ice cream.
OPEN: 11-3 5.30-11 (Sun 12-10.30) **BAR MEALS:** L served all week 12-2 D served all week 6-9.30 Av main course £8
RESTAURANT: L served Sun-Fri 12-2 D served all week 7-9.30 Av 3 course à la carte £26 ☺: Free House ◖: Greene King Old Speckled Hen, Timothy Taylor Landlord, Bass, Abbey Dale Moonshine. **FACILITIES:** Children's licence Garden: Well kept gardens Dogs allowed **NOTES:** Parking 60
ROOMS: 10 bedrooms en suite 2 family rooms s£75 d£85

HASSOP
Map 16 SK27

Eyre Arms ♀
DE45 1NS ☎ 01629 640390 e-mail: nick@eyrearms.com
Dir: On B6001 N of Bakewell

Just a short drive north of Bakewell, this traditional free house was built by the Eyre family in the early 17th century. Oak pews, beams and old photographs create a cosy atmosphere - but the pub also boasts the ghost of a Civil War Cavalier! The garden overlooks rolling Peak District countryside and there are lovely local walks. Typical dishes include steak and kidney pie; trout with almonds and breadcrumbs; and bulgar wheat and walnut casserole.
OPEN: 11.30-3 6.30-11 Closed: 25 Dec **BAR MEALS:** L served all week 12-2 D served all week 6.30-9 ☺: Free House ◖: Marston's Pedigree, Scottish Courage John Smiths, Black Sheep Special.
FACILITIES: Garden **NOTES:** Parking 20

HATHERSAGE
Map 16 SK28

Millstone Inn ♦♦♦♦ 🠒 ♀
Sheffield Rd S32 1DA ☎ 01433 650258 🖷 01433 651664
e-mail: jerry@millstone.fsbusiness.co.uk
web: www.millstoneinn.co.uk
Tastefully furnished former coaching inn with striking views over the picturesque Hope Valley. Chatsworth House, Ladybower Reservoir and the Blue John Mines are among nearby attractions. An atmospheric bar, traditional and innovative dishes, and a popular terrace restaurant specialising in seafood add to the appeal. Try chargrilled salmon with braised lentils; or calves' liver with saffron mash and chick pea relish.
OPEN: 11.30-3 6-11 (Sat 11-11, Sun 12-10.30)
BAR MEALS: L served all week 12-2 D served all week 6-9
RESTAURANT: D served all week 6.30-9.30 ☺: Free House
◖: Timothy Taylor Landlord, Black Sheep, Guest Beers.
FACILITIES: Garden **NOTES:** Parking 50 **ROOMS:** 6 bedrooms en suite

Pick of the Pubs

The Plough Inn ♦♦♦♦ ⊚ ▷ ♀
Leadmill Bridge S32 1BA ☎ 01433 650319
& 650180 📠 01433 651049
e-mail: sales@theploughinn-hathersage.com

Originally a farmstead, this 17th-century stone-built inn is situated in nine acres of its own grounds by the River Derwent. The public rooms are charming, with plenty of exposed beams and brickwork, and in winter welcoming log fires blaze in the grates. The sheltered garden is a delight in summer - with tea served in the afternoons - and a pretty array of flower-filled baskets adorns the inn's external walls. Choice is the key word here, with a good range of hand-pulled ales, 50 malt whiskies, 14 wines by the glass and an extensive menu offering something for everybody - from traditional British cuisine (cod, chips and mushy peas on the bar menu) to modern European (seared scallops on red onion and tomato tarte Tatin with aged balsamic on the restaurant menu). The menus are fairly flexible, but bar food cannot be served in the restaurant during the evening.
OPEN: 11-11 Closed: 25 Dec **BAR MEALS:** L served all week 11.30-2.30 D served all week 6.30-9.30 Sun 12-9 Av main course £10 **RESTAURANT:** L served all week 11.30-2.30 D served all week 6.30-9.30 Sun 12-9 ⊕: Free House ◀: Theakstons Old Peculier, Batemans, Adnams Bitter, Smiles Best. ♀: 14 **FACILITIES:** Garden: Sheltered, south facing garden **NOTES:** Parking 50 **ROOMS:** 5 bedrooms en suite 2 family rooms s£49.50 d£69.50

See advert on this page

HAYFIELD   Map 16 SK08

The Royal Hotel ♀
Market St SK22 2EP ☎ 01663 741721 📠 01663 742997
e-mail: enquiries@royalhayfield.co.uk
Dir: Off A624
A fine-looking, 1755-vintage building in a High Peak village that itself retains much of its old-fashioned charm. The oak-panelled Windsor Bar has log fires when you need them, and serves a constantly changing roster of real ales, bar snacks and selected dishes, while the dining room usually offers sausage and mash, vegetable chow mein, grilled gammon steak, glazed lamb hock, T-bone steak, mixed grill, and wholetail scampi in breadcrumbs. Kinder Scout and the fells look impressive from the hotel patio.
OPEN: 11-11 **BAR MEALS:** L served all week 12-2.15 D served all week 6-9.15 Av main course £7 **RESTAURANT:** L served all week D served all week Av 3 course à la carte £16 ⊕: Free House ◀: Hydes, Tetleys, San Miguel. ♀: 8 **FACILITIES:** Child facs Patio, seats 80 **NOTES:** Parking 70

England

HOGNASTON   Map 16 SK25

Pick of the Pubs

The Red Lion Inn
Main St DE6 1PR ☎ 01335 370396 📠 01335 372145
e-mail: lionrouge@msn.com
Dir: M1 J25 take A52 towards Derby & Ashbourne. Hognaston on B5035
The Red Lion Inn is located in the main street of a picturesque Peak District village overlooking Carsington Water. It's surrounded by attractive countryside and is popular with walkers who stop off for lunch or use the inn as a base for exploring. There's a traditional pub atmosphere in this 17th-century building with its beamed ceilings, open fireplaces and church pew seating. Food here is very much pitched at restaurant diners with value-for-money and choice being the guiding lights of an ever-changing blackboard menu. Expect to be offered dishes as diverse as chicken Roghan Jhosh on the bone, and haggis with "neeps and tatties" from the same menu. Lighter meals include home-made soups with warm bread, or goats' cheese and herb bruschetta salad, flash-fried lamb's liver with crispy bacon and mashed potato, or delicious cod kebabs coated in Thai ginger. The Red Lion is handy for the nearby Peak District National Park.
OPEN: 12-3 6-11 (Closed Mon lunch, Sun eve)
BAR MEALS: L served Tue-Sun 12-2 D served Mon-Sat 6.30-9 Av main course £9.95 **RESTAURANT:** L served Tue-Sun 12-2 D served Tue-Sat 6.30-9 Av 3 course à la carte £18.50 ⊕: Free House ◀: Greene King Old Speckled Hen, Interbrew Bass, Worthington's Creamflow, Marston's Pedigree.
NOTES: Parking 30

HOLLINGTON   Map 10 SK23

Pick of the Pubs

The Red Lion Inn NEW ⌂ ♀
Main St DE6 3AG ☎ 01335 360241 ▤ 01335 361209
e-mail: redlionhollington@ukonline.co.uk
Dir: On A52 between Ashbourne and Derby, turn off at signed Ednaston/Hollington, pub 2m on right
In 1999, The Red Lion almost closed its doors for ever, and it's clearly been a labour of love for proprietor Robin Hunter to turn it back into a thriving village local, which is now winning serious accolades for its food. Set in a rural farming community, and obviously just as popular with villagers as visitors, this 18th-century coaching inn offers a relaxed friendly bar and smarter restaurant. All the details, from the fresh flowers to the friendly, knowledgeable staff, have clearly been given thoughtful attention. Chalk board menus change daily, rely entirely on local produce (although fish comes from a little further afield) and everything - bread, pickles, biscuits and ice cream - is home made. Start off with baked goat's cheese wrapped in smoked pancetta; follow with vanilla-scented monkfish with sesame noodles and tomato salsa; or roasted rack of lamb with star anise. Dessert? White chocolate pannacotta with raspberries should please.
OPEN: 12-3 6-11 Sun 12-10.30 **BAR MEALS:** L served all week 12-2 D served Tues-Sun 6.30-9 Sun 12-2.30 Av main course £6.80 **RESTAURANT:** L served all week 12-2 D served Tues-Sat 6.30-9 Sun 12-2.30 Av 3 course à la carte £25 Av 2 course fixed price £8.95 ◀: Pedigree, Abbot Ale, Bass, Adnams Broadside. ♀: 8 **FACILITIES:** Garden: Large garden, seating and parasols Dogs allowed (not in restaurant) **NOTES:** Parking 30

HOPE   Map 16 SK18

Cheshire Cheese Inn ♀
Edale Rd S33 6ZF ☎ 01433 620381 ▤ 01433 620411
e-mail: cheshire.cheese@barbox.net
Dir: On A6187 between Sheffield & Chapel-en-le-Frith
This 16th-century inn lies on the old trans-Pennine salt route in the heart of the Peak District. The pub owes its name to the tradition of accepting cheese as payment for lodgings. Today it retains a relaxed, unspoilt atmosphere, with open fires, hand-pulled beer and a reputation for good home-made food. Expect peppered pork steak, cream cheese and broccoli bake; or chicken breast with leek and stilton sauce.
OPEN: 12-3 6.30-11 (Sun 12-10.30 all day Sat)
BAR MEALS: L served all week 12-2 D served all week 6.30-9 Sun 12-8.30 Av main course £8 **RESTAURANT:** L served all week 12-2 D served all week 6.30-9 Sun 12-8.30 ▥: Free House ◀: Barnsley Bitter, Wentworthy Pale Ale, Black Sheep Best, Hartington Bitter. ♀: 13 **FACILITIES:** Garden: Paved patio area Dogs allowed Water **NOTES:** Parking 8

LITTON   Map 16 SK17

Red Lion Inn
SK17 8QU ☎ 01298 871458 ▤ 01298 871458
e-mail: redlioninn@littonvillage.fsnet.co.uk
Dir: Just off A623 (Chesterfield -Stockport rd), 1m E of Tideswell
Overlooking the village green, a 17th-century pub where in summer visitors can enjoy a meal under the trees. June is a good time to observe local well-dressing rituals. Many local walks begin and end here, and it is therefore very popular with hikers. Indoors it's all beams and log fires in cosy rooms,
continued

where favourite dishes include rabbit casserole, braised steak in Black Sheep ale, and garlic and rosemary lamb.
OPEN: 12-3 6-11 (Fri-Sun 11-11) **BAR MEALS:** L served all week 12-2 D served Mon-Sat 6-8.30 ▥: Free House ◀: Jennings Bitter, Barnsley Bitter, Shepherd Neame Spitfire, Black Sheep Best.
FACILITIES: Garden: Four picnic tables on village green Dogs allowed Water bowl, Dog chews

LONGSHAW   Map 16 SK27

Fox House ⌂ ♀
Hathersage Rd S11 7TY ☎ 01433 630374 ▤ 01433 637102
Dir: From Sheffield follow A625 towards Castleton.
A delightfully original 17th-century coaching inn and, at 1,132 feet above sea level, one of the highest pubs in Britain. The Longshaw dog trials originated here, after an argument between farmers and shepherds as to who owned the best dog. A simple menu lists sandwiches, starters, Sunday roasts, and mains like chicken and ham pie, ground Scottish beefsteak burger, spicy prawn pasta, and lamb cutlets.
OPEN: 11-11 (Sun 12-10.30) **BAR MEALS:** L served all week 12-5 D served all week 5-10 Sun 12-9.30 Av main course £7 **RESTAURANT:** L served all week 12-5 D served all week 5-10 Sun 12-9.30 ▥: Vintage Inns ◀: Cask Bass, Cask Stones, Cask Tetleys, John Smiths. ♀: 20 **FACILITIES:** Children's licence Garden: Patio area **NOTES:** Parking 80

MATLOCK   Map 16 SK35

The Red Lion ♦♦♦♦
65 Matlock Green DE4 3BT ☎ 01629 584888
Dir: From Chesterfield, A632 into Matlock, on right of road just before junct of A615
This friendly, family-run free house makes a good base for exploring local attractions like Chatsworth House, Carsington Water and Dovedale. Spectacular walks in the local countryside help to work up an appetite for bar lunches, steaks and a wide selection of home-cooked meals. In the winter months, open fires burn in the lounge and games room, and there's a boules area in the garden.
OPEN: 11-11 **BAR MEALS:** L served Tue-Fri, Sun 12-2 D served Tue-Sun 7-9 Sun 12-4 **RESTAURANT:** L served Tue-Fri, Sun 12-2 D served Tue-Sat 7-9 Sun 12-4 ◀: Scottish Courage Courage Directors, John Smiths & Theakstons Bitter, Maston's Pedigree, Guest Ale. **FACILITIES:** Garden: Small, seating area **NOTES:** Parking 20 **ROOMS:** 6 bedrooms en suite 1 family room s£30 d£60 No children overnight

The White Lion Inn
195 Starkholmes Rd DE4 5JA ☎ 01629 582511 ▤ 01629 582511
e-mail: info@whitelion-matlock.com
Dir: Telephone for directions
Right in the heart of the Peak District, with spectacular views over Matlock Bath, this 18th-century inn is the ideal venue for a relaxing break. Close to many beautiful dales and historic buildings, it makes a good starting point. Typical dishes are chargrilled fillet medallions of ostrich, wild mushroom risotto, venison fillet with fondant potato, marinated free-range Norfolk duck breast, and Aberdeen Angus steak. Ragout of mushrooms and baked goats' cheese feature among the appetising starters.
OPEN: 12-3 5-11 (All day Sat-Sun) **BAR MEALS:** L served all week 12-2 D served Mon-Sat 7-9.30 **RESTAURANT:** L served all week 12-2 D served Mon-Sat 7-9.30 Av 3 course à la carte £25 ▥: Burtonwood ◀: Scottish Courage John Smiths, Marston's Pedigree plus guest ales. **FACILITIES:** Garden: Facing over Matlock bath, large boules pitch Dogs allowed Water **NOTES:** Parking 50

RIPLEY
Map 16 SK35

The Moss Cottage ★★
Nottingham Rd DE5 3JT ☎ 01773 742555 ▤ 01773 741063
web: www.mosscottage.net
This red-brick free house specialises in carvery dishes, with
four roast joints each day. The Moss Cottage also offers
regular 'two for the price of one' weekday meals, as well as
blackboard specials and a selection of home-made puddings.
Expect popular menu choices like prawn cocktail or
mushroom dippers; ham, egg and chips; liver and onions; or
battered haddock. Hot puddings include rhubarb crumble and
chocolate fudge cake.
OPEN: 12-3 6-11 (All day wkds & BHs) **BAR MEALS:** L served all
week 12-2.15 D served Mon-Sat 6-9 Sun 12-5
RESTAURANT: L served all week 12-2.15 D served Mon-Sat 6-9
🍴: Free House ◀: Interbrew Bass, Coors Worthington's 1744,
Shepherd Neame. **NOTES:** Parking 52 **ROOMS:** 14 bedrooms
en suite s£40 d£65 No children overnight

ROWSLEY
Map 16 SK26

The Grouse & Claret 🍷
Station Rd DE4 2EB ☎ 01629 733233 ▤ 01629 735194
Dir: On A6 between Matlock & Bakewell
The pub takes its name from a fishing fly, and is a popular
venue for local anglers. It is also handy for touring the Peak
District, the nearby historic towns, and the stately homes of
Haddon Hall and Chatsworth House. The comprehensive
menu offers hot and cold sandwiches, steaks from the grill,
and a varied selection of dishes such as Thai red chicken
curry, avocado and corn bake, and herby lamb in red wine.
OPEN: 11-11 (Sun 12-10.30) **BAR MEALS:** L served all week 12-9
D served all week 12-9 **RESTAURANT:** L served all week 11.30-9
D served all week 🍴: Whampton & Dudley ◀: Marston's Pedigree,
Mansfield, Bank's, Bitter. 🍷: 12 **FACILITIES:** Child facs Garden:
Food served outside, great views **NOTES:** Parking 60 ⊗

SHARDLOW
Map 11 SK43

The Old Crown 🍷
Cavendish Bridge DE72 2HL ☎ 01332 792392
e-mail: bjohns5@aol.com
*Dir: M1 junct 24 take A6 towards Derby. Left before river bridge into
Shardlow*
Atmospheric village pub on the southern side of the River
Trent, built as a coaching inn during the 17th century. Several
hundred water jugs hang overhead throughout the pub's
ceilings, while the walls display an abundance of brewery and
railway memorabilia. A wide range of home-cooked food is
offered from the specials board and a menu of typical pub
fare, and there are two regularly changing guest ales in
addition to the five fixtures.
OPEN: 11.30-3 5-11 Open all day summer (Sun 12-5, 7-10.30)
BAR MEALS: L served all week 12-2 D served Mon-Thu and Sat 5-8
L 12-3 Sun & summer Av main course £6.50 🍴: Free House
◀: Marston's Pedigree, Interbrew Bass, Burtonwood Bitter & Tophat
and 2 guest ales. 🍷: 8 **FACILITIES:** Garden: Very long with a lot of
benches Dogs allowed Water **NOTES:** Parking 25

SOUTH WINGFIELD
Map 16 SK35

The White Hart NEW 🍷
Moorwood Moor DE55 7NU ☎ 01629 534229 ▤ 01629 534229
e-mail: allanwhitehart@w32.co.uk
Dir: Near Wingfield Manor
Classic award-winning country pub at the gateway to the
Derbyshire Peak District, superbly situated for walkers and
cyclists and offering wonderful views across to Wingfield
Manor where Mary Queen of Scots was held captive. A good
reputation for locally-sourced food and home-grown
ingredients guarantees everything from bread to truffles are
made in the White Hart's kitchen. Expect chicken and locally-
supplied black pudding roulade, natural-smoked haddock,
Bakewell pudding, and a range of Derbyshire cheeses.
OPEN: 5-11 (Sat 12-11, Sun 12-10.30) **BAR MEALS:** L served
Sat-Sun D served Mon-Sat 5-9 Sun 12-4 Av main course £9.95
RESTAURANT: L served Sat-Sun 12-2 D served Mon-Sat 5-9 Sun
12-4 Av 3 course à la carte £15.95 ◀: Pedigree, Guinness, guest
beer. 🍷: 10 **FACILITIES:** Garden: Decking area with seating, lawned
area Dogs allowed Chewsticks behind bar **NOTES:** Parking 30

TIDESWELL
Map 16 SK17

The George Hotel 🏠 🍷
Commercial Rd SK17 8NU ☎ 01298 871382 ▤ 01298 871382
e-mail: georgehoteltideswell@yahoo.co.uk
Dir: A619 to Baslow, A623 towards Chapel en le Frith, 0.25m
A 17th-century coaching inn in a quiet village conveniently
placed for exploring the National Park and visiting Buxton,
Chatsworth and the historic plague village of Eyam. Quality
home-cooked food includes venison cooked in red wine
sauce, roast pheasant with bacon, potatoes and mushrooms,
seafood crumble, and whole rainbow trout with almonds.
OPEN: 12-3 6-11 Open al day Sat-Sun (Apr-Sep)
BAR MEALS: L served all week 12-2 D served all week 6-9 All day
Sat-Sun (summer) Av main course £6 **RESTAURANT:** L served all
week 12-2 D served all week 6-9 All day Sat-Sun (summer)
Av 3 course à la carte £12 🍴: Hardy & Hansons ◀: Kimberley Cool,
Olde Trip Bitter, Best Bitter. 🍷: 12 **FACILITIES:** Garden: enclosed
with seating Dogs allowed Fresh water **NOTES:** Parking 25

Three Stags' Heads
Wardlow Mires SK17 8RW ☎ 01298 872268
Dir: Junct of the A623 & B6465 on the Chesterfield/Stockport road
17th-century former farmhouse pub, now combined with a
pottery workshop, located in the limestone uplands of the
northern Peak District. Grade II listed and designated by
English Heritage as one of over 200 heritage pubs throughout
the UK. Well-kept real ales and hearty home-cooked food for
ramblers, cyclists and locals includes oxtail and chestnut stew,
cottage pie, penne la sanchez, chicken chorizo, and game in
season. No children under eight.
BAR MEALS: L served Sat-Sun 12.30-3 D served Fri-Sun 7.30-9.30
🍴: Free House ◀: Abbeydale Matins, Absolution, Black Lurcher,
Ladywell. **FACILITIES:** Dogs allowed **NOTES:** Parking 14 No credit
cards

All AA rated accommodation can also be
found on the AA's internet site
www.theAA.com

 Pubs with this logo do not allow smoking
anywhere on their premises

Room prices show the minimum double and single
rates charged. Room rates in hotels and B&Bs
often vary depending on the facilities, so be sure to
check prices with the establishment before booking

PUB WALK
The Hoops Inn
Horn's Cross - Devon

THE HOOPS INN,
Clovelly, Horn's Cross, nr Bideford
EX39 5DL
☎ 01237 451222
Directions: On the A39 between
Bideford and Clovelly.
*Thatched and cob-walled 13th-century
longhouse set in 16 acres close to the
coast path. Successfully combines old-
world charm with modern pub food, in
particular fresh local fish and game
dishes.*
Open: 8–11 (Sun 8.30–10.30) Closed:
Dec 25
Bar Meals: L served all week 12–3
D served all week 6.30–9.30
Restaurant Meals: L served all week
12–3 D served all week 6.30–9.30 All
day Sat
Children welcome. Dogs allowed.
Garden and parking available.
(for full entry see page 142)

Distance: 2.5 miles (4km) or 6 miles
(10km)
Map: OS Landranger 190
Terrain: Farmland, cliff-top woodpath
Paths: Field and woodland paths,
coast path, lanes
Gradient: Undulating; some fairly
steep sections

*Walk submitted Dr Kit Mayers & checked
by The Hoops Inn*

A delightful rural walk combining bluebell woods, streams and a cliff-top stroll through ancient oak woods, with views across Bideford Bay to Wales and the option of two visits to the sea shore.

From the rear car park, take the short track on the right and go through the gate on the left. Walk ahead through the paddock, bearing slightly left to a stile. Follow the footpath left along field edge, pass a gate and gently uphill towards farm buildings. Cross a stile and turn right along the lane to Northway Farm cottages. Turn sharp left down a lane, signed Unsuitable to Motors, then soon take the arrowed footpath right. Descend steeply on a rough path into Peppercombe Woods.

Veer left to junction with track and turn left down the valley (with the stream on your right). Pass cottages and cross bridge to join another track. Continue downhill to cross stream via bridge, with a ruined mill on right, and go through the gate ahead. (Option - to reach the shore, take the lower track to a gate and continue downhill on a winding path to the beach). Just beyond the gate, take the Coast Path right and climb steps, then ascend (fairly steeply at first) through Sloo Woods for about a mile (1.6km).

(Short walk - turn left, signed 'footpath', uphill over three stiles to lane and turn left. Just beyond Sloo Farm, cross stile on right and retrace steps back to the inn).

Remain on Coast Path and eventually descend shale path (this can be slippery) into Buck Mills village. (Option - turn right downhill to reach shore, waterfall and café). Turn left up the road to first right-hand bend and take the first of three paths here, over a footbridge and past Rose Cottage. Follow path round back of house and climb through wood, keeping stream on right. Where stream divides, cross footbridge and continue through woods to field. Cross stile to the right of farm building ahead and proceed through Lower Worthygate Farm. Follow drive to the lane. Turn left and keep to lane past Higher Worthygate then, just beyond Sloo Farm, cross stile on right and retrace steps back to the inn.

WESSINGTON
Map 16 SK35

The Three Horseshoes NEW
The Green DE55 6DQ
Dir: A615 towards Matlock, 3m after Alfreton, 5m before Matlock
Built in the 17th century, this thoroughly rural pub was once a
centre for horse-trading. It makes an ideal stopping point after
a glorious local walk, or to while away a rainy afternoon over
dominoes and a pint. There's a bar and restaurant menu, with
exemplary use of Peak produce: Derbyshire chicken with
black pudding and apple; or braised shank of lamb with
celeriac purée. If you've been out shooting or fishing, they'll
even cook your catch.
OPEN: 11.30-11 (Sun 12-10.30) Closed Mon in winter
BAR MEALS: L served Tues-Sat, BHs 12-2 D served Tues-Thurs, BHs
5.30-8.30 Sun 12.30-4.45 Av main course £6.80
RESTAURANT: L served Sun in winter D served Fri-Sat 7-9 Sun
12.30-5 Av 3 course à la carte £21 **⚄:** Guinness, Hardys & Hansons
Olde Trip, monthly guest beer. **FACILITIES:** Child facs Garden:
Large gravelled area, seating, grassed area Dogs allowed Biscuits,
water **NOTES:** Parking 18

DEVON

ASHBURTON
Map 03 SX77

The Rising Sun ♦♦♦♦ ⚐ ♀
Woodland TQ13 7JT ☎ 01364 652544 📠 01364 653628
e-mail: mail@risingsunwoodland.co.uk
web: www.risingsunwoodland.co.uk
*Dir: E of Ashburton from A38 take lane signed Woodland/Denbury. Pub
on left approx 1.5m*

Situated in beautiful Devon countryside, the Rising Sun was
once a drovers' inn where animals were allowed to rest en
route to Newton Abbot market from Dartmoor. Largely rebuilt
following a fire in 1989 and very convenient for Exeter,
Plymouth and Torbay. Breast of chicken, fillet of salmon, and
honey roast pork sausages feature on the well-designed
menu, along with creamy fish pie, tempura of vegetables, and
a selection of home-made pies.
OPEN: 11.45-3 Closed Mon lunch in summer ex BHs 6-11 (Sun
12-3, 7-10.30) Closed: 25 Dec **BAR MEALS:** L served Tue-Sun
12-2.15 D served Tue-Sun 6-9.15 Sun 12-3, 7-9.15 Av main course
£8.95 **RESTAURANT:** L served Tue-Sun 12-2.15 D served Tue-Sun
6-9.15 Sun 12-3, 7-9.15 Av 3 course à la carte £15 **⚄:** Free House
⚄: Princetown Jail Ale, IPA, Teignworthy Reel Ale & changing guest
ales. **♀:** 10 **FACILITIES:** Child facs Garden: Patio and lawn with
seating Dogs allowed Water **NOTES:** Parking 30
ROOMS: 6 bedrooms en suite 1 family room s£38 d£60

AVONWICK
Map 03 SX75

The Avon Inn
TQ10 9NB ☎ 01364 73475 e-mail: rosec@beeb.net
Dir: From A38 take South Brent turning, Avonwick signed on B3210
An 18th-century country pub beside the River Avon, with a
large enclosed orchard garden and plenty of moorland walks
nearby. It offers classic French and English cuisine using fresh
local produce prepared by new owner/chef Dominique
Prandi. Prime Devon rump steak, roasted chicken supreme,
and escalope of salmon are among the à la carte main
courses. A cosy bar serves local ales, cider and fine wines,
and there are cream teas in the summer.
OPEN: 11.30-3 6-11 (Sun 12-2.30, 7-10.30) **BAR MEALS:** L served
all week 12-2 D served Mon-Sat 6.30-9.30 Av main course £9
RESTAURANT: L served all week 12-2 D served Mon-Sat 6.45-9.30
⚄: Free House **⚄:** Interbrew Bass, Guest Ale, Bass, Otter Bitter.
FACILITIES: Garden: Large garden, play area Dogs allowed Water
NOTES: Parking 30

AXMOUTH
Map 04 SY29

The Ship Inn ⚐ ♀
EX12 4AF ☎ 01392 21838
Dir: 1m S of A3052 between Lyme and Sidmouth
Creeper-clad family-run inn built soon after the original Ship
burnt down on Christmas Day 1879, and can trace its
landlords back to 1769. There are long views over the Axe
estuary from the beer garden. Well kept real ales complement
an extensive menu including daily blackboard specials where
local fish and game feature, cooked with home-grown herbs.
OPEN: 11-3 6-11 11.30-2.30, 6.30-11 (winter)
BAR MEALS: L served all week 12-2 D served all week 7-9.30
Av main course £8.50 **RESTAURANT:** L served all week 12-2
D served all week 7-9 Av 3 course à la carte £14 **⚄:** Pubmaster
⚄: Otter Bitter, Youngs, Bass. **♀:** 6 **FACILITIES:** Garden: Lawn and
patio area with views over valley Dogs allowed on leads

BANTHAM
Map 03 SX64

Sloop Inn ♀
TQ7 3AJ ☎ 01548 560489 & 560215 📠 01548 561940
*Dir: From Kingsbridge take A379. At rdbt after Churchstow follow signs for
Bantham*
Just a short stroll from the beach, this 16th-century smugglers'
inn features oak beams, a flagstone floor, and a bar made
from half a rowing boat. Fresh local produce, especially
seafood, is to the fore in a comprehensive choice of
blackboard dishes.
OPEN: 11-2.30 6-11 (Sun 12-2.30, 7-10.30) **BAR MEALS:** L served
all week 12-2 D served all week 6.30-9 Av main course £9
RESTAURANT: L served all week 12-2 D served all week 6-9 (Sun
6.30-8.30) Av 3 course à la carte £20 **⚄:** Free House **⚄:** Palmers
IPA, Bass, Palmers Copper Ale. **♀:** 8 **FACILITIES:** Garden: Patio
area with six tables Dogs allowed **NOTES:** Parking 4

Website addresses are included where available.
The AA cannot be held responsible for the
content of any of these websites

England

BERE FERRERS   Map 03 SX46

Olde Plough Inn
PL20 7JL ☎ 01822 840358 e-mail: oldeplough@breathe.com
Dir: A386 from Plymouth, A390 from Tavistock
Originally three cottages, dating from the 16th century, this inn has bags of character, with its old timbers and flagstones, which on closer inspection are revealed to be headstones. To the rear is a fine patio overlooking the River Tavey, and there are lovely walks in the Bere Valley on the doorstep. The are is ideal for birdwatchers. Dishes on offer range through fresh fish, crab, local pies, curries and stir-fries.
OPEN: 12-3 7-11.30 **BAR MEALS:** L served all week 12-2 D served all week 7-9 Av main course £6.75 **RESTAURANT:** L served all week 12-2 D served all week 7-9 ☺: Free House ◀: Sharp's Doom Bar & Sharp's Own, Interbrew Flowers, weekly guest ale.
FACILITIES: Safe beer garden with river views Dogs Water

BICKLEIGH   Map 03 SS90

Fisherman's Cot ♀
EX16 8RW ☎ 01884 855237 ▤ 01884 855241
e-mail: fishermanscot.bickleigh@eldridge-pope.co.uk
Well-appointed thatched inn by Bickleigh Bridge over the River Exe with food all day and large beer garden, just a short drive from Tiverton and Exmoor. The Waterside Bar is the place for snacks and afternoon tea, while the restaurant incorporates a carvery and à la carte menus. Sunday lunch is served, and champagne and smoked salmon breakfast.
OPEN: 11-11 (Sun 12-10.30) **BAR MEALS:** L served all week 12-6 D served all week 6-9.30 Av main course £7.95
RESTAURANT: L served all week 12-10 D served all week ☺: Eldridge Pope ◀: Wadworth 6X, Bass. ♀: 8 **FACILITIES:** Garden: Located on the banks of the river Exe **NOTES:** Parking 100
ROOMS: 21 bedrooms en suite 3 family rooms s£49 d£59 (♦♦♦♦)

BIGBURY-ON-SEA   Map 03 SX64

Pilchard Inn ♀
Burgh Island TQ7 4BG ☎ 01548 810514 ▤ 01548 810514
e-mail: reception@burghisland.com
Dir: From A38 turn off to Modbury, follow signs to Bigbury & Burgh Island

This small 14th-century pub has a stunning beach location in an area of outstanding natural beauty. Suppers, prepared by the kitchen of nearby art-deco Burgh Island Hotel, are available on Thursdays, Fridays and Saturdays. Reasonably-priced mains include spiced sausage, kale and bean soup; and red Thai chicken and pineapple curry. Try a pudding such as apple and rhubarb crumble with warm egg custard; and chocolate and hazelnut crème brûlée.
OPEN: 11.30-11 (Sun 12-10.30) **BAR MEALS:** L served all week 12-2.30 D served Thur-Sat 7-9 Av main course £7.50 ☺: Free House ◀: Sharps, Teignworthy, St Austell. ♀: 7 **FACILITIES:** Children's licence Garden: Terrace overlooking sea, beach Dogs allowed ⊘

BRANSCOMBE   Map 04 SY18

The Fountain Head
EX12 3BG ☎ 01297 680359
Approximately 500 years old, and set among some of the oldest dated houses in Branscombe. Its small interior has flagstone floors and wood-panelling; outside are stools made from tree trunks, and a stream. The dining area was once the village forge and retains its central chimney. Representative dishes include no-nonsense steak and kidney pie and fresh battered cod. Beer comes from the local Branscombe Vale micro-brewery. Popular with hikers and their dogs.
OPEN: 11.30-3 6.30-11 **BAR MEALS:** L served all week 12-2 D served all week 7-9 Av main course £6 ☺: Free House ◀: Guest ales. **FACILITIES:** Food served outside. Dogs allowed Water & biscuits provided **NOTES:** Parking 12

Pick of the Pubs

The Masons Arms ★★ ◉ ⤳ ♀
EX12 3DJ ☎ 01297 680300 ▤ 01297 680500
e-mail: reception@masonsarms.co.uk
See Pick of the Pubs on opposite page

BRAUNTON   Map 03 SS43

The Williams Arms NEW ⤳
Wrafton EX33 2DE ☎ 01271 812360 ▤ 01271 816595
Dir: On A361 between Barnstaple and Braunton
Spacious thatched pub dating back to the 16th century when it was the tavern of a local aristocratic family of the same name. The restaurant includes a carvery serving fresh locally-sourced meat and various vegetable dishes. Specials boards are updated daily, and the menu offers innovative main courses using seasonal produce. Exmoor venison braised in red wine and brandy, scampi platter, breast of chicken and pan-grilled sea bass are prime examples.
OPEN: 11-11 **BAR MEALS:** L served all week 12-2 D served all week 6-10 Sun 12-2.30 Av main course £6.95
RESTAURANT: L served all week 12-2 D served all week 6.30-10 Sun 12-2.30 ◀: Draught Bass, Worthington Creamflow, Tetleys Creamflow. **FACILITIES:** Child facs Children's licence Garden: Large lawned area with picnic tables Dogs allowed Water **NOTES:** Parking 90

The Masons Arms

It's hard to believe that this charming 14th-century creeper-clad inn, originally a cider house, was once a well-documented haunt of smugglers. In recent years it has been updated and substantially improved by its present owners. In the centre of picturesque Branscombe, it is located only a ten-minute stroll from the sea.

The Masons Arms is noted for its charming bar with stone walls, ancient ships' beams, slate floors and a splendid open fireplace, used for spit-roasts on a weekly basis and including Sunday lunch. Accomplished chefs create dishes using carefully selected fresh produce, much of which is locally grown. In good weather lobster and crab – two menu favourites – are landed on Branscombe beach. Meals can be enjoyed in the bar, on the terrace or in the restaurant. Popular snacks at lunchtime range from traditional ploughman's to panini, while dinner brings a more varied menu. Starters might include Thai noodle soup; bouillabaisse; braised field mushrooms; Scottish roll mop herrings; and Atlantic prawn and feta cheese. Main choice range through chick pea and sweet pepper biryani; Thai sour orange chicken curry; crispy fried cod in Mason's ale butter; salmon, mussel, cod and leek stew; roast cushion of salmon; steamed steak and kidney pudding; braised shank of lamb in a red wine reduction; and a wide choice from the house grill. Fish enthusiasts should note that there are always at least three daily fish specials.

OPEN: 11-11 (winter 11-3, 6-11) Times vary, please phone
BAR MEALS: L served all week 12-2 D served all week 7-9
RESTAURANT: D served Tues-Sat 7-8.45
🛢: Free House
🍺: Otter Ale, Masons Ale, Abbot Ale, Branoc and guest ales. ♀: 14
FACILITIES: Garden: Walled terrace with seating for around 100 Dogs allowed Water **NOTES:** Parking 30
ROOMS: 22 bedrooms 19 en suite fr s£30 fr d£50

★★ ◉ 🍽 ♀ Map 04 SY18
EX12 3DJ
☎ 01297 680300
🖷 01297 680500
🌐 reception@masonsarms.co.uk
Dir: Turn off A3052 towards Branscombe, down hill, hotel at bottom of hill

BRENDON — Map 03 SS74

Rockford Inn
EX35 6PT ☎ 01598 741214 📠 01598 741265
e-mail: enquiries@therockfordinn.com
Dir: A39 through Minehead follow signs to Lynmouth. Turn left off A39 to Brendon approx 5m before Lynmouth.

Situated within the spectacular Exmoor National Park, on the banks of the East Lyn River at Brendon, this traditional West Country pub is ideally placed for touring Devon and Somerset on foot or by car. Nearby is the spectacular Doone Valley, made famous by R D Blackmore's classic 19th-century novel *Lorna Doone*. Sample battered cod, home-made cottage pie or Lancashire hotpot at lunchtime. Alternatively, choose local trout, 8oz rump steak or chicken tikka masala in the evening.
OPEN: 12-3 6.30-10.30 **BAR MEALS:** L served all week 12-2.30 D served all week 7-9 Av main course £8 🍴: Free House 🍺: Rockford, Barn Owl, Golden Arrow, Archers.
FACILITIES: Children's licence Garden: Small-beer garden overlooking East Lyn River Dogs allowed Water

BROADHEMPSTON — Map 03 SX86

The Monks Retreat Inn
The Square TQ9 6BN
Dir: From Newton Abbot to Totnes, take right turn through Ippleden and follow signs for Broadhempston.
Apparently a friendly ghost inhabits this inn - certainly it's the sort of place you'd want to linger in: the building (listed as of outstanding architectural interest) is full of fascinating features, including a panelled oak screen typical of ancient Devon houses. Sit by one of the cosy log fires and enjoy good beer, wine, or food including chicken stuffed with crab and served with a lobster bisque, duck breast on stir-fried vegetables, and grilled fresh turbot with mussels and prawns in a citrus butter.
OPEN: 12-2.30 6-11 (Sun 12-3, 7-10.30) **BAR MEALS:** L served Tue-Sun 12-2 D served Tue-Sun 6.30-9.30 12-2.30 7-9 Sun Av main course £9.60 **RESTAURANT:** L served Tue-Sun 12-2 D served Tue-Sun 6.30-9.30 Av 3 course à la carte £21 🍺: Bass, Buttcombe, Fosters. ♀: 7 **FACILITIES:** Children's licence Dogs allowed
NOTES: Parking 2

BUCKFASTLEIGH — Map 03 SX76

Dartbridge Inn
Totnes Rd TQ11 0JR ☎ 01364 642214 📠 01364 643839
e-mail: dartbridge.buckfastleigh@oldenglishinns.co.uk
Dir: A38 onto A384. Inn 200yds on left
Renowned for its colourful floral displays, this beamed inn began life as a teashop and became popular after the completion of the A38 expressway in the early 1970s. Ideally placed on the banks of the River Dart between Exeter and
continued

Plymouth, the pub is handy for Buckfastleigh's steam railway station, as well as for Buckfast Abbey. Expect peppered rump steak; confit of duck; steamed salmon; or broccoli and cream cheese bake.
OPEN: 11-11 Open all day **BAR MEALS:** L served all week 12-2 D served all week 6.30-9 Av main course £10
RESTAURANT: L served all week 12-2 D served all week 7-9.30 🍴: Old English Inns 🍺: Scottish Courage, Abbot Ale, IPA, Otter Ale. ♀: 12 **FACILITIES:** Terrace overlooking front of building **NOTES:** Parking 100

BUCKLAND MONACHORUM — Map 03 SX46

Drake Manor Inn ♀
The Village PL20 7NA ☎ 01822 853892 📠 01822 853892
Dir: Off A386 near Yelverton
A warm welcome is assured at this 16th-century inn. Nestling between the church and the stream, it is named after local resident Sir Francis Drake. Heavy beams and fireplaces with wood-burning stoves are still in evidence, and the pub is renowned for its pretty gardens and award-winning floral displays. Meals include bar snacks, salads, steaks and ploughman's, and daily specials like chicken supreme with mozzarella glaze and leeks.
OPEN: 11.30-2.30 6.30-11 (Sun 12-3, 7-10.30)
BAR MEALS: L served all week 12-2 D served all week 7-10 (Sun 12-2, 7-9.30) **RESTAURANT:** L served all week 7-10 (Sun 12-2, 7-9.30) Av 3 course à la carte £15 🍴: 🍺: Scottish Courage John Smiths & Courage Best, Wadworth 6X, Greene King Abbott Ale, Sharp's Doom Bar. ♀: 9
FACILITIES: Garden: Pretty cottage garden next to stream Dogs allowed Water **NOTES:** Parking 4

BUTTERLEIGH — Map 03 SS90

The Butterleigh Inn
EX15 1PN ☎ 01884 855407 📠 01884 855600
e-mail: info@butterleighinn.co.uk
Dir: 3m from J 28 on the M5 turn R by The Manor Hotel in Cullompton and follow Butterleigh signs
This 400-year old traditional Devonshire free house is very much a friendly local with a homely atmosphere all year round. There's a mass of local memorabilia throughout the pub, and customers can choose from a selection of real ales including Butcombe Bitter, Otter and Tawny. On fine days, the garden with its huge flowering cherry tree is very popular. Booking is recommended for the restaurant, where home-made dishes and daily specials are always available.
OPEN: 12-2.30 6-11 **BAR MEALS:** L served all week 12-2 D served all week 7-9 Av main course £10 **RESTAURANT:** L served all week D served Mon-Sat 7-9 sun 12-2 Av 3 course à la carte £19 🍴: Free House 🍺: Cotleigh Tawny Ale, Abbot Ale, Butcombe Bitter, Ruddles County. **FACILITIES:** Children's licence Garden: Seating available for 30 plus Dogs allowed Water bowl **NOTES:** Parking 50

CHAGFORD — Map 03 SX78

Ring O'Bells ♀
44 The Square TQ13 8AH ☎ 01647 432466 📠 01647 432466
e-mail: info@ringobellschagford.co.uk
Dir: From Exeter take A30 to Whiddon Down Rdbt, take left onto A382 to Mortonhampstead, 3.5m to Easton Cross, T R signed Chagford
Twice destroyed by fire during its long history, this traditional West Country hostelry, once a prison and the site of the stannary courts, is now a handy watering hole for those touring and exploring Dartmoor. Daily changing menus use local produce as often as possible. Farmhouse pie, rabbit and
continued

game pie, steak and kidney pudding, mixed prawn platter, lasagne, and spaghetti bolognaise are among the popular favourites on the menu.
OPEN: 9-3 5-11 (Sun 9-3, 6-10.30) **BAR MEALS:** L served all week 12-2 D served all week 6-9 Av main course £8.95
RESTAURANT: L served all week 12-2 D served all week 6-9
🍺: Free House 🍺: Butcombe Bitter, Dartmoor Ale, Reel Ale, Tetley.
♀: 8 **FACILITIES:** Child facs Children's licence Walled courtyard with lawn & covered area Very dog friendly, water & biscuits provided

Three Crowns Hotel ★★
High St TQ13 8AJ ☎ 01647 433444 & 433441 ▤ 01647 433117
e-mail: threecrowns@msn.com web: www.chagford-accom.co.uk
An impressive, 13th-century, granite-built inn with a wealth of historical associations to investigate. Take young poet and Cavalier Sydney Godolphin, for example, who was shot in the hotel doorway in 1643 and who continues to 'appear', making him the hotel's oldest resident. Period features include mullioned windows, sturdy oak beams and a massive open fireplace. Among chef's specialities are sautéed fillet of pork with mango salsa; roasted breast of duck with plum sauce; and lemon sole poached in white wine with seafood sauce.
OPEN: 8-11.20 day **BAR MEALS:** L served all week 12-3 D served all week 6-9.30 Av main course £6 **RESTAURANT:** L served all week D served all week 6-9.30 Av 3 course à la carte £28.50
Av 3 course fixed price £19.50 🍺: Free House 🍺: Flowers Original, Boddingtons, Bass, Whitbread. **FACILITIES:** Children's licence Dogs allowed **NOTES:** Parking 20 **ROOMS:** 17 bedrooms en suite 3 family rooms s£60 d£74

CHARDSTOCK
Map 04 ST30

The George Inn ◆◆◆
EX13 7BX ☎ 01460 220241 e-mail: info@george-inn.co.uk
Dir: A358 from Taunton through Chard towards Axminster, left at Tytherleigh. Signed from A358.
The George is over 700 years old, has graffiti from 1648 and was once the church school. Underneath is a sealed-off crypt. Two resident ghosts, one a parson, haunt the main entrance and restaurant. On offer from the daily specials are lamb and vegetable pie; Devon pork and apple hotpot; and boeuf bourguignon, while the bar menu stretches to home-made steak and kidney pie; and liver and bacon with mashed potato and onion gravy.
OPEN: 12-2 6-11 (Sat 12-3 6-11, Sun 12-3 7-10.30)
BAR MEALS: L served all week 12-2 D served all week 7-9 Av main course £8.50 **RESTAURANT:** L served all week 12-2 D served all week 7-9 Av 3 course à la carte £19.50 🍺: Free House 🍺: Otter Bitter, Branscombe Vale Best. **FACILITIES:** Garden & Courtyard Food served outside Dogs allowed Water provided/dog chews
NOTES: Parking 25 **ROOMS:** 4 bedrooms en suite s£35 d£50
No children overnight

CHERITON BISHOP
Map 03 SX79

The Old Thatch Inn ▤ ♀
EX6 6HJ ☎ 01647 24204 ▤ 01647 24584
e-mail: mail@theoldthatchinn.f9.co.uk
Dir: 0.5m off A30, 7m SW of Exeter
This charming free house dates from the 16th century, when it welcomed stagecoaches on the London to Penzance run. The pub became a private house in 1915, but was re-licensed in 1974. Local brews including Sharp's Doom Bar and Princetown's Jail Ale accompany the extensive menu, which ranges from ploughman's and light snacks to dishes like sea bass with chilli, ginger and spring onion stuffing; chargrilled venison steak; and goat's cheese and asparagus filo tartlet.

The Old Thatch Inn

OPEN: 11.30-3 6-11 Closed: 25-26 Dec, Nov-Feb Closed Sun eve
BAR MEALS: L served all week 12-2 D served all week 6.30-9
Av main course £11.50 **RESTAURANT:** L served all week 12-2
D served all week 6.30-9 Av 3 course à la carte £23.50 🍺: Free House 🍺: Sharp's Doombar, Otter Ale, Princetown's Jail Ale, Port Stout. ♀: 9 **FACILITIES:** Garden: South facing patio garden Dogs allowed in bar area only **NOTES:** Parking 30

CLEARBROOK
Map 03 SX56

The Skylark Inn ▤
PL20 6JD ☎ 01822 853258 e-mail: skylvic@btinternet.com
Dir: 5m N of Plymouth, just off the A386 to Tavistock Road. Second turn on right signposted for Clearbrook.
The beamed bar with its large fireplace and wood-burning stove characterises this attractive village inn. Although only ten minutes from Plymouth, the Skylark is set in the Dartmoor National Park and is ideal for cyclists and walkers. Good wholesome food is served from an extensive menu that features rainbow trout with potatoes and salad; vegetable stew with dumplings; and a range of shortcrust pastry pies.
OPEN: 11.30-2.30 6-11 (Summer Mon-Sun 11.30-11)
BAR MEALS: L served all week 11.30-2 D served all week 6.30-9
Av main course £8.50 🍺: 🍺: Interbrew Bass, Scottish Courage, Courage Best, Sharpes Special. **FACILITIES:** Garden: Large lawn, patio, tables, chairs, benches Dogs allowed Water Bowls & treats
NOTES: Parking 16

CLOVELLY
Map 03 SS32

Red Lion Hotel ★★
The Quay EX39 5TF ☎ 01237 431237 ▤ 01237 431044
e-mail: redlion@clovelly.co.uk
web: www.redlion-clovelly.co.uk/redlionindex.html
Charming 18th-century hostelry situated right on the beach and the 14th-century harbour wall. Guests staying in the bedrooms can fall asleep to the sound of the sea on the shingle - it's truly an idyllic location. Seafood is a priority on this modern menu, which could include scallops with garlic butter, or baked Cox's apple with a seafood melange to start, and skate wing with Mediterranean vegetables, or seabass with hollandaise to follow.
NOTES: No credit cards

The Rosette is the AA award for food.
Look out for it next to a pub's name

Pubs offering a good choice of fish on their menu

continued

England

CLYST HYDON · Map 03 ST00

Pick of the Pubs

The Five Bells Inn ⧓
EX15 2NT ☎ 01884 277288 📠 01884 277693
e-mail: info@fivebellsclysthydon.co.uk
web: www.fivebellsclysthydon.co.uk
Dir: 10m from Exeter. B3181 towards Cullompton, turn right at Hele Cross towards Clyst Hydon. Continue 2m turn right to Clyst Hydon

This attractive country pub used to be a thatched farm house way back in the 16th century. It started out as a pub early in the 20th century - it takes its name from the five bells in the village church tower - and has never looked back. In fact, if anything it has made rapid strides under its recent owners and has furthered its reputation of cheerful hospitality and good food. Cotleigh Tawny Ale, Otter Bitter and O'Hanlon's are amongst the beers on offer, supported by a range of six malt whiskies and half a dozen wines served by the glass. Light meals are eaten in the bar, which has designated non-smoking areas, or in the raised side garden with its far-reaching country views. The non-smoking restaurant serves a decent selection of grills, specials, vegetarian and fish dishes. Leave space for some delicious puddings, though.
OPEN: 11.30-3 6.30-11 (Winter week days 7-9, Sun 12 open)
BAR MEALS: L served all week 11.30-2 D served all week 7-9 (Sun from 12) Av main course £9 **RESTAURANT:** L served all week 11.30-2 D served all week 7-9 Av 3 course à la carte £17
🍺: Free House ◀: Cotleigh Tawny Ale, Otter Bitter, O'Hanlon's.
⧓: 8 **FACILITIES:** Child facs Garden: Large well kept award winning floral display Dogs allowed Water **NOTES:** Parking 40

COCKWOOD · Map 03 SX98

The Anchor Inn 🗨 ⧓
EX6 8RA ☎ 01626 890203 📠 01626 890355
Dir: Off A379 between Dawlish & Starcross
This lovely 460-year-old smugglers' inn overlooks a landlocked harbour on the River Exe, and is said to be haunted. The low-beamed interior with its two open fireplaces is cosy and inviting in winter, whilst in summer customers spill out onto the verandah and harbour wall. Local fish features strongly on the comprehensive menu, with whole sections devoted to mussels, oysters and scallops. Other choices include venison in rowanberry sauce; and mushroom and asparagus Wellington.
OPEN: 11-11 (Sun 12-10.30) **BAR MEALS:** L served all week 12-3 D served all week 6.30-10 Sun 6.30-9.30 Av main course £6.95
RESTAURANT: L served all week 12-3 D served all week 6.30-10 Sun 6.30-9.30 Av 3 course à la carte £25 🍺: Heavitree ◀: Interbrew Bass, Wadworth 6X, Fuller's London Pride, Otter Ale. ⧓: 10
FACILITIES: Garden: Patio, verandah, overlooks harbour Dogs allowed Water **NOTES:** Parking 15

COLEFORD · Map 03 SS70

Pick of the Pubs

The New Inn ◆◆◆◆ 🗨 ⧓
EX17 5BZ ☎ 01363 84242 📠 01363 85044
e-mail: enquiries@thenewinncoleford.co.uk
See Pick of the Pubs on opposite page

CORNWORTHY · Map 03 SX85

Hunters Lodge Inn 🗨 ⧓
TQ9 7ES ☎ 01803 732204 e-mail: gill.rees@virgin.net
Dir: Off A381 S of Totnes

This country local is tucked away in a peaceful village near the River Dart. The interior is simply furnished, with an open fire burning. Fresh local produce is used in the cooking, with rump of Devon lamb with rosemary jus; spaghetti carbonara; or crevettes sautéed in garlic paprika butter giving an idea of the range. Plenty of good fish and shell fish choices too, and look out for the thunder and lightning ice cream.
OPEN: 11.30-2.30 6.30-11 **BAR MEALS:** L served all week 12-2 D served all week 7-9 Av main course £10 **RESTAURANT:** L served all week 12-2 D served all week 7-9 🍺: Free House ◀: Teignworthy Reel Ale & Springtide, Guest Ales. ⧓: 14 **FACILITIES:** Garden: Large paddock with shaded seating areas Dogs allowed Water, Dog chews
NOTES: Parking 18

CULMSTOCK · Map 03 ST11

Culm Valley Inn ⧓
EX15 3JJ ☎ 01884 840354 📠 01884 841659
A former station hotel in which the owners exposed a long-hidden bar during a renovation re-creating an interwar look. The ever-changing blackboard menu displays a lengthy list of home-made dishes, mostly using locally-grown or raised ingredients, including chicken breast, duck breast and spiced orange reduction, and Aberdeen Angus sirloin steak. Fish and shellfish mostly come from South Devon or Cornwall, including Cornish fix mix, hand-dived scallops, large lemon sole with quince alioli, and Loch Fyne smoked salmon.
OPEN: 12-3 6-11 (Open All Day Sun) Closed: 25 Dec
BAR MEALS: L served all week 12-2 D served Mon-Sat 7-9 Av main course £10 **RESTAURANT:** L served all week 12-2 D served Mon-Sat 7-9 Av 3 course à la carte £21.50 🍺: Free House
◀: O'Hanlons-Blakelys & Wheat Beer, Otter Bright, Oakhill, Exmoor Ale. ⧓: 50 **FACILITIES:** Garden: Old Railway embankment overlooking River Culm Dogs allowed Water **NOTES:** Parking 40 No credit cards

Pick of the Pubs

COLEFORD – DEVON

The New Inn

This cob-built 13th-century free house is full of olde world charm, and set amidst terraced gardens beside the Cole Brook. Original beams and an ancient bar sit comfortably with extensions created from the old barns. Captain, the pea green resident parrot, presides over the bar.

The team, headed by new owners Simon and Melissa Renshaw, are passionate about using local produce and supporting local growers. This leads to an extensive and constantly changing menu. Fish is delivered fresh from Brixham, and all the cheeses in the ploughmans' are made in the West Country. Even the ice cream comes from a farm near Plymouth. Ways to start a meal could include warmed goats' cheese salad; smoked fish platter with dill mayonnaise; or lime and ginger king prawns. The next course might be West Country faggots with creamed potatoes, cabbage and redcurrant gravy; whole grilled trout with almonds, lemon and fries; beef and venison casserole; or fillet of brill stuffed with prawn and cheese. Up to four real ales, including Badger, are generally on offer, along with a thoughtful wine list, and a wide selection of spirits. Light bites, baguettes and tortilla wraps are also available.

OPEN: 12-3 6-11 (Sun 7-10.30)
Closed: 25-26 Dec
BAR MEALS: L served all week 12-2
D served all week 7-10 (Sun 12-2,
7-9.30) Av main course £9
RESTAURANT: L served all week
12-2 D served all week 7-10 (Sun
12-2, 7-9.30) Av 3 course alc £19
🍺: Free House
🍺: Wadworth 6X, Otter Ale, Badger
Bitter, Wells Bombardier. ♀: 7
FACILITIES: Garden: Terraced, paved,
decked area, stream
NOTES: Parking 50
ROOMS: 6 bedrooms en suite
1 family room s£60 d£70

♦♦♦♦ ♀ Map 03 SS70
EX17 5BZ
☎ 01363 84242
📠 01363 85044
📧 enquiries@thenewinncoleford.
co.uk
Dir: From Exeter take A377,
1.5m after Crediton turn left for
Coleford. Pub in 1.5m

Pick of the Pubs

DALWOOD – DEVON

The Tuckers Arms

Although it has witnessed many changes through the centuries, for all its life the inn has been involved in the provision of hospitality, food and drink. The building is a typical Devon longhouse, reputedly dating back about 800 years. Originally it housed the artisans constructing the local church before establishing itself as a welcome destination for weary travellers.

The cosy interior features low beams, flagstone floors and inglenook fireplaces. Old Speckled Hen, Otter Bitter and Palmers IPA are likely to be served in the bar. The blackboard menus frequently list game, fresh fish and locally caught crab, with the range of choices changing daily according to market availability. Starters could include cream of vegetable soup, fresh asparagus with devilled eggs and peppers, and deep-fried queen scallops with tartare sauce. Expect at least three 'fish of the day' dishes, while other main courses could include rack of lamb; sautéed calves' liver with mushrooms, sherry and cream; supreme of duck with green peppercorn and brandy cream sauce; loin of pork with glazed apple and cider; rib-eye steak and mushrooms; and seared fresh salmon with scallions, orange, Pernod and prawns. Finish off with mouthwatering home-made desserts. Country pursuits, including walks, golfing and fishing, are all available nearby. Within easy striking distance are the historic city of Exeter, the antiques capital of Honiton and the coastal resorts of Sidmouth and Lyme Regis, where the cliff paths offer plenty of opportunities for fossil hunting. The covered garden and patio area are the ideal place for lingering over a meal or just a drink on a hot summer's day.

OPEN: 12-3 6.30-11
BAR MEALS: L served all week 12-2 D served all week 7-8.30 Av main course £5.95
RESTAURANT: L served all week 12-2 D served all week 7-9 Av 3 course à la carte £18.95 Av 2 course fixed price £15.95
🍺: Free House
🍺: Otter Bitter, Scottish Courage Courage Directors, Courage Best, O'Hanlons Firefly. 🍷: 8
FACILITIES: Garden: Old English country garden **NOTES:** Parking 6

🍷   Map 04 ST20
EX13 7EG
☎ 01404 881342
🖹 01404 881138
🄴 tuckersarms@aol.com
🅦 www.tuckersarms.co.uk
Dir: Off A35 between Honiton & Axminster

DALWOOD · Map 04 ST20

Pick of the Pubs

The Tuckers Arms ♀
EX13 7EG ☎ 01404 881342 🖹 01404 881138
e-mail: tuckersarms@aol.com web: www.tuckersarms.co.uk
See Pick of the Pubs on opposite page

DARTINGTON · Map 03 SX76

Cott Inn ♀
TQ9 6HE ☎ 01803 863777 🖹 01803 866629
e-mail: djsorton@fsnet.co.uk
Dir: On A384 between Totnes & Buckfastleigh

Picture-postcard pretty, 14th-century stone and cob-built inn, continuously licensed since 1320, with a wonderful 183ft thatched roof - one of the longest in England. Carpeted bar with open fires, a wealth of beams and a comfortable collection of antique and older-style furnishings. Popular buffet-style lunchtime menu; more elaborate evening dishes like wild sea bass dressed with dill and sweet pepper, and beef fillet stuffed with pâté with a rich game jus.
OPEN: 11-11 (Sun 12-10.30) **BAR MEALS:** L served all week 12-2.30 D served all week 6-9.30 Av main course £10
RESTAURANT: L served all week 12-2.30 D served all week 6-9.30
🍽: Old English Inns ◀: Greene King IPA, Old Speckled Hen, Abbots Ale. ♀: 8 **FACILITIES:** Garden: Food served outside Dogs allowed
NOTES: Parking 40

DARTMOUTH · Map 03 SX85

The Cherub Inn ◆◆◆◆ ♀
13 Higher St TQ6 9RB ☎ 01803 832571
e-mail: enquiries@the-cherub.co.uk web: www.the-cherub.co.uk
The Cherub Inn is Dartmouth's oldest building. It dates from about 1380 and survived the threats of fire in 1864, World War II bombing and threatened demolition in 1958 to be finally restored and Grade II listed. Bar meals are available lunchtime and evenings, and the restaurant serves dinner every night, offering a selection of steak, poultry, game and fish dishes. Expect venison steak with apple, cherry and cinnamon sauce, fillet of ostrich with a port and chive sauce, or roast duck breast with a plum ginger and honey glaze, among many popular favourites.
OPEN: 11-11 (Sun 12-10.30) **BAR MEALS:** L served all week 12-2 D served all week 7-9.30 **RESTAURANT:** L served all week D served all week 7-9.30 🍽: Free House ◀: Cherub Best Bitter, Brakspear Bitter, Shepherd Neame Best, Exmoor Ale. ♀: 10
FACILITIES: Dogs allowed

Pick of the Pubs

Royal Castle Hotel ★★★ ♀
11 The Quay TQ6 9PS ☎ 01803 833033 🖹 01803 835445
e-mail: enquiry@royalcastle.co.uk web: www.royalcastle.co.uk
Dir: Centre of Dartmouth, overlooking the river.

In the 1630s two merchants built their neighbouring quayside houses in commanding positions on the Dart estuary. A century later, one had become The New Inn, and by 1782 it had been combined with its neighbour to become The Castle Inn. Further rebuilds incorporated the battlemented turrets and cornice that gave it an appearance worthy of its name. Opposite the bar is the Lydstone Range, forged in Dartmouth over 300 years ago, and on which you can still have your meat roasted during the winter. There is also a bell-board in the courtyard, with each room's bell pitched to a different note. In the upstairs Adam Room Restaurant fish and seafood dishes are always available - an example being mussels, prawns, scallops and razor fish in white wine sauce. Other options are pan-fried chicken breast on green pea and trompette mushroom risotto; rich lamb casserole; and baby pumpkins served with slow-roasted tomato sauce, filled with fresh local vegetables.
OPEN: 11-11 **BAR MEALS:** L served all week 11.30-6.30 D served all week 6.30-10 Av main course £7
RESTAURANT: L served all week 12-2 D served all week 7-9.30 Av 3 course à la carte £28 Av 3 course fixed price £25 🍽: Free House ◀: Exe Valley Dob's Bitter, Courage Directors, Bass.
♀: 12 **FACILITIES:** Dogs allowed Water, Biscuits
NOTES: Parking 14 **ROOMS:** 25 bedrooms en suite 3 family rooms s£85 d£155

DENBURY · Map 03 SX86

The Union Inn ♀
Denbury Green TQ12 6DQ ☎ 01803 812595 🖹 01803 814206
Dir: 2m form Newton Abbot, signed Denbury
A blacksmith's shop and a cartwright's workshop were linked together to form the 400-year-old Union Inn. Inside, you'll find rustic stone walls and a log fire with adjacent settle. The new owners' emphasis is on home-made fresh food, using local ingredients where possible. Lunchtime sandwiches and pub favourites give way to appetising evening choices like tuna steak on spinach with black pepper sauce; vegetable stir-fry; and pork tenderloin with apple, Calvados and sage sauce.
OPEN: 12-3 6-11 (Sat 12-11, Sun 12-10.30) **BAR MEALS:** L served all week 12-2.30 D served Mon-Sat 6-9 Av main course £6
RESTAURANT: L served all week 12-2.30 D served all week 6.30-9 🍽: ◀: Bass, Otter, Greene King, 6X. ♀: 9 **FACILITIES:** Dogs allowed Water/biscuits

DITTISHAM   Map 03 SX85

The Ferry Boat ♀
Manor St TQ6 0EX ☎ 01803 722368
This quiet, traditional pub (the only riverside inn on the River Dart) continues to prove popular with walkers and families. There are tables by the waterfront with views across the river to Greenway House, a National Trust property that was once Agatha Christie's home. The menu of home-cooked food is based on local produce and includes fish pies and crab cakes in season, along with locally caught fresh fish dishes.
OPEN: 11-11 (Sun 12-10.30) **BAR MEALS:** L served all week 12-2.30 D served all week 7-9 Av main course £8 ⊕: ◖: Bass, Stella Artois, Ushers. ♀: 9 **FACILITIES:** Children's licence Riverside pub with tables on the waterfront Dogs allowed Water, dog chews

DODDISCOMBSLEIGH   Map 03 SX88

Pick of the Pubs

The Nobody Inn ♀
EX6 7PS ☎ 01647 252394 🖷 01647 252978
e-mail: info@nobodyinn.co.uk
Dir: From A38 follow signs for Dunchideock and Doddiscombleigh

This charming inn dating from around 1591 has had a curious history including having been the village's unofficial church house. It became The Nobody Inn in reference to an unfortunate incident involving a deceased landlord. It seems when his burial took place they forgot to actually put him into his coffin. There is always quite a gathering at this popular inn, and you'll be spoilt for choice with the unusual local ales, 240 whiskies, 600 wines and 40 local cheeses. It is hardly a surprise, therefore, to discover that the inn has won a lot of accolades for the wine list and cheese board. You could start with the house speciality, the Nobody soup; or try crab crumble, or roast fennel and pommery mustard risotto. Mains could be brace of quail stuffed with rice and apricots; lamb's liver sautéed with thyme, onion and garlic; sliced fillet of beef with creamy tarragon sauce; and herb-crumbled marlin with lightly spiced pepper courgette.
OPEN: 12-2.30 6-11 (Sun 12-3, 7-10.30) Closed: 25-26 & 31 Dec
BAR MEALS: L served all week 12-2 D served all week 7-10 Av main course £9 **RESTAURANT:** D served Tue-Sat 7.30-9
⊕: Free House ◖: Branscombe Nobody's Bitter, Sharp's Doom Bar, RCH East Street Cream, Exmoor Gold. ♀: 20
FACILITIES: Garden: Patio area Dogs allowed in the garden only **NOTES:** Parking 50

DOLTON   Map 03 SS51

Pick of the Pubs

The Union Inn
Fore St EX19 8QH ☎ 01805 804633 🖷 01805 804633
e-mail: theunioninn@dolton.wanadoo.co.uk
Dir: From A361 take B3227 to S Moulton, then Atherington. Left onto B3217 then 6m to Dolton. Pub on right
A 17th-century free house built as a Devon longhouse. Traditionally constructed of cob, the building was converted to a hotel in the mid-19th century to serve the local cattle markets, and it remains a traditional village pub with a cosy atmosphere. With its large Georgian rooms, sash windows and traditional pub interior, it offers a warm welcome to visitors. There's a homely beamed bar, oak settles and sturdy wooden tables, plus good home cooking, especially Sunday roasts and traditional dishes washed down with West Country ales. In the bar you should find baguettes and toasties, as well as local ham and sausage. Restaurant meals might include marinated rib-eye steak, or braised oxtail with red wine.
OPEN: 12-3 6-11 Closed: 1st 2 wks Feb
BAR MEALS: L served Thur-Tue 12-2 D served Thur-Tue 7-10 Sun 12-2.30, 7-9 Av main course £6.95
RESTAURANT: L served Sun 12-2 D served Thu-Tue 7-9 Sun 12-2.30, 7-9 ⊕: Free House ◖: Sharp's Doom Bar, Jollyboat Freebooter, Clearwater Cavalier, St Austell Tribute.
FACILITIES: Child facs Children's licence Garden: Small area with three tables Dogs allowed Dog bed and toys
NOTES: Parking 15

DREWSTEIGNTON   Map 03 SX79

Pick of the Pubs

The Drewe Arms 🐟
The Square EX6 6QN ☎ 01647 281224
Dir: W of Exeter on A30 for 12m. L at Woodleigh junct follow signs for 3m to Drewsteignton
Quintessentially English thatched inn tucked away in a sleepy village square close to the National Trust's Castle Drogo, and plenty of outstanding country walks on and around Dartmoor. Built in 1646, the Drewe Arms is a rare find these days. Formerly run by Mabel Mudge for 75 years, until her retirement in 1996, the pub has changed hands only twice during the last century. The unique interior - virtually unchanged - and timeless atmosphere both in the pub and the village are undoubtedly the key to its success. Traditional ales are drawn direct from the cask, housed in the original 'tap bar' and served through two hatchways. The chef provides first class food, native favourites and international dishes prepared from fresh produce sourced from local independent suppliers. Expect half crispy roast duck, local butcher's sausages, braised lamb shank, Mediterranean chicken bake, and Thai-style red snapper, as well as sandwiches and ploughman's.
OPEN: 11-3 6-11 (Sun 12-3, 7-10.30) **BAR MEALS:** L served all week 12-2 D served all week 6.30-9 Av main course £6.95
RESTAURANT: L served Sun D served all week 6.30-9 ⊕: Whitbread ◖: Bass, Gales HSB and Guest Ales.
FACILITIES: Garden: beer garden, patio, outdoor eating Dogs allowed Water **NOTES:** Parking 12 **ROOMS:** 3 bedrooms 1 en suite s£50 d£70 (♦♦♦♦)

EAST PRAWLE
Map 03 SX73

Pigs Nose Inn NEW
TQ7 2BY ☎ 01548 511209 🖷 01548 511184
e-mail: pigsnose@eclipse.co.uk
The most southerly hostelry in Devon , this 500-year-old smugglers' pub was a noted refuge for shipwrecked sailors. Inside, the bar has a timeless feel to it, with fascinating bric-a-brac and some charming relics. The chef is Italian, so the menu combines traditional English with a dash of Mediterranean. Expect steak and ale pie, spaghetti bolognaise, Cumberland sausages and mash, halibut in a basil sauce, and locally-sourced lamb chops.
OPEN: 12-3 6-11 (12-4 in tourist season) **BAR MEALS:** L served all week 12-2.30 D served all week 6-9 Av main course £7
RESTAURANT: L served all week 12-2.30 D served all week 6-9 Closed Mondays in winter Av 3 course à la carte £13 ◖: Fullers London Pride, Suttons Dartmoor Pride, Eddystone Lighthouse.
FACILITIES: Child facs Children's licence Garden: Tables to front of pub and village green Dogs allowed 'Dog menu', nibbles on the bar
NOTES: Parking 40 No credit cards

EXETER
Map 03 SX99

Red Lion Inn 🍴 ♀
Broadclyst EX5 3EL ☎ 01392 461271
Dir: On the B3181 Exeter to Culompton.
At the centre of a National Trust village, this renowned 16th-century beamed inn has been transformed by the landlady's builder husband. Situated next to the church, it features antique furniture and a cobbled courtyard. Among the kitchen's output you may find roasted sea bream with garlic and parsley butter; wild mushroom nut roast; coq au vin; and Mediterranean vegetable roulade.
OPEN: 11-3 5.30-11 (Sun 12-3, 7-10.30) **BAR MEALS:** L served all week 12-2.30 D served all week 6-9.30 Sun 12-2.30, 7-9
RESTAURANT: L served all week 12-2.3 D served Mon-Sat 6-9.30 Sun 12-2.3, 7-9 🍽: Free House ◖: Bass, Fullers London Pride, O'Hanlons Local Blakelys Red, Speckled Hen. ♀: 7
FACILITIES: Child facs Garden: Small garden with three tables Dogs allowed in garden only. Water & biscuits provided
NOTES: Parking 70

The Twisted Oak NEW ♀
Little John's Cross Hill EX2 9RG
☎ 01392 273666 🖷 01392 277705
e-mail: martin.bullock@virgin.net
Dir: A30 to Okehampton, follow signs for pub

Set in a beautiful part of Ide just outside Exeter, this large pub has been successfully refurbished and turned into a quality, food-driven venue under the new management. There is a choice of dining area - an informal place where you can smoke, relax on the leather sofas and eat; a separate non-smoking lounge bar restaurant; and a more formal, non-smoking, conservatory area, which is adult only during the evenings. During the summer months the huge garden provides al fresco seating and a children's play area.
OPEN: 11-3 6-11 (Sun 6-10.30) **BAR MEALS:** L served all week 12-2.30 D served all week 6-9.30 Av main course £7.50
RESTAURANT: L served all week 12-2.30 D served all week 6-9.30 Av 3 course à la carte £27.50 Av 2 course fixed price £12 ◖: O'Hanlons Firefly, Cotleighs 25, Bass, Pedigree. ♀: 11 **FACILITIES:** Garden: Large mature garden with BBQ **NOTES:** Parking 40

EXMINSTER
Map 03 SX98

Swans Nest ♀
Station Rd EX6 8DZ ☎ 01392 832371
Dir: From M5 follow A379 Dawlish Rd

A much extended pub in a pleasant rural location whose facilities, unusually, extend to a ballroom, dance floor and stage. The carvery is a popular option for diners, with a choice of meats served with freshly prepared vegetables, though the salad bar is a tempting alternative, with over 39 items, including quiches, pies and home-smoked chicken. A carte of home-cooked fare includes grilled lamb steak, Devon pork chop, and five-bean vegetable curry. Interested diners might like to sample 'Plant Pot Pudding', as well as take a look at a jukebox that once belonged to Sir Elton John.
OPEN: 10.30-2.30 Sun 12.2.30 6-11 Sun 7-10.30 Closed: Dec 26
BAR MEALS: L served all week 12-2 D served all week 6-9.45
RESTAURANT: L served all week 12-2 D served all week 6-9.30 🍽: Free House ◖: Otter Bitter, Princetown Jail Ale.
FACILITIES: Garden **NOTES:** Parking 102

EXTON
Map 03 SX98

Pick of the Pubs

The Puffing Billy ◎◎ ♀
Station Rd EX3 0PR ☎ 01392 877888 🖷 01392 876232
e-mail: food@thepuffingbilly.com
Dir: 3m from junct 30 of M5. Take A376 signed Exmouth, pass through Ebford and follow signs for Puffing Billy right into Exton.
Named for its proximity to the Exeter-Exmouth branch line, the 16th-century Puffing Billy enjoys views of the Exe estuary. Since Martin Humphries took over in 2004, he has spent a small fortune installing some superb equipment in the kitchen, and on giving the restaurant and bar a modern, light makeover. He sums up his approach to food thus: "Without good shopping there cannot be good cooking", a phrase which diners can see expressed pictorially in the original artwork on display. Enjoy mackerel rillette with marinated aubergine and tapenade salad; caramelised scallops with truffled baby

continued

continued

England

EXTON continued

leek terrine; confit duck leg and fennel risotto; twice-baked Cornish Blue soufflé with walnuts and French bean salad; slow honey-roasted pork belly with creamed potato and pine nut salad; and Crediton duckling with fondant potato, turnip, apples and fig jus. Rhubarb crumble soufflé with ginger ice cream is a typical dessert.

The Puffing Billy

OPEN: 11-3 6-11 (Sun 12-2.30) Closed: selected days over Christmas **BAR MEALS:** L served all week 12-2.30 D served Mon-Sat 6.30-9.30 Sun 12-2.30 Av main course £11.75 **RESTAURANT:** L served all week 12-2.30 D served Mon-Sat 6.30-9.30 Sun 12-2.30 Av 3 course à la carte £29 🍺: Firefly, Warsteiner, Tetleys. ♀: 12 **FACILITIES:** Child facs Children's licence Garden: Sun terrace, small garden **NOTES:** Parking 30

HARBERTON   Map 03 SX75

The Church House Inn ♀
TQ9 7SF ☎ 01803 863707
Dir: From Totnes take A381 S. Take turn for Harberton on right, adjacent to church in centre of village

Built to house masons working on the church next door (around 1100), the inn has some fascinating historic features, including a Tudor window frame and latticed window with 13th-century glass. The extensive daily menu is supplemented by daily specials and a traditional roast on Sundays. There's plenty of seafood/fish, and a family room. New owners.
OPEN: 12-3 6-11 (Sat 12-4, 6-11 Sun 12-3, 7-10.30)
BAR MEALS: L served all week 12-2 D served all week 6.30-9.30 Carvery on Sun 12-2.30 Av main course £8.95 🍽: Free House 🍺: Marstons Pedigree, Butcombe, Courage Best, Theakstons XB. ♀: 14 **FACILITIES:** Child facs Dogs allowed Water, dog biscuits, food

🍺 Principal Beers for sale

HATHERLEIGH   Map 03 SS50

Tally Ho Inn & Brewery ♀
14 Market St EX20 3JN ☎ 01837 810306
e-mail: adytaylor65@hotmail.com
Great food, good beer, and a welcoming atmosphere are promised at this 15th-century pub located in the heart of the historic town. With its beamed bar and open fires, own ales brewed on site, and prize-winning home-made dishes, it clearly succeeds in its philosophy. In the cosy dining room and beamed bar expect crispy duck breast served with a roasted pepper and red onion chutney, plus Tally Ho sausages made with the house beer.
OPEN: 11-3 6-11.30 (Sun 11-10.30) **BAR MEALS:** L served all week 11-2.30 D served all week 6-9.30 Av main course £7.50
RESTAURANT: L served all week 11-2.30 D served all week 6-9.30 Av 3 course à la carte £20 🍽: Free House 🍺: Cavalier, Courage Best, Oliver's Nectar & Guest ale. **FACILITIES:** Garden: Food served outside Dogs allowed

HAYTOR VALE   Map 03 SX77

Pick of the Pubs

The Rock Inn ★★ ◉ ♀
TQ13 9XP ☎ 01364 661305 🖹 01364 661242
e-mail: inn@rock-inn.co.uk
Dir: A38 from Exeter, at Drum Bridges rdbt take A382 for Bovey Tracey, 1st exit at 2nd rdbt (B3387), 3m left to Haytor Vale.
Old-fashioned values are as important as ever at this cheerful 18th-century coaching inn, and the old stables recall the pub's strategic position on the road between Widecombe-in-the-Moor and Newton Abbot. Modern-day travellers will find nine comfortable en-suite bedrooms, all named after Grand National winners. Open fires, antique tables and sturdy furnishings lend a traditional feel to the rambling bars, but the cooking style is unashamedly modern British, using excellent produce in nicely presented dishes. Lunchtime might bring pancetta and spring onion risotto, or cod and dill fishcakes on salad leaves with French fries. Fresh fish from Brixham makes for good seafood choices such as whole grilled plaice or pan-fried John Dory. Dinner might start with River Teign mussels in chilli, lemon and parsley, followed by shank of Devon Lamb on pureéd potato with wholegrain mustard sauce, and finishing with poached pear in red wine with pannacotta.
OPEN: 11-11 Closed: Dec 25-26 **BAR MEALS:** L served all week 12-2.30 D served all week 6.30-9.30 Av main course £8
RESTAURANT: L served all week 12-2.30 D served all week 7-9 Av 3 course à la carte £24.95 Av 3 course fixed price £18.50 🍽: Free House 🍺: Old Speckled Hen, St Austell Dartmoor Best, Interbrew Bass. **FACILITIES:** Garden: Large well kept
NOTES: Parking 35 **ROOMS:** 9 bedrooms en suite 2 family rooms s£65.50 d£75

HOLBETON   Map 03 SX65

The Mildmay Colours Inn
PL8 1NA ☎ 01752 830248 🖹 01752 830432
e-mail: mildmaycolours@aol.com
Dir: S from Exeter on A38, Yealmpton/Ermington, S past Ugborough & Ermington right onto A379. After 1.5m, turn left, signposted Mildmay Colours/Holbeton
A 17th-century pub, which derives its unusual name from a famous jockey, Lord Anthony Mildmay, whose portrait and

continued

England

silks are hung in the pub. There are simple bar snacks and children's meals, along with daily specials such as nut roast with a sherry cream sauce; Dartmouth smoked chicken salad; local mackerel and salsa sauce; Mildmay Colours beer batter cod; and whole Torbay sole.
OPEN: 11-2 6-11 (Sun 12-3, 7-10.30) **BAR MEALS:** L served all week 12-1.45 D served all week 6-9 Sun 12-2.30 **RESTAURANT:** L served Sun 12-2.30 Av 3 course à la carte £12 🍺: Free House 🍴: Mildmay Colours Bitter & Mildmay SP, Hellican Honey, Keel Over, Betty Stoggs. **FACILITIES:** Garden: Nice flower arrangements, 10 picnic benches Dogs allowed Water **NOTES:** Parking 20

HOLNE   Map 03 SX76

Church House Inn 🍷
TQ13 7SJ ☎ 01364 631208 🖨 01364 631525
Dir: From A38 at Ashburton (Peartree Junction) take road to Dartmoor. Follow road over Holne bridge, up hill and take left turn, signed to Holne.
Tucked away in the tranquil south Devon countryside, this traditional 14th-century free house is on the southeast edge of Dartmoor and offers a warm welcome and old-fashioned service. This is a paradise for outdoor enthusiasts, and the owners have built a reputation for quality local fare. Examples from the blackboard include medallions of beef topped with cheese mousseline, skate wing on braised fennel, baby aubergines with curried vegetable couscous, and cod steak with cream cauliflower purée and pea and herb sauce.
OPEN: 12-2.30 7-11 (Sun 12-3 7-10.30) **BAR MEALS:** L served all week 12-2 D served all week 7-9 Av main course £10 **RESTAURANT:** L served Sun 12-2 D served all week 7-9 Av 3 course à la carte £22 🍺: Free House 🍴: Butcombe, Summerskills, Teignworthy. 🍷: 12 **FACILITIES:** Child facs Garden: Small village green and patio Dogs allowed **NOTES:** Parking 6

HOLSWORTHY   Map 03 SS30

The Bickford Arms NEW ♦♦♦♦
Brandis Corner EX22 7XY ☎ 01409 221318 🖨 01409 220085
e-mail: info@bickfordarms.com
Dir: On A3072 4m from Holsworthy
The Bickford Arms stood on the Holsworthy to Hatherleigh road for 300 years, serving both travellers and locals, before it was completely destroyed by fire in 2003. Totally rebuilt, the pub retains much of its original charm and character, with beams, a welcoming bar and two fireplaces. The bar and restaurant menu offers food prepared with ingredients sourced locally. Extensive choice includes home-made fish pie, lasagne, duck breast, locally landed cod, and chicken curry.
OPEN: 11-11 **BAR MEALS:** L served all week 12-2.30 D served all week 6.30-9.30 Av main course £7 **RESTAURANT:** D served Thur-Sat 7-9 Av 3 course à la carte £25 Av 3 course fixed price £25 🍴: Skinners Betty Stogs, Skinners Figgy Brew, Courage Directors.
FACILITIES: Children's licence Garden: Large beer garden with seating Dogs allowed Water bowl **NOTES:** Parking 50
ROOMS: 5 bedrooms en suite 1 family room s£40 d£60 No children overnight

Rydon Inn and Restaurant NEW 🍷
EX22 7HU ☎ 01409 259444 e-mail: info@rydon-inn.com
Dir: 1m from Holsworthy on A3072
The Rydon is a restored 300-year-old Devon longhouse with high, vaulted pine ceilings, outstanding views, and a lake illuminated at night. Its owners offer more than just traditional pub grub, with the likes of braised Devon lamb shank with garlic mash, rosemary jus and seasonal vegetables; fillets of sea bass with hot mango salsa;

mushroom stroganoff with saffron rice; and more in the same modern British vein.
OPEN: 11-3 5.30-11 **BAR MEALS:** L served all week 12-2 D served all week 6.30-8.45 Av main course £5.95 **RESTAURANT:** L served all week 12-2 D served all week 6.30-8.45 Av 3 course à la carte £22 🍴: Doom Bar, HHH. 🍷: 7 **FACILITIES:** Child facs Children's licence Garden: 1 acre, fenced lake Dogs allowed Water bowls **NOTES:** Parking 50

HONITON   Map 04 ST10

The Otter Inn
Weston EX14 3NZ ☎ 01404 42594
Dir: Just off A30 W of Honiton
On the banks of the idyllic River Otter, this ancient 14th-century inn is set in over two acres of grounds and was once a cider house. Enjoy one of the traditional real ales, try your hand at scrabble, dominoes or cards, or peruse the inn's extensive book collection. A wide-ranging menu caters for all tastes and includes fresh fish, game, steak, vegetarian dishes, bar meals and Sunday lunch.
OPEN: 11-11 (Sun 12-10.30) Dec 25-26 Closed eve **BAR MEALS:** L served all week 12-3 D served all week 6-10 Sun 12-8 **RESTAURANT:** L served all week 12-3 D served all week 6-9 🍺: Free House 🍴: Otter Ale, Flowers IPA, London Pride. **FACILITIES:** Child facs Children's licence Garden: Large with river at bottom Dogs allowed Water **NOTES:** Parking 50

HORNDON   Map 03 SX58

The Elephant's Nest Inn 🍽
PL19 9NQ ☎ 01822 810273 🖨 01822 810273
e-mail: hugh.cook@onetel.net
Dir: Off A386 N of Tavistock

An isolated inn on the flanks of Dartmoor National Park reached via narrow lanes from Mary Tavy. The 16th-century building retains its real fires, slate floors and low beamed ceilings, decorated with loads of elephant memorabilia. The unique name comes from a humourous remark made by a regular about the then, rather portly, landlord. Traditional pub food is served from a daily-changing menu of fresh local produce, plus a range of bar snacks.
OPEN: 12-3 6.30-11 25-26 Dec Closed lunch **BAR MEALS:** L served all week 12-2.15 D served all week 6.30-9 Av main course £8.50 **RESTAURANT:** L served all week 12-2.15 D served all week 6.30-9 Av 3 course à la carte £15 🍺: Free House 🍴: Palmers IPA, Copper, Otter Bright & changing guest ales.
FACILITIES: Garden: Views of Dartmoor, cricket pitch Dogs allowed **NOTES:** Parking 35

🍷 **7** Number of wines by the glass

continued

England

HORNS CROSS
Map 03 SS32

Pick of the Pubs

The Hoops Inn and Country Hotel ★★★ ◉ ⌑ ♀
Clovelly EX39 5DL ☎ 01237 451222 ▤ 01237 451247
e-mail: sales@hoopsinn.co.uk web: www.hoopsinn.co.uk
Dir: On the A39 between Bideford & Clovelly

Having made their way along tortuous footpaths to evade the revenue men, smugglers would share out their spoils in this thatched, cob-walled, 13th-century inn. Set in 16 acres of gardens and meadows on the rugged Atlantic coast, it offers charm galore. Change of ownership has meant new menus, based on the freshest produce Devon can offer, including herbs, fruit and vegetables from the gardens, and a wide choice of wines by the glass from more than 220 bins. Guests may choose to eat in the Bar, Morning Room or Restaurant, where oak-panelled walls, period furniture and tables set with crisp white napkins create just the right level of formality. Seasonal menus feature simple traditional British cooking, such as steak, ale and kidney pudding, but many diners come for the local seafood, typically fried brill, lobster thermidor, roasted fillet of Lundy cod, and seafood pie.
OPEN: 8-11 (Sun 12-10.30) Closed: Dec 25
BAR MEALS: L served all week 12-3 D served all week 6.30-9.30
RESTAURANT: L served all week 12-3 D served all week 6.30-9.30 All day Sat ▥: Free House ◖: Hoops Old Ale, Jollyboat Mainbrace, Normans Conquest, Bass. ♀: 12
FACILITIES: Children's licence Garden: outdoor eating, BBQ Dogs allowed 2.5 acres of gardens & ponds **NOTES:** Parking 100
ROOMS: 13 bedrooms en suite s£65 d£85

See Pub Walk on page 128

HORSEBRIDGE
Map 03 SX47

The Royal Inn ♀
PL19 8PJ ☎ 01822 870214 e-mail: paul@royalinn.co.uk
Dir: South of B3362 Launceston/Tavistock road
The pub, with a façade enlivened by superb pointed arched windows, was once a nunnery. Standing near a bridge built over the Tamar in 1437 by Benedictine monks, it was the Packhorse Inn until Charles I pitched up one day - his seal is in the doorstep. Beef for the steaks, casseroles and stews, and the pheasant and venison on the specials board are all locally supplied. Chilli cheese tortillas are much appreciated. So is the absence of noisy machines.
OPEN: 12-3 6.30-11 Dec 25 Closed eve **BAR MEALS:** L served all week 12-2 D served all week 7-9 Av main course £6
RESTAURANT: L served all week 12-2 D served all week 7-9 Av 3 course à la carte £14 ▥: Free House ◖: Sharp's Doom Bar & Special, Eastreet, Bass, Ring O'Bells. ♀: 12 **FACILITIES:** Garden: Three patio areas Dogs allowed **NOTES:** Parking 30

IVYBRIDGE
Map 03 SX65

Anchor Inn
Lutterburn St, Ugborough PL21 0NG
☎ 01752 892283 ▤ 01752 897449
e-mail: enquiries@anchorugborough.co.uk
Owner Tim Martin has brought international flavours like ostrich, kangaroo and crocodile to this village free house. Beamed ceilings, open fires and real cask ales maintain the traditional welcome, and the Anchor is ideally located for exploring Dartmoor or the South Devon beaches. Food is served everyday with bar menu choices or full à la carte. The pub's trademark dishes are 'Hot Rocks' - steaks cooked at your table with a selection of sauces.
OPEN: 11.30-3 5-11 (Fri-Sat 11.30-11 Sun 12-10.30)
BAR MEALS: L served all week 12-2 D served all week 7-9
RESTAURANT: L served all week 12-2 D served all week 7-9
▥: Free House ◖: Bass, Courage, Directors, local ales.
FACILITIES: Child facs Garden: Small walled area with two tables Dogs allowed Water & biscuits provided **NOTES:** Parking 15

KENTON
Map 03 SX98

Devon Arms ◆◆◆
Fore St EX6 8LD ☎ 01626 890213 ▤ 01626 891678
e-mail: devon.arms@ukgateway.net
Dir: On A379 between Exeter & Dawlish 7m from Exeter, 5m from Dawlish, adjacent to Powderham castle
An old whitewashed coaching house dating from 1592, the Devon Arms was first licensed in 1822 as the Exeter Inn. Renamed in the 1830s, this comfortable free house offers a garden with patio, barbecue, pets' corner and children's play area, as well as six en suite bedrooms. Lunchtime brings baguettes and jacket potatoes, whilst the main menu includes steak and ale pie; smoked haddock fillet; or three cheese pasta and broccoli bake.
OPEN: 11-2.30 6-11 (Sun 12-3, 7-10.30) **BAR MEALS:** L served all week 12-2 D served all week 6.30-9 Sun 7-9 Av main course £8.75
RESTAURANT: L served all week 12-2 D served all week 6.30-9 Sun 7-9 ▥: Free House ◖: Teign Valley Tipple, Whitbread Best, Sharps Doom Bar. **FACILITIES:** Garden: Grassed area and patio with picnic tables Dogs allowed **NOTES:** Parking 20 **ROOMS:** 6 bedrooms en suite 4 family rooms s£35 d£50

KINGSBRIDGE
Map 03 SX74

Church House Inn ⌑ ♀
Churchstow TQ7 3QW ☎ 01548 852237 ▤ 01548 852237
e-mail: zbaker@churchhouseinn.eclipse.co.uk
Dir: 2.5m from Kingsbridge on A379
Set in some lovely Devon countryside on the way to Salcombe, this historic 15th-century inn was originally the site of a rest house for Cistercian monks during the 13th century, and is haunted by the spirit of a shy monk. The ceiling of the inn contains beams from a hospital ship that sailed as part of the Spanish Armada. Look out for sea bass, steak and kidney pie, scallops in cheese and white wine sauce, or smoked salmon. There is also a very popular hot carvery.
OPEN: 11-2 6-11 Extended in summer **BAR MEALS:** L served all week 12-2 D served all week 6.30-9 Extended in summer Av main course £7.50 **RESTAURANT:** L served all week 12-2 D served all week 7-9 Av 3 course à la carte £14 ▥: Free House ◖: Interbrew Bass, Fuller's London Pride, St Austell Dartmoor Best and Guest Ales. ♀: 8 **FACILITIES:** Child facs Garden: Patio with heaters Dogs allowed **NOTES:** Parking 26

The Crabshell Inn
Embankment Rd TQ7 1JZ ☎ 01548 852345 ▤ 01548 852262
Traditionally a watering hole for barge crews, the Crabshell's free moorings are now just as popular with leisure sailors on the Kingsbridge estuary. Customers enjoy the superb views over the estuary, whether from the open-air quayside tables or from the first floor Waterside Restaurant. The extensive menu and specials boards cater for all tastes, from a simple Salcombe crab sandwich to home-cooked dishes like baked rack of lamb, or whole grilled sea bass.
OPEN: 11-11 (Sun 12-10.30) **BAR MEALS:** L served all week 12-2.30 D served all week 6-9.30 Av main course £5.50
RESTAURANT: L served all week 12-2.30 D served all week 6-9.30 Av 3 course à la carte £12.75 ☺: Free House ◀: Bass Bitter, Crabshell Bitter, Old Speckled Hen. **FACILITIES:** Child facs Garden: Patio area with tables & seats Dogs allowed Water **NOTES:** Parking 40

KINGSKERSWELL — Map 03 SX86

Barn Owl Inn ♀
Aller Mills TQ12 5AN ☎ 01803 872130 ▤ 01803 875279
e-mail: barnowl@oldridge-pope.co.uk
web: www.pubswithrooms.co.uk/barnowl.html
This 16th-century former farmhouse at the heart of Devon boasts many charming features, including flagged floors, a black leaded range and oak beams in a high-vaulted converted barn with a minstrel's gallery. Its location is handy for Dartmoor and the English Riviera towns. The menu offers wholesome fisherman's crumble, minted half-shoulder of lamb, and tournedos Rossini. New management.
OPEN: 11-11 (Sun 12-10.30) **BAR MEALS:** L served all week 12-2.30 D served all week 6-9.30 **RESTAURANT:** D served all week 6-9.30 Av fixed price £15 ☺: Eldridge Pope ◀: Bass, 6X, Tetley, Guest Ales. ♀: 14 **FACILITIES:** Garden: Small secluded garden Dogs allowed Water in garden **NOTES:** Parking 30

KINGSTON — Map 03 SX64

The Dolphin Inn
TQ7 4QE ☎ 01548 810314 ▤ 01548 810314
Dir: From A379 Plymouth to Kingsbridge road take B3233 for Bigbury-on-Sea. Follow the brown signs for the Dolphin Inn
Built as somewhere to live by stonemasons constructing the neighbouring church, this 16th-century inn retains all the beams, inglenooks and exposed stonework one would hope to find. A mile from the sea, and only a few to Bigbury Bay where offshore Burgh Island is reachable at high tide only by tractor transport. Home-made dishes making good use of locally caught or grown produce include fisherman's pie, crab bake, liver and onions, bangers and mash, and steaks.
OPEN: 11-3 Jan-Feb, Mon-Fri 12-3 6-11 (Sun 12-3, 7-10.30)
BAR MEALS: L served all week 12-2 D served all week 6-9.30 Sun 7-9; closed Mon in winter Av main course £7.95 ☺: ◀: Butcombe, Four Seasons Ale, Courage Best, Sharps Doom Bar.
FACILITIES: Child facs Garden: Small patio area, large garden, seating Dogs allowed Water provided **NOTES:** Parking 40

◆ Diamond rating for inspected guest accommodation

Do you have a favourite pub that we have overlooked? Please use the Reader's Report form at the back of this guide to tell us all about it

KINGSWEAR — Map 03 SX85

The Ship
Higher St TQ6 0AG ☎ 01803 752348
Dir: Telephone for directions
Historic village pub overlooking the scenic River Dart towards Dartmouth and Dittisham. Located in one of South Devon's most picturesque corners, this tall, character inn is very much a village local with a friendly, welcoming atmosphere inside. Well-prepared fresh food is the hallmark of the menu. Sandwiches, baguettes and pies are available in the bar, while the restaurant menu offers crispy duck with stir-fried vegetables on egg noodles, or oven-baked cod with lemon and lime crust.
OPEN: 12-3 6-11 **BAR MEALS:** L served all week 12.30-2 D served all week 7-9.30 **RESTAURANT:** L served all week 12.30-2 D served all week 7-9.30 ☺: Heavitree ◀: Greene King IPA, Otter, Adnams.
FACILITIES: Patio, several garden tables Dogs allowed Water

LEWDOWN — Map 03 SX48

Pick of the Pubs

The Harris Arms ♀
Portgate EX20 4PZ ☎ 01566 783331 ▤ 01566 783359
e-mail: whiteman@powernet.co.uk
Dir: From A30 take Lifton turning, between Lifton and Lewdown

Nicknamed 'The Gastro-pub on the border', this award-winning 16th-century inn is located on the old A30 close to the boundary between Devon and Cornwall, with wonderful views to Brent Tor. The owners, Rowena and Andy Whiteman, are acknowledged lovers of good food and wine and they have invested a great deal of time and energy in establishing the pub's reputation as an eating place for discerning diners. Having previously run vineyards in France and New Zealand, the Whitemans have devised a wine list that is both eclectic and extensive, with many wines sourced from small producers or ecologically sound wineries. Their objective is to complement the wine by serving what they call 'honest food' using local and seasonal produce. Try pan-fried pork tenderloin, Thai fish casserole, half a Cornish lobster, or breast of guinea fowl with smoked bacon and sage from the specials board. Lighter lunchtime options include fish and chips and a range of filled baguettes.
OPEN: 12-3 5.30-11 (Sun 12-3, 7-10.30 winter 12-3, 6-11)
BAR MEALS: L served all week 12-2 D served all week 6.30-9 Sun 12-2, 7-9 Av main course £8.95 **RESTAURANT:** L served all week 12-2 D served all week 6.30-9 Sun 12-2, 7-9 Av 3 course à la carte £21 ☺: Free House ◀: Skinners Border Bitter, Sharps Doombar, Guinness Extra Cold **FACILITIES:** Child facs Garden: Lawned area with views towards Brentor Dogs allowed
NOTES: Parking 30

LIFTON
Map 03 SX38

Pick of the Pubs

The Arundell Arms ★★★ @@@ ♀
PL16 0AA ☎ 01566 784666 ▤ 01566 784494
e-mail: reservations@arundellarms.com
Dir: *1m off the A30 dual carriageway, 3m E of Launceston*

Owned for 43 years by Anne Voss-Bark, widow of the
BBC's one-time 'Man at Westminster' and subsequently
fishing correspondent for The Times, this creeper-clad,
18th-century coaching inn is in a delightful village on the
edge of Dartmoor. A former owner, William Arundell,
once staked it in a snail race and lost. Anne herself is a
passionate angler, as are many of those who come for
the 20 miles of private fishing, plus shooting, riding and
golf. Both bars - the Courthouse, once the magistrate's
court, and the Arundell - offer meals, while in the
restaurant traditional English and French dishes include
grilled sirloin of Devon beef; fillets of Cornish haddock;
grilled rump of venison; and cured ham, avocado and
rocket salad. The rod and tackle room was once a cock-
fighting pit, one of the few remaining in England.
OPEN: 11.30-3 6-11 **BAR MEALS:** L served all week 12-2.30
D served all week 6-10 Av main course £13
RESTAURANT: L served all week 12.30-2 D served all week
7.30-9.30 Av 3 course à la carte £40 Av 4 course fixed price £35
⊕: Free House ◀: Guest beers. ♀: 9 **FACILITIES:** Child facs
Garden: Terraced garden with fountain Dogs allowed
NOTES: Parking 70 **ROOMS:** 21 bedrooms en suite s£95
d£150

LITTLEHEMPSTON
Map 03 SX86

Tally Ho Inn ▷
TQ9 6NF ☎ 01803 862316 ▤ 01803 862316
Dir: *Off the A38 at Buckfastleigh. A381 between Newton Abbot & Totnes*
A traditional 14th-century inn. In summer the hanging baskets
and flower-filled patio are a delight, while roaring log fires
and cosy corners have their own charm in winter. A great
range of starters, many featuring seafood; chargrills (try the
mixed grill for a real protein fix); chef's dishes of distinction,
such as escalope of pan-fried turkey with orange and brandy
sauce, and oven roasted breast of duckling with cassis and
raspberry sauce; and a good seafood selection. Real ales,
guest beers, selection of malts are all served.
OPEN: 12-3 6-11 (Sun 6-10.30) Closed: Dec 25
BAR MEALS: L served all week 12-2 D served all week 7-9 Sun
12-2.30 Av main course £10.95 ⊕: Free House ◀: London Pride,
Greene King IPA, Whitbread Best Bitter, guest ales.
FACILITIES: Garden: Patio area, picnic benches, grass area Dogs
allowed **NOTES:** Parking 20

LOWER ASHTON
Map 03 SX88

Manor Inn ▷ ♀
EX6 7QL ☎ 01647 252304 e-mail: mark@themanorinn.co.uk
Dir: *A38, Teign Valley turning, follow signs for B3193, pub 5m on right, Just
over the stone bridge*
Picturesque free house set in a Teign Valley village
surrounded by countryside and attractive cottages. The Manor
retains its traditional appeal with blazing log fires in winter
and a sheltered garden with views of fields and hills. All food
is cooked to order, and the comprehensive menu of snacks
and main meals is supplemented by blackboard specials,
including casseroles, game sausages, fresh fish, and curry.
OPEN: 12-2 6.30-11 (Closed Mon ex BHs) **BAR MEALS:** L served
Tue-Sun 12-1.30 D served Tue-Sun 7-9.30 Sun 7-9 Av main course
£7.95 ⊕: Free House ◀: Teignworthy Reel Ale, Princetown Jail Ale,
RCH Pitchfork, changing guest ale. ♀: 10 **FACILITIES:** Sheltered
garden overlooking fields and hills Dogs allowed Water and biscuits
NOTES: Parking 20

LUTON (NEAR CHUDLEIGH)
Map 03 SX97

Pick of the Pubs

The Elizabethan Inn
Fore St TQ13 0BL ☎ 01626 775425 ▤ 01626 775151
e-mail: nick@elizabethaninn.freeserve.co.uk
Dir: *Located between Chudleigh & Teignmouth*
A cosy, country free house dating back to the 16th century,
in a rural farming hamlet that could hardly be more
different from its industrial Bedfordshire namesake. A
frequently changing selection of dishes, made with local
produce wherever possible, may include Exmoor venison
steaks and wild mushrooms; sautéed chicken breast
Toscana; ragout of lamb; Italian-style meatballs and
spaghetti; and lemon sole fillets with prawns. The daily
specials board may feature Hungarian-style beef goulash
soup; Provençale-style local mussels; and Balinese prawn
salad. For vegetarians, the chef likes to produce stuffed red
peppers, and courgette, tomato and mushroom risotto.
Sticky toffee pudding, crème brûlée, and chocolate with
orange and mascarpone cheesecake are typical desserts.
Local cider, Devon and guest beers, and any of 30 malt
whiskies may be enjoyed next to the log fire in the bar.
OPEN: 11-3 6-11 Closed: 26 Dec, 1-2 Jan
BAR MEALS: L served all week 12-2 D served all week 6-9.30
Sun 7-9.30 Av main course £11.95 **RESTAURANT:** L served all
week 12-2 D served all week 6-9.30 Sun 7-9 Av 3 course à la
carte £20 ◀: London Pride, Teignworthy Real Ale, Timothy
Taylor's Landlord, Charleswells Bombardier.
FACILITIES: Garden: Country cottage garden Dogs allowed
Dog bowl **NOTES:** Parking 40

Restaurant and Bar Meal times indicate the times
when food is available. Last orders may be
approximately 30 minutes before the times stated

Most of the pubs in this guide book pride
themselves on the quality of their food. This
may take a little time to prepare

LYDFORD
Map 03 SX58

Pick of the Pubs

Castle Inn ♀
EX20 4BH ☎ 01822 820242 & 820241 🖷 01822 820454
Dir: Off A386 S of Okehampton

This pretty, wisteria-clad inn dates from the 16th century, has a castle next door and one of the nicest beer gardens in the country. No visit would be complete without a look at the impressive Lydford Gorge nearby. The interior oozes atmosphere, with its slate floors, low, lamp-lit beams, decorative plates and huge ancient fireplace. New owners, Richard and Sarah Davies, offer freshly prepared dishes at lunch and dinner. Fresh fish appears daily such as fillet of salmon with coriander dressed noodles and lemon-butter sauce. Starters include warm goat's cheese salad with parma ham or chicken liver and green peppercorn pâté. Main courses include several vegetarian dishes as well as roasts and a confit of duck. Sticky toffee or bread & butter pudding should provide enough calories for the short walk to the gorge and back. The shrub-filled garden is a lovely spot to while away time with a pint, and great for summer dining.
OPEN: 11-11 (Sun 12-10.30) **BAR MEALS:** L served all week 12-2 D served all week 6.30-9 Av main course £8
RESTAURANT: L served all week 12-2 D served all week 6.30-9 🍴: Heavitree 🍺: Fullers London Pride, 6X, Otter Ale. ♀: 13
FACILITIES: Garden: Food served outside. Dogs allowed Allowed in bar & patio **NOTES:** Parking 10

♦ Pubs with Red Diamonds are the top places in the AA's three, four and five diamond ratings

The Hotel Guide — **AA 2006**
Britain's best-selling hotel guide for all your leisure needs.
www.theAA.com

Pick of the Pubs

Dartmoor Inn ◉◉ ♀
EX20 4AY ☎ 01822 820221 🖷 01822 820494
e-mail: karen@dartmoorinn.co.uk
Dir: On A386 S of Okehampton

This 16th-century coaching inn is steeped in history. Set in the pretty village of Lydford on the western side of Dartmoor National Park, it is almost certainly described in Charles Kingsley's novel *Westward Ho!* Original features create a traditional atmosphere while small, intimate dining areas establish a cosy feel. Décor is informally rustic with gentle colours, intricate patchworks and fresh and dried flowers. Log fires in the winter make the bar an inviting place in which to enjoy a pre-dinner drink. Seasonal and locally produced ingredients are turned into an array of Modern British dishes which could include steamed scallops with an oriental dressing, pan fried lambs' kidneys with warm salad leaves, or a mixed grill of sea fishes with garlic and parsley butter. Puddings like honey custard tart with a fruit compote bring meals to a close. Periodically, special themed menus are offered such as 'Lavender Harvest' or 'Stir Fry'. This is enjoyable pub dining of a high standard.
OPEN: 11.30-3 6.30-11 (6-11 in Summer)
BAR MEALS: L served Tue-Sun 12-2.15 D served Tue-Sat 6.30-9.15 Av main course £14.75 **RESTAURANT:** L served Tue-Sun 12-2.15 D served Tue-Sat 6.30-9.15 🍴: Free House 🍺: Interbrew Bass, Otter Ale, Austell Hicks Special & Dartmoor Best. ♀: 6 **FACILITIES:** Garden: Paved area with umbrellas Dogs allowed Water & Food **NOTES:** Parking 35

LYMPSTONE
Map 03 SX98

The Globe Inn 🛏 ♀
The Strand EX8 5EY ☎ 01395 263166
Set in the estuary village of Lympstone, this traditional beamed inn has a good local reputation for seafood. The separate restaurant area serves as a coffee bar during the day. Look out for seafood platter, Thai grilled haddock, bass with plum and ginger sauce, crab sandwiches, tapas, lasagne, and battered fish and chips on Thursdays. Weekend music nights. Quiz night weekly.
OPEN: 11-3 5.30-11 **BAR MEALS:** L served all week 12-2 D served Mon-Sat 6.30-9.30 Av main course £7 **RESTAURANT:** L served all week D served Mon-Sat 7-9.30 Av 3 course à la carte £17
🍴: Heavitree 🍺: London Pride, Otter, Bass, Whitbread Best. ♀: 6
FACILITIES: Dogs allowed Water & treats provided

LYNMOUTH   Map 03 SS74

Pick of the Pubs

Rising Sun Hotel ★★ ☺☺ ♀
Harbourside EX35 6EG ☎ 01598 753223 ▣ 01598 753480
e-mail: risingsunlynmouth@easynet.co.uk
web: www.risingsunlynmouth.co.uk
Dir: *From M5 junct 25 follow Minehead signs. A39 to Lynmouth*

Overlooking Lynmouth's tiny harbour and bay is the Rising Sun, a 14th-century thatched smugglers' inn. In turn, overlooking them all, are Countisbury Cliffs, the highest in England. The building's long history is evident from the uneven oak floors, crooked ceilings and thick walls. Literary associations are plentiful: R D Blackmore wrote some of his wild Exmoor romance, *Lorna Doone*, here; the poet Shelley is believed to have honeymooned in the garden cottage; and Coleridge stayed too. Immediately behind rises Exmoor Forest and National Park, home to red deer, wild ponies and birds of prey. With sea and moor so close, game and seafood are in plentiful supply, and pheasant, venison, hare, wild boar, monkfish, crab or scallops, for example, will appear variously as starter or main course dishes. At night the oak-panelled, candlelit dining room is an example of romantic British inn-keeping at its best.
OPEN: 11-11 (Open all day all year) **BAR MEALS:** L served all week 12-4 D served all week 7-9 Av main course £7
RESTAURANT: L served all week 12-2 D served all week 7-9 Av 3 course à la carte £32 ☺: Free House ◀: Exmoor Gold, Fox & Exmoor Ale, Cotleigh Tawny Ale. **FACILITIES:** Garden: Beautiful terraced garden, sea views **ROOMS:** 16 bedrooms en suite 2 family rooms s£59 d£78 No children overnight

LYNTON   Map 03 SS74

The Bridge Inn
Lynbridge Hill EX35 6NR ☎ 01598 753425 ▣ 01598 753225
e-mail: bridgeinnlynton@hotmail.co.uk
web: www.bridgeinnlynton.co.uk
Dir: *Turn off the A39 at Barbrook onto the B3234. Continue for 1m, located on the right just after the Sunny Lyn camp site.*
Attractive 17th-century riverside inn overlooked by National Trust woodlands. In the cellars the remains of 12th-century salmon fishermen's cottages are still visible, and the unusually shaped windows at the front originally belonged to Charles I's hunting lodge at Coombe House which were salvaged following flood damage in the 1680s. The 1952 Lynmouth Flood destroyed the Lyn Bridge and car park, but most of the pub survived intact. Recent change of hands - reports welcome.
OPEN: 12-3 6-11 (Summer & Xmas open 12-11, Sun 7-10.30-winter)
BAR MEALS: L served all week 12-2.30 D served all week 6-9.30

continued

Sun 7-10.30 (winter) Av main course £8.95
RESTAURANT: L served all week 12-2.30 D served all week 6-9.30
☺: Free House ◀: St. Austell Tribute, Sharps Doombar, Exmoor Fox.
FACILITIES: Children's licence Garden: Patio with picnic tables, benches Dogs allowed **NOTES:** Parking 14

MARLDON   Map 03 SX86

The Church House Inn ♀
Village Rd TQ3 1SL ☎ 01803 558279 ▣ 01803 664865
Dir: *Take Torquay ring road, follow signs to Marldon & Totnes, follow brown signs to Church House Inn*
Originally a 14th-century hostel for the builders of the adjoining village church, boasting beautiful Georgian windows that were added in 1740. With Brixham just down the road, expect at least four choices of fish and seafood, such as monkfish with cherry tomatoes, pine nuts, fresh basil and olive oil; or king prawns pan-fried in coriander, ginger and lime butter. A meaty alternative is shoulder of lamb with a redcurrant, orange and red wine sauce.
OPEN: 11.30-2.30 5-11 (Sat 11-11) (Sun 12-10.30)
BAR MEALS: L served all week 12-2 D served all week 6.30-9.30
RESTAURANT: L served all week 12-2 D served all week 6.30-9.30
◀: Dartmoor Best, Bass, Old Speckled Hen, Greene King IPA. ♀: 10
FACILITIES: Garden: Lawned area, hanging baskets, patios Dogs allowed Water Bowls **NOTES:** Parking 50

MEAVY   Map 03 SX56

The Royal Oak Inn ♀
PL20 6PJ ☎ 01822 852944
Dir: *Off A386 between Tavistock & Plymouth*
Standing on the edge of Dartmoor, between Tavistock and Plymouth, this 12th-century brew house is a popular watering hole for those touring and exploring the National Park. Good quality fare is prepared from produce bought locally, and much of the meat is free-range. A local fishmonger delivers fresh fish from Plymouth. Expect filled baguettes, local pasties and salads at lunchtime, while the evening menu consists of stuffed plaice, lemon butterfly chicken, and salsa sardines.
OPEN: 11-3 6.30-11 (Sun 12-3, 6.30-10.30) **BAR MEALS:** L served all week 12-2 D served all week 6.30-9 No smoking during serving hrs Av main course £5 ☺: Free House ◀: Bass, Princetown Jail Ale, IPA. ♀: 12 **FACILITIES:** Dogs allowed

MOLLAND   Map 03 SS82

The London Inn
EX36 3NG ☎ 01769 550269
Just below Exmoor lies peaceful Molland, and to find its church is to find this 15th-century inn. Historic features abound, but try and picture today's spacious dining room as the original inn, and the bar as the brewhouse. The frequently-changing menu features savoury pancakes, Welsh rarebit, mixed grill, as well as ploughman's, jackets and sandwiches. No credit cards.
OPEN: 11.30-2.30 6-11 (Sun 12-3, 7-10.30) **BAR MEALS:** L served all week 12-2 D served all week 7-9 Av main course £10
RESTAURANT: L served all week D served all week ☺: Free House
◀: Exmoor Ale, Cotleigh Tawny Bitter. **FACILITIES:** Child facs Garden: Dogs allowed Water **NOTES:** Parking 12 No credit cards

 ★ Star rating for inspected hotel accommodation

MORETONHAMPSTEAD
Map 03 SX78

White Hart Hotel NEW ♥
The Square TQ13 8NF ☎ 01647 441340 ▤ 01647 441341
e-mail: whitehart1600@aol.com
Dir: *In Dartmoor National Park, 16m from Exeter*
This grade II listed building was a meeting place for French
officers on parole from Dartmoor's nearby prison during the
Napoleonic Wars. Today's stylish hotel provides both a well-
stocked bar offering lunch and a brasserie serving up a
contemporary combination of dishes: chargrilled aubergine
and brie; pan fried calves' liver with red onion marmalade; or
roast loin of venison with butter beans.
OPEN: 8-12 **BAR MEALS:** L served all week 12-2 Sun 12-2.30
D served all week Av main course £6.50 **RESTAURANT:** L served
Sun 12-2 D served all week 6.30-9 Av 3 course à la carte £21
◑: ◪: Tribute, Dartmoor, Bass, HSD. ♥: 16
FACILITIES: Children's licence Garden: Courtyard with tables Dogs
allowed **NOTES:** Parking 7 **ROOMS:** 21 bedrooms en suite
1 family room s£45 d£90 (★★)

NEWTON ABBOT
Map 03 SX87

The Linny Inn & Hayloft Dining Area ♥
Coffinswell TQ12 4SR ☎ 01803 873192 ▤ 01803 873395
e-mail: markgilstone@aol.com
Dir: *Follow signs from A380*
In a largely-thatched village near Torquay, the Linny dates
from about 1368, but it's been a pub only since 1969 after 15
years as a country club. The name comes from linhay, an
outbuilding, which the snugs originally were. The inn enjoys a
high reputation with a range of tasty starters, pastas, salads,
fresh Torbay fish and vegetarian dishes, as well as succulent
steaks and roasts. A patio leads to the suntrap garden.
OPEN: 11.30-3 6.30-11 (Closed Mon Jan-Feb)
BAR MEALS: L served all week 12-2 D served all week 6.30-9.30
RESTAURANT: 12-2 6.30-9.30 ◑: Free House
◪: Carlsberg-Tetley, Real Ales. **FACILITIES:** Garden
NOTES: Parking 34

The Wild Goose Inn 🐟 ♥
Combeinteignhead TQ12 4RA ☎ 01626 872241
Dir: *From A380 at the Newton Abbot rdbt, take the B3195 Shaldon rd,
signed Milber, for 2.5m into village then right at signpost*
Virtually unchanged since it was first licensed in 1840, the
name of this Devon longhouse immortalises a flock of geese
that used to leap from a high field onto passers-by. Its
peaceful beer garden overlooks a 14th-century church and a
stream winding its way down to the River Teign. A good
choice of traditional home-made food includes traditional
butchers faggots, whole Brixham plaice, and Torbay mussels.
Real ales from West Country micro-breweries.
OPEN: 11.30-2.30 6.30-11 (Sun 12-2.30, 7-10.30)
BAR MEALS: L served all week 12-2 D served all week 7-9.30 Sun
12-2, 7-9.30 Av main course £6.95 **RESTAURANT:** L served all
week 12-2 D served all week 7-10 ◑: Free House ◪: Otter Ale,
Cotleigh, Sharps Bitter, Skinner's Bitter. ♥: 8 **FACILITIES:** Garden:
Overlooking farmyard, small stream & church Dogs allowed Water
NOTES: Parking 40

NEWTON ST CYRES
Map 03 SX89

The Beer Engine 🐟
EX5 5AX ☎ 01392 851282 ▤ 01392 851876
e-mail: enquiries@thebeerengine.co.uk
Dir: *From Exeter take A377 towards Crediton, pub is opposite train station*

A pretty, whitewashed free house, formerly a railway hotel.
The proprietors have been brewing their own beer for 20
years, making it the longest established Devon brewery. As for
food, expect a home-cooked extravaganza: dishes range from
haddock in the landlord's own Brewery Batter (made with
wort) through to African spicy lamb, home-made steak pies,
monkfish in cream and whisky sauce, and plenty of good
vegetarian options. Sunday lunches draw many people.
OPEN: 11-11 (Sun 12-10.30) **BAR MEALS:** L served all week 12-2
D served all week 6.30-9.30 Sun 12-2, 6.30-9 Av main course £7
RESTAURANT: L served all week 12-2 D served all week 6.30-9.30
Sun 12-2, 6.30-9 ◑: Free House ◪: Beer Engine Ales: Piston Bitter,
Rail Ale, Sleeper Heavy. **FACILITIES:** Child facs Garden: Terraced
with paved area, flowers Dogs allowed on leads **NOTES:** Parking 30

Crown and Sceptre
EX5 5DA ☎ 01392 851278
Dir: *2m NW of Exeter on A377*
Twice razed by fire (the last time in 1962), today's pub has
still managed to keep original character with oak beams and
open fires, while summer barbecues and children's play areas
feature among its added attractions. From straightforward bar
meals of pies of the day, curries and 'big plate specials' (such
as the 24oz mixed grill), the dining menu extends to duck
breast with plum sauce, Mexican chilli and grilled steaks with
saucy options such as chasseur and Diane.
OPEN: 11.30-11 (winter 11.30-3 6-11) **BAR MEALS:** L served all
week 12-9 D served all week Av main course £5.95
RESTAURANT: L served all week 12-2 D served all week 6-9
Av 3 course à la carte £15 ◑: Heavitree ◪: Otter Ale plus guest
beers. **FACILITIES:** Garden: Patio area, food served outside
NOTES: Parking 30

Pubs with this logo do not allow smoking
anywhere on their premises

Pubs offering a good choice of fish on
their menu

 Brewery/Company

All AA rated accommodation can also be
found on the AA's internet site
www.theAA.com

Not all of the pubs in the guide are open all
week or all day. It's always best to check before
you travel

NOSS MAYO   Map 03 SX54

Pick of the Pubs

The Ship Inn ♀
PL8 1EW ☎ 01752 872387 ▤ 01752 873294
e-mail: ship@nossmayo.com
Dir: 5m S if Yealmpton on River Yealm estuary
Imposing waterside free house with a terrace overlooking
the scenic estuary. The 16th-century inn is true to its
roots, with wood floors, log fires, comfortable old
furniture, papers and books. There's a good selection of
local and regional beers, and local produce is the
foundation of the daily changing menu. Mainly English
dishes include cheese-topped baked cod, braised shank of
lamb, and loin of Devon pork with winter fruit stuffing
and dry cider sauce.
OPEN: 11-11 **BAR MEALS:** L served all week 12-9.30 D served
all week Av main course £11 ◉: Free House ◖: Tamar,
Shepherd Neame Spitfire Premium Ale, Vail Ale, Butcombe
Blonde. ♀: 10 **FACILITIES:** Garden: Waterside Dogs allowed
downstairs only **NOTES:** Parking 100 ⊚

OTTERY ST MARY   Map 03 SY19

The Talaton Inn ⤳
Talaton EX5 2RQ ☎ 01404 822214 ▤ 01404 822214

Timber-framed, well-maintained 16th-century inn, run by a
brother and sister partnership. A strong seafood emphasis
means that the menu may feature poached salmon
hollandaise, cod and chips, seafood platter, or scampi.
Blackboard specials change regularly, and may include
chicken Wellington or fillet steak Rossini. Good selection of
real ales and malts, and a fine collection of bar games.
OPEN: 12-3 7-11 (12-3 6-11 Summer) **BAR MEALS:** L served all
week 12-2 D served Tue-Sat 7-9.15 (Sun no food eve) Av main course
£7 **RESTAURANT:** L served all week 12-2.15 D served Tue-Sat 7-9.15
(Sun no food eve) ◉: Free House ◖: Otter, Fuller's London Pride,
O'Hanlon's, Badger Tanglefoot. **FACILITIES:** Small courtyard with 4
benches Dogs allowed **NOTES:** Parking 30

PARRACOMBE   Map 03 SS64

Pick of the Pubs

The Fox & Goose ♦♦♦ ♀
EX31 4PE ☎ 01598 763239 ▤ 01598 763621
See Pick of the Pubs on opposite page

PLYMOUTH   Map 03 SX45

Langdon Court Hotel ★★ ◉ ♀
Down Thomas PL9 0DY ☎ 01752 862358 ▤ 01752 863428
e-mail: enquiries@langdoncourt.co.uk
Dir: On A379 from Elburton follow brown tourist signs
Once owned by Henry VIII, this historic, picturesque manor
became the home of his last wife Catherine Parr. The
Elizabethan walled garden is Grade II listed. Close to
outstanding coastal scenery. Primarily a hotel, Langdon Court
offers a comfortable bar with freshly cooked meals and real
ale. Menu includes whole roasted John Dory with shellfish
risotto, rack of Devon lamb, steak and kidney pudding, and
baked cod with saffron mash and brown shrimp salsa.
OPEN: 12-3 6.30-11 Closed: 25-26 Dec **BAR MEALS:** L served all
week 12-2 D served all week 6.30-9.30 Av main course £11
RESTAURANT: L served all week 12-2.30 D served all week
6.30-9.30 Av 3 course à la carte £25 ◉: Free House ◖: Dartmoor
Best, Bass. **FACILITIES:** Garden: Food served outside, Elizabethan
gardens Dogs allowed **NOTES:** Parking 50 **ROOMS:** 17 bedrooms
en suite s£62.50 d£90

POSTBRIDGE   Map 03 SX67

Warren House Inn
PL20 6TA ☎ 01822 880208
Dir: Take B3212 through Moretonhampstead and on for 5m
High up on Dartmoor, this old tin miners' inn was cut off
during the harsh winter of 1963 and supplies were delivered
by helicopter. A peat fire has burned here continuously since
1845. Home-made cauliflower cheese, seafood platter,
mushroom stroganoff, rabbit pie and venison steak in a port
and cranberry sauce feature among the popular dishes. Good
choice of snacks and sandwiches.
OPEN: 11-2.30 6-11 (Sun til 10:30 May-Oct open all day)
BAR MEALS: L served all week 12-2 D served all week 6-9.30
Av main course £5 ◉: Free House ◖: Sharps Doom Bar,
Butcombe Bitter, Badger Tanglefoot, Old Freddy Walker.
FACILITIES: Garden: Food served outside Dogs allowed Water
NOTES: Parking 30

RACKENFORD   Map 03 SS81

The 12th Century Stag Inn ♀
EX16 8DT ☎ 01884 881369
It's hard to imagine a more traditional inn than the Stag,
which as its name proclaims dates from the 12th century, and
which has a thatched roof and all original features, including
beams and open fireplace. There's even a ghost - Tom King,
highwayman. The pub is located opposite a 12th-century
church, and is ideal for families and dog lovers who enjoy
walking. Dishes include home-made pasties, steaks, sticky ribs
and freshly made curries.
OPEN: 11-3.30 6-11 (Open all day in Summer)
BAR MEALS: L served all week 12-3 D served all week 7-10
Av main course £5.99 **RESTAURANT:** L served all week 12-3
D served all week 7-10 ◖: Cotleigh Barn Owl & Tawny, Scottish
Courage John Smith's Smooth. ♀: 10 **FACILITIES:** Two gardens,
overlooking open fields Dogs allowed Water & toys provided
NOTES: Parking 20

Website addresses are included where available.
The AA cannot be held responsible for the
content of any of these websites

Pick of the Pubs

The Fox & Goose

Set in the heart of an unspoilt Exmoor village, this charming free house was originally no more than a couple of tiny thatched cottages serving the local farming community. The landlord enlarged the building to compete with nearby hotels after the narrow gauge Lynton & Barnstaple Railway linked Parracombe with the outside world in 1898.

Then, in 1925, the village's narrow street was sidelined by an early bypass, which may have contributed to the closure of the railway just ten years later. Through all this, the pub has remained a relaxing place where drinkers are welcomed with a selection of local ales including Cotleigh Barn Owl; Dartmoor Best; and Exmoor Gold. Nowadays, the Fox also enjoys a sound reputation for good food, with meals served in the bar, as well as in the non-smoking restaurant and paved courtyard garden overlooking the river. There's a wide selection of dishes to suit all tastes, based on produce from the surrounding farms and the Devon coast. The blackboard menus keep pace with daily changes, which

might include rustic patés, venison, lamb and fillet steak, rich casseroles with tender vegetables, and hearty pies. There are stroganoffs and stirfries, too, and seafood lovers won't be disappointed with a selection that encompasses seasonal crabs and lobster, as well as cod fillet with tiger prawns; skate wing with caper salsa; bouillabaisse; and trout fillet with a muschroom white wine sauce. Four en suite bedrooms make the Fox an ideal touring base and - who knows? - visitors may once again be able to see Exmoor by train. Nearly seventy years after the railway's closure, a short section of line near Parracombe has been reopened, and there are ambitious plans for future extensions.

OPEN: 12-3 6-11
BAR MEALS: L served all week 12-2
D served all week 6-9 Av main
course £11.50
🍺: Free House
🍺: Cotleigh Barn Owl, Carlsberg,
Dartmoor Best, Exmoor Gold. ♀: 10
FACILITIES: Garden: Paved courtyard
overlooking river Dogs allowed
Water, outside **NOTES:** Parking 15
ROOMS: 1 bedroom en suite s£30
d£45 No children overnight

♦♦♦ ♀   Map 03 SS64
EX31 4PE
☎ 01598 763239
📄 01598 763621
Dir: The Fox is 1m from the A39
between Blackmoor Gate (2m)
and Lynton (6m). Signposted to
Parracombe (With a 'Fox &
Goose' sign on approach)

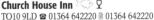

England

RATTERY
Map 03 SX76

Church House Inn 🍽️ ♀
TQ10 9LD ☎ 01364 642220 📠 01364 642220
e-mail: ray12@onetel.com

Dating from 1028, Devon's oldest inn is also one of the oldest in the UK. Large open fireplaces, sturdy oak beams and loads of nooks and crannies. Traditional English pub food includes sandwiches, baguettes, salads and ploughmans. Heartier courses may include citrus and olive lamb shank, chicken in whisky cream sauce, stilton and vegetable crumble, pork and leek sausages, various grills, and a good variety of fish including trout, John Dory, brill, halibut and sea bass. Interesting choice of alcoholic coffees to finish, including Caribbean, Mexican and Gaelic.
OPEN: 11-3 6-11 (Winter 11-2.30, 6.30-10.30)
BAR MEALS: L served all week 12-2 D served all week 7-9
RESTAURANT: L served all week 12-2 D served all week 7-9
🍴: Free House 🍺: St Austell Dartmoor Best, Greene King Abbot Ale, George Gale HSB, Otter Ale. ♀: 8 **FACILITIES:** Children's licence Garden: Large lawn, seating, benches Dogs allowed Water
NOTES: Parking 30

ROCKBEARE
Map 03 SY09

Pick of the Pubs

Jack in the Green Inn 🐮🐮 🍽️ ♀
London Rd EX5 2EE ☎ 01404 822240 📠 01404 823445
e-mail: info@jackinthegreen.uk.com
web: www.jackinthegreen.uk.com
See Pick of the Pubs on opposite page

SALCOMBE
Map 03 SX73

Pick of the Pubs

The Victoria Inn 🍽️ ♀
Fore St TQ8 8BU ☎ 01548 842604 📠 01548 844201
e-mail: info@victoriainnsalcombe.co.uk
See Pick of the Pubs on page 152

SHEEPWASH
Map 03 SS40

Half Moon Inn
EX21 5NE ☎ 01409 231376 📠 01409 231673
e-mail: lee@halfmoon.demon.co.uk
Dir: From M5 take A30 to Okehampton then A386, at Hatheleigh, left onto A3072, after 4m right for Sheepwash

A very popular venue for anglers, this white-painted inn overlooking the village square in a remote Devon village is a Grade II listed building with fishing rights for ten miles of the River Torridge. Inside you'll find slate floors and a huge inglenook fireplace where a log fire burns in cooler weather. Bar snacks are available at lunchtime and a set menu of traditional fare at dinner. Dishes are traditionally English. Over 60 malts and 340 wines are available.
OPEN: 11-2.30 6-11 Closed: 20-27 Dec **BAR MEALS:** L served all week 12-1.45 **RESTAURANT:** D served all week 8 🍴: Free House 🍺: Scottish Courage Courage Best, Sharpe's Own, Greene King Ruddles Best Bitter. **FACILITIES:** Dogs allowed **NOTES:** Parking 30

SIDMOUTH
Map 03 SY18

The Blue Ball ♦♦♦♦ 🍽️ ♀
Stevens Cross, Sidford EX10 9QL
☎ 01395 514062 📠 01395 514062
e-mail: rogernewton@blueballinn.net
Dir: On A3052 approx 12m from Exeter
Run by the same family for over 90 years, this thatched pub dates back to 1385 and is built of cob and flint. Converted from its farmhouse origins, the bar occupies the old dairy, with beams and log fires inside and a garden with a terrace and playhouse outside. Food centres round fresh fish and other local produce, and options range from ploughman's and sandwiches to steak and ale pudding, grilled fillet of fresh salmon, and local sausages.
OPEN: 11-11 Closed: 25 Dec eve **BAR MEALS:** L served all week 11-2 D served all week 6-9.30 Food all day Sun Av main course £7.50
🍴: Pubmaster 🍺: Interbrew Bass & Flowers IPA, Otter Bitter, Greene King Old Speckled Hen, Guest ale each week. ♀: 10
FACILITIES: Child facs Garden: Large colourful gardens, quiet areas Dogs allowed Water **NOTES:** Parking 100 **ROOMS:** 6 bedrooms 4 en suite 1 family room s£30 d£50

Room prices show the minimum double and single rates charged. Room rates in hotels and B&Bs often vary depending on the facilities, so be sure to check prices with the establishment before booking

We only include details of accommodation that has been inspected by the AA (big Stars or Diamonds at the top of an entry), or the RAC, VisitBritain, VisitScotland or WTB (small Stars or Diamonds at the end of an entry)

Jack in the Green Inn

There has been a pub on this site for several centuries, but the name is even older. It has pagan origins associated with spring fertility celebrations, presided over by a character known as the Green Man. The area is also well-known for its cider apple trees.

The Parnells have been here for thirteen years and have built the pub up to be a popular dining venue with their simple philosophy: to serve real food to real people who want to eat and drink in comfortable surrounding and be served by nice people. Whether you're stopping by for a bar snack, or a fuller meal in the restaurant, the quality is evident in everything produced. Start with caramelised scallops with leeks, star anise and orange sauce; or kiln roast salmon with caper and parsley vinaigrette, then continue with stilton and baby leek eccles cake with toasted pine nuts; fillet of sea bass with fragrant rice and soy dip, braised pork belly with roasted vegetables and aubergine caviar, or roast partridge with quince purée and game jus. Tempting desserts include ginger and strawberry mousse, and pear fritters with mulled wine syrup and cinnamon ice cream. The pub is set in four acres of grounds and gardens overlooking East Devon countryside, and in summer you can sit outside and enjoy the view. Extensive but well-chosen wine list.

OPEN: 11-2.30 6-11 (Sun 12-10.30)
Closed: Dec 25 - Jan 5 inclusive
BAR MEALS: L served all week 11-2
D served all week 6-9.30 Sun 12-9.30
Av main course £11
RESTAURANT: L served all week
11-2 D served all week 6-9.30 Fixed
price menu Sun. Sun 12-9.30
Av 3 course à la carte £24
Av 3 course fixed price £23.95
🍺: Free House
🍺: Cotleigh Tawny Ale, Thomas
Hardy Hardy Country, Otter Ale,
Royal Oak. ♀: 12
FACILITIES: Garden: Benches Dogs
allowed Water outside, field for
walks **NOTES:** Parking 120

   Map 03 SY09
London Rd EX5 2EE
☎ 01404 822240
🖹 01404 823445
🄴 info@jackinthegreen.uk.com
🅦 www.jackinthegreen.uk.com
Dir: From M5 take old A30
towards Honiton, signed
Rockbeare

Pick of the Pubs

SALCOMBE – DEVON

The Victoria Inn

Set in the picturesque harbour town of Salcombe, with over 2000 acres of National Trust countryside surrounding it, this newly refurbished inn has a strong focus on food, as well as stunning views of the town from the first floor restaurant.

Fresh local seafood is a regular feature of the daily-changing specials boards, so look out for the award-winning signature dish shellfish chowder; fresh Salcombe white crabmeat platter; pan-fried turbot wrapped in smoked bacon; oven-baked sea bass; grilled John Dory fillet with buttered tagliatelle; Salcombe crabmeat salad with prawns; monkfish tail collops in crispy beer batter; and smoked haddock mornay topped with creamy mashed potato. There is no shortage of non-fish dishes either: home-made chicken and duck liver with wild mushroom, pink peppercorn and brandy pâté; hot leek tart with grilled smoked back bacon; chicken, ham and mushroom pie; slowly roasted half shoulder of Devon lamb; Aune Valley pork and apple sausages; home-made lamb and apricot pie; home-made vegetarian pancakes with Devonshire cheese sauce; and grilled fillet of Aune Valley beef with a wild mushroom, pink peppercorn and port sauce. Desserts might offer up rich hot chocolate mousse with red berry compote; chilled light lemon soufflé with lemon shortbread; and fresh vanilla crème caramel. Following the £125,000 refurbishment in 2004, look out for a new fully-equipped children's activity play area complete with safety surfaces in the large landscaped garden.

OPEN: 11-11 (may close 3-6pm during Winter)
BAR MEALS: L served all week 12-2.30 D served all week 6-9 Av main course £9.95
RESTAURANT: D served all week 7-9
🍺: St Austell Brewery
🍺: St Austell Tribute, Dartmoor Best, St Austell HSD, Black Prince & Tinners. ♀: 9
FACILITIES: Child facs Garden: Large beer garden with play area Dogs allowed Water bowls and free biscuits

🐟 ♀   Map 03 SX73
Fore St TQ8 8BU
☎ 01548 842604
📠 01548 844201
📧 info@victoriainnsalcombe.co.uk
🌐 www.victoriainnsalcombe.co.uk
Dir: Centre of Salcombe, overlooking estuary. 12m from Totnes railway station, 20m from M5 junct 34

England

SLAPTON   Map 03 SX84

Pick of the Pubs

The Tower Inn 🍽 ⚲
Church Rd TQ7 2PN ☎ 01548 580216
e-mail: towerinn@slapton.org
See Pick of the Pubs on page 154

SOURTON   Map 03 SX59

The Highwayman Inn
EX20 4HN ☎ 01837 861243 ▤ 01837 861196
e-mail: info@thehighwaymaninn.net
web: www.thehighwaymaninn.net
Dir: Situated on the A386 Okehampton to Tavistock Rd off main A30 towards Tavistock. Pub is 4m from Okehampton, 12m from Tavistock

A fascinating old inn full of eccentric furniture, unusual architectural designs, and strange bric-a-brac. Since 1959 the vision of Welshman John 'Buster' Jones, and now run by his daughter Sally, it is made from parts of sailing ships, wood hauled from Dartmoor's bogs, and Gothic church arches. Popular with holidaymakers and international tourists, the menu consists of light snacks including pasties, platters and organic nibbles. In the garden, the kids will enjoy Mother Hubbard's Shoe, and the Pumpkin House.
OPEN: 11-2 6-10.30 (Sun 12-2, 7-10.30) Jan & Feb Closed Mons
BAR MEALS: L served all week 11-1.45 D served all week 🍴: Free House 🍺: St Anstell Duchy, Teignworthy. **FACILITIES:** Garden: Tables and Benches Dogs allowed **NOTES:** Parking 150

SOUTH POOL   Map 03 SX74

The Millbrook Inn 🍽 ⚲
TQ7 2RW ☎ 01548 531581 e-mail: cjstarkey@hotmail.com
Dir: Take A379 from Kingsbridge to Frogmore then E
Take the ferry to East Portlemouth, cross over the stepping stones at Waterhead and follow a quiet country lane to this quaint 16th-century village pub. It is cosy and unspoilt inside, with open fires, fresh flowers, cushioned wheelback chairs, and beams adorned with old banknotes and clay pipes. Fish is a speciality, and there's a peaceful sunny rear terrace overlooking a stream with ducks.
OPEN: 12-3 6-11 (open all day Aug, Sun 12-3, 6-10.30)
BAR MEALS: L served all week 12-2 D served all week 7-9 Av main course £7.95 🍴: Free House 🍺: Bass, Sharps Doombar, Otter Ale, Teignworthy Reel. ⚲: 12 **FACILITIES:** Garden: Paved area with canopy available Dogs allowed Water Bowls

SOUTH ZEAL   Map 03 SX69

Oxenham Arms ★★ 🍽
EX20 2JT ☎ 01837 840244 ▤ 01837 840791
e-mail: theoxenhamarms@aol.com
Dir: Just off A30 4m E of Okehampton in the centre of the village
First licensed in 1477, but probably built by monks in the 12th century, the building is scheduled as an Ancient Monument. In the lounge is a stone shaped by prehistoric man, which archaeologists believe the monks built around. Local produce features strongly, with curries and sausages available in the bar. The garden overlooks Cosdon Hill and Cawsand Beacon.
OPEN: 11-2.30 5-11 (All day Sat, Sun 12-2.30, 7-10.30)
BAR MEALS: L served all week 12-1.45 D served all week 6.30-8.45 Summer food all day Sat Av main course £8.50
RESTAURANT: L served all week 12-1.45 D served all week 6.30-8.4 Summer 6-8.45 Av 3 course à la carte £20 🍴: Free House 🍺: Sharp's Doom Bar Bitter, Sharps Special Ale, Archers Golden, Sharps Own. **FACILITIES:** Child facs Garden: Overlooking Cosdon Hill, Cawsand Beacon Dogs allowed Water **NOTES:** Parking 8
ROOMS: 8 bedrooms 7 en suite 3 family rooms s£40 d£50 (★★)

SPREYTON   Map 03 SX69

The Tom Cobley Tavern 🍽
EX17 5AL ☎ 01647 231314
Dir: From Merrymeet rdbt take A3124 N. Right at Post Inn, then 1st right over bridge.

From this pub one day in 1802 a certain Thomas Cobley and his companions set forth for Widecombe Fair, recorded and remembered in the famous song. Today, this traditional village local offers a good selection of bar snacks, lighter fare and home-made main meals, including pies, salads, duck and fish dishes, as well as a good vegetarian selection. Finish off with one of the great ice creams or sorbets, including white chocolate and vodka! The garden is in a pretty setting.
OPEN: 12-2 6-11 (Mon open Summer, BHs)
BAR MEALS: L served Tue-Sun 12-2 D served Tue-Sun 7-9 Av main course £8 **RESTAURANT:** L served Sun 12-2 D served Wed-Sat 7-8.45 🍴: Free House 🍺: Cotleigh Tawny Ale, Interbrew Bass, Tom Lobely Bitter, Doom Bar Tribute. **FACILITIES:** Child facs Garden: Wooden seated area, approx 8 benches **NOTES:** Parking 8
ROOMS: 4 bedrooms 1 family room s£24.50 (♦♦♦)

All AA rated accommodation can also be found on the AA's internet site
www.theAA.com

Pick of the Pubs
SLAPTON – DEVON

The Tower Inn

A charming 14th-century inn approached down a narrow lane in a delightful historic village, and entered through a rustic porch. It owes its name to the ruined tower overlooking the pub's walled garden, now all that remains of the Collegiate Chantry of St Mary whose builders ate and slept within the same four walls as visitors do today.

In far more recent times, during 1943-44, Slapton was invaded by American servicemen, in Britain to practise amphibious landings for the D-Day attack on Normandy beaches. The pub's interior is a fascinating series of low-ceilinged, interconnecting rooms with stone walls and fireplaces, beams, pillars and pews, and decorated with plants, a giant cartwheel, brasses, pictures and violins. Starters from the lunch menu include a platter of locally smoked prawns, mackerel, trout and salmon; pheasant and pistachio terrine with apricot, roasted shallot, cherry tomato and rocket; and twice-baked gruyère and spinach soufflé. Main courses may be beef and ale pie; red wine and plum-braised lamb shank with horseradish creamed potatoes; and

beer-battered cod fillet with potato wedges. There's also a choice of well-filled sandwiches. At dinner, in addition to some of the lunchtime selection, there are different starters like crispy fried duck confit on caramelised vermicelli with cucumber, spring onion and plum sauce; and main courses such as roasted chicken supreme stuffed with mozzarella, sun-dried tomato and basil; crisp-fried red mullet fillets with olive mash, roasted red pepper pesto and rocket; and fillet and sirloin steaks. The daily-changing specials offer yet more possibilities. Traditional bread and butter pudding can be served with ice cream, clotted cream or custard. An excellent range of beers includes ales from Adnams and St Austell, plus local cider, and mulled wine in winter.

OPEN: 12-3 6-11 (Sun 7-10.30)
Closed: Sun & Mon eve in winter
25 Dec
BAR MEALS: L served all week
12-2.30 D served all week 6-9.30
RESTAURANT: L served all week
12-2.30 D served all week 7-9.30
⊞: Free House
◖: Adnams Southwold, Badger
Tanglefoot, St Austell, Tower. ♀: 8
FACILITIES: Child facs Garden:
Beautiful walled garden Dogs
allowed Water, biscuits
NOTES: Parking 6

🐟 ♀   Map 03 SX84
Church Rd TQ7 2PN
☎ 01548 580216
ℯ towerinn@slapton.org
Dir: Off A379 S of Dartmouth,
turn left at Slapton Sands

England

Pick of the Pubs

The Sea Trout ★★ ◉ ♀
TQ9 6PA ☎ 01803 762274 🖷 01803 762506
e-mail: enquiries@seatroutinn.com
web: www.seatroutinn.com
Dir: M5/A38

Situated in the tranquil rural surroundings of the Dart
Valley, this attractive 15th-century inn has a loyal local
following. It's a rambling, whitewashed building with a
relaxed atmosphere; a good combination of comfortable
hotel, elegant restaurant and village pub. Eleven
comfortably furnished en suite bedrooms make this an
ideal base for touring Dartmoor and the South Devon
coast. Dartington Hall is on the doorstep, and Dart Valley
steam trains cover the short journey to Buckfast Abbey.
An interesting bar menu features sausage, kidney &
bacon casserole with parsnip purée, or rump steak with
lyonnaise potatoes and béarnaise sauce, plus other pub
classics such as bangers and mash. The conservatory style
restaurant includes seasonal starters like chargrilled
vegetable tian or seared fillets of brill with crab risotto.
For main courses there's seared fillet of eponymous sea
trout or honey glazed roast Gressingham duck. Round off
with desserts such as fresh fruit salad, raspberry crème
brûlée, or sample some wonderful West Country cheeses.
OPEN: 11-3 6-11 (Sun 12-3, 7-10.30) **BAR MEALS:** L served
all week 12-2 D served all week 7-9 Av main course £8.50
RESTAURANT: L served Sun 12-2 D served all week 7-9
🍽: Palmers ◖: Palmers IPA, Dorset Gold, Palmers Bi-Centenary
'200'. **FACILITIES:** Garden: Large, walled patio garden with
ponds Dogs allowed Water, dog walk map **NOTES:** Parking 80
ROOMS: 11 bedrooms en suite 2 family rooms s£45 d£65

 Brewery/Company

Pick of the Pubs

The Kings Arms Inn ♦♦♦♦ ◁⊃ ♀
EX14 9BS ☎ 01404 881361 🖷 01404 881732
e-mail: info@kingsarms.net web: www.kingsarms.net
Dir: Off A30 to Chard, 6m NE of Honiton

Tucked away at the edge of the Blackdown Hills, you'll find
this long Grade II listed, thatched and whitewashed 16th-
century inn. It boasts an impressive flagstoned walkway
entrance, a medieval oak screen and an original bread
oven, as well as an old grey-painted phone box. The
atmospheric Farmers bar is a lively meeting place, popular
with locals and visitors alike, while the Cotley restaurant bar
offers a wide range of blackboard specials. There's a good
balance of fish, meat and vegetarian dishes; marscapone
and spinach linguini; king prawn thermidor; slow roast belly
of pork; or fillet of beef stroganoff are amongst many
options. Mouthwatering desserts include double chocolate
truffle gateau; and sherry trifle, as well as an excellent
selection of West Country cheeses. Regular skittles matches
and live music add to the lively, vibrant feel.
OPEN: 12-3 6.30-11.30 Closed: Dec 25 **BAR MEALS:** L served
all week 12-1.45 D served all week 6.30-9 Av main course £10.50
RESTAURANT: L served all week 12-1.45 D served all week
6.30-9 Av 3 course à la carte £20 🍽: Free House ◖: Otter Ale,
Exmoor Ale, Scottish Courage John Smiths, O'Hanlon's
Yellowhammer. ♀: 21 **FACILITIES:** Garden: Part lawn part
patio, Seating for 30 Dogs allowed **NOTES:** Parking 45
ROOMS: 3 bedrooms en suite 1 family room s£45 d£70

The Green Dragon Inn ♀
Church Rd TQ6 0PX ☎ 01803 770238 🖷 01803 770238
e-mail: pcrowther@btconnect.com
Dir: Telephone for directions
A smugglers tunnel is said to connect this 12th-century pub to
Blackpool Sands. Certainly the landlord is drawn to the sea:
he's famous for his voyages across the Atlantic. Inside, you'll
find a warm atmosphere and deceptively simple cooking.
Lunchtime snacks include fresh baguettes and locally made
beefburgers, whilst dinner menus allow you to order starters
as light bites (perhaps prawn platter with aïoli and bread or
Dartmouth smoked mackerel). Main courses include Italian
meatloaf, venison pie and lamb shanks.
OPEN: 11-3 5.30-11 (Sun 12-3, 6.30-10.30) **BAR MEALS:** L served
Mon-Sun 12-2.30 D served Mon-Sun 6.30-9
RESTAURANT: L served Mon-Sun 12-2.30 D served Mon-Sun 6.30-9
🍽: Heavitree ◖: Otter, Flowers IPA, Bass, 6x. ♀: 9
FACILITIES: Child facs Small garden at rear; covered patio at front
Dogs allowed **NOTES:** Parking 6

STOKENHAM
Map 03 SX84

Pick of the Pubs

Trademan's Arms ♀
TQ7 2SZ ☎ 01548 580313 ▥ 01548 580313
e-mail: becks@thetradesmansarms.com
Dir: *Just off A379 between Kingsbridge & Dartmouth*

This part-thatched free house dates from 1390 and forms the centrepiece of a picturesque old village that was given to Anne of Cleves by Henry VIII in 1539. Incorporating a former brewhouse and three cottages, the pub takes its name from the tradesmen who used to call at the brewhouse while working in the area. Unpretentious and simply furnished, the interior has a stone fireplace and enjoys fine views of the parish church. Dishes may include rack of Loddiswell lamb in a rosemary and redcurrant sauce; poached chicken breast with a stilton crust in a red wine jus; braised lamb's liver in a red wine gravy with caramelised onions; steak and ale pie; or for the vegetarian, pancake filled with stir-fry vegetables with a parmesan sauce. Interesting puddings, real ales, local cider and a fine range of malt whiskies round things off.
OPEN: 11-3 6-11 (Sun 12-3, 7-10.30) **BAR MEALS:** L served all week 12-2.30 D served all week 6.30-9.30
RESTAURANT: L served all week 12-2.30 D served all week 6.30-9.30 ☺: Free House ◀: South Ham Plymouth Pride & XSB, Brakspear, Bass plus guest ale. ♀: 8 **FACILITIES:** Garden: Raised garden overlooking the valley Dogs allowed Water
NOTES: Parking 14

STRETE
Map 03 SX84

Pick of the Pubs

Kings Arms NEW ⌂◇ ♀
Dartmouth Rd TQ6 0RW ☎ 01803 770377 ▥ 01803 771008
e-mail: kingsarms_devon_fish@hotmail.com
See Pick of the Pubs on opposite page

TEDBURN ST MARY
Map 03 SX89

Kings Arms Inn ⌂◇ ♀
EX6 6EG ☎ 01647 61224 ▥ 01647 61224
e-mail: reception@kingsarmsinn.co.uk
Dir: *A30 W to Okehampton, 1st exit right signed Tedburn St Mary*
Until after the Civil War the pub was the Taphouse Inn, and even today locals refer to this part of the village as Taphouse. Log fires and exposed beams are features of this delightful old building, which sits just off Dartmoor's northern flanks. 'Think global, eat local' says the menu cover, an exhortation
continued

easily met by such possibilities as Thai crab cakes, chicken arrabiata, Devon mushroom pot, and moules marinières. Fresh fish and specials are chalked on the blackboard.

Kings Arms Inn

OPEN: 11-3 6-11 (Open all day Sat and Sun)
BAR MEALS: L served all week 11-2.30 D served all week 6-9.30 Sun 6-8 Av main course £7.75 **RESTAURANT:** L served all week 11-2.30 D served all week 6-9.30 Sun 6-8 ☺: Free House ◀: Interbrew Bass & Worthington Best, Sharps Cornish Coaster, Whitbread Best.
FACILITIES: Child facs Garden: Large lawned gardens, large covered courtyard **NOTES:** Parking 40

THURLESTONE
Map 03 SX64

The Village Inn ♀
TQ7 3NN ☎ 01548 563525 ▥ 01548 561069
e-mail: mike@thurlestone.co.uk
Dir: *Take A379 from Plymouth towards Kingsbridge, at Bantham rdbt go straight over, B3197, then right onto a lane signed Thurlestone 2.5m*

In the same family ownership for over a century, a friendly village local that draws seasonal trade from the nearby coastal path to Bigbury Bay. Once a farmhouse B&B, the 16th-century free house today prides itself on good service, well-kept ales and decent food. Blackboards offer daily choices such as shell-on prawns with garlic mayonnaise, soft poached eggs with grilled smoked bacon and hollandaise sauce on a toasted English muffin, or chargrilled rump of salmon with chived crushed potatoes with crab and coriander beignet. Mark Frith, the head chef, changes the menus regularly.
OPEN: 11.30-3 6-11 (Sun 12-3, 7-10.30, Aug all day)
BAR MEALS: L served all week 12-2 D served all week 6.30-9 Av main course £7.95 ☺: Free House ◀: Palmers IPA, Interbrew Bass, Sharp's Doom Bar & Guest beer. **FACILITIES:** Garden: Outdoor seating, food served outside Dogs allowed Water
NOTES: Parking 50

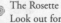
The Rosette is the AA award for food.
Look out for it next to a pub's name

Kings Arms

You can't go wrong with a pub whose kitchen motto is 'keep it fresh, keep it simple'. In the Kings Arms, the only pub in the village, customers are welcome to eat in the traditional terracotta-walled bar with its old photographs of the village and fish prints, or they can opt for the contemporary dining room, enlivened by specially commissioned art.

Menus are based around local and regional produce, and seafood makes up about eighty percent of it. Among the seafood dishes you might find River Yealm oysters with local chipolatats and coarse-grain mustard; grilled fillets of red mullet on warm tomato and mint vinaigrette; seared hand-dived scallops on braised puy lentils with Pedro Xiemenes sherry dressing; Szechwan 'salt and pepper' squid with mooli and carrot salad and sweet soy sauce; Thai-style mussels with coriander, lemon grass and chili; mackerel 'escabeche' with rhubarb jelly; grilled sardines with sea salt, lemon and thyme; Spanish-style roast cod with chorizo, potatoes and peppers; grilled sea bream, pancetta, vanilla, green peppercorn and apple syrup; and Singapore crab with black pepper, steamed pak choi and sesame oil. What's more, they also bake their own bread, brioche, oatcakes and biscuits, and make their own sausages, pickles, relishes and ice creams. At lunchtime you can opt for a light meal like caesar salad with hot smoked salmon; or warm salad of goats' cheese with roasted baby tomato and pesto; or go for a River Yealm's oysters on ice starter, followed by mixed Devon seafood poached in a thin Thai broth.

OPEN: 11.30-2.30, 7-10.30 (Sun 12-3, 6.30-11)
BAR MEALS: L served all week 12-2 D served Mon-Sat 7-9 (Sun 12-3) Av main course £14
RESTAURANT: L served all week 12-2 D served Mon-Sat 7-9 (Sun 12-3) Av 3 course à la carte £25
🍺: Otter Ale, Adnams Bitter, Murphys Stout. ♀: 15
FACILITIES: Children's licence Garden: Patio with parasols, lawn with flowers Dogs allowed
NOTES: Parking 12

NEW 🐟 ♀   Map 03 SX84
Dartmouth Rd TQ6 0RW
☎ 01803 770377
🖷 01803 771008
📧 kingsarms_devon_fish
  @hotmail.com
🌐 www.kingsarms-dartmouth.co.uk
Dir: On A379 Dartmouth-Kingsbridge, 5m from Dartmouth

The Durant Arms

Ashprington, just outside the Elizabethan town of Totnes, is a beautiful South Hams village close to the River Dart and with lovely views over the valley. Here you will find the 18th-century Durant Arms, a locally renowned dining pub, ideal as a base for touring this popular area. The award-winning inn takes its name from the owners of the original village estate.

All food is freshly cooked to order and based on a wide variety of locally sourced meat, fish and vegetables. The comfortable bar is fitted out in traditional style, and serves a good choice of real ales, malt whiskies and wines by the glass, perhaps one of the reds or whites from the local Sharpham Vineyard, just fifteen minutes walk away. There are three separate dining rooms to choose from, all supervised by owners Eileen and Graham Ellis who pride themselves on the quality of service and hospitality. For lovers of traditional cooking there are steak and kidney pie; ham, egg and chips; cottage pie; game pie; lasagnes and salads, as well as a very good choice from the fish specials board, including scallops with tiger prawns; whole grilled lemon sole; halibut with prawns; monkfish with cream and garlic; baked skate and tarragon butter; and plaice roulade with smoked salmon. A pleasant way to end a meal is with one of the fine unpasteurised cheeses made from milk produced by Sharpham's herd of Jersey cows. The tasteful en suite bedrooms, some featuring exposed beams, are individually designed and furnished. A small terrace garden with hardwood furniture and a water feature makes a pleasant alternative to the bars in warm weather.

OPEN: 11.30-2.30 6.30-11 (Sun 12-2.30, 7-10.30)
BAR MEALS: L served all week 12-2.30 D served all week 7-9.15 Av main course £7.95
RESTAURANT: L served all week 12-2 D served all week 7-9.15
🏠: Free House
🍺: Dartmoor Bitter, Tetley, Tribute.
🍷: 8
FACILITIES: Garden: Terraced garden with rosewood furniture Dogs allowed Water **NOTES:** Parking 8
ROOMS: 7 bedrooms en suite s£45 d£70 No children overnight

◆◆◆◆◆ 🍸Map 03 SX86
Ashprington TQ9 7UP
☎ 01803 732240
📧 info@thedurantarms.com
🌐 www.thedurantarms.com
Dir: Leave A38 at Totnes Jct, proceed to Dartington & Totnes, at 1st set of traffic lights right for Knightsbridge on A381, after 1m left for Ashprington

TOPSHAM
Map 03 SX98

Bridge Inn
Bridge Hill EX3 0QQ ☎ 01392 873862 🖥 01392 877497
e-mail: bridge@cheffers.co.uk
Dir: *4m from Exeter city centre*
Four generations of the same family have run this listed 16th-century inn since 1897, and it has remained old-fashioned in the best sense of the word. It sits peacefully beside the River Clyst, while inside are quirky little rooms filled with atmosphere and a bar with a minimum of eight real ales on tap. As this is mainly a drinker's pub food is limited to sandwiches, ploughman's, and hot meat and potato pasties.
OPEN: 12-2 6-10.30 (Sun 7-10.30 Fri-Sat 6-11)
BAR MEALS: L served all week 12-1.45 🍴: Free House
🍺: Branscombe Vale-Branoc, Adnams Broadside, Exe Valley, O'Hanlons. **FACILITIES:** Garden: Benches overlooking River Clyst Dogs allowed Water **NOTES:** Parking 20 No credit cards

The Lighter Inn ♀
The Quay EX3 0HZ ☎ 01392 875439 🖥 01392 876013

The imposing 17th-century customs house on Topsham Quay has been transformed into a popular waterside inn. A strong nautical atmosphere is reinforced with pictures, ship's instruments and oars beneath the pub's wooden ceilings, and the attractive quayside sitting area is popular in summer. Dishes may include whole sea bass or plaice, steaks, curries and salads, or steak, ale and mushroom pie.
OPEN: 11-11 **BAR MEALS:** L served all week 12-2.30 D served all week 6.30-9 (Food all day Jul-Sep) Av main course £7.95
🍴: Woodhouse Inns 🍺: Badger Best, Badger Tanglefoot, Sussex.
FACILITIES: Public Quay Dogs allowed Water provided
NOTES: Parking 40

TORCROSS
Map 03 SX84

Pick of the Pubs

Start Bay Inn 🐟 ♀
TQ7 2TQ ☎ 01548 580553 🖥 01548 580513
e-mail: cstubbs@freeuk.com
Dir: *Between Dartmouth & Kingsbridge on the A379*
Start Bay Inn dates back to the 14th century when local fishermen frequented it. Today the pub is a very successful family business - a success the proprietors attribute to their friendly staff and use of high quality local produce. Everything including the crisps is sourced locally. In fact the landlord takes great delight in scuba diving within Start bay for plaice and scallops, and catching bass by rod and line for customers' pleasure. Thanks to his dedication to serve local produce as freshly as possible, he was featured on Rick Stein's *Local Heroes*

continued

series in 2002. Arrive soon after opening, especially in the summer, to sample cod, haddock and plaice deep-fried in a light batter; or lemon sole, giant prawns, and crab and seafood platters, along with various steaks, freshly-roasted chicken, spinach and mascapone lasagne; and plenty of sandwiches, ploughman's lunches, burgers and other snacks. Locally-made ice creams, and fresh gateaux are among the stars of the dessert menu.
OPEN: 11.30-2.30 6-11 (Summer 11.30-11)
BAR MEALS: L served all week 11.30-2 D served all week 6-10 Sun 12-2.15, winter 6-9.30 🍴: Heavitree 🍺: Interbrew Flowers Original & Bass, Otter Ale. ♀: 8 **FACILITIES:** Child facs Garden: Patio area overlooks Slapton Sands Dogs allowed on leads, Water **NOTES:** Parking 18

TOTNES
Map 03 SX86

Pick of the Pubs

The Durant Arms ♦♦♦♦♦ 🐟 ♀
Ashprington TQ9 7UP ☎ 01803 732240
e-mail: info@thedurantarms.com
web: www.thedurantarms.com
See Pick of the Pubs on opposite page

Rumour NEW ♀
30 High St TQ9 5RY ☎ 01803 864682 🖥 01803 864682
e-mail: philip@eiaddio.com
Set within the walls of old Totnes, Rumour was a Cavalier's house during the Civil War. More recently, the building has been a toffee factory, a coffee bar, a top class restaurant, and finally a wine bar! Rumour still offers coffee and wines, as well as a wide selection of Belgian beers. Local ingredients are used in dishes like roast duck breast; butternut squash, courgette and chestnut stew; and roast cod with rarebit crust.
OPEN: 10-11 (Sun 6-10.30) **BAR MEALS:** L served Mon-Sat D served all week **RESTAURANT:** L served Mon-Sat 12-2.30 D served all week 6-9.30 ♀: 9

The Steam Packet Inn ♦♦♦♦ ♀
St Peter's Quay TQ9 5EW ☎ 01803 863880 🖥 01803 862754
e-mail: steampacket@bucaneer.co.uk
web: www.thesteampacketinn-totnes.co.uk
Dir: *Leave A38 at Totnes junct, proceed to Dartington & Totnes. Straight across lights & rdbt following signs for town centre with river on left, follow The Plains in town centre for 100yds. Pub on river*

The sign for this riverside inn depicts the Amelia, a steam packet ship that regularly called here with passengers, parcels and mail before the days of modern road and rail transport. The inn has great river views, particularly from the restaurant. One menu is served throughout, including fresh fish

continued

England

according to market availability. Typical dishes are steaks, oven-roasted cod with goats' cheese, trio of sausages (also vegetarian), and green Thai vegetable curry.
OPEN: 11-11 (Sun 12-10.30) **BAR MEALS:** L served all week 12-2.30 D served all week 6-9.30 Av main course £12
RESTAURANT: L served all week 12-2.30 D served all week 6-9.30 🍽: Free House 🍷: Scottish Courage Directors, Courage Best, Interbrew Bass & Two Real Ales. **FACILITIES:** Garden: Riverside quay, lights, raised terrace Dogs allowed Water, small dogs in bedroom **NOTES:** Parking 16 **ROOMS:** 4 bedrooms en suite 1 family room d£65

Pick of the Pubs

The White Hart Bar 🍷
Dartington Hall TQ9 6EL ☎ 01803 847111 📠 01803 847107
Dir: Totnes turning on A38 to Plymouth, approx 4m
Set in a stunning location beside the 14th-century Dartington Hall, the White Hart is surrounded by landscaped gardens, ancient deer parkland and woodland. It began life as a private club in 1934 and is now a stylish dining venue with flagstone floors, limed oak settles, roughcast walls and a welcoming atmosphere. Enjoy the range of West Country ales, or choose from an accessible wine list that classifies bottles by their flavours. The innovative menu uses local and organic produce where possible to create dishes with a modern twist. Starters like grilled local goats' cheese on celery, apple and walnut salad, precede main course choices like baked brill with herb crust and asparagus cream sauce; or Moroccan-style Devon lamb casserole with mint and lemon-scented couscous. Finish, perhaps, with a bitter Belgian chocolate tart and clotted cream.
OPEN: 11-11 Closed: 24 Dec-29 Dec **BAR MEALS:** L served all week 12-2.30 D served all week 6-9.30 Av main course £8
RESTAURANT: L served all week 12-2 D served all week 6-9 🍽: Free House 🍷: Princetown Jail Ale, White Hart Ale, Dartmoor IPA. 🍷: 8 **FACILITIES:** Garden: 29 landscaped acres, river walks etc **NOTES:** Parking 250

Cridford Inn 🔷
TQ13 0NR ☎ 01626 853694 📠 01626 853694
e-mail: cridford@eclipse.co.uk
An archetypal thatched country pub, the Cridford Inn had been a nunnery and a farm before finding its present vocation. The building dates from 825 but was remodelled in 1081. Features of the atmospheric interior are rough stone walls, slate floors, and what is believed to be the oldest domestic window in Britain. The landlady is a culinary expert from Kuala Lumpur, so Malaysian specialities such as beef Rendang are offered alongside traditional pub fare.
OPEN: 12-3 7-11 (Open all week Jul-Sep) Closed: 8 Jan- 13 Feb
BAR MEALS: L served all week 12-2.30 D served all week 7-9.30
RESTAURANT: D served all week 7-9.30 🍽: Free House 🍷: Sharpes Own, Badger Best , Trusham Ale, Tinners.
FACILITIES: Child facs Garden: Dogs allowed **NOTES:** Parking 35

Pubs with Red Diamonds are the top
◆ places in the AA's three, four and five diamond ratings

The Maltsters Arms 🍷
TQ9 7EQ ☎ 01803 732350 📠 01803 732823
e-mail: pub@tuckenhay.demon.co.uk
In secluded, wooded Bow Creek off the River Dart, this splendid 18th-century pub is accessible only through high-banked Devon lanes, or by boat for about three hours either side of high tide. It is noted for real charcoal barbeques in the summer, live music events on the quayside, and a daily changing menu of good local produce imaginatively cooked. This may feature grilled whole local trout with toasted almonds and lemon butter, asparagus and pecorino ravioli, veal marsala and chestnut mushroom ragout, or roast half duckling with honey and five spice. There is a good selection of starters and light bites, and some Devonshire real ales.
OPEN: 11-11 **BAR MEALS:** L served all week 12-3 D served all week 7-9.30 Av main course £10 **RESTAURANT:** L served all week 12-3 D served all week 7-9.30 Av 3 course à la carte £18 🍽: Free House 🍷: Princetown Dartmoor IPA, Young's Special, Teignworthy Maltsters Ale, Southams Eddystone. 🍷: 18 **FACILITIES:** Child facs Garden: On quayside Dogs allowed Dog Bowl, Biscuits, lots of pals **NOTES:** Parking 40

Tytherleigh Arms Hotel 🍷
EX13 7BE ☎ 01460 220400 & 220214 📠 01460 220406
e-mail: TytherleighArms@aol.com
Beamed ceilings and huge roaring fires are notable features of this family-run, 17th-century former coaching inn. It is a food-led establishment, situated on the Devon, Somerset and Dorset borders. Fresh home-cooked dishes, using local ingredients, include lamb shank with honey and cider, steaks and fresh seafood such as West Country cod and Lyme Bay scallops. Comprehensive bar snack menu also available.
OPEN: 11-2.30 6.30-11 **BAR MEALS:** L served all week 12-2.30 D served all week 6.30-9 Av main course £8.95
RESTAURANT: L served all week 12-2.30 D served all week 6.30-9 Av 3 course à la carte £16.95 🍽: Free House 🍷: Butcombe Bitter, Exmoor Fox, Murphy's, Boddingtons. **FACILITIES:** Children's licence Garden: Courtyard, very pretty Dogs allowed Water dishes **NOTES:** Parking 60

Pick of the Pubs

The Rising Sun Inn ★★ 🔷 🍷
EX37 9DU ☎ 01769 560447 📠 01769 560764
e-mail: risingsuninn@btopenworld.com
web: www.risinguninn.com
Dir: On A377, Exeter/Barnstaple road, at junct with B3227
Idyllically set beside the River Taw and with a very strong fly fishing tradition, the Rising Sun dates back in part to the 13th century. The traditional flagstone bar is strewn with fishing memorabilia, comfortable chairs and daily papers and magazines for a very relaxing visit. Outside is a sunny raised terrace with beautiful rural views of the valley, and the riverside walk is equally enjoyable before or after a meal. This inn is an excellent base for the touring motorist with several National Trust properties nearby. A choice of à la carte restaurant or regularly updated bar menus feature the best of West Country produce, with seasonal delights like seafood from the North Devon coast, salmon and sea trout from the Taw,

continued

England

game from Exmoor, and local cheeses. The daily changing specials board is often the best place to start looking.
OPEN: 12-3 6-11 (open all day May-Sep)
BAR MEALS: L served all week 12-2 D served all week 6.30-9 Sun 12-2, 6.30-8.30 **RESTAURANT:** L served all week 12-2 D served all week 6.30-8.30 Sun 6.30-8.30 ⊕: Free House
🍺: Cotleigh Tawny Bitter, Barn Owl, Guinness. ♀: 9
FACILITIES: Child facs Children's licence Garden: Patio garden overlooking the river Dogs allowed **NOTES:** Parking 30
ROOMS: 9 bedrooms en suite 1 family room s£49 d£85

WIDECOMBE IN THE MOOR　　　　Map 03 SX77

The Old Inn 🕭
TQ13 7TA ☎ 01364 621207 🖷 01364 621407
e-mail: oldinn.wid@virgin.net
Dir: Telephone for directions

Dating from the 15th century, the Old Inn was partly ruined by fire but rebuilt around the original fireplaces. Two main bars and no fewer than five eating areas offer plenty of scope for visitors to enjoy the extensive selection of home-cooked food on offer. Sustaining main courses include home-made pies; fresh local salmon; and steaks from the grill. There are plenty of vegetarian options such as mushroom stroganoff and lasagne verde.
OPEN: 11-3 7-11 (Summer 6.30-11) Closed: 25 Dec
BAR MEALS: L served all week 11-2 D served all week 7-10 Sun lunch 12-2.30, dinner 7-9.30 Av main course £7.50
RESTAURANT: L served all week 11-2 D served all week 7-10
⊕: Free House 🍺: Interbrew Flowers IPA & Boddingtons.
FACILITIES: Garden: Streams, Ponds, Gazebos Dogs allowed Water
NOTES: Parking 55
See advert on this page

Rugglestone Inn
TQ13 7TF ☎ 01364 621327 🖷 01364 621224
Dir: A38 Drumbridges exit towards Bovey Tracey, left at 2nd rdbt, left at sign Haytor & Widecombe, village is 5m
Surrounded by peaceful moorland, this pretty Dartmoor inn has a large lawned garden with picnic tables. Converted from a farm cottage in 1832, it features open fires, beamed ceilings, real ales straight from the barrel and local farm cider, helping to give the pub its special atmosphere. The menu is typically British, featuring good quality produce. Dishes include steak and kidney pie, liver and bacon and fisherman's pie.
OPEN: 11.30-3 6.30-11 (Sat 11.30-3, Sun 12-3) (Winter 7-11, Sun 10.30) **BAR MEALS:** L served all week 12-2 D served all week 7-9 ⊕: Free House 🍺: Butcombe Bitter, St Austells Dartmoor Best.
FACILITIES: Garden: Large lawn, picnic tables, cover if needed Dogs allowed Water and biscuits **NOTES:** Parking 40

The Old Inn
Widecombe-in-the-Moor
Devon TQ13 7TA
Telephone: 01364 621207　Fax: 01364 621407

A friendly welcome awaits you at our XIV Century Freehouse in the beautiful valley of Widecombe-in-the-Moor.
Still independent and family owned.
Renowned for excellent, home-made food and value for money.
Extensive menu including English and international cuisine
Children's facilities • Large water gardens • Car park at rear
Delightful new conservatory-style Garden Restaurant
Open all year – table reservations recommended

WINKLEIGH　　　　Map 03 SS60

Pick of the Pubs

The Duke of York ♀
Iddesleigh EX19 8BG ☎ 01837 810253 🖷 01837 810253
No juke boxes, fruit machines or karaoke warblings disturb the unspoilt atmosphere of this 15th-century thatched inn, deep in rural mid-Devon. Originally three cottages built for workers restoring the parish church, all the timeless features of a classic country pub are here - heavy old beams, a huge inglenook fireplace with winter fires, scrubbed tables and farmhouse chairs. Popular with all, it offers decent real ales (Cotleigh Tawny, for example) and hearty home cooking, with everything freshly prepared using local produce, such as meat reared on nearby farms. Examples of bar meals taken from the large blackboard menu include crab mayonnaise, or rollmops, with salad; vegetable, chicken or beef curry korma or Madras; and double lamb chop with rosemary and garlic. From the more expensive menu could come a meal of leek and potato soup, pork tenderloin escalopes with sweet and sour sauce, and home-made puddings.
OPEN: 11-11 **BAR MEALS:** L served all week 12-10 D served all week Sun 12-9.30 Av main course £7
RESTAURANT: D served all week 7-10 Sun 7-9.30 Av 3 course à la carte £20 Av 3 course fixed price £20 ⊕: Free House
🍺: Adnams Broadside, Cotleigh Tawny, Guest beers. ♀: 8
FACILITIES: Garden: patio/terrace, outdoor eating Dogs allowed water provided

The Digger's Rest

Originally a Devon cider house, this picturesque country inn offers traditionally drawn Otter ales, home-cooked food and a relaxed, welcoming atmosphere. Its thick 500-year-old walls are built of stone and cob with heavy beams under a thatched roof. Inside, soft furnishings and lighting, and West Country art contrast with antique furniture and a refurbished skittle alley.

The patio garden provides seating for up to forty people and is the perfect setting for alfresco drinking and dining, especially at night when it is attractively lit up. A single menu is offered in the bar and non-smoking restaurant. Weekly changing dishes could include pan-fried scallops with bacon, served with dressed leaves; crab and ginger salad with lemon confit; pan-fried tiger prawns in lemon garlic butter; warm red onion and goat's cheese tart; garlic mushrooms on toast; warm roasted Mediterranean vegetable crostini; chargrilled lamb cutlets with caramelised red onions and yoghurt and mint dressing; steak and kidney pie with a shortcrust pastry, served with fresh vegetables; Devon free-range chicken breast pan-fried with Muscat wine and black pudding; slow cooked lamb shanks in a rich red wine and tomato sauce; penne pasta with mushroom, garlic, parmesan and cream sauce; aubergine and red pepper moussaka, with a ricotta topping; passion fruit crème brûlée; profiteroles and cream with warm chocolate sauce; sticky toffee pudding; and warm raspberry and cinnamon torte.

OPEN: 11-3 6-11 All day Sat-Sun
BAR MEALS: L served all week 12-2 D served all week 7-9.30 (Sun 12-2.30) Av main course £9.50
RESTAURANT: L served all week 12-2 D served all week 7-9.30 (Sun 12-2.30) Av 3 course à la carte £23
🍺: Otter Bitter, Otter Ale, Scatterbrook Devonian. ♀: 10
FACILITIES: Children's licence Garden: Contemporary patio garden, wooden furniture
NOTES: Parking 30

🐟 ♀   Map 03 SY08
EX5 1PQ
☎ 01395 232375
🖹 01395 232711
🖃 bar@diggersrest.co.uk
Dir: 2.5m from A3052

England

WINKLEIGH continued

The Kings Arms ♀
Fore St EX19 8HQ ☎ 01837 83384
Dir: The village is signed off the B3220, Crediton to Torrington road.
An ancient thatched country inn in Winkleigh's central square.
Wood-burning stoves keep the beamed bar and dining rooms warm in chilly weather, and wooden settles and flagstones add to the traditional atmosphere. Great real ales are supplemented by local draught ciders, while darts and dominoes are encouraged, with no juke box or fruit machines. Food served all day includes duck parcel with port sauce; mixed grill; cottage pie; vegetarian shepherd's pie; and salmon fishcakes. Booking recommended at weekends.
OPEN: 11-11 (Sun 12-10.30) **BAR MEALS:** L served all week 11-9.30 D served all week Sun 12-9 Av main course £8.95
RESTAURANT: L served all week 11-9.30 D served all week (Sun 12-9) ☻: Enterprise Inns ◖: Butcombe Bitter, Otter Bitter, Skinners Cornish Knocker. ♀: 8 **FACILITIES:** Child facs Children's licence Garden: Small courtyard to side of property Dogs allowed

WONSON
Map 03 SX68

Northmore Arms
EX20 2JA ☎ 01647 231428
Dir: From M5 take A30 Towards Okehampton. At Merrymeet roundabout (Whiddon Down) take first left on to the old A30 through village then left, then right down lane, left at T Junction 0.75 to Wonson
Located in a very rural corner of Dartmoor, this pub is an ideal destination for ramblers, cyclists and horse riders (own paddock). No juke boxes or one-armed bandits spoil the peace of the place, and visitors find it relaxing to chat to the friendly locals. Bar food is of the traditional variety, with the likes of ham, eggs and chips, and steak and kidney pudding with vegetables, chips and gravy.
OPEN: 11-11 (Sun 12-10.30) **BAR MEALS:** L served all week 12-2.30 D served all week 7-9 Av main course £6 ◖: Adnams, Broadside, Cotley, Tawney & Ex Valley Dob's. **FACILITIES:** Garden: Park for horses large playing area Dogs allowed Water **NOTES:** Parking 8

WOODBURY SALTERTON
Map 03 SY08

Pick of the Pubs

The Digger's Rest NEW ▷ ♀
EX5 1PQ ☎ 01395 232375 ▤ 01395 232711
e-mail: bar@diggersrest.co.uk
See Pick of the Pubs on opposite page

DORSET

ABBOTSBURY
Map 04 SY58

Ilchester Arms
9 Market St DT3 4JR ☎ 01305 871243 ▤ 01305 871225
Rambling 16th-century coaching inn set in the heart of one of Dorset's most picturesque villages. Abbotsbury is home to many crafts including woodwork and pottery. A good area for walkers, and handy for the Tropical Gardens and Swannery.
OPEN: 11-11 (Sun 12-10.30) 25 Dec 12-3, 7-10.30
BAR MEALS: L served all week 12-2 D served all week 7-9 Sun 12-2.30/3 Av main course £7 **RESTAURANT:** L served all week 12-2.30 D served all week 6-9.30 Sun 12-2.30, 7-9 Av 3 course à la carte £18.50 ◖: Gales HSB, Badger Tanglefoot, Courage Best, Tribute. **FACILITIES:** Child facs Children's licence Garden: Dogs allowed **NOTES:** Parking 50

BLANDFORD FORUM
Map 04 ST80

The Crown Hotel ★★★ ♀
West St DT11 7AJ ☎ 01258 456626 ▤ 01258 451084
e-mail: thecrownhotel@blandforddorset.freeserve.co.uk
Dir: M27 W onto A31 to A350 junct, W to Blandford. 100mtrs from town bridge
Classic Georgian coaching inn in the heart of Dorset, on the banks of the River Stour. This inn has plenty of period atmosphere and a separate restaurant. Start with mushroom filled croissant; or goats' cheese and sun-dried tomatoes. Mains include chicken and seafood paella; chargrilled steaks; and grilled lemon sole. Bar snacks, Badger ales and German lagers available in the bar.
OPEN: 10-2.30 6-11 Closed: 25-28 Dec **BAR MEALS:** L served all week 12-2 D served all week 7-9 **RESTAURANT:** D served Sun 7.15-9.15 Av 3 course à la carte £24 Av 3 course fixed price £17.50 ☻: Hall & Woodhouse ◖: Badger Tanglefoot & Best. ♀: 20
FACILITIES: Garden: Food served outside Dogs allowed
NOTES: Parking 70 **ROOMS:** 32 bedrooms en suite 1 family room s£78 d£99

BOURTON
Map 04 ST73

Pick of the Pubs

The White Lion Inn ♀
High St SP8 5AT ☎ 01747 840866 ▤ 01747 841529
e-mail: whitelioninn@bourtondorset.fsnet.co.uk
Dir: Off A303, opposite B3092 to Gillingham

This stone-built village inn should certainly feature in any list of typical English pubs. Here you'll find old beams and flagstones, log fires and real ales, as well as home-cooked English food. Hosts Mike and Scarlett Senior share decades of catering experience - Mike has clocked up more than 40 years of innkeeping, while Scarlett's family has been in the trade for around 100 years. The single menu allows diners to choose between eating in one of the bars, or in the non-smoking restaurant. Lunchtime brings choices like rare roast beef and horseradish on farmhouse bread; and pork, ham and stilton pie with pease pudding mash. The main menu includes roasted tomato, dolcelatte and chive tart; braised lamb shank in red wine sauce; and Herefordshire beef and Guinness pie.
OPEN: 12-3 6-11 (Sun 12-5 Winter, 12-4, 7-10.30 Summer) Closed: 26 Dec **BAR MEALS:** L served all week 12-2 D served all week 7-9 Av main course £9.50 **RESTAURANT:** L served all week 12-2 D served Mon-Sat 7-9 (Sun 12-2.30) ☻: ◖: Fullers London Pride, Greene King IPA & Guest Beer. ♀: 8
FACILITIES: Child facs Garden: Grassed with trees, patio area Dogs allowed Water **NOTES:** Parking 30

PUB WALK

Piddle Inn
Piddletrenthide - Dorset

THE PIDDLE INN,
DT2 7QF
☎ 01300 348468
Friendly riverside village inn that has been a pub since the 1760s, and was once a staging post for the exchange of prisoners from Sherborne and Dorchester. Popular riverside patio.
Open: 12–3 6–11 (Closed Mon lunch)
Bar Meals: L served Tues–Sun 12–2 D served Mon–Sun 6.30–9
Restaurant Meals: L served Tues–Sun 12–2 D served Mon–Sun 6.30–9
Dogs allowed. Garden and parking available.
(for full entry see page 172)

This circular walk around Piddletrenthide offers the chance to savour the peace and beauty of the renowned Piddle Valley. The 15th-century village church has one of Dorset's best towers and nearby is a fine 18th-century manor house.

From the Piddle Inn take the footpath behind the pub, cross the river and head round to the right by the farm outbuildings. On reaching the Cerne Abbas road, turn left and then right after a few paces. Keep straight on along a wide track and when you reach a sign for Kiddles Farm, turn right and follow Church Lane to the junction with the B3143. Turn left and walk towards Alton Pancras for about 160 yards (146m), heading up the track on the right which climbs to Hollery Down. Make for a stile at the top of the track, then walk across the down towards a clump of trees. Draw level with a drinking trough and

continue to the north-east corner of Hollery Down. Follow the hedge on the right to the north-east corner of the next field. Negotiate a sometimes overgrown section of fencing and enter a pretty hilltop meadow known as Watcombe Plain. Exit by the first field gate on the left, beside a small round copse. Stay on the bridleway across the next field and continue to a fork. Veer right down the side of Burnt House Bottom to a concrete drinking trough. Fork left off the track into a sunken area, go through a gate and keep ahead between houses to the B3143. Turn left and follow the road back into the centre of the village, passing Church Lane on your right and the Poachers Inn beyond. Look out for the manor house also on the right. There is a hidden bend here, so take care and stay close to the wall for safety. Pass turnings on the left and right and return to the inn.

Distance: 6 miles (9.7km)
Map: OS Landranger 194
Terrain: Rolling fields, farmland and woodland
Paths: Bridleways, paths and tracks
Gradient: : Gently undulating

Walk submitted by the Piddle Inn, Piddletrenthide

BRIDPORT
Map 04 SY49

The George Hotel ♀
4 South St DT6 3NQ ☎ 01308 423187
Dir: Centre of Bridport, 1.5m from West Bay
Handsome Georgian town house, with a Victorian-style bar and a mellow atmosphere, which bustles all day, and offers a traditional English breakfast, decent morning coffee and a good menu featuring fresh local plaice, rabbit and bacon pie, natural smoked haddock, and avacado and bacon salad. Everything is home-cooked using local produce.
OPEN: 9.30-11.30 (Sun 9.30-10.30) Closed: Dec 25
BAR MEALS: L served all week 12-2.15 D served Wed-Thurs 6-9 Av main course £6.95 ☺: Palmers ◀: Palmers - IPA, Copper & 200, Tally Ho. **FACILITIES:** Dogs allowed Water, biscuits

Pick of the Pubs

Shave Cross Inn ♀
Shave Cross, Marshwood Vale DT6 6HW
☎ 01308 868358 ≣ 01308 867064
e-mail: roy.warburton@virgin.net
See Pick of the Pubs on page 166

The West Bay NEW ▷ ♀
Station Bay, West Bay DT6 4EW
☎ 01308 422157 ≣ 01308 459717
e-mail: Karen.Trimby@btopenworld.com
A traditional bar/restaurant in a picturesque harbour village, within easy reach one way of Dorset's famous Jurassic Coast, now a World Heritage Site, and Chesil Beach the other way. A hostelry since 1739, it offers snacks and light bites, a fish menu incorporating lobster platter, skate wing, 'posh' fish pie, roasted halibut, turbot fillets and many more, and meat courses of Cajun chicken breast stuffed with brie, or guinea fowl on creamed leeks and chives.
OPEN: 11-2.30 6-11 Closed Sun eve **BAR MEALS:** L served all week 12-2.30 D served Mon-Sat Sun 12-2.30 **RESTAURANT:** L served all week 12-2 D served Mon-Sat 6.30-9.30 Av 3 course à la carte £21 ◀: Palmers IPA, Copper Ale, Palmers 200. ♀: 7
FACILITIES: Garden: Front and rear gardens with seating, fountain

BUCKLAND NEWTON
Map 04 ST60

Gaggle of Geese ♀
DT2 7BS ☎ 01300 345249
e-mail: gaggle@bucklandnewton.freeserve.co.uk
Dir: On B3143 N of Dorchester
At the heart of Hardy's Wessex, this pub was known as the Royal Oak until a previous landlord started keeping geese. From just a simple flock has evolved a twice-yearly goose auction that featured in the popular television series, *Tales from Riverside Cottage*. Menus might include crispy battered fillet of cod; spinach and mushroom lasagne; Scottish smoked salmon; and ravioli in tomato sauce. Good range of starters, snacks and sandwiches.
OPEN: 12-2.30 6.30-11 **BAR MEALS:** L served all week 12-2 D served all week 7-10 **RESTAURANT:** L served all week 12-2 D served all week 7-10 ☺: Free House ◀: Badger Dorset Best, Ringwood Best & Fortyniner, Butcombe. ♀: 6 **FACILITIES:** Child facs Garden: Pub on 5 acres. Pond & stream Dogs allowed Water **NOTES:** Parking 30

BURTON BRADSTOCK
Map 04 SY48

Pick of the Pubs

The Anchor Inn ▷ ♀
High St DT6 4QF ☎ 01308 897228 ≣ 01308 897228
e-mail: aex013@dialpipex.xom
Dir: 2m SE of Bridport on B3157 in the centre of the village of Burton Bradstock

The Anchor Inn is a 300-year-old coaching inn set on the beautiful coastline between Lyme Regis and Portland. In keeping with its name, it is full of marine memorabilia: fishing nets are draped across the ceilings, and old fishing tools and shellfish art created by the chef-proprietor can be seen on the walls. Seafood is the house speciality, with sometimes as many as twenty different main fish courses on the menu, especially fresh local scallops, crab and lobster. You can choose between fillet of brill; grilled Cornish mackerel; local trout fillet with a selection of shellfish; and grilled whole local plaice. Meat eaters are not ignored with platters like Barbary duck; beef stroganoff; Cajun blackened fillet; and peppered pork fillet among others. You could also try the steak platter or combinations like grilled red mullet and red bream; baked fresh cod and crab; and sea bass and shellfish - all with a selection of sauces. Several real ales are on sale, and over 50 different Scottish whiskies.
OPEN: 11-11 (Sun 12-10.30) **BAR MEALS:** L served all week 12-2 D served all week 6.30-9 **RESTAURANT:** L served all week 12-2 D served all week 6.30-9 ☺: ◀: Ushers Best, Flowers IPA, Hobgoblin. ♀: 8 **FACILITIES:** Child facs Children's licence Garden: Patio/courtyard Dogs allowed Water
NOTES: Parking 24

 Pubs offering a good choice of fish on their menu

★ Star rating for inspected hotel accommodation

Shave Cross Inn

With its thatched roof and cob and flint walls, the family-run, 13th-century Shave Cross is one of Dorset's hidden treasures. Tucked away down narrow lanes in the heart of the beautiful Marshwood Vale, it used to be where pilgrims and monks stopped on their way to the church of St Candida and St Cross in nearby Whitchurch Canonicorum.

While here, or so the story goes, the monks would have their hair cut in the way only monks did. The churchyard contains the grave of Georgi Markov, Bulgaria's 'most revered dissident', who was assassinated by a Soviet agent on Waterloo Bridge in 1978. In the bar, with a floor made of timeworn blue lias flagstones from Dorset's Jurassic Coast (a World Heritage Site), there's the perfect inglenook fireplace for smoking hams, while the beams in the restaurant come from the rib of an old boat. Owners Roy and Mel Warburton spent a long time in Tobago, returning a few years ago to take over and revive the pub. They brought with them their head chef, creator of the authentic Caribbean cooking on the menu here. Examples include jerk chicken salad with plantain, bacon and aioli; and roast Creole duck with cherry compote. Traditional British tastes are met with freshly battered haddock and chips, rump steak, ploughman's, and fresh crab sandwiches. Local beers come from Branscombe Vale in Devon, and Weymouth's Quay Brewery. The garden has a play area for children, a thatched wishing well and a huge display of flowers and shrubs. The inn is home to the oldest thatched skittle alley in the country, and the old traditions of Morris dancing, folk singing, and ashen-faggot burning on Twelfth Night, are strongly maintained.

OPEN: 10.30-3 5-11 (all day Tue-Sun in Summer, BH Mons)
BAR MEALS: L served Tue-Sun 12-3 D served Tue-Sun 5-9.30 Sun 12-3, 6-8 Summer
RESTAURANT: L served Tue-Sun 12-3 D served Tue-Sat 7-9.30 Sun 6-8 (summer) Av 3 course à la carte £26
🍺: Free House
🍺: Local guest beers, Branoc (Branscombe Valley), Quay Brewery Weymouth. 🍷: 8
FACILITIES: Child facs Children's licence Cottage garden Dogs allowed on leads, water available, not in restaurant **NOTES:** Parking 30

🍷 Map 04 SY49
Shave Cross, Marshwood Vale
DT6 6HW
☎ 01308 868358
📄 01308 867064
✉ roy.warburton@virgin.net
Dir: From Bridport take B3162, 2m turn left signed 'Broadoak/Shave Cross' then Marshwood

The Shave Cross Inn

CATTISTOCK   Map 04 SY59

Fox & Hounds Inn ◆◆◆◆
Duck St DT2 0JH ☎ 01300 320444 ▤ 01300 320444
e-mail: info@foxandhoundsinn.com
web: www.foxandhoundsinn.com

An attractive 16th-century inn set in the beautiful village of Cattistock. Original features include bare beams, open fires and huge inglenooks, one with an original bread oven. It's a fascinating building, full of curiosities such as the 'hidden cupboard', reached by a staircase that winds around the chimney in one of the loft areas. Meals are traditional and home made: typical examples include cottage pie, fresh cod fillet in 'secret batter', pork in cider and apple sauce, lamb shank on mash, and haddock mornay.
OPEN: 12-2.30 7-11 **BAR MEALS:** L served Tue-Sun 12-1.45 D served all week 7-8.45 Av main course £7.95
RESTAURANT: L served Tue-Sun 12-1.45 D served all week 7-8.45
⌷: Palmers Brewery ◀: Palmers IPA, Copper Ale, Gold.
FACILITIES: Large and well maintained garden Dogs allowed Water and biscuits **NOTES:** Parking 12 **ROOMS:** 3 bedrooms 2 en suite 1 family room s£35 d£60

CERNE ABBAS   Map 04 ST60

The Royal Oak ℗
23 Long St DT2 7JG ☎ 01300 341797 ▤ 01300 341814
e-mail: info@royaloakcerneabbas.wanadoo.co.uk
Dir: M5/A37, follow A37 to A352 signposted Cerne Abbas, midway between Sherborne & Dorchester. Pub in centre of village

Thatched 16th-century inn located in a pretty village handy for the Dorset Downs. A previous owner sold the pub, and with the proceeds he purchased 1800 acres of land in the United States, now the site of Capitol Hill. Home-cooked food is served in the cosy interior, including steaks and grills, roast pork fillet, delice of haddock, Italian pasta bake and baked pheasant breasts. There's an attractive courtyard garden.
OPEN: 11-3 6-11 (Open all day summer) **BAR MEALS:** L served all week 12-2 D served all week 6.30-9 Summer 12-2.30 Av main
continued

The Royal Oak at Cerne Abbas
23, Long Street, Dorset DT2 7JG
Tel: 01300 341797   Fax: 01300 341814

Warm, cosy and atmospheric with great food, well kept West Country Ales, a good value wine list, superb coffees, tea, soft drinks to quench all thirsts, and a menu to cater for most appetites and budgets – Scotch beef, local lamb and rare breed pork is hard to beat with fresh fish another Chef's speciality. Childrens menu always available. Air filters maintain a smoke free atmosphere. Flagstone floors, oak beams, antiques – a little gem! Eat al fresco in the attractive courtyard garden.

course £9 ⌷: Free House ◀: Tanglefoot, Badger Best, Fursty Ferret, Stowford Press. ℗: 8 **FACILITIES:** Garden: Courtyard garden with seating and heaters Dogs allowed Water bowl in garden, treats
See advert on this page

CHIDEOCK   Map 04 SY49

The Anchor Inn
Seatown DT6 6JU ☎ 01297 489215
Dir: On A35 turn S in Chideock opp church & follow single track rd for 0.75m to beach
Originally a smugglers' haunt, The Anchor has an incredible setting in a little cove surrounded by National Trust land, beneath Golden Cap, the highest point on the south coast. The wide-ranging menu starts with snacks and light lunches - three types of ploughman's and a range of sandwiches might take your fancy. For something more substantial you could try freshly caught seafood - crab salad, for example - or a choice from their "Dorset meaty masterpieces": a hearty steak and kidney pie or lamb and suet pudding would be typical.
OPEN: 11-3 6-11 (11-11 in Summer, all day Fri-Sun)
BAR MEALS: L served all week 12-2.30 D served all week 6-9 all day w/e, & Summer Av main course £7.50 ⌷: Palmers ◀: Palmers 200 Premium Ale, IPA, Copper Ale. **FACILITIES:** Garden: spectacular views, large cliff terrace Dogs allowed Water, Dog treats
NOTES: Parking 20

Do you have a favourite pub that we have overlooked? Please use the Reader's Report form at the back of this guide to tell us all about it

CHRISTCHURCH   Map 05 SZ19

Fishermans Haunt Hotel ◆◆◆ ♀
Salisbury Rd, Winkton BH23 7AS ☎ 01202 477283
& 484071 ▤ 01202 478883
e-mail: fishermanshaunt@accommodating-inn.co.uk
web: www.accommodating-inns.co.uk/fishermanshaunt.html
Dir: 2.5m north on B3347 (Christchurch/Ringwood rd)
Dating from 1673, this inn overlooks the River Avon and is a
popular place for walkers and anglers, for Winkton has its
own fishery and there are many others locally. The area is
also well endowed with golf courses. The menu offers a daily
fish selection, usually including trout and whole plaice, and
staples such as steak and kidney pie, battered cod, and mixed
grill along with sandwiches and baked potatoes. There's a
more extensive carte menu in the restaurant.
OPEN: 10.30-3 5-11 (Sat 11-11, Sun 12-10.30)
BAR MEALS: L served all week 12-2 D served all week 6-9 Av main
course £7.95 **RESTAURANT:** L served Sat-Sun 12-2 D served Sat-Sun
6-9 Av 3 course à la carte £18 ☺: Gales ◖: Gales GB & HSB,
Ringwood Fortyniner, Interbrew Bass. ♀: 7 **FACILITIES:** Garden:
Food only Dogs allowed Water **NOTES:** Parking 80
ROOMS: 17 bedrooms en suite s£49.50 d£66

The Ship In Distress
66 Stanpit BH23 3NA ☎ 01202 485123 ▤ 01202 483997
e-mail: enquires@shipindistress.com

A 300-year-old smugglers' pub close to Mudeford Quay,
specialising in seafood. Legend says former pub owner,
Mother Sellers, warned smugglers of the coastguards'
presence by wearing a red dress. Nowadays the food
provides the excitement, with a wide range of locally caught
fish and seafood dishes: try blue fin tuna Niçoise; roast
monkfish with asparagus, cherry tomatoes and shallot mash;
or smoked trout and asparagus risotto. Meat and vegetarian
alternatives, plus a wide choice of home-made puddings.
OPEN: 10-11 Closed: Dec 25 **BAR MEALS:** L served all week 12-2
D served all week 7-9.30 (Sun 12-3) Av main course £11.25
RESTAURANT: L served all week 12-2 D served all week 7-9
Av 3 course à la carte £22.50 ☺: Inn Partnership ◖: Ringwood
Best, Fortyniner, Interbrew Bass, Courage Directors.
FACILITIES: Garden: Patio with awning and parasols Dogs allowed
Water, Biscuits **NOTES:** Parking 40

CHURCH KNOWLE   Map 04 SY98

The New Inn ♀
BH20 5NQ ☎ 01929 480357 ▤ 01929 480357
Dir: Telephone for directions
A 16th-century inn of stone and thatch set in a picturesque
village overlooking the Purbeck hills. Maurice and Rosemary
Estop have been in the business for over 30 years and their son
Matthew is head chef. Home-made dishes feature daily
continued

delivered fresh fish, including grilled trout topped with roasted
flaked almonds, haddock in golden batter, roasted cod with
wild mushroom and white wine sauce, grilled sardines, half pint
of whole prawns, and salmon steak with hollandaise and caviar
sauce. Pies, grills and sandwiches also make an appearance.

The New Inn

OPEN: 11-3 6.30-11 **BAR MEALS:** L served all week 12-2.15
D served all week 6-9.15 **RESTAURANT:** L served all week 12-2.15
D served all week 6-9.15 ☺: Inn Partnership ◖: Wadworth 6X, Old
Speckled Hen, Interbrew Flowers Original. **FACILITIES:** Garden: Beer
garden, food served outdoors Dogs allowed only on lead, water
available **NOTES:** Parking 100

CORFE CASTLE   Map 04 SY98

The Greyhound Inn ⌇ ♀
The Square BH20 5EZ ☎ 01929 480205 ▤ 01929 481483
e-mail: mjml@greyhound-inn.fsnet.co.uk
*Dir: W from Bournemouth, take A35, after 5m left onto A351, 10m to Corfe
Castle*
The brooding presence of Corfe Castle forms the dramatic
backdrop to this lively 16th-century inn, and may even have
furnished the stones to build it. There's a good selection of
real ales, and large filled or grilled sandwiches with chunky
chips are an eye-catching feature of the locally-based menu.
Hot dishes include local game casserole and forcemeat
stuffing; hand-made Dorset faggots; and Corfe Castle cod.
Beer, cider and sausage festivals are regular summer events.
OPEN: 11-11.30 **BAR MEALS:** L served all week 12-3 D served all
week 6-9 Jul-Aug food all day Av main course £9.95
RESTAURANT: L served all week 12-3 D served all week 6-9 Jul-Aug
food all day ☺: Enterprise Inns ◖: Fuller's London Pride, Timothy
Taylor Landlord, Black Sheep, Ringwood Best. ♀: 10
FACILITIES: Child facs Garden: BBQ & hog roast in summer; castle
views Dogs allowed Water

CORFE MULLEN   Map 04 SY99

The Coventry Arms NEW ♀
Mill St BH21 3RH ☎ 01258 857284
Dir: On A31 Wimborne-Dorchester road.
A 13th-century pub, formerly a watermill with its own island,
offering beer served direct from the cask. An annual spring beer
festival is an attraction here. The inn specialises in fish and
game from local estates, and most of the produce is sourced
from within the area. Expect oven roasted whole gurnard, pan-
fried fillet of monkfish, honey-glazed duck breast, and
chargrilled Cumberland sausages among the varied specials.
Fish and seafood menu Wednesday and Thursday lunchtime.
OPEN: 11-3 5.30-11 **BAR MEALS:** L served all week 12-2.30
D served all week 6-9.30 All day Sun Av main course £10
RESTAURANT: L served all week 12-2.30 D served all week 6-9.30
All day Sun Av 3 course à la carte £15.50 ◖: HSB, Timothy Taylor
Landlord, Gales Best. ♀: 17 **FACILITIES:** Garden: By riverside,
seating for 150 Dogs allowed **NOTES:** Parking 50

EAST CHALDON
Map 04 SY78

The Sailors Return
DT2 8DN ☎ 01305 853847 ▤ 01305 851677
Dir: 1m S of A352 between Dorchester & Wool

A splendid 18th-century thatched country pub in the village of East Chaldon (or Chaldon Herring - take your pick), tucked away in rolling downland near Lulworth Cove. Considerably extended since the 1930 view on the website. Seafood includes whole local plaice, scallop and mussel stroganoff, and wok-fried king prawns. Alternatives include half a big duck, local faggots, whole gammon hock, and vegetarian dishes. Choose from the blackboard in the beamed and flagstoned bar and eat inside or in a grassy area outside.
OPEN: 11-11 (all day open from Easter-end Sept, Sun 11-10.30)
BAR MEALS: L served all week 12-2 D served all week 6-9
RESTAURANT: L served all week 12-2 D served all week 6-9
Summer 12-9 ⊕: Free House ◀: Ringwood Best, Hampshire Strongs Best Bitter, Badger Tanglefoot. **FACILITIES:** Garden: Grassed area with wooden tables and benches **NOTES:** Parking 100

EAST MORDEN
Map 04 SY99

Pick of the Pubs

The Cock & Bottle ▷ ⬭ ♀
BH20 7DL ☎ 01929 459238
Dir: From A35 W of Poole take right B3075, pub 0.5m on left

Some 400 years ago, this popular pub was a cob-walled Dorset longhouse. It acquired a brick skin around 1800 and remained thatched until 1966. The original interiors remain comfortably rustic with quaint, low-beamed ceilings, attractive paintings and lots of nooks and crannies around the log fires. Additional to the lively locals' bar are a lounge bar and the modern rear restaurant extension; lovely pastoral views over farmland include the pub's paddock, where vintage car and motorcycle meetings are occasionally hosted during the

summer. The experienced chef serves up an appealing mix of traditional and inventive cooking, with the emphasis on fresh local produce where possible. Starters could include butternut squash soup with roast cumin; or confit of potted pheasant and redcurrants. To follow there's braised saddle of wild rabbit cooked in white wine and prunes; or steamed sea bass in a Poole Bay mussel and saffron broth.
OPEN: 11-3 6-11 (Sun 12-3, 7-10.30) **BAR MEALS:** L served all week 12-2 D served all week 6-9 Sun 7-9 Av main course £11
RESTAURANT: L served all week 12-2 D served all week 6-9 Sun 7-9 Av 3 course à la carte £21 ⊕: Hall & Woodhouse ◀: Badger Dorset Best & Tanglefoot & Sussex. ♀: 6
FACILITIES: Garden: Patio, grass area Dogs allowed Water
NOTES: Parking 40

EVERSHOT
Map 04 ST50

Pick of the Pubs

The Acorn Inn ♦♦♦♦ ◉ ▷ ♀
DT2 0JW ☎ 01935 83228 ▤ 01935 83707
e-mail: stay@acorn-inn.co.uk web: www.acorn-inn.co.uk
Dir: A303 to Yeovil, Dorchester Rd, on A37 right to Evershot

Thomas Hardy immortalised this 16th-century stone-built inn, now carefully restored, as The Sow and Acorn in *Tess of the D'Urbervilles*. 'Hanging' Judge Jeffreys may have used the grand hall - today's stylish no-smoking Hardy Restaurant - as a courthouse, while a skittle alley now occupies the old stables. There are two oak-panelled bars - one flagstoned, one tiled - with logs blazing in carved hamstone fireplaces. Most of the food is sourced from within a 15-mile radius. Bar meals include hearty soups, open sandwiches, and dishes such as Greek-style lamb casserole, and Mediterranean vegetable bruschetta with goat's cheese. In the restaurant expect roast fillet of beef; pan-fried pheasant breasts with spiced apricots; Barbary duck with black cherries; and a decent roll-call of fish - sea bass, red mullet, bream and scallops, for example. Vegetarians might try grilled button mushrooms on herbed tagliatelle with stilton and Cornish yarg. Desserts include warm apple charlotte with orange and Calvados sauce.
OPEN: 11.30-11 **BAR MEALS:** L served all week 12-2 D served all week 6.30-9.30 Av main course £8 **RESTAURANT:** L served all week 12-2 D served all week 6.30-9.30 Av 3 course à la carte £25 ⊕: Free House ◀: Fuller's London Pride, Butcombe, Guest Ale. ♀: 9 **FACILITIES:** Garden: Lawned garden with tables and umbrellas Dogs allowed **NOTES:** Parking 40
ROOMS: 10 bedrooms en suite 2 family rooms s£75 d£100

continued

The Kings Arms Inn

East Stour Common SP8 5NB ☎ 01747 838325
e-mail: citsuk@aol.com
Dir: *4m W of Shaftesbury on A30*
This family-run country free house dates back 200 years, and offers a large car park and beer garden. It makes an excellent base for exploring the delights of Dorset's countryside and coast, with plenty of well-loved attractions within reach, including nearby Shaftesbury and the famous Golden Hill. The menu ranges from lunchtime snacks to the likes of lamb shank with mint and onion gravy or vegetable lasagne.
OPEN: 12-2.30 5-11 (Longer hrs summer) Closed: 25 Dec
BAR MEALS: L served Tue-Sun 12-2 D served Tue-Sat 6-8.45
Av main course £9 **RESTAURANT:** L served Tue-Sun 12-2 D served Tue-Sat 6-8.45 No food Mon and Sun evenings ⊕: Free House
◀: London Pride, Palmers Copper Ale, Buttcombe Bitter.
FACILITIES: Child facs Garden: Patio & Sitting area, grassed area Dogs allowed Water **NOTES:** Parking 40

Smiths Arms

DT2 7AQ ☎ 01300 341236
With only room for around six tables, the Smiths Arms is one of the smallest pubs in Britain. It was previously a blacksmiths, and was granted its licence by Charles II. Set on the riverside in the Cerne Valley, this 15th-century thatched pub offers hearty meals including ham and broccoli au gratin, chicken and leek pie, tuna and spicy tomato lasagne, and delicious bread pudding.
OPEN: 11-3 6.30-11 **BAR MEALS:** L served all week 12-2 D served all week 6.30-9.30 Av main course £5.50 ⊕: Free House
◀: Wadworth 6X, Stowford Press Cider. **FACILITIES:** Garden: Seating area by river **NOTES:** Parking 15 No credit cards ⊗

The Drovers Inn ♀

BH21 5ET ☎ 01258 840084 e-mail: info@thedroversinn.net
Dir: *A31 Ashley Heath rdbt, right onto B3081*

Rural 16th-century pub with a fine terrace and wonderful views from the garden. Popular with walkers, its refurbished interior retains plenty of traditional appeal with flagstone floors and oak timbers. Ales include Ringwood's seasonal ales and guest beers. The menu features home-cooked pub favourites: fresh cod in home-made beer batter, curry, steak and kidney pie, and steak and chips.
OPEN: 11.45-11 **BAR MEALS:** L served all week 12-2 D served all week 6-9 all day weekends Av main course £6.95 ⊕: ◀: Ringwood Best, Old Thumper, Ringwood Seasonal Ales, Fortyniner & Guest Beers. ♀: 10 **FACILITIES:** Garden Overlooking surrounding countryside Dogs allowed Water **NOTES:** Parking 50

Loders Arms

DT6 3SA ☎ 01308 422431
Dir: *Off the A3066, 2m NE of Bridport*
Unassuming stone-built local tucked away in a pretty thatched village close to the Dorset coast. Arrive early to bag a seat in the bar or in the homely (and tiny) dining room. Interesting blackboard menus may list fish soup, smoked haddock fishcakes and filled baguettes for bar diners, with the likes of scallops in Pernod, steak and ale pie, rack of lamb, and sea bass with salsa verde available throughout. Lovely garden.
OPEN: 11.30-3 6-11 (Sun 11.30-11) **BAR MEALS:** L served all week 12.30-2 D served all week 7.15-9 Av main course £7.50
RESTAURANT: L served all week 12.30-2 D served all week 7.15-9 ⊕: Palmers Brewery ◀: Palmers Copper, Palmers IPA, Palmers 200.
FACILITIES: Garden: Dogs allowed

The Fox Inn ♦♦♦♦ ⋗ ♀

DT2 7PN ☎ 01258 880328 ▥ 01258 881440
e-mail: foxinnansty@tiscali.co.uk
Dir: *A35 from Dorchester towards Poole for 4m, exit signed Piddlehinton/Athelhampton House, turn left to Cheselbourne, then right. pub in Ansty village, opposite post office.*

This fine-looking, 250-year-old brick and flint dining pub was once home to Charles Hall, founder of Ansty Brewery, later to become Hall & Woodhouse of Blandford Forum. Photos and memorabilia in the bar hark back to this appropriate past. Starters might include haddock and spring onion fishcakes; while mains make good use of local produce including Torbay sole with olive crushed potatoes; and Dorset jugged venison, here casseroled in port with bacon and wild mushroom.
OPEN: 11-11 (Sun 12-10.30) **BAR MEALS:** L served all week 12-2.30 D served all week 6.30-9 Av main course £6.95
RESTAURANT: L served all week 12-2.30 D served all week 6.30-9 Sun 12-3 Carvery Av 3 course à la carte £19 ⊕: Hall & Woodhouse
◀: Badger Tanglefoot, Badger Best, Badger Smooth Seasonal Guest Ale Export. ♀: 8 **FACILITIES:** Garden: Grassed area at front, swimming pool at rear Dogs allowed only in bar
NOTES: Parking 40 **ROOMS:** 12 bedrooms en suite 4 family rooms s£45 d£65

Pilot Boat Inn ♀

Bridge St DT7 3QA ☎ 01297 443157
This busy town centre pub is close to the sea front and has a number of old smuggling and sea rescue connections, but its biggest claim to fame would seem to be as the possible birthplace of the inspiration for Hollywood's favourite super-collie, Lassie. Meals include a range of fish dishes, steaks and

continued

grills, ploughman's, salads, sandwiches and a selection of vegetarian options. Look to the blackboard for specials.
OPEN: 11-11 (Sun 12-10.30) Closed: Dec 25 **BAR MEALS:** L served all week 12-10 D served all week **RESTAURANT:** 12-10 🅶: Palmers 🍺: Palmers Dorset Gold, IPA, 200, Bridport Bitter. 🍷: 8
FACILITIES: Children's licence Garden: Patio Dogs allowed

Victoria Hotel ♦♦♦ 🍽️🍷
Uplyme Rd DT7 3LP ☎ 01297 444801
e-mail: info@vichotel.co.uk
Dir: Telephone for directions
From its elevated position, the Victoria's patio garden has splendid views over an area of outstanding natural beauty. The hotel was built in 1906 at the terminus of the new Bluebell line into Lyme Regis. Fish and seafood from Lyme Bay feature strongly on the menu, in dishes like pan-roasted fillet of Lyme Bay, line-caught seabass, and roasted Cornish monkfish tail. Other options may include slow-roasted free range pork belly with honey, or steak and kidney pud.
OPEN: 11-3 6-11 Closed: Last wk in Jan **BAR MEALS:** L served Tue-Sun 12-2.30 D served Tue-Sun 6.30-9.30 **RESTAURANT:** L served Tue-Sun 12-2.30 D served Tue-Sun 6.30-9.30 Av 3 course à la carte £22.50 🍺: Otter Bitter, Abbot Ale, Marston Pedigree, Bass. 🍷: 8 **FACILITIES:** Children's licence Garden: Patio garden, picturesque views **NOTES:** Parking 18
ROOMS: 7 bedrooms en suite 1 family room s£35 d£55 (♦♦♦)
No children overnight

MARSHWOOD   Map 04 SY39

Pick of the Pubs

The Bottle Inn 🍷
DT6 5QJ ☎ 01297 678254 🖥 01297 678739
e-mail: thebottleinn@msn.com
Dir: On the B3165 Crewkerne to Lyme Regis Road.

The thatched Bottle Inn was first mentioned as an ale house back in the 17th century, and was the first pub in the area during the 18th century to serve bottled beer rather than beer from the jug - hence the name. Standing beside the B3165 on the edge of the glorious Marshwood Vale, its rustic interior has simple wooden settles, scrubbed tables and a blazing fire. Proprietor Shane Pym loves introducing new dishes onto the menu, and recent additions have included local pork tenderloin with a cream and stilton sauce; Highland chicken stuffed with smoked salmon and served with a whisky and mustard sauce; for vegetarians there is aubergine in oregano batter with caramelised onions and goats cheese; and fish lovers will surely go for monkfish with a sun-dried tomato pesto, wrapped in parma ham. Taking the organic food theme to its

continued

furthest reaches, the pub is home to the annual World Stinging-Nettle Eating Championships.
OPEN: 12-3 6.30-11 **BAR MEALS:** L served all week 12-2 D served all week 6.30-9 **RESTAURANT:** L served all week D served all week 🅶: Free House 🍺: Otter Ale, Greene King Old Speckled Hen & Guest ales. 🍷: 7 **FACILITIES:** Garden **NOTES:** Parking 40

MILTON ABBAS   Map 04 ST80

The Hambro Arms 🍷
DT11 0BP ☎ 01258 880233 e-mail: info@hambroarms.co.uk
Dir: A354 Dorchester to Blandford, turn off at Royal Oak
Traditional whitewashed 18th-century thatched pub located in a picturesque landscaped village. Enjoy an appetising bar snack or perhaps, half shoulder of lamb with minted redcurrant sauce, liver and bacon, duck with orange sauce, venison sausages, or grilled sea bass, in the comfortable lounge bar or on the popular patio.
OPEN: 12-3 6.30-11 (May-Sep 11-11) **BAR MEALS:** L served all week 12-2 D served all week 7-9 **RESTAURANT:** L served all week 12-2 D served all week 7-9 🅶: Free House 🍺: Abbot Ale, Ringwood. **FACILITIES:** Dogs allowed in the garden only **NOTES:** Parking 20

MOTCOMBE   Map 04 ST82

The Coppleridge Inn ♦♦♦♦ 🍽️🍷
SP7 9HW ☎ 01747 851980 🖥 01747 851858
e-mail: thecoppleridgeinn@btinternet.com
web: www.coppleridge.com

Seventeen years ago the Coppleridge was a working dairy farm. The farmhouse is now the bar and restaurant, with flagstone floors, stripped pine and delightful views across the Blackmore Vale. Accommodation is provided in converted cowsheds and a function room/civil wedding venue in the 300-year-old threshing barn. Wide-ranging menus offer daily fresh fish and specials such as roast rack of lamb or mixed curry platter. Take a walk in the woods and meadows before eating.
OPEN: 11-3 5-11 (All day Sat & Sun) **BAR MEALS:** L served all week 12-2.30 D served all week 6-9.30 Av main course £8.50 **RESTAURANT:** L served all week 12-2.30 D served all week 6-9.30 Av 3 course à la carte £19.50 🅶: Free House 🍺: Butcombe Bitter, Greene King IPA, Wadworth 6X, Fuller's London Pride. 🍷: 7 **FACILITIES:** Child facs Garden: 15 acres including lawns, wood, pond area Dogs allowed Water provided **NOTES:** Parking 60
ROOMS: 10 bedrooms en suite 3 family rooms s£42.50 d£75 (♦♦♦♦)

> 🚭 Pubs with this logo do not allow smoking anywhere on their premises

England

Marquis of Lorne ♦♦♦♦ ♀
DT6 3SY ☎ 01308 485236 ▤ 01308 485666
e-mail: julie.woodroffe@btinternet.com
web: www.marquisoflorne.com
Dir: 3m E of A3066 Bridport-Beaminster rd. From Bridport North to Beaminster after 1.5m turn right signed Powerstock, West Milton & Mill after 3m at a T jct, pub up hill on left

A 16th-century farmhouse converted into a pub in 1871, when the marquis himself named it to prove land ownership. Membership of the Campaign for Real Food means that much local produce is used. Daily menus offer such dishes as pigeon breast with juniper and red wine sauce, home-made curry, fresh cod fillet, and mushroom and pepper stroganoff. Desserts might be rum and chocolate truffle terrine or twice baked cheesecake. Superb gardens with beautiful views.
OPEN: 11.30-2.30 6.30-11 (Sun all day) **BAR MEALS:** L served all week 12-2 D served all week 6.30-9 (Sun 12-9) Av main course £8
RESTAURANT: L served all week 12-2 D served all week 6.30-9 (Sun 12-9) Av 3 course à la carte £15 ☺: Palmers ◖: Palmers Copper, IPA, 200 Premium Ale. ♀: 8 **FACILITIES:** Garden: Well kept garden with good views & play area Dogs allowed Water **NOTES:** Parking 50 **ROOMS:** 7 bedrooms en suite s£45 d£70

The Three Elms ⌂◠ ♀
DT9 5JW ☎ 01935 812881 ▤ 01935 812881
Dir: From Sherborne, A352 towards Dorchester then A3030. Pub 1m on R

Real ales and locally produced ciders await you at this family-run free house overlooking scenic Blackmore Vale. Stunning views can be enjoyed from the pub garden, and the landlord prides himself on his impressive collection of about 1,600 model cars, as well as number plates from every state in America. Wide-ranging menu includes dishes like rosemary-crusted trout fillet, minted lamb shank, chicken kiev and mixed grill. Extensive range of starters, snacks and sandwiches.
OPEN: 11-2.30 6.30-11 (Sun 12-3, 7-10.30) Closed: 25-26 Dec
BAR MEALS: L served all week 12-2 D served all week 6.30-10 Av main course £7.50 **RESTAURANT:** L served all week 12-2 D served all week 6.30-10 ☺: Free House ◖: Fuller's London Pride, Butcombe Bitter, Otter Ale. ♀: 10 **FACILITIES:** Garden: Dogs allowed **NOTES:** Parking 50

The Smugglers Inn ♀
DT3 6HF ☎ 01305 833125 ▤ 01305 832219
e-mail: smugglersinn@innforanight.co.uk
Dir: 7m E of Weymouth, towards Wareham, pub is signed
This 13th-century inn was the headquarters of notorious French smuggler Pierre Latour, whose wife (the landlord's daughter) was mistakenly shot during a raid on the pub. Her husband was hiding up the chimney. Located on the coastal path, with a stream running through the garden and a play area for children, it's a good stop on a sunny day. The interior is cosy, with bare beams and flagstone floors. A major refurbishment took place in 2005.
OPEN: 11-11 (Sun 12-10.30) Closed Mon-Fri 3-6 Nov-Mar
BAR MEALS: L served all week 12-9.30 D served all week 12-9.30 Sun 12-9 Av main course £7 **RESTAURANT:** L served all week 12 D served all week 9.30 ☺: Woodhouse Inns ◖: Badger Best, Tanglefoot. ♀: 12 **FACILITIES:** Child facs Children's licence Garden: Large lawn with picnic benches & BBQ Dogs allowed Water & Treats **NOTES:** Parking 70

The Thimble Inn
DT2 7TD ☎ 01300 348270
Dir: A35 westbound, right onto B3143, Piddlehinton 4m
Friendly village local with open fires, traditional pub games and good food cooked to order. The pub stands in a pretty valley on the banks of the River Piddle, and the riverside patio is popular in summer. The extensive menu ranges from sandwiches and jacket potatoes to specials: rabbit, mushroom and tarragon pie, or poached rolled sole filled with shrimps and garlic and topped with seafood sauce.
OPEN: 12-2.30 7-11 (Sun 12-2.30 7-10.30) Closed: 25 Dec
BAR MEALS: L served all week 12-2 D served all week 7-9
RESTAURANT: L served all week 12-2 D served all week 7-9
☺: Free House ◖: Badger Best & Tanglefoot, Palmer Copper Ale & Palmer IPA, Ringwood Old Thumper. **FACILITIES:** Garden: Dogs allowed **NOTES:** Parking 50

The Piddle Inn ♀
DT2 7QF ☎ 01300 348468 ▤ 01300 348102
e-mail: info@piddleinn.co.uk
Dir: 7m N of Dorchester on B3143

Taking its name from the river Piddle which flows past the popular beer garden, this friendly village local has been a pub since the 1760s. The head chef sources local markets and suppliers, using the best produce available to prepare the daily-changing dishes. Expect chicken Caesar salad, cheesy pasta bake, home-made steak and ale pie, and fish and chips from a range of dishes.
OPEN: 12-3 6-11 (Closed Mon lunch) **BAR MEALS:** L served Tues-Sun 12-2 D served Mon-Sun 6.30-9 **RESTAURANT:** L served Tues-Sun 12-2 D served Mon-Sun 6.30-9 ☺: Free House ◖: Greene King Old Speckled Hen, IPA, Abbot Ale. ♀: 15
FACILITIES: Garden: 48 seater patio area, riverside Dogs allowed Water **NOTES:** Parking 20 **ROOMS:** 3 bedrooms en suite 1 family room s£40 d£65 (♦♦♦♦)
See Pub Walk on page 164

The Poachers Inn ♦♦♦♦ ⌂◠ ♀
DT2 7QX ☎ 01300 348358 ▤ 01300 348153
e-mail: thepoachersinn@piddletrenthide.fsbusiness.co.uk
web: www.thepoachersinn.co.uk
Dir: 8m from Dorchester on B3143
Following refurbishment, this inn by the River Piddle continues to provide real ales, good food, fires and traditional pub games at the heart of Thomas Hardy country. The riverside patio is especially popular in summer. Daily specials might feature stuffed field mushrooms with parmesan leeks; monkfish baked in parma ham; or scallops and king prawns with chilli jam. Leave room for home-made Dorset apple cake.

continued

OPEN: 12-11 **BAR MEALS:** L served all week 12-6.30 D served all week 6.30-9 Av main course £8.50 **RESTAURANT:** L served all week 12-6.30 D served all week 6.30-9 Av 3 course à la carte £16 ☺: Free House ☜: Carlsberg-Tetley Bitter, Poachers Ale, Scottish Courage John Smiths Smooth, Ringwood Old Thumper. ☘: 10 **FACILITIES:** Child facs Garden: Overlooks river, tables, seating Dogs allowed **NOTES:** Parking 40 **ROOMS:** 21 bedrooms en suite 3 family rooms s£45 d£65

PLUSH — Map 04 ST70

Pick of the Pubs

The Brace of Pheasants ☘

DT2 7RQ ☎ 01300 348357 e-mail: information@thebraceof pheasants.co.uk
Dir: A35 onto B3143, 5m to Piddletrenthide, then R to Mappowder & Plush

Tucked away in a fold of the hills east of Cerne Abbas, is this pretty 16th-century thatched village inn, hidden at the heart of Hardy's beloved county. He is believed to have used Plush as the model for Flintcomb-Ash in *Tess of the d'Urbervilles*. Beginning life as two cottages, the Brace of Pheasants then became a village smithy. Over the years it has been transformed into one of the area's most popular pubs. Inside the ambience is warm and welcoming, with an open fire, oak beams and fresh flowers. Lunch, dinner and bar meals are available, and the choice of menu reflects the changing of the seasons. Among the dishes you may find home-made bangers and mash, fillet steak and "huge" chips, wild mushroom risotto with truffle oil, or a selection of local fresh fish. Fantastic walking country.
OPEN: 12-2.30 7-11 (Sun 12-3 7-10.30) Closed: Dec 25 Closed Mon in winter **BAR MEALS:** L served Tues-Sun 12.30-2.30 D served Tues-Sun 7.30-9.30 Av main course £10.50 **RESTAURANT:** L served Tues-Sun 12-1.30 D served Tues-Sun 7-9.30 Av 3 course à la carte £22 ☺: Free House ☜: Fuller's London Pride, Butcombe Bitter, Ringwood Best, Adnams. ☘: 12 **FACILITIES:** Children's licence Large garden, food served outside Dogs allowed Water **NOTES:** Parking 30

POOLE — Map 04 SZ09

The Guildhall Tavern Ltd

15 Market St BH15 1NB ☎ 01202 671717 ▤ 01202 242346
e-mail: sewerynsevfred@aol.com
Dir: 2mins from Poole Quay
The Gallic nature of this historic former cider house in Poole's Old Town is explained by the names of its owners: Severine and Frederic Grande. For a start, there's bouillabaisse, which one doesn't often see in Britain, and a bilingual French/English specials menu which features mostly locally-landed fresh fish, crab and lobster. The rope-grown mussels travel a bit farther - from the Shetlands. Other mains include pan-fried duck breast, pork fillet with honey and sesame sauce, and vegetarian dishes.
OPEN: 11-3.30 6.30-11 Closed: 1st & 2nd wk in Nov **BAR MEALS:** L served all week 11-2.30 D served all week **RESTAURANT:** L served all week 12-2.30 D served all week 6.30-9.30 ☺: Inn Partnership ☜: Ringwood Best. **NOTES:** Parking 8

POWERSTOCK — Map 04 SY59

Pick of the Pubs

Three Horseshoes Inn ◆◆◆◆ ☘

DT6 3TF ☎ 01308 485328
e-mail: info@threehorseshoesinn.com
web: www.threehorseshoesinn.com
Dir: 3m off A3066 (Bridport/Beaminster rd)

A Victorian inn tucked away in a peaceful corner of West Dorset. The honeyed stone building forms an integral part of a classic English village scene, which is beloved of film producers seeking the spirit, character and essence of rural England. Powerstock is a popular choice with walkers and cyclists, and the pub's delightful garden tends to attract those wishing to savour the glorious view of the coast. With its well-deserved reputation for fine cuisine, it's hardly surprising the Three Horseshoes relies heavily on the use of fresh local produce for its light lunch menu and evening fare. Even the herbs are picked daily from the on-site garden. Grilled garlic tiger prawns and home-made game terrine with Lillian Sarah chutney for a starter, or, for a main course, confit duck leg with a wild damson sauce; pan-fried fillet of sea bass with a chilli and coriander salsa; or home-made venison pie with chips.
OPEN: 11-3 6.30-11 (Sun 12-3 6.30-10.30) **BAR MEALS:** L served all week 12-2.30 D served all week 7-9 Summer 7-9.30, Sun 12-3, 7-8.30 Av main course £9 **RESTAURANT:** L served all week 12-2.30 D served all week 7-9 Summer 7-9.30, Sun 12-3, 7-8.30 Av 3 course à la carte £22 ☺: Palmers ☜: Palmer's IPA, Copper Ale. ☘: 7 **FACILITIES:** Child facs Garden: Large terrace with lower garden for children Dogs allowed Water, food, toys, blankets **NOTES:** Parking 30 **ROOMS:** 3 bedrooms en suite 1 family room d£60

PUNCKNOWLE — Map 04 SY58

The Crown Inn ☘

Church St DT2 9BN ☎ 01308 897711 ▤ 01308 898282
Dir: From A35, into Bridevally, through Litton Cheney. From B3157, inland at Swyre.
There's a traditional atmosphere within the rambling, low-beamed bars at this picturesque 16th-century thatched inn, which was once the haunt of smugglers on their way from nearby Chesil Beach to visit prosperous customers in Bath. Food ranges from light snacks and sandwiches to home-made dishes like lamb chops with mint sauce; mushroom and nut

continued

PUNCKNOWLE continued

pasta with French bread; and tuna steak with basil and tomato sauce.

The Crown Inn

OPEN: 11-3 7-11 (Sun 12-3, 7-10.30 Summer 6.30 opening) Closed: 25 Dec **BAR MEALS:** L served all week 12-2 D served all week 7-9 Summer weekdays from 6.30 Av main course £8 ☺: Palmers ☜: Palmers IPA, 200 Premium Ale, Copper, Tally Ho!. ♀: 10 **FACILITIES:** Garden: Large garden with raised patio area Dogs allowed Water **NOTES:** Parking 12 No credit cards

---

SHERBORNE   Map 04 ST61

The Digby Tap
Cooks Ln DT9 3NS ☎ 01935 813148
e-mail: peter@lefevre.fslife.co.uk
Old-fashioned town pub with stone-flagged floors, old beams and a wide-ranging choice of real ale. A hearty menu of pub grub includes lasagne, steak and kidney pie, rump steak, gammon steak, and plaice or cod. The pub was used as a location for the 1990 TV drama *A Murder of Quality*, that starred Denholm Elliot and Glenda Jackson. Scenes from the film can be seen on the pub walls.
OPEN: 11-2.30 5.30-11 (Sat 6-11, Sun 12-3, 7-10.30) Closed: 1 Jan **BAR MEALS:** L served Mon-Sat 12-1.45 ☺: Free House ☜: Ringwood Best, Sharp's Cornish Coaster & Cornish Jack, St Austell Tinners. **FACILITIES:** Dogs allowed **NOTES:** No credit cards

Half Moon ♀
Half Moon St DT9 3LN ☎ 01935 812017 ▤ 01935 818130
An interesting building constructed from both Cotswold stone and brick and timber, the inn stands close to Sherborne Abbey in the centre of town. There's a choice of real ales and 14 wines by the glass, while food options take in a children's menu, bar snacks, traditional roasts, and a range of platter meals - chargrill, curry, pie and jumbo - (the latter including a giant mixed grill). Fish, vegetarian and salads are also offered.
OPEN: 11-11 (Sun 12-10.30) **BAR MEALS:** L served all week 11-6 D served all week 6-9 Av main course £6.95
RESTAURANT: L served all week 11-3 D served all week 6-9.30 ☺: Eldridge Pope ☜: Interbrew Bass, Wadworth 6X, Butcombe, Ringwood Best. ♀: 14 **FACILITIES:** Garden: Patio area, seating and flowers **NOTES:** Parking 40

Queen's Head
High St, Milborne Port DT9 5DQ
☎ 01963 250314 ▤ 01963 250339
Dir: On A30
Milborne Port has no facilities for shipping, the suffix being Old English for 'borough', a status it acquired in 1249. The building came much later, in Elizabethan times, although no mention is made of it as a hostelry until 1738. Charming and

continued

friendly bars, restaurant, beer garden and skittle alley combine to make it a popular free house in these parts. The new owners offer a sensible range of food.
OPEN: 12-2.30 5.30-11 (Sunday 12-10.30) **BAR MEALS:** L served all week 12-2 D served all week 7-9.30 Av main course £7.50
RESTAURANT: L served all week 12-2 D served all week 7-9.30 Av 3 course à la carte £14 ☺: Enterprise Inns ☜: Butcombe Bitters, old Speckled Hen, Fullers London Pride. **FACILITIES:** Children's licence Garden: patio/terrace, food served outside Dogs allowed Water **NOTES:** Parking 15

Skippers Inn ☜ ♀
Horsecastles DT9 3HE ☎ 01935 812753
e-mail: chrisfrowde@tiscali.co.uk
Dir: From Yeovil A30 to Sherborne

The interior of this end-of-terrace converted cider house is covered in naval memorabilia, and the building is much larger inside than it looks from the outside. The extensive blackboard menu can change by the minute, but there's usually a good selection of fresh fish. Other choices range from snacks and sandwiches to hot dishes such as faggots with red wine and mushroom sauce; and smoked chicken and asparagus.
OPEN: 11-2.30 6-11 Closed: 25 Dec **BAR MEALS:** L served all week 11.15-2 D served all week 6.30-9.30 Sun 12-3, 7-10.30 **RESTAURANT:** L served all week 11.15-2 D served all week 6.30-9.30 Sun 12-2, 7-9 ☺: Wadworth ☜: Wadworth 6X & Henrys IPA, Butcombe Butter & Guest Ales. ♀: 8 **FACILITIES:** Garden: Small garden with shrubs Dogs allowed Water **NOTES:** Parking 30

White Hart
Bishops Caundle DT9 5ND ☎ 01963 23301 ▤ 01963 23301 (by arrangement)
Dir: On A3030 between Sherborne & Sturminster Newton
Located in the heart of the Blackmore Vale, the 16th-century White Hart was reputedly used as a courthouse by the infamous Judge Jeffries. The large enclosed family garden offers beautiful views of the Bullbarrow Hills, as well as play equipment and an adventure trail for children. The extensive menu starts with baguettes, jacket potatoes and ploughman's, whilst hot dishes include pork steak Valentine; spinach and mushroom tagliatelle; and poached salmon supreme.
OPEN: 11.30-3 6.30-11 (Sun 12-3, 7-10.30) **BAR MEALS:** L served all week 12-2 D served all week 6.45-9.30 Av main course £8.50
RESTAURANT: L served all week 12-2 D served all week 6.30-9.30 ☺: Hall & Woodhouse ☜: Badger Best, Tanglefoot, Golden Champion, Sussex Golden Glory. **FACILITIES:** Child facs Garden: Patio area and large grass area with benches Dogs allowed Water provided **NOTES:** Parking 32

SHROTON OR IWERNE COURTNEY   Map 04 ST81

Pick of the Pubs

The Cricketers ◆◆◆◆◆ 🐟 ♀
DT11 8QD ☎ 01258 860421 📠 01258 861800
See Pick of the Pubs on page 176

STOKE ABBOTT   Map 04 ST40

The New Inn
DT8 3JW ☎ 01308 868333
A welcoming 17th-century farmhouse turned village inn, with thatched roof, log fires and a beautiful garden. It offers three real ales, and an extensive menu of light meals such as grilled black pudding with caramelised apples, and cold smoked duck breast with plum chutney, plus a good choice of baguettes, sandwiches and vegetarian dishes. Specials might include pork schnitzel with sweet chili dip, scallops wrapped in bacon, and beef and mushroom pie. Listen out for the singing chef!
OPEN: 11.30-3 7-11 (Winter Mon-Thur 7-10.30) (Sun 12-3, 7-10.30)
BAR MEALS: L served all week 12-2 D served all week 7-9.30
RESTAURANT: L served all week 12-2 D served all week 7-9.30
🍴: Palmers 🍺: Palmers IPA & 200 Premium Ale, Tally Ho.
FACILITIES: Child facs Garden: Large, comfortable, beautiful views Dogs allowed **NOTES:** Parking 25

STOURPAINE   Map 04 ST80

The White Horse Inn NEW ♀
Shaston Rd DT11 8TA ☎ 01258 453535
Dir: *A350 towards Shaftesbury in village of Stourpaine*
Traditional village public house dating back to the early 18th century. Sympathetically extended and refurbished in the last two years, the White Horse is within easy reach of two favourite haunts of walkers - the Roman fort on Hod Hill and the meandering River Stour. Inside are popular pub games, including darts and pool. From the wide-ranging menu expect honey and mint lamb; beef lasagne; cod and chips; pan-fried lambs' liver; and vegetable moussaka.
OPEN: 12-3 6-11 **BAR MEALS:** L served all week 12-2 D served Tues-Sun 6-9 Av main course £8 **RESTAURANT:** L served all week 12-2 D served Tues-Sun 6-9 🍺: Badgers Best, Festive Pheasant, Fursty Ferrett, Sussex. ♀: 8 **FACILITIES:** Child facs Garden: Decked courtyard Dogs allowed **NOTES:** Parking 25

STRATTON   Map 04 SY69

Saxon Arms 🐟 ♀
DT2 9WG ☎ 01305 260020 📠 01305 264225
e-mail: rodsaxonlamont1@yahoo.co.uk
Dir: *3m NW of Dorchester on A37, Saxon Arms is at the back of the village green between the church and new village hall*
A massive thatched roof, a patio overlooking the village green, solid oak beams, flagstone floors and a log-burning stove provide great atmosphere. Menus offer steak and ale pie, local butcher's pork herb sausages, lasagne verdie, and chicken, bacon and tarragon pie, while the specials boards may conjure up scallop & tiger prawn brochette, Portland crab or beef in Guinness casserole. Either way, leave room for one of the many desserts.
OPEN: 11-2.30 5.30-11 **BAR MEALS:** L served all week 11.30-2 D served all week 6.30-9 🍴: Free House 🍺: Fuller's London Pride, Palmers IPA, Saxon Ale. ♀: 8 **FACILITIES:** Garden: Portland stone patio area with table **NOTES:** Parking 35

STUDLAND   Map 05 SZ08

The Bankes Arms Hotel
Watery Ln BH19 3AU ☎ 01929 450225
& 450310 📠 01929 450307
Dir: *B3369 from Poole, across on Sandbanks chain ferry, or A35 from Poole, A351 then B3351*
Close to sweeping Studland Bay, across which can be seen the prime real estate enclave of Sandbanks, is this part 15th-century, creeper-clad inn, once a smugglers' dive. It specialises in fresh fish and seafood, including mussels, kebabs, crab gratin and lobster dishes. Others include game casserole, lamb noisettes in mint, honey and orange sauce, and spicy pork in chilli, coriander and caper sauce. The annual beer festival held in its large garden showcases 60 real ales, music, Morris dancing and stone carving.

The Bankes Arms Hotel

OPEN: 11-11 Closed: Dec 25 **BAR MEALS:** L served all week 12-3 D served all week 6-9.30 (Sun 12-9) 🍴: Free House 🍺: Isle of Purbeck Fossil Fuel, Studland Bay Wrecked, Solar Power.
FACILITIES: Garden: Garden with sea views of the Isle of Wight Dogs allowed **NOTES:** Parking 10

SYDLING ST NICHOLAS   Map 04 SY69

The Greyhound Inn ◆◆◆◆ ♀
DT2 9PD ☎ 01300 341303 📠 01300 341303
e-mail: info@thegreyhounddorset.co.uk
web: www.thegreyhounddorset.co.uk
Dir: *Off A37 Yeovil to Dorchester Road, turn off at Cerne Abbas/Sydling St Nicholas*
Located in one of Dorset's loveliest villages and surrounded by picturesque countryside, this traditional inn is characterised by its relaxed, welcoming atmosphere and delightful walled garden. Fresh home-cooked food served daily includes rib-eye steak, rack of English lamb, pan-fried king scallops with a sweet chilli, roast duck breast with port and redcurrant jus, and goats' cheese topped with pesto and grilled on salad.
OPEN: 11-3.30 6-11 (Sun 12-3.30, 7-11) **BAR MEALS:** L served all week 12-2 D served all week 6-10 **RESTAURANT:** L served all week 12-2 D served all week 6-10 🍴: Free House 🍺: Fuller's London Pride, Palmer IPA, Butcombe. ♀: 12 **FACILITIES:** Garden: Dogs allowed **NOTES:** Parking 24 **ROOMS:** 6 bedrooms en suite No children overnight

Pick of the Pubs

SHROTON OR IWERNE COURTNEY – DORSET

The Cricketers

A classically English pub, built at the turn of the 20th century, The Cricketers is to be found nestling under Hambledon Hill, which is renowned for its Iron-Age hill-forts. Above all a welcoming local, The Cricketers comprises a main bar, sports bar and den, all light and airy rooms leading to the restaurant at the rear. This in turn overlooks a lovely garden, well stocked with trees and flowers.

In fine weather, customers may like to eat outside beneath the clematis-covered pergola which seats 24. Inside, the cricket theme is taken up in the collection of sports memorabilia on display and the hand pumps for the real ales, which are shaped like cricket bats. And during the summer months the local cricket team really do frequent the establishment. The pub is also popular with hikers, lured from the Wessex Way, which runs conveniently through the garden. An extensive menu, serving both the bar and restaurant, offers a good choice of interesting dishes featuring unusual combinations. Typical options are beetroot risotto with pecans and feta cheese, or home-made cod and spring onion fish cakes with peppers, a hint of garlic and lemon mayonnaise. Guests who wish to prolong a pleasurable experience might want to book ahead for the exclusive privilege of staying in the pub's self-contained garden room. It offers attractive five-diamond accommodation with en suite facilities.

OPEN: 11.30-2.30 6.30-11 (Winter Sun eve 7-11)
BAR MEALS: L served all week 12-2 D served all week 6.30-9 Sun 7-9, no food on Sun eve in winter Av main course £6
RESTAURANT: L served all week 12-2 D served all week 6.30-9 (Sun 7-9, no food on Sun eve in winter) Av 3 course à la carte £17
🍴: Free House
🍺: Ringwood 49er, Greene King IPA, Tanglefoot Marstons Pedigree, Wadworth 6X. ♀: 10
FACILITIES: Child facs Garden: Bordered by trees and hedges, herb garden Dogs allowed Water in garden **NOTES:** Parking 19
ROOMS: 1 bedroom en suite s£40 d£70 No children overnight

◆◆◆◆◆ 🐟 ♀ Map 04 ST81
DT11 8QD
☎ 01258 860421
📠 01258 861800
Dir: Off the A350 Shaftesbury to Blandford, signed from Shroton

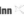
TARRANT MONKTON   Map 04 ST90

Pick of the Pubs

The Langton Arms ◆◆◆◆ ♀
DT11 8RX ☎ 01258 830225 ▤ 01258 830053
e-mail: info@thelangtonarms.co.uk
Dir: A31 from Ringwood, or A357 from Shaftesbury, or A35 from Bournemouth
This is an attractive 17th-century thatched inn occupying a peaceful spot in the village centre close to the church. Well known for its excellent food and an ever-changing range of real ales, The Langton Arms offers a good selection of interesting dishes and, where possible, uses Dorset produce supplied by local farmers. The main menu is divided between starters, Dorset game selection, pub favourites, fish selection, vegetarian selection, steaks and desserts. King prawns in crisp filo pastry, and country farmhouse paté might open a meal, and you could then go on to select from game pie cooked in red wine and redcurrant sauce; pan-fried Dorset lamb's liver with pork and leek sausage and bacon; deep fried battered cod; home-made broccoli, brie and mushroom lasagne; or one of the roasts with green pepper, béarnaise or garlic butter sauce. Desserts like warm chocolate cake; mango mousse; and coffee and walnut pudding should please.
OPEN: 11.30-11 (Sun 12-10.30) **BAR MEALS:** L served all week 11.30-2.30 D served all week 6-9.30 Av main course £8.95 **RESTAURANT:** L served Sun 12-2 D served Wed-Sat 7-9 Av 3 course à la carte £28 Av 3 course fixed price £18.95 ❑: Free House ◖: Hop Back Best, Guest Beers. ♀: 6 **FACILITIES:** Garden: Large beer garden Dogs allowed only in public bar **NOTES:** Parking 100 **ROOMS:** 6 bedrooms en suite s£60 d£80

TOLPUDDLE   Map 04 SY79

The Martyrs Inn ♀
DT2 7ES ☎ 01305 848249 ▤ 01305 848977
e-mail: martyrs@scottz.co.uk
Dir: Off A35 between Bere Regis (A31/A35 Junction)
Tolpuddle is the somewhat unlikely birthplace of the Trades Union Congress. Its seeds were sown in 1834 by six impoverished farm labourers who tried to bargain with local landowners for better conditions. Their punishment was transportation to Australia. Martyrs' memorabilia abounds in the pub. Home-made starters include chicken liver and wild mushroom paté, and garlic mushrooms en croûte; main courses include Tolpuddle sausages with mash and onion gravy, country vegetable pasta bake, and spicy chicken curry with rice and naan bread. There is a play area to keep the children amused.
OPEN: 11-3 6-11 (Etr-Oct open all day all wk)
BAR MEALS: L served all week 12-3 D served all week 6.30-9 Av main course £7.95 **RESTAURANT:** L served all week D served all week ❑: Hall & Woodhouse ◖: Badger Dorset Best & Tanglefoot. ♀: 10 **FACILITIES:** Child facs Garden: Dogs allowed **NOTES:** Parking 25

Pick of the Pubs have that extra special quality that makes them stand out from the crowd. Their entries are highlighted, and may be a full page

TRENT   Map 04 ST51

Rose & Crown Inn ▷
DT9 4SL ☎ 01935 850776 ▤ 01935 850796
e-mail: ian@roseandcrowntrent.co.uk
web: www.roseandcrowntrent.com
Dir: W on A30 towards Yeovil. 3m from Sherborne right to Over Compton/Trent, 1.5m downhill, then right. Pub opp church
Workers building the 15th-century church constructed the oldest part of this thatched pub, which has been considerably added to over the centuries. The France-bound Charles II reputedly hid here, while in the mid 20th-century it was a favoured watering hole of Lord Fisher, the Archbishop of Canterbury who crowned Queen Elizabeth II. Today's visitors can enjoy the likes of moules marinière, seafood mornay or herb-crusted lamb cutlets, while the children play on the climbing frame, swings and slide.
OPEN: 12-3 7-11 (Sun 12-3 only) Closed: 1 Jan
BAR MEALS: L served all week 12-2 D served all week 7-9 Av main course £9 **RESTAURANT:** L served all week 12-2 D served all week 7-9 Av 3 course à la carte £16 ❑: Free House ◖: Otterale, Butcombe Bitter,Dartmoor, Guiness. **FACILITIES:** Child facs Garden: table seating, fish pond, south facing Dogs allowed on lead only, water **NOTES:** Parking 30

WEST BEXINGTON   Map 04 SY58

The Manor Hotel ★★ ▷
DT2 9DF ☎ 01308 897616 ▤ 01308 897704
e-mail: themanorhotel@btconnect.com
Dir: On B3157, 5m E of Bridport
The extraordinary pebbled sweep of Chesil Beach is just 500 yards from this sturdy, handsome and cosily inviting 11th-century manor house, its original flagstones still reassuringly underfoot, and Jacobean oak panelling intact. Whether you pick a traditional bar meal, or lunch or dinner in the elegant restaurant, all is freshly prepared, including starters such as prawn cocktail; and main courses like home-made fish pie, steak and kidney pie (or pudding), liver and bacon.
OPEN: 11-11 (Sun 12-10.30) **BAR MEALS:** L served all week 12-2 D served all week 6.30-9.30 Av main course £9.95 **RESTAURANT:** L served all week 12-2 D served all week 7-9.30 Av 3 course fixed price £19.50 ❑: Free House ◖: Butcombe Gold, Harbour Master. **FACILITIES:** Child facs Garden: Large garden with sea views Dogs allowed Water Bowls **NOTES:** Parking 40 **ROOMS:** 13 bedrooms en suite 3 family rooms s£70 d£110

WEST KNIGHTON   Map 04 SY78

The New Inn
DT2 8PE ☎ 01305 852349
A 200-year-old pub with a listed archway, the New Inn was originally a row of farm cottages. Its rural location makes an ideal base for walks and exploring the surrounding countryside. The regular menu is supplemented by weekly specials, such as moules marinière, and braised beef in red wine and garlic sauce. Among the interesting puddings are kish-mish salad of dried fruit in brandy and rosewater, and squidgy chocolate roll.
OPEN: 11-3 7-11.30 (Winter 12-3, 7-11.30) **BAR MEALS:** L served all week 12-2 D served all week 7-9 Av main course £5 **RESTAURANT:** L served all week 11.30-2 D served all week 7-9 ❑: Pubmaster ◖: Ringwood Best, Old Speckled Hen, Directors. **FACILITIES:** Garden: Fenced area safe for young children Dogs allowed Water **NOTES:** Parking 30

England

WEST LULWORTH
Map 04 SY88

The Castle Inn ⌂ ♀
Main Rd BH20 5RN ☎ 01929 400311 📠 01929 400415
Dir: On the Wareham to Dorchester Rd, left approx 1m from Wareham

In a delightful setting near Lulworth Cove, this family-run thatched village inn lies close to plenty of good walks. The friendly bars offer a traditional atmosphere in which to enjoy a pint of Ringwood Best or Gales' ales. Outside, you'll find large tiered gardens packed with plants, and in summer there's a giant outdoor chess set. The wide-ranging menu includes guinea fowl breast, salmon with hash browns and peas, and a selection of grilled steaks.
OPEN: 11-2.30 6-11 (Winter 12-2.30, 7-11) Closed: 25 Dec
BAR MEALS: L served all week 11-2.30 D served all week 6-10.30
Av main course £7.50 **RESTAURANT:** L served all week D served Fri & Sat 7-9.30 ⊕: Free House ◀: Ringwood Best, Gales, Courage, John Smiths. ♀: 8 **FACILITIES:** Child facs Children's licence Garden: Large tiered garden lots of plants flowers Dogs allowed Water/Food **NOTES:** Parking 30

WEST STAFFORD
Map 04 SY78

The Wise Man Inn ⌂
DT2 8AG ☎ 01305 263694
Dir: 2m from A35

Set in the heart of Thomas Hardy country, this thatched 16th-century pub was originally the village shop and off-licence. It is now a regular stopping-off point for those on the Hardy trail, with the Thomas Hardy cottage and Church of Stinsford not far away. The menu makes full use of good local produce - fresh fish and vegetables, and organic meat. Along with a selection of sandwiches, baguettes, light meals and ploughman's you'll find a blackboard dinner menu of specials in the restaurant.
OPEN: 12-3 6.30-11 (Summer Sat-Sun open all day)
BAR MEALS: L served all week 12-2 D served Mon-Sat 7-9 Sun 12-2.30 **RESTAURANT:** L served all week 12-2 D served Mon-Sat 7-9 Sun 12-2.30 Av 3 course à la carte £12 ⊕: Pubmaster ◀: Ringwood, 2 casked ales each week. **FACILITIES:** Child facs Garden: Large, plenty of seating, secluded Dogs allowed Water & biscuits provided **NOTES:** Parking 25

WEYMOUTH
Map 04 SY67

The Old Ship Inn ⌂ ♀
7 The Ridgeway DT3 5QQ ☎ 01305 812522 📠 01305 816533
Dir: 3m from Weymouth town centre, at bottom of the ridgeway
Thomas Hardy refers to this historic pub in his novels *Under the Greenwood Tree* and *The Trumpet Major*. The terrace offers views over Weymouth, while inside there are copper pans, old clocks and a beamed open fire. A good range of jacket potatoes, baguettes and salads is supplemented by traditional pub favourites. There are also more adventurous dishes like chestnut gnocchi with fresh cranberry and wild mushrooms; and lobster, fresh crab and lime risotto.
OPEN: 12-11 (Sun 12-10.30) **BAR MEALS:** L served all week 12-2.30 D served all week 6-9.30 Av main course £12.50
RESTAURANT: L served Mon-Sat 12-2 D served all week 6-9.30 Av 3 course à la carte £35 Av 3 course fixed price £25 ⊕: Inn Partnership ◀: Greene King Old Speckled Hen, Ringwood Best & guest ales. ♀: 7 **FACILITIES:** Garden: Patio garden with enclosed grass area Dogs allowed Water **NOTES:** Parking 12

WINTERBORNE ZELSTON
Map 04 SY89

Botany Bay Inne
DT11 9ET ☎ 01929 459227
An obvious question: how did the pub get its name? Built in the 1920s as The General Allenby, it was changed about 17 years ago in belated recognition of prisoners from Dorchester jail who were required to spend a night nearby before transportation to Australia. Since no such fate awaits anyone these days, meals to enjoy at leisure include bacon-wrapped chicken breast; steak and kidney pudding; roasted Mediterranean vegetable Wellington; and fish catch of the day. Real ales are locally brewed.
OPEN: 12-3 6-11 (Mon-Sat summer open 10)
BAR MEALS: L served all week 12-2.15 D served all week 6.30-9.30
RESTAURANT: L served all week 12-2.15 D served all week 6.30-9.30 Av 3 course à la carte £16 ◀: Badger Best Bitter, Tanglefoot, Botany Bay Bitter, Fursty Ferret. **FACILITIES:** Children's licence Garden: Paved area with flowers overlooking fields Dogs allowed in bar only; water **NOTES:** Parking 60

CO DURHAM

AYCLIFFE
Map 19 NZ22

The County ♀
13 The Green, Aycliffe Village DL5 6LX
☎ 01325 312273 📠 01325 308780 web: www.the-county.co.uk
Dir: Off the A167 into Aycliffe Village
With its welcoming atmosphere and award-winning village location, this informal free house has twice featured on the BBC's *Food and Drink* programme. Owner Andrew Brown won the first Raymond Blanc scholarship in 1995 so, as you'd expect, all meals are cooked to order from the freshest local ingredients. Smoked salmon and scrambled egg toasted muffin sets the tone of the bar menu, whilst pot-roast pheasant and vegetable moussaka are typical carte dishes.
OPEN: 12-3 5.30-11 (Closed Sun) Closed: 25-26 Dec, 1 Jan
BAR MEALS: L served Mon-Sat 12-2 D served Mon-Sat 6-7 Av main course £13.50 **RESTAURANT:** L served Mon-Sat 12-2 D served Mon-Sat 6-9.30 Av 3 course à la carte £26 ⊕: Free House ◀: Scottish Courage , Wells Bombardier, Jennings Cumberland Ale, Castle Eden & Camerons. ♀: 9 **NOTES:** Parking 30

BARNARD CASTLE
Map 19 NZ01

Pick of the Pubs

The Morritt Arms Hotel ★★★ 🏵 ♀
Greta Bridge DL12 9SE ☎ 01833 627232 📠 01833 627392
e-mail: relax@themorritt.co.uk web: www.themorritt.co.uk
Dir: At Scotch Corner take A66 towards Penrith, after 9m turn at
Greta Bridge. Hotel over bridge on left.

Situated in rural Teesdale, The Morritt Arms has been an inn for two centuries. The present building began life in the 17th century as a farmhouse, although buried underneath are the remains of a Roman settlement. In its busy coaching days The Morritt and other Greta Bridge inns were important overnight stops for the London-Carlisle service. Charles Dickens researched *Nicholas Nicklelby* here in 1839, his stay commemorated by the Dickens Bar, with a famous mural by John Gilroy. The artist, in turn, is remembered in Gilroy's Restaurant, the more formal dining area. Here the carte offers starters of smoked haddock and potato chowder; roast pear and goat's cheese salad with a citrus reduction; seared scallops topped with a lemon crust served with a petit salad and chive oil; sweet melon and poached fruits with a aport and orange syrup; and grilled black pudding with pan-fried foie gras, apricot and saffron chutney and ginger syrup. Main courses include ballantine of chicken with a wild mushroom and tarragon stuffing; cannon of lamb with a red onion crust with basil crushed potatoes and a mint and fevés jus; pan-roasted duck with Parmentier potatoes and sautéed pancetta finished with honey and pepper jus; and risotto of wild mushrooms and artichokes, with deep-fried Swaledale cheese beignets. For more informal meals choose the bar, Pallatts bistro, or the landscaped gardens.
OPEN: 11-11 **BAR MEALS:** L served all week 12-3 D served all week 6-9.30 Sun 6-9 **RESTAURANT:** L served all week 12-3 D served all week 7-9 Sun 7-9 Av 3 course à la carte £30 Av 4 course fixed price £15.95 🍴: Free House 🍺: John Smith's, Timothy Taylor Landlord, Black Sheep Best, Cumberland Ale. ♀: 20 **FACILITIES:** Child facs Children's licence Garden: Terraced, traditional garden with walk ways Dogs allowed Water **NOTES:** Parking 100 **ROOMS:** 23 bedrooms en suite s£65 d£65

COTHERSTONE
Map 19 NZ01

The Fox and Hounds 🐟 ♀
DL12 9PF ☎ 01833 650241 📠 01833 650518
e-mail: ianandnichola@tiscali.co.uk
Dir: 4m W of Barnard Castle. From A66 onto B6277. Cotherstone signed

Set in the heart of Teesdale, this delightful 18th-century

continued

The Fox & Hounds

Cotherstone DL12 9PF
Tel: 01833 650241 Fax: 01833 650518

The Fox & Hounds Country Inn & Restaurant warmly welcomes you to the village of Cotherstone which is situated in beautiful Upper Teesdale.
There are five recently refurbished bedrooms (2004) that include whirlpool baths, electric showers & colour televisions.
Only fresh seasonal produce is used in the kitchen to prepare your menus, which are accompanied by a large range of wines & award winning real ales.

coaching inn is the perfect outdoor holiday base. Both the restaurant and the heavily beamed bar boast welcoming winter fires in original fireplaces. Fresh local ingredients are the foundation of home-made bar meals like pork, sage and apple pie, whilst roast salmon fillet on chive mash; or curried aubergine and cashew nut loaf are typical daily specials.
OPEN: 12-3 6.30-11 Closed: 25-26 Dec **BAR MEALS:** L served all week 12-2 D served all week 7-9 Sun 7-8.30 Av main course £9.90 **RESTAURANT:** L served all week 12-2 D served all week 7-9 Sun 7-8.30 Av 3 course à la carte £18.50 🍴: Free House 🍺: Black Sheep Best, Village Brewer Bull Bitter, Tetley Smoothflow. ♀: 10 **FACILITIES:** Garden: Picnic benches at front in summer Dogs allowed Kennel available **NOTES:** Parking 20
See advert on this page

DURHAM
Map 19 NZ24

Seven Stars Inn ♀
High St North, Shincliffe Village DH1 2NU
☎ 0191 384 8454 📠 0191 386 0640
e-mail: enquiries@sevenstarsinn.co.uk
A little gem tucked away on the edge of picturesque Shincliffe, this quaint inn has remained virtually unaltered since 1724, although tasteful decoration and the addition of antique furnishings have improved levels of comfort for discerning local diners. Pretty in summer with its tubs and window boxes, and cosily lit during the winter, it offers a fine setting for imaginative British cuisine with exotic influences. The bar/lounge menu offers sandwiches, soup, and steak and ale pie, while the restaurant menu (also available in the lounge and bar) has the likes of Thai crab cakes on tomato salad with coriander dressing, Cajun-spiced rump of lamb with tomato and olive ragout, sautéed potatoes and red wine jus, and for

continued

DURHAM continued

pudding a white chocolate and blueberry brûlée. Accommodation is also available in individually-furnished bedrooms.
OPEN: 11.30-11 (Sun 12-10.30) **BAR MEALS:** L served all week 12-2.30 D served all week 6-9.30 Av main course £11 **RESTAURANT:** L served all week 12-2.30 D served all week 6-9.30 Av 3 course à la carte £23 ⊕: Free House ◖: Theakstons Best Bitter, Castle Eden Ale, Blacksheep Bitter, Courage Directors. ♀: 8 **FACILITIES:** Dogs allowed **ROOMS:** 8 bedrooms en suite 1 family room s£40 d£55 (♦♦♦)

Victoria Inn NEW 🐟
86 Hallgarth St DH1 3AS ☎ 0191 386 5269
Dir: In Durham city centre
The interior of this family-run pub has scarcely changed since it opened in 1899, and with no jukebox, music or pool table to spoil things, it's a Durham must. A Grade-II listing embraces the tiny snug and screened off-sales booth. Some people say they've heard 'original customers' ringing the bell-pushes for service, but it can't be for food as there's no kitchen. There are frequently changing guest ales, 40 Scottish malts and 30 Irish whiskies, though.
OPEN: 11.45-3 6-11 ◖: Jarrow Red Ellen, Darwin Ghost, Big Lamp Bitter, Jarrow Bitter. **FACILITIES:** Dogs allowed Water
NOTES: Parking 4 **ROOMS:** 6 bedrooms en suite 1 family room s£40 d£58 (♦♦♦)

FIR TREE   Map 19 NZ13

Duke of York ♦♦♦♦
DL15 8DG ☎ 01388 762848 ▨ 01388 767055
e-mail: suggett@firtree-crook.fsnet.co.uk
Dir: On A68 trunk road to Scotland, 12m W of Durham City

Former drovers' and coaching inn, dating from 1749, on the tourist route (A68) to Scotland, midway between York and Edinburgh. Family owned and run for four generations, it offers an old world atmosphere with 'mouseman' Robert Thompson's furniture and bar fittings, and the proprietor's collection of African memorabilia and Stone Age flints. Best quality local meat, fish and cheeses are used in the dishes, and the home-made soups are particularly popular.
OPEN: 11-2.30 6.30-10.30 **BAR MEALS:** L served all week 12-2 D served all week 6.30-9 Av main course £7.95 **RESTAURANT:** L served all week 12-2 D served all week 6.30-9 Av 3 course à la carte £20 ⊕: Free House ◖: Black Sheep, Worthington. **FACILITIES:** Child facs Children's licence Garden at rear of pub, patio area Dogs allowed Water **NOTES:** Parking 65 **ROOMS:** 5 bedrooms en suite 1 family room s£54 d£78

MIDDLESTONE   Map 19 NZ23

Ship Inn
Low Rd DL14 8AB ☎ 01388 810904
e-mail: graham@snaithg.freeserve.co.uk
Dir: On B6287, Kirk Merrington to Coundon rd
Beer drinkers will appreciate the string of CAMRA accolades received by this family-run pub on the village green. In the last four years regulars could have sampled well over 800 different beers. Ask about the pub's challenge for regulars to send postcards from every country in the world. Home-cooked food in the bar and restaurant. The rooftop patio has spectacular views over the Tees Valley and Cleveland Hills.
OPEN: 4-11 (Thur-Sat 12-11 Sun 12-10) **BAR MEALS:** L served Fri-Sun 12-2.30 D served Mon, Wed-Sat 5-9 (Sun 12-2) Av main course £6 **RESTAURANT:** L served Fri-Sun 12-2.30 D served Mon, Wed-Sat 5-9 (Sun 12-2) ◖: Timothy Taylor Landlord & 5 Guest Ales. **FACILITIES:** Child facs Village green and patio with panoramic views Dogs allowed **NOTES:** Parking 6 No credit cards

MIDDLETON-IN-TEESDALE   Map 18 NY92

The Teesdale Hotel
Market Square DL12 0QG ☎ 01833 640264
& 640537 ▨ 01833 640651
The hotel lies just off the Pennine Way, close to some of Northern England's loveliest scenery. Tastefully modernised, this family-run coaching inn is noted for its striking 17th-century stone exterior. Inside, the friendly atmosphere and cosy log fires simply add to the charm. Old favourites like cottage pie or cod and chips rub shoulders with more adventurous fare, including brie and redcurrant tart; and smoked haddock with poached egg and cheese sauce.
OPEN: 11-11 **BAR MEALS:** L served all week 12-2 D served all week 7-9 **RESTAURANT:** L served Sun 12-1.30 D served all week 7.30-9 ⊕: Free House ◖: Guinness, Tetley Smooth, Jennings Cumberland Ale, Jennings Red Breast. **FACILITIES:** Dogs allowed

NEWTON AYCLIFFE   Map 19 NZ22

Blacksmiths Arms 🐟 ♀
Preston le Skerne, (off Ricknall Lane) DL5 6JH ☎ 01325 314873
As its name suggests, this traditional pub was originally a blacksmith's shop dating from around 1800. Set in isolated farmland, it enjoys an excellent reputation locally as a good dining pub. Fish dishes range from deep fried cod, and fillet of salmon, to orange and tarragon trout, and whole tail breaded scampi. Chef's specialities include sweet chilli pancakes, stir-fry beef cashew, grilled fillet of beef and authentic Italian lasagne.
OPEN: 12-3 6-11 (Sun 12-10.30) Closed: 25 Dec, 1 Jan **BAR MEALS:** L served Tue-Sun 11.30-2 D served Tue-Sun 6-9.30 (Sun 12-2, 7-9) ⊕: Free House ◖: Ever changing selection of real ales. ♀: 10 **FACILITIES:** Child facs Garden: Fully enclosed rural setting, 0.75 acre Dogs allowed Water **NOTES:** Parking 25

ROMALDKIRK   Map 19 NY92

Pick of the Pubs

Rose and Crown ★★ ◉◉ ♀
DL12 9EB ☎ 01833 650213 ▨ 01833 650828
e-mail: hotel@rose-and-crown.co.uk
web: www.rose-and-crown.co.uk
See Pick of the Pubs on opposite page

Rose and Crown

In the 18th century travellers arrived here by coach and four. In transport terms we have moved on, but the appearance of what must be one of the prettiest villages in England can have changed very little. Certainly the inn looks much the same, the stocks and water pump remain standing on the green, while ancient St Romald's church - the Cathedral of the Dale - is still going strong after seven centuries.

So it comes as no great surprise to step inside the inn and discover polished panelling, old beams, gleaming brasses, fresh flowers and maybe the odd creaking stair. Savour the buzz of the wood-panelled bar with its oak settle, daily newspapers, antique prints, carriage lamps and a crackling fire in the dog-grate. In the restaurant are more oak panelling, crisp white tablecloths, sparkling silver and soft lights, while candles in waxy bottles, and pictures of pompous French waiters set the mood in the red-walled Crown Brasserie. Lunch in the bar from the daily changing menu could begin with smoked Loch Fyne salmon, wholemeal blinis and crème fraîche, or home-made corned beef with pickled red cabbage. Try grilled sea bass with tagliatelle of vegetables and fresh herb cream as a main course, or perhaps Mr Slack's pork sausage with black pudding, mustard mash and shallot gravy. In the evening, dinner in the restaurant might consist of matured Cumberland farmhouse ham with fresh figs; followed by crisp roast farm duckling with leek and bacon pudding, apple compote and calvados gravy; and warm lemon tart with vanilla ice cream for pudding. The good selection of wines is tasted and chosen in-house, with many by the glass. Bedrooms, individually decorated with rich fabrics and vibrant colours, all have luxurious modern bathrooms. Book room six if you dare - it has a ghost!

OPEN: 11.30-3 5.30-11 (Closed: Dec 24-26)
BAR MEALS: L served all week 12-1.30 D served all week 6.30-9.30 Av main course £9.50
RESTAURANT: L served Sun only 12-1.30 D served all week 7.30-9 Av 4 course fixed price £26
🍺: Free House
🍺: Theakston Best, Black Sheep Best.
♀: 10
FACILITIES: Child facs Children's licence Garden: Tables at front of Inn Dogs allowed **NOTES:** Parking 24
ROOMS: 12 bedrooms en suite 2 family rooms s£75 d£126

★★ ◎◎ ♀   Map 19 NY92
DL12 9EB
☎ 01833 650213
🖷 01833 650828
📧 hotel@rose-and-crown.co.uk
🌐 www.rose-and-crown.co.uk
Dir: 6m NW from Barnard Castle on B6277

England

SEDGEFIELD — Map 19 NZ32

Dun Cow Inn ◆◆ ☒
43 Front St TS21 3AT ☎ 01740 620894 📠 01740 622163
e-mail: duncowinn@grayner.fsnet.co.uk
Dir: At junct of A177 & A689. Inn in centre of village
An interesting array of bric-a-brac can be viewed inside this splendid old village inn, which has many flower baskets bedecking its exterior in summer. It is also the pub that can claim to be Prime Minister Tony Blair's local, as he is the local MP. This is the pub that hosted Tony's 'million pound lunch' with American President, George W Bush. Typical offerings include Angus sirloin steaks, locally-made sausages, spring lamb cutlets, fresh Shetland mussels, and mushroom stroganoff. Pudding choices often include gooseberry crumble and chocolate fudge cake with butterscotch sauce.
OPEN: 11-3 6.30-11 **BAR MEALS:** L served all week 12-2 D served all week 7-10 Av main course £8.95 **RESTAURANT:** L served all week 12-2 D served all week 7-10 Av 3 course à la carte £19 🖱: Free House ☒: Theakston Best Bitter, John Smiths Smooth, Black Sheeps Bitter & Guest Beers. ☒: 8 **NOTES:** Parking 30
ROOMS: 6 bedrooms en suite s£49.50 d£65

TRIMDON — Map 19 NZ33

The Bird in Hand
Salters Ln TS29 6JQ ☎ 01429 880391
Village pub nine miles west of Hartlepool with fine views over surrounding countryside from an elevated position. There's a cosy bar and games room, stocking a good choice of cask ales and guest beers, a spacious lounge and large conservatory restaurant. Traditional Sunday lunch goes down well, as does breaded plaice and other favourites. In summer you can sit outside in the garden, which has a roofed over area for climbing plants.
OPEN: 12-11 (Sun 12-10.30) Closed Mon-Thurs 4-7
BAR MEALS: L served Tues-Sun 12-3 D served Tues-Sun 7-9
Av main course £3.50 **FACILITIES:** Child facs Garden: Enclosed area with gazebo type roof Dogs allowed **NOTES:** Parking 30

ESSEX

ARKESDEN — Map 12 TL43

Pick of the Pubs

Axe & Compasses 🖱 ☒
High St CB11 4EX ☎ 01799 550272 📠 01799 550906
See Pick of the Pubs on opposite page

BLACKMORE END — Map 12 TL73

Pick of the Pubs

The Bull Inn ☒
CM7 4DD ☎ 01371 851037 📠 01371 851037
Dir: 5m from Braintree 1m from Wethersfield
Off the beaten track in the heart of tranquil north Essex, not far from the showpiece village of Finchingfield, star of a thousand kitchen calendars. This traditional village pub, created from two (possibly) 14th-century cottages and an adjoining barn, is full of original beams and open hearths, and overlooks farmland. Some of the beams may have come from old ships. Herbs used in the kitchen are grown

in the attractive garden. Word of mouth, rather than advertising, guarantees its continuing popularity with locals and visitors. The no-nonsense menu caters for most tastes with a good choice of starters such as crispy mushrooms with a garlic dip, prawn cocktail, or nachos, backed up with main courses including sausage and mash, thatched pie, fish and chips, or rack of lamb. Baked potatoes, toasties and baguettes are available for those taking the light bite route. On Sundays there's a set-price lunch with similar starters, traditional roasts and a selection of sweets of the toffee apple and pecan pie, and chocolate pudding variety.
OPEN: 12-3 6-11 **BAR MEALS:** L served all week 12-3 D served all week 7-9 Sun 12-3, 6-9 Av main course £7.95 **RESTAURANT:** L served Tue-Sun 12-2.30 D served Mon-Sun 6-9 🖱: Free House ☒: Greene King IPA, Abbot Ale, Adnams Best, London Pride. ☒: 6 **FACILITIES:** Child facs Children's licence Garden: Beer garden, outdoor eating, BBQ Dogs allowed Water bowl **NOTES:** Parking 36

BRAINTREE — Map 07 TL72

Pick of the Pubs

The Green Dragon at Young's End 🖱 ☒
Upper London Rd, Young's End CM77 8QN
☎ 01245 361030 📠 01245 362575
e-mail: info@greendragonbraintree.co.uk
Dir: M11 junct 8, A120 towards Colchester. At Braintree bypass, A131 S towards Chelmsford, exit at Youngs End on Great Leighs bypass

The building of a new by-pass has restored the quiet location of this country inn on the old A131 Braintree - Chelmsford road. The former house and stables is now a comfortable venue for good drinking and dining, with winter fires creating a cosy atmosphere in the friendly bars. Quality awards for their cask ales and hygiene standards testify to the owners' commitment to running a good-value, family-friendly hostelry. Plain brick walls and a wealth of old beams characterise the non-smoking Barn and first-floor Hayloft restaurants. The same blackboard and extensive printed menus are available throughout, ranging from light snacks to full meals. Lunchtime brings sandwiches, ploughman's and filled baguettes, with more substantial offerings like Tuscan-style wild rabbit; baked Loch Fyne Queen scallops; and wild Islay venison in red wine. There are daily vegetarian specials, and a range of hot puddings to round off your meal.
OPEN: 12-3 5.30-11 (Sun & BHs 12-11)
BAR MEALS: L served all week 12-2.15 D served all week 6-9.30 Sun 12-9 **RESTAURANT:** L served all week 12-2.15 D served all week 6-9.30 Sun 12-9 Av 3 course à la carte £15 🖱: Greene King ☒: Greene King IPA , Abbot Ale, Ruddles County & Old Speckled Hen. ☒: 8 **FACILITIES:** Garden **NOTES:** Parking 40

continued

Pick of the Pubs

ARKESDEN – ESSEX

Axe & Compasses

Situated in the narrow main street of a captivating village, the Axe ought to have featured on chocolate box lids, although to the best of the owner's knowledge, it hasn't yet. It's an inn of real character, with the central thatched section dating from around 1650. A stream called Wicken Water runs alongside, spanned by footbridges leading to white, cream and pink-washed thatched cottages.

The pub's long-held motto is 'Relax at the Axe', and there's no difficulty in doing so, either in the welcoming bar or laid-back lounge, with easy chairs, sofas, antique furniture, clocks, horsebrasses and maybe the warming glow of an open fire; on a fine day there's always the patio. In the cosy, softly lit separate restaurant area, which seats 50 on various levels, agricultural implements adorn the old beams. The Christou family, who run this Greene King pub, are Greek but there's no overt Hellenic influence on their regularly updated menus, other than authentic moussaka, and lamb kebabs, prepared in a marinade made according to a closely guarded secret recipe, in

the bar. On the carte, starters include lightly-baked fresh mackerel fillet, rolled in oats; sesame goat's cheese with raspberry coulis; and chicken liver and bacon pâté, with Cumberland sauce and hot toast. Main courses include lightly grilled sea bass with leek and potato cake, and lemon parsley butter sauce; pan-fried duck breast with cherry brandy, fat black cherries and creamed parsnip; and medallions of beef fillet with rösti, soft green peppercorns, brandy and cream. Round off with popular desserts from the trolley such as lemon meringue crunch, or mandarin cheesecake. The wine list is split more or less evenly between France and the rest of the world.

OPEN: 11.30-2.30 6-11
BAR MEALS: L served all week 12-2 D served all week 6.45-9.30 Av main course £14.50
RESTAURANT: L served all week 12-2 D served all week 6.45-9.30 Av 3 course à la carte £25
☺: Greene King
◀: Greene King IPA, Abbot Ale & Old Speckled Hen. ♀: 14
FACILITIES: Garden: Patio, seats around 30 people
NOTES: Parking 18

 Map 12 TL43
High St CB11 4EX
☎ 01799 550272
🖹 01799 550906
Dir: From Buntingford take B1038 towards Newport. Then left for Arkesden

Pick of the Pubs
CLAVERING – ESSEX

The Cricketers

It was in this popular 16th-century country pub that, at the age of eight, future celebrity chef Jamie Oliver first started to cook, under the guidance of his parents, Trevor and Sally, who still run it. In the heart of a beautiful and unspoilt Essex village, it is near the cricket pitch and related memorabilia decorates the brick-fronted bar and green-themed restaurant.

In both areas seasonally changing menus are offered, fixed-price in the restaurant, and carte in the bar. Although fresh fish is served every day, Tuesdays are special fish days, with lobsters, crabs and whatever looks good at the market. In the bar, roast joints are carved at lunchtimes from Wednesday to Friday, and on Monday, Wednesday and Sunday evenings. Salads and vegetarian options are also available. Characteristic starters are confit of rabbit served warm with a salad of peas, celery, fresh mint and little gem lettuce with walnut oil dressing; fresh peeled large prawns, grilled and served with a sweet potato and red curry sauce; and blue cheese fritots (a kind of savoury fritter) with green leaf salad and mango and lime chutney. Main courses include medallions of monkfish fillet rolled in chopped herbs served on a light red wine butter sauce; supreme of free range chicken stuffed with cep mushrooms and sliced on to creamy wholegrain mustard sauce; sautéed lambs' kidneys with pease pudding and a devilled sauce; fillet of pork stuffed with a petit ratatouille, wrapped in Serrano ham and served with yellow pimento sauce; and pancakes stuffed with spinach and four cheeses. The home-made dessert menu is equally mouth-watering. Beer drinkers will be interested in the range of bottled English real ales and Suffolk cider.

OPEN: 10.30-11 (Closed: 25-26 Dec)
BAR MEALS: L served all week 12-2 D served all week 7-10
RESTAURANT: L served all week 12-2 D served all week 7-10
🍽: Free House
🍺: Adnams Bitter, Carlsberg-Tetley Tetley Bitter. ♀: 10
FACILITIES: Child facs Garden: A patio and a courtyard
NOTES: Parking 100
ROOMS: 14 bedrooms en suite s£70 d£100 (♦♦♦♦)

♀   Map 12 TL43
CB11 4QT
☎ 01799 550442
🖷 01799 550882
📧 cricketers@lineone.net
🌐 www.thecricketers.co.uk
Dir: From M11 junct 10, A505 E. Then A1301, B1383. At Newport take B1038

BURNHAM-ON-CROUCH   Map 07 TQ99

Ye Olde White Harte Hotel
The Quay CM0 8AS ☎ 01621 782106 🖥 01621 782106
Dir: On high street

Directly overlooking the River Crouch, the hotel dates from the 17th century and retains many original features, including exposed beams. The pub has its own private jetty. The food is mainly English-style with such dishes as roast leg of English lamb, local roast Dengie chicken and seasoning, and grilled fillet of plaice and lemon. There is also a range of bar snacks including toasted and plain sandwiches, and jacket potatoes. **OPEN:** 11-11 **BAR MEALS:** L served all week 12-2 D served all week 7-9 **RESTAURANT:** L served all week 12-2 D served all week 7-9 🍴: Free House 🍺: Adnams Bitter, Crouch Vale Best.
FACILITIES: Jetty over river Dogs allowed **NOTES:** Parking 15

CASTLE HEDINGHAM   Map 13 TL73

The Bell Inn 🍸
St James St CO9 3EJ ☎ 01787 460350 e-mail: bell-inn@ic24.net
Dir: On A1124 N of Halstead, right to Castle Hedingham

Once the principle coaching inn on the Bury St Edmunds to London route, the Bell has been in the same family since 1967 and still has beams, wooden floors, open fires and gravity-fed real ale straight from the barrel. Monday is fish night and among the perennial favourites are sea bass, sea bream, red mullet and sword fish - try them barbecued. Alternatively, choose steak and ale pudding, liver and bacon casserole, shepherd's pie, or red hot beans.
OPEN: 11.30-3 6-11 (Open all day Fri-Sun Sun 12-10.30) Closed: 25 Dec (eve) **BAR MEALS:** L served all week 12-2 D served all week 7-9.30 Sun 7-9 Av main course £7.95 🍴: Grays 🍺: Mild Adnams Broadside, Greene King IPA , Adnams Bitter. 🍸: 7
FACILITIES: Garden: Large walled orchard garden Dogs by arrangement only **NOTES:** Parking 15

CHAPPEL   Map 13 TL82

The Swan Inn
CO6 2DD ☎ 01787 222353 🖥 01787 220012
Dir: Pub visible just off A1124 Colchester-Halstead road, from Colchester 1st left after viaduct

Set in the shadow of a magnificent Victorian railway viaduct, this rambling, low-beamed old free house boasts a charming riverside garden and overflowing flower tubs. Fresh meat and fish arrives daily from Smithfield and Billingsgate markets; typically, the non-smoking seafood restaurant and grill might offer poached Scottish salmon with hollandaise sauce; grilled trout with almonds; calves' liver and bacon; or English pork chops. Daily vegetarian specials, and home-made desserts, too. **OPEN:** 11-3 6-11 (Sat 11-11, Sun 12-10.30) **BAR MEALS:** L served all week 12-2.30 D served all week 6.30-10 (Sun 12-3) Av main course £9.95 **RESTAURANT:** L served all week 12-2.15 D served all week 7-10 Av 3 course à la carte £20 🍴: Free House 🍺: Greene King IPA, Abbot Ale. **FACILITIES:** Garden: Drinks served outside Dogs allowed Water **NOTES:** Parking 55

CLAVERING   Map 12 TL43

Pick of the Pubs

The Cricketers 🍸
CB11 4QT ☎ 01799 550442 🖥 01799 550882
e-mail: cricketers@lineone.net web: www.thecricketers.co.uk
See Pick of the Pubs on opposite page

COLCHESTER   Map 13 TL92

The Rose & Crown Hotel ★★★ 🏨🏨
East St CO1 2TZ ☎ 01206 866677 🖥 01206 866616
e-mail: info@rose-and-crown.com
Dir: From M25 junct 28 take A12 N. Follow Colchester signs
Situated in the heart of Britain's oldest town, this splendid 14th-century posting house retains much of its Tudor character. With ancient timbers, smartly decorated bedrooms, and wide-ranging menus, this popular destination has a daily log fire during the winter season to add to its air of warmth. Part of the bar is made of cell doors from the old jail that was once on the site. The focus is on fresh seafood, with other options such as rack of lamb, calves' liver and bacon, breast of duck with orange sauce, or seared venison fillet.
OPEN: 11-2.30 6-11 **BAR MEALS:** L served all week 12-2 D served all week 7-10 Av main course £7.95 **RESTAURANT:** L served all week 12-2 D served Mon-Sat 7-9.45 🍴: Free House
🍺: Carlsberg-Tetley Tetley's Bitter, Rose & Crown Bitter, Adnams Broadside. **NOTES:** Parking 50 **ROOMS:** 31 bedrooms en suite 2 family rooms s£69 d£86

DEDHAM Map 13 TM03

Marlborough Head Hotel
Mill Ln CO7 6DH ☎ 01206 323250
Dir: E of A12, N of Colchester
Set in glorious Constable country, close to Flatford Mill and peaceful walks, this former wool merchants house dates from 1455. Became an inn in 1704, the year of the Duke of Marlborough's famous victory over the French at the Battle of Blenheim. Extensive menu might feature fisherman's pie, king cod, hot cross bunny, or duck delight.
OPEN: 11-11 Dec 25-26 Closed eve **BAR MEALS:** L served all week 12-3 D served all week 6.30-9.30 Av main course £8.50
RESTAURANT: L served all week 12-2.30 D served all week 7-9.30 Av 3 course à la carte £16 ▣: ◖: Adnams Southwold, Greene King IPA, Adnams Broadside,plus guest. **FACILITIES:** Garden: Beer garden outdoor eating, Dogs allowed in the garden only
NOTES: Parking 28

Pick of the Pubs

The Sun Inn NEW ♦♦♦♦ �‍Y
High St CO7 6DF ☎ 01206 323351
e-mail: info@thesuninndedham.com
Dir: Off A12. Pub opposite church
Owner Piers Baker has created an independently owned free house where a quiet pint goes hand in hand with robust food and wine. He's restored original features such as oak floorboards and the elm bar top, and brought all four open fires back into use. There's an impressive selection of real ales, and a respectable wine list with around half a dozen wines available by the glass. Here you can expect comfortable tables and chairs, with sofas and banquettes to snuggle into whilst reading the newspapers or playing board games. In summer the large walled garden and sun-trapped terrace come into their own for alfresco wining and dining. Locally sourced seasonal ingredients govern the menu of rustic Mediterranean dishes, which might include stuffed roast partridge with thyme and mascarpone; linguine pasta with roasted fennel and garlic; or grilled Tuscan sausages with celeriac and parsnip mash.
OPEN: 11-11 (Sun 12-10.30) Closed: 25-27 Dec
BAR MEALS: L served all week 12-2.30 D served all week 6.30-9.30 Sat-Sun 12-3, Fri-Sat 6.30-10 Av main course £9.75
◖: Adnams, Greene King, Courage. �‍Y: 8 **FACILITIES:** Child facs Children's licence Walled garden: trees, terrace Dogs allowed Water **NOTES:** parking 15 **ROOMS:** 4 bedrooms en suite s£55 d£70

EARLS COLNE Map 13 TL82

The Carved Angel NEW ☺ �‍Y
Upper Holt St CO6 2PG ☎ 01787 222330 ▤ 01787 220013
e-mail: info@carvedangel.com web: www.carvedangel.com
Dir: From A120 take B1024 to Coggeshall, turn right at junct with A1124, pub 300yds on right
This 15th-century coaching inn was once a haven for monks and nuns escaping Henry VIII persecution. These days, it's the setting for a stylish bar and restaurant. Traditional ales from Adnam and Greene King are among favourite tipples, as well as a thorough wine list. The kitchen turns out well-crafted dishes: chicken liver and rosemary terrine to start, perhaps followed by pea risotto with pan fried haloumi and a poached egg; or a mixed seafood tagliatelle.
OPEN: 11.30-3 6.30-11 (Sun 12-3.30 Sun 6.30-10.30) Closed: 26
continued

Dec, 1 Jan **BAR MEALS:** L served all week 12-2 D served all week 7-9 Fri-Sat 7-10, Sun 12-2.30 Av main course £7.50
RESTAURANT: L served all week 12-2 D served all week 7-9 Fri-Sat 7-10, Sun 12-2.30 Av 3 course à la carte £20 Av 3 course fixed price £12.95 ◖: Greene King IPA, Adnams Bitter, Bittburger. �‍Y: 14
FACILITIES: Garden: Secure area at back of pub, tables, decking
NOTES: Parking 50 ⊗

ELSENHAM Map 12 TL52

The Crown
The Cross, High St CM22 6DG ☎ 01279 812827
Dir: M11 junct 8 towards Takeley. L at lights
A pub for 300 years, with oak beams, open fireplaces and Essex pargetting at the front. The menu, which has a large selection of fresh fish, might offer baked trout with toasted almonds, steak and kidney pie, Crown mixed grill with onion rings, a choice of steaks cooked to order, or breast of duck with peppercorn sauce. There's a good choice of vegetarian choices as well, including brie crumble, pasta bake or mushroom stroganoff. Lighter bites and jacket potatoes too.
OPEN: 12-11 (Sun 12-10.30) **BAR MEALS:** L served Mon-Sat 12-9 D served Mon-Sat (Sun lunch 12-3) Av main course £6.50
RESTAURANT: L served Mon-Sat 12-9 D served Mon-Sat Av 3 course à la carte £16 ▣: ◖: IPA, Broadside, Spitfire.
FACILITIES: Garden: enclosed grassed area, tables patio Dogs allowed **NOTES:** Parking 28

FEERING Map 07 TL82

The Sun Inn
Feering Hill CO5 9NH ☎ 01376 570442
Dir: On A12 between Colchester & Witham
You can enjoy up to 20 constantly changing real ales at this lively timbered pub, which also hosts the Feering Beer Festival. The building dates from 1525, although wall carvings removed in the 19th century are believed to have been even older. The menu of substantial pub favourites begins with serve-yourself ploughman's as you like them; hot dishes include lamb rogan josh with rice and naan bread, and cauliflower and cheese grill with chips.
OPEN: 12-3 6-11 (Sun 12-3, 6-10.30) **BAR MEALS:** L served all week 12-2 D served all week 6-9.30 Sun 12-3, 6-9.30 ▣: Free House ◖: Constantly changing guest beers - 6-20 per wk.
FACILITIES: Garden: Enclosed, large lawn, hanging baskets, ducks Dogs allowed Water provided **NOTES:** Parking 19 No credit cards

FELSTED Map 06 TL62

Pick of the Pubs

The Swan at Felsted NEW �‍Y
Station Rd CM6 3DG ☎ 01371 820245 ▤ 01371 821393
e-mail: jono@theswanatfelsted.co.uk
Dir: 8m N of Chelmsford on A130
Rebuilt after a devastating fire in the early 1900s, and rescued from impending closure in 2000 - The Swan has had quite a few rebirths. Today it offers a combination of excellent cuisine, fine wines and well-kept cask ales, achieving a good balance between the traditional English pub and a high quality restaurant. The menus stimulate the taste buds while retaining a simplicity that allows the individual flavour and quality of the fresh ingredients to shine through. Lunchtime choices offer a range of light dishes, while in the evening you are offered an à la carte menu featuring old favourites among others, and
continued

England

regularly changing specials. You could start with pan-fried red mullet fillet with caponata and olive tapenade; or stir-fried five-spice lamb with rocket and almonds. To follow there might be cardamom and ginger marinated pork; or venison steak with braised red cabbage and sultanas, blackberry sauce. To finish, try dark chocolate and coconut delice with lemongrass sorbet; or traditional treacle suet pudding with custard.
OPEN: 11-3 7-11 (Sun 12-6, 5-midnight)
BAR MEALS: L served all week 12-2.45 D served Mon-Sat 6-9.45 Sun 12-4.30 Av main course £12.50
RESTAURANT: L served all week 12-2.45 D served Mon-Sat 6-9.45 Sun 12-4.30 Av 3 course à la carte £22 🛢: Ridleys IPA, Old Bob, Prospect, Guinness. 🍷: 13 **FACILITIES:** Child facs Garden: Enclosed courtyard, patio heaters, parasols Dogs allowed **NOTES:** Parking 6

FINGRINGHOE   Map 07 TM02

The Whalebone
Chapel Rd CO5 7BG ☎ 01206 729307 📠 01206 729307
e-mail: fburroughes1974@aol.com
Dir: Telephone for directions

The 250-year-old Whalebone sits beside the village green and pond, close to the Fingrinhoe Nature Reserve from which the foot ferry crosses the Colne Valley river. Outside is believed to be the oldest oak tree in Essex. With the new owners comes a new menu, featuring dishes such as pigeon breast on bacon and onion compote and juicy liver and bacon on crushed potatoes with Madeira cream sauce.
OPEN: 11-3 5.30-11 (all day Sat-Sun) **BAR MEALS:** L served all week 12-2.30 D served all week 7-9.30 Av main course £8.50 🍺: Free House 🛢: Greene King IPA, Old Speckled Hen & 2 guest beers. **FACILITIES:** Garden: Panoramic views across Colne Valley Dogs allowed Water **NOTES:** Parking 25

GOSFIELD   Map 13 TL72

The Green Man 🍷
The Street CO9 1TP ☎ 01787 472746
Dir: Take A131 N from Braintree then A1017 to village
Traditional yet smart village dining pub that changed hands in October 2004. The menu and daily specials owe much to good fresh produce, whether traditional cod in beer batter, steak and kidney pudding, or more adventurous possibilities such as navarin of lamb with rosemary mash and vegetable spaghetti; honey-glazed duck breast with coriander and oyster mushroom noodles; and char-grilled Mediterranean vegetables with toasted goat's cheese. From end-January to November there's an impressive buffet-style cold table.
OPEN: 11-3 6.15-11 (Sun 12-3, 7-10.30) **BAR MEALS:** L served all week 12-2 D served Mon-Sat 6.45-9 Sun 12-2.30 Av main course
continued

£7.95 **RESTAURANT:** L served all week 12-2 D served Mon-Sat 6.45-9 Sun 12-2.30 🍺: Greene King 🛢: Greene King IPA, Old Speckled Hen & Abbot Ale. 🍷: 9 **FACILITIES:** Child facs Children's licence Garden: 10 Tables, paved patio area Dogs allowed Water **NOTES:** Parking 25

GREAT BRAXTED   Map 07 TL81

Du Cane Arms 🍽 🍷
The Village CM8 3EJ ☎ 01621 891697 📠 01621 890009
e-mail: fred@fredrodford.com
Dir: Great Braxted signed between Witham and Kelvedon on A12

Walkers and cyclists mingle with the locals at this friendly pub, built in 1935 at the heart of a leafy village: handy for the A12 today, it is a popular spot and comes up with a variety of lively real ales and daily fresh fish. Adnams bitter boosts the beer batter for fresh cod or haddock, while the steak and kidney pie is livened up with a splash of Guinness. Thai curries, rack of lamb, and seafood curry are among the other dishes. The garden is ideal for summertime eating.
OPEN: 11.30-3 6.30-11 **BAR MEALS:** L served 12-2 D served all week 6.30-9.30 Winter Sun 12-4.45
RESTAURANT: L served all week 12-2 D served all week 7-9.30 🍺: Free House 🛢: Adnams Bitter, Greene King IPA, John Smiths Smooth. 🍷: 10 **FACILITIES:** Garden: Landscaped, walled garden, seating & umbrellas Well behaved dogs allowed **NOTES:** Parking 25

HARLOW   Map 06 TL41

Rainbow & Dove 🍽
Hastingwood Rd CM17 9JX ☎ 01279 415419 📠 01279 415419
Dir: M11 junct 7, A414 towards Chipping Ongar. L into Hastingwood Rd
Quaint listed inn with many charming features, originally a farmhouse and staging post. It became a pub when Oliver Cromwell stationed his New Model Army on the common here in the 1640s. The Rainbow & Dove was also popular with RAF pilots stationed at North Weald Station during WWII. Relaxed atmosphere inside and good quality bar food. Lots of fresh fish on the specials board, including lemon sole, plaice, cod, haddock, sea bass, and skate.
OPEN: 11.30-3 6-11 **BAR MEALS:** L served all week 11.30-2.30 D served all week 7-9.30 Av main course £6.50 🍺: Inn Business 🛢: Morland Old Speckled Hen, Courage Directors, Bass.
FACILITIES: Garden: Beer garden, BBQ area Dogs allowed **NOTES:** Parking 50

> Not all of the pubs in the guide are open all week or all day. It's always best to check before you travel

England

HORNDON ON THE HILL   Map 06 TQ68

Pick of the Pubs

Bell Inn & Hill House ♀
High Rd SS17 8LD ☎ 01375 642463 📠 01375 361611
e-mail: info@bell-inn.co.uk web: www.bell-inn.co.uk
Dir: Off M25 junct 30/31 signed Thurrock. Lakeside A13 then B1007 to Horndon

When the present family took over this 15th-century former coaching inn in 1938, it retained many original features, including a courtyard balcony where luggage was lifted from coach roofs. Unfortunately, at that stage it had no running water or electricity. Their refurbishment has skilfully maintained original features while injecting modern comforts. The two bars and restaurant offer a good choice of real ales and guest beers, and 16 wines by the glass. Imaginative modern menus are supplemented by daily specials and bar snacks. You could start with squash and rhubarb ravioli with apple remoulade, or smoked mackerel fishcake, and move on to roast pheasant with chorizo and beetroot tart; or roast bacon knuckle with maple butter beans and pancetta velouté. Appearing among the interesting desserts are dark chocolate crème brûlée with orange braised chicory ice cream; and glazed lemon tart with black olives.
OPEN: 11-2.30 5.30-11 (Sat 11-3, 6-11 Sun 12-4, 7-10.30) Closed: 25-26 Dec **BAR MEALS:** L served all week 12-1.45 D served all week 6.45-9.45 Sun food from 7 Av main course £13.95 **RESTAURANT:** L served all week 12-1.45 D served all week 6.45-9.45 Sun food from7 Av 3 course à la carte £25.95 🍴: Free House 🍺: Greene King IPA, Interbrew Bass, Crouchvale Brewers Gold, Ruddles County. ♀: 16 **FACILITIES:** Child facs Garden: Paved courtyard with hanging baskets and tubs Dogs allowed **NOTES:** Parking 50

LANGHAM   Map 13 TM03

The Shepherd and Dog ♀
Moor Rd CO4 5NR ☎ 01206 272711 📠 01206 273136
e-mail: julian@shepherdanddog.fsnet.co.uk
Dir: A12 towards Ipswich, 1st turn on L out of Colchester, signed Langham
A much-loved local, deep in Dedham Vale, this friendly pub has an increasing range of regulars. Foodie theme evenings are a highlight - Indian night, Italian night and fish'n'chip night for example. Good wine and good beer accompany locally sourced ingredients in dishes that encompass fresh market sardines, plaice and skate along with lasagne, various curries, grilled chump of lamb and Sunday lunch with up to four roasts to choose from.
OPEN: 11-3 5.30-11 **BAR MEALS:** L served all week 12-2.15 D served all week 6-10 (Sat 11-11 Sun 12-10.30) Av main course

continued

£8.95 **RESTAURANT:** L served all week 12-2.15 D served all week 6-10 Av 3 course à la carte £17.45 🍴: Free House 🍺: Greene King IPA, Abbot Ale & Ruddles County. ♀: 6 **FACILITIES:** Children's licence Garden: Small fenced garden Dogs allowed **NOTES:** Parking 40

LITTLE CANFIELD   Map 06 TL52

The Lion & Lamb ♀
CM6 1SR ☎ 01279 870257 📠 01279 870423
e-mail: info@lionandlamb.co.uk web: www.lionandlamb.co.uk
Dir: M11 junct 8, B1256 towards Takeley

There's a friendly welcome at this traditional country pub restaurant, with its soft red bricks, oak beams and winter log fires. Handy for Stansted airport and the M11, the pub's charm and individuality make it a favourite for business or leisure. Choices from the bar menu include steak and ale pie, local sausages and York ham salad, while the restaurant offers, perhaps, braised lamb shanks with a ragout of white beans, or wild mushroom risotto. There is a separate fresh fish board.
OPEN: 11-11 (Sun 12-10.30) **BAR MEALS:** L served all week 11-10 D served all week 11-10 (Sun 12-10) Av main course £12.50 **RESTAURANT:** L served all week 11-10 D served all week 11-10 (Sun 12-10) 🍴: Ridley & Sons 🍺: Ridleys IPA, Old Bob, Prospect & Seasonal Beers.. ♀: 10 **FACILITIES:** Child facs Garden: Large enclosed garden overlooking farmland Dogs allowed Water **NOTES:** Parking 50
See advertisement under STANSTED AIRPORT

LITTLE DUNMOW   Map 06 TL62

Flitch of Bacon
The Street CM6 3HT ☎ 01371 820323 📠 01371 820338
Dir: A120 to Braintree for 10m, turn off at Little Dunmow, 0.5m pub
A 15th-century country inn whose name refers to the ancient gift of half a salted pig, or 'flitch', to couples who have been married for a year and a day, and 'who have not had a cross word'. It may now also refer to the new owners, Neil and Theresa Bacon! Reports on this new operation would be welcome.
OPEN: 12-3 5.30-11 (Sun 12-5, 7-10.30 Sat 6-11)
BAR MEALS: L served Tues-Sun 12-2 D served Mon-Sat 7-9 Sun 12-3 Av main course £8 🍴: Free House 🍺: Fullers London Pride, Greene King IPA & regular changing ales. **FACILITIES:** Garden: Paved patio with bench seating Dogs allowed **NOTES:** Parking 6

> We endeavour to be as accurate as possible but changes to times and other information can occur after the guide has gone to press

MANNINGTREE   Map 13 TM13

Pick of the Pubs

The Mistley Thorn  ♀
High St, Mistley CO11 1HE
☎ 01206 392821 ▤ 01206 392133
e-mail: info@mistleythorn.com web: www.mistleythorn.co.uk

Built in 1723, this historic free house in the centre of Mistley stands on the estuary of the River Stour near Colchester. A previous pub on the same site was the scene of 17th-century witch trials conducted by the self-appointed 'Witchfynder General', Matthew Hopkins. After a complete refurbishment a few years ago, the Mistley Thorn became the first completely non-smoking pub in Essex. Owner Sherri Singleton, who is also the proprietor of the Mistley Kitchen cookery school, serves up an accomplished menu. The emphasis is on locally sourced produce with a leaning towards fresh seafood. Imaginative lunchtime dishes include game terrine with spiced green tomato chutney and sourdough toast; and steamed fresh mussels in coconut, coriander, lemongrass and ginger. Evening diners might begin with rosemary grilled chicken livers and bacon on crostini, before moving on to aubergine parmegiana with tallagio and roasted tomato sauce. **OPEN:** 12-11 **BAR MEALS:** L served all week 12-2.30 D served all week 7-10 Av main course £10.95 **RESTAURANT:** L served all week 12-2.30 D served all week 7-9.30 Av 3 course fixed price £13.95 ▤: Free House ◖▮: Greene King IPA, Adnams, St. Peters. ♀: 8 **FACILITIES:** Child facs Dogs allowed **NOTES:** Parking 6

NORTH FAMBRIDGE   Map 07 TQ89

The Ferry Boat Inn
Ferry Ln CM3 6LR ☎ 01621 740208
e-mail: sylviaferryboat@aol.com
Dir: From Chelmsford take A130 S then A132 to South Woodham Ferrers, then B1012. right to village
A 500-year-old traditional weatherboard inn with beams, log fires and a resident ghost. It is tucked away at the end of a lovely village on the River Crouch, next to the marina, and was once a centre for smugglers. These days it is understandably popular with the sailing fraternity. In addition to the extensive menu, daily specials might include
continued

minted lamb chop, grilled sea bass, chicken korma or beef chilli.

OPEN: 11.30-3 6.30-11 (Sun 12-4) **BAR MEALS:** L served all week 12-2 D served all week 7-9.30 Sun 12-2.45, 7-9 **RESTAURANT:** L served all week 12-1.30 D served all week 7-9 Av 3 course à la carte £14 ▤: Free House ◖▮: Greene King IPA, Abbot Ale, Ruddles County. **FACILITIES:** Garden: Acre, grassed, benches Dogs allowed **NOTES:** Parking 30 **ROOMS:** 6 bedrooms en suite 3 family rooms s£35 d£45 (♦♦♦)

PAGLESHAM   Map 07 TQ99

Plough & Sail ♀
East End SS4 2EQ ☎ 01702 258242 ▤ 01702 258242
Charming, weather-boarded, 17th-century dining pub on the bracing Essex marshes, within easy reach of the rivers Crouch and Roach. Inside are pine tables, brasses and low beams, giving the place a quaint, traditional feel. The attractive garden is a popular spot during the summer months. Renowned for its good quality food and fresh fish dishes, including fresh skate, tuna steaks, steak and stilton pie, and Dover sole. **OPEN:** 11.30-3 6.45-11 **BAR MEALS:** L served all week 12-2.15 D served all week 7-9.30 **RESTAURANT:** L served all week 12-2.15 D served all week 7-9.30 ▤: Free House ◖▮: Greene King IPA, Ridleys, Mighty Oak, Fuller's London Pride. ♀: 10 **FACILITIES:** Garden: Large garden with aviary **NOTES:** Parking 30

PATTISWICK   Map 13 TL82

The Compasses ♀
CM77 8BG ☎ 01376 561322 ▤ 01376 564343
e-mail: info@thecompasses.co.uk
Dir: Off A120 between Braintree & Coggeshall
Set in idyllic Essex countryside surrounded by woodland and rolling fields and much extended from the original, this inn dates back to the 13th century. Lighter bar bites are supplemented by the bistro menu by local favourites such as Trucker's Platter, liver and bacon, toad-in-the-hole, braised Scottish steak and kidney pie, and spinach and goats cheese cannelloni. Multi-choice Sunday lunch. Non-smoking in the eating areas. New owners - reports please. **OPEN:** 11-3 6-11 (open all day wknds and in summer) Dec 25 **BAR MEALS:** L served all week 12-2 D served all week 6-9 Av main course £9.50 ▤: Free House ◖▮: Greene King - IPA, Ridley's Pale Island, Maldon Gold. **FACILITIES:** Garden: Beer garden, patio, outdoor eating Child friendly, play area Dogs welcome **NOTES:** Parking 40

    Pubs offering a good choice of fish on their menu

★   Star rating for inspected hotel accommodation

RADWINTER — Map 12 TL63

The Plough Inn ⚲
CB10 2TL ☎ 01799 599222
Dir: 4m E of Saffron Walden, at Junct of B2153 & B2154
An Essex woodboard exterior, old beams and a thatched roof characterise this listed inn, once frequented by farm workers. A recent refurbishment program has added a 50-seat restaurant, and turned the Plough from a purely local village pub into a destination gastro-pub, without losing too much of the village pub feel. A typical menu includes the likes of smoked haddock parcels, lamb noisettes, partridge, duck breast, and a variety of home-made pies.
OPEN: 12-3 6-11 (Sun 12-10.30) **BAR MEALS:** L served all week 12-3.30 D served Mon-Sat 6.30-9 Sun 12-2.30, Sat 6.30-9.30 Av main course £7.95 **RESTAURANT:** L served all week 12-2 D served Mon-Sat 6.30-9 Sun 12-3.30, Sat 6.30-9.30 Av 3 course à la carte £20 🍴: Free House 🍺: Adnams Best, IPA, Woodfordes Wherry, Archers Golden. ⚲: 7 **FACILITIES:** Garden: Patio under pergola, large lawn Dogs allowed Water **NOTES:** Parking 28

SAFFRON WALDEN — Map 12 TL53

The Cricketers' Arms ◆◆◆◆ ⚲
Rickling Green CB11 3YG ☎ 01799 543210 📠 01799 543512
e-mail: reservations@cricketers.demon.co.uk
web: www.cricketersarms.co.uk
Dir: Exit B1383 at Quendon. Pub 300yds on left opp cricket ground
The cricketing connection began in the 1880's when Rickling Green became the venue for London society cricket matches; associations with the England team and the county game are still maintained. This historic inn was built as a terrace of timber-framed cottages, and one menu serves all three dining areas. Choices include seafood lasagne, sweet and sour king prawns, traditional rib-eye steak, and chicken chasseur, with plenty of light bites and snacks.
OPEN: 12-11 Sun 12-22.30 **BAR MEALS:** L served all week 12-2.30 D served all week 7-9.30 Sun 7-9 Av main course £8 **RESTAURANT:** L served all week 12-2.30 D served all week 7-9.30 Sun12-2.30, 7-9 Av 3 course à la carte £30 🍴: Free House 🍺: Greene King IPA, Jennings Cumberland. ⚲: 8 **FACILITIES:** Child facs Garden: Front terrace, Japanese garden Dogs allowed on lead, water **NOTES:** Parking 40 **ROOMS:** 9 bedrooms en suite 1 family room s£65 d£85

SHALFORD — Map 12 TL72

The George Inn
The Street CM7 5HH ☎ 01371 850207 📠 01371 851355
e-mail: info@thegeorgeshalford.com
A hundred years ago there were five pubs in Shalford, but the George Inn, which dates back some 500 years, is the only one now. It's a traditional village pub, with oak beams and open fires, surrounded by lovely countryside. The menu is written up on the blackboard daily, including steaks, chicken breast specialities and popular Oriental and Indian dishes. Fish goes down well too, particularly battered plaice, cod mornay, and salmon en croute.
OPEN: 12-2 6.30-11 Closed Mon evening Nov-Mar **BAR MEALS:** L served all week 12-2.30 Av main course £4.95 **RESTAURANT:** L served all week 12-2.30 D served Mon-Sat 6.30-9.30 Av 3 course à la carte £11.95 🍺: Greene King IPA, Fullers London Pride, Stella Artois, Guiness. **FACILITIES:** Garden: Patio **NOTES:** Parking 25

STANSTED AIRPORT — Map 06 TL52

See **Little Canfield**

Lion & Lamb
Stortford Road (B1256)
Little Canfield
Dunmow
Near Takeley CM6 1SR

Restaurant and Bar now offering Accommodation in conjunction with The White House Luxury Country House

A traditional country restaurant and bar complete with oak beams and a large secluded garden overlooking farmland. Side the B1256 (the old A120) 5 mins from M11–J8 is the Lion & Lamb, a traditional country pub combined with a restaurant serving very modern food all day long – Kangaroo, grilled Dover Sole, pork belly and roasted loin with a pumpkin puree, parsnips and a tarragon jus and wild mushroom risotto just some of the temptations that could be offered. With its oak beams and cosy fireplace, the Lion & Lamb dates back to the 16th century and is very inviting. Bar snacks are available and diners are welcome to eat in the bar, dining area or conservatory. Children are welcome, making the Lion & Lamb a popular choice for family groups.

Tel: 01279 870257 FAX 01279 870423
Email: info@lionandlamb.co.uk
www.lionandlamb.co.uk

STOCK — Map 06 TQ69

The Hoop
21 High St CM4 9BD ☎ 01277 841137 📠 01277 841137
Dir: On B1007 between Chelmsford & Billericay
This 15th-century free house, which stands on Stock's attractive village green, was formerly three weavers' cottages. There's a traditional beamed interior, and a large garden where you can choose from an extensive barbeque menu on summer weekends. The annual beer festival runs for 10 days in late spring and features more than 100 beers from the Orkneys to the West Country. Popular dishes include braised oxtail; cottage pie; grilled skate; and home-cooked ham.
OPEN: 11-11 (Sun 12-10.30) **BAR MEALS:** L served all week 11-2.30 D served all week 6-9 Fri-Sat 11-9; Sun 12-8 Av main course £7 🍴: Free House 🍺: Fuller's London Pride, Hop Back, Adnams Bitter, Shepherd Neame Spitfire Premium Ale. **FACILITIES:** Garden: 30 tables, gazebo & heaters, bar Dogs allowed Water bowl

---

Restaurant and Bar Meal times indicate the times when food is available. Last orders may be approximately 30 minutes before the times stated

---

PUB WALK
The Bell at Sapperton
Sapperton - Gloucestershire

THE BELL AT SAPPERTON,
GL7 6LE
☎ 01285 760298
Directions: Halfway between
Cirencester & Stroud on the A419, take
signs for Sapperton village. The Bell is
in the centre near the church.
*Local pub and fine dining venue,
serving well-kept ales, rough old
scrumpy and adventurous dishes that
appear on a menu alongside more
traditional choices.*
Open: 11–2.30 6.30–11 (Sun times
vary) Closed: 25 Dec, 31 Dec
Bar Meals: L served all week 12–2
D served all week 7–9.30 Sun 7–9
Av main course £13.50
Restaurant Meals: L served all week
12–2 D served all week 7–9.30 Sun 7–9
Av 3 course à la carte £26
No children under 10 after 6.30. Dogs
allowed. Garden and parking available.
(for full entry see page 212)

Distance: 3 miles (4.8km)
Map: OS Landranger 165
Terrain: Valley and woodland.
Paths: Clear paths and tracks - one
lengthy section which can be muddy
Gradient: Moderate climbing

Walk submitted by The Bell, Sapperton

A very pleasant walk in the Sapperton valley, exploring a quiet corner of the Cotswolds between Cirencester and Stroud.

From the pub descend the hill towards 14th-century St Kenhelm's Church, take the footpath to the left of it and go through the kissing gate into the meadow. Follow the unmarked path straight across the bank, keeping the garden of Upper Dorvel House to your right. The garden is extensive and includes some of the distinctive topiary for which Sapperton is noted.

The path runs down to a metal green gate that leads out to a no through road. Descend the steep hill to reach Lower Dorvel House. Turn left at the entrance, heading down a narrow track to pass over a small stream. This is the River Frome. The going can be very wet and muddy here - especially in winter.

Follow the path uphill for about 200yds (183m), keeping left at the fork and climbing steeply to reach another track. Turn sharp left by a large beech tree and follow the track down a slight slope.

Continue through the woods for about 0.5 mile (800m) and remain on the track as you emerge from the trees. Daneway House is seen on your left. Cross a lane to a stile and follow the path with fence to your left, soon reaching a gate. Once through it, turn left and follow the path across Daneway Banks, climbing very gradually to the next stile. Cross the lane into Sicarage Wood.

Follow the stony track through the wood for about 0.5 mile (800m) to a junction of five paths. Take the path to the left, following it down a steep slope to a bridge over the old Thames & Severn Canal. Cross the bridge and turn sharp left at the end of the parapet to join the towpath. Follow this upstream to a narrow wooden footbridge, cross over and continue on the path to the next road. The Daneway pub is in front of you.

Keep ahead on the towpath towards Sapperton, following the path to the tunnel entrance. Leave the canal at this point by crossing the stile into the adjacent meadow. Follow the steep, well-defined path towards a church steeple, rejoin the path encountered earlier in the walk and return to the Bell.

Pick of the Pubs

ANDOVERSFORD – GLOUCESTERSHIRE

The Kilkeney Inn

The rolling Cotswold landscape stretches away from this charming country dining pub located on the main road outside Andoversford. Nigel and Jean White have taken over ownership of the pub since May 2004, following two years when they ran it as managers.

Well worth the drive out from Cheltenham, it's very much a desirable place to eat, but beer drinkers are obviously more than welcome and will find real ales like Hook Norton Best and St Austell's Tribute served in good condition. A wood-burning stove warms the beamed bar whenever there's a hint of a nip in the air, and the atmosphere is welcoming and cosy whatever the weather. The best views of the Cotswolds are from the front of the pub and the mature garden, originally six individual plots belonging to mid-19th century terraced stone cottages. The lunch menu ranges from filled ciabattas, herb sausages in Yorkshire pudding, and warm chicken caesar salad, to the Kilkeney special, a slow-roast shoulder of lamb with smashed root vegetables in a rich red wine and mint glaze. At dinner, try a starter of fried goat's cheese coated with coconut and roasted sweet peppers; marinated breast of cornfed chicken stuffed with brie and pesto; a classic beef bourguinon; and fillet of sea bass baked with sea salt. Puddings along the lines of chocolate and orange cheesecake with fruit sauce, and a basket of figs with raspberry coulis and cream, may be among the dessert choices. It's best to book for any meal, especially traditional Sunday lunch, the monthly fish suppers, and the occasional jazz lunches.

OPEN: 11-3 5-11
BAR MEALS: L served all week 12-2 D served all week 7-9.30 Av main course £10
RESTAURANT: L served all week 12-2 D served all week 7-9.30 Av 3 course à la carte £18
🏠: Free House
🍺: Hook Norton Best, St Austells Tribute & Guest Ales. ⛾: 9
FACILITIES: Garden: Patio, small grassy area **NOTES:** Parking 50

⛾   Map 10 SP01
Kilkeney GL54 4LN
☎ 01242 820341
📄 01242 820133
Dir: On A436 1m W of Andoversford

England

TILLINGHAM
Map 07 TL90

Cap & Feathers Inn
South St CM0 7TH ☎ 01621 779212 ▤ 01621 779212
Dir: From Chelmsford take A414, follow signs for Burnham-on-Crouch, then Tillingham
Originally built in 1500 by Dutch labourers working on land drainage, the classic white-painted, weather-boarded frontage is delightfully unspoiled, as is its timeless old-fashioned, quiet interior, traditional furnishings and unassuming pub food that attracts its fair share of hikers, cyclists, bird-watchers and fishermen. Fresh fish such as bream, skate, plaice, haddock and cod, and locally smoked fish and meats are main stays of the menu, supported by a host of meat pies, hand-made sausages and game in winter. Commendable real ales.
OPEN: 12-2.30 6-11 (Sat 12-11, Sun 12-10.30) 25 Dec closed evening **BAR MEALS:** L served Tue-Sun 12-2 D served Tue-Sun 7-9 Av main course £7.50 **RESTAURANT:** L served Tue-Sun 12-2 D served Tue-Sun 7-9 Av 3 course à la carte £15 ⬡: Crouch Vale ◖: Crouch Vale Best. **FACILITIES:** Garden: Food served outside Dogs allowed **NOTES:** Parking 20

WENDENS AMBO
Map 12 TL53

The Bell
Royston Rd CB11 4JY ☎ 01799 540382
Dir: 3m from Saffron Walden, 2m from Audley End House
Formerly a farmhouse and brewery, this 16th-century timber-framed building is set in a pretty Essex village close to Audley End House. The pub is surrounded by extensive gardens, which have now been landscaped from the summer terrace down to the children's mini golf. The cottage-style rooms have low ceilings and open fires in winter. An allegedly friendly ghost, Mrs Goddard, is also in residence. The kitchen offers smoked haddock florentine; fillet steak with Madeira, mushroom and red wine sauce; and chicken with pan-fried mushrooms in a tarragon sauce.
OPEN: 11.30-2.30 5-11 (Fri-Sun all day) **BAR MEALS:** L served all week 12-2 D served Mon-Sat 6-9 Av main course £8 **RESTAURANT:** L served all week 12-2 D served Mon-Sat 7-9 ⬡: Free House ◖: Adnams Bitter & Broadside, Woodefords Wherry & Nelsons Revenge, Fullers London Pride. **FACILITIES:** Children's licence Garden: Patio with several acres of secluded garden Dogs allowed Water **NOTES:** Parking 40

WICKHAM BISHOPS
Map 07 TL81

The Mitre
2 The Street CM8 3NN ☎ 01621 891378 ▤ 01621 894932
Dir: Off B1018 between Witham and Maldon
Originally the Carpenter's Arms, this friendly pub changed its name in the mid-1890s, presumably to reflect the one-time possession of the village by the Bishops of London. The pub's regular range of meat choices includes mixed grills, pies and curries, steaks, and dishes featuring duck, pork, lamb and chicken. Fish is strongly represented by dishes based on salmon, haddock, cod, snapper, trout, sea bass, mahi mahi, plaice, Dover sole, red mullet and sea bream.
OPEN: 11.30-11 **BAR MEALS:** L served Tues-Sun 12-2 D served Tues-Sun 7-9 Sun 12-3 **RESTAURANT:** L served Tues-Sat 12-2 D served Tues-Sun 7-9 Sun 12-3 ⬡: Ridley & Sons ◖: Ridleys Rumpus, IPA, Old Bob, Tolly. **FACILITIES:** Garden: Enclosed garden with patio and BBQ **NOTES:** Parking 20

GLOUCESTERSHIRE

ALMONDSBURY
Map 04 ST68

The Bowl ★ ★ ♀
16 Church Rd BS32 4DT ☎ 01454 612757 ▤ 01454 619910
e-mail: reception@thebowlinn.co.uk web: www.thebowlinn.co.uk

The Bowl, which is located on the south-eastern edge of the Severn Vale, takes its name from the shape of the land surrounding the Severn Estuary, as seen from the inn. It's a picturesque whitewashed building, originally a terrace of three cottages, and dates from 1550. The bar menu offers snacks, pasta, curry, roast chicken and fish and chips, while Lilies Restaurant might list venison bourguignon, grilled sea bass, and roasted avocado with camembert.
OPEN: 11-3 5-11 (Sun 12-10.30) **BAR MEALS:** L served all week 12-2.30 D served all week 6-10 Sun 12-8 Av main course £8 **RESTAURANT:** L served all week 12-2.30 D served all week 7-10 Av 3 course à la carte £25 ⬡: Free House ◖: Scottish Courage Courage Best, Smiles Best, Wickwar BOB, Moles Best. ♀: 9 **FACILITIES:** Child facs Garden: Patio area at rear. Seating on frontage Dogs allowed **NOTES:** Parking 50 **ROOMS:** 13 bedrooms en suite s£44.50 d£71

ANDOVERSFORD
Map 10 SP01

Pick of the Pubs

The Kilkeney Inn ♀
Kilkeney GL54 4LN ☎ 01242 820341 ▤ 01242 820133
See Pick of the Pubs on opposite page

The Royal Oak Inn ♀
Old Gloucester Rd GL54 4HR ☎ 01242 820335
e-mail: bleninns@clara.net
Dir: 200metres from A40, 4m E of Cheltenham
The Royal Oak stands on the banks of the River Coln, one of a small chain of popular food-oriented pubs in the area. Originally a coaching inn, its main dining room, galleried on two levels, occupies the converted former stables. Lunchtime bar fare of various sandwiches, lasagne and ham, egg and chips (for example), extends in the evening to Chinese crispy duck with lime and soy noodles or roast pork fillet with rosti potato and creamy cider sauce.
OPEN: 11-2.30 5.30-11 **BAR MEALS:** L served all week 12-2.30 D served all week 7-9.30 Av main course £6.50 **RESTAURANT:** L served all week 12-2.30 D served all week 7-9.30 Av 3 course à la carte £15 ⬡: Free House ◖: Hook Norton Best, Tetleys Bitter, Draught Bass. ♀: 8 **FACILITIES:** Garden: Patio area with tables on banks of the river Dogs allowed Water **NOTES:** Parking 44

🍺 Principal Beers for sale

ARLINGHAM　　　　　　　　　Map 04 SO71

Pick of the Pubs

The Old Passage Inn ◆◆◆◆ ◎◎ ⌂ ⌂
Passage Rd GL2 7JR ☎ 01452 740547 ▤ 01452 741871
e-mail: oldpassage@ukonline.co.uk
Dir: Telephone for directions

First class fish and seafood restaurant on the banks of the Severn, Britain's longest river. It is said that St Augustine, the first Archbishop of Canterbury, forded the Severn at Arlingham in 604AD to meet Welsh Christians at the Synod of the Oak. Listen out for the cries of geese and swans as they make their way to the adjacent Slimbridge bird sanctuary. The restaurant is run by Josephine Living-Moore, Patrick Le Mesurier and Raoul Moore. Somerset Moore, one of the owners, was the fish chef at the world renowned Maison Prunier in St James, London. He subsequently promoted and specialised in fresh fish and shellfish, and the next generation of the family has maintained this tradition, offering a superb range of shellfish stored in seawater tanks, the best oysters, lobsters, crabs and mussels supplied by the pick of the market. Organic meats, vegetarian dishes, quality puds and a variety of fine wines add to the experience.
OPEN: 12-3　7-11.30 Closed: Dec 24-30　**BAR MEALS:** L served Tue-Sun 12-2 D served Tue-Sat 7-9　Av main course £14
RESTAURANT: L served Tue-Sun 12-2 D served Tue-Sat 7-9 Av 3 course à la carte £25.50 ▣: Free House ◖: Bass, John Smiths. ⌂: 14　**FACILITIES:** Garden: Mostly grass, bordering river, raised terrace　Dogs allowed　At publican's discretion
NOTES: Parking 60　**ROOMS:** 3 bedrooms en suite s£50　d£90
No children overnight

ASHLEWORTH　　　　　　　　Map 10 SO82

Boat Inn
The Quay GL19 4HZ ☎ 01452 700272 ▤ 01452 700272
e-mail: elisabeth_nicholls@boat-inn.co.uk
With historic connections to King Charles, the Boat stands beside Ashleworth quay and close by the medieval Tithe Barn and former Court House. In the same family for 400 years, it's a gem of a pub with its tiny front parlour, flagstone floors and ancient kitchen range; a magnet to the many walkers exploring the nearby Severn or the village itself (leaflets available from the bar). Interesting real ales from Wye Valley and Church End breweries, dispensed direct from the cask, are ideal to accompany a generously filled roll or ploughman's lunch with pickle. There is plenty of seating outside to enjoy the location. Annual beer festival in late summer.
OPEN: 11.30-2.30　6.30-11 (Winter from 7)　**BAR MEALS:** L served Tues-Sun 12-2　Av main course £1.95 ▣: Free House ◖: Wye Valley, Church End, Arkells, RCH Pitchfork.　**FACILITIES:** Garden: Courtyard garden overlooking river bank　**NOTES:** Parking 10　No credit cards ⊗

⌂ 7　Number of wines by the glass

Website addresses are included where available. The AA cannot be held responsible for the content of any of these websites

Pick of the Pubs

The Queens Arms ⌂⌂ ⌂
The Village GL19 4HT ☎ 01452 700395
Dir: From Gloucester travel N on A417 for 5m. Continue into the middle of Hartpury. Opposite the Royal Exchange turn right at Broad St. to Ashleworth. Pub is 100 yds passed the village

Ashleworth is a delightful village, with rolling hills and the River Severn nearby. As far as the owners can establish, their village centre inn was built in the 16th century, although, as was their wont, the Victorians gave it a bit of a makeover. Thankfully, they didn't (couldn't, more like) touch the original beams or iron fireplaces; the comfy chairs and a collection of antiques in the immaculate bar and dining room came later. The restaurant area is really two intimate rooms, where regular pub grub can be chosen from blackboards. But the specials boards take you into different territory altogether with bouillabaisse, tournedos of monkfish, escalope of springbok, bobotie (also South African), and roasted local partridge. Two beautifully clipped, 200-year-old yew trees dominate the pretty front garden and, at the rear, white cast-iron garden furniture and attractive flower tubs and hanging baskets ornament a flagstoned patio.
OPEN: 12-2.30　7-11 Closed: Dec 25-26
BAR MEALS: L served all week 12-2 D served all week 7-9 Fri-Sat 7-10　Av main course £6.95　**RESTAURANT:** L served all week 12-2 D served all week 7-9 Fri-Sat 7-10 Av 3 course à la carte £19.50 ▣: Free House ◖: Shepherd Neame Spitfire, Donnington BB, S A Brain & Company Rev James, Young's Special. ⌂: 12　**FACILITIES:** Garden with rose bushes, yew trees, patio　**NOTES:** Parking 50 ⊛

AWRE　　　　　　　　　　　Map 04 SO70

The Red Hart Inn at Awre ⌂
GL14 1EW ☎ 01594 510220
Dir: E of A48, with access is from Blakeney or Newnham villages

The history of this cosy traditional free house goes back to
continued

England

1483, when it was built to house workmen renovating the nearby 10th-century church. Close to the River Severn, the setting is ideal for hikers - and there's a map by the front door for inspiration! The charming interior includes flagstone floors and an illuminated well. Favourite dishes include lamb's liver and bacon; and cod, chips and mushy peas.
OPEN: 12-3 6-11 Closed: 23 Jan-5 Feb **BAR MEALS:** L served all week 12-2.30 D served all week 6-9.30 Sun 6-9 Av main course £8.95 **RESTAURANT:** L served all week 12-2.30 D served all week 6-9.30 Sun 6-9 Av 3 course à la carte £16.95 🍴: Free House 🍺: Fuller's London Pride, guest ales from Wye Valley, Wickwar, Goffs. 🍷: 6 **FACILITIES:** Garden: Country garden with seating Dogs allowed Water **NOTES:** Parking 40

BARNSLEY   Map 05 SP00

Pick of the Pubs

The Village Pub 🏵 🍷
GL7 5EF ☎ 01285 740421 🖨 01285 740929
e-mail: reservations@thevillagepub.co.uk
Dir: On B4425 4m NE of Cirencester
There is plenty of atmosphere in the beautifully restored dining rooms at the Village Pub, with their eclectic mix of furniture, flagstone floors, exposed beams and open fires. But despite the mellow-stoned country pub setting, this distinctive dining venue is light years away from the average local. This is an exemplary pub restaurant, perennially busy and renowned locally as one of the best places to eat in the area. The food starts with quality ingredients as the basic premise - locally sourced produce, traceable or organic meats, and fresh seasonal fish from Cornwall - offered from a daily changing menu. Starters might include oxtail soup, smoked chicken and vegetable salad or steamed mussels; mains could be fillet of bream with sweet and sour vegetables or rib eye steak with roast mushrooms. If the New York cheesecake's on the menu don't fail to order it!
OPEN: 11-3.30 6-11 **BAR MEALS:** L served all week 12-3 D served all week 7-10 **RESTAURANT:** L served all week 12-3 D served all week 7-10 🍴: Free House 🍺: Hook Norton Bitter, Wadworth 6X. 🍷: 17 **FACILITIES:** Children's licence Garden: Walled terrace Dogs allowed **NOTES:** Parking 35

BERKELEY   Map 04 ST69

The Malt House ♦♦♦ 🏷
Marybrook St GL13 9BA ☎ 01453 511177 🖨 01453 810257
e-mail: the-malthouse@btconnect.com
web: www.themalthouse.uk.com
Dir: From A38 towards Bristol, from M5 junct 13/14, after approx 8m Berkeley signed, Malthouse on road towards Sharpness

Family-run business within walking distance of Berkeley Castle and its deer park. Also handy for a museum dedicated to the life
continued

---

of Edward Jenner, founding father of immunology. The home-made specials board changes weekly, and the extensive choice of main courses includes grilled red snapper, roasted pork tenderloin, stilton and vegetable crumble, sweet bean curry, beef casserole, and fish pie. Good selection of lunchtime snacks.
OPEN: 12-11 **BAR MEALS:** L served all week 12-2 D served Mon-Sat 6-9 Sun 12-2 Av main course £8 **RESTAURANT:** L served all week 12-2 D served Mon-Sat 6-9 Sun 12-2 Av 3 course à la carte £13.50 🍴: Free House 🍺: Pedigree, Theakstons. **FACILITIES:** Garden: Small garden; Food served outside in summer **NOTES:** Parking 40 **ROOMS:** 9 bedrooms en suite 1 family room s£58 d£75

BIBURY   Map 05 SP10

Catherine Wheel
Arlington GL7 5ND ☎ 01285 740250 🖨 01285 740779
e-mail: catherinewheel.bibury@eldridge-pope.co.uk

Low-beamed 15th-century pub situated in a Cotswold village described by William Morris as the most beautiful in England. Inside is an original ship's timber beam, as well as various prints and photographs of Old Bibury, and blazing log fires in winter. Traditional pub food includes the likes of fresh Bibury trout, salmon and prawns, and tuna steak.
OPEN: 11-11 (Sun 12-10.30) **BAR MEALS:** L served all week 12-2 D served all week 6-9.30 bar snacks 2-6 Av main course £8.95 **RESTAURANT:** L served all week 12-2 D served all week 6-9 🍴: Eldridge Pope 🍺: Adnams, Wadworth 6X. **FACILITIES:** Garden: Food served outside. Vintage orchard Dogs allowed Water provided **NOTES:** Parking 20

BIRDLIP   Map 10 SO91

The Golden Heart 🍷
Nettleton Bottom GL4 8LA ☎ 01242 870261 🖨 01242 870599
Dir: On the main road A417 Gloucester to Cirencester
Glorious country views are afforded from the terraced gardens of this Cotswold stone inn, while inside you will find real fires, real ales and a wide selection of wines. The regular menu is supplemented by a daily blackboard choice. Starters might include Thai steamed seafood dim sum; or devilled whitebait. Follow with kangaroo steak with a date or Madeira sauce; Caribbean minced beef with rice; or a doorstep sandwich.
OPEN: 11-3 5.30-11 (Fri-Sat 11-11, Sun 12-10.30) Closed: Dec 25 **BAR MEALS:** L served all week 12-3 D served all week 6-10 Sun 12-10 **RESTAURANT:** L served all week 12-3 D served all week 6-10 Sun 12-10 🍴: Free House 🍺: Interbrew Bass, Timothy Taylor Landlord & Golden Best, Archers Bitter, Young's Special. 🍷: 10 **FACILITIES:** Child facs Garden: Terrace, 3 levels, large patio area, seating Dogs allowed water **NOTES:** Parking 60

🍺 Principal Beers for sale

BISLEY   Map 04 SO90

The Bear Inn
George St GL6 7BD ☎ 01452 770265
Dir: E of Stroud off B4070
Constructed as a courthouse with meeting rooms for the village in the 16th century, The Bear became an inn around 1766 and has continued as such ever since. Its outstanding features include a huge inglenook fireplace, a bread oven and an old priest hole; though the rock-hewn cellars, including a 60-ft well, are more likely Tudor. Menu items include bear burgers, Bear Necessities (sauté potatoes with various ingredients mixed in) and Bear Essentials such as steak, kidney and Guinness pie.
OPEN: 11.30-3 6-11 (Sun 12-3 Sun 7-10.30) Closed: 25-26 Dec **BAR MEALS:** L served all week 12-2 D served Mon-Sat 7-9 No food Sun pm ⊕: Pubmaster ◖: Tetley, Flowers IPA, Charles Wells Bombardier, Marstons. **FACILITIES:** Garden: Food served outside Dogs allowed **NOTES:** Parking 20

BLEDINGTON   Map 10 SP22

Pick of the Pubs

Kings Head Inn ◆◆◆◆ ♀
The Green OX7 6XQ ☎ 01608 658365 📠 01608 658902
e-mail: kingshead@orr-ewing.com
web: www.kingsheadinn.net
See Pick of the Pubs on opposite page

BLOCKLEY   Map 10 SP13

The Crown Inn & Hotel ★★★
High St GL56 9EX ☎ 01386 700245 📠 01386 700247
e-mail: info@crown-inn-blockley.co.uk

Log fires and friendly staff offer a warm welcome to this 14th-century coaching inn. Untouched by the pace of modern life, the hidden and sleepy village of Blockley is the perfect location from which to explore all that the Cotswolds have to offer. The hotel's non-smoking restaurant offers a balanced blend of traditional and modern cuisine; typical dishes include ricotta and spinach tortellini; hare casserole; and lemon sole roulade with prawns.
OPEN: 12-11 **BAR MEALS:** L served all week 12-2 D served all week 7-9 **RESTAURANT:** L served all week 12-2 D served all week 7-9 Av 3 course à la carte £24.95 Av 3 course fixed price £24.95 ⊕: Free House ◖: Hook Norton Best, Scottish Courage John Smith's, Wadworth 6X. **FACILITIES:** Children's licence Garden: Dogs allowed Water **NOTES:** Parking 40 **ROOMS:** 24 bedrooms en suite 4 family rooms s£59.95 d£90

BROCKWEIR   Map 04 SO50

Brockweir Country Inn
NP16 7NG ☎ 01291 689548
Dir: From Chepstow A446 to Monmouth, 1m after Tintern Bridge on R
This approximately 500-year-old inn is situated at Brockweir, known as the jewel in the Wye Valley. The only pub in the village, it is close to the banks of the river and surrounded by numerous walks and magnificent scenery. Local ales and food are served in a laid-back atmosphere, and the menu features Wye salmon, and local meats and vegetables.
OPEN: 12-3.30 6-11 (Sun 7-11.30) All day Spring-Autumn **BAR MEALS:** L served Tue-Sun 12-2.30 D served Tue-Sat 6-8.30 **RESTAURANT:** 12-2.30 6-9 ⊕: Free House ◖: Butcombe Bitter, Wadworth 6X, Wye Valley Bitter, Bass. **FACILITIES:** Garden: Patio area and beer garden Dogs allowed On leads **NOTES:** No credit cards

---

◆ Pubs with Red Diamonds are the top places in the AA's three, four and five diamond ratings

---

Room prices show the minimum double and single rates charged. Room rates in hotels and B&Bs often vary depending on the facilities, so be sure to check prices with the establishment before booking

---

We only include details of accommodation that has been inspected by the AA (big Stars or Diamonds at the top of an entry), or the RAC, VisitBritain, VisitScotland or WTB (small Stars or Diamonds at the end of an entry)

Disabled people and those with Assist Dogs have new rights of access to pubs, restaurants and hotels under the Disability Discrimination Act of 1 October 2004. For more information see the website at www.drc gb.org/open4all/rights/2004.asp

---

Pick of the Pubs

Kings Head Inn

Set back off a perfect Cotswold village green, with its brook and stone bridge, this 16th-century, honey-coloured stone inn has quickly developed a seriously good reputation. It was once a cider house, and much of the original building has survived - low ceilings, sturdy beams, flagstone floors, exposed stone walls, and big open fireplaces.

Add some solid oak furniture, and the absolutely vital large black kettle hanging in an inglenook, and the result is that unmistakeable English country pub look. Age gives it a head start, naturally, but enthusiastic owners Archie and Nicola Orr-Ewing, now into their sixth year, have made their mark too. In the bar, Hook Norton Best is a mainstay, alongside other real ales, and guests from local micro-breweries. The wine list offers a choice of more than 40 bins, including house wines by the glass. The good quality food is prepared in-house and locally sourced as far as is practicable. Fish has to travel, of course, but it arrives fresh from Cornwall three times a week. The Aberdeen Angus beef comes from the family farm, and the vegetables from the nearby Daylesford Estate. Starters at lunch or dinner might be home-cured gravadlax with warm toast and dressed leaves; and homemade duck spring rolls with sweet chilli sauce. Main courses include grilled mustard and herb chicken breast with purple sprouting broccoli and chorizo parmentier potatoes; roast chump of English lamb with buttered savoy cabbage and celeriac horseradish mash; and smoked haddock and crayfish pie. Twelve lovely bedrooms offer en suite accommodation.

OPEN: 11-2.30 6-11 (Closed: 24-25 Dec)
BAR MEALS: L served all week 12-2 D served all week 7-9.30
RESTAURANT: L served all week 12-2 D served all week 7-9.30
⊕: Free House
◖: Hook Norton Bitter, Shepherd Neam Spitfire, Timothy Taylor Landlord, Adnams. ♀: 8
FACILITIES: Garden: Food served outside in summer
NOTES: Parking 35
ROOMS: 12 bedrooms en suite s£55 d£70 No children overnight

♦♦♦♦ ♀   Map 10 SP22
The Green OX7 6XQ
☎ 01608 658365
🖹 01608 658902
ⓔ kingshead@orr-ewing.com
ⓦ www.kingsheadinn.net
Dir: On B4450 4m from Stow-on-the-Wold

CHEDWORTH   Map 05 SP01

Hare & Hounds
Foss Cross GL54 4NN ☎ 01285 720288 🖷 01285 720488
Dir: On A429 (Fosse Way), 6m from Cirencester

Rustic stone-built pub on a remote stretch of the ancient
Fosse Way, surrounded by beautiful Cotswold countryside.
The 14th-century building features flagged floors, splendid
open fires, a spiral staircase and working bread oven. There's
a daily changing blackboard in addition to the regular menu,
and typical dishes are Geraldo's antipasti, Old Spot sausage
and mash, and baked sultana and orange cheesecake.
OPEN: 11-3 6-11 **BAR MEALS:** L served all week 12-2.30 D served
all week 7-9.45 Av main course £12.95 **RESTAURANT:** L served all
week 11-2.30 D served all week 6.30-9.45 Sun 12-3, 7-9
🍽: 🍺: Arkells 3B JRA. **FACILITIES:** Child facs Large colourful
garden Dogs allowed Water **NOTES:** Parking 80

Seven Tuns ♀
Queen St GL54 4AE ☎ 01285 720242 🖷 01285 720242
e-mail: theseventuns@clara.co.uk
*Dir: A40 then A429 towards Cirencester, after 5m right for Chedworth, 3m
then 3rd turning on right*

Traditional village inn dating back to 1610, and the ideal place
to relax in after an exhilarating walk in the Cotswolds. Handy
also for visiting nearby Chedworth Roman villa which can be
reached on foot. Directly opposite the inn, which takes its
name from seven chimney pots, are a waterwheel, a spring
and a raised terrace for summer drinking. The freshly
prepared daily-changing menu might feature sausages with
mash, fish and chips, salad with chicken, bacon and avacado,
or wild mushroom tagliatelle. Well-kept real ales, South
African BBQ, and a renovated skittle alley.
OPEN: 11-11 (Nov-Mar 11-3, 6-11, Sun 12-10.30)
BAR MEALS: L served all week 12-3 D served all week 6.30-10
Av main course £8.50 **RESTAURANT:** L served all week 12-3
D served all week 6.30-10 Av 3 course à la carte £19 🍽: Free House
🍺: Young's Bitter, Youngs Special, Winter Warmer, Waggledance.
♀: 12 **FACILITIES:** Child facs Garden: 60 seater terrace, heaters,
BBQ Dogs allowed Water, biscuits **NOTES:** Parking 30

CHIPPING CAMPDEN   Map 10 SP13

Pick of the Pubs

The Bakers Arms
Broad Campden GL55 6UR ☎ 01386 840515
Award-winning small Cotswold inn with a great
atmosphere - visitors are welcomed and regulars are
involved with the quiz, darts and crib teams. The
traditional look of the place is reflected in its time-
honoured values, with good meals at reasonable prices
and a choice of four or five real ales. You can go for the
main menu or opt for light bites at lunchtimes. The latter
include sandwiches, ploughman's lunches, warm
baguettes, and giant Yorkshire puddings. Menu starters
could include breaded goats' cheese with redcurrant jelly;
prawn cocktail with marie rose sauce; and deep-fried
camembert with redcurrant jelly. Main courses could
include lasagne verdi; lamb moussaka; chilli con carne;
smoked haddock bake; chicken curry; and Thai red
vegetable curry. On the specials list you may find lamb
shank; bangers and mash; pork chops in cider; and
venison casserole. Toffee and banana sponge; fruit
crumble; hot chocolate fudge cake; and treacle tart are
among the enticing desserts.
OPEN: 11.30-2.30 4.45-11 (Fri-Sat 11.30-11 Sun 12-10.30,
Summer 11.30-11) Closed: 25 Dec 26 Dec closed evening
BAR MEALS: L served all week 12-2 D served all week 6-9
Apr-Oct 12-9 **RESTAURANT:** L served all week 12-2 D served
all week 6-9 🍽: Free House 🍺: Stanway Bitter, Bombardier,
Timothy Taylor Landlord, Donnington BB. **FACILITIES:** Child
facs Garden: Large grassed area Dogs allowed garden only.
Water provided **NOTES:** Parking 30 No credit cards

Pick of the Pubs

Eight Bells ♀
Church St GL55 6JG ☎ 01386 840371 🖷 01386 841669
e-mail: neilhargreaves@bellinn.fsnet.co.uk
web: www.eightbellsinn.co.uk

The inn was built in the 14th century to house the
stonemasons working on the nearby church and to store
the eight church bells. It is a tiny stone-built free house
with two atmospheric bars retaining the original oak
beams, open fireplaces and even a priest's hole. In
summer the pub is hung with attractive flower baskets,
and guests arrive through the cobbled entranceway
where the bars lead into the modern dining room. There
is also an enclosed courtyard with seating in fine weather,
and a beautiful terraced garden overlooking the
almshouses and the church. Freshly prepared local food

continued

England

is offered from a daily-changing seasonal menu, with filled ciabattas at lunchtime, and main menu dishes like ale-poached mackerel with spiced braised onions and parsley butter; coq au vin with smoked bacon, mushrooms and shallots, served with new potatoes; and steamed walnut and syrup sponge with ginger custard.
OPEN: 12-3 5.30-11 (all day Jul-Aug) Closed: 25 Dec
BAR MEALS: L served all week 12-2.30 D served all week 6.30-9.30 Av main course £10 **RESTAURANT:** L served all week 12-2.30 D served all week 6.30-9.30 Av 3 course à la carte £22 🍺: Free House 🍺: Hook Norton Best & Guest Beers, Goff's Jouster, Marston Pedigree. ♀: 8 **FACILITIES:** Child facs Garden: Terrace, courtyard, great views of almshouses Dogs allowed Water **ROOMS:** 7 bedrooms en suite 1 family room s£50 d£80 (♦♦♦♦)

King's Arms NEW ♦♦♦♦ ⓖ ♀
The Square GL55 6AW ☎ 01386 840256 🖷 01386 841598
e-mail: info@thekingsarmshotel.com
web: www.thekingsarmshotel.com
Set in the square of a pretty Cotswold town, this smart 17th-century inn has an air of relaxed elegance. The two dining rooms are spacious, and the lavender-planted courtyard could be a million miles away from worldly bustle. There are plenty of snacks to enjoy with a drink, but the full menu offers celeriac and braised pork ravioli perhaps; or roast mallard breast with creamed cabbage and bacon.
OPEN: 12-11 **BAR MEALS:** L served all week 12-2.30 D served all week 6.30-9.30 Sat-Sun 12-3 **RESTAURANT:** L served all week 12-2.30 D served all week 6.30-9.30 Sat-Sun 12-3 🍺: Johns Smiths, Hook Norton Best. ♀: 14 **FACILITIES:** Child facs Garden: Dogs allowed **NOTES:** Parking 8 **ROOMS:** 11 bedrooms en suite 5 family rooms s£85 d£105

The Noel Arms Hotel ★★★ 🐟
High St GL55 6AT ☎ 01386 840317 🖷 01386 841136
e-mail: reception@noelarmshotel.com
web: www.noelarmshotel.com
Dir: On High St, opposite Town Hall
This 16th-century coaching inn has a great atmosphere. Original oak beams, and an open fire warm the Dover's Bar, where guests can enjoy wide variety of meals and snacks. An à la carte menu is served in the Gainsborough Restaurant, where you might try salmon pavé, stir-fried mange-tout and carrot with lime dressing; tempura vegetables with sweet chilli and tartar sauces; seafood coconut curry; and prawns, squid, cod, tuna and salmon in a mild Sri Lankan sauce with yellow rice. The pub has had many famous visitors down the years, including King Charles II and, more recently, Johnny Depp.
OPEN: 11-11 (Sun 12-10.30) **BAR MEALS:** L served all week 12-2.30 D served all week 6-9.30 Av main course £10
RESTAURANT: L served all week 12-2.30 D served all week 7-9.30 Av 3 course à la carte £25 Av 4 course fixed price £24.50 🍺: Free House 🍺: Hook Norton Generation, Hook Norton Best Bitter, Guinness. **FACILITIES:** Child facs Garden: Courtyard with cast iron & ceramic furniture Dogs allowed **NOTES:** Parking 25 **ROOMS:** 26 bedrooms en suite 1 family room s£90 d£125

The Volunteer Inn ♀
Lower High St GL55 6DY ☎ 01386 840688 🖷 01386 840543
e-mail: saravol@aol.com
A 300-year-old inn where in the mid-19th century the able-bodied used to sign up for the militia - hence its name. In the same family hands for twenty years, its unspoilt local charm attracts many visitors, particularly to the 'olde worlde' rear garden by the River Cam where Aunt Sally is played in

continued

summer. Ramblers set off from here to walk the Cotswold Way refreshed by a pint of one of the six real ales. Food choices include home-made pies and casseroles, honey-roast ham, half-shoulder of lamb cooked in wine and herbs, and goats' cheese baked on puff pastry salad with bacon.
OPEN: 11.30-3 5-11 (Sat 11.30-3, 6-11 Sun 12-3, 7-10.30)
BAR MEALS: L served all week 12-2 D served all week 7-9 Not 25 Dec Av main course £7 🍺: Free House 🍺: Hook Norton Best, North Cotswold Genesis, Stanway Bitter, Wickwar Cotswold Way. ♀: 14 **FACILITIES:** Garden: Large lawn, courtyard with tables and seating Dogs allowed Except in lounge

---

CIRENCESTER   Map 05 SP00

Pick of the Pubs

The Crown of Crucis ★★★ 🐟 ♀
Ampney Crucis GL7 5RS ☎ 01285 851806 🖷 01285 851735
e-mail: info@thecrownofcrucis.co.uk
web: www.thecrownofcrucis.co.uk
Dir: On A417 to Lechlade, 2m E of Cirencester

Standing beside the Ampney Brook at the gateway to the glorious Cotswolds, this classic 16th-century inn overlooks the village cricket green, and on sunny summer days the evocative sound of willow on leather and the quiet stream meandering past the lawns conspire to create a perfect picture of quintessential England. The hotel, which takes its name from the Latin cross or 'crucis' in the nearby village churchyard, provides modern comforts while still retaining the original character. The restaurant offers a large and varied menu using a daily selection of fresh local produce prepared by a team of dedicated and innovative young chefs. Alternatively, the surroundings of the cosy, inviting bar are conducive to relaxing and enjoying traditional home-cooked food available throughout the day. Try whole roasted partridge, crispy duck rolls, or smoked haddock, or look at the daily specials listed on the blackboard. Restaurant main courses include gently braised lamb shank, Crown of Crucis beef fillet, and softly roasted all spice pork belly.
OPEN: 10.30-11 (Sun 12-11) Closed: Dec 25 Dec 24-30 No accommodation **BAR MEALS:** L served all week 12-2.30 D served all week 6-10 **RESTAURANT:** L served all week 12-2.30 D served all week 7-9.30 🍺: Free House 🍺: Wadworth 6X, Archers Village, Scottish Courage John Smith's. ♀: 10 **FACILITIES:** Garden: Riverside Setting Dogs allowed **NOTES:** Parking 70 **ROOMS:** 25 bedrooms en suite 2 family rooms s£60 d£80

♦ Diamond rating for inspected guest accommodation

England

Pick of the Pubs

Wyndham Arms ♀
GL16 8JT ☎ 01594 833666 ▤ 01594 836450
e-mail: nigel@thewyndhamhotel.co.uk
Dir: *In village centre on B4231*

The quintessentially English village of Clearwell in the Royal Forest of Dean takes its name from the Dunraven Well on the hotel boundary. The building itself dates back to the 14th century when it was a manor house; later it was converted into a public house and over the centuries since then it has evolved into a highly civilised small hotel, run with great style and enthusiasm. Beautiful flower displays are an appealing feature. In the Old-Spot restaurant, a three-course meal might comprise pressing of foie gras and baby leeks as a starter, parmesan tart with roasted baby vegetables and mint hollandaise; free range corn fed chicken with sorrel butter and Jerusalem artichoke risotto; Aberdeen Angus fillet with horseradish mash potato; or study of Cornish lamb with garden herb roasted sweetbreads as a main course, and valrhoma chocolate tart for dessert. Local beers are likely to be Freeminer's Bitter and Speculation Ale, brewed in Cinderford on the other side of the Forest.
OPEN: 11-11 (Sun 12-10.30) **BAR MEALS:** L served all week 12-2 D served all week 7-9.30 **RESTAURANT:** L served all week 12-2 D served all week 7-9.30 Sun lunch 12-2.30, dinner 7-9.30
🍴: Free House 🍺: Speculation Bitter, Freeminer Bitter. ♀: 7
FACILITIES: Child facs Garden: Dogs allowed Field for exercise **NOTES:** Parking 50

Restaurant and Bar Meal times indicate the times when food is available. Last orders may be approximately 30 minutes before the times stated

---

Pick of the Pubs have that extra special quality that makes them stand out from the crowd. Their entries are highlighted, and may be a full page

Pick of the Pubs

The Tunnel House Inn NEW
GL7 6PW ☎ 01285 770280 ▤ 01285 770120
e-mail: info@tunnelhouse.com
Dir: *Leave Cirencester on A433 towards Tetbury, after 2m turn right towards Coates, follow signs to Canal Tunnel and Inn*

The Tunnel House is set in an idyllic rural location, nestling between the Cotswold villages of Coates and Tarlton. It is close to the source of the River Thames, and sits besides the Thames and Severn canal. Inside, the bar has a relaxed and welcoming atmosphere, furnished as it is with unique memorabilia collected over the years. Roaring log fires provide comfort and warmth in the winter months, while the garden is a peaceful retreat in the summer. A children's play area, and spectacular walks in the surrounding area add to its popularity. The menu boasts a range of good home cooking using fresh and local produce wherever possible, and updated monthly to make the most of the seasonal variety. You can dine in the restaurant area or relax in the comfortable bar.
OPEN: 11-3 6-11 Open all day Fri-Sun **BAR MEALS:** L served all week 12-2.15 D served all week 6.45-9.15 Av main course £8
🍺: Uley Old Spot, Uley Bitter, Wye Valley Bitter, Archers Village.
FACILITIES: Children's licence Garden: Large area at rear of pub Dogs allowed Water **NOTES:** Parking 50

The Colesbourne Inn ♀
GL53 9NP ☎ 01242 870376 ▤ 01242 870397
e-mail: info@colesbourneinn.com
Dir: *On A435 (Cirencester to Cheltenham road)*
Large log fires, beams, and a large garden overlooking wooded hills are all features of this 17th-century coaching inn. The interior is decorated with a wealth of bric-a-brac, and there are cask ales to sup and traditional food in both lounge bar and dining room. Lunch might offer boiled gammon and wild boar sausages, with favourites at night that take in pan-fired king prawns and scallops, and lamb or beef sizzlers.
OPEN: 11.30-3 6.30-11 **BAR MEALS:** L served Wed-Sun 12-2 D served Mon-Sat 7-9 Av main course £10.95
RESTAURANT: L served Wed-Sun 12-2.30 D served Mon-Sat 7-9.30
🍴: Wadworth 🍺: Wadworth 6X, Henrys IPA. ♀: 6
FACILITIES: Garden: Views overlooking Cotswold countryside Dogs allowed Water, toys **NOTES:** Parking 40

COLN ST ALDWYNS   Map 05 SP10

Pick of the Pubs

The New Inn At Coln ★★ 🏵🏵 ♀
GL7 5AN ☎ 01285 750651 📠 01285 750657
e-mail: stay@new-inn.co.uk web: www.new-inn.co.uk
Dir: *Between Bibury (B4425) & Fairford (A417), 8m E of Cirencester*
The New Inn at Coln was well established long before
Christopher Wren built St Paul's Cathedral. The pub's
creeper-covered façade is a welcoming sight amongst the
Cotswold stone buildings of this pretty village. Flagstone
floors, exposed beams and open fires characterise the
bars, where comfy mate's chairs and bar stools offer a
choice of seating. In summer, meals are served in the
delightful flower-filled courtyard, while the restaurant is a
stylish place to peruse the menus and savour the food in
all seasons. Delights like spicy apricot and cumin lamb
with coconut rice, and New Inn fish and chips with tartare
sauce feature on the bar menu, followed, perhaps, by
banana and rum cheesecake, or apple and cranberry
turnover with crème fraîche. At dinner, the imaginative
restaurant dishes include fillet of beef with fondant
potato, cep fricassee, red onion confit and Madeira jus;
tenderloin of Gloucestershire Old Spot pork with bubble
and squeak, apricot chutney and mild curry cream; and
pan-fried sea bass with orange braised chicory, aubergine
caviar and lemon grass prawns butter sauce. For those
with time to linger, there are several very individual
bedrooms offering en suite facilities along with half-
testers and four-posters, or double and twin beds.
OPEN: 11-11 (Sun 12-10.30) **BAR MEALS:** L served all week
12-2 D served all week 7-9 (Sun 12-2.30, Fri-Sat 7-9.30)
RESTAURANT: L served all week 12-2 D served all week 7-9
Fri-Sat 7-9.30, Sun 12-2.30 Av 3 course à la carte £37 🍴: Free
House 🍺: Hook Norton Best Bitter, Wadworth 6X, Butcombe
Bitter. ♀: 8 **FACILITIES:** Garden: Terrace area Dogs allowed
Water bowls provided **NOTES:** Parking 24
ROOMS: 14 bedrooms en suite s£126 d£196 No children
overnight

COWLEY   Map 10 SO91

Pick of the Pubs

The Green Dragon Inn 🔾 ♀
Cockleford GL53 9NW ☎ 01242 870271 📠 01242 870171
web: www.buccaneer.co.uk

A handsome stone-built inn dating from the 17th century
and located in the Cotswold hamlet of Cockleford. The
fittings and furniture are the work of the 'Mouse Man of

Kilburn' (so-called for his trademark mouse) who lends
his name to the popular Mouse Bar, with its stone-flagged
floors, beamed ceilings and crackling log fires. The weekly
menu includes sandwiches at lunchtime, children's
favourites, and a choice of starters/light meals such as
smoked haddock chowder or Caesar salad. Typical fish
dishes may include fillet of mackerel on ciabatta; stir-fried
smoked eel with black beans and spring onions; Green
Dragon fish pie; and blue swimming crab omelette. Other
important features are the choice of real ales, with a
monthly guest beer; the heated dining terrace; and the
function room/skittle alley. Very popular at weekends.
OPEN: 11-11 (Sun 12-10.30) **BAR MEALS:** L served all week
12-2.30 D served all week 6.30-10.30 (Sat & Sun 12-10) 🍴: Free
House 🍺: Hook Norton, Directors Butcombe, guest ale. ♀: 8
FACILITIES: Children's licence Garden: Dogs allowed Water
NOTES: Parking 100

CRANHAM   Map 10 SO81

The Black Horse Inn 🔾
GL4 8HP ☎ 01452 812217
Dir: *A46 towards Stroud, follow signs for Cranham*
Situated in a small village surrounded by woodland and
commons, a mile from the Cotswold Way and Prinknash
Abbey, this is a traditional inn with two open fires, a stone-
tiled floor and two dining rooms upstairs. On the menu you'll
find all sorts of pies, as well as chops, gammon, salads,
casseroles and a variety of fish dishes including trout with
garlic and herb butter, or fisherman's pie. Any eggs used have
probably come from the pub's own chickens. There's quite a
bit of Morris dancing throughout the season, with the sloping
garden offering lovely views across the valley.
OPEN: 11.30-2.30 6.30-11 (Sun 12-3, 7-10.30) Closed: 25 Dec
BAR MEALS: L served Tue-Sun 12-2 D served Tue-Sun 6.45-9.30
Av main course £8.80 **RESTAURANT:** L served all week D served
Mon-Sat 🍴: Free House 🍺: Wickwar Brand Oak, Archers, Golden
Train & Village, Hancocks HB & Guest Beers. **FACILITIES:** Garden:
Sloping garden with good views Dogs allowed on leads Water
NOTES: Parking 25

DIDMARTON   Map 04 ST88

Pick of the Pubs

The Kings Arms ♦♦♦♦ 🔾 ♀
The Street GL9 1DT ☎ 01454 238245 📠 01454 238249
e-mail: kingsarms@didmarton.freeserve.co.uk
Dir: *M4 junct 18 take A46 N signed Stroud, after 8m take A433
signed Didmarton 2m*
Attractively restored, 17th-century former coaching inn,
originally leased from the Beaufort family of Badminton
for 1000 years at a yearly rent of sixpence. Famous
locally for its annual Rook Night Supper held after
these birds are culled on the sprawling Badminton
Estate. The Edwardian-style interior is cosy and
welcoming all year, especially when the big open
winter fires are blazing away. Both bars support local
breweries, and 12 wines are available by the glass. You
may choose to eat from the diverse and frequently
updated bar snack menu, or have something more
substantial from the main restaurant menu or list of
daily specials. Local game is a speciality, as are roasted
rack of lamb with a herb crust and a light casserole of
vegetables and cider; and mousseline of lemon sole

continued

continued

DIDMARTON continued

with lobster bisque. The beautiful large garden incorporates a boules pitch.

The Kings Arms

OPEN: 11-3 6-11 (Fri-Sat 11-11 Sun 12-10.30)
BAR MEALS: L served all week 12-2 D served all week 7-9.30
Sun 7-9 Av main course £11 **RESTAURANT:** L served all week
12-2 D served all week 7-9.30 Sun 7-9 Av 3 course à la carte £22
⊕: Free House ◀: Uley Bitter, Otter, Laurie Lee Bitter from Uley,
Cotswold Way. ♀: 12 **FACILITIES:** Garden: Enclosed garden,
stone wall, benches Dogs allowed **NOTES:** Parking 28
ROOMS: 4 bedrooms en suite No children overnight

DURSLEY   Map 04 ST79

Pickwick Inn
Lower Wick GL11 6DD ☎ 01453 810259 ▤ 01453 810259
e-mail: enquiries@thepickwickinn.com
Dir: *From Gloucester A38, turn L opposite Berkeley turn off, pub on L*
Built in 1762, this has always been an inn, but has also
doubled as a barber's and a slaughterhouse. The restaurant
was built on in the mid-1980s, and the bar has an Old Codger
Corner especially reserved for elderly regulars. Log burners
warm the building in cooler months. Typical menu includes
Tracy Tupman's honey glazed duck breast, stilton and walnut
pie, mushroom and red pepper stroganoff, Pickwick special
mixed grill, steak and ale pie, and plenty of fish options.
Recent change of management. Lots of live music.
OPEN: 11.30-3 6-11 (Sun 12-3,7-10.30) **BAR MEALS:** L served all
week 11.30-2.30 D served all week 6.30-10 Sun 12-3 Av main course
£10 **RESTAURANT:** L served all week 11.30-2.30 D served all week
6.30-10 Av 3 course à la carte £15 ⊕: Youngs ◀: Youngs Bitter,
Youngs Special, Waggle Dance, Youngs Winter Warmer.
FACILITIES: Child facs Garden: Food served outside. Lawn & flower
beds Dogs allowed Water **NOTES:** Parking 80

EBRINGTON   Map 10 SP14

Ebrington Arms
Ebrington GL55 6NH ☎ 01386 593223 ▤ 01386 593763
Dir: *Telephone for directions*
A charmingly down-to-earth Cotswold village pub dating from
the mid-18th century. Stone floors, inglenook fires and
beautiful surrounding countryside give it plenty of character.
Walkers and others frequent the pub for its locally-brewed
ales and good home-cooked food, including marinated prawn
skewer on a bed of mango and Oriental spiced salad; and
fillet of lamb with rösto potatoes and a red wine jus.
OPEN: 11-2.30 6-11 (open all day from Etr) **BAR MEALS:** L served
Tue-Sun 12-2 D served Tue-Sat 6-9 Av main course £11
RESTAURANT: L served Tue-Sun 12-2 D served Tue-Sat 6-9 Av 3 course
continued

à la carte £22 ⊕: Free House ◀: Hook Norton Best, Fullers London
Pride & Bombadier. **FACILITIES:** Child facs Children's licence Garden:
Lawn and patio area Dogs allowed Water **NOTES:** Parking 12

FORD   Map 10 SP02

Plough Inn ♦♦♦♦
GL54 5RU ☎ 01386 584215 ▤ 01386 584042
e-mail: info@theploughinnatford.co.uk
web: www.theploughinnatford.co.uk
Dir: *4m from Stow-on-the-Wold on Tewkesbury rd*

This 16th-century inn, steeped in history and character,
provides all that one associates with a traditional English pub:
flagstone floors, log fires, sturdy pine furnishings and lively
conversation. Meals made from local produce are cooked to
order, and include half a slow roasted shoulder of lamb,
luxury fish pie, braised beef, and mushroom stroganoff; the
inn is renowned for its fresh, seasonal asparagus.
OPEN: 11-11 (Sun 12-10.30) Closed: 25 Dec
BAR MEALS: L served all week 12-2 D served Mon-Sun 6.30-9
weekends food all day 12-9 **RESTAURANT:** L served all week
11.30-2 D served all week 6.30-9 Food all day Sat-Sun
⊕: ◀: Donnington BB & SBA. **FACILITIES:** Child facs Garden:
Large courtyard, beer garden with heat lamps Dogs allowed Water
NOTES: Parking 50 **ROOMS:** 3 bedrooms en suite 2 family rooms
s£35 d£60 (♦♦♦♦)

FOSSEBRIDGE   Map 05 SP01

Pick of the Pubs

Fossebridge Inn ♀
GL54 3JS ☎ 01285 720721 ▤ 01285 720793
e-mail: info@fossebridge.co.uk www.fossebridgeinn.co.uk
Dir: *From M4 junct 15, A419 towards Cirencester, then A429 towards
Stow. Pub approx 7m on left*

This attractive, family-run inn is situated in the Coln Valley
and has wonderful views of the Cotswolds. The Romans
continued

were the first to settle this site although the extant building is mostly Regency. Ideal for touring Bibury, Northleach and Chedworth, there's a friendly and informal ambience here which never overlooks standards of service and comfort. The atmospheric Bridge bar and restaurant is located in the oldest part of the building dating back to the 15th century. Exposed beams, stone walls, flagstone floors and open fires provide the setting for tempting bar food and fixed price or à la carte menus. Dishes include lots of local produce, with typical examples ranging from smoked salmon with scrambled eggs or home-made cheese and bacon beefburgers with chunky chips on the bar menu, through to dishes like slow roast lamb shank with root vegetables and tangy lemon tartlets, or chilli tiger prawns on coriander noodles on the carte. Pudding might be along the lines of poached pear with chocolate sauce. New management.
OPEN: 11-3 6-11 (Sun eve 7-10.30) **BAR MEALS:** L served all week 12-3 D served all week 6-10 Av main course £11 ⊕: Free House ◀: Youngs, Bass, Youngs Special. ♀: 8 **FACILITIES:** Garden: 3.5 acres, food served outside Dogs allowed **NOTES:** Parking 40

FRAMPTON MANSELL   Map 04 SO90

Pick of the Pubs

The Crown Inn ♀
GL6 8JG ☎ 01285 760601 🖹 01285 760681
Dir: A49 halfway between Cirencester and Stroud

Dating back to the 17th century, and located in the heart of the unspoilt village of Frampton Mansell with the beautiful drama of the Golden Valley unfolding around, is The Crown Inn. It is full of old world charm, with honey-coloured stone walls, beams, and open fireplaces where log fires are lit in winter. There is also plenty of garden seating for the warmer months. Fresh local food with lots of seasonal specials, real ales and a good choice of wines by the glass are served in the restaurant and three inviting bars. Representative dishes include fresh Brixham lemon sole grilled with nut brown butter; fresh monkfish wrapped in pancetta; tandoori prawns on spicy mixed leaves; crab and salmon fish cakes with Thai dressing; and Old Spot pork chops stuffed with apricots, apples, sage and nuts. There are some wonderful walks and cycling routes in the surrounding countryside, and the royal residences of Highgrove and Gatcombe Park are in the neighbourhood.
OPEN: 12-2.30 6.30-11 Closed Sun pm Jan-Easter
BAR MEALS: L served all week 12-2 D served all week 6.30-9.30 Lunch Sat-Sun 12-3, dinner Fri-Sat 6.30-10 Av main

course £10.95 **RESTAURANT:** L served all week 12-2.30 D served all week 6.30-9.30 lunch Sat-Sun 12-3, dinner Fri-Sat 6.30-10 ◀: Courage & real ales. ♀: 8 **FACILITIES:** Child facs Garden: Patio, garden overlooking valley **NOTES:** Parking 100 **ROOMS:** 12 bedrooms en suite s£59 d£80 (♦♦♦♦)

Pick of the Pubs

The White Horse ⊛ ♀
Cirencester Rd GL6 8HZ ☎ 01285 760960
Dir: 6 miles from Cirencester on the A419, towards Stroud

This smart dining pub has a growing reputation for good food and offers a warm welcome even if you just want a quiet drink. A large sofa and comfy chairs encourage the latter, whilst the daily-changing menu based on traceable ingredients will please the hungry and the discerning. A recently installed large lobster tank (no chemicals used) means that fresh Cornish lobsters, crabs, native oysters, clams and mussels are all on their menu. The aim is to serve the seafood as simply as possible to allow the depth of flavours to come through - for example, the oysters are merely opened and served with a red wine and shallot vinegar; and lobsters are accompanied by a straightforward garlic, lemon and herb butter or saffron mayonnaise. Other mains include rib-eye steak with cracked black pepper sauce; veal osso bucco with germolata and saffron risotto; and pan-fried calves' liver with bacon and onion gravy.
OPEN: 11-3 6-11 Closed: 24-26 Dec **BAR MEALS:** L served all week 12-2.30 D served Mon-Sat 7-9.45 Sun 12-3 Av main course £13.50 **RESTAURANT:** L served all week 12-2.30 D served Mon-Sat 7-9.45 Sun 21-3 Av 3 course à la carte £23.50 ◀: Uley Bitter, Hook Norton Best, Arkells Summer Ale. ♀: 7 **FACILITIES:** Garden: Large, attractive, tables Dogs allowed **NOTES:** Parking 40

GLOUCESTER
Map 10 SO81

Queens Head
Tewkesbury Rd, Longford GL2 9EJ
☎ 01452 301882 ▣ 01452 524368 e-mail: queenshead@aol.com
Dir: On the A38 Tewkesbury to Gloucester road in the village of Longford

Festooned with hanging baskets in summer, this 250 year-old pub/restaurant is just out of town. A lovely old locals' bar with flagstoned floor proffers a great range of real ales, while two dining areas tempt with tasty menus. These may include chef's home-made fresh crab cakes with a spicy tomato salsa dressing; or the pub's signature dish of Longford lamb - a kilo joint slowly cooked in mint gravy until it falls off the bone.
OPEN: 11-3 5.30-11 **BAR MEALS:** L served all week 12-2 D served all week 6.30-9.30 Av main course £5.95 **RESTAURANT:** L served all week 12-2 D served all week 6.30-9.30 ☺: Free House
◖: Ringwood, Landlord, Black Sheep, Hook Norton. ♀: 8
NOTES: Parking 40

GREAT BARRINGTON
Map 10 SP21

The Fox ♀
OX18 4TB ☎ 01451 844385 e-mail: info@foxinnbarrington.co.uk
web: www.foxinnbarrington.co.uk
Dir: 3m W on A40 from Burford, turn N signed The Barringtons, pub is 1000yds on right.
Picturesque pub with a delightful patio and large beer garden overlooking the River Windrush - on warm days a perfect summer watering hole. It is very popular with those attending Cheltenham racecourse. Built of mellow Cotswold stone and characterised by low ceilings and log fires, the inn offers a range of well-kept Donnington beers and a choice of food which might include beef in ale pie, local pigeon breasts casseroled with button mushrooms, chicken piri-piri, Thai tuna steak, and spinach, leek and chestnut pie.
OPEN: 11-11 **BAR MEALS:** L served all week 12-2.30 D served all week 6.30-9.30 Sat-Sun 12-9.30 **RESTAURANT:** L served all week 12-2.30 D served all week 6.30-9.30 Sat-Sun 12-9.30
☺: ◖: Donnington BB, SBA. ♀: 7 **FACILITIES:** Very large garden by river & lake, seats 100 people Dogs allowed **NOTES:** Parking 60

GREAT RISSINGTON
Map 10 SP11

The Lamb Inn
GL54 2LP ☎ 01451 820388 ▣ 01451 820724
e-mail: enquiries@thelambinn.com
Dir: Between Oxford & Cheltenham off A40

Make this delightful former farmhouse your base for exploring the picturesque Cotswold countryside on foot and touring the region's famous old towns by car. Among the attractions at this busy inn, parts of which date back 300 years, are part of a Wellington bomber which crashed in the garden in 1943, and a specially installed OS map of the area helpful for walkers. Home-cooked pub food might include pork loin steak on a mustard mash with apple and sage sauce, tagliatelle with spinach, blue cheese and pine nut cream, or chargrilled salmon, tuna and red mullet on noodles.
OPEN: 11.30-2.30 6.30-11 **BAR MEALS:** L served all week 12-2 D served all week 7-9.30 Av main course £9.50
RESTAURANT: L served all week 12-2 D served all week 7-9.30
☺: Free House ◖: Hook Norton, John Smiths & guest ale. ♀: 8
FACILITIES: Child facs Garden: Food served outside. Dogs allowed Water **NOTES:** Parking 15 **ROOMS:** 14 bedrooms en suite s£45 d£65 (♦♦♦♦)

GREET
Map 10 SP03

The Harvest Home ♀
Evesham Rd GL54 5BH ☎ 01242 602430
e-mail: Sworchardbarn@aol.com
Dir: M5 junct 9 take A435 towards Evesham, then B4077 & B4078 towards Winchombe. 200yds from station
Set in the beautiful Cotswold countryside, this traditional country inn draws steam train enthusiasts aplenty, as a restored stretch of the Great Western Railway runs past the end of the garden. Built around 1903 for railway workers, the pub is handy for Cheltenham Racecourse and Sudeley Castle. Expect a good range of snacks and mains, including locally-reared beef and tempting seafood dishes.
OPEN: 12-3 6-11 (Sun 6-10.30) **BAR MEALS:** L served all week 12-2 D served all week 6-9 Av main course £8.95
RESTAURANT: L served all week 12-2 D served all week 6-9 Av 3 course à la carte £17.50 Av 2 course fixed price £5.95
☺: Enterprise Inns ◖: Old Speckled Hen, Goffs Jouster, Deuchars IPA. ♀: 11 **FACILITIES:** Children's licence Garden: Grass area, picnic tables, countryside views Dogs allowed Water
NOTES: Parking 30

The Rosette is the AA award for food. Look out for it next to a pub's name

Pubs offering a good choice of fish on their menu

Pubs with this logo do not allow smoking anywhere on their premises

All AA rated accommodation can also be found on the AA's internet site
www.theAA.com

GUITING POWER
Map 10 SP02

The Hollow Bottom ♦♦♦♦ 🍽 ♀
GL54 5UX ☎ 01451 850392 📠 01451 850945
e-mail: hello@hollowbottom.com web: www.hollowbottom.com
Dir: *Telephone for directions*

There's a horse-racing theme at this 18th-century Cotswold
free house, often frequented by the Cheltenham racing
fraternity. Its nooks and crannies lend themselves to an
intimate drink or meal, and there's also a separate dining
room, plus outside tables for fine weather. Specials include
prawn cocktail on seasonal leaves with a spicy tomato sauce;
breast of pan-fried chicken with stilton, olive oil, tomato and
spring onion; and home-made raspberry cheesecake to finish.
OPEN: 11-11 **BAR MEALS:** L served all week 12 D served all week
9.30 Av main course £9.95 **RESTAURANT:** L served all week 12
D served all week 9.30 Av 3 course à la carte £20 🍽: Free House
🍺: Hollow Bottom Best Bitter, Goff's Jouster, Timothy Taylor
Landlord, Fullers London Pride. ♀: 7 **FACILITIES:** Child facs
Children's licence Garden: Bench, table, patio heaters Dogs allowed
NOTES: Parking 15 **ROOMS:** 4 bedrooms 3 en suite 1 family room
s£45 d£70

HINTON
Map 04 ST77

The Bull Inn ♀
SN14 8HG ☎ 0117 9372332
Dir: *From M4 Junc 18, A46 to Bath for 1m then R, 1m downhill, on R*
The inn is in a lovely setting with a summer terrace to the
front of the building and a large garden with a children's play
area to the rear. The property dates from the 17th century
and has two inglenook fireplaces, original flagstone flooring
and a resident ghost. In addition to the à la carte menu, there
is a large selection of daily specials, served in the restaurant
and bar. Booking is strongly recommended.
OPEN: 12-3 6-11 (Sun 7.30-10.30) **BAR MEALS:** L served all week
12-2 D served all week 6-9 Fri-Sat 9.30 Av main course £9
RESTAURANT: L served Tue-Sun 12-2 D served Mon-Sat 6-9 Fri-Sat
9.30 Av 3 course à la carte £18 🍽: Wadworth 🍺: Wadworth 6X &
Henrys IPA, Wadworth Bishops Tipple, Wadworth Summersault plus
monthly guest ale. ♀: 12 **FACILITIES:** Child facs Garden: Very
large garden Dogs allowed **NOTES:** Parking 50

LECHLADE ON THAMES
Map 05 SU29

The Trout Inn ♀
St Johns Bridge GL7 3HA ☎ 01367 252313 📠 01367 252313
e-mail: chefpjw@aol.com
Dir: *From A40 take A361 then A417. From M4 to Lechlade then A417 to Inn*
Dating from around 1220, a former almshouse with a large
garden on the banks of the Thames. Things are generally
humming here, with tractor and steam events, and jazz and
folk festivals. The interior is all flagstone floors and beams in

a bar that overflows into the old boat-house. The extensive
menus offer choices ranging from appetising small snacks to
pork fillet in a creamy whole-grain mustard sauce; fish pie
with haddock and prawns; and sweetcorn, red pepper and
spinach puff pastry parcel.

The Trout Inn

OPEN: 10-3 6-11 (open all day summer) Closed: 25 Dec
BAR MEALS: L served all week 12-2 D served all week 7-10 Sun
7-9.30 Av main course £11.50 🍽: 🍺: Courage Best, John Smiths,
Bass, Smiles. ♀: 16 **FACILITIES:** Child facs Garden: Food served
outside, overlooking Weir Pool Dogs allowed Water
NOTES: Parking 30

LITTLE WASHBOURNE
Map 10 SO93

Hobnail's Inn ♀
GL20 8NQ ☎ 01242 620237 📠 01242 620458
e-mail: info@hobnailsinn.com
Dir: *From M5 junct 9 take A46 towards Evesham then B4077 to Stow-on-
the-Wold. Inn 1.5 m on L*
Established in 1473, the Hobnails is one of the oldest inns in
the county. Here you'll find winter log fires, as well as lovely
large gardens for warmer days. Tuck yourself into a private
corner, or relax with a pint of ale on one of the leather sofas.
A good range of bar snacks is supplemented by main course
dishes like Barbary duck in plum sauce; poached salmon on
tagliatelle; and spinach and ricotta pasta.
OPEN: 12-3 6-11 (Sat-Sun all day Easter-Sept 11-11)
BAR MEALS: L served all week 12-2 6.30-9 Av main course £10
RESTAURANT: L served Tues-Sun D served Tues-Sun 6.30-9
🍽: Enterprise Inns 🍺: London Pride, Flowers IPA, Hook Norton
Best, Greene King IPA. ♀: 6 **FACILITIES:** Child facs Children's
licence Garden: Large patio area with tables Dogs allowed
NOTES: Parking 80

LONGHOPE
Map 10 SO61

The Glasshouse Inn NEW 🍽
May Hill GL17 0NN ☎ 01452 830529
Traditional pub dating back to 1450 and located in a
wonderful rural setting. Sympathetically extended in recent
years, the inn gets its name from Dutch glassmakers who
settled locally in the 16th century. Inside it's quiet and
dignified without the intrusion of juke boxes or slot machines.
Home-cooked dishes range from chicken breast in bacon with
stilton sauce, and seafood tagliatelle, to vegetable lasagne,
and game casserole with herb dumplings.
OPEN: 11.30-3 6.30-11 **BAR MEALS:** L served Mon-Sat 12-2
D served Mon-Sat 7-9 Av main course £8.50 🍺: Butcombe, Cats
Whiskers, Hook Norton, Archers. **FACILITIES:** Garden: Quiet,
country garden Dogs allowed lunchtimes only **NOTES:** Parking 20

continued

LOWER APPERLEY
Map 10 SO82

The Farmers Arms ⌂ ♀
Ledbury Rd GL19 4DR ☎ 01452 780307 ▤ 01452 780307
e-mail: estopnight99@aol.com
Dir: On B4213 SE of Tewkesbury (off A38)

Popular country pub with an inviting atmosphere, delightfully set between the Cotswolds and the Malvern Hills. Low beams, an open fire and regular guest ales add to the charm and appeal, complementing the extensive menu. Strong emphasis is placed on fresh fish, offering roasted cod, whole Dover sole and whole trout among other dishes. The latest speciality is elver - baby eel - which the landlord imports from Spain and cooks in the traditional Gloucestershire way.
OPEN: 11-2.30 6-11 (Open Mon eve summer hols)
BAR MEALS: L served all week 12-2.15 D served all week 6.30-9.30
Av main course £8 **RESTAURANT:** L served Tues-Sun 12-2.15
D served all week 6.30-9.30 Av 3 course à la carte £16 ⊕: Wadworth
🍺: Wadworth 6X, Henry's Original IPA plus guest beers. ♀: 10
FACILITIES: Garden: Patio enclosed garden Dogs allowed Water
NOTES: Parking 80

LOWER ODDINGTON
Map 10 SP22

Pick of the Pubs

The Fox ♀
GL56 0UR ☎ 01451 870555 ▤ 01451 870666
e-mail: info@foxinn.net
Dir: A436 from Stow-on-the-Wold then right to Lower Oddington

With its mellow stone façade largely hidden by dense Virginia creeper, this 16th-century inn enjoys one of the most idyllic and unspoilt village locations in the Cotswolds; and with its polished flagstone floor, beams, log fires and daily papers in the convivial bar it is probably one of the most cosy and welcoming inns too. Fresh flowers and candles decorate the pine tables, and there are tasteful prints on the rag-washed walls. Well-

continued

kept beers are served, along with good, imaginative food, and there's a respectable wine list. In the summer months, sit out and enjoy a meal on the awning-covered terrace or in the pretty, traditional cottage garden. The menu takes full advantage of fresh local ingredients, and changes regularly with the seasons. You could start with caramelised red onion and stilton tart; or prawn and saffron risotto, and move on to breast of guinea fowl with wild mushrooms and red wine; smoked haddock and leek fishcakes with hollandaise and lemon; braised lamb shank with rosemary red wine; or honey and mustard baked ham with parsley sauce.
OPEN: 12-3 6.30-11 Sat-Sun (12-11) Apr-Oct (12-11) Closed: Dec 25 **BAR MEALS:** L served all week 12-2.30 D served all week 6.30-10 Sun 6.30-9.30 **RESTAURANT:** L served all week 12-2.30 D served all week 6.30-10 Sun 6.30-9.30 ⊕: Free House
🍺: Hook Norton Best, Badger Tanglefoot, Abbot Ale, Ruddles County. ♀: 10 **FACILITIES:** Child facs Garden: Slightly sunken terrace with gas heating Dogs allowed **NOTES:** Parking 14

LYDNEY
Map 04 SO60

The George Inn ♀
St Briavels GL15 6TA ☎ 01594 530228 ▤ 01594 530260
e-mail: mail@ithegeorge.fsnet.co.uk web: www.thegeorgeinn.info
Dir: Telephone for directions

In a quiet village high above the Wye Valley and close to the Forest of Dean, this pub has been a family-run business for the last fourteen years, and overlooks a moody 12th-century castle ruin. The pub possesses an interior of great character, including an 8th-century Celtic coffin lid set into one of the walls. Local produce features high on grills and specials menus. The pub is famous for braised shoulder of lamb and Moroccan lamb, along with popular dishes such as traditional steak and kidney and beef and Guinness pies, and fresh fish such as natural smoked haddock on a bed of spinach with two poached eggs, plaice, fresh red snapper, and sea bass.
OPEN: 11-2.30 6.30-11 **BAR MEALS:** L served all week 11-2.30 D served all week 6.30-9.30 **RESTAURANT:** L served all week 11-2.30 D served all week 6.30-9.30 ⊕: Free House 🍺: RCH Pitchfork, Freeminers, London Pride, Archers. ♀: 10
FACILITIES: Garden: Large courtyard with tables, benches, chess Dogs allowed Water **NOTES:** Parking 20 **ROOMS:** 4 bedrooms en suite 1 family room s£35 d£50 (♦♦♦)

> Pick of the Pubs have that extra special quality that makes them stand out from the crowd. Their entries are highlighted, and may be a full page

MARSHFIELD

Map 04 ST77

The Catherine Wheel

39 High St SN14 8LR ☎ 01225 892220
e-mail: info@thecatherinewheel.co.uk
Dir: Telephone for directions

A friendly country pub that serves a good range of food: calves' liver with caramelised onions and fruit sauce, beef Wellington with black pudding and paté served with red wine jus, and pork tenderloin filled with a prune stuffing wrapped in parma ham with a light stilton sauce are likely dishes. Whole roasted peppers stuffed with goats cheese and topped with a couscous crust is among the vegetarian options.
OPEN: 12-3 5.30-11 (Sat 12-11, Sun 12-10.30) Closed Mon lunch
BAR MEALS: L served all week 12-2 D served Mon-Sat 7-10 Sun 12-7 Av main course £8 **RESTAURANT:** L served all week 12-2 D served Mon-Sat 7-10 Sun 12-7 ☺: Free House ◀: Scottish Courage Courage Best, Abbey Ales Bellringer, Buckleys Best.
FACILITIES: Garden: Patio Area Dogs allowed **NOTES:** Parking 10

The Lord Nelson Inn ♀

1 & 2 High St SN14 8LP ☎ 01225 891820 & 891981
e-mail: clair.vezey@btopenworld.com
Family-run 17th-century coaching inn located in the Cotswolds, in a village on the outskirts of Bath. A friendly atmosphere, various real ales and cosy open fires add to its appeal and character. The menu features medallions of monkfish with a lemon and herb sauce; home-made steak and kidney pudding; and mushroom and goats' cheese filo parcel.
OPEN: 12-2.30 5.30-11 (Sun 12-10.30) **BAR MEALS:** L served all week 12-2 D served all week 6.30-9 Sun 12-3, 6-9 Av main course £9.95 **RESTAURANT:** L served all week 12-2 D served all week 6.30-9 Sun 12-3, 6-9 Av 3 course à la carte £16.95 ◀: Courage Best, Butcombe, Guiness. ♀: 7 **FACILITIES:** Child facs Garden: small patio area with seating Dogs allowed

MEYSEY HAMPTON

Map 05 SP10

The Masons Arms

28 High St GL7 5JT ☎ 01285 850164 ▣ 01285 850164
e-mail: jane@themasonsarms.freeserve.co.uk
Dir: 6m E of Cirencester, off A417, beside the village green
With its origins in the 17th century, this charming village free house is an ideal haven for travellers. Nine individually decorated en suite bedrooms provide a good base for touring local Cotswold beauty spots, while the bar remains a convivial focus of village life. A varied menu of home-made dishes and light bites is served in the bar and restaurant; daily specials might include Italian-style chicken; minted lamb chops; or fresh pan-fried swordfish.
OPEN: 11.30-2.45 Sun 11.30-4 6-11 Sun 7-10.30
BAR MEALS: L served all week 12-2 D served Mon-Sat 7-9.30 Fri/Sat
continued

6.30-9.30 Av main course £6.95 **RESTAURANT:** L served all week 12-2 D served Mon-Sat 7-9.30 Fri/Sat dinner from 6.30 Av 3 course à la carte £18.45 ☺: Free House ◀: Wickwar Cotswold Way, Hook Norton Best, Guest Ales. **FACILITIES:** Garden: Village green beside the pub Dogs allowed Water (£5 charge to stay overnight) **NOTES:** Parking 5 **ROOMS:** 9 bedrooms en suite s£45 d£70 (♦♦♦♦) No children overnight

MINCHINHAMPTON

Map 04 SO80

Pick of the Pubs

The Weighbridge Inn ♀

GL6 9AL ☎ 01453 832520 ▣ 01453 835903
e-mail: enquiries@2in1pub.co.uk
Dir: Situated between Nailsworth and Avening on the B4014

This historic 17th-century free house stands beside the original London to Bristol packhorse trail. In 1822 it became a turnpike with a toll of threepence for a score of pigs, but today it is just a quiet footpath and bridleway. At one time the innkeeper also looked after the weighbridge, which served the local woollen mills, including the now long-disused Longfords Mill, memorabilia from which is displayed around the inn. Behind the scenes there has been careful renovation, but the original features of the bars and the upstairs restaurant, with massive roof beams reaching almost to the floor, remain untouched. The drinking areas are just as cosy while, outside, the patios and arbours offer good views of the surrounding Cotswolds. Meals include lamb shank, chicken cordon bleu, moussaka, salads and jacket potatoes. A firm favourite is the famous 2in1 pie, one half containing your chosen filling, the other brimming with cauliflower cheese.
OPEN: 12-11 (Sun 12-10.30) Closed: 25 Dec & 10 days in Jan
BAR MEALS: L served all week 12-9.30 D served all week 12-9.30 **RESTAURANT:** L served all week 12-9.30 D served all week 12-9.30 ◀: Wadworth 6X, Uley Old Spot & Laurie Lee.
♀: 16 **FACILITIES:** Garden: Two large patios, heaters, awnings, arbors Dogs allowed Water **NOTES:** Parking 50

MISERDEN

Map 04 SO90

The Carpenters Arms ♀

GL6 7JA ☎ 01285 821283 e-mail: bleninns@clara.net
Dir: Leave A417 at Birdlip, B4010 towards Stroud, 3m Miserden signed
Named after the carpenter's workshop on the Miserden Park Estate, this old inn retains its inglenook fireplaces and original stone floors. Worn benches still carry the nameplates used by the locals a century ago to reserve their seats at the bar. Supplemented by daily specials, the main menu includes lamb Wellington, and Cajun-spiced chicken, while the bar list runs to lamb-burgers, fishcakes, Mexican nachos, and pizza.
continued

MISERDEN continued

Good range of vegetarian dishes. The unspoilt village is very popular with film crews.

The Carpenters Arms

OPEN: 11.30-2.30 6.30-11 (Sun 12-3, 7-10.30)
BAR MEALS: L served all week 12-2.30 D served all week 7-9.30
RESTAURANT: L served all week 12-2.30 D served all week 7-9.30
🍺: Free House 🍺: Greene King IPA, Wadworths, Guest Beer. ♀: 8
FACILITIES: Children's licence Garden: Patio area and gardens
Dogs allowed Water **NOTES:** Parking 22

NAILSWORTH   Map 04 ST89

The Britannia ♀

Cossack Square GL6 0DG ☎ 01453 832501 ▤ 01453 872228
e-mail: pheasantpluckers2003@yahoo.co.uk
Dir: In town centre

Impressive 17th-century former manor house occupying a delightful position on the south side of Nailsworth's Cossack Square. The interior is bright and uncluttered with an open-plan design and a blue slate floor. Various modern works of art divide the restaurant from the bar, which is heated by a large open fire. The menu is a blend of modern British and continental food, such as spicy beef Casereccia, goats' cheese crostini, venison medallions, and salmon fishcakes.
OPEN: 11-11 Closed: 25 Dec **BAR MEALS:** L served all week 11-2.45 D served all week 5.30-10 All day Sun
RESTAURANT: L served all week 11-2.45 D served all week 5.30-10 All day Sun Av 2 course fixed price £8.95 🍺: Free House
🍺: Greene King Abbot Ale, Fuller's London pride, Bass. ♀: 12
FACILITIES: Garden: Heated terrace & lawns Dogs allowed Water
NOTES: Parking 100

 Pubs offering a good choice of fish on their menu

Pick of the Pubs

Egypt Mill ★★ ◉ ♀

GL6 0AE ☎ 01453 833449 ▤ 01453 836098
e-mail: reception@egyptmill.co.uk
Dir: M4 junct 18, A46 N to Stoud. M5 junct 13, A46 to Nailsworth

Situated in the charming Cotswold town of Nailsworth, this converted corn mill contains many features of great character, including the original millstones and lifting equipment. The refurbished ground floor bar and bistro enjoy a picturesque setting, and its views over the pretty water gardens complete the scene. There is a choice of eating in the bistro or restaurant, and in both there is a good selection of wines by the glass. For those who like to savour an aperitif before dining, try the large Egypt Mill lounge. Tempting starters might offer ham hock and pea risotto; smoked salmon and avocado parcels; and salmon and lobster sausages. Main courses include the likes of saddle of lamb Greek style; calves' liver and bacon; breast of duck with apple and blackberry risotto; and Brixham fish and potato pie.
OPEN: 7-11 **BAR MEALS:** L served all week 12-2 D served all week 6.30-10 Sat-Sun food served all day 7-9 Av main course £11.50 **RESTAURANT:** L served all week 12-2 D served all week 7-10 Sun food all day -9 Av 3 course à la carte £20 🍺: Free House 🍺: Tetley Smoothflow, Archers Best, Cats Whiskers, Wickwar Cotswold Way. ♀: 10 **FACILITIES:** Child facs Garden: Mill garden, waterside Dogs allowed **NOTES:** Parking 100
ROOMS: 27 bedrooms en suite s£60 d£75

Pick of the Pubs

Tipputs Inn ♀

Bath Rd GL6 0QE ☎ 01453 832466 ▤ 01453 832010
e-mail: pheasantpluckers2003@yahoo.co.uk
Dir: A46, 0.5m S of Nailsworth

The Tipputs, a warm and welcoming 17th-century pub-

continued

restaurant in the heart of the Cotswolds, is owned by Nick Beardsley and Christophe Coquoin. They both started out as chefs together more than 12 years ago, but admit to spending less time in the kitchen these days now that they have to create menus for this and their three other Gloucestershire food pubs. Much of their time is spent on selecting and importing some of their menu ingredients and wines direct from France. Steaks, Tipputs burgers, fettuccini with smoked haddock, and several vegetarian dishes, including penne pasta with wild mushroom cream, are available all day. On the main menu are piri piri chicken; locally caught Bibury trout; marinated and roasted pork ribs; black-eyed bean, lentil and spiced vegetable pasty; and sea bream on toasted ciabattas.

OPEN: 11-11 Closed: 25 Dec **BAR MEALS:** L served all week 11-10 D served all week 11-10 **RESTAURANT:** L served all week 11-10 D served all week Av 2 course fixed price £8.95 ⊕: Free House ⬤: Greene King IPA, Ruddles County & Abbot Ale. ⚲: 12 **FACILITIES:** Garden: Terraced area, heaters, courtyard, grass area Dogs allowed **NOTES:** Parking 75

See advert on this page

NAUNTON   Map 10 SP12

The Black Horse
GL54 3AD ☎ 01451 850565

Renowned for its home-cooked food and Donnington real ales this friendly inn enjoys a typical Cotswold village setting beloved of ramblers and locals alike. The inn provides a traditional English menu featuring liver and bacon, cottage pie, scampi and broccoli and cheese bake.

OPEN: 11.30-3 6-11 (Open all day Sat & Sun) **BAR MEALS:** L served all week 12-2 D served all week 6.30-9.30 **RESTAURANT:** L served all week 12-2 D served all week 6.30-9.30 ⊕: ⬤: Donnington BB, SBA. **FACILITIES:** Garden: Food served outside Dogs allowed **NOTES:** Parking 12

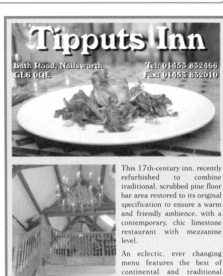

Tipputs Inn

Bath Road, Nailsworth
GL6 0QE

Tel: 01453 832466
Fax: 01453 832010

This 17th-century inn, recently refurbished to combine traditional, scrubbed pine floor bar area restored to its original specification to ensure a warm and friendly ambience, with a contemporary, chic limestone restaurant with mezzanine level.

An eclectic, ever changing menu features the best of continental and traditional British cuisine highlighting top local produce complemented by a well sourced wine list with a wide variety and range by the glass. Jazz evenings and winetasting dinners are a regular feature. Food served all day.

NORTH CERNEY   Map 05 SP00

Bathurst Arms ⚲
North Cerney GL7 7BZ ☎ 01285 831281 ▤ 01285 831887
e-mail: chefpilgrim@aol.com
Dir: 5m N of Cirencester on A435
Former coaching inn with bags of period charm - antique settles on flagstone floors, stone fireplaces, beams and panelled walls. The pretty garden stretches down to the River Churn, and a large barbecue is in use most summer weekends. Among the main dishes you may find a medley of winter root vegetables topped with a cheesy herb and nut crumble, chicken breast stuffed with dates and caramelised onions, marinated strips of venison flash-fried with a sauce of wild berries, chocolate and herbs.

OPEN: 12-3 6-11 (Sun 12-3, 7-10.30) **BAR MEALS:** L served all week 12-2 D served all week 6-9 Av main course £10 **RESTAURANT:** L served all week 12-2 D served all week 7-9.30 ⊕: Free House ⬤: Hook Norton, Cotswold Way, rotating guest beers. ⚲: 10 **FACILITIES:** Child facs Riverside garden with boules pitch Dogs allowed Dog bowl **NOTES:** Parking 40

 Pubs with this logo do not allow smoking anywhere on their premises

Room prices show the minimum double and single rates charged. Room rates in hotels and B&Bs often vary depending on the facilities, so be sure to check prices with the establishment before booking

continued   continued

England

NORTHLEACH Map 10 SP11

The Puesdown Inn ♦♦♦♦

Compton Abdale GL54 4DN ☎ 01451 860262 01451 861262
e-mail: inn4food@btopenworld.com
web: www.puesdown.cotswoldinns.com
***Dir:** Located on A40 between Oxford and Cheltenham*

The emphasis is on hospitality at this traditional Cotswold free house. The former coaching inn is said to date from 1236, and for centuries it has provided a warm welcome to travellers on the old Salt Way between Cheltenham and Burford. Now lovingly refurbished by the proprietors John and Maggie Armstrong, the Puesdown Inn features fresh flowers, new oak flooring, cosy sofas and log fires. The patio and large garden are popular for alfresco dining, and offers stunning views over the surrounding countryside. Lunchtime brings omelettes, sandwiches with chunky chips, and light meals such as warm duck salad; and chargrilled sardines. Dinner in the non-smoking restaurant might begin with root vegetable soup, before continuing with grilled turbot; boiled leg of mutton; or roast aubergine with butternut squash fries. The dessert menu takes in bread and butter pudding, home-made ice creams, and cheeses with home-made chutney.

OPEN: 11-3 6-11 (Open all day Jul-Aug Fri-Sun 11-11)
BAR MEALS: L served all week 12-3 D served all week 6-10.30 Sun 6-10 Av main course £8 **RESTAURANT:** L served all week 12-3 D served Mon-Sat 7-10.30 Av 3 course à la carte £23 **:** Hook Norton, Guest Ales. **:** 7 **FACILITIES:** Patio, wooden furniture, heaters, large garden Dogs allowed Water Bowls
NOTES: Parking 80 **ROOMS:** 3 bedrooms en suite 1 family room s£50 d£80 No children overnight

Do you have a favourite pub that we have overlooked? Please use the Reader's Report form at the back of this guide to tell us all about it

Wheatsheaf Inn ♦♦♦♦

GL54 3EZ ☎ 01451 860244 01451 861037
e-mail: info@wheatsheafatnorthleach.com
web: www.wheatsheafatnorthleach.com

There's plenty of character at this 17th-century Cotswold stone coaching inn, with its flagstone floors, open fires and comfortable en suite bedrooms. A regular guest beer supports Hook Norton and Wadworth ales at the bar; there's also a good selection of wines and malt whiskies. The single menu changes daily, covering the bar, non-smoking restaurant and attractive terraced garden. Typical dishes include pan-fried salmon; courgette and sunblushed tomato cannelloni; and corned beef hash with vegetables.

OPEN: 12-11 **BAR MEALS:** L served all week 12-2.30 D served all week 6.30-9.30 Sun 12-4, 7-9 Av main course £8
RESTAURANT: L served all week 12-2.30 D served all week 6.30-9.30 Sun 12-43, 7-9 Av 3 course à la carte £21 **:** Free House **:** Wadsworth 6X, Hook Norton Best Bitter, guest ales. **:** 12
FACILITIES: Garden: Terraced with beautiful flowers & trees Dogs allowed **NOTES:** Parking 15 **ROOMS:** 8 bedrooms en suite 1 family room s£50 d£60

OAKRIDGE Map 04 SO90

The Butcher's Arms

GL6 7NZ ☎ 01285 760371 01285 760602
***Dir:** From Stroud take A419, left for Eastcombe. Then follow Bisley signs. Just before Bisley turn right to Oakridge. Follow brown signs for pub*

Traditional Cotswold country pub with stone walls, beams and log fires in the renowned Golden Valley. Once a slaughterhouse and butchers shop. A full and varied restaurant menu offers steak, fish and chicken dishes, while the bar menu ranges from ploughman's lunches to home-cooked daily specials.

OPEN: 11-3 6-11 Closed: 25-26 Dec, 1 Jan **BAR MEALS:** L served Tue-Sun 12-2 D served Tue-Sat 6.30-9 **RESTAURANT:** L served Sun 12-3 D served Tue-Sat 7-9 **:** Free House **:** Greene King Abbot Ale, Wickwar BOB, Archers Best, Buttcombe Bitter.
FACILITIES: Garden: Food served outside. Overlooks Golden Valley Dogs allowed except in restaurant **NOTES:** Parking 50

Principal Beers for sale

Disabled people and those with Assist Dogs have new rights of access to pubs, restaurants and hotels under the Disability Discrimination Act of 1 October 2004. For more information see the website at www.drc gb.org/open4all/rights/2004.asp

OLDBURY-ON-SEVERN
Map 04 ST69

The Anchor Inn ♀
Church Rd BS35 1QA ☎ 01454 413331
Dir: From N A38 towards Bristol, 1.5m then R, village signed. From S A38 through Thornbury
This Cotswold stone pub started life as a mill house, with part of the building dating back to 1540. The large garden by a stream has plenty of seats for summer dining, and a boules piste attracts a multitude of teams. The friendly atmosphere is just right for sampling a real ale or one of 12 wines sold by the glass. Indulge in traditional English fare like roast beef, home-made faggots, and chicken and ham pie, before taking the magnificent one-mile stroll to the river Severn.
OPEN: 11.30-2.30 6.30-11 (Sat 11.30-11, Sun 12-10.30)
BAR MEALS: L served all week 11.30-2.30 D served all week 6.30-9.30 Sun 12-3, 6-9 **RESTAURANT:** L served all week 11.30-2.30 D served all week 6.30-9.30 🍴: Free House 🍺: Interbrew Bass, Scottish Courage Theakston Old Peculier, Butcombe Best, Wickwar Bob Best. ♀: 12 **FACILITIES:** Large garden by river, plenty of seats Dogs allowed **NOTES:** Parking 65

PAINSWICK
Map 04 SO80

The Falcon Inn ♀
New St GL6 6UN ☎ 01452 814222 📠 01452 813377
e-mail: bleninns@clara.net
Dir: On A46 in centre of Painswick

Boasting the world's oldest known bowling green in its grounds, the Falcon dates from 1554 and stands at the heart of a conservation village. For three centuries it was a courthouse, but today its friendly service extends to a drying room for walkers' gear. A sampling of dishes from the menu includes whole trout and almonds, gammon and egg, sirloin steak, chilli crust beef fillet, duck leg confit on a bed of sherry and puy lentils with Madeira sauce, penne pasta arrabiatta, stuffed pork loin with apricot and pistachios, steamed sea bass fillet with scallop mousseline, and minted lamb chop with fennel, asparagus and Jerusalem artichoke garnish.
OPEN: 11-11 (Sun 12-10.30) **BAR MEALS:** L served all week 12-2.30 D served all week 7-9.30 Av main course £8
RESTAURANT: L served all week 12-2.30 D served all week 7-9.30 🍴: Free House 🍺: Hook Norton Best, Old Hooky, Wadworth 6X, Greene King IPA. ♀: 10 **FACILITIES:** Children's licence Garden: Courtyard and large bowling green to rear Dogs allowed Water **NOTES:** Parking 35

We endeavour to be as accurate as possible but changes to times and other information can occur after the guide has gone to press

The Royal Oak Inn ♀
St Mary's St GL6 6QG ☎ 01452 813129
e-mail: bleninns@clara.net
Dir: In the centre of Painswick on the A46 between Stroud & Cheltenham

Tucked away behind the church of this conservation village, the Royal Oak features very low ceilings, old paintings and artefacts, and a huge, open fire. In summer, a sun-trap rear courtyard contributes to its atmosphere. Food is a mixture of old favourites (Cumberland sausage and mash; cauliflower cheese; beef curry); specials (lamb and apricot casserole; rabbit and leek pie); grills and vegetarian choices.
OPEN: 11-2.30 5.30-11 (Sun 12-3 Sun 7-10.30)
BAR MEALS: L served all week 12-2.30 D served all week 7-9.30 Av main course £6.50 **RESTAURANT:** L served all week 12-2.30 D served all week 7-9.30 🍴: Free House 🍺: Hook Norton Best, Wadworth 6X, Black Sheep Bitter plus Guest Ales. ♀: 8
FACILITIES: Garden: Patio and courtyard Dogs allowed Water

PAXFORD
Map 10 SP13

Pick of the Pubs

The Churchill Arms ◉ ♀
GL55 6XH ☎ 01386 594000 📠 01386 594005
e-mail: info@thechurchillarms.com
Dir: 2m E of Chipping Campden, 4m N of Moreton-in-Marsh
In the heart of a picturesque north Cotswolds village, the Churchill Arms enjoys glorious views over rolling countryside. Popular with walkers and lovers of outdoor pursuits, the pub offers refreshing ales including Hook Norton bitter, a wide range of wines, and interesting modern pub food. Menus change daily: starters might include cream of cauliflower soup; chicken boudin with button onions and Madeira sauce; marinated salmon with fennel and apple salad; and pigeon breast with mushroom caponata. For your main course, try cod fillet with grain mustard, creamed potatoes and beetroot vinaigrette; rib-eye steak with port and green peppercorn sauce; monkfish with broth of potato, chorizo and butternut squash; or one of several vegetarian options. Puddings such as sticky toffee pudding, red wine and chocolate terrine with baked pears and mascarpone; black coffee jelly with clotted cream, caramelised walnuts and butterscotch sauce will make your meal even more memorable. The Churchill Arms deservedly continues to attract discerning custom.
OPEN: 11-3 6-11 **BAR MEALS:** L served all week 12-2 D served all week 7-9 Av main course £12
RESTAURANT: L served all week 12-2 D served all week 7-9 Av 3 course à la carte £23 🍴: Free House 🍺: Hook Norton Bitter, Arkells, Moonlight. ♀: 10 **FACILITIES:** Garden: 25 Covers, parasols

England

POULTON
Map 05 SP00

The Falcon Inn NEW ♀
London Rd GL7 5HN ☎ 01285 850844 ▨ 01285 850403
e-mail: info@thefalconpoulton.co.uk
Dir: From Cirencester travel E on A417 towards Fairford
At the heart of the Cotswold village of Poulton, the Falcon has
been transformed from a straightforward village local into a
stylish and sophisticated gastro pub which has become very
popular with drinkers and diners from far and wide. Choose
from the lunch menu, perhaps pan-fried fillet of sea bass with
parsnip purée and red wine sauce, or chargrilled shorthorn
rib-eye steak with roasted garlic butter and home-produced
chips. Sandwiches on home-made white bread and an
extensive wine list.
OPEN: 11-3 7-11 (Sun 12-3, 7-10.30) **BAR MEALS:** L served all
week 12-2 D served all week 7-9 Av main course £12
RESTAURANT: L served all week 12-2 D served all week 7-9
Av 3 course à la carte £25 Av 3 course fixed price £20 **🍺:** Hook
Norton Best, Guest ales. **♀:** 8 **FACILITIES:** Dogs allowed
NOTES: Parking 20

REDMARLEY D'ABITOT
Map 10 SO73

Rose & Crown
Playley Green GL19 3NB ☎ 01531 650234
Dir: On the A417 Gloucester to Ledbury, 1m from exit 2 of the M50
This pretty old roadside building, dating from the 1720s with
numerous later additions, is a blaze of summer colour from
hanging baskets and flower troughs, and an array of daffodils
in spring. The dishes on the main menu change very little, but
the daily specials may offer fresh sea bream with lime butter,
Moroccan spiced lamb with couscous or beef and ale
casserole. The prime Herefordshire beef steaks are a further
plus, as are the Sunday roast lunches; booking advisable.
OPEN: 11-2.30 6-11 (Sun 12-10.30) Closed: Dec 25
BAR MEALS: L served all week 12-2 D served Mon-Sat 6.30-9
Av main course £8 **RESTAURANT:** L served all week 12-2 D served
Mon-Sat 6.30-9 Av 3 course à la carte £14.95 **🍺:** Pubmaster
🍺: Interbrew Flowers Original IPA, Young's Special, Wadworth 6X,
Greene King Old Speckled Hen & Ruddles County Ale.
FACILITIES: Garden: Food served outdoors, patio Dogs allowed
Water **NOTES:** Parking 50

SAPPERTON
Map 04 SO90

The Bell at Sapperton ♀
GL7 6LE ☎ 01285 760298 ▨ 01285 760761
e-mail: thebell@sapperton66.freeserve.co.uk
*Dir: Halfway between Cirencester & Stroud A419 take signs for Sapperton
village. The Bell is in the centre near the church.*

Under the capable management of Paul Davidson and Pat
LeJeune, The Bell is both a local pub and a fine dining venue,
continued

thus appealing to a wide clientele. The well-kept local ales are
a major attraction, along with menus that demonstrate Paul
and Pat's laudable commitment to the local sourcing of food.
The pub has won awards for it, and details of main suppliers
are given on the menus. Choices here might include pan-fried
monkfish tail on buttered samphire and crushed new
potatoes; and chargrilled loin of lamb chops with sticky port.
There are always English farmhouse and French artisan
cheeses, and an irresistible choice of desserts.
OPEN: 11-2.30 6.30-11 (Sun times vary) Closed: 25 Dec, 31 Dec
BAR MEALS: L served all week 12-2 D served all week 7-9.30 Sun
7-9 Av main course £13.50 **RESTAURANT:** L served all week 12-2
D served all week 7-9.30 Sun 7-9 Av 3 course à la carte £26 **🍺:** Free
House **🍺:** Uley Old Spot, Hook Norton Best, Buttcombe Best,
Buttcombe Gold. **♀:** 16 **FACILITIES:** Garden: Traditional pub
garden at front, courtyard Dogs allowed Waterbowl
NOTES: Parking 60

See Pub Walk on page 191

SHEEPSCOMBE
Map 04 SO81

The Butchers Arms ♀
GL6 7RH ☎ 01452 812113 ▨ 01452 814358
e-mail: bleninns@clara.net
Dir: 1.5m south of A46 (Cheltenham to Stroud road), N of Painswick

Once used to hang and butcher deer hunted by Henry VIII
from his Royal deer park, this friendly hostelry boasts a sunny
sheltered terrace and panoramic views. Laurie Lee, author of
Cider with Rosie was once a regular. A varied menu includes
blackboard specials like lamb medallions with wholegrain
mash; and stilton, leek and walnut pie; along with salmon and
prawn pancakes at lunchtime, perhaps, and pork chops
braised with potatoes and vegetables in the evening.
OPEN: 11.30-2.30 6-11.30 (Sun 12-3, 7-10.30)
BAR MEALS: L served all week 12-2.30 D served all week 7-9.30
Av main course £7.50 **RESTAURANT:** L served all week 12-2.30
D served all week 7-9.30 **🍺:** Free House **🍺:** Hook Norton Best,
Uley old Spot, Wye Valley, Dorothy Goodbodys Summer Ale. **♀:** 10
FACILITIES: Children's licence Garden: Beer garden, food served
outdoors, patio Dogs allowed in garden and on terrace only, water
NOTES: Parking 16

SHURDINGTON   Map 10 SO91

The Bell Inn
Main Rd GL51 4XQ ☎ 01242 862245 ▤ 01242 862245
Unassuming 18th-century pub by the village green with tables for outside eating in warmer weather. Inside proves somewhat of a surprise - very modern with wood floors, interesting pictures and a nautical theme in the conservatory extension. The menu features old favourites such as ploughman's, rare beef sandwiches and sausage & parsley mash, but there are globally inspired dishes too, as in the braised Moroccan shank of lamb and coconut curried monkfish. Puddings are very tempting.
OPEN: 11-11 **BAR MEALS:** L served all week 12-2.30 D served all week 6.30-9.30 D served all week 12-2.30 D served all week 6.30-9.30 **◖:** Timothy Taylor Best and guest ales. **FACILITIES:** Garden: Very large pebble & grass area Dogs allowed Water **NOTES:** Parking 25

SIDDINGTON   Map 05 SU09

The Greyhound ♀
Ashton Rd GL7 6HR ☎ 01285 653573 ▤ 01285 650054
Dir: A419 from Swindon, turn at sign for industrial estate, L at main rdbt, follow Siddington signs, pub at far end of village on R
Village pub, formally a coach house, built of Cotswold stone with flagstone floors inside. Friendly, relaxed atmosphere.
OPEN: 11.30-2.30 6.30-11 **BAR MEALS:** L served all week 12-2.30 D served all week 6-9 Av main course £7 **⊜:** Wadworth **◖:** Wadworth 6X & Henry's IPA, Badger Tanglefoot. **♀:** 9 **FACILITIES:** Garden: Dogs allowed **NOTES:** Parking 30

SOUTHROP   Map 05 SP10

The Swan at Southrop ♀
GL7 3NU ☎ 01367 850205 ▤ 01367 850555
Dir: Off A361 between Lechlade and Burford

This creeper clad, 16th-century Cotswold pub is situated in an area of Gloucestershire renowned for gentle strolls and picturesque country rambles. Extensive lunch menu offers everything from smoked salmon and scrambled eggs to linguine carbonara. Other options include Lincolnshire poacher cheddar ploughman's, grilled calves' kidney and bacon, and fillet of wild sea bass.
OPEN: 11.30-3.30 6.30-11 **BAR MEALS:** L served all week 12-2 D served all week 7-9 **RESTAURANT:** L served all week 12-2.30 D served all week 7-10 Sun pm closed (winter) **⊜:** Free House **◖:** Hook Norton, Wadworth 6X, Timothy Taylor Landlord, Marstons. **♀:** 10 **FACILITIES:** Dogs allowed

STONEHOUSE   Map 04 SO80

The George Inn ♦♦♦
Bath Rd, Frocester GL10 3TQ ☎ 01453 822302 ▤ 01453 791612
e-mail: enquiries@georgeinn.fsnet.co.uk
web: www.georgeinn.co.uk
Dir: M5 junct 13, take A419 at 1st rdbt - 3rd exit Eastington, left at next rdbt Frocester. Continue for approx 2m. Inn in the village centre
An award-winning village pub in the traditional mould, undisturbed by music or games machines. This former coaching inn has huge inglenook fireplaces and the original stables surrounding the courtyard garden. The food is locally produced and cooked to order: look for British roast beef baguettes, chicken goujons with lemon mayonnaise, and Frocester Fayre faggots with creamy mash, followed by treacle pudding or Gaelic whiskey trifle. Sunday lunch carvery, occasional live music and a warm village welcome.
OPEN: 11.30-2.30 5-11 (Sat-Sun open all day)
BAR MEALS: L served all week 12-2 D served Mon-Sat 6.30-9.30
Sunday carvery 12.30-3 Av main course £10
RESTAURANT: L served all week 12-2 D served Mon-Sat 6.30-9.30
Sunday 12.30-3pm **⊜:** Enterprise Inns **◖:** Smiles Best, Blacksheep, 2 guest beers. **FACILITIES:** Garden: Courtyard, boules pitch
NOTES: Parking 25 **ROOMS:** 8 bedrooms 6 en suite
3 family rooms s£40 d£60

STOW-ON-THE-WOLD   Map 10 SP12

Pick of the Pubs

The Eagle and Child ★★★ ◎◎ ♀
C/o The Royalist Hotel, Digbeth St GL54 1BN
☎ 01451 830670 ▤ 01451 870048
e-mail: info@theroyalisthotel.co.uk
See Pick of the Pubs on page 214

The Unicorn ★★★
Sheep St GL54 1HQ ☎ 01451 830257 ▤ 01451 831090
e-mail: reception@birchhotels.co.uk
Attractive hotel of honey-coloured limestone, hand-cut roof tiles and abundantly flowering window boxes, set in the heart of Stow-on-the-Wold. The interior is stylishly presented with Jacobean pieces, antique artefacts and open log fires. Light meals are served in the bar (sandwiches and salads, plus beef and Guinness stew, and beer-battered fish and chips), and a dinner menu of modern British dishes is available in the elegant Georgian setting of the Shepherd's Restaurant.
OPEN: 12-11 (Winter 12-3, 7-11) **BAR MEALS:** L served all week 12-2 D served all week 7-9 Av main course £11.50
RESTAURANT: D served all week 7-9 **FACILITIES:** Garden: Dogs allowed **NOTES:** Parking 40 **ROOMS:** 20 bedrooms en suite s£60 d£78

 Pubs with this logo do not allow smoking anywhere on their premises

 The Rosette is the AA award for food. Look out for it next to a pub's name

 Brewery/Company

 Principal Beers for sale

Pick of the Pubs
STOW-ON-THE-WOLD – GLOUCESTERSHIRE

The Eagle and Child

The Eagle and Child, the oldest inn in England, is part of the Royalist Hotel. The site is said to date back to 947 AD and was once a hospice to shelter lepers. Historic finds include a 10th-century Saxon shoe, a leper hole, witches' marks in the rooms, a bear pit, thousand-year-old timbers and an ancient frieze.

The Eagle and Child is said to come from the crest of the Earl of Derby (16th century), and the last battle of the English Civil War (1646) was in Stow, hence the hotel's name. Digbeth Street is thought to derive from 'duck bath'. The ducks were said to be running down the street bathed in blood from the Royalist casualties. Niche Hotels have recently taken ownership and their style is to retain period character and provide good, wholesome and contemporary aspects to the food, drink and accommodation. There's a regularly changing choice of beers and a good range of snacks and meals. Starters may include bruschetta of grilled Mediterranean vegetables with pesto and chick peas; warm Thai beef salad or chicken liver and wild mushroom parfait with toasted brioche and chutney. Mains should be along the lines of sea bass, pilaff rice, pak choi, ginger and soy dressing; Braveheart Scottish steak; gammon steak, apple and stilton sauce and bubble and squeak; or lamb's liver served with bacon, champ mash and red wine jus.

OPEN: 11 -11
BAR MEALS: L served all week 12-2.30 D served all week 6-9.30 Sat 6-10 Av main course £9.95
RESTAURANT: L served Tues-Sat 12-2.30 D served Tues-Sat 7-9.30 Av 3 course à la carte £20
🍺: Free House 🍺: Hook Norton Best, Greene King Abbot Ale, Timothy Taylor Landlord, Bass. ♀: 8
FACILITIES: Child facs Garden: Small paved terraced garden Dogs allowed Dog bowls and biscuits
NOTES: Parking 8
ROOMS: 8 bedrooms en suite 2 family rooms s£50 d£90

★★★ ◎◎ ♀ Map 10 SP12
C/o The Royalist Hotel, Digbeth St GL54 1BN
☎ 01451 830670
🖷 01451 870048
🄴 info@theroyalisthotel.co.uk
🅦 www.nichehotels.com
Dir: From the A40 take the A429 towards Stow-on-the-Wold, turn into town and pub is situated by the green on the left.

Map 04 SO80

Pick of the Pubs

Bear of Rodborough Hotel ★★★ ⊕ ♀
Rodborough Common GL5 5DE
☎ 01453 878522 ▨ 01453 872523
e-mail: bookings@cotswold-inns-hotels.co.uk
Dir: From M5 junct 13 follow signs for Stonehouse then Rodborough
Originally built as an ale house in the 17th century, this former coaching inn stands high above Stroud in acres of National Trust parkland. The hotel is worth seeking out for its comfortable accommodation, open log fires, stone walls and solid wooden floors. There is certainly plenty of character here and, like many older buildings, the hotel is reputed to have its own resident ghost. Golden Archers and Uley Bitter are served in the bar, and the elegant non-smoking Box Tree restaurant is just the place to sample the contemporary British menu. Start, perhaps, with assiette of duck, before moving on to main course choices like cannon of lamb with cinnamon and redcurrant glaze; thyme roasted pavé of salmon; and wild mushroom risotto. Dark chocolate fetish heads the dessert menu, with local varieties on the cheese board.
OPEN: 10.30-11 **BAR MEALS:** L served all week 12-2.30 D served all week 6.30-10 Sun 12-2, 6.30-9.30 Av main course £12 **RESTAURANT:** L served Tue-Fri, Sun 12.30-2.30 D served all week 7-9.30 Sun 7-9 Av 3 course à la carte £30 Av 3 course fixed price £28.95 ⊕: Free House ◀: Uley Bitter, Golden Archers, guest ale. ♀: 6 **FACILITIES:** Child facs Garden: Patio area, next to croquet lawn Dogs allowed Water provided **NOTES:** Parking 175 **ROOMS:** 46 bedrooms en suite s£75 d£120

Pick of the Pubs

Halfway Inn ♀
Box GL6 9AE ☎ 01453 832631 ▨ 01453 835275
e-mail: matt_halfwayinn@hotmail.com
Dir: From Cirencester A419 and from Stroud A46

Once a wool store for the drovers of Michinhampton Common, this building has been stunningly converted to create a pub that manages to feel fresh, modern and rustic. There's plenty of bare wood, pine furniture and brightly painted walls, along with a rejuvenated garden for summer drinks and dining. It's a popular destination after a walk on the common, or perhaps a round of golf, and despite a change of hands the reputation for good food remains. The AA rosette-winning menu has a distinctly modern feel. Dishes range from classic combinations such as pan-fried steak with rösti potato,

glazed baby vegetables and port wine, through to internationally inspired dishes - perhaps tuna spring roll with a spiced avocado and aïoli salad or a trio of lobster sausage, salmon fishcake and red mullet fillet with saffron.
OPEN: 12-3 5-11 (summer open all day)
BAR MEALS: L served all week 12-2 D served Mon-Sat 7-9.30 Av main course £11 **RESTAURANT:** L served all week 12-2.30 D served Mon-Sat 7-9.30 Av 3 course à la carte £20 ⊕: Free House ◀: Wickwar Brand Oak Bitter, Hook Norton, Smiles, plus guest ales. **FACILITIES:** Garden: Food served outside. Landscape garden Dogs allowed **NOTES:** Parking 60

The Ram Inn
South Woodchester GL5 5EL ☎ 01453 873329 ▨ 01453 873329
Dir: A46 from Stroud to Nailsworth, right after 2m into S.Woodchester (brown tourist signs)
From the terrace of the 400-year-old Cotswold-stone Ram there are splendid views over five valleys, although proximity to the huge fireplace may prove more appealing in winter. Rib-eye steak, at least two fish dishes, home-made lasagne and Sunday roasts can be expected, washed down by regularly changing real ales such as Uley Old Spot, Wickwar BOB and Archer's Golden. The Stroud Morris Men regularly perform.
OPEN: 11-11 (Sun 12-10.30) **BAR MEALS:** L served all week 12-2.30 D served all week 6-9.30 Sun 12-2.30, 6-8.30 Av main course £7.50 **RESTAURANT:** L served all week 12-2.30 D served all week 6-9.30 Sun 12-2.30, 6-8.30 Av 3 course à la carte £12 Av 2 course fixed price £9.95 ⊕: Free House ◀: Scottish Courage, John Smiths, Uley Old Spot, Wickwar BOB. **FACILITIES:** Garden: 2 large Patio areas, seat approx 120 people Dogs allowed Water **NOTES:** Parking 60

Pick of the Pubs

Rose & Crown Inn
The Cross, Nympsfield GL10 3TU
☎ 01453 860240 ▨ 01453 861564
e-mail: www.gadros@aol.com
Dir: M5 junct 13 off B4066, SW of Stroud

Four hundred-year-old coaching inn of honey-coloured local stone, in the heart of the village close to the Cotswold Way. Possibly the highest pub in the Cotswolds, the Rose & Crown is situated between Stroud and Dursley, and the surrounding views of the Severn are breathtaking. It's a popular watering hole for walkers and cyclists, and all are made welcome by new proprietors, The Gadd Family. Inside, natural stone and wood panelling preserves the inn's original character, with a lovely open fire and traditional draught ales in the bar, and a galleried restaurant reaching up to the old timbers

continued

continued

STROUD continued

in the roof. The kids will enjoy the new playground area, which has a swing, slides and a climbing bridge. **OPEN:** 12-11 **BAR MEALS:** L served all week 12-9.30 D served all week **RESTAURANT:** L served all week 12-9.30 D served all week 🍴: Free House 🍺: Uley Best, Scottish Courage Courage Directors & Best, Hogshead, Otter. **FACILITIES:** Child facs Large, shady garden, stunning views, safe Dogs allowed Water provided **NOTES:** Parking 20

The Woolpack Inn
Slad Rd, Slad GL6 7QA ☎ 01452 813429 🖹 01452 813429
Dir: 2 miles from Stroud, 8 miles from Gloucester
Situated in the Slad valley close to the Cotswold Way, a friendly local that offers good real ales, interesting wine selections and middle-of-the-road food based largely on chargrills and popular daily specials. Tempting starters include smoked mackerel and country pâté, followed by butcher's faggots with mustard mash, beef and ale stew and a mammoth mixed grill. Save room for fruit crumble or treacle sponge. Booking advised for the good-value Sunday roast. **OPEN:** 12-3 5-11 (Open all day Sat & Sun) **BAR MEALS:** L served Tue-Sat 12-2 D served Tues-Sat 6-9 Av main course £8.50 **RESTAURANT:** L served (not avail. on Mon Oct-Apr) 12-2 D served Tues-Sat 6-9 🍴: Free House 🍺: Uley Pig's Ear, Old Spot, Laurie Lee. **FACILITIES:** Garden: Food served outside Dogs allowed Water **NOTES:** Parking 8

TETBURY
Map 04 ST89

Pick of the Pubs

Gumstool Inn 🔴 ♀
Calcot Manor GL8 8YJ ☎ 01666 890391 🖹 01666 890394
e-mail: reception@calcotmanor.co.uk
Dir: 3m W of Tetbury in A4135

The cheerful Gumstool is the integral pub at Calcot Manor Hotel, a charmingly converted 14th-century English farmhouse built of Cotswold stone by Cistercian monks. Ancient barns and stables surround the flower-filled courtyard, while the interior is a truly successful marrying of old and new architectural features. An interesting menu offers a wide choice of dishes: starters-cum-light main courses of devilled lambs' kidneys in a crisp pastry case; fettuccini with wood-roasted pumpkin; and pan-fried local trout fillet. Among the more substantial mains are chargrilled yellow-fin tuna steak with spicy Asian slaw; oak-smoked salmon with Skagen prawns; breast of chicken with roquefort; confit of crisply roasted pork belly; and free-range pork and leek sausages. Orange and

lemon pancakes with crème fraîche, and Scottish fruit and whisky tart with thick cream are on hand to fill any remaining space. **OPEN:** 11.30-2.30 5.30-11 (Sat 11.30-11, Sun 12-10.30) **BAR MEALS:** L served all week 12-2 D served all week 7-9.30 Av main course £9 **RESTAURANT:** L served all week 12-2 D served all week 7-9.30 Av 3 course à la carte £35 🍴: Free House 🍺: Wickwar BOB, Sharps Doombar, Fullers London Pride, Butcombe. ♀: 12 **FACILITIES:** Child facs Garden **NOTES:** Parking 100

Pick of the Pubs

Trouble House Inn ◉◉ ♀
Cirencester Rd GL8 8SG ☎ 01666 502206 🖹 01666 504508
e-mail: enquiries@troublehouse.co.uk
Dir: On A433 between Tetbury & Cirencester
Two successive landlords committed suicide at this aptly named historic Cotswold inn. Then there were the agricultural riots, and the ghostly Lady in Blue. Or could the name simply reflect the nearby area, known as The Troubles, which regularly used to flood? Inside you'll find polished wooden floors, ancient black beams, open fires, pastel-coloured walls and subtle lighting. Wadworth's beers and Henry's IPA are served at the bar, whilst the extensive wine list features choices from most of the world's great wine producing regions. Chef/proprietor Michael Bedford concentrates on providing freshly prepared rustic cooking in a relaxed pub environment. Starters include pea and ham soup; and confit of rabbit with mustard lentils, followed by choices like roast brill with garlic mash; coq au vin; and grilled rump of veal with braised snails in red wine. **OPEN:** 11-3 6.30-11 (Sun 12-3 Oct-May Tue-Sat 7-11) Closed: 25 Dec-5 Jan **BAR MEALS:** L served Tue-Sat 12-2 D served Tue-Sat 7-9.30 **RESTAURANT:** L served Tue-Sun 12-2 D served Tue-Sat 7-9.30 Av 3 course à la carte £28 🍴: Wadworth 🍺: Wadworth 6X & Henrys IPA. ♀: 12 **FACILITIES:** Garden: Benches Dogs allowed none **NOTES:** Parking 30

TEWKESBURY
Map 10 SO83

The Fleet Inn
Twyning GL20 6DG ☎ 01684 274310 🖹 01684 291612
e-mail: fleetinn@hotmail.com
Dir: 0.5m Junction 1 - M50
Idyllically located on the banks of the River Avon, this 15th-century pub with restaurant has lawns and patios that can seat up to 350. Fishing, boules, play area, pet's corner, bird garden, craft shop, tea room and a Japanese water garden are all to hand. The traditional bars and themed areas provide a wide range of dishes. **OPEN:** 11-11 **BAR MEALS:** L served all week 12-2.30 D served all week 6-9.30 **RESTAURANT:** 12-2.30 6-9 Av 3 course à la carte £12 🍴: Whitbread 🍺: Boddingtons, Greene King Abbot Ale & Old Speckled Hen, Wells Bombardier , Fullers London Pride. **FACILITIES:** Garden: Patios and water front garden **NOTES:** Parking 50

> ◆ Pubs with Red Diamonds are the top places in the AA's three, four and five diamond ratings

continued

TODENHAM   Map 10 SP23

Pick of the Pubs

The Farriers Arms NEW ⌂ ♟ ♀
Main St GL56 9PF ☎ 01608 650901 ▤ 01608 650403
e-mail: tom@farriersarms.com
Dir: Follow signs to Todenham, only pub in village
Set right at the heart of the Cotswolds, this cheery
traditional pub has all the features you'd associate with
the country local. This means horse-brasses above the
wood burner, cider flagons adorning the walls and a
dartboard for friendly local-versus-visitor games! There are
also plenty of books, games and colouring materials for
the younger members of the party. A raised patio outside
gives a sense of why this area of England is so rapturously
celebrated. A daily changing specials board makes the
most of local produce: pheasant and bacon terrine with
port and juniper sauce; braised steak and local Hook
Norton ale pie with chips; or local asparagus supper with
gammon or salmon. Desserts are in the traditional home-
made pub favourites line: sticky toffee pudding perhaps,
or banoffee pie. There's also a good range of real ales to
take a pull at, including Wye Valley Butty Bach.
OPEN: 12-3 6.30-11.20 Sun open at 7 Jan-Etr closed Mon lunch
BAR MEALS: L served all week 12-2 D served all week 7-9
Fri-Sat 7-9.30 Av main course £9 **RESTAURANT:** L served all
week 12-2 D served all week 7-9 Fri-Sat 7-9.30 Av 3 course à la
carte £18 ◖: Hook Norton Best, Archers Golden, Wye Valley
Butty Bach, Timothy Taylor Landlord. ♀: 11
FACILITIES: Garden: Raised patio at rear of pub, seating Dogs
allowed Water bowl **NOTES:** Parking 18

TORMARTON   Map 04 ST77

Compass Inn ★★ ♀
GL9 1JB ☎ 01454 218242 ▤ 01454 218741
e-mail: info@compass-inn.co.uk web: www.compass-inn.co.uk
*Dir: From M4 junct 18 take A46 N towards Stroud. After 200 mtrs take first
right then turn towards Tormarion Village, continue for 300 mtrs*
A traditional pub - in the same family for over 40 years - with
extensive facilities including an orangery, 26 bedrooms and
space for functions. It is set in five and a half acres of
beautiful grounds right on the Cotswold Way. Light bites
include jacket potatoes and sandwiches, while the bar menu
offers home-cooked dishes (lamb curry, spinach and ricotta
ravioli) and specials from the blackboard. There is also a daily
carte in the restaurant.
OPEN: 7-11 Closed: 25-26 Dec **BAR MEALS:** L served all week
11-10 D served all week 7-10 Av main course £9
RESTAURANT: L served all week D served all week 7-10
Av 3 course à la carte £22.50 ◷: Free House ◖: Interbrew Bass
& Butcombe, Butcombe Gold. ♀: 7 **FACILITIES:** Garden: Beer
garden and several terraces Dogs allowed Water
NOTES: Parking 200 **ROOMS:** 26 bedrooms en suite
4 family rooms s£69.50 d£79.50

♀ 7   Number of wines by the glass

Website addresses are included where available.
The AA cannot be held responsible for the
content of any of these websites

UPPER ODDINGTON   Map 10 SP22

Pick of the Pubs

Horse & Groom Inn ♀
GL56 0XH ☎ 01451 830584 ▤ 01451 870494
e-mail: info@horseandgroom.uk.com
Dir: 1.5m S of Stow-on-the-Wold, just off the A436

The specials board changes twice a day at this
quintessentially English free house. Located in a pretty
Cotswold village just a couple of miles from Stow-on-the-
Wold, the charming and immaculate 16th-century stone
building features beamed ceilings and flagstone floors,
with open log fires in winter. There's a good selection of
real ales, too, including Hook Norton Best and Wye
Valley Butty Bach. In warmer weather the terrace garden
calls. Just perfect for alfresco summer dining, the tables
overlook dry stone walls and pretty stone-built cottages.
Head chef Jason Brewster uses fresh local ingredients in
his quest to create the best pub food in the Cotswolds;
bread is freshly baked daily, and there's not a bought
pudding in sight! Typical dishes might include pan-fried
sea bass; grilled Cotswold lamb steak with fondant
potatoes; or roast Mediterranean vegetable tower with
goats' cheese.
OPEN: 11-3 5.30-11 Sun 12-10.30 **BAR MEALS:** L served all
week 12-2 D served all week 6.30-9.30 Not Sun night Nov-Feb
Av main course £11 **RESTAURANT:** L served all week 12-2
D served all week 6.30-9.30 Not Sun night Nov-Feb Av 3 course à
la carte £22 ◷: Free House ◖: Wye Valley Butty Bach, London
Pride, Hook Norton Best, Archers Best. ♀: 11 **FACILITIES:**
Child facs Children's licence Garden: Dining terrace
NOTES: Parking 40

WINCHCOMBE   Map 10 SP02

Royal Oak ⌂ ♀
Gretton GL54 5EP ☎ 01242 604999 ▤ 01242 602387
Family-run Cotswold free house with flagstone floors, exposed
beams and lovely views of the Malvern Hills from the
conservatory or garden, at the bottom of which is a restored
steam railway line. A great selection of food ranges through
basket meals, local beef and lamb dishes, and fishy options
such as fresh sea bass baked in garlic lemon butter. New
proprietors welcome all their customers, including the little
ones.
OPEN: 12-3 6-11 (Sun 12-4, 6-11) Closed: Dec 25
BAR MEALS: L served all week 12-2.30 D served all week 6-9
Av main course £6.50 **RESTAURANT:** L served all week 12-2.30
D served all week 6-9.30 (Sun 12-4) ◷: Free House ◖: Goffs
Josster, Hook Norton Landlord and 2 guest. ♀: 8
FACILITIES: Child facs Garden: Orchard, patio, tennis court Dogs
allowed Water **NOTES:** Parking 50

England

WINCHCOMBE continued

The White Hart Inn and Restaurant NEW ♀
High St GL54 5LJ ☎ 01242 602359 🖹 01242 602703
e-mail: enquiries@the-white-hart-inn.com
Dir: In centre of Winchcombe on B4632
A traditional 16th-century coaching inn with a Swedish twist,
the White Hart has been recently refurbished to offer a
beamed bar and Swedish-style restaurant. Enjoy snacks
(antipasti, olives), a pizza or a Swedish hotdog at the bar -
followed by an Italian ice-cream dessert. Dinner in the
restaurant could be Scandinavian seafood platter; or pan-fried
cod with red caviar mashed potato.
OPEN: 8am-midnight Closed: 25 Dec **BAR MEALS:** L served all
week 11-10 D served all week 6-10 **RESTAURANT:** L served all week
11-6 D served all week 6-10 Av 3 course à la carte £25 Av 3 course
fixed price £16.95 **🍺:** Archers Golden, Uley Old Spot, Whittingtons
Cats Whiskers, Greene King IPA. **♀:** 8 **FACILITIES:** Child facs
Children's licence Garden: Patio area Dogs allowed Bowls, towels
NOTES: Parking 12

WITHINGTON   Map 10 SP01

The Mill Inn 🍽️
GL54 4BE ☎ 01242 890204 🖹 01242 890195
Dir: 3m from the A40 between Cheltenham & Oxford
This traditional inn has been serving travellers for over 400
years from its position beside the River Coln in a deep
Cotswold valley. Inside are stone-flagged floors, oak panelling
and log fires, whilst outside is a lawned garden with 40 tables,
providing a peaceful setting for a drink or meal. The menu
has a good fish content, including seafood medley, battered
cod, and stuffed plaice.
OPEN: 11.30-3 6.30-11 (Sun 12-3, 6.30-10.30)
BAR MEALS: L served all week 12-2 D served all week 6.30-9
🍴: Samuel Smith **🍺:** Samuel Smith Old Brewery Bitter, Samuel
Smith Sovereign. **FACILITIES:** Garden: Lawned with 40 tables, trees
and river Dogs allowed Water, biscuits **NOTES:** Parking 80

WOODCHESTER   Map 04 SO80

The Old Fleece 🍽️ ♀
Bath Rd, Rooksmoor GL5 5NB ☎ 01453 872582 🖹 01453 872228
e-mail: pheasantpluckers2003@yahoo.co.uk
Dir: 2m S of Stroud on the A46

Delightful old coaching inn dating back to the 18th century
and built of Cotswold stone with a traditional stone roof. Cosy
log fires add to the inviting atmosphere, and the inn's interior
includes wooden floors, wood panelling and exposed stone.
Impressive menu offers a variety of dishes, including slow
roasted leg of duck with a garlic and rosemary jus; Cajun
chicken served with salsa; Old Fleece steakburger; and
smoked haddock fishcakes with dill and lemon mayonnaise.
continued

Good range of starters and light meals.
OPEN: 11-11 Closed: 25 Dec **BAR MEALS:** L served all week
11-2.45 D served all week 5.30-10 Sat-Sun all day
RESTAURANT: L served all week 11-2.45 D served all week 5.30-10
Sat-Sun all day Av 2 course fixed price £8.95 **🍴:** **🍺:** Interbrew
Boddington & Bass, Greene King Abbot Ale. **♀:** 12
FACILITIES: Garden: Heated terrace Dogs allowed Water provided
NOTES: Parking 40

GREATER LONDON

CARSHALTON   Map 06 TQ26

Greyhound Hotel ♀
2 High St SM5 3PE ☎ 020 8647 1511 🖹 020 8647 4687
e-mail: greyhound@youngs.co.uk
Dir: Telephone for directions
Distinctive white-painted former coaching inn with a
welcoming fire in the bar in cold weather. It is located directly
opposite the ponds in Carshalton Park, five minutes' walk
from the railway station and a short distance from the M23.
Records go back to 1706, when the Greyhound was a centre
for cock-fighters and race-goers. Interesting snacks include
marinated olives, filled ciabatta and home-made houmous.
For something more substantial try slow roast lamb shank or
hake fillet in Young's batter.
OPEN: 11-11 (Sun 12-10.30) **BAR MEALS:** L served all week
12-2.30 D served all week 6.30-9.45 Sun 12-9 Av main course £9
RESTAURANT: L served Sun D served all week 6.30-9.45 Sun 12-9
Av 3 course à la carte £18 **🍴:** Young & Co **🍺:** Youngs Special,
Youngs Winter Warmer, Youngs PA, Youngs AAA. **♀:** 17
FACILITIES: Outside seating area **NOTES:** Parking 46

KESTON   Map 06 TQ46

The Crown ♀
Leaves Green BR2 6DQ ☎ 01959 572920 🖹 01959 572920
Dir: A21 onto A232, then L onto A233, pub 4m
Spitfire sausages and mash with onion gravy and parsnip
crisps, Lancaster hotpot - braised lamb and vegetables with a
potato topping - and Biggin Hill bomber burgers are
appropriately-named selections on the menu at this old pub
not far from Biggin Hill airfield of Battle of Britain fame. There
are good country walks from the pub, which was recently
fully renovated. There is a large restaurant and extensive
garden with play equipment for children.
OPEN: 11.30-11 (Sat-Sun, all week in summer 11-11)
BAR MEALS: L served all week 12 D served Mon-Sat 9.30 Av main
course £7 **RESTAURANT:** L served all week 12 D served Mon-Sat
9.30 Av 3 course à la carte £15 **🍴:** Shepherd Neame **🍺:** Shepherd
Neame Master Brew, Spitfire, Hurlimans, Seasonal Ale. **♀:** 8
FACILITIES: Garden: Very large garden Dogs allowed Water
NOTES: Parking 30

RICHMOND (UPON THAMES)   Plan 2 C2

The White Cross ♀
Water Ln TW9 1TH ☎ 020 8940 6844
Dir: Telephone for directions
Licensed for over two centuries, this Grade II listed pub is set
right beside the River Thames. An old fireplace uniquely fitted
under a window is still lit on winter evenings, and there's an
upstairs area with a balcony overlooking the river. Youngs
Bitter, Summer Waggledance, and Winter Warmer wash down
home-cooked menu choices like curry, steak pie, lasagne, and
chilli con carne.
continued

England

OPEN: 11-11 (Sun 12-10.30) **BAR MEALS:** L served Mon-Sat 12-3.30 (Sun 12-4) D served none Av main course £7 🍴: Young & Co 🍺: Youngs Bitter, Summer Waggledance, Winterwarmer, Pilsner. 🍷: 13 **FACILITIES:** Garden: Large patio overlooking the Thames Dogs allowed Water

The White Swan
Riverside TW1 3DN ☎ 020 8892 2166
e-mail: whiteswan@massivepub.com
A traditional pub, the White Swan has been trading here on the Thames since 1690. Outside is a pleasant riverside garden, which attracts plenty of custom in the summer and is a popular setting for barbecues and family gatherings. The pub fills up rapidly when there is rugby at Twickenham or an annual charity raft race on the river in July. Typical dishes include calves' liver, bacon and mash; cottage pie; fresh beer-battered cod and chips; and sausage and mash.
OPEN: 11-3 5.30-11 (Summer: 11-11, Sun 12-10.30 Fri-Sat 11-11, Sun 12-10.30) **BAR MEALS:** L served all week 12-2.30 D served all week 6-9.30 Sun 12-5 Av main course £7 🍺: IPA, Bombadier, Spitfire, Directors. **FACILITIES:** Garden: 15 benches overlooking river Dogs welcome if on lead and well behaved

GREATER MANCHESTER

The Church Inn 🍷
Ravenoak Rd SK8 7EG ☎ 0161 485 1897 📠 0161 485 1698
e-mail: church_inn@yahoo.co.uk
An old world, proprietor-run pub with a friendly atmosphere, the Church Inn has welcoming log fires in winter and a front patio with tables and chairs for summer use. In addition to Robinsons' ales, two guest beers are offered, plus a wide selection of wines by the glass. Dishes are based on carefully sourced meats and fresh fish according to seasonal availability. The home-made curries are a popular choice.
OPEN: 11-11 (Sun 12-10.30) **BAR MEALS:** L served all week 11.30-2.30 D served Mon-Sat 5.30-8.30 Sun 12-2.30 Av main course £8.50 **RESTAURANT:** L served all week 11.30-2.30 D served Mon-Sat 5.30-8.30 Sun 12-2.30 Av 3 course à la carte £18.50 Av 3 course fixed price £10.95 🍺: Robinsons Best Bitter, Hatters Mild, Robinsons Old Stockport plus 2 guests. 🍷: 18 **FACILITIES:** Garden: Front patio **NOTES:** Parking 70

The Rams Head Inn 🏆 🍷
OL3 5UN ☎ 01457 874802 📠 01457 820978
e-mail: ramsheaddenshaw@aol.com
Dir: From M62 junc 22 towards Oldham
A 400-year-old, farmhouse-style pub with fabulous unspoilt moorland views. Each room has original beams and log fires, but an otherwise modest interior is turned into a treasure trove by collections of fascinating memorabilia. Blackboard menus list everything available, except the desserts, which are on the tables. There's always a good range of fish and seafood; roast suckling pig stuffed with garlic and herbs will probably feature, as will loin of lamb on roasted vegetables, and game, including quail and hare, in season.
OPEN: 12-2.30 6-11 (Sun 12-10.30) Closed: 25 Dec
BAR MEALS: L served Tue-Sun, 12-2.30 D served Tue-Sun, 6-10 (BH Mon 12-3, Sun 12-8.30) Av main course £12.95
RESTAURANT: L served Tue-Sun 12-2.30 D served Tue-Sun 6-10

continued

(BH Mon 12-3, Sun 12-8.30) Av 3 course fixed price £10.95 🍴: Free House 🍺: Carlsberg-Tetley Bitter, Timothy Taylor Landlord, Black Sheep Bitter. 🍷: 8 **NOTES:** Parking 200

Pick of the Pubs

The Metropolitan NEW 🍷
2 Lapwing Ln M20 2WS ☎ 0161 374 9559 📠 0161 282 6544
e-mail: barry_lavin@the-metropolitan.co.uk
Dir: Junct 5 of M60. A5103 turn right onto Barlow Moor Road, then left onto Burton Road. The Metropolitan is at the x-rds - turn right on to Lapwing Lane for car park.
Formerly known as the Midland Hotel, the Metropolitan was built in the Victorian era for the London to Midland Railway. The building was very run down when Simon and Jim Barker took it over in 1997; but, after a sympathetic renovation, it reopened the following year as Didsbury's newest gastro-pub. Now, the huge airy interior with its antique tables and chairs offers a stylish setting for the young, cosmopolitan clientele. The pub does get very busy at peak times, but the recent addition of an outside bar with attractive furniture and patio heaters should help to lessen the crush. Menus vary throughout the day: roast parsnip and courgette soup, served with a roast lamb and mint ciabatta is a typical lunchtime offering. Early evening might bring beef and ginger noodle stir-fry, whilst the full evening menu includes dishes like lamb rump on swede mash; and grilled salt cod.
OPEN: 11.30-11 (Sun 12-10.30) Closed: Dec 25
BAR MEALS: L served all week 1-6 D served all week 6-7 Sun 12-6
RESTAURANT: L served all week 12-6 D served all week 6-9.30 Fri-Sat 12-10 Sun 12-9 🍺: Timothy Taylor Landlord, Deuchars IPA, Hoegarden, Staropramen. 🍷: 8 **FACILITIES:** Garden: Large terrace with furniture and heaters **NOTES:** Parking 75

The Royal Oak
729 Wilmslow Rd M20 6WF ☎ 0161 434 4788
Dir: Wimslow Road Jct 6 M60
Character town pub gutted by fire in 1995 but now fully restored. Inside are Victorian fireplaces and old theatre memorabilia. Sources suggest the pub was once run by an ex-zookeeper who trained a monkey to clear glasses in the bar. Renowned for cheese and pâté lunches, with a daily choice of about 30 cheeses.
OPEN: 11-11 (Sun 12-10.30) **BAR MEALS:** L served Mon-Fri 12-2.15 Av main course £3.95 🍴: W'hampton & Dudley 🍺: Marstons Pedigree, Banks Bitter, plus guest ales.

The White House 🏆 🍷
Blackstone Edge, Halifax Rd OL15 0LG ☎ 01706 378456
Old coaching house, built in 1671, standing high on the Pennines 1,300 feet above sea level, with panoramic views of the moors and Hollingworth Lake far below. The pub is on the Pennine Way, attracting walkers and cyclists who sup on Theakston's and regular guest ales. Fresh fish is a feature of the blackboard specials: cheddar topped grilled haddock, lobster thermidor and chargrilled tuna with balsamic glaze. Alternatives include steaks or lamb Henry.
OPEN: 12-3 6-11 Closed: 25 Dec **BAR MEALS:** L served all week 12-2 D served all week 6.30-9 Av main course £6 🍴: Free House 🍺: Timothy Taylor Landlord, Theakstons Bitter, Exmoor Gold, Blacksheep. **NOTES:** Parking 44

England

Dukes 92
14 Castle St, Castlefield M3 4LZ
☎ 0161 839 8646 📠 0161 832 3595
e-mail: dukes92@freenet.co.uk
Dir: Town centre
Beautifully-restored 19th-century stable building with a vast patio beside the 92nd lock of the Duke of Bridgewater canal, opened in 1762. The interior is full of surprises, with minimalist décor downstairs and an upper gallery displaying local artistic talent. The renowned cheese and pâté counter is a great draw, offering a huge range of British and continental cheeses, along with a salad selection, and a choice of platters for sharing.
OPEN: 11-11 (Fri-Sat 11-12, Sun12-10.30) Closed: 25-26 Dec, 1 Jan
BAR MEALS: L served all week 12-3 D served Sun-Thurs 5-8
RESTAURANT: L served all week 12-3 D served Mon-Fri 5-8
🍴: Free House 🍺: Interbrew Boddingtons Bitter.
FACILITIES: Garden: Large front and back patio with seating
NOTES: Parking 30

The Queen's Arms
6 Honey St, Cheetham M8 8RG ☎ 0161 835 3899
The Queen's is part of a loose grouping of real ale pubs in Manchester's Northern Quarter. The original tiled frontage shows that it was once allied to the long-vanished Empress Brewery. Its clientele spans the socio-economic spectrum from 'suits' to bikers to pensioners, all seemingly happy with the heavy rock on the jukebox. Food is available, but it's the brewed, distilled and fermented products that attract, including an impressive 'menu' of bottled lagers, fruit beers, vodkas and wines.
OPEN: 12-11 (Sun 12-10.30, 25 Dec 12-3, 7.30-10.30)
BAR MEALS: L served all week 12-8 D served all week After 5-bookings preferred Av main course £3.50 🍺: Timothy Taylors Landlord, Phoenix Bantam, changing guest beers.
FACILITIES: Children's licence Garden: Lawn & seated veranda Dogs allowed **NOTES:** No credit cards

The Oddfellows Arms ♀
73 Moor End Rd SK6 5PT ☎ 0161 449 7826
e-mail: amollimited@hotmail.co.uk
A friendly welcome can be expected in this c1650 building, which has had a liquor licence since 1805. It changed its name from 'The Angel Inn' in 1860 to accommodate the Oddfellows Society, a fore-runner of the Trades Unions. Seafood options include lobster and tiger prawn linguini, and Basque seabass with crispy rocket salad. Recent change of ownership - reports welcome.
OPEN: 12-3 5.30-11 (Sun 12-3, 7-10.30) Closed: 25-26 Dec, 31 Dec-1 Jan **BAR MEALS:** L served Tues-Sun 12-2 D served Tues-Sat 6.30-9.30 **RESTAURANT:** L served Sun 12-2 D served Tue-Sat 7-9.30 🍴: Free House 🍺: Adnams Southwold, Marston's Pedigree & Bitter. ♀: 8 **FACILITIES:** Garden: Small patio area Dogs allowed **NOTES:** Parking 21

★ Star rating for inspected hotel accommodation

We endeavour to be as accurate as possible but changes to times and other information can occur after the guide has gone to press

The Roebuck Inn ⌦ ♀
Strinesdale OL4 3RB ☎ 0161 624 7819 📠 0161 624 7819
e-mail: smhowarth1@aol.com
Dir: From Oldham take A62 then A672 towards Ripponden. 1m turn right at Moorside PH into Turf Pit Lane. Pub 1m.
Historic inn located on the edge of Saddleworth Moor in the rugged Pennines, a thousand feet above sea level. Part of the pub used to be used as a Sunday School, while the upstairs lounge served as a morgue. This may explain the presence of the ghost of a girl who drowned in the local reservoir. A look at the specials board may offer sirloin tips in a pepper sauce; chicken breast in bacon with mushroom sauce; or half a roast duck with orange stuffing and Grand Marnier sauce. Plenty of fish and steak dishes also available.
OPEN: 12-2.30 5-12 **BAR MEALS:** L served all week 12-2.15 D served all week 5-9.30 Sun 12-8.15 Av main course £8
RESTAURANT: L served all week 12-2.15 D served all week 5-9.30 (Sun 12-8.15) 🍴: Free House 🍺: Tetleys, guest beer. ♀: 8
FACILITIES: Child facs Garden: Dogs allowed **NOTES:** Parking 40

Pick of the Pubs

The White Hart Inn ◉◉◉ ♀
Stockport Rd, Lydgate OL4 4JJ
☎ 01457 872566 📠 01457 875190
e-mail: charles@thewhitehart.co.uk
Dir: From Manchester A62 to Oldham. Right onto bypass, A669 through Lees. In 500yds past Grotton brow of hill right onto A6050
Originally built by local landowner John Buckley in 1788, the White Hart remained in the Buckley family until 1921. The vast cellars were initially used for brewing the beer; later they did duty as an air raid shelter during the Second World War, whilst the top floor was used as a Home Guard lookout. More recently, three of the pub's regulars inspired the popular BBC TV series *Last of the Summer Wine*. Since 1994, the present owners Charles Brierley and John Rudden have transformed the building into a welcoming gastro-pub with a non-smoking restaurant and a fine wine list. Quick dishes on the combined brasserie and restaurant menu include mouthwatering open sandwiches, and ham, feta and olive omelette. Main course dishes range from grilled halibut with salmon cannelloni, to griddled sweet potatoes with curried leek risotto and cauliflower fritters.
OPEN: 12-11 (Sun 1-10.30) **BAR MEALS:** L served all week 12-2.30 D served all week 6-9.30 Sun 1-7.30
RESTAURANT: L served Sun 1-3.30 D served Tue-Sat 6.30-9.30
🍴: Free House 🍺: Timothy Taylor Landlord, J W Lees Bitter, Carlsberg-Tetley Bitter, Interbrew Bass Bitter. ♀: 10
FACILITIES: Garden: Lawned garden with view of Saddleworth Moor **NOTES:** Parking 70

Mark Addy Public House
Stanley St M3 5EJ ☎ 0161 832 4080
On the banks of the River Irwell close to Salford Quays, a former river-ferry landing stage - where Mark Addy saved 50 passengers from drowning in Victorian times. Up to 50 cheeses from eight countries and eight Belgian pâtés are served with granary bread - and soup in winter. Wine tasting notes accompany: free doggy bags.
OPEN: 11.30-11 Closed: 25/26 Dec, Jan1 **BAR MEALS:** L served all week 11.30-9 D served all week Av main course £5 🍴: Free House 🍺: Boddingtons. **FACILITIES:** Garden: Riverside patio

STALYBRIDGE   Map 16 SJ99

Stalybridge Station Buffet Bar ♀
The Railway Station SK15 1RF ☎ 0161 303 0007
e-mail: esk@buffetbar.co.uk
Unique Victorian railway station refreshment rooms dating
from 1885 and including original bar fittings, open fire and
conservatory. The old living accommodation and first class
ladies' waiting room are used to good effect. There have been
over 4,300 real ales served here in the last six years, and the
bar hosts regular beer festivals and folk nights. Expect pasta
bake, pies and black peas, liver and onions, and sausage and
mash on the bar menu.
OPEN: 11-11 (12-10.30 Sun) Closed: Dec 25 **BAR MEALS:** L served
all week 11-8 Av main course £3 ☺: Free House ◖: Interbrew
Boddingtons, Bass & Flowers, Wadworth 6X, Guest Ales each week.
FACILITIES: Garden: Platform Dogs allowed Water provided
NOTES: Parking 60 No credit cards

STOCKPORT   Map 16 SJ89

The Nursery Inn
Green Ln, Heaton Norris SK4 2NA
☎ 0161 432 2044 ▤ 0161 442 1857
Dir: Green Lane is off Heaton Moor Road. Pass rugby club on Green Lane,
at end on right. Little cobbled road, pub is 100yds on right.
The Nursery Inn was erected in 1939, as might be guessed
from pre-war features such as the wood panelling in the
lounge/dining room. Food is served at lunchtime only -
sandwiches, baguettes, jacket potatoes in the bar, and salads
and hot meals in the restaurant, typically roast chicken and
stuffing, fillet of plaice, and sausage, egg, chips and beans. Its
award-winning beers include a fine selection of Hydes ales.
OPEN: 11.30-11 **BAR MEALS:** L served all week 12-2.30 D served
Fri-Sat 5-8 **RESTAURANT:** L served all week 12-2.30 D served
Fri-Sat 5-8 2 sittings Sun; 12.30 & 2.30 Av 3 course à la carte £14
◖: Hydes Bitter, Hydes Jekylls Gold, Hydes Seasonal Ales, Harp Irish.
FACILITIES: Garden: Bowling green with patio furniture Dogs
allowed except in eating areas **NOTES:** Parking 20 No credit cards

WIGAN   Map 15 SD50

Bird I'th Hand 🔎
Gathurst Rd, Orell WN5 0LH ☎ 01942 212006
Handy for Aintree races, this vibrant pub might once have
been the home of Dr Beecham of 'powders' fame. Home-
made food, freshly made from market produce, characterises
the menu which includes full rack of barbecue pork ribs, lamb
shank, chicken and leek pudding, Cajun salmon and half a
roast chicken. There are also various Oriental dishes and a
good selection of starters. Large garden and play area.
OPEN: 12-11 **BAR MEALS:** L served all week 12-6 D served all
week 6-9 Av main course £6.95 **RESTAURANT:** L served all week
12-6 D served all week 6-9 Av 3 course à la carte £9.95 ◖: John
Smiths, Directors Bitter, guest beer. **FACILITIES:** Garden: Large
garden with BBQ and patio Dogs allowed Water
NOTES: Parking 35

    Pubs offering a good choice of fish on
their menu

Restaurant and Bar Meal times indicate the times
when food is available. Last orders may be
approximately 30 minutes before the times stated

ANDOVER   Map 05 SU34

Wyke Down Country Pub & Restaurant
Wyke Down, Picket Piece SP11 6LX
Dir: 3m fromAndover town centre/A303. Follow signs for Wyke Down
Caravan Park.
Originally a family-owned farm and once used by Irish
navvies who built a railway cutting on the Waterloo line
outside Andover. Opened seven years ago, the restaurant
stands on the site of the old farm buildings. Good selection of
dishes, including roast sultana and nut loaf in wild mushroom
and red wine sauce, 8oz fillet steak topped with melted
stilton, and supreme of chicken filled with brie and
cranberries, wrapped in smoked bacon with a white wine and
mushroom sauce. Each day a variety of fish specials are
available from the blackboard.
OPEN: 12-3 6-11 Closed: Christmas Day, Boxing Day
BAR MEALS: L served all week 12-2 D served all week 6-9 (Fri-Sat
6-9.30, Sun 12-2, 6.30-8.30) Av main course £7
RESTAURANT: L served all week 12-2 D served all week 6-9 (Fri-sat
6-9.30, Sun 12-2, 6.30-8.30) Av 3 course à la carte £20 ◖: Fosters,
Guiness, Real Ale. **FACILITIES:** Garden: Enclosed area with bench
seating **NOTES:** Parking 90 **ROOMS:**

AXFORD   Map 05 SU64

The Crown at Axford ♀
RG25 2DZ ☎ 01256 389492 ▤ 01256 389149
e-mail: thecrowninn.axford@virgin.net
Dir: Telephone for directions
Small country inn set at the northern edge of the pretty
Candover Valley. A selection of real ales is the ideal
accompaniment to ginger and lemongrass chicken skewers,
moules marinière, chilli con carne or barbequed ribs plus
blackboard specials, all cooked to order and served in the two
bars or in the dining area. Pie of the day is always worth a try
too. A large garden for the summer.
OPEN: 12-3 6-11 (Apr-Oct Sat 12-11 Sun 12-10.30)
BAR MEALS: L served all week 12-2.30 D served all week 6.30-9.30
Av main course £8 **RESTAURANT:** L served all week 12-2.30
D served all week 6.30-9 (Fri Sat 9.30, Sun 8.30) ☺: Free House
◖: Becketts Whitewater, Triple FFF Alton Pride, Cheriton Potts Ale,
Wadworth 6X. ♀: 7 **FACILITIES:** Garden: Large Patio and garden
Dogs allowed Water **NOTES:** Parking 30

BASINGSTOKE   Map 05 SU65

Hoddington Arms 🔎 ♀
Upton Grey RG25 2RL ☎ 01256 862371 ▤ 01256 862371
e-mail: monca777@aol.com
Dir: Telephone for directions
Log fires and 18th-century beams contribute to the relaxing
atmosphere at this traditional pub, which is located near the
duck pond at Upton Grey, Hampshire's best kept village for
several years. In addition to a choice of bar snacks and a set
price menu of the day, blackboard specials include the likes of
swordfish with a caper and sun-dried tomato crust, minted
lamb casserole, and home-cooked Hoddington pies. There's
also a peaceful rear terrace and garden.
OPEN: 12-3 6-11 (Sun 7-10.30) **BAR MEALS:** L served Mon-Sun
12-2 D served Mon-Sat 6-9.30 Av main course £8.50
RESTAURANT: L served Mon-Sun 12-2 D served Mon-Sat 6-9.30
Av 3 course à la carte £20 ☺: Greene King ◖: Greene King IPA,
Old Speckled Hen, Ruddles Best, Fosters. ♀: 7 **FACILITIES:** Child
facs Garden: Large patio with play area Dogs allowed Water
NOTES: Parking 30

PUB WALK
The Plough Inn
Sparsholt - Hampshire

THE PLOUGH INN,
Main Street, Sparsholt, SO21 2NW
☎ 01962 776353
Directions: From Winchester take
B3049 (A272) W, take L turn to village
of Sparsholt. The Plough Inn is 1m
down the lane.
*A 200-year-old cottage with a
delightful garden - the perfect spot for
a summer evening drink. Inside, a
bustling bar, a log fire, award-winning
food, Wadworth ales and fine wines.*
Open: 11–3 6–11 (Sun 12–3, 6–10.30)
Closed: 25 Dec
Bar Meals: L served all week 12–2
D served all week 6–9 Av main course
£8.95
Restaurant Meals: L served all week
12–2 D served all week 6–9 Av 3 course
à la carte £25
Children welcome and dogs allowed.
Garden and parking available.
(for full entry see page 243)

Distance: 4 miles (6.4km)
Map: OS Landranger 185
Terrain: Remote, unpopulated
expanses of country - woodland and
downland
Paths: Bridleways, country roads,
woodland tracks and paths
Gradient: Undulating countryside

*Walk submitted by Nick Channer &
checked by The Plough Inn*

The middle stages of this varied and scenic walk are under cover of trees. The route passes through a delightful and ancient coppice on the edge of Farley Mount Country Park. Extending to 1,000 acres, the park is a popular amenity area with a wide variety of wildlife. The views over open countryside near the finish of the walk are some of the most striking in Hampshire.

From the front of the inn turn left and walk up the lane towards Lainston House. At the first junction, bear right and drop down the narrow lane between trees and hedgerows. Pass a path in the right-hand bank. Continue down beyond Dean Hill Cottage to the pretty hamlet of Dean. As the road bends left by Barn Cottage, go straight on along a bridleway running between hedges and trees. Head up the chalk slope and avoid turnings on the left and right.

The path runs through a tunnel of yew trees and passes a turning on the right. Continue on the main bridleway all the way to the road. Bear right and pass several remote houses and barns. Soon the lane becomes enveloped by woodland. Avoid a waymarked path running into the trees, pass a wide entrance to the wood further on and continue until you reach another main gateway. Turn right at this point and follow the winding track through Crab Wood, all the way to the road.

Join forces now with the Clarendon Way, a waymarked trail linking Salisbury and Winchester. The route is named after Clarendon Palace, a hunting lodge for Norman kings. Cross over and join the next section of the route. Keep to the main path and eventually you reach a forest clearing where there is a sign for West Wood.

With the Forestry Commission sign on your left, go straight on along the clear bridleway between silver birch trees. Don't veer over to the track on the left or take the track on the right. Instead, follow the bridleway as it heads for the north-east boundary of West Wood. Eventually the trees thin. On the left are fields and paddocks.

After more than half a mile on the bridlepath you join a track serving various bungalows. Pass the entrance to Little Sheddons and just before reaching the road junction, look for a path veering off half left into the trees. Follow it down to the lane and turn left. Walk back into Sparsholt and return to the inn.

222

BEAUWORTH
Map 05 SU52

The Milburys ♀
SO24 0PB ☎ 01962 771248 📠 01962 7771910
e-mail: info@themilburys.co.uk
Dir: A272 towards Petersfield, after 6m turn right for Beauworth
A rustic hill-top pub dating from the 17th century and named after the Bronze Age barrow nearby. It is noted for its massive, 250-year-old treadmill that used to draw water from the 300ft well in the bar, and for the far-reaching views across Hampshire that can be savoured from the lofty garden. The new owners are South African, and their African Oasis restaurant has a distinctive flavour.
OPEN: 11-11 (Sun 12-10.30) Closed Mon-Thurs 3-5.30 in winter
BAR MEALS: L served all week 12-2 D served all week 6.30-9.30
Av main course £9 **RESTAURANT:** L served all week 12-2 D served all week 6.30-9.30 Av 3 course à la carte £10 🍽: Free House
🍺: Scottish Courage Theakstons Old Peculier, Triple FFF Altons Pride, Deuchars, guest ale. ♀: 8 **FACILITIES:** Garden: Beautiful view of valley Dogs allowed Water provided **NOTES:** Parking 60

BENTLEY
Map 05 SU74

The Bull Inn
GU10 5JH ☎ 01420 22156 📠 01420 520772
Dir: 2m from Farnham on A31 towards Winchester

A welcome refuge from the A31 between Alton and Farnham, a beamed 16th-century inn with open fires and two distinct bars and a restaurant. An extensive selection of pub food complemented by steaks from the chargrill, fresh fish, and innovative restaurant dishes such as smoked salmon and avocado cheesecake with Bloody Mary ice cream and canon of lamb coated in brioche crumbs with an aubergine caviar.
OPEN: 11-11 (Sun 11-10.30) **BAR MEALS:** L served all week 12-2.30 D served all week 6.30-9.30 **RESTAURANT:** L served all week 12-2.30 D served all week 6.30-9.30 🍽: Free House
🍺: Scottish Courage Courage Best, Hogs Back TEA, Young's Bitter, Fullers London Pride. **FACILITIES:** Child facs Garden: Dogs allowed
NOTES: Parking 40

BENTWORTH
Map 05 SU64

The Star Inn 🍽
GU34 5RB ☎ 01420 561224 e-mail: matt@star-inn.com
web: www.star-inn.com
Dir: N of Alton 3m off A339
With its eye-catching floral displays in summer, the Star occupies a charming spot in prime Hampshire countryside. There's a safe, secluded garden, and the pub is handy for the Woodland Trust's property at Home Farm. Choose from the usual favourites on the bar menu (sandwiches, baked potatoes, ploughman's, omelettes), or move up to the separate dining-room menu for liver and bacon with orange,

continued

brandy and oregano; trio of lamb chops with mint and redcurrant gravy; or a good selection of vegetarian dishes. Specials and sweets on the board.

The Star Inn

OPEN: 12-3 5-11 Sat 12-4, 6-11 Sun 12-4, 7-10.30
BAR MEALS: L served all week 12-2 D served all week 6.30-9 Sun 7-9 Av main course £9.50 **RESTAURANT:** L served all week 12-2 D served all week 6.30-9 Sun 7-9 🍽: Free House 🍺: Fullers London Pride, Ringwood Best, Doombar, ESB. **FACILITIES:** Garden: Safe and secluded **NOTES:** Parking 12

Pick of the Pubs

The Sun Inn ♀
Sun Hill GU34 5JT ☎ 01420 562338
See Pick of the Pubs on page 224

BOLDRE
Map 05 SZ39

The Red Lion Inn ♀
Rope Hill SO41 8NE ☎ 01590 673177 📠 01590 676403
Though mentioned in the Domesday Book, today's inn dates from the 15th century when it was formed from two cottages and a stable. Inside you'll find a rambling series of beamed rooms packed with rural memorabilia. The lengthy menu takes in starters and snacks, main courses, pasta dishes, salads and light bites. Specialities include steaks and home-made suet pudding filled with chicken, bacon and mushrooms, plus daily specials such as smoked salmon and crayfish risotto.
OPEN: 11-11 (Sun 12-10.30) **BAR MEALS:** L served all week 12-2.30 D served all week 6.30-9.30 **RESTAURANT:** L served all week 12-2.30 D served all week 6.30-9.30 🍽: ELD 🍺: Bass, Ringwood Best. ♀: 12 **FACILITIES:** Garden: Floral displays Dogs allowed Water **NOTES:** Parking 50

BRAMDEAN
Map 05 SU62

The Fox Inn ♀
SO24 0LP ☎ 01962 771363 e-mail: thefoxinn@callnet.uk.com
Dir: A272 between Winchester and Petersfield
400-year-old village pub situated in the beautiful Meon Valley surrounded by copper beech trees. Produce is locally sourced and a good choice of fresh fish is featured on blackboard menus written up twice a day. Options might include pan-fried wing of skate, baked cod with a herb crust and lemon sauce, roast rack of lamb, fresh battered cod and chips, and fillet steak in a mushroom cream sauce.
OPEN: 11-3 6-11 (Winter open at 6.30) **BAR MEALS:** L served all week 12-2 D served all week 7-9 Av main course £11.95 🍽: Greene King 🍺: Ruddles County & IPA Smooth. ♀: 7
FACILITIES: Garden: Food served outside, patio
NOTES: Parking 25

Pick of the Pubs
BENTWORTH – HAMPSHIRE

The Sun Inn

This delightful flower-decked pub is either the first building you pass as you enter Bentworth from the Basingstoke-Alton road, or the last one out, depending on which way you are travelling, and it always seems to come as a surprise. Originally two cottages, it now has three interconnecting rooms, each with its own log fire and brick and wood floors.

The bar is the middle room, right in front of the door. Pews, settles, and scrubbed pine tables with lit candles in the evening add to the homely atmosphere. Food is hearty and traditional, with beef stroganoff; minted lamb; a range of meat and vegetarian curries; liver and bacon; cheesy haddock bake; filled Yorkshire puddings; braised steak in red wine and mushroom sauce; and Mediterranean lamb. Game in season includes venison cooked in Guinness with pickled walnuts, and pheasant. Everything, from the soup to the desserts, is home made. A thriving free house, it offers eight hand-pumped real ales, including Cheriton Brewhouse Pots Ale, Ringwood's Best and Old Thumper, both from Hampshire breweries, and Brakspear Bitter and Fuller's London Pride. There is much to see and do in the area: Gilbert White's House and the Oates Museum in Selborne are not far away, and neither are Jane Austen's House at Chawton, or the Watercress Line at Alresford. Also within easy reach is Basing House in Old Basing, on the outskirts of Basingstoke.

OPEN: 12-3 6-11 (Sun 12-10.30)
BAR MEALS: L served all week 12-2
D served all week 7-9.30
🍺: Free House
🛢: Cheriton Pots Ale, Ringwood Best & Old Thumper, Brakspear Bitter, Fuller's London Pride.
FACILITIES: Garden: Dogs allowed
Water

☿   Map 05 SU64
Sun Hill GU34 5JT
☎ 01420 562338

BROCKENHURST   Map 05 SU30

The Filly Inn
Lymington Rd, Setley SO42 7UF
☎ 01590 623449 ▣ 01590 622682 e-mail: pub@fillyinn.co.uk

Friendly pub in the heart of the New Forest complete with
George, the resident ghost. The oldest part of the building
dates from the 16th century, and the modern extension was
seamlessly attached. Old beams are hung with animal traps,
and other items on display include swords, bayonets and
agricultural implements. Food options take in curry nights,
summer weekend hog roasts, Sunday carvery, daily fish
specials and succulent steaks. Live music is a feature.
OPEN: 10-11 **BAR MEALS:** L served all week 10-2.15 D served all
week 6.30-10 **RESTAURANT:** L served all week 10-2.15 D served all
week 6.30-10 ⬚: Free House ⬛: Ringwood Best, Old Thumper,
Badger Tanglefoot, London Pride. **FACILITIES:** Child facs Garden:
About 0.75 acres of lawn Dogs allowed Water **NOTES:** Parking 90

BROOK   Map 05 SU21

Pick of the Pubs

The Bell Inn ★★★ 🌀 ⌖
SO43 7HE ☎ 023 80812214 ▣ 023 80813958
e-mail: bell@bramshaw.co.uk web: www.bramshaw.co.uk
Dir: From M27 junct 1 take B3078 signed Brook, 0.5m on right

Throughout its long history - it was established in 1782 -
the Bell has been owned by the same family. A handsome
building with window shutters, an imposing inglenook
fireplace and beamed bedrooms, it makes an ideal base
for touring the New Forest, as well as serving as the 19th
hole for two neighbouring golf clubs. Bar food ranges
from hot and cold snacks (omelettes, sandwiches,
burgers) to daily specials featuring fresh fish and local
game in season. A daily menu offers starters of carrot
and ginger soup; chorizo, tomato and feta cheese salad;
and chicken liver pâté with red onion jam. Among the

continued

generous choice of main courses are mushroom
stroganoff, pheasant and venison sausages, lamb jalfrezi,
and baked mackerel fillet. Caramel apple crème brûlée
with shortbread fingers looks tempting, but then so do all
the other home-made desserts.
OPEN: 11-11 (Sun 12-10.30) **BAR MEALS:** L served all week
12-2.30 D served all week 6.30-9.30 Av main course £10.50
RESTAURANT: L served all week 12-2 D served all week
6.30-9.30 Av 3 course fixed price £31 ⬚: Free House
⬛: Ringwood Best, Courage Best, John Smiths, 6X.
FACILITIES: Child facs Garden: **NOTES:** Parking 60
ROOMS: 25 bedrooms en suite s£65 d£90

BUCKLERS HARD   Map 05 SU40

The Master Builders House Hotel ★★★ 🌀 ⌖
SO42 7XB ☎ 01590 616253 ▣ 01590 616297
e-mail: res@themasterbuilders.co.uk
web: www.themasterbuilders.co.uk
The former house of the master shipbuilder Henry Adams is a
fine 18th-century building in the historic ship-building village
of Buckler's Hard, with a grassy area in front running down to
the Beaulieu River. It has been carefully refurbished to create
a smart hotel and the beamed Yachtsman's Bar. The bar
offers light snacks and a short evening menu with fish pie,
steak, chicken tikka masala and a daily vegetarian dish.
OPEN: 11-11 (Sun 12-10.30) **BAR MEALS:** L served all week
12-2.30 D served all week 7-9 Av main course £8.95
RESTAURANT: L served all week 12-3 D served all week 7-10
Av 3 course à la carte £30 Av fixed price £22.50 ⬚: Free House
⬛: Greene King IPA, Youngs, Tetleys, Broadside. ⌖: 6
FACILITIES: Child facs Garden: Dogs allowed Water
NOTES: Parking 50 **ROOMS:** 25 bedrooms en suite s£135 d£180

BURLEY   Map 05 SU20

The Burley Inn ⌖
BH24 4AB ☎ 01425 403448 ▣ 01425 402058
e-mail: info@theburleyinn.co.uk
Dir: Between the A31 & A35

Where Edwardians once waited to see their doctor, landlady
Janet Miller now asks visitors to be patient while she cooks
their meals freshly to order. 'It's worth the wait', she says.
Sprinkled with foody epigrams, the long and interesting menu
offers snacks, starters and light bites, a good selection of meat,
poultry and fish dishes, home-made pies, bakes and desserts,
with steamed beef suet puddings hailed as classics. Additional
daily specials are also served. In the garden is the famous tree
house where the good doctor once sold cream teas.
OPEN: 10-10.30 (Sun 10-10) **BAR MEALS:** L served all week 12-8.30
D served all week 12-8.30 Av main course £7.95 ⬚: Wadworth
⬛: Wadworth 6X, Henry's IPA & JCB. ⌖: 12 **FACILITIES:** Garden:
Outside terrace Dogs allowed Water **NOTES:** Parking 18

CADNAM   Map 05 SU31

Pick of the Pubs

The White Hart 🐟 ♀
Old Romsey Rd SO40 2NP ☎ 023 80812277
e-mail: whitehart@laurelpubco.com
Dir: M27 junct 1. Just off rdbt to Southampton, left at Cadnam rdbt, then first left.

Quaint chocolate box former coaching inn on the edge of the New Forest, conveniently close to junction 1 of the M27. Rambling interconnected rooms, including a skittle alley, heated by log burner in winter, have a comfortable mix of old and new furniture, tiled floors, and traditional décor; outside, a beautiful garden for al fresco dining in summer. Seasonal food is the attraction here, the extensive menu listing home-cooked dishes, which include lamb shank with rosemary, home-made beef Wellington, and halibut steak with roasted sweet peppers. At lunch there are also bar snacks and light meals such as sandwiches, pastas and salads. Please note that the White Hart is fully non-smoking.
OPEN: 11-11 (Sun 12-10.30) **BAR MEALS:** L served all week 12-5 D served all week 5-10 Sun 12-9.30 Av main course £8
🍴: 🍺: Ringwood Best, Green King Abbot Ale. ♀: 21
FACILITIES: Children's licence Garden: Secluded country garden, with fish pond **NOTES:** Parking 55 ⊗

CHALTON   Map 05 SU71

Pick of the Pubs

The Red Lion 🐟 ♀
PO8 0BG ☎ 023 9259 2246 📠 023 9259 6915
e-mail: redlionchalton@aol.com
Dir: Just off A3 between Horndean & Petersfield. Take Clanfield turning
Records show that the Red Lion, which is probably Hampshire's oldest pub, began life in 1147 as a workshop and residence for the craftsmen building the Norman church opposite. By 1460 it had expanded to become a hostel for church dignitaries, and in 1503 it was granted a licence to sell ale. By the 1700s it was extended again to cope with the growing number of travellers needing accommodation as they journeyed between London and Portsmouth. Imaginative dishes from the daily specials board include venison bourguignon; roast shoulder of lamb with redcurrant sauce; fillet of beef Wellington; grilled butterfish steak with spicy tomato salsa; and Mediterranean stewed fish soup. Typical pub snacks include sandwiches, baguettes, Thai fish cakes and jacket

potatoes. Chicken nuggets, sausages, fish fingers and pizza keep the children happy. There are spectacular views of the South Downs from the large garden.

The Red Lion

OPEN: 11-3 6-11 25-26 Dec closed evening
BAR MEALS: L served all week 12-2 D served Mon-Sat 6.30-9.30 Sun 12-2.30 **RESTAURANT:** L served all week 12-2 D served Mon-Sat 6.30-9.30 🍴: Gales 🍺: Gales Butser, Winter Brew, GB & HSB. ♀: 20 **FACILITIES:** Child facs Garden: Spectacular views over South Downs Dogs welcome in public bar **NOTES:** Parking 80

CHARTER ALLEY   Map 05 SU55

The White Hart
White Hart Ln RG26 5QA ☎ 01256 850048 📠 01256 850524
e-mail: enquiries@whitehartcharteralley.com
web: www.whitehartcharteralley.com
Dir: From M3 junct 6 take A339 towards Newbury. Turn right to Ramsdell. Turn right at church, then 1st left into White Hart Lane

Built in 1819, this village pub originally catered for local woodsmen and coaches visiting the farrier's next door. These days it's popular with cyclists and walkers from Basingstoke and Reading and real ale enthusiasts from all over, having sold more than 600 real ales from around the country in the last 15 years and won many CAMRA awards in recent times. Guest ales change weekly and home-made food is served in generous portions. Look out for steak and stilton pie, White Hart smokie, venison and game pie, and Cajun tuna steak.
OPEN: 12-2.30 7-11 (Sun 12-3, 7-10.30) Closed: Dec 25-26
BAR MEALS: L served all week 12-2 D served Tue-Sat 7-9 No food Sun/Mon evenings Av main course £8 **RESTAURANT:** L served all week 12-2 D served Tue-Sat 7-9 Av 3 course à la carte £16 🍴: Free House 🍺: Timothy Taylor Landlord, Otter Ale, West Berkshire Mild, Butts Jester. **FACILITIES:** Garden: Enclosed sunny position Dogs allowed **NOTES:** Parking 30

continued

CHAWTON
Map 05 SU73

The Greyfriar ♀
Winchester Rd GU34 1SB ☎ 01420 83841
e-mail: info@thegreyfriar.co.uk
Dir: *Chawton lies just off the A31 near Alton. Access to Chawton via the A31/A32 J. Signed Jane Austen's House*
A terrace of cottages in the 16th century, a 'beer shop' by 1847, and from 1871 a proper pub, known as the Chawton Arms. The simple lunch menu offers baguettes, ploughman's, quiches, burgers and breaded scampi tails. The evening menu, which changes most days, might well come up with milk-fed lamb with leeks; fillet of gurnard with tomatoes and olive sauce; and gammon steak with bubble and squeak. Jane Austen's house is opposite.
OPEN: 12-11 (Mon-Fri 12-11, Sun 12-10.30) **BAR MEALS:** L served all week 12-2 D served Mon-Sat 7-9.30 Sun 12-3 Av main course £8.95 **RESTAURANT:** L served all week 12-2 D served Mon-Sat 7-9.30 **⬤:** Fuller's London Pride, Chiswick & ESB, Seasonal Ales. **♀:** 14 **FACILITIES:** Garden: Paved area, sun trap, picnic tables Dogs allowed Water **NOTES:** Parking 16

CHERITON
Map 05 SU52

Pick of the Pubs

The Flower Pots Inn
SO24 0QQ ☎ 01962 771318 📠 01962 771318
Dir: *A272 toward Petersfield, L onto B3046, pub 0.75m on R*
Red brick village pub, originally a farmhouse, built in the 1840s by the head gardener of nearby Avington House. The Flowerpots is a popular venue for supping award-winning beers like Pots Ale or Diggers Gold, brewed in the micro-brewery across the car park. There are two bars: the rustic, pine furnished public bar and the cosy saloon with its comfy sofa. Both have welcoming open fires in winter. Wednesday night is exclusively Punjabi curry night, otherwise simple and honest bar food is the order of the day. Expect the likes of toasted sandwiches, jacket potatoes and tasty hotpots - beef, spicy mixed bean, and lamb and apricot - served with crusty bread, basmati rice, garlic bread or jacket potato. There's also a choice of ploughman's lunches (with cheese, ham or beef), and giant baps filled with steak and onions, cheese, or coronation chicken.
OPEN: 12-2.30 6-11 (Sun 12-3, 7-10.30)
BAR MEALS: L served all week 12-2 D served Mon-Sat 7-9 (Subject to change if busy); Wed curry only, No D BHs Av main course £5.50 **⬤:** Free House **⬤:** Cheriton Pots Ale, Best Bitter, Diggers Gold (Brewed on premises). **FACILITIES:** Garden: Lawns with picnic benches; flowerpots Dogs allowed on leads **NOTES:** Parking 30 No credit cards

CRAWLEY
Map 05 SU43

The Fox and Hounds ♀
SO21 2PR ☎ 01962 776006 📠 01962 776006
e-mail: liamlewisairey@aol.com
Dir: *A34 onto A272 then 1st right into Crawley*
Just north west of Winchester, at the heart of a peaceful Hampshire village, this mock Tudor inn enjoys a burgeoning reputation for simple well-cooked food. Recently restored to former glory, it features beamed rooms warmed by log fires that create a welcoming, lived-in atmosphere. Typical menu choices include Old English sausages on bubble and squeak, steak and ale pie, salmon fillet with hollandaise sauce, dressed crab salad, and pork fillet with black pudding.
OPEN: 12-3 6-11 **BAR MEALS:** L served all week 12-2 D served all week 6-9 **RESTAURANT:** L served all week 12-2 D served all week 7-9 **⬤:** Free House **⬤:** Wadworth 6X, Ringwood Best, Gales HSB, Fullers London Pride. **FACILITIES:** Garden: Small terraced area, family garden to rear **NOTES:** Parking 17

CRONDALL
Map 05 SU74

Pick of the Pubs

The Hampshire Arms ♀
Pankridge St GU10 5QU ☎ 01252 850418 📠 01252 850418
e-mail: paulychef@hantsarms.freeserve.co.uk
See Pick of the Pubs on page 228

DAMERHAM
Map 05 SU11

The Compasses Inn ♦♦♦♦ 🐟 ♀
SP6 3HQ ☎ 01725 518231 📠 01725 518880
e-mail: info@compassesinn.net
Dir: *From Fordingbridge (A338) follow signs for Sandleheath/Damerham. Or signs from B3078*

Located in the village centre overlooking the cricket pitch, this 300-year-old coaching inn has atmosphere a-plenty in both of the bars, and in the cottagey bedrooms which are named after famous trout flies. Real ales, including their own brew and regular guests, accompany locally produced fresh food, with plenty of fish (smoked mackerel, asparagus and horseradish tart), and tasty meat dishes such as beef medallions with Murphy sauce and blue cheese glaze.
OPEN: 11-3 6-11 (All day Sat, Sun 12-4, 7-10.30)
BAR MEALS: L served all week 12-2.30 D served all week 7-9.30 Sun 7-9 Av main course £8 **RESTAURANT:** L served all week 12-2.30 D served all week 7-9.30 Sun 7-9 Av 3 course à la carte £20 **⬤:** Free House **⬤:** Ringwood Best, Hop Back Summer Lightning, Courage Best, Gales Best plus guest. **♀:** 8 **FACILITIES:** Children's licence Garden: Large garden, water feature, by village green Dogs allowed by arrangement **NOTES:** Parking 30
ROOMS: 6 bedrooms en suite 1 family room s£39.50 d£69

Pick of the Pubs

CRONDALL – HAMPSHIRE

The Hampshire Arms

Now in the hands of Alan Piesse, and billing itself as an à la carte restaurant, the 18th-century Hampshire Arms offers exceptional standards of food, wine and service, attracting many accolades and awards as a result. It began life as two cottages, but in its time has also been a courthouse, a post office and a bakery.

Open fires, bare beams, hop bines and candlelight now combine to create a delightfully welcoming atmosphere. In warmer weather you can enjoy an al fresco meal, and a game of pétanque, if you wish, in the large landscaped garden, a river forming one of its boundaries. Otherwise you may eat and drink in the heated covered area, or in the bar, of course, where aromatic lamb stew, crab and prawn linguine, and the Brunch Bowl - potatoes sautéed with garlic and herbs, bacon, eggs, tomatoes and fried bread - are offered. In the ultra-smart, non-smoking restaurant typical starters might include a selection of European cold meats; smooth chicken liver parfait with toasted brioche and caramelised orange; and cassoulet of asparagus and broad beans with tomato concasse and chives. You might then fancy canon of lamb with roast garlic and minted jus; or grilled risotto cakes with parmesan, wild mushrooms and marinated vegetables. Among the fish dishes are mosaic of fish and shellfish with lobster and saffron cream; pan-fried John Dory fillet with fennel and butter sauce; and seared scallops on ribbon vegetables, sesame oil and wasabi. Desserts include whisky and marmalade bread and butter pudding with crème Anglaise.

OPEN: 11-3.30 5.30-11 (all day Sat, Sun 12-10.30)
BAR MEALS: L served Tue-Sun 12-2.30 D served Mon-Sat 7-9 Av main course £13.50
RESTAURANT: L served all week 12-2.30 D served Mon-Sat 7-9 Av 3 course à la carte £27.50
🍺: Greene King
🍺: Greene King IPA, Abbot Ale, Ruddles County. 🍷: 10
FACILITIES: Garden: Large landscaped garden, river at bottom Dogs allowed Water
NOTES: Parking 40

🍷   Map 05 SU74
Pankridge St GU10 5QU
☎ 01252 850418
📧 dining@thehampshirearms.co.uk
Dir: From M3 junct 5 take A287 South towards Farnham. Follow signs to Crondall on R

DOGMERSFIELD
Map 05 SU75

The Queens Head
Pilcot Ln RG27 8SY ☎ 01252 613531 📠 01252 629957
e-mail: chrsh@chrysalispubco.com

A 17th-century coaching inn linked to Katherine of Aragon, set beside a stream and some pretty thatched cottages with Dogmersfield Park and lake close by. An extensive international menu includes grilled lambs' liver and bacon, salmon en croute, honey roast duck, fisherman's pie, and home-made steak and ale pie. Various established favourites can also be found, like jacket potato, ploughman's and freshly baked baguettes.
OPEN: Open all day **BAR MEALS:** L served all week 12-2.15 D served all week 6-9.15 **RESTAURANT:** L served all week 12-2.15 D served all week 6-9.15 Av 3 course à la carte £22 ⊜: Free House ◖: Scottish Courage Courage Best, Adnams Broadside & Guest ale. ♀: 10 **FACILITIES:** Garden: Grass seated area, good views **NOTES:** Parking 20

DOWNTON
Map 05 SZ29

The Royal Oak
SO41 0LA ☎ 01590 642297 📠 01590 641798
e-mail: enquiries@oakdownton.freeuk.com
Dir: Situated on A337 between Lymington & Christchurch.
Recently extensively renovated, the Royal Oak now offers enhanced dining and a new look to the garden, while remaining in all other respects true to its traditional and hospitable atmosphere. It is also more visibly appealing from the road. Dishes range from ciabatta club sandwiches (at lunchtime) to the likes of half shoulder of lamb confit on mint pea mash finished with a redcurrant and rosemary jus.
OPEN: 11.30-2.30 6-11 **BAR MEALS:** L served all week 12-2 D served all week 6-9 Sun 12-2.30, 7-9, Fri-Sat 6-9.30 Av main course £7.95 **RESTAURANT:** 12-2 D served all week 6-9 Sun 12-2.30, 7-9, Fri-Sat 6-9.30 Av 3 course à la carte £20 ⊜: Enterprise Inns ◖: Ringwood Best Bitter, Gales HSB, Whitbread Best Bitter. ♀: 20 **FACILITIES:** Garden: Large grassed area, picnic tables & umbrellas Dogs allowed in the bar only **NOTES:** Parking 40

Do you have a favourite pub that we have overlooked? Please use the Reader's Report form at the back of this guide to tell us all about it

---

Not all of the pubs in the guide are open all week or all day. It's always best to check before you travel

---

DUMMER
Map 05 SU54

The Queen Inn ♀
Down St RG25 2AD ☎ 01256 397367 📠 01256 397601
Dir: From M3 junct 7, follow Dummer signs
You can dine by candlelight at this 16th-century village pub, with its low beams and huge open log fire. Everything is home made, from the soup and light bites to the famous fish and chips with beer batter, pan-fried lamb fillet, and prime steaks. The steak and kidney pudding is only for the heartier appetite! Fresh fish is a speciality. Under new ownership.
OPEN: 11.30-2.30 6-11 (Sun 12-3 7-10.30) **BAR MEALS:** L served all week 12-2.30 D served all week 6-9.30 **RESTAURANT:** L served all week 12-2 D served all week 6-9.30 ⊜: Unique Pub Co ◖: Courage Best & John Smiths, Fuller's London Pride, Old Speckled Hen & Guest ales ♀: 8 **FACILITIES:** Garden: Benches, tables, chairs Dogs allowed (not in bar) **NOTES:** Parking 20

EAST MEON
Map 05 SU62

Ye Olde George Inn
Church St GU32 1NH ☎ 01730 823481 📠 01730 823759
e-mail: yeoldgeorge@aol.com
Dir: S of A272 (Winchester/Petersfield). 1.5m from Petersfield turn left opp church

In a lovely village on the River Meon, a charming 15th-century inn close to a magnificent Norman church, and near to Queen Elizabeth Country Park. Its open fires, heavy beams and rustic artefacts create an ideal setting for relaxing over a good choice of real ales or enjoying freshly prepared bar food.
OPEN: 12-3 6-11 Sat 11-3 **BAR MEALS:** L served all week 12-2 D served all week 7-9 Sun eve no food Av main course £7.95 **RESTAURANT:** L served all week 12-2 D served all week 7-9 No food Sun eve ⊜: Hall & Woodhouse ◖: Badger Best, Tanglefoot & King & Barnes Sussex. **FACILITIES:** Garden: Patio area Dogs allowed **NOTES:** Parking 30

England

Pick of the Pubs

The Chestnut Horse ♀
SO21 1EG ☎ 01962 779257 📠 01962 779037
Dir: From M3 J9 take A33 towards Basingstoke, then B3047. Take 2nd right, then 1st left

A delightful dining pub with a beautiful village setting in the Itchen Valley. There's plenty of 16th-century character in the open fires, and low-beamed ceilings hung with old beer mugs and chamber pots. A good selection of ales is kept, along with a choice of 40-50 malt whiskies. The lunchtime menu offers lasagne, steak and salad, confit of duck or bangers and mash, with perhaps honey and mustard glazed pork loin medallions in the evenings. Ideal walking country.
OPEN: 11-3 5.30-11 (Sun eve Winter closes at 6)
BAR MEALS: L served all week 12-2.30 D served all week 6.30-9.30 Sun 12-4 in winter, 12-8 in summer Av main course £14 **RESTAURANT:** L served all week 12-2.30 D served all week 6.30-9.30 Sun 12-4 winter, 12-8 summer Av 3 course à la carte £25 Av 2 course fixed price £10 😊: Free House 🛢: Interbrew Bass, Scottish Courage Courage Best, Chestnut Horse Special, Fuller's London Pride. ♀: 9 **FACILITIES:** Garden: Decked patio, heaters Dogs allowed Water **NOTES:** Parking 40

The Cricketers Inn
SO21 1EJ ☎ 01962 779353 📠 01962 779010
e-mail: info@cricketers-easton.com
Dir: M3 junct 9, A33 towards Basingstoke, right at Kingsworthy onto B3047. In 0.75m turn right.
Three devoted former customers continue to run this traditional free house in a pretty village close to the River Itchen. Regularly changing guest ales from all over the UK combined with hearty food and a good atmosphere makes it a popular establishment. An extensive bar snack menu and varied carte offer many accomplished dishes, including whole plaice with prawn and lobster bisque sauce, Thai chicken, and the house speciality - ribs with a variety of accompaniments.
OPEN: 12-3 6-11 (Sun 12-3 7-10.30) **BAR MEALS:** L served all week 12-2 D served Mon-Sat 7-9 **RESTAURANT:** L served all week 12-2 D served Mon-Sat 7-9 😊: Free House 🛢: Ringwood, Otter, Changing guest ales. **FACILITIES:** Garden: Paved patio at front Dogs allowed **NOTES:** Parking 16

> Most of the pubs in this guide book pride
> themselves on the quality of their food. This
> may take a little time to prepare

The Northbrook Arms
SO21 3DU ☎ 01962 774150
Dir: Just off A33, 9m S of Basingstoke, 7m N of Winchester, follow Kingsworthy signs from M3

In an idyllic setting adjoining the green and an assortment of thatched cottages, the pub was formerly known as the Plough. Built around 1847, it was once the village shop and bakery and has a skittle alley in converted stables. Home-produced fare includes steak and kidney pie, breast of Barbary duck, vegetable stir fry, cod and chips, and bangers and mash. Handy for Winchester and some of mid-Hampshire's loveliest walks.
OPEN: 12-11 (Sun 12-10.30) **BAR MEALS:** L served all week 12-3 D served all week 6-8.45 😊: Free House 🛢: Gales HSB & GB, Otter Bitter, Ringwood Best, Scottish Courage John Smith's.
FACILITIES: Very large garden, bench seating, volleyball pitch Dogs allowed Water **NOTES:** Parking 30

Pick of the Pubs

Star Inn ♦♦♦♦ 🏨🏨 🍽 ♀
SO51 0LW ☎ 01794 340225 📠 01794 340225
e-mail: info@starinn-uk.com
Dir: 5m N of Romsey off A3057, left for Dunbridge on B3084. Left for Awbridge & Lockerley. Through Lockerley then 1m
An award-winning 16th-century country inn adjoining the village cricket ground, on a quiet road between Romsey with its abbey, and the cathedral city of Salisbury. Dine where you like, in the bar, at dark-wood tables in the main dining room, or outside on the patio, where you can also play chess on a king-sized board. There are two menus, the carte and the classical. The former offers the more sophisticated dishes, which can be eaten as starter or main, like Welsh rarebit tart with smoked haddock and a poached egg; penne pasta with sweet pepper, chickpeas and mushrooms; and pan-fried skate with nut brown butter, caperberries and crispy parma ham. For the enthusiastic fly fisherman, the Star makes a perfect watering hole after a day on the world-famous River Test, or Holbury Lakes. Ringwood Best and guest ales on tap.
OPEN: 11-2.30 6-11 Closed: 26 Dec **BAR MEALS:** L served Tue-Sun 12-2 D served Tue-Sun 7-9 Av main course £10 **RESTAURANT:** L served Tue-Sun 12-2 D served Tue-Sun 7-9 Av 3 course à la carte £25 Av 3 course fixed price £15 😊: Free House 🛢: Ringwood Best plus guest beers. ♀: 10
FACILITIES: Child facs Garden: Patio area, country garden with furniture. Dogs allowed Water bowl **NOTES:** Parking 60
ROOMS: 3 bedrooms en suite 2 family rooms s£50 d£70

EMSWORTH   Map 05 SU70

The Sussex Brewery ♢ ♀
36 Main Rd PO10 8AU ☎ 01243 371533 🖷 01243 379684
Dir: On A259 (coast road), between Havant & Chichester
A fresh 'carpet' of sawdust is laid daily in the bars of this
traditional 17th-century pub that boasts wooden floors, large
open fires and a typically warm welcome. Fully 40 sausage
recipes are on offer, ranging from gluten-free Moroccan lamb
and vegetarian varieties to the full-blown Feathered Platter,
which includes spiced ostrich, garlic chicken, Sussex pigeon
and pheasant. Non sausage-related daily specials might
include fresh local fish, steaks, or rack of lamb.
OPEN: 11-11 **BAR MEALS:** L served all week 12-2.30 D served all
week 7-10 **RESTAURANT:** L served all week 12-2.30 D served all
week 7-10 🍴: Young & Co 🍺: Smiles Best Bitter, Young's PA, AAA &
Special, Timothy Taylor Landlord. ♀: 8 **FACILITIES:** Garden:
Enclosed courtyard garden Dogs allowed Water **NOTES:** Parking 30

EVERSLEY   Map 05 SU76

The Golden Pot ♀
Reading Rd RG27 0NB ☎ 0118 9732104
*Dir: Between Reading and Camberley on the B3272 about 0.25m from
the Eversley cricket ground*

Dating back to the 1700s and located in a famous village
where Charles Kingsley, author of *The Water Babies*, was
once rector, this charming pub hosts a possibly unique rösti
night on Mondays, with live entertainment. A warming fire
connects the bar and restaurant, where good food is cooked
from fresh ingredients. A sample bar menu includes pork
schnitzel Milanaise; and seared tuna and oriental
mayonnaise.
OPEN: 11-3 6-11 Closed: Dec 25, Jan 1 **BAR MEALS:** L served all
week 12-2.15 D served all week 6.30-9.15 Sun lunch 12-2 Av main
course £9.50 **RESTAURANT:** L served Sun-Fri 12-2 D served
Mon-Sat 7-9.15 🍴: Greene King 🍺: Greene King Ruddles Best,
Abbot Ale, Greene King IPA. **FACILITIES:** Garden: Pergola, picnic
tables Dogs allowed in bar only **NOTES:** Parking 30 ⊗

Do you have a favourite pub that we have overlooked?
Please use the Reader's Report form at the back of
this guide to tell us all about it

Pick of the Pubs have that extra special quality
that makes them stand out from the crowd.
Their entries are highlighted, and may be a
full page

FORDINGBRIDGE   Map 05 SU11

The Augustus John ♀
116 Station Rd SP6 1DG ☎ 01425 652098
e-mail: enquiries@augustusjohn.com web: www.augustusjohn.com
Dir: Telephone for directions
The renowned British portrait painter lived in the village and
drank here, long before it became known as a smart dining
pub. Lunches range from sandwiches and baguettes to salads,
by way of jackets and light meals. The carte offers Aberdeen
Angus steaks, rack of Welsh lamb, and fillet of pork
tenderloin, with fresh fish and daily specials on the
blackboard. The new owner has introduced a Thai menu.
OPEN: 11.30-3.30 6-12 **BAR MEALS:** L served all week 11.30-2
D served all week 6.30-9 Sun 7-9 Av main course £10
RESTAURANT: L served all week 11.30-2 D served all week 6.30-9
Av 3 course à la carte £22.50 🍴: Eldridge Pope 🍺: Bass, Tetley,
Flowers IPA, Ringwood Best. ♀: 8 **FACILITIES:** Garden: Dogs
allowed **NOTES:** Parking 40

FRITHAM   Map 05 SU21

The Royal Oak ♀
SO43 7HJ ☎ 02380 812606 🖷 02380 814066
e-mail: royaloakfritham@btopenworld.com
*Dir: M27 junct 1. Follow B3078 signposted Fordingbridge. Continue for 2m
then turn left at x-rds signposted Ocknell & Fritham. Then contiynue to
follow signs to Fritham*

Unaltered for some 100 years, this small, thatched 17th-
century traditional country pub is deep in the New Forest and
maintains its long tradition of preferring conversation to the
distractions of juke box and fruit machines. With open fires
and overlooking the forest and its own working farm, it is
ideally located for walkers and ramblers, with ploughman's
lunches and home-baked quiches to munch on, and home-
made evening meals on two nights per week. The garden has
lovely views of the valley, and a pétanque terrain.
OPEN: 11-3 6-11 (Summer Sat 11-11, Sun 12-10.30)
BAR MEALS: L served all week 12-2.30 D served 2 days a wk winter
only 7-9 Av main course £5 🍴: Free House 🍺: Ringwood Best &
Fortyniner, Hop Back Summer Lightning, Palmers Dorset Gold,
Cheriton Pots Ale. ♀: 7 **FACILITIES:** Large garden, countryside
views, ample benches Dogs allowed Water, biscuits **NOTES:** No
credit cards

Website addresses are included where available.
The AA cannot be held responsible for the
content of any of these websites

England

HAVANT
Map 05 SU70

The Royal Oak ♀
19 Langstone High St, Langstone PO9 1RY
☎ 023 92483125 ▤ 023 9247 6838
Occupying an outstanding position overlooking Langstone
Harbour, this historic 16th-century pub is noted for its rustic,
unspoilt interior. Flagstone floors, exposed beams and winter
fires contrast with the waterfront benches and a secluded
rear garden for alfresco summer drinking. Light lunches such
as rich tomato soup or chicken Caesar salad support a
dinner menu that includes slow-cooked Welsh lamb; baked
salmon fillet; and ham hock with honey mustard.
OPEN: 11-11 (Sun 12-10.30) 25 Dec Closed eve
BAR MEALS: L served all week 12-6 D served all week 6-9 Av main
course £6.95 **RESTAURANT:** L served all week 12-6 D served all
week 6-9 Av 3 course à la carte £13.95 ▤: ◀: Gales HSB, Interbrew
Flowers, Bass, London Pride. ♀: 16 **FACILITIES:** Garden: Patio and
garden, food served outside Dogs allowed Water

HAWKLEY
Map 05 SU72

Hawkley Inn
Pococks Ln GU33 6NE ☎ 01730 827205
Dir: 2mins W of A3 at Liss
Tucked away down narrow lanes on the Hangers Way Path,
an unpretentious rural local with a fine reputation for quality
ale from local micro-breweries and its own cider. Ambitious
bar food offers brie and bacon or spinach and ricotta tart,
duck breast in peppercorn sauce, Mediterranean chicken and
green pesto spaghetti: for traditionalists, sausage and mash
and faggots with onion gravy. Frequent live jazz and blues.
OPEN: 12-2.30 6-11 **BAR MEALS:** L served all week 12-2 D served
Mon-Sat 7-9.30 Av main course £7.95 ◀: RCH East Street Cream,
Itchen Valley Godfathers, Triple FFF Alton's Pride, Ballards Best Bitter.
FACILITIES: Garden: Food served outdoors Dogs allowed Water

HOLYBOURNE
Map 05 SU74

White Hart
GU34 4EY ☎ 01420 87654 ▤ 01420 543982
Dir: Off A31 between Farnham & Winchester
Traditional village inn popular with locals and business guests.
Families are also welcome, and the children can play in the
special play area which has swings and climbing frames. A
good selection of bar food, which may include fish dishes
such as sea bass, grilled trout, and salmon.
OPEN: 11-3 5-11 **BAR MEALS:** L served all week 12-2.30 D served
all week 7-10 Av main course £6 **RESTAURANT:** L served all week
12-2.30 D served all week 7-10 Av 3 course à la carte £12.50
▤: Greene King ◀: Scottish Courage Courage Best, Greene King
Abbot Ale & IPA. **FACILITIES:** Children's licence Large rear garden
Dogs allowed **NOTES:** Parking 40

HOOK
Map 05 SU75

Crooked Billet ♀
London Rd RG27 9EH ☎ 01256 762118 ▤ 01256 761011
e-mail: Richardbarwise@aol.com
*Dir: From M3 take Ring Road. At third rdbt turn right on A30
towards London, pub on left 0.5m by river.*
This traditional pub is over 100 years old; so is the resident
ghost. Barely had the cement set in the early 1900s when a
motorist - drunk, the coroner thought - on his way back from
Cowes Week crashed into the building at 20mph, with fatal

continued

results. A large garden running down to the River Whitewater
incorporates a play area and barbecue, and Morris Men meet
here regularly. Food for all appetites includes meats, grills,
fish, vegetarian, salads, toasties and jackets. Surrey-brewed
Hogs Back TEA from the pump.

Crooked Billet

OPEN: 11.30-3 6-11 **BAR MEALS:** L served all week 12-2.30
D served all week 7-9.30 Av main course £8.50 ▤: Free House
◀: Scottish Courage Courage Best & Directors & John Smith's, Hogs
Back TEA, Timothy Taylors Landord. ♀: 8 **FACILITIES:** Child facs
Garden: Large garden next to Whitewater River Dogs allowed Water
NOTES: Parking 60

HORSEBRIDGE
Map 05 SU33

John O'Gaunt Inn 🐟⋙
SO20 6PU ☎ 01794 388394
*Dir: A3057 Stockbridge to Romsey. Horsebridge is 4m from Stockbridge,
trun right at brown info board.*
Small country inn, five miles north of Romsey, popular with
walkers from the nearby Test Way, fishermen from the River
Test and the winter shooting fraternity. It provides a great
atmosphere for well-kept ales and generously priced food.
The specials board showcases fresh local produce, notably
pheasant, duck, rabbit and pigeon. The main menu offers
traditional pub food and the likes of curried tuna, roast pork
tenderloin, and spinach and ricotta cannelloni.
OPEN: 11-2.30 6.30-11 (Sat-Sun 11-11) Closed: 4-5 Jan
BAR MEALS: L served Tue-Sun 12-2.45 D served Tue-Sat 6-9.30
Av main course £8.95 **RESTAURANT:** L served Tue-Sun 12-2.45
D served Tue-Sat 6-9.45 ▤: Free House ◀: Ringwood Best Bitter,
Ringwood Fortyniner, Palmers IPA. **FACILITIES:** Child facs
Children's licence Garden: Small area with tables, chairs and
umbrellas Dogs allowed **NOTES:** Parking 12

ITCHEN ABBAS
Map 05 SU53

The Trout ♀
Main Rd SO21 1BQ ☎ 01962 779537 ▤ 01962 791046
e-mail: thetroutinn@aol.com
*Dir: Junct 9 off the M3, follow A34, fork of to the right on the A33, follow
signs to Itchen Abbas, pub is 2m on the left.*
A 19th-century coaching inn located in the Itchen Valley
close to the river itself. Originally called The Plough, it is
said to have been the location that inspired Charles
Kingsley to write *The Water Babies*. Freshly cooked,
locally sourced produce is served in the bar and restaurant:
trout, of course, baked whole in a shrimp velouté, and
Hampshire bangers with mash and gravy. An additional
lunchtime selection includes baguettes, wraps, foccacias
and salads.

continued

The Trout

OPEN: 12-3 6-11 (Open all day Sat-Sun) Closed: 25 Dec
BAR MEALS: L served all week 12-2.15 D served all week 6.30-9 Sun
12-8 Av main course £10.50 **RESTAURANT:** L served all week
12-2.15 D served all week 6.30-9 Sun 12-8 ☺: Greene King
🍺: Greene King IPA, Ruddles County, Morland Speckled Hen. ♀: 9
FACILITIES: Child facs Children's licence Garden: Large garden with
lots of seating **NOTES:** Parking 30

LINWOOD   Map 05 SU10

Red Shoot Inn & Brewery
Toms Ln BH24 3QT ☎ 01425 475792
Dir: From M27 take A338, take Salisbury turning and follow brown signs
The unique beauty of the New Forest is all around this
country pub which, despite its out-of-the-way location, has no
trouble attracting customers, especially during the summer.
Standard pub fare includes home-made soups, sizzling steaks,
sandwiches and a wide variety of ploughman's. There are live
bands every Sunday night, a music quiz on Thursdays and
beer festivals in April and October. A micro-brewery on site
produces Forest Gold and Toms Tipple. Muddy boots, children
and dogs with well-behaved owners are all welcomed.
OPEN: 11-3 6-11 (Apr-Oct open all day) **BAR MEALS:** L served all
week 12-2 D served all week 6.30-9.30 Apr-Oct 12-9.30 Av main
course £6.95 **RESTAURANT:** L served all week 12-2 D served all
week 6.30-9.30 Apr-Oct 12-9.30 ☺: Wadworth 🍺: Forest Gold &
Toms Tipple, 6X, Henry's IPA, Henry's Smooth. **FACILITIES:** Garden:
Patio Dogs allowed **NOTES:** Parking 60

LITTLETON   Map 05 SU43

Pick of the Pubs

The Running Horse NEW ♀
88 Main Rd SO22 6QS ☎ 01962 880218 ▤ 01962 886596
e-mail: runninghorse@btconnect.com
Dir: 3m from Winchester, signed from Stockbridge Rd
Come in on a Sunday with the answer to nine down in
the crossword, and friendship with the locals is
guaranteed! Although built two hundred years ago, recent
months have seen a complete revamp of this pretty rural
pub, boarded on either side by stud farms. Modern
décor, including leather tub chairs positioned around a
roaring fire, have added to the attractive ambiance. Food
is taken seriously here by the competent team of chefs,
and produce is well-sourced and of an impeccable
freshness. Dinner could begin with crab soup and crab
dumplings; followed by butternut squash and spinach
risotto with hazelnut vinaigrette; while the popular
Sunday lunch offers a free range loin of pork with 'perfect
crackling' amongst a variety of carnivorous and
vegetarian options, all of which come in both adult and

continued

child size portions. Desserts include lemon posset; and
pineapple tarte Tatin.
OPEN: 11-3 5.30-11 (Sun 12-7.30) **BAR MEALS:** L served all
week 12-2 D served Mon-Sat 6.30-9.30 Sun 12-4 Av main course
£16 **RESTAURANT:** L served all week 12-2 D served Mon-Sat
6.30-9.30 Sun 12-4 Av 3 course à la carte £25.30 🍺: Ringwood
Best, Itchen Valley Fagins. ♀: 15 **FACILITIES:** Children's licence
Garden: Front and back patio, lawn at rear Dogs allowed Water
bowls **NOTES:** Parking 40

LONGPARISH   Map 05 SU44

The Plough Inn ♀
SP11 6PB ☎ 01264 720358 ▤ 01264 720377
Dir: Off A303 4m S of Andover

As it is only 100 yards away from the River Test, this 400-year
old pub is regularly visited by the local duck population. It is
also a popular meeting place for both family and business
get-togethers. Typical menu includes a wide selection of fish,
and game such as venison, partridge, wild boar, and ostrich.
OPEN: 11-3.30 6-11 (11-3, 6-11 in winter) Dec 25-26 closed evening
BAR MEALS: L served all week 12-2.30 D served all week 6.30-9.30
Av main course £5.95 **RESTAURANT:** L served all week 12-2.30
D served all week 6.30-9.30 ☺: Enterprise Inns 🍺: Hampshire
Ironside, Greene King Old Speckled Hen, Ringwood, Warsteiner.
FACILITIES: Children's licence Garden with wooded/secluded area,
wildlife **NOTES:** Parking 60

LYMINGTON   Map 05 SZ39

The Kings Arms ♦♦♦ ♀
St Thomas St SO41 9NB ☎ 01590 672594
Dir: Approaching Lymington from N on A337, head L onto St Thomas St.
Kings Arms 50yds on right

King Charles I is reputed to have patronised this historic
coaching inn, which these days enjoys an enviable reputation
for its cask ales, housed on 150-year-old stillages. Local
Ringwood ales as well as national brews are served. It is a

continued

LYMINGTON continued

real community pub, with a dartboard and Sky TV, and open brick fireplaces used in winter. Good food includes home-cooked beefsteak and ale pie, jumbo cod, and sirloin steak. **OPEN:** 11-11 (Sun 12-10.30) **BAR MEALS:** L served all week 12-2.30 D served all week 6.30-9 Av main course £8 **RESTAURANT:** L served all week 12-2.30 D served all week 6-8.30 ⊜: Whitbread ◖: Weekly rotating guest ales. **FACILITIES:** Garden: beer garden, live entertainment Dogs allowed Water **NOTES:** Parking 8 **ROOMS:** 2 bedrooms en suite s£45 d£60 No children overnight **NOTES:** No credit cards

Mayflower Inn ♀
Kings Saltern Rd SO41 3QD ☎ 01590 672160 ▤ 01590 679180
e-mail: info@themayflower.uk.com
Dir: A337 towards New Milton, left at rdbt by White Hart, left to Rookes Ln, right at mini-rdbt, pub 0.75m
Solidly built mock-Tudor inn by the water's edge with views over the Solent and Lymington River. It's a favourite with yachtsmen and walkers with dogs, and welcomes families with its purpose-built play area for children and summer barbecues, weather permitting. The bar menu offers sandwiches, light meals, main meals and puds. For dinner in the non-smoking restaurant, expect starters such as antipasto platter or seared scallops; and mains like lamb en croûte or roasted duck sizzler. **OPEN:** 11-11 (Sun 12-10.30) **BAR MEALS:** L served all week 12-9.30 D served all week 6.30-9.30 **RESTAURANT:** L served all week 12-9.30 D served all week 6.30-9.30 ⊜: Enterprise Inns ◖: Ringwood Best, Fuller's London Pride, Greene King Abbot Ale & Old Speckled Hen. ♀: 8 **FACILITIES:** Child facs Garden: Large lawns, decking area Dogs allowed Water, baskets **NOTES:** Parking 30

LYNDHURST   Map 05 SU30

New Forest Inn ♀
Emery Down SO43 7DY ☎ 02380 282329 ▤ 02380 283216
Delightfully situated in the scenic New Forest, this rambling inn lies on land claimed from the crown by use of squatters' rights in the early 18th-century. Ale was once sold from a caravan which now forms the front lounge porchway. Lovely summer garden and welcoming bars with open fires and an extensive menu listing local game in season and plenty of fresh fish - whole Dover sole, fresh tuna, monkfish thermidor - alongside traditional pub meals. **OPEN:** 11-11 **BAR MEALS:** L served all week 12-3 D served all week 6-9.30 **RESTAURANT:** L served all week 11-10 D served all week 6-10 ⊜: Enterprise Inns ◖: Ringwood Best, Fullers London Pride, Abbot Ale, Old Hooky. **FACILITIES:** Garden: Food served outside Dogs allowed Water **NOTES:** Parking 20

The Oak Inn ⌇◡
Pinkney Ln, Bank SO43 7FE ☎ 02380 282350
An 18th-century New Forest inn, once a cider house, where ponies, pigs and deer graze outside. Behind the bay windows are antique pine, a traditional woodburner and an extensive collection of bric-à-brac. There is also a large beer garden for fine weather use. A selection of fresh seafood, including lobster, features among an interesting choice of dishes, including the local sausage of the week and the Oak's pie of the day. **OPEN:** 11.30-3 6-11.30 (all day Apr-Oct) (all day Sat-Sun) **BAR MEALS:** L served all week 12-2 D served all week 6-9.30 ⊜: Free House ◖: Ringwood Best, Holdens Black Country, Hop Back Summer Lightening, Young's Best. **FACILITIES:** Garden: Covered area and grassed area Dogs allowed Water **NOTES:** Parking 40

The Trusty Servant
Minstead SO43 7FY ☎ 02380 812137
e-mail: enquiries@trustyservant.co.uk
Popular New Forest pub overlooking the village green and retaining many Victorian features. The famous sign is taken from a 16th-century Winchester scholar's painting portraying the qualities of an ideal college servant. The menu prides itself on its real food, good value and generous portions. You might sample snacks, Tony's home-made pies, steaks from the grill, venison or tenderloin of pork. There's also a good choice of vegetarian dishes, such as sizzling Thai vegetable stir-fry. **OPEN:** 11-11 (Sun 12-10.30) **BAR MEALS:** L served all week 12-9 D served all week 7-10 **RESTAURANT:** L served all week 12-2.30 D served all week 7-10 ⊜: Enterprise Inns ◖: Ringwood Best, Fuller's London Pride, Wadworth 6X, Timothy Taylor Landlord. **FACILITIES:** Garden: Heated barn area seats 30, picnic benches Dogs allowed Water **NOTES:** Parking 16

MAPLEDURWELL   Map 05 SU65

The Gamekeepers ⌇◡ ♀
Tunworth Rd RG25 2LU ☎ 01256 322038 ▤ 01256 322038
e-mail: phil_costello64@hotmail.com
Dir: 3m from junct 6 M3. Turn right at the Hatch pub on A30 towards Hook. Gamekeepers is signposted
A very rural location for this 19th-century pub, which has a large secluded garden and, unusually, a well at its centre. An extensive menu is offered and all the food is made on the premises. Expect the likes of monkfish and tiger prawns in a creamy garlic sauce, duck breast on a bed of ginger and coriander noodles, and tenderloin of pork in sage and onion gravy. Game is also a feature in season. **OPEN:** 12-3 6-11 **BAR MEALS:** L served all week 12-2.30 D served all week 6.30-9.30 Sun 12-3 **RESTAURANT:** L served all week 12-2.30 D served all week 6.30-9.30 Sun 12-3 ⊜: Hall & Woodhouse ◖: Badger Best, Tanglefoot, Sussex Ales, Badgers Smooth. ♀: 12 **FACILITIES:** Garden: Large, secluded garden area Dogs allowed Water **NOTES:** Parking 50

MICHELDEVER   Map 05 SU53

Half Moon & Spread Eagle ♀
Winchester Rd SO21 3DG ☎ 01962 774339 ▤ 01962 774339
e-mail: team@thehalfmoonandspreadeagle.co.uk
Dir: Take A33 from Winchester towards Basingstoke. After 5m turn left after petrol station. Pub 0.5m on right
Old drovers' inn located in the heart of a pretty thatched and timbered Hampshire village, overlooking the cricket green. The pub, comprising three neatly furnished interconnecting rooms, has a real local feel, and has reverted to its old name having been the Dever Arms for eight years. An extensive menu ranges through Sunday roasts, Moon burgers, honeyed salmon supreme with lime courgettes, fresh battered cod, and half shoulder of minted lamb. **OPEN:** 12-3 6-11 **BAR MEALS:** L served all week 12-2 D served all week 6-9 Fri & Sat food served til 9.30 Av main course £8 **RESTAURANT:** L served all week 12-2 D served all week 6-9 (Fri-Sat 6-9.30) Av 3 course à la carte £20 ⊜: Greene King ◖: Greene King IPA Abbot Ale, Wadworth 6X, Tanners Jack. ♀: 8 **FACILITIES:** Child facs Children's licence Garden: Patio area, tables, chairs, grass area Dogs allowed Water provided **NOTES:** Parking 20

◆   Pubs with Red Diamonds are the top places in the AA's three, four and five diamond ratings

England

THE FOX

North Waltham,
Hampshire RG25 2BE

Tel: 01256 397288
email: info@thefox.org

Converted from three flint cottages, built in the early 1600s, this traditional village pub has a warm and welcoming atmosphere, with exposed beams and open wood fires. It is set in large award winning gardens, which are a riot of colour in the summer, with splendid views over the Hampshire countryside.

The cosy Village Bar stocks an excellent range of well kept real ales and offers a traditional 'Bar Snack' menu.

The Restaurant menus feature only the freshest local produce, game and daily delivered fresh fish, all wonderfully cooked and beautifully presented. The menu changes monthly to reflect the seasons. Starters include Seared King Scallops and Stilton & Mushroom Filo Tart. Main courses list the likes of Hampshire Venison, with glazed shallots,

wild mushrooms, savoy, creamed swede and sauté potatoes and a Port glaze, and Sea Bass, steamed with Ginger and Corriander. The puddings, all made daily, including Mango and Passionfruit Pavlova or Crème Brulée with a fruit compote are worth a visit alone.

The food is complemented by an extensive wine list with at least 10 wines available by the glass.

On the 4th Sunday of every month THE FOX features a buffet 'Singapore' Curry Lunch from 12.00–4.00pm.

The FOX is situated at the South edge of North Waltham village, close to J7 on the M3, just off the A30 and A303.

Open 11–11; Food Served 12–2.30 and 6.30–10.00.

grown and all meat and fish free range. Starters include grilled goats' cheese, and home-made soup, while typical examples of main courses are wild mushroom risotto, 8oz fillet of beef, and pan-fried scallops. To follow, expect sticky toffee pudding or lemon crème brûlée.
OPEN: 12-11 (Sun 12-10.30) Closed: 25 Dec, 1 Jan
BAR MEALS: L served all week 12-2 Fri-Sat 12-2.30 Av main course £13 **RESTAURANT:** L served Sun-Thurs 12-2 D served all week 6-9.30 Fri-Sun 12-2.30, 6-10 ◖: Timothy Taylor Landlords, Ringwood Best Bitter, Summer Lightning, London Pride. **FACILITIES:** Garden: Dogs allowed **NOTES:** Parking 40

NEW ALRESFORD   Map 05 SU53

Pick of the Pubs

The Globe on the Lake ♀
The Soke, Broad St SO24 9DB
☎ 01962 732294 ▤ 01962 732221
e-mail: duveen-conway@supanet.com
See Pick of the Pubs on page 236

NORTH WALTHAM   Map 05 SU54

The Fox ◌◌ ♀
RG25 2BE ☎ 01256 397288 ▤ 01256 398564
e-mail: info@thefox.org
Dir: *From M3 junct 7 take A30 towards Winchester. Village signed on R. Take 2nd signed road*

Built as three farm cottages in 1624, this peaceful village pub is situated down a quiet country lane enjoying splendid views across fields and farmland. Its three large flat gardens also have attractive flower beds. The menu changes monthly to reflect the seasonal produce available, but expect dishes such as chicken breast stuffed with parma ham, baby spinach and brie; Hampshire venison on a potato rosti; and a trio of award winning sausages with mash and onion gravy.
OPEN: 11-12 (all day w/end) **BAR MEALS:** L served all week 12.30-2.30 D served all week 6.30-10 (Last orders Sun 8.30) Av main course £10.18 **RESTAURANT:** L served all week 12.30-2.30 D served all week 6.30-10 Av 3 course à la carte £20.75 ▤: ◖: Gales HSB, Oakleaf Farmhouse, Bombardier, Brakespear. ♀: 11
FACILITIES: Child facs Children's licence Garden: Large, flat grass areas, countryside views Dogs allowed Water **NOTES:** Parking 40
See advert on this page

MONXTON   Map 05 SU34

Pick of the Pubs

The Black Swan NEW
High St SP11 8AW ☎ 01264 710260 ▤ 01264 710961

Situated close to the Portway Roman road, and dating from 1662, possibly earlier, the Black Swan was originally known as Ye Swan - the name changed in the mid-19th century when it was a popular watering hole for travellers. During the Second World War it was a haunt of fighter pilots based at nearby Middle Wallop. Unusually, even today, the pub kitchen is located at the front of the pub, while the bars and dining rooms are at the rear. It's quite common for ducks to come waddling in from the direction of the stream at the bottom of the Black Swan's garden. Dishes are home made from the freshest ingredients, and where possible all vegetables are locally

 Pubs offering a good choice of fish on their menu

continued

Pick of the Pubs

NEW ALRESFORD – HAMPSHIRE

The Globe on the Lake

In an outstanding setting on the banks of a reed-fringed lake and wildfowl sanctuary, The Globe is a convivial hostelry facing a prime Hampshire waterscape. The lake was created by Bishop de Lucy in the 12th century as a fish pond, and the great weir remains to this day an outstanding piece of medieval engineering.

An inn on the site since then was probably all but destroyed during Alresford's great fire of 1689. The Globe was rebuilt as a coaching inn, sitting at the bottom of the town's superb Georgian main street. Waterfowl frequent the garden, sunbathing between the picnic benches or by the children's playhouse. Inside the bar, a log fire blazes on cooler days, while a smart dining room and unusual garden room share the stunning outlook over the water. In summer freshly prepared food can be enjoyed in the garden and on the heated rear terrace. The daily changing blackboard features several fish dishes, like tiger prawns cooked with fresh lime and chilli; or fresh fillet of hake in beer batter with home-made

tartare sauce and chips. Other specialities may include Meon Valley pork and leek sausages; Alresford watercress flan with a hint of English mustard; oven-roasted partridge; or sautéed lambs' liver with crispy bacon. At least ten puddings, all at the same price, range from the typically English (bread and butter pudding, custard) to the exotic (citrus meringue crush with kumquat citrus sauce). A mailing list keeps regulars informed of special events, when the chef's team will prepare a menu to suit - such as the Hampshire Food Festival, a musical quiz, or Burns' Night. Real ales, of course, plenty of house wines including one from a Hampshire vineyard, and local apple juice all supplement the perfect views.

OPEN: 11-3 6-11 (Summer wknd 11-11, Winter Sun 12-8) Closed: 25-26 Dec
BAR MEALS: L served all week 12-2 D served all week 6.30-9 wknds 6.30-9.30 Av main course £9.25
RESTAURANT: L served all week 12-2 D served all week 6.30-9 wknds 6.30-9.30
🍺: Unique Pub Co
🍺: Wadworth 6X, Scottish Courage Directors, Henley Brakspear Bitter, Fuller's London Pride. ♀: 20
FACILITIES: Garden: Large lakeside garden Dogs allowed in the garden only Water

♀   Map 05 SU53
The Soke, Broad St SO24 9DB
☎ 01962 732294
🖹 01962 732221
✉ mwjbyrne@aol.com
Dir: Telephone for directions

England

OLD BASING
Map 05 SU65

The Millstone ♀
Bartons Ln RG24 8AE ☎ 01256 331153 & 473560
Dir: From M3 junct 6 follow brown signs to Basing House
Enjoying a charming rural location beside the River Loddon, close to a country park and Old Basing House, close to Hampshire's Civil War ruins, this attractive old building is a popular lunchtime spot for nearby office workers. Typical dishes might include chilli con carne, salmon goujons, lasagne, Thai sweet and sour pork, cod and chips, lamb balti and a traditional Sunday roast. Basket meals, vegetarian options, jacket potatoes and baguettes also feature.
OPEN: 11.30-2.30 6-11 (Fri & Sat 11.30-11, Sun 12-10.30)
BAR MEALS: L served all week 12-2 D served all week 6.30-9 Av main course £5.75 ☺: Wadworth ◀: Wadworth 6X, Wadworth JCB, Henrys Smooth, Beer Blonde & Henrys IPA. ♀: 9
FACILITIES: Garden: Patio and lawn area adjoining river Dogs allowed except when food being served **NOTES:** Parking 50

OVINGTON
Map 05 SU53

Pick of the Pubs

The Bush 🐟 ♀
SO24 0RE ☎ 01962 732764 ▤ 01962 735130
e-mail: thebushinn@wadworth.co.uk
Dir: A31 from Winchester, E to Alton & Farnham, approx 6m turn left off dual carriageway to Ovington. 0.5m to pub

Tucked away down a meandering lane on the Pilgrim's Way, this delightful rose-covered pub must have been a pleasant distraction from spiritual matters. The River Itchen runs at the bottom of the pretty garden, and a gentle riverside stroll will set you up in readiness for a lingering meal. If the landscape looks familiar, it's because more than one film crew has used this spot to give an evocative sense of England's rural charms. Log fires and plenty of old wood furnishings continue the theme inside. The bar serves lunch and dinner; expect simple dishes cooked with flair. The menu makes use of local produce, changing regularly according to availability. Starters may include a home-made smoked trout mousse; or chicken liver paté, followed by mustard and leek crusted roast lamb served on sweet potato and red onion mash; or an old favourite like luxury fish pie.
OPEN: 11-3 6-11 (Sun 12-3, 7-10.30) Closed: Dec 25
BAR MEALS: L served all week 12-2 D served Mon-Sat 6.30-9.30 Av main course £12.25 ☺: Wadworth ◀: Wadworth 6X, IPA & Farmers Glory, JCB & occasional guest beers. ♀: 12
FACILITIES: Pretty garden alongside river Dogs allowed Water **NOTES:** Parking 40

OWSLEBURY
Map 05 SU52

The Ship Inn ♀
Whites Hill SO21 1LT ☎ 01962 777358 ▤ 01962 777458
e-mail: theshipinn@freeuk.com
Dir: M3 junct 11 take B3335. Follow Owslebury signs

Wonderful views of the South Downs to the Solent can be enjoyed from this 300 year-old inn, standing high on a chalk ridge. Old ship's timbers and an open fire create a warm atmosphere. Daily menus might include Shetland mussels with herbs and cream; Gressingham duck breast with honey-roasted butternut squash; and tagliatelle with feta, roasted peppers and spiced tomato sauce. Good selection of baguettes at lunchtime. Popular with families.
OPEN: 11-3 6-11 (Sun 12-10.30, Sat Apr-Sep 11-11 Jul-Aug 11-11 all week) **BAR MEALS:** L served all week 12-2 D served all week 6.30-9.30 Sun lunches to 3 Av main course £8.95
RESTAURANT: L served all week 12-2 D served all week 6.30-9.30 Sun lunch 12-3, dinner 6.30-9 Av 3 course à la carte £19.95 ☺: Greene King ◀: Greene King IPA, Morland Original & Ruddles County, Pots, Abbots. ♀: 12 **FACILITIES:** Child facs Garden with BBQ, pond, horse park Dogs allowed Water **NOTES:** Parking 50

PETERSFIELD
Map 05 SU72

The Good Intent ♀
40-46 College St GU31 4AF ☎ 01730 263838 ▤ 01730 302239
e-mail: pstuart@goodintent.freeserve.co.uk

Candlelit tables, open fires and well-kept ales characterise this 16th-century pub, and in summer, flower tubs and hanging baskets festoon the front patio. Regular gourmet evenings are held and there is live music on Sunday evenings. Sausages are a speciality (up to 12 varieties) alongside a daily pie and the likes of seafood chowder and Thai fish curry. As members of the Campaign For Real Food they have well-established links with the local junior school.
OPEN: 11-3 5.30-11 **BAR MEALS:** L served all week 12-2.30 D served all week 6-9.30 **RESTAURANT:** L served all week 12-2 D served all week 6-9.30 ☺: Gales ◀: Gale's HSB, GB, Buster. **FACILITIES:** Garden: Small patio with lots of flowers Dogs allowed Water **NOTES:** Parking 10

237

PETERSFIELD continued

The Trooper Inn
Alton Rd, Froxfield GU32 1BD ☎ 01730 827293 ▤ 01730 827103
e-mail: info@trooperinn.com web: www.trooperinn.com
Dir: From A3/A272 Winchester exit, towards Petersfield then left at the 1st rndt towards Steep. Stay on this road for 3m and pub is on right.
An upgraded roadside inn enjoying an isolated downland position west of Petersfield, the Trooper is also known as 'The Pub at the Top of the Hill'. There is a relaxed atmosphere throughout the spacious, rustic, pine-furnished interior. Guest ales and decent wines by the glass accompany home-cooked food, like Aberdeen Angus fillet steak; duck breast with spiced apricots in a white wine sauce; pork medallions with wild mushrooms; and spinach and ricotta ravioli.
OPEN: 12-3 6-12 Closed: Dec 25-6, Jan 1 **BAR MEALS:** L served all week 12-2 D served all week 7-9.30 **RESTAURANT:** L served all week 12-2 D served all week 7-9.30 🍽: Free House ◀: Ringwood Best, Fortyniner, Interbrew Bass, guest ales. **FACILITIES:** Garden: Attractive gardens **NOTES:** Parking 30 **ROOMS:** 8 bedrooms en suite s£69 d£89 (♦♦♦♦)

The White Horse Inn
Priors Dean GU32 1DA ☎ 01420 588387 ▤ 01420 588387
e-mail: info@stuartinns.com
Dir: A3/A272 to Winchester/Petersfield. In Petersfield left to Steep, 5m then right at small X-rds to E Tisted, 2nd drive on right

Also known as the 'Pub With No Name' as it has no sign, this splendid 17th-century farmhouse was originally used as a forge for passing coaches. The blacksmith sold beer to the travellers while their horses were attended to. Hearty pub grub nowadays includes ciabattas, fillet steaks and beer-battered fish. Special fresh fish dishes are available on Fridays and Saturdays.
OPEN: 11-2.30 6-11 (Sun 12-4.30, 7-10.30) **BAR MEALS:** L served all week 12-2.30 D served Mon-Sat 7-9.30 **RESTAURANT:** L served all week 12-2.30 D served Mon-Sat 7-9.30 🍽: Gales ◀: No Name Best, No Name Strong, Fullers London Pride, Bass.
FACILITIES: Garden: Dogs allowed Water, dog biscuits
NOTES: Parking 60

PILLEY
Map 05 SZ39

The Fleur de Lys ♀
Pilley St SO41 5QG ☎ 01590 672158
Arguably the oldest in the New Forest, tracing its origins back to 1096, this traditional thatched pub has a stone flagged hallway, low beamed ceilings and open log fires. Fresh food is prepared daily using local suppliers, and results include Lolly's fish or steak, kidney and Guinness pies, pork hocks and half shoulders of lamb. Fish from the specials board and a variety of inspired dishes with oriental influences keep customers - and the kitchen - on their toes.
OPEN: 11-2.30 5.30-11 (Sun 12-3, 7-10.30) 25 Dec Closed eve
BAR MEALS: L served all week 12-2 D served all week 6.30-9.30 (Sun 7.30-9.30) Av main course £6.75 **RESTAURANT:** 12-2 6.30-9.30 🍽: ◀: Ringwood Best, plus guest ales.
FACILITIES: Garden: Food served outside Dogs allowed Water
NOTES: Parking 18

PORTSMOUTH & SOUTHSEA
Map 05 SZ69

The Wine Vaults ♀
43-47 Albert Rd, Southsea PO5 2SF
☎ 023 92864712 ▤ 023 92865544 e-mail: winevaults@freeuk.com
Originally several Victorian shops, now converted into a Victorian-style alehouse with wooden floors, panelled walls, and seating from old churches and schools. Partly due to the absence of a jukebox or fruit machine, the atmosphere here is relaxed and there is a good range of real ales and good-value food. A typical menu includes beef stroganoff, Tuscan vegetable bean stew, grilled gammon steak, salads, sandwiches, and Mexican specialities. Look out for celebs appearing at the local theatre.
OPEN: 12-11 (12-10.30 Sun) Closed: 1 Jan **BAR MEALS:** L served all week 12-9.30 D served all week **RESTAURANT:** L served all week 12-9.30 D served all week 🍽: Free House ◀: Hop Back Gilbert's First Brew & Summer Lightning, Scottish Courage Best, Fuller's London Pride. ♀: 20 **FACILITIES:** Children's licence Garden: Patio area Dogs allowed

ROCKBOURNE
Map 05 SU11

Pick of the Pubs

The Rose & Thistle 🐟 ♀
SP6 3NL ☎ 01725 518236
e-mail: enquiries@roseandthistle.co.uk
See Pick of the Pubs on opposite page

ROCKFORD
Map 05 SU10

The Alice Lisle NEW ♀
Rockford Green BH24 3NA ☎ 01425 474700 ▤ 01425 483332
Well-known New Forest pub with landscaped gardens overlooking a lake, popular with walkers and visitors to the region. It was named after the widow of one of Cromwell's supporters who gave shelter to two fugitives from the Battle of Sedgemoor. Choose from a varied menu which might include salmon and crab cakes, honey minted lamb shoulder, liver and bacon, and Mexican enchilada. There's a good range of starters and children's dishes.
OPEN: 11-3 5.30-11 (Sun all day) **BAR MEALS:** L served all week 12-2 D served all week 6-9 Sun 12-8 Av main course £7
RESTAURANT: L served all week 12-2 D served all week 6-9 Sun 12-8 🍽: Gales ◀: HSB, Gales, Ringwood, Winter Brew. ♀: 7
FACILITIES: Child facs Children's licence Garden: Large garden with lots of seating, aviary Dogs allowed **NOTES:** Parking 150

Pick of the Pubs

The Rose & Thistle

Nearly 200 years ago, two long, low 16th-century cottages were converted to create this village pub, which still displays many of its original features. Conveniently placed for visiting the New Forest, Salisbury, Breamore House and Rockbourne's very own Roman villa, it's a picture postcard pub if ever there was one, with a stunning rose arch, flowers around the door and a delightful setting at the top of a street of thatched cottages and period houses.

Inside, the low-beamed bar and dining area are furnished with country-house fabrics, polished oak tables and chairs, cushioned settles and carved benches, with even more homely touches created by floral arrangements and magazines. Open fires make it a cosy retreat in cold weather, while the summer sun encourages visitors to sit in the neat front garden where they can watch the feathery goings-on in the quaint dovecote. For the last 13 years landlord Tim Norfolk has maintained his tradition of serving fine fresh food, good ales and some very decent wines from Europe, South America, South Africa and the Antipodes. Bar snacks and lunch favourites -

locally made sausages, stir-fried garlic prawns, and bacon and mushrooms on toast, for example - are supplemented by a good choice of blackboard specials including fresh fish. Veal escalope with walnut and roquefort sauce; venison with cider and fruit chutney; and a variety of steaks and sauces are usually available at dinner, while for vegetarians there's vegetable stir-fry with a mixture of nuts, and herb and garlic tagliatelle with a julienne of vegetables. Tim knows which puddings are popular - they're all there: sticky toffee and date, steamed syrup sponge, bread and butter and chocolate roulade. On Sundays there's traditional roast rare sirloin of beef with Yorkshire pud.

OPEN: 11-3 6-11 (Sun 12-10.30)
Oct-Apr closed Sun from 8
BAR MEALS: L served all week
12-2.30 D served all week 6.30-9.30
(Sun seasonal variation) Av main
course £10
RESTAURANT: L served all week
12-2.30 D served all week 6.30-9.30
(Sun seasonal variation) Av 3 course
à la carte £16
🍺: Free House
🍺: Fuller's London Pride, Adnams
Broadside, Wadworth 6X, Hop Back
Summer Lightning. ♀: 18
FACILITIES: Children's licence
English country garden
NOTES: Parking 28

🐟 ♀   Map 05 SU11
SP6 3NL
☎ 01725 518236
🅔 enquiries@roseandthistle.co.uk
Dir: Follow Rockbourne signs
from B3078 & A354

England

Pick of the Pubs

The Dukes Head ♀
Greatbridge Rd SO51 0HB ☎ 01794 514450

This rambling 400-year-old pub, covered in flowers during the summer, is just a stone's throw from the Test, England's premier trout river. Food is largely locally sourced, respects the seasons as far as possible, and is freshly prepared. Several menus are offered: monthly carte, daily fish, mid-week special, snack lunch, evening bar snack and the 'Unchangeable' which, in addition to an interesting half-dozen starters, offers main courses of curry of the day; Périgord duck leg confit; and in a twist on what you might expect, coq au vin blanc. From the carte come oxtail cottage pie; slow-braised belly of pork stuffed with apples, celery, plums and pancetta; and beef fillet bourguignonne. Brandade of mackerel is one of four fish starters that could precede whole pan-fried trout meunière; roasted monkfish on the bone; or fresh cod fillet in tempura, on the specialist fish menu.
OPEN: 11-11 **BAR MEALS:** L served Mon-Sun 12-2.30 D served Tue-Sat 6-8 (No lunch Sun) **RESTAURANT:** L served all week 12-2.30 D served Tue-Sat 6-9 (Fri-Sat 6-9.30) Av 2 course fixed price £12.50 ⌷: Free House ◖: Fuller's London Pride, Ringwood Best Bitter, Courage Directors. ♀: 8
FACILITIES: Garden: Large garden near river, approx 60 seats Dogs allowed **NOTES:** Parking 50

The Mill Arms ◌ ♀
Barley Hill, Dunbridge SO51 0LF ☎ 01794 340401
e-mail: themillarms@btconnect.com web: www.millarms.co.uk
This attractive 18th-century coaching inn enjoys a reputation for good food, fine wines and a solid selection of real ales. Surrounded by colourful gardens, the building retains its flagstone floors, oak beams and large open fireplaces. The varied menus range from favourites like ham, egg and chips to more contemporary fare: expect pork loin stuffed with apricot and thyme; or balsamic roasted vegetables with Parmesan crust and salad.
OPEN: 12-3 6-11 (open all day Fri-Sun) **BAR MEALS:** L served all week 12-2.30 D served all week 6-9.30 Av main course £10 **RESTAURANT:** L served all week 12-2.30 D served all week 6-9.30 Av 3 course à la carte £10 ⌷: Free House ◖: Ringwood Best, Hampshire Meddler, guest ales. ♀: 8 **FACILITIES:** Garden: Large garden, patio area Dogs allowed Water **NOTES:** Parking 90

Pick of the Pubs

The Three Tuns NEW ♀
58 Middlebridge St SO51 8HL
☎ 01794 512639 ▤ 01794 514524
e-mail: threetunsromsey@aol.co.uk
Dir: Situated on Romsey bypass 0.5m from main entrance of Broadlands Estate.
Around 400 years old, centrally placed in this old market town, with its fine abbey, and a short walk from the front gates of Broadlands, country seat of Earl Mountbatten. High quality local ingredients form the basis of all meals, typified by seared scallops with sweetcorn fritters as a starter, then sirloin of beef with caramelised onions and blue cheese, followed by chocolate brownie with vanilla ice cream. Game comes from the Broadlands estate.
OPEN: 12-11 **BAR MEALS:** L served all week 12-2 D served Mon-Sat 7-9.30 Closed Sun evening Av main course £12
RESTAURANT: L served all week 12-2 D served Mon-Sat 7-9.30 Closed Sun evening Av 3 course à la carte £29 ◖: Ringwood Best, Gale's HSB. ♀: 8 **FACILITIES:** Garden: Patio outside Dogs allowed **NOTES:** Parking 20

The Castle Inn ♀
1 Finchdean Rd PO9 6DA ☎ 023 9241 2494 ▤ 023 9241 2494
e-mail: rogerburrell@btconnect.com
Dir: N of Havant take B2149 to Rowlands Castle. Pass green, under rail bridge, pub 1st on left opp Stansted Park
A Victorian building directly opposite Stansted Park, part of the Forest of Bere. Richard the Lionheart supposedly hunted here, and the house and grounds are open to the public for part of the year. Traditional atmosphere is boosted by wooden floors and fires in both bars. Menu options include pies, lasagne, curry, steaks, local sausages, and chilli.
OPEN: 11-11 (Sun 12-10.30) **BAR MEALS:** L served all week 12-6 D served summer-all week, winter Tues-Sat 6-10 Sun 12-3 Av main course £7 **RESTAURANT:** L served all week 12-6 D served Summer-all, Winter-Tue-Sat 6-9 Sun 12-3 Av 3 course à la carte £17.50 ⌷: Gales ◖: Gales Butser, HSB & GB. **FACILITIES:** Garden: Grassed area with benches **NOTES:** Parking 30

The Fountain Inn ♦♦♦♦
34 The Green PO9 6AB ☎ 023 9241 2291 ▤ 023 9241 2291
e-mail: fountaininn@amserve.com
Once a coach house, and now a lovingly refurbished Georgian building on a village green. Owned by one-time Van Morrison band member Herbie Armstrong, who holds frequent live music gigs here. Menus from a Savoy-trained chef offer 'real' corned beef, parsnip and carrot hash; and potted Selsey crab and prawns at both lunchtime and dinner. Some dishes, like beetroot risotto, broad beans and parmesan, for instance, appear for dinner only.
OPEN: 12-2.30 5-11 (Fri-Sun 12-11) **BAR MEALS:** L served Tue-Sun 12-3 D served Tue-Sat 6.30-9.30 **RESTAURANT:** L served Tue-Sun 12-3 D served Tue-Sat 6.30-9.30 ⌷: Greene King ◖: Ruddles IPA, Abbot, Ruddles Cask. **FACILITIES:** Child facs Garden: Enclosed back garden, eight tables Dogs allowed **NOTES:** Parking 20 **ROOMS:** 4 bedrooms en suite 1 family room s£25 d£50

♦ Diamond rating for inspected guest accommodation

 Principal Beers for sale

England

ST MARY BOURNE Map 05 SU45

The Bourne Valley Inn
SP11 6BT ☎ 01264 738361 ▤ 01264 738126
e-mail: bournevalleyinn@wessexinns.fsnet.co.uk
Located in the charming Bourne valley, this popular
traditional inn is the ideal setting for conferences, exhibitions,
weddings and other notable occasions. The riverside garden
abounds with wildlife, and children can happily let off steam
in the special play area. Typical menu includes deep-fried brie
or a cocktail of prawns, followed by rack of lamb with a
redcurrant and port sauce, salmon and prawn tagliatelle,
steak and mushroom pie, crispy haddock and chips, and
warm duck salad.
OPEN: 11-11 **BAR MEALS:** L served all week 12-2 D served all
week 7-9 **RESTAURANT:** L served all week 12-2 D served all week
7-9.30 ☻: Free House ◖: Draught Bass, Flowers, Brakspeare.
FACILITIES: Child facs Children's licence Garden: Riverside,
secluded garden Dogs allowed Water & biscuits provided
NOTES: Parking 50 **ROOMS:** 9 bedrooms en suite s£50 d£60
(♦♦♦)

The George Inn
SP11 6BG ☎ 01264 738340 ▤ 01264 738877
Dir: M3 J8/A303, then A34 towards Newbury. Turn at Whitchurch & follow
signs for St Mary Bourne
Listed village inn in the picturesque Tarrant valley, with a bar
full of cricket memorabilia, one dining room decorated with
regimental battle scenes, and another one with a mural of the
River Test. Expect steak and Tanglefoot pie, fajitas, and local
sausage and mash, served indoors or in the courtyard patio.
OPEN: 11-3 5-11 (Open all day Sat-Sun in Summer)
BAR MEALS: L served all week 12-2 D served all week 7-9.30
Av main course £8 **RESTAURANT:** L served all week 12-3.30
D served all week 7-9.30 ☻: Hall & Woodhouse ◖: Badger Best &
Tanglefoot. **FACILITIES:** Garden: Patio, courtyard Dogs allowed
Water bowl, biscuits **NOTES:** Parking 40

SELBORNE Map 05 SU73

The Selborne Arms NEW ▷ ☖ ♀
High St GU34 3JR ☎ 01420 511247 ▤ 01420 511754
Dir: From A3 follow B3006, pub is on the left in centre of village
A traditional village pub, 17th-century in origin, known for its
friendly atmosphere and good food; the latter is sourced
extensively from Hampshire growers and suppliers, and all
GM-free. Plenty of light lunch choices include breaded plaice
goujons; half roast duck with orange and elderflower sauce;
locally made Toulouse sausages and mash; and home-made
curry. Much the same line-up at dinner, with the addition of
chargrilled sirloin of English beef. Blackboards list specials
and desserts.
OPEN: 11-3 6-11 (Sun 12-10.30) (Fri 5.30-11)
BAR MEALS: L served all week 12-2 D served all week 7-9 Av main
course £7.50 ◖: Courage Best, Ringwood 49er, Cheriton Pots, local
guest ales. ♀: 9 **FACILITIES:** Garden: Large grassed area, trees,
patio Dogs allowed in the garden only, on leads **NOTES:** Parking 7

SOUTHAMPTON Map 05 SU41

The Cowherds ♀
The Common SO15 7NN
Dir: From J13 on M3, follow signs for Southampton onto the A33. The
Cowherds is on the right hand side of the avenue (A33) after 1.5 miles
Located at the heart of Southampton Common, the Cowherds
offers easy access to both countryside and city. It was once a
popular haunt of cattle drovers en route to London - hence

continued

the name. Inside is a variety of charming traditional features,
including open fires, oak beams, flagstone floors and wood
panelling, with hops hanging from the ceiling. Try the ham
hock with a creamy wholegrain mustard sauce, 8oz sirloin
grilled to individual preference, or the pork, apple and
Somerset cider sausages with cheddar mash.
OPEN: 12-11 (Sun 12-10.30) **RESTAURANT:** L served all week
D served all week Av 3 course à la carte £16.70 ☻: Vintage Inns
◖: Tetley Bitter, Cask Bass. ♀: 16 **FACILITIES:** Garden: Patio with
floral displays **NOTES:** Parking 60

St Jacques Bar & Restaurant ♀
Romsey Rd, Copythorne SO40 2PE ☎ 023 8081 2321
& 8081 2800 ▤ 023 8081 2158
Dir: On A31 between Cadnam & Ower, of M27 between junctions 1 & 2
Once called The Old Well, this large pub and restaurant
caters for visitors to the New Forest. Set in attractive
surroundings, it offers comfortable seating and a wide choice
of well-cooked food. Light bites might include sausages and
mash, cottage pie, and ham with eggs and chips, while the
restaurant carte offers braised oxtail in a red wine sauce,
breast of duckling with orange sauce, and seabass with king
scallops. The Sunday lunch attracts diners from far and wide.
OPEN: 11-3 5.30-11 (Sun 12-10.30) **BAR MEALS:** L served all
week 12-2.15 D served all week 6-9 Av main course £9
RESTAURANT: L served all week 1-2.15 D served all week 6-9.30
Av 3 course à la carte £20.50 Av 2 course fixed price £10 ☻: Free
House ◖: Ringwood Best. **FACILITIES:** Children's licence Garden
NOTES: Parking 100

Pick of the Pubs

The White Star Tavern & Dining Rooms ♀
28 Oxford St SO14 3DJ ☎ 023 8082 1990 ▤ 023 8090 4982
e-mail: manager@whitestartavern.co.uk
Dir: Exit M3 junct 13. Take A33 to Southampton, head towards Ocean
Village and Marina.

This former seafarers' hotel, located in this historic and
sensitively restored part of the city, is close to the city
centre and the marina and has a lovely cosmopolitan
atmosphere. It has been stylishly renovated to
incorporate a good blend of old and new, with its cosy
bar area with original flagstone floors and fireplaces,
and a stylish panelled dining room with huge windows.
The tavern prides itself on a frequently changing
modern British menu using fresh and locally sourced
ingredients. Quality dishes include starters like
chargrilled sardines with a chorizo salad, followed by
rib-eye steak and chips with roasted field mushrooms,
tomato and aged balsamic vinegar, and desserts like
chocolate cappuccino mousse. On sunny days patrons
can enjoy a cocktail and watch the world go by while

continued

England

SOUTHAMPTON continued

dining at pavement tables on Southampton's restaurant row.
OPEN: 12-11 Closed: 25-26 Dec, 1 Jan **BAR MEALS:** L served all week 12-3 D served all week 6-9.30 Fri and Sat 6-10, food all day Sun Av main course £10 **RESTAURANT:** L served all week 12-3 D served all week 6.30-10.30 Sun 12-9 Av 3 course à la carte £25 ●: London Pride, Bass. ♀: 8

SPARSHOLT — Map 05 SU43

Pick of the Pubs

The Plough Inn ◇ ♀
Main Rd SO21 2NW ☎ 01962 776353 ▤ 01962 776400

See Pub Walk on page 222
See Pick of the Pubs on opposite page

STEEP — Map 05 SU72

Pick of the Pubs

Harrow Inn ♀
GU32 2DA ☎ 01730 262685
Dir: *Off A3 to A272, left through Sheet, take road opp church (school lane) then over A3 by-pass bridge*
Fans of this well-known unspoilt gem which has been in the McCutcheon family since 1929, will be saddened to know that the popular landlady Ellen McCutcheon is no more. However the good news is that her daughters, who have worked here since they left school and took over the running of the pub last year, are determined to keep things exactly as that grand old lady would have wanted them. Tucked away down a sleepy lane outside Petersfield, the tile-hung 500-year-old building and its delightful cottage garden are popular with walkers following the Hangers Way. The two characterful bars, each with scrubbed wooden tables, boarded walls and seasonal flower arrangements, are the perfect environment to relax over a decent pint of local ale. The cooking has now been taken over by Nisa McCutcheon, and she intends to keep serving home cooked food just like before. So, little has altered over the years - and why should it? A true survivor, the Harrow remains, as ever, resistant to change.
OPEN: 12-2.30 6-11 (Sat 11-3, 6-11, Sun 12-3, 7-10.30) Closed Sun eve Oct-Apr Closed: Dec25 evening **BAR MEALS:** L served all week 12-2 D served all week 7-9 ◉: Free House ●: Ringwood Best, Cheriton Diggers Gold & Pots Ale, Ballards Best. **FACILITIES:** Garden: Wild cottage garden Dogs allowed on lead, water available **NOTES:** Parking 15

STOCKBRIDGE — Map 05 SU33

Mayfly ♀
Testcombe SO20 6AZ ☎ 01264 860283 ▤ 861304
Dir: *Between A303 & A30, on A3057*
The Mayfly has one of the prettiest locations in Hampshire, on an island between the River Test and another little river to the rear. Access from the car park is via a small bridge. The current licensees have been here 19 years, and they offer a buffet-style selection of hot and cold meats, quiches and pies,
continued

along with a few hot daily specials. The pub is ideal for walkers on the nearby Test Way.

Mayfly

OPEN: 10-11 **BAR MEALS:** L served all week 11.30-9 D served all week Av main course £8 ◉: Enterprise Inns ●: Wadworth 6X, Interbrew, Abbot Ale, HSB. ♀: 20 **FACILITIES:** Garden: Riverside Garden Dogs allowed **NOTES:** Parking 48

The Peat Spade ♀
Longstock SO20 6DR ☎ 01264 810612
e-mail: peat.spade@virgin.net
Dir: *Telephone for directions*
Tucked away in the Test Valley close to Hampshire's finest chalk stream is this red-brick and gabled Victorian pub with unusual paned windows. It offers an informal atmosphere, a decent pint of Hampshire ale, and a satisfying meal: salmon, haddock and scallop fish pie; local pork medallions with hoi sin sauce; or baked goat's cheese with sweet potatoes and parsley oil dressing. Good use of local organic produce.
OPEN: 11.30-3 6.30-11 Closed: Dec 25-26 & 31Dec-1 Jan Sun closed eve **BAR MEALS:** L served Tue-Sun 12-2.30 D served Tue-Sun 7-9.30 **RESTAURANT:** L served Tue-Sun 12-2 D served Tue-Sun 7-9.30 ◉: Free House ●: Ringwood Best, Ringwood 49er & guest ales. **FACILITIES:** Garden: Raised terrace, teak seating, lawn area Dogs allowed on a lead **NOTES:** Parking 22 No credit cards

STRATFIELD TURGIS — Map 05 SU65

The Wellington Arms ★★★ ♀
RG27 0AS ☎ 01256 882214 ▤ 01256 882934
e-mail: wellington.arms@virgin.net
Dir: *On A33 between Basingstoke & Reading*
Standing at an entrance to the ancestral home of the Duke of Wellington, this 17th-century former farmhouse is now a Grade II listed hotel with some period bedrooms in the original building. Well-kept real ales go down well with a good range of eating options, including roasted vegetable lasagne, steak and mushroom pie, lime-scented chicken breast, parmesan crusted cod with dauphinoise potatoes, half-shell green lipped mussels, and smoked haddock with mash, cheese sauce and poached egg.
OPEN: 11-11 (Sun 12-10.30) **BAR MEALS:** L served all week 12-2.30 D served all week 6-10 Sun 9.30 Av main course £9 **RESTAURANT:** L served Sun-Fri 12-2 D served Mon-Sat 6.30-9.30 Av 3 course à la carte £27 ◉: Woodhouse Inns ●: Badger Best Bitter & Tanglefoot. **FACILITIES:** Child facs Garden: Patio area with grass area to side and rear Dogs allowed **NOTES:** Parking 60 **ROOMS:** 30 bedrooms en suite 2 family rooms s£95 d£105

 Brewery/Company

Pick of the Pubs

SPARSHOLT – HAMPSHIRE

The Plough Inn

The Plough, in the same village as the well-known agricultural college, is close enough to Winchester to draw many of its well-heeled citizens out for a meal or just a drink. It seems to have started life about 200 years ago as a coach house for Sparsholt Manor on the other side of the road, becoming an alehouse just 50 years later.

From the outside, you can see that it has been much extended but, once inside, the main bar and dining areas blend together very harmoniously, helped by judicious use of farmhouse-style pine tables, a mix of wooden and upholstered seats, collections of agricultural implements, stone jars, wooden wine box end-panels and dried hops. The dining tables to the left of the entrance have a view across open fields to wooded downland, and it's at this end you'll find a blackboard menu offering lighter dishes exemplified by peppered tomato and olive pasta; spicy oriental beef noodles; salmon and smoked haddock lasagne; and chilli and chickpea cakes with avocado salsa. The menu board at

the right-hand end of the bar offers meals of a slightly more serious nature - maybe breast of chicken filled with mushrooms on a garlic and bacon sauce; lamb shank with braised red cabbage and rosemary jus; pan-fried tuna with crushed new potatoes and olives in herb oil, and several other fish dishes. Lunchtime regulars know that 'doorstep' is the most apt description for the tasty sandwiches. Puddings include fruit crumbles, or British cheeses as a popular alternative. Wadworth of Devizes supplies the real ales and there's a good wine selection. Booking is definitely advised for any meal. There's a good-sized car park and a delightful garden.

OPEN: 11-3 6-11 (Sun 12-3, 6-10.30)
Closed: 25 Dec
BAR MEALS: L served all week 12-2
D served all week 6-9 Av main
course £8.95
RESTAURANT: L served all week
12-2 D served all week 6-9
Av 3 course à la carte £25
🍺: Wadworth
🍺: Wadworth Henry's IPA, 6X,
Farmers Glory & Old Timer. ♀: 12
FACILITIES: Child facs Garden:
Patio, Lawn, Play Area Dogs allowed
on leads **NOTES:** Parking 90

🌳 ♀   Map 05 SU43
Main Rd SO21 2NW
☎ 01962 776353
📠 01962 776400
Dir: From Winchester take
B3049 (A272) W, L to Sparsholt.
Inn 1m

England

TANGLEY
Map 05 SU35

The Fox Inn ♀
SP11 0RY ☎ 01264 730276 📠 01264 730478
e-mail: thefoxinn@computorpost.net
Dir: 4m N of Andover
The 300-year-old brick and flint cottage that has been the Fox
since 1830 stands on a small crossroads, miles, it seems, from
anywhere. The blackboard menu offers reliably good
lunchtime snacks and imaginative evening dishes. Enjoy a
drink the tiny, friendly bar, and enjoy a meal in the
unpretentious restaurant. Dishes are based on the finest local
produce. Recent change of ownership.
OPEN: 12-3 6-11 Sun 7-10.30 **BAR MEALS:** L served all week 12-2
D served all week 6-9 Sun 7-9 **RESTAURANT:** L served all week
12-2 D served all week 6-9 🍽: Free House 🍺: Flowers IPA, Fullers
London Pride, Bass, Adnams. ♀: 12 **FACILITIES:** Children welcome
Garden: Front patio Dogs allowed Water provided
NOTES: Parking 50

TICHBORNE
Map 05 SU53

Pick of the Pubs

The Tichborne Arms
SO24 0NA ☎ 01962 733760 📠 01962 733760
e-mail: n.burt@btinternet.com
*Dir: Off A31 towards Alresford, after 200yds right at sign for
Tichborne*

A heavily thatched free house in the heart of the Itchen
Valley, dating from 1423 but destroyed by fire and rebuilt
three times; the present red-brick building was erected in
1939. An interesting history is attached to this idyllic rural
hamlet, which was dramatised in the feature film *The
Tichborne Claimant*. The pub displays much memorabilia
connected with the film's subject, Tom Castro's
impersonation and unsuccessful claim to the title and
estates of Tichborne. Real ales straight from the cask are
served in the comfortable atmospheric bars, and all food
is home made. Traditional choices range from steak, ale
and stilton pie; crab salad; pheasant casserole; chicken,
tarragon and mushroom pie; and fish pie to toasted
sandwiches and filled jacket potatoes. Expect hearty old-
fashioned puddings. A large, well-stocked garden is ideal
for summer eating and drinking, with a beer festival the
first weekend in June. New owners Nigel and Sarah Burt.
OPEN: 11.30-2.30 6-11 **BAR MEALS:** L served all week
12-1.45 D served all week 6.30-9.45 🍽: Free House
🍺: Ringwood Best, Wadworth 6X, Otter Ale, Several Guest
Beers. **FACILITIES:** Garden: Large country garden seats around
70 Dogs allowed Water, biscuit **NOTES:** Parking 30

UPPER FROYLE
Map 05 SU74

The Hen & Chicken Inn ♀
GU34 4JH ☎ 01420 22115 📠 01420 23021
e-mail: bookings@henandchicken.co.uk
Dir: 2m form Alton, on A31 next to petrol station
A 16th-century inn, once the haunt of highwaymen and
retaining a traditional atmosphere enhanced by large open
fires, panelling and beams. Close by is the delightful old
Georgian town of Farnham, famous for its castle, Maltings arts
complex and various listed buildings. The tempting menu has
everything from fillet of halibut, chargrilled rib eye steak, and
rich venison casserole, to Cumberland sausages, and penne
pasta. Specials might include risotto of Cornish crab and
grilled marlin loin.
OPEN: 11-3 5.30-11 (Fri-Sat 11-11 Sun 12-10.30)
BAR MEALS: L served all week 12-2.30 D served all week 6-9 Sun
12-9 Av main course £7.50 **RESTAURANT:** L served all week
12-2.30 D served all week 6-9 Sun 12-9 Av 3 course à la carte £22
🍽: Hall & Woodhouse 🍺: Badger Best, Tanglefoot, King & Barnes
Sussex Ale. ♀: 8 **FACILITIES:** Child facs Large garden, food served
outside Dogs allowed none **NOTES:** Parking 36

WARSASH
Map 05 SU40

The Jolly Farmer Country Inn ♀
29 Fleet End Rd SO31 9JH ☎ 01489 572500 📠 01489 885847
e-mail: mail@thejollyfarmeruk.com
*Dir: Exit M27 Junct 9, head towards A27 Fareham, turn right onto Warsash
Rd. Follow for 2m then left onto Fleet End Rd*

Not far from the Hamble river, this pub has an Irish landlord
with a famous sense of humour - you can't miss the multi-
coloured classic car parked outside. The pub also has its own
golf society and cricket team. The bars are furnished in rustic
style with farming equipment on walls and ceilings, there's a
patio for al fresco eating, and a purpose-built children's play
area. The menu offers local fish, salads and grills, as well as
specialities like medallions of beef fillet with brandy and
peppercorn sauce.
OPEN: 11-11 **BAR MEALS:** L served all week 12-2.30 D served all
week 6-10 **RESTAURANT:** L served all week 12-2.30 D served all
week 6-10 🍽: Whitbread 🍺: Gale's HSB, Fuller's London Pride,
Interbrew Flowers IPA. **FACILITIES:** Child facs Garden: Large play
area Dogs allowed Water **NOTES:** Parking 50

See advert on opposite page

> Most of the pubs in this guide book pride
> themselves on the quality of their food. This
> may take a little time to prepare

The Jolly Farmer Country Inn

Fleet end Road, Warsash, Hampshire SO31 9JH   Tel/Fax: 01489 572500/885847

Martin & Cilla O'Grady and Staff Welcome you to ...

The Jolly Farmer Inn at Warsash offers a superb Menu every lunchtime and evening. Among the many choices are succulent steaks, locally caught seafood dishes and our daily specials board.

To complement the food we have a selection of Traditional Real Ales and an excellent Wine List.

Outside, there is a large Beer Garden, Patio Area and ample parking. For children we have a purpose built play area.

• COUNTRY INN ACCOMMODATION • OPEN ALL DAY •

WELL   Map 05 SU74

The Chequers Inn ♀
RG29 1TL ☎ 01256 862605 ▤ 01256 862133
e-mail: chequers.odiham.wi@freshnet.uk.com
Dir: From Odiham High St turn right into Long Lane, follow for 3m, left at T jct, pub 0.25m on top of hill
A charming, old-world 17th-century pub with a rustic, low-beamed bar, replete with log fire, scrubbed tables, and vine-covered front terrace, set deep in the heart of the Hampshire countryside. Choose from a menu including spinach and feta cheese parcel, spicy Thai chicken, duck breast topped with red wine and plum sauce, Cumberland sausage wheel, grilled cod, or trout stuffed with feta cheese and apricots.
OPEN: 12-3 6-11 (Sat 12-11, Sun 12-10.30) **BAR MEALS:** L served all week 12-2.30 D served all week 6.30-9.30 Sat-Sun 12-3.30, Sun 6.30-8.30 Av main course £9 **RESTAURANT:** L served all week 12-2.30 D served all week 6.30-9.30 Sat-Sun 12-3.30, Sun 6.30-8.30 🍺: Hall & Woodhouse ◀: Gribble Inn Fursty Ferret, Badger Tanglefoot & Best. ♀: 8 **FACILITIES:** Garden: Food served outside Dogs allowed Biscuits, water **NOTES:** Parking 30

WHERWELL   Map 05 SU34

The White Lion ♀
Fullerton Rd SP11 7JF ☎ 01264 860317 ▤ 01264 860317
Dir: A303 W signed Wherwell
Set in the delightful Test Valley, famous for its fly and course fishing, parts of the White Lion date back to before the Civil War. Allegedly, one of Cromwell's cannon balls hit the front door, while another shot down the chimney and is still on display today. Beef rogan josh, and sausages from Robinsons, the renowned Stockbridge butcher, are boosted by specials

continued

---

like crab in season, pork casserole and traditional fish bake.
OPEN: 11-2.30 6-11 (Sat 11-3 Sun 12-3 Sun 7-10.30, Mon-Tue 7-11)
BAR MEALS: L served all week 12-2 D served all week 7-9 Sun 12-2, 7-8.30 Av main course £8.50 **RESTAURANT:** L served all week 12-2 D served all week 7-9 Sun 12-2, 7-8.30 Av 3 course à la carte £17.50
🍺: Punch Taverns ◀: Ringwood Best Bitter, Tetley Smooth Flow, Bass Bitter. ♀: 7 **FACILITIES:** Garden: Enclosed courtyard seating for 50 Plus Dogs allowed **NOTES:** Parking 40

WHITCHURCH   Map 05 SU44

Pick of the Pubs

The Red House Inn ⊛ ♀
21 London St RG28 7LH ☎ 01256 895558
Dir: From M3 or M4 take A34 to Whitchurch
A busy 16th-century coaching inn with quaint flagstones and gnarled beams, the Red House is set near the centre of this small Hampshire town. The friendly, open plan layout includes a locals' bar and a stylish dining room with stripped pine floor, large mirror and old fireplace. This is one of the growing group of chef-owned free houses where diners can expect to find first-rate ingredients cooked in an imaginative modern style. The varied menu might feature starters like sesame-seared tuna carpaccio with honey and mustard vinaigrette; hand-made tortellini filled with crab, spinach and mascapone cheese; and marinated halloumi cheese with roast peppers, pesto and yoghurt dressing. Mains might include roast fillets sea bream with prawn pannacotta; sirloin steak with garlic and peppercorn sauce; thin slices of pork tenderloin with creamed leeks; and aubergine parmesana

continued

England

WHITCHURCH continued

topped with mozzarella. A short walk will bring you to southern England's only working silk mill, delightfully located on the River Test.
OPEN: 11.30-3 6-11 (Sun 12-3, 7-10.30)
BAR MEALS: L served all week 12-2 D served all week 6.30-9.30 **RESTAURANT:** L served all week 12-2 D served all week 6.30-9.30 ⊜: Free House ◖: Cheriton Diggers Gold & Pots Ale, Itchen Valley Fagins, Hop Back Summer Lightning. ⊻: 7
FACILITIES: Large garden, 25 seat patio Dogs allowed except in restaurant **NOTES:** Parking 25

Watership Down Inn ⊻
Freefolk Priors RG28 7NJ ☎ 01256 892254
e-mail: mark@watershipdowninn.co.uk
Dir: On B3400 between Basingstoke & Andover
Enjoy an exhilarating walk on Watership Down before relaxing with a pint of well-kept local ale at this homely 19th-century inn named after Richard Adams' classic tale of rabbit life. The menu choices range from sandwiches, jacket potatoes, salads and ploughman's through to liver and bacon casserole, sausage and mash, mushroom stroganoff, Somerset chicken, and braised lamb shank in a red wine gravy. Just don't expect any rabbit dishes!
OPEN: 11.30-3.30 6-11 **BAR MEALS:** L served all week 12-2.30 D served all week 6-9.30 (Sun 12-2.30 & 7-8.30) ⊜: Free House ◖: Oakleaf Bitter, Butts Barbus Barbus, Triple FFF Pressed Rat & Warthog, Hogs Back TEA. ⊻: 8 **FACILITIES:** Child facs Garden: Beer garden, patio, heaters **NOTES:** Parking 18

WHITSBURY   Map 05 SU11

The Cartwheel Inn ◌⊳ ⊻
Whitsbury Rd SP6 3PZ ☎ 01725 518362
e-mail: info@thecartwheelinn.co.uk
Dir: From Ringwood follow A338 to Salisbury. After 8m turn off at Fordingbridge North and Whitsbury. Turn into 4th road on right (Alexandria rd), continue to end and turn right, Inn is 3m
Handy for exploring the New Forest, visiting Breamore House and discovering the remote Mizmaze on the nearby downs, this extended, turn-of-the-century one-time wheelwright's and shop has been a pub since the 1920s. Venue for a beer festival held annually in August, with spit-roast pigs, barbecues, Morris dancing and a range of 30 real ales. Popular choice of well kept beers in the bar too. Home-made food on daily specials boards - steak and kidney pudding, fisherman's pie and chicken curry. Like their postcard says: "Off the beaten track, but never in a rut!"
OPEN: 11-3 5.30-11 (All day Sun) **BAR MEALS:** L served all week 12-2 D served all week 6-9 Av main course £7.50 ⊜: ◖: Ringwood 49er, Old Thumper, Ringwood Best, Ringwood Seasonal. ⊻: 20
FACILITIES: Garden: Lawn, rockery borders Dogs allowed Water, Biscuits **NOTES:** Parking 25

WICKHAM   Map 05 SU51

Greens Restaurant & Pub ◌⊳ ⊻
The Square PO17 5JQ ☎ 01329 833197
e-mail: DuckworthGreens@aol.com
Dir: 2m from M27. On corner of historic Wickham Square
Prominently located pub on the corner of Wickham's picturesque square, run by Frank and Carol Duckworth for 20 years. It is well-known for its charity events. The interior is light and airy, enhanced by the popular no-smoking policy. Food prepared from fresh ingredients includes a set lunch, and carte options of baked monkfish tail with saffron creamed potatoes, and honey roast lamb shank with red wine sauce.
OPEN: 11-3 6-11 (Summer Sun all day) **BAR MEALS:** L served Tues-Sun 12-2 D served Tues-sun 6-9 Sun 12-3, 6-9 Av main course £11 **RESTAURANT:** L served Tues-Sun 12-2 D served Tues-Sun 6-9 Sun 12-3, 6-9 Av 3 course à la carte £22.50 Av 3 course fixed price £12.95 ⊜: Free House ◖: Fullers London Pride, Hopback Summer Lightning, Youngs Special, Guiness. ⊻: 10 **FACILITIES:** Garden: Safe area, views & access to River Meon Dogs allowed Water outside **NOTES:** Parking 200 ⊗

WINCHESTER   Map 05 SU42

The Westgate Hotel ◆◆◆ ◌⊳ ⊻
2 Romsey Rd SO23 8TP ☎ 01962 820222 📠 01962 820222

The hotel stands at the top end of Winchester's main shopping street, opposite the medieval West Gate and historic Great Hall. The popular bar serves home-cooked meals by day. The hotel also houses The Gourmet Rajah, an innovative Indian restaurant. Expect a mix of English, Indian and Bangladeshi; chicken anjali in lemongrass and lime sauce perhaps, or bhindi gosht (steamed lamb cooked with okra). Tempting desserts include saffron and honey cheesecake.
OPEN: 11-11 **BAR MEALS:** L served all week 12-2.30 D served Mon-Sat 6.30-9.30 Av main course £5.25 **RESTAURANT:** L served Mon-Sat 12-2.30 D served Mon-Sat 6.30-9.30 Av 3 course à la carte £18 ⊜: Eldridge Pope ◖: Interbrew Flowers, Ringwood Best, Pride of Romsey. ⊻: 7 **ROOMS:** 8 bedrooms 6 en suite d£65 No children overnight

---

★ Star rating for inspected hotel accommodation

⊻ 7 Number of wines by the glass

Room prices show the minimum double and single rates charged. Room rates in hotels and B&Bs often vary depending on the facilities, so be sure to check prices with the establishment before booking

We only include details of accommodation that has been inspected by the AA (big Stars or Diamonds at the top of an entry), or the RAC, VisitBritain, VisitScotland or WTB (small Stars or Diamonds at the end of an entry)

PUB WALK

The Saracen's Head Inn
Symond's Yat - Herefordshire

THE SARACEN'S HEAD,
HR9 6JL
☎ 01600 890435
Riverside inn on the bank of the River Wye, next to the hand ferry that has been used for the last 250 years.
Open: 11–11
Bar Meals: L served all week 12–2.30 D served all week 7–9.15 Av main course £8
Restaurant Meals: L served all week 12–2.30 D served all week 7–9.15
Av 3 course à la carte £20
Dogs allowed. Garden and parking available.
(for full entry see page 255)

Distance: 3 miles/4.8km
Map: Explorer OL 14
Terrain: Scenic Wye valley
Paths: Riverside and disused railway tracks
Gradient: Level ground by the River Wye

Walk submitted and checked by the Saracens Head Inn

The Forest of Dean and the glorious Wye Valley are renowned for their natural beauty, breathtaking views and miles of winding woodland trails just waiting to be discovered. Many writers and poets, including Wordsworth, have been inspired by the region's distinctive charm and magic and today it is a Mecca for outdoor enthusiasts.

Walking is one of the main pursuits here and this scenic linear route is one of the most popular in the area. When the walk is finished, return to the Saracens Head Inn via the local ferry service which operates on the Wye between mid February and the end of November. There is a small charge.

From the inn turn left and head south with the River Wye on your right. Keep on the lane and pass through the Royal Hotel car park - formerly the local railway station. Take the old railway track at the far end of the car park and soon you reach the Wye rapids on your right - a popular playground for canoeists and kayakers.

Take the lower track here and continue with the Forest of Dean on your left and the River Wye on your right. After about 1.5 miles (2.4km) you come to Biblins Bridge, a wire suspension footbridge spanning the Wye. On your left here is the Lady Park Wood Nature Reserve. Cross the bridge and turn right, reaching Biblins Youth Campsite.

Continue north, passing a little waterfall on your left, as well as some toilets. Pass the canoe launch point at the edge of the campsite, with some small cliffs on your left and the river on your right. The track narrows here. With the roar of the rapids audible, take the lower track or remain on the same track. The former climbs some steps, the latter passes Woodlea Hotel before both reach a lane. Turn right here and the ferry across the Wye will be found on the right, a few yards down the lane. Use it to return to the inn.

England

WINCHESTER continued

Pick of the Pubs

The Wykeham Arms ♀
75 Kingsgate St SO23 9PE ☎ 01962 853834 ▤ 01962 854411
Dir: *Near Winchester College & Winchester Cathedral*
Diligence pays off when seeking the 'Wyk' in Winchester's
old back streets. When, at last, you open the curved,
glazed doors into this historic pub's main bar you enter
not just a local, but an institution. Its two bars are nearly
always full of people talking, laughing and warming their
behinds at the open fires. Photographs, paintings and
ephemera fill most vertical surfaces, and a walking stick
collection hangs from a ceiling. Recycled Winchester
College desks, set inkwell to inkwell, allow lovers to gaze
at one another. Willie Whitelaw carved 'Manners Makyth
Man' on one. Both bars lead to small, intimate dining
areas, and the food is very good: exemplars from a daily
menu are chicken liver parfait with tomato and mustard;
mushroom and walnut paté; roast rack of Hampshire
down lamb with dauphinoise potatoes; whole baked
lemon sole with fondant potato, asparagus and
hollandaise; crème brûlée; and sticky toffee pudding. Wyk
cottage pie is a lunchtime favourite. Some 80 wines are
kept, with up to 20 by the glass.
OPEN: 11-11 (Sun 12-10.30) Closed: 25 Dec
BAR MEALS: L served all week 12-2.30 D served Mon-Sat
6.30-8.45 Sun 12-1.30 **RESTAURANT:** L served all week 12-2.30
D served Mon-Sat 6.30-8.45 Av 3 course à la carte £25 ⬗: Gales
🍺: Butser Bitter, Special, HSB, Gales Best. ♀: 18
FACILITIES: Garden: Small walled garden 12 tables, seats 55
Dogs allowed **NOTES:** Parking 12 **ROOMS:** 14 bedrooms
en suite s£55 d£90 (♦♦♦♦) No children overnight

WOODLANDS   Map 05 SU31

The Game Keeper
268 Woodlands Rd SO40 7GH ☎ 023 80293093
e-mail: mfa@thegamekeeper.fsworld.co.uk
Dir: *M27 J2 follow signs for Fawley (A326). At 1st rndbt after the Safeway
rndbt turn R, then next L. 1m on L*
Backing onto open fields on the very edge of the New Forest,
this 150-year-old extended cottage is the perfect resting place
after a long forest walk. Comfortable modernised interior and
traditional pub food.
OPEN: 11-11 **BAR MEALS:** L served all week 12-2.30 D served all
week 6.30-9 Av main course £5.50 **RESTAURANT:** 12-2 D served
all week 6.30-9.30 ⬗: Wadworth 🍺: Wadworth 6X, IPA, JCB &
Guest. **FACILITIES:** Garden: patio Dogs allowed
NOTES: Parking 40

ASTON CREWS   Map 10 SO62

Pick of the Pubs

The Penny Farthing Inn NEW ▷
HR9 7LW ☎ 01989 750366 ▤ 01989 750922
Dir: *5m E of Ross-on-Wye*

Located 5 miles east of Ross-on-Wye, and set on a hill
with beautiful views of the Malvern Hills, the Black Hills
and the Forest of Dean, this used to be an old coaching
inn. There are lots of nooks and crannies filled with oak
beams, antiques and saddlery, and some parts of the
building are over 300 years old. The new proprietors took
in November 2004, and they suspect the presence of a
friendly ghost; making the atmosphere even friendlier,
warm and inviting are the two cheerful real flame log fires
and the pleasant staff. Food is an interesting mixture of
Mediterranean and other international influences. You'll
find plenty of fish, including mussels, monkfish, sea bass,
tuna, salmon and trout on the menu, and specials might
include Mediterranean seafood salad with balsamic; Thai
fishcakes with date and lime chutney; Cajun spiced
swordfish with Sri Lankan chutney; and barramundi steak
with fresh ginger and coriander butter.
OPEN: 12-3 6.30-11 (Open all day Fri-Sun May-Sept)
BAR MEALS: L served all week 12-2 D served all week 12-9
Av main course £10 **RESTAURANT:** L served all week 12-2
D served all week 6.30 Sun 12-3 Av 3 course à la carte £22.50
🍺: John Smiths, Abbott Ale, Wadworth 6X.
FACILITIES: Garden: Large sloping garden, benches Dogs
allowed **NOTES:** Parking 50

AYMESTREY   Map 09 SO46

Pick of the Pubs

The Riverside Inn ♀
HR6 9ST ☎ 01568 708440 ▤ 01568 709058
e-mail: theriverside@btinternet.com
See Pick of the Pubs on opposite page

Pick of the Pubs
AYMESTREY – HEREFORDSHIRE

The Riverside Inn

An attractive half-timbered Welsh longhouse, dating from 1580, set on the banks of the River Lugg in the heart of the Welsh Marches. The inn's location halfway along the Mortimer Way is great for walkers - circular walks range from six to 15 miles; anglers will enjoy the mile of private fly fishing for brown trout and grayling.

The interior, with its low beams and log fires, provides a relaxing atmosphere reflecting 400 years of hospitality. Richard and Liz Gresko take a serious approach to food, using locally-grown produce if possible, including vegetables, salads and herbs from their own gardens. Real ales and ciders from local brewers are carefully selected, and good wines match specialities such as home-made steak and kidney pudding in the bar, or roast haunch of local venison on sweet and sour red cabbage in the restaurant. The terraced and landscaped garden overlooks the river.

OPEN: 11-3 6-11 Open All day in summer Closed: Dec 25
BAR MEALS: L served all week 12.30-2 D served all week 7-9.30 Av main course £7.95
RESTAURANT: L served all week 12-2.30 D served all week 7-9.30
🍺: Free House
🍺: Wye Valley Seasonal, Wood Seasonal. 🍷: 7
FACILITIES: Terraced garden. Overlooks river, landscaped Dogs allowed Water, Food Bowls
NOTES: Parking 40

🍷   Map 09 SO46
HR6 9ST
☎ 01568 708440
📄 01568 709058
✉ theriverside@btinternet.com
Dir: On A4110 18m N of Hereford

England

BODENHAM   Map 10 SO55

England's Gate Inn
HR1 3HU ☎ 01568 797286 📠 01568 797768

A pretty black and white coaching inn dating from around
1540, with atmospheric beamed bars and blazing log fires in
winter. A picturesque garden attracts a good summer
following, and so does the food. The menu features pan fried
lamb steak with apricot and onion marmalade, roasted breast
of duck with parsnip mash and spinach and wild rice cakes
with peppers on a chilli and tomato salsa.
OPEN: 11-11 (Sunday 12-10.30) **BAR MEALS:** L served all week
12-2.30 D served all week 6-9.30 Av main course £9.95
RESTAURANT: L served all week 12-2.30 D served all week 6-10 Sun
12-3, 6-9 Av 3 course à la carte £15 ⊕: Free House ◀: Marston's
Pedigree, Wye Valley Bitter & Butty Bach. **FACILITIES:** Garden: Large
sunken garden with large patio area Dogs allowed Water
NOTES: Parking 100

CANON PYON   Map 09 SO44

The Nags Head Inn ◆◆◆ 🖙
HR4 8NY ☎ 01432 830252
Dir: Telephone for directions
More than four hundred years old, with flagstone floors, open
fires and exposed beams to prove it. A comprehensive menu
might entice you into starting with slices of smoked salmon
drizzled with brandy, lemon and cracked pepper, then to
follow with medallions of lamb in a sticky Cumberland sauce,
breast of Gressingham duck in a rich morello cherry sauce, or
butterflied sea bass on sauteed strips of carrot and chopped
coriander. Vegetarian options include stuffed peppers and
tagliatelle. Curry nights and Sunday carvery. The large garden
features a children's adventure playground.
OPEN: 11-2.30 6-11 **BAR MEALS:** L served Tue-Sun 12-2.30
D served all week 6.30-9.30 Sun 12-9 Av main course £5.95
RESTAURANT: L served Tue-Sun 12-2.30 D served all week 6.30-9.30
Sun 12-9 Av 2 course fixed price £8.95 ⊕: Free House ◀: Fuller's
London Pride, Boddingtons, Flowers, Nags Ale. **FACILITIES:** Child
facs Garden: Beer garden, patio, table seating for 60
NOTES: Parking 50 **ROOMS:** 6 bedrooms en suite 1 family room
s£40 d£50

CAREY   Map 10 SO53

Cottage of Content 🍴
HR2 6NG ☎ 01432 840242 e-mail: swolf@sjsw.freeserve.co.uk
*Dir: From A40 W of Ross-on-Wye take A49 towards Hereford. Follow signs
for Hoarwithy, then Carey*
Originally three cottages, this is a charming Wye Valley inn,
dating from 1485, in an attractive rural setting by a stream.
Typical daily specials include tempura-battered hake with
lettuce and sweet soy dressing, and chicken breast with a

continued

mango, coconut and chilli sauce. Vegetarian dishes are always
available, such as brie, potato, courgette and almond crumble.

Cottage of Content
OPEN: 12-2.30 6.30-11 (Sun 12-3) **BAR MEALS:** L served all week
12-2 D served all week 7-9.30 Av main course £12
RESTAURANT: L served all week 12-2 D served all week 7-9.30 à la
carte only evenings ⊕: Free House ◀: Hook Norton, Wye Valley.
🍷: 10 **FACILITIES:** Garden: Dogs allowed on leads
NOTES: Parking 30

DORMINGTON   Map 10 SO54

Yew Tree Inn 🖙
Len Gee's Restaurant, Priors Frome HR1 4EH
☎ 01432 850467 📠 01432 850467 e-mail: len@lengees.info
web: www.lengees.info
*Dir: A438 Hereford to Ledbury, turn at Dormington towards Mordiford,
0.5m on left.*
This former hop pickers' pub has fantastic panoramic views
over Hereford towards the Black Mountains of Wales. With
many country walks in the surrounding area, it is the ideal
place to take a relaxing stroll before enjoying a home-cooked
meal in Len Gee's restaurant. The menu features classic
European dishes, as well as a splendid carvery, with four
joints of meat and a wide selection of vegetables. For
something a little different, try the tempting fish specials,
including baked red snapper with lime butter and chargrilled
shark with chilli oil and peppers.
OPEN: 12-2 7-11 (Closed Tue Jan-Mar) **BAR MEALS:** L served all
week 12-2 D served all week 7-9 Av main course £8.95
RESTAURANT: L served all week 12-2 D served all week 7-9
Av 3 course à la carte £14.95 Av 3 course fixed price £14.95 ⊕: Free
House ◀: Ruddles Best, Wye Valley, Greene King Old Speckled Hen.
FACILITIES: Child facs Terraced garden with views of Black
Mountains Dogs allowed Waterbowls **NOTES:** Parking 40

DORSTONE   Map 09 SO34

The Pandy Inn
HR3 6AN ☎ 01981 550273 📠 01981 550277
e-mail: magdalena@pandyinn.wanadoo.co.uk
Dir: Off B4348 W of Hereford
Oliver Cromwell was a frequent visitor to the Pandy, the
oldest inn in Herefordshire, built in 1186 to house workers
building Dorstone Church. Robert de Brito, who built the inn,
did it as penance for his part in the murder of Thomas A
Becket. Alongside the usual pub favourites, the South African
owners offer traditional dishes from back home (bobotie and
tomato bredie) along with Herefordshire rump steak, poached
salmon, or lamb's liver with mash and onions, plus various
hot and cold desserts.
OPEN: 12-3 6-11 (Open all day May-Oct) Mon closed Oct-May
BAR MEALS: L served all week 12-3 D served all week 6-9.30

continued

England

Av main course £9.50 **RESTAURANT:** L served all week 12-3
D served all week 6-11 Av 3 course à la carte £16 🍴: Free House
🍺: Wye Valley Bitter, Butty Bach. **FACILITIES:** Children's licence
Garden: Large garden, 19 tables views of Dorstone Hill Dogs allowed
NOTES: Parking 20

FOWNHOPE   Map 10 SO53

The Green Man Inn 🍷
HR1 4PE ☎ 01432 860243 📠 01432 860207
e-mail: info@thegreenmaninn.co.uk
Dir: From M50 take A449 then B4224 to Fownhope
This white-painted 15th-century coaching inn has a host of
beams inside and out. Set in an attractive garden close to the
River Wye, it's an ideal base for walking, touring and salmon
fishing. The extensive menu has something for everyone, with
a range of filling sandwiches, jacket potatoes, burgers and
ciabatta melts. Then there are hand-made pies, gourmet grills,
and main course favourites like sausages and mash. All this,
and sticky puddings too!
OPEN: 11-11 (Sun12-10.30) **BAR MEALS:** L served all week
12-2.30 D served all week 6-9 Sun 12-3, 6-9
RESTAURANT: L served Sun 12-2.30 D served all week 6-9 Sun
12-3, 6-9 Av 3 course à la carte £12.15 🍴: Free House 🍺: John
Smith's Smooth, Samuel Smith. 🍷: 8 **FACILITIES:** Garden: Lawn
area with seating overlooks countryside Dogs allowed
NOTES: Parking 80 **ROOMS:** 23 bedrooms en suite 5 family rooms
s£44.50 d£72.50 (★★)

HAMPTON BISHOP   Map 10 SO53

The Bunch of Carrots 🍷
HR1 4JR ☎ 01432 870237 📠 01432 870237
e-mail: bunchofcarrotts@buccaneer.co.uk
Dir: From Hereford take A4103, A438, then B4224
Friendly pub with real fires, old beams and flagstones. Its
name comes from a rock formation in the River Wye which
runs alongside. There is an extensive menu plus a daily
specials board, a carvery, salad buffet and simple bar snacks.
OPEN: 11-3 6-11 **BAR MEALS:** L served all week 12-2.30 D served
all week 6-10 (Sun 9) **RESTAURANT:** L served all week 12-2
D served all week 6-10 🍴: Free House 🍺: Bass, Hook Norton,
Directors, Butcombe. 🍷: 11 **FACILITIES:** Garden: Dogs allowed
NOTES: Parking 100

HEREFORD   Map 10 SO53

Pick of the Pubs
The Ancient Camp Inn ◎ 🏠
Ruckhall HR2 9QX ☎ 01981 250449 📠 01981 251581
e-mail: reservations@theancientcampinn.co.uk
Dir: Take A465 from Hereford, then B4349. Follow signs 'Belmont
Abbey/Ruckhall'
This is a family-run restaurant situated spectacularly on
the banks of the River Wye, four miles west of the city of
Hereford. Known to be a cider house dating from the
19th century, the inn takes its name from an Iron Age fort,
the site of which stands in the grounds. From its elevated
position some 70 feet above the Wye, it offers stunning
views across the river and Golden Valley from the terrace
in summer. The low-beamed interior, with its stone-
flagged floors, simple furnishings and log fires, provides a
warm and welcoming atmosphere through the long
winter evenings. Choose your meal from the bar lunch on
the blackboard, or make a selection from the restaurant

menu which changes daily. Sample dishes include pan-
seared duck foie with onion marmalade and granary
toast, and slow-roast Gloucester Old Spot belly pork with
red cabbage. Amaretto spumoni is a well-loved dessert.

The Ancient Camp Inn

OPEN: 12-3 7-11 (Closed Sun eve Closed: 3 weeks Feb)
BAR MEALS: L served Tue-Sun 12-2 D served Tue-Sat 7-9
Av main course £10.40 **RESTAURANT:** L served Tue-Sun 12-2
D served Tue-Sat 7-9 Av 3 course à la carte £26 🍴: Free House
🍺: Wye Valley Real Ales. **FACILITIES:** Garden: Terrace
overlooking the River Wye, tables **NOTES:** Parking 30
ROOMS: 5 bedrooms en suite s£60 d£70 No children
overnight 🚭

The Crown & Anchor 🍷
Cotts Ln, Lugwardine HR1 4AB ☎ 01432 851303 📠 01432 851637
e-mail: c_a@oz.co.uk
Dir: 2m from Hereford on A438. Left into Lugwardine down Cotts Lane
Old Herefordshire-style black-and-white pub with quarry tile
floors and a large log fire, just up from the bridge over the
River Lugg. Among the many interesting specials you might
find fillets of Torbay sole with mussels and white wine,
mushrooms in filo pastry with wild mushroom and marsala
sauce, seafood tagliolini, supreme of chicken stuffed with wild
mushrooms and chestnuts with cranberry and white wine
sauce, or Brother Geoffrey's pork sausages with juniper and
red wine sauce and mash. A long lunchtime sandwich list.
OPEN: 12-11 Closed: 25 Dec **BAR MEALS:** L served all week 12-2
D served all week 7-10 Av main course £9 🍴: Enterprise Inns
🍺: Worthington Bitter, Theakstons XB, Timothy Taylors Landlord,
Marstons Pedigree. 🍷: 8 **FACILITIES:** Garden: Patio area with
tables and lots of plants **NOTES:** Parking 30

KIMBOLTON   Map 10 SO56

Pick of the Pubs
Stockton Cross Inn 🐟
HR6 0HD ☎ 01568 612509
e-mail: enquiries@stocktoncross.co.uk
Dir: On the A4112 off A49 between Leominster and Ludlow
A picturesque black and white building, regularly
photographed by tourists and featured on calendars and
chocolate boxes, Stockton Cross is a drovers' inn dating
from the 17th century. It is set beside a crossroads where
alleged witches, rounded up from the surrounding
villages such as Ludlow, were hanged, a grisly historical
aspect belied by the peace and beauty of the setting.
Good home cooking is the proud boast of owner Stephen
Walsh, whose specialist vegetarian menu is proving a
great success. Using all local produce, his lunch and

continued   *continued*

KIMBOLTON continued

evening choices include pan-fried halibut with a creamy white wine and prawn sauce; half a free-range Aylesbury duckling served with a rich orange sauce; and tagine of lamb with apricots, honey and flaked almonds. There is also a pretty country garden with umbrellas and two trees.

Stockton Cross Inn

OPEN: 12-3 7-11 **BAR MEALS:** L served all week 12-2.15 D served Tues-Sat 7-9 Sun 12-2.30 Av main course £12 **RESTAURANT:** L served all week 12-2.15 D served Tues-Sat 7-9 Not Sun or Mon eve Av 3 course à la carte £20 🍽: Free House ◀: Wye Valley Butty Bach, Wye Valley pale Ale, Teme Valley This, Flowers Best Bitter. **FACILITIES:** Garden: Pretty country garden with seating, parasols Dogs allowed Water bowls **NOTES:** Parking 30

KINGTON   Map 09 SO25

Pick of the Pubs

The Stagg Inn & Restaurant ◉◉ ♀

Titley HR5 3RL ☎ 01544 230221 📠 231390
e-mail: reservations@thestagg.co.uk
Dir: Between Kington & Presteigne on the B4355

Surrounded by the magnificent countryside of the Welsh Borders, the Stagg Inn is within easy reach of the region's numerous attractions. Just yards away is the route of the Mortimer Trail, linking Ludlow with Kington and crossing some of Britain's loveliest landscapes, while nearby is the spectacular and much longer Offa's Dyke National Trail. The romantic ruins of a country house and England's highest golf course are also easy to find. The pub's chef/proprietor Steve Reynolds has tried to retain an authentic feel, using local stone and items of furniture acquired in the area's well-known antique markets. Sample pork chop with mustard mash, or smoked haddock risotto from the lunch/bar snack menu, or opt for Aylesbury duck breast, Herefordshire rump steak, wild sea bass fillet, or stuffed pork tenderloin in the restaurant. An 80-bin wine list includes wines from Uraguay and the Lebanon, and there are up to 20 regional cheeses.
OPEN: 12-3 6.30-11 (Sun 12-3) Closed: 1st 2wks Nov & 1wk Feb **BAR MEALS:** L served Tue-Sun 12-2 D served Tue-Sat 6.30-10 Av main course £8.50 **RESTAURANT:** L served Tue-Sat 12-2 D served Tue-Sat 6.30-10 Av 3 course à la carte £24 🍽: Free House ◀: Hobsons Town Crier, Hobsons Old Henry, Hobsons Best Bitter, Bass. ♀: 10 **FACILITIES:** Child facs Garden: Small garden with herbs and vegetables Dogs allowed **NOTES:** Parking 20

LEDBURY   Map 10 SO73

The Farmers Arms ♀

Horse Rd, Wellington Heath HR8 1LS ☎ 01531 632010
Dir: Telephone for directions

Handy for the breathtaking high ground of the Malvern Hills and the seductive charms of Ross and the Wye Valley, this popular country inn offers a varied menu, with dishes cooked daily on the premises. Recent change of ownership, so readers reports are welcome.
OPEN: 12-3 6-11 **BAR MEALS:** L served all week 12-2 D served all week 7-10 **RESTAURANT:** L served all week 12-2 D served all week 7-10 🍽: Free House ◀: Fuller's London Pride, Hancocks HB plus guest ales. ♀: 8 **FACILITIES:** Children's licence Garden: Patio area small grassed area with rockery **NOTES:** Parking 40

Pick of the Pubs

The Feathers Hotel ★★★ ◉ 🛏 ♀

High St HR8 1DS ☎ 01531 635266 📠 01531 638955
e-mail: mary@feathers-ledbury.co.uk
web: www.feathers-ledbury.co.uk
Dir: S from Worcester A449, E from Hereford A438, N from Gloucester A417.

The Feathers, dating from 1564, is a distinctive building on Ledbury High Street with a striking black and white frontage. The fine old inn retains it oak beams, panelled walls and open log fires, and naturally enough there is a resident ghost. Meals are served in Quills Restaurant (available for private dining), Fuggles Brasserie (festooned with Fuggles hops), and the Top Bar, where lunchtime sandwiches and Herefordshire ciders are available along with a good choice of real ales. There is also a function room licensed for civil weddings. Daily fish dishes might include line-caught Cornish sea bass with tomato and vanilla butter sauce, and chargrilled monkfish tail with crab and saffron sauce. Locally sourced meats are also a feature, including Herefordshire beef, lamb, duck and pheasant. Lighter or vegetarian meals and steaks from the chargrill increase the choice. Afternoon tea is a treat by the fire in the reception lounge.
OPEN: 11-11 (Sun 12-10.30) **BAR MEALS:** L served all week 12-2 D served all week Av main course £13 **RESTAURANT:** L served all week 12-2 D served all week 7-9.30 Av 3 course à la carte £25 🍽: Free House ◀: Coors Worthington's Bitter, Interbrew Bass, Fuller's London Pride, Greene King Old Speckled Hen. ♀: 18 **FACILITIES:** Garden: Courtyard garden, fountain, gazebo **NOTES:** Parking 30 **ROOMS:** 19 bedrooms en suite 3 family rooms s£79.50 d£105

The Talbot ♀

14 New St HR8 2DX ☎ 01531 632963 📠 01531 633796
e-mail: talbot.ledbury@wadworth.co.uk
Dir: Follow Ledbury signs, turn into Bye St, 2nd left into Woodley Rd, over bridge to junct, left into New St. Talbot on right

Take a step back in time at this historic black-and-white coaching inn dating from 1596. The oak-panelled dining room, with its fine carved overmantle, was once the scene of fighting between Roundheads and Cavaliers - the musket-holes are still visible today. A good choice of local ales and wines by the glass accompanies avocado with prawns and ginger mayonnaise; Herefordshire steaks; or grilled salmon steak with Vermouth, cream and chive sauce.
OPEN: 11.30-3 5-11 **BAR MEALS:** L served all week 12-2 D served all week 6.30-9 **RESTAURANT:** L served all week 12-2 D served all week 6.30-9 🍽: Wadworth ◀: Wadworth 6X & Henrys Original IPA, Wye Valley Butty Bach,. ♀: 6 **NOTES:** Parking 10

The Trumpet Inn

Trumpet HR8 2RA ☎ 01531 670277 e-mail: aa@trumpetinn.com
Dir: *4 miles from Ledbury, on the X-roads of the A438 and A417*
This traditional black and white free house dates back to the
late 15th century. The former coaching inn and post house
takes its name from the days when mail coaches blew their
horns on approaching the crossroads. The cosy bars feature a
wealth of exposed beams, with open fireplaces and a separate
non-smoking dining area. Light sandwich lunches and salad
platters complement main dishes like salmon fishcakes;
kleftiko; or vegetable stroganoff.
OPEN: 8-2.30 6-11 (Apr-Oct 8-11) **BAR MEALS:** L served all week
8-2 D served all week 6-9 **RESTAURANT:** L served all week 8-2
D served all week 6-9 🛢: Free House 🍺: Interbrew Flowers IPA,
Scottish Courage John Smith's, Castle Eden Ale, Wye Valley HPA &
Butty Bach. **FACILITIES:** Garden: Small paddock adjacent to pub,
sun trap Dogs allowed Water **NOTES:** Parking 60

The Verzon ★★ ◉ ▷ ♀

Trumpet HR8 2PZ ☎ 01531 670381 🖹 01531 670830
e-mail: info@theverzon.co.uk web: www.theverzon.co.uk
Dir: *Situated 2.5 miles west of Ledbury on the A438 towards Hereford*
Georgian country house hotel and former farmhouse which
stands in over four acres of countryside with views of the
Malvern Hills. Versatile facilities include a large function room,
private deck terrace and a comfortable lounge with open fire.
Braised shank of lamb, pan-fried wild sea bass, duck leg
confit, grilled vegetable lasagne, tatin of white chicory, and
tournedos of Herefordshire beef give a good choice.
OPEN: 8-11 **BAR MEALS:** L served all week 12-2 D served all week
7-9 Sun 12-2.30 Av main course £14.50 **RESTAURANT:** L served all
week 12-2 D served all week 7-9 Sun 12-2.30 Av 3 course à la carte
£26 🍺: Wye Valley Bitter, Butty Bach, Tetley Smoothflow. ♀: 7
FACILITIES: Children's licence Garden: Large terrace and lawn,
views of Malvern Hill **NOTES:** Parking 80 **ROOMS:** 8 bedrooms
en suite 1 family room s£60 d£78

LEINTWARDINE   Map 9 SO47

The Jolly Frog NEW ▷ ♀

The Todden SY7 0LX ☎ 01547 540298 🖹 01547 540105
e-mail: jaynejollyfrog@aol.com
Dir: *1m from Leintwardine on the A4113 towards Ludlow*
Until five years ago it was called, somewhat curiously, The
Cottager's Comfort, although it's always been The Poker to
locals, because a red-hot one used to warm up the beer. It is
run as a pub-restaurant, with an emphasis on fresh fish and
shellfish. Daily changing dishes appear on the blackboard,
and there are new guest real ales every week. There's a
'million dollar view' over the valley from the outside decking.
OPEN: 12-2.30 6-10.30 (May be open 7 day in summer)
BAR MEALS: L served Tues-Sun D served Tues-Sat Av main course
£11 **RESTAURANT:** L served Tues-Sun 12-2.30 D served Tues-Sat
6-9.30 Av 3 course à la carte £20 Av 3 course fixed price £14
🍺: Guest beers. ♀: 12 **FACILITIES:** Child facs Children's licence
Garden: Landscaped and decked Dogs allowed **NOTES:** Parking 20

LEOMINSTER   Map 10 SO45

The Grape Vaults ♀

Broad St HR4 8BS ☎ 01568 611404 e-mail: jusaxon@tiscali.co.uk
An unspoilt pub with a small, homely bar complete with real
fire - in fact it's so authentic that it's Grade II-listed, even
down to the fixed seating. Real ale is a popular feature, and
includes microbrewery ales. The good food includes turkey
and ham pie, bubble and squeak, steak and ale pie, and
various fresh fish dishes using cod, plaice, salmon and
continued

whitebait. No music, darts, gaming machines, or alcopops!
OPEN: 11-11 **BAR MEALS:** L served Mon-Sat 12-2 D served
Mon-Sat 5.30-9 No food Sun 🛢: 🍺: Banks Bitter, Pedigree, Banks
Original & Guest Ales. ♀: 6 **FACILITIES:** Dogs allowed Water
NOTES: No credit cards

The Royal Oak Hotel ★★ ◉ ♀

South St HR6 8JA ☎ 01568 612610 🖹 01568 612710
e-mail: reservations@theroyaloakhotel.net
web: www.theroyaloakhotel.net
Dir: *Town centre, near A44/A49 junct*

Coaching inn dating from around 1733, with log fires,
antiques and a minstrels' gallery in the original ballroom. The
pub was once part of a now blocked-off tunnel system that
linked the Leominster Priory with other buildings in the town.
Good choice of wines by the glass and major ales, and a
hearty menu offering traditional British food with a modern
twist. Under new ownership.
OPEN: 10-2.30 6-11 (Sun 12-10.30) **BAR MEALS:** L served all
week 12-2.30 D served all week 6-9 **RESTAURANT:** L served Sun
12-2 D served all week 7-9.30 Av 3 course à la carte £25 Av 3 course
fixed price £19.95 🛢: Free House 🍺: Brains SA, Wood Special
Bitter, Shepherd Neame Spitfire, Fuller's London Pride. ♀: 10
FACILITIES: Dogs allowed Water **NOTES:** Parking 30
ROOMS: 18 bedrooms en suite 2 family rooms s£50 d£66

LITTLE COWARNE   Map 10 SO65

The Three Horseshoes Inn ▷ ♀

HR7 4RQ ☎ 01885 400276 🖹 01885 400276
Dir: *Off A456 (Hereford/Bromyard). At Stokes Cross, take turning signed
Little Cowarne/Pencombe*

Named after the horses brought for shoeing at the next-door
blacksmiths', and an alehouse for nearly 200 years. This
country inn offers home-made food using local produce,
which can be served in the bar or the garden room as well as
in the restaurant. A selection of typical dishes includes braised
shoulder of Herefordshire lamb with garlic and rosemary
sauce; steak and Wye Valley ale pie; and Shropshire Blue
continued

LITTLE COWARNE continued

cheesecake with spiced pears. Sandwiches and other light bites are also available.
OPEN: 11-3 6.30-11 (Closed Sun eve in Winter) Closed: Dec 25 **BAR MEALS:** L served all week 12-2 D served all week 6.30-9.30 (Sun 12-3, Summer Sun eve 7-9) Av main course £6.50 **RESTAURANT:** L served all week 12-2 D served all week 6.30-9.30 Av 3 course à la carte £17.50 Av fixed price £10 ⊕: Free House ◀: Marston's Pedigree, Greene King Old Speckled Hen, Websters Yorkshire Bitter, Wye Valley Bitter. ♀: 6 **FACILITIES:** Garden: Patio/Lawn area with seating, flower beds Dogs allowed Water **NOTES:** Parking 50 **ROOMS:** 2 bedrooms en suite s£32.50 d£27.50 (♦♦♦♦)

MADLEY   Map 09 SO43

The Comet Inn
Stoney St HR2 9NJ ☎ 01981 250600
e-mail: thecometinn@yahoo.co.uk
Dir: Approx 6m from Hereford on the B4352
Located on a prominent corner position and set in two and a half acres, this black and white 19th-century inn was originally three cottages, and retains many original features and a roaring open fire. A simple, hearty menu includes steak and ale pie, shank of lamb, grilled gammon, chicken curry, cod in crispy batter, mushroom stroganoff, and a variety of steaks, baguettes, and jacket potatoes.
OPEN: 12-2 7-11 (Open all day Fri-Sun & BH's) Restricted Winter Mon Lunch **BAR MEALS:** L served all week 12-2 D served Mon-Sun 7-9.30 Av main course £5 **RESTAURANT:** L served all week 12-2 D served Mon-Sat 7-9.30 ⊕: Free House ◀: Hook Norton Best Bitter, Wye Valley Bitter, Tetley Smooth Flow, Carlsberg Tetley. **FACILITIES:** Child facs Garden: Large garden with shrubs **NOTES:** Parking 40

MICHAELCHURCH ESCLEY   Map 09 SO33

The Bridge Inn ♀
HR2 0JW ☎ 01981 510646 🖷 01981 510646
e-mail: embengiss@yahoo.co.uk
Dir: From Hereford take A465 towards Abergavenny, then B4348 towards Peterchurch. Turn L at Vowchurch for village
By Escley Brook, at the foot of the Black Mountains and close to Offa's Dyke, there are 14th-century parts to this oak-beamed family pub: the dining room overlooks the garden, abundant with rose and begonias, and the river - an ideal area for walkers and nature lovers. Speciality dishes include steak and kidney with crispy dumplings.
OPEN: 12-2.30 6-11 (Sun 12-10.30) Closed: 25 Dec
BAR MEALS: L served Tue-Sun 12-2 D served all week 7-9.15 **RESTAURANT:** L served Tue-Sun 12-2 D served all week 7-9.30 ⊕: Free House ◀: Wye Valley Beers, Interbrew Flowers, Adnams. ♀: 12 **FACILITIES:** Garden: Large riverside patio, fenced garden, heaters Dogs allowed Water **NOTES:** Parking 25

MUCH MARCLE   Map 10 SO63

The Scrumpy House Bar & Restaurant
The Bounds HR8 2NQ ☎ 01531 660626
e-mail: matt@scrumpyhouse.co.uk
Dir: Approx 5 miles from Ledbury & Ross-on-Wye on A449, follow signs to Cidermill
A renovated hay barn on the site of a family-run cider mill with a bar and restaurant separated by a woodburner in the fireplace. Over 20 different ciders are offered alongside local bitters and a varied wine list. All food is prepared on the premises, including 16 kinds of ice cream, and fresh fish on

continued

Friday from Grimsby. Favourite dishes include award-winning local bangers and oven-baked sea bass stuffed with home-grown herbs.
OPEN: 11-3 7-12 (Fri-Sat 12-2.30, 6.30-12) Closed: 25-26 Dec **BAR MEALS:** L served all week 12-2 D served Wed-Sat 7-9.30 Av main course £8 **RESTAURANT:** L served all week 12-2.30 D served Wed-Sat 7-11 Av 3 course à la carte £22 ⊕: Free House ◀: Hook Norton, Guest ales. **FACILITIES:** Garden: Patio, Food served outside **NOTES:** Parking 30

The Slip Tavern ♀
Watery Ln HR8 2NG ☎ 01531 660246 🖷 01531 660700
e-mail: thesliptavern@aol.com
Dir: Follow signs off A449 at Much Marcle junction

Curiously named after a 1575 landslip which buried the local church, this country pub is delightfully surrounded by cider apple orchards. An attractive conservatory overlooks the award-winning garden, where summer dining is popular, and there's also a cosy bar. It's next to Westons Cider Mill, and cider is a favourite in the bar.
OPEN: 11.30-2.30 5.30-11 Closed Mon lunch (Sun 12-3, 7-10.30) **BAR MEALS:** L served Tues-Sun 11.30-2.30 D served Tues-Sat 6.30-9 Av main course £7 **RESTAURANT:** L served Tues-Sun 11.30-2 D served Tues-Sat 6.30-9.30 Av 3 course à la carte £18 ⊕: Free House ◀: John Smiths, Tetleys Smooth Flow, Guest Ales. ♀: 8 **FACILITIES:** Garden: Large terrace seating 50, lawns/flowerbeds **NOTES:** Parking 45

ORLETON   Map 09 SO46

The Boot Inn
SY8 4HN ☎ 01568 780228 🖷 01568 780228
e-mail: thebootorleton@hotmail.com
Dir: Follow A49 S from Ludlow (approx 7m) to B4362 (Woofferton), 1.5m off B4362 turn left. The Boot Inn is in the centre of the village

Relaxed and welcoming, this black and white timbered inn dates from the 16th century. In winter a blazing fire in the inglenook warms the bar, where an appetising selection of snacks and sandwiches extends the menu along with a list of

continued

specials: vegetable lasagna, individual beef Wellington, seafood pancakes, pan-fried lamb's kidneys all make an appearance, backed up by real ales and cider are on tap. Behind the pub is the smallest house in Herefordshire. **OPEN:** 12-3 6-11 (Sun 12-3, 6-10.30) **BAR MEALS:** L served Tue-Sun 12-2 D served all week 7-9 Av main course £9.50 **RESTAURANT:** L served Tue-Sun D served all week 7-9 Av 3 course à la carte £16 ⊕: Free House ⬦: Hobsons Best, Local Real Ales, Woods, Wye Valley. **FACILITIES:** Child facs Children's licence Garden: Lawn, BBQ area Dogs allowed Water **NOTES:** Parking 20

PEMBRIDGE   Map 09 SO35

New Inn ⏛

Market Square HR6 9DZ ☎ 01544 388427 📠 01544 388427
Dir: From M5 junct 7 take A44 W through Leominster towards Llandrindod Wells
Worn flagstone floors and open fires characterise this unspoilt black and white timbered free house. Formerly a courthouse, the building dates from the early 14th century. It lies close to the village centre and, in summer, customers spill out into the pub's outdoor seating area in the Old Market Square. Expect lamb and vegetable hotpot; cream cheese and spinach lasagne; and trout fillets in lemon butter.
OPEN: 11-2.30 6-11 (12-3 in summer) **BAR MEALS:** L served all week 12-2 D served all week 7-9.30 Sun 12-9 **RESTAURANT:** 12-2 7-9.30 ⊕: Free House ⬦: Fuller's London Pride, Kingdom Bitter, Wood Shropshire Lad, Black Sheep Best. ⏛: 6 **FACILITIES:** Garden: Patio, seating under the Market Sq **NOTES:** Parking 25

ROSS-ON-WYE   Map 10 SO52

Pick of the Pubs

The Moody Cow 🍴 ⏛
Upton Bishop HR9 7TT ☎ 01989 780470
See Pick of the Pubs on page 256

SELLACK   Map 10 SO52

Pick of the Pubs

The Lough Pool Inn ⊛ ⏛
HR9 6LX ☎ 01989 730236 📠 01989 730462
Dir: A49 from Ross-on-Wye towards Hereford. Take road signed Sellack/Hoarwithy.
Black and white, half-timbered pubs are a familiar sight in Herefordshire. This one, with its flagstones, beams and open fires, sets a distinctly friendly tone. In the 19th century it was a butchers' shop with a licence to sell beer brewed on the premises. The remote location doesn't deter the die-hard followers of Stephen Bull. This renowned ex-London chef considers it very much a food pub, taking pride in the use of local produce. That said, he's equally excited about the 'wet' side of the business, especially its ciders, perries, ales and wines. The restaurant is at the rear of the pub, where the daily carte is honest, rustic, and eminently satisfying. Delights include terrine of ham hock with roast onions; or deep-fried haggis fritters with beetroot relish. Mains are along imaginative lines, like pan-fried skate wing on noodles; or melting 8-hour roast lamb with white bean, chorizo and saffron stew.
OPEN: 11.30-2.30 6.30-11 (Sun 12-2 7-10.30) Closed: 25 Dec, 26 Dec (eve) **BAR MEALS:** L served all week 12-2 D served all week 7-9.15 Av main course £12.50 **RESTAURANT:** L served

all week 12-2 D served all week 7-9.15 Av 3 course à la carte £22 ⊕: Free House ⬦: Wye Valley, Scottish Courage John Smiths, Greene King Ruddles Country & Old Speckled Hen. ⏛: 10 **FACILITIES:** Garden: Lawn outside pub Dogs allowed water **NOTES:** Parking 40

SYMONDS YAT (EAST)   Map 10 SO51

The Saracens Head Inn ♦♦♦♦ 🍴 ⏛
HR9 6JL ☎ 01600 890435 📠 01600 890034
e-mail: email@saracensheadinn.co.uk
web: www.saracensheadinn.co.uk

A riverside inn, formerly a cider mill, on the east bank of the Wye where it flows through a picturesque gorge. It is handy for exploring this unspoiled area, and just over a mile from the Welsh border. A wide range of home-made bar food and restaurant dishes is offered, including traditional pork and leek sausages, seared tuna loin, braised lamb shank, steak and kidney pie, and field and forest mushroom casserole.
OPEN: 11-11 **BAR MEALS:** L served all week 12-2.30 D served all week 7-9.15 Av main course £8 **RESTAURANT:** L served all week 12-2.30 D served all week 7-9.15 Av 3 course à la carte £20 ⊕: Free House ⬦: Scottish Courage Theakstons Best & Old Peculier, Old Speckled Hen, Wye Valley Hereford Pale Ale, Marston's Pedigree. ⏛: 7 **FACILITIES:** Garden: 2 riverside terraces Dogs allowed Bowls **NOTES:** Parking 38 **ROOMS:** 11 bedrooms en suite 1 family room s£45 d£70
See Pub Walk on page 247

TILLINGTON   Map 09 SO44

The Bell 🍴
HR4 8LE ☎ 01432 760395 📠 01432 760580
e-mail: beltill@aol.com
Popular family-run pub in an area renowned for its apple orchards and fruit farms - a good base for exploring the scenic countryside of the Welsh Borders. Plenty of character features inside, including an English oak floor in the lounge bar. Good and appetising menu features Badnage chicken fillet with sausage and thyme stuffing, salmon fillet and prawns in lemon and white wine, pork and Little Dilwyn Farm cider pie, and savoy cabbage and potato bake. There's also a good lunchtime snack menu that offers sandwiches, baguettes, soup and jackets.
OPEN: 11-3 6-11 (All day Sat-Sun) **BAR MEALS:** L served all week 12-2.15 D served Mon-Sat 6-9.15 Sun 12-2.30 Av main course £8.50 **RESTAURANT:** L served all week 12-2.15 D served Mon-Sat 6-9.15 Av 3 course à la carte £18 ⬦: London Pride, Hereford Bitter, local ales. **FACILITIES:** Child facs Garden: Small paved area & large lawn with tables Dogs allowed in public bar **NOTES:** Parking 60

continued

The Moody Cow

The Moody Cow is an old stone-built inn with a patio area out front offering plenty of shaded seating in summer, assuming there's some sun! The no-nonsense philosophy behind the running of this popular inn goes like this: simple, fresh home-made food presented well in comfortable surroundings at a sensible price, and served by obliging people.

In the rustic bar, with exposed stone walls and farmhouse seating, local Wye Valley bitter figures among the real ales, alongside a good selection of wines by the glass. Beyond the bar are two further rooms: the Fresco is set up for informal eating at wooden tables with raffia chairs and cow-themed displays; and the Snug where you can relax with a drink on comfy sofas by the wood-burning fire. The restaurant, on two levels and forming one leg of an L, is a converted barn with blue glazing, exposed beams and carpeted floors. To ensure consistency it offers just one menu throughout,

from which come starters of soup of the day (perhaps French onion gratinée, or bouillabaisse); Moody's Caesar salad with anchovy fillets, garlic croutons and fresh parmesan; a 'decent' wedge of deep-fried brie with cranberry and red wine sauce; and pasta carbonara. Mains ('the ones we've never changed') include good old bangers and mash with onion gravy; chicken or prawn jalfrezi; canon of lamb en croute; fresh boneless sea bass; and guinea fowl casserole. The day's fresh fish and other specials which are chalked on the blackboard might be wild mushroom risotto, or chilli con carne.

OPEN: 12-2.30 6-11 (Sun 12-3)
BAR MEALS: L served Tues-Sun 12-2 D served Tues-Sat 6-9.30 Av main course £10.95
RESTAURANT: L served Tues-Sun 12-2 D served Tues-Sat 6-9.30
Av 3 course à la carte £22
Av 3 course fixed price £11.95
🍺: Free House
🍺: Nine Lives, Hook Norton Best, Wye Valley Best. ♀: 7
FACILITIES: Child facs Garden: Patio area with iron table, chairs, parasols Dogs allowed Water provided
NOTES: Parking 40

🐟 ♀   Map 10 SO52
Upton Bishop HR9 7TT
☎ 01989 780470

England

ULLINGSWICK   Map 10 SO54

Pick of the Pubs

Three Crowns Inn @@ ♀
HR1 3JQ ☎ 01432 820279 ▤ 01432 820279
e-mail: info@threecrownsinn.com
Dir: *From Burley Gate rdbt take A465 toward Bromyard, after 2m L to Ullingswick, L after 0.5m, pub 0.5m on R*

An unspoilt country pub in deepest rural Herefordshire, where food sources are so local their distance away is referred to in fields, rather than miles. A hand-written sign even offers to buy surplus garden fruit and veg from locals. Parterres in the garden give additional space for growing more varieties of herbs, fruit and vegetables that are not easy, or even possible, to buy commercially. There's even a pea whose provenance can be traced back to some that Lord Carnarvon found in a phial in Tutankhamun's tomb. The menus change daily, but there is always fish, such as line-caught poached monkfish and proscuito with celeriac mousse and haricot blanc. Soufflés often appear too. Meat dishes have included braised belly of Berkshire pork, marinated lamb rumb with kidney kebab, and confit of Gressingham duck. Tuesday tasting evenings feature a set four-course dinner that changes week by week, with wines normally sold only by the bottle, available by the glass.
OPEN: 12-2.30 7-11 (May-Aug 12-3, 6-11) Closed: 2wks from Dec 25 **BAR MEALS:** L served all week 12-3 D served all week 7-10.30 **RESTAURANT:** L served all week 12-2 D served all week 7-9.30 ▥: Free House ◖: Hobsons Best, Wye Valley Butty Bach & Dorothy Goodbody's. ♀: 9 **FACILITIES:** Child facs Garden: Formal garden with patio, heaters Dogs allowed except when food is being served in bar **NOTES:** Parking 20

WALTERSTONE   Map 09 SO32

Carpenters Arms ♀
HR2 0DX ☎ 01873 890353
Dir: *Off the A465 between Hereford & Abergavenny at Pandy*

There's plenty of character in this 300-year-old free house located on the edge of the Black Mountains where the owner, Mrs Watkins, was born. Here you'll find beams, antique settles and a leaded range with open fires that burn all winter. Popular food options include beef and Guinness pie; beef lasagna; and thick lamb cutlets. Ask about the vegetarian selection, and large selection of home-made desserts.
OPEN: 12-3 7-11 **BAR MEALS:** L served all week 12-3 D served all week 7-9.30 **RESTAURANT:** L served all week 12-3 D served all week 7-9.30 ▥: Free House ◖: Wadworth 6X.
FACILITIES: Garden: Dogs allowed by arrangement
NOTES: Parking 20 No credit cards

WELLINGTON   Map 10 SO44

The Wellington
HR4 8AT ☎ 01432 830367 e-mail: thewellington@hotmail.com
Dir: *Take Wellington turning between Hereford & Leominster on the A49*
Victorian country pub with original fireplaces, antique furniture and a good selection of real ales and local ciders, many of which are showcased at the inn's annual beer festival. Bar meals include fish and chips, roasted smoked ham, and steak and Guinness pie, with restaurant options like Barbary duck breast; pan-fried calves' liver; and baked smoked haddock. St George's Day and St Patrick's Day celebrations are a popular fixture.

continued

OPEN: 12-3 6-11 (Sun 12-3, 7-10.30) **BAR MEALS:** L served Tue-Sun 12-2 D served Mon-Sat 7-9 Av main course £12
RESTAURANT: L served Tue-Sun 12-2 D served Mon-Sat 7-9 Av 3 course à la carte £22 ◖: Hobsons, Wye Valley Butty Bach, Guest Real Ales. **FACILITIES:** Child facs Garden: Beer garden, play area, ample seating Dogs allowed Water **NOTES:** Parking 20

WEOBLEY   Map 09 SO45

Pick of the Pubs

The Salutation Inn ♦♦♦♦ @ ▷
Market Pitch HR4 8SJ ☎ 01544 318443 ▤ 01544 318405
e-mail: salutationinn@btinternet.com
Dir: *In village centre opposite Broad Street, 10m NNW of Hereford*

A popular pub, in a pretty medieval village in a county famous for its cattle, apple orchards and hops. The 500-year-old black and white timber-framed building and adjoining cottage have been tastefully converted from an old ale and cider house. After a long walk or bike ride you can eat well but informally in the traditional lounge bar, with a pint of Wye Valley Butty Bach to hand. The stylish Oak Room restaurant promises modern British-style dishes carefully prepared with fresh local ingredients. You should find starters like grilled field mushroom or pearls of haggis. Main courses may include chicken supreme with wild mushroom and smoked bacon, honey glazed breast of duck, or fillet of sea bass and lobster medallion.
OPEN: 11-11 (Sun 12-10.30) **BAR MEALS:** L served all week 12-2.30 D served all week 7-9.30 Av main course £9
RESTAURANT: L served all week 12-2.30 D served all week 7-9 Av 3 course à la carte £25 ▥: Free House ◖: Hook Norton Best, Coors Worthington's Creamflow, Wye Valley Butty Bach, Fullers London Pride. **FACILITIES:** Children's licence Garden: Patio area with tables and umbrellas Dogs allowed Water **NOTES:** Parking 14 **ROOMS:** 4 bedrooms en suite 1 family room s£51 d£76

WHITNEY-ON-WYE   Map 09 SO24

Rhydspence Inn ★★ ▷
HR3 6EU ☎ 01497 831262 ▤ 01497 831751
e-mail: info@rhydspence-inn.co.uk
Dir: *N side of A438 1m W of Whitney-on-Wye*

The Rhydspence was originally a manor house, built in 1380, with additions from the 17th and 20th centuries. For hundreds of years the inn was used by Welsh and Irish drovers taking the Black Ox Trail to markets as far away as London. Food options include Caribbean beef in the elegant dining room or Hereford rabbit in the brasserie and bar, all overlooking the Wye Valley. There is also a good choice of grills.

continued

England

WHITNEY-ON-WYE continued

OPEN: 11-2.30 7-11 Closed: 2 wks in Jan **BAR MEALS:** L served all week 11-1.45 D served all week 7-8.45 Av main course £7 **RESTAURANT:** L served all week 11-1.45 D served all week 7-8.45 Sun lunch 12-2 Av 3 course à la carte £24 ❂: Free House ❚: Robinsons Best, Interbrew Bass. **FACILITIES:** Garden: 2/3 acres, mostly lawn **NOTES:** Parking 30 **ROOMS:** 7 bedrooms en suite s£42.50 d£85

WOOLHOPE Map 10 SO63

The Crown Inn ◗ ♀
HR1 4QP ☎ 01432 860468 ▤ 01432 860770
e-mail: thecrowninn1382@aol.com
Dir: From Hereford take B4224 to Mordiford, left immediately after Moon Inn. Crown Inn in village centre
Parts of this mainly 18th-century inn date back to about 1520 as indicated by a mounting block at the front of the original building bearing this date. Located in a beautiful conservation area close to Hereford, Ross-on-Wye and Ledbury. The owners offer an extensive menu which includes steak, stout and mushroom pie; chicken, leek and stilton vol-au-vent; salmon and broccoli au gratin; and lamb and cranberry casserole. Various light bites and home-made desserts.
OPEN: 12-3 6.30-11 (Sun 7-11, Winter 7-11 Mon-Fri) Closed: 25 Dec **BAR MEALS:** L served all week 12-2 D served all week 6.30/7-9.30 Av main course £7.95 **RESTAURANT:** L served all week 12-2 D served all week 6.30/7-9.30 Av 3 course à la carte £17 ❂: Free House ❚: Smiles Best, Wye Valley Best, Cats Whiskers, Worthington Creamflow. ♀: 6 **FACILITIES:** Garden: Garden front and back with heaters Dogs allowed Water **NOTES:** Parking 30

HERTFORDSHIRE

ALDBURY Map 06 SP91

The Greyhound Inn ◗ ♀
19 Stocks Rd HP23 5RT ☎ 01442 851228 ▤ 01442 851495
Recently refurbished pub overlooking the village pond in Aldbury, a recent finalist in the Best Kept Village awards. The Chiltern Hills are close by, so The Greyhound is understandably popular with walkers. One menu is offered throughout, and seafood figures strongly with dishes like monk fish wrapped in parma ham; or smoked haddock on herb potato cakes with poached egg and horseradish hollandaise. Food can also be served in the courtyard outside.
OPEN: 11-11 Closed: 25 Dec **BAR MEALS:** L served all week 12-2.30 D served Mon-Sat 7-10 Av main course £13 **RESTAURANT:** L served all week 12-2.30 D served Mon-Sat 7-10 Av 3 course à la carte £18 ❂: Hall & Woodhouse ❚: Badger Best, Tanglefoot, Champion, IPA. ♀: 10 **FACILITIES:** Garden: Courtyard, Food served outside Dogs allowed Water **NOTES:** Parking 9

The Valiant Trooper ♀
Trooper Rd HP23 5RW ☎ 01442 851203 ▤ 01442 851071
Dir: A41 at Tring junct, follow railway station signs, 0.5m and at village green turn right then 200yds on left
Family-run free house in a pretty village surrounded by the Chiltern Hills, where hikers, cyclists and dogs are all made welcome. Local and guest beers feature, and interesting daily specials from the blackboard are hot and spicy chicken stir fry; beef fillet stroganoff; steak, kidney and ale pie; and shark and tuna Breton. The Duke of Wellington is rumoured to have held a tactical conference at the pub - hence the name.
OPEN: 11-11 (Sun 12-10.30) **BAR MEALS:** L served all week

continued

12-2.30 D served Tue-Sat 6.30-9.15 **RESTAURANT:** L served Tue-Sun 12-2 D served Tue-Sun 6.30-9.15 ❂: Free House ❚: Fuller's London Pride, Scottish Courage John Smith's, Marston's Pedigree, Greene King Ruddles Best. **FACILITIES:** Child facs Garden: Large grassed area with picnic tables Dogs allowed Water **NOTES:** Parking 36

ARDELEY Map 12 TL32

The Jolly Waggoner
SG2 7AH ☎ 01438 861350
Cream-washed 500-year-old pub with open beams, roaring fires, antique furniture and a popular cottage garden. The inn also benefits from a lovely village setting and a variety of local walks. All the food is home-made from fresh ingredients, with everything from appetising sandwiches to à la carte dining. Fish is something of a speciality, like dressed crab salad, halibut and sea bass. Alternatively, try loin of lamb, calves' liver or steak and kidney pie.
OPEN: 12-2.30 6.30-11 (Open BH Mon, closed Tue after BH) **BAR MEALS:** L served Tue-Sun 12-2 D served Tue-Sat 6.30-9 Av main course £12 **RESTAURANT:** L served Sun 12.30-2 D served Tue-Sat 6.30-9 Av 3 course à la carte £27.50 ❂: Greene King ❚: Greene King IPA & Abbot Ale. **FACILITIES:** Garden: Pretty cottage garden, wooden fruniture **NOTES:** Parking 15

ASHWELL Map 12 TL23

Bushel & Strike ♀
Mill St SG7 5LY ☎ 01462 742394 ▤ 01462 743768
e-mail: graeme@375aol
Wooden floors, leather chesterfields and open fires in winter characterise the main bar of this popular inn, which stands in the shadow of Ashwell's Norman church tower. The restaurant is a conversion of the old school hall with its vaulted roof and oak floor. Try a traditional lamb and vegetable-filled Hertfordshire pasty, braised lamb shank on ratatouille, seafood pie, or chicken breast with a wild mushroom and basil mousse. Spotted Dick and apple crumble are often among the sweet selections.
OPEN: 11.30-3 6-11 (all day Sun) **BAR MEALS:** L served all week 12-2.30 D served all week 7-9.30 Sun 12-4, 7-9 Av main course £7.50 **RESTAURANT:** L served all week 12-2.30 D served all week 7-9.30 Av 3 course à la carte £19 ❂: Charles Wells ❚: Charles,Old Speckled Hen, Broadside, Bombadier. ♀: 7 **FACILITIES:** Child facs Garden: Large garden, patio, tables, benches Dogs allowed in bar only Water **NOTES:** Parking 40

The Three Tuns ♀
High St SG7 5NL ☎ 01462 742107 ▤ 01462 743662
e-mail: claire@tuns.co.uk
There are many original features in this 19th-century inn, providing an old-world atmosphere in the heart of Ashwell village. The freshly prepared menu changes daily and includes salads, ploughman's and baguettes as well as specials. Starters include devilled whitebait; herrings in Madeira; and home-made soup. Follow with a main course such as fresh Nile perch fillet with a tomato and herb sauce; pot-roast partridge with pork and leek stuffing; and pasta bake.
OPEN: 11-11 (Sun 12-10.30) **BAR MEALS:** L served all week 12-2.30 D served all week 6.30-9.30 **RESTAURANT:** L served all week 12-2.30 D served all week 6.30-9.30 ❂: Greene King ❚: Greene King IPA, Ruddles, Abbot. ♀: 7 **FACILITIES:** Child facs Garden: Large, terrace at top, seats around 100 Dogs allowed **NOTES:** Parking 20

England

AYOT ST LAWRENCE   Map 06 TL11

Pick of the Pubs

The Brocket Arms ♀
AL6 9BT ☎ 01438 820250 ⧠ 01438 820068
See Pick of the Pubs on page 260

BARLEY   Map 12 TL43

The Fox & Hounds
High St SG8 8HU ☎ 01763 848459 ⧠ 01763 849274
Dir: A505 onto B1368 at Flint Cross, pub 4m
Set in a pretty village, this former 17th-century hunting lodge
is notable for its pub sign which extends across the lane. It
has real fires, a warm welcome and an attractive garden. The
menu offers a good range of dependable choices, including
lemon chicken, steak and ale pie, cheese and bacon burger,
mushroom stroganoff, and good old fish and chips.
OPEN: 12-11 (Sun 12-10.30) **BAR MEALS:** L served all week 12-10
D served all week 12-10 Sun 12-9 **RESTAURANT:** 12-10 12-10
⊕: Punch Taverns ◀: IPA, 6X, Adnams Bitter, Adnams Broadside.
FACILITIES: Garden: L shaped garden with tables and chairs Dogs
allowed **NOTES:** Parking 25

BEDMOND   Map 06 TL00

The Swan ♀
Bedmond Rd, Pimlico HP3 8SH
☎ 01923 263093 ⧠ 0118 375 1555
e-mail: courtangie@hotmail.com
Dir: Between Hemel Hempstead and Watford

An attractive, traditional pub, whose whitewashed front is
adorned with colourful hanging baskets. Outside is a large
lawn, play area and adults-only patio. Inside, you'll find a
warm welcome and a wide selection of traditional pub food.
Bar meals include burgers, jacket potatoes and sandwiches,
with French fish soup, roast lamb, scampi and chips or pan-
fried chicken and bacon from the main menu.
OPEN: 11-11 (Sun 12-10.30) **BAR MEALS:** L served all week 12-3
D served all week 6.30-9.30 Sun 12-8.30 Av main course £9
RESTAURANT: L served all week 12-3 D served all week 6.30-9.30
Sun 12-8.30 ◀: Mr Chubbs Lunchtime Bitter, Abbot Ale, Fullers
London Pride. ♀: 8 **FACILITIES:** Garden **NOTES:** Parking 70

> Restaurant and Bar Meal times indicate the times
> when food is available. Last orders may be
> approximately 30 minutes before the times stated

BUNTINGFORD   Map 12 TL32

The Sword in Hand ⌦ ♀
Westmill SG9 9LQ ☎ 01763 271356
e-mail: heather@swordinhand.ndo.co.uk
Dir: Off A10 1.5m S of Buntingford
A 14th-century pub once home to a Scottish noble family
when it was known as The Old House. The inn is reputedly
haunted by the ghost of one the descendents who died of
smallpox in a small, airless attic. The dining room overlooks
open countryside and offers a regularly changing menu
incorporating fresh, local ingredients: pan-fried veal escalope,
crispy fried pork fillet, garlic and herb roasted rack of lamb,
and swordfish steak.
OPEN: 12-3 5-11 (Open Mon L in Summer)
BAR MEALS: L served Tue-Sun 12-2.30 D served Tue-Sun 6.30-9.30
Sun 12-5 (12-7 summer) Av main course £10
RESTAURANT: L served Tue-Sun 12-2.30 D served Tue-Sun
6.30-9.30 Av 3 course à la carte £20 ⊕: Free House ◀: Greene
King IPA, Young's Bitter, Shephard & Neame Spitfire & Guest Ales.
FACILITIES: Child facs Large garden beautiful view, patio area,
pergola Dogs allowed **NOTES:** Parking 25

COTTERED   Map 12 TL32

The Bull at Cottered
Cottered SG9 9QP ☎ 01763 281243
Dir: On the A507 in Cottered between Buntingford & Baldock
Traditional local occupying a picturesque village setting, with
low-beamed ceilings, pub games, cosy fires and antique
furniture inside. The menu offers the likes of fresh fishcakes,
rack of lamb, calves' liver with onion gravy, fillet of chicken in
cream sauce, and steak and kidney pie. Sandwiches, jacket
potatoes and ploughman's are also available. There's a new
restaurant extension with access to alfresco dining area.
OPEN: 12-2.30 6.30-11 Sun 7-10.30 **BAR MEALS:** L served all
week 12-2 D served all week 6.30-9 Sun 12-2, 7-9 Av main course
£12 **RESTAURANT:** L served all week 12-2 D served all week 6.30-9
Sun 12-2, 7-9 Av 3 course à la carte £22.50 Av 3 course fixed price
£20 ⊕: Greene King ◀: Greene king IPA & Abbot Ale.
FACILITIES: Garden: Large well kept garden, wooden furniture
NOTES: Parking 35

FLAUNDEN   Map 06 TL00

The Bricklayers Arms ♀
Hogpits Bottom HP3 0PH ☎ 01442 833322 ⧠ 834841
e-mail: goodfood@bricklayersarms.co.uk
*Dir: M1 junct 8 through Hemel Hempstead to Bovington then follow
Flaunden sign.*

Tucked away in deepest rural Hertfordshire, this award-
winning country pub has been extensively renovated and
refurbished. With its low beams, exposed brickwork and open

continued

Pick of the Pubs

AYOT ST LAWRENCE – HERTFORDSHIRE

The Brocket Arms

A delightful 14th-century inn standing in the village that was home to George Bernard Shaw for 40 years until his death in 1950. Before the Reformation, the building formed the monastic quarters for the Norman church. Among the legendary tales associated with it is the one about Henry VIII who supposedly wooed his sixth wife, Catherine Parr, in the nearby manor house.

There are many charming features inside the pub, including low oak beams, and an inglenook fireplace, while outside is an extensive walled garden that makes a glorious sun trap. Traditional English game and home-cooked dishes characterise the bar menu - among them perhaps sandwiches of fresh roast meats, and steak and kidney pie. The lunch menu might begin with vegetarian Brocket pasta, or salmon tartare, and move on to game pie with a crusty pastry, tortellini with salmon in a cream and cheesy sauce, or roast chicken. The dinner menu moves up a notch, with roasted goats' cheese, or flat mushrooms with garlic, red pepper and mozarella cheese to start; followed by main courses like venison marinaded in a juniper berry and red wine sauce; roast pheasant with a redcurrant and port sauce; tournedos Rossini topped with pâté and port sauce; vegetarian stroganoff with tumeric rice; sea bass grilled with garlic, lemon, spring onion and ginger; and salmon cutlets with a dill and cream sauce.

OPEN: 11-11
BAR MEALS: 12-2.30 7.30-10
RESTAURANT: 12-2.30 7.30-10
🍺: Free House
🍺: Greene King Abbot Ale & IPA, Adnams Broadside, Fullers London Pride, Youngs IPA.
FACILITIES: Garden: Large walled garden with tables Dogs allowed Must be supervised
NOTES: Parking 6

♀   Map 06 TL11
AL6 9BT
☎ 01438 820250
🖹 01438 820068

FLAUNDEN continued

fires, it is popular with walkers and locals, as well as those who enjoy relaxing in the sunny and secluded garden in the summer months. Hearty vegetables accompany dishes such as Scotch beef with black peppercorn sauce; lamb confit; and sea bass with red pepper sauce.
OPEN: 11.30-11.30 **BAR MEALS:** L served all week 12-2 D served all week 6-9.30 **RESTAURANT:** L served all week 12-3 D served all week 6-9.30 ☺: Free House ⬤: Old Speckled Hen, Brakspear Bitter, Ringwood Old Thumper, Marston's Pedigree. ♀: 12
FACILITIES: Sunny & secluded garden Dogs allowed Water, biscuits **NOTES:** Parking 40

HARPENDEN Map 06 TL11

Gibraltar Castle ▷◁ ♀
70 Lower Luton Rd AL5 5AH ☎ 01582 460005 📠 01582 462589
e-mail: gibraltar.castle@ntlworld.com
Bustling Fuller's pub located opposite parkland in Batford. The pub may be up to 350 years old, and is believed to be the only pub with this name in the UK. It was allegedly owned by an ex-governor of Gibraltar. In the past it was used as a magistrates' court, and the remnants of an old cell are to be found in the beer cellar. Blackboard menu offers a wide range of imaginative fresh fish dishes, depending on market availability, with other choices such as chicken and mushroom pie, lasagne, lamb shank, chicken stuffed with brie, and goats' cheese, walnut and almond salad.
OPEN: 11.30-11 25 Dec open 12-2 only **BAR MEALS:** L served all week 12-2.30 D served Mon-Sat 6-9 (Sun 12-4) Av main course £9 **RESTAURANT:** L served all week 12-2.30 D served Mon-Sat (Sun 12-4) ☺: Fullers ⬤: Fuller's London Pride, ESB, Chiswick Bitter, Honey Dew & Red Fox. ♀: 7 **FACILITIES:** Garden: Flower lined rear garden, patio at front Dogs allowed Water **NOTES:** Parking 25

HEMEL HEMPSTEAD Map 06 TL00

Pick of the Pubs

Alford Arms ♀
Frithsden HP1 3DD ☎ 01442 864480 📠 01422 876893
e-mail: info@alfordarmsfrithsden.co.uk

Award-winning Victorian pub with a modern feel heightened by scrubbed wooden tables and fresh flowers. In fine weather customers opt for afternoon tea served on the sun-trap terrace, many of them having just explored the extensive beech woodland of the Ashridge Estate nearby. Ivinghoe Beacon, marking the end of the Ridgeway National Trail, is also a short distance away. An imaginative selection of blackboard specials and an appetising takeaway menu are among the key attractions here. The

pub is also renowned for its high-quality, organic, free-range and locally sourced produce. Listed among a varied choice of small plates are caper berries; pressed game terrine with sherry roasted figs; and pancetta, leek and parmesan risotto, while main courses might include crispy chicken on herb polenta cake with smoked bacon, wild mushroom and red onion; beer-braised beef stew with herb dumplings; and smoked haddock on colcannon with poached egg and chive butter sauce.
OPEN: 11-11 (Sun 12-10.30) Closed: 25-26 Dec
BAR MEALS: L served all week 12-2.30 D served all week 7-10 (Sun 12-3) Av main course £11.75 **RESTAURANT:** L served all week 12-2.30 D served all week 7-10 (Sun 12-3) Av 3 course à la carte £22.25 ☺: Free House ⬤: Marstons Pedigree, Brakspear, Interbrew Flowers & Morrells Oxford Blue. ♀: 15
FACILITIES: Garden: Terrace with tables over-looking green Dogs allowed Water provided **NOTES:** Parking 25

HEXTON Map 12 TL13

The Raven ♀
SG5 3JB ☎ 01582 881209 📠 01582 881610
e-mail: jack@ravenathexton.f9.co.uk web: www.theraven.co.uk
Dir: 5m W of Hitchin. 5m N of Luton, just outside Barton le Clay

Named after Ravensburgh Castle up in the neighbouring hills, this neat 1920s pub has comfortable bars and a large garden with terrace and play area. The traditional pub food menu is more comprehensive than many, with baguettes, filled jackets, pork ribs, steaks from the Duke of Buccleuch's Scottish estate, surf and turf, ribs, hot chicken and bacon salad, Mediterranean pasta bake and a whole lot more. Daily specials are on the blackboard.
OPEN: 11-3 6-11 (Sun 12-10.30, Sat 11-11) **BAR MEALS:** L served all week 12-2 D served all week 6-10 Sat-Sun 12-9 Av main course £9 **RESTAURANT:** L served all week 12-2 D served all week 6-10 Av 3 course à la carte £15 ☺: Enterprise Inns ⬤: Greene King Old Speckled Hen, Fullers London Pride, Greene King IPA. ♀: 24
FACILITIES: Child facs Garden: Table & chair seating for 50 Dogs allowed in the garden only. Water provided **NOTES:** Parking 40

> ◆ Pubs with Red Diamonds are the top places in the AA's three, four and five diamond ratings

> Not all of the pubs in the guide are open all week or all day. It's always best to check before you travel

continued

HINXWORTH   Map 12 TL24

Three Horseshoes ♀
High St SG7 5HQ ☎ 01462 742280
Dir: E of A1 between Biggleswade and Baldock
Thatched 18th-century country pub with a dining extension
into the garden. Parts of the building date back 500 years,
and the walls are adorned with pictures and photos of the
village's history. Samples from a typical menu include lamb
cutlets with champ; rainbow trout with almonds; sea bass
provençale; steak and Guinness pie; bacon and cheese pasta
bake; and roasted Tuscan red peppers.
OPEN: 11.30-2.30 6-11 (Sun 12-3, 7-10.30) **BAR MEALS:** L served
all week 12-2 D served Mon-Sat 7-9 Av main course £7.50
RESTAURANT: L served all week 12-2 D served Mon-Sat 7-9
Av 3 course à la carte £18 ⊕: Greene King ◀: Greene King IPA,
Abbot Ale, Tanners Jack. ♀: 6 **FACILITIES:** Large rustic garden with
trees and a pétanque area Dogs allowed in the garden only
NOTES: Parking 16

HITCHIN   Map 12 TL12

The Greyhound ♦♦♦ ▷ ♀
London Rd, St Ippolyts SG4 7NL ☎ 01462 440989
e-mail: greyhound@freenet.co.uk

The Greyhound was rescued from dereliction by the present
owner who previously worked for the London Fire Brigade,
and is now a popular, family-run hostelry surrounded by
pleasant countryside yet handy for the M1 and Luton Airport.
The food is good, wholesome and unpretentious, offering the
likes of fresh fish, rabbit pie, faggots, steak and ale pie and
home-made lasagne.
OPEN: 11:30-2.30 5-11 Closed: Dec 25-26 **BAR MEALS:** L served
all week 12-2 D served Mon-Sat 7-9 Av main course £8.75
RESTAURANT: L served all week 12-2 D served Mon-Sat 6-9
Av 3 course à la carte £16 ⊕: Free House ◀: Adnams, Guest.
♀: 8 **NOTES:** Parking 25 **ROOMS:** 4 bedrooms en suite s£35
d£35 No children overnight

 Pubs offering a good choice of fish on
their menu

 Pubs with this logo do not allow smoking
anywhere on their premises

All AA rated accommodation can also be
found on the AA's internet site
www.theAA.com

HUNSDON   Map 06 TL41

Pick of the Pubs

The Fox and Hounds NEW ▷ ♀
2 High St SG12 8NH ☎ 01279 843999 ⬛ 01279 841092
Dir: Within 10m of Harlow, Hertford, Bishops Stortford, Ware.
A welcoming inn tucked away in rural England, in the
sleepy village of Hunsdon nestling in the heart of
Hertfordshire countryside. The atmosphere is informal
and friendly, and there is large attractive garden with
patio area and tables. The bar is stocked with most of the
best locally brewed real ales. The menus are succinct, but
succulent. Starters could be wild garlic leaf soup; salad of
smoked trout with new potatoes and spring onions;
linguine with clams, chilli, garlic and parsley; moules
marinieres; and sauté of squid, chorizo and piquillo
peppers. Mains could be wild mushroom risotto; baked
fillet of cod with spiced chickpeas and gremolata; côte de
boeuf, hand cut chips and sauce béarnaise; salt marsh
lamb rump and braised savoy cabbage; veal T-bone steak,
sauté potatoes, broad beans and salsa verde; calves' liver
with duck fat potato cake; and Cumberland sausages,
mash and onion gravy.
OPEN: 12-4 6-11 (Sun 12-6 BH 12-4) Closed: 1 week in Jan
BAR MEALS: L served Tue-Sat 12-3.30 D served Tue-Sat 6-10.30
Sun 12-4 Av main course £9.75 **RESTAURANT:** L served Sun
12-4 D served Fri-Sat 7 Av 3 course à la carte £35 ◀: Adnams
Bitter, Adnams Broadside, Guiness. ♀: 7 **FACILITIES:** Child
facs Large, attractive quiet garden and patio area Dogs allowed

KIMPTON   Map 06 TL11

The White Horse ♀
22 High St SG4 8RJ ☎ 01438 832307 ⬛ 01438 833842
e-mail: thewhitehorsepub@aol.com

Dating from the mid-1500s, this popular low-roofed pub
features a priest hole behind the bar, and on winter evenings
welcomes customers with a roaring log fire. Located in a
delightful country village, it also has a decked garden for
dining outside. The varied menu features Highland steak,
gammon platter, supreme chicken parcel, haddock and chips,
plus Mexican, Chinese and Indian choices and a number of
vegetarian options. The area is great for walking.
OPEN: 12-2.30 6-11 (Sat 12-3, 6-11, Sun 12-4, 7-10.30)
BAR MEALS: L served Tues-Sun 12-2 D served Tues-Sat
RESTAURANT: L served Tues-Sun 12-2 D served Tues-Sat 7-9
◀: Scottish Courage Courage Directors, Interbrew Bass, McMullen
Original AK. ♀: 8 **FACILITIES:** Garden: Decked area, tables & chairs
NOTES: Parking 10

LITTLE GADDESDEN — Map 11 SP91

The Bridgewater Arms NEW 🐟 ⚥
HP4 1PD
Dir: 6m from Berkhampstead
Set in 4500 acres of National Trust land, the Bridgewater Arms dates from the 18th century. Beer was brewed here until the end of the 19th century, and part of the building was also used as the village school - hence the present day 'School Room' restaurant. Sandwiches, jacket potatoes and hot meals are served in the bar, whilst restaurant diners can expect whole roast partridge, seafood risotto, and roasted vegetable and brie Wellington.
OPEN: 11-11 **BAR MEALS:** L served all week 12-2.30 D served all week 6-9.30 Sun 12-8.30 Av main course £7
RESTAURANT: L served all week 12-2.30 D served all week 6-9.30 Sun 12-8.30 Av 3 course à la carte £20 ◖: Greene King IPA, Abbot Ale, seasonal guest beers. ⚥: 9 **FACILITIES:** Garden: Spacious garden, well maintained, benches Dogs allowed Water
NOTES: Parking 35

LITTLE HADHAM — Map 06 TL42

The Nags Head 🐟 ⚥
The Ford SG11 2AX ☎ 01279 771555 ▤ 01279 771555
e-mail: robinsonmark2002@yahoo.co.uk
Dir: M11 junct 8 take A120 towards Puckeridge & A10. Left at lights in Little Hadnam. Pub 0.75m on right
This 16th-century former coaching inn has also been a brewery, bakery and Home Guard arsenal in its time. Internal features are an oak-beamed bar and a restaurant area with open brickwork and an old bakery oven. Fish is a speciality with 22 fish main courses on offer: try red snapper with Portuguese sauce; seafood platter; or poached skate wing with a black butter. Vegetarian options include Thai red curry.
OPEN: 11-3 6-11 (Sun 12-3.30 7-10.30) Dec 25-26 Closed eve
BAR MEALS: L served all week 12-2 D served Mon-Thurs 6-9 Sun 7-9, Fri-Sat 6-9.30 Av main course £8.50 **RESTAURANT:** L served all week 12-2 D served Mon-Thurs 6-9 Sun 7-9, Fri-Sat 6-9.30 Av 3 course à la carte £15 ◖: Greene King ◖: Greene King Abbot Ale, IPA, Old Speckled Hen & Ruddles County Ale, Marstons Pedigree.
FACILITIES: Garden: Patio area at front of pub; courtyard Dogs allowed Water

MUCH HADHAM — Map 06 TL41

Jolly Waggoners ⚥
Widford Rd SG10 6EZ ☎ 01279 842102 ▤ 01279 842102
e-mail: Jollywaggoners@btinternet.com
Dir: On B1004 between Bishops Stortford & Ware
Daily fresh fish features on the evening menu at this Victorian pub built from two older cottages. A large open fire and beamed interior lend character to the non-smoking bar, and there are no noisy games machines to disturb the atmosphere. From the specials board expect several choices of fish, plus roast meats and grills, and the likes of omelettes, curries, pork Wellington and vegetarian dishes, all home made. Classic car meet held on each third Sunday.
OPEN: 12-2.30 6.30-11 (Sun 12-3, 7-10.30) **BAR MEALS:** L served all week 12-2 D served all week 6.30-9 Av main course £6
RESTAURANT: L served all week 12-2.30 D served all week 6.30-9 Av 3 course à la carte £15 Av 2 course fixed price £5.95
◖: McMullens ◖: McMullens Original AK & Country Best Bitter, Scottish Courage Courage Directors. ⚥: 8 **FACILITIES:** Garden: picnic area with seating for over 40 people Dogs allowed Water
NOTES: Parking 40

OLD KNEBWORTH — Map 06 TL22

The Lytton Arms 🐟 ⚥
Park Ln SG3 6QB ☎ 01438 812312 ▤ 01438 817298
e-mail: thelyttonarms@btinternet.com
Dir: From A1(M) take A602. At Knebworth turn right at rail station. Follow Codicote signs. Pub 1.5m on right

The pub was designed around 1877 by Lord Lytton's brother-in-law, who happened to be the architect Sir Edwin Lutyens, replacing the previous inn, now a residence next door. Also next door, but in a much grander way, is the Lytton estate, the family home for centuries. On the simple but wide-ranging menu are Mrs O'Keefe's flavoured sausages; chicken or vegetable balti; honeyroast ham; chargrilled lamb's liver and bacon; and fisherman's pie.
OPEN: 11-11 (Sun 12-10.30) **BAR MEALS:** L served Mon-Sat 12-2.30 Sun 12-5 D served Mon-Sat 7-9.30 **RESTAURANT:** L served Mon-Sun 12-2.30 D served Mon-Sat 6.30-9.30 Sun 12-5 ◖: Free House ◖: Fuller's London Pride, Adnams Best Bitter, Broadside, Wherry. ⚥: 30 **FACILITIES:** Children's licence Garden: Large umbrella protected decking Dogs allowed Water
NOTES: Parking 40

POTTERS CROUCH — Map 06 TL10

The Hollybush ⚥
AL2 3NN ☎ 01727 851792 ▤ 01727 851792
Dir: Ragged Hall Ln off A405 or Bedmond Ln off A4147
Picturesque, attractively furnished country pub with quaint, white-painted exterior and large, enclosed garden. Close to St Albans with its Roman ruins and good local walks. An antique dresser, a large fireplace and various prints and paintings help give the inn a delightfully welcoming atmosphere. Food is simple and unfussy, with a range of ploughman's, burgers, platters and toasted sandwiches. Smoked and peppered mackerel fillet, pasties and salads also feature.
OPEN: 11.30-2.30 6-11 (Sun 12-2.30, 7-10.30)
BAR MEALS: L served Mon-Sat 12-2 ◖: Fullers ◖: Fullers Chiswick Bitter, Fullers London Pride, ESB & Seasonal Ales. ⚥: 7
FACILITIES: Garden **NOTES:** Parking 50

PRESTON — Map 06 TL12

The Red Lion
The Green SG4 7UD ☎ 01462 459585 ▤ 01462 442284
e-mail: janebaerlein@hotmail.com
Bought from Whitbread's in 1983, the Red Lion was the first community-owned pub in Britain. When the pub was threatened with closure, local people funded the purchase and renovation to ensure a continuing focal point for their village. Now, this award-winning free house offers a range of guest ales and a regularly changing menu board that includes

continued

England

PRESTON continued

home-made pies, seasonal game, fresh fish and vegetarian options, as well as a selection of home-made puddings.

The Red Lion

OPEN: 12-2.30 5.30-11 **BAR MEALS:** L served all week 12-2 D served Wed-Sat, Mon 7-9 Av main course £5.95 ⊕: Free House ◄: Greene King IPA & Changing real ales. **FACILITIES:** Garden: Dogs allowed Water **NOTES:** Parking 60 No credit cards

---

RICKMANSWORTH   Map 06 TQ09

The Rose and Crown NEW ♀
Harefield Rd WD3 1PP ☎ 01923 897680
e-mail: chipiehall@aol.com
Dir: 2m from Rickmansworth
The Rose and Crown is a 16th-century farmhouse with a clubby atmosphere, thanks to the many social activities held here. It is run by four devoted pub professionals who place a strong emphasis quality home cooked food, ever-changing real ales, and an adventurous wine list. Expect potted chicken liver pâté with red onion marmalade; slow roasted belly pork with mash, nutmeg spinach and apple sauce; and lemon tart with mint cream.
OPEN: 12-11 (Sun 12-10.30) **BAR MEALS:** L served all week 12-5 D served all week 5-10 Sun 12-4, 7-10 Av main course £5.50 **RESTAURANT:** L served all week 12-3 D served all week 7-10 Sun 12-4, 7-10 Av 3 course fixed price £12.50 ◄: Regularly changing bitters. ♀: 11 **FACILITIES:** Garden: Large garden with seating and BBQ area Dogs allowed water **NOTES:** Parking 70

ROYSTON   Map 12 TL34

Pick of the Pubs

The Cabinet Free House and Restaurant NEW ◉ ♀
High St, Reed SG8 8AH ☎ 01763 848366 📠 01763 849407
e-mail: thecabinet@btopenworld.com
Dir: 2m N of Royston just off the A10
Here's a pub that touches lofty heights - literally, because it is the highest point between the UK and the Ural mountains in Russia, as the crow flies. The Cabinet is a 16th-century pub that Paul Bloxham has transformed into foodie heaven. Everything is seasonal, and based on interesting French, British and the transatlantic inspirations. For example, you can start with gambas à la plancha - large tiger prawns cooked with garlic butter and lemon; or steamed Thai style mussels. To follow you could choose between brochette of salmon, scallop, tiger prawns with champagne risotto and tomato fondue; Breckland duck breast with honey-roasted root vegetables and ginger jus; and rocket and preserved lemon risotto,

continued

lemon cream and baked blue cheese phyllos. Finish with Tahitian vanilla bean crème brûlée with confit citrus fruits and almond lace tuile, or apple and blackberry crumble (from the Cabinet's gardens) with custard.

The Cabinet Free House and Restaurant

OPEN: 12-3 6-11 (Open all day Sat-Sun summer) Closed: 25-26 Dec **BAR MEALS:** L served Tue-Sun 12-2.30 D served Tue-Sat 6-10 12-3.30 Sunday **RESTAURANT:** L served Tue-Sun 12-2.30 D served Tue-Sat 6-10 Closed Sun evening Av 3 course à la carte £28 Av 3 course fixed price £13.95 ⊕: Free House ◄: London Pride, Green King IPA,. ♀: 50 **FACILITIES:** Garden: 1 acre of countryside Dogs allowed **NOTES:** Parking 40

ST ALBANS   Map 06 TL10

Rose & Crown ♀
10 St Michael St AL3 4SG ☎ 01727 851903 📠 01727 761775
e-mail: ruth.courtney@ntlworld.com
Traditional 16th-century pub situated in a beautiful part of St Michael's 'village', opposite the entrance to Verulanium Park and the Roman Museum. It has a classic beamed bar with a huge inglenook, and a summer patio filled with flowers. The pub offers a distinctive range of American deli-style sandwiches, which are served with potato salad, kettle crisps and pickled cucumber. The Cotton Club, for example, has a roast beef, ham, Swiss cheese, mayo, tomato, onion, lettuce and horseradish mustard filling.
OPEN: 11.30-3 5.30-11 (Open all day Sat-Sun)
BAR MEALS: L served Mon-Fri 12-2 D served Mon-Sat (L served Sat-Sun 12.30-2.30) **RESTAURANT:** 12-2 6-8.30 Sun 12-2.30 ⊕: Punch Taverns ◄: Adnams Bitter, Carlsberg-Tetley Tetley Bitter, Fuller's London Pride, Courage Directors. ♀: 8
FACILITIES: Children's licence Garden: Walled garden, tables, hanging baskets etc Dogs allowed Water **NOTES:** Parking 6

STOTFOLD   Map 12 TL23

The Fox & Duck ♀
149 Arlesey Raod SG5 4HE ☎ 01462 732434 📠 01462 835962
e-mail: foxandduck@cragg-inns.co.uk
Set on a large site, this picturesque family pub has a big garden, a children's playground, a caravan site, weekly football matches, and regular barbecues. Children's birthday parties catered for. A sample menu selection includes 8oz fillet steak with stilton and madeira, sizzling black bean chicken, medallions of pork with honey and ginger, and a wide range of home-made soups and pâtés.
OPEN: 12-3 5-11 (Sat 12-11, Sun 12-10.30) **BAR MEALS:** L served all week 12-2 D served all week 5-8 Av main course £5.50 **RESTAURANT:** L served all week 12-2 D served all week 6-9 Av 3 course à la carte £21 ⊕: Greene King ◄: Greene King Old Speckled Hen & IPA. **FACILITIES:** Garden: Food served outdoors Dogs allowed **NOTES:** Parking 40

TEWIN
Map 06 TL21

The Plume of Feathers ♀
Upper Green Rd AL6 0LX ☎ 01438 717265 🖹 01438 712596
Dir: E from A1(M) junct 6 toward WGC, follow B1000 toward Hertford, Tewin signed on left

Built in 1596, this historic inn, firstly an Elizabethan hunting lodge and later the haunt of highwaymen, boasts several ghosts including a 'lady in grey'. Interesting menus change daily, and now include a tapas bar from noon till close. Other options available are Moroccan spiced baby shark with king prawns and couscous, honey-roast duck with sweet potato wontons, and slow-roasted belly pork with bacon and cabbage. Be sure to book in advance.
OPEN: 11-11 **BAR MEALS:** L served all week 11 D served Mon-Sat 11 (Sun 12-4) Av main course £10 **RESTAURANT:** L served all week 11 D served Mon-Sat 11 (Sun 12-4) Av 3 course à la carte £20 🍴: Greene King 🍺: IPA, Abbot Ales, Stella Artois, Kronenberg 1664. ♀: 30 **FACILITIES:** Garden: View of country side Dogs allowed garden only, water **NOTES:** Parking 40

WALKERN
Map 12 TL22

The White Lion ♀
31 The High St SG2 7PA ☎ 01438 861251 🖹 01438 861160
e-mail: bar@whitelionwalkern.com
Dir: B1037 from Stevenage
Traditional 16th-century former coaching inn set in rolling Hertfordshire countryside. The extensive pub garden offers the chance to relax with a cold beer or a glass of wine on warm summer days, while in winter the bar, with its cosy open fire, is the obvious place to be. Alternatively, the informal, smoke-free restaurant offers an appetising menu with options such as Somerset chicken, fillet of salmon, stuffed peppers ricardo and casserole of the day.
OPEN: 12-11 **BAR MEALS:** L served all week 12-2.30 D served Tues-Sat 6-9.30 Sun 12-5 Av main course £8 **RESTAURANT:** L served all week 12-2.30 D served Tues-Sat 6-9.30 Av 3 course à la carte £15 🍴: Greene King 🍺: Greene King IPA & Abbot Ale, Guinness. ♀: 8 **FACILITIES:** Child facs Garden: Large mature garden and patio **NOTES:** Parking 30

WELLPOND GREEN
Map 06 TL42

The Kick & Dicky ♦♦♦♦
SG11 1NL ☎ 01920 821424
Dir: Telephone for directions
Formerly the Nag's Head, this unusually named pub is a family-run free house in a sleepy hamlet in pretty rolling countryside, half a mile off the A120. Just before this guide went to press there was a change of hands, so readers reports are especially welcome.
OPEN: 12-2.30 6-11 **BAR MEALS:** L served Tue-Sun 12-2 D served
continued

Mon-Sat 6.30-9.30 Av main course £6.95 **RESTAURANT:** L served Tue-Sun 12-2 D served Mon-Sat 6.30-9.30 Av 3 course à la carte £18 🍴: Free House 🍺: Greene King IPA & Ruddles County. **FACILITIES:** Child facs Garden: Lawn, full size boules pitch, Patio **NOTES:** Parking 28 **ROOMS:** 5 bedrooms en suite 1 family room s£50 d£70

WESTON
Map 12 TL23

The Rising Sun 🍽
21 Halls Green SG4 7DR ☎ 01462 790487 🖹 01462 790846
e-mail: mike@therisingsun-hallsgreen.co.uk
Dir: A1(M) junct 9 take A6141 towards Baldock. Turn right towards Graveley. In 100yds take 1st left.
Set in picturesque Hertfordshire countryside, the Rising Sun offers a regularly changing menu. Starters include stilton mushrooms, and salmon fishcakes with dill sauce. Main courses include chargrilled steaks, salmon with dill and mustard sauce, and smoked fish crumble. A huge choice of sweets, and blackboard specials change daily. The owners say that their pub may be hard to find on your first visit, but that it's well worth the trouble.
OPEN: 11-2.30 6-11 (Open all day Sat & Sun Apr-Sep)
BAR MEALS: L served all week 12-2 D served all week 6-9
RESTAURANT: L served all week 12-2 D served all week 6-9 Sun 12-8 🍴: McMullens 🍺: McMullen Original AK Ale, Fosters, Macs Country Best. **FACILITIES:** Garden: Well maintained with plenty of play equipment Dogs allowed in bar only **NOTES:** Parking 40

KENT

BIDDENDEN
Map 07 TQ83

Pick of the Pubs

The Three Chimneys ♀
Biddenden Rd TN27 8LW ☎ 01580 291472
Dir: On A262 between Biddenden & Sissinghurst
Built in 1420, this public house and restaurant is full of character. The name is derived from a story about French prisoners during the Seven Years War (1756-1763): it seems the prisoners from Sissinghurst Castle were allowed to go only as far as a junction defined as the 'Trois Chemins' (three lanes), which has been translated back into English as 'The Three Chimneys'. A friendly sentry lit the candelabra in the window by the front door to indicate to the prisoners that no English officials were inside. The pub retains its original small-room layout, with old settles, low beams, wood-panelled walls, flagstone floors and warming fires. Food is freshly cooked to order from a menu of around 10 starters and nine main courses chalked up on the blackboard. You could start with Three Chimneys-style crab, avocado, poached salmon and Icelandic prawn cocktail, and go on to duck leg confit on creamed potato and braised puy lentils; or sautéed lambs liver and bacon with mash with a port and red onion gravy.
OPEN: 11.30-3 6-11 (Sun 12-3, 7-10.30) Closed: 25 Dec
BAR MEALS: L served all week 12-1.50 D served all week 6-9.45 Sun 7-9 Av main course £13.95 **RESTAURANT:** L served all week 12-1.50 D served all week 6-9.45 🍴: Free House 🍺: Adnams, Spitfire, Harveys Best, Porter. ♀: 10 **FACILITIES:** Garden: View of fields, nuttery at bottom of garden Dogs allowed **NOTES:** Parking 70

PUB WALK
The Castle Inn
Chiddingstone - Kent

THE CASTLE INN,
Chiddingstone, TN8 7AH
☎ 01892 870247
Directions: S of B2027 between
Tonbridge & Edenbridge
*Much used as a film set, the Castle
dates back to 1420, and is full of nooks
and crannies. The beamed bar, vine-
hung orchard and good ales are
popular features. Good reputation for
food, with typical bar meals alongside
more sophisticated dishes.*
Open: 11–11
Bar Meals: L served all week 11–9.30
D served all week Sun 12–6
Restaurant Meals: L served
Wed–Mon 12–2 D served Wed–Mon
7.30–9.30 Av 3 course à la carte £25
Av 3 course fixed price £17.50
Children welcome and dogs allowed.
Garden available.
(for full entry see page 269)

DISTANCE: 4.5 miles (7.2km)
MAP: OS Explorer 147
TERRAIN: Woodland and farmland
PATHS: roads, sometimes muddy
paths and tracks
GRADIENT: One steep climb

*Walk submitted by the Castle Inn,
Chiddingstone*

This delightful walk passes close to historic Hever Castle, in Tudor times the home of the Boleyn family and later the property of William Waldorf Astor, who spent a fortune on restoring it. He also built the village of Hever in Tudor style.

With the Castle Inn behind you and St Mary's Church on your right, take the road skirting the lake, keeping Chiddingstone Castle away to your left. Go over Gilwyns crossroads and straight ahead along the undulating road for about half a mile (800m).

When the road turns sharp left, go through an opening in the fence on your right to a path cutting through the grounds of Hever Castle. The path runs alongside a fence, next to a wood, with a private road to your left. Cross the road by a picturesque rustic bridge and continue between fences to a path crossing Hever churchyard to a lychgate. Noted for its slender spire, the church contains the tomb of Sir Thomas Bullen, father of Anne Boleyn, Henry VIII's mistress and then his tragic queen.

Make for the lychgate and turn left. When the road bends sharp right by the Henry VIII Inn, continue straight ahead via a path, passing the village school on your left. Follow the path to a quiet road and turn left. On reaching a junction, turn left over a stile and continue by a hedge. Turn right, skirt a wood and continue by hedging to a stile. Cross it, passing woodland on the right to reach the private road encountered early in the walk.

Don't join the road; instead turn right and follow a path alongside fencing. Cross the next road to a gate and go straight ahead between fences along the field edge. Turn right on reaching a wood, then sharp left, over a small footbridge and up a steep path. When the path reaches a track, turn left - if it is muddy here then take the parallel track on the left. Pass alongside a half-timbered house called Withers and turn left down the road. Follow it for about 0.5 mile (800m) to reach Gilwyns crossroads again. Turn right and return to the inn.

England

BOSSINGHAM
Map 07 TR14

The Hop Pocket
The Street CT4 6DY ☎ 01227 709866 🖹 01227 709866
e-mail: forgan50@aol.com
Birds of prey and an animal corner for children are among the more unusual attractions at this family pub in the heart of Kent. Canterbury is only five miles away and the county's delightfully scenic coast and countryside are within easy reach. All meals are cooked to order, using fresh produce. Expect fish pie, supreme of chicken, spicy salmon, Cajun beef, chilli nachos and fish platter. Extensive range of sandwiches and omelettes.
OPEN: 11-3 6.30-11 **BAR MEALS:** L served Tue-Sun 12-2.30 D served Mon-Sun 7-9.15 Sunday 12-3 & 6.30-9 Av main course £6.50 **RESTAURANT:** L served Tue-Sun 12-2 D served Mon-Sun 7-9.15 Av 3 course à la carte £16.50 🍺: London Pride, Shepherd Neame Admiral, Master Brew, Adnams. **FACILITIES:** Garden: Dogs allowed **NOTES:** Parking 30 No credit cards

BOUGH BEECH

See **Hever**

The Wheatsheaf

Hever Road, Bough Beech
Kent TN8 7NU

Tel: 01732 700254

BOYDEN GATE
Map 07 TR26

Pick of the Pubs

The Gate Inn 🍷
North Stream CT3 4EB ☎ 01227 860498
Dir: From Canterbury on A28 turn L at Upstreet
This rural retreat is surrounded by marshland and pasture, with a beautiful garden overlooking a stream

continued

populated by ducks and geese. On display is the Chislet Horse, which the locals will explain better than this guide! Inside, quarry-tiled floors and pine furniture feature in the family-friendly interconnecting bars. It might be a challenge to decide on what to eat, since the huge menu offers a wide range of snacks and sustaining meals. There are 17 sandwich fillings (from home-cooked ham and double Gloucester cheese to black pudding); 9 different 'ploughpersons'; jacket potatoes with 16 different fillings; and 'Gateburgers' filled with various delights. A similarly tempting range of side orders includes garlic bread, sausages on sticks and nachos. There is a selection of wines by the glass and local beers.

The Gate Inn

OPEN: 11-2.30 6-11 (Sun 12-4, 7-10.30)
BAR MEALS: L served all week 12-2 D served all week 6-9 Av main course £5.95 🍴: Shepherd Neame 🍺: Shepherd Neame Master Brew, Spitfire & Bishops Finger, Seasonal Beers. 🍷: 11 **FACILITIES:** Child facs Garden: By the side of stream Dogs allowed Water & dog biscuits **NOTES:** Parking 14 No credit cards

BRABOURNE
Map 07 TR14

The Five Bells 🍷
The Street TN25 5LP ☎ 01303 813334 🖹 01303 814667
e-mail: fivebells@aol.com
Dir: 5m E of Ashford

Named long ago when the village church couldn't manage a campanological octave (it can now), this 16th-century inn was once the village poorhouse. Old beams, an inglenook fireplace, traditional upholstery and no piped music help create a welcoming and hospitable atmosphere in Alex Ash and Nigel Bull's latest venture. Extensive menus include fresh fish of the day, crispy fried chicken strips, various grills, snacks, salads and a children's menu. Delightful garden.
OPEN: 11.30-3 6.30-11 **BAR MEALS:** L served all week 12-2 D served all week 6.30-9.30 Av main course £8

continued

BRABOURNE continued

RESTAURANT: L served all week 12-2 D served all week 6.30-9.30 Sun 12-2.30, 6.30-9.30 Av 3 course à la carte £14 **⊜:** Free House **🍺:** Shepherd Neame Master Brew, London Pride, Greene King IPA, Adnams. **🍷:** 12 **FACILITIES:** Child facs Garden: Lawn, seating for 80 persons Dogs allowed Water **NOTES:** Parking 65

BROOKLAND Map 07 TQ92

Woolpack Inn

TN29 9TJ ☎ 01797 344321

Built in 1410 and known to generations of smugglers in this wild English Channel hinterland, although these days the group huddled in the corner are probably birdwatchers. Many of the pub's original beams were sourced from shipwrecks. Wholesome home-made pub food includes sausages, chips and peas, lamb shank, lasagne, a pint of prawns with brown bread, steaks, and the usual sandwiches, jackets and ploughman's. See the blackboard for daily specials, including game when available.

OPEN: 11-3 6-11 (Sat 11-11, Sun 12-10.30) **BAR MEALS:** L served all week 12-2 D served all week 6-9 Sat-Sun 12-9 **⊜:** Shepherd Neame **🍺:** Shepherd Neame Spitfire Premium Ale, Master Brew Bitter. **FACILITIES:** Child facs Garden: Large secluded beer garden with 18 tables Dogs allowed Water **NOTES:** Parking 80

BURHAM Map 06 TQ76

The Golden Eagle

80 Church St ME1 3SD ☎ 01634 668975 📠 01634 668975

e-mail: kathymay@btconnect.com

Dir: *S from M2 junct 3 or N from M20 junct 6 on A229, signs to Burham*

Set on the North Downs with fine views of the Medway Valley, this traditional free house has a friendly and informal atmosphere. The appearance of an old-fashioned English inn is belied by the fact that the kitchen specialises in oriental cooking, with an extensive menu that includes dishes from China, Malaysia, Thailand and Singapore. House specials include pork babibangang, king prawn sambal, wor-tip crispy chicken, vegetarian mee goreng, and chicken tom yam. As you would expect, vegetarians are well catered for.

OPEN: 11-3 6.15-11 Closed: 25-26 Dec **BAR MEALS:** L served Mon-Sat 12-2 Sun 12-2.30 D served 7-10 Mon-Sat Av main course £7.95 **RESTAURANT:** L served all week 12-2 Sun 12-2.30 D served all week 7-10 Sun 7-9.30 Av 3 course fixed price £18 **⊜:** Free House **🍺:** Wadworth 6X, Boddingtons. **NOTES:** Parking 45

> The Rosette is the AA award for food. Look out for it next to a pub's name

CANTERBURY Map 07 TR15

The Chapter Arms 🍷

New Town St, Chartham Hatch CT4 7LT

☎ 01227 738340 📠 01227 732536

e-mail: chapterarms@clara.co.uk

Dir: *3m from Canterbury. Off A28 in Chartham Hatch*

A flower-bedecked free house on the Pilgrims' Way with a garden featuring fish ponds and fruit trees. The property was once three cottages owned by Canterbury Cathedral's Dean and Chapter - hence the name. Daily menus rely on plenty of excellent fresh fish. Other choices might be slow roast shoulder of local pork with apple sauce, pan-fried beef fillet strips on rosti with rose peppercorn sauce, or roast pepper, aubergine and cherry tomato tart, topped with goats' cheese. Lighter snacks too, such as filled baps.

OPEN: 11-3 6.30-11 (Sun 12-10.30) Closed: 25 Dec (eve)
BAR MEALS: L served al 12-2 D served all week 7-9 Sun 12-2.30, afternoon tea 3-5 and BBQ 7-9 Av main course £8
RESTAURANT: L served all week 12-2 D served all week 7-9 Sun afternoon tea 3-5 Av 3 course à la carte £22.50 **⊜:** Free House **🍺:** Shepherd Neame Master Brew, Cambrinus Herald, Harveys Sussex Best, Adnams. **🍷:** 8 **FACILITIES:** Child facs Garden: 1 acre of lawn, fish ponds & flower beds Dogs allowed Water
NOTES: Parking 40

Pick of the Pubs

The Dove Inn 🍷

Plum Pudding Ln, Dargate ME13 9HB

☎ 01227 751360 📠 01227 751360

e-mail: nigel@thedoveinn.fsnet.co.uk

Not far from Canterbury, tucked away in a sleepy hamlet on the delightfully named Plum Pudding Lane, the Dove is the sort of pub you dream of having as your local: roses round the door, a simple interior (stripped wooden floors and plain tables), tip-top Shepherd Neame ales, and a relaxed atmosphere. On top of all this, it has astonishingly good food. Blackboard menus feature fresh fish from Hythe and local game expertly prepared by talented chef/proprietor Nigel Morris. An inspiring selection of snacks might include salt cod served on a chorizo, flageolet and tomato sauce; cassoulet; or a warm salad of marinated chicken scented with mint. Full meals could begin with whole pan-fried crevettes flavoured with pickled ginger and garden herbs; or glazed goat's cheese served on a tomato and red onion salad seasoned with pesto. For main courses, expect roast breast of duck served on a bed of crushed new potatoes flavoured with tapenade; or whole pan-fried sole flavoured with a caper, shallot and herb butter.

continued

England

OPEN: 11-3 6-11 **BAR MEALS:** L served Tue-Sun 12-2
D served Wed-Sat 7-9 Av main course £7.25
RESTAURANT: L served Tue-Sun 12-2 D served Wed-Sat 7-9
Av 3 course à la carte £25 🍴: Shepherd Neame 🍺: Shepherd
Neame Master Brew. ♀: 10 **FACILITIES:** Garden: Dogs
allowed Chews, water **NOTES:** Parking 14

The Old Coach House ♀

A2 Barnham Downs CT4 6SA ☎ 01227 831218 ▤ 01227 831932
Dir: 7M S of Canterbury on A2. Turn at Jet petrol station.
A former stop on the original London to Dover coaching
route, and listed in the 1740 timetable, this inn stands some
300 metres from the Roman Way. Noteworthy gardens with
home-grown herbs and vegetables, weekend spit-roasts, and
unabashed continental cuisine mark it as an auberge in the
finest Gallic tradition. Food options include seafood, venison
and other game in season, plus perhaps rib of beef with
rosemary, pot au feux, and grilled lobster with brandy sauce.
OPEN: 11-11 **BAR MEALS:** L served all week 12-2.30 D served all
week 6.30-9 **RESTAURANT:** L served all week 12-2 D served all
week 6.30-9 🍴: Free House 🍺: Interbrew Whitbread Best Bitter.
FACILITIES: Garden **NOTES:** Parking 60 ⊗
ROOMS: 10 bedrooms en suite 2 family rooms d£55 (★★)

The Red Lion NEW 🍴 ♀

High St, Stodmarsh CT3 4BA ☎ 01227 721339 ▤ 01227 721339
e-mail: tiptop-redlion@hotmail.com
Dir: From Canterbury take A257 towards Sandwich, left into Stodmarsh.
Known to locals as The Old Junk Shop because of its antiques,
the Red Lion was built in 1475 and until relatively recently was
surrounded by hop fields. Lunches are served every day, with
Sunday roasts alternating weekly between beef, pork and
lamb. Among the fish dishes might be scallops with chopped
chives and ginger wine sauce; grilled sardines stuffed with
fresh garlic and marinated apricots; and Bantry Bay mussels.
OPEN: 10.30-11.30 **BAR MEALS:** L served all week 12.30-2.15
D served Mon-Sat 7.30-9.15 Av main course £15
RESTAURANT: L served all week 12.30-9.15 D served Mon-Sat
7.30-9.15 Av 3 course à la carte £27 🍺: Greene King IPA, Ruddles
Country, Speckled Hen. ♀: 7 **FACILITIES:** Garden: Garden with
large antique forge fire Dogs allowed

Pick of the Pubs

The White Horse Inn ⊕ 🍴 ♀

53 High St, Bridge CT4 5LA
☎ 01227 830249 ▤ 01227 832814
e-mail: thewaltons_thewhitehorse@hotmail.com
Dir: 3m S of Canterbury, just off A2. 15m N of Dover
This medieval and Tudor building was originally a staging
post close to a ford on the main Dover to Canterbury road.
An enormous log fire burns in the beamed bar during the
winter months, whilst the extensive garden is popular for al
fresco dining on warmer days. Fullers and Shepherd
Neame are amongst the real ales served in the bar, with up
to ten wines available by the glass. You'll find a strong
emphasis on food, with seasonal dishes created from the
best local ingredients. Choose between the relaxed
blackboard bar menu, and more formal dining in the non-
smoking restaurant. A range of lunchtime baguettes and
ploughman's is supplemented by pan-fried scallops salad;
smoked eel mousse with pickled beetroot; baked stilton
soufflé, mussels steamed in leek and cider cream; beer-
battered cod with chips and tartare sauce; Moroccan spiced

lamb with roast winter squash, apricot and coriander
couscous. Suppliers are named to indicate the serious
attention paid to good, wholesome seasonal produce.
OPEN: 11-3 6-11 (Sun 12-5) Closed: 25 Dec, 1Jan
BAR MEALS: L served all week 12-2 D served Mon-Sat 6.30-9
Av main course £8 **RESTAURANT:** L served Tues-Sun 12-2
D served Tues-Sat 7-9 Av 3 course à la carte £28 Av 3 course
fixed price £24.50 🍺: Shepherd Neame Masterbrew, Greene
King Abbot Ale, Fullers London Pride, Greene King IPA. ♀: 10
FACILITIES: Child facs Garden: Large grass area, mature trees,
benches Dogs allowed in the bar only **NOTES:** Parking 20 ⊗

CHIDDINGSTONE   Map 06 TQ54

Pick of the Pubs

Castle Inn ♀

TN8 7AH ☎ 01892 870247 ▤ 01892 870808
e-mail: info@castleinn.co.uk web: www.castleinn.co.uk
Dir: S of B2027 between Tonbridge & Edenbridge

Such is the appeal of the Castle's mellow brick exterior
that it has served as a much favoured film set. The
building dates back to 1420, and is still full of nooks and
crannies, period furniture and curios. Outside, a vine-
hung courtyard has its own garden bar. Real ales, such as
Larkins Traditional, rub shoulders with an outstanding,
vast wine list. The inn also has a strong reputation for its
cooking. The bar menu offers typical pub snacks, while
the Fireside Menu provides informal dinners in the saloon
bar. At the top end of the dining range, a small, very
individual restaurant caters for more special occasions.
Dishes are priced individually, or any three courses can
be selected for a fixed price - truly excellent value. Roast
foie gras, chargrilled marlin steak with mussels and clams,
and vanilla crème brûlée and a glass of house wine will
still leave change from £30.
OPEN: 11-11 **BAR MEALS:** L served all week 11-9.30 D served
all week Sun 12-6 **RESTAURANT:** L served Wed-Mon 12-2
D served Wed-Mon 7.30-9.30 Av 3 course à la carte £25
Av 3 course fixed price £17.50 🍴: Free House 🍺: Larkins
Traditional, Harveys Sussex, Young's Ordinary, Larkins Porter.
♀: 10 **FACILITIES:** Child facs Children's licence Garden: Patio,
lawn, sheltered, bar Dogs allowed Water and chews
See Pub Walk on page 266

Do you have a favourite pub that we have overlooked?
Please use the Reader's Report form at the back of
this guide to tell us all about it

---

continued

CHILHAM   Map 07 TR05

The White Horse ♀
The Square CT4 8BY ☎ 01227 730355
Dir: *Take A28 from Canterbury then A252, 1m turn left*
One of the most photographed pubs in Britain, The White
Horse stands next to St Mary's church facing onto the 15th-
century village square, where the May Fair is an annual event.
The pub offers a traditional atmosphere and modern cooking
from a monthly-changing menu based on fresh local produce.
Dishes include fillet steak poached in red wine, and cod and
smoked haddock fishcakes served with a sweet chilli sauce.
OPEN: 11-11 (Every day breakfast 8.30-10 Sun 12-10.30, Jan-Feb
12-3, 7-11) **BAR MEALS:** L served all week 12-3 D served Tue-Sat
5.30-9 🍴: Free House 🍺: Flowers Original Fullers London Pride,
Greene King Abbot Ale, Adnams Best. **FACILITIES:** Garden:

CHILLENDEN   Map 07 TR25

Griffins Head ♀
CT3 1PS ☎ 01304 840325 📠 01304 841290
Dir: *A2 from Canterbury towards Dover, then B2046. Village on right*

A Kentish Wealden hall house, dating from 1286, with a lovely
garden. Once occupied by monks who farmed the
surrounding land, it features inglenook fireplaces, beamed
bars, fine Kentish ales and home-made food. Typical dishes
include home-made pies, local game in season, lasagne,
cottage pie, roulade of pork with mozzarella and parma ham,
and fresh local cod. A vintage car club meets here on the first
Sunday of every month.
OPEN: 10.30-11 **BAR MEALS:** L served all week 12-2 D served
Mon-Sat 7-9.30 **RESTAURANT:** L served Sun-Fri 12-2 D served
Mon-Sat 7-9.30 🍴: Shepherd Neame 🍺: Shepherd Neame. ♀: 10
FACILITIES: Garden: Large country garden, bat & trap pitch
NOTES: Parking 25

♀ **7**   Number of wines by the glass

DARTFORD   Map 06 TQ57

The Rising Sun Inn ♦♦♦
Fawkham Green, Fawkham DA3 8NL
☎ 01474 872291 📠 01474 872779

A pub since 1702, The Rising Sun stands on the green in a
picturesque village not far from Brands Hatch. Inside you will
find an inglenook log fire and a cosy restaurant. Starters
include crispy soy duck; stilton and bacon field mushrooms;
and tempura tiger prawns. Follow pork loin with honey
and herb crust; Portuguese chicken piri-piri; or sea bass fillets
with mango and garlic beurre. There is also an extensive
range of steaks.
OPEN: 11.30-11 (Sun 12-10.30) **BAR MEALS:** L served all week
12-6.30 D served all week 6.30-9.30 Sun 12-9 Av main course £10
RESTAURANT: L served all week 12-2.15 D served all week
6.30-9.30 Sun 12-9 Av 3 course à la carte £22 🍴: Free House
🍺: Scottish Courage Courage Best, Courage Directors, London Pride,
Timothy Taylors Lanlords. **FACILITIES:** Garden: Garden & patio with
seating **NOTES:** Parking 30 **ROOMS:** 5 bedrooms en suite
1 family room No children overnight

DEAL   Map 07 TR35

The King's Head
9 Beach St CT14 7AH ☎ 01304 368194 📠 01304 364182
e-mail: booking@kingsheaddeal.co.uk
Dir: *A249 from Dover to Deal, on seafront*

Traditional 18th-century seaside pub, overlooking the seafront
and situated in one of the south-east's most picturesque coastal
towns. Deal's famous Timeball Tower is a few yards away and
the pub is within easy reach of Canterbury, Walmer Castle and
the Channel Tunnel. Bar meals include steaks, sandwiches and
seafood, and there is a daily-changing specials board.
OPEN: 10-11 (Sun 12-10.30) **BAR MEALS:** L served all week
11-2.30 D served all week 6-9 Jun-Sep food 11-9 Av main course
£5.95 🍴: Free House 🍺: Shephard Neame Master Brew, Courage
Best, Spitfire, Fullers London Pride. **FACILITIES:** Garden: Seafront
terrace **ROOMS:** 14 bedrooms en suite 5 family rooms s£40 d£50
(♦♦♦)

DOVER
Map 07 TR34

The Clyffe Hotel
High St, St Margaret's at Cliffe CT15 6AT
☎ 01304 852400 ▤ 01304 851880
e-mail: stay@theclyffehotel.com web: www.theclyffehotel.com
Dir: 3m NE of Dover
Quaint Kentish clapperboard building dating back to the late
16th-century. In its time it has been a shoemaker's and an
academy for young gentlemen. Just a stone's throw from the
Saxon Shore Way and the renowned White Cliffs of Dover.
The main bar and neatly furnished lounge lead out into the
delightful walled rose garden. Seared fillet of tuna and lightly
steamed halibut are among the seafood specialities; other
options include pan-fried chicken breast, and penne pasta.
OPEN: 11-3 5-11 (Sun 12-10.30) **BAR MEALS:** L served all week
11-2.30 D served all week 6-9.30 (no food Sun eve) Av main course
£6.95 **RESTAURANT:** L served all week 12-2.30 D served all week
6.30-9.30 (no food Sun eve) Av 3 course à la carte £20 ⊖: Free
House ◖: Interbrew Bass, Boddingtons, Fullers London Pride.
FACILITIES: Child facs Children's licence Garden: Traditional
English walled garden Dogs allowed **NOTES:** Parking 20

EYNSFORD
Map 06 TQ56

Malt Shovel Inn ♀
Station Rd DA4 0ER ☎ 01322 862164 ▤ 01322 864132
Dir: A20 to Brands Hatch, then A225, 1m to pub

Close to the River Darenth, this charming village pub is very
popular with walkers and those visiting the Roman villa in
Eynsford, or Lullingstone Castle. Fish is very well represented
on the menu, and dishes may include grilled monkfish, best
smoked Scotch salmon, whole lobster, sea bass, tiger prawns,
tuna, plaice, trout, skate or dressed baby crab. Rack of ribs,
venison pie, leek and lentil lasagne, and vegetable curry also
turn up on a typical menu.
OPEN: 11-11 **BAR MEALS:** L served all week 12-3 D served all
week 7-10 **RESTAURANT:** L served all week 12-3 D served all week
7-10 ⊖: Free House ◖: Greene King Old Speckled Hen, Harvey's
Armada, Fullers London Pride & ESB, Timothy Taylor Landlord.
NOTES: Parking 35

FAVERSHAM
Map 07 TR06

The Albion Tavern
Front Brents, Faversham Creek ME13 7DH
☎ 01795 591411 ▤ 01795 591587
e-mail: albiontavern@tiscali.co.uk
*Dir: From Faversham take A2 W. In Ospringe turn R just before Ship Inn,
at Shepherd Neame Brewery 1m turn L over creek bridge*
A quaint, white-weatherboarded gem built in 1748
overlooking historic Faversham Creek. On the opposite bank
stands Britain's oldest brewery, Shepherd Neame, which owns

continued

the Albion. The small bar has a distinct nautical atmosphere
with a hammock, old photographs of boats and other
artefacts. The attractive, contemporary menu offers dishes like
roasted vegetable tart with salad and new potatoes; hot herby
chicken with chorizo salad and cayenne potatoes; and grilled
sea bass on roasted Mediterranean vegetables.

The Albion Tavern

OPEN: 11-3 6-11 (Sun 12-10.30) **BAR MEALS:** L served all week
12-2.30 D served Mon-Sat 6.30-9.30 Av main course £5
RESTAURANT: L served all week 12-2.30 D served Mon-Sat
6.30-9.30 Sun L 12-3, Av 3 course à la carte £16 ⊖: Shepherd
Neame ◖: Spitfire, Master Brew, Orangeboom, Hurliman Shepherd
Neame. **FACILITIES:** Child facs Garden: Dogs allowed Water
NOTES: Parking 20

Shipwrights Arms ♀
Hollowshore ME13 7TU ☎ 01795 590088
*Dir: A2 through Osprince then right at rdbt. Turn right at T-junct then left
opp Davington School & follow signs*
A classic pub on the Kent marshes, first licensed in 1738, and
once a haunt of pirates and smugglers. There are numerous
nooks and crannies, and Kent-brewed real ales are served
traditionally by gravity straight from the cask. The self-
sufficient landlord generates his own electricity and draws
water from a well. Home-cooked food might include
mushroom stroganoff, and sausage and mash, with an
emphasis on English pies and puddings during the winter.
OPEN: 12-3 6-11 (Sun 12-3, 6-10.30) Summer wknds open all day
BAR MEALS: L served Tue-Sun 12-2.30 D served Tue-Sat 7-9
Av main course £6.50 ⊖: Free House ◖: Local Beers.
FACILITIES: Garden: Large open area adjacent to Faversham Creek
Dogs allowed **NOTES:** Parking 30

FOLKESTONE
Map 07 TR23

The Lighthouse ◆◆◆◆
Old Dover Rd, Capel le Ferne CT18 7HT
☎ 01303 223300 ▤ 01303 256501 web: www.lighthouse-inn.co.uk
From its cliff top vantage point, this former wine and alehouse
enjoys breathtaking sea views. Dover and the Channel Tunnel
are within easy reach, so the inn's eight en-suite bedrooms
are popular with continental travellers. An extensive menu is
served in the bar and non-smoking restaurant. Traditional
favourites like chilli con carne and gammon steak rub
shoulders with à la carte choices including vegetable
stroganoff, and poached salmon with prawn and mushroom
sauce.
BAR MEALS: L served all week 12-2.15 D served all week 5.30-9 Sun
12-8.30 **RESTAURANT:** L served all week 12-2.15 D served all week
5.30-9 Sun 12-8.30 Av 3 course à la carte £17 ◖: Abbot Ale, Greene
King IPA, Guest Ales, Ramsgate No5. **FACILITIES:** Child facs
Garden: lawn, large patio **NOTES:** Parking 80
ROOMS: 8 bedrooms en suite 2 family rooms s£45 d£55

England

FORDCOMBE   Map 06 TQ54

Chafford Arms 🔍 ♀
TN3 0SA ☎ 01892 740267 📠 01892 740703
e-mail: bazzer@chafford-arms.fsnet.co.uk
Dir: *On B2188 (off A264) between Tunbridge Wells & E Grinstead*

This old-fashioned tile-hung village pub has been run by the
same landlord for 38 years. It was built in 1851 for the local
paper works for the Royal Mint. For starters expect Greenland
prawns with mayonnaise; or crispy coated camembert. Main
courses might be lamb chops; grilled Dover sole, or
vegetarian quiche. There's a good range of snacks, and the
added treat of a pretty enclosed, award-winning garden.
OPEN: 11.45-11 (All day Sat) **BAR MEALS:** L served all week
12.30-2 D served Tue-Sat 7.15-9 Av main course £7.95
RESTAURANT: L served all week 12.30-2 D served Tue-Sat 7.15-9
Av 3 course à la carte £15.50 🍺: Enterprise Inns 🍺: Larkins Bitter,
Wadworth 6X. ♀: 9 **FACILITIES:** Garden: Enclosed garden, patio
Dogs allowed Water **NOTES:** Parking 16

FORDWICH   Map 07 TR15

The Fordwich Arms ♀
King St CT2 0DB ☎ 01227 710444 📠 01227 712811
Dir: *From A2 take A28, on approaching Sturry turn R at 'Welsh Harp' pub
into Fordwich Rd*
Solid Tudor-style pub situated opposite the tiny, half-timbered
15th-century town hall, a reminder of the days when
Fordwich was a borough (it is now supposedly England's
smallest town). It offers a large bar with log-burning fires, an
oak-panelled dining room and delightful riverside patio and
garden for summer sipping. Modern menu encompasses
Moroccan-style lamb with apricots, almonds, spices and
herbs; half-shoulder of garlic- and herb-crusted lamb; and
chicken with bacon, mushroom and brie stuffing.
OPEN: 11-11 (Sun 12-3, 7-10.30) **BAR MEALS:** L served all week
12-2.30 D served Mon-Sat 6.30-9.30 **RESTAURANT:** L served all
week 12-2.30 D served Mon-Sat 6.30-9.30 Av 3 course à la carte £17
🍺: Whitbread 🍺: Interbrew Flowers Original & Boddingtons Bitter,
Shepherd Neame Masterbrew, Wadworth 6X,. ♀: 10
FACILITIES: Garden: Terrace, River Stour runs along garden Dogs
allowed **NOTES:** Parking 12

We only include details of accommodation that
has been inspected by the AA (big Stars or
Diamonds at the top of an entry), or the
RAC, VisitBritain, VisitScotland or WTB
(small Stars or Diamonds at the end of an entry)

GOUDHURST   Map 06 TQ73

Pick of the Pubs

Green Cross Inn 🔍
TN17 1HA ☎ 01580 211200 📠 01580 212905
Dir: *Tonbridge A21 toward Hastings, left into A262 towards Ashford,
in 2m into Station road, Goudhurst on the R*
Food orientated pub in a delightful unspoiled corner of
Kent, ideally placed for visiting Tunbridge Wells, the
Ashdown Forest and the remote fenland country of
Pevensey Levels. The dining-room is prettily decorated
with fresh flowers and white linen table cloths, and the
whole pub is being upgraded by the chef-proprietor.
Fresh seafood is the house speciality here, with all dishes
cooked to order and incorporating the freshest
ingredients. Main courses in the bar range from home-
made steak, kidney and mushroom pie with shortcrust
pastry, to calves' liver and bacon lyonnaise. Restaurant
fish dishes might include fillet of turbot with spinach and
a creamy cheese sauce, grilled lemon sole with home-
made tartare sauce, and Cornish cock crab with fresh
dressed leaves.
OPEN: 11-3 6-11 Sun Closed eve in winter
BAR MEALS: L served all week 12-2.30 D served Mon-Sat
7-9.45 Av main course £10.65 **RESTAURANT:** L served all
week 12-2.30 D served Mon-Sat 7-9.45 Av 3 course à la carte £24
🍺: Free House **FACILITIES:** Garden: Patio area Well behaved
dogs only in pub **NOTES:** Parking 26

Pick of the Pubs

The Star & Eagle Hotel ◆◆◆◆ 🔍 ♀
High St TN17 1AL ☎ 01580 211512 📠 01580 212444
e-mail: StarandEagle@btconnect.com
web: www.starandeagle.co.uk
Dir: *Just off A21 to Hastings. Take A262 into Goudhurst. The Star &
Eagle is at top of hill next to the church.*

Was this 14th-century, heavily beamed building once a
monastery? Locals believe so, citing as proof vaulted
stonework and an underground tunnel from the cellars to
a point beneath the neighbouring parish church. During
the 18th century the inn became the headquarters of the
'Hawkhurst Gang', whose members robbed and terrorised
the surrounding district. Located at the highest point of
the village, the inn enjoys magnificent views across the
orchards and fast-disappearing hopfields of the Kentish
Weald. The bar and refectory menu is characterised by a
variety of well-prepared dishes, mostly Mediterranean/
English in character. Fish is well represented - try
chef/owner Enrique's creamy cod, smoked haddock and

continued

salmon pie. Other possibilities are ginger chicken; fillet of beef Wellington; pot roast shoulder of lamb Spanish style; and Aberdeen Angus rib-eye steak. Lighter meals include mussels and chips, and cannelloni. Enrique does a mean treacle sponge and bread and butter pudding too.
OPEN: 11-11 (Sun 12-3 6.30-10.30) **BAR MEALS:** L served all week 12-2.30 D served all week 7-9.30 (Sun 7-9) Av main course £9 **RESTAURANT:** L served all week 12-2.30 D served all week 7-9.30 Sun 7-9 Av 3 course à la carte £25 ⌂: Free House 🍺: Flowers Original & Bass Bitter, Adnams Bitter.
FACILITIES: Garden: Sunny terrace with great view of the Weald **NOTES:** Parking 25 **ROOMS:** 10 bedrooms 8 en suite d£70 No children overnight

---

GRAVESEND   Map 06 TQ67

The Cock Inn
Henley St, Luddesdowne DA13 0XB
☎ 01474 814208 📠 01474 812850
e-mail: andrew.r.turner@btinternet.com
Dir: Telephone for directions
Traditional English alehouse, dating from 1713, serving plenty of real ale and a range of local and West Country ciders. The menu encompasses a good choice of doorstep sandwiches, and dishes such as venison and redcurrant open pie, fillet of cod, or lamb shank with mint sauce. The inn is set in the beautiful Luddesdowne Valley making it an ideal watering hole for walkers. Under 18's are not permitted in the bars.
OPEN: 12-11 (Sun 12-10.30) **BAR MEALS:** L served all week 12-8 Sun 12-4 ⌂: Free House 🍺: Adnams Southwold, Adnams Broadside Shepherd Neame Masterbrew, Goacher's Real Mild Ale, Harvey Best Bitter. **FACILITIES:** Garden: Dogs allowed Dog biscuits on sale **NOTES:** Parking 60

HARRIETSHAM   Map 07 TQ85

The Pepper Box Inn
ME17 1LP ☎ 01622 842558 📠 01622 844218
e-mail: pbox@nascr.net
Dir: Take the Fairbourne Heath turning from A20 in Harrietsham and follow for 2m to crossroads, straight over follow for 200 yds, pub on L

A delightful 15th-century country pub enjoys far-reaching views over the Weald of Kent from its terrace, high up on the Greensand Ridge. The pub takes its name from an early type of pistol, a replica of which hangs behind the bar. Typical dishes might include pot-roasted lamb shanks, local seasonal game, sea bass and Thai-style monkfish.
OPEN: 11-3 6.30-11 **BAR MEALS:** L served all week 12-2.15 D served Tue-Sat 7-9.45 Sun L 12-3 Av main course £10.50 **RESTAURANT:** L served Tue-Sat 12-2 D served Tue-Sat 7-9.45 ⌂: Shepherd Neame 🍺: Shepherd Neame Master Brew, Bishops Finger, Spitfire. **FACILITIES:** Garden: Country cottage garden with terrace Dogs allowed **NOTES:** Parking 30

HAWKHURST   Map 07 TQ73

Pick of the Pubs

The Great House 🏠 ♀
Gills Green TN18 5EJ ☎ 01580 753119 📠 01622 851881
See Pick of the Pubs on page 274

HERNHILL   Map 07 TR06

Pick of the Pubs

Red Lion ♀
The Green ME13 9JR ☎ 01227 751207 📠 01227 752990
e-mail: theredlion@lineone.net
Dir: S of A299 between Faversham & Whitstable

Visitors to this historic inn will find a good range of local guest ales on tap with a monthly changing menu and bar blackboards listing a good range of daily specials. Well-flavoured, robust dishes include Thai chicken; braised beef in ale and mushrooms; poached salmon with a creamy herb sauce; roast vegetable tartlet; and seafood crumble. For dessert the options include waffles with ice cream and chocolate sauce; bread and butter pudding; and apple and fruit crumble. Meals are taken in the bar at rustic pine tables in front of roaring fires in winter and cooling draughts in the summer; all part of the charm of this handsome, half-timbered 14th-century hall house, which overlooks the village green towards the historic church. Masterbrew is always on tap, along with guest ales like Speckled Hen and Spitfire.
OPEN: 11.30-3 6-11 (Sun 12-3.30, 7-10.30) Closed: 25 Dec & 26 Dec, 1 Jan eves **BAR MEALS:** L served all week 12-2.30 D served all week 6-9.30 Av main course £8 **RESTAURANT:** L served (Sat & Sun only) 12-2.30 D served Fri-Sat 6-9.30 ⌂: Free House 🍺: Shepherd Neame Master Brew & 2 Guest beers. ♀: 6 **FACILITIES:** Garden: Food served outside, attractive garden **NOTES:** Parking 40

★ Star rating for inspected hotel accommodation

♦ Diamond rating for inspected guest accommodation

We endeavour to be as accurate as possible but changes to times and other information can occur after the guide has gone to press

The Great House

Wonderfully atmospheric 16th-century free house with lots of character and history. It was once a haunt of smugglers who today would struggle to recognise its warm and comfortable ambience. A pretty garden filled with mature trees and shrubs also yields many of the herbs used in the preparation of food here, together with seasonal and local produce.

An informal brasserie menu is one of the main attractions at the Great House, which tends to draw discerning diners from quite a way away. Expect fresh crayfish flambéed in cognac; onions and tomato fine tart; foie gras and black truffle tartines; assiette de charcuterie; Mediterranean fish soup with croutons and gruyere cheese; sautéed king prawns Asian style; and pan-fried sweetbread salad among the starters. To follow there could be roasted salmon with creamy leeks and coriander seeds; pan-fried local rib-eye steak or rump steak with gratin dauphinois and salad; veal rib and mash potatoes; roast breast of duck with basquaise white beans and port reduction; wild pigeon breasts and confit legs with mushroom risotto; baby spinach risotto with comte cheese and confit lemon; halibut cassolette with fresh market vegetables; fresh lobster bouillabaisse; and wild venison stew slow cooked in red wine as main courses. Various light bites, an extensive and impressive wine list and an appetising selection of French cheeses are further reasons to seek this popular place out, and then linger a while.

OPEN: 12-3 5.30-11 (Sat 12-11, Sun 12-10.30)
BAR MEALS: L served all week 12-3 D served all week 6.30-10 Sun 12-9.30 Av main course £8
RESTAURANT: L served all week 12-3 D served all week 7-9.30 Sun 12-9 Av 3 course à la carte £25 Av 2 course fixed price £23
🍺: Harveys, Guinness, Leffe. ♀: 12
FACILITIES: Children's licence
Garden: Pretty garden with shrubs, mature trees **NOTES:** Parking 40

🐟▷♀   Map 07 TQ73
Gills Green TN18 5EJ
☎ 01580 753119
🖹 01622 851881
Dir: Just off A229 between Cranbrook and Hawkhurst

HEVER
Map 06 TQ44

The Wheatsheaf
Hever Rd, Bough Beech TN8 7NU
☎ 01732 700254 📠 01732 700141
Dir: M25 & A21 exit for Hever Castle & follow signs. 1m past Castle on R

Originally built as a hunting lodge for Henry V, this splendid medieval pub boasts lofty timbered ceilings and massive stone fireplaces, as well as oddities like the mounted jaw of a man-eating shark and a collection of musical instruments. In the winter enjoy roast chestnuts and mulled wine, while the lovely gardens are at their best in summer. The Wheatsheaf has a well-deserved reputation for good food; expect smoked turkey salad, pork dijonaise, New Zealand hoki fish, minted lamb shank, crispy well-cooked duck, local pork and herb sausages, and leek and cheese quiche. Tasty snacks and light lunches available too.
OPEN: 11-11 **BAR MEALS:** L served all week 12-10 D served all week 12-10 **RESTAURANT:** L served all week 12-10 D served all week 12-10 🍴: Free House 🍺: Harveys Sussex Bitter, Shepherds Neame, Greene King Old Speckled Hen. **FACILITIES:** Garden: Sheltered, seats, benches Dogs allowed Water **NOTES:** Parking 30
See advertisement under BOUGH BEECH

IDEN GREEN
Map 06 TQ73

The Peacock ♀
Goudhurst Rd TN17 2PB ☎ 01580 211233
Dir: A21 Tunbridge Wells to Hastings, A262, 1.5m past Goudhurst
Grade II listed building dating from the 14th century with low beams, an inglenook fireplace, old oak doors, real ales on tap, and a wide range of traditional pub food. A large enclosed garden with fruit trees and picnic tables on one side of the building is popular in summer, and there's also a patio. Recent change of management.
OPEN: 12-11 (Sun 12-10.30) **BAR MEALS:** L served all week 12-2.45 D served Mon-Sat 6-8.45 Sun 12-3 Av main course £6.95 **RESTAURANT:** L served all week D served all week 🍴: Shepherd Neame 🍺: Shepherd Neame Master Brew, Spitfire and seasonal ales. ♀: 8 **FACILITIES:** Garden: Patio seats 20, large garden with fruit trees Dogs allowed Water **NOTES:** Parking 50

> ♦ Pubs with Red Diamonds are the top places in the AA's three, four and five diamond ratings

IGHTHAM
Map 06 TQ55

Pick of the Pubs

George & Dragon ♀
The Street TN15 9HH ☎ 01732 882440 📠 01732 883209
Dir: From M20, A20 then A227 towards Tonbridge
A beautiful Tudor country pub, dating from 1515, with beams and inglenook fireplaces. Among its many claims are: the Earl of Stafford lived here, the peripatetic Queen Elizabeth I visited it, Guy Fawkes hatched the Gunpowder Plot next door, and the Duke of Northumberland was imprisoned in the old restaurant for being a plot collaborator. There are several comfortable bars, a beer garden and an excellent restaurant offering a varied, season-following menu. The fresh fish catch of the day always appears, along with seafood risotto timbale, classic fillet of beef Wellington, spinach tortilla wraps, bowl of green-lipped mussels in a Thai broth, grilled lamb, and ginger-steamed salmon. Close by is Ightham Mote, a 14th-century manor and one of England's oldest continuously inhabited houses.
OPEN: 11-11 (Sun 12-10.30) Closed: 25-26 Dec eve, 1 Jan eve **BAR MEALS:** L served all week 12-3 D served all week 6.30-9.30 **RESTAURANT:** L served all week 12-3 D served all week 6.30-9.30 🍴: Shepherd Neame 🍺: Shepherd Neame Master Brew, Spitfire, Bishops Finger & Seasonal Ale. ♀: 20 **FACILITIES:** Garden: Patio Dogs allowed **NOTES:** Parking 20

Pick of the Pubs

The Harrow Inn
Common Rd TN15 9EB ☎ 01732 885912
Dir: 1.5m from Borough Green on A25 to Sevenoaks, signed Ightham Common, turn left into Common Road, 0.25m on left
Within easy reach of both M20 and M26 motorways, yet tucked away down country lanes close to the National Trust's Knole Park and Igtham Mote, this Virginia creeper-clad stone inn clearly dates back to the 17th century and beyond. The bar area comprises two rooms with a great brick fireplace, open to both sides and piled high with blazing logs; meanwhile the restaurant boasts a vine-clad conservatory that opens to a terrace that's ideal for summer dining. Menus vary with the seasons, and seafood is a particular speciality: fish aficionados can enjoy dishes such as crab and ginger spring roll; swordfish with Cajun spice and salsa; or pan-fried fillets of sea bass with lobster cream and spinach. Other main courses have included Bishops Finger (one of Shepherd Neame's fine beers) baked sausage with gammon, fennel, red onions and garlic; and tagliatelle with a wild mushroom, fresh herb, lemongrass and chilli ragoût. Look out for the grass floor!
OPEN: 12-3 6-11 (Sun 12-3 only) Closed: Dec 26 Jan 1, BH Mon **BAR MEALS:** L served Tues-Sat 12-2 D served Tues-Sat 6-9 Av main course £9.95 **RESTAURANT:** L served Tue-Sun 12-2 D served Tue-Sat 6-9 Av 3 course à la carte £23 🍴: Free House 🍺: Greene King Abbot Ale, IPA,. **FACILITIES:** Garden: Terrace **NOTES:** Parking 20

IVY HATCH

Map 06 TQ55

Pick of the Pubs

The Plough
High Cross Rd TN15 0NL ☎ 01732 810100
Dir: M25 junct 5, A25 towards Borough Green, follow Ivy Hatch signs
The Plough is set deep in Kent countryside just a quarter of a mile from the National Trust's 14th-century Ightham Mote. It has been trading as a pub/restaurant for over 25 years, but has recently had a change of hands. It is still a very food oriented establishment seating over 70 people and specialising in game and seafood. There is an extensive wine list (over 70 wines) with 20 available by the glass. Typical starters from the carte menu are potted shrimps, or oysters served on ice with lemon wedges, red onion and wine vinegar marmalade. Mains might offer roast rack of lamb, chargrilled rump steak, and medley of pan-fried seafood with chanterelles, ginger sauce, rocket and watercress. A vegetarian alternative might be filo pastry rolls filled with mozzarella and sun blushed tomatoes. The pub has a large garden, safe for children, with seating for fine weather use.
OPEN: 12-3 6-11 **BAR MEALS:** L served all week 12-2.30 D served Wed-Sat 6-9 Sun 12-4 Av main course £7.50
RESTAURANT: L served all week 12-3 D served all week 7-11 Av 3 course à la carte £20 ⊞: Free House ◼: Harveys, Hogsback. ⬭: 18 **FACILITIES:** Garden: Large garden safe for children Dogs allowed in the garden only **NOTES:** Parking 30

LAMBERHURST

Map 06 TQ63

The Swan at the Vineyard NEW ⬭
The Down TN3 8EU ☎ 01892 890170 ⬚ 01892 890401
With a large village green at the front and acres of Kentish vineyard to the rear, the Swan declares that it is 'not a traditional pub grub place', so don't expect jacket potatoes or chips. Instead choose from a comprehensive menu featuring Mediterranean vegetables with blue stilton creamed fondue; grilled sea-bass fillet with Cajun coriander prawns; and veal escalope poached in milk, garlic and nutmeg with dauphinoise potato. Award-winning English wines are attractively priced.
OPEN: 12-3 6-11 Sun 12-5 (closed Sun eve)
BAR MEALS: L served all week 12-2.15 D served Mon-Sat 6-9.30 Av main course £9 **RESTAURANT:** L served all week 12-2.15 D served Mon-Sat 6-9.30 Av 3 course à la carte £20 ◼: Harveys Best, Adnams Broadside, Bombadier, Adnams Regatta. ⬭: 7
FACILITIES: Child facs Garden: Secure grassed and patio area with seating Dogs allowed Water bowls **NOTES:** Parking 30

LINTON

Map 07 TQ75

The Bull Inn ⬭
Linton Hill ME17 4AW ☎ 01622 743612 ⬚ 01622 749513
e-mail: thebullinlinton@yahoo.co.uk
Dir: S of Maidstone on A229 Hastings road
Traditional 17th-century coaching inn in the heart of the Weald with stunning views from the glorious garden. Popular with walkers and very handy for the Greensand Way. Large inglenook fireplace and a wealth of beams inside, as well as tunnels which once led to the nearby church. A tasty bar menu includes lasagne; spinach and ricotta tortellini; cod and chips; and bubble and squeak, as well as sandwiches, baguettes, and ploughmans. The restaurant menu has the likes of seafood stir fry; salmon and cod duo; trout and almonds; and beef Wellington.

OPEN: 11-3 6-11 (Sun 12-10.30, Sat 11-11) **BAR MEALS:** L served all week 12-2.30 D served Mon-Sat 7-9.30 (Sun 12-3.30) Av main course £7 **RESTAURANT:** L served Mon-Sun 12-2.30 D served all week 7-9.30 (Sun 12-3.30) Av 3 course à la carte £25 Av 2 course fixed price £10.95 ⊞: Shepherd Neame ◼: Shepherd Neame Master Brew & Spitfire, Seasonal Ale. ⬭: 7 **FACILITIES:** Garden: Large garden, ample seating, stunning views Dogs allowed **NOTES:** Parking 30

LITTLEBOURNE

Map 07 TR25

Pick of the Pubs

King William IV
4 High St CT3 1UN ☎ 01227 721244 ⬚ 01227 721244
Dir: From A2 follow signs to Howletts Zoo. After zoo & at end of road, pub is straight ahead

Located just outside the city of Canterbury, the King William IV overlooks the village green and is well placed for Sandwich and Herne Bay. With open log fires and exposed oak beams, this friendly inn is a good place for visitors and locals. New owners Karen Leonard and Tim Philpott offer a choice of wholesome food.
OPEN: 11-11 Sun 12-10.30 **BAR MEALS:** L served all week 12-2.30 D served Mon-Sat 6-9 no evening meal Sun-Mon Av main course £10 **RESTAURANT:** L served all week 12-2.30 D served all week 6-9 ⊞: Free House ◼: Shepherd Neame Master Brew Bitter, Scottish Courage John Smith's, Adnams Bitter.
FACILITIES: Child facs **NOTES:** Parking 15

MAIDSTONE

Map 07 TQ75

Pick of the Pubs

The Ringlestone Inn ♦♦♦♦♦ ⬭
Ringlestone Hamlet, Nr Harrietsham ME17 1NX
☎ 01622 859900 ⬚ 01622 859966
e-mail: bookings@ringlestone.com web: www.ringlestone.com
Dir: Take A20 E from Maidstone/at rdbt opp Great Danes Hotel turn to Hollingbourne. Through village, right at x-rds at top of hill
A carved inscription on the inn's impressive oak sideboard reads: 'A ryghte joyouse and welcome greetynge to ye all'. The unknown chiseller left his enduring message in 1632, a hundred and one years after this hospice for monks was built, by which time it was already an alehouse. Some things haven't changed since, like the brick and flint walls, the floors and oak beams, and the furniture, which clearly predates G-Plan by centuries. Even 'new' tables in the dining room were made out of timbers from an 18th-century Thames barge. The weekday lunchtime menu offers salads, sizzlers, stir-

continued

continued

fries, pastas, and the Ringlestone's 'famous' pies. Candlelit suppers can be eaten in the refurbished, non-smoking restaurant or behind the inglenook fireplace. Shredded beef brisket with rösti; grilled swordfish steak; sausage and mash; and aubergine stuffed with feta are some of the main courses. A leaflet entitled Spirits Aplenty recounts shiver-inducing ghostly tales.

The Ringlestone Inn

OPEN: 12-11 Closed: 25 Dec **BAR MEALS:** L served all week 12-2.30 D served all week 7-10 Av main course £11.95 **RESTAURANT:** L served all week 12-2.30 D served all week 7-10 🍺: Shepherd Neame Bishops Finger & Spitfire, Greene King Abbot Ale, Theakston Old Peculiar. ♀: 40 **FACILITIES:** Child facs Children's licence Garden: Five acres of landscaped gardens, seating Dogs allowed at manager's discretion **NOTES:** Parking 70 **ROOMS:** 3 bedrooms en suite 1 family room s£89 d£99

MARKBEECH   Map 06 TQ44

The Kentish Horse
Cow Ln TN8 5NT ☎ 01342 850493
Surrounded by Kent countryside, this pub is popular with ramblers, cyclists and families. The inn dates from 1340 and is said to have a smuggling history; it also boasts a curious street-bridging Kentish sign. The wide-ranging menu offers fresh starters such as Greek feta salad, or pint of shell-on prawns, followed by spinach and ricotta cannelloni; sausage and mash with onion gravy; and steak and Guinness pie. Regular folk festivals and other events.
OPEN: 12-11 (Sun 12-10.30) **BAR MEALS:** L served all week 12-2.30 D served Tues-Sat 7-9.30 (Sun L 12-3.30) **RESTAURANT:** L served all week 12-2.30 D served Tue-Sat 7-9.30 Sun L (12-3.30) 🍺: Harvey's Larkins, plus guest ales. **FACILITIES:** Child facs Garden: Big garden with spectacular veiws Dogs allowed Water, biscuits **NOTES:** Parking 40

NEWNHAM   Map 07 TQ95

Pick of the Pubs

The George Inn ♀
44 The Street ME9 0LL ☎ 01795 890237 🖷 01795 890726
Dir: Between Sittingbourne & Faversham
The George, dating from 1540, is a country inn with a large beer garden in the ancient parish of Newnham. Originally a farm dwelling, it was licensed in 1718, during the reign of George I, and subsequently became a coaching inn. Despite the passing of the centuries, the inn retains much of its historic character with beams, polished wooden floors, inglenook fireplaces and candlelit tables.

continued

In addition to the regular range of beers there's a changing winter/summer ale. Food is served in the bar and 50-seater restaurant. Bar snacks range from sandwiches to sausage and mash, while main meals might include pan-fried fillet of sea bass with fresh asparagus and hollandaise sauce, or shoulder of lamb with thyme, redcurrant and port sauce. Regular events include live jazz, 60's music nights, quizzes and murder mystery evenings.
OPEN: 11-3 6.30-11 **BAR MEALS:** L served all week 12-2 D served all week 7-9.30 Av main course £10 **RESTAURANT:** L served all week 12-2.30 D served all week 7-9.45 Av 3 course à la carte £20 🍺: Shepherd Neame 🍺: Shepherds Neame Master Brew, Spitfire, Bishops Finger, seasonal ale. ♀: 8 **FACILITIES:** Garden: Food served outside **NOTES:** Parking 25

PENSHURST   Map 06 TQ54

Pick of the Pubs

The Bottle House Inn ☜ ♀
Coldharbour Rd TN11 8ET ☎ 01892 870306 🖷 01892 871094
e-mail: info@thebottlehouseinnpenshurst.co.uk
See Pick of the Pubs on page 278

The Leicester Arms
High St TN11 8BT ☎ 01892 870551 🖷 01892 870554
Dir: Take the 2nd exit off A21 and follow signs to Penhurst Place

Once part of the Penshurst Place estate, the Leicester Arms was named after Viscount De L'isle, Earl of Leicester, who was grandson of the former owner. Richard Burton and Elizabeth Taylor stayed here while filming *Anne of a Thousand Days* at nearby Hever Castle. Ideally located for visiting a variety of well-established tourist attractions, this picturesque watering hole has a large secluded garden and fine views over pretty meadows. A tempting sample menu includes roast loin of pork with crackling and roast potatoes, fillet of poached salmon with a bearnaise sauce, chicken breast filled with smoked bacon and mushrooms, and steak and ale pie.
OPEN: 11-11 **BAR MEALS:** L served all week 12-9.30 D served all week 12-9.30 **RESTAURANT:** L served all week 12-9.30 D served all week 12-9.30 🍺: Enterprise Inns 🍺: Old Speckled Hen, Shepherd Neame, Master Brew, Fullers London Pride. **FACILITIES:** Garden: Lawns to the river, views over Medway Valley Dogs allowed Water & Biscuits **NOTES:** Parking 35
See advertisement under TONBRIDGE

 Brewery/Company

Pick of the Pubs

The Bottle House Inn

Highly regarded, characterful dining pub run for many years by the friendly Meer family. It is believed to have been built in 1492 as a barn on the South Park estate, once owned by Lord Hardinge, a British diplomat and viceroy of India who was instrumental in securing that country's support for Britain in World War I.

Over the years it has been a row of cottages, forge, shoemender's and small shop, finally becoming a pub in 1938. During the subsequent refurbishment hundreds of old bottles were found, so locals were hardly taxed when later asked to think of a suitable name. The kitchen has been extended at least twice since then, but people still refer to the pub as the Tardis when they see the limited working space. The daily-changing menu offers considerable choice with, as far as possible, everything made from locally supplied fresh produce. With about twenty starters, one could have trouble choosing: shall it be authentic Vietnamese spring rolls with chilli jam; whitebait with garlic mayonnaise; or hot roquefort, spinach and onion tart? Among the twenty-five meat dishes are fillet steak with boursin wrapped in bacon en croûte; 'famous' Speldhurst sausages; and herb- and garlic-crusted rack of lamb with port and redcurrant sauce. Fish runs to a dozen or so options, including fillet of local trout with dill and mustard sauce; lemon sole stuffed with scallops and crab; Thai red monkfish and king prawn curry; and coconut salmon, banana fritters and chilli glaze. Vegetarians may go for brie, pesto and cherry tomato filo tart; roasted vegetable lasagne; or three-cheese omelette. Among the delicious puds are strawberry cheesecake with fruit coulis; and banoffee pie.

OPEN: 11-11 (Sun 12-10.30) Closed: Dec 25
BAR MEALS: L served all week 12-10 D served all week 12-10 (Sun 12-9) Av main course £10.50
RESTAURANT: L served all week 12-10 D served all week 12-10 (Sun 12-9.30) Av 3 course à la carte £21
🛢: Free House
🍺: Larkins Ale, Harveys Sussex Best Bitter. ♀: 8
FACILITIES: Child facs Children's licence Garden: Front raised terrace garden and side patio Dogs allowed Water **NOTES:** Parking 36

🐟 ♀ Map 06 TQ54
Coldharbour Rd TN11 8ET
☎ 01892 870306
📠 01892 871094
✉ info@thebottlehouseinn
penshurst.co.uk
Dir: From Tunbridge Wells take A264 W then B2188 N

PENSHURST continued

Pick of the Pubs

The Spotted Dog ♀
Smarts Hill TN11 8EE ☎ 01892 870253 ▧ 01892 870107
See Pick of the Pubs on page 280

PLUCKLEY   Map 07 TQ94

Pick of the Pubs

The Dering Arms ♀
Station Rd TN27 0RR ☎ 01233 840371 ▧ 01233 840498
e-mail: jim@deringarms.com
Dir: M20 junct 8, A20 to Ashford. Then R onto B2077 at Charing to Pluckley

The Dering Arms was built in the 1840s, originally as a hunting lodge serving the Dering Estate, once one of the largest of its kind. The impressive building with its curved Dutch gables and uniquely arched windows was built as a replica of the main manor house. Chef/patron James Buss has run this distinctive inn with passion and flair for over 20 years. Ale from Goacher's micro-brewery in Maidstone complements the daily specials, and an impressive wine list supports the popular gourmet evenings. The extensive menus reflect James's own love of fresh fish and seafood, making good use of fresh vegetables from the family farm and herbs from the pub garden. Starters could include smoked mackerel in creamy cheese sauce; soft herring roes; sardines grilled with rosemary butter; half a pint of prawns; and sautéed chicken liver. From the main list come grilled fillet of salmon; tuna steak; duck confit; and rib-eye steak. Desserts offer vanilla ice cream with hot espresso coffee; chestnut, chocolate and brandy cake; and lemon posset.
OPEN: 11-3 6-11 Closed: 26-29 Dec **BAR MEALS:** L served all week 12-2 D served Mon-Sat 7-9.30 Av main course £14 **RESTAURANT:** L served all week 12-2 D served all week 7-9.30 Av 3 course à la carte £24 ▣: Free House ◀: Goacher's Dering Ale, Maidstone Dark, Gold Star, Old Ale. ♀: 7 **FACILITIES:** Garden: Small grassed area with picnic tables Dogs allowed Water **NOTES:** Parking 20

The Rose and Crown ♀
Munday Bois TN27 0ST ☎ 01233 840393 ▧ 01233 756530
e-mail: helen@roseandcrown.biz
An ale house since 1780, the Rose and Crown is located in a remote hamlet in the heart of the Weald of Kent - *Darling Buds of May* country. The bar menu offers home-made cottage pie, cauliflower cheese, Aberdeen Angus half-pound burger, and Mundy Bois mixed grill, plus various toasties, baguettes and sandwiches. From the restaurant come roasted rack of Romney lamb, fillet of monkfish, and chicken breast wrapped in bacon and tarragon sauce.
OPEN: 11.30-3 6-11 (Fri-Sun 11.30-11) **BAR MEALS:** L served all week 12-2.30 D served all week 7-9.30 **RESTAURANT:** L served all week 12-2.30 D served all week 7-9.30 ▣: Free House ◀: Master Brew, Wadworth 6X. ♀: 10 **FACILITIES:** Child facs Garden: Food served outside. Picnic tables Dogs allowed in the garden only Water provided **NOTES:** Parking 30

ST MARGARET'S AT CLIFFE   Map 07 TR34

The Coastguard NEW 🔍
St Margaret's Bay CT15 6DY ☎ 01304 853176
e-mail: thecoastguard@talk21.com
Dir: 2m off the A258 between Dover and Deal.
Once the haunt of smugglers, the Coastguard is Britain's nearest pub to France, just 20 miles across the English Channel. Home at different times to the likes of Noel Coward, Ian Fleming and Peter Ustinov, St Margaret's Bay is situated on a scenic stretch of Kentish coastline known during the Second World War as 'Hellfire Corner'. The pub serves fresh local produce, using local ingredients from quality suppliers. Expect roast local skate, casserole of wild boar, and pan-fried Sussex chicken breast.
OPEN: 11-11 (Sun 12-10.30) Dec 25 12-3 **BAR MEALS:** L served all week 12.30-2.45 D served all week 6.30-8.45 Later times available by arrangement Av main course £9 **RESTAURANT:** L served all week 12.30-2.45 D served all week 6.30-8.45 Private dining available with bespoke menu Av 3 course à la carte £17 ◀: Gadds of Ramsgate, Hopdaemon, Adnams, Caledonian. **FACILITIES:** Garden: Large secure garden on waters edge Dogs allowed water bowls **NOTES:** Parking 50

SANDWICH   Map 07 TR35

George & Dragon Inn NEW 🔍 ♀
Fisher St CT13 9EJ ☎ 01304 613106 ▧ 01304 621137
Dir: Between Dover and Canterbury
An attractive, heavily beamed period pub/restaurant in a pretty Sandwich back street, with an open log fire in winter. A varied menu includes plenty of fresh fish, such as turbot, red snapper, and Thai-style mussels, as well as rack of lamb, breast of duckling, Mediterranean vegetable tatin, pizzas galore, baguettes and ciabattas, but definitely 'no chips'. Daily specials could include sausage casserole with wholegrain mustard mash. Good choice of real ales.
OPEN: 11-3 6-11 Closed: 26 Dec **BAR MEALS:** L served all week 12-2.15 D served all week 6-9.15 Sun 7-9.15 Av main course £8 **RESTAURANT:** L served all week 12-2.15 D served all week 6-9.15 Sun 7-9.15 Av 3 course à la carte £19 ◀: Shepherd Neame Master Brew, Youngs Special, Harveys Sussex Best, Adnams Broadside. ♀: 6 **FACILITIES:** Garden: York stone paved area Dogs allowed Water

Pick of the Pubs

PENSHURST – KENT

The Spotted Dog

When the trees are bare, this 15th-century, typically Kentish weatherboarded pub enjoys fine views over the Weald from the rear terrace. In summer the trees are thick with foliage, but it's still a lovely spot for a drink or meal. The rambling interior cuts the mustard too, with beams, four open fireplaces, tiled and oak floors, and those little nooks and crannies that just seem to crop up in old pubs.

Deciding where and what to eat is simple, as the single menu offers both traditional favourites and dishes that might be regarded as more sophisticated, applies throughout the pub, and covers lunchtimes and evenings. For those who like their food straight, there are staples like ham, eggs and chips, and fish and chips, although some qualification might be necessary: the ham is honey-baked, the eggs free-range, and the fish is beer-battered cod. But for those who want to push their culinary boundaries, head chefs Wayne Birch and James Chalkin and their team have the answer in such starters as caramelised shallot tarte tatin with gorgonzola and wild rocket;

home-made chicken liver parfait with plum chutney and toasted brioche; and salmon and dill fishcakes on fine beans with tomato and lemon butter sauce. Main courses include slow-braised belly of pork, butter beans and peas; and pan-fried salmon fillet with creamed leeks and lentil and red wine sauce. On the specials board are grilled whole lemon sole with garlic and hazelnut butter; duck breasts with turnip gratin, savoy cabbage and swede purée; and roasted rump of lamb, grilled Mediterranean vegetables and red wine sauce. And finally, home-made sticky toffee pudding; bread and butter pudding and white and dark chocolate mousse tart with chantilly cream.

OPEN: 11-3 Sun 12-10.30, Sat 11-11 6-11 (Seasonal times vary, ring for details)
BAR MEALS: L served all week 12-2.30 D served all week 7-9.30 Sun 12-6 Av main course £10
RESTAURANT: L served all week 12-2.30 D served all week 7-9.30 Sun 12-6
🍺: Free House
🍺: Harveys Best, Larkins Traditional, guest ale (changes regularly). ♀: 9
FACILITIES: Garden: Terraced garden with views of Medway Valley Dogs allowed Water **NOTES:** Parking 60

♀   Map 06 TQ54
Smarts Hill TN11 8EE
☎ 01892 870253
🖷 01892 870107
Dir: Off B2188 between Penshurst & Fordcombe

SANDWICH continued

St Crispin Inn ♀
The Street, Worth CT14 0DF ☎ 01304 612081 📠 01304 614838
e-mail: job.tob@virgin.net
Dir: *Village of Worth 1.5m from Sandwich. To Deal rd off A258, continue through village to primary school. Pub on left*
King William III was on the throne when the first licence was granted for the St Crispin Inn in 1604. Situated on a coastline once frequented by smugglers and now the site of fascinating bird sanctuaries, the pub includes an oak-beamed restaurant, a spacious bar and cosy open fires. Favourite dishes are lamb in coconut and black pepper; steak, mushroom and ale pie; cod in beer batter; and spinach and feta goujons. Sandwiches, ciabattas and baguettes are also available.
OPEN: 12-2.30 6-11 (Sat 12-3, Sun 16-6) **BAR MEALS:** L served all week 12-2 D served all week 6-9.30 (Sun 12-3 only) Av main course £5.95 **RESTAURANT:** L served all week 12-2 D served all week 6-9.30 Av 3 course à la carte £11.95 🍺: Shepherd Neame Master Brew, Wadworth 6X, Theakston Old Peculier, Wells Bombardier. ♀: 8 **FACILITIES:** Child facs Large garden with flower borders seats 100 Dogs allowed **NOTES:** Parking 30

SELLING
Map 07 TR05

The Rose and Crown
Perry Wood ME13 9RY ☎ 01227 752214
e-mail: rich-jocie@supanet.com
Dir: *A28 to Chilham, right at Shottenden turning, right at Old Plough x-rds, next right signed Perry Wood. Pub at top of hill*
Set amid 150 acres of woodland, on the top of Crown Hill, this 16th-century pub is decorated with hop garlands and a unique corn dolly collection. It has log fires and a very attractive garden with a vine-clad gazebo and patio heaters. A menu of pies, curries and fisherman's fancy is supplemented by specials such as fishcakes with tomato and herb sauce, beef in red wine, and stilton, asparagus and broccoli pancake.
OPEN: 11-3 6.30-11 Closed: 25-26 Dec pm only, 1 Jan pm only
BAR MEALS: L served all week 12-2 D served Sat 7-9.30 Av main course £8 **RESTAURANT:** L served all week 12-2 D served Tue-Sat 7-9.30 Av 3 course à la carte £16 🍺: Free House 🍺: Adnams Southwold, Harveys Sussex Best Bitter, Goacher's Real Mild Ale. **FACILITIES:** Garden: Prize-winning garden, patio, heaters Dogs allowed Water, biscuit on arrival **NOTES:** Parking 25

SEVENOAKS
Map 06 TQ55

The White Hart Inn NEW 🔍 ♀
Tonbridge Rd TN13 1SG ☎ 01732 452022
e-mail: sportingheros@btclick.com
A 16th-century inn close to Knole House, one of Kent's most famous and historic homes, noted for its glorious deer park. The pub's attractive garden, spacious terrace and traditional period interior draw customers from all corners of the county. The menu offers everything from shank of lamb with garlic mash, and breast of chicken in artichoke sauce, to steak and kidney pudding, and beer-battered cod. Bloomer sandwiches, ploughman's and baguettes make good snacks.
OPEN: 11-4 6-12 **BAR MEALS:** L served all week 12-2.30 D served Mon-Sat 6-9.30 Sun 12-4.30 Av main course £8.50
RESTAURANT: L served all week 12-2.30 D served Mon-Sat 6-9 Sun 12-4.30 Av 3 course à la carte £21 🍺: Harveys Sussex, Shepherd Neame Spitfire, Adnams Best. ♀: 8 **FACILITIES:** Child facs Children's licence Garden terrace and beer garden to seat 130 **NOTES:** Parking 50

SMARDEN
Map 07 TQ84

The Bell ♀
Bell Ln TN27 8PW ☎ 01233 770283

Built in the year 1536, the Bell was originally a farm building on a large estate. It was used as a blacksmiths forge right up until 1907, but it had also been an alehouse since 1630. A typical menu includes seared king scallops with spinach and a crab sauce, chargrilled chicken breast with mozzarella, basil and wild mushroom sauce, gammon steak with beetroot mash and parsley sauce, and tournedos of monkfish Rossini.
OPEN: 12-3 5.30-11(Fri-Sat 12-11 Sun 12-10.30)
BAR MEALS: L served all week 12-2.30 D served Sun-Thurs 6.30-9.30 Fri-Sat 6.30-10 Av main course £11
RESTAURANT: L served all week 12-2.30 D served Sun-Thurs 6.30-9.30 Fri-Sat 6.30-10 🍺: Free House 🍺: Shepherd Neame Master Brew Spitfire, Interbrew Flowers IPA, Fuller's London Pride. **FACILITIES:** Garden **NOTES:** Parking 30

Pick of the Pubs

The Chequers Inn ♦♦♦♦ ♀
The Street TN27 8QA ☎ 01233 770217 📠 01233 770623
e-mail: jan-mick@supernet.co.uk
Dir: *Through Leeds village, left to Sutton Valence/Headcorn then left for Smarden. Pub in village centre*
The Chequers is an atmospheric 14th-century inn with a clapboard façade, situated in the centre of one of Kent's prettiest villages close to the ancient parish church. The inn has its own beautiful landscaped garden with a large duck pond and an attractive courtyard - the perfect setting for drinks or a meal. Bar meals, real ales and a good choice of wines by the glass are served in the low beamed bars. Two separate restaurants offer the same delicious food prepared from fresh local produce: fillet steak with port and stilton sauce; and breast of chicken with mozzarella and tarragon are typical. If you fancy staying over and making the most of this delightful spot, there are four en suite bedrooms with beams and antique furniture.
OPEN: 11-11 (Sun 12-10.30) **BAR MEALS:** L served all week 12-2.30 D served all week 6-9.30 **RESTAURANT:** L served all week 12-2.30 D served all week 6.30-9.30 🍺: Free House 🍺: Harveys, IPA Bass, Abbot, Ruddles. ♀: 9 **FACILITIES:** Child facs Garden: Landscaped garden with natural pond Dogs allowed **NOTES:** Parking 15 **ROOMS:** 4 bedrooms en suite 1 family room

Pubs offering a good choice of fish on their menu

SNARGATE   Map 07 TQ92   TONBRIDGE

The Red Lion
TN29 9UQ ☎ 01797 344648
Few pubs invite you to picnic in their garden, but then they
don't serve food at this one. Instead there's an emphasis on
excellent ales, poured straight from the cask and served over
the original marble-topped counter. Doris Jemison's family
has run this free house since 1911, and little has changed here
in fifty years. The result is delightfully nostalgic: expect bare
floorboards, a real fire, wartime memorabilia and traditional
games like shove ha'penny or toad-in-the-hole. Chickens,
guinea fowl and bantams roam in the pretty cottage garden.
OPEN: 12-3 7-11 (Sun 12-3, 7-10.30) ⊕: Free House
🍺: Goachers Fine Light, Goachers Mild, Hop Daemon Golden Braid,
Hop Daemon Skrimshander. **FACILITIES:** Garden: Cottage garden
with free range hens & bantams **NOTES:** Parking 15 No credit cards

STALISFIELD GREEN   Map 07 TQ95

The Plough Inn 🍴 ⌺
ME13 0HY ☎ 01795 890256 ▤ 01795 890940
Dir: A20 to Charing, on dual carriageway turn left for Stalisfield
Originally a farmhouse, this 15th-century free house inn has
been unspoilt by time, and boasts a lady ghost among its
original beams and log fires. Set in a pretty village on top of
the North Downs, it is run by Italian owners who hold regular
theme evenings from their homeland. Interesting menus are
supplemented by the specials, which might include gravadlax,
baked cod fillet with pancetta and mozzarella, chicken
supreme in a white wine cream sauce or smoked haddock
with leek mash. The Plough featured in an episode of the TV
series, *The Darling Buds of May.*
OPEN: 12-3 7-11 **BAR MEALS:** L served Tue-Sun 12-2.30 D served
Tue-Sun 7-9.30 Sun 12-3, 7-10.30 **RESTAURANT:** L served Tue-Sun
12-3 D served Tue-Sun 7-9.30 Av 3 course à la carte £14.45 ⊕: Free
House 🍺: Adnams Bitter, Wadworth 6X. ⌺: 8
FACILITIES: Garden: Large beer garden, excellent view Dogs
allowed **NOTES:** Parking 100

TENTERDEN   Map 07 TQ83

White Lion Inn ♦♦♦♦ ⌺
57 High St TN30 6BD ☎ 01580 765077 ▤ 01580 764157
e-mail: whitelion@celticinnspubs.co.uk web: www.celticinns.co.uk
Dir: On the A28 Ashford/Hastings road
A 16th-century coaching inn on a tree-lined street of this old
Cinque Port, with many original features retained. The area is
known for its cricket connections, and the first recorded
county match between Kent and London was played here in
1719. The menu offers plenty of choice, from calves' liver and
bacon, shoulder of lamb, and Cumberland cottage pie to tuna
pasta bake and various ploughman's.
OPEN: 7am-11 **BAR MEALS:** L served all week 12-2.30 D served
all week 6-9.30 Sun 6-8.30 Av main course £7.95
RESTAURANT: L served all week 12-2.30 D served all week 6-9.30
Sun 6-8.30 Av 3 course à la carte £20 ⊕: Lionheart 🍺: Greene
King IPA, Adnams Broadside,. ⌺: 12 **FACILITIES:** Garden: Large
patio area with tables and chairs Dogs allowed, accomodated
overnight **NOTES:** Parking 30 **ROOMS:** 15 bedrooms en suite
2 family rooms s£64 d£84

TONBRIDGE

See **Penshurst**

The Leicester Arms

High Street, Penshurst, Kent, TN11 8BT

Tel: 01892 870551

TUNBRIDGE WELLS (ROYAL)   Map 06 TQ53

Pick of the Pubs

The Beacon ♦♦♦♦ 🍴 ⌺
Tea Garden Ln, Rusthall TN3 9JH
☎ 01892 524252 ▤ 01892 534288
e-mail: beaconhotel@btopenworld.com
web: www.the-beacon.co.uk
Dir: From Tunbridge Wells take A264 towards E Grinstead. Pub 1m on L

The Beacon was built in 1895 as the country home of Sir
Walter Harris, a lord-lieutenant of the City of London. He
chose a great spot. Sitting regally on a sandstone outcrop,

continued

🍺 Principal Beers for sale

the extensive grounds include lakes, woodland walks and a chalybeate spring that predated the famous one in Tunbridge Wells. Harris used his contacts to employ the best craftsmen, their work still evident in the fireplaces, ceilings and marvellous stained glass window in the restaurant. The bar and restaurant menu goes in for long, mouth-watering descriptions, such as leek, potato and apricot galette with sesame-fried broccoli florets, brie and tarragon sauce; and baked salmon fillet with green pea cream infused with dill and honey-glazed carrot parisienne. A specials board lists the day's fresh fish. The view from the dining terrace remains unaltered since a Victorian guidebook declared it as being 'as beautiful as any England affords'.
OPEN: 11-11 (Sun 12-10.30) **BAR MEALS:** L served all week 12-2.30 D served all week 6.30-9.30 **RESTAURANT:** L served all week 12-2.30 D served all week 6-9.30 ☻: Free House ◖: Harveys Best, Timothy Taylor Landlord, Breakspear Bitter. ♀: 10 **FACILITIES:** Children's licence Decking area, 17 acres of garden Dogs allowed Water, Biscuits **NOTES:** Parking 40 **ROOMS:** 3 bedrooms en suite s£68.50 d£97

The Crown Inn ♀
The Green, Groombridge TN3 9QH ☎ 01892 864742
e-mail: crowngroombridge@aol.com
Dir: Take A264 W of Tunbridge Wells, then B2110 S
A cosy and inviting 16th-century inn situated by the village green and once frequented by the Groombridge smugglers, one of whom went on to become a cartographer and surveyor. Sir Arthur Conan Doyle wrote of seeing a ghost at the Crown in his story *The Valley of Fear*. In winter there's a huge open fire in the beamed bar, and in summer a popular garden. Traditional bar food plus various salads with chips, filled bagels and steak and mushroom pie washed down with local real ales from Harveys or Larkins. Evening fare in the restaurant may be diced curried lamb, seared salmon, beef chilli, or sirloin steak.
OPEN: 11-3 6-11 (Summer Fri-Sun open all day)
BAR MEALS: L served all week 12-3 D served Mon-Sat 7-9 Sun 12-3
RESTAURANT: L served all week 12-3 D served Mon-Sat 7-9
Av 3 course à la carte £25 ☻: Free House ◖: Harveys IPA, Greene King IPA & Abbot Ale, Larkins. ♀: 8 **FACILITIES:** Child facs Garden: Benches, overlooks village green Dogs allowed Water bowls **NOTES:** Parking 35

Pick of the Pubs

The Hare on Langton Green ♀
Langton Rd, Langton Green TN3 0JA
☎ 01892 862419 ▤ 01892 861275
e-mail: hare@brunningandprice.co.uk
Dir: On A264 W of Tunbridge Wells
A large Tudorbethan-style pub in a well-to-do Tunbridge Wells suburb. There was once another pub on the site, but it was demolished in 1900 after a fire revealed that it was probably about to fall down anyway. Was the fire the reason a woman holding a child haunts the cellar and main staircase? History doesn't say. On the comfortably comprehensive daily-changing menu starters and main dishes might include smoked duck with pink and orange grapefruit salad; grilled goats cheese with a beetroot and coriander salsa; lemon sole grilled with tequila, lime and coriander butter; braised shoulder of local lamb with roasted new potatoes; Moroccan vegetable stew with feta cheese and cherry tomato cous cous; or slow roast belly

pork with spinach, dauphinoise potatoes, apple sauce & red wine sauce. Light bites and sandwiches are also available. In addition to Greene King beers, there's an impressive range of malt whiskies and wines by the glass.
OPEN: 12-11 (Sun 12-10.30) **BAR MEALS:** L served all week 12-9.30 D served all week 12-9.30 Av main course £8.95
RESTAURANT: L served all week 12-9.30 D served all week Av 3 course à la carte £20 ☻: ◖: Greene King IPA & Abbot Ale. ♀: 16 **FACILITIES:** Garden: Long terrace overlooking Langton Green Dogs allowed **NOTES:** Parking 15

Pick of the Pubs

Sankeys ♀
39 Mount Ephraim TN4 8AA
☎ 01892 511422 ▤ 01892 511450
e-mail: seafood@sankeys.co.uk
Dir: On A26

An informal, privately run bar and brasserie, specialising in seafood, that has become a Tunbridge Wells institution. Guy Sankey is a dedicated importer of rare beers from around the world, although he refuses to stock any made under licence in the UK. The wine list offers quality wines at reasonable prices, including around a dozen by the glass. Recent major renovations have led to many improvements in layout and facilities, but the cluttered, cosy, relaxed atmosphere has been skilfully maintained. 'Disgusted of Tunbridge Wells', that legendary grumbler, would for once surely have approved. Steps lead from the street down to old cellars that open onto a sheltered garden with an electric canopy, patio heaters and a charcoal barbecue for summer Sunday roasts. A sensibly priced menu brings diners the best of British seafood, purchased direct from sources in Cornwall, the Shetlands, the Scottish west coast and Ireland. Try braden rost and braden orach, respectively kiln-roasted, or traditional Loch Fyne smoked salmon with whisky horseradish sauce.
OPEN: 11-3.30 6-12 (Open all day in summer) Closed: 25-26 Dec **BAR MEALS:** L served all week 12-2.30 D served all week 7-10 **RESTAURANT:** L served all week 12-2.30 D served all week 7-10 Av 3 course à la carte £25 ☻: Free House ◖: Timothy Taylor Landlord, Larkins Traditional Bitter, Harveys Sussex Best. ♀: 11 **FACILITIES:** Garden: Patio, seats 50, heated

Most of the pubs in this guide book pride themselves on the quality of their food. This may take a little time to prepare

continued

England

WESTERHAM — Map 06 TQ45

The Fox & Hounds 🐟 ⬤
Toys Hill TN16 1QG ☎ 01732 750328 📠 01732 750941
e-mail: hickmott1@hotmail.com
A traditional family-run country pub surrounded by the National Trust's 450-acre Toys Hill woodland estate. Beautiful gardens outside, open fires and comfortable old furniture inside, with no loud music, gaming machines or even smokers to upset the convivial atmosphere. From the menu comes beef and stilton pie, North African lamb stew, chicken mozzarella, and at least five fish dishes including seafood platter. Chartwell, Sir Winston Churchill's home, is nearby.
OPEN: 11.30-2.30 6-11 All day Sun (open all day, Apr-Oct) Closed: Dec 25 **BAR MEALS:** L served all week 12-2.30 D served Tue-Sat 6-9.30 Sun 12-4 Av main course £9.25 **RESTAURANT:** L served all week 12-2.30 D served Tue-Sat 6-9.30 Sun 12-4 Av 3 course à la carte £20 ⬤: Greene King ◀: Greene King IPA, Abbot Ale, Ruddles County. ⬤: 9 **FACILITIES:** Garden: Large woodland, numerous tables with shade Dogs allowed at discretion of innkeeper
NOTES: Parking 15 ⊗

WEST MALLING — Map 06 TQ65

Pick of the Pubs

The Farmhouse NEW ⬤
97 The High St ME19 6NA ☎ 01732 843257 📠 01622 851881
See Pick of the Pubs on opposite page

WHITSTABLE — Map 07 TR16

Pick of the Pubs

The Sportsman 🍴 🐟
Faversham Rd CT5 4BP ☎ 01227 273370 📠 01227 262314
Reached via a winding lane across open marshland from Whitstable, and tucked beneath the sea wall, the Sportsman may seem an unlikely place to find such good food. The rustic yet comfortable interior, with its wooden floors, stripped pine furniture and interesting collection of prints has a warm and welcoming feel. The full range of Shepherd Neame ales is served, including seasonal brews, and there is an excellent wine list. The daily menu is based on local produce. Fish dishes make up half of the menu - for example rock oysters or smoked eel for starters, perhaps followed by poached smoked haddock with curried carrot sauce, or grilled red mullet with green olive tapenade. Other dishes might be roast chicken and foie gras terrine; roast Rye scallops with black pudding and apple; crispy duck, smoked chilli salsa and sour cream; or confit pork belly with apple sauce. The pub is ideally positioned for walkers on the Saxon Shore Way.
OPEN: 12-3 6-11 (all day Sun) Closed: 25 Dec
BAR MEALS: L served Tue-Sun 12-2 D served Tue-Sat
RESTAURANT: L served Tue-Sun 12-2 D served Tue-Sat 7-9 12-3 Sun ⬤: Shepherd Neame ◀: Shepherd Neame Late Red, Spitfire, Masterbrew, Porter. **FACILITIES:** Garden: Dogs allowed on leads **NOTES:** Parking 25

WROTHAM — Map 06 TQ65

The Green Man 🐟
Hodsoll St, Ash-cum-Ridley TN15 7LE ☎ 01732 823575
e-mail: the.greenman@btopenworld.com
Dir: Off A227 between Wrotham & Meopham
A family run 300-year-old pub located in the picturesque village of Hodsoll Street on the North Downs. An extensive menu is prepared to order using fresh local produce, and includes a wide variety of fish (especially on Wednesday, fish night) including mixed fish grill; haddock on Bombay potatoes, lamb shank, roast duck, and chicken stuffed with king prawns. Those who enjoy a good pint will be pleased with the well-kept cellar.
OPEN: 11-2.30 6.30-11 (Fri & Sat 11-11, Sun 12-10.30)
BAR MEALS: L served all week 12-2 D served all week 6.30-9.30 (Sun 6.30-9) Av main course £12 **RESTAURANT:** L served all week 12-2 D served all week 6.30-9.30 (Sun 6.30-9) Av 3 course à la carte £20 ⬤: Enterprise Inns ◀: Youngs Bitter, Fuller's London Pride, Harveys, Flowers Original. **FACILITIES:** Children's licence Garden: Large grassed area with many picnic benches Dogs allowed water
NOTES: Parking 42 ⊗

WYE — Map 07 TR04

The New Flying Horse ⬤
Upper Bridge St TN25 5AN ☎ 01233 812297 📠 01233 813487
e-mail: newflyhorse@shepherd-neame.co.uk
A 400-year-old Shepherd Neame inn, characterised by low ceilings, black beams and an open fire, tucked away in a pretty village beneath the North Downs. The restaurant serves some excellent dishes, using mainly local produce when available. The attractive patio and large garden are popular for summer drinks.
OPEN: 11-11 Closed 3-5.30 Winter **BAR MEALS:** L served all week 12-2 D served all week 6-9 **RESTAURANT:** L served all week 12-2.30 D served all week 6-9 ◀: Masterbrew Spitfire, Plus guests.
FACILITIES: Garden: Dogs allowed

Room prices show the minimum double and single rates charged. Room rates in hotels and B&Bs often vary depending on the facilities, so be sure to check prices with the establishment before booking

Pick of the Pubs

WEST MALLING – KENT

The Farmhouse

The Farmhouse dates from the Elizabethan era and over the years has served both travellers to and the inhabitants of the Kent village of West Malling. In keeping with modern trends, today it is a gastro-pub with a warm, inviting atmosphere and food that is cooked from fresh, seasonal, local produce. Fish - like halibut, seabass, fresh lobster, crayfish, oysters, and langoustine - is in plentiful supply.

The lunch menu offers light bites (roasted goats cheese and Bayonne ham salad; and paupiette of smoked salmon and trout mousseline) - along with the usual panninis (like steak melt, and smoked salmon) and tapas (Bayonne ham and pimento crostini; and fresh prawns and mayo). The dinner menu could start with pan-fried foie gras with grape and armagnac; Scottish smoked salmon and crique Ardechoise; or assiette of charcuterie. For a main course you could try local grilled Limousin beef with various sauces; pan-fried fillet of salmon, salsa verde and crushed new potatoes; roasted chicken breast with stilton, parma ham and creamed mash; roasted fillet of halibut, creamed leek mash and chive beurre blanc; or baby spinach and Comte cheese risotto. The home-made desserts include organic plum crème brûlée; chocolate mousse; peach tatin; French tarte au citron; and a specialty sorbet. Watch out for the themed evenings - in the past there have been Spanish, Moroccan, Burgundy and Alsace themes.

OPEN: 12-3 5.30-11 Sat 12-11, Sun 12-10.30
BAR MEALS: L served all week 12 D served all week 6.30 (Sun 12-9.30) Av main course £8
RESTAURANT: L served all week 12-3 D served all week 7-9.30 (Sun 12-9) Av 3 course à la carte £25 Av 2 course fixed price £23
🍺: Harveys, Guinness. ♀: 12
FACILITIES: Children's licence Garden: Spacious beer garden
NOTES: Parking 50

NEW ⋈ ♀   Map 06 TQ65
97 The High St ME19 6NA
☎ 01732 843257
🖷 01622 851881
Dir: On High St in West Malling

PUB WALK

The Shireburn Arms
Clitheroe - Lancashire

THE SHIREBURN ARMS,
Whalley Road, Hurst Green, BB7 9QJ
☎ 01254 826518
Believed to have been the inspiration for Tolkien's Hobbiton, with blazing fires, low beams and real ales. Traditional food and snacks are served in the comfortable bar and smart restaurant. 18 individually-styled bedrooms.
Open: 11–11
Bar Meals: L served all week 12–2 D served all week 5.30–9.30 Sun 12–9 Av main course £7.95
Restaurant Meals: L served all week 12–2 D served all week 5.30–9.30 Av 3 course à la carte £20 Av 4 course fixed price £17.95
Dogs allowed. Garden and parking available.
(for full entry see page 288)

DISTANCE: 4 miles (6.4km)
MAP: OS Explorer OL 41
TERRAIN: Parkland, farmland, a river valley
PATHS: Drives, tracks and field paths
GRADIENT: Undulating

Walk submitted by
The Shireburn Arms

A very attractive and interesting walk in a part of Lancashire that may well have been the inspiration for Middle-earth in JRR Tolkien's epic 'Lord of the Rings.' Tolkien's son, a priest in training, was evacuated to a seminary next door to nearby Stonyhurst College, a Roman Catholic school and part of the route. Another of his son's was a teacher here and Tolkien was a regular visitor.

From the entrance to the Shireburn Arms Hotel, walk along the B6243 road, passing the war memorial, and turn into Avenue Road. Continue through the village, passing the Bayley Arms pub and some almshouses and then take the drive towards Stonyhurst College.

Turn sharp right at a statue and follow the drive to the bottom end of several lakes where it turns left. At the road junction turn right, then take the waymarked path on the right at a bend, following it to a driveway running between two large gate posts.

Keep ahead alongside the college and pass the church. Keep left, passing some observatories to reach a bend near some barns on the left. Leave the drive here and pass through a gate to join a track. Cut across farmland for about 1/2 mile (800m) to reach the B6243.

Turn right, then left into a field, passing through the right-hand gate. Follow an indistinct path to the right of a hedgerow, cross a stile and then descend to the left towards Fox Fields Farm. Pass through a gap in the hedge to the right of the farm and then through the farmyard. Follow the drive to the right, heading for the banks of the River Ribble.

Turn right, following the riverside Ribble Way and continue ahead beside the water for almost 1/2 mile (800m), eventually passing the aqueduct bridge. Follow the path over a footbridge beneath trees, then up a stepped hillside to reach a stile. Follow the waymarks, ascending through pasture, and make for the hotel, passing just to the right of it.

LANCASHIRE

BILSBORROW
Map 18 SD53

Owd Nell's Tavern
Guy's Thatched Hamlet, Canal Side PR3 0RS
☎ 01995 640010 🖷 01995 640141
e-mail: info@guysthatchedhamlet.com
web: www.guysthatchedhamlet.com
Dir: Telephone for directions

A great venue for families, this famous thatched tavern stands on a picturesque stretch of the Lancaster Canal. The 16th-century former farmhouse offers a wide choice of cask kept ales, 50 malt whiskies and 40 wines by the glass. A good choice of traditional, wholesome food and an appetising selection of seafood and shellfish are among the promised fare. Home-made beef steak and kidney pudding, and local game in season are popular choices.
OPEN: 11-11 Closed: 25 Dec **BAR MEALS:** L served all week 11-9 D served all week 11-9 Av main course £5.50
RESTAURANT: L served all week 12-2.30 D served all week 5.30-10.30 Sunday 12-10.30 Av 3 course à la carte £12.50 Av 2 course fixed price £6.95 ⊕: Free House ◖: Boddingtons Bitter, Jennings Bitter, Copper Dragon, Balck Sheep. ♀: 40 **FACILITIES:** Child facs Garden: Patio areas by the Lancaster Canal, 200 seats Dogs allowed Water **NOTES:** Parking 300

See advert on this page

BLACKBURN
Map 18 SD62

Pick of the Pubs

Millstone Hotel ★★ 🏵🏵 ▷ ♀
Church Ln, Mellor BB2 7JR
☎ 01254 813333 🖷 01254 812628
e-mail: millstone.reception@shirehotels.co.uk
web: www.millstonehotel.co.uk
Dir: From M6 junct 31 take A59 towards Clitheroe, past British Aerospace. Right at rdbt signed Blackburn/Mellor. Next rdbt 2nd left. Hotel at top of hill on right
This old inn stands in the heart of the Ribble Valley, surrounded by some of England's finest countryside and yet within an hour's drive of over six premier league football teams. It was the original flagship of Daniel Thwaites's Blackburn brewery, and the old man himself keeps a watchful eye on the place from his resting place in the graveyard next door. Developed from a 17th-century tithe barn, the building retains original oak beams, linenfold panelling and the circular grinding-stone incorporated in the façade, which gives the hotel its name. Good value food is served in the bar and restaurant. Typical dishes are fresh cod fillet in Lancaster

Drink
Eat
Sleep
Play
Shop
Dance

Open All Day Everyday
Family Owned & Run Thatched Hamlet
Free from the Brewer – wide range of Independent Brewers Ales
An ever-changing selection with "The Landlords Choice" on at £1.30 Mon–Fri
Cask Marque 2004 & "Ask if it's Cask" Supporters
Big Screen TV, Conference Facilities
Canalside Patios & Duck Watching, Tavern Deck Patio Area
Cricket Ground, Floodlit Crown Green Bowling Green & Thatched Pavilions
Guy's Lodge – All room's with Spa's available
Guy's Thatched Hamlet, Canalside, Bilsborrow, Nr Garstang, PR3 0RS
Tel: (01995) 640010 www.guysthatchedhamlet.com

bomber beer batter; linguini and woodland mushrooms; and Farnsworth of Whalley pork sausages.
OPEN: 11-11 (Sun 12-10.30) **BAR MEALS:** L served all week 12-2.15 D served Mon-Sat 6.30-9.15 Sunday 12-9 Av main course £8.95 **RESTAURANT:** L served all week 12-2.15 D served Mon-Sat 6.30-9.15 Sunday 12-9 Av 3 course à la carte £24.95 Av 3 course fixed price £24.95 ⊕: Shire Hotels ◖: Thwaites, Warsteiner, Lancaster Bomber, Thwaites Original Cash Bitter. ♀: 12 **NOTES:** Parking 45 **ROOMS:** 24 bedrooms en suite 1 family room s£51 d£82 No children overnight

BLACKO
Map 18 SD84

Moorcock Inn ▷
Gisburn Rd BB9 6NG ☎ 01282 614186 🖷 01282 614186
e-mail: boo@patterson1047.freeserve.co.uk
Dir: M65 junct 13, take A682 to Blacko
Family-run country inn with traditional log fires and good views towards the Pendle Way, ideally placed for non-motorway travel to the Lakes and the Yorkshire Dales. Home-cooked meals are a speciality, with a wide choice including salads and sandwiches, and vegetarian and children's meals. Tasty starters like cheesy mushrooms, and garlic prawns are followed by lasagne, various steak choices, pork in orange and cider, and trout grilled with lemon and herb butter.
OPEN: 12-2 6-9 (All day Sat and Sun, Sun close at 8)
BAR MEALS: L served all week 12-2 D served Tues-Sun 12-7.30 **RESTAURANT:** L served all week 12-2.30 D served Tues-Sun 6-9 Sun 12-6 ⊕: Thwaites ◖: Thwaites, Best Bitter, Smooth, Warfsteiner. **FACILITIES:** Garden: Picnic benches, beautiful views Dogs allowed Water, food **NOTES:** Parking 80

continued

England

CARNFORTH   Map 18 SD47

Dutton Arms ♥
Station Ln, Burton LA6 1HR ☎ 01524 781225 ▤ 01524 782662
Dir: From M6 take A6 signed Milnthorpe (Kendal), 3m before Milnthorpe turn right signed Burton/Holme
Built in 1860 to serve the nearby mainline railway, this Victorian free house was formerly the Station Hotel. Here you'll find Boddington's and Black Sheep ales, as well as a regular guest beer and a decent choice of wines by the glass. Seafood is a speciality, and a single menu is served in the bar and non-smoking restaurant. Choices include grilled mackerel with garlic butter; and seared marlin with saffron rice and chargrilled peppers.
OPEN: 10-11 **BAR MEALS:** L served all week 11-9.30 D served all week 11-9.30 Sun 11-8 Av main course £10
RESTAURANT: L served all week 12-9 D served all week 11-9 Sun 12-8 Av 3 course à la carte £18 Av 3 course fixed price £13.95
🍽: Free House ◀: Interbrew Boddingtons, Black Sheep & Guest Beer. ♀: 15 **FACILITIES:** Child facs Garden: Lawned area with adventure playground Dogs allowed Water **NOTES:** Parking 30

CHIPPING   Map 18 SD64

Dog & Partridge
Hesketh Ln PR3 2TH ☎ 01995 61201 ▤ 01995 61446
Dating back to 1515, this comfortably modernised rural free house in the Ribble Valley enjoys wonderful views of the surrounding fells. The barn has been converted into an additional dining area, where the emphasis is on home-made food using local produce. Choose from bar snacks, or à la carte in the restaurant. The latter includes broccoli and stilton pancakes; roast Lancashire beef; and poached salmon with prawn sauce. Vegetarians are well catered for.
OPEN: 11.45-3 6.45-11 (Sun 11.45-10.30) **BAR MEALS:** L served all week 12-1.45 D served all week **RESTAURANT:** L served all week 12-1.30 D served all week 7-9 Sun lunch 12-3, carte menu 3.30-8.30 Av 3 course à la carte £20 Av 4 course fixed price £14.75 🍽: Free House ◀: Carlsberg-Tetley. **NOTES:** Parking 30

CLITHEROE   Map 18 SD74

Pick of the Pubs

Assheton Arms ♥
Downham BB7 4BJ ☎ 01200 441227 ▤ 01200 440581
e-mail: asshetonarms@aol.com
Dir: From A59 to Chatburn, then follow Downham signs

Named after Lord Clitheroe's family, which owns the whole village, although fans of the BBC TV drama series *Born and Bred* may know this pub better as the Signalman's Arms, and the picturesque village of

Downham as Ormston. The single bar and sectioned rooms are furnished with solid oak tables, wingback settees, window seats, the original stone fireplace, and a large blackboard listing the range of daily dishes on offer. Typical are starters/snacks such as Morecambe Bay shrimps, mixed Chinese dim sum, and stilton pâté. From the grill come ham with free range eggs; Glen Fyne steaks; and lamb cutlets, while home-made chicken and mushroom pie; chilli con carne; lobster Thermidor; and courgettes Italian-style appear in the entrées section of the comprehensive menu. The pub is well placed for a wild moorland walk up Pendle Hill, which looms high above the village.
OPEN: 12-3 7-11 (summer Sun open all day) Closed: 1st wk in Jan **BAR MEALS:** L served all week 12-2 D served all week 7-10 Av main course £8.75 🍽: Enterprise Inns ◀: Marstons Pedigree, Marston Bitter, Mansfield Bitter. ♀: 18 **FACILITIES:** Child facs Dogs allowed **NOTES:** Parking 12

The Shireburn Arms ★★ ♀
Whalley Rd, Hurst Green BB7 9QJ
☎ 01254 826518 ▤ 01254 826208
e-mail: steve@shireburnarmshotel.com
web: www.shireburnarmshotel.com
Dir: Telephone for directions
The Shireburn, the village of Hurst Green and nearby Stonyhurst College all allegedly provided inspiration for the books of J R R Tolkien. Certainly the blazing fires, low beams and real ales of this 17th-century inn do little to dispel the rumour. The menu ranges from sandwiches and snack options like prawn platter or hot pot of mushrooms, to liver and onions, or brie & broccoli pithivier.
OPEN: 11-11 **BAR MEALS:** L served all week 12-2 D served all week 5.30-9.30 Sun 12-9 Av main course £7.95
RESTAURANT: L served all week 12-2 D served all week 5.30-9.30 Av 3 course à la carte £20 Av 4 course fixed price £17.95 🍽: Free House ◀: Scottish Courage Theakstons Best Bitter, Mild & Guest Cask Ales. ♀: 10 **FACILITIES:** Child facs Garden: Patio garden, seating for 60 people **NOTES:** Parking 100 **ROOMS:** 18 bedrooms en suite 3 family rooms s£50 d£70

See Pub Walk on page 286

DARWEN   Map 15 SD62

Old Rosins Inn ♀
Treacle Row, Pickup Bank, Hoddlesden BB3 3QD
☎ 01254 771264 ▤ 01254 873894
Dir: M65 junct 5, follow Haslingden signs. Right after 2m signed Egworth. 0.5m right & then 0.5m
The original inn, set in the heart of the Lancashire Moors, has been extended to provide a variety of facilities. New owners have worked on updating both the inside and outside of the business. Readers reports are welcome.
OPEN: 11-11 (Sun 12-10.30) **BAR MEALS:** L served all week 12-9 D served all week 12-9 Av main course £8.50
RESTAURANT: L served all week 12-9 D served all week 12-9 Av 3 course à la carte £25 🍽: Jennings ◀: Directors, John Smiths cask, Theakstons. ♀: 20 **FACILITIES:** Garden: Lawns and shrubbery, food served outdoors Dogs allowed at manager's discretion only **NOTES:** Parking 200

 The Rosette is the AA award for food.
Look out for it next to a pub's name

continued

FENCE   Map 18 SD83

Fence Gate Inn ♀
Wheatley Lane Rd BB12 9EE ☎ 01282 618101 ▤ 01282 615432
Dir: *From M65 L 1.5m, set back on right opposite T-junction for Burnley*

An extensive property, the Fence Gate Inn was originally a collection point for cotton delivered by barge and distributed to surrounding cottages to be spun into cloth. Food is served both in the bar and the Topiary Brasserie. Highlights are a selection of sausages starring Lancashire's champion leek and black pudding with a hint of sage. There is a good choice of pasta, and medallions of organic Salmesbury pork fillet.
OPEN: 12-11 **BAR MEALS:** L served all week 12-2.30 D served all week 6.30-9.30 **RESTAURANT:** L served all week 12-2.30 D served all week 6.30-9.30 ◷: Free House ◑: Theakston, Directors, Deuchers. ♀: 16 **FACILITIES:** Garden: patio, outdoor eating Dogs allowed at manager's discretion **NOTES:** Parking 100

FORTON   Map 18 SD45

Pick of the Pubs

The Bay Horse Inn ⤳ ♀
LA2 0HR ☎ 01524 791204 ▤ 01524 791204
e-mail: wilkicraig@aol.com
Dir: *1 m S off Junct 33 of M6*
Judging from the notes that feature on the menu and wine list of the Bay Horse Inn, the surrounding area (called Bay Horse) is not only picturesque but also anecdotally interesting. For further information you can visit the inn and read for yourself. If that doesn't tickle your curiosity, then the good range of malt whiskies is bound to, and so will the food: the inn specialises in simple, fresh and imaginative dishes from an award-winning chef who is wholly self-taught. Starters could be grilled goat's cheese niçoise with sun blushed tomatoes, fresh anchovy fillet and black olives; and terrine of Goosnargh chicken, Garstang blue cheese and Waberthwaite air-dried ham, served with pear and saffron chutney. Mains include poached fillet of smoked Fleetwood haddock; Lancashire hot pot with pickled red cabbage; roast fillet of Cumbrian fellbred beef; fillet of Lytham sea bass with potato purée and grilled asparagus; and Bay Horse fish pie.
OPEN: 12-3 6.30-11 (Sun 12-5, 8-10.30)
BAR MEALS: L served Tue-Sun 12-1.45 D served Tue-Sat 7-9.15 Av main course £14 **RESTAURANT:** L served Tue-Sun 12-1.45 D served Tue-Sat 7-9.15 (Sun 12-3, closed eve) Av 3 course à la carte £25 Av 3 course fixed price £17.50 ◑: Wadworth 6X, Everards Tiger, Twaites Lancaster Bomber. **FACILITIES:** Garden: Large rustic garden with views **NOTES:** Parking 30

GOOSNARGH   Map 18 SD53

The Bushell's Arms ⤳ ♀
Church Ln PR3 2BH ☎ 01772 865235 ▤ 01772 865235
Dir: *Take A6 N to Garstang, right onto Whittingham Lane, after 3m left into Church Lane. The pub is on right of village green*
Dr Bushell was a philanthropic Georgian who built his villagers not just a hospital but this pub too. It seems that patients at the hospital were entitled to a daily pint of beer at the pub. The owner previously managed an IT company, but has had a long-standing ambition to become a publican. A collection of main courses may include chicken breast filled with smoked Lancashire cheese and spinach and wrapped in bacon; oven roasted ham hock on a bramley apple fritter, The Bushell's pie of the day, or spinach and ricotta cheese cannelloni. Ideal walking country.
OPEN: 12-2.30 5-11 **BAR MEALS:** L served Tue-Sun 12-2 D served Tue-Sat 6-9 Sun 12-8 Av main course £8.50
RESTAURANT: L served Tue-Sun 12-2 D served Tue-Sat 6-9 Sun 12-8 Av 3 course à la carte £15 ◷: Enterprise Inns ◑: Timothy Taylor Landlord, Abbot Ale, Old Speckled Hen, Black Sheep. ♀: 25 **FACILITIES:** Garden: Secluded garden with lawns & flower beds Dogs allowed Water & Toys **NOTES:** Parking 10

Ye Horns Inn ⤳ ♀
Horns Ln PR3 2FJ ☎ 01772 865230 ▤ 01772 864299
e-mail: info@yehornsinn.co.uk web: www.yehornsinn.co.uk
Dir: *From M6 junct 32 take A6 N towards Garstang. Right at lights onto B5269 towards Goosnargh. In Goosnargh follow Inn signs*

Elizabeth and Mark Woods have been welcoming guests to this 18th-century, black and white coaching inn for over 20 years. Warming open fires, original beams and luxurious furnishings await you indoors, whilst the patio and outdoor seating area is perfect for summer days. Located in a peaceful country setting, the pub serves fish dishes like home-made salmon fishcakes, and fresh battered cod with mushy peas.
OPEN: 11.30-3 6-11 (Ex Mon) **BAR MEALS:** L served Tue-Sun 12-2 D served all week 7-9.15 Av main course £9.50
RESTAURANT: L served Tue-Sun 12-2 D served all week 7-9.15 Av 3 course à la carte £18.50 Av 5 course fixed price £19.50 ◷: Free House ◑: Flowers IPA, Tetleys. ♀: 8 **FACILITIES:** Garden: Large patio area, tables, seating, pond, lawn **NOTES:** Parking 70
ROOMS: 6 bedrooms en suite s£59 d£79 (♦♦♦♦)

HASLINGDEN   Map 15 SD72

Farmers Glory ⤳
Roundhill Rd BB4 5TU ☎ 01706 215748 ▤ 01706 215748
Dir: *On A667 8 miles from Blackburn, Burnley and Bury, 1.5m from M66*
Stone-built 300-year-old pub situated high above Haslingden on the edge of the Pennines. Formerly a coaching inn on the ancient route to Whalley Abbey, it now offers locals and

continued

England

HASLINGDEN continued

modern A667 travellers a wide-ranging traditional pub menu of steaks, roasts, seafood, pizzas, pasta, curries and sandwiches. Live folk music every Wednesday, and a large beer garden with ornamental fishpond.

Farmers Glory

OPEN: 12-3 7-11.30 **BAR MEALS:** L served all week 12-2.30 D served all week 7-9.30 **RESTAURANT:** L served all week 12-2.30 D served all week 7-9.30 Av 3 course à la carte £13.50 ☺: Pubmaster ☜: Carlsberg-Tetley Tetley Bitter, Marston's Pedigree, Greene King IPA, Jennings. **FACILITIES:** Child facs Garden: 0.5 acre, fixed seating, ornamental fish pond **NOTES:** Parking 60

HESKIN GREEN   Map 15 SD51

Farmers Arms ⬩

85 Wood Ln PR7 5NP ☎ 01257 451276 ▤ 01257 453958
e-mail: andy@farmersarms.co.uk
Dir: On B5250 between M6 & Eccleston
Long, creeper-covered country inn with two cosy bars decorated in old pictures and farming memorabilia. Once known as the Pleasant Retreat, this is a family-run pub proud to offer a warm welcome. Typical dishes include steak pie, fresh salmon with prawns and mushroom, halibut, rack of lamb and chicken curry.
OPEN: 12-11 (Sun close 10.30) **BAR MEALS:** L served all week 12-9.30 D served all week Av main course £7.50
RESTAURANT: L served all week 12-9.30 D served all week Av 3 course à la carte £13 ☺: Enterprise Inns ☜: Timothy Taylor Landlord, Pedigree, Black Sheep, Interbrew Boddingtons. ⬩: 7
FACILITIES: Garden: Dogs allowed **NOTES:** Parking 50
ROOMS: 5 bedrooms en suite (♦♦♦)

HEST BANK   Map 18 SD46

Hest Bank Hotel ⬩⬦

2 Hest Bank Ln LA2 6DN ☎ 01524 824339 ▤ 01524 824948
e-mail: hestbankhotel@hotmail.com
Dir: From Lancaster take A6 N, after 2m left to Hest Bank
Originally named the Sands Inn and once a staging post for coaches crossing Morecambe Bay from Grange-Over-Sands, this canal-side hotel was first licensed in 1554 to brew mead ale, sack, and honey beer as well as sell cooked game. These days it provides freshly prepared food sourced mostly from local suppliers. Expect fresh haddock, cajun dusted fresh salmon, home-made steak, mushroom and ale pie, lambs' liver and bacon, and chargrilled pork chop.
OPEN: 11.30-11 (Sun 12-10.30) **BAR MEALS:** L served all week 12-9 D served all week (No food Christmas Day) Av main course £5.95 **RESTAURANT:** L served all week 12-9 D served all week Av 3 course à la carte £13 Av 2 course fixed price £5.95 ☺: Punch Taverns ☜: Interbrew Boddingtons, Timothy Taylor Landlord, Green King IPA, guest beers. **FACILITIES:** Garden: Canalside, benches, lawn & patio area **NOTES:** Parking 20

HORNBY   Map 18 SD56

The Castle Hotel NEW ★★ ⬤⬤ ⬩

Main St LA2 8JT
A former coaching inn, the Castle is a Grade II listed building situated in the village of Hornby in the lovely Lune Valley. The Castle Barns menu ranges from panninis, soup and sandwiches to pub favourites like beer-battered haddock with mushy peas and chips, and beef braised in Black Sheep ale. Outside, there is a patio and barbeque area with seating. The hotel also has a fine dining restaurant called The Vanilla Room.
OPEN: 11-11 **BAR MEALS:** L served all week 12-6 D served all week 6-9 Av main course £8.95 **RESTAURANT:** L served all week 3-6 D served all week 6-9 Av 3 course à la carte £15.20 ☜: Black Sheep, Boddingtons. ⬩: 12 **FACILITIES:** Child facs Children's licence Patio area with BBQ, seating **NOTES:** Parking 30
ROOMS: 8 bedrooms en suite 3 family rooms s£50 d£60

LANCASTER   Map 18 SD46

The Stork Inn

Conder Green LA2 0AN ☎ 01524 751234 ▤ 01524 752660
e-mail: the.stork@virgin.net
Dir: M6 junct 33 take A6 north. L at Galgate & next L to Conder Green
White-painted coaching inn spread along the banks of the Conder Estuary, with a colourful 300-year-history that includes several name changes. The quaint sea port of Glasson Dock is a short walk along the Lancashire Coastal Way, and the Lake District is easily accessible. Seasonal specialities join home-cooked food like steak pie, locally-smoked haddock, salmon fillet with bonne femme sauce, and Cumberland sausage with onion gravy and mashed potatoes.
OPEN: 11-11 (Sun 12-10.30) **BAR MEALS:** L served all week 12-2.30 D served all week 6.30-9 Av main course £6.95
RESTAURANT: L served all week 12-2.30 D served all week 6-9 ☺: Free House ☜: Boddingtons, Pedigree, Black Sheep.
FACILITIES: Garden: Large seating area with wishing well Dogs allowed Water **NOTES:** Parking 35

The Sun Hotel and Bar NEW ⬩

LA1 1ET ☎ 01524 66006
Dir: 6m from junct 33 of M6
A listed building dating back to the 1600s, retaining much of its original character. It is handy for exploring the ancient city of Lancaster, with its Castle and Maritime Museum, and the town of Carnforth, used in the filming of *Brief Encounter* in the 1940s. An extensive and wide-ranging choice of beers, a limited breakfast menu, and lunch dishes like cheese and onion pie, lasagne, and seafood crepes. Cheeseboard only in the evening.
OPEN: 11-11 **BAR MEALS:** L served all week 12-3 D served none Av main course £6 ☜: Thwaites Lancaster Bomber, Titanic Iceberg, Leifmans Frambozen. ⬩: 16

Pick of the Pubs

The Waterwitch ⬩

The Tow Path, Aldcliffe Rd LA1 1SU
☎ 01524 63828 ▤ 01524 34535
Dir: 6m from junct 33 of M6.
The Waterwitch is situated beside the Lancaster Canal and takes its name from three longboats that worked the canal in the late 18th century. Two hundred years later the pub was created from a tasteful conversion of old stables which retain the original building's exterior profile, stone walls and interior slab floors. In just a few years it

continued

has acquired celebrity status and a fistful of awards, while remaining a true pub with the broad appeal of a wine bar and restaurant. Its current owners started as real ale specialists; then the drinks list expanded to include everything from Armagnac to Zambucca. A celebrated team of chefs have found success with their menus, and the wine list has grown accordingly. Among the dishes are crab and mango reattie; and fillet of sea bass wrapped in parma ham, studded with rosemary and served with lemon buerre blanc. The canal-side garden provides a beautiful setting for over 200 people.

OPEN: 11-11 **BAR MEALS:** L served all week 12-3 D served all week 6-9.30 Sun lunch 12-5, dinner 6-9 Av main course £12.50 **RESTAURANT:** L served all week D served all week Av 3 course à la carte £20 Av 3 course fixed price £18.50 **◖:** Thwaites Lancaster Bomber, Warsteiner, Konic Ludwig. **♀:** 27 **FACILITIES:** Seating outside by canal

---

PARBOLD   Map 15 SD41

Pick of the Pubs

The Eagle & Child ◝ ♀
Maltkiln Ln L40 3SG ☎ 01257 462297 ▤ 01257 464718
www.ainscoughs.co.uk
Dir: 3m from M6 junct 27. Over Parbold Hill, follow signs for Bispham Green on right

Many years ago the villagers called this pub the Bird and Bastard, not apparently, after the landlords of the time, but as a nose-tappingly knowing reference to the implausible story local landowner Lord Derby concocted to cover up the outcome of his illicit liaison with a village girl. New landlord David Anderson may tell you the full story while maintaining a proprietorial eye on the pub's long-standing reputation for good food and drink. Flagged floors, coir matting and oak settles grace the interior, and there's also a no-smoking room. Starters include seafood ceviche; lamb and thyme pasty; and crispy duck and chorizo salad, while main course options include monkfish in creamy pepper sauce; roast breast of duck, orange and port sauce; Cajun steak kebab and chilli rice; and vegetable korma. The bar menu offers pub favourites such as steak and real ale pie; and grilled gammon and pineapple.

OPEN: 12-3 5.30-11 (Sun 12-10.30) **BAR MEALS:** L served all week 12-2 D served Mon-Thurs 6-8.30 Fri-Sat 6-9 Sun 12-8.30, Av main course £12 **RESTAURANT:** L served all week 12-2 D served Mon-Thurs 6-8.30 Fri & Sat 6-9, Sun 12-8.30 Av 3 course à la carte £20 **◖:** Free House **◖:** Moorhouses Black Cat, Thwaites Bitter, 5 changing guest beers. **♀:** 6 **FACILITIES:** Garden: Large patio, wooden benches, bowling green Dogs allowed **NOTES:** Parking 50

PRESTON   Map 18 SD52

Pick of the Pubs

Cartford Country Inn & Hotel ♀
Little Eccleston PR3 0YP ☎ 01995 670166 ▤ 01995 671785
e-mail: cartfordhotel@tiscali.co.uk

This old, pleasantly rambling three-storey inn guards a historic toll bridge over the tidal River Wyre, a few miles upstream from its entry into the Irish Sea near Fleetwood. Co-owner Tracy Mellodew's great grandfather was once the landlord here, so four generations on her family has come full circle. Inside, an open log fire may be blazing, and there's always pool, darts or dominoes to be played while enjoying a pint of Dishy Debbie, one of several real ales brewed behind the pub by the Hart brewery. A good range of food on the bar menu includes sandwiches, pizzas (evenings only), jacket potatoes, salads, chicken and bacon pasta, lamb Henry and seafood platter. Various specials might include curries, and lemon sole with crabmeat. The choice for vegetarians has recently been extended. Meals can also be taken outside overlooking the river, along part of which runs a four-mile walk that conveniently starts and finishes at the pub.

OPEN: 12-3 6.30-11 Closed: Dec 25 **BAR MEALS:** L served Mon-Sat 12-2 D served all week 6.30-9.30 Av main course £5.50 **RESTAURANT:** 12-2 6.30-9.30 **◖:** Free House **◖:** Hart Beers, Fullers London Pride, Moorhouse, Guest ales. **FACILITIES:** Child facs Dogs allowed **NOTES:** Parking 60 **ROOMS:** 6 bedrooms en suite s£36.95 d£48.95 (♦♦♦)

◆ Diamond rating for inspected guest accommodation

We only include details of accommodation that has been inspected by the AA (big Stars or Diamonds at the top of an entry), or the RAC, VisitBritain, VisitScotland or WTB (small Stars or Diamonds at the end of an entry)

Disabled people and those with Assist Dogs have new rights of access to pubs, restaurants and hotels under the Disability Discrimination Act of 1 October 2004. For more information see the website at www.drc gb.org/open4all/rights/2004.asp

RIBCHESTER — Map 18 SD63

The White Bull ⚲
Church St PR3 3XP ☎ 01254 878303
e-mail: emily.jason@virgin.net
Dir: Leave A59 towards Ribchester, follow signs for Roman Museum.
Established in 1707, partly on the site of an old Roman town, this Grade II listed courthouse is soaked in antiquity. Cask beers accompany the likes of duck breast with chargrilled pineapple, fruit salsa and plum sauce; Thai chicken and prawn curry; whole baked trout in sea salt and dill; or locally produced sausages with mash and onion gravy. An ideal base for walkers in the Ribble Valley.
OPEN: 12-11 Sun 12-10.30 **BAR MEALS:** L served all week 12-9 D served Mon-Sat 12-9 Sun 12-8 Av main course £6.50
RESTAURANT: L served all week 12-9 D served Mon-Sat 12-9 Sun 12-8 Av 3 course à la carte £14 🍴: 🍺: Interbrew Boddingtons Bitter, Black Sheep Best, Bombadier, Abbots Ale. ⚲: 10 **FACILITIES:** Child facs Garden: Seating for 40 overlooking roman ruins
NOTES: Parking 14

SLAIDBURN — Map 18 SD75

Hark to Bounty Inn
Townend BB7 3EP ☎ 01200 446246 🖷 01200 446361
e-mail: manager@hark-to-bounty.co.uk
Dir: From M6 junct 31 take A59 to Clitheroe then B6478

A family-run 13th-century inn known as The Dog until 1875 when Bounty, the local squire's favourite hound, disturbed a post-hunt drinking session with its loud baying. The squire's vocal response obviously made a lasting impact. View the ancient courtroom, last used in 1937. Traditional favourites like home-made steak and kidney pie, and vegetable and cheese crumble, are supplemented by pastas and curries from the chalkboards. New owners are Vicki and Nicholas Hay.
OPEN: 11-11 **BAR MEALS:** L served all week 12-2 D served Mon-Sat 6-9 all day Sunday **RESTAURANT:** L served Tue-Sun 12-2 D served Tue-Sat 6-9 all day Sunday 🍴: Scottish Courage 🍺: Theakston Old Peculier, Scottish Courage Courage Directors & 1 guest ale (changed monthly). **FACILITIES:** Children's licence Garden: Large enclosed area Dogs allowed except during food service **NOTES:** Parking 25

 Pubs offering a good choice of fish on their menu

We endeavour to be as accurate as possible but changes to times and other information can occur after the guide has gone to press

TUNSTALL — Map 18 SD67

Pick of the Pubs

The Lunesdale Arms NEW
LA6 2QN ☎ 015242 74203 🖷 015242 74229
e-mail: info@thelunesdale.co.uk
Located in the beautiful Lune Valley, this pub is bright, airy and cheerful with a warmth that, no doubt, comes in part from the pub's ever-popular landlady. All food is freshly prepared, with meat largely from local farms, most of the salad leaves and vegetables grown organically, and all of the bread made in their own kitchens. Food ranges from lighter bites at lunchtime to the full three courses for dinner. Interesting midday choices include carrot and artichoke soup; organic purple sprouting broccoli, wholegrain mustard and cheddar cheese tart; and prawns and marie rose open sandwich. Evening starters could be chicken liver parfait with red onion jam; or houmous with marinated red peppers. To follow, you could try chicken breast with home-made basil pesto, sunblushed tomato and herby cheese; or local lamb's liver with bacon and crispy onions with mash. Puddings might be cardamom, crème fraîche and honey cheesecake; or the house special sticky toffee pudding.
OPEN: Closed: 25-26 Dec **BAR MEALS:** L served Tues-Sun 12-2 D served Tues-Sun 6-9 **RESTAURANT:** L served Tues-Sun 12-2 D served Tues-Sun 6-9 Av 3 course à la carte £18.50 🍺: Black Sheep, Dent Aviator, Guinness. **FACILITIES:** Terrace Dogs allowed **NOTES:** Parking 25

WHALLEY — Map 18 SD73

Pick of the Pubs

Freemasons Arms 🐟 ⚲
8 Vicarage Fold, Wiswell BB7 9DF ☎ 01254 822218
e-mail: freemasons@wiswell.co.uk
See Pick of the Pubs on opposite page

Pick of the Pubs

The Three Fishes NEW 🐟 ⚲
Mitton Rd, Mitton BB7 9PQ ☎ 01254 826888 🖷 01254 826026
Dir: 3m from Whalley Village, signed to Stonyhurst.
After many years of neglect, the Three Fishes is once again refreshing travellers and visitors in the Ribble Valley. This is a place full of mystery and legend; and, if you enjoy country pursuits, local heritage, or simply relaxing amidst stunning countryside, then you'll find the area has plenty to offer. Founded at least 400 years ago, the Three Fishes has been carefully restored as a non-smoking pub, and its traditional rustic interior has been given a strongly contemporary twist. The menu embraces regional dishes and British classics. Lunchtime sandwiches and hot oven bottoms combine robust flavours like ox tongue and pickled beetroot, whilst main course dishes are just as distinctive. Try slow baked pigs' trotters with chicken and black pudding stuffing; Bowland lamb hotpot with pickled red cabbage; or celeriac dabs, pearl barley and button mushroom broth.
OPEN: 12-11 Sun 12-10.30 Closed: Dec 25
BAR MEALS: L served all week 12-2 D served all week 6-9 Fri-Sat 6-9.30, Sun 12-8.30 Av main course £8.50 🍺: Thwaites Traditional, Thwaites Bomber, Moorhouse's Black Cat Mild & guest beer every month. ⚲: 8 **FACILITIES:** Child facs Children's licence Garden: Fabulous views of The Ribble Valley Dogs allowed **NOTES:** Parking 55 🚭

Pick of the Pubs
WHALLEY – LANCASHIRE

Freemasons Arms

At least two hundred years old, this traditional country dining pub is set in the quiet village of Wiswell, not far from Whalley in the lovely Ribble Valey. Numerous walks in the area take in some stunning views of the countryside.

Formerly housing the monks from nearby Whalley Abbey, it was converted at some point into a pub, and was believed to have hosted secret freemasons' meetings, hence the name. Today it has a reputation for good ales and fine food, served in the spacious bar area, and in a more refined upstairs dining room. The extensive menu includes many fish specials, such as deep-fried cod; grilled salmon; grilled sea bass; gratin of mixed seafood; and deep-fried tempura of monkfish. Other dishes appearing on the interesting menu are slow roast joint of lamb with flageolet beans and rosemary sauce; grilled fillet steak with port and stilton sauce;

Goosnargh duck breast with spiced plum compote and red wine jus; dry cured Bowland knuckle of ham, braised in cider with a mustard and parsley cream sauce; chicken liver pâté with spiced apple chutney; Goosnargh chicken pot roasted with mushrooms, cream and white wine. Puddings are in the same tantalizing vein, with the likes of chocolate sponge with hot chocolate sauce and clotted cream; individual Bakewell tart; sticky toffee pudding; glazed figs in mascapone and maple syrup; cider and apple crumble; banana filo parcels with Galliano sauce; golden syrup sponge; and vanilla crème brûlée.

OPEN: 12-3 6-11 Closed: 25-26 Dec, 1-2 Jan
BAR MEALS: L served Wed-Sun 12-2 D served Wed-Sun 6-9.30 (Sun 12-8) Av main course £10
RESTAURANT: L served Wed-Sun 12-2 D served Wed-Sun 6-9.30 (Sun 12-8) Av 3 course à la carte £20 Av 2 course fixed price £9.95
🏠: Free House
🍺: Bowland Brewery Hen Harrier, Black Sheep Bitter, Moorhouse Pride of Pendle, Guinness. ♀: 15
FACILITIES: Seating outside

〰️🐟 ♀   Map 18 SD73
8 Vicarage Fold, Wiswell BB7 9DF
☎ 01254 822218
✉ freemasons@wiswell.co.uk
Dir: From A59, onto A671, Wiswell is 1st left

England

WHITEWELL   Map 18 SD64

Pick of the Pubs

The Inn At Whitewell 🏠 ⌁
Forest of Bowland BB7 3AT
☎ 01200 448222 📠 01200 448298
Dir: From B6243 follow Whitewell signs

A slightly eccentric inn, packed with a haphazard arrangement of furnishings and bric-a-brac, that stands on the east bank of the River Hodder at the heart of the Forest of Bowland. Parts of the building date back to the 1300s, at which time it would have been the forest-keeper's house. Outside are two acres of riverside grounds incorporating an extensive herb garden, which keeps the kitchen well supplied. The comprehensive bar lunch and supper menus are supplemented by daily specials. Fish pie is a lunchtime favourite, while Bowland venison with figs and juniper jus is a speciality at dinner. Other food options range through substantial sandwiches, traditional home-made puddings and fine hand-made cheeses. A la carte dining is available at night in a relaxing atmosphere where no-one stands on ceremony - a fine old inn.

OPEN: 11-3 6-11 **BAR MEALS:** L served all week 12-2 D served all week 7.30-9.30 **RESTAURANT:** D served all week 7.30-9.30 😊: Free House ◀: Marston's Pedigree, Interbrew Boddingtons Bitter, Timothy Taylors Landlord. ⌁: 16 **FACILITIES:** Garden: 2 acres running to river bank, herb garden Dogs allowed **NOTES:** Parking 65 **ROOMS:** 23 bedrooms en suite s£70 d£96 No children overnight

WRIGHTINGTON   Map 15 SD51

Pick of the Pubs

The Mulberry Tree ⊚⊚ ▷⌁ ⌁
WN6 9SE ☎ 01257 451400 📠 01257 451400
Dir: M6 junct 27 into Mossy Lea Rd, 2m on right

Built in 1832 as a wheelwright's, later a brewery and blacksmith, The Mulberry Tree opened in April 2000. It was set up by former Roux brothers' head chef Mark Prescott - ranked in Great Britain's top ten of contemporary chefs - and James Moore, so it is no surprise that The Mulberry Tree is a sought-after venue for discerning diners. Customers from near and far feel at home in its clean, airy space whilst choosing from a veritable feast of options. The bar menu has speciality sandwiches (lunchtime only); starters that may include potted Morecambe Bay shrimps with bloody mary dressing; and main choices among deep-fried cod and chips; and seared tikka marinated salmon with cardamom-scented rice cake. The dinner menu offers similarly accomplished dishes, like slow braised lamb shank with puy lentils; and roast breast of Goosnargh duck with black pudding; or you can keep it simple but pricey with Iranian Sevruga caviar, followed by fresh lobster with champagne and herb sauce.

OPEN: 12-3 6-11 Closed: 26 Dec, 1 Jan **BAR MEALS:** L served All 12-2 D served All 6-9.30 All day Sun, Fri-Sat 6-10 Av main course £14.50 **RESTAURANT:** L served all week 12-2 D served all week 6-10 Sun 12-3 Av 3 course à la carte £28 😊: Free House ◀: Interbrew Flowers IPA,. ⌁: 8 **NOTES:** Parking 100

YEALAND CONYERS   Map 18 SD57

The New Inn
40 Yealand Rd LA5 9SJ ☎ 01524 732938
e-mail: charlottepinder@hotmail.com
Dir: M6 junct 35, follw signs for Kendal (A6) approx 3m, go past Holmere Hall, next junct on left, up hill turn left at T-junct. Pub is on left .

Picturesque village setting for a 17th-century inn with a beamed bar and large stone fireplace. Alongside the cask conditioned ales are mulled wine in winter and home-made lemonade in summer, plus around 30 malt whiskies and wines from around the world. Home-cooked fayre is available all day everyday, with dishes ranging from beef in beer, stuffed field mushroom, and fresh fillet of salmon, to fillet and sirloin steaks or roasted duck and guinea fowl.

OPEN: 11.30-11 (Sun 12-10.30) **BAR MEALS:** L served all week 11.30-9.30 D served all week Sun 12-9.30 Av main course £8.95 **RESTAURANT:** L served all week 11.30-9.30 D served all week 11.30-9.30 Sun 12-9.30 😊: Frederic Robinson ◀: Hartleys XB, Robinson's Seasonal Bitter, Old Tom. **FACILITIES:** Garden: quiet and private Dogs allowed Water **NOTES:** Parking 50

continued

LEICESTERSHIRE

BRUNTINGTHORPE
Map 11 SP68

Joiners Arms NEW
Church Walk LE17 5QH ☎ 0116 247 8258
e-mail: stephen@thejoinersarms-bruntingthorpe.co.uk
Dir: 4m from Lutterworth
Demure whitewashed walls and small paned windows belie the Joiners' contemporary interior. Indeed, only a discreet hanging sign betrays the fact that this is a pub at all! The recently refurbished building boasts a new tiled floor, restored natural oak beams, and a new bar area. This is very much a food-orientated establishment, and the freshly prepared dishes include slow-roasted lamb shank; aubergine with ratatouille and mozzerella; and herb-crusted halibut. **OPEN:** 12-1.45 6.30-11 **BAR MEALS:** L served Tues-Sun 12-1.45 D served Tues-Sat 6.30-9.30 Sun 12-1.45 Av main course £11.50 **RESTAURANT:** L served Tues-Sun 12-1.45 D served Tues-Sat Av 3 course à la carte £22.50 ◖: Greene King IPA, Murphys, John Smiths. ☿: 8 **NOTES:** Parking 15

CASTLE DONINGTON
Map 11 SK42

Pick of the Pubs

The Nag's Head
Hilltop DE74 2PR ☎ 01332 850652
See Pick of the Pubs on page 296

CROXTON KERRIAL
Map 11 SK82

Peacock Inn
1 School Ln NG32 1QR ☎ 01476 870324 ▤ 01476 870171
e-mail: peacockcroxton@globalnet.co.uk
web: www.peacockcroxton.co.uk
Dir: Situated on A607, 3m from Junct with A1
300-year-old coaching inn situated on the edge of the Vale of Belvoir with its historic castle only a mile away. Noted for its lovely views and garden, the pub attracts walkers, equestrians and anglers. Everything is prepared on the premises and the menu is noted for its quality fish and chips. Other options may include Aberdeen Angus steak, lasagne and a range of celebrated Sunday roasts. The salad dressing, made from the chef's own recipe, is a particular favourite with customers. **OPEN:** 12-3.30 6-11 **BAR MEALS:** L served all week 12-3.30 D served all week 6.30-10 **RESTAURANT:** L served all week 12-3.30 D served all week 6.30-10 ◗: Free House ◖: Scottish Courage John Smith's, Timothy Taylor Landlord and guest beers. **FACILITIES:** Children's licence Garden: 1.5 acres of landscaped garden Dogs allowed Water **NOTES:** Parking 40

EAST LANGTON
Map 11 SP79

Pick of the Pubs

The Bell Inn
Main St LE16 7TW ☎ 01858 545278 ▤ 01858 545748
A creeper-clad, 16th-century listed building tucked away in a quiet village with good country walks all around. The cosy inn has a pretty walled garden, low beams and an open log fire. Peter Faye and Joy Jesson took over running the pub a few years ago, and have carried out a refurbishment that leaves the pub looking bright and cheerful. The Langton micro-brewery operates from

outbuildings, and produces two regular brews as well as seasonal ales. There's a wide range of food on menus in both the Long Bar and non-smoking Green Room, from starters and light bites to more hearty fare: signature dishes include beer-battered cod with home-cut chips and mushy peas; parisienne rib-eye steak with mushrooms and tomatoes in a balsamic syrup; and chicken breast on a warm nicoise salad. Vegetarian choices may include wild mushroom pancake; roasted red pepper filled with brown rice, hazelnut and onion; and stilton and celeriac savoury torte.
OPEN: 12-2.30 7-11 Closed: Dec 25 **BAR MEALS:** L served all week 12-2 D served Mon-Sat 7-9.30 Sun 12-2.30 **RESTAURANT:** L served all week D served Mon-Sat ◗: Free House ◖: Greene King IPA & Abbot Ale, Langton Bowler Ale & Caudle Bitter. **FACILITIES:** Garden: Large sunny aspect at front of pub, lawned **NOTES:** Parking 20

FLECKNEY
Map 11 SP69

The Old Crown
High St LE8 8AJ ☎ 0116 2402223
e-mail: old-crown-inn@fleckney7.freeserve.co.uk
Close to the Grand Union Canal and Saddington Tunnel, a traditional village pub that is especially welcoming to hiking groups and families. Noted for good real ales and generous opening times (evening meals from 5pm) offering a wide choice of popular food or, as the landlady says, food your grandmother would cook. Choose from a variety of platters, grills, baguettes, burgers, jacket potatoes and more. Chef's specials include lamb in a red wine and plum sauce; poached salmon; lamb and mint pudding; and pork in a mushroom and brandy sauce. The garden has lovely views of fields and the canal, as well as a pétanque court.
OPEN: 11-11 (Sun 12-10.30) **BAR MEALS:** L served all week 12-2 D served Tue-Sat 5-9 Av main course £8 **RESTAURANT:** L served all week 12-2 D served Tue-Sat 8-9 ◗: Everards Brewery ◖: Everards Tiger & Beacon, Scottish Courage Courage Directors, Adnams Bitter, Greene King Abbot Ale. **FACILITIES:** Child facs Garden: Very large, wonderful views Dogs allowed Water **NOTES:** Parking 60 No credit cards

GRIMSTON
Map 11 SK62

The Black Horse
3 Main St LE14 3BZ ☎ 01664 812358 ▤ 01664 813138
e-mail: joe.blackhorsepub@virgin.net
Dir: Telephone for directions
A traditional 16th-century coaching inn displaying much cricketing memorabilia in a quiet village with views over the Vale of Belvoir. Plenty of opportunities for country walks, or perhaps a game of pétanque on the pub's floodlit pitch. Dishes include devilled whitebait with freshly twisted lemon and lime; local lamb cutlets with honey and mint sauce; five cheese and spinach canneloni; and giant Yorkshire pudding with mustard mash, Lincolnshire sausages and black pudding. Extensive sweet menu changes weekly.
OPEN: 12-3 6-11 **BAR MEALS:** L served all week 12-2 D served Mon-Sat 6.30-9.30 Av main course £8.95 **RESTAURANT:** L served all week 12-2 D served Mon-Sat 6.30-9.30 Av 3 course à la carte £15.15 ◗: Free House ◖: Belvoir, Greene King, Marstons Pedigree, Archers. ☿: 6 **FACILITIES:** Child facs Children's licence Garden: Large beer garden, floodlights Dogs allowed Water **NOTES:** Parking 30

continued

Pick of the Pubs
CASTLE DONINGTON – LEICESTERSHIRE

The Nag's Head

Originally the site of a farm, the pub is a simple whitewashed building with low beamed ceilings and coal fires in a hilltop location on the edge of Castle Donington. The Nag's Head was a gradual conversion of four farm cottages and dates back over a hundred years.

It was a popular watering hole with the RAF in World War II, and these days provides an ideal refreshment stop en route to the East Midlands airport or the nearby motor racing circuit. In addition to the real ales on offer in the bar there's a choice of 30 malt whiskies, and in summer you can sit outside in the garden, which is a small enclosed area with a boules pitch. The dining room is spacious and well presented, and there's a bistro feel to its colour-washed walls and plain scrubbed tables. The flexible menu offers snacks and sandwiches 12-2pm and 5.30-7pm, such as smoked salmon with crème fraîche on salad baguette, or Lincolnshire sausage with mash and onion gravy. If you're after the full three courses, starters take in seared scallops with balsamic vinegar, and garlic and cream mushrooms - dishes that can also be taken as snacks. An interesting choice of main courses lists sliced fillet of beef in Cajun spices with tzatziki dressing, and monkfish with stir-fried oriental vegetables. Vegetarian alternatives might include aubergine, black olive and polenta layer with sun-dried tomato dressing. Treacle oat tart and chocolate rum torte are among the tempting selection of home-made puddings, served with custard or cream.

OPEN: 11.30-2.30 5.30-11 (Sun 12-3, 7-10.30) Closed: 26 Dec-4 Jan
BAR MEALS: L served Mon-Sat 12-2 D served Mon-Sat 5.30-7 Av main course £14
RESTAURANT: L served Mon-Sat 12-2 D served Mon-Sat 5.30-9.30
🍴: W'hampton & Dudley
🍺: Bank's Bitter, Marston's Pedigree, Mansfield Cask Bitter.
FACILITIES: Garden: Small enclosed area with boules pitch Dogs allowed
NOTES: Parking 20

Map 11 SK42
Hilltop DE74 2PR
☎ 01332 850652

England

HALLATON   Map 11 SP79

Pick of the Pubs

The Bewicke Arms ♀
1 Eastgate LE16 8UB ☎ 01858 555217 📠 01858 555598
www.bewickearms.co.uk
Dir: S of A47 between Leicester & junct of A47/A6003

On Easter Monday 1770, a local chatelaine was saved from being gored by a raging bull when a hare ran across the bull's path. Driving a tank through the conventions of gratitude, she arranged for two hare pies and a generous supply of ale be made available to the parish poor each succeeding Easter Monday. The Bewicke Arms plays host to this annual orgy of beer and hare pie - nowadays beef - guzzling. For the rest of the year, this refurbished 400-year-old thatched inn serves Langton's Caudle Bitter amongst others and good, robust meals such as chilli con carne with real steak, and local gammon - the real thing - with hordes of home-made chips. The climbing frame and gardens are child friendly, as indeed are the foot-long fish fingers offered on the junior menu. Other menu highpoints include Mediterranean vegetable and potato bake, chicken with boursin cream sauce, and salmon fillet with spring onion mash, asparagus and prawn sauce.
OPEN: 12-3 6-11 (Open all day Sun, Winter months 7-11) Closed: Easter Monday **BAR MEALS:** L served all week 12-2 D served Mon-Sat 7-9.30 Food on Sun May-Oct Av main course £8.95
RESTAURANT: L served all week 12-2 D served Mon-Sat 7-9.30
🍺: Free House 🍻: Grain Store Brewery, IPA Flowers, Grainstore Triple B, Guest beers. ♀: 18 **FACILITIES:** Garden: Patio with picnic benches, enclosed with pond **NOTES:** Parking 20

HATHERN   Map 11 SK52

The Anchor Inn ♀
Loughborough Rd LE12 5JB ☎ 01509 842309
e-mail: stevejvincent@aol.com
Dir: M1 junct 24, take A6 towards Leicester, 4.5m on left
Hathern's oldest pub, the Anchor was originally a coaching inn, with stables accessed through an archway off what is now the A6. It offers snacks galore, with vegetarian options, and a bar/restaurant menu presenting pasta, fish, and steaks, known here as Anchor Inn sizzlers. House specialities include supreme of chicken, and Barnsley lamb chop, pork chop and duck breast - all pan fried. Unquestionably family-friendly, with a fenced-off children's play area in the large garden.
OPEN: 11-11 (Jan-Mar Mon-Wed closed 3-5)
BAR MEALS: L served all week 12-9 D served all week 12-9
RESTAURANT: L served all week 12-9.30 D served all week 12-9.30
🍺: Scottish & Newcastle 🍻: John Smiths, Pedigree & Guest Beers.
♀: 8 **FACILITIES:** Child facs Children's licence Garden: Large garden, fenced area **NOTES:** Parking 100

HOSE   Map 11 SK72

Rose & Crown
43 Bolton Ln LE14 4JE ☎ 01949 860424
e-mail: brian@rosehose.freeserve.co.uk
Dir: Off A606 N of Melton Mowbray
Two hundred-year-old pub in the picturesque Vale of Belvoir, renowned for its real ales and good food. It has a large lounge bar with open fires, a heavily beamed restaurant and, weather permitting, outside eating on the patio. The bar menu offers large filled baps, baguettes and baked potatoes, while the main menu takes in gammon and pineapple, chicken tikka, steak and Guinness pie, and Mediterranean vegetable bake.
OPEN: 12-2.30 7-11 (Sun 12-3, 7.30-10.30) Mon-Wed Closed lunch
BAR MEALS: L served Fri-Sun 12-2.30 D served Thurs-Sat 7-9
RESTAURANT: L served Fri-Sun 12-2.30 D served Thu-Sat 7-9
🍺: Free House 🍻: Greene King IPA & Abbot Ale, Belvoir Mild, Guest. **FACILITIES:** Garden: Large grassy area, tables, sheltered patio Dogs allowed **NOTES:** Parking 30

KEGWORTH   Map 11 SK42

Cap & Stocking
20 Borough St DE74 2FF ☎ 01509 674814
Dir: Village centre (chemist on left. Turn left, left again to Borough St)
A traditional, unspoilt country pub with comfortable, old-fashioned rooms and authentic features. Its award-winning garden has a barbecue area and pétanque piste, as well as a children's play area. Appetising food includes soups, rolls (some hot) and burgers for the snack seeker; pizzas and ploughman's for those with a little more appetite; and, for the truly hungry, Hungarian goulash, chicken curry, beef stroganoff, or vegetarian green lentil curry. Thai chicken, and minty lamb appear as specials. Bass is served from the jug.
OPEN: 12 (Sun 12-2.30, 7-10.30) **BAR MEALS:** L served all week 12-1.45 D served all week 6-7.45 Sun 12-2.30 Av main course £5.90
🍺: Punch Taverns 🍻: Bass & Greene King IPA.
FACILITIES: Garden: Enclosed walled garden, patio, conservatory Dogs allowed Water **NOTES:** Parking 4

LOUGHBOROUGH   Map 11 SK51

The Swan in the Rushes ♀
21 The Rushes LE11 5BE ☎ 01509 217014 📠 01509 217014
e-mail: tynemill@tynemill.co.uk
Dir: On A6 (Derby road)
A 1930s tile-fronted real ale pub with two drinking rooms, a cosmopolitan atmosphere and no frills. The oldest of The Tynemill independent chain pubs, it always offers ten ales, including six guests, and hosts two annual beer festivals, acoustic open-mic nights, folk club, and skittle alley. The simple menu lists dishes like Lincolnshire sausages, chilli, Kefalonian meat pie, or vegetables à la crème, with baguettes, jacket potatoes, and ploughman's also available.
OPEN: 11-11 (Sun 12-10.30) **BAR MEALS:** L served all week 12-2.30 D served Mon-Fri 6-8.30 Av main course £5.95 🍺: Tynemill Ltd 🍻: Archers Golden, Castle Rock Gold, Castle Rock Harvest Pale, Adnams Bitter. ♀: 17 **FACILITIES:** Car park with outdoor seating area Dogs allowed Water if required **NOTES:** Parking 16

Pick of the Pubs have that extra special quality that makes them stand out from the crowd. Their entries are highlighted, and may be a full page

MEDBOURNE — Map 11 SP89

The Nevill Arms
12 Waterfall Way LE16 8EE ☎ 01858 565288 ▤ 01858 565509
e-mail: nevillarms@hotmail.com
Dir: A508 from Northampton to Market Harborough, then B664 for 5m.
Left for Medbourne
Warm golden stone and mullioned windows make this traditional old coaching inn, in its riverside setting by the village green, truly picturesque. The popular pub garden has its own dovecote and is a great attraction for children who like to feed the ducks. A choice of appetising home-made soups, spicy lamb with apricots, smoked haddock and spinach bake, and pork in apple cream and cider are typical examples of the varied menu.
OPEN: 12-2.30 6-11 (Sun 12-3, 7-10.30) 25 Dec, 31 Dec Closed eve
BAR MEALS: L served all week 12-2 D served all week 7-9.45 Sun 12-3 & 7-9.30 Av main course £6.50 ⊜: Free House ◖: Fuller's London Pride, Adnams Bitter, Greene King Abbot Ale, Guest Beers.
FACILITIES: Child facs Garden: Edges the river bank, with picnic benches **NOTES:** Parking 30

MELTON MOWBRAY — Map 11 SK71

Anne of Cleves House ♀
12 Burton St LE13 1AE ☎ 01664 481336
e-mail: anneofcleves@btconnect.com
Dir: Next to church

Fine old 14th-century building once used to house chantry priests. After Henry VIII dissolved the monasteries it was given to Anne of Cleves as part of her divorce settlement, and it is under a local heritage protection order. Log fires in winter and a picturesque garden for summer enjoyment. The menu includes home-made steak and kidney pie, traditional lasagne, and chicken breast on penne with roasted pepper, tomato and basil sauce.
OPEN: 10.30-11 (Sun 12-4, 7-10.30) **RESTAURANT:** L served all week 12-2 D served Tue-Sat 7-9 Wknd lunch 12.15-2 ⊜: Everards Brewery ◖: Everards Tiger Best, Everards Original, Guest ale.
FACILITIES: Garden: Dogs allowed Water if asked
NOTES: Parking 20

MOUNTSORREL — Map 11 SK51

The Swan Inn
10 Loughborough Rd LE12 7AT
☎ 0116 2302340 ▤ 0116 2376115 e-mail: swan@jvf.co.uk
web: www.jvf.co.uk/swan
Dir: On A6 between Leicester & Loughborough
A privately-owned free house and former coaching inn, and proud acquirer of many accolades for its beers and food since opening in 1990. Within granite walls, flagstone floors and exposed beams, food is freshly cooked: the menu changes
continued

---

weekly, always maintaining a part-international theme with enchiladas and a range of pastas, as well as the more traditional beef casseroled in Old Peculier with onions; seared pigeon breast; and fish of the day. Salads, French toasted sandwiches, baguettes and nachos are also available.
OPEN: 12-2.30 5.30-11 (Sat all day & Sun 12-3, 7-10.30)
BAR MEALS: L served all week 12-2 D served Mon-Sat 6.30-9.30 Av main course £8 **RESTAURANT:** L served all week 12-2 D served Mon-Sat 6.30-9.30 Av 3 course à la carte £16 ⊜: Free House ◖: Theakston Best, XB, Old Peculier, Ruddles County.
FACILITIES: Garden: Quiet, secluded riverside Dogs allowed
NOTES: Parking 12

OADBY — Map 11 SK60

Pick of the Pubs

Cow and Plough NEW ♀
Gartree Rd, Stoughton Farm LE2 2FB
☎ 0116 272 0852 ▤ 0116 272 0852
e-mail: enquiries@steaminbilly.co.uk
Dir: 3m S of Leicester off A6, close to BUPA Hospital
The Cow and Plough has an interesting history, and an atmosphere to match. Housed in an old farm dairy, it was the brainchild of licensee Barry Lount. In 1989, he approached the owners of Stoughton Grange Farm who were then in the process of opening the farm to the public. Barry suggested that an old type pub selling real ale would fit in with their plans, and fortunately they agreed. Today the pub, which produces its own Steamin' Billy beers - named after the owner's Jack Russell - is a very popular place and has won many awards and accolades for its hospitality and beer. The ingredients used in the cooking are organic and locally produced wherever possible, as they themselves put it: "from farm to fork - the simplest way." You could start with flowerpot-baked brioche with sautéed chicken liver and sage, follow it up with chargrilled rump of aged William's farm beef, and finish with fragrant Thai rice pudding and lychee compote.
OPEN: 12-3 5-11 (Open all day Sat-Sun)
BAR MEALS: L served Tues-Sun 12-3 D served Tues-Sun 6.30-9.30 Sun 12-5 **RESTAURANT:** L served Tues-Sun 12-3 D served Tues-Sat 6.30-9.30 Sun 12-5 Av 3 course à la carte £20.25 ◖: Steamin Billy Bitter, Steamin Billy Mild, Skydiver, London Pride. ♀: 8 **FACILITIES:** Garden: Large patio and courtyard area Dogs allowed **NOTES:** Parking 100

OLD DALBY — Map 11 SK62

Pick of the Pubs

The Crown Inn
Debdale Hill LE14 3LF ☎ 01664 823134
e-mail: thecrownolddalby@btconnect.com
Dir: A46 turn for Willoughby/Broughton. R into Nottingham Ln, then L to Old Dalby
Dating back to 1509, a classic creeper-covered, old-style pub in extensive gardens and orchards, with small rooms, all with open fires. Undisturbed by background music or video games, you can eat, play solitaire or dominoes, or just stare into a pint of decent real ale in peace here. If the food doesn't come from Leicestershire, and admittedly the fish doesn't because it is landed in Brixham, the county's suppliers are otherwise
continued

England

wholeheartedly supported. Filled ciabattas and sandwiches are available in the bar and the restaurant offers starters such as chicken roulade; prawn hollandaise; and egg boudin which, for the uninitiated, is a poached egg on mixed salad leaves, with sauté potatoes, crispy smoked bacon and black pudding. Main courses include spicy jerk pork; magret of duck; classic daube of beef; and fish of the day. In summer the gardens are full of flowers, shrubs, hanging baskets and pot plants.

OPEN: 12-3 6-11 (Winter 12-2.30, 6.30-11) 25-26 Dec, 1 Jan Closed in eve **BAR MEALS:** L served Tues-Sun 12-2.30 D served Mon-Sat 7-9.30 Av main course £13.50

RESTAURANT: L served Tues-Sun 12-2.30 D served Tue-Sat 7-9.30 Av 3 course à la carte £22.50 Av 3 course fixed price £12.95 ⊕: Free House ⬤: Wells Bombardier, Hook Norton, Scottish Courage Directors Castle Rock Hemlock.

FACILITIES: Garden: 3/4 acre formal garden. Patio Dogs allowed Water **NOTES:** Parking 32

REDMILE   Map 11 SK73

Pick of the Pubs

Peacock Inn
Church Corner NG13 0GB ☎ 01949 842554 ▤ 01949 843746
e-mail: info@thepeacockinnredmile.co.uk
Dir: From A1 take A52 towards Nottingham

The Peacock Inn is a 16th-century stone-built pub with a lovely beamed interior and open fireplaces. Located in the pretty village of Redmile, it sits beside the Grantham Canal in the Vale of Belvoir, only two miles from the picturesque castle. It has a local reputation for good quality food, and offers a relaxed and informal setting for wining, dining and socialising. The menus include dishes based on local seasonal produce: from the restaurant you might find lamb shank roasted in an apricot and rosemary licquor; tuna loin on black olive chorizo, with French bean salad and chilli and lime salsa; and local rabbit and woodland mushrooms in a fresh thyme, mustard, wine and cream sauce. From the bar menu expect Cumberland sausage with onion gravy and mash, Thai-style chicken and saffron rice, and sirloin steak Diane. Guest ales like Bombadier, Timothy Taylor Landlord and Tetley Cask are on tap.

OPEN: 11-11 (Sun 12-10.30) **BAR MEALS:** L served all week 12-2.30 D served all week 9.30 Av main course £12

RESTAURANT: L served all week 12-2.30 D served all week 7-9.30 ⊕: ⬤: Timothy Taylor Landlord, Bombardier.

FACILITIES: Garden **NOTES:** Parking 24

SADDINGTON   Map 11 SP69

The Queens Head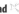
Main St LE8 0QH ☎ 0116 2402536
Dir: Between A50 & A6 S of Leicester, NW of Market Harborough
Traditional prize-winning English pub with terrific views from the restaurant and garden over the Saddington Reservoir. Specialises in real ale and very good food, with four specials boards to supplement the evening menu. Foil-cooked cod fillet, roast Banbury duck, lamb shank with garlic mash, steak and ale pie, monkfish medallions with parma ham, and pan-fried tuna steak with sweet pepper and oyster sauce guarantee something for everyone.

OPEN: 12-3 5.30-11 (Summer all day wknds)
BAR MEALS: L served all week 12-2 D served Mon-Sat 6.30-9.30 Sun lunch 12.30-4 Av main course £6.50 **RESTAURANT:** L served all week 12-2 D served Mon-Sat 6.30-9.30 Av 3 course à la carte £20 ⊕: Everards Brewery ⬤: Everards Tiger Best & Beacon Bitter + Guests. **FACILITIES:** Garden: Stunning views of reservoir and countryside **NOTES:** Parking 50

SILEBY   Map 11 SK61

The White Swan
Swan St LE12 7NW ☎ 01509 814832 ▤ 01509 815995
Beyond the unassuming exterior of this 1930s free house lies a book-lined non-smoking restaurant and homely bar with open fire. There are always lunchtime snacks, hot filled baguettes and home-made rolls, alongside a more extensive menu that changes every week. Typical choices include salmon and prawn pasta with cheese sauce; mixed vegetable crumble with salad and potatoes; and hot potato skins with onions, bacon and cheddar cheese.

OPEN: 11.45-3 7-11 (Closed Mon am, Sun pm) Closed: 1-7 Jan
BAR MEALS: L served Tue-Sun 12-2 D served Tue-Sat 7-10
RESTAURANT: L served Tue-Sun 12-2 D served Tue-Sat 7-10 ⊕: Free House ⬤: Marston's Pedigree, Carlsberg-Tetley Ansells, Banks, Fuller's London Pride. **FACILITIES:** Garden: Small secluded courtyard **NOTES:** Parking 10

SOMERBY   Map 11 SK71

The Old Brewery
High St LE14 2PZ ☎ 01664 454777 ▤ 01664 454165
Dir: Between Melton Mowbray & Oakham off the A606 at Leesthorpe
Holder of the record for brewing the strongest beer in the world, (a mind pummelling 23% ABV!) this 15th-century coaching inn offers eight traditional cask ales. In addition to fine ale, the pub is also known for its food. Typical menu includes lemon sole, breaded haddock, and battered cod. Lots of good walking country around. Live music every Saturday.
OPEN: 12-2.30 6.30-11 (Sun 12-10.30) **BAR MEALS:** L served Tues-Sun 12-2 D served Tues-Sat 7-9 Av main course £5.95 **RESTAURANT:** L served Tue-Sun D served Tue-Sat Av 3 course à la carte £6 ⊕: Free House ⬤: Bass, Worthington Smooth.
FACILITIES: Garden: Food served outside Dogs allowed on lead only **NOTES:** Parking 50

Stilton Cheese Inn ♀
High St LE14 2QB ☎ 01664 454394
Located at the heart of a working village in scenic countryside, this quaint sandstone building dates from the 16th century. The same menus service both bar and restaurant areas, with a varied selection of dishes on the specials boards. You'll find grilled Dover sole; whiting fillets in prawn sauce; grilled T-bone steak with mushrooms, tomato and salad garnish;

continued

SOMERBY continued

Somerby sausages and mash; and spinach and vegetable pakoras.

Stilton Cheese Inn

OPEN: 12-3 6-11 **BAR MEALS:** L served all week 12-2 D served all week 6-9 Sun 7-9 **RESTAURANT:** L served all week 12-2 D served all week 6-9 ☺: Free House ☗: Grainstore Ten Fifty, Brewster's Hophead, Belvoir Star, Carlsberg-Tetley Tetley's Cask. ♀: 10 **FACILITIES:** Garden: Small patio, seats around 20 **NOTES:** Parking 14

STATHERN
Map 11 SK73

Pick of the Pubs

AA Pub of the Year for England 2005-06

Red Lion Inn ⊛ ⤳ ♀
Red Lion St LE14 4HS ☎ 01949 860868 🖹 01949 861579
e-mail: info@theredlioninn.co.uk
Dir: From A1, A52 towards Nottingham, L signed Belvoir Castle/Redmile. 2-3m turn to Stathern on left
The young team at the Red Lion is passionate about traditional pub values, aiming to serve excellent food, beer and wine in a friendly and enjoyable atmosphere. Following a complete refurbishment in 2002, you'll discover a traditional stone-floored bar and an informal lounge with a comfy sofa, magazines and newspapers. There's also an informal dining area and an elegant dining room. Besides the hand-pumped local beers, speciality beers and bottled ciders are also on offer. Seasonal highlights include mulled wine and roast chestnuts by the open fire in winter, and homemade lemonade or Pimms cocktails to wash down summer barbecues in the enclosed rear garden. Produce from the best local suppliers is used to create a daily-changing menu, which might include Toulouse sausage, mashed potato and onion gravy; aubergine, tomato and chickpea bake; crab and penne pasta; and pan-fried scallops with rocket and crispy bacon, supplemented by snacks and nibbles, and set lunches.
OPEN: 12-3 6-11 (Sat 12-11, Sun 12-5.30) Closed: 26 Dec, 1 Jan **BAR MEALS:** L served all week 12-2 D served Mon-Sat 7-9.30 Sun 12-3 Av main course £10.50 **RESTAURANT:** L served all week 12-2 D served Mon-Sat 7-9.30 Sun 12-3 Av 3 course fixed price £14.50 ☺: ☗: Grainstore Olive Oil, Brewster's VPA, Exmoor Gold. London Pride. ♀: 8 **FACILITIES:** Child facs Garden: Patio garden, tables & chairs, heaters, BBQ Dogs allowed Water **NOTES:** Parking 25

THORPE LANGTON
Map 11 SP79

Pick of the Pubs

The Bakers Arms
Main St LE16 7TS ☎ 01858 545201
Dir: Take A6 S from Leicester then left signed 'The Langtons'
A thatched pub set in a pretty village, with plenty of period charm and an enthusiastic following. The first class modern pub food is one of the key attractions, though this remains an informal pub rather than a serious dining pub or restaurant. An intimate atmosphere is created with low beams, rug-strewn quarry-tiled floors, large pine tables, and open fires. Fish dishes include whole baked sea bass with mussels and saffron potatoes, cod fillet with Welsh rarebit crust and pesto mash, supreme of salmon with creamed leeks and prawn jus, and monkfish with parma ham and tapenade. Meat eaters might enjoy breast of chicken filled with salmon and Ricotta cheese, or roast shank of lamb with shallots in a red wine sauce. Vegetarians choices include filo parcel filled with goats' cheese and roasted vegetables. The area is popular with walkers, riders and mountain bikers.
OPEN: 12-3 6.30-11 (closed all Mon, Tue-Fri lunch, Sun eve) **BAR MEALS:** L served Sat-Sun D served Tue-Sat 6.30-9.30 Av main course £14 **RESTAURANT:** L served Sat-Sun 12-2.15 D served Tue-Sat 6.30-9.30 Av 3 course à la carte £24 ☺: Free House ☗: Langton Brewery, Bakers Dozen Bitter.
FACILITIES: Garden: Cottage style **NOTES:** Parking 12

WOODHOUSE EAVES
Map 11 SK51

The Wheatsheaf Inn ⤳ ♀
Brand Hill LE12 8SS ☎ 01509 890320 🖹 01509 890891
e-mail: wheatsheaf.woodhouse@virgin.net
web: www.wheatsheafinn.net
Dir: M1 junct 22 follow directions for Quorn

Local quarrymen built this as their own pub around 1790, with its distinctive archway through to what is now the car park and garden. In addition to daily specials, the varied, attractively presented menu offers Maryland chicken burger, barbecued minty lamb chops, salmon and asparagus fishcakes, and spicy sausages and mash with onion gravy. Fresh fish is supplied daily from Leicester fish market, and there are sandwiches, ciabattas and baguettes.
OPEN: 12-2.30 6-11 **BAR MEALS:** L served Mon-Sat 12-2 D served Mon-Sat 7-9.30 Sat-Sun 12-2.30 Av main course £9 **RESTAURANT:** L served all week 12-2 D served Mon-Sat 7-9.30 (Sun L 12-2.30) ☺: Free House ☗: Greene King Abbot Ale, Interbrew Bass, Timothy Taylor Landlord, Adnams Broadside. ♀: 14 **FACILITIES:** Garden: Enclosed patio with seating, picnic tables Dogs allowed Water **NOTES:** Parking 70

WYMONDHAM   Map 11 SK81

Pick of the Pubs

The Berkeley Arms ♀
59 Main St LE14 2AG ☎ 01572 787587 📠 01572 787587
e-mail: dawnpetherick@handbag.com

Equidistant from Oakham and Melton Mowbray in the heart of the county's largely unsung countryside, this chef-managed country inn has become a favoured dining destination since refurbishment several years ago. Its interior comprises a village bar of exposed stonework and original beams hung with dried hops, a carpeted, non-smoking dining-room with well-spaced pine tables and a garden that is popular with families and walkers in summer. The landlord prides himself on utilising the best available locally produced meats, poultry and fresh herbs on monthly menus that are a modern mix of traditional and trendy. Typically, bar lunches might include garlic chicken and chorizo sausage with roast tomato and basil ciabatta and cornbeef hash with fired egg and herb butter sauce. At night, begin perhaps with pancetta with honey-glazed baby pears, herb and walnut dressing before seared calves' liver on a truffle spinach with horseradish mash and truffle oil. For dessert, chocolate cappucino mousse or sticky toffee sponge.

OPEN: 12-3 6-11 (Closed Mon & Tue Lunch)
BAR MEALS: L served Thu-Sun 12-2 D served Sat 6-9
Av main course £8.50 **RESTAURANT:** L served Wed-Sun 12-2
D served Wed-Sat 6-9 Av 3 course fixed price £14 ⏣: Pubmaster
◖: Marstons Pedigree, Greene King IPA & Guest Ale. ♀: 10
FACILITIES: Garden: Food served outside Dogs allowed
NOTES: Parking 40

LINCOLNSHIRE

ALLINGTON   Map 11 SK84

The Welby Arms ♀
The Green NG32 2EA ☎ 01400 281361 📠 01400 281361
Dir: From Grantham take either A1 north, or A52 west. Allington 1.5m

With its views across the village green towards Allington Manor, this proper village pub provides a quiet retreat for travellers from the nearby A1, and lies within easy reach of South Lincolnshire's historic houses and market towns. The constantly changing menu might include halibut fillet with pesto and cheese crumb crust, slow braised lamb shank, and medallions of pork with a Dijon mustard sauce. There's also a tempting array of home-made sweets.

OPEN: 12-2.30 6-11 (Sun 12-4 6-10.30) **BAR MEALS:** L served all
week 12-2 D served all week Av main course £8.50
RESTAURANT: L served all week 12-2 D served all week 6.30-9.30
Sun 8.30-9 ⏣: Free House ◖: Scottish Courage John Smith's,
Interbrew Bass, Timothy Taylor Landlord, Greene King Abbot. ♀: 8
FACILITIES: Garden: Terrace with benches and parasols Dogs
allowed in the garden only **NOTES:** Parking 35

ASWARBY   Map 12 TF03

The Tally Ho Inn ◆◆◆
NG34 8SA ☎ 01529 455205 📠 01529 455773
web: www.tally-ho-aswarby.co.uk
Dir: From A1 at Grantham onto A52 towards Boston, then left onto A15
towards Sleaford. Pub 5m S of Sleaford

Part of the Aswarby Estate in deepest rural Lincolnshire, this
continued

The Tally Ho Inn
Aswarby, Nr. Sleaford, NG34 8SA
Tel: (01529) 455205   Fax: (01529) 455773
Email: enquire@tally-ho-aswarby.co.uk
www.tally-ho-aswarby.co.uk

The Tally Ho is a top-of-the-range 17th Century hostelry in a parkland setting on the A15 just a few miles from the market town of Sleaford. Offering traditional restaurant fayre, excellent bar food, well-kept real ales, fine wines, comfortable Bed & Breakfast accommodation and a delightful ambience created by sturdy old wooden pillars & beams, exposed stonework, log fires and a wealth of pictures, ornaments and brasses.

17th-century coaching inn has exposed stone walls, oak beams and open log fires. Tables outside, under the fruit trees, overlook sheep-grazing meadows. The menu changes every few weeks, and features old favourites like Dickens suet pudding filled with braised beef and mushrooms cooked in ale, and smoked haddock stack with potato rösti, asparagus and fried egg. Lighter options are also available at lunchtime.

The Tally Ho Inn

OPEN: 12-3 6-11 (Sun 12-3, 7-10.30) **BAR MEALS:** L served all
week 12-2 D served all week 6-9.30 Sun 7-9 Av main course £9.50
RESTAURANT: L served Mon-Sun 12-2 D served Mon-Sun 6-9.30
Sun 7-9 Av 3 course à la carte £20 ⏣: Free House ◖: Bass,
Adnams, Tiger. **FACILITIES:** Garden: Old English garden, overlooks
parkland etc Dogs allowed **NOTES:** Parking 40
ROOMS: 6 bedrooms en suite s£40 d£60 No children overnight
See advert on this page

🛢 Brewery/Company

England

BARNOLDBY LE BECK   Map 17 TA20

Pick of the Pubs

The Ship Inn 🏠 ⓨ
Main Rd DN37 0BG ☎ 01472 822308 ▤ 01472 811148
e-mail: silgy386@aol.com
Dir: Off A46/A18 SW of Grimsby
The Ship Inn has been a pub since 1730, and lies on the edge of the Lincolnshire Wolds and the outskirts of Grimsby. Both the coast and the countryside nearby are perfect for exploring on foot and by car. The bar itself is filled with an assortment of fascinating bric-a-brac, and outside there is a beautiful garden. As the pub owners have their own fishing vessels, and the landlord personally has had thirty years of experience on the sea, it's not surprising that fish is their speciality. A growing seafood section boasts tuna, halibut, plaice, Dover sole, ling, haddock, mackerel, salmon, skate, turbot, scallops, cod and dogfish - the list is most impressive. These options change weekly, and might also include sausage and mash, fillet steaks, game pie, and beef stroganoff. You can also expect to find chicken, leek and smoked bacon casserole; steak and kidney pie; and vegetable cobbler. For something lighter, try one of the freshly-made sandwiches or baguettes.
OPEN: 12-3 6-11 **BAR MEALS:** L served all week 12-2 D served all week 7-9.30 Sun 12-2.30 Av main course £11 **RESTAURANT:** L served all week 12-2 D served all week 7-9.30 Av 3 course à la carte £20 ⓔ: Punch Taverns ◖: Black Sheep Best, Timothy Taylor Landlord, Carlsberg-Tetley Tetley's Smooth, Boddingtons. ⓨ: 8 **FACILITIES:** Garden: Shaded & secluded with hanging baskets Dogs allowed Water **NOTES:** Parking 30

BOURNE   Map 12 TF02

Black Horse Inn NEW ⓨ
Grimsthorpe PE10 0LY ☎ 01778 591247 ▤ 01778 591373
e-mail: dine@blackhorseinn.co.uk
Dir: 4m from Bourne
Built in the early part of the 18th century as a coaching inn attached to Grimsthorpe Castle, the Black Horse Inn was billeted by Number 1 Parachute Squadron during both World Wars. A courtyard garden is one of several popular features, and dishes on the extensive menu are prepared using fresh, locally sourced produce. Traditionals include steak and ale pie, sausage and mash, and smoked duck breast.
OPEN: 12-2 6-12 Closed: 1 Jan **BAR MEALS:** L served all week 12-2 D served all week 6-9 Sun 12-3 Av main course £9.50 **RESTAURANT:** L served all week 12-2 D served all week 6-9 Sun 12-3 Av 3 course à la carte £22.50 ⓔ: Free House ◖: Black Dog, Tribute, Bombadier, Red Squall. ⓨ: 8 **FACILITIES:** Garden: Open but enclosed, overlooks castle Dogs allowed in the garden only **NOTES:** Parking 50

◆ Diamond rating for inspected guest accommodation

Website addresses are included where available. The AA cannot be held responsible for the content of any of these websites

The Wishing Well Inn
Main St, Dyke PE10 0AF ☎ 01778 422970 ▤ 01778 394508
Dir: Take A15 towards Seaford, Inn is situated in first village that is entered
Named after the wishing well in the smaller of its two restaurants, this village free house dates back 300 years. There's a wealth of old oak beams, as well as two inglenook fireplaces in the bar and restaurant areas. A daily specials board supports a menu of pub favourites that include home-made pies; steaks; crispy coated fish medley; and sausages, egg and chips. An attractive beer garden backs onto the children's play area.
OPEN: 9-11 **BAR MEALS:** L served all week 12-9 D served all week Av main course £9 **RESTAURANT:** L served all week 12-2 D served all week 7-9 ⓔ: Free House ◖: Greene King Abbot Ale, Everards Tiger Bitter, 3 Guest's. **FACILITIES:** Child facs Children's licence Garden: Large garden with patio Dogs allowed Water bowls **NOTES:** Parking 100

BRIGG   Map 17 TA00

The Jolly Miller 🏠
Brigg Rd, Wrawby DN20 8RH ☎ 01652 655658 ▤ 01652 657506
Dir: 1.5m E of Brigg on the A18, on left
Popular country inn a few miles south of the Humber Estuary. The pleasant bar and dining area are traditional in style, and there's a large beer garden. The menu offers a good range of food with most dishes under £5. Tuck into a chip butty; vegetable burger bap; home-made curry; or steak with onion rings. Puddings include hot chocolate fudge cake and banana split. Play area and children's menu.
OPEN: 12-11 Tue 3-11 **BAR MEALS:** L served all week 12 D served all week 8 Sun 12-4.30 Av main course £4.95 ⓔ: Free House ◖: Guiness, and two changing guest ales. **FACILITIES:** Child facs Garden: outdoor eating, patio Dogs allowed Fresh water outside **NOTES:** Parking 40

COLEBY   Map 17 SK96

The Bell Inn ⓨ
3 Far Ln LN5 0AH ☎ 01522 810240 ▤ 01522 811800
Dir: 8m S of Lincoln on A607. In Coleby village turn right at church.
One of the three original buildings that became today's rural Bell Inn actually was a pub, built in 1759. The dining area is also divisible by three - a brasserie, a restaurant, and a terrace room. Main courses may include braised shoulder of lamb on Greek-style potatoes; steamed steak and mushroom pudding; and smoked tofu and sweet potato strudel. A separate fish and seafood menu may offer grilled haddock on a sweet potato, goat's cheese and aubergine gâteau.
OPEN: 11.30-3 5.30-11 (Sun 11.30-10.30) Closed: 2-11 **BAR MEALS:** L served all week 12-2.30 D served all week 5.30-9 (Sun 12-8) **RESTAURANT:** L served all week 12-2.30 D served all week 5.30-9.30 Av 3 course à la carte £25 Av 3 course fixed price £15.95 ⓔ: Pubmaster ◖: Interbrew Bass, Carlsberg-Tetley Bitter, Batemans XB, Wadworths 6X. ⓨ: 7 **FACILITIES:** Garden: Enclosed by fence, decking area, heaters Dogs allowed **NOTES:** Parking 40

CONINGSBY   Map 17 TF25

The Lea Gate Inn ⓨ
Leagate Rd LN4 4RS ☎ 01526 342370 ▤ 01526 345468
e-mail: theleagateinn@hotmail.com
web: www.the-leagate-inn.co.uk
Dir: Off B1192 just outside Coningsby
The oldest licensed premises in the county, dating from 1542, this was the last of the Fen Guide Houses that provided shelter before the treacherous marshes were drained. The

continued

oak-beamed pub has a priest's hole and a very old inglenook fireplace among its features. The bar menu includes Lea Gate fish pie; honey-glazed duck breast with Cumberland sauce; and mushroom stroganoff with rice and salad.

The Lea Gate Inn

OPEN: 11.30-2.30 6.30-11 (Sun 12-2.30, 6.30-10.30)
BAR MEALS: L served all week 12-2 D served all week 6.30-9.30 Av main course £8 **RESTAURANT:** L served all week D served all week 6.30-9.15 Av 3 course à la carte £16 ☺: Free House ⬛: Scottish Courage Theakstons XB, Marston's Pedigree. ♀: 7 **FACILITIES:** Child facs Garden: Large garden with children's play area **NOTES:** Parking 60 **ROOMS:** 8 bedrooms en suite 1 family room s£52.50 d£70 (♦♦♦♦)

CORBY GLEN
Map 11 TF02

The Coachman Inn ♀
NG33 4NS ☎ 01476 550316 ▤ 01476 550184
Dir: 4m E of A1 on the A151 towards Bourne

Old coaching inn complete with beams, woodburners and open fires, plus a newly-landscaped garden. An imaginative range of freshly-prepared dishes and a daily-changing menu includes baked seabass with lime butter, rack of lamb with herb crust, grilled rib-eye steak with pink peppercorn sauce, fillet of salmon with Punjabi spices, and wild mushroom risotto with balsamic dressing. Cabaret nights and a more spacious dining room have proved popular.
OPEN: 11.30-3 6-11.30 **BAR MEALS:** L served all week 12-2 D served all week 7-9 (Sun 12-2.30) Av main course £9 **RESTAURANT:** L served all week 12-2 D served all week 7-9 (Sun 12-2.30) Av 3 course à la carte £14 ☺: Free House ⬛: Fullers London Pride, Abbott Ale, Guest ales. ♀: 6 **FACILITIES:** Large garden: patio and landscaped garden Dogs allowed Water, Dog Biscuits **NOTES:** Parking 30

Not all of the pubs in the guide are open all week or all day. It's always best to check before you travel

---

DONINGTON ON BAIN
Map 17 TF28

The Black Horse ♦♦♦ 🐾 ♀
Main Rd LN11 9TJ ☎ 01507 343640 ▤ 01507 343640
e-mail: mike@blackhorse-donington.co.uk
Ideal for walkers, this old-fashioned country pub is set in a small village in the heart of the Lincolnshire Wolds on the Viking Way. A large grassed area surrounded by trees is ideal for enjoying a drink or dining al fresco on sunny days. Dining options include the non-smoking dining room, the Blue Room, and the Viking Snug. Recent change of management.
OPEN: 12-3 6-11 Rest: 25 Dec Closed eve **BAR MEALS:** L served all week 12-2 D served all week 7-9 Sat-Sun 7-9.30
RESTAURANT: L served all week 12-2 D served all week 7-9 Sat-Sun 7-9.30 ☺: Free House ⬛: John Smiths, Greene King, Theakstons. **FACILITIES:** Garden: Large grassed area surrounded by trees Dogs allowed Water provided **NOTES:** Parking 80
ROOMS: 8 bedrooms en suite 2 family rooms s£27 d£45

EWERBY
Map 12 TF14

The Finch Hatton Arms
43 Main St NG34 9PH ☎ 01529 460363 ▤ 01529 461703
e-mail: bookings@finchhatton.fsnet.co.uk
Dir: From A17 to Kirkby-la-Thorne, then 2m NE. Also 2m E of A153 between Sleaford & Anwick
Originally known as the Angel Inn, this 19th-century pub was given the family name of Lord Winchelsea, who bought it in 1875. After a chequered history and a short period of closure, it reopened in the 1980s and these days offers pub, restaurant and hotel facilities. It is a very popular venue for meals, offering an extensive and varied menu to suit all tastes and budgets, but with its traditional ale and regular customers it retains a 'local' atmosphere.
OPEN: 11.30-2.30 6.30-11 Closed: 25-26 Dec
BAR MEALS: L served all week 11.30-2 D served all week 6.30-10 Sun 6.30-9.30 **RESTAURANT:** L served all week 11.30-2 D served all week 6.30-10 Sun 6.30-9.30 Av 3 course à la carte £18 ☺: Free House ⬛: Everards Tiger Best, Dixons Major, guest beer.
FACILITIES: Child facs Garden **NOTES:** Parking 60
ROOMS: 8 bedrooms en suite s£40 d£66 (★★)

FREISTON
Map 12 TF34

Kings Head
Church Rd PE22 0NT ☎ 01205 760368
Dir: From Boston take A52 towards Skegness. 3m turn right at Haltoft End to Freiston
Once two cottages, this friendly village pub has won awards both for its well-kept cellar and the glorious displays of hanging baskets and window boxes outside. Inside, you can relax by an open fire and enjoy simple, wholesome bar food. Specials change weekly and may include rabbit pie; or fresh Grimsby haddock served with home-made chips. Classic puddings also feature. Birdwatchers come from far and near to visit the RSPB reserve at Freiston Shore.
OPEN: 11-2.30 7-11 (Sun 12-3 7.30-10.30) **BAR MEALS:** L served Tues-Sun 12-2 D served Tues-Sat 7-9 Sun 12-3 Av main course £6 **RESTAURANT:** L served Tue-Sun 12-2 D served Wed-Sat 7-9 Sun 12-3 Av 3 course à la carte £16 Av 2 course fixed price £6 ☺: Batemans ⬛: Batemans XB & Dark Mild, Worthington Cream Flow. **NOTES:** Parking 30 No credit cards

---

🍺 Principal Beers for sale

FROGNALL

Map 12 TF11

The Goat ⛯ ♀

155 Spalding Rd PE6 8SA ☎ 01778 347629
e-mail: graysdebstokes@btconnect.com
Dir: A1 to Peterborough, A15 to Market Deeping, old A16 to Spalding, pub about 1.5m from junct of A15 & A16

Welcoming country pub dating from the 17th century, with an open fire, large beer garden and plenty to amuse the kids. Real ale is taken seriously, with four different guest cask ales each week. Also on offer are more than fifty single malt whiskies, plus mulled wine in winter and sangria in summer. The chef's home-made selection includes pork in sweet and sour sauce, trout with almonds, curry of the day, and leek and mushroom crumble.
OPEN: 11-2.30 6-11 (Sun 12-3, 7-10.30 Sun open all day (summer)) Closed: 25 Dec **BAR MEALS:** L served all week 12-2 D served all week 6.30-9.30 Av main course £8 **RESTAURANT:** L served all week 12-2 D served all week 6.30-9.30 Av 3 course à la carte £15 ⊕: Free House ◀: 4 Guest Cask Ales change each week. ♀: 16 **FACILITIES:** Child facs Garden: Covered patio, beer garden, seats approx 90 **NOTES:** Parking 50

GEDNEY DYKE

Map 12 TF42

The Chequers ♀

PE12 0AJ ☎ 01406 362666 ▤ 01406 362666
Dir: From King's Lynn take A17, 1st rndbt after Long Sutton, B1359
In a pretty village close to the Wash, this 18th-century country inn serves a good selection of food. Local quails eggs with bacon; or bang bang chicken, and fish specials like marinated loin of tuna with tomato salsa; or baked seabass with lobster fish cake are popular. Lincolnshire pork and leek sausages; and wild mushroom gateau crêpe with parmesan shavings are non-fish options. Well-chosen ales, patio garden and outdoor eating in summer.
OPEN: 12-2 7-11 (Sun 12-2 7-10.30) Closed: 26 Dec
BAR MEALS: L served Tue-Sun 12-2 D served Tue-Sun 7-9 Sun 12-2.30 Av main course £9.95 **RESTAURANT:** L served Tue-Sun 12-2 D served Tue-Sun 7-9 Sun Lunch 12-2.30 Dinner 7-9 Av 3 course à la carte £22 Av 3 course fixed price £25 ⊕: Free House ◀: Adnams Best, Greene King Abbot Ale. ♀: 10
FACILITIES: Garden: Beer garden, patio, food served outside **NOTES:** Parking 25

GRANTHAM

Map 11 SK93

The Beehive Inn

10/11 Castlegate NG31 6SE ☎ 01476 404554
Dir: A52 to town centre, L at Finkin St, pub at end
Grantham's oldest inn (1550) is notable for having England's only living pub sign - a working beehive high up in a lime tree. Otherwise, this simple town hostelry offers a good pint

continued

of Newby Wyke and good-value, yet basic bar food. Kids will enjoy the bouncy castle that appears during the summer.
OPEN: 11-11 **BAR MEALS:** L served all week 12-1.50 D served Tue-Thurs Av main course £4 ⊕: Free House ◀: Newby Wyke Real Ales, Everards. **FACILITIES:** Garden: Enclosed, block paved patio Dogs allowed Water

HECKINGTON

Map 12 TF14

The Nags Head ♀

34 High St NG34 9QZ ☎ 01529 460218
Dir: 5m E of Sleaford on A17
Overlooking a village green boasting the only eight-sailed windmill in the country. This listed, white-painted coaching inn, built in 1645, was reputedly visited by highwayman Dick Turpin after stealing some horses. He was later captured in York. On the menu: home-made pies, including chicken and stilton, beef and ale, and homity; salmon, scampi, mussels, haddock and sea bass. Patio garden with lots of tables and play area.
OPEN: 11-3 5-11 **BAR MEALS:** L served all week 12-2 D served all week 7-9 ⊕: Punch Taverns ♀: 15 **FACILITIES:** Garden: Patio with lots of tables **NOTES:** Parking 50

LINCOLN

Map 17 SK97

Pyewipe Inn

Fossebank, Saxilby Rd LN1 2BG
☎ 01522 528708 ▤ 01522 525009
e-mail: enquiries@pyewipeinn.co.uk web: www.pyewipeinn.co.uk
Dir: Out of Lincoln on A57 past Lincoln A46 Bypass, pub signed after 0.5m

The Pyewipe is an 18th-century alehouse on the Roman Fossedyke Canal, set in four acres with great views of the city and the cathedral - a 20-minute walk along the Fossedyke. All food from pâté to ice cream is freshly prepared from local sources and is offered from a daily board in the bar or seasonal carte in the restaurant. Look out for lamb fillet on a bed of spring onion mash with a mint glaze, deep-fried goats' cheese with red pepper and tomato salsa, peppered fillet steak with spinach and au poivre sauce, and chicken breast wrapped in parma ham with a stilton sauce. The outdoor area seats up to 200.
OPEN: 11-11 (Mon-Sat 11-11, Sun 12-10.30)
BAR MEALS: L served all week 12-9.30 D served all week Sun 12-9
RESTAURANT: L served all week 12-9.30 D served all week Sun 12-9 ⊕: Free House ◀: Timothy Taylor Landlord, Greene King Abbot Ale, Interbrew Bass & Flowers Original, Wadworth 6X.
FACILITIES: Garden: 200 seats along river. Patio, grassy areas Dogs allowed **NOTES:** Parking 100

♀ 7   Number of wines by the glass

The Victoria

6 Union Rd LN1 3BJ ☎ 01522 536048
Dir: From city outskirts follow signs for Cathedral Quarter. 2mins walk from all major up-hill car parks
Situated right next to the Westgate entrance of the Castle and within a stone's throw of Lincoln Cathedral, a long-standing drinkers' pub with a range of real ales, including six changing guest beers, as well as two beer festivals a year. It also offers splendid meals made from exclusively home-prepared food including hot baguettes and filled bacon rolls, Saturday breakfast and Sunday lunches. House specials include sausage and mash, various pies, chilli con carne and home-made lasagne.
OPEN: 11-11 (Sun 12-10.30) **BAR MEALS:** L served all week 12-2.30 Sat 11.-2.30 Sun 12-2, Av main course £4.50
RESTAURANT: L served Sun 12-2 ☺: Tynemill Ltd ◀: Timothy Taylor Landlord, Batemans XB, Castle Rock Snow White, Guest Beers.
FACILITIES: Garden: Patio area, in the lee of castle wall Dogs allowed, but not inside during food service

Pick of the Pubs

Wig & Mitre ◎ ♀

30/32 Steep Hill LN2 1TL ☎ 01522 535190 📠 01522 532402
e-mail: email@wigandmitre.com web: www.wigandmitre.com
Dir: Adjacent to cathedral & castle car park, at top of Steep Hill
Situated between the castle and the cathedral in the heart of medieval Lincoln, this is a reassuringly civilised pub-restaurant. A haven of peace, free of music and amusement machines, it offers continuous service from 8am to around midnight, 365 days of the year. Many 14th-century timbers have survived in the evocative interior. The pub is justifiably popular for its food and selection of real ales, as well as almost three dozen wines by the glass. Food service begins with breakfast sandwiches or the traditional 'full English', whilst a range of toasted sandwiches and light meals is always on offer. Main course dishes might include halibut with saffron; glazed duck breast with butternut squash and pine kernels; or flat parsley, shallot and Parmesan tart with plum tomatoes and basil. Raspberry and mascarpone crème brûlée, and bread and butter pudding with crème Anglaise are amongst the tempting desserts.
OPEN: 8am-midnight **BAR MEALS:** L served all week 8am-11pm D served all week 8am-11pm Av main course £13.95
RESTAURANT: L served all week 8am-11pm D served all week 8am-11pm Av 3 course à la carte £27.50 Av 3 course fixed price £14.95 ☺: Free House ◀: Greene King, Marstons Pedigree, Black Sheep Special & Ruddles Best. ♀: 34 **FACILITIES:** Child facs Dogs allowed

LOUTH Map 17 TF38

Masons Arms ♀

Cornmarket LN11 9PY ☎ 01507 609525 📠 0870 7066450
e-mail: ron@themasons.co.uk web: www.themasons.co.uk

Situated in the Cornmarket, this former posting inn dates from 1725 and some relics of its past association with the Masons can be found on doors and windows. There is a 'downstairs' for informal eating and an 'upstairs' where the à la carte menu features steaks, sautéed duck breast, and fresh Bateman's beer-battered Grimsby haddock. Well-kept real ales complement the mainly traditional fare.
OPEN: 10-11 12-10.30 (Sun 12-10.30) **BAR MEALS:** L served all week 12-2 D served Wed-Sat 6-8.30 Av main course £5.95
RESTAURANT: L served Sun 12-2 D served Fri-Sat 7-9.30 ☺: Free House ◀: Timothy Taylor Landlord, Marston's Pedigree, Batemans XB Bitter, XXXB. ♀: 9 **FACILITIES:** Child facs Children's licence

NEWTON Map 12 TF03

The Red Lion 🍴

NG34 0EE ☎ 01529 497256 e-mail: therednewton@tiscali.co.uk
Dir: 10m E of Grantham on A52
Dating from the 17th century, The Red Lion is particularly popular with walkers and cyclists, perhaps because the flat Lincolnshire countryside makes for easy exercise. Low beams, exposed stone walls and an open fire in the bar help to create a very atmospheric interior. Popular dishes include haddock in beer batter, lemon sole with parsley butter sauce, breadcrumbed scampi, and home-made steak and ale pie. The carvery serves cold buffets on weekdays, hot ones on Friday and Saturday evenings, and Sunday lunchtime.
OPEN: 12-3 6-11 (Sun 12-4, 7-10.30) Mon-Tues 7-11 Closed: 25 Dec, 1 Jan **BAR MEALS:** L served all week 12-2 D served Mon-Sun 7-9
RESTAURANT: L served Sun 12-2 D served Mon-Sat 7-9 ☺: Free House ◀: Weekly guest ale, Greene King IPA, Everards.
FACILITIES: Garden: Patio area with lawn, shrubs Dogs allowed Water **NOTES:** Parking 40

Disabled people and those with Assist Dogs have new rights of access to pubs, restaurants and hotels under the Disability Discrimination Act of 1 October 2004. For more information see the website at www.drc gb.org/open4all/rights/2004.asp

Pick of the Pubs have that extra special quality that makes them stand out from the crowd. Their entries are highlighted, and may be a full page

PARTNEY
Map 17 TF46

Red Lion Inn
PE23 4PG ☎ 01790 752271 🖹 01790 753360
Dir: On A16 from Boston, or A158 from Horncastle
Parts of this Lincolnshire inn date back 400 years, but reports of a ghost seem to be unsubstantiated. All the pub's food is home made and freshly cooked to order using local produce wherever possible. The comprehensive menu offers a selection for vegetarians, steaks, main courses and daily specials. Typical dishes are vegetable and cheese roast; lamb moussaka; and salmon and prawns in dill sauce, plus traditional roasts for Sunday lunch.
OPEN: 11-3 7-11 (Sun 12-2.30, 7-10.30, closed Mon-Tue) Closed: 25 Dec **BAR MEALS:** L served Wed-Sun 12-2 D served all week 7-9.30 **RESTAURANT:** L served Wed-Sun 12-2 D served Mon-Sun 7-9.30
🍴: Free House 🍺: Bateman, Tom Woods, XXXB, Tetleys.
FACILITIES: Garden **NOTES:** Parking 40

RAITHBY
Map 17 TF36

Red Lion Inn
PE23 4DS ☎ 01790 753727
Dir: Take A158 from Horncastle, right at Sausthorpe, keep left into Raithby

Traditional beamed black-and-white village pub, parts of which date back 300 years. Log fires provide a warm welcome in winter. A varied menu of home-made dishes includes seabass with lime stir fry vegetables, roast guinea fowl with tomato, garlic and bacon, and medallions of beef with peppercorn sauce.
OPEN: 12-3 7-11 **BAR MEALS:** L served Thu-Sun 12-2.30 D served Wed-Mon 7-9.30 Av main course £8
RESTAURANT: L served Sat-Sun 12-2.30 D served Wed-Mon 7-10
🍴: Free House 🍺: Raithby, Thwaites, Tetley, Batemans XB.
FACILITIES: Food served outside. Terrace patio **NOTES:** Parking 20 No credit cards

2006
The
Golf Course
Guide

Britains best-selling Golf Course Guide featuring over 2,500 courses.

AA

www.theAA.com

SKEGNESS
Map 17 TF56

The Vine Hotel ★★★
Vine Rd, Seacroft PE25 3DB ☎ 01754 763018
& 610611 🖹 01754 769845 e-mail: info@thevinehotel.com
Dir: From centre of Skegness follow signs for Gibraltor Point and Seacroft Golf Club

Ivy-covered Victorian hotel, converted from a farmhouse and bought by Harry Bateman in 1928. Now this charming hostelry offers a fine selection of Bateman ales, silver service in the restaurant and comfortable accommodation, attracting lots of weddings. Once a haunt of poet Alfred Lord Tennyson, who has given his name to The Tennyson Lounge. Also the haunt of a variety of ghosts including a walled-up customs and excise man. Specialities include Grimsby fish and chips, and Batemans beef and ale pie.
OPEN: 11-11 (Sun 12-10.30) **BAR MEALS:** L served all week 12-2.15 D served all week 6-9.15 Sat-Sun all day
RESTAURANT: L served all week 12.30 D served all week 6.30-9.15 Sun 12-2.30 🍴: Free House 🍺: Batemans XB & XXXB, Mild, Batemans Blackbeard. **FACILITIES:** Children's licence Secluded garden: Dogs allowed **NOTES:** Parking 50 **ROOMS:** 24 bedrooms en suite 3 family rooms s£50 d£84

SOUTH WITHAM
Map 11 SK91

Blue Cow Inn & Brewery
High St NG33 5QB ☎ 01572 768432 🖹 01572 768432
e-mail: richard@thirlwell.fslife.co.uk
web: www.thebluecowinn.co.uk
Dir: Between Stamford & Grantham on A1
Situated on the borders of Lincolnshire and Rutland, this once-derelict inn stands close to the source of the River Witham, which flows down to Lincoln. Named after the landlord, Thirlwell's real ales are brewed on the premises - with guided tours of the micro-brewery an added attraction. Eclectic menus embrace Thai seafood curry and Malaysian chicken satay along with home-made pub pie, fresh Grimsby fish, and British steak grills.
OPEN: 12-11 **BAR MEALS:** L served all week 12-2.30 D served all week 6-9.30 **RESTAURANT:** L served all week 12-2.30 D served all week 6-9.30 🍴: Free House 🍺: Own beers. **FACILITIES:** Garden: Seating for 32 Dogs allowed Water **NOTES:** Parking 45 **ROOMS:** 6 bedrooms en suite 2 family rooms s£40 d£45 (♦♦♦)

STAMFORD
Map 11 TF00

The Bull & Swan Inn NEW ♦♦♦ ♀
24a High St, St Martin's PE9 2LJ ☎ 01780 763558 🖹 01780 763558
e-mail: bullandswan@btconnect.com
Dir: From A1 rdbt with B1081, towards Stamford, pub is on the right
A 17th-century coaching inn on the Great North Road, and close to historic Burghley House. Log fires in winter and live

continued

music once a week help to make this a popular watering hole. Freshly cooked lunchtime dishes include fillet of Cajun spiced chicken breast with mayonnaise, breaded wholetail scampi, and locally produced pork chop, while the specials menu delivers chargrilled sirloin steak, and traditional cured ham.
OPEN: 11.30-2.30 5-11 Open all day Sat-Sun Closed Mon lunch
BAR MEALS: L served Tues-Sun 12-2 D served Mon-Sat 6.30-9 Av main course £10 **RESTAURANT:** L served Tues-Sun 12-2 D served Mon-Sat 6.30-9.30 Av 3 course à la carte £20 ▪: Jennings Cumberland, Greene King Abbot Ale, Adnams Bitter, guest ales.
♀: 12 **FACILITIES:** Garden: Patio garden with seating for 50 Dogs allowed **NOTES:** Parking 112 **ROOMS:** 6 bedrooms 5 en suite 5 family rooms s£55 d£60 No children overnight

Pick of the Pubs

The George of Stamford ★★★ ◉ ⌂ ♀
71 St Martins PE9 2LB ☎ 01780 750750 🖷 01780 750701
e-mail: reservations@georgehotelofstamford.com
web: www.georgehotelofstamford.com
Dir: From Peterborough take A1 N. Onto B1081 for Stamford, down hill to lights. Hotel on left
Magnificent, essentially 16th-century coaching inn with log fires, oak-panelled restaurants, a walled monastery garden and a cobbled courtyard. On entering The George two doors greet the customer, one marked 'London', the other 'York'. These lead to two panelled rooms originally used as waiting rooms for passengers while the horses were changed in the hotel courtyard. Forty coaches a day once stopped here - twenty up and twenty down. The style of food at The George is essentially traditional, with the emphasis on the best of all things British, utilising the freshest possible ingredients. Various menus are available - a typical example being the bistro-style restaurant where the food ranges from the very best Italian pastas to fish and chips. Seafood plays a key role in the restaurant where lobster is available throughout the year. Try the Brittany seafood platter - an abundance of shellfish, including lobster, crab, oysters and the like.
OPEN: 11-11 (Sun 12-11) **BAR MEALS:** L served all week 11.30-2.30 Av main course £6.50 **RESTAURANT:** L served all week 12.30-2.30 D served all week 7.30-10.30 Av 3 course à la carte £33 Av 2 course fixed price £17.50 ◉: Free House ▪: Adnams Broadside, Fuller's London Pride, Greene King Ruddles Bitter. ♀: 15 **FACILITIES:** Child facs Garden: Sunken lawn, 200 year-old Mulberry tree Dogs allowed dog pack, towel, blanket, feeding mat **NOTES:** Parking 120 **ROOMS:** 47 bedrooms en suite 20 family rooms s£78 d£115

WOODHALL SPA   Map 17 TF16

Village Limits Motel
Stixwould Rd LN10 6UJ ☎ 01526 353312 🖷 01526 353312
e-mail: enquiries@villagelimits.com
Dir: On reaching roundabout on main street of Woodhall Spa follow directions for Petwood Hotel. 500 yds further on same road
The once-fashionable Woodhall Spa, with its grand hotels, grew up after iodine- and bromide-rich waters were discovered by chance in the 19th century. Traditional pub food in the motel's restaurant and bar includes steaks, grilled gammon, chargrilled chicken, wholetail scampi, grilled rainbow trout, battered and smoked haddock, and salads. Real ales include Tom Wood's Best Bitter from the Highwood brewery, Barnetby. In World War II, the famous Dambusters requisitioned nearby Petwood House for their Officers' Mess.
OPEN: 12-2.30 6-11 **BAR MEALS:** L served all week 12-2 D served

continued

all week 6-9 **RESTAURANT:** L served all week 12-2 D served all week 6.30-9 ◉: Free House ▪: Bateman XB, Black Sheep Best, Barnsley Bitter, Carlsberg-Tetley Tetley's Smooth Flow.
FACILITIES: Garden: Enclosed garden with superb views
NOTES: Parking 30 **ROOMS:** 8 bedrooms en suite 1 family room (♦♦♦♦)

WOOLSTHORPE   Map 11 SK83

Rutland Arms
NG32 1NY ☎ 01476 870111
Better known to locals as the 'Dirty Duck' (or the 'Mucky Duck', or 'Muddy Duck'!), this mid-18th-century family pub sits at the side of the Grantham canal, in the shadow of Belvoir Castle.
OPEN: 11-3 6-11 (Sat 11-11 Sun 12-10.30) **BAR MEALS:** L served all week 12-3 D served all week 6-9 Av main course £5.50 **RESTAURANT:** L served all week 11-3 D served all week 6-9.30 Av 3 course à la carte £12 ◉: Free House ▪: Interbrew Bass, Robinsons. **FACILITIES:** Garden **NOTES:** Parking 100

LONDON

E1

Prospect of Whitby ♀   Plan 2 F4
57 Wapping Wall E1W 3SH ☎ 020 7481 1095 🖷 020 7481 9537
Originally known as The Devil's Tavern, this famous 16th-century inn has been a meeting place for sailors and was also a gruesome setting for public executions. Samuel Pepys was a regular here before the tavern was renamed in 1777. Today, old ships timbers retain the seafaring traditions of this venerable riverside inn, which also boasts a rare pewter bar counter. Expect beef Wellington, minted lamb loins, and a good selection of fish dishes.
OPEN: 11.30-11 **BAR MEALS:** L served all week 11.30-9 D served all week Sun 12-9 Av main course £6.45 **RESTAURANT:** L served Sun-Fri D served Mon-Sat ◉: Scottish & Newcastle ▪: London Pride, Youngs, Speckled Hen, Directors. ♀: 16 **FACILITIES:** Garden: Paved, riverside Dogs allowed

Town of Ramsgate ♀   Plan 2 F4
62 Wapping High St E1W 2NP ☎ 020 7481 8000
Dir: 0.3m from Wapping Tube Station and Tower of London
A 500-year-old pub close to The City, decorated with bric-a-brac and old prints. Judge Jeffries was caught here while trying to flee the country and escape the kind of justice he dealt out. Press gangs used to work the area, imprisoning men overnight in the cellar. The new owners continue to offer real ale and value for money bar food, which can be enjoyed on the decked terrace overlooking the river Thames.
OPEN: 12-11 (Sun 12-10.30) **BAR MEALS:** L served all week 12 D served all week 9 (Sun12-8) Av main course £6 ▪: Adnams, Youngs, Fullers London Pride. ♀: 7 **FACILITIES:** Garden: Dogs allowed

---

★ Star rating for inspected hotel accommodation

 Pubs offering a good choice of fish on their menu

PUB WALK

The Seven Stars
London WC2

THE SEVEN STARS,
53 Carey Street, WC2A 2JB
☎ 020 7242 8521
Nearest tube: Chancery Lane or Temple
*Early 17th-century hostelry with two
narrow rooms, a tiny Tudor staircase
leading to the loos, and well-kept
Adnams ales. Freshly-made food from
cookery-writer and TV personality Roxy
Beaujolais is well worth trying.*
Open: 11–11 Closed: Bank Holidays
Bar Meals: L served all week 12–5
D served all week 5–9 Av main course
£8
Dogs allowed.
(for full entry see page 333)

Distance: 1 mile/1.6km
Terrain: Level surfaces and pavements
Gradient: No hills

*Walk submitted & checked by the
Seven Stars*

A fascinating walk through the streets of the capital, taking in Lincoln's Inn Fields and the Royal Courts of Justice.

From The Seven Stars turn right and walk along to the junction with Portugal Street. Turn left, passing the London School of Economics. Take a moment to look around the newly pedestrianised area of Houghton Street and Clare Market, then swing right into Sheffield Street leading to Portsmouth Street, passing the Old Curiosity Shop, immortalised by Charles Dickens in his novel of the same name.

Ahead now is Lincoln's Inns Fields, created by Inigo Jones. Cross it to the fascinating Sir John Soane's Museum. With the museum on your left, continue along Lincoln's Inn Fields and then swing right. On the left now is Lincoln's Inn, established in 1422. This is the oldest of the four Inns of Court - the centre of all things legal. It is where young barristers study before embarking on a career in law. If time allows and opening hours permitting, visit the Old Hall where Shakespeare's 'A Midsummer Night's Dream' was first performed, as well as Lincoln's Inn Chapel.

Just south of Lincoln's Inn is the delightful 17th-century New Square. Look for More's Passage or the more easterly gate by the porter's lodge and return to Carey Street. Turn left, head south along Bell Yard, then west along Fleet Street to reach the Royal Courts of Justice. Designed in the late 19th century by the architect George Edmund Street, this huge building is one of the best examples of High Victorian Gothic. Such was the scale of the building that the construction of it virtually drained parliament's budget. However, work was eventually completed and today it serves as a monument to Street's skill and ingenuity. Inside is a lofty concourse leading to ornately finished courts, high vaulted ceilings and dark corridors.

Walk through the concourse, up a flight of steps and out through the north door into Carey Street. Almost directly opposite this exit is The Seven Stars where the walk started.

E3

Pick of the Pubs

The Crown ♀ Plan 2 F4
223 Grove Rd E3 5SN ☎ 020 8981 9998 📠 020 8980 2336
e-mail: crown@singhboulton.co.uk
web: www.singhboulton.co.uk
Dir: *Nearest tube: Mile End Central Line & District line. Buses 277 to Victoria Park*
A beautifully restored listed building, The Crown overlooks Victoria Park. Owned by Geetie Singh, it is one of the UK's first two Soil Association-certified pubs; Geetie owns the other one too. Certification means that all the food is organic, apart from that hunted or fished, and drink too, except whisky and tequila. Even the fish are from sustainable sources and clean waters, a policy approved by the Marine Conservation Society. You may dine in the bar or the no-smoking restaurant upstairs - same food, same price, but different styles of service, although friendly and efficient in both. There's no music, jukebox, pinball machines or TV. The regional European food is presented on seasonal menus that change twice daily. Pan-fried red mullet with linguine, lemon and chilli sauce; roast cod in salsa verde with mussel stew; and home-smoked lamb fillet with potato, aubergine and feta gratin give you a flavour of what's available.
OPEN: 12-11 (Mon 5-11, Wknd phone for details) Closed: 25-26 Dec **BAR MEALS:** L served Tue-Sun 12.30-3.30 D served Mon-Sat 6.30-10.30 (Sun 12.30-4, 6.30-10) Av main course £12 **RESTAURANT:** L served Tue-Sun 12.30-3.30 D served Mon-Sat 6.30-10.30 (Sun 12.30-4, 6.30-10) ⊕: Free House ◀: Pitfield Eco Warrior & East Kent Goldings, St Peters Best, SB Best. ♀: 12 **FACILITIES:** Child facs Children's licence Garden: Paved area, 2 balconies Dogs allowed Water Bowls

E14

Pick of the Pubs

The Grapes 🐦 ♀ Plan 2 G4
76 Narrow St, Limehouse E14 8BP
☎ 020 7987 4396 📠 020 7987 3137
Dir: *Docklands Light Railway stations: Limehouse or West Ferry*

Charles Dickens once propped the bar up here, and so taken was he by its charms that the pub appears, thinly disguised, as The Six Jolly Fellowship Porters in his novel *Our Mutual Friend*. While the novelist might still recognise the interior, the surroundings have changed dramatically with the development of Canary Wharf and the Docklands Light Railway. However, the tradition of old-fashioned

values is maintained by the provision of the best cask conditioned ales in the atmospheric bar downstairs, while in the tiny upstairs restaurant only the freshest fish is served. This is a fish lover's paradise with a menu that includes sea bass, monkfish, Dover sole and halibut, all available with a range of different sauces. Meat eaters and vegetarians should not, however, be deterred from experiencing this evocative slice of old Limehouse; traditional roasts are served on Sundays, and sandwiches and salads are always available.
OPEN: 12-3 5.30-11 (Sat 12-11, Sun 12-10.30) Closed: BHs Rest: Closed **BAR MEALS:** L served all week 12-2 D served Mon-Sat 7-9 Sun 12-3.30 Av main course £6.50
RESTAURANT: L served Mon-Fri 12-2.15 D served Mon-Sat 7.30-9.15 Sunday roast only 12-3.30 Av 3 course à la carte £30 ⊕: ◀: Adnams, Marstons Pedigree, Carlsberg-Tetley Tetley's Bitter, Interbrew Bass. ♀: 6 **FACILITIES:** Small deck outside by river Dogs allowed Water

EC1

Pick of the Pubs

The Bleeding Heart Tavern ⊛ ♀ Plan 1 E4
19 Greville St EC1N 8SQ ☎ 0207 2428238 📠 8311402
e-mail: bookings@bleedingheart.co.uk
Dir: *Close to Farringdon Station, at corner of Grenville St and Bleeding Heart Yard*
There's been a tavern here since 1746, and although the promise of 'drunk for a penny, dead drunk for twopence' no longer holds quite true, plenty of the spirit of old London has been maintained in this scrubbed-up, contemporary version. Inside is a happy blend of smart and rustic; glass, original stone and wooden floors. The dining room houses a 65-seater restaurant, where a French-style rotisserie and grill allows attention to be focused on providing happy carnivores with a glorious array of meats. Spit-roast ale-fed pigs - fed, incidentally, on the same Adnam's beer they serve the customers - are a speciality, but look out for pot-roast Norfolk pigeon; or Suffolk Blackface burger on sourdough. Vegetarian options are few but thoughtful: roast beetroot, red wine and barley risotto, for example. Supplementing the range of well-kept Adnam's ales - Fisherman and Regatta are two seasonal visitors - is an impressive list of wines.
OPEN: 11-11 Closed: Sat/Sun, BHs, 10 days at Xmas
BAR MEALS: L served Mon-Fri 11-3 D served Mon-Fri 6-10.30 Av main course £9 **RESTAURANT:** L served Mon-Fri 12-3 D served Mon-Fri 6-10.30 Av 3 course à la carte £19 ⊕: Free House ◀: Adnams Southwold Bitter, Broadside & Fisherman. ♀: 17 **NOTES:** Parking 20

Pick of the Pubs

The Eagle ♀ Plan 1 E4
159 Farringdon Rd EC1R 3AL ☎ 020 7837 1353
Dir: *Angel/Farringdon Stn. North end Farringdon Road*
In 1990, The Eagle became the first of the genre of smart eating and drinking establishments we know as the gastropub. Back then London's trendies would not have done their chilling out in the drab Farringdon Road, but a lot of Fleet River water has flowed under its pavements since then, and Clerkenwell is now considered by some the capital's new Soho. The Eagle has remained one of

continued

continued

EC1 continued

the neighbourhood's top establishments - no mean feat, given the competition today. The airy interior has a wooden-floored bar and dining area, a random assortment of furniture, and an open-to-view kitchen which produces a modern, creative daily-changing menu with a pretty constant Southern European/South American/Pacific Rim theme. Seen frequently are gazpacho Andaluz; bruschetta with spiced aubergines, roast cherry tomatoes and mozzarella; sardines stuffed with breadcrumbs, capers, pine-nuts and raisins; and cuttlefish stew with chilli, garlic, parsley onions and broad beans. Draught and bottled beers, and an international wine list are all well chosen.

OPEN: 12-11 Closed: 1Wk Xmas, BHs **BAR MEALS:** L served all week 12.30-3 D served Mon-Sat 6.30-10.30 Sun 12.30-3.30 Av main course £9 **RESTAURANT:** L served all week D served Mon-Sat ☺: Free House ☜: Wells Eagle IPA & Bombardier. ♀: 14 **FACILITIES:** Dogs allowed

Pick of the Pubs

The Jerusalem Tavern   Plan 1 F4
55 Britton St, Clerkenwell EC1M 5NA
☎ 020 7490 4281 ▤ 020 7490 4281
e-mail: beers@stpetersbrewery.co.uk
Dir: 100 metres NE of Farringdon tube, 300 metres N of Smithfield

Named after the Priory of St John of Jerusalem, this historic tavern has been in four different locations since it was established in the 14th century. The current building dates from 1720, when a merchant lived here, although the frontage dates from about 1810, by which time it was the premises of one of Clerkenwell's many watch and clockmaker's workshops. A fascinating and wonderfully vibrant corner of London that has only recently been 'rediscovered', centuries after Samuel Johnson, David Garrick and the young Handel used to drink in this tavern. Its dark, dimly-lit Dickensian bar, with bare boards, rustic wooden tables, old tiles, candles, open fires and cosy corners, is the perfect film set - and that is what is has been on many occasions. The Jerusalem Tavern, a classic pub in every sense of the description, is open every weekday and offers the full range of bottled beers from St Peter's Brewery (which owns it), as well as a familiar range of pub fare, including game pie, risotto, sausage and mash, and various roasts.

OPEN: 11-11 Closed: 25 Dec & BH Mon's
BAR MEALS: L served all week 12-3 D served Sat 6-10 Av main course £6.95 **RESTAURANT:** L served all week D served Sat Av 3 course à la carte £14.85 ☺: St Peters Brewery ☜: St Peters (complete range).

Pick of the Pubs

The Peasant ♀   Plan 1 D3
240 St John St EC1V 4PH ☎ 020 7336 7726 ▤ 020 7490 1089
e-mail: gapstairs@aol.com
Dir: Nearest tube: Angel & Faringdon Rd. On corner of St John St & Percival St

In the heart of the Clerkenwell Building dating back to 1860, this award-winning pub retains many original Victorian features including the lovingly restored mahogany horseshoe bar with its original inlaid mosaic floor, and a fabulous conservatory. The upstairs restaurant has had similar treatment, and is beautifully lit by period chandeliers. An interesting choice of bar food includes a vegetable mezze; smoked haddock and Greenland prawn fish pie with steamed curly kale; prawn and pickled ginger spring rolls; and slow-cooked pork belly on braised red cabbage with tomato and cardamom jus. From the inventive modern menu upstairs, expect fennel and sweet corn fritters with sautéed spinach and spiced coconut sauce; roast wild Scottish venison with Jerusalem artichoke purée and stilton fondue; pan-fried sea bass on Swiss chard and soba noodles; and braised lamb shank on sweet potato purée with bok choi and oyster sauce. Desserts include dark chocolate and date meringue tart; and toasted stöllen with cinnamon and pine nut ice cream.

OPEN: 11-11 Mon-Fri Closed: Christmas Eve to 02/01
BAR MEALS: L served Sun-Fri 12-3 D served Mon-Sat 6-11 Sunday 12-4 Av main course £8 **RESTAURANT:** L served Tue-Fri 12-3.30 D served Tue-Fri 6.30-11 Av 3 course à la carte £25 ☺: Free House ☜: Bombardier, Watt Tyler, Spitfire, Leffe. ♀: 12 **FACILITIES:** Garden terrace Dogs allowed

The Well ♀   Plan 1 F5
180 Saint John St, Clerkenwell EC1V 4JY
☎ 020 7251 9363 ▤ 0207 404 2250
e-mail: drink@downthewell.co.uk
Dir: Telephone for directions

A gastro-pub where the emphasis is on modern European and Mediterranean-style food served on two floors. The lower ground features the leather-panelled aquarium bar with exotic tropical fish occupying huge tanks set into the walls. Try the crispy pork belly with roasted leeks, Jerusalem artichokes and pied bleu mushrooms with a mustard and brandy cream sauce; or slow-roasted rib eye steak with dauphinoise potatoes, roasted garlic and crispy bacon. Many wines by the glass, and European bottled beers.
OPEN: 11-12 (Sun 11-10.30) **BAR MEALS:** L served Mon-Sun 12-3 D served Mon-Sun 6-10.30 Food served all day Sat-Sun Av main course £12.50 **RESTAURANT:** L served Mon-Sun 12-3 D served Mon-Sun 6-10.30 Av 3 course à la carte £20 ☜: San Miguel, Lowenbrau, Paulaner, Red Stripe. ♀: 15 **FACILITIES:** Children's licence

Ye Olde Mitre   Plan 1 E4
1 Ely Court, Ely Place, By 8 Hatton Garden EC1N 6SJ
☎ 020 7405 4751

The pub has been standing here since 1546, and is located just off Holborn Circus at the edge of The City. Mentioned in two of Shakespeare's plays, it retains its historic atmosphere along with the preserved trunk of a cherry tree that Elizabeth I is thought to have danced around. The pub is famous for its toasted sandwiches served with real ales pulled from hand pumps. Other bar snacks include pork pies, Scotch eggs and sausages.
OPEN: 11-11 Open wkend 7-8 Aug Closed: 25 Dec, 1 Jan, BHs
BAR MEALS: L served Mon-Fri (Snack menu) 11-9.30
☺: ☜: Adnams Bitter, Adnams Broadside, Tetleys, guest ales.
FACILITIES: Outside drinking area and courtyard

England

EC2

Old Dr Butler's Head
Plan 1 F4
Mason's Av, Coleman St, Moorgate EC2V 5BY
☎ 020 7606 3504 ▤ 020 7600 0417
Dir: *Telephone for directions*
Dr Butler sold 'medicinal ale' from taverns displaying his sign. This, the only survivor, was rebuilt after the Great Fire of London, while the frontage is probably Victorian. Pub lunches are served in the pleasantly Dickensian gas-lit bar, where Shepherd Neame real ales are on tap, and steak and suet pudding is a speciality. More intimate dining areas, including a carvery, are upstairs, where dinner is by arrangement. The City empties at weekends, so the pub closes.
OPEN: 11-11 Mon-Fri **BAR MEALS:** L served Mon-Fri 12-3 D served Arrangement only Av main course £7.95 ▥: Shepherd Neame ◀: Shepherd Neame Spitfire, Bishops Finser Master Brew, Sheperds Neame Best.

EC4

The Black Friar
Plan 1 F3
174 Queen Victoria St EC4V 4EG ☎ 020 7236 5474
Located on the site of Blackfriar's monastery, where Henry VIII dissolved his marriage to Catherine of Aragon and separated from the Catholic church. The pub has made several TV appearances because of its wonderful Art Noveau interior. It is close to Blackfriars Bridge and gets very busy with after-work drinkers. A traditional-style menu includes the likes of steak and ale pie, sausage and mash, and sandwiches.
OPEN: 11.30-11 (Sat 11.30-11, Sun 12-9.30) **BAR MEALS:** L served all week 12-9 D served all week 12-9 ▥: ◀: Fullers London Pride, Adnams, Timothy Taylor, Speckled Hen. **FACILITIES:** Garden: Patio with plantation in the centre ⊛

The Centre Page ♀
Plan 1 F3
29 Knightrider St EC4V 5BH ☎ 020 7236 3614 ▤ 020 7236 3614
e-mail: centre.page@btinternet.com
Dir: *Telephone for directions*
Situated in the shadow of St Paul's Cathedral, this historic pub used to be known as the Horn Tavern and was mentioned by Charles Dickens in *The Pickwick Papers*, and in Samuel Pepys' diary. Menu may include lasagne verde, Thai fishcakes, hot and spicy chicken burger, Cumberland sausage, or spinach and ricotta cannelloni.
OPEN: 11-11 (Closes 8pm wknds, for hire at wknds)
BAR MEALS: L & D served all week 12-close **RESTAURANT:** L & D served all week 12-close (Sun 9-close) ▥: Free House ◀: Fullers London Pride, Pedigree, John Smith Bombardier. ♀: 11

The Old Bank of England ♀
Plan 1 E4
194 Fleet St EC4A 2LT ☎ 020 7430 2255 ▤ 020 7242 3092
e-mail: oldbankofengland@fullers.co.uk
Dir: *Pub located right of the courst of justice*
Magnificent building, formerly the Law Courts branch of the Bank of England, set between the site of Sweeney Todd's barbershop and his mistresses' pie shop, under which their unfortunate victims were butchered before being cooked and sold in Mrs Lovett's pies. The bar menu ranges from light snacks to the likes of fishcakes, cod and chips, and bangers and mash. Also a selection of meat pies.
OPEN: 11-11 (closed wknds, BHs) Restricted: weekends, BH's
BAR MEALS: L served Mon-Fri 12-9 D served Mon-Thurs Av main course £7.50 ▥: Fullers ◀: Fuller's London Pride, ESB, Chiswick Bitter. ♀: 10

Ye Olde Cheshire Cheese
Plan 1 E4
Wine Office Court, 145 Fleet St EC4A 2BU
☎ 020 7353 6170 ▤ 020 7353 0845
A pub has stood on this site since 1538 and the present building, one of London's few remaining chop houses, was rebuilt after the Great Fire of 1666. It's a character setting, full of nooks and crannies, and has a long history of entertaining literary greats - Arthur Conan Doyle, Yeats and Dickens to name but a few. Food includes traditional steak and kidney pudding, roast beef and fish and chips.
OPEN: 11-11 Closed: Christmas & BHs **BAR MEALS:** L served all week 12-2.30 D served Mon-Sat 12-9.30 Av main course £5
RESTAURANT: L served all week 12-9 D served Mon-Sat Av 3 course à la carte £21 ▥: Samuel Smith ◀: Samuel Smith Old Brewery Bitter.

N1

The Albion ♀
Plan 2 F4
10 Thornhill Rd, Barnsbury N1 1HW
☎ 020 7607 7450 ▤ 020 7607 8969
Dir: *Telephone for directions*
An ivy-clad pub of uncertain antiquity with a warren of homely rooms. The pub often plays host to local TV celebrities. Baguettes, burgers and jacket potatoes of choice clutter the chalkboards. Starters and 'lite bites' include spinach and roquefort tart, and Thai fishcakes, with main dishes represented by beef and Theakston pie, minted lamb shoulder, and Louisiana meatballs, with vegetarian Cajun cream linguini, or rarebit strudel. Grilled steaks with multifarious side orders: outdoor eating in fine weather.
OPEN: 12-11 (Sun 12-10.30) **BAR MEALS:** L served all week 12-3 D served all week 6-9.30 (Sun 12-5 6-9.30) Av main course £7.95
RESTAURANT: L served all week 12-3 D served all week 6-9.30
▥: ◀: Fuller's London Pride, Theakstons. **FACILITIES:** Garden:

Pick of the Pubs

The Barnsbury NEW ♀
Plan 2 F4
209-211 Liverpool Rd, Islington N1 1LX
☎ 020 7607 5519 ▤ 020 7607 3256
e-mail: info@thebarnsbury.co.uk
The Barnsbury, in the heart of Islington, is a welcome addition to the London scene as a gastropub that gets both the prices and food right. The recent addition of a walled garden has added a secluded and sought-after summer oasis for al fresco dining. The food is cooked from daily supplies of fresh produce which have been bought direct from the market, resulting in interesting menus with a slight nod to international cuisine. Starters include leek and smoked haddock chowder; Welsh rarebit crouton with scallops and tiger prawns, and Thai fragrant salad; and chargrilled halloumi, aubergine, parsley and harissa oil. Mains include choices like roast chicken breast with pappardelle and wild mushroom sauce; chargrilled rib-eye steak with béarnaise sauce, chips and salad; and goat's cheese and ricotta ravioli, artichokes and sun dried tomatoes. Desserts range through lemon mousse brûlée; French apple tart with butterscotch sauce and Calvados crème fraiche; and chocolate mousse with oranges in grand Marnier.
OPEN: 12-11 **BAR MEALS:** L served all week 12-2.45 Av main course £12 ◀: Timothy Taylor Landlord, Fullers London Pride, guest ale. ♀: 12 **FACILITIES:** Child facs Walled garden, seating

N1 continued

The Compton Arms ♀
Plan 2 F4

4 Compton Av, Off Canonbury Rd N1 2XD ☎ 020 7359 6883
e-mail: thecomptonarms@ukonline.co.uk
The best kept secret in N1. A late 17th-century country pub in the middle of town with a peaceful, rural feel, frequented by a mix of locals, actors and musicians. Real ales from the hand pump, and good value steaks, mixed grill, big breakfast and Sunday roast. One local described the Compton Arms as "an island in a sea of gastro-pubs". Expect a busy bar when Arsenal are at home.
OPEN: 12-6 6-11 Closed: 25 Dec (afternoon)
BAR MEALS: L served all week 12-2.30 D served all week 6-9 Av main course £5.95 ◉: Greene King ◖: Greene King IPA, Abbot Ale, Moorlands, plus guest ale. **FACILITIES:** Garden: Courtyard

The Crown ♀
Plan 2 F4

116 Cloudsley Rd, Islington N1 0EB
☎ 020 7837 7107 ▤ 020 7833 1084
e-mail: crown.islington@fullers.co.uk
London's beer drinkers are usually happy to head for a Fuller's pub like the Grade II-listed Crown. To add to the appeal, it has a wealth of period features, and a modern menu designed for the diversity of tastes in this upmarket residential district. Alongside traditional chargrilled regular and veggie sausages and mash, there's open scallop and asparagus ravioli with chive cream sauce, pan-fried fillet of pork with savoy cabbage, bacon and fondant potato, various casseroles, and the Crown's own burger.
OPEN: 12-11 (Sun 12-10.30) Closed: 25 Dec
BAR MEALS: L served all week 12-3 D served all week 6-10 Sat 12-4,6-10, Sun 12-5,6-9 Av main course £9 ◉: Fullers ◖: Fullers London Pride, Honey Dew, Kirin, Staropramen & Guest ale. ♀: 10
FACILITIES: Garden: Patio with six tables

Pick of the Pubs

The Drapers Arms ◉♀
Plan 2 F4

44 Barnsbury St N1 1ER ☎ 020 7619 0348 ▤ 020 7619 0413
e-mail: info@thedrapersarms.co.uk
Dir: Turn R outside Tube St, along Upper Street. Opposite Town Hall
Smart Islington gastro-pub offering one menu throughout, though it is preferable to book the upstairs dining room which attracts a good crowd - celebrities from television, politics and the arts among others. Downstairs there is plenty of wood in evidence from the floor to the furniture and fires burning in winter. A range of appetising starters includes roast scallops, shaved fennel, watercress and pink grapefruit, and crispy five spice pork belly with Thai green salad. For a main course, try grilled maize-fed chicken with baba ghanoush, cracked wheat and lemon yogurt; wild boar sausages, bubble and squeak, and grilled apples; chargrilled haunch of venison with pumpkin mash and shitake mushroom jus; or roast swordfish with a saffron and shellfish stew. To follow, savour the delights of rhubarb and plum crumble; warm Bakewell with custard; sticky toffee pudding or lemon posset tart with cinnamon and pistachio biscuits.
OPEN: 11-11 (Sun 12-10.30) Closed: 24-27 Dec, 1 & 2 Jan
BAR MEALS: L served all week 12-3 D served Mon-Sat 7-10 Av main course £12.50 **RESTAURANT:** L served Sun 12-4 D served Mon-Sat 7-10.30 ◖: Old Speckled Hen, Courage, Budvar & Corona. ♀: 18 **FACILITIES:** Garden: Dogs allowed

Pick of the Pubs

The Duke of Cambridge ♀
Plan 2 F4

30 St Peter's St N1 8JT ☎ 020 7359 3066 ▤ 020 7359 1877
e-mail: duke@singhboulton.co.uk
web: www.singhboulton.co.uk
Award-winning community pub with an eclectic mix of locals, just a stone's throw from Battersea Park and two of London's most famous river crossings - Albert Bridge and Battersea Bridge. Also handy for the Almeida Theatre and Saddlers Wells. The Duke of Cambridge is Britain's first organic pub, offering a twice daily-changing menu characterised by uncomplicated British food and regional Mediterranean influences. Expect pan-fried red mullet, chargrilled chicken thighs, and roast vegetable parmigiana.
OPEN: 12-11 (Sun 12-10.30) Closed: Dec 25-26, Jan 1
BAR MEALS: L served all week 12.30-3 D served all week 6.30-10.30 (Sun 12.30-3.30, 7-10) (Sat 12.30-3.30) Av main course £12 **RESTAURANT:** L served all week 12.30-3 D served all week 6.30-10.30 (Sun 12.30-3.30, 7-10) ◉: Free House ◖: Eco Warrior, St Peter's Best Bitter, East Kent Golding. ♀: 12
FACILITIES: Children's licence Garden: Small courtyard and front paved area Dogs allowed Dog bowls

The House ◉♀
Plan 2 F4

63-69 Canonbury Rd N1 2DG ☎ 020 7704 7410 ▤ 020 7704 9388
e-mail: info@inthehouse.biz
This pub has only been operating since October 2002, and already it has been awarded an AA Rosette, won an award for Gastropub of the Year, and been featured in a celebrity cookbook. The team behind this success story consists of Barnaby Meredith who holds the fort at the front of house, and who has clocked up ten years of Swiss and British hospitality experience, and Jeremy Hollingsworth, a Michelin starred chef, who works wonders in the kitchen. Everything is home made, and listed on the seasonally changing à la carte menu for both lunch and dinner. Signature dishes include savoy cabbage à l' ancienne with tomato sauce; and game terrine, vegetable à la Greque, and spiced pear chutney. The tempting desserts include a baked-to-order Bramley apple pie with clotted cream; and hot Valrhona chocolate pudding with vanilla ice cream, among other favourites.
OPEN: 12-11 (Sun 12-10.30, Mon 5-11) Closed: 24-46 Dec
BAR MEALS: L served Tues-Sun 12-2.30 D served all week 5.30-10.30 (Sun 12-3.30, Sat 6.30-10.30, Sun 6.30-9.30) Av main course £14 **RESTAURANT:** L served Tues-Sun 12-2.30 D served all week 5.30-10.30 Sat-Sun 12-3.30, Sat 6.30-10.30, Sun 6.30-9.30 Av 3 course à la carte £25.50 Av 3 course fixed price £14.95 ◖: Adnams, Hoegaarden. ♀: 8 **FACILITIES:** Garden: Decked terrace & paved front garden

The Northgate ♀
Plan 2 F4

113 Southgate Rd, Islington N1 3JS
☎ 020 7359 7392 ▤ 020 7359 7393
This popular pub was transformed from a run-down community local into a friendly modern establishment serving excellent food. A regular guest beer, two real ales, and a good mix of draught lagers and imported bottled beers. The menu changes daily, and might include smoked haddock fishcake, slow-roast tomatoes with lemon butter; roast confit duck leg, mustard mash and savoy cabbage; and roast aubergine, goats' cheese and onion tart with mixed leaves.
OPEN: 5-11 (Sat 12-11, Sun 12-10.30) Closed: 24-26 Dec, 1 Jan
BAR MEALS: L served Sat, Sun 12-4 D served all week 6.30-10.30 (Sun 6.30-9.30) Av main course £11 **RESTAURANT:** L served Sun 12-4 D served all week 6.30-10.30 (Sun 6.30-9.30) Av 3 course à la

continued

carte £20 ⊕: Punch Taverns ◖: Adnams Bitter, Fuller's London Pride & Guest ales. ♀: 9 **FACILITIES:** Garden: Patio with seating Dogs allowed Water, Biscuits

N6

Pick of the Pubs

The Flask ♀ — Plan 2 E5
Highgate West Hill N6 6BU ☎ 020 8348 7346
e-mail: info@theflaskhighgate.co.uk
A 17th-century former school in one of London's loveliest villages. Dick Turpin hid from his pursuers in the cellars, and TS Elliot and Sir John Betjeman enjoyed a glass or two here. The interior is listed and includes the original bar with sash windows which lift at opening time. Enjoy a glass of good real ale, a speciality bottled beer (choice of 15), or a hot toddy while you peruse the menu, which changes twice a day. Choices range through sandwiches and platters to chargrills and home-made puddings.
OPEN: 11-11 (Nov-Mar open 12 noon) Dec 31 Closed eve
BAR MEALS: L served all week 12-3 D served all week 6-10 Sun 12-4, 6-9.30 Av main course £8 ⊕: ◖: Adnams, Tim Taylor Landlord, Caledonian IPA, Harveys Sussex. ♀: 12
FACILITIES: Garden: A large terrace at the front of the pub Dogs allowed Water, Doggie Snacks

N19

Pick of the Pubs

The Landseer ♀ — Plan 2 E5
37 Landseer Rd N19 4JU
Sunday roasts are a speciality at this unpretentious gastro pub. Tucked off the main road opposite the park, The Landseer is popular with its local clientele. Well-kept beers like Marston's Pedigree, Courage Director's and Kronenbourg are supported by a range of over a dozen wines served by the glass. This is an ideal spot to relax with the weekend papers, or while away an evening with one of the pub's extensive library of board games. Weekend lunches and daily evening meals are served from separate bar and restaurant menus. Steak and Guinness sausage with mash and gravy, or penne with roast vegetables and chilli are typical choices in the bar. Meanwhile, the restaurant menu begins with French onion soup, or rabbit rillettes with sweet pepper coulis. Main courses include roast cod, chorizo, butter beans and mash; cassoulet; and herb-crusted rack of lamb with ratatouille.
OPEN: 12-11 (Mon-Fri open from 5) Closed: Christmas Day
BAR MEALS: L served Sat, Sun 12-5 D served all week 6-10 Sun 6-9.30 Av main course £9 **RESTAURANT:** L served Sat/Sun 12-5 D served all week 6-10 Sun 12.30-5 & 6-9.30 ⊕: Free House ◖: Marston's Pedigree, Courage Directors. ♀: 11
FACILITIES: Children's licence Garden: Pavement area between pub and park Dogs allowed

We only include details of accommodation that has been inspected by the AA (big Stars or Diamonds at the top of an entry), or the RAC, VisitBritain, VisitScotland or WTB (small Stars or Diamonds at the end of an entry)

Pick of the Pubs

St Johns ♀ — Plan 2 E5
91 Junction Rd, Archway N19 5QU
☎ 020 7272 1587 ⓕ 020 76872247
The exterior of this Victorian street corner pub is pure Albert Square, yet the airy bar and spectacular dining room attract trendy North London thirty-somethings. Beyond the long, attractively converted bar, owner Nic Sharp has transformed the adjoining snooker hall into a vast, comfortable restaurant - idiosyncratic decor, solid oak and pine tables, deep red walls hung with modern works of art and comfy settees around the fire. You'll need to book - and be sure to come hungry: St John's portions are lavish, the food's very good, and the happy staff generate a relaxed atmosphere. Starters like terrine of serrano ham, chorizo, chicken and rabbit or chargrilled mackerel fillets are chalked up on huge daily-changing blackboards. Main courses might be chargrilled sea bass with red onion potato cake, or chicken with mussels and tarragon. If you've space, dark chocolate and Amaretto tart will round things off nicely.
OPEN: 11-11 (Sun 12-10.30) Closed: Dec 25-26, Jan 1
BAR MEALS: L served Tue-Sun 12-3 D served Mon-Sun 6.30-11 Av main course £11 **RESTAURANT:** L served Tue-Sun 12-3 D served Mon-Sun 6.30-11 Av 3 course à la carte £20
⊕: ◖: Marston's Pedigree, Fuller's London Pride, Adnam's Broadside. ♀: 10 **FACILITIES:** Dogs allowed

NW1

Pick of the Pubs

The Chapel ♀ — Plan 1 B4
48 Chapel St NW1 5DP ☎ 020 7402 9220 ⓕ 020 7723 2337
e-mail: thechapel@btconnect.com
Dir: By A40 Marylebone Rd & Old Marylebone Rd junct. Off Edgware Rd by tube station
There's a relaxed, informal atmosphere at this bright and airy Marylebone gastropub with stripped floors and pine furniture. The open-plan building derives its name from nothing more than its Chapel Street location, although it used to be called The Pontefract Castle. The daily chalkboard menus give the place an Anglo-Mediterranean feel, with food served throughout, including in the attractive tree-shaded garden. On any given day expect starters such as crostini with roasted vegetables and mozzarella; and salmon fishcakes with rocket salad and tzatziki. Follow with chargrilled côte de beouf with gratin potatoes and béarnaise sauce; grilled bison fillet with both French and haricot beans, rosemary and balsamic jus; and grilled gilt-head bream with mash, asparagus and tartare sauce. Leave space for chocolate, almond and apricot tart. Greene King IPA and Adnams ales and an extensive wine list.
OPEN: 12-11 (Sun 12-10.30) Closed: 24 Dec-2 Jan
BAR MEALS: L served all week 12-2.30 D served all week 7-10 (Sun 12.30-3, 7-10) **RESTAURANT:** L served all week 12-2.30 D served all week 7-10 (Sun 12.30-3, 7-10) ⊕: Punch Taverns ◖: Greene King IPA, Adnams. ♀: 8 **FACILITIES:** Garden: Paved area, shaded by large tree, with tables Dogs allowed

♀ 7 Number of wines by the glass

NW1 continued

Crown & Goose
Plan 2 E4
100 Arlington Rd NW1 7HP ☎ 020 7485 2342 ▤ 020 7485 2342
Dir: Nearest tube: Camden Town
One of the original gastro-pubs with a relaxed atmosphere attracting a fashionable media crowd. The food has an Anglo-Mediterranean flavour with bar snacks like potato skins and ciabatta rolls, and daily specials often feature fish. A typical menu includes chargrilled tuna with mixed pepper salsa; pork chop with apple sauce; gigot lamb with Greek salad and new potatoes; beer battered cod and chips; and fragrant Thai fish or chicken stew with coconut and rice.
OPEN: 11-11 (Sun 12-10.30) Closed: 25 Dec **BAR MEALS:** L served all week 12-3 D served all week 6-10 Av main course £7
RESTAURANT: L served all week 12-3 D served all week 6-10 Av 3 course à la carte £15 ⊕: Free House ◀: Fuller's London Pride, and guest ales.

Pick of the Pubs

The Engineer ♀
Plan 2 E4
65 Gloucester Av, Primrose Hill NW1 8JH
☎ 020 7722 0950 ▤ 020 7483 0592
e-mail: info@the-engineer.com
Dir: Nearest tube: Camden Town/Chalk Farm, on the corner of Princess Rd and Gloucester Ave
Situated in a very residential part of Primrose Hill close to Camden Market, this unassuming corner street pub, built by Isambard Kingdom Brunel in 1841, attracts a discerning dining crowd for imaginative and well-prepared food and its friendly, laid-back atmosphere. Inside it is fashionably rustic, with a spacious bar area, sturdy wooden tables with candles, simple decor and changing art exhibitions in the restaurant area. A walled, paved and heated garden to the rear is extremely popular in fine weather. A first-class, fortnightly-changing menu features an eclectic mix of inspired home-made dishes and uses organic or free-range meats. Typical examples could be organic cheeseburger, baker fries, sweet tomato relish; salmon fillet wrapped in parma ham, with mash and Swiss chard; red braised belly pork with aromatic broth and rice noodles; fillet of seabass with wok-fried white beans, sweet pickled onions and soy dressing; and savoy cabbage parcel of shitake and water chestnut, green beans and ginger dressing. Excellent Sunday brunch.
OPEN: 9-11 **BAR MEALS:** L served all week 12-3.30 D served all week 7-11 Sun 12.30-4.30 Av main course £13.50
RESTAURANT: L served all week 12-3.30 D served all week 7-11 Sun 12.30-4.30 Av 3 course à la carte £25 ⊕: ◀: Erdinger, Leffe, Timothy Taylor Landlord, Hook Norton. ♀: 10
FACILITIES: Child facs Children's licence Garden: Attractive garden, tables and seating aprx 100 Dogs allowed Water bowls

The Globe ♀
Plan 1 B4
43-47 Marylebone Rd NW1 5JY
☎ 020 7935 6368 ▤ 020 7224 0154
Dir: At the corner of Marylebone Rd and Baker St, opposite Baker St tube station.
Built in 1735, the Globe Tavern is contemporary with the adjoining Nash terraces and the Marylebone Road itself. The first omnibus service from Holborn stopped here, and the Metropolitan Railway runs beneath the road outside. The pub retains much of its 18th-century character and proudly serves traditional English fare. Bombardier and London Pride are amongst the ales that accompany dishes like sausages, mash
continued

and onion gravy; oak smoked salmon fishcake; and spicy five-bean shepherd's pie.
OPEN: 11-11 (Sun 12-10.30) Closed: 25 Dec **BAR MEALS:** L served all week D served all week Mon-Sat 11-10, Sun 12-8 Av main course £5.50 ⊕: ◀: Scottish Courage Directors, Bombadier, Youngs, London Pride. ♀: 17 **FACILITIES:** Outside seating area with benches

Pick of the Pubs

The Lansdowne ♀
Plan 2 E4
90 Gloucester Av, Primrose Hill NW1 8HX
☎ 020 7483 0409 ▤ 0207 5861723
e-mail: thelansdowne@hotmail.co.uk
In 1992, Amanda Pritchett started The Lansdowne as one of the earliest dining pubs in Primrose Hill. Stripping the pub of its fruit machines, TVs and jukebox, she brought in solid wood furniture and back-to-basics décor; today, it blends a light, spacious bar and outdoor seating area with a slightly more formal upper dining room. All that apart, however, its success depends on the quality of its cooking. All food is freshly prepared on the premises, using organic or free-range ingredients wherever possible, and portions are invariably generous. The seasonal menu offers dishes like spiced red lentil soup with Greek yoghurt; home-cured bresaola with rocket, capers and Parmesan; pan-fried sardines on toast with watercress; confit pork belly with prunes, potatoes and lardons; poached sea trout with crushed herb potatoes; polenta with roast pumpkin, buffalo mozzarella and walnut; hot chocolate fondant with double cream; and peached poached in saffron with yoghurt and nuts.
OPEN: 12-11 Mon 5-11, Sun 12-10.30 Closed: 25/26 Dec
BAR MEALS: L served Tue-Sun 12.30-3 D served Mon-Sun 7-10 Sun 12.30-3.30 & 7-9.30, Pizza 12.30-6 7-10 Av main course £12
RESTAURANT: L served Sun 1-3 D served Tue-Sat 7-10 Av 3 course à la carte £23 ⊕: Bass ◀: Staropramen, IPA, Tiger Bitter. ♀: 8 **FACILITIES:** Picnic tables at front of pub Dogs allowed dog bowls

The Lord Stanley ♀
Plan 2 E4
51 Camden Park Rd NW1 9BH
☎ 0207 428 9488 ▤ 020 7209 1347
In the mid-1990s, the Lord Stanley was stripped and re-kitted in a gastro-pub garb that has served the pub well. At an open grill, food is produced in full view - a typically modern idiom producing, perhaps, chicken with mango salsa. Other dishes include seasonal soups, steaks, pasta or sausages with various accompaniments. Monday night jazz.
OPEN: 12-11 Closed: 26 Dec & 1 Jan **BAR MEALS:** L served Tue-Sun 12.30-3 D served all week 7-10 Av main course £11
RESTAURANT: L served Tue-Sun 12.30-3 D served all week 7-10 ⊕: Free House ◀: Young's Special, Adnams Broadside, Abbot Ale.
FACILITIES: Garden: Food served outside Dogs allowed

The Queens ♀
Plan 2 E4
49 Regents Park Rd, Primrose Hill NW1 8XD
☎ 020 7586 0408 ▤ 020 7586 5677
e-mail: mail@thequeens49.fsnet.co.uk
Dir: Nearest tube - Chalk Farm
In one of London's most affluent and personality-studded areas, this Victorian pub looks up at 206ft-high Primrose Hill. Main courses may include seared calve's liver with bacon and sage mash, roast vegetable Yorkshire pudding, smoked chicken with mango and mange-tout peas, and whole roasted plaice with prawns and pancetta. On Sundays there's a
continued

selection of roasts, as well as fish, pasta and salad. Beers include Youngs and guests.
OPEN: 11-11 (Sun 12-10.30) **BAR MEALS:** L served all week 12-3 D served all week 7-10 (Sun 7-9) Av main course £11.50
RESTAURANT: L served all week 12-3 D served all week 7-10 (Sun 7-9) Av 3 course à la carte £25 ⊜: Youngs ◖: Youngs & guest ales.
⚲: 12 **FACILITIES:** Dogs allowed Water provided

NW3

The Flask ♀ Plan 2 E5
14 Flask Walk, Hampstead NW3 1HE ☎ 020 7435 4580
e-mail: flask@youngs.co.uk
Dir: Nearest tube: Hampstead. Turn L, then L again for Flask Walk
Friendly local with a fascinating clientele - writers, poets, actors, tourists, locals, workmen, shopkeepers, office-workers, professors and medics. The name reflects the time when flasks were made on site for the healing waters of the Hampstead spa. Dishes range through home-made soup, pies and burgers, fish and chips, chicken and leek pie, sausage and mash and various pastas.
OPEN: 11-11 (Sun 12-11) **BAR MEALS:** L served all week 12-3 (Sun 12-4) D served Tue-Sat 6-8.30 Av main course £6.50
RESTAURANT: L served all week 12-3 D served Tue-Sat 6-8.30 Av 3 course à la carte £11 ⊜: Young & Co ◖: Young's Special, Winter Warmer & Waggle Dance. ⚲: 17 **FACILITIES:** Dogs allowed on lead

The Holly Bush ♀ Plan 2 E5
Holly Mount, Hampstead NW3 6SG
☎ 020 7435 2892 ▤ 020 7431 2292
e-mail: hollybush@btconnect.com
Once the home of English portraitist George Romney, the Holly Bush became a pub after his death in 1802. The building was recently investigated by ghostbusters looking for a spooky barmaid, but more tangible 21st-century media celebrities are easier to spot. Staple fare includes saltmarsh lamb cutlets with hazelnut and rosemary stuffing; rabbit in mustard and Pilsner sauce; and vegetarian sausages with cheddar mash and red onion gravy. Real ales from Adnams and Harveys.
OPEN: 12-11 **BAR MEALS:** L served all week 12.30-4 D served all week 6.30-10 Sat 12-10, Sun 12-9 Av main course £9.50
RESTAURANT: L served Sat-Sun 12.30-10 D served all week Sun 12.30-9 Av 3 course à la carte £25 ⊜: ◖: Harveys Sussex Best, Adnams Bitter & Broadside, Lowenbrau, London Pride. ⚲: 12
FACILITIES: Child facs Garden: Small area outside pub with seating & tables Dogs allowed

Spaniards Inn ♀ Plan 2 E5
Spaniards Rd, Hampstead NW3 7JJ
☎ 020 8731 6571 ▤ 020 8731 6572
The birthplace of highwayman Dick Turpin, this former tollhouse is a famous landmark beside Hampstead Heath. The poet Keats was once a regular; Bram Stoker mentioned the place in *Dracula*, and it is still much frequented by celebrities to this day. Traditional British fare is on offer, such as fish and chips, sausage and mash, and steamed steak and kidney pudding. In summer the stone flagged courtyard provides a shady retreat.
OPEN: 11-11 (Sun 12-10.30) **BAR MEALS:** L served all week 11-10 D served all week 11-10 Av main course £7
RESTAURANT: L served all week D served all week 5-9
⊜: ◖: Fullers London Pride, Adnams Best & monthly changing guest ales. **FACILITIES:** Garden: Flagstone shaded courtyard Dogs allowed Auto dog wash **NOTES:** Parking 40

Ye Olde White Bear ♀ Plan 2 E5
Well Rd, Hampstead NW3 1LJ ☎ 0207 4353758
Victorian pub with a Hampstead village feel and varied clientele from dustmen to Hollywood stars. Friendly and traditional, there has been a pub on this site since 1704. Lots of theatrical memorabilia, and a patio at the rear. All day bar food includes steak and Guinness pie, home-made cheeseburger, vegetarian lasagne, cod in beer batter, and tuna steak.
OPEN: 11-11 **BAR MEALS:** L served all week 9 D served all week 9 Av main course £7.75 **RESTAURANT:** L served all week D served all week ⊜: ◖: Fuller's London Pride, Youngs, Abbot. ⚲: 12
FACILITIES: Garden: Courtyard with seating&benches to front Dogs allowed Water provided

NW5

Dartmouth Arms NEW ◖◗ ♀ Plan 2 E5
35 York Rise NW5 1SP ☎ 020 7485 3267
e-mail: info@dartmoutharms.co.uk
Dir: 5min walk for Hampstead Heath.
Fortnightly quizzes, regular wine and bistro evenings, and knitting club meetings are popular fixtures at this pub close to Hampstead Heath. Walkers caught in the rain often make their way here to dry off by the fire and enjoy something from the imaginative menu. Honey glazed pork chops with sautéed new potatoes, braised red cabbage and juniper gravy; and roasted organic salmon fillet with mash, baby spinach and hollandaise sauce might feature.
OPEN: 11-11 (Sat-Sun open 10) Sun close 10.30
BAR MEALS: L served all week 11-3 D served all week 6-10 Sat-Sun 10-10 Av main course £7.50 ◖: Adnams. ⚲: 11
FACILITIES: Dogs allowed Dog bowl

Pick of the Pubs

The Junction Tavern NEW ♀ Plan 0
101 Fortess Rd NW5 1AG
☎ 020 7485 9400 ▤ 020 7485 9401
Dir: Between Kentish Town and Tufnell Park tube stations.
Situated halfway between Kentish Town and Tufnell Park underground stations, the Junction Tavern is also handy for the vibrant delights of nearby Camden and the green spaces of Parliament Hill and Hampstead Heath. This is a comfortable and friendly neighbourhood gastro-pub offering a daily changing seasonal menu and a good selection of real ales. In fact, the pub is the venue for an annual beer festival held on August bank holiday. Enthusiasts mingle in the conservatory or heated beer garden, choosing from a range of 50-plus ales which come from regional breweries and are served straight from the cask. To accompany a plentiful supply of beer, the inn offers an extensive lunch and dinner menu, with dishes including dressed Dorset crab with celeriac remoulade and watercress salad; salt beef sandwich on rye with chips, cornichons and mustard pickle; pot-roast maize-fed chicken breast with boulangère potatoes and spinach; and wild mushroom and cep risotto.
OPEN: 12-11 (Sun 12-10.30) Closed: 24-26 Dec, 1 Jan
BAR MEALS: L served all week 12-3 D served all week 6.30-10.30 Sun 12-4, 6.30-9.30 Av main course £11
RESTAURANT: L served all week 12-3 D served all week 6.30-10.30 Sun 12-4, 6.30-9.30 Av 3 course à la carte £23 ◖: Caledonian Deuchars IPA, guest ales. ⚲: 12
FACILITIES: Garden: Large, 100 seat garden, heated umbrellas Dogs allowed Water, biscuits

NW5 continued

Pick of the Pubs

The Vine
Plan 2 E5
86 Highgate Rd NW5 1PB
☎ 020 7209 0038 🖷 020 7209 3161
e-mail: info@thevinelondon.co.uk
Dir: Telephone for directions
What looks like a Victorian pub on the outside has a very contemporary feel on the inside, with its copper bar, wooden floors, huge mirrors and funky art. Not far from Hampstead Heath, the Vine is billed as a bar, restaurant and garden, and the latter is a great asset - fully covered in winter. Rooms are also available upstairs for private meetings or dinner parties. Lunch, dinner and weekend brunch menus are offered, the latter including eggs Benedict, burgers and roast cod. Bar snack favourites include fish cakes, chicken satay and tempura sweetcorn, while restaurant fare features crispy duck pancakes with watercress, ginger and mango salsa, cassoulet, risottos and classic dishes like calves' liver with dried prosciutto, potato rösti and Madeira jus.
OPEN: 12-11 Closed: 26 Dec **BAR MEALS:** L served all week 12.30-3 D served all week 6.30-10.30 Av main course £10.50
RESTAURANT: L served all week 12.30-3.30 D served all week 6.30-10.30 Av 3 course à la carte £22.50 🍴: Punch Taverns
🍺: Stella Artois, San Miguel, Fullers London Pride & guest ales.
FACILITIES: Pretty garden: ideal for weddings
NOTES: Parking 4

NW6

The Salusbury Pub and Dining Room ♀
Plan 2 D4
50-52 Salusbury Rd NW6 6NN ☎ 020 7328 3286
e-mail: thesalusbury@aol.com
Dir: 100m L out of Queens Park tube & train station
The Salusbury is a gastropub that attracts its fair share of big names in fashion and media circles to leafy Brondesbury. You don't have to be famous to enjoy a satisfying meal, though, starting perhaps with pan-fried squid with chilli and rocket, or linguini with clams and broccoli, and continuing with calves' liver à la Veneziana, or braised lamb shank with shallots and blackcurrants.
OPEN: 12-11 (Sun 12-10.30) Closed: 25-26 Dec
BAR MEALS: L served Tues-Sun 12.30-3.30 D served all week 7-10.15 Sun 7-10 Av main course £11 **RESTAURANT:** L served Tue-Sun 12.30-3.30 D served all week 7-10.15 Sun until 10 Av 3 course à la carte £20.25 🍺: Broadside, Bitburger, Guiness. ♀: 7
FACILITIES: Dogs allowed

NW8

Pick of the Pubs

The Abbey Road Pub ♀
Plan 2 E4
63 Abbey Rd NW8 0AE ☎ 020 7328 6626 🖷 020 7625 9168
Situated in a leafy area of St Johns Wood, a compact and informal dining pub with a tiny open-plan kitchen that takes its food, though not itself, seriously. Expect nothing short of well-prepared fresh ingredients along with decent pints of real ale and numerous house wines served by the glass. A sample menu features Thai fishcakes with sweet chilli dressing; spiny artichoke, rocket and lentil salad with olive dressing; or potato gnocchi with butternut squash,

sage and parmesan. For more substantial dishes try roast free range chicken with flageolet beans and roast garlic, duck breast with smashed celeriac, or fillet of sea bass with beetroot, mizuna and horseradish. Try the wonderfully named rhubarb Eton mess for pudding.
OPEN: 12-11 Closed: Dec 25 **BAR MEALS:** L served all week 12.30-3.30 D served all week 7-10.30 (Sun 12-4) Av main course £13 **RESTAURANT:** L served all week 12-3 D served all week 6.30-10.30 Av 3 course à la carte £30 Av 3 course fixed price £11.75 🍴: Free House 🍺: Greene King IPA.
FACILITIES: Garden: Food served outside

NW10

The Greyhound NEW 🥢 ♀
Plan 2 D4
64-66 Chamberlayne Rd NW10 3JJ
☎ 020 8969 8080 🖷 020 8969 8081
e-mail: greyhoundnw10@aol.com
This new pub was created from a derelict building, much to the delight of the locals, who have been flocking in ever since. Customers range from a smattering of supermodels to young families and older couples, all clearly enjoying the friendly atmosphere. There's an eclectic wine list, and a menu each for the bar and dining room. The kitchen offers intelligent, gastro-pub fodder; butternut squash risotto; home-made beef burger; or Toulouse sausages with red wine lentils.
OPEN: 11-11 (Mon 6-11 Fri-Sat 11-12, Sun 11-10.30) Closed: 25-26 Dec, 1 Jan **BAR MEALS:** L served Tues-Sun 12.30-3.30 D served all week 6.30-10 Sun 12.30-7 Av main course £6.50
RESTAURANT: L served Tues-Sun 12.30-3.30 D served all week 6.30-10.30 Sun 12.30-7 Av 3 course à la carte £22.50 🍺: Guinness, guest ales. ♀: 14 **FACILITIES:** Garden: Tranquil urban space, plants, heaters, BBQ Dogs allowed Water

William IV Bar & Restaurant 🥢 ♀
Plan 2 D4
786 Harrow Rd NW10 5JX ☎ 020 8969 5944 🖷 020 8964 9218
Dir: Telephone for directions

The William IV enjoys a strong local following of people drawn to the revitalized interior including a music-orientated bar (Virgin Records around the corner), and modern European food. A very flexible array of dishes typically includes chargrilled sirloin steak with chips and beetroot pesto; baked plaice with green beans; and pea, broad bean and mint tart. Plenty of fish too.
OPEN: 12-11 (Thu-Sat 12-12, Sun 12-10.30) Closed: Dec 25 & Jan 01 **BAR MEALS:** L served all week 12-3 D served all week 6-10.30 Sun 12-4.30 Av main course £10 **RESTAURANT:** L served all week 12-3 D served all week 6-10.30 Av 3 course à la carte £16 🍴: Free House 🍺: Fuller's London Pride, Greene King IPA, Interbrew Bass, Brakspear. ♀: 12 **FACILITIES:** Garden: Large beer garden Dogs allowed except in the evening

continued

SE1

The Anchor ♀
Plan 1 F3

Bankside, 34 Park St SE1 9EF ☎ 020 7407 1577
& 7407 3003 📠 020 7407 7023
e-mail: 0977anchor@thespiritgroup.com

In the shadow of the Globe Theatre, this historic pub lies on one of London's most famous tourist trails. Samuel Pepys supposedly watched the Great Fire of London from here in 1666, and Dr Johnson was a regular, with Oliver Goldsmith, David Garrick and Sir Joshua Reynolds. The river views are excellent, and inside are black beams, old faded plasterwork, and a maze of tiny rooms. A varied menu includes fish and chips, pan-fried halibut with olives, and cod in crispy bacon served on wilted spinach.
OPEN: 11-11 (Sun 12-10.30) **BAR MEALS:** L served all week 11.30-8.30 D served all week **RESTAURANT:** L served all week 12-2.30 D served all week 5-10 🍽: 🍺: Wadworth 6X, Scottish Courage Courage Directors, Greene King IPA. **FACILITIES:** Garden: Patio overlooking the River Thames

Pick of the Pubs

The Anchor & Hope ☺☺ ♀
Plan 1 E2

36 The Cut SE1 8LP ☎ 020 7928 9898 📠 020 7928 4595
Considering that it's an award-winning gastropub which has picked up many accolades for its cooking in a short space of time, the Anchor and Hope is a remarkably down-to-earth and friendly place. Children with parents, and dogs with owners are all made welcome. If the weather permits, pavement seating allows you to watch the world go by as you enjoy a pint of Eagle IPA or one of twelve wines sold by the glass. Some of the less expensive wines are sold by the carafe - half a bottle for half the price of a full one - an honest approach appreciated by the pub's faithful diners. The short menu, too, is refreshingly unembroidered, with straightforward dish descriptions and most of the prices in whole pounds. The menu changes with every lunch and dinner, and features quality British produce and unusual but hearty rustic dishes. Two or three desserts complete the picture.
OPEN: 11-11 (Mon 5-11) **BAR MEALS:** L served Tue-Sat 12-2.30 D served Mon-Sat 6-10.30 reduced menus 2.30-6 **RESTAURANT:** L served Tue-Sat 12-2.30 D served Mon-Sat 6-10.30 🍺: Bombadier, Eagle IPA, Erdinger, Kirin. ♀: 12 **FACILITIES:** Garden: Pavement Seating Dogs allowed

All AA rated accommodation can also be found on the AA's internet site
www.theAA.com

The Bridge House Bar & Dining Room ♀
Plan 1 G2

218 Tower Bridge Rd SE1 2UP
☎ 020 7407 5818 📠 020 7407 5828
Dir: 5 min walk from London Bridge/Tower Hill tube stations
The nearest bar to Tower Bridge, The Bridge House has great views of the river and city and is handy for London Dungeons, Borough Market, Tate Modern, London Eye, Globe Theatre and Southwark Cathedral. It comprises a bar, dining room and new café, plus facilities for private functions. Typical dishes are chargrilled steak, beer battered haddock, and calves' liver with black pudding, smoked bacon, parsley mash and red wine gravy.
OPEN: 11.30-11 (Sun 12-10.30) Closed: 25-26 Dec, 1 Jan **BAR MEALS:** L served all week 11.30-10 D served all week 5-10 Sun 12-9.30 **RESTAURANT:** L served all week 12-4 D served all week 6-10 🍽: Adnams 🍺: Adnams Best Bitter, Adnams Broadside. ♀: 16

Pick of the Pubs

The Fire Station ☺ ♀
Plan 1 D2

150 Waterloo Rd SE1 8SB
☎ 020 7620 2226 📠 020 7633 9161
e-mail: firestation@wizardinns.co.uk
Close to Waterloo Station, and handy for the Old Vic Theatre and the Imperial War Museum, this remarkable conversion of a genuine early-Edwardian fire station has kept many of its former trappings intact. The rear dining room faces the open kitchen. An interesting menu includes dishes such as Fire Station avocado Caesar salad; baked cod with cheese polenta and pimento and pesto dressing; and roast spiced pork belly with sticky rice and pak choi. Alternatively try Tandoori seared yellowfin tuna loin, calves' liver with bacon and mustard mash, or lemon sole with Jerusalem artichokes. There are also imaginative midweek and Sunday set-price lunches.
OPEN: 11-11 (Sun 12-10.30) Closed: 25/26 Dec **BAR MEALS:** L served all week 12-5.30 D served all week 5.30-10.30 **RESTAURANT:** L served all week 12-2.45 D served all week 5-11 (Sat 12-11, Sun 12-9.30) 🍽: 🍺: Adnams Best Bitter, Fuller's London Pride, Young's Bitters, Shepherd Neame Spitfire. ♀: 8

Pick of the Pubs

The George Inn
Plan 1 G3

77 Borough High St SE1 1NH
☎ 020 7407 2056 📠 020 7403 6956
e-mail: info@georgeinn-southwark.co.uk
Dir: London Bridge tube station, take Borough High Street exit, turn L, 200 yrds on left hand side.
The only remaining galleried inn in London, this striking black and white building dates back at least to 1542 when it numbered one William Shakespeare among its clientele; there is a long tradition of open-air theatre in the yard. Dickens mentioned it in *Little Dorrit*, and his original life assurance policy is displayed along with 18th-century rat traps. In the 18th and 19th centuries the George was a renowned focus of merriment during the Southwark Fair, and a famous coaching terminus until the railways arrived. Taken over by the National Trust in the 1930s, the George has fading plasterwork, black beams and a warren of tiny rooms. Food can be enjoyed here or in the large cobbled courtyard, with a straightforward choice including steak, mushroom and ale pie, roast sirloin of

continued

SE1 continued

beef, and gammon steak. Decent ales include Fuller's London Pride, George Inn Ale, and Marston's Pedigree. Now popular with tourists, this is still a 'real' olde English pub with plenty of buzz.
OPEN: 11-11 (Sunday 12-10.30) Closed: 25 Dec
BAR MEALS: L served all week 12-3 D served Mon-Sat Sun 12-4 Av main course £5.45 **RESTAURANT:** D served Mon-Sat 5-10 Av 3 course fixed price £8.45 🍴: 🍺: Fuller's London Pride, Greene King Abbot Ale, George Inn Ale, Marstons Pedigree.
FACILITIES: Garden: Large courtyard, picnic tables, enclosed

The Market Porter 🍷   Plan 1 F3
9 Stoney St, Borough Market, London Bridge SE1 9AA
☎ 020 7407 2495 📠 020 7403 7697
Dir: *Close to London Bridge Station*
Traditional tavern serving a market community that has been flourishing for about 1,000 years. Excellent choice of real ales. Worth noting is an internal leaded bay window unique in London. The atmosphere is friendly, if rather rough and ready, and the pub has been used as a location in *Lock, Stock and Two Smoking Barrels*, *Only Fools and Horses*, and *Entrapment*. Menu includes bangers and mash, roasted lamb shank, beetroot and lemon marinated salmon, and a hearty plate of fish and chips. Early morning opening.
OPEN: 6.30-8.30 11-11 (Sat 11-11 Sun 12-10.30)
BAR MEALS: L served Mon-Sun 12-2.30 5-8.30
RESTAURANT: L served Mon-Fri 12-2.30 5.30-8.30 🍴: Free House 🍺: Harveys Best, Scottish Courage Courage Best, Lands End To John O'Groats. 🍷: 6

The Old Thameside   Plan 1 F3
Pickford's Wharf, Clink St SE1 9DG
☎ 020 7403 4243 📠 020 7407 2063
Just two minutes' walk from Tate Modern, the Millennium Bridge and Shakespeare's Globe, this former spice warehouse is also close to the site of England's first prison, the Clink. The pub features a large outdoor seating area that overhangs the River Thames, and the friendly staff are always happy to point bewildered tourists in the right direction! Traditional pub fare includes fish and chips, sausage and mash, curries and vegetarian pies.
OPEN: 12-11 Closed: 25 Dec **BAR MEALS:** L served all week 12-5 Av main course £6.95 🍺: Fuller's London Pride, Adnams Bitter.
FACILITIES: Children's licence Beer Garden on the River

SE5

Pick of the Pubs

The Sun and Doves 🍷   Plan 2 F3
61-63 Coldharbour Ln, Camberwell SE5 9NS
☎ 020 7924 9950 📠 020 7924 9330
e-mail: mail@sunanddoves.co.uk
Attractive Camberwell venue known for good food, drink and art - all with a contemporary flavour. For a London pub it also has a decent sized garden, great for the summer months. Drinks options range from Fairtrade coffee and herbal infusions to draught ales and champagne, including plenty of wines by the glass. The menu is stylishly simple, with a daily soup and stew, and snacks like marinated olives and nachos. Otherwise there's a choice of starters/light meals including hot sandwiches, eggs Benedict, and cured meats and pickles.

Grills and mains take in speciality skewers - marinaded ingredients (chicken, swordfish, halloumi) grilled on a beech skewer - alongside Cumberland sausage and mash, and fish in beer batter. There are cool side orders too, like fat chips; rocket, Parmesan and pine nut salad, and rustic bread with roast garlic and olive oil. The pub also showcases local artists, many pretty well known.
OPEN: Mon-Thu 12-11, Fri-Sat 12-12, Sun 12-10.30 Closed: 25/26 Dec **BAR MEALS:** L served all week 12-10.30 D served all week 12-10.30 Sun 12-9 Av main course £8 **RESTAURANT:** L served all week 11-11 D served all week Av 3 course à la carte £18 🍴: Scottish & Newcastle 🍺: Greene King Old Speckled Hen, Scottish Courage John Smith's Smooth. 🍷: 8
FACILITIES: Child facs Garden: Secluded, spacious, sosouth-facing Dogs allowed Water bowl in garden

SE10

The Cutty Sark Tavern   Plan 2 G3
4-6 Ballast Quay, Greenwich SE10 9PD ☎ 0208 858 3146
Originally the Union Tavern, this 1695 waterside pub was renamed when the world famous tea-clipper was dry-docked upriver in 1954. Inside, low beams, creaking floorboards, dark panelling and from the large bow window in the upstairs bar, commanding views of the Thames, Canary Wharf and the Millennium Dome. Well-kept beers, wines by the glass and a wide selection of malts. Bangers and mash, seafood and vegetarian specials and Sunday roasts. Busy at weekends, especially on fine days.
OPEN: 11-11 (Sun 12-10.30) **BAR MEALS:** L served all week 12 D served all week 9 🍺: Fullers London Pride, Staropramen, Adnams Broadside. **FACILITIES:** Children's licence

Greenwich Union Pub   Plan 2 G3
56 Royal Hill SE10 8RT ☎ 020 8692 6258 📠 8305 8625
e-mail: andy@meantimebrewing.co.uk
Dir: *Close to Greenwich station*
Comfortable leather sofas and flagstone floors help to keep the original character of this refurbished pub intact. Interesting beers (including chocolate and raspberry!) and a beer garden make this a popular spot. Try a foccacia sandwich; pearl barley risotto with courgette and radicchio; or chicken with spicy broccoli and sweet shallots. The Meantime Brewery Co, which brews the beers on offer, was the only UK brewery to win awards at the 2004 Beer World Cup.
OPEN: 11-11 (Sat 10-11, Sun 10-10.30) **BAR MEALS:** L served Mon-Sun 12.30-10 D served Mon-Sun Sat-Sun 10-9 🍺: White Beer, Golden Beer, Blonde Ale, Red Beer. **FACILITIES:** Children's licence Garden: Beer garden, tables and chairs Dogs allowed Water

Pick of the Pubs

North Pole Bar & Restaurant 🔍 🍷   Plan 2 G3
131 Greenwich High Rd, Greenwich SE10 8JA
☎ 020 8853 3020 📠 020 8853 3501
e-mail: north-pole@btconnect.com
See Pick of the Pubs on opposite page

Do you have a favourite pub that we have overlooked? Please use the Reader's Report form at the back of this guide to tell us all about it

continued

Pick of the Pubs

North Pole Bar & Restaurant

Three venues in one: the stylish Piano Restaurant with resident ivory-tinkler in the evenings; funky cocktail bar; and basement night club. In 2004 the whole building was refurbished to a high standard, and now includes a VIP bar for private parties.

The restaurant takes pride in offering modern European cooking with a French twist, typified by starters of foie gras-stuffed ballottine of duck with apricot, orange and grape honey; and oxtail risotto with herbs and parmesan. Among the main courses are pan-fried skate wing with wild mushroom, root vegetable, pesto and Madeira jus; chump of English lamb with potato dauphinoise, green beans and rosemary jus; and confit leg and roast breast of pheasant, asparagus and bacon wrapped in savoy cabbage, with apple purée and red wine sauce.

Puddings include chocolate marquis with hazelnuts praline, and cassis coulis. A long wine list even draws on Lebanon, a relatively unusual source. Draught lagers or Guinness will have to suffice for real ale lovers, although fans of classic crooners are well catered for. Tribute acts are a regular fixture each month, and have included Dean Martin, Tom Jones and Frank Sinatra. What could be a better accompaniment to these ersatz singers than a cocktail or two from an extensive list that offers the Rat Pack Manhattan, the Foxy Brown, and Sex at the Pole!

OPEN: 12-12
BAR MEALS: L served all week 12-3
D served all week Av main course £6
RESTAURANT: L served Sun 12-4
D served all week 6-11 Av 3 course à la carte £25 Av 3 course fixed price £17.50
🛢: Free House
🍺: Stella Artois, Staropramen, Budvar, Hoegarden. ⌕: 20
FACILITIES: Child facs

  Plan 2 G3
131 Greenwich High Rd,
Greenwich SE10 8JA
☎ 020 8853 3020
▤ 020 8853 3501
🅔 north-pole@btconnect.com

SE16

The Mayflower 🐟 ♀ — Plan 2 F3
117 Rotherhithe St, Rotherhithe SE16 4NF
☎ 020 7237 4088 🗐 020 7064 4710
Dir: Exit A2 at Surrey Keys roundabout onto Brunel Rd, 3rd left onto Swan Rd, at T jct left, 200m to pub on right
From the patio of the Mayflower Inn you can still see the renovated jetty from which the eponymous 'Mayflower' embarked on her historic voyage to the New World. The pub has maintained its links with the famous ship through a range of memorabilia, as well as its unusual licence to sell both British and American postage stamps. Pub fare includes stuffed pork loin; and Cajun chicken supreme.
OPEN: 11-3 6-11 (Sun 12-10.30, May-Oct 11-11)
BAR MEALS: L served all week 12-2.30 D served all week 6.30-9.30 (Sun 12-4) Av main course £5 **RESTAURANT:** L served Mon-Sun 12-2.30 D served Mon-Sat 6.30-9.30 (Sun 12-4) 🍴: Greene King
🍺: Greene King Abbot Ale, IPA, Old Speckled Hen. ♀: 30
FACILITIES: Jetty over river, Food served outside Dogs allowed

SE21

The Crown & Greyhound ♀ — Plan 2 F2
73 Dulwich Village SE21 7BJ ☎ 020 8299 4976 🗐 020 8693 8959
With a tradition of service and hospitality reaching back to the 18th century, the Crown and Greyhound counts Charles Dickens and John Ruskin amongst its celebrated patrons. Modern day customers will find three bars and a restaurant in the heart of peaceful Dulwich Village. The weekly-changing menu might feature bean cassoulet with couscous; or an 8oz Angus burger with Cheddar cheese and potato wedges. There are daily salads, pasta and fish dishes, too.
OPEN: 11-11 (Sun 12-10.30) **BAR MEALS:** L served all week 12-10 D served all week Sun 12-9 Av main course £7
RESTAURANT: L served all week 12-10 D served all week Sun 12-9
🍺: Fuller's London Pride & guest ales. ♀: 10 **FACILITIES:** Garden: 2 levels, paved with trees and BBQ area Dogs allowed

SE22

Pick of the Pubs

Franklins 🌳 ♀ — Plan 2 F2
157 Lordship Ln, Dulwich SE22 8HX ☎ 020 8299 9598
e-mail: franklins@madasafish.com
Perhaps a little more bar/restaurant than pub, there are nonetheless real ales and lagers on tap here, including Young's, Kronenbourg and Guinness. The upwardly mobile and appreciative clientele enjoy the no-frills short menu, where prices are both reasonable and refreshingly devoid of the ubiquitous 95p. An interesting selection of starters may include smoked quail, rocket and olives, tongue, watercress and horseradish. Follow these with kidneys, chard and mustard; or roast monkfish, lentils and bacon. Specialities are Old Spot belly, stuffed cabbage and black pudding; scallops, pea shoots and bacon; and wood pigeon, beetroot and shallots. For dessert, gingerbread ice cream or rhubarb trifle may be two of the half dozen choices. From Monday to Friday set lunch menus allow the option of two or three courses, with three courses being only £3 the dearer.
OPEN: 12-12 Closed: 25-26, 31 Dec, 1 Jan
BAR MEALS: L served all week 12-4 D served all week 6-10.30 (Sun 1-10.30) Av main course £12.50 **RESTAURANT:** L served all week 12-4 D served all week 6-10.30 (Sun 1-10.30) Av 3 course à la carte £24 Av 3 course fixed price £12 🍴: Free House 🍺: Youngs, Estrella, Guinness. ♀: 11 **FACILITIES:** Child facs Dogs allowed

SW1

The Albert ♀ — Plan 1 D2
52 Victoria St SW1H 0NP ☎ 020 7222 5577
& 7222 7606 🗐 020 7222 1044
e-mail: thealbert.westminster@thespiritgroup.com
Dir: Nearest tube - St James Park
Built in 1854, this Grade II Victorian pub is named after Queen Victoria's husband, Prince Albert. The main staircase is decorated with portraits of British Prime Ministers, from Salisbury to Blair, and the pub is often frequented by MPs. To make sure they don't miss a vote, there's even a division bell in the restaurant. The pub was the only building in the area to survive the Blitz of WWII, with even its old cut-glass windows remaining intact. The traditional menu includes a carvery, buffet, a selection of light dishes and other classic fare. Recent change of hands.
OPEN: 11-11 (Sun 12-10.30) Closed: 25 Dec **BAR MEALS:** L served all week 11-10 D served all week **RESTAURANT:** L served all week 12-9.30 D served all week 5-9.30 🍴: 🍺: Bombadier, Courage Directors & Best, London Pride, John Smiths. ♀: 14

The Buckingham Arms ♀ — Plan 1 D2
62 Petty France SW1H 9EU ☎ 020 7222 3386
e-mail: buckinghamarms@youngs.co.uk
Dir: St James's Park tube
Known as the Black Horse until 1903, this elegant, busy Young's pub is situated close to Buckingham Palace. Popular with tourists, business people and real ale fans alike, it offers a good range of simple pub food, including the 'mighty' Buckingham burger, nachos with chilli, chicken ciabatta and old favourites like ham, egg and chips in its long bar with etched mirrors.
OPEN: 11-11 (Sat & Sun 12-5.30) **BAR MEALS:** L served all week 12-2.30 D served Mon-Fri 6-9 Av main course £4 🍴: Young & Co 🍺: Youngs Bitter, Special & Winter Warmer. ♀: 11
FACILITIES: Dogs allowed

The Clarence ♀ — Plan 1 D3
55 Whitehall SW1A 2HP ☎ 020 7930 4808 🗐 020 7321 0859
Dir: Between Big Ben & Trafalgar Sq
This apparently haunted pub, situated five minutes' walk from Big Ben, the Houses of Parliament, Trafalgar Square and Buckingham Palace, has leaded windows and ancient ceiling beams from a Thames pier. Typical of the menu choice are sausage and mash; pesto penne pasta with brie or chicken; and pie of the day. Daily specials also available. The pub has a friendly atmosphere and is handy for the bus and tube.
OPEN: 10-11 **BAR MEALS:** L served all week all day D served all week Av main course £6.95 **RESTAURANT:** L served all week D served all week 🍴: 🍺: Bombardier, Fullers London Pride, Youngs & Guest ale. ♀: 17

The Grenadier ♀ — Plan 1 B2
18 Wilton Row, Belgravia SW1X 7NR
☎ 020 7235 3074 🗐 020 7235 3400
Regularly used for films and television series, the ivy-clad Grenadier stands in a cobbled mews behind Hyde Park Corner, largely undiscovered by tourists. Famous patrons have included King George IV and Madonna! Outside is the remaining stone of the Duke's mounting block. Expect traditional favourites on the blackboard, and keep an eye out for the ghost of an officer accidentally flogged to death for cheating at cards.
OPEN: 12-11 (Sun 12-10.30 and BHs) **BAR MEALS:** L served all week 12-2.30 D served all week Av main course £6.65
RESTAURANT: L served all week 12-1.30 D served all week 6-8.30 Av 3 course à la carte £30 🍴: 🍺: Youngs, Fuller's London Pride, Bombardier. ♀: 8

Nags Head
Plan 1 B2

53 Kinnerton St SW1X 8ED ☎ 020 7235 1135
Whether or not it really is London's smallest pub - and it could easily be - the Nag's Head is definitely compact and bijou. In a quiet mews near Harrods, its front and back bars, connected by a narrow stairway, both serve the full Adnams range. Favourites include real ale sausages with mash and beans, steak and mushroom pie, shepherd's pie and chilli con carne, supplemented by roasts and specials, such as pork, turkey and cranberry pie.
OPEN: 11-11 (Sun 12-10.30) **BAR MEALS:** L served all week 11-9.30 D served all week Av main course £7 ⊕: Free House ◀: Adnams Best, Broadside, Fisherman & Regatta. **NOTES:** No credit cards

The Orange Brewery ♀
Plan 1 C1

37-39 Pimlico Rd SW1 W8NE ☎ 020 7730 5984
Dir: Nearest tube: Sloane Square or Victoria
The name comes from local associations with Nell Gwynne, a 17th-century purveyor of oranges and a favourite of Charles II. The building dates from 1790, and fronts onto an appealing square. Beers are brewed in the cellar, including SW1, SW2 and Pimlico Porter, and regulars will find a different guest beer every month. Expect traditional pub food; steak, Guinness and suet pudding, chicken curry, or scampi and chips are favourites.
OPEN: 11-11 (Sun 12-10.30, bar food all day) 24 Dec Close at 6 **BAR MEALS:** L served all week 11.30-9.30 D served all week Av main course £6 ⊕: ◀: Theakston Best, Greene King IPA, Old Speckled Hen, Bombadier. ♀: 16 **FACILITIES:** Dogs allowed

The Wilton Arms
Plan 1 B2

71 Kinnerton St SW1X 8ED ☎ 020 7235 4854 ◫ 020 7235 4895
e-mail: wilton@shepherd-neame.co.uk
Dir: Telephone for directions
Early 19th-century pub named after the 1st Earl of Wilton but known locally as 'The Village Pub'. It is adorned with flower-filled baskets and window boxes, and a conservatory covers the old garden. Inside, high settles and bookcases create individual seating areas, all air-conditioned. Real ales and home cooking are served, including a selection of daily specials, all-day dishes (bangers and mash; smoked salmon platter) and favourites like burgers and fish and chips.
OPEN: 11-11 Sun (12-10.30) **BAR MEALS:** L served Mon-Sat 12-3.45 D served Mon-Fri 5.30-10 No food Sun ⊕: Shepherd Neame ◀: Spitfire, Holsten, Orangeboom, Bishops Finger.

SW3

Pick of the Pubs

The Admiral Codrington 🐟 ♀
Plan 1 B2

17 Mossop St SW3 2LY ☎ 020 7581 0005 ◫ 020 7589 2452
e-mail: admiralcodrington@longshotplc.com
Dir: Telephone for directions
No prizes for guessing what this pub is popularly known as locally - yes, of course, The Cod. And, perhaps not surprisingly, one of the equally popular main dishes is The Admiral's Cod. Although this old Chelsea pub was given a complete makeover that resulted in a smart new look when it re-opened, it still retains a relaxed and homely feel. The bar has large sofas for you to flop in while enjoying a good ale or wine. The emphasis is on serving quality food in comfortable surroundings, and the restaurant is bright and warm, with a large skylight to let the sun in on the bare wooden floor. Food is well turned

out modern British fare - expect tasty home-made delights like linguini of Cornish crab; crispy salmon and smoked haddock fishcake; aromatic steamed seabass; and beer battered plaice. Virtually all the well-chosen wines are available by the glass.
OPEN: 11.30-11 (Sun 12-10.30) **BAR MEALS:** L served all week 12-2.30 D served all week Av main course £11 **RESTAURANT:** L served all week 12-2.30 D served all week 7-10.30 Av 3 course à la carte £25 ⊕: Free House ◀: Stella, Heineken, Becks, Cobra. ♀: 20 **FACILITIES:** Garden: Beer garden/patio

The Builders Arms ♀
Plan 1 B1

13 Britten St SW3 3TY ☎ 020 7349 9040
e-mail: buildersarms@geronimo-inns.co.uk
Conveniently situated for rest and refreshment after shopping in the Kings Road, and close to St Luke's church, the Physic Garden and Chelsea Farmers' Market. Starters might include eggs Benedict; and crab and avocado tian; while seared salmon fillet, Builders Arms Cajun-spiced beefburger, and slow-roasted lamb shank feature as main courses. Popular terrace for alfresco enjoyment.
OPEN: 11-11 (Sun 12-10.30) 25 Dec 7-11 **BAR MEALS:** L served all week 12-3 D served all week 7-10 (Sat 12-3.30, Sun 12-4) **RESTAURANT:** L served all week 12-2.30 D served all week 7-9.45 Sat 12-3, Sun 12-4, 7-9.15 ♀: 16 **FACILITIES:** Dogs allowed water

Pick of the Pubs

The Coopers of Flood Street ♀
Plan 1 B1

87 Flood St, Chelsea SW3 5TB
☎ 020 7376 3120 ◫ 020 7352 9187
e-mail: drinks@thecoopers.co.uk
Dir: From Sloane Square tube station, straight onto Kings Road. Travel approx 1m W, opposite Waitrose supermarket, left and half way down Flood Street.
A quiet backstreet Chelsea pub close to the Kings Road and the river. Celebrities and the notorious rub shoulders with the aristocracy and the local road sweeper in the bright, vibrant atmosphere, while the stuffed brown bear, Canadian moose and boar bring a character of their own to the bar. Food is served here and in the quiet upstairs dining room, with a focus on meat from the pub's own organic farm. The fresh, adventurous menu also offers traditional favourites that change daily: seared king scallops and chorizo; grilled chicken, bacon, avocado and sunblushed tomato salad might precede chargrilled harissa lamb steak with Moroccan vegetable couscous; bangers and mash with onion gravy; and ricotta and spinach tortellini. Spotted dick with custard, and chocolate fudge cake with cream bring their own sweet pleasures. Good staff-customer repartee is always entertaining.
OPEN: 11-11 Closed: 25-26 Dec, 1 Jan & Good Friday **BAR MEALS:** L served all week 12.30-3 D served Mon-Sat 6.30-9.30 Not Sun evening Av main course £8 ⊕: Young & Co ◀: Youngs Special, Youngs Bitter, Winter Warmer, Seasonal Ales. ♀: 13 **FACILITIES:** Dogs allowed Dogs on a lead

Restaurant and Bar Meal times indicate the times when food is available. Last orders may be approximately 30 minutes before the times stated

continued

SW3 continued

SW4

Pick of the Pubs

The Cross Keys
Plan 2 E3
1 Lawrence St, Chelsea SW3 5NB
☎ 020 7349 9111 📠 020 7349 9333
e-mail: cross.keys@fsmail.net
Dir: Walking from Sloane Square, walk down Kings rd, turn left onto Old Church st, then left onto Justice Walk and then right
A fine Chelsea pub dating from 1765 which has been a famous bolthole for the rich and famous since the 1960s. The stylish interior includes a Bohemian-style banqueting room and open-plan conservatory, plus a restaurant and a first-floor gallery that is adorned with works of modern art. There is a modern European flavour to the menu, although Sunday is mainly traditional with some adventurous forays. The set meals offer good value around dishes likes smoked duck terrine, Toulouse sausages with mash, and date and pecan sponge pudding for lunch. Evening fare differs only in the extra choice on the carte: asparagus and broad bean risotto, or deep-fried Oriental samosas, followed by grilled marinated lamb steak, or baked tranche of cod with seafood linguine.
OPEN: 12-11 (Sun 12-10) Closed: Dec 25-26 Jan1, Easter Mon **BAR MEALS:** L served all week 12-3 D served all week 6-8 Av main course £14 **RESTAURANT:** L served Mon-Sun 12-3 D served Mon-Sun 7-11 Av 3 course à la carte £30 Av 0 course fixed price £17.50 🍽: 🍺: Courage Directors, John Smiths, Kronenberg 1664, Guiness.

The Crown at Chelsea ♀
Plan 1 A1
153 Dovehouse St, Chelsea SW3 6LB
☎ 020 7352 9505 📠 020 7352 9535
Dir: Just off Fulham Road, beside Royal Marsden Hospital
Traditional London pub located between the Royal Marsden and Brompton Hospitals. Popular with locals including celebrities and musicians who live in the area, it is known for its quality food and real ales. Big bites include lemon chicken supreme, and Hawaiian gammon, while lighter snacks come in the guise of filled potato skins, and baked potatoes. Daily specials also served.
OPEN: 11-11 (Sun 12-10.30) **BAR MEALS:** L served Mon-Fri 12-3 D served Mon-Fri 6-9.30 Av main course £6.95 **RESTAURANT:** 12-2.30 🍽: Enterprise Inns 🍺: Adnams Best, Fullers London Pride, Stella Artois, Carlsberg. ♀: 8

The Phene Arms
Plan 1 B1
Phene St, Chelsea SW3 5NY ☎ 020 7352 3294 📠 020 7352 7026
e-mail: info@phenearms.com
Dir: 200 yds from Kings Road.
Hidden away down a quiet Chelsea cul-de-sac, a short stroll from The Embankment, this welcoming neighbourhood pub has a charming roof terrace and large garden for summer alfresco eating. Food options range from Jerusalem salad, burgers and Cumberland sausage through to oven-baked cod and fillet steak.
OPEN: 11-11 (Sun 12-10.30) **BAR MEALS:** L served all week 12-4 D served Tue-Sun 4-10 Av main course £8 **RESTAURANT:** L served only avail. for large pre-booked groups D served all week 7-10 Av 3 course à la carte £22 🍽: Free House 🍺: Adnams Bitter Broadside, Guiness, Grolsch, Greene King Old Speckled Hen.
FACILITIES: Garden: Quiet fenced garden Dogs allowed
NOTES: Parking 2

Pick of the Pubs

The Belle Vue 🐾 ♀
Plan 2 E3
1 Clapham Common Southside SW4 7AA
☎ 0207 498 9473 📠 0207 627 0716
e-mail: sean@sabretoothgroup.com

An independently owned freehouse overlooking the 220 acres of Clapham Common, one of South London's largest green spaces. Free internet access makes it a great place to catch up on work or leisure pursuits, with a coffee, hot snack or some tapas-style nibbles close at hand. A daily changing bistro-style lunch and dinner menu specialises in fish and shellfish, such as pan-fried giant tiger prawns in Thai spices; grilled marlin steak with pepper sauce; dressed Cornish crab salad; and chef's special fish pie. Other possibilities are braised leg of rabbit; steak and kidney pie; Thai green chicken curry; and Mediterranean vegetarian lasagne. Sunday lunch is very popular, and in addition to all the regular roasts are fish and vegetarian dishes. The wine list features over 25 wines and champagnes by the glass, and Harvey's Sussex Bitter is the house real ale.
OPEN: 11-11 (Sun 12-10.30) Closed: 25-26 Dec
BAR MEALS: L served all week 12.30-3.30 D served all week 6.30-10 All day Sat-Sun Av main course £8.50 🍽: Free House 🍺: Harveys Sussex Bitter. ♀: 35

The Coach & Horses
Plan 2 E3
173 Clapham Park Rd SW4 7EX
☎ 020 7622 3815 📠 020 7622 3832
e-mail: info@barbeerian-inns.com
Dir: 5 mins walk from Clapham High Street and Clapham Common Tube
Despite its city location, this attractive coaching inn feels like a country pub. It draws a wide clientele, from locals to trendy young professionals. As the owner says: "Fine wines and Guinness sold in equal amounts." Good roast dinners make it particularly busy on Sundays, whilst Saturday is barbeque day. Samples from a specials board include chicken kebabs, marinated in lemon and fresh herbs with wild rice, warm pitta and coriander chutney; chunky vegetable stew with herb dumplings; or hearty fish pie with a puff pastry lid.
OPEN: 11-11 (Sun 12-10.30) Closed: 25-26 Dec
BAR MEALS: L served all week 12.30-2.30 D served all week 6-9.30 Sat 12.30-3, 6-9; Sun 12.30-5, 7-9 Av main course £7.50 🍺: London Pride, Adnams. **FACILITIES:** Garden: Large patio in front of pub seats 64 Dogs allowed Water bowls

The Royal Oak ⚲
Plan 2 E3

8-10 Clapham High St SW4 7UT ☎ 020 7720 5678
Dir: Telephone for directions
Set in the heart of Clapham, the Royal Oak is a traditional London pub that includes the modern tradition of a large screen TV for sporting events, and a funky gastro-pub interior that belies its rather drab exterior. A typical menu includes rib of English beef and horseradish, mushroom and tarragon sausage toad in the hole, and chicken and leek pie.
OPEN: 12-11 (Sun 12-10.30) **BAR MEALS:** L served all week 12-6 D served all week 6-10.30 Av main course £7 ⊕: ◖: Adnams Broadside, Adnams Bitter, Hoegarden. ⚲: 8 **FACILITIES:** Children's licence Dogs allowed

The Windmill on the Common ★★★ ⚲ Plan 2 E2
Clapham Common South Side SW4 9DE
☎ 020 8673 4578 ▤ 020 8675 1486
e-mail: windmillhotel@youngs.co.uk
Dir: 5m from London - Northern Line for tube and just off South Circular 205 where the 205 meets the A24 at Clapham.
The original part of this unusually-named pub was known as Holly Lodge and at one time was the property of the founder of Youngs Brewery. The varied menu offers such dishes as steak and ale pie, salmon fillet, lamb moussaka, chicken stir-fry with vegetables, bangers and mash, Thai fishcakes, and Windmill burger with bacon, cheese and onions.
OPEN: 11-11 (Sun 12-10.30) **BAR MEALS:** L served all week 12-3 D served all week 6-10 Sat 12-10, Sun 12-9 Av main course £7 ⊕: Young & Co ◖: Youngs Bitter, Guiness. ⚲: 17 **FACILITIES:** Children's licence Benches in outside area, not grassed Dogs allowed None **NOTES:** Parking 20 **ROOMS:** 29 bedrooms en suite s£99 d£115

SW6

Pick of the Pubs

The Atlas ⚲
Plan 2 D3

16 Seagrave Rd, Fulham SW6 1RX
☎ 020 7385 9129 ▤ 020 7386 9113
e-mail: theatlas@btconnect.com
Dir: 2mins walk from West Brompton underground
In a fashionable area of London where so many pubs have been transformed into trendy diners or restaurants, here is a hostelry that remains true to its cause. The large bar area - split into drinking and eating sections - attracts what in rural enclaves would be called outsiders, but to be a local here you can even come from Chelsea, Hammersmith or Hampstead. Dinner menus might feature pan-roast wild sea bass fillet and couscous salad with parsley, mint, red onion and lime zest and chilli yoghurt; Tunisian beef tagine with dates, pistachios, almonds, cumin and tomatoes, lemon rice with toasted coriander seed and parsley and mixed leaves; and grilled lamb chops with rosemary and lemon zest, roast garlic mashed potatoes with mustard seed, tomato and chilli jam. One of the few pubs in London to have a walled beer garden.
OPEN: 12-11 (Sun 12-10.30) Closed: 24 Dec-1 Jan, Easter **BAR MEALS:** L served all week 12.30-3 D served all week 7-10.30 (Sun 7-10) Av main course £10.50 ⊕: Free House ◖: Wells Bombardier, Fuller's London Pride, Brakspear, Adnams Broadside. ⚲: 13 **FACILITIES:** Garden: Large suntrap, heaters, awning

The Imperial ⚲
Plan 1 B1

577 Kings Rd SW6 2EH ☎ 020 7736 8549 ▤ 7731 3874
Dir: Telephone for directions
Mid 19th-century food pub in one of London's most famous and fashionable streets, with a paved terrace at the back. Vibrant and spacious inside, with wooden floors, striking features, and a lively and varied clientele. A selection of pizzas, sandwiches, salads, and burgers feature on the popular menu. Look out for the wild boar sausage with bubble and squeak.
OPEN: 11-11 Closed: BHs **BAR MEALS:** L served Mon-Sat 12-2.30 D served Mon-Fri 7-9.30 Av main course £6 ◖: Haggards Imperial Ale. ⚲: 8 **FACILITIES:** Garden: Paving, seven benches, plants, lights Dogs allowed

Pick of the Pubs

The Salisbury Tavern ⚲
Plan 2 D3

21 Sherbrooke Rd SW6 7HX
☎ 020 7381 4005 ▤ 020 7381 1002
e-mail: thesalisburytavern@longshotplc.com
Since this sister pub to Chelsea's famous Admiral Codrington opened in 2003, it has quickly established itself as one of Fulham's most popular bar-restaurants. Its elegantly simple, triangular bar and dining area, fitted out with high-backed banquettes as well as individual chairs, is given a lofty sense of space by a huge skylight. Modern European menus offer a great selection of snacks, such as ricotta and spinach ravioli; tempura squid and sweet chilli sauce; hand-cut chips with dipping sauce; and cocktail sausages with honey and wholegrain mustard dressing. More substantial are full, all-day English breakfast; home-made cottage pie; Scottish rib-eye burger with chips; and, on Sundays only, traditional roast beef, Yorkshire pudding and fresh market vegetables. On the main menu are crispy salmon and smoked haddock fishcakes; chargrilled swordfish; braised belly of pork; and the Salisbury's signature dish, fillet of beef Wellington (for two).
OPEN: 11-11 Closed: 24-26 Dec **BAR MEALS:** L served all week 12-2.30 D served all week 6-9 Av main course £12.50 **RESTAURANT:** L served all week 12-2.30 D served all week 7-11 Av 3 course à la carte £25 Av 3 course fixed price £17.50 ◖: Fullers Pride, Bombadier, Pilsner, Urqual. ⚲: 27 **FACILITIES:** Children's licence

SW6 continued

Pick of the Pubs

The White Horse ♀ — Plan 1 A1
1-3 Parson's Green, Fulham SW6 4UL
☎ 020 7736 2115 📠 020 7610 6091
e-mail: whitehorsesw6@btconnect.com
Dir: 140 mtrs from Parson's Green tube
This coaching inn has stood on this site since at least
1688, and has advanced impressively since then, with its
polished mahogany bar and wall panels, open fires and
contemporary art on the walls. A large modern kitchen
is behind the imaginative, good value meals served in
the bar and Coach House restaurant. For lunch, you
might try basil-infused seared tuna with Greek salad, or
pork sausages with mash, summer cabbage and beer
onion gravy. In the evening there might be smoked
salmon with avocado and a wasabi cream, or braised
lamb shank with preserved lemon couscous. Every dish
from the starters through to the desserts comes with a
recommended beer or wine, and the choice of both is
considerable.
OPEN: 11-11 (Sun 11-10.30) **BAR MEALS:** L served all week
11-3.30 D served all week 6-10.30 Av main course £8.25
RESTAURANT: L served all week 12-3.30 D served all week
6-11 Av 3 course à la carte £20 🍺: Adnams Broadside, Fullers
ESB, Harveys Sussex Best Bitter, Oakam JHB. ♀: 20
FACILITIES: Garden: 80 seats in front of pub overlooking Green
Dogs allowed

SW7

The Anglesea Arms ♀ — Plan 1 A1
15 Selwood Ter, South Kensington SW7 3QG
☎ 020 7373 7960 📠 020 7370 5611
e-mail: enquiries@angleseaarms.com
Dir: Telephone for directions
This pub has an interior little changed since 1827, though the
dining area has proved a popular addition with its panelled
walls and leather-clad chairs. The new head chef has
introduced exciting daily menus using seasonal produce.
Along with a varied choice of sandwiches might come Dorset
crab on sourdough bread; cepes and baby spinach fettuccine
with truffle oil; or Anglesea burger with gruyere and bacon.
Great London beers, including Fuller's London Pride.
OPEN: 11-11 (Sun 12-10.30) Closed: Xmas pm only
BAR MEALS: L served all week 12-3 D served all week 6.30-10
Sat-Sun 12-close Av main course £9 **RESTAURANT:** L served all
week 12-3 D served all week 6.30-10 Sat 12-10, Sun 12-9 Av 3 course
à la carte £19 🍺: Free House 🍺: Fuller's London Pride, Youngs
Bitter, Adnams Bitter, Broadside. ♀: 10 **FACILITIES:** Garden:
Terrace at front and side of the pub Dogs allowed Water

Pick of the Pubs

Swag and Tails ♀ — Plan 1 B2
10/11 Fairholt St SW7 1EG
☎ 020 7584 6926 📠 020 7581 9935
e-mail: theswag@swagandtails.com
web: www.swagandtails.com
See Pick of the Pubs on opposite page

SW8

The Masons Arms ♀ — Plan 2 E3
169 Battersea Park Rd SW8 4BT
☎ 020 7622 2007 📠 020 7622 4662
e-mail: themasonsarms@ukonline.co.uk
Dir: Opposite Battersea Park BR Station
More a neighbourhood local with tempting food than a
gastro-pub, the worn wooden floors and tables support
refreshingly delightful staff and honest, modern cuisine. Here
you'll find a warm and welcoming atmosphere, equally suited
for a quiet romantic dinner, partying with friends, or a family
outing. Open fires in winter and a summer dining terrace.
Daily changing menus feature escobar fillet with paw paw and
cucumber salad, pan-fried blackened tuna, and spinach and
duck spring roll.
OPEN: 12-11 (Sun 12.30-10.30) **BAR MEALS:** 12-3 6-10 (Sun
12.30-4, 6.30-9) Av main course £19 **RESTAURANT:** 12-3 6-10 Sun
12.30-4, 6.30-9.30 Av 3 course à la carte £19 🍺: Free House
🍺: Adnams. ♀: 12 **FACILITIES:** Garden: Food served outdoors,
cobbled patio Dogs allowed water bowls

SW10

Pick of the Pubs

The Chelsea Ram ♀ — Plan 2 E3
32 Burnaby St SW10 0PL ☎ 020 7351 4008 📠 020 7351 5557
Dir: Nearest tube - Earls Court
A busy neighbourhood gastro-pub located just off the
beaten track close to Chelsea Harbour and Lots Road. It
offers a distinct emphasis on fresh produce, including
market fish and meat from Smithfield. The set monthly
menu has a manifestly modern flavour, exemplified by
interesting and eclectic starters like smoked haddock and
potato tart, or salad of wood pigeon and quail's eggs.
Main dishes, which include special market selections from
the blackboard, range through braised lamb shanks with
olive oil mash, Chelsea Ram salad with grilled chicken,
bacon avocado and sour cream dressing, and bangers
and mash with roast field mushrooms and spinach. Baked
peppers are suitable for vegetarians, while Sunday roasts
might finish with puddings like glazed lemon tart with
lemon sorbet, and sticky toffee pudding.
OPEN: 11-11 (Fri 11-11, Sun 12-10.30) **BAR MEALS:** L served
all week 12-3 D served all week 6.30-10 Sun 12-3.30, 7-9.30
Av main course £10.50 **RESTAURANT:** L served all week 12-3
D served all week 6.30-10 Sun 12-3.30, 7-9.30 Av 3 course à la
carte £20 🍺: Young & Co 🍺: Youngs Bitter, Special & Winter
Warmer. ♀: 16 **FACILITIES:** Outside seating area at front
Dogs allowed

The Rosette is the AA award for food.
Look out for it next to a pub's name

Room prices show the minimum double and single
rates charged. Room rates in hotels and B&Bs
often vary depending on the facilities, so be sure to
check prices with the establishment before booking

Pick of the Pubs

Swag and Tails

It's hard to believe that this almost rustic, or as Annamaria Boomer Davies, the proprietor, puts it 'neighbourhood' pub is five minutes walk away from Harrods, Harvey Nichols, the V&A and Hyde Park. Obviously oblivious to the hustle and bustle around, this pretty flower-decked Victorian pub sits in a quiet back street off Knightsbridge.

Over the last fifteen years, the owners have created a successful and welcoming pub-restaurant with a discerning local trade. Real ales and good quality food are served in a warm, relaxing environment, with high standards of service by efficient staff. A decent wine list features a dozen wines by the glass - including champagne. Open fires, original panelling and pine tables complement the stripped wooden floors, whilst the windows with their attractive 'swag and tailed' curtains set the scene in which to savour freshly prepared seasonal dishes inspired by Mediterranean cuisine. Starters could include pan-seared foie gras with pear compote and spiced red wine reduction; and wok-fried squid with chillis and lime and a mizuna and mango salad. Seared fillet of gilt head bream with sweet potato mash, red pepper and tomato salsa; roast fillet of cod with braised puy lentil and vegetable fricassee; braised lamb shank with tomatoes and black olives; and slow roast duck's leg with orange, thyme and onions are among the main offerings. For simpler food, there are also choices like classic burger in a sesame bap; and sirloin steak on granary bread. White chocolate bavarois with poached blood oranges and a sesame tuille; date sponge pudding; and steamed lemon sponge with plum and honey ice cream might be hard to resist. A selection of teas, coffees and liqueurs provides a rounded choice.

OPEN: 11-11 Closed: all BHs
BAR MEALS: L served Mon-Fri 12-3 D served Mon-Fri 6-10 Av main course £12.95
RESTAURANT: L served Mon-Fri 12-3 D served Mon-Fri 6-10 Av 3 course à la carte £26.75
🍺: Free House
🍺: Adnams Bitter, Wells Bombardier Premium Bitter, Scottish Courage John Smiths Smooth. ♀: 13
FACILITIES: Dogs allowed in eve

⊚ ♀   Plan 1 B2
10/11 Fairholt St SW7 1EG
☎ 020 7584 6926
🖷 020 7581 9935
ⓔ theswag@swagandtails.com
ⓦ www.swagandtails.com
Dir: 4mins walk from Harrods

England

SW10 continued

Pick of the Pubs

The Hollywood Arms NEW ♀   Plan 1 A1
45 Hollywood Rd SW10 9HX
☎ 020 7349 7840 ▤ 020 7349 7841
e-mail: hollywood.arms@virgin.net
Dir: 1min from Chelsea and Westminster Hospital

The first balloon to successfully cross the channel was launched from this site, an unusual distinction for any pub. These days, tucked just off the buzz of Fulham and the Kings Road, it caters to a young, vibrant crowd, while still maintaining something of a traditional atmosphere. The frequently changing menus offer a smartly updated version of classic pub dishes: bangers, mustard mash and gravy; the delightfully named Chelsea Cowboy Brunch (a vast fry-up); pea and asparagus risotto with organic poached egg; and peppered tuna, bok choi and creamed potatoes. Desserts include a selection of home-made ice creams with Mars Bar sauce, and Granny Morrison's apple and thyme pie. There is plenty of organic produce and vegetarian options and, unusually for a city pub, all vegetables are carefully sourced from one farm.
OPEN: 4-11 (Sat-Sun 12-11) **BAR MEALS:** L served Sat-Sun 12-3 D served all week 7-10 Sun 12-8 Av main course £10
RESTAURANT: L served Sat-Sun 12-3 D served all week 7-10 Sun 12-8 ◖: Guinness, London Pride. ♀: 11
FACILITIES: Dogs allowed

Pick of the Pubs

Lots Road Pub and Dining Room NEW ♀ Plan 2 E3
114 Lots Rd, Chelsea SW10 0RJ
Situated at the heart of Chelsea's bustle, the light, spacious chic of Lots Road has been gaining platitudes from far and wide. This is just the establishment the term gastro-pub was coined for - a smart, comfortable, well-designed space which segues smoothly between jaunty bar area and the more secluded and grown-up restaurant. Slate grey and cream walls and wooden tables create a pared-down feel, and attentive staff are set on making you feel comfortable. There's an excellent wine list, and cocktails both quirky and classic. The menu changes daily, and offers plenty of imaginative, modern dishes. Start with the likes of cod fish cakes; or red onion, pepper and mozzarella tart; before tucking into slow cooked pork belly with grilled herb polenta; or braised lamb shank on dauphinoise potatoes. Puddings are delightfully rich - think brownies with chocolate ice cream - and the more restrained will enjoy cheeses served with Bath Olivers.

OPEN: 11-11 **BAR MEALS:** L served all week 12-10.30 D served all week 12-10.30 Sun 12-10 Av main course £10
RESTAURANT: L served all week 12-10.30 D served all week 12-10.30 Sun 12-10 Av 3 course à la carte £20 ◖: Wadworth 6X, London Pride, Adnams, Guinness. ♀: 28 **FACILITIES:** Dogs allowed Bowl

The Sporting Page   Plan 1 A1
6 Camera Place SW10 0BH ☎ 020 7349 0455 ▤ 020 7352 8162
e-mail: sportingpage@frontpagepubs.com
Dir: Telephone for directions
A smart Chelsea pub in a quiet side street, all varnished wood and sporting scenes. Apparently it sells more Bollinger than any other pub in the country, but then given its King's Road/Fulham Road catchment area, it would. Modern British food includes grilled tuna with celeriac skordalia, platter of smoked fish with summer salad, Cumberland sausages with spring onion mash, and the locally renowned Chelsea burger. The large screen TV explains why it's popular with ticketless Chelsea fans.
OPEN: 11-11 (Sun 12-10.30) Closed: 25-26 Dec
BAR MEALS: L served all week 12-2.30 D served Mon-Fri 7-10
◖: Front Page Pubs Ltd ◖: Shepherd Neame Spitfire Premium Ale, Charles Wells Bombardier, Fuller's London Pride.
FACILITIES: Garden: terrace Dogs allowed

SW11

The Castle ♀   Plan 2 E3
115 Battersea High St SW11 3HS
☎ 020 7228 8181 ▤ 020 7924 5887 e-mail: thecastle@tiscali.co.uk
Dir: Approx 10min walk from Clapham Junction
Built in the mid-1960s to replace an older coaching inn, this ivy-covered pub tucked away in 'Battersea Village', has rugs and rustic furnishings on bare boards inside, and an outside enclosed patio garden. A typical menu offers fresh salmon and dill fishcakes; Cajun chicken sandwich; organic lamb steak; and fresh swordfish steak with avocado salsa.
OPEN: 12-11 (Sun 12-10.30 Good Friday 12-10.30) Closed: 25-26 Dec **BAR MEALS:** L served all week 12-3 D served all week 7-9.45 Sun lunch 12.30-4.30 dinner 6-9.30 Av main course £8.50 ◖: Young & Co ◖: Youngs Bitter & Special, Goddard's Winter Warmer. ♀: 13
FACILITIES: Garden: Patio at back of pub with 6 tables Dogs allowed **NOTES:** Parking 6

Duke of Cambridge ♀   Plan 2 E3
228 Battersea Bridge Rd SW11 3AA
☎ 020 7223 5662 ▤ 020 7801 9684
e-mail: info@geronimo-inns.co.uk
An award-winning community pub with an eclectic mix of locals and just a stone's throw from Battersea Park and two of London's most famous Thames crossings - Battersea Bridge and Albert Bridge. Popular Saturday brunch menu and traditional Sunday roasts. The interesting range of dishes includes bacon wrapped venison steaks, sea bass fillet with pesto and tomato roulade, and chicken breast stuffed with mushrooms. The Duke of Cambridge supports the Haven trust breast cancer support centres by making a donation every time one its designated dishes, which are healthy and carcinogen free, is sold.
OPEN: 11-11 **BAR MEALS:** L served all week 12-2.30 D served all week 7-9.45 Sun 12-4 Av main course £9.50
RESTAURANT: L served all week 12-3 D served all week 7-9.45 Sun 6-9.30 Av 3 course à la carte £16 ◖: Young & Co ◖: Youngs Bitter & Special, Stella, Fosters, Guiness. ♀: 14 **FACILITIES:** Garden: Beer garden, patio, food served outdoors, BBQ Dogs allowed

continued

England

The Fox & Hounds ♀   Plan 2 E3
66 Latchmere Rd, Battersea SW11 2JU
☎ 020 7924 5483 ▤ 020 7738 2678
e-mail: foxandhoundsbattersea@btopenworld.com
*Dir: From Clapham Junction left down St John's Hill, up Lavender Hill, left
at the 1st lights into Latchmere Rd. Pub is 200 yds on left.*
A late 19th-century free house, restored rather than
refurbished, with a walled garden, extensive patio planting
and a covered and heated seating area. Fresh ingredients
are delivered daily from London's markets, and the
Mediterranean-style menu changes accordingly. Start,
perhaps, with parsnip, celery and gorgonzola soup before
moving on to smoked salmon salad; pan-fried pork chops;
or fettuccine with roast sweet peppers. Warm pear and
hazelnut tart with cream is amongst the desserts.
OPEN: 12-3 5-11 (Sat 12-11, Sun 12-10.30, Mon 5-11) Closed: Easter
Day, 24 Dec- 1 Jan **BAR MEALS:** L served Tue-Sun 12.30-3
D served all week 7-10.30 🍽: Free House 🍺: Interbrew Bass,
Harveys Sussex Best Bitter, Fullers London Pride. ♀: 12
FACILITIES: Garden: Walled garden, covered area with heaters

SW13

The Bull's Head ♀   Plan 2 D3
373 Lonsdale Rd, Barnes SW13 9PY
☎ 020 8876 5241 ▤ 020 8876 1546
e-mail: jazz@thebullshead.com
Facing the Thames and established in 1684, the Bull's Head has
become a major venue for mainstream modern jazz and blues.
Nightly concerts draw music lovers from far and wide, helped
in no small measure by some fine cask-conditioned ales, over
200 wines, and more than 80 malt whiskies. Traditional home-
cooked meals are served in the bar, with dishes ranging from
haddock and crab to a variety of roasts and pies. Popular
home-made puddings. An intrinsic feature of the pub is the
Thai menu, available throughout the pub in the evening.
OPEN: 11-11 (Sun 12-10.30) Closed: 25 Dec **BAR MEALS:** L served
all week 12-3 D served all week 6-11 Av main course £5
RESTAURANT: D served all week 6-11 🍽: Young & Co
🍺: Young's Special, Bitter, Winter Warmer. ♀: 32
FACILITIES: Garden: Patio Dogs allowed

SW18

Pick of the Pubs

The Alma Tavern NEW ♀   Plan 2 E3
499 Old York Rd, Wandsworth SW18 1TF
☎ 020 8870 2537 ▤ 020 8488 6603
e-mail: drinks@thealma.co.uk
Dir: Opposite Wandsworth town rail station
Step off the train at Wandsworth Town and you can't
(indeed, shouldn't) miss this pub/brasserie/restaurant
built around 1900. Standing imposingly on a corner,
surmounted by a dome, at street level its shiny green wall
tiles are punctuated only by the door. The bright and airy
central bar can be all things to all people: a civilised place
for a frothing morning cappucino, a soup with crusty
French bread, a plate of barbecued peri peri sardines, or
a pint of Young's. In the terracotta-coloured restaurant an
all day menu (that changes every couple of months)
offers rabbit and mustard stew with parsley and pancetta
dumplings; spiced chickpea and coriander cakes; Alma
burger with brie, bacon and fries; and herb-baked
butterfly sea bass. Aficionados say it is the place for a
fantastic breakfast at the weekend.

continued

OPEN: 10-11 (Sun 12-10.30) Closed: 26 Dec
BAR MEALS: L served all week 12-10 D served all week 7-10
Av main course £8.75 **RESTAURANT:** L served all week 12-10
D served all week 7-10 Av 3 course à la carte £16 🍽: Young &
Co 🍺: Youngs Bitter, Youngs Special, Youngs Winter warmer,
Youngs guest/seasonal ales. ♀: 12

Pick of the Pubs

The Freemasons NEW ♀   Plan 2 E3
2 Northside, Wandsworth Common SW18 2SS
☎ 020 7326 8580 ▤ 020 7223 6186
e-mail: info@freemasonspub.com

The aim of this stylish, popular pub is to get back to
basics: to provide excellent, affordable food while
maintaining all the ambiance of the friendly local. To
judge by the response, it's something the denizens of
Wandsworth have been longing for. The space has been
considered well, and with details like a round, black
walnut bar, an open kitchen, modern art on the walls and
plenty of sofas to settle into, it's clearly a million miles
from the chain-pub. Both food and drink are taken
seriously, and there's a lengthy, eclectic wine list as well
as daily changing menus. Kick off with fresh Asian squid
and glass noodle salad; and move on to grilled minted
lamb steak with pepperonata, red wine jus and tsatziki.
There's plenty of Mediterranean-style snacks for the
smaller appetite; perhaps houmous with Turkish bread; or
rocket and parmesan salad.
OPEN: 12-11 (Sun 12-10.30) Closed: 25-26 Dec, 1 Jan
BAR MEALS: L served all week 12.30-3 D served all week
6.30-10 Sun 12.30-4, 6.30-9.30 Av main course £10.50
RESTAURANT: L served all week 12.30-3 D served all week
6.30-10 Sun 12.30-4, 6.30-9.30 Av 3 course à la carte £20
🍺: Timothy Taylor, Tiger Ale, Guinness. ♀: 20
FACILITIES: Garden benches in front Dogs allowed Water

The Old Sergeant   Plan 2 D2
104 Garrett Ln, Wandsworth SW18 4DJ
☎ 020 8874 4099 ▤ 020 8874 4099
Traditional, friendly and oozing with character, The Old
Sergeant enjoys a good reputation for its beers, but also
offers some good malt whiskies. It's a good place to enjoy
home-cooked food too: the menu could include salmon fish
cakes with a sweet chili sauce, duck and orange sausages with
coriander mash and gravy, or Thai fishcakes. One of the first
pubs bought by Young's in the 1830s.
OPEN: 11-11 (12-10.30 Sun) **BAR MEALS:** L served all week
12-2.30 D served all week 7-10 (all day Sun) Av main course £7.50
RESTAURANT: L served Mon-Fri D served Mon-Fri 🍽: Youngs
🍺: Youngs Ordinary, Youngs Special. **FACILITIES:** Garden: Dogs
allowed dog bowl

England

SW18 continued

The Ship Inn ♀   Plan 2 E3
Jew's Row SW18 1TB ☎ 020 8870 9667 ▤ 020 8874 9055
e-mail: drinks@theship.co.uk
Dir: *Wandsworth BR station nearby. On S side of Wandsworth Bridge*
Situated next to Wandsworth Bridge on the Thames, the Ship
exudes a lively, bustling atmosphere. The saloon bar and
extended conservatory area lead out to a large beer garden,
and in the summer months an outside bar is open for
business. There is a popular restaurant, and all-day food is
chosen from a single menu, with the emphasis on free-range
produce from the landlord's organic farm. Expect the likes of
lamb cutlets, chargrilled marlin fillet, shepherds pie, and
peppers stuffed with hazelnuts and goats cheese.
OPEN: 11-11 (Sun 11-10.30) **BAR MEALS:** L served all week 12-10
D served all week 7-10.30 Sun 7-10 Av main course £9
RESTAURANT: L served all week 12-10.30 D served all week Sun
12-10 Av 3 course à la carte £18 ⊕: Young & Co ◖: Youngs: PA,
SPA, Waggle Dance, Winter Warmer. ♀: 15 **FACILITIES:** Garden:
Food served outside Dogs allowed Water provided

SW19   Map 06 TQ27

The Brewery Tap ♀   Plan 2 D2
68-69 High St, Wimbledon SW19 5EE ☎ 020 8947 9331
e-mail: thebrewerytap@hotmail.com
Small, cosy one-room pub, big on sports like football, rugby
and cricket. It is also the closest pub to the Wimbledon tennis
championships. Breakfast is served till 12.30pm, and snacks
take in wooden platters, sandwiches and salad bowls. More
substantial lunches are hot salt beef, and bangers and mash
(with veggie sausage alternative). The only evening food is
tapas on Wednesday. Special events are held for Burns' Night,
Bastille Day etc.
OPEN: 11-11 (Sun 11-10.30, 25 Dec 12-2) **BAR MEALS:** L served
all week 11-2.30 Av main course £7.50 ⊕: Enterprise Inns
◖: Fuller's London Pride, Adnams, Guest Beers. ♀: 13
FACILITIES: Dogs allowed Water

W1

The Argyll Arms ♀   Plan 1 C4
18 Argyll St, Oxford Circus W1F 7TP ☎ 020 7734 6117
Dir: *Nearest tube - Oxford Circus*
A tavern has stood on this site since 1740, but the present
building is mid-Victorian and is notable for its stunning floral
displays. There's a popular range of sandwiches and the hot
food menu might offer vegetarian moussaka, beef and
Guinness pie, chicken and leek pie, and haddock and lasagne.
OPEN: 11-11 (Sun 12-10.30) Closed: 25 Dec **BAR MEALS:** L served
all week 11-10 D served all week (Sun 11-9) Av main course £6.95
RESTAURANT: L served All day Sun 12-9 ⊕: ◖: Tetley, Bass,
Fullers London Pride, Greene King IPA & Guest Beers. ♀: 15

French House ♀   Plan 1 D4
49 Dean St, Soho W1D 5BG ☎ 020 7437 2477 ▤ 020 7287 9109
Small but very historic pub which has stayed much as it was
in the 1950s when the likes of Dylan Thomas, Francis Bacon
and Brendan Behan, as well as many other colourful actors,
artists and writers, used it as a regular haunt. President De
Gaulle supposedly wrote a famous speech in the restaurant.
Weekly-changing menu might include pheasant, crepenette of
slow-cooked venison, wild turbot, and suckling pig with black
pudding, apple sauce and celeriac.
OPEN: 11-11 (Sun 12-10.30) Closed: 25 Dec **BAR MEALS:** L served
Mon-Sat 12-3 No food Sun Av main course £5
RESTAURANT: L served Mon-Sun 12-3 D served Mon-Sat 5.30-11
Av 3 course à la carte £25 ⊕: Courage ♀: 22

Red Lion   Plan 1 C3
No 1 Waverton St, Mayfair W1J 5QN
☎ 020 7499 1307 ▤ 020 7409 7752
e-mail: gregpeck@redlionmayfair.co.uk
Dir: *Nearest tube - Green Park*
Built in 1752, The Red Lion is one of Mayfair's most historic
pubs. Originally used mainly by 18th-century builders, the
clientele is now more likely to be the rich and famous of
Mayfair, yet the friendly welcome remains. The pub was used
as a location in the recent Brad Pitt and Robert Redford
movie, *Spy Game*. The bar menu has a traditional pub feel,
offering the likes of steak and stilton pie, Cumberland
sausage, chicken masala, rack of pork ribs, and steak
sandwich. Piano music on Saturday nights.
OPEN: 11.30-11.20 Closed: 25-26 Dec, 1 Jan **BAR MEALS:** L served
all week 12-2.30 D served all week 6-9.45 **RESTAURANT:** L served
all week 12-2.30 D served all week 6-9.45 Av 3 course à la carte £25
⊕: ◖: Greene King IPA, London Pride/Bombadier, Youngs Ordinary,
Marstons Pedigree

Zebrano   Plan 1 C3
14-16 Gantan St W1V 1LB ☎ 020 7287 5267 ▤ 020 7287 2729
e-mail: info@freedombrew.com
Dir: *5 min walk from Oxford Circus Tube*
The second of the Fulham-based Freedom Brewing
Company's new micro-brew bars, this popular watering hole
opened in 1999, taking advantage of the growing demand for
fresh, hand-crafted beer. The bar sells a range of six ales, as
well as offering a varied choice of freshly prepared salads,
sandwiches, tortilla wraps and main dishes. Expect fish and
chips, baked chicken with steamed greens, Thai spiced
mussels, and lamb steak with grilled vegetables.
OPEN: 11-11 (Thu-Sat 11-12) Closed: 25-26 Dec, 1 Jan
BAR MEALS: L served Mon-Sat 12-5 D served Mon-Sat 6-10
Av main course £6.50 ⊕: ◖: Freedom Beers.

England

W2

Pick of the Pubs

The Cow 🐟 ♀   Plan 2 D4
89 Westbourne Park Rd W2 5QH
☎ 020 7221 5400 🖹 020 7727 8687
e-mail: thecow@btconnect.com
Dir: Nearest tubes - Royal Oak & Westbourne Park
Once known as the Railway Tavern, the pub was
reputedly renamed after a former landlady with attitude.
An equally plausible explanation is that drovers and their
livestock passed this way headed east to London's
Smithfield Market. Whatever, 'eat heartily and give the
house a good name' is the sound philosophy of the pub,
which specialises in oysters, Guinness and Cuban cigars.
Seafood figures strongly, and a seafood platter for two
includes native and rock oysters, whole crab, prawns,
clams, whelks and winkles. Other favourites are the Cow
fish stew, and grilled razor clams with chilli, garlic and
parsley. Alternatively, try blackboard specials like lamb's
kidney, black pudding and mustard sauce, or slow
roasted belly of Old Spot pork with wild mushrooms.
Arrive early for a good table (preferably in the upper
dining room) as it gets very busy. Drinks include Fuller's
beers on tap and some fairly priced wines.
OPEN: 12-11 Closed: 25 Dec **BAR MEALS:** L served all week
12-3.30 D served all week 6-10.30 Av main course £12
RESTAURANT: L served Sat-Sun 12.30-3.30 D served all week
6.30-10.30 🍷: Free House 🍺: London Pride, Guiness,
Hoegarden, Budvar. ♀: 10

The Prince Bonaparte ♀   Plan 2 D4
80 Chepstow Rd W2 5BE ☎ 020 7313 9491 🖹 020 7792 0911
A first-generation gastro pub where Johnny Vaughan filmed
the Strongbow ads. Renowned for its Bloody Marys, good
music and quick, friendly service, the pub proves popular with
young professionals and has DJ nights on Fridays and
Saturdays. The building is Victorian, with an airy and open
plan interior. Typical meals include sausages and mash,
tomato and mozzarella bruschetta, sea bass with spinach, and
spicy chicken gnocchi.
OPEN: 12-11 (Close 10.30 Sun) Closed: 25-26 Dec, 1 Jan
BAR MEALS: L served all week 12.30-3 D served all week 6.30-10
Av main course £8.50 **RESTAURANT:** L served all week 12.30-3
D served all week 6.30-10 (Sun 6.30-9) Av 3 course à la carte £20
🍷: Bass 🍺: Fullers London Pride, Staropramen, Caffreys. ♀: 13

The Westbourne ♀   Plan 2 D4
101 Westbourne Park Villas W2 5ED
☎ 020 7221 1332 🖹 020 7243 8081
*Dir: On corner of Westbourne Pk Rd and Westbourne Pk Villas - 2min
drive form Portobello Rd*
Classic Notting Hill pub/restaurant favoured by bohemian
clientele, including a sprinkling of celebrities. Sunny terrace
is very popular in summer. Tempting, twice-daily-changing
menu is listed on a board, and might include baked filo roll
with butternut squash, ricotta, sage & nutmeg ; pot roasted
pheasant with bacon, shallots, oyster mushrooms, garlic
mash & winter greens; or fillet of seabass baked with
lentils, chicory, thyme, white wine & Vermouth.
OPEN: 12-11 (Mon 5-11 only, Sun 12-10.30) Closed: 24 Dec-2 Jan
BAR MEALS: L served Tue-Sun 12.30-3.30 D served all week 7-10.15
Fri-Sun 7-9.30 Av main course £12 **RESTAURANT:** L served
Tues-Sun 12.30-3.30 D served all week 7-10.15 Fri-Sun 7-9.30
Av 3 course à la carte £22 Av 2 course fixed price £10.50 🍷: Free
continued

House 🍺: Leffe, Warsteiner, Hoegaarden, Old Speckled Hen.
FACILITIES: Garden: Large terrace with tables & chairs Dogs
allowed Water

W4   Map 06 TQ27

Pick of the Pubs

The Devonshire House ◉ ♀   Plan 2 C3
126 Devonshire Rd, Chiswick W4 2JJ
☎ 020 8987 2626 🖹 020 8995 0152
e-mail: info@thedevonshirehouse.co.uk
Dir: 150yds off Chiswick High Road. 100 yds from Hogarth rdbt & A4
"Laid back and unpretentious" perfectly describes
London's latest gastro-pub The Devonshire House, which
is located in the quiet leafy district of Chiswick. Previously
the Manor Tavern, the Devonshire House was extensively
refurbished and transformed in 2003 by its two new
owners (who have Marco Pierre White on their CVs) to an
attractive, light and airy bar and restaurant. The menu is
an interesting mix of modern British and Mediterranean
dishes, and changes daily depending upon what fresh
produce is available. Lunch is a casual affair, divided into
starters, brunches, main courses and desserts; and dinner
is served predominantly à la carte. Start perhaps with
cappuccino of mushroom soup with white truffle oil; or
home-cured beef bresola with Italian salad. Move on to
sauté baby plaice with Montpellier butter; rib-eye of
Scottish beef with sauté haricot beans; or roast fillet of
wild bass with braised gems and artichoke. Puddings
might include steamed chocolate sponge with chocolate
sauce; and Bakewell tart with fresh double cream.
OPEN: 12-12 (Sun 12-11.30) Closed: 25 Dec, 1 Jan,
BAR MEALS: L served Tue-Sun 12-2.30 D served Tue-Sun
7-10.30 (Sun 12-3.30) Av main course £12.50
RESTAURANT: L served Tue-Sun 12-2.30 D served Tue-Sun
7-10.30 (Sun 12-3.30) Av 3 course à la carte £24.40
🍺: Hoegaarden, Guinness. ♀: 17 **FACILITIES:** Children's
licence Garden: Terraced courtyard with trees, heating

The Pilot ♀   Plan 2 C3
56 Wellesley Rd W4 4BZ ☎ 020 8994 0828 🖹 020 8994 2785
e-mail: the.pilotpub@ukonline.co.uk
Dir: Telephone for directions
A large garden makes this Chiswick pub a real winner,
especially in summer, while indoors the atmosphere is always
friendly and welcoming. The new licensee, while not ignoring
more traditional fare, has introduced an exciting menu which
includes pan-seared bison with sweet potato, spring onion
hash and red wine jus; steamed barracuda on jasmine rice
cooked in Asian crab broth with pak choi; and stuffed baby
squid with wild rice and chorizo on tomato, anchovy and
caper sauce.
OPEN: 12-11 (Sun 12-10.30) Closed: 25-27 Dec, 1 Jan
BAR MEALS: L served Mon-Sun 12-3.30 D served Mon-Sun 6.30-10
(Sun 12.30-4, 6.30-9.30) Av main course £9.50
RESTAURANT: L served all week 12-3.30 D served all week 6.30-10
Av 3 course à la carte £18.50 🍺: Adnams, Staropramen ♀: 10
FACILITIES: Garden: Large garden, capacity for 60 seated

> Pubs with Red Diamonds are the top
> ♦ places in the AA's three, four and five
> diamond ratings

329

England

W5

The Red Lion ♀
Plan 2 C3
13 St Mary's Rd, Ealing W5 5RA
☎ 0208 5672541 🗎 0208 840 1294
e-mail: red.lionealing@bt.click.com
Dir: Telephone for directions
The pub opposite the old Ealing Studios, the Red Lion is
affectionately known as the 'Stage Six' (the studios have five),
and has a unique collection of film stills celebrating the Ealing
comedies of the 50s. Sympathetic refurbishment has
broadened the pub's appeal, and the location by Ealing Green
has a leafy, almost rural feel, plus there's an award-winning
walled garden. Pub food ranges through oysters, burgers,
bangers and mash, and fillet steak.
OPEN: 11-11 (Sun 12-10.30) **BAR MEALS:** L served all week
12-2.30 D served Mon-Sat 7-9.30 ⊕: Fullers ◀: Fullers London
Pride, Chiswick, ESB, Stella Artois. ♀: 50 **FACILITIES:** Garden:
Walled Garden, can seat 60 Dogs allowed Water

The Wheatsheaf ♀
Plan 2 C4
41 Haven Ln, Ealing W5 2HZ ☎ 020 8997 5240
Dir: 1m from A40 junct with North Circular
Just a few minutes from Ealing Broadway, this large Victorian
pub has a rustic appearance inside. Ideal place to enjoy a big
screen sporting event or a warm drink among wooden floors,
panelled walls, beams from an old barn, and real fires in
winter. Traditional pub grub includes cottage pie; beer
battered cod and chips; steak, ale and mushroom pie; pork
and leek sausage and mash; and vegetable lasagne.
OPEN: 11-11 (Sun 12-10.30) **BAR MEALS:** L served all week 12-9
D served Mon-Sat Sun 12-5 Av main course £6.25 ⊕: Fullers
◀: Fullers London Pride, ESB & Chiswick, Seasonal ales. ♀: 10
FACILITIES: Garden: Side alleyway Dogs allowed

W6

Pick of the Pubs

Anglesea Arms ⊛ ♀
Plan 2 D3
35 Wingate Rd W6 0UR ☎ 020 8749 1291 🗎 020 8749 1254
e-mail: angleseaarms@hotmail.com
Real fires and a relaxed, smokey atmosphere are all part
of the attraction at this traditional corner pub. Behind the
Georgian façade the decor is basic but welcoming, and
the place positively hums with people eagerly seeking out
the highly reputable food. A range of simple, robust
dishes might include starters like pigeon, duck and foie
gras terrine, Anglesea charcuterie platter and butternut
squash and goats' curd risotto. Among main courses
could be slow-cooked belly of pork, Brittany 'Cotriade'
fish stew, pot-roast stuffed saddle of lamb, and toasted
sea bass with saffron potatoes. Puddings are also
exemplary: expect poached pear, brandy snap and pear
sorbet; chocolate, pecan and hazelnut 'brownie' cake with
vanilla ice cream; or perhaps buttermilk pudding with
pineapple and almond biscotti. A savoury alternative
might be Cornish yarm with chutney and water biscuits.
OPEN: 11-11 (Sun 12-10.30) Closed: 24-31 Dec
BAR MEALS: L served all week 12.30-2.45 D served all week
7-10.45 Sun lunch 12.30-3.30, Dinner 7-10.15 Av main course
£11.50 **RESTAURANT:** L served all week 12.30-2.45 D served
all week 7-10.45 Sun lunch 12.30-3.30, dinner 7-10.15 Av 3 course
à la carte £20 Av 3 course fixed price £12.95 ⊕: Free House
◀: Greene King Old Speckled Hen, Fuller's London Pride.
♀: 15 **FACILITIES:** Dogs (not in restauraunt)

The Stonemasons Arms ♀
Plan 2 D3
54 Cambridge Grove W6 0LA ☎ 020 8748 1397 🗎 020 8846 9636
e-mail: stonemasons@ukonline.co.uk
Trendy, welcoming London gastro-pub with wooden floors
and trestle tables, serving modern, honest British cuisine.
Sample such delights as home-made fish pie with salad;
poached smoked haddock with crème fraîche and parmesan
sauce, roast new potatoes and watercress salad; grilled beef
burger with hummus, salad and chips; and hoi sin chargrilled
leg of lamb steak with sautéed spinach. Extensive wine list.
OPEN: 12-11 (Sun 12-10.30) Closed: Dec 25, Jan 1
BAR MEALS: L served Mon-Fri 12-3 D served all week 6.30-10 Sat
12.30-3.30, 6.30-10. Sun 12.30-3.30, 6.30-9.30 Av main course £9.25
RESTAURANT: L served Mon-Fri 12-3 D served all week 6.30-10 Sat
12.30-3.30, 6.30-10. Sun 12.30-3.30, 6.30-9.30 Av 3 course à la carte
£20 ⊕: Free House ◀: Adnams, Marstens Pedigree. ♀: 16
FACILITIES: Food served outdoors

Pick of the Pubs

The Thatched House ♀
Plan 2 D3
115 Dalling Rd W6 0ET ☎ 020 8748 6174 🗎 020 8563 2735
e-mail: thatchedhouse@establishment.ltd.uk
This trendy sister pub to the Chelsea Ram, the Thatched
House, in a leafy Hammersmith backwater, is not
thatched at all - nor do the Mediterranean-style features
of a 'modern British' menu evoke the English countryside.
Cosmopolitan gastro-pub fare delivers monthly changing
menus of freshly prepared modern dishes. Expect the
likes of roasted red pepper soup, seared scallops with
ginger and stir-fried vegetables, and American-style
doughnuts with coffee cream and chocolate sauce. The
popular English breakfast salad is borrowed from Gary
Rhodes: grilled black pudding and sausage with bacon
and poached egg on crisp salad leaves. There is a full
range of Youngs' beers on tap plus some 20 wines-by-
glass on the list. The pub also acts as a gallery for artists'
as the walls are decorated with paintings for sale.
OPEN: 11-11 (Sun 12-10.30) **BAR MEALS:** L served all week
12-3 D served all week 6-10 Av main course £9
RESTAURANT: L served all week 12-2.30 D served all week
7-10 Av 3 course à la carte £22 ⊕: Young & Co ◀: Youngs
Bitter, Special & Guest beer. **FACILITIES:** Garden: Food served
outside Dogs allowed

W8

The Churchill Arms ♀
Plan 2 D3
119 Kensington Church St W8 7LN ☎ 020 7727 4242
Dir: Off A40 (Westway). Nearest tube-Notting Hill Gate
Thai food is the speciality at this traditional 200-year-old pub,
with strong emphasis on exotic chicken, beef, prawn and pork
dishes. Try Kaeng Panang curry with coconut milk and lime
leaves, or Pad Priew Wan stir-fry with sweet and sour tomato
sauce. Oriental feasts notwithstanding, the Churchill Arms has
many traditional British aspects including oak beams, log fires
and an annual celebration of Winston Churchill's birthday.
OPEN: 11-11 (Sun 12-10.30) **BAR MEALS:** L served all week
12-9.30 D served Mon-Sat Av main course £5.85
RESTAURANT: L served all week 12-9.30 D served Mon-Sat Av fixed
price £5.85 ⊕: Fullers ◀: Fullers London Pride, ESB & Chiswick
Bitter & seasonal ales. ♀: 12 **FACILITIES:** Garden: converted to
conservatory, food served Dogs allowed (water)

The Scarsdale NEW ♀   Plan 2 D3
23A Edwardes Square, Kensington W8 6HE
☎ 020 7937 1811 📠 020 7938 2984
A 19th-century, free-standing local with a stone forecourt
enclosed by railings, just off Kensington High Street. The
Frenchman who developed the site was supposedly one of
Bonaparte's secret agents. There's so much about this place,
not least its intriguing mix of customers, that ensures you
don't forget which part of London you are in. The food is
modern European and highly praised, but the stupendous
Bloody Marys are the real talking point.
OPEN: 12-11 (Sun 12-10.30) Closed: 25-26 Dec
BAR MEALS: L served all week 12-10 D served all week 12-10 Sun
12-9 **RESTAURANT:** L served all week 12-2.30 D served all week
6-10 Sun 12-3, 6-9 Av 3 course à la carte £23 🍺: London Pride, Old
Speckled Hen, Youngs, Greene King IPA. ♀: 20
FACILITIES: Garden: Stone forecourt with tables, chairs, heaters
Dogs allowed **NOTES:** No credit cards

The Windsor Castle ♀   Plan 2 D4
114 Campden Hill Rd W8 7AR ☎ 0207 243 9551
Dir: From Notting Hill Gate tube station take south exit towards Holland
Park, left opposite Pharmacy
Built around 1830, this pub takes its name from the royal
castle, which could once be seen from the upper-floor
windows. Unchanged for years, it boasts oak panelling and
open fires, and is reputedly haunted by the ghost of Thomas
Paine, author of The Rights of Man, whose bones are
allegedly buried in the cellar. A good variety of food is served
in the bar, from speciality sausages and mash, to salads,
sandwiches, snacks like half-a-dozen oysters, and lamb with
roasted vegetables.
OPEN: 12-11 (Sun 12-10.30) **BAR MEALS:** L served all week 12-4
D served all week 5-10 Sat 12-10, Sun 12-9 Av main course £8
🍺: 🍺: Staropramen, Timothy Taylor Landlord, Fullers London Pride,
Adnams Broadside. ♀: 10 **FACILITIES:** Garden: Ivy covered walled
garden, seating, bar(summer) Dogs allowed Dog Bowl

W9

The Waterway NEW ♀   Plan 2 D4
54 Formosa St W9 2JU ☎ 020 7266 3557 📠 020 7266 3547
e-mail: olly&tridge@thebury.co.uk
Trendy Maida Vale restaurant and bar in a canal-side setting.
The bar is a great place to relax with its comfy sofas and open
fires, and there is an interesting choice of drinks, including
cocktails and champagne by the glass. The restaurant menu
might offer citrus cured organic salmon; apple glazed confit
pork belly with caraway creamed savoy cabbage, grain
mustard and mashed potatoes; and pain perdue with black
figs, port and bay leaf.
OPEN: 12-11 **BAR MEALS:** L served all week 12.30-3.30 D served
all week 6.30-10.15 Sun 12.30-4, 7-9.45 Av main course £13
RESTAURANT: L served all week 12.30-3.30 D served all week
6.30-10.15 Sun 12.30-4, 7-9.45 Av 3 course à la carte £21
🍺: Guinness, Hoegaarden. ♀: 10 **FACILITIES:** Garden: Dogs

W10

Golborne Grove ♀   Plan 2 D4
36 Golborne Rd W10 5PR ☎ 020 8960 6260 📠 020 8960 6961
Dir: R out of the station onto Ladbroke Grove, 1st left up to Portobello Rd.
Left at Portobello Rd and follow road until Golborne Res. Turn R
Popular gastro-pub at the north end of Notting Hill, with a
ground floor bar and private function room upstairs. Photos
of local architecture, 1920's Venetian mirrors and squashy
60's sofas contribute to an appealing interior. In addition to

continued

the choice of beers, there's a cocktail menu and a reasonable
wine list. Typical dishes are chargrilled organic rib-eye steak
with rustic fries and salad, and pan-fried fillet of Atlantic
halibut with roasted butternut squash.
OPEN: 12-11 (Sat 12-12, Sun 12-10.30) Closed: 25-26 Dec, 1 Jan
BAR MEALS: L served all week 12.30-3.45 D served all week
6.30-10.15 Av main course £11.50 **RESTAURANT:** L served all week
12.30-3.45 D served all week 6.30-10.15 Av 3 course à la carte £25
🍺: Free House 🍺: Fuller's London Pride. ♀: 10
FACILITIES: Child facs Dogs allowed

The North Pole ♀   Plan 2 D4
13-15 North Pole Rd W10 6QH
☎ 020 8964 9384 📠 020 8960 3774
e-mail: northpole@massivepub.com
Dir: 2 mins off A40 White City 10 mins walk from White City tube station.
Turn R, past BBC Worldwide, R at 2nd traffic lights, 200yds on R.
A modern gastro-pub with large windows and bright decor.
Expect leather sofas, armchairs, daily papers, a good range of
wines by the glass and a lively atmosphere in the bar.
Separate bar and restaurant menus continue to show real
interest, and dishes are modern and simply described. 'Small
Plates' may include seared scallops with pineapple salsa,
chicken Caesar salad and rocket and parmesan salad. 'Main
Flavours' include rib-eye steak with roasted potatoes and
asparagus risotto.
OPEN: 12-11 (Sun 12-10.30) **BAR MEALS:** L served all week 12-3
D served all week 6-9.30 Sun Lunch 12-4 Dinner 6-9.30 Av main
course £10 **RESTAURANT:** L served all week 12-3 D served all week
6-9.30 Av 3 course à la carte £20 🍺: Free House 🍺: Bombadier.
♀: 13 **FACILITIES:** Dogs allowed None

Pick of the Pubs

Paradise by Way of Kensal Green ♀   Plan 2 D4
19 Kilburn Ln, Kensal Rise W10 4AE
☎ 020 8969 0098 📠 020 8960 9968
e-mail: paradise.bywayof@virgin.net
A truly eclectic pub atmosphere with bare boards, bric-à-
brac, oriental tapestries and wrought iron chandeliers
creating a Bohemian setting for working artists, musicians
and actors. The unusual name derives from the last line
of G K Chesterton's poem 'The Rolling English Road', and
there are plenty of original Victorian features in keeping
with its late 19th-century origins. The food at this lively
venue stands up well to the demands placed on it by
weekly live jazz and special events like weddings, but
don't expect bar snacks or too much flexibility. The self-
styled gastro-pub serves classy food from the carte, such
as parma ham with rocket and roasted figs, or crispy fried
squid salsa to start, followed by monkfish and mussels in
a creamy garlic sauce with linguine, and Moroccan spiced
haddock with roast vegetable couscous.
OPEN: 12-11 (Sun 12-10.30) Closed: 25 Dec & Jan 1
BAR MEALS: L served all week 12-4 D served all week 7.30-11
Av main course £12 **RESTAURANT:** L served all week 12.30-4
D served all week 7.30-11 (Sun 12.30-9) Av 3 course à la carte
£20 Av 2 course fixed price £18 🍺: Free House 🍺: Shepherds
Neame Spitfire, Hoegarden, Stella Artois. ♀: 8
FACILITIES: Children's licence Garden: Courtyard Dogs
allowed Water provided

W11

Pick of the Pubs

The Ladbroke Arms ♀   Plan 2 D4
54 Ladbroke Rd W11 3NW
☎ 020 7727 6648 📠 020 7727 2127
e-mail: enquiries@ladbrokearms.com
One of London's trendiest districts is the location of this pub, close to Holland Park and fashionable Notting Hill, renowned for its street market, chic restaurants and film location image. A broad spectrum of regulars, including the young well-heeled, is drawn to the chatty atmosphere, and seating areas which encompass the popular front courtyard and a split-level dining area to the rear. The menu changes daily, and offers imaginative but not outlandish choices: confit tuna with garlic lentils, soft boiled egg and bottarga, or prawns wrapped in betel leaves (Miang Gung) to start perhaps, then linguini with sweet tomato and basil, or pan-fried salmon with proscuitto, pea and mint risotto. Don't leave without trying banana cake with mascarpone sorbet and custard, or blood orange and chocolate parfait.
OPEN: 11-11 (Sat-Sun 12-11) Closed: Dec 25
BAR MEALS: L served all week 12-2.30 D served all week 7-9.45 (Sat-Sun 12-3) Av main course £12.50
RESTAURANT: D served Same as bar 🍺: Free House
🍺: Greene King & Abbot Ale, Fuller's London Pride, Adnams.
FACILITIES: Dogs allowed

The Pelican ♀   Plan 2 D4
45 All Saints Rd W11 1HE ☎ 020 7792 3073 📠 020 7792 1134
e-mail: thepelican@btconnect.com
Built as a pub in 1869, The Pelican organic pub is spread over two floors and has a ground floor bar with outside seating on All Saints Road. There's a wide choice of real ales and over 50 organic wines; upstairs, the dining room is bright, with a view of the working kitchens. The menu changes twice daily. Typical choices include crab and parsley risotto, grilled swordfish, and roast lamb chump.
OPEN: 12-11 Closed: Dec 25&26 Rest: Mon Closed morning
BAR MEALS: L served all week 12-4 D served all week 6-10 Av main course £7 **RESTAURANT:** L served Tues-Sun 12.30-3 D served all week 6.30-10.30 🍺: Free House 🍺: Bombadier, plus guests. **FACILITIES:** Dogs allowed

W14   Map 02 XX00

Pick of the Pubs

The Cumberland Arms ♀   Plan 2 D3
29 North End Rd, Hammersmith W14 8SZ
☎ 020 7371 6806 📠 020 7371 6848
e-mail: thecumberlandarmspub@btconnect.com
Mellowed furniture, stripped floorboards and large windows are the staple features at this popular and very spacious gastro-pub close to Olympia. The Cumberland Arms reopened as an independent establishment in 2002, and since then it has built up a good reputation as a London boozer frequented by local residents and office workers. Even beer and food critics have been known to grow rather fond of the place. Menus offer a daily-changing selection of Italian, Spanish and North African dishes, with lighter fare including tapas, risottos and pastas. Main courses are typified by the likes of grilled

rib-eye steak with grilled sweet potato, beetroot and red onion salad with salsa fresca; and pan-roasted mackerel fillets with paprika, couscous salad with apricot and cucumber, spring onion and coriander yoghurt.
OPEN: 12-11 Closed: 23 Dec-2 Jan **BAR MEALS:** L served all week 12.30-3 D served all week 7-10.30 Sun 12.30-3, 7-10
RESTAURANT: L served all week 12.30-3 D served all week 7-10.30 Sun 12-3.30, 7-10 🍺: Hoegaarden, London Pride, Deuchars Caledonian. ♀: 12 **FACILITIES:** Garden: 12 wooden tables, tiled courtyard Dogs allowed Water

Pick of the Pubs

The Havelock Tavern ♀   Plan 2 D4
57 Masbro Rd, Brook Green W14 0LS
☎ 020 7603 5374 📠 020 7602 1163
Dir: Nearest tubes: Shepherd's Bush & Olympia
Unlike some gastropubs, which cynics have been known to say are just restaurants in old pub buildings, The Havelock is still run very much as a boozer - but with the good food. It has been under the same ownership/management team since 1996, the year it re-opened in its current guise. In West Ken's flatland, midway between Shepherd's Bush Green and Olympia, this typical street-corner, yellow-brick London pub is popular with lunchtime customers who want a quick one-course meal before returning to work. In the evenings, when it gets busy again, it recognises the needs of those wanting to eat more substantially with a reasonably priced, ever-rolling two/three course menu. Typically, there's wild mushroom risotto with rocket, parmesan & truffle oil; slow roast belly of pork with mash and red cabbage; pan-fried sea trout with spinach; chargrilled Bavette steak; or roast chump of lamb, green beans, red lentil Dhal and minted yoghurt; and always at least one vegetarian starter and main course.
OPEN: 11-11 (Sun 12-10.30) Closed: Xmas 5 days
BAR MEALS: L served all week 12.30-2.30 D served all week 7-10 Sun 12-3, 7-10 Av main course £9.50 🍺: Free House 🍺: Brakspear, Marston's Pedigree, Fuller's London Pride. ♀: 11
FACILITIES: Garden: Small walled garden, pergola **NOTES:** No credit cards

WC1

Pick of the Pubs

Cittie of Yorke ♀   Plan 1 E4
22 High Holborn WC1V 6BN
☎ 020 7242 7670 📠 020 7405 6371
A pub has stood on this site since 1430. In 1695, it was rebuilt as the Gray's Inn Coffee House and the large cellar bar dates from this period. The panelled front bar features an original chandelier and portraits of illustrious locals, including Dickens and Sir Thomas More. In addition to a variety of sandwiches, salads and soups, six hot dishes are freshly prepared each day.
OPEN: 11.30-11 (Closed Sun) Closed: Dec 25-26
BAR MEALS: L & D served all week 12-9 Av main course £5 🍺: Samuel Smith 🍺: Samuel Smith Old Brewery Bitter.

♀ 7   Number of wines by the glass

continued

England

Pick of the Pubs

The Lamb ℞   Plan 1 E4
94 Lamb's Conduit St WC1N 3LZ ☎ 020 7405 0713
This building was first recorded in 1729, was 'heavily improved' between 1836-1876, and frequented by Charles Dickens when he lived nearby in Doughty Street (now housing the Dickens Museum). This really is a gem of a place, with its distinctive green-tiled façade, very rare glass snob screens, dark polished wood, and original sepia photographs of music hall stars who performed at the nearby Holborn Empire. The absence of television, piped music and fruit machines allows conversation to flow, although there is a working polyphon. Home-cooked bar food includes a vegetarian corner (vegetable curry, or burger), a fish choice including traditional fish and chips; and steaks from the griddle, plus pies and baked dishes from the stove. Favourites are steak and ale pie (called the Celebration 1729 pie); sausage and mash; liver and bacon; and fried egg and chips. For something lighter, try a ploughman's or a vegetable samosa.
OPEN: 11-11 (Sun 12-4, 7-10.30) **BAR MEALS:** L served all week 12-2.30 D served Mon-Sat 6-9 No dinner Sun Av main course £6.50 ⊕: Young & Co ◖: Youngs (full range). ℞: 13 **FACILITIES:** Garden: Patio with benches and out-door heaters Dogs allowed Water bowl

The Museum Tavern   Plan 1 D4
49 Great Russell St WC1B 3BA ☎ 020 7242 8987
Built long before the British Museum, which is just across the road, this historic inn first opened its doors in 1723. Real ales from the pump and wines by the glass. Food all day.
OPEN: 11-11 (Sun 12-10.30) **BAR MEALS:** L served all week 11-4 D served all week 5-10 Av main course £6.50 ◖: Fullers London Pride, Theakstons, Courage Directors. **NOTES:** No credit cards

The Perseverance ℞   Plan 1 E4
63 Lambs Conduit St WC1N 3NB
☎ 020 7405 8278 ▤ 020 7831 0031
A Central London haven of good food, fine wine and abundant conviviality. The elegant, candlelit dining room upstairs offers six starters: home-made gnocchi, courgettes and mussels, maybe, while mains might include gilt-head sea bream with globe artichokes, confit potatoes and red wine sauce, or daube of pork with cep casserole. Sunday lunch requires booking.
OPEN: 12-11 Closed: Xmas **BAR MEALS:** L served Sun-Fri 12.30-3 D served Mon-Sat 7-10 **RESTAURANT:** L served Sun-Fri 12.30-3 D served Mon-Sat 7-10 Av 3 course à la carte £25 Av 3 course fixed price £22 ⊕: ◖: Scottish Courage Courage Directors.

WC2

The Lamb and Flag ℞   Plan 1 D3
33 Rose St, Covent Garden WC2E 9EB
☎ 020 7497 9504 ▤ 020 7379 7655
Dir: Telephone for directions
Licensed during the reign of Elizabeth 1, the Lamb and Flag exudes a strong atmosphere, with low ceilings and high-backed settles both striking feaures of the bar. In 1679 the poet Dryden was almost killed in a nearby alley. These days office workers and Covent Garden tourists throng the surrounding streets. Typical examples of the varied menu include mince beef and onion pie with mash, cauliflower cheese, and toad in the hole.
OPEN: Mon-Thur 11-11 (Fri-Sat 11-10.45, Sun 12-10.30) Closed:
continued

25-26 Dec, Jan 1 **BAR MEALS:** L served all week 12-3 Sat-Sun 12-5 Av main course £4.95 ◖: Scottish Courage Courage Best & Directors, Young's PA & Special, Charles Wells Bombardier. ℞: 10

Pick of the Pubs

The Seven Stars   Plan 1 E4
53 Carey St WC2A 2JB ☎ 020 7242 8521
e-mail: nathansilver@btconnect.com
The Seven Stars, one of London's oldest public houses, was built in 1602, the last year of the reign of Elizabeth I. And the name might have given it its luck - because it survived the Great Fire of London in 1666, which destroyed nearly everything around. The Grade II listed building has two narrow rooms, complete with Irish linen lace curtains and a tiny Elizabethan staircase. Today it is near the Royal Courts of justice and is popular with litigants, barristers and reporters. This highly individual free house serves Adnams' and Harvey's ales, along with either Young's or Fuller's. The colourful landlady Roxy Beaujolais, author and television presenter, does all the cooking herself. The blackboard menu changes daily and the specials are well worth looking into. Delights on offer could include chargrilled sirloin and salad; lamb steak with barley; and roast chicken with warm bread salad. Lighter dishes include charcuterie with sourdough bread and a little pot of mustard, and elegant club sandwiches.
OPEN: 11-11 Closed: Bank Holidays **BAR MEALS:** L served all week 12-5 D served all week 5-9 Av main course £8 ⊕: Free House ◖: Adnams Best, Broadside, Fuller's London Pride, Harveys. **FACILITIES:** Dogs allowed Water
See Pub Walk on page 308

MERSEYSIDE

BARNSTON   Map 15 SJ28

Fox and Hounds ℞
Barnston Rd CH61 1BW ☎ 0151 6487685 ▤ 0151 648 0872
e-mail: ralphleech@hotmail.com
Dir: From M53 junct 4 take A5137 to Heswell. R to Barnston on B5138

Situated in the conservation area of Barnston, the decor of this pub is true to its origins, featuring an assortment of 1920s/1930s memorabilia - look out for the collection of police helmets! Much of the Edwardian building's character has been preserved, including pitch pine woodwork and leaded windows. Alongside a superb range of bar snacks - platters, baked potatoes and toasted ciabattas - daily specials might include beef pie, fish of the day or lasagne.
OPEN: 11-11 (Sun 12-10.30) **BAR MEALS:** L served all week 12-2 D served none Mother's Day and 1st Jan Av main course £5.75
continued

BARNSTON continued

☺: Free House ◀: Websters Yorkshire Bitter, Theakston, Best & Old Peculier, Marstons Pedigree & two guest beers. ♀: 12 **FACILITIES:** Garden: Lots of flowers & baskets Dogs allowed except at lunchtime **NOTES:** Parking 60

LIVERPOOL   Map 15 SJ39

Everyman Bistro ♀
9-11 Hope St L1 9BH ☎ 0151 708 9545 ▤ 0151 708 9545
e-mail: info@everyman.co.uk
Dir: Town centre. Bistro in basement of Everyman Theatre building, on Hope St. which runs between the two cathedrals
Situated beneath the famous Everyman Theatre, this has been Liverpool's best-known venue for 35 years. An eclectic mix of media folk, students and academics are attracted by the range of local and guest real ales, as well as by the high quality, low price menu. Fresh seasonal ingredients underpin main course dishes like warm sausage and potato salad; roast salmon fillet with gazpacho mayonnaise; and spinach and feta filo pie. **OPEN:** 12-12 (Thur-Fri 12-2, Sat 11-2) Closed: BHs **BAR MEALS:** L served Mon-Sat 10-5 D served Mon-Sat 5-11.30 Av main course £7.50 **RESTAURANT:** L served Mon-Sat 12-4 D served Mon-Sat 4 Av 3 course à la carte £12 ☺: Free House ◀: Cains, Black Sheep, Derwent Pale, Teachers Pet. ♀: 11

Ship & Mitre
133 Dale St L2 2JH ☎ 0151 236 0859 ▤ 0151 236 0855
e-mail: Dave@shipandmitre.co.uk web: www.shipandmitre.co.uk
Dir: 5mins from Moorfields Underground and Lime St Station
Award-winning pub in the heart of bustling Liverpool. Built in the art deco style of the 1930s and boasting the city's largest and most varied range of independent or micro-brewery ales; regular beer festivals. Choose something from the frequently-changing menu; perhaps chicken and mushroom pie or cassoulet. There is always a selection of sausages, provided by a local butcher, as well as at least three vegetarian options. **OPEN:** 11.30-11 (Sat 12-11, Sun 12.30-10.30) Closed: Dec 25-26, Jan 1 **BAR MEALS:** L served all week 11.30-2.30 D served all week 5-8 ☺: Free House ◀: Roosters, Salopian, Hyde's Mild, Hydes Miller. **FACILITIES:** Dogs allowed **NOTES:** No credit cards

ST HELENS   Map 15 SJ59

Pick of the Pubs

The Red Cat
8 Red Cat Ln WA11 8RU ☎ 01744 882422 ▤ 01744 886693
e-mail: redcat@amserve.net
Dir: From A580/A570 Junct follow signs for Crank
The Red Cat is reputedly linked to local witch Isobel Roby, who was executed in 1612. Witches often keep 'familiars' - small-time demons in the shape of domestic pets - and Roby's red cat was, of course, the colour associated with the devil! It will come as no surprise that the 700 year-old building is said to be haunted but, nowadays, the pub restaurant offers well-sourced, home-cooked food. Appetisers like Caesar salad with smoked chicken; Bury black pudding with bacon and pepper sauce; or salmon and parsley fishcakes herald a decent range of main course dishes. Expect slow roast lamb with rosemary gravy; wild Lune salmon with poached samphire and sorrel sauce; or hand-made noodles with roast vegetables with garlic bread and salad. Desserts like glazed summer berries with vanilla ice cream; or glazed figs with

mascarpone and maple syrup round off the meal.
OPEN: 12-11 (Sun 12-10.30) **BAR MEALS:** L served Wed-Sun 12-2 D served Wed-Sun 6-9.30 Av main course £8.95 **RESTAURANT:** L served Wed-Sun 12-2 D served Wed-Sun 6-9.30 ☺: Inn Partnership ◀: Carlsberg-Tetley Greenalls Bitter, Scottish Courage Theakston Best Bitter, Greene King Old Speckled Hen. **FACILITIES:** Dogs allowed Water **NOTES:** Parking 60

SOUTHPORT   Map 15 SD31

The Berkeley Arms NEW ♦♦
19 Queens Rd PR9 9HN web: www.berkeley-arms.com
Part of the Berkeley Arms Hotel, just off Southport's famous Lord Street. There are never fewer than eight real ales on sale at any one time here, which gives the pub a shrine-like status among beer drinkers. Bar meals are available only in the evenings, so when better to have one of the Berkeley's range of home-made pizzas, whose excellence is revered throughout West Lancashire.
OPEN: 12-11 **BAR MEALS:** D served Tues-Sun 5-9.30 Av main course £3.95 ◀: Adnams Southwold, Banks Bitter, Hawkshead Bitter, Sandgrounder. **FACILITIES:** Child facs Garden: Paved, south facing beer garden with seating Dogs allowed **NOTES:** Parking 9 **ROOMS:** 11 bedrooms en suite 1 family room s£25 d£50

NORFOLK

BAWBURGH   Map 13 TG10

Kings Head ♀
Harts Ln NR9 3LS ☎ 01603 744977 ▤ 01603 744990
e-mail: anton@kingshead-bawburgh.co.uk
Dir: From A47 W of Norwich take B1108 W
The charming King's Head, named after Edward VII, has been sitting on the banks of the restful Yare river since the 17th century. That such an old building survives, given its fabric of wood, horsehair and dung, is food for thought - but one best put aside in order to enjoy the real food. Start perhaps with Martini prawn, crayfish cocktail, pickled cucumber and lemon perhaps; Peruvian escabeche of whitebait with coriander, chillies and red onion; or rustic pork, pistachio, cranberry and fig terrine. Main courses include calves' liver with rich fava beans, pancetta, sausage, Chianti and oregano ragout; or crispy pork belly, spiced Puy lentils and gingery Asian greens. Finish with peach Melba and home-made vanilla ice cream; or hot chocolate fondant with vanilla mascarpone and kirsch cherries.
OPEN: 11.30-11 (Sun 12-10.30) Closed: 25-27 Dec(eve) 1 Jan(eve) **BAR MEALS:** L served all week 12-2 D served Tues-Sat 6.30-9.30 **RESTAURANT:** L served all week 12-2 D served all week 6.30-9.30 ☺: Free House ◀: Adnams, Woodforde's Wherry, Green King IPA, Courage Directors. ♀: 15 **FACILITIES:** Children's licence Garden: Secluded, landscaped garden with flower beds **NOTES:** Parking 100

 The Rosette is the AA award for food.
Look out for it next to a pub's name

Do you have a favourite pub that we have overlooked? Please use the Reader's Report form at the back of this guide to tell us all about it

continued

PUB WALK

Titchwell Manor Hotel
Titchwell - Norfolk

TITCHWELL MANOR HOTEL,
Titchwell, PE31 8BB
☎ 01485 210221
Directions: A149 (coast rd) between Brancaster & Thornham.
Attractive Victorian manor house particularly popular with families. Wonderful views of the beach, and next door to a famous RSPB reserve. Well known for seafood among other well-cooked meals.
Open: 11–11
Bar Meals: L served all week 12–2 D served all week 6.30–9.30
Restaurant Meals: L served all week 12–2 D served all week 6.30–9.30
Children welcome and dogs allowed.
Garden and parking available.
(for full entry see page 350)

Magnificent coastal views, abundant bird-life and Roman remains all add to the pleasure of this coastal walk.

From the hotel turn right along the A149 to a bridle path (Gipsy Lane) at the end of the village. The bank here is part of the local sea defences. Follow the right of way for about 0.75mile/1.2km to reach the beach by the Royal West Norfolk Golf Club. On the shore are the remains of trees that grew here some 6,000 years ago. Keep ahead along the beach, looking out for sandpipers, plovers and dunlin searching for food on the shoreline.

Turn right to join a road heading towards Brancaster and when you see the church and village buildings, turn left along the edge of reed beds, following the board walk to the National Trust harbour at Brancaster Staithe. Soon you reach redundant whelk sheds looking across to the nature reserve on Scolt Head Island, an important breeding ground. Fishermen supply Titchwell Manor with fresh crab,

lobster, mussels and oysters from this stretch of coast.

From the harbour walk inland to the A149 and turn right towards Brancaster village. There is a pavement here. The fields beside the road represent the site of an old Roman fort known as Branodunum from which Brancaster takes its name. The fort's walls were 11ft thick and backed by ramparts with a wide ditch. Branodunum was built to guard the approaches of The Wash and during the Roman Occupation it became a well-fortified base with naval patrols and a garrison for a cavalry regiment.

As well as offering stunning views of the sea, this final stretch of the walk reveals rows of picturesque cottages lining the road. Walk back to the hotel at Titchwell and you may be lucky enough to witness thousands of geese flying low overhead as they return from their feeding grounds to roost on the mud flats.

Distance: 5 miles (8km)
Map: OS Landranger 250
Terrain: Coastal - marshes and reedbeds.
Paths: Pavements, boardwalk (can be slippery after rain) and quiet coastal roadway
Gradient: Flat, no hills

Walk submitted and checked by Margaret Snaith of Titchwell Manor

BINHAM   Map 13 TF93

Chequers Inn
Front St NR21 0AL ☎ 01328 830297
e-mail: steve-thechequers@btconnect.com
Dir: *On B1388 between Wells-next-the-Sea & Walsingham*
Possibly dating back to the mid-16th century, the Chequers
Inn was originally a trade guildhall, with many stones from
the nearby priory used in its construction. The pub has the
unusual distinction of being owned by a village charity and
leased from them. The constantly changing menu offers a
range of starters and light meals, including smoked salmon
and whitebait. Main course options might be Cromer crab,
penne pasta, and Norfolk pork sausages with cream mash.
OPEN: 11.30-2.30 6-11 (Sun 12-2.30, 7-10.30)
BAR MEALS: L served all week 12-2 D served all week 6-9 Av main
course £9.50 **RESTAURANT:** L served all week 12-2 D served all
week 6-9 ☺: Free House ◖: Varying range of East Anglian beers
(approx. 80). **FACILITIES:** Garden: Beer garden, food served
outdoors **NOTES:** Parking 20

BLAKENEY   Map 13 TG04

The Kings Arms 🐟 ☺ ♀
Westgate St NR25 7NQ ☎ 01263 740341 ▤ 01263 740391
e-mail: kingsarms.blakeney@btopenworld.com
This grade II listed free house is located on the beautiful
North Norfolk coast, close to the famous salt marshes. The
Kings Arms is an ideal centre for walking, or perhaps a ferry
trip to the nearby seal colony and world-famous bird
sanctuaries. Locally-caught fish and seasonal seafood feature
on the menu, plus local game, home-made pies and pastas.
OPEN: 11-11 **BAR MEALS:** L served all week 12-9.30 D served all
week 12-9.30 Sun 12-9 ☺: Free House ◖: Greene King Old
Speckled Hen, Woodfordes Wherry Best Bitter, Marston's Pedigree,
Adnams Best Bitter. ♀: 12 **FACILITIES:** Child facs Garden: Very
safe large patio and grass area Dogs allowed Water
NOTES: Parking 10

Pick of the Pubs

White Horse Hotel 🐟 ☺ ♀
4 High St NR25 7AL ☎ 01263 740574 ▤ 01263 741303
e-mail: enquiries@blakeneywhitehorse.co.uk
Dir: *From A148 (Cromer to King's Lynn rd) take A149 signed
Blakeney.*

Blakeney is a pretty little spot, with narrow streets lined
with flint-built cottages running down to a small harbour.
This 17th-century coaching inn is set just 100 yards from
the tidal quay, with soothing watery views right outside.
Local bird colonies are waiting to be explored, and you
can while away the hours catching gilly crabs. Not

surprisingly, given this proximity to the sea, seafood is a
speciality, including lobster, whitebait, crab, mussels, sea
bass, Dover sole and sea trout. The house style leans
towards simplicity, making the most of fresh local
produce. Bar meal options range from filled ciabattas and
granary sandwiches to cockle chowder or Norfolk lamb
hotpot. The restaurant, overlooking a courtyard where the
stagecoaches once arrived, is served by a carte offering
Moroccan-spiced chicken breast with pickled lemon; or
grilled halibut with prawns.
OPEN: 11-3 6-11 (Sun 12-3, 7-10.30) Closed: 7-21 Jan
BAR MEALS: L served all week 12-2 D served all week 6-9
Av main course £10 **RESTAURANT:** D served all week 7-9
Av 3 course à la carte £27 ☺: Free House ◖: Adnams Bitter,
Adnams Broadside, Woodfordes Wherry, Woodfordes Nelson.
♀: 12 **FACILITIES:** Garden: Courtyard, picnic tables and
umbrellas **NOTES:** Parking 14

BLICKLING   Map 13 TG12

Pick of the Pubs

The Buckinghamshire Arms
Blickling Rd NR11 6NF ☎ 01263 732133
Dir: *From Cromer (A140) take exit at Aylsham onto B1354*

'The Bucks', a late 17th-century coaching inn by the gates
of Blickling Hall (NT), is Norfolk's most beautiful inn, say
its owners. Anne Boleyn's ghost is said to wander in the
adjacent courtyard and charming garden. The lounge bar
and restaurant, with their solid furniture and wood-
burning stoves, are appealing too. Meals can be taken in
either, with menus offering fresh local food served in both
traditional and modern ways, with starters such as brie
wedge in beer batter; baked crab; and Waldorf salad.
Sample main courses, all served with salad or vegetables,
new potatoes or chips, include venison with port and
blackberries; grilled whole lemon sole; home-made
lasagne; sautéed lambs' kidneys with Marsala; and
salmon and prawn tagliatelle. The Victorian cellar houses
real ales from Norfolk, Suffolk and Kent.
OPEN: 11.30-3 6.30-11.30 Sun 12-3, 7-10.30 Closed: 25 Dec
BAR MEALS: L served all week 12-2 D served all week 7-9
Av main course £8.95 **RESTAURANT:** L served all week 12-2
D served all week 7-9 Av 3 course à la carte £17.40 ☺: Free
House ◖: Adnams, Woodforde's. **FACILITIES:** Garden:
Sheltered garden & lawn, picnic tables Dogs allowed Water
NOTES: Parking 60 **ROOMS:** 3 bedrooms en suite s£45 d£75
(♦♦♦♦) No children overnight

continued

England

BRANCASTER STAITHE — Map 13 TF74

Pick of the Pubs

AA Seafood Pub of the Year for England 2005-06

The White Horse ★★ @ ⌐ ⌐ ☖ ♀
Main Rd PE31 8BY ☎ 01485 210262 ▤ 01485 210930
e-mail: reception@whitehorsebrancaster.co.uk
web: www.whitehorsebrancaster.co.uk
Dir: Mid-way between King's Lynn & Wells-next-the-sea on the A149

The view over the tidal marshes from the restaurant (and bedrooms) of this stylish dining pub are fantastic. Small boats are moored everywhere, some marooned on the mud, others upturned, looking for all the world like the Peggotty family's home in *David Copperfield*. Scrubbed pine tables, high-backed settles, an open log fire in winter and cream walls contribute to the bright, welcoming atmosphere. Adnams and Woodforde's real ales add to the relaxed ambience. The pub's enviable reputation is based partly on its fresh seafood, which can be enjoyed in the airy conservatory restaurant, the bar, or on the sun deck. Generally available, season permitting, are haddock chowder, lemon sole, sea bass, cod, local oysters and mussels, and smoked salmon and herring roes. In addition, there may be grilled pork and leek sausages and mash; rump of English lamb with sweet red onion confit and creamed leek tartlet; or garlic-creamed polenta with chargrilled vegetables.
OPEN: 11-11 (Sun 12-10.30) **BAR MEALS:** L served all week 12-2 D served all week Av main course £8.50
RESTAURANT: L served all week 12-2 D served all week 6.45-9 Av 3 course à la carte £24 ☖: Free House ☖: Adnams Best Bitter, Fullers London Pride, Woodfordes Nelsons Revenge, Woodfordes Wherry. ♀: 12 **FACILITIES:** Garden: Sun deck terrace overlooking tidal marshes Dogs allowed
NOTES: Parking 80 **ROOMS:** 15 bedrooms en suite 3 family rooms s£45 d£90 No children overnight

BRISTON — Map 13 TG03

The John H Stracey ♦♦♦ ♀
West End NR24 2JA ☎ 01263 860891 ▤ 01263 862984
e-mail: thejohnhstracey@btinternet.com

A 16th-century inn, renamed in the mid-1970s after the famous British welterweight champion, who used to spar with the then owner's son. Characterful interior, with log fire and knick-knacks. The wide choice of straightforward pub food includes ploughman's, sandwiches, 'lite bites', steaks cooked in various styles, home-made steak and ale pie, duck à l'orange, curries, pastas, scampi, lobster, Dover sole and

continued

salads. Vegetarian and children's selections too. Old Speckled Hen and Ruddles County in the bar.
OPEN: 11-2.30 6.30-11 (Sun 12-2.30 7-10.30)
BAR MEALS: L served all week 12-2 D served all week 6.30-9.30 Av main course £8 **RESTAURANT:** L served all week 12-2 D served all week 6.30-9.30 ☖: Free House ☖: Greene King Old Speckled Hen & IPA, Greene King Ruddles County,. **FACILITIES:** Garden: Bench tables on grass **NOTES:** Parking 30 **ROOMS:** 3 bedrooms 1 en suite s£26.50 d£53

BURNHAM MARKET — Map 13 TF84

Pick of the Pubs

The Hoste Arms ★★ @@ ⌐ ⌐ ♀
The Green PE31 8HD ☎ 01328 738777 ▤ 01328 730103
e-mail: reception@hostearms.co.uk
web: www.hostearms.co.uk
Dir: Signed off B1155, 5m W of Wells-next-the-Sea

A popular country dining pub and hotel, the Hoste Arms was originally built as a manor house in 1550. Over the centuries it has variously been a court house and livestock market, and did brisk trade for a period as a Victorian brothel. The inn was rescued in 1989 by its current owners, following 130 years of decline, and is now beautifully presented with striking interior design. There is a non-dining village bar, several interlinked dining areas, the first floor Gallery Restaurant, and a secret walled garden for outside eating and drinking. Specialities of the house are Burnham Creek oysters and Brancaster mussels, perhaps served steamed in white wine with cream. Other options range through beef burgers with crispy bacon, cheddar and relish; and fried squid with oriental salad and pomegranate and paprika syrup. Magnificent new toilet facilities have recently been installed, including a gossip area in the ladies'.
OPEN: 11-11 **RESTAURANT:** L served all week 12-2 D served all week 7-9 Av 3 course à la carte £27.50 ☖: Free House ☖: Woodforde's Wherry Best, Greene King Abbot Ale & IPA, Adnams Best Bitter, Adnams Broadside. ♀: 11
FACILITIES: Garden: Grassy area, seating for 100, outside heaters Dogs allowed Dog bowls, blanket if requested
NOTES: Parking 45 **ROOMS:** 36 bedrooms en suite 1 family room s£82 d£114 No children overnight

> Not all of the pubs in the guide are open all week or all day. It's always best to check before you travel

BURNHAM THORPE — Map 13 TF84

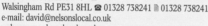

Pick of the Pubs

The Lord Nelson
Walsingham Rd PE31 8HL ☎ 01328 738241 🖷 01328 738241
e-mail: david@nelsonslocal.co.uk
web: www.nelsonslocal.co.uk

Built around 1637, this unspoilt gem was originally The Plough, but was renamed after England's most famous seafarer's victory at the Battle of the Nile in 1798. Our Horatio was born in the village rectory in 1758 and later used to eat and drink here, once treating villagers to a farewell dinner before returning to sea in 1792. Inside, the atmosphere is timeless, with huge high-backed settles, old brick floors and open fires. From the Suffolk brewery Woodforde's comes Nelson's Revenge (for what, we wonder), or you can sample 'Nelson's Blood' - a secret, rum-based concoction made on the premises. Lunchtime brings hot and cold sandwiches, salads, and light and not-so-light meals. Dinner might feature tempura of king prawns with sweet chilli basil sauce; red mullet with ratatouille sauce; or guinea fowl breast with braised red cabbage and Madeira. Families are warmly welcomed, and children will enjoy the huge garden with climbing frame, wooden play area and basketball net.
OPEN: 11-3 6-11 (Sun 12-3, 6.30-10.30 winter 12-2.30 Tue-Fri)
BAR MEALS: L served all week 12-2 D served Mon-Sat 7-9 closed Mon in winter Av main course £12.95
RESTAURANT: L served all week 12-2 D served Mon-Sat 7-9 closed Mon in winter Av 3 course à la carte £23.40 ⊕: Greene King ▣: Greene King Abbot Ale & IPA, Woodforde's Wherry, Nelsons Revenge, Old Speckled Hen (summer only). ♀: 11
FACILITIES: Child facs Very large garden seating, childrens play area, bbq Dogs allowed Water, No dogs in restauraunt
NOTES: Parking 30

CLEY NEXT THE SEA — Map 13 TG04

Pick of the Pubs

The George Hotel ◆◆◆◆
High St NR25 7RN ☎ 01263 740652 🖷 01263 741275
e-mail: thegeorge@cleynextthesea.com
See Pick of the Pubs on opposite page

All AA rated accommodation can also be found on the AA's internet site
www.theAA.com

COLKIRK — Map 13 TF92

The Crown ♀
Crown Rd NR21 7AA ☎ 01328 862172 🖷 01328 863916
e-mail: thecrown@paston.co.uk
Dir: 2m from B1146 Fakenham-Dereham rd

A quietly-located inn in a country village with plenty of enjoyable walks nearby. Open fires in winter, and a sunny terrace on warmer days make this a popular haunt with a lively atmosphere. The menu offers oriental tiger prawns and mushrooms, pan-fried chicken fillet, and various steaks, plus blackboard specials like fruity pork curry, chicken with stilton sauce, and fillet of salmon with lemon sauce.
OPEN: 11-2.30 6-11 **BAR MEALS:** L served all week 12-1.45 D served all week 7-9.30 Av main course £7.95
RESTAURANT: L served all week 12-1.45 D served all week 7-9.30
⊕: Greene King ▣: Greene King - IPA, Abbot Ale & guest beers.
♀: 25 **FACILITIES:** Garden; Dogs allowed **NOTES:** Parking 30

COLTISHALL — Map 13 TG21

Pick of the Pubs

Kings Head ♀
26 Wroxham Rd NR12 7EA
☎ 01603 737426 🖷 01603 736542
Dir: A47 Norwich ring road onto B1150 to North Walsham at Coltishall. Right at petrol station, follow rd to right past church, on right next to car park
This 17th-century free house stands on the banks of the River Bure, right in the heart of the Norfolk Broads. Hire cruisers are available at nearby Wroxham, and fishing boats can be hired at the pub. If you prefer to stay on dry land you'll find a warm welcome at the bar, with a range of real ales that includes Adnams Bitter, Directors and Marston's Pedigree. There's an inviting menu, too, served in both the bar and the non-smoking restaurant. Starters like smoked Scottish salmon with scrambled eggs; and potted chicken liver pâté with toasted focaccia precede an appetising choice of main courses. Try local rabbit in white wine and cream; potato mille feuille of wild mushrooms with Jerusalem artichokes and butter sauce; braised oxtail in Beaujolais; or wild sea bass with scallops. Desserts include poached pears in shortcake biscuits.
OPEN: 11-3 6-11 (Sun all day) Closed: 26 Dec
BAR MEALS: L served all week 12-2 D served all week 7-9 Av main course £7.50 **RESTAURANT:** L served all week 12-2 D served all week 7-9 Av 3 course à la carte £22.50 ⊕: Free House ▣: Adnams Bitter, Directors, Marston's Pedigree. ♀: 10
NOTES: Parking 20

Pick of the Pubs

CLEY NEXT THE SEA – NORFOLK

The George Hotel

Set within the beautiful and historic village of Cley-next-the-sea, not far from Cley's famous windmill, the George Hotel is a classic Edwardian Norfolk inn. A rambling country property full of character with a modern twist, it is located close to the sea and marshes. The first naturalist trust was formed here in 1926, and the area's wildlife reserves boast abundant bird life and local seal colonies.

The bar is fitted with solid oak floors and wood burner. The George has an excellent reputation for freshly prepared food made from the finest seasonal ingredients supplied from the local area. The dinner menu starts with steamed black mussels with black beans, garlic and coriander; pressed terrine of guinea fowl, duck livers and pigeon breast; salad of Cromer crab, avocado and pink grapefruit; and oysters served with lemon and tarragon olive oil. Mains include white bean and coriander sausage with tomato and basil; whole black sea bream baked with fresh herbs; Dijon peppered chicken with tagliatelle; steak, kidney and Guinness pudding served with potatoes and fresh vegetables. Puddings might be sticky toffee pudding; Eton mess; or honey and lavender crème brûlée.

OPEN: 11-3 6-11 (all day Apr-Oct & Bank Hols)
BAR MEALS: L served all week 12-2.30 D served all week 6.30-9 Av main course £10.95
RESTAURANT: L served all week 12-2.30 D served all week 6.30-9
🍺: Free House
🍺: Greene King IPA, Abbot Ale & Old Speckled Hen, Adnams Bitter, Woodforde's Wherry. ♀: 8
FACILITIES: Child facs Garden: Mature garden Dogs allowed
NOTES: Parking 15
ROOMS: 12 bedrooms en suite d£50

♦♦♦♦ 🐟 ♀ Map 13 TG04
High St NR25 7RN
☎ 01263 740652
🖺 01263 741275
📧 thegeorge@cleynextthesea.com
Dir: On A149 (coast road). Village centre

DEREHAM　　　　　　　　　　　Map 13 TF91

Yaxham Mill ◆◆◆ 🐾
Norwich Rd, Yaxham NR19 1RP
☎ 01362 851182 ▤ 01362 631482
e-mail: reservations@yaxhammill.com web: www.yaxhammill.com
A converted windmill in the middle of open Norfolk
countryside and dating back to 1810. The miller's house and
chapel have been transformed into a restaurant and bar with
two well-appointed guest rooms above. Menus cater for all
tastes, with grilled lemon sole, minted lamb steak, sweet and
sour chicken, and chilli con carne among other dishes. Home-
made pies, including steak and kidney and cottage, are
something of a speciality.
OPEN: 12-3 7-11.30 (Summer open all day)
BAR MEALS: L served Tue-Sun 12-2 D served all week 7-9 Av main
course £6.95 **RESTAURANT:** L served Tue-Sun 12-2 D served all
week 7-9 Av 3 course à la carte £12 🍺: Carlsberg, Tetley, guest ales.
FACILITIES: Garden: Lawn, picnic tables **NOTES:** Parking 40
ROOMS: 8 bedrooms en suite 2 family rooms s£40 d£60 No
children overnight

EATON　　　　　　　　　　　　Map 13 TG20

The Red Lion 🐾 ♀
50 Eaton St NR4 7LD ☎ 01603 454787 ▤ 01603 456939
Dir: Off the A11
A 17th-century coaching inn with lots of beams and plenty of
character. Dutch gables, panelled walls and inglenook
fireplaces add to the charm of the place. A covered terrace
enables customers to enjoy one of the real ales or sample the
extensive wine list alfresco during the summer months. The
extensive lunch menu offers everything from roast chicken
with smoked bacon and deep-fried North Sea skate, to fresh
fillet of Lowestoft plaice and Hungarian beef steak goulash.
OPEN: 11-3 6-11 (Sun 12-3, 7-10.30) **BAR MEALS:** L served all
week 12-2.15 D served all week 7-9 **RESTAURANT:** L served all
week 12-2 D served all week 7-9 🍺: Free House 🍺: Theakston
Bitter, Scottish Courage Courage Best, Courage Directors, Greene King
IPA. **FACILITIES:** Garden: Covered patio area & covered terrace
NOTES: Parking 40

ERPINGHAM　　　　　　　　　　Map 13 TG13

Pick of the Pubs

The Saracen's Head
NR11 7LZ ☎ 01263 768909 ▤ 01263 768993
e-mail: saracenshead@wolterton.freeserve.co.uk
web: www.saracenshead-norfolk.co.uk
*Dir: A140, 2.5m N of Aylsham, left through Erpingham, (pass Spread
Eagle on left) follow signs to Calthorpe. Through Calthorpe 1m on
right (in field) (do not bear right to Aldburgh)*
Those who know their Italian architecture will see how
the former coach house to Wolterton Hall, the Walpole
family seat, was modelled on a Tuscan farmhouse. In
warm and hearty Robert Dawson-Smith's hands for nearly
20 years, the Saracen's Head is known as north Norfolk's
'Lost Inn', standing as it does in the middle of nowhere.
No piped music, no fruit machines; indeed, no chips, peas
or scampi, just seasonally changing menus reflecting
Robert's enduring passion for "cooking up some of
Norfolk's most delicious wild and tame treats". A
blackboard-derived special could feature starters of crispy
fried aubergine with garlic mayonnaise; Saracent 'gamey'
pate; and lamb Bolognese tarts with pesto mayonnaise;

follow-up dishes might be baked Cromer crab with
mushrooms and sherry; roast Norfolk pheasant with
Calvados and cream; and roasted fennel with tomato and
goats' cheese. The delightful courtyard and walled garden
are open during the spring and summer.

The Saracen's Head

OPEN: 12-3 6-11.30 (Sun 12-3, 7-10.30) Closed: 25 Dec
BAR MEALS: L served all week 12.30-2 D served all week 7.30-9
Av main course £10.95 **RESTAURANT:** L served all week
12.30-2 D served all week 7.30-9 Av 3 course à la carte £23.25
🍺: Free House 🍺: Adnams Bitter, Woodforde's Wherry.
FACILITIES: Garden: Beautiful sheltered courtyard garden Dogs
allowed Water **NOTES:** Parking 50 **ROOMS:** 6 bedrooms
en suite 1 family room s£50 d£85 (◆◆◆◆) No children
overnight

FAKENHAM　　　　　　　　　　Map 13 TF92

The Wensum Lodge Hotel
Bridge St NR21 9AY ☎ 01328 862100 ▤ 01328 863365
e-mail: enquiries@wensumlodge.fsnet.co.uk
Dir: 20m from Norwich, 20m from Kings Lynn
Originally built around 1750 as the grain store to Fakenham
Mill, this privately-owned establishment opened as a
restaurant in 1983. It later became the Wensum Lodge Hotel,
taking its name from the river it overlooks. Friendly service
and quality home-cooked food, with two dozen wines to
choose from. The à la carte menu may start with warm bacon
and avocado salad, and continue with classic dishes like pork
tenderloin in mixed herbs, or peppered fillet of lamb.
Vegetarians are well catered for, with their own menu.
OPEN: 11-11 **BAR MEALS:** L served all week 11.30-3 D served all
week 6.30-9.30 (Sun 12-3, 6.30-9) Av main course £8
RESTAURANT: L served all week 11.30-3 D served all week
6.30-9.30 (Sun 12-3, 6.30-9) Av 3 course à la carte £25 🍺: Free
House 🍺: Greene King Abbot Ale & IPA, Old Mill Bitter, Carling.
FACILITIES: Garden: Small garden with stream **NOTES:** Parking 20
ROOMS: 17 bedrooms en suite 2 family rooms s£55 d£80 (★★)

The White Horse Inn ◆◆◆◆ 🐾
Fakenham Rd, East Barsham NR21 0LH
☎ 01328 820645 ▤ 01328 820645
e-mail: subalpine19@whsmith.net.co.uk
Dir: 1.5m N of Fakenham on the minor road to Little Walsingham.
Ideally located for birdwatching, walking, cycling, fishing, golf
and sandy beaches, this refurbished 17th-century inn offers en
suite rooms and a characterful bar with log-burning
inglenook. Good range of beers and malt whiskies. Fresh
ingredients are assured in daily specials, with fish especially
well represented. Typical choices include chicken breast
stuffed with stilton, peppered mackerel fillets, sweet and sour
pork, and venison steak. There is also a grill menu.

continued　　　　　　　　　　　　　　　*continued*

Birdwatching tours can be arranged. New owners.

The White Horse Inn

OPEN: 11.30-3 6.30-11 **BAR MEALS:** L served all week 12-2
D served all week 7-9.30 Av main course £9
RESTAURANT: L served all week 12-2 D served all week 7-9.30
🍴: 🍺: Adnams Best, Adnams Broadside, Tetley, Wells Eagle IPA.
FACILITIES: Child facs Garden: Patio area & enclosed courtyard
NOTES: Parking 50 **ROOMS:** 3 bedrooms en suite 1 family room
s£40 d£60

GREAT RYBURGH   Map 13 TF92

The Boar Inn

NR21 0DX ☎ 01328 829212 📠 01328 829421
Dir: Off A1067 4m S of Fakenham
The village, deep in rural Norfolk, has one of the county's
unusual round-towered Saxon churches. Opposite is the 300-
year-old Boar, dispensing a good variety of food, including
beef Madras with rice, sweet and sour chicken with noodles,
plaice fillet with prawns in mornay sauce, scallops, lemon sole,
and prime Norfolk steaks. Specials include skate wing with
garlic and herb butter, and wild boar steak with cranberry and
red wine jus. Bar/alfresco snacks and children's meals.
OPEN: 11-2.30 6.30-11 (All day 1 May-30 Sep)
BAR MEALS: L served all week 12-2 D served all week 7-9.30
RESTAURANT: L served all week 12-2 D served all week 7-9.30
Av 3 course à la carte £15 🍴: Free House 🍺: Adnams & guest ale.
FACILITIES: Child facs Garden: Food served outside.
NOTES: Parking 30 **ROOMS:** 5 bedrooms en suite 2 family rooms
s£30 d£50 (♦♦♦)

HAPPISBURGH   Map 13 TG33

The Hill House 🍴

NR12 0PW ☎ 01692 650004 📠 01692 650004
Dir: 5m from Stalham, 8m from North Walsham
16th-century coaching inn with original timbers situated in an
attractive North Norfolk coastal village. Sir Arthur Conan Doyle
stayed here and was inspired to write a Sherlock Holmes story
called 'The Adventure of The Dancing Men'. Changing guest
ales; good value bar food; large summer garden. Look out for
steaks, chicken breast with leek and stilton, or seafood platter,
plus various Greek, Italian and French dishes. Beer festival
each June, on the Summer Solstice.
OPEN: 12-3 (Thu-Sun all day) 7-11 (Summer all day) 25 Dec Closed
eve **BAR MEALS:** L served all week 12-2.30 D served all week
7-9.30 **RESTAURANT:** L served all week 12-2.30 D served all week
7-9.30 🍴: Free House 🍺: Shepherd Neame Spitfire, Buffy's,
Woodforde's Wherry , Adnams Bitter. **FACILITIES:** Child facs Large
garden by the sea Dogs allowed Water **NOTES:** Parking 20

HETHERSETT   Map 13 TG10

Kings Head

36 Norwich Rd NR9 3DD ☎ 01603 810206
Dir: Old Norwich Road just off B1172 Cringleford to Wymondham road.
5m SW of Norwich

This former manorial cottage dates back to the 17th century.
Here, local constables arrested killer James Johnson for the
murder of a glove-maker; he was tried and hanged in 1818.
Today, the pub's garden with its trees, benches and tables
offers a more tranquil setting for alfresco summer dining. The
varied menus range from toasted sandwiches and jacket
potatoes to hot dishes like steak and kidney pie, scampi and
chips, and moussaka with green salad.
OPEN: 11-2.30 5.30-11 (all day Sat Sun 12-4 6.30-11.30)
BAR MEALS: L served all week 12-2 D served Mon-Sun 6.30-9 (Sun
12-2.30, 7-9) Av main course £7.50 **RESTAURANT:** L served all
week 12-2 D served Mon-Sun 6.30-9.30 (Sun 12-2.30, 7-9)
Av 3 course à la carte £18 🍴: Unique Pub Co 🍺: Adnams Best
Bitter, Greene King Abbot Ale, IPA, Tetley Smoothflow.
FACILITIES: Child facs Garden: Seating surrounded by trees,
benches & tables Dogs allowed Water **NOTES:** Parking 20

HEVINGHAM   Map 13 TG12

Marsham Arms Freehouse ♦♦♦♦ 🍴 ♀

Holt Rd NR10 5NP ☎ 01603 754268 📠 01603 754839
e-mail: nigelbradley@marshamarms.co.uk
web: www.marshamarms.co.uk
Dir: 4m N of Norwich Airport on B1149 through Horsford

Victorian philanthropist and landowner Robert Marsham
built what is now the Marsham Arms as a hostel for poor
farm labourers, and some original features remain -
including the large open fireplace. Cabaret and live music
often feature in the function suite. A good range of
traditional pub fare is offered, including roast salmon,
minted lamb casseroles, sausage and mash, chicken in
bacon and mushroom sauce, and steak and kidney pie.
Plenty of fresh fish.

continued

HEVINGHAM continued

OPEN: Open all day Closed: 25 Dec **BAR MEALS:** L served all
week 11-3 D served all week 6-9.30 Sun 12-3, 6.30-9 Av main course
£8.95 **RESTAURANT:** L served all week 12-3 D served all week
6-9.30 Sun 6.30-9 Av 3 course à la carte £18.50 ⊕: Free House
◀: Adnams Best, Woodforde's Wherry Best Bitter, Mauldens,
Interbrew Bass. ♀: 8 **FACILITIES:** Child facs Garden: Large lawn
with patio with covered area **NOTES:** Parking 100
ROOMS: 11 bedrooms en suite 8 family rooms s£54.50 d£85

See advertisement under NORWICH

HEYDON — Map 13 TG12

Earle Arms ♀
The Street NR11 6AD ☎ 01263 587376 e-mail: haitchy@aol.com
Dir: Signed off the main Holt to Norwich rd, between Cawston & Corpusty
Heydon is a privately owned village with the lord of the
manor still in residence. The pub dates from the 17th century
and overlooks the village green. The interior retains a timeless
quality, with log fires, attractive wallpapers, prints and a
collection of bric-a-brac. There are two rooms, one with
service through a hatch, and more tables outside in the pretty
back garden. The bar menu offers proper home-cooked food
with local fish figuring strongly.
OPEN: 12-3 6-11 (Sun 12-3, 7-10.30) **BAR MEALS:** L served all
week 12-2 D served all week 7-8.30 **RESTAURANT:** L served all
week ⊕: Free House ◀: Adnams, Woodfordes Wherry, Adnams
Broadside, Bass. **FACILITIES:** Garden: Marquee, lawn
NOTES: Parking 20 No credit cards

HOLKHAM — Map 13 TF84

Pick of the Pubs

Victoria at Holkham NEW ★★ ⊛⊛ ♀
Park Rd NR23 1RG ☎ 01328 711008 ▤ 01328 711009
e-mail: victoria@holkham.co.uk
Dir: On A149, 3m W of Wells-next-the-Sea
Located on the North Norfolk coast, the Victoria Hotel is
part of the Holkham Estate, home to the Earls of Leicester,
since the 1700s. Situated about 10 minutes walk away
from the beach, the hotel was built in 1838 and, after
years of being leased out, was taken back by the family
and re-opened after extensive refurbishment in 2001.
Many of the bedrooms have views across the Holkham
Nature Reserve, and have been individually designed with
furniture sourced from Rajasthan in India. The restaurant
offers fresh, local food including game and beef from the
estate and seafood from the coast, complemented by a
well-balanced global wine list and local ales. Starters
could include local crab with green herb purée; and
risotto of Thornham mussels, saffron and chives. Mains
include grilled sea bream with spaghetti of vegetables;
organic chicken breast saltimbocca with cannellini beans;
and saddle of Holkham venison.
OPEN: 12-12 **BAR MEALS:** L served all week D served all
week Av main course £10 **RESTAURANT:** L served all week
12-2.30 D served all week 7-9.30 Av 3 course à la carte £25
◀: Adnams Best, Woodfordes Wherry, Branthill Best, Nelsons
Revenge. ♀: 12 **FACILITIES:** Child facs Children's licence
Garden: Beer and herb garden with seasonal BBQ Dogs allowed
Water bowls **NOTES:** Parking 50 **ROOMS:** 14 bedrooms
en suite 3 family rooms s£90 d£110

HORSEY — Map 13 TG42

Nelson Head ⟡
The Street NR29 4AD ☎ 01493 393378
Dir: On coast rd (B1159) between West Somerton & Sea Palling
Located on a National Trust estate, which embraces nearby
Horsey Mere, this 17th-century inn will, to many, epitomise
the perfect country pub. It enjoys the tranquility of a
particularly unspoilt part of the Norfolk coast - indeed,
glorious beaches are only half an hour's walk away - and the
sheltered gardens look out towards the dunes and water
meadows. Fresh cod, plaice and home-made fish and prawn
pie are usually available. Local beers are Woodforde's Wherry
and Nelson's Revenge.
OPEN: 11-3 6-11 Winter hrs vary **BAR MEALS:** L served all week
12-2 D served all week 6-8.30 **RESTAURANT:** L served all week
12-2 D served all week 6-8.30 ⊕: Free House ◀: Woodforde's
Wherry & Nelson's Revenge, Greene King IPA. **FACILITIES:** Garden:
Sheltered with a range of amazing views **NOTES:** Parking 30 No
credit cards

HORSTEAD — Map 13 TG21

Recruiting Sergeant ♀
Norwich Rd NR12 7EE ☎ 01603 737077 ▤ 01603 738827
Dir: On the B1150 between Norwich & North Walsham
The name of this inviting country pub comes from the
tradition of recruiting servicemen by giving them the King or
Queen's shilling in a pint of beer. It offers good food, ales and
wines in homely surroundings with a patio and lawned
garden for alfresco dining. The menu is ever changing, with
inventive dishes such as fresh oysters with a tabasco, lime and
red onion dressing, duck breast on an apple and potato rosti
and chicken breast stuffed with mozzarella and chorizo. There
is also a vast daily specials menu, including fish and
vegetarian dishes.
OPEN: 11-11 **BAR MEALS:** L served all week 12-2 D served all
week 6.30-9.30 **RESTAURANT:** L served all week 12-2 D served all
week 6.30-9.30 ⊕: Free House ◀: Adnams, Woodefordes, Greene
King Abbot Ale, Scottish Courage. ♀: 13 **FACILITIES:** Garden: Large
patio, seats approx 40, enclosed lawn Dogs allowed Water
NOTES: Parking 50

ITTERINGHAM — Map 13 TG13

Pick of the Pubs

Walpole Arms ♀
NR11 7AR ☎ 01263 587258 ▤ 01263 587074
e-mail: goodfood@thewalpolearms.co.uk
web: www.thewalpolearms.co.uk
*Dir: Leave Aylsham in Blickling direction. After Blickling Hall take 1st
right to Itteringham*
A pub since 1836, but the building is older. It was once
owned by Robert Horace Walpole, a direct descendant of
Britain's first prime minister. It has all the traditional
things looked for in an 18th-century country pub, such as
oak beams and log fires but, perhaps paradoxically, in
many ways the Walpole Arms is bang up-to-date as the
result of a major transformation carried out at the behest
of joint owner Richard Bryan. Work finished just hours
before his long-standing friend, Loyd Grossman,
performed the opening ceremony. Richard spent ten
years as producer of BBC TV's *Masterchef*, enabling him
to channel his lifelong passion for food into something he
could literally get his teeth into. The other co-owner, Keith

continued

England

Reeves, is a highly respected wine merchant, and he it is one must thank for the comprehensive wine list. All the food is freshly bought and prepared, so if mussels are on the menu it's because those from nearby Morston are at their best; if venison is being served, the kitchen team will tell you exactly how it was reared, slaughtered and hung at Gunton Hall. Other items on the menu might be tagine of lamb shank with roast vegetable couscous; coddle of smoked haddock, leeks, spinach, potatoes and gruyère cheese; and Loch Duart salmon with risotto of crayfish and saffron. To follow, American cheesecake with raspberry coulis; Christmas pudding ice cream in a brandy snap; and port-marinated stilton with oatcakes and grapes.

Walpole Arms

OPEN: 12-3 6-11 (Summer open all day Sat, Sun) (Winter Sun 7-10.30) **BAR MEALS:** L served all week 12-2 D served Mon-Sat 7-9.30 Sunday 12.30-2.30 Av main course £8.50
RESTAURANT: L served Wkds 12-2 D served Mon-Sat 7-9.30 Sun 12.30-2.30 Av 3 course à la carte £22 🍴: 🍺: Adnams Broadside & Bitter, Woodfordes Wherry Best Bitter & Walpole. 🍷: 12 **FACILITIES:** Child facs Garden: 2 large grassy areas with tables, patio area Dogs allowed Water **NOTES:** Parking 100

KING'S LYNN   Map 12 TF62

The Stuart House Hotel, Bar & Restaurant NEW ★★
35 Goodwins Rd PE30 5QX ☎ 01553 772169 📠 01553 774788
e-mail: reception@stuarthousehotel.co.uk
web: www.stuarthousehotel.co.uk
Small family-run hotel, bar and restaurant quietly situated close to the centre of the medieval town and historic port of King's Lynn. The bar is well known for the quality of its real ale, and the annual King's Lynn Beer Festival is held in a marquee in the grounds at the end of July. Menus offer a good choice of steaks, vegetarian dishes, curries, pasta, and fish and chips.
OPEN: 6-11 **BAR MEALS:** L served Sunday D served all week 7-9.15 (Lunch available for pre-booked parties of 12 or more) Av main course £8.50 **RESTAURANT:** 7-9.15 D served all week 7-9.15 Lunch available for pre-booked aprties of 12 or more Av 3 course à la carte £23.95 🍴: Free House 🍺: Adnams, Woodfordes, Greene King, Oakham JHB. **FACILITIES:** Children's licence Garden: Small beer garden **NOTES:** Parking 30
ROOMS: 18 bedrooms en suite 2 family rooms s£64 d£85
No children overnight

The Tudor Rose Hotel
St Nicholas St PE30 1LR ☎ 01553 762824 📠 01553 764894
e-mail: enquiries@tudorrose-hotel.co.uk
Dir: Hotel is off Tuesday Market Place in the centre of Kings Lynn
Built by a local wool merchant and situated in the heart of King's Lynn, the oldest part of this historic inn dates back to 1187 and was originally part of the winter palace of a Norfolk bishop. The Dutch gable extension of 1645 remains one of the best examples of its kind in the town. Cosy snug and medieval-style tapestries inside. Dishes range from steak and kidney pie and ham, egg and chips to Mexican chilli and prawn salad. Various light bites and starters and a good choice of well-kept beers, whiskies and popular wines.
OPEN: 11-11 (Sun 7-10.30) **BAR MEALS:** L served Mon-Sat 12-2 D served Mon-Sat 7-9 **RESTAURANT:** L served Sun 12-3 D served Mon-Sat 7-9 🍴: Free House 🍺: Fullers London Pride & 3 guest ales. **FACILITIES:** Garden **ROOMS:** 13 bedrooms 11 en suite 1 family room s£45 d£60 (★★)

LARLING   Map 13 TL98

Angel Inn 🍷
NR16 2QU ☎ 01953 717963 📠 01953 718561
A 17th-century former coaching inn close to Norwich and Bury St Edmunds, with a comfortable lounge bar with wheel back chairs and oak-panelled settle. A collection of more than 100 water jugs and a warming wood-burning stove add to the charm. Whenever possible, local produce is used in the preparation of lunchtime and evening dishes, which might include lamb chops, seafood platter and chicken korma. The largest annual beer festival in Norfolk is held in August.
OPEN: 10-11 **BAR MEALS:** L served Sun-Sat 12-2 D served Sun-Sat 6.30-9.30 Fri 23-2.30, 6.30-10, Sat 12-10, Sun 12-9.30 Av main course £7.95 **RESTAURANT:** L served all week 12-2 D served all week 6.30-9.30 Fri 12-2.30, 6.30-10, Sat 12-10, Sun 12-9.30 Av 3 course à la carte £15 🍴: Free House 🍺: Adnams Bitter, Buffy's Bitter, Wolf Bitter, Caledonian Deuchars IPA. 🍷: 7 **FACILITIES:** Child facs Large garden garden tables **NOTES:** Parking 100

LITTLE FRANSHAM   Map 13 TF91

The Canary and Linnet
Main Rd NR19 2JW ☎ 01362 687027 📠 01362 687021
e-mail: ben@canaryandlinnet.co.uk
Dir: Situated on A47 between Dereham and Swaffham
Pretty former blacksmith's cottage with exposed beams, low ceilings, inglenook fireplace and a conservatory dining area overlooking the rear garden. Food is offered in the bar, restaurant or garden from daily specials, carte or bar menu. Typical dishes include cod in beer batter, steak and ale pie, salmon fillet with wholegrain mustard sauce, medallions of pork in a stilton sauce, or smoked haddock with spinach and cheddar. A selection of malt whiskies.
OPEN: 12-3 6-11 (Sun 12-3 7-10) **BAR MEALS:** L served Mon-Sun 12-2 D served all week 6-9.30 **RESTAURANT:** L served Mon-Sun 12-2 D served Mon-Sun 6-9.30 🍴: Free House 🍺: Greene King IPA, Tindall's Best, Adnams Bitter, Wolf. **FACILITIES:** Garden: Dogs allowed **NOTES:** Parking 70

◆ Pubs with Red Diamonds are the top places in the AA's three, four and five diamond ratings

Room prices show the minimum double and single rates charged. Room rates in hotels and B&Bs often vary depending on the facilities, so be sure to check prices with the establishment before booking

LITTLE WALSINGHAM — Map 13 TF93

The Black Lion Hotel
Friday Market Place NR22 6DB ☎ 01328 820235 ▤ 01328 821407
e-mail: blacklionwalsingham@btinternet.com
web: www.blacklionwalsingham.com
Dir: From Kings Lynn, A148 and B1105, from Norwich A1067 and B1105.
The northern end of the hotel was built in the 14th century to accommodate King Edward III on his numerous pilgrimages to the shrine of Our Lady at Walsingham. Nowadays the hotel caters for discerning diners and drinkers. Besides a range of appetising bar snacks, the menu offers delicious dishes like venison medallions with roquefort cheese and walnuts; grilled skate with orange and capers; or sage Derby and baby cauliflower vol-au-vents with cheddar gratin.
OPEN: 11.30-3 6-11 (Easter-Oct 11.30-11 Sat 11.30-11, Sun 12-10.30)
BAR MEALS: L served all week 12-2 D served all week 7-9.30
Av main course £8.50 **RESTAURANT:** L served all week D served all week 7-9.30 Av 3 course à la carte £18 ⊖: Free House ◖: Greene King IPA, Carlsberg Tetley Bitter, Abbott Ale. **FACILITIES:** Garden: Courtyard garden, Picnic tables, Dogs allowed Water, food
ROOMS: 8 bedrooms en suite 1 family room s£48.50 d£70 (♦♦♦♦)

MARSHAM — Map 13 TG12

The Plough Inn
Old Norwich Rd NR10 5PS ☎ 01263 735000 ▤ 01263 735407
e-mail: enquiries@ploughinnmarsham.co.uk
Dir: Telephone for directions

Smart, traditional 18th-century country pub and restaurant close to the historic town of Aylsham and ideally placed for the Norfolk Broads. Good base for fishing and walking. A typical menu includes home-made pies, vegetarian options, and fish choices such as seafood pasta, battered cod, or fillet with salmon in a dill sauce. Musical entertainment on the first, third and last Fridays of the month.
OPEN: 12-3 5-11 (Sun 12-3 6-10.30) Dec 25 Closed from 3
BAR MEALS: L served all week 12-2.30 D served all week 6.30-9
Av main course £8.95 **RESTAURANT:** L served Mon-Sat 12-2.30 D served all week 6.30-9 Av 3 course à la carte £16.75 Av 3 course fixed price £11.95 ⊖: Free House ◖: Greene King IPA, John Smiths, Greens Gluten and Wheat Free Beer lager and stout.
FACILITIES: Garden: Large lawned garden, trees & shrubs Dogs are welcome in the garden **NOTES:** Parking 80 **ROOMS:** 11 bedrooms en suite 2 family rooms s£40.50 d£50 (♦♦♦♦)

 Pubs offering a good choice of fish on their menu

MUNDFORD — Map 13 TL89

Crown Hotel
Crown Rd IP26 5HQ ☎ 01842 878233 ▤ 01842 878982
Dir: A11 to Barton Mills interception, A1065 to Brandon & Mundford
In 1652, the Crown was a famous hunting inn. In later years, the building played host to the local magistrates, and has even acted as a doctors' waiting room. Its most unusual feature, in these pancake-flat parts, must be that it is set into a hill! Food is served in the bar, and a more elaborate menu is available in the restaurant; perhaps smoked duck and kumquat terrine, followed by baked local trout.
OPEN: 11-11 **BAR MEALS:** L served all week 12-3 D served all week 7-10 Av main course £7.50 **RESTAURANT:** L served all week 12-3 D served all week 7-10 Av 3 course à la carte £19.50 ⊖: Free House ◖: Courage Directors, Marston Pedigree, Archers, Greene King IPA & Guest ales. **FACILITIES:** Garden: beer garden patio, food served outside Dogs allowed **NOTES:** Parking 30

NORWICH — Map 13 TG20
See entry under Hevingham

Marsham Arms Free House & Inn
Holt Road, Hevingham, Norwich NR10 5NP
Tel: 01603 754268 Fax: 01603 754839
email: NigelBradley@marshamarms.co.uk

A taste of the country, fresh air, fresh food and the warmth of a cosy fire. Our aim is to practice the forgotten art of simple pleasures. Well-crafted real ales, outstanding food, freshly and expertly prepared by our staff, warm comfortable hotel rooms and the peace of the Norfolk countryside.

Wine and dine in our various bar areas – traditional, family or non-smoking. Choose from our Specials Boards or our wide menu of dishes freshly prepared from local ingredients. We are noted for our fish dishes, meat & poultry specialities, and vegetarian fayre.

We value your custom and want you to return again and again to stay, dine or sup our local real ales. Our bars, conference, function and hotel rooms provide you – the business or holiday traveller – with all you need to enjoy your stay.

Adam & Eve
Bishopsgate NR3 1RZ ☎ 01603 667423 ▤ 01603 667438
e-mail: theadamandeve@hotmail.com
First recorded as an alehouse in 1249, the Adam & Eve was used by workmen constructing the nearby cathedral. Labour was cheap as the men were paid in bread and ale! Today, the pub is acknowledged as one of the ten most haunted buildings in Norwich. The varied menu offers the likes of Elizabethan pork, beef and mushroom pie, salmon goujons, and sausages in rich onion sauce.
OPEN: 11-11 (Sun 12-10.30) Closed: 25-26 Dec, 1 Jan

continued

BAR MEALS: L served all week 12-7 Sun 12-2.30 Av main course £5.75 🍴: 🍺: Adnams Bitter, Scottish Courage Theakston Old Peculiar, Greene King IPA, Wells Bombadier. 🍷: 10 **NOTES:** Parking 10

Ribs of Beef 🍷
24 Wensum St NR3 1HY ☎ 01603 619517 📠 01603 625446
e-mail: roger@cawdron.co.uk
Welcoming riverside pub incorporating remnants of the original 14th-century building destroyed in the Great Fire in 1507. Once used by the Norfolk wherry skippers, it is still popular among boat owners cruising the Broads. The lunchtime menu offers a wide range of sandwiches, burgers and jacket potatoes, as well as Thai fish cakes, seafood platter with aioli, tempura vegetables, a savoury tart of the day, and a choice of omelettes.
OPEN: 11-11 **BAR MEALS:** L served all week 12-2.30 D served by arrangement Av main course £5.95 🍴: Free House 🍺: Woodforde's Wherry, Adnams Bitter, Adnams Broadside, Marston's Pedigree & Elgoods Mild. 🍷: 8 **FACILITIES:** Riverside jetty

REEDHAM   Map 13 TG40

Pick of the Pubs

Railway Tavern 🍷
17 The Havaker NR13 3HG ☎ 01493 700340
e-mail: railwaytavern@tiscali.co.uk

A classic Victorian station pub in the middle of the Norfolk Broads, with as many summer visitors arriving by boat as by car. Good home-cooked meals are served in the restaurant, bar or beer garden, from a varied and innovative menu. Starters may include orange and Cointreau pâté; baked feta with olives and red peppers; and red Thai salmon fishcakes with coriander and lemongrass mayonnaise. Main courses include home-made fish and beef and ale pies; fillet of beef Wellington; wild mushroom risotto with rocket and shaved parmesan; and haloumi salad with chargrilled vegetables. Weekly fish specials could be mixed seafood tagliatelle; skate wing; or salmon en croûte. Poached pears with cinnamon cream, and apple and blackberry crumble are among the tasty sweets. The pub serves Humpty Dumpty beers brewed in the village. It also plays host to beer festivals in April and September, when real ale lovers can line their stomachs with roast hog then sample some of the 70 Norfolk brews on offer.
OPEN: 11-3 6-11 (Fri-Sun 11-11) **BAR MEALS:** L served all week 11.30-3 D served all week 6-9 Av main course £8.50 **RESTAURANT:** L served all week 11.30-3 D served all week 6-9.30 (Fri-Sun all day) Av 3 course à la carte £15 🍴: Free House 🍺: Adnams, plus guest ales. 🍷: 12 **FACILITIES:** Child facs Children's licence Garden: converted stable block Dogs allowed Water provided **NOTES:** Parking 20

The Reedham Ferry Inn
Ferry Rd NR13 3HA ☎ 01493 700429 & 700999 📠 01493 700999
e-mail: reedhamferry@aol.com
Dir: 6m S of Acle follow signs from Acle or Loddon (Acle to Beccles rd)

Quaint 17th-century inn in lovely Norfolk Broads country and associated with the last working chain ferry in East Anglia. With the same name over the door for well over fifty years, this is one of the longest running family inns in East Anglia. Typical fare ranges from salads, baguettes, sausage and chips and pizzas, to Chinese style king ribs, lasagne al forno, or half roast chicken with bacon and stuffing. The specials boards are always worth examining.
OPEN: 11-3 6.30-11 (Sun 12-10.30) Open all day all year **BAR MEALS:** L served Mon-Sat 12-2 D served all week 7-9 (Sun 12-9) Av main course £7.95 **RESTAURANT:** L served Mon-Sat 12-2 D served all week 7-9 (Sun 12-9) 🍴: Free House 🍺: Woodforde's Wherry, Adnams - Best & Broadside, Greene King Abbot Ale.
FACILITIES: Garden: Beside the River Yare on the Norfolk Broads Dogs allowed Water provided **NOTES:** Parking 50

REEPHAM   Map 13 TG12

The Old Brewery House Hotel
Market Place NR10 4JJ ☎ 01603 870881 📠 01603 870969
Dir: Off the A1067 Norwich to Fakenham rd, B1145 signed Aylsham
A grand staircase, highly polished floors and wooden panelling characterise this fine hotel, originally built as a private residence in 1729. It became a hotel in the 1970s, retaining many of its Georgian features. Alongside the real ales and fine wines is a bar menu of fresh dishes.
OPEN: 11-11 (Sun 12-10.30) **BAR MEALS:** L served all week 12-2 D served all week 6.30-9.30 Sun lunch 12-2.15, dinner 7-9 Av main course £7 **RESTAURANT:** L served all week 12-2 D served all week 6.30-9.30 Av 3 course à la carte £20 🍴: Free House 🍺: IPA, Greene King Abbot Ale, Adnams & Old Speckled Hen. **FACILITIES:** Garden: Garden with pond & benches Dogs allowed **NOTES:** Parking 80

RINGSTEAD   Map 12 TF74

Pick of the Pubs

Gin Trap Inn ♦♦♦♦ 🏅🏅 🍽
High St PE36 5JU ☎ 01485 525264 📠 01485 525264
e-mail: info@gintrapinn.co.uk
See Pick of the Pubs on page 346

Website addresses are included where available. The AA cannot be held responsible for the content of any of these websites

Pick of the Pubs

Gin Trap Inn

Originally known as The Compasses, this award-winning 18th-century coaching inn changed its name to the Gin Trap in the early 1970s. Nearby is the scenic North Norfolk Coast, renowned for its miles of empty beaches, historic houses and tranquil country walks.

Chef Andy Bruce, who has been at the Gin Trap for more than 12 months, has certainly made his mark on the pub's menus, helping to establish a reputation for good eating. The bar offers traditional ales and house wines which complement the likes of ploughman's, sandwiches, granary baps, burgers, and bangers and mash. The restaurant menu is in another league altogether, and may start with large tiger prawns cooked in garlic butter and olive oil; Gin Trap home-cured salmon with dill, brandy and Dijon mustard; and hot game spring roll with a beetroot salad. To follow you could try Gin Trap mussels with various sauces; baked line caught halibut with fresh asparagus, fondant potato and beurre noisette; roasted partridge with braised Savoy cabbage and rosemary roasted potatoes; braised shank of lamb with caramelised onion mashed potato, broccoli and red wine jus; breast of duck and confit of leg with a peach and red onion tart; seared calves' liver with braised baby lettuce; or seared Cajun tuna with aubergine relish, galette potato and lemon oil. Watch out for the themed evenings.

OPEN: 11-3 6-11 (open all day summer)
BAR MEALS: L served all week 12-2 D served all week 6-9 Av main course £10.50
RESTAURANT: L served all week 12-2 D served all week 6-9 Av 3 course à la carte £20
🍺: Free House
🍺: Adnams Best, Woodfordes Wherry, Abbot, plus guest ales.
FACILITIES: Garden: Patio, food served outside **NOTES:** Parking 50
ROOMS: 3 bedrooms en suite No children overnight

♦♦♦♦ ◉◉ ⌖   Map 12
TF74
High St PE36 5JU
☎ 01485 525264
🖷 01485 525321
ℯ gintrap@aol.com
Dir: Take A149 from Kings Lynn to Hunstanton, after 15m right at Heacham

SALTHOUSE
Map 13 TG04

The Dun Cow
Coast Rd NR25 7XG ☎ 01263 740467
Dir: On A149 coast road, 3m E of Blakeney, 6m W of Sheringham

Overlooking some of the country's finest freshwater marshes, the front garden of this attractive pub is inevitably popular with birdwatchers and walkers. The bar area was formerly a blacksmith's forge, and many original 17th-century beams have been retained. Children are welcome, but there's also a walled rear garden reserved for adults. The menu includes snacks, pub staples like burgers and jacket potatoes, and main courses like gammon steak, pasta and meatballs, plaice and chips, and lasagne.
OPEN: 11-11 (Sun 12-10.30) **BAR MEALS:** L served all week 12-8.30 D served all week 12-9 Av main course £7 🍽: Pubmaster 🍺: Greene King IPA & Abbot Ale, Adnams Broadside.
FACILITIES: Garden: Large garden overlooking marshes Dogs allowed **NOTES:** Parking 8

SCULTHORPE
Map 13 TF83

Sculthorpe Mill
Lynn Rd NR21 9QG ☎ 01328 856161 📠 01328 853549
e-mail: sculthorpe@mill4228.fsnet.co.uk
Dir: 0.25m off A148, 2m from Fakenham
This charming 18th-century watermill is set in beautiful riverside gardens, ideal for alfresco summer drinking. Relax in the comfortable bar with a pint of real ale, or head upstairs to the non-smoking restaurant with its beams and polished floors. The bar menu includes light snacks and pub favourites like ham, egg and chips, while restaurant diners can expect roast Gressingham duck; grilled tuna steak; or sautéed vegetables and goat's cheese in a filo pastry basket.
OPEN: 11-3 6-11 (Summer 11-11) **BAR MEALS:** L served all week 12-2.30 D served Mon-Sat 6.30-9.30 Av main course £5.75
RESTAURANT: L served all week 12-2.30 D served Mon-Sat 7-9.30 Av 3 course à la carte £22 🍽: Free House 🍺: Fosters, Greene King IPA, Old Speckled Hen. **FACILITIES:** Garden: Dogs allowed
NOTES: Parking 60

SNETTISHAM
Map 12 TF63

Pick of the Pubs

The Rose & Crown ★★ 🌐 ⏵ ♀
Old Church Rd PE31 7LX ☎ 01485 541382 📠 01485 543172
e-mail: info@roseandcrownsnettisham.co.uk
web: www.roseandcrownsnettisham.co.uk
See Pick of the Pubs on page 348

STIFFKEY
Map 13 TF94

Pick of the Pubs

Stiffkey Red Lion ♀
44 Wells Rd NR23 1AJ ☎ 01328 830552 📠 01328 830882
e-mail: mail@redlion.freeserve.co.uk
Dir: Take A149 from Wells toward Sheringham, 4m on L
Rustic 16th-century brick-and-flint cottage standing amid rolling Norfolk countryside. Popular with walkers, birdwatchers, holidaymakers and devoted fish fanciers, the many charms of this welcoming watering-hole include fresh fish from King's Lynn, crab from Cromer, mussels from local beds, and first-rate ales from East Anglian brewers like Woodfordes, Elgoods, Adnams and Greene King. The interior comprises three wooden-floored or quarry-tiled rooms with open fires and a simple mix of wooden settles, pews and scrubbed tables. Ever-changing blackboard menus may list deep-fried Blakeney whitebait, Stiffkey mussels, and grilled local fish, alongside hearty home-made steak and kidney pie, hand-made sausages with mash, and seared local venison with a port and plum compôte. Lighter bites include home-made soup and imaginative salads. After a day on the beach or strolling the Peddars Way, this is a good stop for families who have use of a large and airy rear conservatory with access to the terraced garden.
OPEN: 11-3 6-11 **BAR MEALS:** L served all week 12-2 D served all week 6-9 Av main course £7.95
RESTAURANT: L served all week D served all week 🍽: Free House 🍺: Woodforde's Wherry, Adnams Bitter, Greene King Abbot Ale. **FACILITIES:** Garden: Terraced patio & garden overlooking valley Dogs allowed Water **NOTES:** Parking 40

STOKE HOLY CROSS
Map 13 TG20

Pick of the Pubs

The Wildebeest Arms 🌐🌐 ♀
82-86 Norwich Rd NR14 8QJ
☎ 01508 492497 📠 01508 494353
e-mail: wildebeest@animalinns.co.uk
A passion for fine food underpins the operation of this unusually named dining pub, situated just two miles south of Norwich. Formerly the Red Lion, the pub was renamed after an erstwhile landlord whose nicknames included 'the wild man' and 'beasty'. The old pub was opened up some years ago to create a wonderful space with working fireplaces at both ends and a horseshoe bar in the middle. If the interior is striking and sophisticated, the casual and relaxed atmosphere attracts a good range of clients from country and city alike. Good quality local produce forms the basis of dishes like chargrilled rib-eye steak with aioli and house chips; twice-baked goats cheese soufflé; and grilled black bream with chorizo bubble and squeak, courgette tagliatelle and red pepper fondue. Desserts are just as appetising, with choices like glazed mango tart, and raspberry and redcurrant parfait.
OPEN: 12-3 6-11 (Sun 12-3 7-10.30) Closed: Dec 25-26
BAR MEALS: L served All D served All Av main course £13.95
RESTAURANT: L served all week 12-2 D served all week 7-10 Av 3 course à la carte £25 🍽: Free House 🍺: Adnams. ♀: 12 **FACILITIES:** Child facs Garden: Beer garden, beautifully landscaped **NOTES:** Parking 40

The Rose & Crown

Long, white and covered in roses in the summer, this family-run pub is very much a village local at heart. People from all walks of life come in for a drink, and maybe to tune in to the older regulars grumbling about the tides, the government or indeed, vine weevils.

Situated opposite the village cricket pitch, it was built in the 14th century to house craftsmen building Snettisham's amazing church, which Simon Jenkins in his book *England's Thousand Best Churches* claims has one of the country's finest stained-glass windows. These days Jeannette and Anthony Goodrich oversee a popular and hospitable operation, as they have done for over ten years. The three bar areas all have timbered ceilings, open fires and marvellous worn pamment-tiled floors. Friday and Saturday nights are very popular, and as Jeannette says "feel like a huge private party." Good quality food is enormously important here, with a regularly changing menu presenting such pleasures as pan-fried grey mullet, ratatouille and parma ham; braised lamb shank with root vegetable broth and minty mash; and roast teriyaki duck breast, with sticky black rice and shiitake mushrooms. Rose and Crown 'Classics' include chargrilled burger with streaky bacon, red onion relish and cheese; fish and chips with minted mushy peas; and grilled pork and Cox apple sausages, mustard mash, and cider pan gravy. Puddings are very desirable too. A shorter all-day menu is also available.

OPEN: 11 -11 (Sun 12-10.30)
BAR MEALS: L served all week 12-2
D served all week 6.30-9 (Sat-Sun 2.30, Fri & Sat 9.30) Av main course £10
RESTAURANT: L served all week 12-2
D served all week 6.30-9 Set menu Mon-Fri except BH Av 3 course à la carte £20 Av 2 course fixed price £10
🍴: Free House 🍺: Adnams Bitter & Broadside, Interbrew Bass, Fuller's London Pride, Greene King IPA. ♀: 20
FACILITIES: Child facs Garden: Large walled garden, seating & shade Dogs allowed Water **NOTES:** Parking 70
ROOMS: 11 bedrooms en suite
4 family rooms s£60 d£80

★★ ⊛ ⌇ ♀   Map 12 TF63
Old Church Rd PE31 7LX
☎ 01485 541382
🖹 01485 543172
📧 info@roseandcrownsnettisham.co.uk
🌐 www.roseandcrownsnettisham.co.uk
Dir: N from King's Lynn on A149 signed Hunstanton. Inn in village centre between market square & church

STOW BARDOLPH
Map 12 TF60

Pick of the Pubs

The Hare Arms 🍴 ♟
PE34 3HT ☎ 01366 382229 📠 01366 385522
e-mail: trishmc@harearms222.fsnet.co.uk
Dir: From King's Lynn take A10 to Downham Market. After 9m village signed on left

This attractive ivy-clad pub, set just off the A10 between Ely and King's Lynn, took its name from the surrounding Hare estate - the family have lived in this village for generations - over 200 years ago. Today there's a non-smoking conservatory and terrace overlooking the garden, where peacocks and chickens roam freely, and the old coach house and stables have been converted to a function room. The relaxed, welcoming atmosphere attracts all sorts of people, from villagers and landowners to business folk, and celebrities like Johnny Depp, Winona Ryder, and Robbie Williams. The extensive bar menu is divided between fish, meats, steaks, vegetarian, sandwiches, jacket potatoes, ploughman lunches, daily specials, and salads. The restaurant menu might include starters like crispy prawns; Thai caramelised pork; and goat's cheese salad. Mains might offer lemon sole with parsley butter; chicken with coriander and chilli; sea bass with celeriac veloute; and lamb cutlets. There's a dessert trolley in the restaurant with a tempting range.
OPEN: 11-2.30 6-11 (Sun 12-2.30 7-10.30) Closed: 25-26 Dec
BAR MEALS: L served all week 12-2 D served all week 7-10
Av main course £9 **RESTAURANT:** L served Sun only 12-2
D served Mon-Sat 7-9.30 Av 3 course à la carte £32.50
Av 3 course fixed price £22.50 🍺: Greene King 🍺: Greene King, Abbot Ale, IPA & Old Speckled Hen, Tanners Jack + guest.
♟: 7 **FACILITIES:** Garden: Picnic tables, chickens, peacocks
NOTES: Parking 50

SWANTON MORLEY
Map 13 TG01

Darbys Freehouse 🍴
1&2 Elsing Rd NR20 4NY ☎ 01362 637647 📠 01362 637987
Dir: From A47 (Norwich to King's Lynn) take B1147 to Dereham
Converted from two cottages in 1988 but originally built as a large country house in the 1700s, this popular freehouse opened when the village's last traditional pub closed. Named after the woman who lived here in the 1890s and farmed the adjacent land. Stripped pine tables, exposed beams and inglenook fireplaces enhance the authentic country pub atmosphere. Up to eight real ales are available, and home-cooked food includes pigeon breast, steak and mushroom pudding, pesto pasta and salmon fillet.
OPEN: 11.30-3 6-11 (Sat 11.30-11, Sun 12-10.30) Dec 25 Closed Eve
BAR MEALS: L served all week 12-2.15 D served all week 6.30-9.45
RESTAURANT: L served all week 12-2.15 D served all week
6.30-9.45 🍺: Free House 🍺: Woodforde's Wherry, Badger
Tanglefoot, Adnams Broadside, plus three guest beers.
FACILITIES: Garden: beer garden, outdoor eating, Dogs allowed
NOTES: Parking 75

Restaurant and Bar Meal times indicate the times
when food is available. Last orders may be
approximately 30 minutes before the times stated

THOMPSON
Map 13 TL99

Pick of the Pubs

Chequers Inn ◆◆◆◆ 🍴
Griston Rd IP24 1PX ☎ 01953 483360 📠 01953 488092
e-mail: richard@chequers_inn.wanadoo.co.uk
Dir: Between Watton and Thetford off A1075

Historic 17th-century pub which over the years has been a manor court, doctor's surgery and meeting room. It is understood to take its name from the method used at one time of counting money on a chequered cloth to make counting easier. Many original features remain, including exposed beams and a timber and thatched roof swooping almost to the ground. Situated opposite the village cricket pitch, the Chequers offers an ideal base from which to visit Sandringham, nearby bird reserves, and the lovely North Norfolk beaches, not to mention the walkers' dream that is the Peddars Way. Mouth-watering examples from the specials board include seafood mixed grill, medallions of ostrich with wild mushroom and Madeira sauce, skate wing with black butter and capers, and baked avacado pear stuffed with crab and baked with course grain mustard and cheddar cheese sauce. Steaks, omelettes, jacket potatoes, and ploughman's too.
OPEN: 11.30-2.30 6.30-11 (Sun 12-3, 6.30-10.30)
BAR MEALS: L served all week 12-2 D served all week
6.30-9.30 Av main course £7.95 **RESTAURANT:** L served all week 12-2 D served all week 6.30-9.30 🍺: Free House
🍺: Fuller's London Pride, Adnams Best, Wolf Best, Greene King IPA. **FACILITIES:** Child facs Garden: Childrens climbing frame lawned area Dogs allowed Water, Sweeties **NOTES:** Parking 35
ROOMS: 3 bedrooms en suite 1 family room s£40 d£60
(◆◆◆◆)

THORNHAM
Map 12 TF74

Pick of the Pubs

Lifeboat Inn ★★ 🏵 🍴 ♟
Ship Ln PE36 6LT ☎ 01485 512236 📠 01485 512323
e-mail: reception@lifeboatinn.co.uk
web: www.lifeboatinn.co.uk
Dir: A149 to Hunstanton, follow coast rd to Thornham, pub 1st left
A 16th-century inn overlooking the salt marshes and Thornham Harbour. Despite being extended, its original character has been retained. Numerous attractions lie within easy reach, including Thornham beach, Blakeney, Cley, Sandringham and Nelson's birthplace at Burnham Thorpe. For the more adventurous there are facilities for dinghy sailing at Brancaster Staithe and windsurfing at

continued

England

THORNHAM continued

Hunstanton. Inside the Lifeboat the warm glow of paraffin lamps enhances the welcoming atmosphere, while the adjoining conservatory is renowned for its ancient vine and adjacent walled patio garden. The best available fish and game feature on the frequently changing menus in the form of traditional country fare. Bowls of steaming mussels are legendary, harvested daily by local fishermen. Among the more popular dishes in the bar are pan-fried liver; roulade of chicken, smoked ham and spinach; roast loin of pork; and Lifeboat fish pie.

Lifeboat Inn

OPEN: 11-11 **BAR MEALS:** L served all week 12-2.30 D served all week 6.30-9.30 Av main course £10
RESTAURANT: D served all week 7-9.30 Av 3 course fixed price £27 💷: Free House 🍺: Adnams, Woodforde's Wherry, Greene King Abbot Ale. 🍷: 10 **FACILITIES:** Child facs Garden: Enclosed wall patio garden Dogs allowed Water provided **NOTES:** Parking 100 **ROOMS:** 22 bedrooms en suite 2 family rooms s£59 d£78

THORPE MARKET   Map 13 TG23

Green Farm Restaurant & Hotel ★★
North Walsham Rd NR11 8TH ☎ 01263 833602 📠 01263 833163
e-mail: enquiries@greenfarmhotel.co.uk
web: www.greenfarmhotel.co.uk
Dir: Situated on A149

Conveniently situated for exploring the Norfolk Broads, or the historic houses at Blickling, Felbrigg and Sandringham, this 16th-century flint-faced former farmhouse features a pubby bar and an interesting menu. Typical dishes may include grilled marinated breast of duck served on a herbal ratatouille with a sage and balsamic jus, roasted pork cutlet with a sweet pepper crust and spicy garlic and okra sauce, baked fillet of turbot filled with spring onion and prawn mousseline wrapped in filo pastry, or baked cherry tomato and sweet

continued

onion tartlet topped with brie and served with a tomato salsa.
OPEN: 11-2 6.30-11 (Sun 12-2 6.30-8.30) **BAR MEALS:** L served Wed-Sun 12-2 D served all week 6.30-8.30 Av main course £9.95 **RESTAURANT:** L served Wed-Sun 12-2 D served all week 7-8.30 💷: Free House 🍺: Greene King IPA, Abbot, Wolf Bitters, St Peter's Best. **FACILITIES:** Garden: Food served outside Dogs allowed at manager's discretion **NOTES:** Parking 80 **ROOMS:** 20 bedrooms en suite s£59.50 d£70

TITCHWELL   Map 13 TF74

Pick of the Pubs

Titchwell Manor Hotel ★★ 🏵🏵 🍴
PE31 8BB ☎ 01485 210221 📠 01485 210104
e-mail: margaret@titchwellmanor.com
web: www.titchwellmanor.com
Dir: A149 (coast rd) between Brancaster & Thornham
This delightful family-run hotel in the peaceful village of Titchwell is ideal for touring the north Norfolk coastline and RSPB reserve. Smart public rooms include a lounge, relaxed informal bar, and a delightful conservatory restaurant. From its pretty walled garden the sea views are glorious, and the sea is also a major influence on the menus with Brancaster oysters, Norfolk smoked eel, crab, lobster, mussels, haddock, kippers, and wild sea bass often featuring. The cooking is skilled and interesting, with desserts like dolcelatta cheesecake with balsamic figs and black pepper brandy snap. Dinner could start with squid sauté with chilli and lime, bean shoot and lotus root salad with sweet and sour cucumber; follow it up with slow roast belly pork, fondant potato, purple sprouting broccoli, coarse mustard jus, and toffee apples; and finish with white chocolate and blood orange tart. There is a proper children's menu with lots of choice.
OPEN: 11-11 **BAR MEALS:** L served all week 12-2 D served all week 6.30-9.30 **RESTAURANT:** L served all week 12-2 D served all week 6.30-9.30 💷: Free House 🍺: Greene King IPA & Abbot Ale. **FACILITIES:** Child facs Garden: Large walled garden, summerhouse Dogs allowed Water, kennel **NOTES:** Parking 50 **ROOMS:** 16 bedrooms en suite 6 family rooms

See Pub Walk on page 335

UPPER SHERINGHAM   Map 13 TG14

The Red Lion Inn 🍴
The Street NR26 8AD ☎ 01263 825408
Dir: A140 (Norwich to Cromer) then A148 to Sheringham/Upper Sheringham
About 300 years old, flint-built, with original floors, natural pine furniture, a large wood-burning stove, and a Snug Bar haunted by a female ghost. Local produce is used extensively, with fish, including plaice, haddock, halibut, cod and crab, featuring in a big way. Other options are liver and bacon in port and orange gravy, steak and ale pie; Thai red chicken curry; a half pheasant in cranberry sauce; and chicken stuffed with prawns on a crab sauce.
OPEN: 11.30-3 6.30-11 (Summer hols open all day Sun)
BAR MEALS: L served all week 12-2 D served all week 6.30-9
RESTAURANT: L served all week 12-2 D served all week 6.30-9
💷: Free House 🍺: Woodforde's Wherry, Greene King IPA.
FACILITIES: Garden: Large lawned area with fruit trees Dogs allowed Water **NOTES:** Parking 16 No credit cards

WARHAM ALL SAINTS
Map 13 TF94

Pick of the Pubs

Three Horseshoes
NR23 1NL ☎ 01328 710547
Dir: From Wells A149 to Cromer, then right onto B1105 to Warham
This charming free house opened as an alehouse in 1725, and has remained one ever since. It has one of the best original interiors in the area, with gaslights in the main bar, scrubbed deal tables, and a grandfather clock that was made in nearby Dereham in 1830. Local ales are served directly from the cask. You can while away the afternoon playing a vintage one-armed bandit downstairs, or, in sunny weather, make the most of a sheltered lawn for some alfresco dining. In keeping with the vintage surrounds, the menu serves up classic English fodder, Mrs Beeton-style. Expect plenty of game and stews, and no chips. Dishes may include grilled herring in lemon; neck of lamb hotpot; and an outstanding range of pies. As you might guess, puddings are not to be missed, with a wide range of fragrant jammy sponges and spotted dick to challenge the waistband!
OPEN: 11.30-2.30 6-11 (Sun 12-3 6-10.30)
BAR MEALS: L served all week 12-1.45 D served all week 6-8.30
Av main course £7.50 🍺: Free House 🍴: Greene King IPA, Woodforde's Wherry. **FACILITIES:** Garden: Grassed area with seating; enclosed courtyard Dogs allowed Water, Dog food and biscuits **NOTES:** Parking 50 No credit cards

WELLS-NEXT-THE-SEA
Map 13 TF94

Pick of the Pubs

The Crown Hotel 🏆
The Buttlands NR23 1EX ☎ 01328 710209 📠 01328 711432
e-mail: reception@thecrownhotelwells.co.uk
web: www.thecrownhotelwells.co.uk
Dir: 10m from Fakenham on B1105
The Crown is a former coaching inn overlooking the tree-lined green known as The Buttlands. Stylish contemporary décor works well with the old-world charm of the 17th-century building. Diners can be sure of freshly prepared food from the best ingredients and flavours from around the world. In the bar, with its mellow colour palette, old beams and open fire, you can choose from filled rolls or light savoury dishes like mozzarella and roasted pepper bruschetta. Or go for Chris's Black Slate (Asian salmon belly, grilled chorizo, marinated chicken wings, seafood spring roll, and smoked chicken and peanut salad). Heartier options are Holkham venison casserole, tempura of haddock with sweet potato chips, or a gourmet cheeseboard. For more formal dining, the two or three-course restaurant menu offers terrine of lamb shank and sweetbreads with brioche toast; pan-fried halibut with citrus braised fennel; and chocolate brownie with vanilla ice cream.
OPEN: 11-11 **BAR MEALS:** L served all week 12-2 D served all week 6-9 **RESTAURANT:** D served all week 7-9 🍺: Free House 🍴: Adnams Bitter, Adnams Broadside, Adnams Guest Ale. 🏆: 12 **FACILITIES:** Child facs Children's licence Decking area Dogs allowed on leads/water bowls

WEST BECKHAM
Map 13 TG13

The Wheatsheaf 🏆
Manor Farm, Church Rd NR25 6NX ☎ 01263 822110
Dir: 2m inland from Sheringham on A148
Former manor house converted to a pub in 1984 and retaining many original features. Sample one of the real ales from Woodfordes Brewery and relax in the large garden where a fully-restored gypsy caravan is on display. On summer evenings you can even enjoy a game of floodlit pétanque. Great pub atmosphere inside and a mix of traditional pub food and more adventurous specials. Expect pan-fried lemon sole with hot tartare sauce, baked duck breast in puff pastry stuffed with mushroom and thyme pate, or brie-stuffed chicken supreme on lavender risotto.
OPEN: 11.30-3 6.30-11 (Winter 12-3, 6.30-11)
BAR MEALS: L served Tues-Sun 12-2 D served Tues-Sat 6.30-9
Av main course £7.50 **RESTAURANT:** L served Tues-Sun 12-2
D served Tues-Sat 7-9 🍺: Free House 🍴: Woodforde's Wherry Best Bitter, Nelson's Revenge, Norfolk Nog, Greene King IPA & Guest Ales. 🏆: 7 **FACILITIES:** Child facs Garden: Large garden with gazebo and covered patio Dogs allowed Water **NOTES:** Parking 50

WINTERTON-ON-SEA
Map 13 TG41

Fishermans Return 🏆
The Lane NR29 4BN ☎ 01493 393305 📠 01493 393951
e-mail: fishermans_return@btopenworld.com
Dir: 8m N of Gt Yarmouth on B1159

This 300-year-old brick and flint pub is within walking distance of long beaches and National Trust land, where you can enjoy bird or seal watching. Dogs are also welcome. There is a vast choice of malts and ciders, and a good, traditional menu with dishes such as Whitby scampi, burgers and seafood special omelette, plus daily specials. Good-value snacks include baked potatoes, toasted sandwiches, fish pie, and chilli con carne.
OPEN: 11-2.30 6.30-11 (Sat 11-11, Sun 12-10.30)
BAR MEALS: L served all week 12-2 D served all week 6.30-9
Av main course £8.50 🍺: Free House 🍴: Woodforde's Wherry & Norfolk Nog, Adnams Best Bitter & Broadside and Greene King IPA & Guest Ales. 🏆: 10 **FACILITIES:** Child facs Garden: Large enclosed, with tables, play equipment Dogs allowed Water & chews
NOTES: Parking 50

> Not all of the pubs in the guide are open all week or all day. It's always best to check before you travel

England

WIVETON
Map 13 TG04

Wiveton Bell
Blakeney Rd NR25 7TL ☎ 01263 740101
e-mail: enquiries@wivetonbell.co.uk
Picturesque village inn close to the green and church, with
cosy beamed bar and spacious non-smoking conservatory
restaurant. The owner is Danish so expect some native
influence here, though the ingredients are largely local.
Dishes might include pork tenderloin, venison steak with a
cranberry and ginger sauce, chicken stir-fry in noodles, cod
fillet in home-made batter, and mussels and crab in season.
OPEN: 12-2.30 6.30-11 (Closed Sun eve & Mon in winter) Closed 2
wks Jan/Feb **BAR MEALS:** L served all week 12-2 D served all week
7-9 **RESTAURANT:** L served all week 12-2 D served all week 7-9
🍺: Free House ◀: Woodeforde's Nelson's Revenge, Adnams Bitter.
FACILITIES: Garden: Grass lawn and tables Dogs allowed Water
NOTES: Parking 5

WOODBASTWICK
Map 13 TG31

The Fur & Feather ♀
Slad Ln NR13 6HQ ☎ 01603 720003 📠 01603 722266
Dir: 1.5m N of B1140, 8m NE of Norwich
An idyllic country pub in a peaceful location, it was originally
two farm cottages and now boasts three cosy bar areas and a
smart restaurant. Next door is Woodforde's Brewery, and all
eight ales are offered here, served straight from the cask. One
of these features in the inn's signature dish of Nogin Yorky, a
giant Yorkshire pudding filled with steak and mushrooms
cooked in Norfolk Nog. From an interesting menu expect five
bean enchilada, Bastwick burger, fish pie, or lamb's liver and
bacon. Jackets, sandwiches and baguettes also available.
OPEN: 11.30-3 6-11 (Summer Mon-Sat 11.30-11, Sun 11.30-11)
BAR MEALS: L served all week 12-2 D served all week 6-9 Av main
course £11 **RESTAURANT:** L served all week 12-2 D served all week
6-9 🍺: Woodforde's ◀: Woodforde's Wherry, Great Eastern,
Norfolk Nog, Nelsons Revenge. ♀: 8 **FACILITIES:** Garden: Large
garden with fenced pond **NOTES:** Parking 100

🍺 Principal Beers for sale

We only include details of accommodation that
has been inspected by the AA (big Stars or
Diamonds at the top of an entry), or the
RAC, VisitBritain, VisitScotland or WTB
(small Stars or Diamonds at the end of an entry)

The
Bed & Breakfast
Guide
2006

**Britain's best-selling
B&B guide featuring
over 4,000 great
places to stay.**

AA

www.theAA.com

WRENINGHAM
Map 13 TM19

Pick of the Pubs

Bird in Hand ♀
Church Rd NR16 1BH ☎ 01508 489438 📠 01508 488004
Dir: 6m S of Norwich on the B1113
An eclectic mixture of styles characterises this interesting
pub-restaurant in the heart of the Norfolk countryside.
The quarry-tiled bar features an attractive open-beamed
roof, whilst diners can choose between the elegant
Victorian-style dining room and the more traditional
farmhouse restaurant. Fresh fish is bought from an old-
established Norwich fishmonger who specialises only in
top quality fish from Lowestoft and delivers on a daily
basis. Meat comes from a local butcher. The menus are
written to include an assortment of traditional favourites
combined with a choice of more adventurous dishes
which have the chef's reputation for flair and innovation
stamped on them. Diner profiling also helps the Bird in
Hand to recognise its customer requirements. Traditional
bar favourites might include seared breast of
Gressingham duck on a pool of mixed peppercorn and
orange sauce and flavoured with Cointreau, chargrilled
thick-cut salmon steak with a white wine cream sauce,
and oven-roasted bell peppers stuffed with couscous,
spring onions, mozzarella cheese and basil served with
pesto. Alternatively, try slow-braised game casserole,
baked herb pancakes, pan-fried veal escalope, flaked
pieces of salmon, cod, haddock and peeled prawns, or
braised lamb's liver and kidneys in sweet and sour sauce
with strips of peppers and shallots served with wild rice.
For something lighter, baguettes and jacket potatoes.
OPEN: 11.30-3 6-11 **BAR MEALS:** L served all week 12-2
D served all week 6-9.30 Av main course £7.95
RESTAURANT: L served all week 12-2 D served all week 6-9.30
🍺: Free House ◀: Adnams, Woodforde's Wherry, Fullers
London Pride, Marstons Pedigree John Smiths Smooth. ♀: 8
FACILITIES: Garden: Landscaped beer garden Dogs allowed in
the garden only **NOTES:** Parking 55

NORTHAMPTONSHIRE

ASHBY ST LEDGERS
Map 11 SP56

The Olde Coach House Inn ♀
CV23 8UN ☎ 01788 890349 📠 01788 891922
e-mail: oldcoachhouse@traditionalfreehouses.com
Dir: M1 junct 18 follow A361/Daventry signs.Village on L
A late 19th-century farmhouse and outbuildings, skilfully
converted into a pub with dining areas, accommodation and
meeting rooms, set in a village that dates way back to the
Domesday Book of 1086. The village was home to Robert
Catesby, one of the Gunpowder plotters. Beer is taken
seriously here, with up to eight regularly changing real ales
and legendary beer festivals. The pub also serves fresh, high
quality food in comfortable surroundings, featuring game
casserole, seafood linguine, massive mixed grills, Australian
butterfish, grilled seabass, and summer barbecues.
OPEN: 12-11 (Sun 12-10.30) **BAR MEALS:** L served all week
12-2.30 D served all week 6-9.30 **RESTAURANT:** L served all week
12-2 D served all week 6-9.30 🍺: Free House ◀: Everards Original,
Everards Tiger, Fuller's London Pride, Hook Norton Best. ♀: 8
FACILITIES: Child facs Garden: Landscaped garden Dogs allowed
Water **NOTES:** Parking 50

PUB WALK
The Falcon Inn
Fotheringhay - Northamptonshire

THE FALCON INN,
Fotheringhay, PE8 5HZ
☎ 01832 226254
Directions: N of A605 between
Peterborough & Oundle.
*Attractive 18th-century stone-built inn
close to the site of Fotheringhay
Castle. Sit in the local's tap room, the
smart dining room or conservatory
extension, and choose food from
blackboard or seasonal carte.*
Open: 11.30–3 6–11 (Sun
12–3,7–10.30)
Bar Meals: L served all week 12–2.15
D served all week 7–9.30
Restaurant Meals: L served all week
12–2.15 D served all week 6.30–9.30
Av 3 course à la carte £25 Av 2 course
fixed price £12.50
Garden and parking available.
(for full entry see page 357)

Distance: 6 miles (9.7km)
Map: OS Landranger 227
Terrain: Low-lying water meadonws,
pasture and parkland
Paths: Field paths, tracks and
bridleways. Some road walking
Gradient: Mainly level ground

Walk submitted by Nick Channer

Cross picturesque water meadows and pasture on this gentle walk by the Nene.

From the pub turn right and take the turning opposite, signposted Nassington. Cross the Willow Brook and take a waymarked footpath on the right to the far boundary, crossing into the next field by an oak tree. Follow the clear path diagonally right towards farm outbuildings.

With the house facing you, veer right, then left alongside the buildings, keeping three trees over to the right in the field. Follow the clear path towards hedge and trees, making for the field's left-hand corner. Cross a wooden footbridge and aim diagonally across the field to a dismantled railway track. Cross over and follow a grassy track through the fields to a footbridge spanning the River Nene.

Walk along to the next bridge and cross the river by Elton Lock. Make for the village green at Elton and turn right at the road. Turn right after a few paces into Chapel Lane and head out of the village, passing alongside Elton Park and some cottages and then continue on a bridleway. Cross a wooden footbridge and then ascend a slope towards trees. Make for a gate and join a track leading to a woodland path. Keep ahead.

Emerge from the trees, follow the field edge to a mast in the corner, drop down the bank to a gate and turn right. Make for two kissing gates, cross the A605 to two more gates and then turn right in the field. Look for a stile in the boundary, with two gates just beyond it. Turn right and follow the road round to the left. Turn right at the Nene Way sign, pass under the A605 and keep right in front of Eaglethorpe Mill.

Turn left immediately beyond it, cross a stile and veer away from the water to a stile and footbridge. Continue ahead to Warmington Lock. Veer slightly left towards Fotheringhay Church and join a track. When it bends right, go straight on along the field path to the next track. Turn left, pass sheep pens and head for the site of Fotheringhay Castle. Turn right here, follow the track and return to the pub.

Pick of the Pubs

BULWICK – NORTHAMPTONSHIRE

The Queen's Head

Overlooking the village church, this charming country pub is thought to have been a pub since the 17th century, although parts of the building date back to 1400. The name comes from the Portuguese wife of Charles II, Katherine of Braganza, who was well known for her very elaborate hair-dos.

The cosy interior boasts four open fireplaces, wooden beams and flagstone floors in a warren of small rooms. Relax by the fire or on the patio with a pint of quality ale from Newby Wyke, Shepherd Neame, Spitfire or a local Rockingham ale, and some hearty pub food. Start with white bean and parsley soup, with a deep fried poached egg; tian of smoked halibut with crab, gazpacho and lemon oil; or red onion marmalade and tomato confit tart. Continue with vanilla roasted monk fish tail with spinach, fondant potato and spiced port jus; roast medallions of roast beef with roasted red onions, potato and bacon cake and bordelaise sauce; or trio of salmon, cod and sea bass, with horseradish and crayfish purée and thermidor sauce. For a truly traditional pub meal try one of the selection of home-made pies or a ploughman's. Look out for special events or themed evenings, usually revolving around special days such as Valentine's Day, Mothering Sunday, or St Patrick's Day, but sometimes just for the fun of it. For example, the Horseshoe Throwing Competition and Hog Roast on the last May Bank Holiday.

OPEN: 12-2.30 6-11
BAR MEALS: L served Tue-Sun 12-2.30 D served Tue-Sat 6-9.30 Sunday lunch 12-3 Av main course £5.95
RESTAURANT: L served Tue-Sun 12-2.30 D served Tue-Sat 6-9.30 Sunday lunch 12-3 Av 3 course à la carte £20.50
🏠: Free House
🍺: Timothy Taylor Landlord, Newby Wyke, Shepherd Neame, Spitfire, Rockingham ale. ♀: 9
FACILITIES: Child facs Garden: Patio area Dogs allowed Water
NOTES: Parking 40

🐟 ♀   Map 11 SP99
Main St NN17 3DY
☎ 01780 450272
Dir: Just off A43, between Corby and Stamford

England

ASHTON
Map 11 SP74

The Old Crown ♀
1 Stoke Rd NN7 2JN ☎ 01604 862268
Dir: 5 mins from junct 15 off the A1. 1m from A508 from Roade Village, 5 mins from National Waterways Museum at Stoke Bruerne

Attractive 17th-century inn with traditional beamed interior and walls decorated with many prints and mirrors. Outside there are two attractively-planted gardens for alfresco dining. Snacks such as soups, sandwiches and salads are available, along with main courses like seared fennel-crusted tuna on Mediterranean couscous; charred aubergine and coconut curry; five-herb roasted chicken breast with potato and celeriac mash; and steamed steak, mushroom, bacon, stilton and herb suet pudding.
OPEN: 12-3 6-11 open all day Sat-Sun **BAR MEALS:** L served Mon-Sun 12-2.30 D served Mon-Sat 6.30-9 Sun lunch 12-3 Av main course £7.95 **RESTAURANT:** L served Mon-Sun 12-2.30 D served Mon-Sat 6.30-9 Sun lunch 12-3 **◖:** Charles Wells, Bombardier, Fosters, Red Stripe. **♀:** 7 **FACILITIES:** Garden: Two large gardens, seating, heaters **NOTES:** Parking 20

BADBY
Map 11 SP55

The Windmill Inn
Main St NN11 3AN ☎ 01327 702363 ▤ 01327 311521
e-mail: windmill_badby@fsmail.net
Dir: M1 junct 16 take A45 to Daventry then A361 S. Village 2m

Traditional thatched pub dating back to the 17th century, with beamed and flagstone bars and a friendly, relaxed atmosphere. Close by are Blenheim Palace and Warwick Castle, and a few hundred yards away is the only thatched youth hostel in England and Wales. A varied menu includes fish kebabs in a Thai marinade; steak and kidney pudding; Cajun-style chicken supreme; and baked fillet of cod with olive oil, garlic and herbs.
OPEN: 11.30-3.30 5.30-11 **BAR MEALS:** L served all week 12-2 D served all week 7-9.30 **RESTAURANT:** L served all week 12-2 D served all week 7-9.30 **☺:** Free House **◖:** Bass , Flowers, Brains, Wadworth 6X. **FACILITIES:** Garden: Front of pub, adjacent to village, 10 tables Dogs allowed **NOTES:** Parking 25

BULWICK
Map 11 SP99

CASTLE ASHBY
Map 11 SP85

CHACOMBE
Map 11 SP44

CLIPSTON
Map 11 SP78

The Bulls Head
Harborough Rd LE16 9RT ☎ 01858 525268
Dir: On B4036 S of Market Harborough
American airmen once pushed coins between the beams as a good luck charm before bombing raids, and the trend continues with foreign paper money pinned all over the inn. In addition to its good choice of real ales, the pub has an amazing collection of over 500 whiskies. The menu offered by the new tenants includes shark steaks, whole sea bass, hot toddy duck, and steak pie.
OPEN: 11.30-3 5.30-11 (Open Sat & Sun all day in summer) Mon Closed Lunch **BAR MEALS:** L served all week 12-2 D served all week 6.30-9 Sat 6.30-9.30 Av main course £7.95
RESTAURANT: L served all week 11.30-2 D served all week 6.30-9.30 Av 3 course à la carte £17.50 **☺:** Free House **◖:** Tiger, Becon, Guest Beers & Seasonal. **FACILITIES:** Children's licence Garden: Patio & lawned aarea Dogs allowed **NOTES:** Parking 40

CRICK
Map 11 SP57

The Red Lion Inn
52 Main Rd NN6 7TX ☎ 01788 822342 ▤ 01788 822342
Dir: From M1 junct 18, 0.75m E on A428
A thatched, stone-built coaching inn dating from the 17th century, with beams and open fires. The Marks family, landlords here for 25 years, give their regulars and visitors exactly what they want - a friendly atmosphere, real ales and traditional food. The daily home-made steak pie is a lunchtime favourite, while fillet and sirloin steaks are a speciality in the evening. Fish eaters will find trout, stuffed lemon sole, salmon and seafood platter.
OPEN: 11-2.30 6.15-11 (Sun 12-3, 7-10.30) **BAR MEALS:** L served all week 12-2 D served Mon-Sat 6.30-9 Sun 12-2 Av main course £6.85 **☺:** Wellington Pub Co **◖:** Websters, Marston's Pedigree, Hook Norton Best, Greene King Old Speckled Hen.
FACILITIES: Garden: Terrace, picnic tables, chairs etc Dogs allowed Water **NOTES:** Parking 40

Pick of the Pubs

CASTLE ASHBY – NORTHAMPTONSHIRE

Falcon Hotel

There's a myriad of activities to enjoy if you're staying in this lovely inn. From clay pigeon shooting to Shakespeare in nearby Stratford-upon-Avon, you certainly won't be bored, but that's not to suggest that the hostelry itself lacks charm.

In tranquil village surroundings, the Falcon is perhaps the archetypal Northamptonshire country-cottage hotel. Attentive, knowledgeable service is the hallmark of the establishment, with owners Michael and Jennifer Eastick bringing a distinctly personal touch to proceedings. In the 60-seat restaurant everything is prepared from fresh ingredients. The fixed-price lunch menu offers salad of home-cured gravad lax, with artichokes and olives, breast of guinea fowl, with tarragon mousse and parma ham, and grilled pavé of salmon, topped with a mustard and herb crust. At dinner try spiced mussel broth, followed perhaps by pan-fried fillet of venison; seared king scallops, black pudding and pancetta torte; or grilled sea bass. Bedrooms are comfortable and are split between the inn itself and a cottage next door. Situated minutes from Castle Ashby House, the Falcon is within easy walking distance of the magnificent grounds of the home of the Marquss of Northampton, whose family has owned the 10,000 acre estate for over four centuries.

OPEN: 12-3 6-11 (Hotel bar 12-2, 7-11)
BAR MEALS: L served all week 12-2 D served all week 7-9.30 Av main course £9
RESTAURANT: L served all week 12-2 D served all week 7-9.30
🍴: Old English Inns
🍺: Scottish Courage John Smith's, Greene King Ruddles County & IPA.
🍷: 8
FACILITIES: Garden: Food served outdoors, herb garden
NOTES: Parking 60
ROOMS: 16 bedrooms en suite s£95 d£120

★★ 🏵 🍷   Map 11 SP85
NN7 1LF
☎ 01604 696200
🖨 01604 696673
Dir: A428 between Bedford & Northampton. Opposite war memorial

EAST HADDON
Map 11 SP66

Red Lion Hotel ✦ ♀
NN6 8BU ☎ 01604 770223 ▤ 01604 770767
Dir: *7m NW of Northampton on A428, 8m from junct 18 of M1. Midway between Northampton & Rugby.*
Near to Althorpe Park, this 17th-century thatched inn boasts a walled side garden filled with lilac, roses and fruit trees. The cosy interior has oak panelled settles and cast-iron framed tables. The bar menu offers hearty choices like ploughman's; smoked haddock and spinach lasagne; and Thai fish cakes with home-made mango chutney. In the dining room, try smoked trout and cucumber tian with gazpacho dressing; or Gressingham duck breast on red cabbage with orange sauce.
OPEN: 11-2.30 6-11 Closed: Dec 25 **BAR MEALS:** L served all week 12.15-2 D served Mon-Sat 7-9.30 **RESTAURANT:** L served all week 12.15-2 D served Mon-Sat 7-9.30 Av 3 course fixed price £21
🍽: Charles Wells 🍺: Wells Eagle IPA, & Bombardier, Adnams Broadside, Red Stripe. ♀: 7 **FACILITIES:** Child facs Garden: Large lawns overlooking hills and valleys Assistance dogs only in bar
NOTES: Parking 40

FARTHINGSTONE
Map 11 SP65

The Kings Arms
Main St NN12 8EZ ☎ 01327 361604 ▤ 01327 361604
e-mail: paul@kingsarms.fsbusiness.co.uk
Dir: *From M1 take A45 W, at Weedon join A5 then right on road signed Farthingstone*
This cosy 18th-century Grade II listed inn is tucked away in unspoilt countryside near Canons Ashby (NT), adorned with a collection of stone gargoyles. Excellent real ales can accompany the short menu, with its British cheese platters, sausage and mash, and Yorkshire pudding filled with steak and kidney or beef in Guinness. The landlord also sells cheeses and a variety of speciality regional foods including wild boar sausages, venison and Loch Fyne salmon.
OPEN: 12-3 7-11 (Lunchtime wknds only) Mon-Fri open evenings only **BAR MEALS:** L served Sat-Sun 12-2 D served none Some Friday evening specials 7.30-10 Av main course £6.70 🍺: Free House
🍺: Timothy Taylor Landlord, Jennings Bitter, Adnams, Brakspear Bitter.
FACILITIES: Garden: Many plants, herb garden, innovative design Dogs allowed Water **NOTES:** Parking 20 No credit cards

FOTHERINGHAY
Map 12 TL09

Pick of the Pubs

The Falcon Inn ◉ ♀
PE8 5HZ ☎ 01832 226254 ▤ 01832 226046
web: www.huntsbridge.com
Dir: *N of A605 between Peterborough & Oundle*
Overlooking Fotheringhay church and close to the site of Fotheringhay Castle, where Mary Queen of Scots was beheaded and Richard III was born is this attractive 18th-century stone-built inn. Set in a garden recently redesigned by landscape architect Bunny Guinness, The Falcon and chef/patron Ray Smikle are members of the Huntsbridge Inns group, each member producing innovative yet affordable food in a relaxing pub environment. For this dedication to good food they also hold an AA rosette. Settle down in the locals' tap bar, the smart rear dining room or the conservatory extension, and choose from the blackboard snack selection or the seasonal carte. Typical dishes are mozzarella, fig, candied pecan and avocado salad with crème fraîche and caviar;

continued

crab and saffron tart with green bean salad and tomato salad; penne pasta with cannelloni beans; roast garlic raddichio with oven-dried tomatoes; calves' liver with olive oil mashed potato, bacon and spinach; and desserts like sticky toffee pudding with rum and raisin ice cream; and tiramisu.

The Falcon Inn

OPEN: 11.30-3 6-11 (Sun 12-3,7-10.30)
BAR MEALS: L served all week 12-2.15 D served all week 7-9.30
RESTAURANT: L served all week 12-2.15 D served all week 6.30-9.30 Av 3 course à la carte £25 Av 2 course fixed price £12.50 🍺: Free House 🍺: Adnams Bitter, Greene King IPA, Scottish Courage John Smith's, Nethergate. ♀: 15
FACILITIES: Garden: Good views over historic Fotheringhay Church **NOTES:** Parking 30
See Pub Walk on page 353

GRAFTON REGIS
Map 11 SP74

The White Hart ♀
Northampton Rd NN12 7SR ☎ 01908 542123
e-mail: alan@pubgraftonregis.co.uk
Dir: *M1 junct 15 on A508 between Northampton & Milton Keynes*

Set in the historic village of Grafton Regis, where Edward IV married Elizabeth Woodville in 1464, the White Hart is a stone-built thatched pub that has been licensed since 1750. The restaurant menu might list garlic and mushroom chicken; fillet steak Diane; or fresh fillet of plaice Italian style. From the lounge menu, you can choose from the likes of steak and kidney pie; fresh battered cod, haddock or plaice; or grilled gammon steak. Round off with citrus fruit Bavarois, or caramel amaretti délice.
OPEN: 12-2.30 6-11 (Sun 12-2.30, 7-10.30) **BAR MEALS:** L served Tue-Sun 12-2 D served Tue-Sun 6-9.30 (Sun 12-2, 7-9)
RESTAURANT: L served Tue-Sun 12-1.30 D served Tue-Sat 6.30-9 🍺: Free House 🍺: Greene King, Abbot Ale & IPA. ♀: 14
FACILITIES: Garden: Large floral garden, food served at lunchtime Dogs allowed Water **NOTES:** Parking 40
See advert on page 361

Pick of the Pubs

George and Dragon

An attractive, honey-stoned, 16th-century pub tucked away by the church in a pretty village protected by Conservation Area status. Formerly a free house, the pub is owned by the Everard brewery of Leicester.

It is well placed for motorists on the M40, who can turn off at Junction 11 two miles away, and also popular with the business community in nearby Banbury, who can easily make it for lunch or a drink here and back for the afternoon. There's a welcoming feel to its three comfortable bars, with low beams, simple wooden chairs and settles, log fires, and warm terracotta decor. Blackboards list an interesting selection of food, from sandwiches, filled jacket potatoes, and pasta dishes such as tagliatelle with chicken, bacon and leek, to scampi; sirloin and fillet steaks; salmon and tuna in a cream and dill sauce; shepherd's pie; and vegetable lasagne. A perennial favourite with George and Dragon regulars is deep-fried haddock, chips and mushy peas. Some dishes come and go as the weather changes, so a cold winter's day might prompt the preparation of green Thai prawn curry. The Northamptonshire countryside is a delightful area to explore and is well placed for visits to Oxfordshire. New landlord.

OPEN: 12-11 Sun 12-10.30
BAR MEALS: L served all week 12-2.30 D served Mon-Sat 6.30-9.30 Av main course £9
RESTAURANT: L served all week 12-2.30 D served Mon-Sat 7-9.30
🍺: Free House
🍺: Theakston Best, Scottish Courage Courage Directors
FACILITIES: Garden
NOTES: Parking 40

Map 11 SP44
Silver St OX17 2JR
☎ 01295 711500
🖹 01295 710516
@ thegeorgeanddragon
@msn.com
Dir: From M40 take A361 to Daventry, 1st right to Chacombe, 2nd left in village

GREAT OXENDON
Map 11 SP78

The George Inn ♀
LE16 8NA ☎ 01858 465205 🖳 01858 465205
Dir: Telephone for directions
A country dining pub on the main A508, The George dates in part from the 16th century. It maintains a traditional atmosphere with log fires in the bar and a Victorian-style restaurant. A well-lit car park is provided, and a conservatory overlooks the large formal gardens and patio. Typical dishes are roast cod with black olives and sun-dried tomato mash; and crisp belly pork on buttered noodles, with spinach, mushrooms & black bean sauce.
OPEN: 11.30-3 6-11 **BAR MEALS:** L served all week 12-2.30 D served Mon-Sat 7-10 (Closed Sun pm) Av main course £9.95 **RESTAURANT:** L served Tues-Sun 12-2.30 D served Mon-Sat 7-10 Sun night closed Av 3 course à la carte £30 ☺: Free House 🍺: Interbrew Bass, Adnams Bitter. ♀: 9 **FACILITIES:** Child facs Garden: Large formal, large patio for dining Dogs allowed Water **NOTES:** Parking 34

HARRINGTON
Map 11 SP78

The Tollemache Arms ♀
High St NN6 9NU ☎ 01536 710469 🖳 01536 713447
e-mail: enquiries@tollemache-harrington.co.uk
Dir: 6m from Kettering, off A14. Follow signs for Harrington

Situated near to Harrington airfield and museums is this pretty, thatched 16th-century village inn originally belonging to the Knights of St John. It was named in the 19th century, after a local vicar who was the incumbent for 60 years. In addition to ales from Wells and Greene King, freshly prepared food made from local produce is served throughout the character bars and restaurant. Typical dishes include chilli beef stir fry, Cajun pork, Moroccan lamb, steak and stilton cobbler, mushroom and brie stroganoff, haddock in parsley sauce, and selection of grills, sandwiches and baguettes. Popular Sunday lunch menu.
OPEN: 12-3 6-11 (open all day Sun) 25, 26 Dec, 1 Jan Closed eve **BAR MEALS:** L served all week 12-2.30 D served all week 7-9 Av main course £8.50 **RESTAURANT:** L served Mon-Sat 12-2.30 D served all week 7-9 ☺: Charles Wells 🍺: Wells Eagle IPA & Bombardier Premium Bitter, Adnams Broadside & Old Speckled Hen. ♀: 6 **FACILITIES:** Garden: Garden overlooking countryside **NOTES:** Parking 60

The White Hart
Northampton Rd, Grafton Regis NN12 7SR
Tel: 01908 542123   www.pubgraftonregis.co.uk

Grafton Regis is a small village located on the main A508 midway between Milton Keynes and Northampton. This small friendly village with approximately 96 residents is home to *The White Hart*, a small 16th Century Stone, Thatched property owned by the same family for almost 9 years. Alan one of the owners is also the main Chef, ensuring quality food at all times.

Although we are a Free House we choose to use Green King as our supplier for our beers, we serve a very nice well kept IPA. The Abbots pretty good too, we only stock 2 main real ales usually, as we like to look after them and turn them over, to ensure you get the perfect pint every time, we sometimes have a third usually in the summer months and occasionally at Christmas.

We have just been awarded by Green King brewery the title of
Catering Pub of the Year
winning first place from over 700 outlets!!!

HARRINGWORTH
Map 11 SP99

The White Swan
Seaton Rd NN17 3AF ☎ 01572 747543 🖳 01572 747323
e-mail: thewhiteswan@fsmail.net
Dir: Off B672 NE of Corby

Photographs recalling the nearby World War II airbase decorate the bar of this stone-built 15th century coaching inn. The prettily-situated free house also displays an old collection of craftsman's tools and memorabilia. There's a nice selection of well-kept real ales, and the constantly changing blackboard menu is complemented by a carte that offers pan-roast loin of lamb, roast hazelnut and dill risotto, chicken Harringworth supreme, and pan-fried saddle of venison.
OPEN: 11-2 6.30-11 (Sat 11.30-3, Sun 12-4, 7-10.30) Closed: 25 Dec, 1 Jan **BAR MEALS:** L served all week 12-2 D served all week 7-9 Av main course £7.95 **RESTAURANT:** L served all week 12-2 D served all week 7-9 ☺: Free House 🍺: Timothy Taylor Landlord, Greene King Old Speckled Hen and Guest Ales.
FACILITIES: Garden: Patio **NOTES:** Parking 10

KETTERING
Map 11 SP87

The Overstone Arms ♀
Stringers Hill, Pytchley NN14 1EU
☎ 01536 790215 ▤ 01536 791098
Dir: 1m from Kettering, 5m from Wellingborough
The 18th-century coaching inn is at the heart of the village
and has been home to the Pytchley Hunt, which over the
years has attracted many royal visitors. Years ago guests
would travel up from London, staying here or at Althorp Hall,
mainly for the hunting. Despite its rural location, the pub is
just a mile from the busy A1-M1 link road (A14). Home-made
pies, grilled trout, steaks, lasagne and curry are typical.
OPEN: 12-2.30 7-11 Closed: 1 Jan **BAR MEALS:** L served all week
12-2 D served all week 7-9.30 Av main course £7.50
RESTAURANT: L served all week 12-2 D served all week 7-9.30
◉: ◀: Greene King, Marston's Pedigree, Interbrew Bass, Adnams
Bitter. ♀: 8 **FACILITIES:** Garden **NOTES:** Parking 50

LOWICK
Map 11 SP98

The Snooty Fox ◉ ♀
NN14 3BH ☎ 01832 733434 ▤ 733931
e-mail: thesnootyfox@btinternet.com
Dir: Off the A14 5 m E of Kettering on A6116. Straight over at 1st
roundabout and L into Lowick
Exquisite carved beams are among the more unusual features
at this 16th-century building which has been a pub since 1700.
Originally the manor house, it is supposedly haunted by a
horse and its rider killed at the Battle of Naseby. The new
operators now specialise in grill and rotisserie cooking, so
check out the rack of Cornish lamb, Gloucester Old Spot pork
belly, sirloin steaks, and others. Fresh Cornish fish is also a
feature, as is a good wine list.
OPEN: 12-3 6-11 25-26 Dec & 1 Jan Closed eve
BAR MEALS: L served all week 12-2 D served all week 6.30-9.30
Av main course £11 **RESTAURANT:** L served all week 12-2
D served all week 6.30-9.30 Av 3 course à la carte £25 ◀: Jennings
Cumberland, Greene King Ipa, Fullers London Pride, Morland Old
Speckled Hen & Morland Original. ♀: 7 **FACILITIES:** Garden:
Small lawned area at front of property Dogs allowed
NOTES: Parking 100

MARSTON TRUSSELL
Map 11 SP68

Pick of the Pubs

The Sun Inn ★★ ◉ ♥♀
Main St LE16 9TY ☎ 01858 465531 ▤ 01858 433155
e-mail: manager@suninn.com
Dir: S of A4304 between Market Harborough & Lutterworth
This 17th-century coaching inn has a lot to offer - an
original red brick bar, roaring real coal winter fires, a
friendly welcome, well-kept ales and a carefully chosen
wine list. Add to that a non-smoking restaurant, and a
cuisine - for which chef/patron Paul Elliot holds an AA
rosette - to suit all tastes, and you have the perfect place
for an evening out. Start, perhaps, with terrine of foie
gras and duck confit; roasted hand-dived scallop with
oriental salmon and pak choi; or polenta crisps and
salsa. Mains could be herb crusted rack of lamb with
creamed fresh peas; fresh lobster with herb butter and
dressed beef fillet with horseradish
rarebit; and pan-fried sea trout with herb scented spring
vegetable risotto. Vanilla pannacotta and black peppered
strawberries; hot liquorice soufflé, prune and Armagnac

continued

ice cream; and millefeuilles' of crepes, custard cream,
redcurrants, and raspberry coulis are typical desserts. In
summer, meals are also served on the paved front patio.
OPEN: 12-2 6-11 Closed: Dec 26, Jan 2
BAR MEALS: L served Mon-Sun 12-1.45 D served all week
7-9.30 Sun 12-2 Av main course £10.95
RESTAURANT: L served Mon-Sun 12-1.45 D served all week
7-9.30 Sun 12-2 Av 3 course à la carte £28 Av 3 course fixed price
£22 ◉: Free House ◀: Guiness, Ruddles,. ♀: 8
FACILITIES: Front patio, seating for 20 **NOTES:** Parking 60
ROOMS: 20 bedrooms en suite 2 family rooms s£59 d£69

NORTHAMPTON
Map 11 SP76

The Fox & Hounds ♀
Main St, Great Brington NN7 4JA
☎ 01604 770651 ▤ 01604 770164
e-mail: althorpcoachinn@aol.com
Dir: Telephone for directions

Dating from the 16th century, this much photographed stone
and thatch coaching inn stands on the Althorp Estate,
ancestral home of the Spencer family. Its many charms
include a pretty courtyard and garden, real fires, numerous
guest ales and a reputation for quality food. Jacket potatoes
and ciabatta sandwiches feature on the snack menu; other
meals include Kinsale seafood pie; pan-fried kangaroo; and
spinach, tomato and mozzarella pudding.
OPEN: 11-11 (Sun 12-10.30) **BAR MEALS:** L served all week
12-2.30 D served all week 6.30-9.30 Sun 12-2.30, 6.30-8.30 Av main
course £6.85 **RESTAURANT:** L served all week 12-2.30 D served all
week 6.30-9.30 Sun 12-2.30, 6.30-8.30 Av 3 course à la carte £19.95
◀: Green King IPA, Speckled Hen, Fullers London Pride, Abbot Ale.
♀: 8 **FACILITIES:** Garden: Secluded wall area, lots of trees, seating
Dogs allowed Water bowls, toys, dog chews **NOTES:** Parking 50

OUNDLE
Map 11 TL08

The Mill at Oundle ♀
Barnwell Rd PE8 5PB ☎ 01832 272621 ▤ 01832 272221
e-mail: reservations@millatoundle.com
Dir: A14 Thrapston exit, A605 toward Peterborough, 8m Oundle turning,
1m to pub
Set on the banks of the River Nene, this converted watermill
dates back to the Domesday Book. These days it comprises a
waterside bar and two restaurants. La Trattoria offers an
open air eating area with river views; the Granary on the top
floor has high ceilings and oak beams. The menu ranges
through grills, Tex Mex dishes, fish and pasta to Caribbean
chicken, home-made lasagne, and the speciality sausage of
the day.
OPEN: 12-3 6.30-11 (Summer all day Sat-Sun) Closed: Dec 26-27
BAR MEALS: L served all week 12-2 D served all week 6.30-9 (Sun

continued

6.30-8.30) Av main course £8.95 **RESTAURANT:** L served all week 12-2 D served all week 6.30-9 (Sun 6.30-8.30) ☺: Free House ◖: Scottish Courage Theakston Best & XB, Marston's Pedigree. ♀: 12 **FACILITIES:** Child facs Garden: Terraces overlooking River Nene **NOTES:** Parking 80

The Montagu Arms ⌇⌇☞ ♀
Barnwell PE8 5PH ☎ 01832 273726 ▤ 01832 275555
e-mail: ianmsimmons@aol.com
Dir: Off A605 opposite Oundle slip Rd, access to A605 via A14 or A1
One of Northamptonshire's oldest inns, the Montagu Arms was originally three cottages dating from 1601, housing the workmen building the nearby manor house. The inn has a large garden, well equipped for children's play, and overlooks the brook and village green of the royal village of Barnwell. An extensive menu serving the bar and restaurant ranges through snacks and sharing platters, to Rutland sausages and mash, stuffed chicken, and crispy fish pie.
OPEN: 12-3 6-11 (Sat-Sun all day) **BAR MEALS:** L served all week 12-2.30 D served all week 7-10 Av main course £5
RESTAURANT: L served all week 12-2.30 D served all week 7-10 Av 3 course à la carte £15 ☺: Free House ◖: Adnams Broadside, Interbrew Flowers IPA & Original, Hop Back Summer Lightning, Fullers London Pride. ♀: 14 **FACILITIES:** Child facs Garden: Large lawn, ample benches, pétanque Dogs allowed Water **NOTES:** Parking 25

SIBBERTOFT   Map 11 SP68

The Red Lion ♀
43 Welland Rise LE16 9UD ☎ 01858 880011 ▤ 01858 880011
e-mail: andrew@redlion880011.wanadoo.co.uk
Dir: From Market Harborough take A4304, then A50. After 1m turn L
Friendly and civilised 300-year-old pub which has recently been refurbished. Among many features thankfully retained are the oak beams and open fires. Try pheasant with haggis parfait and Drambuie sauce; forest mushroom crumble with savoury white wine cream; roast Gressingham duck breast with caramelised orange and cumin jus; or whole sea bass steamed with white wine and Thai herbs. A very extensive wine list and an appetising choice of home-made desserts are further bonuses.
OPEN: 12-2 6.30-11 (Sun 7-10.30) **BAR MEALS:** L served Wed-Sun 12-2 D served all week 6.30-9.45 Lunch 12-3 Av main course £10 **RESTAURANT:** L served Wed-Sun 12-2 D served all week 6.30-9.45 Sun L 12-3 Av 3 course à la carte £18 ☺: Free House ◖: Adnams Bitter, Gales HSB, Bass, Hoegaarden. ♀: 10
FACILITIES: Child facs Garden: Patio area, lawn
NOTES: Parking 15

STOKE BRUERNE   Map 11 SP74

The Boat Inn ⌇☞
NN12 7SB ☎ 01604 862428 ▤ 01604 864314
e-mail: info@boatinn.co.uk web: www.boatinn.co.uk
Dir: 4m from junct 15 M1. Signed A508 Stoke Bruerne. Continue through village, 0.75m turn right into village, over canal bridge and car park is on right.
Traditional thatched canalside inn run by the same family since 1877, located by a working lock and opposite a popular canal museum. Inside are cosy bars with open fires and flagstones. Dishes range from steak and ale pie or BBQ chicken to tiger prawns with pasta, or spinach and ricotta cannelloni. The "Boatmans Meal" includes whole lobster thermidor, supreme of chicken chasseur, and cod loin in white wine and shallot sauce. Good range of jacket potatoes filled with Greenland prawns and chicken tikka mayonnaise.

continued

The Boat Inn

OPEN: 9-11 (3-6 closed Mon-Thu in winter) **BAR MEALS:** L served all week 9.30-9 D served all week Av main course £7
RESTAURANT: L served Tue-Sun 12-2 D served all week 7-9 Sun 12-2. 6.30-8.30. Fixed price menu £22.50 Sat night. Av 3 course fixed price £18 ☺: Free House ◖: Banks Bitter, Marstons Pedigree, Adnams Southwold, Frog Island Best. **FACILITIES:** Children's licence Garden: Table and grass area by canal Dogs allowed Water
NOTES: Parking 50

SULGRAVE   Map 11 SP54

The Star Inn
Manor Rd OX17 2SA ☎ 01295 760389 ▤ 01295 760991
Dir: M1 junct 15A follow signs for Silverstone race circuit or M40 junct 11 follow A422 to Brackley. Follow brown signs for Sulgrave Manor

A 17th-century inn with real ales (Hook Norton) and good food from chef/proprietor Jamie King and his team. The cosy bar area has flagstone floors and a large inglenook fireplace, and in summer there's a vine-covered patio. The same menu is served in the bar and no-smoking dining room, offering the likes of Oathill Farm gammon steak, Bury black pudding hash with a poached egg and mustard sauce, Sulgrave lamb chops with watercress and artichoke hearts, or wild sea bass with tomato, fennel and potato salad.
OPEN: 11-2.30 6-11 (Sun 12-5 only) Closed: 25-26 Dec Rest: Closed Mon Lunchtimes **BAR MEALS:** L served Tue-Sun 12-2 D served Tue-Sat 6.30-9 (Sun 12.30-3) Av main course £9.50
RESTAURANT: L served Tue-Sun 12-2 D served Tue-Sat 6.30-9.30 (Sun 12.30-3) Av 3 course à la carte £18 ☺: Hook Norton ◖: Hook Norton Best, Old Hooky, Generation, & Haymaker.
FACILITIES: Garden: Vine covered patio with wooden benches & lawn Dogs allowed Water, dogs in bar by prior arrangement
NOTES: Parking 20

Pubs offering a good choice of fish on their menu

WADENHOE
Map 11 TL08

Pick of the Pubs

The King's Head 🐟
Church St PE8 5ST ☎ 01832 720024
This friendly free house is a 16th-century inn, stone-built and partially thatched, standing by the River Nene in a pretty village setting. There is seating by the river and moorings for boats. Inside you'll find oak beams, quarry-tiled floors and an inglenook fireplace. The public bar, popular with locals, is the perfect place for a pint of Adnams, while the lounge bar and cottage room provide a relaxing atmosphere for a meal. The chef landlord excels in curries, sauces and seafood. You might try Thai-style crab and scallop cakes with hollandaise sauce, or marlin steak pan-fried with garlic and whole baby sweetcorn, and don't miss out on the delicious home-made puddings. Traditional pub skittles is a feature at the King's Head, and there is also a function room - the Old Sty - which really did used to be the pub's pigsty.
OPEN: 12-3 6.30-11 All day on wknds during sunny weather (Sun 12-4 Closed Sun eve in winter) **BAR MEALS:** L served all week 12-2 D served Wed-Sat 7-9 (Sun 12-2)
RESTAURANT: L served all week D served Wed-Sat 7-9
🍺: Free House 🍺: Adnams, Timothy Taylor Landlord, Oakham JHB, Adnams Broadside. **FACILITIES:** Garden: Large paddock, courtyard, patio, seating Dogs allowed Water
NOTES: Parking 20

WESTON
Map 11 SP54

Pick of the Pubs

The Crown 🍷
Helmdon Rd NN12 8PX ☎ 01295 760310 📠 01295 760310
e-mail: thecrown-weston@tiscali.co.uk

The first documented evidence of The Crown pins the year down to 1593. It has been a hostelry since the reign of Elizabeth I, and its first recorded owner was All Souls College, Oxford. On a more sinister note, Lord Lucan was allegedly spotted in the inn on the night after his nanny was murdered, quietly enjoying a pint. Nearby attractions are Sulgrave Manor, ancestral home of George Washington, and Silverstone race circuit. A typical menu might start with goat's cheese and sun-dried tomato tart and salad; or moules marinière and warm French bread. Mains range from the simple Charolais minute steak and caramelised onion baguette; to lamb casserole with mint and apricots, vegetables and herb mash; and wild mushroom risotto, tomato and rocket salad. Desserts take

in a selection of ice creams and sorbets, as well as raspberry crème brûlée; and hot chocolate soufflé. Food is prepared from fresh ingredients, and the pub has a 25 bin wine list.
OPEN: 6-11 (Fri 12-3, Sat 12-3.30 Sun 12-10.30)
BAR MEALS: L served Fri-Sun 12-2.30 D served Wed-Sat 6-9.30 Av main course £7.50 🍺: Greene King IPA , Hook Norton Best, Bombardier, Black Sheep. 🍷: 6 **FACILITIES:** Garden: Small garden at front with tables Dogs allowed water
NOTES: Parking 10

WOODNEWTON
Map 11 TL09

The White Swan
22 Main St PE8 5EB ☎ 01780 470381
Dir: 5m off A605/A47
Welcoming village local comprising a simple, single oblong room, one end focusing on the bar and wood-burning stove, the other set up as a dining area. The regularly changing blackboard menu may offer home-made soup, fresh cod fillet in beer batter; stuffed chicken with stilton, bacon and port sauce; beef stroganoff, curries and steaks. Finish with a traditional home-made sweet, like fruit crumble or sticky toffee pudding. Recent change of hands.
OPEN: 12-2.30 6-11 (Fri from 6, Sat from 6.30, Sun to 3.30)
BAR MEALS: L served Wed-Sun 12-1.45 D served Tue-Sat 7-9 (Sun 12-2.30) **RESTAURANT:** L served Wed-Sun 12-1.45 D served Tue-Sat 7-9 Sun 12-2.30 🍺: Free House 🍺: Adnams, London Pride, Bass, Batemans. **FACILITIES:** Garden **NOTES:** Parking 20

NORTHUMBERLAND

ALLENHEADS
Map 18 NY84

The Allenheads Inn
NE47 9HJ ☎ 01434 685200 📠 01434 685200
e-mail: theallenheadsinn@yahoo.co.uk
Dir: From Hexham take B6305, then B6295 to Allenheads
Situated in the remote high country of the North Pennines, perfect for walking and exploring, this 18th-century pub is full of charm and character. A useful watering hole for those using the coast-to-coast cycle route, the Allenheads has a friendly, welcoming atmosphere. Relax in the popular Antiques Bar, or the unusually-named Forces Room, and enjoy steak pie, lasagne, battered cod or one of the pub's seasonal specials.
OPEN: 12-4 7-11 (Fri-Sat 12-11, Sun 12-10.30)
BAR MEALS: L served all week 12-2.30 D served all week 7-9 Av main course £5.50 **RESTAURANT:** L served Sun 12-2.30
🍺: Free House 🍺: Greene King Abbott Ale, Tetley Bitter, Timothy Taylor Landlord, Black Sheep Bitter and Guest Ales.
FACILITIES: Garden **NOTES:** Parking 10

ALNWICK
Map 21 NU11

Masons Arms 🍷
Stamford, Nr Rennington NE66 3RX
☎ 01665 577275 📠 01665 577894
e-mail: bookings@masonsarms.net web: www.masonsarms.net
Dir: NE of Alnwick on B1340, 0.5m past Ronnington
This 200-year-old coaching inn has been tastefully modernised, and is known by the local community as Stamford Cott. It is a useful staging post for visitors to Hadrian's Wall, Lindisfarne and the large number of nearby golf courses. The same substantial home-cooked food is

continued

continued

available in the bar and non-smoking restaurant, using the best of local produce. Expect Northumbrian sausage ring; grilled lemon sole; and spinach and ricotta cannelloni.

Masons Arms

OPEN: 12-2 6.30-11 (Sun 12-2 7-10.30) **BAR MEALS:** L served all week 12-2 D served all week 6.30-9 Av main course £7.50 **RESTAURANT:** L served all week 12-2 D served all week 7-9 Av 3 course à la carte £15.75 ⊜: Free House 🍺: Scottish Courage John Smith's, Theakston Best, Secret Kingdom, Gladiator. ♀: 12 **FACILITIES:** Children's licence Garden: Grassed area with fountain and seating Dogs allowed **NOTES:** Parking 50 **ROOMS:** 11 bedrooms en suite 3 family rooms d£32.50 (♦♦♦♦)

BAMBURGH   Map 21 NU13

Lord Crewe Arms Hotel ★★

Front St NE69 7BL ☎ 01668 214243 🖹 01668 214273 e-mail: lca@tinyonline.co.uk Historic coaching inn named after Lord Crewe, who was one of the Prince Bishops of Durham. Perfect base for touring Northumberland, exploring the Cheviot Hills and visiting nearby Holy Island. Good, wholesome pub food ranges from local kipper pâté, wild boar and apple sausages and pan-fried supreme of chicken, to breast of guinea fowl with an apricot, apple and raisin stuffing. **OPEN:** 12-3 6-11 Closed: Jan-Feb **BAR MEALS:** L served all week 12-2.30 D served all week 6.30-9 Av main course £7.25 **RESTAURANT:** L served all week 12-2.30 D served all week 6.30-9 Av 3 course à la carte £25 ⊜: Free House 🍺: Interbrew Bass, Black Sheep Best, Fullers London Pride. **FACILITIES:** Garden: Food served outside **NOTES:** Parking 20 **ROOMS:** 18 bedrooms 17 en suite s£52 d£98

Pick of the Pubs

Victoria Hotel ★★ ♀

Front St NE69 7BP ☎ 01668 214431 🖹 01668 214404 e-mail: enquiries@victoriahotel.net web: www.victoriahotel.net
See Pick of the Pubs on page 364

BELFORD   Map 21 NU13

Blue Bell Hotel ★★★

Market Place NE70 7NE ☎ 01668 213543 🖹 01668 213787 e-mail: bluebell@globalnet.co.uk web: www.bluebellhotel.com *Dir: Off A1 25m from Berwick, 15m from Alnwick* A long-established and creeper-clad coaching inn located in the centre of Belford. Just off the A1 it makes a convenient base for exploring Northumberland's magnificent coastline and the Cheviot Hills. The inn offers a friendly, relaxed atmosphere, and a good range of real ales. Choices from the

continued

menu in the elegant restaurant may include tournedos of Aberdeen Angus steak with wild mushroom sauce, and roasted monkfish in a light tomato concassé, while lamb balti, chicken fajitas, and steak and kidney pie with Newcastle brown are typical of the bar and buttery. Three acres of garden with an orchard and vegetable garden.

Blue Bell Hotel

OPEN: 11-2.30 6.30-11 **BAR MEALS:** L served all week 11-2 D served all week 6.30-9 Av main course £8.50 **RESTAURANT:** L served all week 12-2 D served all week 7-9 Av 3 course à la carte £25 ⊜: Free House 🍺: Interbrew Boddingtons Bitter, Northumbrian Smoothe, Calders, Tetleys Smooth. **FACILITIES:** Child facs Garden: 3 acres **NOTES:** Parking 17 **ROOMS:** 17 bedrooms en suite 3 family rooms s£44 d£88

BERWICK-UPON-TWEED   Map 21 NT95

The Rob Roy 🍴 ♀

Dock Rd, Tweedmouth TD15 2BE ☎ 01289 306428 🖹 01289 303629 e-mail: therobroy@btinternet.com *Dir: Exit A1 2m S of Berwick at A1167 signed Scremerston, to rdbt signed Spittal, then right. 1m to Albion PH, left, 1m to pub*

Originally a riverside cottage built about 150 years ago, the Rob Roy was converted in the 1970s and has earned itself a fine reputation for fresh local seafood over the years. The bar has exposed stone walls, an open log fire and some striking salmon fishing paraphernalia, and serves said seafood, Border meats, snacks and sandwiches. More seafood specialities, including local fresh fish and shellfish, are served in the restaurant. **OPEN:** 12-2.30 7-11 Closed: 3wks Feb or Mar. Xmas & New Year Closed: Wed lunch Nov-Mar **BAR MEALS:** L served Mon, Wed-Sun 12-2 D served Mon, Wed-Sun 7-9 (Sun 7-8.30) Av main course £8.50 **RESTAURANT:** L served Wed-Mon 12-1.45 D served Wed-Mon 7-9.30 Av 3 course à la carte £25 ⊜: Free House 🍺: Tennants 70/-. ♀: 8 **ROOMS:** 5 bedrooms en suite 1 family room s£38 d£50 (♦♦♦♦) No children overnight

Pick of the Pubs

BAMBURGH – NORTHUMBERLAND

Victoria Hotel

This exuberant stone-built Northumbrian hotel has been substantially refurbished and now boasts 29 bedrooms and an indoor children's play area. The modern brasserie with its stylish domed glass ceiling serves up food of a similarly modern bent, with starters like Seahouses smoked haddock fishcakes served with a salsa vierge, or tian of Farne Island crab with tiger prawns and black olive tapenade.

Main courses include Cajun-spiced Gressingham duck breast on a creamed leek & orange sauce, or darn of wild salmon on baby spinach with red wine and thyme sauce. Glazed lemon tart with raspberries, dark chocolate mousse with creme Anglaise and blackcurrant sorbet, and a selection of Northumbrian cheeses might be chosen to round off the meal. Service is friendly and attentive and the location - close to the famous castle and overlooking Bamburgh's historic village

green - is very appealing. The building may be cool and modernised but the welcome is warm and traditional. The hotel is popular as a base for golfing breaks, as there are a lot of courses along this spectacular stretch of coastline. The nearest course is Bamburgh, in the heart of the village, which provides an 18-hole course for golfers of all standards. The area has also become popular with fans of Harry Potter, as nearby Alnwick Castle was used as a location in the recent films.

OPEN: 11-11 (Fri-Sat 11-12)
BAR MEALS: L served all week 12-9 D served all week 7-9 Av main course £6
RESTAURANT: L served Sun 12-2 D served all week 7-9 Av 3 course à la carte £22
🍺: Free House
🍺: John Smiths, Theakstons Cool Keg, plus guest ales. ♀: 20
FACILITIES: Dogs allowed Water provided **NOTES:** Parking 6
ROOMS: 29 bedrooms en suite s£44 d£78

★★ ♀   Map 21 NU13
Front St NE69 7BP
☎ 01668 214431
📄 01668 214404
📧 enquiries@victoriahotel.net
🌐 www.victoriahotel.net
Dir: In centre of Bamburgh village green

BLANCHLAND
Map 18 NY95

Lord Crewe Arms ★★
DH8 9SP ☎ 01434 675251 ▤ 01434 675337
e-mail: lord@crewearms.freeserve.co.uk
web: www.lordcrewehotel.com
Dir: 10m S of Hexham via B6306
Once the abbot's house of Blanchland Abbey, this is one of England's oldest inns. Antique furniture, blazing log fires and flagstone floors make for an atmospheric setting. Wide-ranging, good-value bar and restaurant menus with specials offer filled rolls, salads, savoury bean hot pot, and game pie. Watch out, there are lots of ghosts!
OPEN: 11-11 **BAR MEALS:** L served all week 12-2 D served all week 7-9 Av main course £7 **RESTAURANT:** L served Sun 12-2 D served all week 7-9.15 Av 4 course fixed price £30 ⊕: Free House ⚫: Black Sheep, Wylam Gold, John Smiths, Guiness.
FACILITIES: Large garden Dogs allowed **NOTES:** Parking 20
ROOMS: 21 bedrooms en suite 4 family rooms s£80 d£120

CARTERWAY HEADS
Map 19 NZ05

Pick of the Pubs

The Manor House Inn 🐟 ♀
DH8 9LX ☎ 01207 255268
Dir: A69 W from Newcastle, left onto A68 then S for 8m. Inn on right.

This small family-run free house enjoys spectacular views across open moorland and the Derwent Reservoir from its lonely position high on the A68. The cosy stone-walled bar, with its log fires, low-beamed ceiling and massive timber support, offers a good range of well-kept real ales and around 70 malt whiskies. Built circa 1760, the inn has a succession of dining areas, and a huge collection of mugs and jugs hangs from the beams in the candlelit restaurant. Typical dishes include Cumberland sausage and mash; panfried scallops with chili jam; filo baskets of king prawns and mussels; roast duck breast; and various steaks. Home-made puddings are a feature, as is the choice of up to 16 local cheeses.
OPEN: 11-11 **BAR MEALS:** L served all week 12-9.30 D served all week 12-9 Av main course £11 **RESTAURANT:** L served all week 12-2.30 D served all week 7-9.30 (Sun 9) Av 3 course à la carte £22.50 ⊕: Free House ⚫: Theakstons Best, Mordue Workie Ticket, Greene King Ruddles County, Scottish Courage Courage Directors. ♀: 12 **FACILITIES:** Children's licence Garden: Small picnic area Dogs allowed **NOTES:** Parking 60
ROOMS: 4 bedrooms en suite s£38 d£60 (♦♦♦♦)

 Brewery/Company

CHATTON
Map 21 NU02

The Percy Arms Hotel ♀
Main Rd NE66 5PS ☎ 01668 215244 ▤ 01668 215277
Dir: From Alnwick take A1 N, then B6348 to Chatton

Traditional 19th-century forming coaching inn, situated in the heart of rural Northumberland. Expect a warm, traditional pub welcome, as well as a selection of fine beers, wines and tempting food. Bar menu includes Aberdeen Angus steaks, deep-fried haddock, steak and kidney pie and a wide selection of fish and seafood dishes. Bar games include snooker, pool and darts, but those who wish to can still enjoy a quiet pint in comfort.
OPEN: 11-11 (Sun12-10.30) **BAR MEALS:** L served all week 12-2 D served all week 6.30-9 **RESTAURANT:** L served all week 12-2 D served all week 6.30-8.30 ⊕: Jennings ⚫: Jennings Beers. ♀: 8 **FACILITIES:** Child facs Children's licence Garden: patio/terrace, front beer garden **NOTES:** Parking 30

CHRISTON BANK
Map 21 NU22

Blink Bonny NEW 🐟 ♀
NE66 3ES
Dir: From Denwick take B1340 for 8m, pub on left at T-junct within Christon Bank
Named after the famous racehorse, the Blink Bonny is a traditional stone-built village pub, just two miles from the sea. The proprietors pride themselves on their Northumbrian hospitality, welcoming regulars and visitors alike, and have built up a good reputation for their food. Locally caught fresh fish is a key feature, including seafood platter with Greek salad and fresh baked bread; pint o' prawns; Thai mussels, and Blink Bonny crab cakes.
OPEN: 5-12 **BAR MEALS:** L served Sat-Sun 12-3 D served all week 6.30-9 Av main course £10 **RESTAURANT:** L served Sat-Sun 12-2.30 D served Mon-Sat 6.30-9 Sun 12-3 Av 3 course à la carte £20 Av 2 course fixed price £8.50 ⚫: John Smiths Smooth, Northumbrian Smooth, Worthingtons Creamflow, Guinness.
FACILITIES: Child facs Children's licence Garden: Grassed, enclosed garden, tables Dogs allowed Fresh water **NOTES:** Parking 22

CORBRIDGE
Map 21 NY96

The Angel of Corbridge 🐟 ♀
Main St NE45 5LA ☎ 01434 632119 ▤ 01434 633496
e-mail: info@theangelofcorbridge.co.uk
Dir: 0.5m off A69, signed Corbridge
Stylish 17th-century coaching inn overlooking the River Tyne. Relax with the daily papers in the wood-panelled lounge or attractive bars, or enjoy a home-made dish or two from the extensive menu choice. Options include pan-fried chicken
continued

CORBRIDGE continued

breast with spicy cous cous, salmon and lemon fish cakes and risotto of asparagus and leek.
OPEN: 11-11 (Sun 11-10.30) **BAR MEALS:** L served all week 12-2.30 D served Mon-Sat 6-9.30 Av main course £15
RESTAURANT: L served all week 12-2.30 D served Mon-Sat 6-9.30 Av 3 course à la carte £25 ☺: Free House ◑: Black Sheep Best, Mordue, Boddingtons. ♀: 10 **FACILITIES:** Children's licence Garden: Walled garden with seats and grassed area Dogs allowed Water **NOTES:** Parking 25

CRASTER   Map 21 NU21

Cottage Inn ♀
Dunstan Village NE66 3SZ ☎ 01665 576658 🖷 01665 576788
e-mail: enquiries@cottageinnhotel.co.uk
Dir: NW of Howick to Embleton road
In an area of outstanding natural beauty, easily accessible from the A1, this 18th-century inn is located in a hamlet close to the sea. There is a beamed bar, Harry Hotspur Restaurant, conservatory, loggia and patio. One menu serves all - a comprehensive choice of snacks, full meals, kids' and vegetarian options, supplemented by daily specials. Local ingredients are used wherever possible in dishes such as seafood platter, Craster fish stew and whole joint of lamb.
OPEN: 11-12 **BAR MEALS:** L served all week 12-2.30 D served all week 6-9.30 Av main course £9.50 **RESTAURANT:** L served all week 12-2.30 D served all week 6-9.30 ☺: Free House ◑: Belhaven 80/-, Wylam Bitter, John Smiths. ♀: 12 **FACILITIES:** Child facs Garden: Patio area with 6 acres of lawn & woodland **NOTES:** Parking 60 **ROOMS:** 10 bedrooms en suite s£39 d£69 (◆◆◆)

Jolly Fisherman Inn 🍷
Haven Hill NE66 3TR ☎ 01665 576461
e-mail: muriel@silk827.fsnet.co.uk
Genuine local situated in a tiny fishing village famous for the kipper sheds that produce the world renowned Craster kippers. The pub is handy for local walks, visiting Dunstanburgh Castle and exploring the scenic delights of Northumberland and the Scottish Borders. The menu takes in hot drinks, sandwiches, toasties and light bites, plus house specialities like home-made Craster kipper pâté and home-made crabmeat soup with whisky and cream.
OPEN: 11-3 6.30-11 (all day Jun-Aug) **BAR MEALS:** L served all week 11-2.30 Sun 12-2.30 Av main course £3 ☺: Punch Taverns ◑: Balck Sheep, John Smith's, Directors. **FACILITIES:** Garden by the sea Dogs allowed **NOTES:** Parking 10 No credit cards

> ♀ 7   Number of wines by the glass

> Restaurant and Bar Meal times indicate the times when food is available. Last orders may be approximately 30 minutes before the times stated

> Most of the pubs in this guide book pride themselves on the quality of their food. This may take a little time to prepare

EGLINGHAM   Map 21 NU11

Tankerville Arms 🍷
NE66 2TX ☎ 01665 578444 🖷 01665 578444
Dir: B6346 from Alnwick

Picturesquely located in the foothills of the Cheviots, this traditional stone-built pub has a good reputation for its real ales and food. The local castles (including Alnwick, featured in the Harry Potter movies), countryside and beaches make it a favourite with walkers and cyclists. Expect smoked fish chowder; steak and Black Sheep ale pie; and smoked duck with roasted vegetables and thyme sauce. Good range of soups, salads and sandwiches.
OPEN: 12-2 7-11 (Times may vary, ring for details) Closed: 25 Dec
BAR MEALS: L served all week 12-2 D served all week 6-9 Av main course £8 **RESTAURANT:** L served all week 12-2 D served all week 6-9 Av 3 course à la carte £18 ☺: Free House ◑: Greene King Ruddles Best, Scottish Courage Courage Directors, Black Sheep Best, Mordue Workie Ticket. **FACILITIES:** Child facs Garden: Country garden, seating for 25, good views **NOTES:** Parking 15

ETAL   Map 21 NT93

Black Bull 🍷
TD12 4TL ☎ 01890 820200 🖷 07092 367 733
e-mail: blackbulletal@aol.com
Dir: 10m N of Wooler right off A697, left at Jct for 1m then left into Etal.
How many thatched pubs are there in Northumberland? Answer, one, and this 300-year-old hostelry by the ruins of Etal Castle is it. Not far away flows the River Till, the grand walking country of the Cheviots is on the doorstep. Traditional pub food includes mince and dumpling, chilli con carne, steak and black pudding pie, deep-fried scampi, and several vegetarian options, including vegetable goulash. Have a hot filled baguette or a sandwich at lunchtime.
OPEN: 11-3.30 5.30-11 (Open all day summer Closed Mon in winter) **BAR MEALS:** L served all week 12-2 D served all week 6-9 All day in summer Av main course £6 **RESTAURANT:** L served all week 11.30-2.30 D served all week 6-9.30 All day in summer Av 3 course à la carte £13.95 ☺: Pubmaster ◑: Jennings, Deuchers, John Smith Smooth, Fosters. **FACILITIES:** Child facs Children's licence Garden: Grass area with tables, chairs, gazebo, BBQ **NOTES:** Parking 10

FALSTONE   Map 21 NY78

The Blackcock Inn ◆◆◆ ♀
NE48 1AA ☎ 01434 240200 🖷 01434 240200
e-mail: blackcock@falstone.fsbusiness.co.uk
Dir: Off unclassified rd from Bellingham (accessed from A68 or B6320)
A traditional 18th-century stone-built free house, close to Kielder Reservoir and Forest, with some lovely walks accessible from the village. The pub is also handy for the

continued

Rievers Cycle Route. The homely bar with its exposed beams and wide range of real ales, together with the non-smoking restaurant, combine to make this a firm favourite with locals and visitors alike.
OPEN: 12-2 7-11 (Longer hrs in summer) **BAR MEALS:** L served all week 12-2 D served all week 7-8.30 Sun 12-2, 7-8.30 Av main course £8 **RESTAURANT:** L served Wed-Sun 12-2 D served all week 7-8.30 Av 3 course à la carte £16 ⊕: Free House ◖: Blackcock Ale, Theakston Cool Cask, Magnet Ale, John Smiths. ♀: 8
FACILITIES: Child facs Garden: lawn, flower beds, picnic benches Dogs allowed **NOTES:** Parking 20 **ROOMS:** 6 bedrooms 4 en suite 1 family room s£40 d£60

Pick of the Pubs

The Pheasant Inn ♦♦♦♦
Stannersburn NE48 1DD ☎ 01434 240382 ▤ 01434 240382
e-mail: enquiries@thepheasantinn.com
web: www.thepheasantinn.com
See Pick of the Pubs on page 368

GREAT WHITTINGTON   Map 21 NZ07

Pick of the Pubs

Queens Head Inn
NE19 2HP ☎ 01434 672267
Dir: Off A68 & B6318 W of Newcastle upon Tyne
At the heart of Hadrian's Wall country this old pub/restaurant, once a coaching inn, radiates a welcoming atmosphere in comfortable surroundings of beamed rooms, oak settles and open fires. In addition to Black Sheep beers there are some three dozen wines of choice and nearly as many malt whiskies. Menus combine the best of local and European ingredients, without losing touch with the classics. Expect the likes of seared fillet of salmon with ratatouille and a tomato and herb couscous or herb crusted rack of lamb with a basket of turned roast vegetables with a rosemary and redcurrant jus. Speciality dishes could include breast of wood pigeon on a black pudding mash with a tomato salsa, roast garlic and Burgundy, or prime fillet steak topped with a mushroom and stilton sabayon served on a Madeira sauce. A long and beguiling Sunday lunch menu begins with something like deep-fried black pudding with beetroot relish, or warm ciabatta bread with smoked mackerel and a coarse wholegrain mustard. Follow with anything from traditional roast sirloin with Yorkshire pudding and gravy to roast vegetable and nut gateau with roast garlic coulis, or seared fillet of salmon on a tagliatelle of vegetables.
OPEN: 12-3 6-11 **BAR MEALS:** L served Tues-Sun 12-2 D served Tues-Sun 6.30-9 Av main course £10
RESTAURANT: L served Tues-Sun 12-2 D served Tues-Sun 6.30-9 Av 3 course à la carte £20 ⊕: Free House ◖: Black Sheep, Queens Head, Hambleton. **FACILITIES:** Garden: Drinks served in the garden **NOTES:** Parking 20

HALTWHISTLE   Map 21 NY76

Milecastle Inn
Military Rd, Cawfields NE49 9NN ☎ 01434 321372
e-mail: clarehind@aol.co.uk
Dir: Leave A69 into Haltwhistle. Pub approx 2m at junct with B6318
Spectacular views from the gardens towards Hadrian's Wall are a treat for tourists arriving at this stone-built rural inn.
continued

Even scenery-hardened locals are probably aware of how lucky they are to have such a backdrop to their eating and drinking. The beamed bar has open fires and even a resident ghost. New owners have developed a menu strong on the likes of game pie, venison, pheasant, steaks, gammon, Whitby scampi, seafood medley and other fish, as well as vegetarian dishes.

Milecastle Inn

OPEN: 12-9 (Nov-Mar 12-3, 6-9 Nov-Mar 12-3 6-11)
BAR MEALS: L served all week 12-3 D served all week 6-9 Food when open Av main course £7.95 ⊕: Free House ◖: Big Lamp, Prince Bishop, Carlsberg-Tetley. **FACILITIES:** Garden: Walled seats 25, overlooks Hadrians Wall **NOTES:** Parking 30

HAYDON BRIDGE   Map 21 NY86

The General Havelock Inn ♀
Ratcliffe Rd NE47 6ER ☎ 01434 684376 ▤ 01434 684283
e-mail: GeneralHavelock@aol.com
Dir: On A69, 7m west of Hexham

Built as a private house in 1840, this roadside free house takes its name from a British Army officer. The non-smoking restaurant in a converted barn overlooks the River Tyne, as does the tranquil south-facing patio framed by trees and potted plants. Locally sourced ingredients are the foundation of dishes like pan-fried sea bass with ratatouille; beef, Guinness and wild mushroom stew with mash; and roast duck leg on sautéed potatoes and watercress salad.
OPEN: 12-2.30 7-11 **BAR MEALS:** L served Tue-Sun 12-2 D served Tue-Sat 7-9 Av main course £7 **RESTAURANT:** L served Tue-Sun 12-2 D served Tue-Sat 7-9 Av 3 course à la carte £22.75 Av 3 course fixed price £15.25 ⊕: Free House ◖: Hesket Newmarket, Wylam Magic, Helvellyn Gold, Mordue Al Wheat Pet. ♀: 9
FACILITIES: Child facs Children's licence Garden: Patio area on river bank, lots of plants Dogs allowed

 Brewery/Company

The Pheasant Inn

Enjoy the traditional warmth and friendly atmosphere of this cosy stone-walled pub, owned by the Kershaw family since 1985. It began life as a large farmstead, but for over 250 years one room was always used as a bar. Around the walls old photos record local people engaged in long-abandoned trades and professions.

Robin and Irene Kerhsaw's wholesome food may be eaten al fresco in the pretty garden courtyard, in either of the bars or in the restaurant, with its mellow pine furniture and warm terracotta walls. The bar menu changes daily according to season, but traditional favourites like home-made soups, steak and kidney pie, lasagne, freshly prepared salads, ploughman's and sandwiches are always available. Main menu starters include roast tomato and red pepper soup, and sweet marinated herrings, while main courses include roast Northumbrian lamb with rosemary and redcurrant jus; fresh fish of the day from North Shields; hearty home-made game and mushroom pie; and pan-fried breast of marinated chicken with honey-roasted peppers. Vegetarian and salad choices are also plentiful. Round off with sticky toffee pudding, or lemon and lime cheesecake. Traditional Sunday lunches come with all the trimmings, and, again, vegetarians are well looked after. Timothy Taylor's Landlord and 35 malt whiskies are served in the bars. Close by is Kielder Water, the largest artificial lake in Europe, and some of Northumberland's most unspoilt countryside. Guests staying overnight may book one of eight en suite bedrooms, grouped around a small courtyard, and which look out over that same wonderful landscape.

OPEN: 11-3 6-11 (opening times vary, ring for details) Closed: Dec 25-26
BAR MEALS: L served all week 12-2.30 D served all week 7-9 Av main course £9.50
RESTAURANT: L served all week 12-2.30 D served all week 7-9 Av 3 course à la carte £18.50
🏠: Free House
🍺: Theakston Best, Marstons Pedigree, Timothy Taylor Landlord, Greene King Old Speckled Hen.
FACILITIES: Child facs Grassed courtyard, stream running through Dogs allowed by arrangement only
NOTES: Parking 30
ROOMS: 8 bedrooms en suite 1 family room s£40 d£70

◆◆◆◆   Map 21 NY78
Stannersburn NE48 1DD
☎ 01434 240382
📠 01434 240382
📧 enquiries@thepheasantinn.com
🌐 www.thepheasentinn.com
Dir: From A68 onto B6320, or from A69, B6079, B6320, follow signs 'Kielder Water'

HEDLEY ON THE HILL   Map 19 NZ05

Pick of the Pubs

The Feathers Inn
NE43 7SW ☎ 01661 843607 ▤ 01661 843607

From its hilltop position, this small stone-built free house overlooks the splendid adventure country of the Cheviots. The three-roomed pub is well patronised by the local community, but strangers too, are frequently charmed by its friendly and relaxed atmosphere. Families are welcome, and a small side room can be booked in advance if required. Old oak beams, coal fires and rustic settles set the scene and there's a good selection of traditional pub games like shove ha'penny and bar skittles. The stone walls are decorated with local photographs of rural life. Although the pub has no garden, food and drinks can be served at tables on the green in good weather. The menus change regularly, and the imaginative home cooking includes an extensive choice of vegetarian meals. Expect spiced lentil and vegetable hotpot with naan bread, gingered salmon cakes with coriander salsa, pork casseroled with tarragon and Dijon mustard, and seafood pancake. An appetising range of puddings. Coach parties by arrangement.
OPEN: 12-3 6-11 (Sun 12-3, 7-10.30) Closed: 25 Dec
BAR MEALS: L served Sat-Sun 12-2.30 D served Tue-Sun 7-9
🍺: Free House 🍺: Mordue Workie Ticket, Big Lamp Bitter, Fuller's London Pride, Yates Bitter. **FACILITIES:** Children's licence Tables outside at the front Dogs allowed Water
NOTES: Parking 12

HEXHAM   Map 21 NY96

Pick of the Pubs

Dipton Mill Inn ♀
Dipton Mill Rd NE46 1YA ☎ 01434 606577
e-mail: ghb@hexhamshire.co.uk
Dir: 2m S of Hexham on HGV route to Blanchland (B6306)
Quintessential English country pub, formerly part of a farm, with a millstream running through the garden and cosy fires enhancing the feel and atmosphere of the bar in winter. Perfect for walking, exploring the rugged countryside around Hadrian's Wall and visiting an assortment of other Roman sites in the area. Alternatively, you could play golf nearby or enjoy an afternoon at Hexham races just down the road before spending your winnings at the Dipton Mill, enjoying one of the locally-brewed Hexhamshire beers. Food is served evenings and lunchtimes with all dishes being freshly prepared.

Perhaps sample mince and dumplings, lamb leg steak in wine and mustard sauce, haddock baked with tomato and basil, or pork fillet with apple, orange and ginger. To follow, try plum crumble or raspberry roulade. Round off with a tempting selection of cheeses, including Northumberland oak-smoked, Coquetdale, and white stilton with apricot.
OPEN: 12-2.30 6-11 (Sun 12-3, 7-10.30) Oct-Etr closed Sun eve
Closed: 25 Dec **BAR MEALS:** L served all week 12-2.15
D served all week 6.30-8.30 Sun 12-2.15 Av main course £6.25
🍺: Free House 🍺: Hexhamshire Shire Bitter, Old Humbug, Devil's Water, Devil's Elbow & Whapweasel. ♀: 16
FACILITIES: Children's licence Garden: Grassed and terraced area, small aviary **NOTES:** No credit cards

Miners Arms Inn ♀
Main St, Acomb NE46 4PW ☎ 01434 603909
Dir: 17m W of Newcastle on A69, 2m W of Hexham.
Close to Hadrian's Wall in a peaceful village, this charming 18th-century pub has stone walls, beamed ceilings and open fires. Real ales are a speciality, as is good home-cooked food. There is no jukebox or pool table, so visitors will have to entertain themselves with conversation, and some choices from a menu that includes lasagne, curry, Italian chicken, steak and kidney pie, chilli, and a special trifle. Good setting for cyclists and walkers, and the garden has an aviary.
OPEN: 12-11 (Sun 12-10.30 -11 Easter, Summer, Xmas Hols 12-11 all wk) **BAR MEALS:** L served all week 12-9 D served all week 5-9 Sun 12-5 Av main course £5.25 **RESTAURANT:** L served all week 12-9 D served all week 5-9 Sunday 12-5 🍺: Free House 🍺: Jennings Best, Yates, Durham White Velvet, Boddingtons. ♀: 7
FACILITIES: Child facs Garden: Secluded sun trap beer garden, seating, BBQ Dogs allowed Water and biscuits **NOTES:** No credit cards

The Rose & Crown Inn ♀
Main St, Slaley NE47 0AA ☎ 01434 673263
A 200-year-old listed building combining the charm of a traditional country inn with modern service and comfort. Conveniently situated for exploring Keilder Forest and the delights of the Borders, as well as the Roman sites of Vindolanda and Housesteads. Handy, too, for fishing, horse-riding, hunting, sailing and shooting. Appetising food is on offer and among the dishes on the menu you might find beef casserole, turkey and ham pie, poached chicken breast and salmon and mushroom tagliatelle.
OPEN: 12-3 6-11 (Sun 12-3 7-10.30) **BAR MEALS:** L served all week 12-2 D served all week 7-9 Av main course £6.95
RESTAURANT: L served all week 12-2.15 D served all week 6.30-9.30 Av 3 course a la carte £16 🍺: Free House
🍺: Woodpecker, Jennings, plus guest ales. **FACILITIES:** Garden: Food served outside **NOTES:** Parking 36 **ROOMS:** 3 bedrooms en suite s£25 d£50 (♦♦♦)

 Pubs with this logo do not allow smoking anywhere on their premises

Website addresses are included where available. The AA cannot be held responsible for the content of any of these websites

continued

LONGFRAMLINGTON Map 21 NU10

Pick of the Pubs

The Anglers Arms
Weldon Bridge NE65 8AX
☎ 01665 520271 570655 📠 01665 570041
e-mail: johnyoung@anglersarms.fsnet.co.uk

The warm and friendly ambience at this traditional old coaching inn, dating from the 1760s, is not only thanks to the personal attention from the staff, but also from those nice little touches one finds at every corner. The ornaments, antiques, quaint pieces of bric-a-brac including hand painted wall tiles, and interesting items of fishing memorabilia make this place so special. Speaking of fishing, residents may do so for free on the inn's own one-mile stretch of river. Typical dishes at the bar, or in the decidedly sophisticated old Pullman railway carriage restaurant, are home-made steak and ale pie, Northumbrian sausage Lyonnaise, mixed grill, steaks, grilled rainbow trout, and balti curry. For some, a hot beef sandwich with rich onion gravy and French fries might be sufficient, with one of the ever-changing real ales.
OPEN: 11-3 6-11 **BAR MEALS:** L served all week 12-2 D served all week 6-9.30 Sun 12-9 **RESTAURANT:** L served all week 12-2 D served all week 6-9.30 🍺: Worthington, Carling, Boddingtons & 3 Guest Ales. **FACILITIES:** Child facs Children's licence Garden: Well-tended 0.5 acre garden with play park Dogs allowed **NOTES:** Parking 30

Granby Inn ♀
Front St NE65 8DP ☎ 01665 570228 📠 01665 570736
Dir: On A697, 11m N of Morpeth

A friendly 200-year-old coaching inn that retains much of its original character, including fine old oak beams. Set in the heart of Northumberland, between the Cheviots and the coast, this family-run business specialises in good home-cooked food: grilled trout, glazed lamb cutlets, steak au

continued

poivre, grilled ham. These might be followed by toffee and pecan sponge pudding or sherry trifle. Lighter bites include sandwiches, pasta and omelettes.
OPEN: 11-3 6-11 Closed: 25-26 Dec **BAR MEALS:** L served all week 11.30-2 D served all week 6-9.30 (Sun 12-3, 7-10.30) Av main course £8.35 **RESTAURANT:** L served all week 11.30-2 D served all week 6-9.30 (Sun 12-3, 7-10.30) 🍺: Free House 🍺: Stones Best Bitter, Worthington E. ♀: 11 **NOTES:** Parking 20

LONGHORSLEY Map 21 NZ19

Linden Tree ★★★ 🏵🏵
Linden Hall NE65 8XF ☎ 01670 500033 📠 01670 500001
e-mail: stay@lindenhall.co.uk web: www.lindenhall.co.uk
Dir: Off A1 on A697, 1m N of Longhorsley

Originally two large cattle byres, this popular bar takes its name from the linden trees in the grounds of Linden Hall Hotel, an impressive Georgian mansion. Straightforward meals range from aubergine and broccoli bake, braised lamb shank, or medallions of pork, to grilled salmon, or poached smoked cod fillets.
OPEN: 11-11 (Sun 12-10.30) **BAR MEALS:** L served all week 12-2 D served all week 6-9.30 (Sun 12-4,6-9) Av main course £7.50 **RESTAURANT:** L served all week 12-2 D served all week 6-9.30 (Sun12-4, 6-9) Av 3 course à la carte £15 🍺: Free House 🍺: Worthingtons, Worthington 1744, Pedigree, Carling. **FACILITIES:** Child facs Children's licence Garden: Large open court yard Dogs allowed Water in garden **NOTES:** Parking 200
ROOMS: 50 bedrooms en suite s£48 d£58

LOW NEWTON BY THE SEA Map 21 NU22

The Ship Inn
The Square NE66 3EL ☎ 01665 576262
e-mail: forsythchristine@hotmail.com
Dir: NE from A1 at Alnwick
The village of Low Newton was purpose-built as a fishing village in the 18th century and is in the shape of an open-sided square. The unspoilt Ship overlooks the green and is just a stroll away from the beach. Bustling in summer and a peaceful retreat in winter, it offers a menu that includes plenty of fresh, locally caught fish and shellfish, venison rump steaks, Greek salad with houmous, and maybe Ship Inn trifle with ratafia and Madeira to finish.
OPEN: 11-4 (During school holidays open all day) 6.30-11 **BAR MEALS:** L served all week 12-2.30 6.30-8 Av main course £10 🍺: Free House 🍺: Original Northumberland, Black Sheep, Guest beers. **FACILITIES:** Garden: Food served outside Dogs allowed Water provided **NOTES:** No credit cards

 Principal Beers for sale

England

NEWTON ON THE MOOR
Map 21 NU10

Cook and Barker Inn
NE65 9JY ☎ 01665 575234 ▤ 01665 575234
Dir: 0.5m from A1 S of Alnwick

Traditional Northumbrian inn located in a picturesque village with outstanding views over the coast. Good quality fare and a welcoming atmosphere make this a popular dining destination. Real ales and a dozen house wines accompany the lunch bar menu. In the evening, you could enjoy Northumbrian game terrine with red onion and beetroot chutney; Mediterranean fish soup with Pernod and basil; char-grilled sardines; or west coast scallops with black pudding and fresh pea purée.
OPEN: 12-3 6-11 **BAR MEALS:** L served all week 12-2 D served all week 6-9 Single menu lunch only Av main course £7.95
RESTAURANT: L served all week 12-2 D served all week 7-9 Av 3 course à la carte £27.50 Av 3 course fixed price £8 ⊕: Free House ◖: Timothy Taylor Landlord, Theakstons Best Bitter, Fuller's London Pride, Batemans XXXB. ♀: 12 **FACILITIES:** Garden: Pretty area with lots of space for children **NOTES:** Parking 60

ROWFOOT
Map 21 NY66

The Wallace Arms
NE49 0JF ☎ 01434 321872 ▤ 01434 321872
e-mail: www.thewallacearms@aol.com
The pub was rebuilt in 1850 as the Railway Hotel at Featherstone Park station, when the now long-closed Haltwhistle-Alston line (today's South Tyne Trail) was engineered. It changed to the Wallace Arms in 1885. All around is great walking country, and just half a mile away is Featherstone Castle in its beautiful parkland. Nothing pretentious on the menu, just good, modestly-priced haddock fillet in beer batter, salmon fillet in lemon and tarragon sauce, steak and ale pie, grilled sirloin steak, and smoked haddock and prawn pasta. There are light snacks, burgers and sandwiches, if you prefer.
OPEN: 11-3 4-11 (opening times vary, ring for details)
BAR MEALS: L served all week 12-2.30 D served all week 6-9 Av main course £6.50 **RESTAURANT:** L served all week 12-2.30 D served all week 6-9 Av 3 course à la carte £18 ⊕: Free House ◖: Hook Norton Old Hooky, Young's Special, Greene King IPA, Greene King Abbot Ale. **FACILITIES:** Garden: Large lawn surrounded by stone wall **NOTES:** Parking 30

Pick of the Pubs have that extra special quality that makes them stand out from the crowd. Their entries are highlighted, and may be a full page

WARDEN
Map 21 NY96

The Boatside Inn
NE46 4SQ ☎ 01434 602233 601061
Dir: Just off A69 west of Hexham, follow signs to Warden Newborough & Fourstones

Attractive stone-built inn situated where the North and South Tyne rivers meet, beneath Warden Hill Iron Age fort. The name refers to the rowing boat that ferried people across the river before the bridge was built. It is a popular destination for walkers, promising real ale and good food cooked from local produce. Dishes include seafood stew, battered haddock, and slow roast lamb shoulder. There is also a garden with a lawn area and barbecue.
OPEN: 11-3 6-11 **BAR MEALS:** L served all week 12-2 D served all week 6.30-9.30 Av main course £8 **RESTAURANT:** L served all week 12-2 D served all week 6.30-9.30 ⊕: Free House ◖: Jennings, Cumberland, Caerons Trophy, Worthington.
FACILITIES: Garden: Paved patio with lawn area, hanging baskets Dogs allowed Water **NOTES:** Parking 70

WARENFORD
Map 21 NU12

Pick of the Pubs

Warenford Lodge
NE70 7HY ☎ 01668 213453 ▤ 01668 213453
e-mail: warenfordlodge@aol.com
Dir: 100yds E of A1, 10m N of Alnwick

This 200-year-old coaching inn stands near the original toll bridge over the Waren Burn. Formerly on the Great North Road, the building is now just a stone's throw from the A1. Inside, you'll find thick stone walls and an open fire for colder days; in summer, there's a small sheltered seating area, with further seats in the adjacent field. The Dukes of Northumberland once owned the pub, and its windows and plasterwork still bear the family crests. Visitors and locals alike enjoy the atmosphere and award-winning

continued

England

WARENFORD continued

Northumbrian dishes: try Seahouses kippers with creamy horseradish sauce; venison pudding with lemon suet crust and fresh vegetables; or roast pork hock with wine and herbs. Vegetarians are well catered for, with interesting dishes like beetroot and potato gratin; artichoke and leek pancakes; and celeriac pan Haggarty with fresh tomato sauce. Book ahead to avoid disappointment.
OPEN: 12-2 7-11 Closed Sun Eve, Mon-Tue (Nov-Easter) Closed: 25/26 Dec, 1 Jan-31 Jan **BAR MEALS:** L served Sun 12-1.30 D served Tues-Sun 7-9.30 Av main course £8.50 **RESTAURANT:** L served Sun 12-1.30 D served Tues-Sun 7-9.30 Av 3 course à la carte £16.50 ⊕: Free House ◀: Scottish Courage John Smith's. ⛿: 8 **FACILITIES:** Garden: Small, sheltered seating area Dogs allowed Water in the car park **NOTES:** Parking 60

regularly changing blackboard menus. Smoked salmon with scrambled eggs and hot granary toast is amongst the breakfast options; later, you might pop in for a Somerset brie, plum tomato and basil sandwich, although the main menu is also on offer throughout the day. Expect portabello mushroom and tarragon ravioli with poached egg and melting gruyère; rack of lamb with anchovies and garlic; and lemon sole in sea salt and lime with beurre noisette. Finish, perhaps, with home-made honeycomb and caramel crème brûlée.
OPEN: 8am-midnight **BAR MEALS:** L served all week 8-11 D served all week 8-11 Av main course £13.50 **RESTAURANT:** L served all week 8-11 D served all week 8-11 Av 3 course à la carte £25.50 Av 3 course fixed price £14.95 ⊕: Free House ◀: Greene King Ruddles Best, Scottish Courage John Smith's, Black Sheep Special. ⛿: 22 **FACILITIES:** Child facs Children's licence Garden: Terrace & lawns Dogs allowed **NOTES:** Parking 30

NOTTINGHAMSHIRE

BEESTON   Map 11 SK53

Pick of the Pubs

Victoria Hotel ⛿
Dovecote Ln NG9 1JG ☎ 0115 925 4049 ▤ 0115 922 3537
e-mail: hopco.victoriabeeston@virgin.net
Dir: M1 junct 25, A52 E. right at Nurseryman PH, right opp Rockaway Hotel into Barton St, 1st left
The Victoria dates from 1899 when it was built next to Beeston Railway Station, and the large, heated patio garden is still handy for a touch of train-spotting. It offers an excellent range of traditional ales, continental beers and lagers, farm ciders, a good choice of wines by the glass and over 100 single malt whiskies. Dishes on the menu might include Lincolnshire sausages, smoked chicken and bacon pasta, Dartmouth smokehouse kiln-roasted salmon, and brie, mushroom and cranberry Wellington with hazelnuts.
OPEN: 11-11 (Sun 12-10.30) Closed: 26 Dec
BAR MEALS: L served all week 12-8.45 D served all week Sun 12-7.45 Av main course £7.95 **RESTAURANT:** L served all week D served all week 12-8.45 Sun 12-7.45 Av 3 course à la carte £15 ⊕: Tynemill Ltd ◀: Batemans XB, Draught Bass, Castle Rock Hemlock, Everards Tiger & at least 6 Guests. ⛿: 30 **FACILITIES:** Garden: Large patio next to railway, with heaters Dogs allowed **NOTES:** Parking 10

CAUNTON   Map 17 SK76

Pick of the Pubs

Caunton Beck ⛿
NG23 6AB ☎ 01636 636793 ▤ 01636 636828
e-mail: email@wigandmitre.com
Dir: 5m NW of Newark on A616
It's rare to find a country pub that opens for breakfast at 8am and carries on serving until around midnight every day of the year. But then, this is no ordinary free house. The civilised pub-restaurant is built around a 16th-century cottage, set amid herb gardens and a dazzling rose arbour. Black Sheep Special, Ruddles and Greene King beers complement an extensive international wine list and

CAYTHORPE   Map 11 SK64

Black Horse Inn ▷◌
NG14 7ED ☎ 0115 966 3520
Dir: 12m from Nottingham off road to Southwell (A612)
Three generations of the same family have run this small, beamed country pub where old-fashioned hospitality is guaranteed. It has its own small brewery, producing Caythorpe Dover Beck bitter, a coal fire in the bar, and delicious home-cooked food prepared from seasonal ingredients. Fresh fish is a speciality; other choices might include Chinese dim sum; king prawns in garlic and cream sauce; fillet steak; and omelettes with various fillings.
OPEN: 12-3 5.30-11 (Sat 6-11, Sun 7-10.30) **BAR MEALS:** L served Tue-Sat 12-1.45 D served Tue-Fri 7-8.30 **RESTAURANT:** L served Tue-Sat 12-1.45 D served Mon-Sat 7-8.30 ⊕: Free House ◀: Interbrew Bass, Adnams Bitter, Greene King Abbot Ale, Black Sheep. **FACILITIES:** Garden: Lawned area with tables Dogs allowed Water **NOTES:** Parking 30 No credit cards

COLSTON BASSETT   Map 11 SK73

Pick of the Pubs

The Martins Arms Inn ▷◌ ⛿
School Ln NG12 3FD ☎ 01949 81361 ▤ 01949 81039
Dir: Off A46 between Leicester and Newark
Set in this lovely village in the stunning Vale of Belvoir, the Martin's Arms has been a popular alehouse since 1844. In fact so much so that this classic award-winning inn has featured on both local and national television from time to time. The listed building has a country house feel to it, with period furnishings, traditional hunting prints and seasonal fires in the Jacobean fireplace. The acre of landscaped grounds - backing on to National Trust land - includes a herb garden and well-established lawns. Regional ingredients are a feature of the menu, with a classic ploughman's lunch comprising Melton Mowbray pork pie, Colston Bassett stilton or cheddar, home-cured ham, pickles and bread. Alternatively, take your pick from the following: sesame baked halibut; beer braised pheasant; seared rump of lamb; walnut crusted cod; and beef and oyster pie; with desserts like Pedro Ximenez sherry trifle; cranberry, orange and port jelly; and mincemeat date and brandy pudding to tempt any doubters.
OPEN: 12-3 6-11 (Sun 7-10.30) 25 Dec Closed eve

continued

continued

England

BAR MEALS: L served all week 12-2 D served Mon-Sat 6-10 Av main course £13 **RESTAURANT:** L served all week 12-2 D served Mon-Sat 6-9 Sun 12-1.30 Av 3 course à la carte £30 ⊕: Free House ◑: Marston's Pedigree, Interbrew Bass, Greene King Abbot Ale, Timothy Taylor Landlord. ♀: 7 **FACILITIES:** Garden: Acre of landscaped garden with 80 covers Dogs allowed only in garden; water available **NOTES:** Parking 35

ELKESLEY
Map 17 SK67

Pick of the Pubs

Robin Hood Inn ♢ ♀
High St DN22 8AJ ☎ 01777 838259
e-mail: robinhooda1@clara.co.uk
Dir: 5m S of Worksop A1 between A57 junct's
Parts of this unassuming village inn date back to the 14th century. For over 20 years it has been run by enthusiastic landlord/chef Alan Draper who keeps it spruce and retains its attractive, homely feel. Ceilings and floors are deep red, while the green walls are adorned with pictures of food. The comprehensive menu is available in both the bar and restaurant, and includes a selection of light bites, sandwiches and baguettes. Main courses on the blackboard might feature chargrilled breast of chicken, plum tomato and chorizo sausage sauce; or lamb curry flavoured with coriander, tomato, garlic and ginger on basmatic rice and spinach. Fresh fish dishes are also displayed on blackboards according to availability, among them lemon sole, sea bass and monkfish. Freshly made cafetiere coffee, a pot of Darjeeling tea, and hot chocolate with whipped cream are also served.
OPEN: 11.30-3 6.30-11 **BAR MEALS:** L served Tue-Sun 12-2 D served Mon-Sat 7-9.30 Av main course £9.50 **RESTAURANT:** L served Tue-Sun 12-2 D served Mon-Sat 7-9.30 ⊕: Enterprise Inns ◑: Boddingtons Bitter, Marston's Pedigree, Carlsberg-Tetley Bitter. ♀: 8 **FACILITIES:** Garden **NOTES:** Parking 40

HALAM
Map 17 SK65

The Waggon and Horses NEW ♀
The Turnpike, Mansfield Rd NG22 8AE
☎ 01636 813109 ▤ 01636 816228
A small, food-led pub with Thwaites-led real ales. Helpful descriptions appear below each dish on the menu, thus oriental-style duck pancakes are 'bursting with flavour, oozing with juices'. Main courses include slow-roasted lamb shoulder with redcurrant, garlic, rosemary and fresh mint sauce ('we'd never consider taking this off the menu'); calves' liver with caramelised onion, crispy bacon and rich ale and thyme sauce; and home-made herb and ricotta ravioli with sweet pepper and butter sauce.
OPEN: 11.30-3 5.30-11 (All day Sat-Sun) **BAR MEALS:** L served all week 12-2.15 D served Mon-Sat 6-9.15 Sun 12-2.45 Av main course £11 **RESTAURANT:** L served all week 12-2.15 D served Mon-Sat 6-9.15 Sun 12-2.45 Av 3 course à la carte £19.50 ◑: Thwaites Bomber, Thwaites Original, Warsteiner, Thwaites Smooth. ♀: 8 **FACILITIES:** Garden: Cobbled patio **NOTES:** Parking 20

KIMBERLEY
Map 11 SK44

The Nelson & Railway Inn
12 Station Rd NG16 2NR ☎ 0115 938 2177
Dir: 1m N of M1 junct 26
The landlord of 34 years gives this 17th-century pub its distinctive personality. Next door is the Hardy & Hanson brewery that supplies many of the beers, but the two nearby railway stations that once made it a railway inn are now sadly derelict. A hearty menu of pub favourites includes soup, ploughman's, and hot rolls, as well as grills and hot dishes like home-made steak and kidney pie; gammon steak; and mushroom stroganoff.
OPEN: 11-11 (Sun 12-10.30) **BAR MEALS:** L served all week 12-2.30 D served all week 5.30-9 (Sun 12-6) **RESTAURANT:** L served all week 12-2.30 D served all week 5.30-9 (Sun 12-6) ⊕: Hardy & Hansons ◑: Hardys, Hansons Best Bitter, Classic, Cool & Dark. **FACILITIES:** Children's licence Garden: Food served outdoors, patio/terrace Dogs allowed water provided **NOTES:** Parking 50

LAXTON
Map 17 SK76

The Dovecote Inn ♀
Moorhouse Rd NG22 0NU ☎ 01777 871586 ▤ 01777 871586
e-mail: dovecoteinn@yahoo.co.uk
Dir: Telephone for directions
Set in the only village that still uses the 'three field system', (pop into the local Visitor Centre to find out what that is), this 18th-century pub is an ideal stopping point for walkers. Dishes on offer include chicken stuffed with asparagus in a smokey bacon and cream sauce; roast rack of lamb in a rosemary, mint, onion and mushroom gravy; and mushroom stroganoff and seafood platter. There is also a range of light bites - baguettes, sandwiches and jacket potatoes.
OPEN: 11.30-3 6.30-11.30 (Fri-Sat 6-11.30) **BAR MEALS:** L served all week 12-2 D served all week 6.30-9.30 Av main course £9 **RESTAURANT:** L served all week 12-2 D served all week 6.30-9.30 ⊕: Free House ◑: Mansfield Smooth, Banks Smooth, Marston's Pedigree. ♀: 10 **FACILITIES:** Garden: Table & chairs in front garden Dogs allowed **NOTES:** Parking 45 **ROOMS:** 2 bedrooms en suite s£35 d£50 (♦♦♦♦)

NORMANTON ON TRENT
Map 17 SK76

The Square & Compass ♀
Eastgate NG23 6RN ☎ 01636 821439 ▤ 01636 822796
e-mail: info@squareandcompass.co.uk
Dir: Off A1 & B1164 N of Newark-on-Trent

Full of charm and character, this beamed pub is approximately 500 years old, and is said to be haunted by the spirit of a traveller who was hanged for stealing. Inside, traditional ales and home-cooked fare add to the appeal, with

continued

NORMANTON ON TRENT continued

everything from fish dishes to all types of game. A typical menu includes battered cod, mixed grill, vegetable lasagne, and rack of loin ribs. Plenty of starters, too, and a good selection of baguettes and bar meals.
OPEN: 12-11 **BAR MEALS:** L served all week 12-2.30 D served all week 5.30-9 Sat-Sun 12-9 Av main course £7
RESTAURANT: L served all week 12-2.30 D served all week 5.30-9 All dat Sat-Sun ⏣: Free House ◖: Wells Bombadier Premium, Shepherd Neame Spitfire, Adnams Best, Black Sheep. ♀: 6
FACILITIES: Child facs Garden: Beer garden, ample seating, parasols
NOTES: Parking 80

NOTTINGHAM   Map 11 SK53

Cock & Hoop ♀
25 High Pavement NG1 1HE ☎ 0115 852 3231 ▤ 0115 852 3236
e-mail: drink@cockandhoop.co.uk

Traditional Victorian alehouse characterized by tasteful antiques, a real fire, a cellar bar and some striking bespoke artwork. The imaginatively designed menu might include Thai fish cakes with wild herb salad and chilli jam; pan-roasted calves' liver with smoked bacon and sage mash; and duck cassoulet with Toulouse sausage. To follow you could try milk chocolate and raspberry parfait, or plum and almond tartlet with freshly churned vanilla ice cream.
OPEN: 12-11 (Open til 1am Fri-Sat) Closed: 25-26 Dec
BAR MEALS: L served all week 12-10 D served all week Av main course £8.95 ◖: Deuchars IPA, Cock & Hoop, London Pride, Timothy Taylors Landlord. ♀: 7 **FACILITIES:** Dogs allowed Water ⊗

Fellows Morton & Clayton ♀
54 Canal St NG1 7EH ☎ 0115 950 6795 ▤ 0115 953 9838
e-mail: info@fellowsmortonandclayton.co.uk
Dir: Telephone for directions
Atmospheric city centre pub surrounded by the impressive Castle Wharf Complex, with a cobbled courtyard overlooking the canal. It is a regular Nottingham in Bloom award winner. Favourite dishes are Howard's Bubble and Willans' Squeak served with crusty bread, breast of chicken with prawns and cream cheese, salmon with peppercorns and spiced yoghurt served with asparagus, and beany vegetable hot-pot with parsley dumplings.
OPEN: 11-11 (Sun 12-10.30 Fri-Sat close at - 12)
BAR MEALS: L served all week 11-9 D served Tue-Sat
RESTAURANT: L served all week 11.30-2.30 D served Tue-Sat 5.30-9.30 ⏣: Free House ◖: Timothy Taylor Landlord, Fuller's London Pride, Castle Eden Ale, Mallard Bitter. ♀: 6
FACILITIES: Garden: Paved area & decked courtyard
NOTES: Parking 4

Ye Olde Trip to Jerusalem ♀
1 Brewhouse Yard, Castle Rd NG1 6AD
☎ 0115 9473171 ▤ 0115 950 1185
e-mail: yeoldtrip@hardysandhansons.plc.uk
Allegedly Britain's oldest pub, and also one of the most unusual, with parts of it penetrating deep into the sandstone of Castle Rock. Most gustatory wishes are met by a menu which runs from sandwiches, jackets, burgers and salads, to main courses typified by giant meat or vegetable-filled Yorkshire puddings, chicken tikka masala, salmon Florentine, steak and Kimberley ale pie, and red pepper and mushroom lasagne (one of several vegetarian options).
OPEN: 11-11 (Sun 12-10.30) **BAR MEALS:** L served all week 11-6 D served snacks only Sun-Fri 6-10 (Sun 12-6) Av main course £7
⏣: Hardys & Hansons Kimberley Best Bitter, Best Mild, Ye Olde Trip Ale,Guest Beers. ♀: 11 **FACILITIES:** Children's licence Garden: Seating in front & rear courtyard Dogs allowed outside only

SOUTHWELL   Map 05 SK65

French Horn ♀
Main St, Upton NG23 5ST ☎ 01636 812394 ▤ 01636 815497
e-mail: ross@bchef.wanadoo.co.uk
Originally a farmhouse, dating from the 18th century, the pub is handy for the racecourse and Southwell Minster. It offers real ales, a dozen wines by the glass and a collection of rare Irish malts. Seafood is a speciality, with the likes of roasted sea bass à la Basquaise or fettucine of blue swimmer crab. Other options include Gloucester Old Spot pork chop and pickled red cabbage, with treacle tart and English custard to finish.
OPEN: 11.30-3 5.30-11 **BAR MEALS:** L served all week 12-2.15 D served all week 6-9.30 Sun 12-4 Av main course £10.50
RESTAURANT: L served Wed-Sun 12-2.15 D served Wed-Sun 7-9.30 Sun 12-2.30, 6-8.30 Av 3 course à la carte £23 Av 3 course fixed price £18 ◖: Directors, Adnams, Boddingtons, John Smith Cask. ♀: 12
FACILITIES: Child facs Children's licence Dogs allowed Water
NOTES: Parking 100

SUTTON BONINGTON   Map 11 SK52

Star Inn ◆◆◆
Melton Ln LE12 5RQ ☎ 01509 852233
Dir: A6 toward Loughborough, 0.33m left to Kingston, over canal, right to Sutt Bonn, over crossroad, 1m Star on left

Whitewashed walls and flowering window boxes and tubs add a touch of colour to this picturesque inn, affectionately known as 'The Pit House'. The owners promise to cater to families, and those seeking a relaxed, quiet pint in a friendly atmosphere. Children are welcome to play in the garden, while parents enjoy a drink on the rear terrace. Straightforward yet appetising pub food includes casseroles, grills, pies, pasta bakes, and fresh fish and chips. Evening specials include Burgundy chicken breast, tuna provençale, and Dijon pork.

continued

OPEN: 11-11 **BAR MEALS:** L served all week 11-3 D served Mon-Sat 6-9 Sun 12-6 Av main course £6.95 **RESTAURANT:** L served all week 11-3 D served Mon-Sat 6-9 Sun 12-6 ☺: Enterprise Inns ◖: Interbrew Bass, Deuchars and guest ale. **FACILITIES:** Child facs Garden: Terrace, benches, large lawn Dogs allowed Water **NOTES:** Parking 70 **ROOMS:** 2 bedrooms en suite 2 family rooms s£45 d£45

THURGARTON
Map 17 SK64

The Red Lion
Southwell Rd NG14 7GP ☎ 01636 830351
Dir: On A612 between Nottingham & Southwell

This 16th-century inn was once a monks' alehouse. Pub food can be enjoyed in the bar, restaurant or garden. Main courses include chicken curry; three cheese and broccoli pasta bake; and grilled fresh salmon. For a lighter option, try a salad with roast ham or poached salmon and prawn; or the cheese platter with local blue stilton. Look out for the 1936 newspaper cutting reporting the murder of a previous landlady by her niece!
OPEN: 11.30-2.30 6.30-11 (Open all day Sat-Sun & BHs) **BAR MEALS:** L served all week 12-2 D served all week 7-9.30 Sat-Sun 12-9.30 **RESTAURANT:** L served all week 12-2 D served all week 7-10 ☺: Free House ◖: Greene King Abbot Ale, Jenning Cumberland, Carlsberg-Tetley, Black Sheep. **FACILITIES:** Large spacious garden: well kept **NOTES:** Parking 40

TUXFORD
Map 17 SK77

Pick of the Pubs

The Mussel & Crab ♀
NG22 0PJ ☎ 01777 870491 🖷 01777 871096
e-mail: musselandcrab1@hotmail.com
web: www.musselandcrab.com
Dir: From the Ollerton/Tuxford Junction of the A1 & the A57 go N on the B1164 to Sibthorpe Hill and the pub is 800 yds on the right.
As its name suggests, fish and seafood dominate the menu at this quirky pub, though its location is far from the sea. Architectural features include a fabulous curved zinc bar, a traditional restaurant and a Mediterranean Room, which is complemented by the Piazza Room (where trees and murals combine to create a courtyard effect indoors), the Roof Garden and Alfresco Terrace. For your amusement, you can play liar dice, admire the fish in the gents' toilets, and sit yourself down on the large carved wooden hands in the bar area. Up to 22 blackboards are in operation at any given time and the dishes change constantly. Expect the likes of crab chowder; tempura prawns; seafood tower; avruga caviar; baked cod; and monkfish wrapped in bacon and served with mushroom and rich red wine sauce. Non-

continued

fishy alternatives might be roast Gressingham duck, or leek and thyme risotto with rocket.

The Mussel & Crab

OPEN: 11.30-2.30 6-11 **BAR MEALS:** L served all week 11.30-2 D served all week 6.30-10 **RESTAURANT:** L served all week 12-2 D served all week 6.30-10 Sun 6.30-9 Av 3 course à la carte £25 ☺: Free House ◖: Carlsberg-Tetley Tetley Smooth, Tetley Cask. ♀: 15 **FACILITIES:** Garden: Food served outside, patio area Dogs allowed **NOTES:** Parking 74

WALKERINGHAM
Map 17 SK79

The Three Horse Shoes
High St DN10 4HR ☎ 01427 890959
Dir: 3m from Gainsborough, Lincs

Hanging baskets festoon this quiet village pub, and bedding plants bring colour to the garden. Lunchtime specials include liver and onions, ploughman's salad, and pork steaks with apple sauce and cheese, while the main menu offers home-made steak pie, chicken Ceylon, and mushroom stroganoff.
OPEN: 11.30-3 6-11 **BAR MEALS:** L served Wed-Sun 12-2 D served Wed-Sat 7-9 Sun 12-3 **RESTAURANT:** L served Sun 12-2 D served Mon-Sat 7-9 ☺: Free House ◖: Stones, Worthington, plus guest ale. **FACILITIES:** Child facs Children's licence Garden **NOTES:** Parking 40

WELLOW
Map 17 SK66

Olde Red Lion
Eakring Rd NG22 0EG ☎ 01623 861000
Dir: From Ollerton on the A616 to Newark after 2m, Wellow village turn R.
400-year-old pub opposite the maypole in a quiet Nottinghamshire village; popular with walkers. Unspoilt atmosphere; traditional pub food.
OPEN: 11.30-3.15 6-11 (all day wknds) **BAR MEALS:** L served all week 11.30-2.30 D served all week 6-10 Av main course £5 **RESTAURANT:** L served all week 11.30-2.30 D served all week 6-10 Av 3 course à la carte £12 ☺: Free House ◖: Castle Eden, Bromsbrooke, plus guests. **FACILITIES:** Garden: beer garden, patio, outdoor eating **NOTES:** Parking 24

PUB WALK

The Turf Tavern
Oxford - Oxfordshire

THE TURF TAVERN,
4 Bath Place, off Holywell, OX1 3SU
☎ 01865 243235
Directions: Off Holywell Street, near the Broad Street end, on the right.
In the heart of Oxford, approached through hidden alleyways, this very popular pub lies in the shadow of the colleges. In the summer relax in the sheltered courtyards.
Open: 11–11 (Sun 12–10.30)
Bar Meals: L served all week 12–7.30
D served all week Av main course
£5.95
Restaurant Meals: L served all week
D served Sun (Roast)
(for full entry see page 393)

Distance: 2.25 miles (3.6km)
Map: OS Cityranger 164
Terrain: Cityscape.
Paths: Pavements, firm paths and tow path
Gradient: Level ground, no hills

Walk submitted by Nick Channer

Likened by Thomas Hardy's Jude to 'the heavenly Jerusalem' and made even more famous throughout the world in recent years by Colin Dexter's fictional sleuth Inspector Morse, Oxford's history, beauty and tradition are admired in every corner of the land.

From the inn make for the Sheldonian Theatre, designed by Christopher Wren and opened in 1669. Close by are the buildings of the Bodleian Library, the second largest library in Britain. Also near is the Radcliffe Camera, named after Dr John Radcliffe, physician to Queen Anne. Radcliffe left money for the building of the first round library in the country.

Cross Radcliffe Square to Brasenose College and bear left into Brasenose Lane. Walk along to Turl Street, then veer right and head for Broad Street where you can visit the world-famous Blackwell's Bookshop. Head west along Broad Street to St Giles, Oxford's widest street. Charles I drilled his men here during the Civil War.

Bear left and walk along to Carfax Tower where Charles II was proclaimed King in 1660. Continue ahead into St Aldates and pass the Town Hall. Opposite is the Tourist Information Centre. Further along is the entrance to Christ Church, the largest college in Oxford and founded in 1525 by Cardinal Wolsey. This is also the city's Cathedral and open to the public.

Leave Christ Church by the Meadows exit and walk straight ahead down the tree-lined New Walk. On reaching the Thames, swing left and follow the towpath. Veer left at the point where the Cherwell flows into the Thames. There is a steeply arched footbridge here. Follow the tree-lined path between meadows and sports fields, passing the Broad Walk on the left. Leave the riverbank and pass into Rose Lane via wrought-iron gates. At the main junction turn right towards Magdalen Bridge.

On the right here is the entrance to the University Botanic Garden, established on the site of a 13th-century Jewish burial ground. It is the oldest botanic garden in Britain and in over 300 years plants have been grown here for both teaching and research at the University.

Have a look at nearby Magdalen College bell tower - here, during the Civil War, Royalist forces hurled rocks down on to the heads of Parliamentarians below. Return to the Botanic Garden, cross the road and bear right into Queen's Lane. Continue into New College Lane to the outstanding Bridge of Sighs. This 1914 structure, a replica of its Venice namesake, connects the north and south quadrangles of Hertford College. Ahead is the Sheldonian Theatre and on the right is the Turf Tavern.

England

OXFORDSHIRE

ABINGDON
Map 05 SU49

The Merry Miller ♀
Cothill OX13 6JW ☎ 01865 390390 ▤ 01865 390040
e-mail: rob@merrymiller.fsbusiness.co.uk
Dir: *1m from the Marcham interchange on the A34*
Alongside beams, flagstones, and log fires, which one might reasonably expect in a 17th-century pub, an inventory of features here must include its risqué prints. Overall, the interior is redolent more of Tuscany than the granary it once was, which at least ensures that the pasta dishes feel at home. But lunch, if not pasta, could just as easily be pie of the day, wholetail scampi and chips, or chicken pistou, while dinner might be characterised by braised half shoulder of lamb, smoked haddock and leek fishcakes, steak and kidney casserole, or brie and broccoli pithivier.
OPEN: 12-11 (Sun 12-10.30) **BAR MEALS:** L served all week 12-2.45 D served all week 6.30-9.45 Sun all day Av main course £10.95 **RESTAURANT:** L served all week 12-2.45 D served all week 6.30-9.45 ⊕: Greene King ◀: Greene King IPA & Old Speckled Hen. ♀: 15 **FACILITIES:** Garden: small patio garden, 20 parasol-covered seats Dogs allowed **NOTES:** Parking 60

ADDERBURY
Map 11 SP43

The Red Lion ♀
The Green OX17 3LU ☎ 01295 810269 ▤ 01295 811906
Dir: *Off M40 3 m from Banbury*
Established in 1669, the Red Lion is a fine stone-built coaching inn on the Banbury to Oxford road, overlooking the village green. Once known as the King's Arms, it had a tunnel in the cellar used by Royalists in hiding during the Civil War. Enter the rambling, beamed interior to find daily newspapers, real ales, good wines and a varied menu offering the likes of home-made fish cakes with salad and salsa.
OPEN: 11-11 (Sun 12-10.30) **BAR MEALS:** 12-3 D served all week 7-9.30 Sat-Sun and BH 12-9.30 **RESTAURANT:** 12-3 7-9.30 ◀: Greene King IPA, Hook Norton, Abbot Ale, Ruddles County. ♀: 11 **FACILITIES:** Garden: Patio at front and back of pub **NOTES:** Parking 30

ARDINGTON
Map 05 SU48

Pick of the Pubs

The Boars Head ♦♦♦♦ ⊛⊛ ♀
Church St OX12 8QA ☎ 01235 833254 ▤ 01235 833254
e-mail: info@boarsheadardington.co.uk
See Pick of the Pubs on page 378

BAMPTON
Map 05 SP30

The Romany
Bridge St OX18 2HA ☎ 01993 850237 ▤ 01993 852133
e-mail: romany@barbox.net
A shop until 20 years ago, The Romany is housed in an 18th-century building of Cotswold stone with a beamed bar, log fires and intimate dining room. The choice of food ranges from bar snacks and bar meals to a full à la carte restaurant menu, with home-made specials like hotpot, Somerset pork, and steak and ale pie. There is a good range of vegetarian choices. Regional singers provide live entertainment a couple of times a month.
OPEN: 11-11 **BAR MEALS:** L served all week 12-2 D served all week 6.30-9 Av main course £6 **RESTAURANT:** L served all week 12-2 D served all week 6.30-9 ⊕: Free House ◀: Archers Village, plus guests. **FACILITIES:** Child facs Garden: Food served outside Dogs allowed Water **NOTES:** Parking 8

BANBURY
Map 11 SP44

The George Inn
Lower St, Barford St Michael OX15 0RH ☎ 01869 338226
Handy for both Banbury and Oxford, this 300-year-old thatched village pub features old beams, exposed stone walls and open fireplaces. It stands in a large garden, with a patio and orchard, overlooking open countryside. Live music is an established tradition, and the pub hosts a variety of rock, folk and solo artists. There's a good choice of real ales, and options from the single menu include baguettes, baked potatoes, pasta, pies, and fish and chips.
OPEN: 12-3 7-11 (Sun 12-4) **BAR MEALS:** 7-9 ⊕: Free House ◀: Timothy Taylor Landlord, IPA, Copper Ale, Greene King. **FACILITIES:** Garden: Patio, orchard, food served outside Dogs allowed **NOTES:** Parking 20 No credit cards

Pick of the Pubs

The Wykham Arms ♀
Temple Mill Rd, Sibford Gower OX15 5RX
☎ 01295 788808 ▤ 01295 788806
Dir: *Between Banbury and Shipston off B4035*
A pretty 17th-century village pub, until recently known as The Inn at Sibford Gower, and then the Moody Cow. Built of mellow Hornton stone with a thatched roof and a gorgeous setting overlooking rolling Oxfordshire countryside, it has been transformed into a stylish gastropub by chef owner Ian Wallace. Although there is an upmarket, modern feel throughout the rambling series of five rooms, you can still expect original features such as slate floors, exposed stone, sturdy pine furnishings, tasteful prints and inglenook fireplaces. Beers like Hook Norton are served along with a short, carefully chosen menu: starters like black pudding and bacon salad, mains of blade of slow-cooked Lighthorne lamb, or wild bass and steamed greens with a white wine and butter sauce, and puddings like baked vanilla cheesecake will reassure locals and destination diners alike.
OPEN: 12-3 6-11.30 **BAR MEALS:** L served Tues-Sun 12-2.30 D served Tues-Sat 6-9.30 Av main course £12 **RESTAURANT:** L served Tues-Sun 12-2.30 D served Tues-Sat 7-9.30 Sun 12-3 Av 3 course à la carte £22 ⊕: Free House ◀: Hook Norton Best, Old Hooky, Generation. ♀: 12 **FACILITIES:** Children's licence Garden: Views of village and hills **NOTES:** Parking 30

Pick of the Pubs
ARDINGTON – OXFORDSHIRE

The Boars Head

Tucked away beside the church, the pretty 400-year-old Boars Head is situated within the beautifully maintained Lockinge Estate, laid out in the 19th century by Lord Wantage. Although dining is important, it's still very much the village local - as it has been for the past 150 years.

Log fires blaze when they should, candles are lit in the evenings, and there are always fresh flowers. Fish dishes are a house speciality, with supplies from Cornwall arriving daily. The words 'fresh', 'locally grown', and 'seasonal' underpin the innovative, refreshingly unwordy menus, and from bread to ice creams, pasta to pastries, everything is home made. Typical starters are deep fried goats' cheese with roasted tomato compote; poached egg salad with black pudding and bacon; terrine of foie gras, poached pears in saffron and chilli with salad; assiette of tuna fish and potato bhaji; and ballontine of duck, five spice salad and parsnip cream. Main dishes include fillet of sea bass with spinach and mussel stew; feuillete of Cornish brill and spinach with girolles and tomato butter sauce; seared Newlyn cod with chorizo, caramelised sweetbreads and shiraz sauce; breast of Gressingham duck with cracked pepper, celeriac rosti and roasted salsify; and medallions of roe deer with sweet and sour beetroot spaetzli and port glaze. Desserts could include prune and almond tart with armagnac ice cream, and lemon tart with lemon curd ice cream.

OPEN: 12-3 6.30-11
BAR MEALS: L served all week 12-2.30 D served all week 7-10
RESTAURANT: L served all week 12-2.30 D served all week 7-10
🍺: Free House
🍺: Hook Norton Old Hooky, West Berkshire Berwery Dr. Hexter's, Warsteiner, Butts Brewery. ♀: 8
FACILITIES: Child facs Garden: Patio area, three tables **NOTES:** Parking 10
ROOMS: 3 bedrooms en suite 1 family room s£65 d£85

♦♦♦♦ ◉◉ ♀ Map 05 SU48
Church St OX12 8QA
☎ 01235 833254
🖹 01235 833254
📧 info@boarsheadardington.co.uk
Dir: Off A417 E of Wantage

England

BANBURY continued

Ye Olde Reindeer Inn NEW
47 Parsons St OX16 5NA ☎ 01295 264031 📠 01295 264018
e-mail: tonypuddifoot@aol.com
Dir: One mile from M40 junct 11, in town centre just off market square
Oliver Cromwell stayed in the Reindeer during the Battle of
Edge Hill in 1642, and royalty, as well as the merely plain rich,
used the magnificent Globe Room on their way to and from
the capital. The original panelling was removed from here
before the First World War and stored in London, finally being
returned in 1964. The menu comprises hot or toasted
sandwiches, ploughman's, omelettes, salads and other snacks,
with daily specials.
OPEN: 11-11 **BAR MEALS:** L served Mon-Sat 11-2.30 D served
Mon-Sat 11-2.30 Sun 12-3 Av main course £4.95
RESTAURANT: L served all week 12-2 D served all week 12-2 Sun
12-3 ☺: Hook Norton ◀: Hook Norton, Best , Hook Norton
Haymaker, Hook Norton Old. **FACILITIES:** Child facs Garden:
Courtyard, tables and chairs Dogs allowed Water
NOTES: Parking 14

BARNARD GATE   Map 05 SP41

The Boot Inn 🏠 ♀
OX29 6XE ☎ 01865 881231 e-mail: info@theboot-inn.com
Dir: Off the A40 between Witney & Eynsham
Not surprisingly, this popular pub is renowned for its
collection of boots and other footwear donated to the pub by
various celebrity pop groups, sportsmen and actors - among
them The Bee Gees, George Best and Jeremy Irons. Acquired
by Australian-born chef Craig Foster in 2003, the Boot offers a
cosy bar and secluded dining areas. Typical lunch menu
features traditional gammon, pot-roasted half shoulder of
lamb, chargrilled rump steak, and beer battered cod.
OPEN: 11-3 6-11 (Open all day in summer)
BAR MEALS: L served all week 12-2.30 D served all week 7-9.30
Av main course £12.95 **RESTAURANT:** 7-9.30 ☺: Free House
◀: Hook Norton Best, Adnams Best, Fullers London Pride, Youngs
Best. ♀: 7 **FACILITIES:** Garden **NOTES:** Parking 20

BECKLEY   Map 05 SP51

Pick of the Pubs

The Abingdon Arms ◉ ♀
High St OX3 9UU ☎ 01865 351311
e-mail: chequers89@hotmail.com
Dir: Junct 8 M40 follow signs at Headington rdbt for Beckley

In the pretty village of Beckley, this pub provides a warm
welcome to walkers and birdwatchers enjoying the
Otmoor countryside. Enjoy the views on the patio whilst

sipping a pint of Brakspear's ale, or refuel with some
quality pub food. There is an inventive, regularly changing
menu - up to six specials are available too. At lunchtime,
the emphasis is on superior pub fare: ham, free range
eggs and chips; beer battered haddock; or a ciabatta
sandwich should set you up for an afternoon in the
outdoors. The dining menu offers an interesting range of
starters and snacks: baby calamari pan fried in ginger,
soy, coriander and lime; Bantry Bay mussels in a range of
sauces; and roasted field mushrooms with gorgonzola
and herb crust. Main courses might include fajitas with
guacamole, salsa and cheese; confit of duck with plum
and port sauce; and goats' cheese and broccoli frittata
with Greek salad.
OPEN: 12-3 6-11 (Open all day Sat & Sun)
BAR MEALS: L served all week 12-2.30 D served Mon-Sat
7-9.30 (Sun 12-3) Av main course £10 **RESTAURANT:** L served
all week 12-2.30 D served Mon-Sat 6.30-8.30 ☺: Brakspear
◀: Brakspears Bitter, Brakspear Special & Brakspear Guest. ♀: 8
FACILITIES: Garden: Terraced patio with good views
NOTES: Parking 20

BLACK BOURTON   Map 05 SP20

Pick of the Pubs

The Vines ◆◆◆◆ ♀
Burford Rd OX18 2PF ☎ 01993 843559 📠 01993 840080
e-mail: vinesrestaurant@aol.co.uk
web: www.vinesblackbourton.co.uk
Dir: From A40 Witney, take A4095 to Faringdon, then 1st right after
Bampton to Black Bourton

Not only is this traditional Cotswold stone building
ideally placed for those on business in Oxford, Swindon,
Witney or Brize Norton, it is also a perfect base for
exploring the beautiful Cotswolds. Guests are welcomed
in the lounge area of the restaurant where they can
relax on comfortable sofas, beside a log fire in winter.
The restaurant area was designed and decorated by
John Clegg of the BBC's Real Rooms team, and here
you can enjoy lunch or dinner from the à la carte or
special daily menus. Starters could include chicken and
bacon salad; spicy tiger prawns; and mozzarella and
proscuitto salad, with main choices like roasted fillet of
halibut; braised shank of lamb; fillet of salmon with leaf
parsley; risotto caponata; crispy duck breast; and rib-
eye steak and chunky chips. The cellar offers a choice
of over 36 wines including from the local vineyard.
OPEN: 12-3 6-11 (Sun 12-10.30) **BAR MEALS:** L served
Tue-Sun 12-2 D served Mon-Sun 6.30-9.30 Closed Mon lunch
Av main course £9 **RESTAURANT:** L served Tue-Sun 12-2

continued

continued

England

BLACK BOURTON continued

D served Tue-Sun 6.30-9.30 Closed Mon lunch ☺: Free House
🍺: Old Hookey, Tetley Smooth, Carlsberg-Tetley. ♀: 7
FACILITIES: Children's licence Garden: Large lawn area,
seating, 'Aunt Sally' facility Dogs allowed in the garden only
NOTES: Parking 70 **ROOMS:** 6 bedrooms en suite
1 family room s£60 d£70

BLOXHAM   Map 11 SP43

The Elephant & Castle
OX15 4LZ ☎ 01295 720383
e-mail: elephant.bloxham@btinternet.com
Dir: Just off A361
The arch of this 15th-century, Cotswold-stone coaching inn
still straddles the former Banbury to Chipping Norton
turnpike. Locals play darts or shove-ha'penny in the big
wood-floored bar, whilst the two-roomed lounge boasts a
bar-billiards table and a large inglenook fireplace. The
reasonably priced menu starts with a range of sandwiches
and crusty filled baguettes, whilst hot dishes include pub
favourites like breaded haddock, crispy battered cod, scampi
and a seafood platter.
OPEN: 10-3 5-11 (Sat, Sun-open all day) **BAR MEALS:** L served
Mon-Sat 12-2 Av main course £5 **RESTAURANT:** L served Mon-Sat
12-2 ☺: Hook Norton 🍺: Hook Norton Best Bitter, Hook Norton
Seasonal Ales, Guest Ales. **FACILITIES:** Garden: Raised lawn in
flower filled garden, patio Dogs allowed Water **NOTES:** Parking 20

BRIGHTWELL BALDWIN   Map 05 SU69

Pick of the Pubs

The Lord Nelson Inn 🛏️♀
OX9 5NP ☎ 01491 612497 🖂 01491 612118
Dir: Off the B4009 between Watlington & Benson

Originally a thatched cottage, this 18th-century inn is
situated opposite the church in the hamlet of Brightwell
Baldwin. In 1905 it was forced to close by the local lord to
prevent his workers from drinking, and it remained closed
for 66 years, reopening in 1971. The cosy interior is filled
with antique furniture, comfy sofas, open fires and a
splendid inglenook fireplace - perfect for recuperating
after a country walk. During summer the pretty garden,
with its weeping willow and rear terrace, is a popular
place to eat al fresco. Real ales from the West Berkshire
Brewery are served in the beamed bar, and there is a
comprehensive wine list with 20 wines available by
the glass. All the food is freshly cooked to order, using
local produce where possible. Typical weekly specials are

crown of local pheasant with orange sauce; and whole
roasted sea bass with rosemary.
OPEN: 11-3 6-11 **BAR MEALS:** L served all week 12-2.30
D served all week 6-10.30 **RESTAURANT:** L served all week
12-2.30 D served all week 6-10.30 (Sun 7-10) Av 3 course à la
carte £23 Av 2 course fixed price £10.95 ☺: Free House
🍺: Hook Norton, Loddon, West Berkshire Brewery. ♀: 20
FACILITIES: Garden: Lawn terrace and borders Dogs allowed
Dog Bowls **NOTES:** Parking 20

BRITWELL SALOME   Map 05 SU69

Pick of the Pubs

The Goose NEW ◉◉◉ ♀
OX49 5LG ☎ 01491 612304 🖂 01491 613945
e-mail: thegooseatbritwellsalome@fsmail.net
Dir: 1.5 from Watlington on B4009 towards Benson & Wallingford
An ancient Roman road known as The Ridgeway runs
right through the charmingly named Britwell Salome.
Once home to three pubs, The Goose is now the only
survivor. This brick and flint 16th-century inn is reportedly
haunted by a pilgrim who never completed his journey.
These days, it's popular with walkers, and can provide
maps for three different local routes, depending on your
stamina. The sunny patio garden is decked with hanging
baskets and fragrant with climbing roses - you can dine al
fresco and be lulled by the piped music. The refreshingly
unwordy menu has some treats in store - wild mushroom
soup with cep powder and white truffle oil; skewered
prawns mpumalanga (just ask!); Cape Malay chicken
curry; and smoked haddock omelette are among the
dishes on offer. The local Hook Norton Best is always
available, along with frequently changing guest beers.
OPEN: 12-3 6.30-11 Closed Sun eve **BAR MEALS:** L served
all week 12-2.30 D served Mon-Sat 7-9 Sun 12-3 Av main course
£10 **RESTAURANT:** L served all week 12-2.30 D served
Mon-Sat 7-9 Sun 12-3 Av 3 course à la carte £30 Av 3 course
fixed price £18 ☺: Free House 🍺: Hook Norton Best Bitter,
guest beer. ♀: 17 **FACILITIES:** Garden: Suntrap garden, teak
furniture, umbrellas Dogs allowed in garden only
NOTES: Parking 35

BROADWELL   Map 05 SP20

The Five Bells Broadwell
GL7 3QS ☎ 01367 860076 e-mail: trevorcooper@skynow.net
*Dir: A361 from Lechlade to Burford, after 2m R to Kencot Broadwell, then
R after 200m, then R at crossrds*
Attractive 16th-century Cotswold stone inn overlooking the
manor and parish church. The bars are full of character with
beams and flagstones, and the conservatory leads to a pretty
garden. An extensive choice of dishes includes salmon and
prawn gratin, pheasant in red wine, and steak and kidney pie.
OPEN: 11.30-2.30 7-11 (Sun 12-3, 7-10.30) Closed: 25 & 26 Dec,
closed Mon except BHs **BAR MEALS:** L served Tue-Sun 12-1.45
D served Tue-Sat 7-9 Av main course £7.50
RESTAURANT: L served Tue-Sun 12-1.45 D served Tue-Sat 7-9
Av 3 course à la carte £13.50 ☺: Free House 🍺: Interbrew Bass
Bitter, Archers Village. **FACILITIES:** Garden: Quiet, peaceful Dogs
allowed **NOTES:** Parking 30

continued

BROUGHTON
Map 11 SP43

Saye and Sele Arms NEW
Main Rd OX15 5ED ☎ 01295 263348 ▤ 01295 272012
e-mail: mail@sayeandselearms.co.uk
Dir: 3m from Banbury Cross
Licensed for 300 years, the Saye & Sele is just five minutes'
walk from Broughton Castle, a popular film location
(*Shakespeare in Love, Edward VIII*). The pub is known for its
food but maintains a good mix of regulars/diners. Choose
between snacks, main meals and specials such as faggots and
mash with mushy peas or chicken cordon bleu. There is a
sheltered garden and a terraced area with seating for 50 plus.
OPEN: 11.30-2.30 Sat 11.30-3 7-11 Sun 12-3 7-10.30
BAR MEALS: L served all week 12-2 D served Mon-Sat 7-10
Av main course £7 **RESTAURANT:** L served all week 12-2 D served
Mon-Sat 7-10 Av 3 course à la carte £17 Av 3 course fixed price £10.95
◀: Wadworth 6X, Adnams Southwold, 2 guest beers.
FACILITIES: Garden: Terraced area with seating for 50+ Dogs
allowed in garden only (ex assistance dogs) **NOTES:** Parking 30

BURCOT
Map 05 SU59

The Chequers ▷ ♀
OX14 3DP ☎ 01865 407771 ▤ 01865 407771
e-mail: info@marlowesltd.co.uk
Dir: On A415 (Dorchester/Abingdon rd)
Partly dating back to the 16th century and originally a staging
post for barges on the Thames. A varied menu might include
bacon, mushroom and pine nut salad; seared salmon with
charred potatoes, braised leek, orange and ginger; braised
shank of lamb; pan-fried duck breast with red cabbage and
garlic mash; and Thai spiced salmon on noodles with stir fry
vegetables and sweet chilli sauce. Good choice of real ales,
and German draught lagers.
OPEN: 12-3 6-11 Closed Sun eve **BAR MEALS:** L served all week
12-2.30 D served Mon-Sat 6-9.30 Av main course £8.75
RESTAURANT: L served all week 12-2.30 D served Mon-Sat 6-9.30
Av 3 course fixed price £17.50 ◉: Free House ◀: Scottish Courage
Directors, Marstons Pedigree, Scottish Courage Best. ♀: 21
FACILITIES: Garden: Large garden with lots of seating
NOTES: Parking 35

BURFORD
Map 05 SP21

Golden Pheasant ★★ ♀
91 High St OX18 4QA ☎ 01993 823223 ▤ 01993 822621
e-mail: robrichardson.goldenpheasant-burford.co.uk
Dir: M40 junct 8 and follow signs A40 Cheltenham into Burford
Mellow Cotswold stone forms the backdrop for this well-
established 17th-century inn at the heart of picturesque
Burford. An informal atmosphere and a friendly welcome
await both guests and locals in the brasserie-style lounge bar
and restaurant where the food has a well-deserved
reputation. Designed to suit a variety of tastes, the menu
might include duck breast; risotto with wild mushrooms;
paella; braised ham hock; and salmon, crab and red snapper
fishcakes.
OPEN: 9-11 **BAR MEALS:** L served all week 12-2.30 D served all
week 6.30-9.30 **RESTAURANT:** L served all week 12-2.30 D served
all week 6.30-9 Av 3 course à la carte £25 ◉: ◀: Abbot, IPA. ♀: 7
FACILITIES: Garden: Patio Dogs allowed at the manager's discretion
NOTES: Parking 12 **ROOMS:** 10 bedrooms en suite s£60 d£85

Pick of the Pubs

The Inn for All Seasons ★★ ♀
The Barringtons OX18 4TN ☎ 01451 844324 ▤ 01451 844375
e-mail: sharp@innforallseasons.com
web: www.innforallseasons.com
Dir: 3m W of Burford on A40
A Grade II-listed, Cotswolds coaching inn that has served
travellers on the London to Wales road since the 16th
century. Behind it, stone used for St Paul's Cathedral was
quarried. Close by is the Sherborne Estate (NT) with its
remarkable collection of early spring flowers. Within its
solid walls is a treasure-trove of ancient oak beams,
inglenooks and contemporary furniture. There are several
guest ales, among them always a Wychwood from nearby
Witney, and a large selection of wines by the glass. The
Sharp family has owned the Inn since 1986; Matthew
Sharp, the chef, has worked with the Roux Brothers and
Anton Mosimann, at the Ritz in both London and Paris - the
list goes on. Good connections with the right people in
Brixham guarantee a wonderful supply of fish for dishes
such as whole roast John Dory on egg noodles with red
wine and shallot sauce; flash-fried squid with lime and baby
spinach leaf salad; whole grilled lobster with lemon rice
and sweet mustard and brandy sauce; and we mustn't
forget classic battered cod with home-made chunky chips
and tartare sauce. Alternatively, there are plenty of
succulent meat dishes, including crisp confit of Gloucester
pork on lemon dauphinoise potatoes, with shallot and red
wine sauce; noisettes of braised Cotswold lamb with carrots
and coriander; and roast breast of Gressingham duck on
steamed pak choi with Thai spiced dressing and basmati
rice. Vegetarians are catered for with imaginative offerings
such as baked butternut squash and sunflower seed risotto
with parmesan shavings. For dessert try champagne and
lemon syllabub with a coconut biscuit crust. The ten en
suite bedrooms are spacious and comfortably furnished.
OPEN: 11-2.30 6-11 (Sun 12-3, 7-10.30)
BAR MEALS: L served all week 11.30-2.30 D served all week
6.30-9.30 Sun 12-2.30, 7-9 Av main course £9.95
RESTAURANT: L served all week 11.30-2.30 D served all week
6.30-9.30 Sun 12-2.30, 7-9 Av 3 course à la carte £18.50 ◉: Free
House ◀: Wadworth 6X, Interbrew Bass, Wychwood, Badger.
♀: 15 **FACILITIES:** Child facs Garden: Small grass area, tables,
good views Dogs allowed Water **NOTES:** Parking 80
ROOMS: 10 bedrooms en suite 2 family rooms s£50 d£90

Pick of the Pubs

The Lamb Inn ★★★ ◉◉ ♀
Sheep St OX18 4LR ☎ 01993 823155 ▤ 01993 822228
e-mail: info@lambinn-burford.co.uk
Dir: From M40 junct 8 follow A40 & Burfordsigns. Off High Street
If your idea of a traditional English inn includes stone
flagged floors, real ale and log fires, you'll not be
disappointed at the Lamb. With its 500 years of history,
this honey-coloured stone-built coaching inn lies just off
the centre of Burford, whilst still having easy access to the
shops. In summer you can visit the walled cottage garden,
admire the herbaceous borders and perhaps take lunch
on the lawn. But there's nothing old-world about the
menus, which present a delicious blend of English and
international cooking. The chef uses locally produced
meat, cheese and vegetables whenever possible, as well
as organic meat and fish when available. Menus are

continued

England

BURFORD continued

changed regularly, and include smoked haddock and trout risotto; vine tomato, halloumi and basil tart; middle eastern lamb shank with pepper couscous; confit of duck with a warm salad; sausage and mash with onion gravy; pancakes with apple and raspberry; and pecan pie with prune and Armagnac ice cream.

The Lamb Inn

OPEN: 11-11 (Sun 12-10.30) **BAR MEALS:** L served all week 12-2.30 D served all week 6.30-9.30 Sat-Sun 12-3 Av main course £10 **RESTAURANT:** L served all week 12.30-2.30 D served all week 7-9.30 Sun 12-3 Av 3 course fixed price £32.50 ⊞: Free House ◀: Wadworth 6X, Hook Norton Best, Adnams. ♀: 14 **FACILITIES:** Child facs Garden: walled cottage garden Dogs allowed Water **ROOMS:** 15 bedrooms en suite s£115 d£145

CHADLINGTON
Map 10 SP32

The Tite Inn ♀
Mill End OX7 3NY ☎ 01608 676475 ▤ 0870 7059308
e-mail: willis@titeinn.com web: www.titeinn.com
Dir: 3m S of Chipping Norton
Run by the same family for 20 years, here is a pub at the heart of village life, not least as a rendezvous for the local investors' club. The lunch menu features bobotie (a sweet and spicy meatloaf), chicken jalfrezi and other hot dishes, as well as ploughman's and sandwiches. In the evening, look for boeuf bourguignonne, lambs' kidneys braised in red wine, and duck sausages with cranberry and brandy sauce. Five draught beers are always available.
OPEN: 12-2.30 6.30-11 (Sun 12-3, 7-10.30) Closed: Dec 25-26 **BAR MEALS:** L served Tue-Sun 12-2 D served Tue-Sun 7-9 Av main course £8.95 **RESTAURANT:** L served Tue-Sun 12-2 D served Tue-Sat 6.30-9 Av 3 course à la carte £16.85 ⊞: Free House ◀: Youngs, Butcombe, 3 guest beers. ♀: 8 **FACILITIES:** Garden: Large beer garden, outstanding views Dogs allowed Water provided **NOTES:** Parking 30

CHALGROVE
Map 05 SU69

Pick of the Pubs

The Red Lion Inn ♀
The High St OX44 7SS ☎ 01865 890625
e-mail: annie@redlionchalgrove.co.uk
Dir: B480 from Oxford Ring road, through Stadhampton, left then right at mini-rdbt, at Chalgrove Airfield right fork into village
It might seem strange that a pub should be owned by a church, but the Red Lion Inn has been since 1637. Back then it provided free dining and carousing for the church

continued

---

wardens. Parts of this lovely cream-painted and beamed pub even date back to the 11th century. The emphasis today is on a warm welcome, a good pint of real ale, and both traditional and imaginative eating. A bar menu offers the simple favourites of beer-battered fish and chips with mushy peas; traditional cottage pie with vegetables; and sandwiches and jacket potatoes. Dinner menu choices are varied and reasonably priced: you may start with Red Lion baby gem Caesar salad; terrine of ham hock and foie gras with onion and orange marmalade; and seafood chowder with caviar sour cream. Puddings include glazed lemon and lime meringue tart with berries and raspberry sorbet; and sticky toffee pudding with butterscotch bananas and vanilla ice cream.

The Red Lion Inn

OPEN: 12-3 6-11 Sun 7-10.30 (Winter 12-2.30) Closed: 1 Jan **BAR MEALS:** L served all week 12-2.30 D served Mon-Sat 6.30-9 Dinner 6.30-9.30 Fri-Sat. No food Sun eve Av main course £8.50 **RESTAURANT:** L served all week 12-2.30 D served Mon-Sat 7-9 7-9.30 Fri-Sat. No food served on Sun Av 3 course fixed price £18.50 ⊞: Free House ◀: Fuller's London Pride, Adnams Best, Timothy Taylors Landlord. ♀: 7 **FACILITIES:** Large garden with seating Dogs allowed Water

---

CHARLBURY
Map 11 SP31

Pick of the Pubs

The Bull Inn ♀
Sheep St OX7 3RR ☎ 01608 810689
e-mail: info@bullinn-charlbury.com
Dir: On A40 at Oxford right to Woodstock, thru Woodstock & after 1.5m left to Charlbury
A 16th-century coaching inn with a smart stone exterior on the main street of Charlbury, a beautifully preserved Cotswold town surrounded by lovely countryside. It is a fine stone-built inn with a lovely location close to Woodstock and only 15 minutes from Oxford by train to Charlbury Station. The interior is full of period character, with exposed beams and inglenook fireplaces, where log fires burn in cooler weather. There's a traditional bar with wooden floors and a tastefully furnished lounge and dining room. Outside, the vine-covered terrace is a delightful spot to sit and enjoy a drink or a meal in summer weather. Food is served in both the bar and restaurant, with options ranging from lunchtime baguettes in the bar, to more serious options.
OPEN: 12-3 6-11 (Sat 11-11, Sun 12-3, 6-10.30) **BAR MEALS:** L served Tues-Sun 12-2 D served Tues-Sat 7-9 summer D available Mon & Sun Av main course £12 **RESTAURANT:** L served Tues-Sun booking only 12-2 D served Tues-Sat 7-9.30 Sun 12-2.30 ⊞: Free House ◀: Greene King IPA, Abbot Ale, Hooky. ♀: 6 **FACILITIES:** Garden: Terrace **NOTES:** Parking 14

CHECKENDON — Map 05 SU68

The Highwayman ♀
Exlade St RG8 0UA ☎ 01491 682020 ▤ 01491 682229
e-mail: thehighwayman@skyeinns670.fsnet.co.uk
Dir: On A4074 Reading to Wallingford Rd

An early 17th-century listed inn which has recently undergone a major refurblishment programme. The emphasis in the character bar is on wooden floors and open fireplaces. The famous Maharajah's Well nearby is surrounded by numerous walks in the glorious Chiltern beechwoods. Seared salmon fillet, pan-fried calves' liver, and honey mustard and lemon chicken escalope are typical examples from the inviting menu.
OPEN: 12-3 6-11 (Sat-Sun & BH all day) 25 Dec Closed pm
BAR MEALS: L served all week 12-3 D served all week 7-9.30
RESTAURANT: L served all week 12-2.30 D served all week 7-9.30
▤: Free House ◀: Fuller's London Pride, Loddon Ferryman's Gold, Butlers Brewers & guest ale. **FACILITIES:** Garden: Dogs allowed courtyard only **NOTES:** Parking 30 **ROOMS:** 4 bedrooms en suite (♦♦♦♦)

CHINNOR — Map 05 SP70

Pick of the Pubs

Sir Charles Napier ◉◉ ▷ ♀
Spriggs Alley OX39 4BX ☎ 01494 483011 ▤ 01494 485311
web: www.sircharlesnapier.co.uk
Dir: M40 junct 6 to Chinnor. Turn right at rdbt, up hill to Spriggs Alley

Surrounded by miles of glorious beech woods, which cry out to be discovered on foot, this is very much a people's pub. Inside is a welcoming atmosphere with huge fires and comfortable sofas. French windows overlook the terrace where lunch is served in the summer beneath vines and wisteria. Carpets of bluebells nearby and the whiff of wild garlic in April and May remind visitors that this is the heart of the countryside. As if that isn't enough, you may be lucky enough to spot one or more of the 160 breeding pairs of red kites in the area. An exhaustive wine list complements the blackboard dishes and imaginative seasonal menus. Potted shrimps on toasted brioche; or Thai chicken soup might precede organic salmon, creamed leeks, crayfish and tomato; Gressingham duck breast with plums in red wine; or traditional roast grouse with bread sauce. Round off with a selection of English and French cheeses.
OPEN: 12-3.30 6.30-12 closed Mon, Sun Night Closed: 25-26 Dec
BAR MEALS: L served Tue-Sat 12-2.30 D served Tues-Thurs 7-9.30
No bar food Sun Av main course £10.50 **RESTAURANT:** L served Tue-Sat 12-2.30 D served Tue-Sat 7-10 Sun 12-3.30 Av 3 course à la carte £30 Av 2 course fixed price £16.50 ▤: Free House
◀: Wadworth 6X, Wadwoth IPA. ♀: 15 **FACILITIES:** Garden: Large garden and terrace **NOTES:** Parking 50

CHIPPING NORTON — Map 10 SP32

The Chequers ♀
Goddards Ln OX7 5NP ☎ 01608 644717 ▤ 01608 646237
e-mail: enquiries@chequers-pub.co.uk
web: www.chequers-pub.co.uk
Dir: Town centre, next to theatre

Located next door to the renowned theatre, this 16th-century inn is popular with locals and theatre-goers alike. Log fires, low ceilings and soft lighting make for a cosy atmosphere in the bar while, by contrast, the courtyard restaurant is wonderfully bright and airy. Well-kept real ale, good wines and decent coffee are served along with freshly prepared dishes. These include shellfish with noodles, spinach and mushroom lasagne, Gloucester Old Spot pork and leek sausage, home-cooked honey and cider ham, and butternut squash risotto.
OPEN: 11-11 (Sun 11-10.30) Closed: 25 Dec **BAR MEALS:** L served all week 12-2.30 D served Mon-Sat 6-9.30 (Sun 12-5) Av main course £8.50 **RESTAURANT:** L served all week 12-2.30 D served Mon-Sat 6-9 Sun 12-5 Av 3 course à la carte £17 ▤: Fullers ◀: Fuller's Chiswick Bitter, London Pride & ESB, Organic Honeydew. ♀: 18

CHISLEHAMPTON — Map 05 SU59

Coach And Horses Inn ♦♦♦ ▷ ♀
Watlington Rd OX44 7UX ☎ 01865 890255 ▤ 01865 891995
e-mail: enquiries@coachhorsesinn.co.uk
Situated in quiet countryside just seven miles from the centre of Oxford, this 16th-century former coaching inn retains plenty of character. There are beams, log fires, and an old bread oven, and the building is said to be haunted by a young girl killed during the Civil War. Specialities include a slow-roasted half shoulder of lamb; asparagus Provençale pancakes; and fresh Scottish salmon on spinach with lemon butter sauce.
OPEN: 11.30-3 6-11 **BAR MEALS:** L served all week 12-2 D served Mon-Sat 7-10 **RESTAURANT:** L served all week 12-2 D served Mon-Sat 7-10 ▤: Free House ◀: Hook Norton Best, Interbrew Flowers Original. ♀: 8 **FACILITIES:** Garden: Landscape courtyard, large lawn area Dogs allowed Water **NOTES:** Parking 40
ROOMS: 9 bedrooms en suite 1 family room No children overnight

> ♀ **7** Number of wines by the glass

> Room prices show the minimum double and single rates charged. Room rates in hotels and B&Bs often vary depending on the facilities, so be sure to check prices with the establishment before booking

England

CHRISTMAS COMMON   Map 05 SU79

The Fox and Hounds ♀
OX49 5HL ☎ 01491 612599 ▤ 01491 614642
Dir: M40 Junct 5, 2.5 miles to Christmas Common (On road to Henley)
Charming 500-year-old pub painstakingly transformed in 2001 into a stylish dining pub with an immaculate interior, a large restaurant with open-plan kitchen, and four cosy bar areas. An imaginative menu includes roasted free range chicken breast, lemon sole, braised lamb shank, pork, turkey and apricot roulade, and cod fillet marinated in coriander, lemon and lime. Bar meals from Welsh rarebit to doorstep sandwiches.
OPEN: 11.30-3 6-11 Open all day Sat-Sun **BAR MEALS:** L served all week 12-2.30 D served Mon-Sun 7-9.30 Sun 12-3, Sun closed pm Nov-Mar. Av main course £12 **RESTAURANT:** L served all week 12-2.30 D served Mon-Sun 7-9.30 Av 3 course à la carte £22.50
⊞: Brakspear ◖: Brakspear Bitter, Organic, Special & seasonal beers. ♀: 11 **FACILITIES:** Garden: Small herb garden, seating for 40/50 Dogs allowed Water **NOTES:** Parking 30

CHURCH ENSTONE   Map 11 SP32

Pick of the Pubs

The Crown Inn ◉ ⌇◇
Mill Ln OX7 4NN ☎ 01608 677262 ▤ 01608 677394
e-mail: tcwarburton@btopenworld.com
Dir: Telephone for directions
The 17th-century Crown was built as an inn from Cotswold stone, its interior walls as bare as those outside, but they keep it comfortably warm or cool, as required. Award-winning chef/proprietor Tony Warburton, and his wife Caroline, have worked in top-class catering establishments abroad and locally, and it's clear from their daily menus that the use of fresh, mostly local, produce is important to them. Start with avocado, bacon, dolcelatte and walnut salad; or parma ham, deep-fried goat's cheese, beans and red wine syrup; or even a simple cream of tomato soup. Consult the menu again for maybe beef curry and rice; pork loin, cabbage, bacon and cider cream; or in-season game. Fish and seafood are a speciality, typically fillet of salmon with couscous, crème fraîche and red pepper dressing; and fillet of turbot with chive beurre blanc. Spend a sunny lunchtime or evening in the picturesque cottage garden.
OPEN: 12-3 6-11 (Sun 12-3) **BAR MEALS:** L served Tue-Sun 12-2 D served Tue-Sat 7-9 Av main course £8.50 **RESTAURANT:** L served Tue-Sun 12-2 D served Tue-Sat 7-9 Av 3 course à la carte £19.50 ⊞: Free House ◖: Hook Norton Best Bitter, Shakespeare Spitfire, Timothy Taylor Landlord. **FACILITIES:** Garden: Small cottage garden Dogs allowed Water **NOTES:** Parking 8

CHURCH HANBOROUGH   Map 11 SP41

Pick of the Pubs

The Hand & Shears ♀
OX29 8AB ☎ 01993 883337 ▤ 01993 881392
Dir: From A40 Eynsham rdbt follow signs for The Hanboroughs. Turn left at sign for Church Hanborough, follow road through village, pub on right opposite church.
Believed to be the only establishment so named in Britain, the Hand & Shears is a stylish pub-restaurant situated opposite the village green and 11th-century church.

There's a good choice of real ales, and the brasserie-style food attracts people from a broad catchment area. Favourite lunchtime dishes include large soup with bread and butter; baked gammon, egg and chips; Spanish omelette; and linguine carbonara with mushrooms. Popular in the evening are home-made beefburger; bubble and squeak and fried eggs with tomato, red onion and mushroom chutney; and seared salmon with watercress sauce. Wines come mostly from Latin countries, although the French and South Africans have got their feet in the door. The pub is also a great base for circular walks and cycle routes, and is particularly popular with admirers of the bluebells in Pinsley Woods.

The Hand & Shears

OPEN: 11-3 6-11 (Open all day Easter-end Summer) **BAR MEALS:** L served all week 12-2.30 D served Mon-Sat 6-9.30 Sun 12-6 Av main course £8.50 **RESTAURANT:** L served all week 12-2.30 D served Mon-Sat 6-9.30 Sun 12-6 ⊞: ◖: Hook Norton Best Bitter, Hobgoblin, Fiddlers Elbow, Adnams. ♀: 7 **FACILITIES:** Child facs Benches outside the front of the pub Dogs allowed Water **NOTES:** Parking 40

CLIFTON   Map 11 SP43

Pick of the Pubs

Duke of Cumberland's Head ⌇◇
OX15 0PE ☎ 01869 338534 ▤ 01869 338643
Dir: A4260 from Banbury, then B4031 from Deddington
Built in 1645, originally as cottages, this thatched stone pub is named after Prince Rupert, Count Palatine of the Rhine, who led his uncle Charles I's troops at the nearby Battle of Edge Hill, and received the dukedom for his success as a military leader. The story goes that important strategic decisions about the Civil War were made by soldiers sitting around the pub's inglenook fireplace. The bar menu has a good choice of starters and main courses, including Inverawe smoked trout, and braised beef in beer. In the restaurant, a short but interesting menu features starters of salmon and crab risotto, and eggs Benedict; mains of roast loin of lamb with port and redcurrant sauce, and monkfish with saffron and red pepper dressing; and puddings such as home-made honey and ginger cheesecake, and orange Grand Marnier. There's a large garden and a barbecue that comes into play in summer.
OPEN: 12-2.30 6.30-11 (W/end 12-3) Closed Mon Lunch Closed: Dec 25 **BAR MEALS:** L served Tue-Sun 12-2 D served all week 6-9 Av main course £10 **RESTAURANT:** L served Wed-Sun 12-2 D served Wed-Sat 7-9.30 Av 2 course fixed price £15 ⊞: ◖: Hook Norton, Adnams, Deuchers Black Sheep. **FACILITIES:** Garden: beer garden, outdoor eating, BBQ Dogs allowed **NOTES:** Parking 20

continued

CRAY'S POND   Map 05 SU68

Pick of the Pubs

The White Lion NEW ♀
Goring Rd, Goring Heath RG8 7SH
☎ 01491 680471 📠 01491 681654
e-mail: reservations@innastew.com
Dir: From M4 junct 11 follow signs to Pangbourne, cross toll bridge to Whitchurch, go N for 3m into Crays Pond
The White lion is a 250-year-old pub, well known - or 'notorious' as the owner prefers to call it - for its very low ceilings. It is home to the Woodcote Rally, the third biggest steam fair in England, and is situated on the edge of the Chilterns. Surrounded by lovely woods, it is only about a mile from the River Thames and is a very popular place with walkers. Starters could include chicken liver pâté with onion marmalade; grilled Manx kipper with caper and parsley butter; or sweet red onion tart Tatin. Mains range from skate tangine with couscous and tzatziki, to calves' liver and bacon with mash, and roast butternut squash risotto with wild mushrooms and parmesan. Puddings are along the lines of apple and mincemeat filo with custard tart and apple sorbet; and poire belle Hélène. The bar menu offers some interesting snacks like pickled chillis, deep-fried broad beans, steak sandwich, aubergine and red pepper terrine with black olive tapenade, and ground fillet burger with chilli jam.
OPEN: 8.30am-11pm Closed Sun eve 25-26 Dec, 1 Jan
BAR MEALS: L served Tues-Sun 12-2.30 D served Tues-Sat 6-9.30 Av main course £13 **RESTAURANT:** L served Tues-Sun 12-9.30 D served Tues-Sat 6-9.30 Sun 12-2.30 Av 3 course à la carte £25 🍺: IPA, Abbot Ale, Hooky, Gales. ♀: 12
FACILITIES: Garden: Large garden, patio with heaters Dogs allowed **NOTES:** Parking 30

and the appeal is enhanced by soft furnishings and warm colours. The pub caters for a wide cross section of locals as well as being a popular destination for lovers of good food. Freshly-prepared meals with full service might produce starters like smoked duck breast on a mixed leaf salad, or timbale of salmon, crab and prawns, followed by monkfish in smoked bacon with saffron sauce, or Thai chicken curry, and perhaps profiteroles with Chantilly cream and a rich chocolate sauce. A good range of Havana cigars, ports and brandies.
OPEN: 12-11 (Sun 12-10.30) **BAR MEALS:** L served all week 12-2.30 D served all week 6-9.30 **RESTAURANT:** L served all week 12-3 D served all week 6-9 🍺: Morrells 🍺: IPA, Old Speckled Hen, Abbot Ale, Old Hooky. **FACILITIES:** Garden: Food served outdoors, patio, BBQ Dogs allowed Water, toys **NOTES:** Parking 60

The Vine Inn ♀
11 Abingdon Rd OX2 9QN ☎ 01865 862567 📠 01865 862567
Dir: A420 from Oxford, right onto B4017
An old village pub whose name, when you see the frontage, needs no explanation. A typical menu here could include lamb shank with a red wine and mint sauce, pan-fried fillet steak with brandy and mushroom sauce, and the day's fresh fish. There's also a good range of snacks. Children love the huge garden. In 1560, the suspicious death of a local earl's wife first had people asking 'Did she fall, or was she pushed?'
OPEN: 11-3 6-11 (Sat 11-11 Sun 12-10.30) **BAR MEALS:** L served all week 12-2.15 D served Mon-all 6.30-9.15 Sun 12-7 Av main course £7.50 **RESTAURANT:** L served all week 12-2.15 D served all week 6.30-9.15 Sun 12-7 Av 3 course à la carte £20 🍺: Punch Taverns 🍺: Adnams Bitter, Carlsberg-Tetleys Tetleys Bitter, Hook Norton, guest beers. ♀: 7 **FACILITIES:** Child facs Children's licence Garden: Fenced with tables and chairs & lawn area Dogs allowed Water **NOTES:** Parking 45

CUMNOR   Map 05 SP40

Pick of the Pubs

Bear & Ragged Staff ♀
28 Appleton Rd OX2 9QH ☎ 01865 862329 📠 01865 865947
Dir: A420 from Oxford, right to Cumnor on B4017

A 700-year-old pub dating back to Cromwell's days, and allegedly haunted by the mistress of the Earl of Warwick. Cromwell's brother Richard is believed to have chiselled out the royal crest from above one of the fireplaces. The wooden décor, including beams and floors, and two of the original massive fireplaces add to the atmosphere,

DEDDINGTON   Map 11 SP43

Pick of the Pubs

Deddington Arms ★★★ ◉ ♀
Horsefair OX15 0SH ☎ 01869 338364 📠 01869 337010
e-mail: deddarms@oxfordshire-hotels.co.uk
web: www.deddington-arms-hotel.co.uk
Dir: A43 to Northampton, B4100 to Aynho, B4031 to Deddington. M40 junct 11 to Banbury. Follow signs for hospital, then towards Adderbury & Deddington, on A4260.
The hotel overlooks the market square in Deddington, a gateway to the Cotswolds, and the only English parish with a coat of arms. From its timbered bars, with open fires blazing away when you need them, it has offered a warm welcome to travellers and locals for 400 years. A bar meal could be a sandwich or something hot and more substantial like a chicken curry, lamb cutlets or smoked haddock. Starters in the smart air-conditioned restaurant might be salmon rillette with scampi and yellow pepper essence; duck and ginger parcels with oriental dressing; or sautéed pigeon breast with apple and bacon salad and port jus. Main courses include pheasant breast with bubble and squeak, smoked bacon and thyme mousse, and Madeira jus; fillet of beef, garlic mash, carrot broth and seared foie gras; and sun-dried tomato and basil risotto with chive beurre blanc. The wine

continued   *continued*

DEDDINGTON continued

list ranges the world. Among the 27 spacious bedrooms are cottage suites and some with four-posters.

Deddington Arms

OPEN: 11-11 **BAR MEALS:** L served all week 12-2 D served all week 6.30-9 Av main course £9 **RESTAURANT:** L served all week 12-2 D served all week 6.30-10 Sun 7-9 Av 3 course à la carte £27 ⊕: Free House ◀: Carlsberg-Tetleys Tetleys Bitter, Green King IPA, Deuchars. ⬚: 8 **NOTES:** Parking 36 **ROOMS:** 27 bedrooms en suite 3 family rooms s£85 d£95

The Unicorn ⬚
Market Place OX15 0SE ☎ 01869 338838 ▤ 01869 338592
e-mail: carol@putland.com
Dir: 6m S of Banbury on A4260
Exposed beams and an open fire set the tone in the bar of this 17th-century coaching inn. For warmer days there's a garden with lawns, flowerbeds and a barbecue. Back indoors there are two restaurants, one non-smoking, with the snug reserved for smokers to enjoy the contemporary English cooking. Expect roasted quail with fresh date stuffing; griddled halibut with gazpacho sauce; or vegetable tartlets with goat's cheese.
OPEN: 12-11 (Sun 12-10.30) **BAR MEALS:** L served all week 12-2.30 D served Mon-Sat 6.30-9 Sun 12-3, No D Sun winter Av main course £8.50 **RESTAURANT:** L served all week 12-2.30 D served all week 6-9.30 Sun 12-3. No D Sun winter Av 3 course à la carte £17 ◀: Hook Norton, Fullers London Pride. ⬚: 8 **FACILITIES:** Garden: Walled, secret garden, lawns, flowerbeds

DORCHESTER (ON THAMES)   Map 05 SU59

Pick of the Pubs

The George ★★★ ⊕ ⬚
25 High St OX10 7HH ☎ 01865 340404 ▤ 01865 341620
e-mail: thegeorgehotel@fsmail.net
Dir: From M40 junct 7, A329 S to A4074 at Shillingford. Follow Dorchester signs. From M4 junct 13, A34 to Abingdon then A415 E to Dorchester
Historic features throughout this 15th-century hostelry, the centrepiece of the village, include the inglenook fireplaces of Potboys Bar and a fine vaulted ceiling in the hotel restaurant. Bar menus change daily with a weather eye to high quality fresh produce from near and far. Starters might include roast plum tomato soup and rabbit confit with mustard sauce, followed by boar and apple sausages with chive mash, wild mushroom and basil tagliatelle, and grilled salmon fillet with sauce vierge. Dinner menus offer chargrilled scallops with pancetta, roast peppered saddle of lamb, home-made

blueberry ice cream and commendable British farmhouse cheeses.

The George

OPEN: 11.30-11 (Sun 12-10.30) Closed: X-mas to New Year **BAR MEALS:** L served all week 12-2.15 D served all week 7-9.45 Sun 7-9.30 **RESTAURANT:** L served all week 12-2.15 D served all week 7-9.45 Av 3 course à la carte £25 ⊕: ◀: Brakspear. ⬚: 12 **FACILITIES:** Garden: Large lawn area **NOTES:** Parking 60 **ROOMS:** 17 bedrooms en suite 1 family room s£70 d£95 No children overnight

Pick of the Pubs

The White Hart ★★★ ⊕⊕ ⬚
High St OX10 7HN ☎ 01865 340074 ▤ 01865 341082
e-mail: whitehart@oxfordshire-hotels.co.uk
web: www.oxfordshire-hotels.co.uk
Dir: A4074 Oxford to Reading, 5M junct 7 M40 A329 to Wallingford

Providing a warm welcome to travellers for around 400 years, including the many thousands who must have arrived by stage-coach during its coaching inn days. Today it has a noted restaurant, and comfortable bars with old beams and log fires. The lunchtime-only menu offers just three starters, main courses and desserts, while the imaginative carte doubles your choice. Begin with terrine of local rabbit, with foie gras, winter vegetables, a celeriac rémoulade and chargrilled brioche; or mussel and clam chowder with saffron rouille and caviar croûte. Follow with Gressingham duck breast with sweet potato mash, deep-fried lemon ice cream and an Asian emulsion; or twice-baked broccoli and stilton soufflé with almond-crushed new potatoes, and tomato and basil coulis. Among the freshly prepared home made desserts might be millefeuille of marshmallow mousse chocolate and sablé biscuits with raspberry jam syrup; and apple and meringue tart with crumble ice cream and Calvados Anglaise.

continued

continued

OPEN: 11-11 **BAR MEALS:** L served all week 12-2.30 D served all week 6.30-9.30 **RESTAURANT:** L served all week 12-2.30 D served all week 6.30-9.30 Av 3 course fixed price £12.50 ⊞: Free House ◖: Greene King, Marstons Pedigree, St Austell Tribute, Deucars Caledeonian IPA. ♀: 12 **NOTES:** Parking 28 **ROOMS:** 28 bedrooms en suite 4 family rooms

---

DUNS TEW
Map 11 SP42

The White Horse Inn ♀
OX25 6JS ☎ 01869 340272 ▤ 01869 347732
e-mail: info@whitehorsedunstew.com
Dir: M40 junct 11, A4260, follow Deddington signs, then onto Duns Tew
Log fires, oak panelling and flagstone floors create a cosy atmosphere appropriate for a 17th-century coaching inn. A selection of main courses includes fillet of beef topped with stilton and a red wine sauce, roasted Cotswold duck with parsnip pureé, marinated venison casserole, cod fillet in a Florentine sauce, and marinated lamb tagine with rice. Lighter meals may include chicken and bacon Caesar salad, chargrilled tuna loin salad, or grilled sausages with mash. **OPEN:** 12-11 (Sun 12-10.30) **BAR MEALS:** L served all week 12-2.45 D served all week 6-9.45 **RESTAURANT:** L served all week 12-2.45 D served all week 6-9.45 ⊞: Old English Inns ◖: Greene King IPA, Batemans XXXX, Ruddles County, Abbot Ale. ♀: 10 **FACILITIES:** Garden: Patio area enclosed by bushes Dogs allowed Water **NOTES:** Parking 25

EAST HENDRED
Map 05 SU48

The Wheatsheaf ♀
Chapel Square OX12 8JN ☎ 01235 833229 ▤ 01235 821521
e-mail: thewheatsheaf@easthendred.wanadoo.co.uk
Dir: 2m from the A34 Milton interchange

In a pretty village close to the Ridgeway path, this 16th-century pub was formerly used as a courthouse. Spit-roasts and barbecues are popular summer features of the attractive front garden, which overlooks the village. In the bar and restaurant you'll find specials boards and a single menu that changes every month. Expect fishcakes with caper and dill sauce; roast pepper, mushroom and goat's cheese salad; and crispy duck leg with haricot bean cassoulet. **OPEN:** 12-3 6-11 (All day Sat, Sun, BHS) **BAR MEALS:** L served all week 12-2.30 D served Mon-Sat 6.30-9.30 Sun 12-3 Av main course £7.95 **RESTAURANT:** L served all week 12-2.30 D served Mon-Sat 6.30-9.30 Sun 12-3 ⊞: Greene King ◖: Greene King Abbot Ale, IPA, Morland, plus guest ales. ♀: 7 **FACILITIES:** Garden: Garden seating 80, enclosed aviary Dogs allowed Water **NOTES:** Parking 12

 Principal Beers for sale

FARINGDON
Map 05 SU29

The Lamb at Buckland ◉ ♀
Lamb Ln, Buckland SN7 8QN ☎ 01367 870484 ▤ 01367 870675
e-mail: enquiries@thelambatbuckland.co.uk
Dir: Just off A420 3m E of Faringdon
The Lamb stands on the very edge of the Cotswolds, with spectacular views across the Thames flood plain. It is a stone-built, 18th-century inn serving real ales, decent wines and restaurant quality food. The imaginative menu is supplemented by daily specials, including fish, and quality local ingredients are to the fore. Typical are medallions of Kelmscott pork with creamy Dijon mustard sauce, and local pheasant served with wild mushroom risotto and Madeira sauce.
OPEN: 10.30-3 5.30-11 Closed: 24 Dec-7 Jan
BAR MEALS: L served Tue-Sun 12-2 D served Tue-Sat 6.30-9.30
RESTAURANT: L served Tue-Sun 12-2 D served Tue-Sat 6.30-9.30
⊞: Free House ◖: Hook Norton, Adnams Broadside, Arkells 3Bs.
♀: 12 **FACILITIES:** Child facs Garden: Food served outside. Dogs allowed in the garden only **NOTES:** Parking 50

Pick of the Pubs

The Trout at Tadpole Bridge ◇ ♀
Buckland Marsh SN7 8RF ☎ 01367 870382
e-mail: info@trout-inn.co.uk
Dir: Halfway between Oxford & Swindon on the A420, take rd signed Bampton, pub is approx 2m
Chef/patron Chris Green bought this 17th-century pub deep in the countryside on the south bank of the River Thames in 1996. First a coal storage house, then cottages, it became an inn towards the end of the 19th century. Now tastefully transformed into a light and airy hostelry, it has polished wooden tables, oak beams, flagstone floors, a roaring log fire in winter, and a very pretty riverside garden. Isolated it may be, but its popularity is in no small measure due to the well-above average food, stylishly cooked using fresh local produce. Delights include starters such as pheasant, prune and foie gras terrine with chilled parsnip purée; and carpaccio of beef with rocket and parmesan. Follow with roast rump of lamb with Puy lentil casserole and dauphinoise potatoes; or chargrilled Aberdeen Angus sirloin with garlic and parsley butter, roasted tomato and mushrooms.
OPEN: 11.30-3 6-11 Closed Sun eve Closed: 25,31 Dec, 1 Jan, 1st wk in Feb **BAR MEALS:** L served all week 12-2 D served Mon-Sat 7-9 **RESTAURANT:** L served all week 12-2 D served Mon-Sat 7-9 ⊞: Free House ◖: Archers Village Bitter, Youngs PA Bitter, Bûtts Barbus, West Berkshire Brewery Mr Chubbs Lunchtime Bitter. ♀: 10 **FACILITIES:** Garden next to the River Thames Dogs allowed Water **NOTES:** Parking 70 **ROOMS:** 6 bedrooms en suite s£55 d£80 (♦♦♦♦)

FIFIELD
Map 10 SP21

Merrymouth Inn ♀
Stow Rd OX7 6HR ☎ 01993 831652 ▤ 01993 830840
e-mail: tim@merrymouthinn.fsnet.co.uk
Dir: On A424 between Burford (3m) & Stow-on-the-Wold (4m)
The Merrymouth takes its name from the Murimouth family who were feudal lords of Fifield. The inn dates back to the 13th century and has a wonderful vaulted cellar, while a secret passage to Bruern Abbey is rumoured. A blackboard of fresh fish and vegetarian dishes supplements the Merrymouth menu, options from which might include smoked haddock with Welsh rarebit, hake with cheese and herb crust, and

continued

FIFIELD continued

breast of chicken with gruyère and mushrooms.

Merrymouth Inn

OPEN: 12-2.30 6-10.30 (Closed Sun eve in winter)
BAR MEALS: L served all week 12-2 D served all week 6.30-9 Sun 7-8.30 Av main course £10.50 **RESTAURANT:** L served all week 12-2 D served all week 6.30-9 Sun 7-9 Av 3 course à la carte £20 ⊜: Free House ◀: Hook Norton Best Bitter, Adnams Broadside. ♀: 7 **FACILITIES:** Child facs Garden: Small patio & enclosed garden at pubs front Dogs allowed **NOTES:** Parking 70

FILKINS   Map 05 SP20

The Five Alls ♀

GL7 3JQ ☎ 01367 860306 ▯ 01367 860776
web: www.dursley-cotswolds-uk.com/five-alls.htm
Dir: A40 exit Burford, Filkins 4m, A361 to Lechlade

Set in a peaceful Cotswold village just outside Lechlade, this popular pub is offering home-made fare such as steak and kidney pudding, beef and Guinness pie, jerk chicken, mussels, chicken and mushroom pie, seabass with watercress, prawn curry, various sandwiches, and various steaks. The lawned garden has an over-sized chess set, quoits and a patio for a summer snack outdoors.
OPEN: 11-3 6-11 **BAR MEALS:** L served all week 11.30-2 D served all week 7-9.30 **RESTAURANT:** L served all week 11.30-2 D served all week 7-9.30 ⊜: Free House ◀: Hook Norton Best, Old Hooky. ♀: 8 **FACILITIES:** Garden: Large lawned garden with patio **NOTES:** Parking 100

FRINGFORD   Map 11 SP62

The Butchers Arms 🐟

OX27 8EB ☎ 01869 277363
Dir: 4m from Bicester on A421 towards Buckingham
Flora Thompson mentioned this traditional village pub in her 1939 novel *Lark Rise to Candleford*, all about life on the Northamptonshire/Oxfordshire border. A good selection of

fresh fish and other seafood, including mussels, crab and king prawns, is offered, as well as liver, bacon and onions, peppered fillet steak, half a roast duck, and steak and kidney pie. Pumps display Adnams Broadside and Marston's Pedigree labels. From the patio watch the cricket during the summer.

The Butchers Arms

OPEN: 12-3 6-11 (Sun 12-10.30) **BAR MEALS:** L served all week 12-2 (Sun 12-3) D served all week 7-10 Av main course £8.95 **RESTAURANT:** L served all week 12-2 D served all week 7-10 Av 2 course fixed price £9.95 ⊜: Punch Taverns ◀: Deaughars IPA, Interbrew Bass, Marstons Pedigree, Adnams Broadside. **FACILITIES:** Dogs allowed on leads in the bar **NOTES:** Parking 40

FYFIELD   Map 05 SU49

The White Hart ♀

Main Rd OX13 5LW ☎ 01865 390585 ▯ 01865 390671
Dir: Just off A420, 8m SW of Oxford
A wonderful old chantry house erected in 1442 to house five people engaged to pray for the soul of the lord of Fyfield manor. It has retained many original features, but now offers succour of a different kind. Food ranges from seared escalopes of salmon or pan-fried swordfish to aubergine stuffed with grilled Mediterranean vegetables or breast of duck with orange and fennel sauce. The extensive gardens include a children's play area.
OPEN: 11-3 6-11 **BAR MEALS:** L served all week 12-2 D served all week 7-10 Av main course £9 **RESTAURANT:** L served all week 12-2 D served all week 7-10 Av 3 course à la carte £16 ⊜: Free House ◀: Hook Norton, Wadworth 6X, Scottish Courage Theakstons Old Peculier, Fuller's London Pride. **FACILITIES:** Large garden: ample tables Dogs allowed Water provided **NOTES:** Parking 40

GORING   Map 05 SU68

Miller of Mansfield ♀

High St RG8 9AW ☎ 01491 872829 ▯ 01491 874200
Dir: From Pangbourne A329 to Streatley, then R on B4009, to Goring
An eighteenth-century, ivy-clad former coaching inn in the Goring Gap, the point where the River Thames flows between the Chilterns and the Berkshire Downs. In addition to the oak-beamed bar, where you can have full meals and snacks, there is a separate restaurant with a substantial menu, serving grilled duck breast with orange sauce; pork tenderloin with Calvados, apple and cream; and pan-fried sea bass with butter sauce. English roasts are available for Sunday lunch.
OPEN: 11-11 (Sun 12-10.30) **BAR MEALS:** L served all week 12-2 D served all week 6.30-10 Sun 12-4, 6.30-9.30 Av main course £9.50 **RESTAURANT:** L served all week 12-2 D served all week 7-10 Av 3 course à la carte £17.50 ⊜: Free House ◀: Greene King Old Speckled Hen, Brakspear Bitter, Adnams Best. **FACILITIES:** Child facs Dogs allowed Water **NOTES:** Parking 8

continued

GREAT TEW   Map 11 SP42

Pick of the Pubs

The Falkland Arms ♀

OX7 4DB ☎ 01608 683653 ▤ 01608 683656
e-mail: sjcourage@btconnect.com
Dir: Off A361, 1.25m, signed Great Tew
This 500-year-old inn takes its name from Lucius Carey,
2nd Viscount Falkland, who inherited the manor of Great
Tew in 1629. Nestling at the end of a charming row of
Cotswold stone cottages, the Falkland Arms is a classic:
flagstone floors, high-backed settles and an inglenook
fireplace characterise the intimate bar, where a huge
collection of beer and cider mugs hangs from the ceiling.
Home-made specials such as beef and ale pie or salmon
and broccoli fishcakes supplement the basic lunchtime
menu, served in the bar and the pub garden. In the
evening, booking is essential for dinner in the small, non-
smoking dining room. Expect parsnip soup or grilled
goats' cheese salad, followed by chicken breast with bacon
and mushrooms in shallot sauce; salmon and prawns with
lemon and dill sauce; or mushroom and herb stroganoff.
OPEN: 11.30-2.30 6-11 (Sat 11.30-3, Sun 12-3,7-10.30) 25/26
Dec & 1 Jan Closed eve **BAR MEALS:** L served all week 12-2
D served Mon-Sat Av main course £8 **RESTAURANT:** L served
all week 12-2 D served Mon-Sat 7-8 Av 3 course à la carte £20
🍺: Wadworth 🍴: Wadworth 6X & Henry's IPA. ♀: 12
FACILITIES: Garden: Landscaped garden. Food served at
lunchtime Dogs allowed on lead, water

HAILEY   Map 11 SP31

Pick of the Pubs

Bird in Hand ♀

Whiteoak Green OX29 9XP
☎ 01993 868811 868321 ▤ 01993 868702
e-mail: welcome@birdinhandinn.co.uk
Dir: From Witney onto B4022, through Hailey, inn 1m N
Classic Cotswold stone inn set in the Oxfordshire
countryside just outside the village of Hailey. It is a Grade
II listed building dating from the 16th century, with a
beamed interior and huge inglenook fireplaces. Log fires
provide a warm welcome in winter, while in summer
there are delightful arrangements of locally grown flowers
inside, and a pleasant garden if you prefer to sit outside.
The restaurant offers imaginative cooking using local
produce. Innovations include Saturday brunch and a
special Monday menu for locals. A popular choice from
the carte might be seafood bouquet, with tiger prawns,
smoked salmon, pine nuts and parmesan on a nest of
noodles; rack of herb crusted Cotswold Lamb on a bed of
beetroot mash and rich gravy; and chocolate and orange
mousse with orange coulis. Monthly themed special
events are held, such as a Burns night and barbecues.
OPEN: 11-11 **BAR MEALS:** L served all week 12-3 D served all
week 6-9 Fri-Sat dinner 6-10, 12-6 cold suppers until 9 Av main
course £8 **RESTAURANT:** L served all week 12-3 D served all
week 6-9 Fri-Sat 10, Sun 12-6 cold supper til 9 🍺: Heavitree
🍴: Worthingtons, Adnams, Old Speckled Hen. ♀: 8
FACILITIES: Garden: Food served outside. Patio & lawn areas
Dogs allowed in the garden only **NOTES:** Parking 100

HENLEY-ON-THAMES   Map 05 SU78

Pick of the Pubs

The Five Horseshoes ♀

Maidensgrove RG9 6EX ☎ 01491 641282 ▤ 01491 641086
Dir: A4130 from Henley, onto B480

A 17th-century vine-covered inn located high above
Henley with breathtaking views over the valley below. Red
kites regularly soar overhead and deer from nearby
Stonor Park can be spotted from the garden, yet this
idyllic spot is only 10 minutes' drive along a twisty road
from Henley-on-Thames. There is a fascinating collection
of curios on display in the low-beamed bar, from old
tools and banknotes to firearms and brasses. The interior
exudes old-world charm, with its wood-burning stove and
rustic stripped tables, just the place to relax over a pint of
Brakspear Special and a plate of superior food. The
regularly changing menu offers the likes of crab cakes,
mussel ravioli, Stonor venison pie topped with cheesy
creamed potatoes, and lamb's liver on mustard mash with
rich onion gravy. Favourite finishes include home-made
banoffee pie or spotted dick and custard.
OPEN: 11-3 6-11 Closed evenings Oct-Jun
BAR MEALS: L served Mon-Fri 12-2 12-2.30 Sat, 12-3 Sun
D served all week 6.30-9.30 Av main course £8
RESTAURANT: L served Mon-Fri 12-2 12-2.30 Sat, 12-3 Sun
D served all week 6.30-9 Av 3 course à la carte £18 Av 3 course
fixed price £14.95 🍺: Brakspear 🍴: Brakspear Ordinary &
Special. ♀: 14 **FACILITIES:** Garden: 2 gardens lovely views
Dogs allowed Water **NOTES:** Parking 85

The Golden Ball

Lower Assendon RG9 6AH ☎ 01491 574157 ▤ 01491 574157
e-mail: thegoldenball@tiscali.co.uk
Dir: A4130, right onto B480, pub 300yds on left
Dick Turpin hid in the priest hole at this 400-year-old building
tucked away in the Stonor Valley close to Henley. It has a
traditional pub atmosphere with well-used furnishings, open
fire, exposed timbers, brasses and a collection of old bottled
ales. Well-kept beer and home-cooked food are served, and
there's a south-facing garden with plenty of garden furniture
and undercover accommodation. Favourite fare includes
sausage and mash, fish pie and lasagne.
OPEN: 11-3 6-11 **BAR MEALS:** L served all week 12-2 D served all
week 7-9 Av main course £7 🍺: Brakspear 🍴: Brakspear Bitter &
Special, 2 monthly seasonal beers. **FACILITIES:** Child facs Garden:
Large south facing garden Dogs allowed water outside, hitching rail
NOTES: Parking 50

HENLEY-ON-THAMES continued

HOOK NORTON — Map 11 SP33

Pick of the Pubs

Three Tuns Foodhouse NEW ♀
5 The Market Place RG9 2AA ☎ 01491 573260
e-mail: thefoodhouse@aol.co.uk
Dir: *Situated in Market Place, in front of the town hall.*
One of Oxfordshire's more distinctive pubs, the Three
Tuns Foodhouse began life as a gallows mortuary where
bodies were brought after public execution. In the 21st
century, the inn is a far from cry from those grim days; as
well as being a pub, it doubles as a showroom for a local
antique dealer, so don't be surprised to find an eclectic
range of rather quirky antiques, including Chinese
benches, items of church furniture, chairs from the 1950s
and 60s, and various pictures and prints. Another
intriguing feature is the modern garden bar, decorated
with striking cow parsley wallpaper. The landlord buys his
produce from London suppliers and local farmers'
markets and the cleverly designed menu is characterised
by dishes such as roast Cornish red mullet, new season
purple sprouting broccoli and caper dressing; Spanish
white onion and parmesan tart; and free-range guinea
fowl breast, baked mash and shallot gravy.
OPEN: 12-3 5.30-11 **BAR MEALS:** L served all week D served
all week Av main course £12.50 **RESTAURANT:** L served all
week 12-2.30 D served all week 6-10 Av 3 course à la carte
£23.50 🍺: Brakspear, Hoegaarden. ♀: 8
FACILITIES: Garden: Courtyard garden Dogs allowed Water
NOTES: Parking 300

Pick of the Pubs

The White Hart Hotel ◉◉ 🏠 ♀
High St, Nettlebed RG9 5DD ☎ 01491 642145 📠 01491 649018
e-mail: Info@whitehartnettlebed.com
Dir: *On the A4130 between Henley-on-Thames and Wallingfrod*
A beautifully restored brick and flint building dating from
the 17th century and used as a billeting house for loyalist
Cavalier troops during the English Civil War. In more
recent times the village was acquired by Robert Fleming,
whose grandson was Ian, creator of James Bond. Fleming
senior extended the White Hart in 1913, and the
architect's drawings are still on show at the County
Archives in Oxford. The pub looks very different today, its
chic bar, restaurant and bistro attracting those who are
seeking stylish surroundings and a welcoming ambience.
Dishes might include seared fillet of salmon with spiced
chick pea; pork and apple sausages with mashed potato,
onions and mustard sauce; steamed breast of chicken
with pearl barley risotto and sage jus; and glazed
butternut and onion tart with pickled mushrooms and
rocket salad.
OPEN: 7am-11 **BAR MEALS:** L served all week 12-2.30
D served all week 6-10 **RESTAURANT:** L served all week
D served all week 7-9 Sun 12-5 Av 3 course à la carte £17
Av 3 course fixed price £14.95 🍺: Brakspear, Guiness. ♀: 12
FACILITIES: Child facs Children's licence Garden: large lawned
area with seating **ROOMS:** 12 bedrooms en suite
3 family rooms s£60 d£60

 The Rosette is the AA award for food.
Look out for it next to a pub's name

Pick of the Pubs

The Gate Hangs High ♦♦♦♦
Whichford Rd OX15 5DF ☎ 01608 737387 📠 01608 737870
e-mail: gatehangshigh@aol
Dir: *Off A361 SW of Banbury*
A charming country pub set in beautiful countryside near
the Rollright stones and the idyllic village of Hook Norton,
home to the famous brewery and source of the tip-top
ales served in the bar. The pub is on the old Wales to
Banbury drovers' road and there was once a tollgate
outside, which was said to hang high so that all the ducks
and geese and small animals could roam freely but large
beasts had to stop and pay the toll. It is also said that
Dick Turpin frequented the place when he was lying low.
The bar has a long, low beamed ceiling, a copper hood
over the hearth in the inglenook fireplace and a brick-
built bar counter with festoons of hops above. Typical
dishes include barbeque ribs, braised rabbit, salmon and
prawn fishcakes, and corned beef hash.
OPEN: 12-3 6-11 (Sun, 12-4, 7-10.30) **BAR MEALS:** L served
all week 12-2.30 D served all week 6-10 Sun 12-3, 7-9 Av main
course £7.95 **RESTAURANT:** L served all week 12-2.30
D served all week 6-10 Sun 12-10.30 Av 3 course à la carte £18
Av 3 course fixed price £12.95 🍷: Hook Norton 🍺: Hook
Norton - Best, Old Hooky, Haymaker & Generation.
FACILITIES: Garden: Wonderful views overlooking fields;
courtyard Dogs allowed Water **NOTES:** Parking 30
ROOMS: 4 bedrooms en suite 1 family room s£40 d£40

Sun Inn ♀
High St OX15 5NH ☎ 01608 737570 📠 01608 737535
e-mail: enquiries@the-sun-inn.com
Dir: *5m from Chipping Norton, 8m from Banbury, just off A361*
Stuart and Joyce Rust have taken over the Sun Inn after a
two-year break from the trade - they were at the Gate Hangs
High for over fourteen years. It's a traditional Cotswold stone
inn with oak beams, flagstone floors and an inglenook
fireplace, close to the Hook Norton Brewery. The same menu
is offered in the bar or candlelit restaurant, including shank of
lamb with mustard mash, and sea bass with spinach and
Mediterranean tomato sauce.
OPEN: 11.30-3 6-11.30 **BAR MEALS:** L served all week 12-2
D served all week 7-9.30 **RESTAURANT:** L served all week 12-2
D served all week 7-9.30 🍷: Hook Norton 🍺: Hook Norton Best
Bitter, Old Generation, Mild & Double Stout. **FACILITIES:** Garden:
Patio area, walled **NOTES:** Parking 20

KELMSCOT — Map 05 SU29

The Plough Inn 🐾
GL7 3HG ☎ 01367 253543 📠 01367 252514
e-mail: plough@kelmscottgl7.fsnet.co.uk
Dir: *From M4 onto A419 then A361 to Lechlade & A416 to Faringdon, pick
up signs to Kelmscot*
A sympathetically restored 17th-century inn, popular with the
walking and boating fraternity, in an attractive village close to
Kelmscot Manor and the Thames. Expect the likes of grilled
cod fillets with ginger and spring onion mash, herb crust and
mild curry cream, or medallions of Scottish beef served with
pan-fried foie gras, celeriac mash, beetroot purée and roast
shallot and Madeira jus. There is a lawn and patio area for
outdoor eating in warmer weather.

continued

The Plough Inn

OPEN: 11-3 7-11 (Sun 12-3, 7-10.30) **BAR MEALS:** L served all week 12-2.30 D served all week 7-9 **RESTAURANT:** L served all week 12-2.30 D served all week 7-9 🍴: Free House 🍺: Hook Norton, Guest beers, Timothy Taylor, Wychwood. **FACILITIES:** Child facs Garden: Grassed area with patio Dogs allowed Water provided **NOTES:** Parking 4

KINGSTON LISLE — Map 05 SU38

The Blowing Stone Inn ♀
OX12 9QL ☎ 01367 820288 📠 01367 821102
e-mail: luke@theblowingstoneinn.com
web: www.theblowingstoneinn.co.uk
Dir: B4507 from Wantage toward Ashbury/Swindon, after 6m right to Kingston Lisle

Combining modern times with old-fashioned warmth and hospitality, this attractive country pub derives its name from the Blowing Stone, located on the outskirts of the village. Popular with walkers and horse racing fans, it is run by Radio Five Live racing presenter Luke Harvey and his sister. Menu choices include pork loin steak with honey and mustard glaze and butterflied chicken with a garlic and mushroom sauce. **OPEN:** 12-2.30 6-11 (Open all day Fri-Sun) **BAR MEALS:** L served all week 12-3 D served all week 7-9.30 Av main course £10.50 **RESTAURANT:** L served all week 12-2.30 D served all week 7-9.30 🍴: Free House 🍺: Courage Best, Fuller's London Pride & Guest Beers. ♀: 7 **FACILITIES:** Child facs Large garden with pond and fountain Dogs allowed Water **NOTES:** Parking 30

LEWKNOR — Map 05 SU79

The Leathern Bottel ♀
1 High St OX49 5TW ☎ 01844 351482
Run by the same family for more than 25 years, this 16th-century coaching inn is set in the foothills of the Chilterns. Walkers with dogs, families with children, parties for meals or punters for a quick pint are all made equally welcome. In winter there's a wood-burning stove, a good drop of
continued

Brakspears ale, nourishing specials and a quiz on Sunday. Summer is the time for outdoor eating, the children's play area, Pimm's and Morris dancers.

The Leathern Bottel

OPEN: 10.30-3 6-11 **BAR MEALS:** L served all week 12-2 D served all week 7-9.30 Av main course £6.95 🍴: Brakspear 🍺: Brakspear Ordinary, Special. ♀: 12 **FACILITIES:** Garden: Large garden enclosed with hedge Dogs allowed Water **NOTES:** Parking 35

LOWER SHIPLAKE — Map 05 SU77

The Baskerville Arms ♀
Station Rd RG9 3NY ☎ 0118 940 3332 📠 0118 940 7235
e-mail: enquiries@thebaskerville.com
Dir: Just off the A4155, 1.5m from Henley.
There's a relaxed and welcoming atmosphere at the brick-built Baskerville Arms, which stands on the popular Thames Path just a few minutes from historic Henley-on-Thames. Light meals and snacks are served in the bar, with regular summer Sunday barbecues in the attractive garden. A meal in the restaurant might start with sautéed pigeon breasts, and continue with pan-fried sea bass; traditional cassoulet; or wild mushroom gateau. Booking is essential during Henley Regatta in early July. **OPEN:** 11.30-2.30 6-11 (Fri 11.30-2.30, 5.30-11.30 Sun 11.30-2.30, 5.30-11) **BAR MEALS:** L served all week 12-2 D served Mon-Sat 7-9.30 Sun last orders 2.30 Av main course £7.50 **RESTAURANT:** L served Mon-Sun 12-2 D served Mon-Sat 7-9.30 Av 3 course à la carte £20 Av 3 course fixed price £19.50 🍺: London Pride, Brakspear, Castlemaine & Hoppit. ♀: 8 **FACILITIES:** Child facs Garden: Spacious garden with play area & BBQ Dogs allowed **NOTES:** Parking 12

LOWER WOLVERCOTE — Map 05 SP40

The Trout Inn ♀
195 Godstow Rd OX2 8PN ☎ 01865 302071
Dir: From A40 at Wolvercote rdbt (N of Oxford) follow signs for Wolvercote

A riverside inn which has associations with Matthew Arnold,
continued

LOWER WOLVERCOTE continued

Lewis Carroll and Colin Dexter's Inspector Morse. Constructed in the 17th century from the ruins of Godstow Abbey, its rich history includes being torched by Parliamentarian troops. A good choice of food offers baked whole trout with garlic mushrooms and cheddar mash, lemon chicken, beef, mushroom and Bass pie, or Cumberland sausage wrapped in Yorkshire pudding, with liver and bacon.
OPEN: 11-11 **BAR MEALS:** L served all week D served all week 🍴: Vintage Inns 🍺: Interbrew Bass, Fuller's London Pride.
FACILITIES: Garden **NOTES:** Parking 100

MARSTON
Map 05 SP50

Victoria Arms 🍷
Mill Ln OX3 0PZ ☎ 01865 241382 e-mail: kyffinda@yahoo.co.uk
Dir: From A40 follow signs to Old Marston, sharp right into Mill Lane, pub in lane 500yrds on left.
Friendly country pub situated on the banks of the River Cherwell, occupying the site of the old Marston Ferry that connected the north and south of the city. The old ferryman's bell is still behind the bar. Popular destinations for punters, and fans of TV sleuth Inspector Morse, as the last episode used this as a location. Typical menu includes lamb cobbler, steak and Guinness pie, spicy pasta bake, battered haddock, and ham off the bone.
OPEN: 11.30-11 (Oct-Apr closed afternoons)
BAR MEALS: L served all week 12-2.30 D served all week 6-9 Sun 12-6 Av main course £5.95 🍴: Wadworth 🍺: Henrys IPA, Wadworth 6X, JCB, guest beers. 🍷: 15 **FACILITIES:** Child facs Garden: Food served outside. Patio & lawn area Dogs allowed **NOTES:** Parking 70

MIDDLETON STONEY
Map 11 SP52

The Jersey Arms ★★ 🍷
OX25 4AD ☎ 01869 343234 ▦ 01869 343565
e-mail: jerseyarms@bestwestern.co.uk web: www.jerseyarms.co.uk
Dir: 3m from junct 9/10 of M4 3m from A34 on B430

This charming family-run free house was formerly a coaching inn. The cosy bar offers a good range of popular pub food with the extensive menu supplemented by daily blackboard specials. In the beamed and panelled Livingston's restaurant with its Mediterranean terracotta décor, the cosmopolitan brasserie-style menu features dishes like salad Niçoise; spinach and cream cheese pancakes; and duck confit with cherry and cinnamon sauce.
OPEN: 12-11 **BAR MEALS:** L served all week 12-2.15 D served all week 6.30-9.30 Av main course £10 **RESTAURANT:** L served all week 12-2.15 D served all week 6.30-9.30 Av 3 course à la carte £21 🍴: Free House 🍺: Interbrew Flower, Bass. **FACILITIES:** Garden: Courtyard garden **NOTES:** Parking 50 **ROOMS:** 20 bedrooms en suite 4 family rooms s£85 d£95

MURCOTT
Map 11 SP51

The Nut Tree Inn 🍴 🍷
Main St OX5 2RE ☎ 01865 331253 ▦ 01865 331977
Dir: Off B4027 NE of Oxford via Islip & Charlton-on-Moor
A 14th-century thatched country inn, dating back to 1360. Set in a country idyll (six acres of gardens, duck pond, donkeys, geese, peacocks and chickens), this pub exudes rustic charm: bare beams, wood-burning stoves in inglenooks, real ales and home-cooked meals. The extensive menu ranges from good-value 'Nuttie Butties', light bites and grills to dishes including Oxfordshire lamb shoulder in red wine gravy; and brie and pepper Wellington.
OPEN: 12-3 6-11 (Sun 12-5) **BAR MEALS:** L served Tue-Sat 12-2.30 D served Tue-Sat 6-9 Sun 12-3 **RESTAURANT:** L served Tue-Sun 12-2.30 D served Tue-Sat 6-9 Sun 12-3 Av 3 course à la carte £20 🍴: Free House 🍺: Hook Norton, Adnams. 🍷: 6
FACILITIES: Child facs Garden: Fenced and hedged with trees and lawns Dogs allowed Kennel **NOTES:** Parking 40

NORTH MORETON
Map 05 SU58

The Bear 🍷
High St OX11 9AT ☎ 01235 811311
Dir: Off A4130 between Didcot & Wallingford
15th-century inn on the village green, with exposed beams, open fireplaces and a cosy, relaxed atmosphere. Hook Norton ales.
OPEN: 12-3 6.30-11 **BAR MEALS:** L served Tue-Sun 12-2.30 D served Tue-Sat 7-9 **RESTAURANT:** L served Tue-Sun 12-2.30 D served Tue-Sat 7-9 🍴: Free House 🍺: Hook Norton Best Bitter, Interbrew Bass & Hancocks HB. **FACILITIES:** Garden: Beer garden, food served outdoors, patio Dogs allowed in the garden only **NOTES:** Parking 50 ⊗

NUFFIELD
Map 05 SU68

The Crown at Nuffield
RG9 5SJ ☎ 01491 641335 ▦ 01491 641335
e-mail: simonlinda@supanet.com
Dir: Follow Henley signs, then Wallingford rd on L past turning for village
Heavily beamed 17th-century pub, originally a waggoners' inn. Located in the wooded country of the Chilterns, on the route of the Ridgeway long-distance trail. The bistro-style restaurant combines contemporary decor with tradition.
OPEN: 11.30-2.30 6.30-11 (Open all day-Summer, Wkds Sun 12-3)
BAR MEALS: L served all week 12-2 D served all week 6.30-9.30 (Sun 12-3) Av main course £8.50 **RESTAURANT:** L served all week 12-2 D served all week 6.30-9.30 (Sun 12-3) Av 3 course à la carte £16 🍴: Brakspear 🍺: Brakspear, Brakspears Bitter, Special, Fosters.
FACILITIES: Garden: Dogs allowed **NOTES:** Parking 40

OXFORD
Map 05 SP50

The Anchor
2 Hayfield Rd, Walton Manor OX2 6TT ☎ 01865 510282
e-mail: anchorhay@aol.com
Dir: A34 Oxford Ring Road(N), exit Peartree Roundabout, 1.5m then R at Polstead Rd, follow rd to bottom, pub on R
Local resident T E Lawrence (of Arabia) once frequented this friendly 1930s pub. Nowadays you'll find a relaxed atmosphere, and good food and drink. The wide-ranging menu offers pub favourites such as steak and ale pie, sausage and mash, and fish and chips.
OPEN: 12-11 (Mon-Sat 12-11, Sun 12-10.30) **BAR MEALS:** L served all week 12-2.30 D served all week 6-9 Av main course £5.95 🍴: Wadworth 🍺: Wadworth 6X, Henrys IPA, JCB.
FACILITIES: Garden: Patio at front and rear of pub Dogs allowed on leads Water **NOTES:** Parking 15

England

Turf Tavern ♀
4 Bath Place, off Holywell St OX1 3SU
☎ 01865 243235 ▧ 01865 243838
e-mail: turftavern.oxford@laurelpubco.com
Situated in the heart of Oxford, approached through hidden alleyways and winding passages, this famous pub lies in the shadow of the city wall and the colleges. It is especially popular in the summer when customers can relax in the sheltered courtyards. Eleven real ales are served daily, from a choice of around 500 over a year, along with some typical pub fare. The pub has been featured in TV's *Inspector Morse*, and was frequented by JRR Tolkien.
OPEN: 11-11 (Sun 12-10.30) **BAR MEALS:** L served all week 12-7.30 D served all week Av main course £5.95
RESTAURANT: L served all week D served Sun (Roast)
▥: ◖: Traditional Ales, changing daily. ♀: 6 **FACILITIES:** Garden: Patio area with lights, heaters coal fires Dogs allowed
See Pub Walk on page 376

The White House
2 Botley Rd OX2 0AB ☎ 01865 242823 ▧ 01865 793331
e-mail: thewhitehouseoxford@btinternet.com
Dir: 2 minutes walk from rail station
Set back from a busy road, this pub was once a tollhouse where people crossed the river to enter Oxford. The menu may include roast fillet of salmon with roast peppers and fresh herbs, sautéed calves' liver with onion sauce, pork cutlets cooked in beer with cabbage and bacon, or wild mushroom ravioli.
OPEN: 11-11 Closed: Dec 25 **BAR MEALS:** L served all week 12-2.30 D served all week 6.30-9.30 Av main course £6
RESTAURANT: L served all week 12-2.30 D served all week 6-9.30 Av 3 course à la carte £25 ▥: Punch Taverns ◖: Wadworth 6X, Greene King Abbot Ale, Fullers London Pride, Hook Norton.
FACILITIES: Garden: Dogs allowed **NOTES:** Parking 15

PISHILL   Map 05 SU78

Pick of the Pubs

The Crown Inn ♀
RG9 6HH ☎ 01491 638364 ▧ 01491 638364
e-mail: jc@capon.fsnet.co.uk web: www.crownpishill.co.uk
See Pick of the Pubs on page 394

RAMSDEN   Map 11 SP31

The Royal Oak ▷ ♀
High St OX7 3AU ☎ 01993 868213 ▧ 01993 868864
Dir: From Witney take B4022 toward Charlbury, then turn right before Hailey, and go through Poffley End.

A 17th-century free house, the Royal Oak was originally a
continued

coaching inn - small wonder that there are still nosebags available for hungry passing horses. Human diners are catered for even more impressively with dishes cooked from local and organic produce where possible. The wine list has been extended to include more than a hundred bottles, with over twenty available by the glass. Starters could range from chicken liver parfait flavoured with Cognac and raisins; to baked aubergine with sun-dried tomato and feta cheese in a tomato sauce. The follow up could be fillet of salmon with a pink pepper and whisky sauce; moules a la marinière; or chargrilled Aberdeen Angus fillet steak with a brandy, green pepper, Madeira and cream sauce. Don't forget to examine the list of desserts on the blackboard menu. Lighter bites are available on the bar menu at lunchtime.
OPEN: 11.30-3 6.30-11 Closed: Dec 25 **BAR MEALS:** L served all week 12-2 D served all week 7-10 Av main course £10
RESTAURANT: L served all week 12-2 D served all week 7-10
▥: Free House ◖: Hook Norton Old Hooky, Best, Adnams Broadside, Youngs Special. ♀: 20 **FACILITIES:** Garden: Flagstone courtyard garden Dogs allowed Water **NOTES:** Parking 20

ROKE   Map 05 SU69

Home Sweet Home ♀
OX10 6JD ☎ 01491 838249 ▧ 01491 835760
Dir: Just off B4009 from Benson to Watlington, signed on B4009
Long ago converted from adjoining cottages by a local brewer, this pretty 15th-century inn stands in a tiny hamlet surrounded by lovely countryside. A wealth of oak beams and the large inglenook fireplace dominate a friendly bar with an old-fashioned feel. Owned and run by Andrew Hearn, who also runs The Horns at Crazies Hill, the menu has a commitment to good, hearty pub eating. Look out for pork and leek sausages with spring onion mash and onion gravy; pan-fried calves' liver with bacon and black pudding; fresh fish of the day; and tuna and chili fish cakes with red Thai cream sauce. Real ale fans will enjoy the beer festival at the end of May. Spit roast over fire available.
OPEN: 11-2.30 6-11 (Sun 12-3, closed Sun eve) Closed: Dec 25-26 Rest: Sun Closed eve **BAR MEALS:** L served all week 12-2 D served Mon-Sat 6-9 Av main course £9 **RESTAURANT:** L served Mon-Sun 12-2 D served Mon-Sat 7-9 ▥: Free House ◖: London Pride, Loddon Brewery Beers- Hoppit, Feremans Gold. ♀: 10
FACILITIES: Garden: Dogs allowed Water **NOTES:** Parking 60

ROTHERFIELD PEPPARD   Map 05 SU78

The Greyhound
Gallowstree Rd RG9 5HT ☎ 0118 9722227 ▧ 0118 9722227
e-mail: kwhitehouse@thegreyhound-peppard.com
Dir: 4 miles from Henley on Thames
A picture-postcard, 400-year-old village inn with a splendid front garden with tables and parasols. Owned since mid-2002 by a Savoy Hotel-trained chef, it offers French/English-style meals in both the beamed, candle-lit bar, with woodblock floor, and open brick fireplace, and in the restaurant. This is in the adjacent, and impressive, converted timber barn and a typical option might be fillet steak, with chestnut, mushroom and brandy cream sauce. Prawn stir-fry is a likely bar meal.
OPEN: 11-3 6-11 (Sat till 12, Sun till 8) **BAR MEALS:** L served all week 12-2.30 D served all week 7-9.30 **RESTAURANT:** L served Mon 12-2.30 D served Mon 7-9.30 Av 3 course à la carte £18.50
▥: Free House ◖: Brakspear, Fuller's London Pride, San Miguel.
FACILITIES: Garden: Dogs allowed **NOTES:** Parking 40

🛢 Brewery/Company

Pick of the Pubs

The Crown Inn

The old maps do spell this village's name with the extra 's' that wags will add on, and it probably does therefore mean what you are thinking. The theory is that, having climbed up the steep hill from Henley-on-Thames, waggon drivers would stop at the inn for a quick one, giving their horses time to relieve themselves.

This area was one of the few strongholds of Catholicism during Henry VIII's reign. Spookily, the inn is said to be haunted by a priest who took refuge in the pub's priest hole (reputedly the country's largest). Legend has it that, hiding from religious persecution, he instead met his doom quite differently - nobly saving a serving wench from a drunken assailant. In the sixties, quite a different atmosphere prevailed, with such luminaries as George Harrison, Ringo Starr and Dusty Springfield playing in the hip nightclub housed in the barn.

These days, the eclectic food is a big part of the agenda of this pretty pub. Menus change seasonally, and a meal could begin with dolcelatte, wild mushrooms and tarragon filo parcel with a plum compote, or roast chicken and basil risotto with parsnip crisps. Follow on with king scallops and tiger prawns sautéed in a Thai dressing; or pan-fried calves' liver with smoked bacon and fried onions. Home-made puddings include chocolate and pecan sponge with espresso custard; and coconut rice pudding with glazed fruits.

OPEN: 11.30-2.30 6-11 (Sun 12-3, 7-10.30) Closed: 25-26 Dec, 1 Jan
BAR MEALS: L served all week 12-2 D served all week 7-9.30 (Sun 12-3, 7-9) Av main course £10
RESTAURANT: L served all week 12-2 D served all week 7-9.30
Av 3 course à la carte £23.50
🍺: Free House
🍺: Brakspears. 🍷: 8
FACILITIES: Garden: Extensive gardens overlooking the valley
NOTES: Parking 60

🍷   Map 05 SU78
RG9 6HH
☎ 01491 638364
📠 01491 638364
📧 jc@capon.fsnet.co.uk
🌐 www.crownpishill.co.uk
Dir: On B480 off A4130, NW of Henley-on-Thames

England

SHENINGTON
Map 11 SP34

The Bell ♀
OX15 6NQ ☎ 01295 670274
e-mail: the_bellshenington@hotmail.com
Dir: M40 junct 11 take A422 towards Stratford. Village signed 3m N of Wroxton

Overlooking a splendid village green surrounded by mellow stone houses, this comfortable and welcoming 300-year-old inn is handy for exploring the Oxfordshire countryside and the nearby Cotswolds. The pub promises home-cooked food prepared on the premises, and offers a blackboard menu which changes regularly. Specialities include casseroles, authentic curries, game in season, and salmon in dill sauce. Expect lemon tart or sticky toffee pudding to follow.
OPEN: 12-2.30 7-11 **BAR MEALS:** L served Tue-Sun 12-2 D served all week 7-11 Av main course £8.45 **RESTAURANT:** L served Tues-Sun 12-2 D served all week 7-10 Av 3 course à la carte £15
⊕: Free House ◖: Hook Norton, Flowers. ♀: 8
FACILITIES: Garden: Beer garden, outdoor eating, Dogs allowed

SHIPTON-UNDER-WYCHWOOD
Map 10 SP21

Pick of the Pubs

The Shaven Crown Hotel ♀
High St OX7 6BA ☎ 01993 830330 ▤ 01993 832136
e-mail: relax@shavencrown.co.uk
See Pick of the Pubs on page 396

SOUTH MORETON
Map 05 SU58

The Crown Inn ⌇ ♀
High St OX11 9AG ☎ 01235 812262
Dir: From Didcot take A4130 towards Wallingford. Village on right
Friendly village pub located midway between Wallingford and Didcot. It prides itself on its home-prepared food, and has real ale on tap. Monday night is quiz night, and during the summer the garden is very popular especially with families. Dishes include steaks, shoulder of lamb, fresh battered haddock, and salmon fillet hollandaise.
OPEN: 11-3 5.30-11 (Sun 12-3, 7-10.30) Closed: Dec 25-26
BAR MEALS: L served all week 12-2 D served all week 7-9.30
Av main course £8.95 **RESTAURANT:** L served all week 12-2
D served all week 7-9.30 Av 3 course à la carte £15 ⊕: Wadworth
◖: Wadworth 6X & Henrys IPA, guest beers. ♀: 8
FACILITIES: Garden: 2 areas with bench style seating Dogs allowed
Water **NOTES:** Parking 30

◆ Diamond rating for inspected guest accommodation

The Perch and Pike

South Stoke
Oxfordshire
RG8 0JS

Tel: 01491 872415
Fax: 01491 875852

Email:
helpdesk@perchandpike.com

SOUTH STOKE
Map 03 SU58

The Perch and Pike
RG8 0JS ☎ 01491 872415 ▤ 01491 875852
e-mail: eating@perchandpike.com
Dir: On The Ridgeway between Reading and Oxford

The Perch and Pike, just two minutes' walk from the River Thames, was the village's foremost beer house back in the 17th century. There is plenty of atmosphere in the original pub and in the adjoining barn conversion, which houses the 42-seater restaurant. Food ranges from a selection of sandwiches to the likes of smoked haddock and salmon fish cakes, and venison with celeriac mash and Madeira jus.
OPEN: 12-3 Sun 6-11 (Open all day) **BAR MEALS:** L served all week 12-3 D served all week 6-10 Sun variation Av main course £9.50
RESTAURANT: L served all week 12-3 D served Mon-Sat 6-10
Av 3 course fixed price £19 ⊕: Brakspear ◖: Brakspear beers.
FACILITIES: Child facs Children's licence Garden: Tiered, grassed area with benches Dogs allowed Water bowls **NOTES:** Parking 50
See advert on this page

The Shaven Crown Hotel

Believed to be one of the ten oldest inns in England, The Shaven Crown is steeped in history, having been built as a hospice to the neighbouring Bruern Monastery. Built of honey-coloured Cotswold stone around a medieval courtyard, parts of it, including the gateway, are up to 700 years old.

Following the Dissolution of the Monasteries, Queen Elizabeth I used it as a hunting lodge before giving it to the village in 1580, when it became the Crown Inn. It was not until 1930 that a brewery with a touch of humour changed the name to reflect the tonsorial hairstyles adopted by monks. The leader of the British Fascists, Oswald Mosley, was held under house arrest here during World War II. Not surprisingly none of the rooms is named after him, whereas the small and cosy drinking area with a log fire is, as you might expect, called the Monks Bar (and it serves Oxfordshire real ales). Bar food includes salads and pastas, steak and kidney pie, oak-smoked sausage and mash, and chicken curry. The carte offers starters of deep-fried brie with raspberry coulis; and roast carrot and parsnip salad with walnut dressing. Popular main courses are pheasant casserole with winter vegetables; venison steak with wild mushroom and chive sauce; trio of fresh fish with rocket dressing; and, for vegetarians, goat's cheese tart with red pepper coulis. Pre-dinner drinks can be taken in the impressive Great Hall, and there's an à la carte menu in the intimate candlelit dining room. Outside, apart from the enclosed courtyard, is a tree-dotted lawned area.

OPEN: 12-2.30 5-11
BAR MEALS: L served all week 12-2 D served all week 6-9.30 Av main course £10.95
RESTAURANT: L served Sun 12-2 D served all week 7-9
🍴: Free House
🍺: Hook Norton Ales, Archers & Wychwood. ♀: 10
FACILITIES: Child facs Garden: Enclosed courtyard, lawned area with trees Dogs allowed Water
NOTES: Parking 15

♀   Map 10 SP21
High St OX7 6BA
☎ 01993 830330
📄 01993 832136
📧 relax@theshavencrown.co.uk
Dir: On A361, halfway between Burford and Chipping Norton opposite village green and church

England

STADHAMPTON   Map 05 SU69

Pick of the Pubs

The Crazy Bear Hotel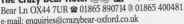
Bear Ln OX44 7UR ☎ 01865 890714 ▤ 01865 400481
e-mail: enquiries@crazybear-oxford.co.uk
Dramatically restored 16th-century coaching inn with a
rural location 15 minutes' drive from Oxford and four
miles from junction 7 of the M40. For a small hotel it is
full of surprises, including draught champagne, house-
flavoured vodkas, 18 wines by the glass and a superb
cigar selection in the bar. The flamboyant refurbishment
has resulted in two award winning dining rooms, one
serving modern British cooking (hand dived scallops and
Gloucester pig's trotter), and the other offering a Thai-
style brasserie (chicken or mushroom satay, rich and sour
soup, green chicken curry and marinated roast duck). The
choice of food is really extensive and includes an all day
menu ranging through sandwiches, frogs' legs, shepherd's
pie and burgers. The garden has palm trees, a large pond
and seating for 40, and accommodation is provided in Art
Deco doubles, designer suites and private cottages.
OPEN: 11-11 **BAR MEALS:** L served all week 12-10 D served
all week 12-10 Av main course £11.50 **RESTAURANT:** L served
all week 12-3 D served all week 6-10 Sun 12-4.30 Av 3 course à la
carte £35 Av 3 course fixed price £15 ⊕: Free House ◀: Old
Speckled Hen, IPA, Guinness. ⬗: 18 **FACILITIES:** Garden:
Landscaped garden, terrace with large tables
NOTES: Parking 50 **ROOMS:** 17 bedrooms en suite
2 family rooms s£65 d£110 No children overnight

STANTON ST JOHN   Map 05 SP50

Star Inn ⬗
Middle Rd OX33 1EX ☎ 01865 351277 ▤ 01865 351006
e-mail: stantonstar@supanet.com
Dir: B4027 Stanton exit, 3rd left into Middle Rd, pub 200yds on left

Although the Star is only a short drive from the centre of
Oxford, this popular pub still retains a definite 'village' feel.
The oldest part of the pub dates from the early 17th century,
and in the past, the building has been used as a butcher's
shop and an abattoir. The garden is peaceful and secluded. A
varied menu features shoulder of lamb in redcurrant &
rosemary, spinach and mushroom strudel, and roast
vegetable and goast cheese tart.
OPEN: 11-2.30 6.30-11 **BAR MEALS:** L served all week 12-2
D served all week 6.30-9.30 Av main course £7.95 ⊕: Wadworth
◀: Wadworth 6X, Henrys IPA & JCB. ⬗: 7 **FACILITIES:** Child facs
Garden: Large secure garden Dogs allowed Water bowls
NOTES: Parking 50

Pick of the Pubs

The Talk House
Wheatley Rd OX33 1EX ☎ 01865 351648 ▤ 01865 351085
e-mail: talkhouse@t-f-h.co.uk
Dir: Stanton-St-John signed from the Oxford ring road
The Talk House is a cleverly converted 17th-century inn
located within easy reach of Oxford and the A40. It
comprises three bar and dining areas, all with a Gothic
look and a welcoming atmosphere. Business, wedding
and function bookings are catered for, and The Snug is
ideal for private parties of eight to 15, with its own
fireplace and private bar. An interesting modern menu
reflects global influences with starters such as Thai crab
cakes, smoked salmon blinis, crispy aromatic duck, and
chicken satay skewers. Main courses show equal diversity
with The Envy of India (chicken Madras on a bed of
Basmati rice served with poppadoms and mango
chutney), and Becky's fur & feather casserole (braised
rabbit, venison and pheasant in a port and red wine gravy
with herb dumplings). Bed and breakfast accommodation
is also offered in four chalet-style rooms situated around
the attractive rear courtyard.
OPEN: 12-3 5.30-11 (Open all day in Summer Easter wknd-Oct)
BAR MEALS: L served all week 12-2 D served all week 7-10
(Sun 12-9) **RESTAURANT:** L served all week 12-2 D served all
week 7-10 (Sun 12-9) ⊕: Free House ◀: Hook Norton Best
Bitter, Tetley's Cask Ale, Burton Ale. **FACILITIES:** Garden:
Courtyard garden **NOTES:** Parking 60 **ROOMS:** 4 bedrooms
en suite (♦♦♦)

STEEPLE ASTON   Map 11 SP42

Red Lion ⬗
South Side OX25 4RY ☎ 01869 340225
e-mail: redlion@leorufus.co.uk
Dir: Off A4260 between Oxford & Banbury
A 17th-century pub with a 30-seat, oak-framed garden room
restaurant. The lunchtime choice ranges from hot sandwich
plates - filled fresh-baked baguettes with straw fries - through
appetisers and light bites such as cod and pancetta fishcake,
or pork and chicken liver pâté, to more substantial entrées.
These are similar to dinner dishes, which might include
steaks, pot-roasted local pheasant, and wild mushroom
risotto.
OPEN: 11-3 6-11 (Sun 12-4, 7-10.30) **BAR MEALS:** L served
Tue-Sun 12-2 D served Tue-Sat 7-9 Sun 12-2.30 Av main course £11
RESTAURANT: L served Tue-Sun 12-2 D served Tue-Sat 7-9.15
Av 3 course à la carte £22.50 ⊕: Free House ◀: Hook Norton.
⬗: 7 **FACILITIES:** Garden: Floral terrace Dogs allowed
NOTES: Parking 15

STOKE ROW   Map 05 SU68

Pick of the Pubs

Crooked Billet ⬗
RG9 5PU ☎ 01491 681048 ▤ 01491 682231
See Pick of the Pubs on page 399

 Pubs offering a good choice of fish on
their menu

SUTTON COURTENAY
Map 05 SU59

Pick of the Pubs

The Fish 🐟 ♀
4 Appleford Rd OX14 4NQ ☎ 01235 848242 🖶 01235 848014
e-mail: mike@thefish.uk.com
Dir: From A415 in Abingdon take B4017 then left onto B4016 to village

The emphasis is very much on food at this unassuming late 19th-century brick-built pub-restaurant, although drinkers are welcome at the bar. The Fish is located a short stroll from the Thames in the heart of this beautiful and historic village - Asquith and George Orwell are both buried here. Good value bistro lunches are served in the all-purpose front bar, as well as outside in the attractive garden in fine weather. Expect modern versions of classic dishes, with a strong emphasis on fresh seafood, and frequently changing menus that reflect seasonal availability. Start, perhaps, with smoked salmon fishcakes, or an Italian salad with prosciutto and mixed charcuterie, before moving on to stronger fare like lobster with herb mayonnaise, mixed shellfish and salads; rack of lamb with grain mustard and Madeira sauce; and aubergine gratinée with goat's cheese, new potatoes and salad.
OPEN: 12-3.30 6-11 (Sat 6.30-11) Closed: 2 days between Xmas & New Year **BAR MEALS:** L served all week 12-2 D served Mon-Sat Av main course £15 **RESTAURANT:** L served all week 12-2 D served Mon-Sat 7-9 Sun 12-2.30, Sat 7-9.30 Av 3 course à la carte £27 Av 3 course fixed price £15 ⬡: Greene King ◀: Greene King IPA. ♀: 10 **FACILITIES:** Garden: Large enclosed lawn with flower beds, patio Dogs allowed Water **NOTES:** Parking 30

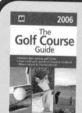

2006
The Golf Course Guide
Britains best-selling Golf Course Guide featuring over 2,500 courses.
www.theAA.com **AA**

SWALCLIFFE
Map 11 SP33

Stag's Head ♀
OX15 5EJ ☎ 01295 780232 🖶 01295 788977
e-mail: stagsheadswalcliffe@dial.pipex.com
Dir: 6M W of Banbury on the B4035

Believed to have been built during the reign of Henry VIII, this thatched pub enjoys picture postcard looks and a pretty village setting. An apple tree in the landscaped garden was reputedly grown from a pip brought back from the Crimean War, and its fruit is still used in home-made puddings. The menu offers Thai chicken green curry, 'Catch of the Week', Scotch fillet steak, or 'Let It All Hang Out' lasagne.
OPEN: 12-2.30 6.30-11 Closed Sun eve **BAR MEALS:** L served Tues-Sun 12-2.15 D served Tues-Sat 7-9.30 Sun 12-4 Av main course £12.45 **RESTAURANT:** L served Tues-Sun 12-2.15 D served Tues-Sat 7-9.30 Sun 12-3 ⬡: Free House ◀: Brakspears PA, Wychwood Seasonal, Spinning Dog Brewery, Black Sheep. ♀: 7
FACILITIES: Child facs Garden: Beautiful terraced garden with play area Dogs allowed Water, biscuits

SWERFORD
Map 11 SP33

Pick of the Pubs

The Mason's Arms ◉
Banbury Rd OX7 4AP ☎ 01608 683212 🖶 01608 683105
See Pick of the Pubs on page 400

SWINBROOK
Map 10 SP21

The Swan Inn
OX18 4DY ☎ 01993 822165
Dir: A40 towards Burford & Cheltenham straight over rdbt right for Swinbrook. Pub over bridge on left
With its flagstone floors, antique furnishings and open fires, the 400-year-old Swan is full of charm and character and sits next to the River Windrush, a setting that cannot fail to impress. Plenty of scenic walks and popular tourist attractions close by. Choose cottage pie, spaghetti bolognese or deep fried whitebait with horseradish from the snack menu, followed perhaps by sirloin steak, Norfolk chicken cooked with tarragon or pan-fried trout with dried fruits.
OPEN: 11.30-3 6.30-11 Closed: 25 Dec **BAR MEALS:** L served all week 12-2 D served Mon-Sat 7-9 **RESTAURANT:** L served all week 12-2 D served Mon-Sat 7-9 ⬡: Free House ◀: Greene King IPA, Old Speckled Hen, Wadworth 6X, Archers. **FACILITIES:** Garden: Large garden with Cotswold stone walls Dogs allowed Water provided **NOTES:** Parking 10

Pick of the Pubs

Crooked Billet

Hidden away down a single-track lane in deepest Oxfordshire, The Crooked Billet is full of rustic charm. It dates back to 1642 and was once the haunt of highwayman Dick Turpin, who, forced to hide here from local law enforcers, whiled away the hours by courting the landlord's pretty daughter, Bess. Many of its finest features are unchanged, including the low beams, tiled floors and open fires that are so integral to its character.

In recent years, the focus has become distinctly food-driven, and it attracts many local celebrities, including several introduced to it by the late George Harrison. Kate Winslet famously held her wedding reception here and, from the lowbrow (cast of Eastenders) to the highbrow (Jeremy Paxman), it continues to draw the well heeled and well known. Extensive, carefully thought-out menus are created by award-winning chef/proprietor Paul Clerehugh, with local produce and organic fare being the mainstay of his kitchen, to the extent that he will even swap a lunch or dinner for the locals' excess veg. Dishes are tantalising, complex and well-balanced. You could begin with a charcuterie board offering wild pig and pepper salami; British 'Parma' ham and pacato chorizo amongst other porcine delights; or opt for home cured gravad lax salmon on fennel and shallot compote. To follow, there's an excellent range of fish mains, including seared blue fin tuna with steamed glass noodles; as well as a hare bourguignonne braised in burgundy with celeriac mash. There are also several original vegetarian options: perhaps sage and pecorino polenta with warm asparagus and artichoke heart salad. Matching the food standards is a thoughtful wine list. The beautiful garden overlooks farmland, making this a wonderful rustic getaway.

OPEN: 12-11 (Sun 12-10.30)
BAR MEALS: L served all week 12-2.30 D served all week 7-10
RESTAURANT: L served all week 12-2.30 D served all week 7-10 All day Sun
🍺: Brakspear
🍺: Brakspear Bitter. ⬛: 12
FACILITIES: Beautiful, rustic garden overlooks farmland
NOTES: Parking 50 ⊗

🍽 🍷 Map 05 SU68
RG9 5PU
☎ 01491 681048
📄 01491 682231
Dir: From Henley to Oxford A4130. Turn left at Nettlebed for Stoke Row

399

Pick of the Pubs
SWERFORD – OXFORDSHIRE

The Mason's Arms

Set on the edge of the Cotswolds, and built of the honey-coloured stone so evocative of that area, this pretty pub is now three hundred years old. It's set just a stone's throw from the Hook Norton Brewery, and a pint of Hook Norton Best can be enjoyed in the garden, while admiring the rural views.

Inside, recent years have seen something of an updating from its days as the local Masonic Lodge; plenty of contemporary comfort has been provided without sacrificing anything in the way of traditional charm. Despite all these virtues, it's the food that really stands out here. With a chef/proprietor who has worked with Marco Pierre White and Gordon Ramsay, it is not surprising to discover wonderful dishes, unusual flavour combinations and frequently changing menus that make the most of seasonal produce. A typical meal could begin with deep fried, polenta-coated goat's cheese, poached figs and mango salsa; or duck and pistachio terrine with piccalilli and toasted brioche.

You could move on to chargrilled leg of pork, served with Tuscan-style bean and tomato stew and chorizo; a pan-fried fillet of bream on mint and pea risotto; or slow roast shin of beef, horseradish mash, stir-fried savoy cabbage and red wine jus. Smaller appetites might appreciate the simpler bar menu, with plenty of rustic favourites including shepherd's pie; ploughman's lunches and salads, washed down with a pint of real ale. Appealing desserts include a treacle and lemon tart with vanilla ice cream; and gooseberry and elderflower fool with shortbread biscuits. There's a good range of malt whiskies to round things off. With food this good, it's little surprise that booking is suggested.

OPEN: 10-3 6-11 Closed: 25-26 Dec
BAR MEALS: L served Mon-Sun 12-2.15 D served Mon-Sun 7-9.15 (Sun lunch 12-3) Av main course £7
RESTAURANT: L served all week 12-2.15 D served all week 7-9.15 Av 3 course à la carte £20 Av 3 course fixed price £9.95
🍺: Free House
🍺: Hook Norton Best.
FACILITIES: Children's licence Garden: Large grassed area, with seating, views Dogs allowed in pub by arrangement only Water
NOTES: Parking 50

Map 11 SP33
Banbury Rd OX7 4AP
☎ 01608 683212
📄 01608 683105
Dir: Between Banbury and Chipping Norton A361

England

TADMARTON
Map 11 SP33

The Lampet Arms ◆◆◆ ♀
Main St OX15 5TB ☎ 01295 780070 ▤ 01295 788066
Dir: Take the B4035 from Banbury to Tadmarton for 5m
Victorian-style building named after Captain Lampet, the local
landowner who built it. The captain mistakenly believed he
could persuade the council to have the local railway line
directed through the village, thereby increasing trade. Typical
menu choices include the likes of casserole, vegetable
lasagne, salmon steak and fish pie.
OPEN: 12-3 5-11 (Sun 12-4, 7-10.30) **BAR MEALS:** L served all
week 12-2.30 D served all week 6.30-9.30 Av main course £6
RESTAURANT: L served all week 12-2 D served all week 6.30-9.30
🍴: Free House 🍺: Scottish Courage, Hook Norton, Theakstons,
Directors. **FACILITIES:** Garden: Dogs allowed **NOTES:** Parking 18
ROOMS: 4 bedrooms en suite 3 family rooms s£43 d£60

THAME
Map 05 SP70

The Swan Hotel ♀
9 Upper Hight St OX9 3ER ☎ 01844 261211 ▤ 01844 261954
e-mail: swanthame@hotmail.com
Dir: Telephone for directions
Former coaching inn dating from the 16th century,
overlooking the market square at Thame. The Tudor-painted
ceiling is a feature of the upstairs restaurant, while downstairs
in the cosy bar there is an open fire. The pub specialises in
real ale, and there are always several on tap. Typical dishes
served here include steak sandwich with mustard, onions,
salad, cheese and chips; steak and kidney pudding; and pork
and leek sausages with mash and red onion gravy.
OPEN: 11-11 Closed: 25-26 Dec **BAR MEALS:** L served all week
12-2.30 D served all week 7-9 Av main course £6.95
RESTAURANT: L served Wed-Sun 12-2 D served all week Tues-Sat 7-9.30
Sunday 12-2 Av 3 course à la carte £25 🍴: Free House 🍺: Hook
Norton, Timothy Taylor Landlord, Brakspears, Shepherd Neame
Spitfire. ♀: 9 **FACILITIES:** Dogs allowed Water
NOTES: Parking 200

TOOT BALDON
Map 05 SP50

Pick of the Pubs

The Mole Inn NEW ♀
OX44 9NG ☎ 01865 340001 ▤ 01865 343011
e-mail: info@themoleinn.com
Dir: 5m from Oxford City Centre

Formerly known as the Crown Inn, this stone-built, Grade
II listed pub has been the subject of an extensive
renovation programme in recent years. The top-notch
makeover has earned the pub a glowing and well

deserved reputation, due in no small measure to the
efforts of award-winning chef/host Gary Witchalls. Inside,
a great deal of care and attention has been lavished on
this classic old local, and now customers can relax in
black leather sofas amid stripped beams and solid white
walls. The dining areas are equally striking with their
intimate lighting and terracotta floors. Gary's inspired
menu draws plenty of foodies from nearby Oxford and
further afield, tempted by roast shoulder of Oxfordshire
lamb, colcannon, root vegetable and rosemary jus; calves'
liver with smoked bacon mash and French beans; and
wing of skate on the bone with fennel and orange risotto.
OPEN: 11-11 Closed: 25 Dec, 1 Jan **BAR MEALS:** L served all
week 12-9.30 D served all week 7-9.30 Sun 12-9 Av main course
£12 **RESTAURANT:** L served all week 12-2.30 D served all
week 7-9.30 Sun 12-9 Av 3 course à la carte £23 🍺: Hook
Norton, London Pride, Directors, Guinness. ♀: 11
FACILITIES: Garden: Extensive garden with seating
NOTES: Parking 30

WANTAGE
Map 05 SU38

The Hare ♀
Reading Rd, West Hendred OX12 8RH
☎ 01235 833249 ▤ 01235 833268
Dir: Situated at West Hendred on A417
A late 19th-century inn mid-way between Wantage and
Didcot, modernised in the 1930s by local brewers, Morland,
and featuring a colonial-style verandah and colonnade. Inside
it retains the more original wooden floors, beams and open
fire. New owners in early 2005 include new manager Sonia
Agostini - reports please.
OPEN: 11.30-2.30 5.30-11 (Fri-Sun 11.30-11)
BAR MEALS: L served all week 12-2 D served all week 7-9
RESTAURANT: L served all week 12-2 D served all week 7-9
🍴: Greene King 🍺: Greene King Abbot Ale, IPA, Morland Original.
FACILITIES: Garden: Food served outside Dogs allowed during the
day Water **NOTES:** Parking 37

WHEATLEY
Map 05 SP50

Bat & Ball Inn ◌ ♀
28 High St OX44 9HJ ☎ 01865 874379 ▤ 01865 873363
e-mail: bb@traditionalvillageinns.co.uk
Dir: Through Wheatley towards Garsington, left signed Cuddesdon
Do not be surprised to discover that the bar of this former
coaching inn is packed to the gunnels with cricketing
memorabilia. The owners claim that their collection puts to
shame even that of Lords cricket ground! The comprehensive
menu, supplemented by daily specials, is likely to feature
steaks, fresh-baked pie of the day, herb-battered fresh cod,
and maybe chargrilled Toulouse sausages. Lighter meals
include home-made lasagne, lamb Peshwari, and warm
spinach and pancetta salad.
OPEN: 11-11 (Sun 11-10.30) Closed: Dec 26, Jan 1
BAR MEALS: L served all week 12-2.45 D served all week 6.30-9.45
(Sun 12-9.45) **RESTAURANT:** L served all week 12-2.45 D served all
week 6.30-9.45 (Sun 12-9.45) Av 3 course à la carte £25 Av 3 course
fixed price £14.50 🍴: Marstons 🍺: Marston's Pedigree & Original,
LBW and guest ale. ♀: 12 **FACILITIES:** Child facs Garden: Patio
with good views of Oxfordshire downs Dogs allowed Water Bowls
NOTES: Parking 20

♀ 7   Number of wines by the glass

continued

England

WITNEY
Map 05 SP31

The Bell Inn
Standlake Rd, Ducklington OX29 7UP
☎ 01993 702514 ▤ 01993 706822
Dir: One mile south of Witney in Ducklington village off A415
Nearly 700 years have passed since the men building the adjacent church also erected their own living accommodation. Their hostel eventually became the Bell, and much extended over the years, it even embraces William Shepheard's former brewery, which closed in 1886. Today it is a popular, traditional village local, with many original features - and a collection of some 500 bells. Home-made pies, stews and burgers are a speciality, with a pig roast on Boxing Day.
OPEN: 12-3 5-11 (Fri-Sun 12-11) Closed: Dec 25 Rest: 25, 26 Dec & 1 Jan closed eve **BAR MEALS:** L served all week 12-2 D served Mon-Sat 6-9 Av main course £9 **RESTAURANT:** L served all week 12-2 D served Mon-Sat 6-9 Av 3 course à la carte £16 ◀: Greene King, IPA & Old Speckled Hen, Morland Original, Guiness.
FACILITIES: Child facs Garden: Terrace at front and rear of pub seating 50 **NOTES:** Parking 12

WOODSTOCK
Map 11 SP41

Pick of the Pubs

Kings Head Inn ♦♦♦♦ ⊛ ♀
Chapel Hill, Wootton OX20 1DX ☎ 01993 811340
e-mail: t.fay@kings-head.co.uk web: www.kings-head.co.uk
Dir: 1.5m N of Woodstock off the A44. In the centrte of the village near the church.
The King's Head is a listed 17th-century mellow Cotswold stone building in this conservation village, which has won best kept small Oxfordshire village five times. What's more, it is also located in an Area of Outstanding Natural Beauty. Winter brings cosy log fires, and in summer you can enjoy peaceful meals in the garden. Making it even more attractive to some, it is completely non-smoking throughout and almost all its menu is gluten-free. Imaginative dishes that have earned an AA Rosette are served in both the restaurant and the bar, based on modern British ideas with some Mediterranean and other influences. Starters might include pâté of marinated olives in Waberthwaite ham with an antipasta; toasted goat's cheese on a rotunda of roasted plum, beef and cherry tomatoes; and rosette of muscovado and lime cured Scottish salmon. Mains dishes could be chargrilled medallions of pork fillet on red onion marmalade; Cantonese braised leg and roasted breast of Gressingham duck; and vegetable Mediterraneo.
OPEN: 11-2 6.30-11 Closed: Dec 25 **BAR MEALS:** L served Tue-Sun 12-2 D served Tue-Sat 7-9 Av main course £12.50 **RESTAURANT:** L served Tue-Sun 12-2 D served Tue-Sat 7-9 Av 3 course à la carte £23 ◀: Free House ◀: Wadworth 6X, Greene King Triumph, Ruddles Country, Hook Norton. ♀: 7
FACILITIES: Garden: Beer garden, food served outdoors **NOTES:** Parking 8 **ROOMS:** 3 bedrooms en suite s£55 d£70 No children overnight ⊛

WOOLSTONE
Map 05 SU28

The White Horse ♦♦♦♦ ♀
SN7 7QL ☎ 01367 820726 ▤ 01367 820566
e-mail: raybatty@aol.com
Attractive beamed and thatched 16th-century village inn, just five minutes' walk from the Uffington White Horse and Ancient Monument. Bar food includes salads, ploughman's lunches and freshly cooked cod and chips. In the restaurant expect calves' liver, rack of lamb, steaks, and baked swordfish.
OPEN: 11-3 6-11 (Sun 12-3 7-10.30) **BAR MEALS:** L served all week 11-3 D served all week 6-9.30 Av main course £6 **RESTAURANT:** 12-3 6-10 Av 3 course à la carte £20 ◀: Free House ◀: Arkells, Hook Norton Best, Moonlight, Hognorton.
FACILITIES: Garden **NOTES:** Parking 80 **ROOMS:** 6 bedrooms en suite s£50 d£65

WYTHAM
Map 05 SP40

White Hart ⌐◠ ♀
OX2 8QA ☎ 01865 244372 e-mail: dapeev@aol.com
Dir: Just off A34 NW of Oxford
Often used in the television series *Inspector Morse*, this creeper-covered gastropub is set in the pretty, thatched village of Wytham. The attractive free house, which is owned by Oxford University, features open winter fires and flagstone floors. Outside, a Mediterranean-style terrace is a delightful spot in summer. The contemporary menu features dishes like pink duck breast with potato fondant and parsnip purée; and free range chicken with butter beans and white wine cream.
OPEN: 12-3 6-11 (Summer-Sat 12-11, Sun 12-10.30)
BAR MEALS: L served all week 12-3 D served Mon-Sat 7-10 Av main course £12 **RESTAURANT:** L served All 12-3 D served Mon-Sat 7-10 Av 3 course à la carte £22.50 ◀: ◀: Old Speckled Hen, Hook Norton, Star Pramen, Leffe. ♀: 20 **FACILITIES:** Garden: Mediterranean Terrace **NOTES:** Parking 80 ⊛

RUTLAND

BARROWDEN
Map 11 SK90

Exeter Arms ♀
LE15 8EQ ☎ 01572 747247 e-mail: info@exeterarms.com
Dir: Off A47 half way between Peterborough and Leicester
Once a smithy, then the village dairy, the Exeter Arms was also a coaching inn before it became the village pub. Nestling in the Welland Valley overlooking the village green and duck pond, this 17th-century inn now offers cosy bars where the home-brewed family of 'Boys' beers is served. Specialities include fish and game when seasonally available, and a choice of traditional roast dishes on Sundays. Non-smoking throughout, and regular live music.
OPEN: 12-2 6-11 (Sun & BHs 7-10.30) **BAR MEALS:** L served Tue-Sun 12-2 D served Tue-Sat 7-9 Av main course £11 **RESTAURANT:** L served Tue-Sun 12-2 D served Tue-Sat 7-9 Av 3 course à la carte £17 ◀: ◀: Own Beers: Beach Boys, Bevin Boys, Farmers Boy, Boys With Attitude. ♀: 10 **FACILITIES:** Garden: 1/2 acre. Over looks Welland Valley Dogs allowed except at bar or in eating area.Water **NOTES:** Parking 15 ⊛

CLIPSHAM — Map 11 SK91

Pick of the Pubs

The Olive Branch
Main St LE15 7SH ☎ 01780 410355 📠 01780 410000
e-mail: info@theolivebranchpub.com
Dir: 2m off A1 at Stretton junct, 10m N of Stamford
In 1999, three young men with the help of local villagers, friends and family saved the 19th-century Olive Branch from closure. The name was chosen after the local squire gave the alehouse to the disgruntled villagers when he closed the original pub. Back to the present, the inn is now a highly successful business, and has picked up a lot of awards and accolades for its quality wines and fine food. An attractive front garden and terrace, and an interior full of locally made furniture including a rare 'nurdling chair', and artists' works (all for sale) set the scene. The cooking is strongly based around local produce and seasonality, with anything from a steak sandwich made from Rearsby bread and local beef, to venison pie with game from the local shoots. Even puddings like apple and Calvados crumble with hot Clipsham custard are made from local fare.
OPEN: 12-3.30 6-11 (Sun 12-10.30 only, summer Sat 12-11)
Closed: 26 Dec 1 Jan **BAR MEALS:** L served all week 12-2
D served all week 7-9.30 Sun 12-3, 7-9 Av main course £11.50
RESTAURANT: L served all week 12-2 D served all week 7-9.30
Sun 12-3, 7-9 Av 3 course à la carte £22.50 Av 3 course fixed
price £15 🍴: 🍺: Grainstore 1050 & Olive Oil, Fenland,
Brewster's, VPA. ♀: 15 **FACILITIES:** Child facs Garden:
Gravelled area, pergola, BBQ area, lawn Dogs allowed
NOTES: Parking 15

COTTESMORE — Map 11 SK91

The Sun Inn ♀
25 Main St LE15 7DH ☎ 01572 812321
e-mail: lindmann.london@btinternet.com
Dir: 3m from Oakham
Dating back to 1610, this whitewashed thatched pub boasts oak beams and a cosy fire in the bar. New owners offer a well-priced menu supplemented by specials: chicken, leek and ham pie; grilled tuna steak with chilli dip; steaks and grills. Lunchtime snacks include baguettes; ham, eggs and chips; and ploughmans. Apparently the ghost of a young girl is sometimes seen behind the bar.
OPEN: 11-2.30 6.30-11 (Sat-Sun all day, Fri 11-3)
BAR MEALS: L served Mon-Sun 12-2.15 D served Mon-Sun 6-9
(Fri-Sat 5.30-9.30, Sun 12-8.30) Av main course £6
RESTAURANT: L served Mon-Sun 12-2 D served Mon-Sat 7-9
🍴: Everards Brewery 🍺: Adnams Bitter, Everards Tiger, Marston's
Pedigree, Scottish Courage Courage Directors. ♀: 9
FACILITIES: Garden: Patio area with water feature Dogs allowed
NOTES: Parking 15

EMPINGHAM — Map 11 SK90

White Horse Inn ★★ ♀
Main St LE15 8PS ☎ 01780 460221 📠 01780 460521
e-mail: info@whitehorserutland.co.uk
web: www.whitehorserutland.co.uk
Dir: From A1 take A606 signed Oakham & Rutland Water
Stone-built 17th-century former courthouse close to Rutland Water, Western Europe's largest man-made lake. The comfortable, cosy atmosphere is complemented by hearty

continued

meals and a well-stocked bar. Dishes served in the non-smoking restaurant might include seafood pancake, mixed roast platter with a Yorkshire pudding, Rutland chicken wrapped in smoked bacon with a Rutland cheese sauce, and leek and mushroom carbonara. Baguettes and sandwiches at lunchtime. Bedrooms include a honeymoon four-poster.

White Horse Inn

OPEN: 8am-11pm **BAR MEALS:** L served all week 12-2.15
D served all week 7-9.30 (Sun 12-9) **RESTAURANT:** L served all
week 12-2.15 D served all week 7-9.30 (Sun 12-9) 🍴: 🍺: John
Smith's, Greene King Old Speckled Hen, Ruddles Best, Abbot Ale.
♀: 7 **FACILITIES:** Child facs Garden: Small sheltered garden,
seating **NOTES:** Parking 60 **ROOMS:** 13 bedrooms en suite
3 family rooms s£50 d£65

EXTON — Map 11 SK91

Fox & Hounds ♀
19, The Green LE15 8AP ☎ 01572 812403 📠 01572 812403
This late 17th-century former coaching inn stands on Exton's village green. There's a large walled garden for al fresco summer dining, and the pub is just a short drive from Rutland Water. Jacket potatoes and filled ciabattas feature on the casual lunch menu, beside an extensive choice of traditional Italian pizzas. Other dishes include marinated lamb shank with rosemary on a fluffy mash potato, Grasmere Lincolnshire sausages with mashed potato and onion gravy, and Aberdeen Angus sirloin steak served with a port and Stilton sauce.
OPEN: 11-3 6-11 Sun 12-3, 7-10.30 **BAR MEALS:** L served all
week 12-2 D served Mon-Sat 6.30-9 No food Sun eve Av main course
£9 **RESTAURANT:** L served all week 12-2 D served all week 6.30-9
Av 3 course à la carte £17 🍴: Free House 🍺: Greene King IPA,
Grainstore Real Ales, John Smiths Smooth. ♀: 8 **FACILITIES:** Child
facs Garden: Large walled garden & patio area Dogs allowed Water
NOTES: Parking 20

LYDDINGTON — Map 11 SP89

Pick of the Pubs

Old White Hart ♀
51 Main St LE15 9LR ☎ 01572 821703 📠 01572 821965
e-mail: mail@oldwhitehart.co.uk
Dir: From A6003 between Uppingham & Corby take B672
Set amongst the sandstone cottages of rural Lyddington, this honey-coloured stone free house lies close to Rutland Water and some good walks. The 17th-century building has retained its original beamed ceilings, stone walls and open fires, and is surrounded by well-stocked gardens. Greene King and Timothy Taylor are amongst the beers on offer, whilst wine drinkers can choose from over half a dozen varieties by the glass. Interesting, freshly prepared

continued

England

LYDDINGTON continued

food is served in the cosy main bar, as well as in the adjoining non-smoking restaurant. The snack menu includes smoked Rutland trout with horseradish; a warm salad of herb crostini and grilled goat's cheese; and White Hart sausages with mustard mash. Blackboard specials could include oriental pork belly with pak choi and ginger dressing; or loin of lamb with a redcurrant jus. The rear garden features ten pétanque pitches, a heated patio and a summer marquee.
OPEN: 12-3 6.30-11 Closed: 25 Dec **BAR MEALS:** L served all week 12-2 D served Mon-Sat 6.30-9 Sun 12-2.30 Av main course £11 **RESTAURANT:** L served all week 12-2 D served Mon-Sat 6.30-9 Sun 12-2.30 Av 3 course à la carte £20 Av 3 course fixed price £12.95 ⊕: Free House ⬛: Greene King IPA & Abbot Ale, Timothy Taylor Landlord, Fullers London Pride. ♀: 7
FACILITIES: Child facs Garden: Beer garden, heated patio area, marquee Dogs allowed Water **NOTES:** Parking 50

OAKHAM   Map 11 SK80

Barnsdale Lodge Hotel ★★★ ◉ ▷◌ ♀
The Avenue, Rutland Water, North Shore LE15 8AH
☎ 01572 724678 ▤ 01572 724961
e-mail: enquiries@barnsdalelodge.co.uk
web: www.barnsdalelodge.co.uk
An Edwardian-style hotel overlooking Rutland Water in the heart of this picturesque little county. Its rural connections go back to its 17th-century origins as a farmhouse, but nowadays the Barnsdale Lodge offers modern comforts and hospitality. Real ales including local brews are served in the bar, with dishes such as pan-fried salmon on saffron mash with crayfish sauce; and risotto of Provencal vegetables, parmesan shavings and herb oil.
OPEN: 7-11 **BAR MEALS:** L served all week 12.15-2.15 D served all week 7-9.45 **RESTAURANT:** L served all week 12.15-2.15 D served all week 7-9.45 ⊕: Free House ⬛: Rutland Grainstore, Marstons Pedigree, Scottish Courage Courage Directors, Theakston Best Bitter. ♀: 8 **FACILITIES:** Child facs Garden: Courtyard, established garden with lawns Dogs allowed Water, field for walks
NOTES: Parking 280 **ROOMS:** 46 bedrooms en suite 4 family rooms

The Blue Ball ♀
6 Cedar St, Braunston-in-Rutland LE15 8QS ☎ 01572 722135
Dir: From A1 take A606 to Oakham. Village SW of Oakham. Pub next to church.
Thatched and beamed village inn full of interconnecting rooms, formerly called The Globe, dating from the 1600s, and reputedly Rutland's oldest pub. Typical dishes include Gressingham duck breast in red wine and raspberry sauce, chargrilled pork loin steak topped with melted stilton on an apple mash in red wine sauce, and roulade of plaice fillet stuffed with salmon mousseline on rosti with tomato sauce. Vegetarian choices also available. New owners.
OPEN: 12-3 6-11 (Sun 12-5) **BAR MEALS:** L served all week 12-2 D served all week 6-9.30 Av main course £7 **RESTAURANT:** L served all week 12-2 D served all week 6-9.30 (Sun 12-3) Av 3 course à la carte £18 ⊕: Free House ⬛: Fullers London Pride, Greene King IPA, Grainstore 1050, Guest beer. ♀: 10
FACILITIES: Children's licence Garden: decking area Dogs allowed **NOTES:** Parking 8

Pick of the Pubs

The Finch's Arms ♀
Oakham Rd, Hambleton LE15 8TL
☎ 01572 756575 ▤ 01572 771142
A simple stone-built, 17th-century inn in a sleepy village on a long tongue of land jutting into Rutland Water. Before the reservoir was created, Colin and Celia Crawford's pub looked out over a deep wooded valley, but these days it has stunning views over Europe's largest man-made lake. The story goes that a 17th-century landowner called Finch moved the pub stone by stone to its present position so that it was several miles away from his Palladian pile, in order to deter his estate workers from getting habitually drunk. The comfortable bar area has typical pub furniture, wooden floors and open fires, while in the stylish Garden Room restaurant, from which doors lead out to the pleasant summer patio, cane is the furniture of choice. While absorbing the vista across the water, tuck into bar snacks such as corned beef hash with fried eggs, countryside poultry terrine, or marinated scallops. A very similar menu is available in the evening, offering interesting dishes such as roast chicken breast with sauce Basquaise, braised gigot of lamb, pan-fried sea bass, whole lemon sole with parsley butter, pan-fried lamb's liver with pancetta, grain mustard mash and red wine sauce, and confit salmon cooked in duck fat. Menus change frequently, inspired by the four French, two English and one Spanish chef. The bar is a good source of real ales, among them Greene King Abbot Ale, Scottish Courage, Theakston Best, and Timothy Taylor Landlord.
OPEN: 10.30-3 6-11.30 **BAR MEALS:** L served all week 12-2.30 D served all week 7-9.30 Av main course £8.50 **RESTAURANT:** L served all week 12-2.30 D served all week 7-9.30 Av 3 course à la carte £16 ⊕: Free House ⬛: Greene King Abbot Ale, Scottish Couage Theakston Best Bitter, Timothy Taylor Landlord. **FACILITIES:** Garden: Large garden, patio, overlooks Rutland water **NOTES:** Parking 40

The Grainstore Brewery
Station Approach LE15 6RE ☎ 01572 770065 ▤ 01572 770068
e-mail: grainstorebry@aol.com
Dir: Beside Oakham railway station

Founded in 1995, Davis's Brewing Company is housed in the three-storey Victorian grain store next to Oakham railway station. Finest quality ingredients and hops are used to make the beers that can be sampled in the pub's Tap Room. Filled baguettes and stilton and pork pie ploughman's are of secondary importance, but very tasty all the same. Go for the brewery tours and blind tastings; or attend the annual beer festival during the August Bank Holiday.
OPEN: 11-11 **BAR MEALS:** L served all week 11-2.15 Av main

continued

course £7 ☺: Free House ◀: Grainstore Cooking Bitter, Triple B, Ten Fifty, Steaming Billy Bitter. **FACILITIES:** Dogs allowed Water, biscuit **NOTES:** Parking 8

Pick of the Pubs

The Old Plough
2 Church St, Braunston LE15 8QY
☎ 01572 722714 📠 01572 770382
e-mail: info@oldplough.co.uk

An old coaching inn that has kept its traditional identity despite being tastefully modernised. This genteel and very popular country pub dates back to 1783, and its village location makes it handy for visiting the lovely Georgian town of Oakham, as well as touring the rest of the old county of Rutland. Owners Claire and David host lots of speciality evenings and various weekend entertainments, and their enthusiasm for good food extends to candle-lit dinners in the picturesque conservatory, as well as light lunches on the terrace. Expect favourites like liver, bacon and onions, and Cajun chicken, as well as steak and kidney pudding, Braunston chicken stuffed with creamy cheese, trio of sausages with mustard mash and Calvados sauce, mushroom stroganoff, salmon en croûte, and beer-battered cod fillet. Regular guest ales.
OPEN: 11-3 6-11 (Fri-Sun 11-11) **BAR MEALS:** L served all week 12-2.30 D served all week 6-9.30 **RESTAURANT:** L served all week 12-2.30 D served all week 6-9.30 Av 3 course à la carte £16.95 ☺: Free House ◀: Boddingtons, Bass Cask, Greene King IPA, Grainstone. **FACILITIES:** Child facs Garden: Food served outside, garden terrace Dogs allowed
NOTES: Parking 30

STRETTON   Map 11 SK91

Pick of the Pubs

The Jackson Stops Inn NEW ♀
Rookery Rd LE15 7RA ☎ 01780 410237 📠 01780 410280
e-mail: James@JacksonStops-Inn.fsnet.co.uk
Dir: 0.5m from A1
For those keen on tracking down uniquely named pubs, this is a winner. You can guarantee nowhere else will have acquired its name by virtue of an estate agent sign that once hung outside for so long that locals dispensed with the original moniker of The White Horse Inn! The thatched stone inn actually dates from the 17th century, and has plenty of appealing features: log fires, scrubbed wood tables and no fewer than four dining rooms, as well as a 90-bin wine list. The cooking itself is distinctive and memorable. Home-cured salmon with blinis and crème

fraîche could be followed up with a melting osso buco Milanaise (braised shin of veal with saffron risotto); then an iced mocha parfait with hot doughnuts. Cheeses are not only hand crafted but come direct from the Paris Cheese Market, while the truffles with your coffee are all home made.

The Jackson Stops Inn

OPEN: 12-2.30 6.30-11 Closed: 26 Dec-New Year
BAR MEALS: L served Tues-Sun 12-2 D served Tues-Sat 7-10 Av main course £12 **RESTAURANT:** L served Tues-Sun 12-2 D served Tues-Sat 7-10 Av 3 course à la carte £22.50
◀: Oakham Ales JHB, Aldershaws Old Boy, Adnams Broadside, Timothy Taylor Landlord. ♀: 10 **FACILITIES:** Garden
NOTES: Parking 20

Pick of the Pubs

Ram Jam Inn ♀
The Great North Rd LE15 7QX
☎ 01780 410776 📠 01780 410361 e-mail: rji@rutnet.co.uk
Dir: On A1 n'bound carriageway past B1668, through service station into car park
The inn is thought to have got its current name some time during the 18th century. It was then that the pub sign advertised 'Fine Ram Jam', though few people, if indeed anyone, are sure what that might have been. These days, the informal café-bar and bistro exude warmth, and make this is a popular stop. The patio overlooks the orchard and paddock, and in fine summer weather is set for alfresco dining. The comprehensive all-day menu offers everything from cakes and pastries to sandwiches and Earl Grey tea. Examples from the range include goats' cheese salad served on a bed of mixed leaves and shredded beetroot with a red onion relish; Rutland sausages made to the Ram Jam's own recipe and served with mashed potato, caramelised onions and a red wine gravy; and tomato and bean casserole served with cowboy bread.
OPEN: 7-11 Closed: 25 Dec **BAR MEALS:** L served all week 12-9.30 D served all week Av main course £8.95
RESTAURANT: L served all week 12-9.30 D served all week ☺: Free House ◀: Fuller's London Pride, Scottish Courage John Smith's Cask and Smooth. ♀: 8 **FACILITIES:** Child facs Garden: Patio set for open air dining Dogs allowed
NOTES: Parking 64

Pubs offering a good choice of fish on their menu

continued

WHITWELL — Map 11 SK90

Noel Arms Inn
Main St LE15 8BW ☎ 01780 460334 ▧ 01780 460531
Dir: *From A1 take A606 to Oakham*
Country pub near Rutland Water with a cosy lounge in the original thatched building and a more modern bar. Dishes range from bangers and mash at lunchtime, to roast monkfish with sauté potatoes, spinach and braised leek, and rack of English lamb with Mediterranean vegetables and rosemary and lentil jus.
OPEN: 11-11 (Breakfast 7.30-9.30) **BAR MEALS:** L served all week 12-9.30 D served all week Av main course £8.50
RESTAURANT: L served all week 12-9.30 D served all week Av 3 course à la carte £18 ⊕: Free House ◀: Marstons Pedigree, Adnams Broadside, Old Speckled Hen and John Smiths.
FACILITIES: Garden: BBQ Dogs allowed **NOTES:** Parking 60

WING — Map 11 SK80

The Cuckoo Inn
3 Top St LE15 8SE ☎ 01572 737340
Dir: *A6003 from Oakham, turn R then L*
Four miles from Rutland Water, a part-thatched 17th-century coaching inn noted for unusual guest ales from micro-breweries: the pub has a rose garden and barbecue. Home-cooked food is notably good value: steak and kidney pie; lamb casserole - supplemented by some authentic Indian dishes such as chicken Madras and lamb rogan josh.
OPEN: 11.30-2.30 6.30-11 (Sun 12-4, 7-10.30) Closed Tue lunch
BAR MEALS: L served Wed-Mon 11.30-2.30 D served all week 6.30-9 Av main course £6.25 ⊕: Free House ◀: Grainstore ales and guests from micro-breweries. **FACILITIES:** Garden: BBQ, outdoor eating, floral display Dogs allowed **NOTES:** Parking 20 No credit cards

Pick of the Pubs

Kings Arms ◆◆◆◆ ▷ ♀
Top St LE15 8SE ☎ 01572 737634 ▧ 01572 737255
e-mail: info@thekingsarms-wing.co.uk
web: www.thekingsarms-wing.co.uk
See Pick of the Pubs on opposite page

SHROPSHIRE

BISHOP'S CASTLE — Map 15 SO38

Boars Head ◆◆◆ ▷ ♀
Church St SY9 5AE ☎ 01588 638521 ▧ 01588 630126
e-mail: sales@boarsheadhotel.co.uk
Dir: *In town centre*
One of Bishop's Castle's oldest buildings, this former coaching inn received its first full licence in 1642. Legend tells that it escaped burning during the Civil War because half the King's men were drinking here, while the rest were out vandalising the town. The exposed beams are genuine, and a chimney contains a priest hole. The inn is celebrated for its lunchtime steak, chicken and sausage sizzlers, while scrumpy pork, lamb shank, salmon béarnaise, and paella appear on the carte.
OPEN: 11.30-11 (Sun 12-10.30) **BAR MEALS:** L served all week 12-2 D served all week 6.30-9.30 (Sun 12-9.30) Av main course £6
RESTAURANT: L served all week 12-2 D served all week 6.30-9.30 Av 3 course à la carte £20 ⊕: ◀: Scottish Courage Courage Best & Courage Directors & regular guests. ♀: 8
FACILITIES: Child facs Children's licence **NOTES:** Parking 20
ROOMS: 4 bedrooms en suite 1 family room s£38 d£65

The Three Tuns Inn ♀
Salop St SY9 5BW ☎ 01588 638797
Dir: *22m SW of Shrewsbury*
A traditional timber-framed, town centre inn established in 1625, and a brewery since 1642. New owners are offering snacks, sandwiches, ploughman's and beer-battered cod and chips at lunchtime, with bangers and mash, mushroom risotto, braised lamb shank, fish pie, and home-made lasagne in the evenings. Traditional roast beef and lamb on Sundays. Today's home-brewed line-up includes Tuns XXX, Cleric's Cure and Scrooge. You can arrange a tour of the brewery and associated museum.
OPEN: 12-11 (Sun 12-10.30) **BAR MEALS:** L served all week 12-2 D served Mon-Sat 7-9.30 Mon all day, Sun 12-3.30 Av main course £7.50 **RESTAURANT:** L served all week 12-2.30 D served all week 12-9.30 ⊕: Free House ◀: Tuns XXX, Steamer, Scrooge, Clerics Cure (all by Three Tuns). ♀: 7 **FACILITIES:** Child facs Garden: Beer garden, patio Dogs allowed **NOTES:** Parking 6

BURLTON — Map 15 SJ42

Pick of the Pubs

The Burlton Inn ▷ ♀
SY4 5TB ☎ 01939 270284 ▧ 01939 270204
e-mail: bean@burltoninn.co.uk
Dir: *8m N of Shrewsbury on A528 towards Ellesmere*

This classy free house is a contemporary interpretation of an 18th-century inn, with a fresh looking dining area and a soft furnished space for relaxation, as well as a traditional bar - the perfect place for a pint of Proud Salopian, or one of the many guest beers. A good choice of food is offered, including snacks and sandwiches and a list of starters doubling as light meals: maybe tandoori chicken skewer, potted prawns, or pear, watercress and blue cheese salad. Among the main courses are a choice of steaks, a popular pie, and slow cooked shoulder of lamb. On the specials board you might find fresh monkfish fillet with a mango and lime cream sauce. Outside there is a lovely patio area, carefully planted to provide a blaze of colour in summer.
OPEN: 11-3 6-11 (Sun 12-3 7-10.30) Closed: Dec 25-26 Jan 1
BAR MEALS: L served all week 12-2 D served all week 6.30-9.45 (Sun 7-9.30) Av main course £10.95 **RESTAURANT:** L served all week 12-2 D served all week 6.30-9.45 (Sun 7-9.30) ⊕: Free House ◀: Banks, Greene King Abbot Ale, Wye Valley Bitter, Salopian Brewing. ♀: 11 **FACILITIES:** Garden: South facing patio and grass area with tables Dogs allowed Dogs allowed at discretion of landlord **NOTES:** Parking 40
ROOMS: 6 bedrooms en suite s£50 d£80 No children overnight (◆◆◆◆)

♀ 7	Number of wines by the glass

Kings Arms

The Goss family - David, Gisa and son James - took over here in May 2004, and are successfully maintaining the same high standards as their predecessors. The Kings Arms was built in 1649 from local stone and Collyweston roof slates; the bar, in the oldest part, is very atmospheric, with flagstones, low beams and large open fires.

The extensive menu served throughout the inn, restaurant, bar and garden, changes monthly according to seasonal availability. Starters such as langoustine ravioli with English asparagus topped with saffron and vanilla cream; pan-fried foie gras with pommes maxime; and San Danielle parma ham in an insalata mista might be followed by dill poached lobster, monkfish, or lemon sole, roast rib of beef, belly pork, lamb shoulder, calves'

liver, Aberdeen Angus rib eye steak, steak and kidney pie, or Grasmere sausages and mash. Vegetarians will find a choice of at least two dishes. In addition to the monthly menu a daily changing specials board increases the choice. All speciality breads, sauces, chutneys, dips and desserts (except ice cream and sorbets) are made in house. On offer too are some fine wines and beers from Oakham's Grainstore brewery.

OPEN: 12-3 6-11 (all day wknds)
BAR MEALS: L served all week 12-2
D served all week 6-9 Av main
course £11.95
RESTAURANT: L served all week
12-2 D served all week 6.30-9
Av 3 course à la carte £24
🍺: Free House
🍻: Timothy Taylor Landlord,
Marstons Pedigree, Grainstore
Cooking, guest beer. ♀: 7
FACILITIES: Garden: Large lawn
NOTES: Parking 25
ROOMS: 7 bedrooms en suite
4 family rooms s£60 d£70

◆◆◆◆ 🐟 ♀ Map 11 SK80
Top St LE15 8SE
☎ 01572 737634
▤ 01572 737255
📧 info@thekingsarms-wing.co.uk
🌐 www.thekingsarms-wing.co.uk
Dir: 1m off A6003 between
Uppingham & Oakham

PUB WALK
The Church Inn
Ludlow - Shropshire

THE CHURCH INN, LUDLOW
Buttercross SY8 1AW
☎ 01584 872174
Directions: Town centre
Open: 11–11
Bar Meals: L served all week 12–2
D served all week 6.30–9 Av main
course £5.95
Restaurant Meals: L served all week
12–10 D served all week Av 3 course à
la carte £15
Notes: Children & dogs welcome.
(For full entry see page 411)

Distance: 6 miles (9.7km)
Map: OS Landranger 203
Terrain: Fields and pasture.
Paths: Field paths, tracks and
bridleways
Gradient: Mainly flat

Walk submitted by Nick Channer

Enjoy this pleasant walk in the fields and pastures below the hilltop town of Ludlow.

From the pub make for the castle entrance in the town centre, keep right of it and follow the Mortimer Trail down to Dinham Bridge over the River Teme. Cross over and follow the road round to the right. Pass a row of stone cottages and then take the lane signposted Priors Halton.

Swing right just before Cliffe Hotel and go diagonally right in the field towards woodland. Descend steeply to a stile in the field corner, cross a footbridge and a second stile and keep right in the next field. Make for the next stile and keep ahead for some time until you draw level with a farm over to the left.

Turn left to a waymark, footbridge and stile in the boundary and then head slightly right. Cross into the next field, maintain the same direction and join a grassy track in the corner. Turn right after a few paces and follow a firm track towards Bromfield.

On reaching the A49 turn right, re-cross the Teme and pass the Cookhouse pub. Follow the A49, turning right just beyond the Bromfield village sign to follow a bridleway running parallel to the road. Keep on the grassy track to a bridleway sign by a road junction and turn right. Follow the Shropshire Way south, pass under power lines and swing left at the next waymark.

Keep Ludlow church tower ahead in the distance and pass to the right of some farm outbuildings. Join a track and continue to the next farm buildings. Cross an intersection, make for a gate and waymark and pass a school. The track graduates to a tarmac lane before reaching the road. Turn right towards Ludlow town centre.

Turn right at a bus stop and head diagonally left across the field, in line with the Castle. Go through a kissing gate into the next pasture and cross a footbridge. Make for the next gate and footbridge and walk along to the road.

Go straight ahead and when the road curves right, keep ahead. Climb some steps, turn left into Upper Linney, then right to the parish church. From St Laurence make for the town centre and return to the pub.

England

CHURCH STRETTON · Map 15 SO49

The Royal Oak
Cardington SY6 7JZ ☎ 01694 771266

Reputedly the oldest pub in Shropshire, dating from 1462, this Grade II listed pub is all atmosphere and character. Nestling in the out-of-the-way village of Cardington, the pub, with its low beams, massive walls and striking inglenook, is a great place to seek out on cold winter days. In the summer it is equally delightful with its peaceful garden and patio. The proprietors offer packed lunches on request and a free walkers' guide to the area.
OPEN: 12-2 7-11 (Sun 12-3, 7-10.30) **BAR MEALS:** L served Tue-Sun 12-2 D served Tue-Sat 7-9 Av main course £7.50
RESTAURANT: L served Tue-Sun 12-2 D served Tue-Sat 7.30-9
🍴: Free House 🍺: Hobsons Best Bitter, Duck and Dive, Golden Arrow, Timothy Taylor Landlord. **FACILITIES:** Garden: Patio, food served outdoors **NOTES:** Parking 30

CLEOBURY MORTIMER · Map 10 SO67

Pick of the Pubs

The Crown Inn ♦♦♦♦ ◉ 🔗 ♀
Hopton Wafers DY14 0NB ☎ 01299 270372 🖷 01299 271127
web: www.crownathopton.co.uk
Dir: On A4117 8m E of Ludlow, 2m W of Cleobury Mortimer

Located in a sleepy hollow, this former coaching inn has been lovingly restored to an excellent standard and is surrounded by immaculate gardens with its own duck pond. The 16th-century free house was once owned by a nearby estate, and the informal Rent Room bar recalls the days when rents were collected here from the local tenants. The inn boasts two inglenook fireplaces, exposed timbers, original stonework and an elegant dining room. Bedrooms are individually furnished for maximum guest comfort, and all offer en suite facilities. The kitchen offers imaginative dishes using fresh seasonal ingredients, with

the main menu enhanced by separate blackboard and fresh fish menus. Expect salmon, crevettes, silver bream, scallops, monkfish, haddock, halibut, red mullet and trout to feature on the fish menu. The Crown Inn makes a perfect base for exploring the beauty, history and secrets of south Shropshire.
OPEN: 12-3 6-12 **BAR MEALS:** L served all week 12-2.30 D served all week 6-9.30 Sun lunch 12-3, dinner 7-9 Av main course £9 **RESTAURANT:** L served all week 12-2.30 D served all week 7-9.30 Av 3 course à la carte £21.95 🍴: Free House 🍺: Timothy Taylor Landlord, Hobsons Best + guest beers.
♀: 10 **FACILITIES:** Child facs Garden: 3 large patios, nature garden with pond **NOTES:** Parking 40 **ROOMS:** 7 bedrooms en suite s£50 d£85

The Kings Arms Hotel ♀
DY14 8BS ☎ 01299 270252 🖷 01299 271968
Dir: Take A456 from Kidderminster the A4117 to Cleobury Mortimer
Simple victuals have given way to steak and kidney pie, and braised duck breast in Grand Marnier, as this 18th-century inn has moved with the times. The oak floors, exposed beams and fine inglenook fireplace remain a pleasant setting for popular choices of food that might also include fish pie, battered haddock, and various home-made pâtés.
OPEN: 11.30-11 (Sun 12-10.30) **BAR MEALS:** L served 11.30-3.30 D served Mon-Wed, Fri-Sat 6.30-9
RESTAURANT: L served all week 12-3 D served Mon-Wed, Fri-Sat 7-9 🍺: Hobsons Best, & guest ales. **FACILITIES:** Garden: Food served outside. Dogs allowed **NOTES:** Parking 4

CLUN · Map 09 SO38

The Sun Inn
10 High St SY7 8JB ☎ 01588 640559 🖷 01588 640277
e-mail: osburnejame@btconnect.com
Set in 'the quietest place under the sun at Clun', this 15th-century inn is full of character and old world features. There is a locals' bar with a friendly atmosphere and a lounge serving freshly prepared home-cooked food. Favourite dishes include haddock, scampi, and beef and Guinness pie. In fine weather food and drinks can be enjoyed outside on the patio.
OPEN: 12-3 5-11 (Closed Wed lunch) **BAR MEALS:** L served Thu-Tue 12-1.45 6-8.45 Sun 12-3, 7-10.30 Av main course £8
RESTAURANT: D served all week 6-8.45 Sun 7-8.30 Av 3 course à la carte £20 🍺: Hobsons Bitter, Banks Bitter, Banks Original,.
FACILITIES: Patio Dogs allowed except in eating area
NOTES: Parking 6

COCKSHUTT · Map 15 SJ42

The Leaking Tap NEW 🔗 ♀
Shrewsbury Rd SY12 0JQ ☎ 01939 270636 🖷 01939 270746
e-mail: nicklaw@btconnect.com
This friendly pub in the centre of Cockshutt village features beamed bars and log fires, and serves a selection of guest ales and food cooked from local produce. Lunchtime or evening menus are available, including a vegetarian selection, might include oven-baked salmon with roasted fennel; almond crusted fish cakes; and baked cod with herbs and stilton.
OPEN: 12-3 6-11 **BAR MEALS:** L served all week 12-2 D served Mon-Sat 6-9.30 Sun 12-2 **RESTAURANT:** L served all week 12-2 D served Mon-Sat 6-9.30 🍺: Banks Bitter, Banks Original, Guest Beers. ♀: 12 **NOTES:** Parking 24

continued

CRAVEN ARMS — Map 09 SO48

The Sun Inn ⌖ ♀
Corfton SY7 9DF ☎ 01584 861239 & 861503
e-mail: normanspride@aol.com
Dir: on the B4368 7m N of Ludlow
Family-run pub in beautiful Corvedale, first licensed in 1613. Landlord Norman Pearce brews his own Corvedale beers, using local borehole water, and sells them bottled and from the barrel. Landlady Teresa Pearce cooks all the meals, which are served with four to six vegetables or a freshly cut salad, and the produce is locally sourced. Dishes include beef in Corvedale Ale, and lamb Shrewsbury. The pub puts on small beer festivals at Easter and August bank holidays.
OPEN: 12-2.30 6-11 **BAR MEALS:** L served all week 12-2 D served all week 6-9 (Sun 12-3, 7-9) **RESTAURANT:** L served all week 12-2 D served all week 6-9.30 (Sun 12-3, 7-9) ⌖: Free House ◖: Corvedale Normans Pride, Secret Hop, Dark & Delicious, Julie's Ale. ♀: 14 **FACILITIES:** Child facs Children's licence Garden: 4 benches with tables, pretty views Dogs allowed Water **NOTES:** Parking 30

CRESSAGE — Map 10 SJ50

Pick of the Pubs

The Riverside Inn ♀
Cound SY5 6AF ☎ 01952 510900 ▤ 01952 510926
Dir: On A458 7m from Shrewsbury, 1m from Cressage
In three acres of garden alongside the River Severn, this extensively refurbished coaching inn offers river view dining both outdoors and in a modern conservatory. The single menu serves both dining areas and spacious bar, furnished and decorated in haphazard country style. Traditional pub dishes include hot crab pâté and mushrooms with Shropshire blue cheese, followed by local lamb noisettes with parsnip chips, and salmon fishcakes with hollandaise. Exotic alternatives follow the lines of Peking duck pancakes with hoisin sauce, "Pee-kai" chicken breasts with satay sauce, and spinach, sorrel and mozzarella parcels.
OPEN: 12-3 6-11 (Open all day Sat-Sun from May-Sept)
BAR MEALS: L served all week 12-2.30 D served all week 6.30-9.30 **RESTAURANT:** L served all week 12-2.30 D served all week 7-9.30 ⌖: Free House ◖: Shropshire Gold, Worthington, various cask ales & regular guest beers. ♀: 6
FACILITIES: Garden: Beer garden, patio overlooking River Severn Dogs allowed **NOTES:** Parking 52

HODNET — Map 15 SJ62

The Bear Hotel ★★
TF9 3NH ☎ 01630 685214 ▤ 01630 685787
e-mail: info@bearhotel.org.uk
web: www.bearhotel.org.uk
Dir: Jct of A53 & A442, turn R at rdbt, hotel on sharp corner in village.
An illuminated cellar garden, once a priest hole, is one of the more unusual attractions at this 16th-century coaching inn. There was also a bear pit in the car park until 1970. Hodnet Hall Gardens are close by. An extensive menu includes bar snacks and restaurant meals, with steak options featuring prominently as well as dishes like Caesar salad or deep-fried brie to start, and baked pheasant or salmon en croute as mains. Renowned for medieval banquets in the baronial hall.
OPEN: 10.30-11 (Sun 12-10.30) Restricted Bank holidays
BAR MEALS: L served all week 12-2 D served all week 6.30-9.30 (Sun to 2.45 & 9) Av main course £11 **RESTAURANT:** L served all
continued

week 12-2 D served all week 6.30-9.30 Sun to 2.45 & 9 Av 3 course à la carte £17 ⌖: Free House ◖: Theakston, John Smiths.
FACILITIES: Garden: Large lawn area, shrubs and hedges Dogs allowed in the garden only **NOTES:** Parking 70
ROOMS: 8 bedrooms en suite 2 family rooms s£42.50 d£60

IRONBRIDGE — Map 10 SJ60

The Grove Inn & Fat Frog ♦♦♦
10 Wellington Rd, Coalbrookdale TF8 7DX
☎ 01952 433269 ▤ 01952 433269 e-mail: frog@fat-frog.co.uk
Dir: J6 M54, follow signs for Ironbridge.
Tucked away in a basement of the Grove hotel, the Fat Frog Restaurant brings a Provençale flavour to the Ironbridge Gorge. With its red check tablecloths, the restaurant is filled with French murals, mannequins and skeletons - not to mention the resident ghost! Owner/chef Johnny Coleau serves a varied selection of English, continental and vegetarian dishes that include fillet au poivre; supreme de saumon citron; and entrecôte forestière.
OPEN: 12-2.30 5.30-11 (Sun 12-5.30) **BAR MEALS:** L served all week 12.30-2 D served Mon-Sat 6.30-8.30 (Sun 12-3) Av main course £8.95 **RESTAURANT:** L served all week 12.30-2 D served Mon-Sat 7-9.30 (Sun 12-3) Av 3 course fixed price £21.50 ⌖: Free House ◖: Banks Original, Traditional, Harp Irish, Hoegarden.
FACILITIES: Garden: Large lawned flowered garden Dogs allowed Water, food if required **NOTES:** Parking 12 **ROOMS:** 5 bedrooms en suite 2 family rooms s£30 d£45

Pick of the Pubs

The Malthouse ♦♦♦♦ ♀
The Wharfage TF8 7NH ☎ 01952 433712 ▤ 01952 433298
e-mail: enquiries@malthousepubs.co.uk
web: www.malthousepubs.co.uk
Dir: Telephone for directions
Originally known as the Talbot, this delightful old building on the banks of the River Severn has been an inn since the 1800s. The village of Ironbridge, a designated UNESCO World Heritage Site, is renowned for its spectacular natural beauty and award-winning museums - 10 in all - offering a wide variety of hands-on displays and special events. Close by is a choice of very pleasant woodland and riverside walks, and the picturesque towns of Bridgnorth and Ludlow are within easy reach. The Malthouse has twice been extensively refurbished, and now offers six rooms above a popular jazz bar where live music is played from Wednesday to Saturday. The bar menu ranges from salmon fish cakes and dry beef curry to poached chicken casserole and rack of barbecue pork ribs. Roast duck breast, pan-fried sea bass and fillet of lamb are typical examples of the restaurant dishes.
OPEN: 11-11 (Sun 12-3 6-10.30) Closed: 25 Dec
BAR MEALS: L served all week 12-2.30 D served all week 6-9.30 **RESTAURANT:** L served all week 12-2 D served all week 6.30-9.45 ⌖: Inn Partnership ◖: Flowers Original, Boddingtons, Tetley. ♀: 10 **FACILITIES:** Child facs Garden **NOTES:** Parking 15 **ROOMS:** 6 bedrooms en suite 2 family rooms s£59 d£69

Do you have a favourite pub that we have overlooked? Please use the Reader's Report form at the back of this guide to tell us all about it

LLANFAIR WATERDINE
Map 09 SO27

Pick of the Pubs

The Waterdine ◆◆◆◆◆ 🏵🏵 ♀
LD7 1TU ☎ 01547 528214 📠 01547 529992
e-mail: info@waterdine.com
Dir: 4m NW of Knighton, just off the Newtown road, turn right in
Lloyney, over bridge, follow to village, last on left opp church
The Waterdine started supplying scrumpy to sheep
drovers and farmers in the mid-16th century. In the early
1950s John (later Lord) Hunt planned what was to
become the most famous mountaineering expedition of
all time, the 1953 conquest of Everest. The old black
beams in the bar have recently been painted white, and it
looks a lot brighter as a result. There are two dining
rooms, one looking out over the lovely countryside.
Chef/owner Ken Adams's highly productive gardens are
the source of many of the ingredients that find their way
into his cooking, exemplified by dishes such as Bayonne
ham with celeriac remoulade; lightly cured loin of
Gloucester Old Spot pork, black pudding and olive and
herb potatoes; and rice pudding and prune crème brûlée.
Wood's of Craven Arms supplies the real ales. Beyond the
River Teme at the foot of the garden, again with superb
views, is Wales.
OPEN: 12-3 7-11 Closed: 1 wk Winter 1wk Spring Sunday
closed eve **BAR MEALS:** L served Tue-Sun 12-1.45 Av main
course £13.50 **RESTAURANT:** L served Tue-Sun 12-1.45
D served Tue-Sat 7-9 Av 3 course à la carte £25.50 🍺: Free
House ◀: Wood Shropshire Legends, Parish Bitter & Shropshire
Lad. ♀: 8 **FACILITIES:** Garden: Quiet walled garden, good
views Dogs allowed Water **NOTES:** Parking 12
ROOMS: 3 bedrooms en suite s£40 d£95 No children
overnight

LUDLOW
Map 10 SO57

The Church Inn ◆◆◆◆ ♀
Buttercross SY8 1AW ☎ 01584 872174 📠 01584 877146
web: www.thechurchinn.com
Dir: Town centre
Down the ages this inn has been occupied by a blacksmith,
saddler, druggist and barber-surgeon, and since being an inn
its name has changed several times. It sits on one of the
oldest sites in Ludlow, where nowadays it enjoys a good
reputation for traditional pub food and good beer including
Hobsons Town Crier and Hook Norton. Expect the likes of
lasagne, scampi, chilli, and gammon.
OPEN: 11-11 **BAR MEALS:** L served all week 12-2 D served all
week 6.30-9 Av main course £5.95 **RESTAURANT:** L served all
week 12-10 D served all week Av 3 course à la carte £15 🍺: Free
House ◀: Hobsons Town Crier, Hook Norton Old Hooky,
Weetwood, Wye Valley Bitter. ♀: 14 **FACILITIES:** Dogs allowed
ROOMS: 9 bedrooms en suite 1 family room s£35 d£60
See Pub Walk on page 408

Room prices show the minimum double and single
rates charged. Room rates in hotels and B&Bs
often vary depending on the facilities, so be sure to
check prices with the establishment before booking

The Cookhouse Cafe Bar ◆◆◆◆ 🏵🏵 ♀
Bromfield SY8 2JR ☎ 01584 856565 & 856665 📠 01584 856661
e-mail: info@theclive.co.uk web: www.theclive.co.uk
Dir: Located 2m N of Ludlow on A49 between Hereford and Shrewsbury

The Cookhouse Café Bar is part of a complex which includes
the Clive Restaurant with rooms and function facilities in a
former farmhouse and outbuildings. The name reflects the
building's association with Robert Clive, who laid the
foundations of British rule in India. Some 250 years on we
find brasserie-style cooking exemplified by smoked haddock
rarebit on dressed tomato salad, and Nash venison sausages
with mixed berry sauce, broccoli and mash.
OPEN: 11-11 (Sunday 12-10.30) Closed: 25-26 Dec
BAR MEALS: L served all week 12-3 D served all week 6-10
RESTAURANT: L served all week 12-3 D served all week 6-10
Av 3 course à la carte £25 Av 3 course fixed price £25 🍺: Free House
◀: Hobsons Best Bitter, Interbrew Worthington Cream Flow, Caffreys.
♀: 8 **FACILITIES:** Child facs Courtyard and beer lawn
NOTES: Parking 100 **ROOMS:** 15 bedrooms en suite
6 family rooms s£50 d£70

Pick of the Pubs

The Roebuck Inn ◆◆◆◆ 🏵🏵 🍴
Brimfield SY8 4NE ☎ 01584 711230 📠 01584 711654
e-mail: himleylimes@aol.com
Dir: Just off the A49 between Ludlow & Leominster
This country inn dating back to the 15th century offers
cosy bars with inglenooks and wood panelling, a bright,
airy dining room and comfortable bedrooms. Imaginative
food uses locally-sourced ingredients and a daily, home-
baked selection of breads. Starters and light meals might
include lemon spiced gravadlax; pan-seared scallops;
goats' cheese fritters; or smoked chicken ravioli. Main
courses range from roast rack of lamb or chicken breast
to glazed chilli and ginger salmon or steamed fillets of
sole. For dessert, try plum and almond crumble tartlet;
chocolate, amaretti and rum mousse; or a home-made ice
cream. An impressive selection of cheeses is available: try
Hereford Hop, Worcester Gold Smoked or Mrs Bells Blue,
served with home-made fruit bread, oatcakes, chutney,
grapes and celery.
OPEN: 11.30-3.30 6.30-11 **BAR MEALS:** L served all week
12-2.30 D served all week 7-9 Sun lunch 12-3.30 Av main course
£13.50 **RESTAURANT:** L served all week 12-3.30 D served all
week 7-9.30 Sun lunch 12-3.30 Av 3 course à la carte £23.50
Av 2 course fixed price £11.50 🍺: Free House ◀: Bank's Bitter,
Camerons Strongarm, Marstons Pedigree plus guests.
FACILITIES: Garden: Enclosed courtyard **NOTES:** Parking 25
ROOMS: 3 bedrooms en suite d£70 No children overnight

England

LUDLOW continued

Pick of the Pubs

Unicorn Inn 🐟 ♀
Corve St SY8 1DU ☎ 01584 873555 📠 01584 876268
Dir: A49 to Ludlow

Dating from the early 17th century, this low, attractive timber-framed building backs on to the once flood-prone River Corve. During the great flood of 1885 a photograph was taken of men sitting drinking around a table in the bar while water lapped the doorway. Apparently it wasn't unusual for empty beer barrels to float out of the cellar and down the river. Log fires in winter and the sunny riverside terrace in summer prove very appealing. Both bar and restaurant menus are served at lunch and dinner 364 days per year. The candlelit restaurant dining room offers good British and European dishes with fillet of beef, mixed peppers and onion souvlaki; roulade of chicken and apricots with cambozala cheese sauce; and lamb Shrewsbury. In the bar you could try duck Koresh with chelo - an Iranian dish served with basmati rice - or the more prosaic battered cod, salad and chips.
OPEN: 12-3 6-11 (Sun 12-3.30, 7-10.30) Closed: Dec 25
BAR MEALS: L served all week 12-2.15 D served all week 6-9.15 Sun (6.30-9.15) Av main course £7 **RESTAURANT:** L served all week 12-2.15 D served all week 6-9.15 Sun D 6.30 Av 3 course à la carte £22.50 🍺: Free House 🍺: Hancocks HB, Timothy Taylor's Landlord, Fuller's London Pride, Three Tuns Castle Steamer. ♀: 8 **FACILITIES:** Garden: Patio garden overlooks river Dogs allowed Water **NOTES:** Parking 3

MADELEY
Map 10 SJ60

The New Inn
Blists Hill Victorian Town, Legges Way TF7 5DU
☎ 01952 588892 📠 01785 252247
e-mail: sales@jenkinsonscaterers.co.uk
Dir: Between Telford & Broseley
Here's something different - a Victorian pub that was moved brick by brick from the Black Country and re-erected at the Ironbridge Gorge Open Air Museum. The building remains basically as it was in 1890, and customers can buy traditionally brewed beer at five-pence farthing per pint - roughly £2.10 in today's terms - using pre-decimal currency bought from the bank. The mainly traditional menu includes home-made soup, steak and kidney pudding, and ham and leek pie.
OPEN: 11-4 Closed: 24-25 Dec, 1 Jan **BAR MEALS:** L served all week 12-3 **RESTAURANT:** L served all week 12-3 🍺: 🍺: Banks Bitter, Banks Original, Pedigree. **FACILITIES:** Child facs Garden **NOTES:** Parking 300

MARTON

The Sun Inn NEW ♀
SY21 8JP ☎ 01938 561211 e-mail: info@suninn.biz
Dir: On B4386 Shrewsbury to Montgomery road, in centre of Marton opposite village shop.
Located in the small village of Marton and surrounded by glorious Shropshire countryside stretching to the Welsh hills, the home of this historic pub is understood to date back to about 1760. Prior to getting its licence in 1860 it was the the village rectory. Built of local mudstone, the inn retains many of its original features with a refurbished dining area offering a more contemporary feel and serving modern European and traditional food cooked to order from fresh ingredients by an award-winning chef. Venison sausages, fillet of cod, mushroom and bacon pasta and cauliflower cheese and ciabatta are typical examples of the bar lunch menu.
OPEN: 12-2 7-11 **BAR MEALS:** L served 12-2 D served Tues-Sat Sun 12-2.30 **RESTAURANT:** L served Wed-Sun 12-2 D served Tues-Sat 7-9.30 Sun 12-2.30 Av 3 course à la carte £20 🍺: Hobsons Best Bitter. ♀: 7 **NOTES:** Parking 38

MORVILLE
Map 10 SO69

The Acton Arms 🐟
WV16 4RJ ☎ 01746 714209 📠 01746 714102
e-mail: acton-arms@madfish.com
Dir: On A458, 3m W of Bridgnorth
Reputedly haunted by Richard Manners, last prior of Morville Priory, the Acton Arms is the target of many specialist ghosthunters and is understood to be one of Britain's most haunted pubs. There are plenty of spirits behind the bar, too, and elsewhere a wide choice of meals and snacks. Try grilled whole trout with almonds and lemon; steak and Guinness pie, or traditional lasagne. For something lighter, there are various snacks, baked jacket potatoes and baguettes.
OPEN: 11.30-2.30 6-11 (All day in summer and Sat/Sun)
BAR MEALS: L served all week 12-2 D served all week 6-9 All day Sat/Sun Av main course £7.50 **RESTAURANT:** L served all week 12-2.30 D served all week 7-9.30 All day Sat/Sun Av 3 course à la carte £14 🍺: Whampton & Dudley 🍺: Bank's Hanson's Mild & Banks Bitter. **FACILITIES:** Child facs Garden: Large area with benches & seats Dogs allowed Water **NOTES:** Parking 40

MUCH WENLOCK
Map 10 SO69

The George & Dragon ♀
2 High St TF13 6AA ☎ 01952 727312
e-mail: miltonmonk@btconnect.com
Dir: On A458 halfway between Shrewsbury & Bridgnorth
There's a remarkable collection of brewery memorabilia, including over 500 water jugs hanging from the ceiling, in this historic Grade II listed building. Adjacent to the market square, Guildhall and ruined priory, the inn's cosy and inviting atmosphere makes this an obvious choice for locals and visitors alike. Expect a good range of popular dishes, with snacks (sandwiches, baguettes, ploughmans etc) at lunch time, with thai chicken curry; chicken breast in apricot, mead and cream; or salmon poached in dill and white wine for dinner.
OPEN: 12-11 **BAR MEALS:** L served Mon-Sun 12-2 D served Mon-Tue, Thu-Sat 6-9 **RESTAURANT:** L served Mon-Sun 12-2 D served Mon-Tue, Thu-Sat 6.30-9 Av 3 course à la carte £18 🍺: 🍺: Greene King Abbot Ale, IPA, Hobsons Town Crier, Timothy Taylors Landlord. ♀: 8

England

Longville Arms

Longville in the Dale TF13 6DT ☎ 01694 771206 ▤ 01694 771742
Dir: *From Shrewsbury take A49 to Church Stretton, B4371 to Longville*
Prettily situated in a scenic corner of Shropshire, ideally
placed for walking and touring, this welcoming country inn
has been carefully restored and now includes a 70-seat dining
room. Solid elm or cast-iron-framed tables, oak panelling and
wood-burning stoves are among the features that help to
generate a warm, friendly ambience inside. Favourite main
courses on the bar menu and specials board include steak
and ale pie, chicken wrapped in bacon and stuffed with pâté,
smoked haddock, mixed fish platter, or a range of steaks.
OPEN: 12-3 7-11 (Sat & Sun all day in summer)
BAR MEALS: L served all week 12-2.30 D served all week 7-9.30
Av main course £8.50 **RESTAURANT:** L served all week 12-2.30
D served all week 7-9.30 Av 3 course à la carte £15 ⬡: Free House
⬤: Scottish Courage Courage Directors, John Smith's & Courage Best,
Theakstons Best, Wells Bombardier. **FACILITIES:** Garden: Patio area
Dogs allowed **NOTES:** Parking 40

The Talbot Inn ♦♦♦ ♀

High St TF13 6AA ☎ 01952 727077 ▤ 01952 728436
e-mail: the_talbot_inn@hotmail.com
web: www.the-talbot-inn.com

Dating from 1360, the Talbot was once a hostel for travellers
and a centre for alms giving. The delightful courtyard was
used in the 1949 Powell and Pressburger film *Gone to Earth*.
Daily specials highlighted on the varied menu may include
steak and kidney pie, baked seabass, and Shropshire pie.
OPEN: 11-3 6-11 (Sun 12-3, 7-10.30 Summer, Sat-Sun 11-11) Closed:
25 Dec **BAR MEALS:** L served all week 12-2.30 D served all week
7-9.30 **RESTAURANT:** L served all week 12-2.30 D served all week
7-9.30 ⬡: Free House ⬤: Bass. ♀: 28 **FACILITIES:** Garden:
Paved courtyard Dogs allowed in the garden only **NOTES:** Parking 5
ROOMS: 6 bedrooms en suite

Pick of the Pubs

Wenlock Edge Inn

Hilltop, Wenlock Edge TF13 6DJ
☎ 01746 785678 ▤ 01746 785285
e-mail: info@wenlockedgeinn.co.uk
Dir: *4.5m from Much Wenlock on B4371*

This inn perches at one of the highest points of Wenlock
Edge's dramatic wooded ledge. Originally a row of 17th-
century quarrymen's cottages, the cosy interior contains a
small country-style dining room and several bars, one
with a wood-burning stove. Outside, a furnished patio
takes full advantage of the views stretching across
Apedale to Caer Caradoc and the Long Mynd. Start your
meal with Bantry Bay mussels; home-made chicken liver
pâté; or oak smoked salmon, followed by a hearty main
course like home-made steak and ale pie or roast
vegetable and blue stilton wellington. Puddings include
warm chocolate brioche pudding with rich chocolate
sauce; and the pub favourite sticky toffee pudding with
home-made toffee sauce. The lunchtime menu offers
freshly baked baguette sandwiches as well as a range of
hot dishes.
OPEN: 12-3 7-11 **BAR MEALS:** L served Wed-Sun 12-2
D served Wed-Sat 7-9 Sun 12-3 Av main course £8.50
RESTAURANT: L served Wed-Sun 12-2 D served Wed-Sat 7-9
Sun 12-3 ⬡: Free House ⬤: Hobsons Best & Town Crier,
Salopian Shropshire Gold, Three Tuns Brewery Edge Ale exclusive
to Wenlock Edge Inn. **FACILITIES:** Garden: Patio area with
furniture, stunning views Dogs allowed Water, toys, chews
NOTES: Parking 50

MUNSLOW Map 10 SO58

Pick of the Pubs

The Crown Country Inn ♦♦♦♦ ♀

SY7 9ET ☎ 01584 841205 ▤ 01584 841255
e-mail: info@crowncountryinn.co.uk
See Pick of the Pubs on page 414

Pick of the Pubs

The Crown Country Inn

Lying below the rolling hills of Wenlock Edge in the Vale of the River Corve, the three-storey Crown, a listed Tudor inn, was once a 'Hundred House' where courts sat and passed judgement on local villains. With many of its original features intact, such as the sturdy oak beams, flagstone floors and the prominent large inglenook fireplace in the main bar area, it doesn't take much to imagine how it must have felt to be on trial.

Perhaps the black-clothed Charlotte sometimes seen in the pub was sentenced here. By the way, ladies going to powder their nose may run into her. Chef and owner Richard Arnold has been cooking professionally for more than twenty years, and for ten has been a Master Chef of Great Britain. His commitment to excellent Shropshire produce is evident from his menus, which also list his many local suppliers. In the Corvedale restaurant starters of griddled pavé of smoked organic salmon with horseradish potatoes and roquette pesto; and risotto of leeks and pecorino cheese topped with toasted pine kernels, signpost his approach. He produces main dishes such as breast of Aylesbury duckling with fondant potato, truffled cream cabbage, and sweet raspberry vinegar jus; grilled Hereford sirloin or fillet steak with flat mushroom, grilled tomato and straw potatoes; and fillet of Devon sea bass with ragout of prawns, tomato and rice grain pasta, and roquette aioli. For desserts try iced hazelnut praline parfait with prunes cooked in orange syrup. Sunday menus are more limited in choice, but just as appetising. If you want to see the beauty of one of England's undiscovered counties, a walk up on Wenlock Edge or the Long Mynd will pay dividends.

OPEN: 12-2 6.30-11 Closed: 25 Dec
BAR MEALS: L served Tue-Sun 12-2 D served Tue-Sun 6.30-9 Av main course £11
RESTAURANT: L served Tue-Sun 12-2 D served Tue-Sun 6.30-9 Av 3 course à la carte £25
🍽: Free House
🍺: Holden's Black Country Bitter, Black Country Mild, Woods Parish Bitter, Holden's Golden Glow & Holden's Special Bitter. ♈: 7
FACILITIES: Child facs Children's licence Garden: Large garden with grassed and patio areas Dogs allowed Water **NOTES:** Parking 20
ROOMS: 3 bedrooms en suite 1 family room s£40 d£60 ⊗

♦♦♦♦ ♈   Map 10 SO58
SY7 9ET
☎ 01584 841205
🖷 01584 841255
✉ info@crowncountryinn.co.uk
Dir: On B4368 between Craven Arms & Much Wenlock

NESSCLIFFE
Map 15 SJ31

The Old Three Pigeons Inn ♀
SY4 1DB ☎ 01743 741279 ▤ 01743 741259
Dir: On A5 London road, 8m W of Shrewsbury
A 600-year-old inn built of ship's timbers, sandstone, and wattle and daub, set in two acres of land looking towards Snowdonia and the Bretton Hills. There is a strong emphasis on fish, with a choice of many seasonal dishes, and it is a venue for gourmet club and lobster evenings. Characteristic dishes include seafood platter, duck and cranberry, braised oxtails, liver and bacon, and oak-smoked haddock.
OPEN: 12-3 6-11 **BAR MEALS:** L served all week 12-2.30 D served all week 6.30-9.30 Av main course £7 **RESTAURANT:** L served all week 12-2.30 D served all week 6.30-9.30 Av 3 course à la carte £18
▣: Free House ◄: Shropshire Gold, Archers & guest ale. ♀: 10
FACILITIES: Garden: Lawn, lake, excellent views Dogs allowed
NOTES: Parking 50

NORTON
Map 10 SJ70

Pick of the Pubs

The Hundred House Hotel ★★ ◉◉ ⌂ ♀
Bridgnorth Rd TF11 9EE
☎ 01952 730353 0845 6446 100 ▤ 01952 730355
e-mail: reservations@hundredhouse.co.uk
web: www.hundredhouse.co.uk
See Pick of the Pubs on page 416

NORTON IN HALES
Map 15 SJ73

The Hinds Head
TF9 4AT ☎ 01630 653014 ▤ 01630 653014
e-mail: thehindshead@nortoninhales.freeserve.co.uk
Dir: Norton in Hales is about 3m NE of Market Drayton

An 18th-century coaching inn located by the parish church. It has been much extended, with a conservatory built out over the old courtyard, but the bars retain their original atmosphere. The pub attracts regular custom from three counties, and rewards them with pan-roasted turbot with scallops, langoustine and hollandaise with shellfish liquor; local partridge pot-roasted with baby vegetables and finished with bitter chocolate; or crispy skin salmon with lemon mash, griddled scallions and salsa verde.
OPEN: 12-2 6.30-11 **BAR MEALS:** L served Tue-Sun 12-2 D served Tue-Sun 7-10 Av main course £11 **RESTAURANT:** L served Tue-Sun 12-2 D served Tue-Sun 7-10 (Sun 7-9) Av 3 course à la carte £20
▣: Free House ◄: Timothy Taylor's Landlord, Worthington 1744, Badger Best, Hook Norton Generation. **FACILITIES:** Paved walled patio **NOTES:** Parking 20

OSWESTRY
Map 15 SJ22

Pick of the Pubs

The Bradford Arms Hotel ♦♦♦♦
Llanymynech SY22 6EJ ☎ 01691 830582 ▤ 01691 830728
e-mail: info@bradfordarmshotel.com
web: www.bradfordarmshotel.com
Dir: On A483 in village centre

A coaching inn originally, but by the age of the car it belonged to the Earl of Bradford, the man responsible for its Edwardian makeover. More recent improvements have endowed it with five tastefully furnished en suite bedrooms and a spacious conservatory. In the comfortable bar and lounge, softly lit with open fires, the range of draught beers on offer will satisfy any real ale aficionado, and the excellent selection of ports, malts and liqueurs will similarly please those who know their stuff. The menu offers an enterprising selection of modern English and European dishes, such as tartare of beef fillet, sun-blushed tomatoes and parmesan with mustard gazpacho; seared fillet of Welsh beef with dauphinoise potato, confit of shallots, mustard rarebit and red wine jus; and wild sea bass, fennel and crab risotto, crab beignet and chive beurre blanc. Check the blackboard for other fresh fish options.
OPEN: 12-2 7-11 (Fri-Sat 7-10.30) Closed: 25-28 Dec, 1 Jan
BAR MEALS: L served Tues-Sat 12-2 Av main course £8
RESTAURANT: D served Tues-Sat 7-9 Fri-Sat 7-9.30 Av 3 course à la carte £23.50 Av 3 course fixed price £15.95 ▣: Free House
◄: Greene King Abbot Ale, Shepherd Neame Bishops Finger, Archers, Golden Ale. **FACILITIES:** Garden: Courtyard with tables and chairs Dogs allowed only in bar **NOTES:** Parking 20
ROOMS: 5 bedrooms en suite 1 family room s£40 d£65 No children overnight

---

♦ Pubs with Red Diamonds are the top places in the AA's three, four and five diamond ratings

---

We only include details of accommodation that has been inspected by the AA (big Stars or Diamonds at the top of an entry), or the RAC, VisitBritain, VisitScotland or WTB (small Stars or Diamonds at the end of an entry)

Pick of the Pubs

The Hundred House Hotel

Surely not, you might think, as you read the words Temperance Hall on the Art Nouveau stained-glass front doors. Don't worry, you're in the right place, but you just have to be prepared for quirkiness in this fine, creeper-clad old building. As one guest recently wrote: "There's something refreshing and interesting around every corner".

Lovingly run by the Phillips family, the main part is Georgian, but the half-timbered, thatched barn in the courtyard is 14th century, and was used as a courthouse in medieval times. Downstairs is an amazing interconnecting warren of lavishly decorated bars and dining rooms with quarry-tiled floors, exposed brickwork, beamed ceilings and oak panelling and, everywhere you look, aromatic bunches of drying herbs and flowers. Mellow brick, stained glass, Jacobean panelling, open log fires and cast-iron cooking pots from Ironbridge create, to quote another guest, "A haven of kindness, comfort and service". Food is in the modern English/Continental style, everything according to season where possible. Stocks, pies and pasta are all home made. In the bar/brasserie, among many other dishes, you can order Thai chicken curry; traditional steak and kidney pie; and beef and venison pie. Daily specials might include grilled Dover sole, or loin of pork stuffed with apple and sage and wrapped in bacon, while on the carte look for roast rack of Shropshire lamb with savoury lentils, roast peppers and rosemary jus; and grilled beef fillet with braised ox cheek and mushrooms with rösti and red wine sauce. But old faithfuls like traditional steak, kidney and stout pie; home-made lasagne; and pork sausages with mash and gravy are there too. Quirkiness extends to one of the bedrooms - it has a swing.

OPEN: 11-3 6-11 (Sun 11-10.30)
Closed: 25/26 Dec eve
BAR MEALS: L served all week 12-2.30 D served all week 6-10 (Sun 12-2.30, 7-8.45)
RESTAURANT: L served all week 12-2.30 D served Mon-Sat 6-10
Av 3 course à la carte £25
🍺: Free House
🍺: Phillips Heritage, Higate Saddlers & Old Ale, Robinsons Bitter, Phillips Mild. ♀: 12
FACILITIES: Garden: Large water garden, herb and rose garden Dogs allowed in the garden only
NOTES: Parking 40
ROOMS: 10 bedrooms en suite 3 family rooms s£85 d£125

★★ ◉◉ ⬭ ♀ Map 10 SJ70
Bridgnorth Rd TF11 9EE
☎ 01952 730353
🖷 01952 730355
✉ reservations@hundredhouse. co.uk
🌐 www.hundredhouse.co.uk
Dir: On A442, 6m N of Bridgnorth, 5m S of Telford centre

England

SHIFNAL
Map 10 SJ70

Odfellows Wine Bar ♀
Market Place TF11 9AU ☎ 01952 461517 ▤ 01952 463855
e-mail: odfellows@odley.co.uk
Dir: *3rd exit from mway rdbt, at next rdbt take 3rd exit, past petrol station, round bend under railway bridge, bar on left*

Owner Matt Jones has fun with the name's odd spelling, offering at lunchtime Od sandwiches, Od burgers, Od omelettes and Od bangers and mash. This quirky, much-loved wine bar has an elevated dining area leading into an attractive conservatory. Each of the four seasonal menus produces one of the following: carpaccio of beef with Tabasco and mustard dressing; spaghetti puttanesca; duck and Toulouse sausage cassoulet; and smoked haddock and mussel chowder.
OPEN: 12-2.30 5.30-11 (Sun & Fri open all day) Closed: 25-26 Dec, 1 Jan **BAR MEALS:** L served all week 12-2.30 D served all week 7-10 (Sun 12-9.30) Av main course £10.95 **RESTAURANT:** L served all week 12-2.30 D served all week 7-10 (Sun 12-9) Av 3 course à la carte £20 ⦿: Free House ◖: Bathams, Enville, Holdens, Salopian. ♀: 12
NOTES: Parking 35 **ROOMS:** 7 bedrooms en suite 2 family rooms s£45 d£55 No children overnight (♦♦♦)

SHREWSBURY
Map 15 SJ41

Pick of the Pubs

The Armoury ♀
Victoria Quay, Victoria Av SY1 1HH
☎ 01743 340525 ▤ 01743 340526
e-mail: armoury@brunningandprice.co.uk
The original armoury building, abandoned in 1882, did not stand on this site. It was 'moved' from the Armoury Gardens in 1922, owing to the scarcity of building materials after World War I. It was a bakery until 1974 and thereafter a warehouse. In 1995 it was renovated, opened as a pub and renamed The Armoury. With its riverside location and large warehouse windows, it makes an impressive pub. There have been some alterations following a recent change of hands: there is no separate restaurant now, but a no-smoking area of the pub, and the same menu is served throughout. Typical dishes from the daily selection include home-made beef burger; free range chicken breast with cider; seared tuna with niçoise salad; and pasta with olives and cherry tomatoes. A good choice of drinks includes a range of real ales, 50 malt whiskies, 20 bourbons, and 16 wines available by the glass.
OPEN: 12-11 (Mon-Sat 12-11, Sun 12-10.30) Closed: 25-26 Dec
BAR MEALS: L served all week 12-9.30 D served all week 6-9.30 (Sun 12-9) Av main course £8.95
RESTAURANT: L served all week D served all week
⦿: ◖: Wood Shropshire Lad, Phoenix Arrona IPA Deuchard, Caledonian, Roosters Cream. ♀: 16

The Mytton and Mermaid Hotel NEW ★★★ ⊚⊚ ♀
Atcham SY5 6QG ☎ 01743 761220 ▤ 01743 761292
e-mail: admin@myttonandmermaid.co.uk
web: www.myttonandmermaid.co.uk
This stylish Grade II listed country house hotel stands on the banks of the River Severn. There's a choice of real ales in the bar, with its log fires and comfortable sofas, whilst candles and freshly cut flowers decorate the tables in the elegant non-smoking restaurant. Seasonal menus incorporate the local ingredients that inspire modern British dishes like pot-roasted guinea fowl; cauliflower cheese risotto; and grilled sea bass on black olive mash.
OPEN: All day **BAR MEALS:** L served all week 12-2.30 D served all week 6.30-10 Av main course £9 **RESTAURANT:** L served all week 12-2.30 D served all week 7-10 Av 3 course à la carte £27.50 Av 3 course fixed price £27.50 ◖: Shropshire Lad, Ruddles, Salopian Icon, Courage Directors. ♀: 12 **FACILITIES:** Garden: On banks of River Severn **NOTES:** Parking 80 **ROOMS:** 20 bedrooms en suite 4 family rooms s£60 d£90 No children overnight

The Plume of Feathers ♦♦♦ ♀
Harley SY5 6LP ☎ 01952 727360 ▤ 01952 728542
e-mail: feathersatharley@aol.com
Nestling at the foot of Wenlock Edge, this 17th-century inn started life as a pair of cottages, though the present name was not recorded until 1842. Look for the Charles I oak bedhead, full size cider press and inglenook fireplace. The menu reflects whatever is in season, such as whole grilled Brixham plaice with garlic, crayfish butter and glazed lemon; and seared breast of duck.
OPEN: 12-3 6-11 (Sat, Sun and summer 12-11)
BAR MEALS: L served all week 12-2 D served all week 6.30-9.30 (Sun 12-4, 6.30-8) Av main course £6 **RESTAURANT:** L served all week 12-3 D served all week 6-9 (Sun 12-4, 6-9) Av 3 course à la carte £21 ⦿: Free House ◖: Worthingtons, Old Speckled Hen, Directors, guest beers. ♀: 8 **FACILITIES:** Child facs Children's licence Garden: Lawned area, wooden tables, chairs & parasols
NOTES: Parking 70 **ROOMS:** 9 bedrooms en suite 3 family rooms s£45 d£55

White Horse Inn
Pulverbatch SY5 8DS ☎ 01743 718247
Dir: *7m past the Nuffield Hospital*
Some 8 miles south of Shrewsbury off the A49, a cruck-structured building houses this fine old inn which was mentioned in the Domesday Book. Up to 40 main dishes on offer every day, ranging from salmon, plaice and haddock in various guises to home-made steak and ale pie, whole lamb shanks and half a dozen speciality curries. Grills include chicken, gammon and various cuts of steak: a daily special might be beef bourguignon.
OPEN: 12-2.30 6-11 **BAR MEALS:** L served all week 12-2.30 D served all week 7-9.30 Av main course £7.50
RESTAURANT: L served all week 12-2 D served all week 7-9.30 Av 3 course à la carte £15.95 ⦿: Enterprise Inns ◖: Local Salopian ales. **FACILITIES:** Garden: Patio area, seats 12 Dogs allowed Water **NOTES:** Parking 50

UPPER AFFCOT
Map 09 SO48

The Travellers Rest Inn ♀
SY6 6RL ☎ 01694 781275 ▤ 01694 781555
e-mail: reception@travellersrestinn.co.uk
Dir: *Situated alongside A49 5m S of Church Stretton*
Traditional south Shropshire inn between Church Stretton and Craven Arms. Customers travel some distance to enjoy the friendly atmosphere, great range of real ales and good pub

continued

England

UPPER AFFCOT continued

meals, with food served until 9pm. Food options include cottage pie, traditional gammon, 6-7oz fillet of plaice, and broccoli and cheese bake, with worthy desserts like hot chocolate fudge cake. **OPEN:** 11-11 (Sun 12-10.30) **BAR MEALS:** L served all week 11.30-8.30 D served all week 11.30-8.30 Sun 12-8.30 Av main course £8.50 ◄: Wood Shropshire Lad, Hobsons Best Bitter, Bass, Guinness. ♀: 14 **FACILITIES:** Children's licence Garden: Dogs allowed on leads **NOTES:** Parking 50

WENTNOR   Map 15 SO39

The Crown Inn ◇

SY9 5EE ☎ 01588 650613 📠 01588 650436
e-mail: crowninn@wentnor.com
Dir: From Shrewsbury A49 to Church Stretton, follow signs over Long Mynd to Asterton, right to Wentnor
Outdoor enthusiasts of all persuasions will appreciate the location of this 17th-century coaching inn below the Long Mynd. Its homely atmosphere, which owes much to log fires, beams and horse brasses, makes eating and drinking here a pleasure. Meals are served in the bar or separate non-smoking restaurant. Typical daily changing, traditional home-made dishes include pork tenderloin filled with marinated fruits; pan-fried breast of duck with a burnt orange sauce; and grilled sea bass with couscous.
OPEN: 12-3 7-11 (Sat 12-11, Sun 12-10.30 Summer wknds all day) Closed: 25 Dec **BAR MEALS:** L served all week 12-2 D served all week 6-9 Sat-Sun 12-9 Av main course £6 **RESTAURANT:** L served all week 12-2 D served all week 6-9 Sat-Sun 12-9 ☺: Free House ◄: Hobsons, Greene King Old Speckled Hen, Three Tuns, Wye Valley. **FACILITIES:** Garden: Lawned area with benches **NOTES:** Parking 20 **ROOMS:** 4 bedrooms en suite s£30 d£53 (★★★★) No children overnight

WESTON HEATH   Map 10 SJ71

Pick of the Pubs

The Countess's Arms ♀

TF11 8RY ☎ 01952 691123 📠 01952 691660
e-mail: thecountesssarms@hotmail.com
Dir: 1.5m from Weston Park. Turn off A5 onto A51 towards Newport

In the owners' own words, 'a large contemporary eatery in a refurbished traditional pub', very popular particularly for jazz night on Fridays. Customers in the spacious gallery bar can look down on the blue glass mosaic-tiled bar below. The Earl of Bradford owns it - the family seat is Weston Park down the road. A stylish, modern approach mixes old favourites such as faggots, mushy peas and mash, with poached seabass with shiitake mushrooms, chickpea and

continued

spinach curry, and Cajun-spiced chicken salad.
OPEN: 12-11 (Sun 12-10.30) **BAR MEALS:** L served all week 12-2.30 D served all week 6-9.30 Av main course £8.95 **RESTAURANT:** L served all week 12-2.30 D served all week 6-9.30 ☺: Free House ◄: Flowers Original, Deuchars IPA, Timothy Taylor Landlord, Woods Shropshire Lad. ♀: 10 **FACILITIES:** Child facs Garden: Large grassed area with play area **NOTES:** Parking 100

WHITCHURCH   Map 15 SJ54

The Horse & Jockey

Church St SY13 1LB ☎ 01948 664902 📠 01948 664902
e-mail: andy-thelwell@yahoo.co.uk
Dir: In town centre next to church
Coaching inn built on Roman ruins and extended between the 17th and 19th centuries. Inside you'll find exposed beams, an open fire and a menu offering a vast array of dishes. You can select from the carte, grill or easy eating menus, plus there's a list of pizzas. Typical dishes might be stuffed best end of lamb with honey and port sauce; pan-fried chicken with brandy, cream and coarse grain mustard, and mushroom tortellini.
OPEN: 11.30-2.30 6-11 **BAR MEALS:** L served Tues-Sun 11.30-2.30 D served Tues-Sun 6-10 **RESTAURANT:** L served Tues-Sun 11.30-2.30 D served Tues-Sun 6-10 ☺: Pubmaster ◄: Interbrew Worthington, Scottish Courage John Smith's, Fosters. **FACILITIES:** Garden: Patio and grassed area, with wooden benches **NOTES:** Parking 10

Willeymoor Lock Tavern ♀

Tarporley Rd SY13 4HF ☎ 01948 663274
Dir: 2m N of Whitchurch on A49 (Warrington/Tarporley)
A former lock keeper's cottage idyllically situated beside the Llangollen Canal. Mrs Elsie Gilkes has been licensee here for some 25 years. Low-beamed rooms are hung with a novel teapot collection, there are open log fires and a range of real ales. Deep-fried fish and a choice of grills rub shoulders with traditional steak pie, chicken curry and vegetable chilli. Other options include salad platters, children's choices and gold rush pie for dessert.
OPEN: 12-2.30 6-11 (Sun 12-2.30 7-10.30) Closed: 25 Dec **BAR MEALS:** L served all week 12-2 D served all week 6-9 7pm on Sun in winter **RESTAURANT:** L served all week 12-2 D served all week 6-9 ☺: Free House ◄: Guest Ales, Abbeydale, Moonshine, Weetwood. ♀: 8 **FACILITIES:** Garden: Besides canal, enclosed play area **NOTES:** Parking 50 No credit cards

WOORE   Map 15 SJ74

Swan at Woore ♀

Nantwich Rd CW3 9SA ☎ 01630 647220
Dir: A51 Stone to Nantwich road 10m from Nantwich in the village

Refurbished 19th-century dining inn by the A51 near Stapley

continued

England

Water Gardens. Four separate eating areas lead off from a central servery. Daily specials boards supplement the menu, which might include crispy confit of duck, slow roast knuckle of lamb, roasted salmon on vegetable linguine, or red onion and garlic tarte Tatin. There's a separate fish menu, offering grilled red mullet fillets, perhaps, or seared tuna on roasted sweet peppers. New owners welcome children.
OPEN: 12-3 5-12 Closed: Dec 25 **BAR MEALS:** L served Mon-Fri 12-2.30 D served Mon-Fri 6-9.30 ☺: Inn Partnership ◀: Marston's Pedigree, Boddingtons, John Smiths. **FACILITIES:** Garden: Food served outside, small lawn **NOTES:** Parking 40

WORFIELD
Map 10 SO79

The Dog Inn & Davenport Arms
Main St WV15 5LF ☎ 01746 716020 ▤ 01746 716050
e-mail: thedog@tinyworld.co.uk
Dir: On the Wolverhampton road turn L opposite the Wheel pub over the bridge and turn R in to the village of Worfield the Dog is on the L. Tourist signs on the A454 & A442
The Dog is an ancient pub nestling in a picturesque village of handsome houses close to the River Worfe. The list of licensees near the entrance dates back to 1820. Spick-and-span with a tiled floor and light pine furnishings inside, it offers tip-top Butcher's Ales (brewed at the Munslow Arms) and a short menu listing home-cooked dishes. Choose from a varied menu that offers dishes such as pasta de casa, country vegetable and mixed bean casserole, lamb chops, baby squid in Mediterranean tomato, classic lobster thermidor, or oven-roasted chicken breast.
OPEN: 12-2.30 7-11 **BAR MEALS:** L served all week 12-2 D served all week 7-9.30 **RESTAURANT:** L served all week 12-2 D served all week 7-9.30 ☺: Free House ◀: Courage Directors, Wells Bombardier, Highgate Mild, Courage Best. **FACILITIES:** Children's licence Garden: Dogs allowed **NOTES:** Parking 8

SOMERSET

APPLEY
Map 03 ST02

Pick of the Pubs

The Globe Inn 🐟
TA21 0HJ ☎ 01823 672327
Dir: From M5 junct 26 take A38 towards Exeter. Village signed in 5m
This quirky slate and cob-built pub on the Somerset Devon border is 500 years old, and stands in glorious walking countryside. The pub is quirky because not only does it have a large collection of Corgi and Dinky cars and Titanic memorabilia, it also features series of 1930s ceramics and old advertising posters and enamel signs from the 20s, 30s and 40s. What's more, they now have a whole new room designed to look like a 1930s railway waiting room. As far as the food goes, specials change every week, and you might be offered a choice between lamb braised with chilli, garlic, spring onions, mushrooms, peppers, honey and soy sauce served with rice; or sweet and sour king prawns wrapped in filo pastry, deep fried and served on a bed of rice with sweet and sour rice. Port and cranberry sorbet, or Irish cream liqueur ice cream are suitable desserts.
OPEN: 11-3 6.30-11 (Closed Mon) **BAR MEALS:** L served Tue-Sun 12-2 D served Tue-Sun 7-10 Av main course £8.50
RESTAURANT: L served Tue-Sun D served Tue-Sun 7-10 Av 3 course à la carte £20 ☺: Free House ◀: Cotleigh Tawny, Palmers IPA, Palmers 200, Exmoor Ales & other Cotleigh Ales.
FACILITIES: Child facs Large garden overlooking countryside Dogs allowed Garden only **NOTES:** Parking 30

ASHCOTT
Map 04 ST43

The Ashcott Inn ♀
50 Bath Rd TA7 9QQ ☎ 01458 210282 ▤ 01458 210282
Dir: M5 J23 follow signs for A39 to Glastonbury
Dating back to the 16th century, this former coaching inn has an attractive bar with beams and stripped stone walls, as well as quaint old seats and an assortment of oak and elm tables. Outside is a popular terrace and a delightful walled garden. A straightforward menu offers 'Home Favourites' such as Cumberland sausages, pasta carbonara, Spanish omelette and steak baguette, while poultry and seafood choices include chicken provençal, tuna steak with salad, or chicken tikka masala. Vegetarians may enjoy mushroom stroganoff with gherkins and capers, or stilton and walnut salad.
OPEN: 11-11 **BAR MEALS:** L served all week D served all week Av main course £7 **RESTAURANT:** L served all week 12-2.45 D served all week 5.30-9.30 Av 3 course à la carte £17 ☺: Heavitree ◀: Otter. ♀: 12 **FACILITIES:** Garden: Large seclude area, shaded with large trees **NOTES:** Parking 50

Ring O'Bells 🐟 ♀
High St TA7 9PZ ☎ 01458 210232 e-mail: info@ringobells.com
web: www.ringobells.com
Dir: From M5 follow signs A39 & Glastonbury. N off A39 at post office follow signs to church and village hall
A traditional village pub, under the same ownership since 1987, the Ring O'Bells is run by three partners as a real family concern. It has won many awards for its quality ales, good food and friendly service. The menu is supplemented by the daily specials board. Options might include fruity West Indian chicken, Korean-style pork fillet, stuffed aubergines, or haddock smokie.
OPEN: 12-3 7-11 (Sun 7-10.30) Closed: 25 Dec
BAR MEALS: L served all week 12-2 D served all week 7-10 Av main course £6.75 **RESTAURANT:** L served all week 12-2 D served all week 7-10 Av 3 course à la carte £14.50 ☺: Free House ◀: Regular Guest Ales & Beers. ♀: 7 **FACILITIES:** Child facs Garden: Large, enclosed garden, grass, patio **NOTES:** Parking 25

ASHILL
Map 04 ST31

Square & Compass
Windmill Hill TA19 9NX ☎ 01823 480467
Dir: Turn off A358 at Stewley Cross service station (Ashill) 1m along Wood Road, behind service station
There's a warm, friendly atmosphere at this traditional free house, beautifully located overlooking the Blackdown Hills in the heart of rural Somerset. Lovely gardens make the most of the views, and the refurbished bar area features hand-made furniture. A good choice of home-cooked food, including beef casserole with cheesy dumplings; tasty shortcrust game pie; and duck breast with port and orange sauce.
OPEN: 12-2.30 6.30-11 (Sun 7-11) **BAR MEALS:** L served all week 12-2.30 D served all week 7-10 Av main course £7.50 ☺: Free House ◀: Exmoor Ale & Gold Moor Withy Cutter, Wadworth 6X, Branscombe Bitter, Exmoor Ale. **FACILITIES:** Child facs Garden: Very large garden, patio area, amazing views Dogs allowed **NOTES:** Parking 30

> Pick of the Pubs have that extra special quality that makes them stand out from the crowd. Their entries are highlighted, and may be a full page

PUB WALK
The Fountain Inn
Wells - Somerset

THE FOUNTAIN INN,
1 St Thomas Street, Wells, BA5 2UU
☎ 01749 672317
Directions: City centre, at jct of A371 & B3139.
Close to the cathedral, an inn with a good reputation for food and wine, as well as locally-brewed and other ales. Unpretentious ground floor bar with fires, and an upstairs restaurant where a more sophisticated menu is served.
Open: 10.30–2.30 6–11 (Sun 12–3, 7–10.30) Closed: 25–26 Dec
Bar Meals: L served all week 12–2.30 D served all week 6–10 (Sun 12–2.30, 7–9.30) Av main course £7.95
Restaurant Meals: L served all week 12–2.30 D served all week 6–10 (Sun 12–2.30, 7–9.30) Av 3 course à la carte £20 Av 2 course fixed price £7.95 Children welcome. Parking available. (for full entry see page 440)

Distance: 6 miles (9.7km)
Map: OS Landranger 141
Terrain: Rolling Mendip country – rolling hills and wooded combes
Paths: Roads, bridleways and paths
Gradient: Some moderate climbing

Walk submitted by Nick Channer & checked by The Fountain Inn

Explore the magnificent Mendips on this glorious country walk.

From the pub turn into Vicar's Close and make for a narrow alleyway and some steps at the top. Turn right at the road and then left into College Road. Follow it to the A39. Turn right and swing left into Walcombe Lane, passing Walcombe Farmhouse. Keep right at the fork and then turn right at the next junction. Take the bridleway on the right, further up the hill. Before proceeding put your dog's lead on, as you will be passing near a pheasant farm. Follow the sunken woodland path and turn sharp right at a junction, following the path along the grassy slopes and round to the right by a footpath sign. Keep to the hedgerow on the right and head for an intersection of tracks further down.

Turn left, pass Pen Hill Farm and continue ahead on the tarmac track. Pass a house called Gollege and continue to a T junction. Turn left and walk along to the A39. Cross over by a cottage, turn right and follow the path down the field boundary to a gate. Keep ahead along the woodland edge with a stream on the right. Cross stream on stepping stones, then cross a footbridge and follow the path just inside the trees. Re-enter the woodland and ascend the grassy slope to a seat round a tree.

Turn right here and keep a house on the left. Follow until you reach a junction. Turn left, proceed until you meet a main path, then turn right. Follow the grassy path to a stile. Cross the field, keeping to the left perimeter. Avoid the first stile and cross the second. Turn right and skirt the field to a kissing gate. Follow stone steps down through trees to a stream and cross a stone bridge.

Go over the junction and uphill, signposted Hawkers Lane. On reaching the field edge, keep left to a stile and cut through trees and alongside a fence. Pass through a wrought iron kissing gate and continue ahead in the field. Pass a gate on the right and follow the hedge as it curves left in line with the boundary. Walk down towards some houses and reach the road. Cross stile, turn left and cut through the housing estate to the B3139. Turn right here and return to the Fountain Inn.

England

AXBRIDGE   Map 04 ST45

Lamb Inn
The Square BS26 2AP ☎ 01934 732253 ▤ 01934 733821
Parts of this rambling 15th-century free house were once the guildhall, but it was licensed in 1830 when the new town hall was built. Standing across the medieval square from King John's hunting lodge, the pub's comfortable bars have log fires; there's also a skittle alley and large terraced garden. Snacks and pub favourites support contemporary home-made dishes like pan-fried salmon in cheese and chive coating; and Mediterranean roasted vegetable pancakes in stilton sauce.
OPEN: 11.30-11 (Mon-Wed, 11.30-3,6-11) **BAR MEALS:** L served all week 12-2.30 D served Mon-Sat 6.30-9.30 ▤: ◖: Butcombe, Butcombe Gold Fosters, Guest Beers. **FACILITIES:** Garden: Patio at front of pub, landscaped garden Dogs allowed

The Oak House ♀
The Square BS26 2AP ☎ 01934 732444 ▤ 01934 733112
Dir: From M5 junct 22, follow signs for Cheddar Gorge and Caves. Turn onto A371 to Cheddar/Wells, then left at Axbridge. All roads lead to The Square.
Parts of the house date back to the 11th century, with exposed beams, massive inglenook fireplaces and an ancient well linked to the Cheddar Caverns. The bar is small and intimate, while in the bistro food is served in an informal atmosphere. Sirloin and gammon steaks, Cumberland sausages and Cajun chicken share the menu with 'family favourites' like fisherman's pie, pork and cider casserole, leek and potato bake and blackboard specials.
OPEN: 11-11 (Sun 11-10.30) **BAR MEALS:** L served all week 12-2.30 D served all week 6.30-9.30 Av main course £8
RESTAURANT: L served all week 12-3 D served all week 6.30-9.30 (Sun 6-9) Av 3 course à la carte £20 ▤: ◖: Timothy Taylor, Butcombe. ♀: 8 **FACILITIES:** Child facs

BATH   Map 04 ST76

The Old Green Tree ♀
12 Green St BA1 2JZ ☎ 01225 448259
Dir: Town centre
18th-century, three-roomed, oak-panelled pub, loved for its faded splendour, dim and atmospheric interior and a front room decorated with World War II Spitfires. Menus include basic pub fare - soup, bangers and mash ('probably the best sausages in Bath'), rolls and salads, steak and ale pie, and the more exotic roasted vegetable risotto with melted brie. Often six or seven local real ales are served, with German lager, local cider, and an array of malts, wines and good coffee.
OPEN: 11-11 (Sun 12-10.30) Closed: 25-26 Dec, 1 Jan
BAR MEALS: L served Mon-Sun 12-2.45 Av main course £6
▤: Phoenix Inns ◖: Bench Mark, Brand Oak Bitter, Pitchfork, Mr Perrretts Stout & Summer Lightning. **FACILITIES:** Dogs allowed (manager's discretion only) **NOTES:** No credit cards

Pack Horse Inn
Hods Hill, South Stoke BA2 7DU
☎ 01225 832060 ▤ 01225 830075
e-mail: jess@packhorseinn.free-online.co.uk
Dir: 2.5m from Bath city centre, via the A367(A37). Turn onto B3110 towards Frome. South Stoke turning on right.
This country inn maintains a tradition of hospitality that dates back to the 15th century. It was built by monks to provide shelter for pilgrims and travellers, and still has the original bar and inglenook fireplace. Outside an extensive garden overlooks the surrounding countryside. All the meals are home made, from sandwiches and snacks to main courses of spinach, pea and forest mushroom risotto; Normandy chicken,
continued

or pepper smoked mackerel fillet with horseradish sauce.

Pack Horse Inn

OPEN: 11.30-2.30 6-11 (Sun all day) **BAR MEALS:** L served all week 12-2 D served Tues-Sat 6-9 Av main course £6.75 ▤: ◖: Bass, Scottish Courage Courage Best, Wadworth 6X. **FACILITIES:** Children's licence Garden: Country garden overlooking countryside Dogs allowed Water

The Star Inn ♀
23 Vineyards BA1 5NA ☎ 01225 425072
e-mail: landlord@star-inn-bath.co.uk
Often described as a rare and unspoilt pub of outstanding historic interest and listed on the National Inventory of Heritage Pubs, this 18th-century listed building stands amid Bath's glorious Georgian architecture. Famous for its pints of bass served from the jug and including many original features such as 19th-century Gaskell and Chambers bar fittings and a lift to transport barrels from the cellar. Large selection of rolls available at lunchtime. Ask about Abbey Ales brewery tours.
OPEN: 12-2.30 5.30-11 All day Sat-Sun ◖: Bellringer, Bass, XXXB, Timothy Taylor Landlord. ♀: 6

BECKINGTON   Map 04 ST85

Pick of the Pubs

Woolpack Inn ♀
BA11 6SP ☎ 01373 831244 ▤ 01373 831223
e-mail: 6534@grenneking.co.uk
Dir: Just off A36 near junction with A361
Standing on a corner in the middle of the village, this charming, stone-built coaching inn dates back to the 1500s. Inside there's an attractive, flagstoned bar and outside at the back, a delightful terraced garden. The new owner's lunch menu offers soup and sandwich platters, and larger dishes such as home-made sausages and mash; fresh herb and tomato omelette; steak and ale pie; and beer-battered cod and chips. Some of these are also listed on the evening bar menu, alongside others such as grilled sirloin steak; wild mushroom risotto; baked breast of pheasant with stilton and spinach stuffing; braised belly of pork with apple and sage mash, brandy and peppercorn sauce; fresh fish of the day; and vegetable and goat's cheese pie with stir-fried savoy cabbage and tomato gravy. A short list of puddings includes home-made apple crumble with vanilla ice cream.
OPEN: 11-11 (Sun 12-10.30) **BAR MEALS:** L served all week 12-2.30 D served all week 6.30-9.30 Sun 6.30-9 Av main course £10.95 **RESTAURANT:** L served Sun 12-2.30 D served all week 6.30-9.30, Av 3 course à la carte £20 ▤: Old English Inns ◖: Greene King IPA, Abbot Ale, Speckled Hen. ♀: 8
FACILITIES: Child facs Garden: Terrace garden Dogs allowed none **NOTES:** Parking 12

BICKNOLLER

Map 03 ST13

The Bicknoller Inn NEW ⬡ ♀
32 Church Ln TA4 4EL ☎ 01984 656234
A 16th-century thatched country inn set around a courtyard
with a large garden under the Quantock Hills. Inside you'll
find traditional inglenook fireplaces, flagstone floors and oak
beams, as well as a new theatre-style kitchen and restaurant.
Meals range from sandwiches and pub favourites like hake in
beer batter (priced for an 'adequate' or 'generous' portion),
to the full three courses with maybe smoked salmon; chicken
supreme cooked in red wine, and warm treacle tart.
OPEN: 12-3.30 6-12 **BAR MEALS:** L served all week 12-3 D served
all week 6.30-9.30 Av main course £10 **RESTAURANT:** L served all
week 12-3 D served all week 6.30-9.30 Av 3 course à la carte £30
⬤: Wadworth 6X, Palmers Copper, Palmers IPA, 2 guest beers.
♀: 10 **FACILITIES:** Child facs Garden: Dogs allowed Water
NOTES: Parking 20

BLAGDON

Map 04 ST55

The New Inn ⬡ ♀
Church St BS40 7SB ☎ 01761 462475 ▤ 01761 463523
e-mail: the.new-inn@virgin.net
Dir: From Bristol take A38 S then A368 towards Bath
Open fires, traditional home-cooked food, and magnificent
views across fields to Blagdon Lake are among the attractions
at this welcoming 17th-century inn, tucked away near the
church. A hearty pub food menu offers lamb chops, Mexican
chilli, battered cod and chips, grilled rainbow trout, beef and
Butcombes pie, and a selection of filled rolls, jacket potatoes,
ploughmans' and basket meals.
OPEN: 11.30-2.30 7-10.30 (times vary, contact for details)
BAR MEALS: L served all week 12-2 D served all week 7-9 Av main
course £7.15 ⬤: Wadworth ⬤: Wadworth 6X, Henry's IPA. ♀: 8
FACILITIES: Garden: Food served outside. Picnic benches Dogs
allowed in the garden only **NOTES:** Parking 40

BLUE ANCHOR

Map 03 ST04

The Smugglers NEW ⬡
TA24 6JS ☎ 01984 640385 ▤ 01984 641697
e-mail: simonandsuzie@aol.com
Dir: Off A3191, midway between Minehead and Watchet
Just 30 yards from the sandy bay, this 300-year-old inn is
reputedly linked to the local abbey by an underground
tunnel. Open fires now warm the two eating areas and, in fine
weather, diners spill out into the large walled garden.
Extensive menus feature a range of pasta, pizzas and
speciality sausages, with fixed-price options, too. Expect baked
halibut with Welsh rarebit crust; miniature lamb and mint
torte; and wild mushroom and roquefort pitivier.
OPEN: 12-11 (12-3, 6-11 Nov-Feb) **BAR MEALS:** L served all week all
day D served all week all day Av main course £8.50
RESTAURANT: L served Sun 12-3 D served Thurs-Sun 7-10 Av 3 course
fixed price £23.95 ⬤: Smuggled Otter, Otter Ale. **FACILITIES:** Child
facs Children's licence Garden: Large, well maintained walled garden,
benches Dogs allowed Water **NOTES:** Parking 30

BRADFORD-ON-TONE

Map 04 ST12

White Horse Inn ⬡ ♀
Regent St TA4 1HF ☎ 01823 461239 ▤ 01823 461872
e-mail: donna@pmccann1.wanadoo.co.uk
Dir: N of A38 between Taunton & Wellington
The stone-built White Horse stands opposite the church in the
heart of this delightful thatched village, with its Post Office

continued

and general stores. Expect a friendly welcome and good value
food, washed down with London Pride or Cotleigh Tawney
ales. Bar snacks, daily blackboard specials and a full
restaurant menu feature dishes like guinea fowl; rib-eye and
stilton crumble; and baked bream with thyme. There's an
extensive vegetarian selection, too.
OPEN: 11.30-3 5.30-11 (Summer Sat-Sun open all day)
BAR MEALS: L served all week 12-2 D served all week 6.30-9
Av main course £7.50 **RESTAURANT:** L served all week 12-2
D served all week 6.30-9 ⬤: Enterprise Inns ⬤: Cotleigh Tawney,
John Smith's, London Pride, Directors. **FACILITIES:** Garden: Large,
neat garden Dogs allowed **NOTES:** Parking 20

BUTLEIGH

Map 04 ST53

The Rose & Portcullis ♀
Sub Rd BA6 8TQ ☎ 01458 850287 ▤ 01458 850120
Dir: Telephone for directions

A 16th-century free house, drawing its name from the local
lord of the manor's coat of arms. Thatched bars and an
inglenook fireplace are prominent features of the cosy
interior. Large bar and dining room menus are on offer daily.
Typical hot food choices include omelettes, burgers, fish,
curry, steaks, hot baguettes, jacket potatoes, ploughman's,
salads, and vegetarian choices.
OPEN: 12-3 6-11 **BAR MEALS:** L served all week 12-2 D served all
week 7-9 **RESTAURANT:** L served all week 12-2 D served all week
7-9 ⬤: Free House ⬤: Interbrew Flowers IPA, Butcombe Bitter,
Archers Best. ♀: 7 **FACILITIES:** Child facs Garden: Dogs allowed
NOTES: Parking 50

CHEW MAGNA

Map 04 ST56

Pick of the Pubs

The Bear and Swan NEW ♀
South Pde BS40 8SL
The Bear and Swan had a complete face lift six years ago
when the current proprietors turned it into the light airy,
oak beamed gastro-pub that it is today. The bar has a
large open fire, comfy chairs and tables, real ales, and a
good selection of fine wines and beers. A big screen
shows requested sports games. The restaurant offers a
daily changing menu made from the finest locally sourced
produce, along with an à la carte menu with a large range
of fish, game, seafood, local meats and vegetarian dishes.
A lunchtime menu in the bar highlights filled baguettes,
soups and old favourites like locally made sausages, mash
and mustard gravy; and gammon, free range eggs and
chips. This list changes daily, too, to ensure that only the
freshest produce is used. Fish aficionados will find
different surprises everyday - from wild seabass served

continued

with prawn spring roll and sweet chilli sauce to brochette of scallops wrapped in smoky bacon with mixed leaves.
OPEN: 12-11 (Sun 12-10.30) **BAR MEALS:** L served all week 12-2 D served Mon-Sat 7-9.30 Av main course £6.50
RESTAURANT: L served all week 12-2 D served Mon-Sat 7-9.30 Av 3 course à la carte £25 **◖:** Butcombe Bitter, Courage Best. **♀:** 10 **FACILITIES:** Garden: Seating area, beautifully designed Dogs allowed Water bowls **NOTES:** Parking 15

Pony & Trap ♀
Newtown BS40 8TQ ☎ 01275 332627
A warm welcome and traditional home-cooked food await visitors to this unspoiled 200-year-old country pub. There's a wide range of real ales, keg and traditional ciders at the bar, and the large garden at the back offers sensational views over the surrounding countryside. A constantly changing menu of appetising meals ranges from country pies, casseroles and curries to fresh fish, pasta and vegetarian dishes. Small portions are provided for children.
OPEN: 12-3 7-11 (Fri-Sat 5-11) **BAR MEALS:** L served all week 12-2 D served all week 7-9.30 Fri-Sat 5-9.30 **RESTAURANT:** L served all week 12-2 D served all week 7-9.30 **◖:** Punch Taverns **◖:** Bass, Butcombe Bitter. **FACILITIES:** Garden: Terraced area overlooking garden and valley Dogs allowed Water **NOTES:** Parking 50

CLAPTON-IN-GORDANO   Map 04 ST47

The Black Horse ♀
Clevedon Ln BS20 7RH ☎ 01275 842105

Built in the 14th-century, a genuinely unspoilt, traditional country inn with flagstone floors, wooden settles and a large open fireplace. For a while it housed village miscreants, and one window still has prison bars on it. Simple bar food includes various ploughman's, hot filled baguettes, chilli and home-made soups. There is a large beer garden with a children's play area. Ideal area for walks.
OPEN: 11-2.30 5-11 (All day Fri-Sun) **BAR MEALS:** L served Mon-Sat 12-2 No food Sun Av main course £5.50 **◖:** Enterprise Inns **◖:** Scottish Courage Courage Best, Smiles Best, Interbrew Bass, Fuller's London Pride. **FACILITIES:** Garden: Large garden, patio Dogs allowed **NOTES:** Parking 40 No credit cards

CLUTTON   Map 04 ST65

Pick of the Pubs

The Hunters Rest ◆◆◆◆ ♀
King Ln, Clutton Hill BS39 5QL
☎ 01761 452303 ▤ 01761 453308
e-mail: info@huntersrest.co.uk web: www.huntersrest.co.uk
See Pick of the Pubs on page 424

COMBE HAY   Map 04 ST75

Pick of the Pubs

The Wheatsheaf Inn ⌂⇨ ♀
BA2 7EG ☎ 01225 833504 ▤ 01225 833504
e-mail: jakic@btclick.com
Dir: *From Bath take A369 (Exeter rd) to Odd Down. Left at park towards Combe Hay. Follow for 2m to thatched cottage & turn left*

This pretty, black and white timbered free house nestles on a peaceful hillside, close to the route of the former Somerset Coal Canal. Just two miles south of Bath off the A367, the 17th-century building is decorated with flowers in summer, and the attractively terraced garden is an ideal spot for alfresco summer dining. The rambling, unspoilt bar is furnished with massive wooden tables and sporting prints, and there's also an open log fire in cold weather. An integral part of the local community, this picturesque setting has also featured as a BBC TV documentary location. The varied blackboard menu features ploughman's lunches, as well as home-cooked dishes such as pies and seasonal local game. Typical choices might include steak and kidney pie or lamb and apricot pie, whilst the daily fresh fish specials range from John Dory or sea bass to mussels, scallops or cod.
OPEN: 11-3 6-11 (Fri-Sat 11-11, Sun 12-10.30 Easter-Sep all dya everyday) Closed: 25-26 Dec **BAR MEALS:** L served all week 12-2.30 D served all week 6.30-9.30 **RESTAURANT:** L served all week 12-2 D served all week 6.30-9.30 **◖:** Free House **◖:** Speckled Hen, Barnstormer, Doom Bar, Tunnel Vision. **♀:** 6 **FACILITIES:** Garden: Large south facing garden Dogs allowed on leads **NOTES:** Parking 100

CRANMORE   Map 04 ST64

Strode Arms ♀
BA4 4QJ ☎ 01749 880450 ▤ 01749 880823
Dir: *S of A361, 3.5m E of Shepton Mallet, 7.5m W of Frome*
Rambling, mostly 15th-century building, formerly a farmhouse and coaching inn, with a splendid front terrace overlooking the village duck pond. Spacious bar areas are neatly laid-out with comfortable country furnishings and warmed by open log fires. Both the varied printed menu and daily specials draw local diners and visitors to the nearby East Somerset Railway. From the board order, perhaps, smoked haddock and cod fishcakes, peppered rib of beef with a shallot and red wine sauce, braised lambs' heart with lemon and lime stuffing and, for pudding, a home-made coconut and orange tart.
OPEN: 11.30-2.30 6-11 Oct-Mar closed Sun evening
BAR MEALS: L served all week 12-2 D served Mon-Sat 6.30-9 Av main course £8 **RESTAURANT:** L served all week 12-2 D served Mon-Sat 6.30-9 **◖:** Wadworth **◖:** Henry's IPA, Wadworth 6X, JCB. **♀:** 7 **FACILITIES:** Garden: Beer garden, patio, outdoor eating Dogs allowed **NOTES:** Parking 24

Pick of the Pubs

CLUTTON – SOMERSET

The Hunters Rest

When the Earl of Warwick built The Hunter's Rest Inn, as a hunting lodge for himself in around 1750, he picked his spot perfectly - the beautiful countryside high on Clutton Hill has commanding views over the Cam Valley to the Mendip Hills and over the Chew Valley to the port of Bristol.

Later it became a tavern for the local north Somerset coal-mining community. The coal is long gone, and the new clientele can now expect the character and atmosphere of a delightful country inn combined with high standards and amenities. In summer the landscaped gardens can be explored by way of their miniature railway, or over a cooling drink. Food includes a wide selection of cold meats, oggies, grills, and mains, with vegetarian dishes well represented, and a separate children's menu. Specials might include sea bass fillet with lemon butter sauce; bacon wrapped chicken with wild mushroom risotto; ham and free-range eggs, chips and salad; smoked haddock fishcakes, dill mayonnaise; pork loin, cider and mustard sauce; lamb shank, rosemary and garlic gravy; roast pepper and goats cheese salad, balsamic dressing; local sausages, spring onion mash, shallot gravy; and tuna steak, lime, chilli and coriander butter, green salad. Desserts like apple crumble pie and chocolate indulgence are perennially popular. Five individually decorated bedrooms with stunning bathrooms offer a serious temptation to stay.

OPEN: 11.30-3 6-11 (All day Sun in summer)
BAR MEALS: L served all week 12-2 D served all week 6.30-9.45 (Sun 12-2.30, 6.30-9) Av main course £8
RESTAURANT: L served all week 12-2 D served all week 6.30-9.45 Av 3 course à la carte £15
🍺: Free House
🍺: Interbrew Bass, Otter Ale, Courage Best, Wadworth 6X. ♀: 14
FACILITIES: Child facs Garden: Large landscaped areas with country views Dogs allowed Water
NOTES: Parking 80
ROOMS: 5 bedrooms en suite 2 family rooms s£60 d£85

♦♦♦♦ ♀   Map 04 ST65
King Ln, Clutton Hill BS39 5QL
☎ 01761 452303
📄 01761 453308
🄴 info@huntersrest.co.uk
Ⓦ www.huntersrest.co.uk
Dir: Follow signs for Wells A37 through village of Pensford, at large rdbt turn left towards Bath, after 100 mtrs right into country lane, pub 1m up hill

CREWKERNE

Map 04 ST40

The Manor Arms ◆◆◆ ☼

North Perrott TA18 7SG ☎ 01460 72901 📠 01460 74055
e-mail: bookings@manorarmshotel.co.uk
Dir: *From A30 take A3066 towards Bridport. N Perrott 1.5m*
On the Dorset-Somerset border, this 16th-century Grade II
listed pub and its neighbouring hamstone cottages overlook
the village green. The popular River Parrett trail runs by the
door. The inn has been lovingly restored and an inglenook
fireplace, flagstone floors and oak beams are among the
charming features inside. Bar food includes fillet steak
medallions, pan-fried whole plaice, shank of lamb, and
chicken supreme.
OPEN: 11-11 (Sun 12-2.30 7-10.30) **BAR MEALS:** L served all week
12-2 D served all week 7-9.30 **RESTAURANT:** L served all week
12-2 D served all week 7-9.30 ⊕: Free House ◀: Butcombe, Otter,
Fullers London Pride, 5 guest ales. ☼: 8 **FACILITIES:** Child facs
Garden: Secluded, lawn, Large wooden tables **NOTES:** Parking 30
ROOMS: 8 bedrooms en suite 1 family room s£45 d£58

CROSCOMBE

Map 04 ST54

The Bull Terrier ◆◆◆

Long St BA5 3QJ ☎ 01749 343658
e-mail: barry.vidler@bullterrierpub.co.uk
Dir: *Half way between Wells & Shepton Mallet on the A371*
Formerly known as the 'Rose and Crown', the name of this
unspoiled village free house was changed in 1976. First
licensed in 1612, this is one of Somerset's oldest pubs. The
building itself dates from the late 15th century, though the
fireplace and ceiling in the inglenook bar are later additions.
One menu is offered throughout, including ginger chicken;
bacon, mushroom and tomato pasta special; hot smoked
mackerel with horseradish; and vegan tomato crumble.
OPEN: 12-2.30 7-11 (Sun 12-2.30, 7-10.30) **BAR MEALS:** L served
all week 12-2 D served all week 7-9 Av main course £6.25
RESTAURANT: L served all week 12-2 D served all week 7-9
Av 3 course à la carte £14.50 ⊕: Free House ◀: Butcombe,
Courage Directors, Marston's Pedigree, Greene King Old Speckled
Hen. **FACILITIES:** Garden: Patio, walled garden Dogs allowed
Water bowls **NOTES:** Parking 3 **ROOMS:** 2 bedrooms en suite
s£30 d£50 No children overnight

CROWCOMBE

Map 03 ST13

Carew Arms ⛫ ☼

TA4 4AD ☎ 01984 618631 📠 01984 618428
e-mail: info@thecarewarms.co.uk
Dir: *Village is 10 miles from both Taunton and Minehead, off A358*

Set in glorious Somerset countryside, this friendly pub offers
local beers, including Exmoor and Otter Ales. These
accompany hearty meals such as local venison fillets with
continued

braised cabbage and field mushrooms; tender brisket of beer
with colcannon potatoes; and confit of duck legs with
parmentier potatoes & damson chutney. A particular speciality
is The Carew Arms shepherd's pie. Fresh fish choices usually
include mussels, Dover sole, king scallops and sea bass.
OPEN: 11-3 6-11 (Sat-Sun Apr-Sep phone for details)
BAR MEALS: L served all week 12-2 D served all week 7-9.30
Av main course £8 **RESTAURANT:** L served all week 12-2.30
D served Mon-Sat 7-10 Av 3 course à la carte £24 ⊕: Free House
◀: Exmoor Ale, Otter Ale, Cotleigh Ales. ☼: 8
FACILITIES: Garden: Beautiful garden with countryside views Dogs
allowed **NOTES:** Parking 40

DINNINGTON

Map 04 ST41

Dinnington Docks

TA17 8SX ☎ 01460 52397 📠 01460 52397
e-mail: hilary@dinningtondocks.co.uk
Dir: *On A303 between South Petherton & Ilminster*
Formerly the Rose & Crown, and licensed for over 250 years,
this traditional village pub is situated on the old Fosse Way,
and has a very relaxed atmosphere and friendly locals. Rail or
maritime enthusiasts will enjoy the large collection of
memorabilia, and it's an ideal location for cycling and
walking. Roast lunch available every day, along with local
beers and ciders. Channel 4's *Time Team* used the pub as its
base while filming a programme on mosaics found in a
nearby field.
OPEN: 11.30-3.30 6-11 **BAR MEALS:** L served all week 12-2.30
D served all week 6-9.30 Av main course £6.50
RESTAURANT: L served all week 12-2.30 D served all week 6-9.30
Av 3 course à la carte £12.50 ⊕: Free House ◀: Butcombe Bitter,
Wadworth 6X, Guest Ales. **FACILITIES:** Child facs Garden: Large
garden with children's play area Dogs allowed Water provided
NOTES: Parking 30

DITCHEAT

Map 04 ST63

The Manor House Inn ☼

BA4 6RB ☎ 01749 860276 📠 0870 286 3379
e-mail: themanorhouseinn@ditcheat.co.uk
Dir: *from Shepton Mallet take Castle Cary road, after 3m right to Ditcheat*

Over the years since its first appearance as The White Hart,
this red-brick pub has had a number of names, but the
current owners choose to subtitle it "The Heart of Somerset
Hospitality." There are flagstone floors, and a menu that
offers the likes of lamb and mint sausages, grilled calves' liver
with bacon on bubble and squeak cake, wild mushroom and
brandy risotto, and individual aubergine charlotte with spicy
vegetable filling. There are also light luncheons, ciabattas, and
specials.
OPEN: 12-2.30 7-10 **BAR MEALS:** L served all week 12-2.30
D served all week 6-10 Sun 12-2.30, 7-9 Av main course £10
continued

England

DITCHEAT continued

RESTAURANT: L served all week 12-2 D served all week 7-9.30 Sun 12-2.30, 7-9 Av 3 course à la carte £19.50 ☺: Free House ☖: Butcombe, Scottish Courage John Smith's & Guest Ales. ♀: 19 **FACILITIES:** Garden: Dogs allowed Water, toys **NOTES:** Parking 25

EAST COKER
Map 04 ST51

Pick of the Pubs

The Helyar Arms ♦♦♦♦ ☺ ♀
Moor Ln BA22 9JR ☎ 01935 862332 ◻ 01935 864129
e-mail: info@helyar-arms.co.uk web: www.helyar-arms.co.uk
Dir: 3m from Yeovil. Take A57 or A30 and follow East Coker signs
A 'real food inn', this charming 15th-century inn was reputedly named after Archdeacon Helyar, a chaplain to Queen Elizabeth I. A Grade II listed building, it dates back in part to 1468. Log fires warm the old world bar, while the separate restaurant was restored from an original apple loft. The kitchen makes full use of local produce, especially cheeses, beef and bread, with suppliers given credit on the menus. From a selection that also includes grills and pasta dishes, you'll find starters like soused herring fillets; or baked fresh figs, followed by such mains as salmon fish cake; beetroot tarte Tatin; coq au vin; or sautéed loin of Somerset free-range pork. Don't forget to look up the daily special list of desserts which supplements those on the menu: expect blackberry crème brûlée or hot valrhona chocolate fondant pudding, plus a choice of ice creams.
OPEN: 11-3 6-11 (Sun 12-3,6-10.30) **BAR MEALS:** L served all week 12-2.30 D served all week 6.30-9.30 Sun 12-4.30 Jan-Apr Av main course £11 **RESTAURANT:** L served all week 12-2.30 D served all week 6.30-9.30 Sun 12-4.30 Jan-Apr Av 3 course à la carte £20 ☺: Punch Taverns ☖: Bass, Flowers IPA, Butcombe Bitter. ♀: 30 **FACILITIES:** Child facs Garden: Grassed area seats 40 Dogs allowed **NOTES:** Parking 40
ROOMS: 6 bedrooms en suite 3 family rooms s£59 d£70

EXFORD
Map 03 SS83

Pick of the Pubs

The Crown Hotel ★★★ ☺☺ 〜 ♀
TA24 7PP ☎ 01643 831554 ◻ 01643 831665
e-mail: info@crownhotelexmoor.co.uk
web: www.crownhotelexmoor.co.uk
Dir: From M5 junct 25 follow Taunton signs. Take A358 then B3224 via Wheddon Cross to Exford

This 17th-century pub, reputedly Exmoor's oldest, is set in

three acres of water gardens and woodland, with its own stabling and stretch of salmon fishing in the heart of Exmoor National Park. At one time it used to provide livery for up to forty horses, being the mid way point for pilgrims from Taunton to Barnstaple. Today, the pub serves food in both the cosy bar and smart non-smoking dining room that makes imaginative use of good quality local produce. Expect starters like half pint prawns with marie rose sauce; grilled goat's cheese, red onion marmalade and pickled walnuts; and chicken liver parfait with onion marmalade. Mains might include battered cod with chips and peas; beef teriyaki with stir-fry; braised lamb shank with spring onion mash and a red wine jus; and game pie with spiced red cabbage. Rum and raisin cream pot; and sticky toffee pudding should prove irresistible. Many of the recently refurbished en suite bedrooms offer superb views of the surrounding moorland scenery.
OPEN: 11-3 6-11 **BAR MEALS:** L served all week 12-2 D served all week 6.30-9.30 **RESTAURANT:** L served Sun 12-2 D served all week 7-9 ☺: Free House ☖: Exmoor Ale, Gold & Stag, Cotleigh Tawny, Cotleigh 25th Anniversary Brew. ♀: 8 **FACILITIES:** Garden: Water garden, next to stream Dogs allowed Water **NOTES:** Parking 20 **ROOMS:** 17 bedrooms en suite 1 family room

---

FAULKLAND
Map 04 ST75

The Faulkland Inn ♀
BA3 5UH ☎ 01373 834312 e-mail: thefaulklandinn@onetel.com
Dir: On the A366 between Radstock and Trowbridge, 17m from Bristol & the M4/M5

Former coaching inn, under new ownership, set in a village complete with a green, stocks, standing stones and pond. A number of guest ales and food specials appeal to the returning customers. There is a bar menu offering light and simple dishes, combined with more traditional favourites, and a carte serving larger dishes in the evening. Typical dishes include beef wellington with red wine jus, grilled calves' liver and smoked bacon with parsnip bubble and squeak, and a range of specials and vegetarian options are available.
OPEN: 12-3 6-11 (Sun 12-3, 6.30-10.30) **BAR MEALS:** L served all week 12-2 D served all week 7-9.30 Av main course £6 **RESTAURANT:** L served all week 12-2 D served all week 7-9.30 ☺: Free House ☖: Butcombe. ♀: 8 **FACILITIES:** Garden: Food served outside, skittle alley **NOTES:** Parking 30

 Pubs offering a good choice of fish on their menu

---

continued

Tuckers Grave

Faulkland BA3 5XF ☎ 01373 834230
Tapped ales and farm cider are served at Somerset's smallest pub, a tiny atmospheric bar with old settles. Lunchtime sandwiches and ploughman's lunches are available, and a large lawn with flower borders makes an attractive outdoor seating area. The grave in the pub's name is the unmarked one of Edward Tucker, who hung himself here in 1747.
OPEN: 11-3 6-11 Closed: Dec 25 ◖▪: Interbrew Bass, Butcombe Bitter. **FACILITIES:** Garden: Large lawns with flower borders Dogs allowed Water

---

FITZHEAD　　　　　　　　　　　　　Map 03 ST12

Fitzhead Inn ◆◆◆

TA4 3JP ☎ 01823 400667

Juwards Honiton ales join Cotleigh Tawny and Exmoor Fox in the bar of this 250-year-old pub, hidden away in the Vale of Taunton. Whisky drinkers can choose from a range of 36 malts, whilst seven en-suite bedrooms and a courtyard garden complete the picture. Appetising dishes like pan-seared venison with roasted onions and mushrooms; cod fillet with herb crust on a saffron sauce; and roasted rack of lamb on ratatouille are featured on the menu.
OPEN: 12-3 7-11 (Closed Mon-Sat Lunch) Closed: 25-26 Dec
BAR MEALS: L served Sun D served all week 7-9.45 (Sun 7-9.30) Av main course £10 **RESTAURANT:** L served Sun 12-2 D served all week 7-9.45 Av 3 course à la carte £20 ◖: Free House ◖▪: Cotleigh Tawny, Fuller's London Pride, Juwards Ales, Interbrew Bass.
FACILITIES: Child facs Garden: Courtyard Dogs allowed
ROOMS: 7 bedrooms en suite 1 family room s£35 d£50
NOTES: No credit cards

FRESHFORD　　　　　　　　　　　　Map 04 ST76

The Inn at Freshford ♀

BA2 6EG ☎ 01225 722250 ▤ 01225 723887
Dir: 1m from A36 between Beckington & Limpley Stoke
With its 15th-century origins, and log fires adding to its warm and friendly atmosphere, this popular inn in the Limpley Valley is an ideal base for walking, especially along the Kennet & Avon Canal. Extensive gardens. The à la carte menu changes weekly to show the range of food available, and a daily specials board and large children's menu complete the variety. Typical home-made dishes are pâtés, steak and ale pie, lasagne and desserts; a nice selection of fish dishes includes fresh local trout.
OPEN: 11-3 6-11 **BAR MEALS:** L served all week 12-2 D served all week 6-9 **RESTAURANT:** L served all week 12-2 D served all week 6-9 ◖: Latona Leisure ◖▪: Wadworth 6X, Butcombe Bitter, Interbrew Bass, Scottish Courage Courage Best. ♀: 12
FACILITIES: Garden: Large terraced garden Dogs allowed Water
NOTES: Parking 60

FROME　　　　　　　　　　　　　　Map 04 ST74

Pick of the Pubs

The Horse & Groom ⌣◎ ♀

East Woodlands BA11 5LY ☎ 01373 462802 ▤ 01373 462802
e-mail: horse.and.groom@care4free.net
Dir: A361 towards Trowbridge, cross B3092 rdbt, take immediate right towards East Woodlands, pub 1m on left

This friendly inn can be found at the end of a single-track lane, surrounded by fields and woods. Before becoming a pub it was a smallholding, and in the bar a framed lease suggests it became The Horse & Jockey (which is why regulars call it The Jockey) in 1785. A photograph obviously taken much later still shows pigsties in what's now the secluded award-winning garden. Huge flagstones form the floor of the bar, and there's a secure stableyard outside if you want to arrive by horse. Regulars, some busy playing dominoes, will attest to the presence of a friendly pair of ghosts. Three menus, updated on a rolling basis, offer a vast choice. The main menu, for example, might list roast haunch of venison with blueberries; smoked artichoke heart and potato filo tart; or beef fillet with Black Forest ham and mozzarella. Desserts and luxurious coffees are also worth consideration.
OPEN: 11.30-2.30 6.30-11 (Sun 12-3, 7-10)
BAR MEALS: L served Tue-Sun 12-2 D served Tue-Sat 6.30-9 (Sun 12-2.30) Av main course £8.50 **RESTAURANT:** L served Tue-Sun 12-2 D served Tue-Sat 6.30-9 (Sun 12-2.30) Av 3 course à la carte £18.50 ◖: ◖▪: Wadworth 6X, Butcombe Bitter, Branscombe Branoc, Archers Golden. ♀: 7
FACILITIES: Garden: Large garden with fruit trees and 7 tables Dogs allowed Water **NOTES:** Parking 20

♀ **7** Number of wines by the glass

FROME continued

Pick of the Pubs

The Talbot 15th-Century Coaching Inn ◆◆◆◆
Selwood St, Mells BA11 3PN
☎ 01373 812254 ▤ 01373 813599
e-mail: roger@talbotinn.com web: www.talbotinn.com
Dir: From A36(T), R onto A361 to Frome, then A362 towards
Radstock, 0.5m then L to Mells 2.5m

Rambling 15th-century, stone coaching inn entered
through an archway into an informally planted cobbled
courtyard, incorporating a beautiful vine-covered pergola,
and laid out with Provençal-style chairs and tables. Inside
the inn itself are lots of little terracotta-painted, stone-
floored bars and eating areas, including a restaurant with
low oak-beamed ceilings, stripped pews, wheelback
chairs, candles in bottles, and fresh flowers on the tables.
A small corridor leads to another restaurant at the front.
English/French-influenced lunch and dinner menus offer a
good selection of largely locally sourced meat, fish, game
and vegetarian dishes. Starters include fine chicken liver
parfait with spiced apple chutney and toast; and fresh
Devon mussels cooked in white wine and onions.
Examples of main courses include confit leg of Barbary
duck with braised red cabbage and peppercorn sauce;
grilled bratwurst with garlic mash and coarse grain
mustard sauce; steamed steak and kidney pudding; and
wild mushroom and asparagus tagliatelle in a herb cream
sauce. Accommodation is offered in eight individually
styled rooms.
OPEN: 12-2.30 6.30-11 (Sun 12-3 7-10.30) Closed: 25-26 Dec
BAR MEALS: L served all week 12-2 D served all week 7-9
Av main course £7.50 **RESTAURANT:** L served all week 12-2
D served all week 7-9 Av 3 course à la carte £21 ⊟: Free House
◀: Butcombe Bitter & guest ales. **FACILITIES:** Garden: Cottage
garden Dogs allowed Water **NOTES:** Parking 10
ROOMS: 8 bedrooms en suite 2 family rooms s£75 d£95

HASELBURY PLUCKNETT   Map 04 ST41

Pick of the Pubs

The White Horse at Haselbury 🐟 ♀
North St TA18 7RJ ☎ 01460 78873
e-mail: haselbury@btconnect.com
Dir: Just off A30 between Crewkerne & Yeovil on B3066
After 20 years of trading as the Haselbury Inn, the White
Horse has now returned to its original name. A major
refurbishment has given the building a fresh, warm
feeling whilst preserving the original character of exposed

stone, brickwork and open fires. Owners Patrick and Jan
Howard have created 'a restaurant that sells good real
ale', and they've successfully introduced a complete no-
smoking policy throughout the bar-restaurant. The
modern English cuisine is founded on locally-sourced
fresh ingredients. Fish specials might include baked cod
with pesto crust; poached salmon with wine and berries;
or grilled turbot with chargrilled Mediterranean
vegetables. Other options range from rack of lamb on
cheddar and rosemary rösti to creamy vegetable crumble
in rich cheese sauce. There's also a set lunch menu, and
early bird dinners are served until 8.00pm; booking is
recommended at busy times.

The White Horse at Haselbury

OPEN: 11.45-2.30 6-11 **BAR MEALS:** L served all week 12-2
D served all week 6.30-9.30 Sun 12-3 Av main course £9
⊟: Free House ◀: Palmers IPA, Otter Ale. ♀: 10
FACILITIES: Garden: Small cottage style garden
NOTES: Parking 12 ⊗

HINTON BLEWETT   Map 04 ST55

Ring O'Bells ♀
BS39 5AN ☎ 01761 452239 ▤ 01761 451245
e-mail: jonboy2ringer@aol.com
Dir: 11 miles S of Bristol on A37 toward Wells, small road signed in
Clutton & Temple Cloud
On the edge of the Mendips, this 200-year-old pub offers
good views of the Chew Valley. An all-year-round cosy
atmosphere is boosted by a log fire in winter, and a wide
choice of real ales. The bar-loving shove ha'penny players
attract a good following. Good value dishes include beef in
Guinness served in a giant Yorkshire pudding, and Persian
chicken curry. Young children should enjoy the Tyke's
Playhouse in the enclosed garden.
OPEN: 11-3.30 5-11 (Sat 11-4, 6-11 Sun 12-4, 7-10.30)
BAR MEALS: L served all week 12-2 D served all week 6.30-10
RESTAURANT: L served all week 12-2 D served all week 7-10 (Sat
12-2.30, 12-2.30) ⊟: Free House ◀: Buttcombe, Wadworth 6X,
Fuller's London Pride, Wickwar BOB. **FACILITIES:** Child facs
Garden: Enclosed garden with lovely views Dogs allowed Water
NOTES: Parking 20

HINTON ST GEORGE   Map 04 ST41

Pick of the Pubs

The Lord Poulett Arms ◆◆◆◆ 🐟 ♀
High St TA17 8SE ☎ 01460 73149 e-mail: shill@datrix.co.uk
web: www.lordpoulettarms.com
See Pick of the Pubs on opposite page

continued

Pick of the Pubs

HINTON ST GEORGE – SOMERSET

The Lord Poulett Arms

Set in one of Somerset's prettiest villages, this thatched pub, built in 1680, has been restored by its owners, Michelle Paynton and Stephen Hill, using the beautiful local Ham stone.

Charming original features such as flagstone floors and fireplaces, making five in all including a 11ft wide inglenook, have been revealed during the refurbishment. In keeping with its venerable old age, the inn has been furnished with period country antiques. It pretty garden has a formal area with pergola, herb garden and boules piste, with a pretty meadow containing fruit trees, hammock and an ancient fives wall. Real ales are served from the barrel, and the monthly-changing menu places a strong emphasis on local, fresh, seasonal and often organic produce, including a great selection of fish and shellfish.

Choices might include chowder of monkfish tail with langoustines, shallots and smoked bacon; fillet of sea bream with a lemon and samphire risotto; sweet soy-glazed bacon loin with a faggot and champ; smoked organic salmon, chive, crème fraîche, and wild rocket pesto; braised pork shoulder with carrot mash; lamb and kidney suet pudding; and steamed fillet of organic salmon and mussels with sweet garlic sauce. Anyone looking for things to do nearby will be pleased to discover the National Trust property of Montacute House, the Fleet Air Arm Museum, and Worldwide Butterflies.

OPEN: 12-3 6.30-11
BAR MEALS: L served all week-12-2 D served all week 7-9 Av main course £11
RESTAURANT: L served all week 12-2 D served all week 7-9 Av 3 course à la carte £20
⊕: Free House
▄: Butcombe Bitter, Hopback, Otter, Branscombe. ♀: 7
FACILITIES: Garden: fruit trees and poleta wall Boules piste Dogs allowed Water bowl
NOTES: Parking 10
ROOMS: 4 bedrooms en suite 4 family rooms s£48 d£72

◆◆◆◆ ⌦ ♀ Map 04 ST41
High St TA17 8SE
☎ 01460 73149
📧 shill@datrix.co.uk
🌐 www.lordpoulettarms.com
Dir: 2m N of Crewkerne, 1.5m S of A303

HOLCOMBE
Map 04 ST64

The Ring O'Roses NEW ★★ ♀
Stratton Rd BA3 5EB ☎ 01761 232478 ▤ 01761 233737
e-mail: info@ringoroses.co.uk
Dir: On A367 to Stratton on The Fosse, take hidden left turn opposite Downside Abbey signed Holcombe, take next right, pub 1.5m on left
This country inn boasts a large garden with views of nearby Downside Abbey and the Somerset countryside. The lunch menu runs to various sandwiches and wraps, while the evening choice is supplemented by a specials board: start with crispy squid with sweet chilli dip; or asparagus tips with tomato and basil hollandaise sauce, and move on to grilled Scottish salmon with cucumber and prawn cream; pork stroganoff; or spinach and ricotta ravioli.
OPEN: 11.30-11 (Sat 11.30-2.30, 6.30-11 Sun 12-2.30, 7-10.30)
BAR MEALS: L served all week 12-2 D served all week 7-9 Sun 12-1.30, 7-8.30 Av main course £13.50 **RESTAURANT:** L served all week 12-2 D served all week 7-9 Sun 12-1.30, 7-8.30 Av 3 course à la carte £22 ◀: Otter Ale, Otter Bitter, Guinness. ♀: 7
FACILITIES: Large garden with views over Somerset Dogs allowed
NOTES: Parking 40 **ROOMS:** 8 bedrooms en suite 1 family room s£65 d£85 No children overnight

ILCHESTER
Map 04 ST52

Ilchester Arms ♦♦♦♦ ♀
The Square BA22 8LN ☎ 01935 840220 ▤ 01935 841353
Dir: From A303 take A37 to Ilchester/Yeovil, left towards Ilchester at 2nd sign marked Ilchester. Hotel 100yds on right
First licensed in 1686, this elegant Georgian building was owned between 1962 and 1985 by the man who developed Ilchester cheese. Brendan McGee, the head chef, and his wife Lucy are well settled in now, enabling Brendan to create an extensive bistro menu offering pan-fried fillet of red snapper, rich lamb casserole, and vegetable moussaka. Sandwiches, paninis, salads, the house burger, and beef and ale pie are available at the bar.
OPEN: 11-11 Closed: 26 Dec **BAR MEALS:** L served all week 12-2.30 D served Mon-Sat 7-9.30 (Sun 12-2.30) Av main course £8
RESTAURANT: L served all week 12-2.30 D served Mon-Sat 7-9.30 (Sun 12-2.30) Av 3 course à la carte £21.50 ☺: Free House
◀: Buttcombe, Flowers IPA & regularly changing ales from local breweries. **FACILITIES:** Child facs Children's licence Garden: Enclosed, walled English garden **NOTES:** Parking 15
ROOMS: 7 bedrooms en suite 2 family rooms s£60 d£75

ILMINSTER
Map 04 ST31

New Inn
Dowlish Wake TA19 0NZ ☎ 01460 52413
Dir: From Ilminster follow signs for Kingstone then Dowlish Wake
A 350-year-old stone-built pub tucked away in a quiet village close to Perry's thatched cider mill. There are two bars with woodburning stoves, bar billiards and a skittle alley. The menu features local produce and West Country specialities, including fish, steaks and home-made pies.
OPEN: 11-3 6-11 (Sun 12-3, 7-10.30) **BAR MEALS:** L served all week 12-2.30 D served Tue-Sat 6-9.30 ☺: Free House
◀: Butcombe Bitter, guest beers. **FACILITIES:** Garden: Beer garden, food served outdoors Dogs allowed **NOTES:** Parking 50

Pubs with this logo do not allow smoking anywhere on their premises

KILVE
Map 03 ST14

The Hood Arms ♦♦♦♦ ▷◇ ♀
TA5 1EA ☎ 01278 741210 ▤ 01278 741477
e-mail: easonhood@aol.com
Dir: Off A39 between Bridgwater & Minehead

This traditional, friendly 17th-century coaching inn is set among the Quantock Hills and provides thirsty walkers with traditional ales (try Exmoor ale). Kilve Beach, within easy walking distance, is famous for its strange 'moonscape' landscape and fossils. A good range of fresh fish is always available, and non-fish choices might include spinach and stilton lasagne or steak and ale pie. Completely refurbished in 2004.
OPEN: 11-3 6-11 **BAR MEALS:** L served all week 12-2.30 D served all week 6.15-9.30 (Winter 7-8.30) Av main course £8.95
RESTAURANT: L served all week 12-2 D served all week 7-9 Winter 7-8.30 Av 3 course à la carte £20 ☺: Free House ◀: Doom Bar, Cotleigh Tawney Ale, Tribute, Exmoor Ale. ♀: 6 **FACILITIES:** Child facs Garden: Walled garden with patios and play area Dogs allowed in some areas, Water **NOTES:** Parking 40 **ROOMS:** 10 bedrooms en suite 4 family rooms s£42 d£72

LANGLEY MARSH
Map 03 ST02

The Three Horseshoes
TA4 2UL ☎ 01984 623763 ▤ 01984 623763
e-mail: marellahopkins@hotmail.com
Dir: M5 junct 25 take B3227 to Wiveliscombe. Turn right up hill at traffic lights. From square turn right and follow Langley Marsh signs, 1m
Time stands still at this handsome 17th-century red sandstone free house, which has had only four landlords during the last century. Here customers benefit from traditional opening hours, beer straight from the barrel - and child-free bars! The landlord's wife prepares fresh, home-cooked meals, incorporating local ingredients and vegetables from the pub garden. Typical dishes on the specials board might include baked black bream with cider and rosemary; pan-fried duck breast with port and honey; and butterbean bourguignon.
OPEN: 12-2.30 7-11 (Sun eve 7-9, in off season) Closed: Early July
BAR MEALS: L served Tues-Sun 12-1.45 D served Tues-Sun 7-9 (Sun eve 7-9) Av main course £7.75 **RESTAURANT:** L served all week D served all week ☺: Free House ◀: Palmer IPA, Otter Ale, Fuller's London Pride, Adnams Southwold. **FACILITIES:** Garden: Enclosed garden with outdoor seating Dogs allowed Water & tethering rings in car park **NOTES:** Parking 6

LANGPORT
Map 04 ST42

The Old Pound Inn ♦♦♦
Aller TA10 0RA ☎ 01458 250469 ▤ 01458 250469
Built as a cider house, the Old Pound Inn dates from 1571 and retains plenty of historic character with oak beams, open fires

continued

and a garden that used to be the village pound. It's a friendly pub with a good reputation for its real ale and home-cooked food, but also provides function facilities for 200 with its own bar. Whimsically named dishes include portly venison, horsy wild boar, and fruit 'n' nut trout.
OPEN: 11-11 **BAR MEALS:** L served all week 12-2.45 D served all week 6-9.45 **RESTAURANT:** L served all week 12-2.45 D served all week 6-9.45 ◼: Butcombe, Butcombe Gold, Yorkshire Bitter, Courage Best. **FACILITIES:** Garden: The old village pound Dogs allowed **NOTES:** Parking 30 **ROOMS:** 6 bedrooms en suite

Rose & Crown
Huish Episcopi TA10 9QT ☎ 01458 250494
Dir: Telephone for directions
Traditional thatched pub which has been in the same family for 140 years. Known locally as 'Eli's - the name of the present owner's father - the Rose & Crown is renowned for its Gothic-style windows and stone-flagged cellar which acts as the bar. Close by are the Somerset Wetlands and the River Parrett Trail, popular with long-distance hikers. A typical menu offers apple, pork and cider cobbler, creamy chicken and broccoli casserole, and roasted vegetable and cheddar tart.
OPEN: 11.30-2.30 5.30-11 (Fri-Sat 11.30-11, Sun 12-10.30) 25 Dec closed eve **BAR MEALS:** L served all week 12-2 D served Mon-Sat 6-7.30 Av main course £6.50 ◼: Free House ◼: Teignworthy Reel Ale, Mystery Tor, Hop Back Summer Lightning, Butcombe Bitter.
FACILITIES: Garden: Mainly lawns, seating, play area Dogs allowed Water **NOTES:** Parking 50 No credit cards

LEIGH UPON MENDIP
Map 04 ST64

The Bell Inn ♀
BA3 5QQ ☎ 01373 812316 ▤ 01373 812434
Dir: Follow the Frome Rd towards Radstock, turn towards Mells and then Leigh-upon-Mendip

The Bell is a 17th-century inn located in the centre of the village on the edge of the Mendip Hills. It was built by the masons who constructed the parish church and who donated the fireplace in the main bar while they were lodging here. Home-cooked dishes include lamb shank, Normandy pork, chicken parmigiana and wild mushroom carbinara. A three-mile walk around the lanes starts and finishes as the pub. Have a go at skittles, pool, darts or shove ha'penny.
OPEN: 12-3 6-11 **BAR MEALS:** L served all week 12-2 D served all week 6.30-9.30 (Sun 12-2.30) Av main course £8
RESTAURANT: L served all week 12-2 D served all week 6.30-9 (Sun 12-2.30) Av 3 course à la carte £16 ◼: Wadworth ◼: Wadworth 6X, Butcombe Bitter, Wadworths JCB, Henrys IPA. ♀: 9
FACILITIES: Child facs Garden: Patio area, grassed area with flower borders Dogs allowed only in skittle alley **NOTES:** Parking 24

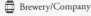
🍺 Brewery/Company

LITTON
Map 04 ST55

The Kings Arms
BA3 4PW ☎ 01761 241301
Full of nooks and crannies, this 15th-century local at the heart of the Mendips has a large garden with a stream running through it, and boasts a separate children's play area and outdoor eating. Menus offer smoked haddock fish pie, home-made chilli, and steak, mushroom and Guinness pie. Kings Arms Platters include pigman's platter - jumbo pork Lincolnshire sausage with eggs and chips.
OPEN: 11-2.30 6-11 (Sun 12-3 7-10.30) **BAR MEALS:** L served all week 12-2.30 D served all week 6.30-10 Av main course £8 ◼: Free House ◼: Bass, Butcombe, Wadworth 6X, Flowers.
FACILITIES: Garden: Dogs allowed in garden only, on lead at all times. **NOTES:** Parking 50

LOVINGTON
Map 04 ST53

Pick of the Pubs

The Pilgrims NEW ▷◁ ♀
BA7 7PT ☎ 01963 240597 e-mail: thejools@btinternet.com
Dir: From A303 take A37 to Lyford, right at lights, 1.5m to The Pilgrims on B3153.
Billing itself as the 'pub that thinks it's a restaurant', The Pilgrims has won many awards. All the food is home made, except the sausages and ice cream. Like most of the ingredients, their transport costs are low: the cheeses are all West Country; bacon comes from Bridport; smoked fish from Hambridge; wet fish from Brixham. Trio of smoked salmon, trout and eel feature as a starter, often sharing the menu with grilled goat's cheese, pesto and sunblushed tomatoes. Sea fish feature prominently, so if you find the likes of sautéed monkfish and scallops with smoked bacon and wild mushrooms; or pan-fried sea bass on celeriac mash with fennel Pernod sauce appealing, head for Lovington. Alternatives include rack of lamb with rich redcurrant and rosemary gravy; and free-range chicken savoyarde with parmesan crust in gruyère and tarragon sauce. Families are welcome, but there's no children's menu since, in the owners' experience, children rarely like them!
OPEN: 12-3 7-11 Closed: Oct **BAR MEALS:** L served Wed-Sun 12-2 D served Tues-Sat 7-9.30 No Av main course £15
RESTAURANT: L served Wed-Sun 12-2 D served Tue-Sat 7-9.30 No Av 3 course à la carte £25 ◼: Cottage Brewing, Champflower, Stowford Press Cider. ♀: 12 **FACILITIES:** Child facs Children's licence Garden: Fenced patio Dogs allowed **NOTES:** Parking 30 ⊛

LOWER VOBSTER
Map 04 ST74

Pick of the Pubs

Vobster Inn ♀
BA3 5RJ ☎ 01373 812920 ▤ 812350
e-mail: vobsterinn@bt.com
Dir: 4m W of Frome
A 17th-century inn of Mendip stone set in four acres of rolling countryside, including a large garden complete with barbecue and established boules pitch. Fresh fish is the speciality of the house, delivered from Cornwall and Devon five times a week to the inn. The owners are also keen supporters of local suppliers and use locally

continued

LOWER VOBSTER continued

produced meats. The cooking is simple, and the menu might start with moules marinere; Thai spiced crab and vegetable spring rolls; and plate of Italian cured meats. The seafood selection could offer you whole Brixham sea bream oven roasted with thyme, garlic and chilli; barramundi fillet with Asian salad; and grilled large whole lemon sole. Meateaters could try Malaysian chicken Kapitan curry; or lamb shank in shiraz gravy. The pudding menu runs to lemon and lime cheesecake; kaffir lime leaf and lemongrass crème brûlée; and classic tiramisu.
OPEN: 12-3 7-11 (Closed Sun eve Jan-Feb)
BAR MEALS: L served all week 12-2 D served all week 7-10 Av main course £10.50 **RESTAURANT:** L served all week 12-2 D served all week 7-11 ⊕: Free House ◖: Butcombe, Scottish Courage Courage Best, Wadworth 6X, London Pride. ♀: 8 **FACILITIES:** Garden: Boule court, 10 tables Dogs allowed Water **NOTES:** Parking 45

LUXBOROUGH   Map 03 SS93

Pick of the Pubs

The Royal Oak Inn
TA23 0SH ☎ 01984 640319 📠 01984 641561
e-mail: info@theroyaloakinnluxborough.co.uk
Dir: From A38 at Washford take minor road S through Roadwater
A 14th-century inn very much at the heart of the local community and farming life in the small Exmoor hamlet of Luxborough. The Blazing Stump bar refers to a parsimonious former landlord who fed the fire only one log at a time. Renovation has left the rustic character intact, with a large open fireplace, low beams and slate floor in the main bar, and tastefully decorated dining areas: the Green Room is ideal for intimate candlelit dinners, the Red Room is perfect for family gatherings or parties, and the Dining Room itself is just off the bar. The fine food and well-kept ales have a well-deserved reputation. Dishes are freshly cooked to order from top quality local produce, and a specials board of daily fish dishes and seasonal specialities is offered in addition to the regular menu. The suntrap courtyard patio makes a delightful setting for a meal or peaceful drink.
OPEN: 12-2.30 6-11 (Mon-Wed 6-10.30, Sun 7-10.30)
BAR MEALS: L served all week 12-2 Av main course £12.95 **RESTAURANT:** L served all week 12-2 D served all week 7-9 Av 3 course à la carte £25 ⊕: Free House ◖: Tawney, Palmer 200, Exmoor Gold, Palmers IPA. **FACILITIES:** Garden: Courtyard garden Dogs allowed Water provided **NOTES:** Parking 18 **ROOMS:** 12 bedrooms 11 en suite s£55 d£65 (♦♦♦)

Not all of the pubs in the guide are open all week or all day. It's always best to check before you travel

Website addresses are included where available. The AA cannot be held responsible for the content of any of these websites

LYNG   Map 04 ST32

Rose & Crown
East Lyng TA3 5AU ☎ 01823 698235
e-mail: derek.mason@btinternet.com
Historic coaching inn, dating from the 13th century, set among the Somerset Levels. The atmosphere is relaxed, and in warmer weather you can sit outside. A menu of typical pub food - ploughman's, omelettes, steaks and scampi - is supplemented by specials such as beef or vegetable curry, chilli, pork chops and pasta and tuna bake. A good choice of popular puddings is offered too, including fresh fruit crumbles, pavlova and treacle tart.
OPEN: 11-2.30 6.30-11 **BAR MEALS:** L served all week 12-1.45 D served all week 7-9 (Sun 12-1.45, 7-8.30) Av main course £7 **RESTAURANT:** L served all week 12-1.45 D served all week 7-9 (Sun 12-1.45, 7-8.30) ⊕: Free House ◖: Butcombe Bitter & Gold, Palmer 200 Premium Ale. **FACILITIES:** Garden: Large garden, approx 8 tables **NOTES:** Parking 40

MARSTON MAGNA   Map 04 ST52

The Marston Inn
BA22 8BX ☎ 01935 850365 📠 01935 850397
Dir: Telephone for directions
Grade II listed building close to Yeovilton Air Museum, and handy for the link road to the West Country. The oldest parts of the inn are reputed to be haunted, and there's a skittle alley for the energetic. The menu offers rump steak with stilton sauce, chicken breast grilled with mushrooms, seafood fettuccine, and ham and eggs, washed down with seasonal guest ales.
OPEN: 12-2.30 6-11 Open all day Sat, Sun 12-10.30 Jun-Sep open 3pm **BAR MEALS:** L served all week 12-2 D served Mon-Sat 6-9.30 Av main course £5.95 **RESTAURANT:** L served all week 12-2 D served Mon-Sat 6-9.30 Av 3 course à la carte £15 ⊕: ◖: Banks Bitter, Worthington Cream Flow, Seasonal Guest Ale. **FACILITIES:** Garden: Walled patio area, secure play area Dogs allowed Water & Toys **NOTES:** Parking 16

MARTOCK   Map 04 ST41

The Nag's Head Inn
East St TA12 6NF
Dir: Telephone for directions
A 200-year-old former cider house set in a picturesque village in rural south Somerset. Al fresco eating and drinking is encouraged in the landscaped garden and huge orchard area, with the home-made food being much sought after locally. Lamb shanks, venison casserole, various Thai and other oriental dishes, and delicious steaks are also available in the bar and restaurant. Readers reports welcome.
OPEN: 12-2.30 6-11 Open all day Sat-Sun **BAR MEALS:** L served Mon-Sun 12-2 D served Mon-Sat 6-9 **RESTAURANT:** L served Mon-Sun 12-2 D served Mon-Sat 6-8.30 ◖: Tanglefoot, Worthington, Stella Artois, Carling. **FACILITIES:** Garden: Landscaped garden with flower beds Dogs allowed Water, Biscuits **NOTES:** Parking 25

MONKSILVER   Map 03 ST03

Pick of the Pubs

The Notley Arms ♀
TA4 4JB ☎ 01984 656217
See Pick of the Pubs on opposite page

Pick of the Pubs

MONKSILVER – SOMERSET

The Notley Arms

A 19th-century English country dining pub on the edge of Exmoor with some interesting African influences, the Notley Arms is named after a prominent local family. It was once connected with old Cleeve Abbey, and started out, as many pubs did, as a resting place for visiting monks.

Building on a reputation for good home cooking, owners Jane and Russell Deary have made this a dining destination with a great range of food on offer. The Dearys have come from Zimbabwe where they were farmers and ran a country club. They clearly relate to the farming community and other food producers in their region, and have a policy of local sourcing for their ingredients, which include Somerset lamb, Exmoor sirloin steaks, and fresh fish and seafood from Cornwall for their daily changing selection. They are also introducing some Zimbabwean and South African dishes such as

ostrich fillet (reared in Devon), and biltong, air-dried beef, produced by a fellow Zimbabwean in Torquay. These delicacies are offered alongside house favourites such as butternut squash soup, Lancashire hotpot, fresh pasta, and treacle tart with clotted cream. All the meals are freshly prepared on the premises. The pub is set in a delightful garden bordered by a stream. Dogs are welcome and you can tie your horse up outside when you come in for refreshment. Children, too, will be happily occupied in the garden in summer and in the children's room with books and games in the winter.

OPEN: 12-2.30 6.30-11
BAR MEALS: L served all week 12-2 D served all week 7-9.30 Weekdays in winter 7-9
🍽: Unique Pub Co
🍺: Exmoor Ale, Wadworth 6X, Smiles Best. ♀: 10
FACILITIES: Well tended garden bordered by stream Dogs allowed on lead, water provided
NOTES: Parking 26

♀   Map 03 ST03
TA4 4JB
☎ 01984 656217
Dir: Telephone for directions

England

MONTACUTE
Map 04 ST41

Pick of the Pubs

The Phelips Arms 🐟◇ ♀
The Borough TA15 6XB ☎ 01935 822557 📠 01935 822557
e-mail: infophelipsarms@aol.com
Dir: From Cartgate rdbt on A303 follow signs for Montacute
A 17th-century listed ham stone building overlooking the
village square and close to historic Montacute House
(NT), where the emphasis is on the quality of the food;
everything is prepared on the premises using the best
local and West Country produce. The menu features an
eclectic selection of dishes cooked in a robust style,
examples of which are pan-fried tuna loin with chilli,
coriander and garlic butter; oven roasted rack of lamb
with crushed sweet potato and port sauce; braised rabbit
with chestnut mash, bacon lardons and thyme gravy; and
grilled fillets of John Dory with saffron mash. There is a
small but delicious pudding menu, and the already
extensive wine list is continually growing. For warm days
there is a beautifully laid out garden. The pub was a
location for the film version of *Sense and Sensibility*.
OPEN: 11.30-2.30 6-11 Closed: 25 Dec **BAR MEALS:** L served
all week 12-2 D served Tue-Sat 7-9 Av main course £12
RESTAURANT: L served all week 12-2 D served Tue-Sat 6-9
Av 3 course à la carte £21 🍽: Palmers ◀: Palmers IPA & 200
Premium Ale, Copper Ale. ♀: 35 **FACILITIES:** Garden:
Secluded, sheltered & beautiful walled garden Dogs allowed
Water **NOTES:** Parking 40

NORTH CURRY
Map 04 ST32

The Bird in Hand 🐟◇ ♀
1 Queen Square TA3 6LT ☎ 01823 490248
Friendly 300-year-old village inn, with large stone inglenook
fireplaces, flagstone floors, exposed beams and studwork.
Cheerful staff provide a friendly welcome, and the place is
atmospheric at night by candlelight. The pub is close to the
Somerset Levels and moors, yet only ten minutes' from
junction 25 of the M5. Blackboard specials concentrate on
local produce, and a good choice of constantly changing
seafood includes sea bass, sea bream, red snapper, crevettes,
cod and mussels.
OPEN: 12-3 6-11 25 Dec Closed eve **BAR MEALS:** L served all
week 12-2 D served all week 7-9.30 **RESTAURANT:** L served all
week 12-2 D served all week 7-9.30 🍽: Free House ◀: Badger
Tanglefoot, Exmoor Gold, Otter Ale, Cotleigh Barn Owl. ♀: 6
FACILITIES: Dogs allowed **NOTES:** Parking 20

NORTON ST PHILIP
Map 04 ST75

Pick of the Pubs

George Inn ♀
High St BA2 7LH ☎ 01373 834224 📠 01373 834861
e-mail: georgeinnnsp@aol.com
web: www.thegeorgeinn-nsp.co.uk
*Dir: From Bath take A36 to Warminster, after 6m take A366 on right
to Radstock, village 1m*
Dating back to the 14th century and built originally as a
monastic guest house for Carthusian monks, this
handsome inn has been lovingly and sympathetically
restored. It was already famous as an historic inn in the
19th and early 20th centuries, appearing frequently in

watercolours, engravings and photographs. In more
recent years it has often been used as a film location -
Albert Finney leapt from the gallery here in *Tom Jones*
and the Italian director Pasolini used the top floor for
scenes from *Canterbury Tales*. *The Remains of the Day*,
Persuasion and *Moll Flanders* have also been filmed at
the George. Imaginative menus complement the very
agreeable surroundings. Begin, perhaps, with spicy pot of
prawns, chicken liver parfait, or stuffed mushrooms, then
follow through with individual beef wellington with a red
wine jus; lamb shank with a mint gravy; whole trout
topped with toasted almonds; or blackened chicken with
a mango salsa and fries.

George Inn
OPEN: 11-2.30 5.30-11 (summer only) **BAR MEALS:** L served
all week 12-2 D served all week 7-9.30 Av main course £7.25
RESTAURANT: L served all week 12-2 D served all week 7-9.30
Av 3 course à la carte £25 🍽: Wadworth ◀: Wadworth 6X,
Henrys IPA, Wadworth, J.C.B. **FACILITIES:** Garden: Terrace
garden overlooking village green Dogs allowed
NOTES: Parking 26

NUNNEY
Map 04 ST74

The George at Nunney ★★ 🐟◇ ♀
Church St BA11 4LW ☎ 01373 836458 📠 01373 836565
e-mail: enquiries@georgeatnunneyhotel.wanadoo.co.uk
Dir: 0.5m N off A361, Frome/Shepton Mallet
The garden was used in the Middle Ages as a place of
execution, but this rambling old coaching inn is deservedly
popular. Set in a historic conservation village, it serves a wide
choice of food. Big steaks, mixed grill, steak and ale pie, and
double chicken breasts with choice of sauces, plus a separate
fish menu including brill, sea bass, hake, red mullet and fresh
dressed crabs.
OPEN: 12-3 5-11 **BAR MEALS:** L served all week 12-2 D served all
week 7-9 Av main course £8 **RESTAURANT:** L served all week 12-2
D served all week 7-9 Av 3 course à la carte £18 Av 3 course fixed
price £12 🍽: Free House ◀: Highgate Brewery Saddlers Best Bitter,
Wadworth 6X, Interbrew Bass and Guest Ales. ♀: 8
FACILITIES: Child facs Garden: Walled cottage type garden with
seating **NOTES:** Parking 30 **ROOMS:** 10 bedrooms 9 en suite
2 family rooms s£56 d£72

OVER STRATTON
Map 04 ST41

The Royal Oak
TA13 5LQ ☎ 01460 240906 📠 01460 242421
e-mail: chris&jill@the-royal-oak.net
Dir: A3088 from Yeovil, L onto A303, Over Stratton on R after S Petherton
A welcoming old thatched inn built from warm hamstone, full
of blackened beams, flagstones, log fires, pews and settles -

continued

continued

with the added attraction of a garden, children's play area and barbecue. Real ales, including Tanglefoot, from the Badger brewery in Blandford Forum, supplement traditional menus of fish pie, salmon with saffron hollandaise, and game cobblers with chive and horseradish scones. Traditional Sunday roast.
OPEN: 11-3 6-11 (wkds all day) **BAR MEALS:** L served all week 12-2.30 D served all week 6.30-9.30 **RESTAURANT:** L served all week 12-2.30 D served all week 6.30-9.30 ⊜: Woodhouse Inns ⬛: Badger Best, Tanglefoot, Sussex Best Bitter.
FACILITIES: Garden: Dogs allowed Water **NOTES:** Parking 70

PITNEY   Map 04 ST42

Pick of the Pubs

The Halfway House ♀
TA10 9AB ☎ 01458 252513
Dir: On B3153 between Langport and Somerton
This is a pub largely dedicated to the promotion of real ale as produced by the many excellent micro-breweries in Somerset, Devon and Wiltshire. There are always six to ten of these available in tip-top condition. There is also an excellent choice of bottled continental beers. This delightfully old-fashioned rural pub draws customers from a huge area. Three homely rooms boast open fires, books and games, but no music or electronic games. Home-cooked meals (except Sundays when it is too busy with drinkers) include soups, local sausages, sandwiches and a good selection of curries and casseroles in the evening.
OPEN: 11.30-3 5.30-11 (Sun 12-3, 7-10.30) Closed: 25 Dec
BAR MEALS: L served Mon-Sat 12-2.30 D served Mon-Sat 7-9.30 Av main course £6 ⊜: Free House ⬛: Butcombe Bitter, Teignworthy, Otter Ale, Cotleigh Tawny Ale. ♀: 8
FACILITIES: Garden: Dogs allowed Water **NOTES:** Parking 30

PORLOCK   Map 03 SS84

The Ship Inn
High St TA24 8QD ☎ 01643 862507 ▤ 01643 863224
e-mail: mail@shipinnporlock.co.uk
web: www.shipinnporlock.co.uk
Dir: A358 to Williton, then A39 to Porlock

Many travellers have been welcomed to this 13th-century inn, including Wordsworth, Coleridge and even Nelson's press gang. Nestling at the foot of Porlock's notorious hill, where Exmoor tumbles into the sea, its thatched roof and traditional interior provide an evocative setting for a meal, drink or overnight stay. Meals range through ploughman's, light bites and dishes such as home-made steak, mushroom and ale pie; cider mussels, and roasted vegetable lasagne.
OPEN: 11-11 (Sun 12-11) **BAR MEALS:** L served all week 12-2
continued

D served all week 6.30-9 Sundays 12.30-2.30
RESTAURANT: L served Sun 12-2 D served all week 7-9 Sun 12.30-2.30, 7-9 ⊜: Free House ⬛: Cotleigh Barn Owl, Bass, Courage Best, Regular Guest Ales eg Snowy (Cotleigh).
FACILITIES: Child facs Garden: Dogs allowed Water provided
NOTES: Parking 40 **ROOMS:** 10 bedrooms 8 en suite 3 family rooms (♦♦♦)

PRIDDY   Map 04 ST55

New Inn ♀
Priddy Green BA5 3BB ☎ 01749 676465
Dir: From M4 junct 18 take A39 right to Priddy 3m before Wells. From junct 19 through Bristol onto A39. From M5 junct 21 take A371 to Cheddar, then B3371

Overlooking the village green high up in the Mendip Hills, this old, former farmhouse is popular with walkers, riders and cavers, and once served beer to the local lead miners. A typical dinner menu features liver and bacon, chargrilled steaks, Brixham plaice, and fillet of pork with braised red cabbage, plus New Inn pies, including a vegetarian version, various jacket potatoes, omelettes and toasties. Skittle alley. Priddy hosts the 'friendliest folk festival in England' every July.
OPEN: 12-3 7-11 **BAR MEALS:** L served all week 12-2 D served all week 7-9.30 Av main course £5.25 **RESTAURANT:** L served all week 12-2 D served all week 7-9.30 ⊜: Free House ⬛: Interbrew Bass, Fuller's London Pride, Wadworth 6X, New Inn Priddy.
FACILITIES: Garden: Large garden with skittle alley Dogs allowed Water **NOTES:** Parking 30

RODE   Map 04 ST85

The Mill at Rode ♀
BA11 6AG ☎ 01373 831100 ▤ 01373 831144
e-mail: info@themillatrode.co.uk
Dir: 6m from Bath
Riverside bar in a contemporary conversion of a former mill, surrounded by fabulous walking country (guide available at the bar). Quite the cultural centre, it provides space for the work of local artists and live music on Friday nights. Regular events include a beer festival and duck race, and private parties, receptions and conferences are catered for. Dishes include chicken roulade, pork medallion, and vegetable wellington, and there's a kids' menu with organic options.
OPEN: 12-11 **BAR MEALS:** L served all week 12 D served all week 10 Av main course £10 **RESTAURANT:** L served all week D served all week 10 Av 3 course à la carte £20 Av 3 course fixed price £11.50 ⬛: Butcombe Bitter, Erdinger, Guinness, guest beers. ♀: 17
FACILITIES: Child facs Garden: Riverside garden with adult only island **NOTES:** Parking 72

⬛ Principal Beers for sale

England

RUDGE
Map 04 ST85

The Full Moon at Rudge ♦♦♦♦ 🐟 ♀
BA11 2QF ☎ 01373 830936 📠 01373 831366
e-mail: enquiries@thefullmoon.co.uk
Dir: From A36 (Bath/Warminster rd) follow signs for Rudge
Strategically placed since the early 1700s at the crossing of two old drove roads, this venerable inn retains its small, stone-floored rooms furnished with scrubbed tables. Modern British cooking at lunchtime includes Full Moon smokie (smoked fish); home-cooked Wiltshire ham, eggs and chips; chicken korma with rice; and tagliatelle carbonara. Main courses served at dinner include escalope of pork; pigeon breast; blackened tuna with chilli butter; avocado and prawn salad; and veggie pancakes. Great views of Westbury White Horse.
OPEN: 11-11 **BAR MEALS:** L served all week 12-2.30 D served all week 6.30-9.30 **RESTAURANT:** L served all week 12-2.30 D served all week 6.30-9.30 Av 3 course à la carte £18.95 ⊕: Free House ◀️: Butcombe Bitter, Wadworth 6X, Timothy Taylor, Worthington Cream Flow. ♀: 7 **FACILITIES:** Garden: Garden to rear of pub with wall and fence Dogs allowed **NOTES:** Parking 50
ROOMS: 17 bedrooms en suite 1 family room s£52.50 d£74.50

SHEPTON MALLET
Map 04 ST64

Pick of the Pubs

The Three Horseshoes ♀
Batcombe BA4 6HE ☎ 01749 850359 📠 01749 850615
Dir: Take A359 from Frome to Bruton. Batcombe signed on right
A 16th-century, honey-coloured stone pub in a pretty village below the Dorset Downs. Terracotta walls, exposed stripped beams, and a fine stone inglenook are to be found in the long, low main bar where home-brewed Bats in the Belfry is one of the real ales on tap. The seasonal menus offer half a dozen choices at each course, sample starters including tian of Cornish crab and prawns with dill crème fraîche; and salad of seared pigeon breast with elderberry dressing. Among the main courses may be chicken roulade filled with pistachio and spinach mousse, dauphinoise potatoes and Madeira sauce; and rack of lamb with boulangère potatoes and red wine jus. Home-made terrine of kiwi fruit and mango sorbet is a refreshing dessert. Sandwiches and a bar menu are also available, the latter offering duck cassoulet with crusty bread. The lovely rear garden overlooks the 15th-century tower of the parish church.
OPEN: 12-3 6.30-11 **BAR MEALS:** L served all week 12-2 D served all week 7-9.30 Av main course £9.95
RESTAURANT: L served all week 12-2 D served all week 7-9.30 Sat-Sun 12-2.30, Sun & Thurs 7-9 Av 3 course à la carte £24.95 ⊕: Free House ◀️: Butcombe Bitter, Bats in the Belfry.
FACILITIES: Child facs Garden: Pretty garden, large patio with heaters Dogs allowed Water **NOTES:** Parking 25

Pick of the Pubs

The Waggon and Horses 🐟 ♀
Frome Rd, Doulting Beacon BA4 4LA
☎ 01749 880302 📠 01749 880602
e-mail: SJCOOKE@hotmail.co.uk
Dir: 1.5m N of Shepton Mallet at X-rds with Old Wells-Frome road, 1m off A37
An 18th-century coaching inn at the heart of artistic life in its rural community. The upstairs skittle alley doubles as a

concert hall and gallery, with regular exhibitions and monthly jazz sessions. Customers travel quite a distance to enjoy the food, which takes in traditional pub fare as well as continental specials. The bar offers varying range of real beers, a good choice of wines by the glass, and local Somerset Royal cider brandy. Owners Simon and Clare are committed to local produce with an emphasis on rare breeds and organic meat. Speciality dishes include Somerset eel and local game, along with a diverse selection of other local products.

The Waggon and Horses

OPEN: 11.30-3 6-11 (open all day Fri-Sun in summer)
BAR MEALS: L served all week 11.30-2.30 D served all week 6-9.30 Food served all day Sat-Sun in summer Av main course £10 **RESTAURANT:** L served all week 11.30-2.30 D served all week 6-9.30 Food served all day Sat-Sun in summer Av fixed price £10 ⊕: ◀️: Wadworth 6X, Greene King IPA, Butcombe. ♀: 12 **FACILITIES:** Child facs Children's licence Very big garden, 20 tables Dogs allowed **NOTES:** Parking 35

SHEPTON MONTAGUE
Map 04 ST63

The Montague Inn
BA9 8JW ☎ 01749 813213 📠 01749 813213
Dir: R off A371 between Wincanton & Castle Cary tow Shepton Montague
This comfortably refurbished, stone-built village inn nestles in rolling unspoilt Somerset countryside on the edge of sleepy Shepton Montague. Tastefully decorated throughout, with the homely bar featuring old dark pine and an open log fire, and a cosy, yellow-painted dining room. Menu choices include bacon and brie ciabatta, Scottish venison steak, home-made pies, mushroom lasagne, and organic lamb. The attractive summer terrace with rural views is perfect for summer.
OPEN: 11-2.30 6-11 **BAR MEALS:** L served Tue-Sun 11-2 D served Tue-Sat 7-9 (Sun 12-2) Av main course £7 **RESTAURANT:** L served Tue-Sun 11-2 D served Tue-Sat 7-9 (Sun 12-2) Av 3 course à la carte £21 ⊕: Free House ◀️: Greene King IPA, Butcombe Gold, Abbot Ale & Guest Beer. **FACILITIES:** Garden: Raised area overlooks countryside, lawn below Dogs allowed Beer garden
NOTES: Parking 30

SPARKFORD
Map 04 ST62

The Sparkford Inn
High St BA22 7JH ☎ 01963 440218 📠 01963 440358
e-mail: sparkfordinn@sparkford.fsbusiness.co.uk
Dir: Just off A303, 400yds from rdbt at Sparkford
A 15th-century former coaching inn with beamed bars and a fascinating display of old prints and photographs. It is set in an attractive garden just off the A303 between Wincanton and Yeovil. The restaurant offers a popular lunchtime carvery, light meals and a full evening menu, featuring steaks from the grill.

continued

continued

England

Dishes include marinated Cajun chicken breast; smoked haddock and bacon au gratin; and bean and celery chilli. **OPEN:** 11-3 5.30-11 (Summer 11-11) **BAR MEALS:** L served all week 12-2 D served all week 7-9.30 **RESTAURANT:** L served all week 12-2 D served all week 7-9.30 🍺: Free House 🍴: Interbrew Bass, Otter Ale, Butcombe Bitter, Greene King Abbot.
FACILITIES: Child facs Garden: Dogs allowed **NOTES:** Parking 50
ROOMS: 10 bedrooms en suite 3 family rooms s£40 d£55 (♦♦♦)

STANTON WICK
Map 04 ST66

Pick of the Pubs

The Carpenters Arms 🐟 ♀
BS39 4BX ☎ 01761 490202 ▤ 01761 490763
e-mail: carpenters@buccaneer.co.uk
web: www.the-carpenters-arms.co.uk
Dir: A37 to Chelwood rdbt, then A368 8m S of Bath - A368
In its tranquil hamlet overlooking the Chew Valley, this charming stone-built free house was formerly a row of miners' cottages. Behind the pretty façade with its climbing roses and colourful flower tubs, you'll find a comfortable bar with low beams and a chatty, music-free atmosphere. There are warming winter fires and, in summer, guests can enjoy the delights of al fresco meals on the spacious garden patio. The Cooper's Parlour, with an extensive daily chalkboard, is the focus of imaginative snacks and bar food. Starters like leek and parmesan tartlet; and terrine of venison and Madeira with Cumberland sauce precede an appetising range of main dishes: wild boar and apple sausages on spring onion mash; steak, mushroom and Butcombe ale pie; and Thai chicken curry with steamed coriander rice are typical. A daily specials list extends the choice.
OPEN: 11-11 (Sun 12-10.30) Closed: 25/26 Dec
BAR MEALS: L served all week 12-2 D served all week 7-10 Sun 7-9 Av main course £12.95 **RESTAURANT:** L served all week 12-2 D served all week 7-10 Sun 7-9 Av 3 course à la carte £12.95 🍺: Buccaneer Holdings 🍴: Butcombe Bitter, Scottish Courage Courage Best, Wadworth 6X. ♀: 12 **FACILITIES:** Landscaped garden. Patio area, pond, heaters Dogs allowed Water **NOTES:** Parking 200 **ROOMS:** 12 bedrooms en suite 1 family room s£67 d£94.50 (♦♦♦♦)

STAPLE FITZPAINE
Map 04 ST21

Pick of the Pubs

The Greyhound Inn ♦♦♦♦ 🐟 ♀
TA3 5SP ☎ 01823 480227 ▤ 01823 481117
e-mail: stay@the-greyhoundinn.com
Dir: From M5, take A358 E, signed Yeovil, after 1m turn right, signed Staple Fitzpaine, at t-junct take left, pub is on right at x-rds
There's a warm welcome for everyone at this attractive 16th-century free house with its flagstone bars and open winter fires. The inn takes its name from the men on horseback who dispatched news before the days of Royal Mail. Nowadays the well-kept ales include Exmoor, Otter and TGI Wallop, as well as a national guest beer; traditional Somerset cider is also available on hand pump. The comprehensive menu features a variety of dishes using the finest local Somerset ingredients, including local cheeses, pork, beef and lamb. Specials are carefully chosen to take advantage of the changing seasons, and fish is freshly delivered each morning from Brixham.

Typical seafood dishes include smoked haddock and mussel chowder; salmon gravlax timbale; and crab farcie with citrus dressing. In the summer months you can enjoy the large split level beer garden that surrounds the inn.
OPEN: 12-2.30 6-11 (All day Sun, Fri 5.30-11)
BAR MEALS: L served all week 12-2 D served all week 7-9 Fri-Sat 7-9.30 **RESTAURANT:** 7-9 🍺: Free House 🍴: Otter, Adnams Broadside, London Pride, Castle Eden. ♀: 7
FACILITIES: Child facs Garden: Split level, all round the Inn Dogs allowed on leads. Water **NOTES:** Parking 60
ROOMS: 4 bedrooms en suite s£55 d£80

STOGUMBER
Map 03 ST03

The White Horse
High St TA4 3TA ☎ 01984 656277 ▤ 01984 656277
Dir: From Taunton take A358 to Minehead. After approx 8m turn left to Stogumber for 2m into centre of village. Right at T-junct and right again. Pub is oppposite church.
A mile down a pretty country lane from the West Somerset Steam Railway station, this traditional village free house incorporates the historic village Market Hall. The extensive menu includes local fish and steaks, washed down with Cotleigh Tawny Bitter, Greene King and local guest beers. Like other local pubs, the White Horse once brewed Stogumber ale, which could allegedly cure anything.
OPEN: 11-2.30 6-11 (open all day Thu-Sun)
BAR MEALS: L served all week 12-2 D served all week 7-9.30 Av main course £6 **RESTAURANT:** L served all week 12-2 D served all week 7-9.30 🍺: Free House 🍴: Cotleigh Tawny Bitter, Marstons Pedigree, Greene King, Abbot Ale. **FACILITIES:** Garden: Enclosed patio Dogs allowed Water, bedrooms by arrangement
NOTES: Parking 5 **ROOMS:** 3 bedrooms en suite 1 family room s£27 d£54 (♦♦♦) No children overnight

STOKE ST GREGORY
Map 04 ST32

Rose & Crown ♀
Woodhill TA3 6EW ☎ 01823 490296 ▤ 01823 490996
e-mail: info@browningpubs.com
Dir: M5 junct 25, follow A358 towards Langport, bear left at Thornfalcon, then left again, follow signs to Stoke St Gregory
The pub has been in the same family for over 25 years and is proud of its reputation for good food, local produce and a warm reception. It is set in the Somerset Levels at the heart of the willow industry, and is on the River Parrett Trail. Both the lunch bar menu and the dinner carte offer a good choice of dishes, perhaps fillet of haddock with Somerset rarebit, scrumpy chicken, or three-cheese tagliatelle.
OPEN: 11-3 7-11 Dec 25 Closed eve **BAR MEALS:** L served all week 12.30-2 D served all week 7-9.30 Sun 12-2 Av main course £9 **RESTAURANT:** L served all week 12.30-2 D served all week 7-10 Av 3 course à la carte £22.50 🍺: Free House 🍴: Exmoor Fox, & Stag, Guest Ales. ♀: 8 **FACILITIES:** Garden: Pretty patio area with tables **NOTES:** Parking 20

 Brewery/Company

Pick of the Pubs have that extra special quality that makes them stand out from the crowd. Their entries are highlighted, and may be a full page

continued

TAUNTON   Map 04 ST22

Queens Arms

Pitminster TA3 7AZ ☎ 01823 421529 📠 01823 451529

In 1086 the Domesday Book recorded this ancient building as
a mill, which for nearly 800 years it remained before
becoming a pub. Local (ie Somerset, Bristol and Devon) real
ales are available, as well as an extremely varied menu.
Almost everything is home made with locally purchased
ingredients. Starters include medley of tempura vegetables
and chicken satay, and to follow could come vegetable, brie
and cranberry crumble, black-fin shark steak in creamy
peppercorn sauce, or chicken curry.
OPEN: 11-11 (Sun 12-10.30) **BAR MEALS:** L served all week 12-2
D served Tue-Sat 6.30-9 Av main course £7 🍴: Enterprise Inns
🍺: Butcombe Bitter, Butcombe Gold, Cotleigh Tawny, Otter Bitter.
FACILITIES: Garden: South facing terrace and lawned area Dogs
allowed Water bowl in bar **NOTES:** Parking 20

TRISCOMBE   Map 04 ST13

Pick of the Pubs

The Blue Ball ♀

TA4 3HE ☎ 01984 618242 📠 01984 618371

Dir: From Taunton follow A358 past Bishops Lydeard to Minehead
Hidden away down a narrow lane in both the Quantock Hills,
this 'old pub' is actually a converted 18th-century thatched
barn. Inside are A-frame wood ceilings, solid beech
furniture, lavish carpets and furnishings, log fires and,
from the windows, breathtaking views south to the
Blackdown Hills. A team of talented chefs makes
absolutely everything except butters and oil, using
ingredients from mostly local suppliers, all of whom are
chosen with considerable care. For a three-course lunch
try crab tian with Thai dressing; venison sausages with
spring onion mash and mustard sauce; and cinnamon
pannacotta with blackberry compote. Alternatively, in the
evening, there may be hand-dived seared scallops with
black pudding and chorizo dressing; pot-roasted rack of
lamb with roasted swede, quince and sage aioli; and
nougatine parfait with mango and mint salsa. Meals are
also served in the garden and on the patio. West Country
real ales are available.
OPEN: 12-3 7-11 Jan to Mar closed Sun eve & Mon Closed: 25
Dec **BAR MEALS:** L served all week 12-2 D served all week
7-9.30 Sun D 7-9 (Apr-Dec) **RESTAURANT:** L served all week
12-2 D served all week 7-9.30 Sun D 7-9 (Apr-Dec) Av 3 course à
la carte £22 🍴: Free House 🍺: Cotleigh Tawny, Exmoor Gold
& Stag, Butcombe, Sharps. ♀: 10 **FACILITIES:** Garden: New
patio and lawn area with views of Exmoor Dogs allowed Water
NOTES: Parking 20

WAMBROOK   Map 04 ST20

The Cotley Inn 🍽️

TA20 3EN ☎ 01460 62348 📠 01460 68833
e-mail: sue-cotley@ticali.co.uk
Dir: Take A30 from Chard, then take the Wanbrook rd at the toll house.
Situated in an area renowned for good walks, close to the
Devon border and the Lyme Bay coastline, the cosy bar and
adjoining dining room of this traditional stone-built inn offer a
choice of full meals, specials and light snacks. The 'small eats'
menu includes beef lasagne, devilled kidneys with rice, and
smoked trout with a spring onion dip. There are fish and
chicken dishes too, and among the main courses are

continued

peppered rump steak and Cotley mixed grill.

The Cotley Inn

OPEN: 11-3 7-11 **BAR MEALS:** L served all week 12-2 D served all
week 7-10 (Sun D 7-9) Av main course £9 **RESTAURANT:** L served
all week 12-2 D served all week 7-10 (Sun D 7-9) Av 3 course à la carte
£15 🍴: Free House 🍺: Otter Ale, Interbrew Boddingtons Bitter, Otter
Bitter, Steela. **FACILITIES:** Children's licence Garden: Patio area,
tables & chairs; beer garden Dogs allowed Water **NOTES:** Parking 40

WASHFORD   Map 03 ST04

The Washford Inn

TA23 0PP ☎ 01984 640256
e-mail: washfordinn@freedomnames.co.uk
A pleasant family inn located beside Washford Station, a stop
on the West Somerset Railway between Minehead and
Bishop's Lydeard - the longest privately-owned line in Britain.
A service runs all year, using both diesel and nostalgic old
steam locos. A good range of beers and a simple menu of
proven pub favourites such as omelette and chips, grilled
steaks, and all-day breakfast. Chicken nuggets, sausages or
pizzas for young trainspotters.
OPEN: 12-11 (Winter 11-3, 5-11) **BAR MEALS:** L served all week
12-2.30 D served all week 5.30-9 Av main course £7.50
RESTAURANT: L served all week 12-2.30 D served all week 5-9
🍴: Scottish & Newcastle 🍺: Adnams Broadside, Old Speckled Hen,
Theakstons Best Mild,. **FACILITIES:** Child facs Garden: Seating area
with good veiw of steam railway Dogs allowed **NOTES:** Parking 40

WATERROW   Map 03 ST02

The Rock Inn ♦♦♦ ♀

TA4 2AX ☎ 01984 623293 📠 01984 623293
Dir: From Taunton take B3227. Waterrow approx 14m W

400-year-old former smithy and coaching inn built into the
rock face, in a lovely green valley beside the River Tone. Sit in
the peaceful bar, with the winter log fire and traditional
furnishings, and sample the appetising menu including steaks
and various home-made dishes.

continued

OPEN: 12-3 6-11 (Sun 7-10.30) **BAR MEALS:** L served all week 12-2.30 D served all week 6-9.30 Sun 7-9 Av main course £8.50
RESTAURANT: L served all week 12-2.30 D served all week 6-9.30
☺: Free House ◖: Cotleigh Tawny, Exmoor Gold, Otter Ale. ♀: 15
FACILITIES: Children's licence Dogs allowed **NOTES:** Parking 20
ROOMS: 7 bedrooms en suite 1 family room s£35 d£70

WELLS
Map 04 ST54

The City Arms ♀
69 High St BA5 2AG ☎ 01749 673916 🖷 01749 672901
e-mail: query@thecityarmsatwells.co.uk
At the heart of the historic cathedral city, this was a jail in
Tudor times. Today, as a free house, it provides a warm
welcome, offering a range of fine ales, and a menu featuring
freshly cooked, often seasonal, local produce. Dishes might
include steak and mushroom pudding; baked salmon en
croute with asparagus and red pepper beurre blanc; and
Aberdeen Angus steaks. Hot chilli; cauliflower cheese; and
Whitby scampi are popular bar snacks.
OPEN: 9-11 **BAR MEALS:** L served all week 9 D served all week 10
RESTAURANT: L served all week 12 D served all week 6-9
◖: Butcombe, Greene King, Sharps. ♀: 16 **FACILITIES:** Children's
licence Garden: Dogs allowed

Pick of the Pubs

The Fountain Inn & Boxer's Restaurant ♀
1 Saint Thomas St BA5 2UU ☎ 01749 672317 🖷 01749 670825
e-mail: eat@fountaininn.co.uk

See Pub Walk on page 420
See Pick of the Pubs on page 440

The Pheasant Inn ♀
Worth, Wookey BA5 1LQ ☎ 01749 672355
e-mail: pheasant@dsl.pipex.com
Dir: *W of Wells on the B3139 towards Wedmore*
Popular country pub at the foot of the Mendips, where you
can enjoy some impressive views and relax with a pint of real
ale beside a welcoming log fire. The menu ranges through
light bites, a pasta and pizza section, and dishes such as slow
roast lamb shank with minty Somerset sauce, and escalope of
pork with cider and sage cream sauce. Friday night is fish
night, and there are some great home-made puddings.
OPEN: 11-3 6-11 (Sun 12-3, 6.30-10.30) **BAR MEALS:** L served all
week 12-2 D served all week 6.30-9.30 Sun 7-9
RESTAURANT: L served all week 12-2 D served all week 6.30-9.30
Sun 7-9 ☺: Enterprise Inns ◖: Butcombe, Greene King Old
Speckled Hen, Pedigree, Butcombe Blond. ♀: 1
FACILITIES: Children's licence Garden: Garden with tables and
umbrellas Dogs allowed **NOTES:** Parking 28

WEST CAMEL
Map 04 ST52

The Walnut Tree
Fore St BA22 7QW ☎ 01935 851292 🖷 01935 851292
e-mail: info@thewalnuttreehotel.com
web: www.thewalnuttreehotel.com
Dir: *Off A303 between Sparkford & Yeovilton Air Base*

Close to the border between Dorset and Somerset, this well-
kept inn is in a quiet village. The Leyland Trail passes close by
and brings plenty of walkers. The cosily carpeted lounge bar,
the restaurant and the bistro entice the hungry with
blackboards offering smoked duck breast with caramelised
onions in an apple and brandy sauce; venison fillet on
dauphinoise potatoes in a port and redcurrant sauce; and filo
parcels filled with mature cheddar cheese and a red onion
compôte on a tomato and basil sauce.
OPEN: 11-3 6.30-11.30 (Closed Sun eve, Mon lunch) Closed: 25-26
Dec **BAR MEALS:** L served Tue-Sun 12-2 D served Mon-Sat 6-9.30
Av main course £12.95 **RESTAURANT:** L served Tue-Sun 12-2
D served Mon-Sat 7-9.30 Av 3 course à la carte £22 ☺: Free House
◖: Butcombe Bitter, Otter Ale & Bitter. **FACILITIES:** Tranuil garden
NOTES: Parking 40

Pick of the Pubs

WELLS – SOMERSET

The Fountain Inn

When members of the cathedral choir want to escape for a quick drink at this popular 16th-century pub/restaurant, they apparently say "Just popping out to the library". Sorry chaps, your secret's out. The inn was built to house labourers and stonemasons working on the cathedral, just 50 yards away.

Owners Adrian and Sarah Lawrence arrived here in 1981, having fallen in love with Wells during a day out in the car. Gradually they shifted the inn's focus from drink to food, creating, in effect, a gastropub before the word was coined, and in the years since they have earned a well-deserved reputation. The unpretentious ground floor bar serves Butcombe Bitter, brewed the other side of the Mendips. The bar menu offers main courses of beef, ale and mushroom pie; beer-battered cod and chips; crispy tortilla basket with tender chicken pieces marinated in chilli oil; and roasted penne pasta bake with melted mozzarella. In Boxer's Restaurant upstairs, starters include smoked salmon timbale filled with cream cheese, tuna and lime; and roasted vegetable patties seasoned with Cajun spices and served with sweet pepper chilli relish. Main courses include pork tenderloin stuffed with dates and bacon, wrapped with smoked bacon slices and served with sage, garlic and mustard sauce; and grilled fillet of sea bass marinated in citrus juices, served on cumin-roasted vegetables. For a dessert with a kick go for baked alaska laced with strawberry vodka. An affordable wine list leans towards Spain.

OPEN: 10.30-2.30 6-11 (Sun 12-3, 7-10.30) Closed: 25-26 Dec
BAR MEALS: L served all week 12-2.30 D served all week 6-10 (Sun 12-2.30, 7-9.30) Av main course £7.95
RESTAURANT: L served all week 12-2.30 D served all week 6-10 (Sun 12-2.30, 7-9.30) Av 3 course à la carte £20 Av 2 course fixed price £7.95
🍺: Butcombe Bitter, Interbrew Bass, Scottish Courage Courage Best.
♀: 23
FACILITIES: Child facs
NOTES: Parking 24

♀ Map 04 ST54
1 Saint Thomas St BA5 2UU
☎ 01749 672317
📠 01749 670825
✉ eat@fountaininn.co.uk
Dir: City centre, at A371 & B3139 junct. Follow The Harringtons signs. Inn on junct of Tor St & St Thomas St

England

WEST HUNTSPILL — Map 04 ST34

Pick of the Pubs

Crossways Inn 🐟 ♀
Withy Rd TA9 3RA ☎ 01278 783756 📠 01278 781899
e-mail: crossways.inn@virgin.net
Dir: On A38 3.5m from M5 junct 22/23

A much lived-in atmosphere strikes you on entering this 17th-century coaching inn on the old Taunton to Bristol road. In an age when UPVC replacement windows seem to be the norm, maybe this feeling is in part due to its old wooden sash windows, and panelled walls. A large fireplace in the central bar has built-in seating, there are old high-back settles, and an assortment of other furniture to deploy when drinking one of the West Country real ales (in a piped music-free environment, please note). The young and enthusiastic kitchen team produces home-made food for a daily changing menu offering corned beef hash with onion gravy, local faggots and marrowfat peas, Madras curry, Greek spiced lamb, sea bass and rainbow trout. Tuscan bean stew would suit vegetarians. Puddings include lemon cheesecake, and chocolate pecan fudge cake. There's a family room, skittle alley and safe rear garden.
OPEN: 12-3 5.30-11 (Sun 12-4.30, 7-10.30) Closed: 25 Dec
BAR MEALS: L served all week D served all week 6.30-9 (Sun; roast served 12-2.30, full menu 12-2, 7-9) Av main course £6.20 **RESTAURANT:** L served all week 12-2 D served all week 6.30-9 ⊕: Free House ◖: Interbrew Bass, Flowers IPA, Fuller's London Pride. ♀: 8 **FACILITIES:** Garden: Seating, food served outside Dogs allowed water **NOTES:** Parking 60

WHEDDON CROSS — Map 03 SS93

The Rest and Be Thankful Inn ◆◆◆◆ 🐟
TA24 7DR ☎ 01643 841222 📠 01643 841813
e-mail: enquiries@restandbethankful.co.uk
web: www.restandbethankful.co.uk
Dir: 5m S of Dunster
Coachmen, passengers and their horses would have been grateful for a break at this old coaching inn, nearly 1000 feet up in Exmoor's highest village. Old world charm blends with friendly hospitality in the cosy bar and spacious restaurant, where both traditional and contemporary food is served. Bar snacks range from soup to steaks, while house specials include macaroni or cauliflower cheese, beef lasagne, and breadcrumbed fillet of plaice.
OPEN: 9.30-2.30 6.30-11 (Winter 7pm Opening)
BAR MEALS: L served all week 12-2 D served all week 7-9 Av main course £7 **RESTAURANT:** L served all week 12-2 D served all week 7-9 Av 3 course à la carte £12.50 ⊕: Free House ◖: Tawny, Worthington Bitter, Abbott Ale, Tribute. **FACILITIES:** Child facs Garden: Paved Patio **NOTES:** Parking 50 **ROOMS:** 5 bedrooms en suite 1 family room s£32 d£64

WITHYPOOL — Map 03 SS83

Pick of the Pubs

Royal Oak Inn ★★ ◉ ♀
TA24 7QP ☎ 01643 831506 📠 01643 831659
e-mail: roy.bookings@ccinns.com
See Pick of the Pubs on page 442

WOOKEY — Map 04 ST54

The Burcott Inn ♀
Wells Rd BA5 1NJ ☎ 01749 673874
Dir: 3m from Wells on the B3139
A convenient stop for visitors to Wells or the Mendip Hills, this stone-built roadside inn is characterised by beams, open fires, pine settles and settles. Freshly prepared food is available in the bars, restaurant or large garden. The menu includes roasted duck breast, fresh steamed salmon steak, battered cod fillet, and lasagne. French sticks, sandwiches and salads are also available. Try your hand at the traditional pub games.
OPEN: 11.30-2.30 6-11 Closed: 25/26 Dec, 1 Jan
BAR MEALS: L served all week 12-2.30 D served Tue-Sat 6.30-9.30 Av main course £7.50 **RESTAURANT:** L served all week 12-2 D served Tue-Sat 6.30-9.30 Av 3 course à la carte £17.50 ⊕: Free House ◖: Teignworthy Old Moggie, Cotleigh Barn Owl Bitter, RCH Pitchfork, Branscombe BVB. ♀: 6 **FACILITIES:** Garden: Large garden, beautiful views **NOTES:** Parking 30

WOOLVERTON — Map 04 ST75

Red Lion ♀
Bath Rd BA2 7QS ☎ 01373 830350 📠 01373 831050
Dir: On the A36 between Bath & Warminster
Once a court room, with possible connections to Hanging Judge Jeffries, this 400-year-old building has lovely slate floors and an open fire. It is decorated in Elizabethan style and is an ideal place to enjoy real ales, country wines and good home cooking. Look out for steak and 6X ale pie, roasted lamb shoulder, ocean lasagne, smoked haddock and asparagus tart, butterflied chicken fillet, and a selection of hot rolls, jacket potatoes and sandwiches.
OPEN: 11.30-11 (Sun 12-10.30) **BAR MEALS:** L served all week 12-2.30 D served all week 6-9 Av main course £6.75 ⊕: Wadworth ◖: Wadworth 6X, Henry's IPA, Wadworth JCB & Seasonal, Guest Beers. ♀: 30 **FACILITIES:** Garden: Large garden, benches Dogs allowed Water **NOTES:** Parking 40

YARLINGTON — Map 04 ST62

The Stags Head Inn
Pound Ln BA9 8DG ☎ 01963 440393
Dir: Leave A303 at Wincanton A371 junct. From slip road turn left and follow signs to Castle Carey for 3m. Turn left off A371. Follow unclassified roads signed Yarlington, take 2nd right into village. Pub is opposite church.
Halfway between Wincanton and Castle Cary lies this completely unspoilt country inn with flagstones, real fires and no electronic intrusions. The menu includes steaks and seafood among other options, and all produce is fresh, delivered daily.
OPEN: 12-2.30 6-11 (Close 3pm on Sat-Sun) Closed: 25 Dec
BAR MEALS: L served Tue-Sun 12-2 D served Tue-Sat 7-9 Av main course £10.45 ◖: Greene King, IPA, Bass & weekly changing guest beer. **FACILITIES:** Garden: Lawned, heated patio, stream, fruit trees Dogs allowed Water, dog menu **NOTES:** Parking 20

Pick of the Pubs

WITHYPOOL – SOMERSET

Royal Oak Inn

With an ever-growing reputation as a sporting hotel for its hunting, shooting, and walking in the Exmoor National Park, this 300-year-old inn continues to generate its own long and colourful history. R D Blackmore stayed here whilst writing the classic *Lorna Doone*, and the hotel was once owned by spymaster Maxwell Knight.

Under the current owner, Gail Slogget, it goes from strength to strength. The two bars - Residents' and Jake's - reflect Exmoor's sporting life. The Rod Room is chock-full of fishing memorabilia; in both beamed bars, warmed by open fires, a wealth of good food created from local produce accompanies real ales and guests like Exmoor Ale and Exmoor Gold, as well as a fine range of whiskies and an impressive wine list. You can dine in the bar or in the strikingly decorated dining room. As many of the ingredients as possible are sourced locally, so starters can include trout pâté, Thai crab cakes, pan-seared pigeon breast, aromatic duck samosas, and duck liver parfait followed by main courses like pan-fried fillet of pork with caramelised apple and Calvados sauce, breast of free-range duck with a black cherry jus, tian of crayfish, duck leg confit, or roast rack of lamb. To finish, there's apple strudel, pears poached in red wine or a good selection of local cheeses. Stay over in one of the eight comfortable bedrooms and bring a copy of R. D. Blackmore's *Lorna Doone* with you: the beamed ceilings, log fires and friendly staff contribute to a wonderful atmosphere that is sure to work its magic on you.

OPEN: 11-2.30 6-11
BAR MEALS: L served all week 12-2 D served all week 6.30-9.30
RESTAURANT: L served all week 12-2 D served all week 7-9.30
Av 3 course à la carte £2
🏠: Free House
🍺: Courage Directors, Exmoor Ale, John Smiths. ♀: 16
FACILITIES: Dogs allowed Kennels if needed **NOTES:** Parking 20
ROOMS: 8 bedrooms 7 en suite s£50 d£65

★★ ♀　　　　　Map 03 SS83
TA24 7QP

☎ 01643 831506
🖷 01643 831659
📧 roy.bookings@ccinns.com
Dir: From M5 through Taunton on B3224, then B3223 to Withypool

England

STAFFORDSHIRE

ALREWAS
Map 10 SK11

The Old Boat ♀
DE13 7DB ☎ 01283 791468 ▤ 01283 792886
e-mail: mat@oldboat.co.uk

Standing on the Trent and Mersey Canal, the pub was originally used by canal construction workers and bargemen. The snug at the end of the bar was once the cellar, where casks of ale were rolled off the barges and kept cool in up to two feet of water. Typical dishes include roast Packington pork belly with sage and apple mash; roast lamb with braised red onions; and grilled turbot with sautéed cabbage and chorizo. **OPEN:** 11.30-3.30 6.30-11.30 Closed Mon in winter (Sun 12-2.30, 6-9.30) **BAR MEALS:** L served all week 12-2.30 D served all week 7-10 Sun12-3 Av main course £5.95 **RESTAURANT:** L served all week 12-2.30 D served all week 7-9 Sun 12-3 Av 3 course à la carte £20 ⊞: ◖: Marston's Pedigree, Directors, Hobgoblin, Butcombe Blond. ♀: 8 **FACILITIES:** Garden: Large lawn by canal **NOTES:** Parking 40

ALSAGERS BANK
Map 15 SJ74

The Gresley Arms
High St ST7 8BQ ☎ 01782 720297 ▤ 01782 720297
A 200-year-old pub in a semi-rural location set between two country parks, making it a popular stopping off point for walkers and cyclists. It is a friendly local, with a traditional bar, separate lounge and large family room, serving real ale and real food at a reasonable price. The menu encompasses basket meals (chicken, scampi, beefburger), steaks with sauces, light bites, main meals and daily specials, such as braised lamb shank, and tagliatelle nicoise. **OPEN:** 12-3 6-11 (All day Sat-Sun) **BAR MEALS:** L served all week 12-2.30 D served all week 6-9.30 (12-9.30 Sat-Sun) Av main course £6 **RESTAURANT:** L served all week 12-3 D served all week 6-9.30 (12-9.30 Sat-Sun) Av 3 course à la carte £12 ◖: 6 guest beers. **FACILITIES:** Garden: Large garden, mountain views Dogs allowed **NOTES:** Parking 30 No credit cards

★ Star rating for inspected hotel accommodation

We only include details of accommodation that has been inspected by the AA (big Stars or Diamonds at the top of an entry), or the RAC, VisitBritain, VisitScotland or WTB (small Stars or Diamonds at the end of an entry)

ALTON
Map 10 SK04

Bulls Head Inn
High St ST10 4AQ ☎ 01538 702307 ▤ 01538 702065
e-mail: janet@alton.freeserve.co.uk
Traditional beers, home cooking and well-equipped accommodation are provided in the heart of Alton, less than a mile from Alton Towers theme park. Oak beams and an inglenook fireplace set the scene for the old world bar, the cosy snug and the country-style restaurant. Menus offer the likes of sirloin steak, deep fried breaded plaice, lasagne verde, steak, ale and mushroom pie, and hunters chicken. **BAR MEALS:** L served Mon-Fri 12-2 D served all week 6.30-9.30 **RESTAURANT:** D served all week 6.30-9.30 ⊞: Free House ◖: Interbrew Bass, Coors Worthington's, Fuller's London Pride. **NOTES:** Parking 15

ANSLOW
Map 10 SK22

The Burnt Gate Inn ♀
Hopley Rd DE13 9PY ☎ 01283 563664
e-mail: theburntgateinn@aol.com
Dir: From Burton take B5017 towards Abbots Bromley. At top of Henhurst Hill turn right Inn on Hopley Road, 2m from town centre
Taking its unique name from a tollgate burnt down to make way for arable land, this extended and refurbished award-winning pub retains much charm and original character. The bar and restaurants have dark wood beams and there is an open coal fire in the bar. In addition to traditional steaks, the menu also has venison sausages on celeriac and apple mash, pork chop with apple, pear and sage sauce, salmon fillet with a soft orange and herb crust, and a good selection of desserts. Sandwiches and Staffordshire oatcake stacks too. **OPEN:** 11.30-3 6-11 (Sun 12-3, 6.30-10.30) **BAR MEALS:** L served all week 11.30-2.15 D served Mon-Sat Av main course £7 **RESTAURANT:** L served all week 11.30-2.15 D served Mon-Sat 6-9 Av 3 course à la carte £20 Av 3 course fixed price £12.95 ◖: Pedigree (Cask ales), guest beers. ♀: 8 **FACILITIES:** Dogs allowed Water **NOTES:** Parking 26

BURTON UPON TRENT
Map 10 SK22

Burton Bridge Inn ♀
24 Bridge St DE14 1SY ☎ 01283 536596
Dir: Telephone for directions
With its own brewery at the back, this is one of the oldest pubs in the area. The unspoilt old-fashioned interior has oak panelling, feature fireplaces, and a distinct lack of electronic entertainment. A full range of Burton Bridge ales is on tap, and the menu includes straightforward meals like roast pork, jacket potatoes, or beef cobs, as well as traditional filled Yorkshire puddings. Long alley skittles upstairs. **OPEN:** 11.30-2.30 5-11 (Sun 12-2.30, 7-10.30) **BAR MEALS:** L served Mon-Sat 11.30-2 Av main course £3.50 ⊞: ◖: Burton Bridge Gold Medal Ale, Burton Bridge Festival Ale, Burton Bridge Golden Delicious & Bridge Bitter. ♀: 15 **FACILITIES:** Garden: Dogs allowed Water **NOTES:** No credit cards

Disabled people and those with Assist Dogs have new rights of access to pubs, restaurants and hotels under the Disability Discrimination Act of 1 October 2004. For more information see the website at www.drc gb.org/open4all/rights/2004.asp

PUB WALK

The Junction Inn
Norbury Junction - Staffordshire

THE JUNCTION INN,
Norbury Junction ST20 0PN
☎ 01785 284288
Directions: From M6 take road for Eccleshall, L at Gt Bridgeford & head for Woodseaves, L there & head for Newport, L for Norbury Junction.
Near the Shropshire Union Canal, this pub was originally built in the heyday of canal traffic. It was the junction of the Shropshire and now disused Shrewsbury and Newport canals.
Open: 11–11 (12–10.30 Sun)
Bar Meals: L served all week 11–9 D served all week 11–9
Restaurant Meals: L served all week 12–9 D served all week 12–9
Av 3 course à la carte £12
Dogs allowed. Garden and parking available.
(for full entry see page 446)

Distance: 2.75 miles (4.4km)
Map: OS Landranger 127
Terrain: Farmland and woodland
Paths: Country lanes, tracks and canal towpath
Gradient: Gently undulating, no steep hills

Walk submitted by Nick Channer

The outward leg of this attractive walk skirts an extensive area of woodland before joining the towpath of the Shropshire Union Canal, returning to Norbury Junction along a pleasant, leafy stretch of the waterway, with views of the Wrekin away to the west.

Leave the pub by turning right and crossing the 66-mile Shropshire Union Canal. Pass the maintenance yard and here the scene is alive with moored narrow boats. Walk ahead along the road and on the left is the entrance to Norbury Manor. Continue down the lane towards the woodland. The canal embankment, known as Shelmore Great Bank, can be seen on the right.

Follow the road between the trees, passing a white cottage on the right. As the road bends sharp right, go straight on to follow a track running along the edge of Shelmore Wood. Further on you join a firm track running alongside a row of oak trees. Soon you come to a junction with a concrete drive. Continue ahead, with the outline of

Norbury Park on the left.

Shortly you reach a brick and stone cottage by the road. Turn right and walk down through the woodland. Go through the tunnel under the canal and then bear immediately left over a stile. A flight of steps takes you to the towpath of the Shropshire Union Canal. Turn left and follow the canal along the top of the embankment. This is Shelmore Great Bank and was built in order to avoid the route of the canal cutting through Lord Anson's estate at Norbury Park. Lord Anson was particularly anxious to ensure that the pheasants, reared for shooting, were not disturbed, and no doubt he exercised his power and influence to stop the canal from running across his land.

On the westerly horizon you can see the distinctive outline of the Wrekin, Shropshire's highest hill. Continue on the towpath, pass an iron milepost, then cross a stone bridge at the junction of the Shropshire Union Canal and the remains of an old disused canal to Newport. A few paces beyond it is the Junction Inn.

BUTTERTON

Map 16 SK05

The Black Lion Inn ♀
ST13 7SP ☎ 01538 304232 e-mail: blacklioninn@hotmail.com
Dir: From A52 (between Leek & Ashbourne) take B5053

This charming, 18th-century village inn lies on the edge of the Manifold valley, in the heart of the Peak District's walking and cycling country. Winter fires add to the pleasure of a well-kept pint. The popular bar menu includes pies and steaks, as well as lamb casserole, spinach and ricotta cannelloni, and plenty of interesting fish dishes. A comfortable base from which to explore the National Park.
OPEN: 12-3 7-11 Mon Closed lunch **BAR MEALS:** L served Wed-Sun 12-1.45 D served all week 7-8.45 **RESTAURANT:** L served Tues-Sun 12-2 D served all week 7-9.30 ⊕: Free House ◖: Scottish Courage Theakston Best, Greene King, Titanic. ♀: 10
FACILITIES: Garden: Beer garden **NOTES:** Parking 30

CAULDON

Map 16 SK04

Yew Tree Inn
ST10 3EJ ☎ 01538 308348 ▤ 01782 212064
Dir: Between A52 and A523, 4.5m from Alton Towers
A 300-year-old pub with plenty of character and lots of fascinating artefacts, including Victorian music boxes, pianolas, grandfather clocks, a crank handle telephone, a pub lantern and an award-winning landlord who's been here for over forty years! Interesting and varied snack menu consists of locally made, hand-raised pork pies, sandwiches, rolls and quiche. Banana split and home-made fruit crumble feature.
OPEN: 10-2.30 6-11 (Sun 12-3, 7-10.30) **BAR MEALS:** L served Snacks available during opening hours ⊕: Free House ◖: Burton Bridge, Grays Mild, Bass. **FACILITIES:** Dogs allowed Water
NOTES: Parking 50 No credit cards

CHEADLE

Map 10 SK04

The Queens At Freehay
Counslow Rd, Freehay ST10 1RF
☎ 01538 722383 ▤ 01538 722383
Dir: 4m from Alton Towers
The current proprietors bought the Queens in 1999, when it was rather run down, though it had had a good reputation for its food. Since then the pub, which is a couple of miles from Alton Towers, has re-established itself as an eating house with a nice, friendly, easy going atmosphere. Freshly cooked meals include fish and game daily specials, maybe pan-fried halibut with stir-fried vegetables, along with light bites and choices from the grill.
OPEN: 12-2.30 6-11 Closed: 25-26 Dec, 31 Dec (eve), 1 Jan (eve)
BAR MEALS: L served all week 12-2 D served all week 6-9.30 (Sun 12-2.30, 6.30-9.30) Av main course £8.95 **RESTAURANT:** L served all week 12-2 D served all week 6-9.30 Av 3 course à la carte £15.95
continued

⊕: Free House ◖: Draught Bass, Draught Worthington Bitter.
FACILITIES: Garden: Small garden with four benches
NOTES: Parking 30

ECCLESHALL

Map 15 SJ82

The George ♀
Castle St ST21 6DF ☎ 01785 850300 ▤ 01785 851452
e-mail: information@thegeorgeinn.freeserve.co.uk
Dir: 6m from M6 junct 14

A family-run, 16th-century former coaching inn with its own micro-brewery, where the owners' son produces award-winning Slater's ales. Occasional beer festivals are held, and the menu features a wide variety of dishes, including spicy chilli tortillas; fish stew; roast salmon with hoi sin sauce, chive mash and stir-fry veg; and cod in Slater's ale batter. There's a selection of salads, baked potatoes and sandwiches too.
OPEN: 11-11 (12-10.30 Sun) Closed: 25 Dec **BAR MEALS:** L served all week 12-9.30 D served all week 6-9.30 (Sun 12-8.30) Av main course £9.50 **RESTAURANT:** L served all week 12-2.30 D served all week 6-9.45 ⊕: Free House ◖:- Slaters Ales. **FACILITIES:** Dogs allowed **NOTES:** Parking 30

LEEK

Map 16 SJ95

Abbey Inn ♀
Abbey Green Rd ST13 8SA ☎ 01538 382865 ▤ 01538 398604
e-mail: martin@abbeyinn.co.uk
Dir: Telephone for directions
Set in beautiful countryside on the Staffordshire moorlands, this 17th-century inn is on the outskirts of Leek, and handy for the potteries of Stoke-on-Trent. It is also conveniently close to Alton Towers and Tittesworth Reservoir, and with its spacious bars and restaurant, and large terrace, it is an ideal destination for a meal or a drink.
OPEN: 11-2.30 6.30-11 (Sun 12-3 7-10.30) **BAR MEALS:** L served all week 11-2 D served all week 6.30-9 Av main course £4 ⊕: Free House ◖: Interbrew Bass. ♀: 8 **FACILITIES:** Children's licence Garden **NOTES:** Parking 30

Ye Olde Royal Oak
Wetton DE6 2AF ☎ 01335 310336 ▤ 01335 310287
e-mail: brian@rosehose.wanadoo.co.uk
Dir: A515 twrds Buxton, left after 4 miles to Manifold Valley-Alstonfield, follow signs to Wetton village,
Formerly part of the Chatsworth estate, this stone-built inn dates back over 400 years and has wooden beams recovered from oak ships at Liverpool Docks. It is now home to the World Annual Toe Wrestling Championships in June. The Tissington walking and cycling trail is close by, and the pub's moorland garden includes a camper's croft. Sample the landlord's collection of over 40 single malts, then tuck into steak and Guinness pie, wild mushroom lasagne, mixed grill,
continued

LEEK continued

or filled Staffordshire oatcakes.
OPEN: 12-3 Closed Tues lunch 7-11 Open all day Sat-Sun (Etr-Sep)
BAR MEALS: L served Wed-Mon 12-2 D served Wed-Mon 7-9
RESTAURANT: L served Wed-Mon 12-2 D served Wed-Mon 7-9
Av 3 course à la carte £12.70 ⊜: Free House ⊄: Adnams Bitter,
Greene King Abbot, guest beer. **FACILITIES:** Garden: Grassed area,
patio, tables & seating Dogs allowed Water **NOTES:** Parking 20

Three Horseshoes Inn ★★ ⊕ ⬩ ⦿ ♀
Buxton Rd, Blackshaw Moor ST13 8TW
☎ 01538 300296 ▤ 01538 300320 web: www.threeshoesinn.co.uk
Dir: Telephone for directions
A sprawling creeper-covered inn geared to catering for visitors
and locals in three smart eating outlets. Choose from the
traditional décor and food of the bar carvery, the relaxed
atmosphere of the brasserie, and the more formal restaurant.
The award-winning menu offers dishes ranging from
traditional (tournedos Rossini; bangers and mash) to steamed
monkfish in banana leaf or Thai duck curry.
OPEN: 12-3 6-11 **BAR MEALS:** L served all week 12-2 D served all
week 6.30-9 (Sun 12-3, 6-8.30) Av main course £7.25
RESTAURANT: L served Sun 12.30-1.30 D served Sun-Fri 6.30-9
Av 3 course à la carte £24 Av 0 course fixed price £15 ⊜: Free House
⊄: Theakstons XB Courage Directors, Morland Old Speckled Hen,
Kronenbourg 1664. ♀: 12 **FACILITIES:** Child facs Garden
NOTES: Parking 100 **ROOMS:** 7 bedrooms en suite

NEWCASTLE-UNDER-LYME   Map 10 SJ84

Mainwaring Arms ♀
Whitmore ST5 5HR ☎ 01782 680851 ▤ 01782 680224
e-mail: info@mannersrestaurant.co.uk

A welcoming old creeper-clad inn on the Mainwaring family
estate. Crackling log fires set the scene at this very traditional
country retreat, where daily blackboard specials support the
popular bar menu. Expect freshly-made sandwiches, home-
made steak and kidney pie, pork and leek sausages with chive
mash, grilled plaice with mustard sauce, or battered cod with
chips and mushy peas.
OPEN: 12-11 (Sun 12-10.30) **BAR MEALS:** L served all week
12-2.30 D served all week 6-8.30 Av main course £5 ⊜: Free House
⊄: Boddingtons, Marstons Pedigree, Bass plus guest ales.
FACILITIES: Garden: Patio seats 25-30, food served outside Dogs
allowed only when food service is over **NOTES:** Parking 60

Pubs with this logo do not allow smoking
anywhere on their premises

NORBURY JUNCTION   Map 15 SJ72

The Junction Inn
ST20 0PN ☎ 01785 284288 ▤ 01785 284288
Dir: From M6 take road for Eccleshall, left at Gt Bridgeford & head for
Woodseaves, left there & head for Newport, left for Norb Junct
Not a railway junction, but a beautiful stretch of waterway
where the Shropshire Union Canal meets the disused
Newport arm. The inn offers fabulous views and a great stop
off point for canal walkers. Food ranges from baguettes,
burgers and basket meals to grills and home-made pies.
Popular options are sizzling chicken fajitas, giant battered cod
and a gargantuan mixed grill. Caravans are welcome and
canal boat hire is available.
OPEN: 11-11 (12-10.30 Sun) **BAR MEALS:** L served all week 11-9
D served all week 11-9 **RESTAURANT:** L served all week 12-9
D served all week 12-9 Av 3 course à la carte £12 ⊜: Free House
⊄: Banks Mild, Banks Bitter, Junction Ale and guest ales.
FACILITIES: Child facs Garden: Scenic garden with fabulous views
Dogs allowed Water provided **NOTES:** Parking 100
See Pub Walk on page 444

ONECOTE   Map 16 SK05

Jervis Arms ⬩⦿
ST13 7RU ☎ 01538 304206
Convenient for visitors from Leek or Ashbourne, this 17th-
century inn set in the Peak National Park has a large
streamside garden kitted out with swings and slides. Some
500 guest ales have featured over the past five years to
accompany home-cooked steak and ale pie, lamb shank,
battered cod, BBQ tuna, popular roasts, and Chinese plum
and ginger duck. Additional menu items to satisfy vegetarians
and children. Two annual beer festivals, one of which includes
a duck race.
OPEN: 12-3 7-11 (6 in Summer, 6-11 Sat, all day Sun)
BAR MEALS: L served all week 12-2 D served all week 7-10 (Sun
12-9.30) ⊜: Free House ⊄: Interbrew Bass, Sarah Hughes Dark
Ruby Mild, Titanic Iceberg, 3 Guest beers. **FACILITIES:** Child facs
Garden: Large beer garden, river Dogs allowed Water
NOTES: Parking 50

ONNELEY   Map 15 SJ74

Pick of the Pubs

The Wheatsheaf Inn ♀
Barhill Rd CW3 9QF ☎ 01782 751581 ▤ 01782 751499
e-mail: thewheatsheaf.inn@virgin.net
Dir: On A525 between Madeley & Woore, 6.5m W of Newcastle-
under-Lyme
Overlooking the local golf course and village cricket
ground, this recently renovated wayside inn has been a
hostelry since 1769. Solid oak beams, roaring log fires and
distinctive furnishings are a fine setting for some fine
dining. Specials include Chateaubriand roast, steamed
halibut steak on buttered spinach, pan-fried kangaroo,
and chicken breast in smoked bacon with creamy grape
and cheese sauce. Bar meals also available.
OPEN: 12-2.30 6-11 **BAR MEALS:** L served all week 12-2.30
D served all week 6-9.30 Av main course £6
RESTAURANT: D served all week 6.30-9.30 Av 3 course à la
carte £15 ⊜: Free House ⊄: Bass, Worthington, Guest Ales.
FACILITIES: Garden: Food served outside Dogs allowed in the
garden only **NOTES:** Parking 60

England

STAFFORD
Map 10 SJ92

Pick of the Pubs

The Hollybush Inn 🐟 ♀
Salt ST18 0BX ☎ 01889 508234 🖹 01889 508058
e-mail: geoff@hollybushinn.co.uk web: www.hollybushinn.co.uk
See Pick of the Pubs on page 448

Pick of the Pubs

The Moat House ★★★★ 🏵🏵 ♀
Lower Penkridge Rd, Acton Trussell ST17 0RJ
☎ 01785 712217 🖹 01785 715344
e-mail: info@moathouse.co.uk web: www.moathouse.co.uk
Dir: M6 J13 towards Stafford, 1st R to Acton Trussell
Grade II listed mansion dating back to the 15th century
and situated behind its original moat. Quality bedrooms,
conference facilities and corporate events are big
attractions, and with four honeymoon suites, the Moat
House is a popular venue for weddings. Inside are oak
beams and an inglenook fireplace, and the bar and food
trade brings in both the hungry and the curious who like
to savour the charm and atmosphere of the place. Major
refurbishments have contributed a stylish lounge area
serving brasserie-style food. Among the more popular
dishes are rocket and goats' cheese soup or tuna spring
roll, followed by braised shank of lamb with bubble and
squeak and a rosemary jus; seared seabass with fennel,
baby spinach and a mussel nage; or plaice fillets with
crab mousse, asparagus and saffron broth. If there's room
afterwards, try bread and butter pudding, steamed treacle
sponge or chocolate fudge brownie.
OPEN: 10-11 Closed: 25-26 Dec, 1-2 Jan
BAR MEALS: L served Mon-Sat 12-2.15 D served Sun-Fri 6-9.30
Av main course £12.50 **RESTAURANT:** L served all week 12-2
D served all week 7-9.30 Av 3 course à la carte £34.50
Av 3 course fixed price £29.50 🍺: Free House 🍺: Bank's Bitter,
Marston's Pedigree, Murphys. ♀: 13 **FACILITIES:** Children's
licence Garden: Adjoining the Moated Manor, overlooks moat
NOTES: Parking 200 **ROOMS:** 32 bedrooms en suite
4 family rooms s£125 d£135

STOURTON
Map 10 SO88

The Fox Inn 🐟 ♀
Bridgnorth Rd DY7 5BL ☎ 01384 872614
& 872123 🖹 01384 877771
e-mail: fox-inn-stourton@dial.pipex.com
Dir: 5m from Stourbridge centre. On A458 Stourbridge to Bridgnorth road.
Remote 18th-century pub with a warm atmosphere from,
attracting walkers from many nearby rambling areas. The pub
still has many of its original features, and is located in
beautiful countryside near Kinver village. Large gardens
complete with weeping willow and hanging baskets in
summer, smart conservatory, good value food including a
wide variety of fish.
OPEN: 11.30-3 5-11 (Sat-Sun 11-11) **BAR MEALS:** L served all
week 12.30-2.15 D served Tue-Sat Late Sun lunch 3-5.30pm
RESTAURANT: L served Tue-Sun 12-9.30 D served Tue-Sat 7-9.30
Sun 12.30-5.15 Av 3 course à la carte £18 Av 3 course fixed price
£13.95 🍺: Bathams Ale, Enville Ale, Murphy's, Boddingtons. ♀: 8
FACILITIES: Garden: 2 acres of garden with patio and seating
NOTES: Parking 75

TATENHILL
Map 10 SK22

Horseshoe Inn ♀
Main St DE13 9SD ☎ 01283 564913 🖹 01283 511314
Dir: From A38 at Branston follow signs for Tatenhill
Probably five to six hundred years old, this historic pub
retains much original character, including evidence of a
priest's hiding hole. In winter, log fires warm the bar and
family area. In addition to home-made snacks like chilli con
carne, and Horseshoe brunch, there are sizzling rumps and
sirloins, chicken curry, moussaka, battered cod with chips and
mushy peas, and a pasta dish of the week. And specials too -
beef bourguignon, or steak and kidney pudding, for instance.
OPEN: 11-11 **BAR MEALS:** L served all week 12-9.30 D served all
week 12-9.30 Sun 12-9 Av main course £5.95
RESTAURANT: L served all week 12-9.30 D served all week 12-9.30
🍺: W'hampton & Dudley 🍺: Marstons Pedigree. ♀: 9
FACILITIES: Child facs Small enclosed garden with fish pond Dogs
allowed Water **NOTES:** Parking 70

TUTBURY
Map 10 SK22

Pick of the Pubs

Ye Olde Dog & Partridge Inn
High St DE13 9LS ☎ 01283 813030 🖹 01283 813178
e-mail: info@dogandpartridge.net
Dir: On A50 NW of Burton-on-Trent (signed from A50 & A511)
A beautiful period building resplendent in its timbers and
whitewashed walls, with abundant flower displays
beneath the windows. The inn has stood in this charming
village since the 15th century when Henry IV was on the
throne. Its connection with the village sport of bull-
running brought it into prominence, and it remains a
focus of local activity. During the 18th century it became a
coaching inn on the route to London. Five hundred years
of offering hospitality has resulted in a well-deserved
reputation for good food and restful public areas. Two
smart eating outlets ensure that all tastes are catered for.
In the Carvery, a grand piano plays while diners choose
from an extensive menu, and time and space should be
found for mouthwatering desserts.
OPEN: 11-11 Closed 25-26 Dec Closed eve **BAR MEALS:** L served all
week 11.30-11 D served all week 🍺: Free House 🍺: Marston's
Pedigree, Courage Director's. **FACILITIES:** Garden: Food served
outside **NOTES:** Parking 100

🍺 Principal Beers for sale

Pick of the Pubs

The Holly Bush Inn

The thatched Holly Bush is generally recognised as being the second pub in the country to have been licensed. This was sometime during Charles II's reign (1660-1685), but the building itself is much older, possibly going back to 1190. It boasts another distinction too: when landlord Geoff Holland's son became a joint licensee at the age of 18 years and 6 days, he was the youngest person ever to be granted a licence.

In the Domesday Book the village of Salt was recorded as Selte, which in Old English meant a salt pit, even though there's no written evidence of workings within the parish. Heavy carved beams, open fires, attractive prints and cosy alcoves characterise the comfortably old-fashioned interior. One of Geoff's proud boasts is that all produce used in the kitchen can be traced to its source, usually local. Also interesting is the fact that all waste food is recycled in the pub's own worm farm. Although traditional British dishes are at the heart of the operation, Greek lamb manages to sneak on to the main menu alongside steamed steak and kidney pudding; braised venison with chestnuts and celery; and poached fillet of plaice with white wine and prawn sauce. The specials boards change every session and might include a second lamb dish called Gloucestershire squab pie, in which tender lamb is layered with apples and flavoured with nutmeg and allspice. Also possible are Staffordshire oatcakes stuffed with bacon and cheese; Scottish mussels steamed with cider and cream; and the mixed grill, which even includes sirloin steak. Lunchtime offerings include triple-decker sandwiches, jacket potatoes, toasties, vegetarian options and a full range of desserts. In summer there are jazz concerts and hog roasts in the large secluded beer garden.

OPEN: 12-9.30 Sun-Thurs, 12-11 Fri-Sat
BAR MEALS: Food served 12-9.30 Sun-Thurs, 12-11 Fri-Sat Av main course £9.50
🍺: Free House
🍺: Adnams, Pedigree & Guest Ales.
🍷: 12
FACILITIES: Garden: Large lawned garden with seatings Dogs allowed Water provided **NOTES:** Parking 25

🍷   Map 10 SJ92
Salt ST18 0BX
☎ 01889 508234
📄 01889 508058
📧 geoff@hollybushinn.co.uk
🌐 www.hollybushinn.co.uk
Dir: Telephone for directions

WATERHOUSES   Map 16 SK05

Ye Olde Crown
Leek Rd ST10 3HL ☎ 01538 308204 📠 01538 308204

A traditional village local, Ye Olde Crown dates from around 1648 when it was built as a coaching inn. Sitting on the bank of the River Hamps, it's also on the edge of the Peak District National Park and the Staffordshire moorlands. Inside are original stonework and interior beams, and open fires are lit in cooler weather. A recent change of ownership has meant some major refurbishment of the pub, and a new car park. Readers reports are welcome.
OPEN: 11.30-3 6.30-11 (Sun 12-3, 6.30-11) **BAR MEALS:** L served all week D served all week 12-9 food available all day Av main course £7 **RESTAURANT:** L served all week 12-9 D served all week 12-9 Av 3 course à la carte £16 🍴: Free House ◀: Carlsberg-Tetley Tetley Bitter, Burton Ale, Pedigree, Marston Bitter. **FACILITIES:** Child facs Tables outside Dogs allowed **NOTES:** Parking 30

WOODSEAVES   Map 15 SJ72

The Plough Inn
Newport Rd ST20 0NP
Dir: 5m from Newport, Shropshire, 3m from Eccleshall, Stafford on the 519 Newport Rd
Built in the mid-18th century for workers constructing the nearby canal, the Plough is a traditional country pub with winter fires and hanging baskets for the summer. There's a good selection of real ales, and the bar menu features favourites like sausages, mash and red wine gravy. The restaurant menu offers more adventurous options like deep-fried goat's cheese with ratatouille and chargrilled potatoes; or pan-fried duck with cranberry and orange sauce.
OPEN: 12-3 6-11 **BAR MEALS:** L served Thur-Sun 12-2.30 D served Tues-Sat 6-9.30 Sun 12-4 (6-8.30 in summer) Av main course £8 **RESTAURANT:** L served Thurs-Sun 12-2.30 D served Tues-Sat (Sun in summer) 6-9.30 Sun 12-2.30, 6-8.30 Av 3 course à la carte £16 ◀: Spitfire, 6X, Grumpy Chef, Titanic Full Kiln Ale.
FACILITIES: Garden with wooden benches, flower beds **NOTES:** Parking 30

> Not all of the pubs in the guide are open all week or all day. It's always best to check before you travel

> Room prices show the minimum double and single rates charged. Room rates in hotels and B&Bs often vary depending on the facilities, so be sure to check prices with the establishment before booking

WRINEHILL   Map 15 SJ74

The Crown Inn
Den Ln CW3 9BT ☎ 01270 820472 📠 01270 820472
e-mail: mark_condliffe@hotmail.com
Dir: Telephone for directions

In the same family for nearly thirty years, this is a pub that serves food, not a restaurant that serves beer. Food, nevertheless, plays a vital part in the Crown's excellent local reputation. Possibilities from the menu include oven-baked haddock with stilton and cream, and mustard-glazed pork steaks topped with a caramelised apple slice. The excellent vegetarian choices include red pepper Moroccan style, Mediterranean vegetable lasagne, five bean casserole or winter squash gratin. There is a good range of steak dishes and light bites.
OPEN: 12-3 6-11 (Sun 12-4, 6-10.30) Closed: 25-26 Dec
BAR MEALS: L served Tue-Sun 12-2 (Sun 12-3.30) D served all week 6.30-9.30 (Sun 6-9) Av main course £7.50 ◀: Marstons Pedigree, Adnams Bitter, Timothy Taylor Landlord & Guest Beers.
FACILITIES: Garden: Secluded lawn area with benches
NOTES: Parking 36

YOXALL   Map 10 SK11

The Crown
Main St DE13 8NQ ☎ 01543 472551
Dir: On A515 N of Lichfield
In a picturesque village, this pub is reputedly over 250 years old: its name possibly deriving from its former use as the local courthouse. Within easy reach of Uttoxeter racecourse and Alton Towers it's a great spot to enjoy locally sourced, home-cooked food prepared by the landlord. Expect the regularly changing menu to offer such lunchtime bites as a breakfast brunch and hot filled baguettes, whilst evening options such as steak and Guinness pie are supplemented by offerings posted on the chalkboard.
OPEN: 11.30-3 5.30-11 (Sat-Sun & BHs open all day)
BAR MEALS: L served all week 12-2 D served Mon-Sat 6.30-9 Av main course £6.50 🍴: Marstons ◀: Marston's Pedigree, Stella Artois. **FACILITIES:** Garden: Dogs allowed **NOTES:** Parking 20

> Pubs offering a good choice of fish on their menu

> Pick of the Pubs have that extra special quality that makes them stand out from the crowd. Their entries are highlighted, and may be a full page

SUFFOLK

ALDEBURGH
Map 13 TM45

The Mill Inn
Market Cross Place IP15 5BJ ☎ 01728 452563 ▤ 01728 451923
web: www.themillinn.com
Dir: Follow Aldeburgh signs from A12 on A1094. Pub last building on left

Occupying a seafront position, this genuine traditional
fisherman's inn is frequented by the local lifeboat crew, those
visiting the North Warren bird reserve, and walkers from
Thorpness and Orford. Opposite is the 17th-century Moot
Hall. Good value food ranges from baguettes, crab salads and
sandwiches to seafood lasagne and a choice of steaks. The
emphasis is very much on locally caught fish. Recent change
of landlord.
OPEN: 11-3 6-11 (11-11 summer) **BAR MEALS:** L served all week
12-2 D served Tue-Sat 7-9 No evening meal Sun
RESTAURANT: L served Tue-Sun 12-2 D served Tue-Sat 7-9
🍴: Adnams 🍺: Adnams Bitter, Broadside, Regatta & Fisherman,
OLD. **FACILITIES:** Dogs allowed Water

ALDRINGHAM
Map 13 TM46

The Parrot and Punchbowl Inn & Restaurant 🐟 ♀
Aldringham Ln IP16 4PY ☎ 01728 830221
e-mail: paul@parrotandpunchbowl.fsnet.co.uk
*Dir: On B1122 1m from Leiston, 3m from Aldeburgh, on X-rds to
Thorpeness*

In addition to a parrot, the colourful pub sign shows a
boatload of pirates and barrels of contraband hooch, for this
16th-century establishment was once a smugglers' local. The
wide-ranging bar menu offers Parrot sandwiches and Parrot
jackets! A light lunch might feature freshly made pie of the
day, or Adnam's (the Southwold brewery) battered cod and
chips, while mains include honey-roasted Barbary duck breast
with a mixed-fruit tartlet, and creamy, wild mushroom risotto.
OPEN: 11.30-3 5.30-11 (Sun 12-3, 7-10.30) Winter 12-3 all week
BAR MEALS: L served every day 12-2.30 D served every day

continued

6.30-9.30 7pm Sun Av main course £5 **RESTAURANT:** L served
every day 12-2.30 D served every day 6.30-9.30 7pm Sun Av 3 course
à la carte £20 Av 2 course fixed price £10.50 🍴: Enterprise Inns
🍺: Adnams, London Pride, Guest beer. ♀: 10
FACILITIES: Garden: Family garden, walled and shaded Dogs
allowed Water bowls **NOTES:** Parking 60

BARNBY
Map 13 TM49

Pick of the Pubs

The Swan Inn 🐟
Swan Ln NR34 7QF ☎ 01502 476646 ▤ 01502 562513
Dir: Just off the A146 between Lowestoft and Beccles

Arguably one of Suffolk's foremost fish restaurants - the
menu lists up to 80 different seafood dishes - the Swan
still looks on itself as a traditional village pub with a
strong local following. The distinctive pink-painted
property dates from 1690, and can be found in the
picturesque village of Barnby, which nestles in its rural
surroundings. Owned by a family of Lowestoft fish
wholesalers, it comprises a village bar that is at the centre
of local activities, and the rustic Fisherman's Cove
restaurant, with its low beams and nautical memorabilia.
The menu is a fish-lovers delight: starters include smoked
sprats, smoked trout pâté and Italian seafood salad, while
main dishes range from monkfish tails in garlic butter, to
crab gratin and whole grilled turbot. Meat lovers are not
left out: various steaks are offered along with home-
cooked gammon salad.
OPEN: 11-3 6-12 **BAR MEALS:** L served all week 12-2
D served all week 7-9.30 **RESTAURANT:** L served all week 12-2
D served all week 7-9.30 🍴: Free House 🍺: Interbrew Bass,
Adnams Best, Broadside, Greene King Abbot Ale.
FACILITIES: Garden: Food served outside, colourful
NOTES: Parking 30

BILDESTON
Map 13 TL94

The Crown Hotel
104 High St IP7 7EB ☎ 01449 740510 ▤ 01449 741583
e-mail: hayley@thecrown.plus.com
Dir: On B1115 between Hadleigh & Stowmarket
A beautiful 15th-century half-timbered former coaching inn
with oak-beamed bars and lounge, maintaining its original
charming character. Originally a wool merchants, it claims to
be one of the most-haunted pubs in Britain. The menu is
governed by the seasons, using the best local produce
available. Confit rabbit terrine, cockle and parsley risotto and
warm chocolate fondant are mixed with classic dishes such as
steak and kidney pudding or fish and chips.
OPEN: 10-3 6-11 (Sat 10-11) **BAR MEALS:** L served all week 12-3

continued

D served all week 7-10 Sun 7-9.30 Av main course £10
RESTAURANT: L served all week 12-3 D served all week 7-10 Sun
7-9.30 Av 3 course à la carte £23 🍴: Free House 🍺: Adnams,
Broadside, Moletrap. **FACILITIES:** Child facs Garden: Rear of hotel,
quiet & peaceful, grassed, flat Dogs allowed **NOTES:** Parking 30

BRANDESTON   Map 13 TM26

The Queens Head ♀
The Street IP13 7AD ☎ 01728 685307
e-mail: stensethhome@aol.com
Dir: From A14 take A1120 to Earl Soham, then S to Brandeston
A village pub dating back 400 years, with wooden panelling,
quarry tile floors and open fires. The menu might offer such
dishes as Moroccan lamb tagine; Barbary duck breast glazed
with honey and mustard, served on roast vegetables with
plum and red wine sauce; and sea trout fillet served on sauté
potatoes with onion chutney and Pernod sauce. Vegetarian
options include mushroom and mascarpone lasagne and
tagliatelle with roasted vegetables.
OPEN: 11.30-3 6-11 (Sun 12-3, 7-10.30) Jan-Mar Closed on Sun eve
BAR MEALS: L served all week 12-2 D served all week 6.30-9
Av main course £9.95 **RESTAURANT:** L served all week D served all
week Av 3 course à la carte £18.95 🍴: Adnams 🍺: Adnams
Broadside, & Bitter seasonal ale. ♀: 8 **FACILITIES:** Garden: Mostly
lawn with flower beds Dogs allowed Water **NOTES:** Parking 30

BROCKLEY GREEN   Map 12 TL74

Pick of the Pubs

The Plough Inn 🏨 ♀
CO10 8DT ☎ 01440 786789 🖶 01440 786710
e-mail: hundonplough@yahoo.co.uk
Dir: Take B1061 from A143, approx 1.5m beyond Kedington

This friendly, family-run free house started life as a small
alehouse serving the local farming community. Recent
expansion projects have successfully blended old and
new, creating a mellow, rustic interior featuring old oak
beams and soft red brickwork. There are cosy log fires in
winter, whilst in summer the attractive terrace and large
garden command superb views over the surrounding
countryside. Greene King IPA and Adnam's Best head the
list of well-kept cask ales, whilst other tastes are catered
for with around 30 malt whiskies and a dozen wines
served by the glass. The bar menu features soups,
sandwiches and ploughman's, supported by simple hot
dishes like pot-roasted lamb shank. For more formal
occasions in the non-smoking restaurant, try pan-fried
scallops on baby leaves with fresh lime and coriander
butter; wild mushroom crêpes with fresh tomato sauce; or
roast rack of lamb with basil and redcurrant jus.

OPEN: 12-2.30 5-11 **BAR MEALS:** L served all week 12-2
D served all week 7-9.30 **RESTAURANT:** L served all week 12-2
D served all week 7-9.30 Sun 12-2.30, 7-9 🍴: Free House
🍺: Greene King IPA, Adnams Best, Fuller's London Pride,
Woodforde's Wherry Best Bitter. ♀: 12 **FACILITIES:** Garden: A
large lawn bordered by shrubs Dogs allowed Water bowls
NOTES: Parking 50

BROME   Map 13 TM17

Pick of the Pubs

Cornwallis Country Hotel ♀
IP23 8AJ ☎ 01379 870326 🖶 01379 870051
e-mail: info@thecornwallis.com web: www.thecornwallis.com
Dir: Just off A140 at Brome, follow B1077 to Eye. Pub 30 metres on L

This handsome looking building dating from 1561 is the
one-time Dower House to Brome Hall. Within its 20
peaceful acres are an avenue of limes, some impressive
yew topiary and a pretty water garden, while inside many
of the original beams, panels and oak and mahogany
settles remain from earliest times. In the log-fired Tudor
Bar look into the murky depths of a 60-foot well. Virtually
everything emanating from the kitchen uses fresh, mostly
locally supplied ingredients, whether it's roasted cod with
chorizo mash, wilted spinach and cockles; winter warmer
sausages with braised vegetables; or cannelloni of
butternut squash and amaretto with ginger and onion
marmalade, salsify and crispy leeks. The same applies to
steak, kidney and Adnam's ale pudding; mussels with
Thai curry broth and seaweed focaccia; and open ravioli
of chicken with baby leeks, marinated peppers and pesto
cream. Refreshing desserts include strawberry and vanilla
pannacotta with lavender sorbet, and a selection of
Scottish cheeses.
OPEN: 11-11 **BAR MEALS:** L served all week 12-2.30 D served
all week 6-9.30 Av main course £10 **RESTAURANT:** L served
all week 12-2.30 D served all week 6-9.30 Av 3 course fixed price
£27 🍴: Free House 🍺: Adnams, Greene King IPA, St Peters
Best. ♀: 16 **FACILITIES:** Garden: 21 acres of gardens, pond
Dogs allowed Water **NOTES:** Parking 400

continued

England

BURY ST EDMUNDS   Map 13 TL86

The Linden Tree
7 Out Northgate IP33 1JQ ☎ 01284 754600
Dir: *Opposite railway station*
Built to serve the railway station, this is a big, friendly
Victorian pub, with stripped pine bar, dining area, non-
smoking conservatory and charming garden. The family-
orientated menu ranges from beef curry, home-made pies,
and liver and bacon, to crab thermidor, fresh sea bass, and
mushroom and lentil moussaka. Youngsters will go for the
burgers, scampi, quorn or pork chipolatas. Freshly filled
ciabattas at lunchtime. Recent change of landlord, but still a
Greene King pub.
OPEN: 11-3 5-11 Closed: Xmas for 2 days **BAR MEALS:** L served
all week 12-2 D served all week 6-9.30 Sun and BH 12-3 & 6-9
(Sunday lunch not roast) Av main course £8.99
RESTAURANT: L served all week 12-2 D served all week 6-9.30 Sun
12-3 & 6-9 ☺: Greene King ◀: Greene King, IPA, Abbot Ale,
Ruddles County & Old Speckled Hen. **FACILITIES:** Child facs Large
garden: picnic tables, play area

The Nutshell
17 The Traverse IP33 1BJ ☎ 01284 764867
Unique pub measuring 15ft by 7ft, and said to be Britain's
smallest. Somehow more than 100 people and a dog
managed to fit inside in the 1980s. The bar's ceiling is covered
with paper money, and there have been regular sightings of
ghosts around the building, including a nun and a monk who
apparently weren't praying! No food is available, though the
pub jokes about its dining area for parties of two or fewer.
OPEN: 12-11pm ☺: Greene King ◀: Greene King IPA & Abbot Ale,
Guest Ales. **FACILITIES:** Dogs allowed **NOTES:** No credit cards

Old Cannon Brewery NEW ◆◆◆◆ ♀
86 Cannon St IP33 1JR ☎ 01284 768769 ⓘ 01284 701137
Dir: *From A14 follow signs to Bury St Edmunds town centre, at 1st rdbt*
take 1st left into Northgate St, then 1st right into Cadney Ln, left at end
onto Cannon St, pub 100yd on left.
Affectionately known as 'The Old Can', this solid and spacious
former beer house and brewery was built in 1845. It boasts
what must be a unique conversation piece in the bar - a
mirror-polished, stainless steel mash tun and boiler, the
source of some terrific real ales. The innovative menu offers
roasted duck breast with sloe gin and blackberry sauce;
Gunner's Daughter ale sausages and onion gravy; and grilled
red snapper.
OPEN: 12-3 5-11 (Sun 12-3 7-10.30) Closed: 25 Dec, 1 Jan
BAR MEALS: L served Tues-Sun 12-2 D served Tues-Sat 6.30-9.30
Av main course £12 **RESTAURANT:** L served Tues-Sun 12-2
D served Tues-Sat 6.30-9.30 Av 3 course à la carte £20 ◀: Old
Cannon Best Bitter, Old Cannon Gunner's Daughter, Adnams Bitter,
seasonal Old Cannon beers. ♀: 7 **FACILITIES:** Garden
NOTES: Parking 7 **ROOMS:** 5 bedrooms en suite s£49 d£62 No
children overnight

The Six Bells at Bardwell ◆◆◆◆ 🍴 ♀
The Green, Bardwell IP31 1AW
☎ 01359 250820 ⓘ 01359 250820
e-mail: sixbellsbardwell@aol.com
web: www.sixbellsbardwell.co.uk
Dir: *From A143 take turning marked Six Bells & Bardwell Windmill, 1m on*
left just before village green
This low-beamed village pub, dating back to the 1500s,
featured in the classic BBC comedy series *Dad's Army*. It's
handy for visiting various historic houses in the area, as well
as walking or cycling in nearby Thetford Forest. The dinner

continued

menu offers dishes such as Suffolk loin of pork steaks;
chargrilled fillet of red snapper with pesto salsa; and breast of
chicken with warm artichoke salad. Comfortable cottage-style
accommodation is available in the converted barn.
OPEN: 6.30-10.30 (Fri-Sat 6-11) Closed Sun Dec-Jan Closed: 23
Dec-3 Jan **BAR MEALS:** D served all week 6.30-8.30 Av main
course £10.95 **RESTAURANT:** D served all week 6.45-8.30
Av 3 course fixed price £17.50 ☺: Free House ◀: Boddingtons.
♀: 7 **FACILITIES:** Garden: Courtyard area with seating, water
feature **NOTES:** Parking 40 **ROOMS:** 10 bedrooms en suite
1 family room s£49.50 d£65 No children overnight

The Three Kings ◆◆◆◆
Hengrave Rd, Fornham All Saints IP28 6LA
☎ 01284 766979 ⓘ 01284 723308
e-mail: enquiries@the-three-kings.com
Plenty of exposed wood and interesting artefacts create a
traditional atmosphere at this pretty pub. Bedroom
accommodation is also provided in converted Grade II listed
outbuildings. Food is served in the bar, conservatory,
restaurant and courtyard. There are at least four fresh grilled
fish dishes every day, a choice of steaks, and old favourites
like steak and ale pie or liver and bacon.
OPEN: 11-11 (Sun 12-10.30) **BAR MEALS:** L served all week
11.30-2 D served all week 5.30-9.30 Sun 12-2.30, 6-8.30 Av main
course £5.95 **RESTAURANT:** L served Tue-Sun 12-2 D served
Tue-Sat 7-8.30 Sun 12-2.30 ☺: Greene King ◀: Greene King IPA &
Abbot. **FACILITIES:** Children's licence Garden: Patio area, benches
Dogs allowed Water offered **NOTES:** Parking 28
ROOMS: 9 bedrooms en suite 2 family rooms s£55 d£75

CAVENDISH   Map 13 TL84

Bull Inn 🍴 ♀
High St CO10 8AX ☎ 01787 280245
Dir: *A134 Bury St Edmunds to Long Melford, R at green, pub 5m on R*
A Victorian pub set in one of Suffolk's most beautiful villages,
with an unassuming façade hiding a splendid 15th-century
beamed interior. Expect a good atmosphere and decent food,
with the daily-changing blackboard menu listing perhaps
curries, shank of lamb, fresh fish and shellfish, and a roast on
Sundays. Outside there's a pleasant terraced garden.
OPEN: 11-3 6-11 (Sun 12-4) **BAR MEALS:** L served Mon-Sun 12-2
D served Mon-Sat 6.30-9 (Sun 12-2.30) Av main course £7.95
RESTAURANT: L served Mon-Sat 12-2 D served Mon-Sat 6.30-9 (Sun
12-2.30) Av 3 course à la carte £18 ☺: Adnams ◀: Adnams Bitter &
Broadside; Nethergate Suffolk County. **FACILITIES:** Patio Dogs
allowed **NOTES:** Parking 30

CHELMONDISTON   Map 13 TM23

Butt & Oyster ♀
Pin Mill Ln IP9 1JW ☎ 01473 780764 ⓘ 01473 780764
The role of this 16th-century pub on the eerie Suffolk coast
has always been to provide sustenance for the local bargees
and rivermen whose thirst for beer is near legendary. Today,
with its character still thankfully intact, the Butt & Oyster is a
favourite haunt of locals, tourists and sailors. A mixture of
seafood and traditional dishes characterises the menu,
including toad in the hole, steak and kidney pie and scampi
and chips.
OPEN: 11-11 (Sun 12-10.30) Dec 25-26 Dec 31 Closed eve
BAR MEALS: L served all week D served all week (Food served all
day, Sun 12-9.30) ☺: Pubmaster ◀: IPA, Adnams, Broadside,
Greene King. **FACILITIES:** Garden: outdoor eating, riverside Dogs
allowed in the garden only, Water **NOTES:** Parking 40

CHILLESFORD — Map 13 TM35

The Froize Inn ♀

The Street IP12 3PU ☎ 01394 450282 e-mail: dine@froize.co.uk
Dir: *Located on B1084 between Woodbridge (8m) and Oxford (3m).*
Built on the site of Chillesford Friary, this distinctive red-brick
building dates back to around 1490 and stands on today's
popular Suffolk Coastal Path. Inside, you will find a traditional
English pub with a modern dining room. The emphasis of the
menu is on rustic English and continental dishes, using
locally-sourced ingredients - fish and seafood, vegetables, and
game in the winter. Choices may include baked Scottish
salmon, devilled kidneys, local dressed crab or lobster salad.
OPEN: 11.30-2.30 6.30-11 Closed Mon **BAR MEALS:** L served
Tues-Sun 12-2 D served Thur-Sat 7-8.30 Av main course £10
RESTAURANT: L served Tue-Sun 12-2 D served Thu-Sat 7-8.30
🍽: Free House 🍺: Adnams. ♀: 11 **FACILITIES:** Garden: Large
fenced area with outside seating **NOTES:** Parking 70 ⊗

COCKFIELD — Map 13 TL95

Three Horseshoes ◑⟡ ♀

Stow's Hill IP30 0JB ☎ 01284 828177 ▤ 01284 828177
e-mail: john@threehorseshoespub.co.uk
Dir: *A134 towards Sudbury, then left onto A1141 towards Lavenham*

This former long hall built around 1350 still has an oak king-
post supporting its massive beams and vaulted ceilings,
making it one of the oldest in Suffolk. Eat in the restaurant,
bar or conservatory with views over rolling countryside. A
good selection of starters precedes steaks, mixed grills, fish,
pies and vegetarian dishes. Specialities include chargrilled
pork loin, tournedos, braised lamb shank, and various curries.
OPEN: 11-3 6-11 (Sun 10.30) **BAR MEALS:** L served Wed-Mon
12-2 D served Wed-Mon 6-9.30 (Sun 12-3, 7-9) Av main course £7.50
RESTAURANT: L served Wed-Mon 12-2.30 D served Wed-Mon
7-9.30 (Sun 12-2.30, 7-9) Av 3 course à la carte £16 Av 3 course fixed
price £12.95 🍽: Free House 🍺: Adnams, Horseshoes Bitter,
Directors, Theakstons XB & Black Bull. ♀: 9 **FACILITIES:** Child facs
Enclosed garden with gazebo and water feature Dogs allowed Water
NOTES: Parking 90

COTTON — Map 13 TM06

Pick of the Pubs

The Trowel & Hammer Inn

Mill Rd IP14 4QL ☎ 01449 781234 ▤ 01449 781765
Dir: *From A14 signs to Haughley, Bacton, then L for Cotton.*
Hidden away down Mill Road, but worth the effort of
finding, this newly thatched, wisteria-covered pub dates
back some 550 years. Merchants and cotton traders
heading inland from the coast used to call here, and

Milton drank in the bar when he lived in Stowmarket.
The modern bar adds to the amenities without
detracting from the traditional style; old oak timbers,
red carpets and imaginative lighting make for a relaxed
atmosphere. The daily-changing, unpretentious menus
offer a wide choice of freshly-cooked food. There is a
different, interesting home-made soup everyday, and
other lighter dishes include home-made creamy salmon
mousse; chilli prawns in filo pastry with lobster tails;
and houmous and taramasalata with pitta bread. For
something more substantial there is wild boar steak
with cider and mustard sauce; venison and apricot
sausages; and roasted fillet of cod with Mediterranean
vegetables from a long, tempting list. Real ales come
from Suffolk's Adnams, Mauldens and Nethergate.

The Trowel & Hammer Inn

OPEN: 11-11 **BAR MEALS:** L served all week 12-2 D served all
week 6-9 food all day Sun Av main course £7.50
RESTAURANT: L served all week 12-2 D served Mon-Sat 6-9
🍽: Free House 🍺: Adnams Bitter, Greene King IPA & Abbot
Ale, Nethergates, Mauldons. **FACILITIES:** Child facs Garden:
Large garden with swimming pool Dogs allowed Water, biscuits
NOTES: Parking 50

DUNWICH — Map 13 TM47

Pick of the Pubs

The Ship Inn ◑⟡

St James St IP17 3DT ☎ 01728 648219 ▤ 01728 648675
e-mail: shipinn@tiscali.co.uk
Dir: *N on A12 from Ipswich through Yoxford, right signed Dunwich*
Dunwich, a famous seaport before the sea swept it
away in the Middle Ages, is now merely an attractive
seaside village. All that is left of its former glory (in 630
it was the seat of the East Anglian bishopric) are the
friary ruins, and of course the Ship Inn. This old
smugglers' haunt exudes great warmth and character,
and is noted for traditional food and local ales. As one
would expect, fresh local fish features prominently on
the menu, including cod, mackerel, prawns, scampi, and
fishcakes. The specials board may supplement these
with sole, haddock, sardines and crab according to
availability, and in fine weather the Dunwich fish can be
eaten in the garden. Non-fish dishes include, bacon and
walnut salad; black pudding with apple cider and
wholegrain mustard sauce; steak and ale casserole; pork
in peach and Madeira sauce; and several salads. Real
ales are from Suffolk's own Adnams and Mauldons.
OPEN: 11-11 (Sun 12-10.30) **BAR MEALS:** L served all week
12-3 D served all week 6-9 Sat-Sun 12-6 bar meals, dinner 6-9

continued   *continued*

England

England

DUNWICH continued

RESTAURANT: L served all week 12-3 D served all week 6-9 Sat-Sun 12-6 bar meals, dinner 6-9 🍴: Free House 🍺: Adnams, Mauldons. **FACILITIES:** Garden: Large terraced area Dogs allowed **NOTES:** Parking 10

EARL SOHAM
Map 13 TM26

Victoria
The Street IP13 7RL ☎ 01728 685758
Dir: From the A14 at Stowmarket, Earl Soham is on the A1120 heading towards Yoxford
Backing on to the village green, this friendly, down-to-earth pub has its own brewery attached to the rear of the building. Traditional pub fare is on offer, like home-made chilli, baked gammon, various meat and game casseroles, curries, and smoked salmon salad, along with such light lunches as macaroni cheese, filled jacket potatoes, toasted sandwiches and various ploughman's. Home-made desserts include sponge pudding and treacle, and walnut tart.
OPEN: 11.30-3 6-11 (Sun 12-3, 7-10.30) **BAR MEALS:** L served all week 11.30-2 D served all week 6-10 Av main course £6.75 🍴: Free House 🍺: Earl Soham-Victoria Bitter, Albert Ale, & Gannet Mild (all brewed on site). Earl Soham Porter, Edward Ale.
FACILITIES: Garden: Benches at front and rear of pub Dogs allowed garden only **NOTES:** Parking 25

ERWARTON
Map 13 TM23

The Queens Head
The Street IP9 1LN ☎ 01473 787550
Dir: From Ipswich take B1456 to Shotley
There's a relaxed and intimate atmosphere here, with magnificent views over the surrounding countryside and across the Stour estuary. Low oak-beamed ceilings make this handsome 16th-century Suffolk free house an atmospheric stop for a pint of locally-brewed Adnams or Greene King ales. The wide-ranging menu includes traditional hot dishes, sandwiches, or a ploughman's lunch. Meanwhile, the specials boards offer choices like roast partridge; cod and prawn mornay; or ratatouille pudding with spicy tomato sauce.
OPEN: 11-3 6.30-11 (Sun 12-3, 7-10.30) Closed: 25 Dec
BAR MEALS: L served all week 12-2.45 D served all week 7-9.30 Av main course £7.95 **RESTAURANT:** L served all week 12-2.45 D served all week 7-9.30 🍴: Free House 🍺: Adnams Bitter & Broadside, Greene King IPA. **FACILITIES:** Garden
NOTES: Parking 30

EYE
Map 13 TM17

The White Horse Inn ♦♦♦♦
Stoke Ash IP23 7ET ☎ 01379 678222 📠 01379 678800
e-mail: mail@whitehorse-suffolk.co.uk
web: www.whitehorse-suffolk.co.uk
Dir: On the main A140 between Ipswich & Norwich
A 17th-century coaching inn set amid lovely Suffolk countryside. The heavily-timbered interior accommodates an inglenook fireplace, two bars and a restaurant. There are seven spacious motel bedrooms in the grounds, as well as a patio and secluded grassy area. An extensive menu is supplemented by lunchtime snacks, grills and daily specials from the blackboard. Grilled liver and crispy bacon; mushroom and cashew nut stroganoff; and salmon filo wraps are typical.
OPEN: 11-11 (Sun 11-10.30) **BAR MEALS:** L served all week 11-9.30 D served all week 11-9.30 **RESTAURANT:** L served all week

continued

11-9.30 D served all week 11-9.30 🍴: Free House 🍺: Adnams, Greene King Abbot, IPA Smooth. **FACILITIES:** Child facs Children's licence Garden: Patio & grass area **NOTES:** Parking 60
ROOMS: 7 bedrooms en suite 1 family room

FRAMLINGHAM
Map 13 TM26

The Station Hotel ♀
Station Rd IP13 9EE ☎ 01728 723455
Dir: Bypass Ipswich towards Lowestoft on A12
Since trains stopped coming to Framlingham in 1962 the buildings of the former station hotel have been put to good use. One is a vintage motorcycle repair shop, while another is an antique bed showroom. The hotel has established itself as a popular destination, with a good reputation for seafood and locally brewed beers. New owners took over in 2004, so look out for their adventurous menu.
OPEN: 12-2.30 5-11 **BAR MEALS:** L served all week 12-2 D served all week 7-9.30 Av main course £8.75 **RESTAURANT:** L served all week 12-2 D served all week 7-9.30 Av 3 course à la carte £15 Av 0 course fixed price £8.75 🍴: Free House 🍺: Earl Soham Victoria, Albert & Mild. **FACILITIES:** Garden: Pond, patio Dogs allowed Water, Biscuits **NOTES:** Parking 20

FRAMSDEN
Map 13 TM15

The Dobermann Inn
The Street IP14 6HG ☎ 01473 890461
Dir: S off A1120 (Stowmarket/Yoxford)
Previously The Greyhound, the pub was renamed by its current proprietor, a prominent breeder and judge of Dobermanns. The thatched roofing, gnarled beams, open fire and assorted furniture reflect its 16th-century origins. Food ranges from sandwiches and salads to main courses featuring game from a local estate in season. Reliable favourites include steak and mushroom pie, Dover sole, and sirloin steak. Vegetarians can feast on mushroom stroganoff or spicy nut loaf, and then indulge in the legendary banana split!
OPEN: 12-3 7-11 Closed: 25 & 26 Dec **BAR MEALS:** L served Tue-Sun 12-2 D served all week 7-10
RESTAURANT: L served all week 12-2 D served all week 7-10 🍴: Free House 🍺: Adnams Bitter & Broadside, Greene King Abbot Ale, Mauldons Moletrap Bitter. **FACILITIES:** Garden: Small beer garden, BBQ, shrubs, stream Dogs allowed Water
NOTES: Parking 27 No credit cards

GREAT GLEMHAM
Map 13 TM36

The Crown Inn ♀
IP17 2DA ☎ 01728 663693
Dir: A12 Ipswich to Lowestoft, in Stratford-St-Andrew L at Shell garage. Crown 1.5m
Cosy 17th-century village pub overlooking the Great Glemham Estate and within easy reach of the Suffolk Heritage Coast. You can eat in the extensively renovated bars and large flower-filled garden, where moussaka, carbonnade of beef, Somerset lamb casserole, roasted vegetables with pasta, and spinach and feta cheese tart from the specials menu might be followed by fresh fruit pavlova or traditional sherry trifle.
OPEN: 11.30-2.30 6.30-11 (Closed Mon) **BAR MEALS:** L served Tue-Sun 11.30-2.30 D served Tue-Sun 6.30-10 Av main course £8 🍴: Free House 🍺: Greene King Old Speckled Hen & IPA. ♀: 7 **FACILITIES:** Child facs Garden: Large lawn, flower border, picnic table Dogs allowed **NOTES:** Parking 20

🛢 Brewery/Company

HADLEIGH
Map 13 TM04

The Marquis of Cornwallis ♀
Upper St, Layham IP7 5JZ ☎ 01473 822051 ▤ 01473 822051
e-mail: marquislayham@aol.com
Dir: 3m from A12 between Colchester & Ipswich take B1070 towards Hadleigh. Upper Layham 1m before Hadleigh

Standing in two acres of gardens overlooking the River Brett, this 16th-century free house offers a truly traditional welcome to all. The low beamed ceilings and candle-lit interior set the tone for enjoying the well kept ales, country wines and traditional meals. Bar snacks and home-made pies are popular options from the single menu, served in the bar and non-smoking restaurant. Other choices include baked pink trout; grilled pork steak with apples; and macaroni cheese.
OPEN: 12-3 6-11 (Sun 12-10.30) **BAR MEALS:** L served all week 12-2.30 D served all week 7-9.30 Av main course £8.15
RESTAURANT: L served all week 12-2.30 D served all week 7-9.30 Av 3 course à la carte £16.15 ☺: Free House ◀: Adnams & Broadside, Greene King IPA & Abbot Ale. ♀: 9 **FACILITIES:** Garden: 2 acres, overlooking River Brett & Valley Dogs allowed Water **NOTES:** Parking 30

HALESWORTH
Map 13 TM37

Pick of the Pubs

The Queen's Head ♀
The Street, Bramfield IP19 9HT
☎ 01986 784214 ▤ 01986 784797 e-mail: qhbfield@aol.com
Dir: 2m from A12 on the A144 towards Halesworth
A renowned dining pub, the Queen's Head is a lovely old building located in the centre of Bramfield village. It is on the Suffolk Heritage Coast, just 15 minutes from Southwold. The pub garden is overlooked by the thatched village church, which has an unusual separate round bell tower. Inside you'll find scrubbed pine tables, exposed beams, a vaulted ceiling in the bar and enormous fireplaces. There is a daily changing menu based on carefully sourced ingredients from small local suppliers and organic farms. Starters, all served with home-made bread, might include herring fillets with a honey, mustard and dill marinade. Main courses take in squash with curry nut stuffing, tomato and basil sauce (among an interesting vegetarian selection); lamb à la grecque; and fresh cod with a crispy cheese and garlic topping. A good variety of puddings includes apple crumble and chocolate and brandy pot.
OPEN: 11.45-2.30 6.30-11 (Sun 12-3, 7-10.30) Closed: 26 Dec
BAR MEALS: L served all week 12-2 D served all week 6.30-10 Sun 7-9 Av main course £3.10 ☺: Adnams ◀: Adnams Bitter & Broadside. ♀: 7 **FACILITIES:** Child facs Garden: Enclosed garden with seating, willow dome Dogs allowed Water **NOTES:** Parking 15

HITCHAM
Map 13 TL95

The White Horse Inn NEW
The Street IP7 7NQ ☎ 01449 740981 ▤ 01449 740981
e-mail: lewis@thewhitehorse.wanadoo.co.uk
Dir: 13m from Ipswich and Bury St. Edmonds 7m from Stowmarket and Hadleigh
This semi-detached Grade II listed building in two storeys is the only pub in Hitcham, and estimated in parts to be around 400 years old. The family run pub has a welcoming atmosphere where you can relax and enjoy home-cooked food washed down by one of the large selection of wines. Please note that from November to April this pub is closed on Mondays and Tuesdays.
OPEN: 12-3 6-11 Nov-Apr Closed Mon and Tue
BAR MEALS: L served all week 12-2 D served all week 6-9 Av main course £8 **RESTAURANT:** L served all week 12-2 D served all week 6-9 Fri-Sat dinner 6-9.30 Av 3 course à la carte £20 Av 3 course fixed price £15 ◀: IPA, Adnams Best Bitter, London Pride, Woodfordes Wherry. **FACILITIES:** Garden: Lawned area with tables and parasols Dogs allowed water bowl **NOTES:** Parking 25

HOLBROOK
Map 13 TM13

Pick of the Pubs

The Compasses
Ipswich Rd IP9 2QR ☎ 01473 328332 ▤ 01473 327403
Dir: From A137 S of Ipswich, take B1456/B1080
Holbrook is bordered by the rivers Orwell and Stour, and this traditional country pub, which dates back to the 17th century, is on the Shotley peninsula. For several decades the inn was a staging post between London and Ipswich and the area is still popular with visitors. The menu is varied and appetising; it's also reasonably priced, with only one steak dish topping the £10 mark. Good fish options include grilled or battered cod or haddock, fish pie, and seafood lasagne. Special mains are chicken Alex, a boneless chicken breast in the pub's gourmet sauce of white wine, bacon, mushrooms and cream; kleftico, a large lamb joint slowly cooked in red wine and herbs, served with chive and onion mash; stroganoffs, carbonades, goulashes - the list continues and not to the exclusion of favourites such as ham, egg and chips. Some courses are offered in smaller portions at lower prices, leaving space for cheese and biscuits or dessert.
OPEN: 11-2.30 6-11 (Sun 12-3, 6-10.30) Closed: 25-26 Dec, 1 Jan **BAR MEALS:** L served all week 11.30-2.15 D served all week 6-9.15 (Sun food times, 12-2.15, 6-9.15)
RESTAURANT: L served all week 11.30-2.15 D served all week 6-9.15 (Sun food times, 12-2.15, 6-9.15) Av 3 course à la carte £17 Av 3 course fixed price £18 ☺: Pubmaster ◀: Carlsberg, Greene King IPA, Adnams Bitter, Kronenbourg & Guest Ales. **FACILITIES:** Garden: Six picnic benches, children's play area Dogs allowed Water Bowl **NOTES:** Parking 30

All AA rated accommodation can also be found on the AA's internet site
www.theAA.com

Pubs with Red Diamonds are the top
♦ places in the AA's three, four and five diamond ratings

England

HONEY TYE
Map 13 TL93

The Lion ♀
CO6 4NX ☎ 01206 263434 🖂 01206 263434
Dir: On A134 between Colchester & Sudbury

Low-beamed ceilings and an open log fire are charming features of this traditional country dining pub on the Essex/Suffolk border. The menu is concise yet offers enticing choices: seared breast of pigeon or deep-fried sardines could lead on to baked breast of chicken filled with green pesto and mozzarella, or duo of duck sausages with orange-scented sweet potato. Fish such as grilled darne of salmon, baked rainbow trout, or roast fillets of sea bass are also available; a couple of thoughtful vegetarian options complete the picture.
OPEN: 11-3 5-11 (Sun 12-10.30) **BAR MEALS:** L served all week 12-2 D served all week 6-9.30 SUn 12-9.30 **RESTAURANT:** L served all week 12-2 D served all week 6-9.30 Sun 12-9.30 🍴: Free House ◀: Greene King IPA, Adnams Bitter, Guest ale.
FACILITIES: Garden: Patio with tables and umbrellas Dogs allowed
NOTES: Parking 40

HORRINGER
Map 13 TL86

Pick of the Pubs

Beehive ♀
The Street IP29 5SN ☎ 01284 735260 🖂 01638 730416
Dir: From A14 1st turn for Bury St Edmunds, sign for Westley & Ickworth Park
On the High Street in Horringer near Bury St Edmunds stands this charming converted, Victorian flint and stone cottage. Full of period features, the Beehive is near the National Trust's Ickworth House. A succession of cosy dining areas is furnished with antique pine tables and chairs. In season, visitors head for the tables on the patio and the picnic benches in the walled beer garden. The proprietors keep apace with changing customer tastes, offering well-chosen seasonal produce and daily changing menus. For example you may find goblet of prawns with mixed leaves and tomato mayo, followed by home-made pork, sun-ripened tomato and paprika sausages on creamy mash and, to finish, meringue 'floating island' with fruit compote. If it's just a snack you are after you, cannot go wrong with Suffolk ham with French bread, salad & chutneys, or the selection of French cheeses, pickles and apple.
OPEN: 11.30-2.30 7-11 Closed: Dec 25-26
BAR MEALS: L served all week 12-2 D served Mon-Sat 7-9.45
RESTAURANT: L served all week 12-2 D served all week 7-9.45
🍴: Greene King ◀: Greene King IPA & Abbot Ale, Guest beers.
FACILITIES: Garden: Patio, picnic benches, walled garden Dogs allowed Garden only **NOTES:** Parking 30

HOXNE
Map 13 TM17

The Swan ♀
Low St IP21 5AS ☎ 01379 668275 e-mail: info@hoxneswan.co.uk
15th-century Grade II listed building formerly known as Bishop's Lodge. Inside, the restaurant and front bar boast a 10ft inglenook fireplace, ornate beamed ceilings and old planked floors, while the garden, overshadowed by a huge willow tree, extends to the River Dove. Food ranges from lunchtime snacks to main dishes including rabbit casserole, Sussex stew trencher (beef stew in a big Yorkshire pudding), roasted monkfish with vine leaves and prosciutto, and winter vegetable shepherds pie.
OPEN: 11.30-3 6-11 (Sun 12-10.30) **BAR MEALS:** L served all week 12-2.30 D served all week 7-9.30 Sun 12-4, 7-9 Av main course £7 **RESTAURANT:** L served all week 12-2.30 D served all week 7-9.30 Sun 12-4, 7-9 🍴: Enterprise Inns ◀: Adnams Best Bitter, Adnams Broadside, Bass, Black Sheep & Guests. ♀: 8
FACILITIES: Garden: Riverside at rear of pub; 25-acre lawn & trees Dogs allowed Water **NOTES:** Parking 40

ICKLINGHAM
Map 13 TL77

Pick of the Pubs

The Red Lion 🐟 ♀
The Street IP28 6PS ☎ 01638 717802 🖂 01638 515702
Dir: On A1101 between Mildenhall & Bury St Edmunds

A sympathetically restored, 16th-century thatched country inn set back from the road behind a grassed area with flower beds and outdoor furniture. The interior, glowing by candlelight in the evening, features exposed beams, a large inglenook fireplace, wooden floors, and antique furniture. Real ales and a good choice of country wines and fruit pressés are offered in the bar. It is particularly well known for fresh fish and seafood, delivered daily from Lowestoft, and game. Among the 15-20 varieties of fish on offer, depending on the season, are mussels, oysters, scallops, plaice, and sea bass. The seasonal game menu includes pheasant, guinea fowl, venison and mixed game grill. The regular carte offers a good choice, including mixed seafood hors d'oeuvre; lamb's liver and kidneys; and recent additions featuring springbok, bison and kangaroo. Bar options include sausages and mash, crayfish cocktail, gammon steak and steak and ale pie.
OPEN: 12-3 6.30-11 (Sun 7-10.30) Closed: 25 Dec
BAR MEALS: L served all week 12-2.30 D served all week 6.30-10 Sun evening 7-9 **RESTAURANT:** L served all week 12-2.30 D served all week 6.30-10 Sun evening 7-9 🍴: Greene King ◀: Greene King Abbot Ale & IPA, Norlands Speckled Hen. ♀: 15 **FACILITIES:** Garden: Large lawn with parasols, river at rear **NOTES:** Parking 50

IXWORTH
Map 13 TL97

Pykkerell Inn
38 High St IP31 2HH ☎ 01359 230398 🖷 01359 230398
Dir: A14 trunk rd/jct Bury St Edmunds central to A143, towards Diss
Attractive 16th-century coaching inn with original beams,
inglenook fireplace, wood-panelled library room, and 14th-
century barn enclosing a patio with barbecue. Menu boards
highlight fresh fish, such as sea bass on basil mash with herb
dressing, alongside steak and ale pie, venison with red wine
and mushroom sauce, and lamb chops.
OPEN: 12-3 6-11 **BAR MEALS:** L served all week 12-2.30 D served
all week 7-10 Av main course £7.95 **RESTAURANT:** L served all
week 12-2.30 D served all week 6-10 Av 3 course à la carte £20
Av 3 course fixed price £15 🍴: Greene King 🍺: Greene King IPA &
Abbot Ale. **FACILITIES:** Garden: Food served outside. Courtyard
Dogs allowed **NOTES:** Parking 30

KERSEY
Map 13 TM04

The Bell Inn
The Street IP7 6DY ☎ 01473 823229
Dir: Follow A1141 from Bury St Edmunds thru Lavenham
Surrounded by thatched cottages, the 14th-century Bell stands
next to a ford that crosses the main street of this picturesque
Suffolk village. Largely beamed within, the large winter log
fire is a focal point. Home-made fare includes warming soups
in winter and pies such as steak and Guinness, fisherman's
and chicken and mushroom. Well-kept cask ales and a warm
family-friendly atmosphere.
OPEN: 12-3 7-11 Sun-Mon Closed eve **BAR MEALS:** L served all week
12-2 D served all week 7-9 Av main course £8 **RESTAURANT:** L served
all week 12-2 D served all week 7-9 🍴: Enterprise Inns 🍺: Adnams
Bitter & Broadside. **FACILITIES:** Garden: Double patio, food served
outside **NOTES:** Parking 15

KETTLEBURGH
Map 13 TM26

The Chequers Inn
IP13 7JT ☎ 01728 723760 & 724369 🖷 01728 723760
e-mail: info@thechequers.net
Dir: From Ipswich A12 onto B1116, left onto B1078 then right through Easton

The Chequers is set in beautiful countryside on the banks of
the River Deben. The landlord serves a wide range of cask
ales, including two guests. In addition to snack and restaurant
meals, the menu in the bar includes local sausages and ham
with home-produced free-range eggs. The riverside garden
covers two acres and can seat up to a hundred people.
OPEN: 12-2.30 6-11 **BAR MEALS:** L served all week 12-2 D served
all week 7-9.30 Sun lunch 12-2, dinner 7-9 Av main course £6.75
RESTAURANT: L served all week 12-2 D served all week 7-9.30 Sun
lunch 12-2, dinner 7-9 Av 3 course à la carte £15.50 🍴: Free House
🍺: Greene King IPA, Shepherd Neame Spitfire, Black Dog Mild & Two
Guest Ales. **FACILITIES:** Child facs Garden: Two acre riverside
garden, large terrace Dogs allowed **NOTES:** Parking 40

LAVENHAM
Map 13 TL94

Pick of the Pubs

Angel Hotel ★★ ◉ 🍷
Market Place CO10 9QZ ☎ 01787 247388 🖷 01787 248344
e-mail: angellav@aol.com
web: www.theangelhotel-lavenham.co.uk
See Pick of the Pubs on page 458

LAXFIELD
Map 13 TM27

Pick of the Pubs

The Kings Head
Gorams Mill Ln IP13 8DW ☎ 01986 798395
Virtually unchanged since Victorian times, and dating back
in part to 1400, this charming inn is known locally as The
Low House. A series of small rooms is furnished with
high-backed settles and wooden seats, while quarry-tiled
floors and an open fire that blazes away except on the
hottest days, all add to the charming atmosphere. Beer is
served from the tap room, while a separate dining room
offers more comfortable seating. Outside, a large lawned
garden surrounded by shrubbed beds and with a perfect
view of the old thatched roof, offers the chance of al
fresco dining and drinking. Lunchtime choices include
sandwiches and ploughman's as well as steak and ale pie,
cottage pie, and sausages and mash, while in the
evenings the menu moves up a notch to offer rack of
lamb, baked duck breast, medallions of fillet steak, and
roast guinea fowl. Desserts include sticky toffee pudding
and bread and butter pudding, and everything is made
on the premises.
OPEN: 12-3 6-11 (Sun 12-3, 7-11) **BAR MEALS:** L served all
week 12-2 D served all week 7-9 No food on Sun evening in
winter Av main course £7.50 **RESTAURANT:** L served all week
12-2 D served all week 7-9 Sun lunch 12.30-2.30, fixed menu
Mon-Thu eve in winter Av 3 course à la carte £15 Av 3 course
fixed price £12 🍴: Adnams 🍺: Adnams Best & Broadside,
Adnams Seasonal Ales & Guest ale. **FACILITIES:** Garden: Large
lawned area with lots of benches Dogs allowed
NOTES: Parking 30 No credit cards

LEVINGTON
Map 13 TM23

The Ship Inn 🍷
Church Ln IP10 0LQ ☎ 01473 659573
Dir: Off the A14 towards Felixstowe. Nr Levington Marina
This charming 14th-century thatched pub overlooks the River
Orwell, and there are pleasant walks in the surrounding
countryside. The Ship is already popular with birdwatchers
and yachting folk, and is fast establishing a reputation for
fresh, home-made dishes. Fish and seafood both feature
strongly; mussels have their own speciality menu, with
crevettes, lobster, crab, haddock, tuna and monkfish all
making an appearance when available. The main menu
changes twice daily.
OPEN: 11.30-3 6.30-11 **BAR MEALS:** L served all week 12-2
D served Mon-Sat 6.30-9.30 (Sun 12-3) **RESTAURANT:** L served all
week 12-2 D served all week 6.30-9.30 (Sun 12-3) 🍴: Pubmaster
🍺: Greene King IPA, Adnams Best & Broadside. 🍷: 8
FACILITIES: Garden: Patio area front and back Dogs allowed Water
NOTES: Parking 70

Pick of the Pubs

LAVENHAM – SUFFOLK

Angel Hotel

Originally licensed in 1420, this inn is surrounded by 300 historical buildings in Lavenham, England's best-preserved medieval town. The building retains many original features such as exposed timbers, a Tudor shuttered shop window and a rare fully pargetted ceiling, added around 1650, in the residents' sitting room. Eight en suite bedrooms enable excellent dinner, bed and breakfast packages to be offered.

The Angel is a bustling pub with local real ales, an extensive wine list and a good selection of malt whiskies. The warm and friendly atmosphere is helped by the open plan layout and a no-smoking policy that applies throughout. Children are also well catered for. In summer, food is served on the front terrace, overlooking the market place, and in the rear lawned garden. The award-winning restaurant and bar menu - holder of an AA rosette - changes daily. All food is prepared on the premises from fresh ingredients, delivered daily by carefully chosen local suppliers. There are always home-made soups, pies and casseroles, fresh fish, game in season and vegetarian dishes. Starters could be tomato salad with feta cheese and basil; chicken liver pâté; and sweet-cured herrings with honey, mustard and dill. Main courses like steak and ale pie; lamb casserole with butterbeans and sweet potatoes; baked aubergine with curried chickpeas and vegetable topping; honey roast duck breast with plum and ginger sauce; and grilled sea bass fillet with prawn, lemon and chive risotto are perennially popular.

OPEN: 11-11 (Sun 12-10.30) Closed: 25-26 Dec
BAR MEALS: L served all week 12-2.15 D served all week 6.45-9.15 Av main course £10
RESTAURANT: L served all week 12-2.15 D served all week 6.45-9.15 Av 3 course à la carte £18
🍺: Free House
🍻: Adnams Bitter, Nethergate, Greene King IPA, Abbot Ale & Old Growler. ♀: 9
FACILITIES: ch facs Children's licence Garden: Lawn and patio area with tables and seating
NOTES: Parking 105
ROOMS: 8 bedrooms en suite 1 family room s£55 d£80

★★ ◎ ♀   Map 13 TL94
Market Place CO10 9QZ
☎ 01787 247388
🖹 01787 248344
e angellav@aol.com
w www.theangelhotel-lavenham. co.uk
Dir: On A1142, between Bury St Edmunds & Sudbury

LIDGATE   Map 12 TL75

Pick of the Pubs

The Star Inn
The Street CB8 9PP ☎ 01638 500275 ▤ 01638 500275
e-mail: tereaxon@aol.com
Dir: *From Newmarket, clocktower in High st, follow signs toward Clare on B1063. Lidgate 7m from Newmarket*

A seemingly traditional English pub that also houses a much-loved Spanish restaurant. It has proved particularly popular with trainers on Newmarket race days, and with dealers and agents from all over the world during bloodstock sales. Star of the Star is undoubtedly the owner, a Catalan landlady who has made her mark with Spanish dishes sharing space with some imaginative international and British choices. The pretty pink-painted Elizabethan building is made up of two cottages with gardens front and rear; inside, two traditionally furnished bars with heavy oak and pine furniture lead into a fairly simple dining room. The menu offers appealingly hearty food, just the thing after a day at the races: grilled squid, paella Valenciana, lamb kidneys in sherry, or scallops Santiago may all be on the menu. Friendly staff are on hand if any translation is required.
OPEN: 11-3 5-11 Closed: 25-26 Dec, 1 Jan
BAR MEALS: L served all week 12-2 D served Mon-Sat 7-10
RESTAURANT: L served all week 12-2 D served Mon-Sat 7-10
🍺: Greene King ◀: Greene King IPA, Old Speckled Hen & Abbot Ale. **FACILITIES:** Garden **NOTES:** Parking 12

MELTON   Map 13 TM25

Wilford Bridge
Wilford Bridge Rd IP12 2PA ☎ 01394 386141
Dir: *Head to the coast from the A12, follow signs to Bawdsey & Orford, cross railway lines, next pub on left*

Fish dishes and chargrills are specialities at this pub, just

continued

down the road from the famous Saxon burial ship at Sutton Hoo (NT). Examples include Dover sole, pan- or deep-fried skate wing, deep-fried sprats, chargilled chicken piri piri, rib-eye and T-bone steaks, and lamb cutlets. Other menu choices include home-made steak Guinness and mushroom pie, beef burgers, and spinach and ricotta cannelloni. Supreme of pheasant, and sea bass sometimes appear as daily specials.
OPEN: 11-3 6.30-11 (Open all day Sat-Sun) Closed: 25-26 Dec
BAR MEALS: L served all week 11.30-2 D served all week 6.30-9.30 food served all day Sat-Sun Av main course £8.95
RESTAURANT: L served all week 11.30-2 D served all week 6.30-9.30 Food served all day Sat-Sun Av 3 course à la carte £17.85
🍺: Free House ◀: Adnams Best, Broadside, Scottish Courage John Smith's + guest Ales. **FACILITIES:** Garden: Patio, seats up to 30 people Dogs allowed Water available **NOTES:** Parking 40

MONKS ELEIGH   Map 13 TL94

Pick of the Pubs

The Swan Inn
The Street IP7 7AU ☎ 01449 741391 ▤ 01449 741391
Dir: *On the B1115 between Sudbury & Hadleigh*
The thatch and cream façade of this part-14th century free house blends easily with the 'Suffolk pink' wash of its medieval neighbours in the middle of the village. Like nearby Lavenham, Monks Eleigh was founded on the prosperous local wool trade, which explains the impressive nature of some of these properties. The original building was open to the roof and evidence of the smoke hole still exists. Wattle and daub panels were discovered in one room during renovations, and the main restaurant, with its magnificent open fireplace, may have been used as the manorial court. Menus change daily, making use of seasonal local produce. A typical meal might start with dressed Cromer crab, before moving on to pan-fried guinea fowl; or filo parcel of goats' cheese, sun-dried tomato and pesto. A glazed lemon tart or a trio of cheeses might round off the evening.
OPEN: 12-3 7-11 Closed: 21 Sep-5 Oct, 25-26 Dec
BAR MEALS: L served Wed-Sun 12-2 D served Wed-Sun 7-9.30 Av main course £12 **RESTAURANT:** L served Wed-Sun 12-2 D served Wed-Sun 7-9.30 Av 3 course à la carte £20 🍺: Free House ◀: Greene King IPA, Adnams Bitter & Broadside. 🍷: 20
FACILITIES: Garden **NOTES:** Parking 10

NAYLAND   Map 13 TL93

Pick of the Pubs

Anchor Inn NEW
26 Court St CO6 4JL ☎ 01206 262313 ▤ 01206 264166
e-mail: enquiries@anchornayland.co.uk
The Anchor Inn, with the river Stour right on its doorstep, is the only pub in this picturesque Suffolk village. Dating back to the 15th century, it is reported to be the last remaining place from where press gangs recruited their 'volunteers'. Today this is an entirely non-smoking pub, and offers a superb bar with a lively warm atmosphere, fine ales and good food. The inn has its own smokery, and produce from the smokehouse is often featured on the menu, including fish and cheeses. Starters can include Anchor smoked platter; spiced tiger prawns; or guacamole and lentil stuffed chargrilled sweet peppers. Main dishes might be Anchor sausage of the day served

continued

NAYLAND continued

with leek and bacon mash; wild mushroom open lasagne with aubergine and truffle olive oil sauce; and braised lamb shank with crushed new potatoes, carrot and swede purée. A selection of pistachio parfait; steamed honey, lemon and ginger pudding with lemon curd ice cream; and plum and almond tart with cinnamon cream will be found on the dessert list.
BAR MEALS: L served all week 12-2 D served all week 6.30-9 Sun 12-3 Av main course £8.50 **RESTAURANT:** L served all week 12-2 D served all week 6.30-9 Sun 12-3 Av 3 course à la carte £17.50 **FACILITIES:** Garden: Riverside terrace Dogs allowed Water **NOTES:** Parking 10 😊

ORFORD   Map 13 TM45

Pick of the Pubs

The Crown and Castle NEW ★★ ◉◉ ♀
IP12 2LJ ☎ 01394 450205
e-mail: info@crownandcastle.co.uk
Dir: From A12 take B1078 to Orford. Pub is 50m from the Castle
With a picture-book Norman Castle just yards away, the Crown and Castle hotel stands on the corner of Orford's atmospheric old market square. Guests can enjoy an al fresco meal in the south-facing garden in the summer. The cheerful, friendly service and relaxed ambience make this a popular pub. The informal and lively Trinity bistro uses local produce including Butley-Orford oysters, asparagus, lobster and loganberries in season. The dinner menu, awarded two AA rosettes for excellence, is divided between 'raw' (beef fillet carpaccio); 'cold' (Orford-smoked trout and salmon with beetroot relish); and 'hot' (Suffolk guineafowl, Puy lentils and gingery greens). Well-behaved' dogs and children are welcome in designated areas of the inn.
OPEN: 12-3 7-11 (Sun 7-10.30) Closed: 19-22 Dec, 3-4 Jan
BAR MEALS: L served all week 12.15-2.15 D served all week Av main course £11.95 **RESTAURANT:** L served all week 12.15-2.15 D served all week 7-9.30 Av 3 course à la carte £25 🍺: IPA Greene King, Aspalls Cider, Mild Greene King. ♀: 18
FACILITIES: Garden: Paved terrace, food outside in summer Dogs allowed Water, treats **NOTES:** Parking 18
ROOMS: 18 bedrooms en suite 1 family room s£90 d£90 No children overnight

Jolly Sailor Inn 🍺
Quay St IP12 2NU ☎ 01394 450243 📠 0870 128 7874
e-mail: jacquie@jollysailor.f9.co.uk
Dir: On B1084 E of Woodbridge, Orford signed from A12 approx 10m
Until the 16th century Orford was a bustling coastal port. This ancient, timber-framed smugglers' inn stood on the quayside - but, as Orford Ness grew longer, the harbour silted up and fell out of use. Nevertheless, the pub still serves visiting yachtsmen, and local fishermen supply fresh fish to the kitchen. There's also a daily roast, and other dishes might include seasonal local pheasant in red wine; or fresh pasta with a choice of sauces.
OPEN: 11.30-2.30 7-11 **BAR MEALS:** L served all week 12-2 D served all week 7.15-8.45 Av main course £5.95 🍺: Adnams 🍺: Adnams Bitter & Broadside. **FACILITIES:** Garden: Food served outside Dogs allowed in the public bar on lead only **NOTES:** No credit cards

King's Head 🍺
Front St IP12 2LW ☎ 01394 450271
e-mail: ian_thornton@talk21.com
Dir: From Woodbridge follow signs for Orford Castle along the B1084 through Butly and Chillesford onto Orford
Atmospheric 13th-century inn with a smuggling history, located a short walk from the quay. The interior includes a beamed bar serving Adnams ales, and a wood-floored restaurant offering plenty of local produce. Typical starters include locally smoked mackerel with a salad garnish, and deep-fried brie with a Cumberland sauce, followed perhaps by 'boozy beef' (made with steak and Adnams ale), seafood platter, or Orford-made salmon fish cakes. Bar snacks include sandwiches, burgers and things with chips.
OPEN: 11.30-3 6-11 **BAR MEALS:** L served all week 12-2 D served all week 6-9 Sun 12-2.45, 7-9 Av main course £7.75
RESTAURANT: L served all week 12-2 D served all week 6-9 Sun 12-2.30, 7-9 Av 3 course à la carte £15 🍺: Adnams 🍺: Adnams Bitter, Adnams Broadside, Adnams Regatta, Adnams Fisherman.
FACILITIES: Garden: Large grassed area with flower border Dogs allowed Water **NOTES:** Parking 20

POLSTEAD   Map 13 TL93

Pick of the Pubs

The Cock Inn 🍺
The Green CO6 5AL ☎ 01206 263150 📠 01206 263150
e-mail: mail@cockinn.info
Dir: Colchester/A134 towards Sudbury then right, follow signs to Polstead

Originally a 17th-century farmhouse, the pub has oak beams, quarry-tiled floors and a Victorian restaurant extension. It overlooks the green in a lovely village at the heart of Constable country, and with some of Suffolk's prettiest landscapes right on the doorstep, it's not surprising that the pub attracts its fair share of cyclists and ramblers. The menu changes frequently and there's always a great choice. A Suffolk huffer might suffice: these large, soft white baps come with a myriad choice of fillings. The list of starters may feature home-made soup of the day, devilled whitebait with tartare dip, or minted lamb pieces. Mains range from home-made chilli con carne, and beer-marinated duck breast, to jumbo sausage and sirloin steak. You'll also find fresh fish dishes, and a good selection for vegetarians. Families are especially welcome - there's a children's menu and an award-winning garden with a water feature and hanging baskets.
OPEN: 11-3 6-11 Open all day Sat-Sun (Apr-Sep) (Sun-BHS 12-3, 6-10.30) **BAR MEALS:** L served Tues-Sun 11.30-2.30 D served Tues-Sun 6.30-9.30 Sun 12-2.30, 6.30-9 Av main course £7 **RESTAURANT:** L served Tue-Sun 11.30-2.30 D served

England

Tues-Sun 6.30-9.30 Sun 12-2.30, 6.30-9 Av 3 course à la carte £15
⌂: Free House ◖: Greene King IPA, Adnams, Tetley Smooth,
Guinness. **FACILITIES:** Child facs Garden: Picnic tables, water
feature Dogs allowed Water and treats **NOTES:** Parking 20

RAMSHOLT — Map 13 TM34

Pick of the Pubs

Ramsholt Arms
Dock Rd IP12 3AB ☎ 01394 411229
*Dir: End of lane on beach at Ramsholt, signed off B1083 Woodbridge
to Bawdsey*
Enjoying a glorious, unrivalled position on a tidal beach
overlooking the River Deben, this 18th-century, pink-
washed former farmhouse, ferryman's cottage and
smugglers' inn is the perfect summer evening destination
for a pint on the terrace to watch the glorious sunset over
the river. Expect a civilised atmosphere, picture windows,
Adnams ales, and good home-cooked food, in particular
fish and seafood in summer and local game in winter.
Blackboard dishes could include cod and chips, local
lobster, Cromer crab, whole Dover sole, roast partridge
and decent pies.
OPEN: 11.30-11 (Sun 12-10.30) **BAR MEALS:** L served all
week 12-3 D served all week 6.30-9 Av main course £8
RESTAURANT: L served all week 12-3 D served all week 6.30-9
⌂: Free House ◖: Adnams, Greene King, Woodfords,
Nethergates. **FACILITIES:** Garden: Food served outside. Large
garden, estuary Dogs allowed Water provided
NOTES: Parking 60

REDE — Map 13 TL85

The Plough
IP29 4BE ☎ 01284 789208
Dir: On the A143 between Bury St Edmunds and Haverhill
Picture-postcard half-thatched 16th-century pub set beside a
pond on the village green. Worth the effort in finding for the
freshly prepared food served in rambling low-beamed bars.
An adventurous array of blackboard-listed dishes may include
rabbit wrapped in bacon with a mustard sauce, stuffed pigeon
with lentils, grilled tuna with salmoriglio, monkfish Creole, or
venison steak with wild mushroom gravy.
OPEN: 11-3 6.30-11 **BAR MEALS:** L served all week 12-2 D served
Mon-Sat 7-9 **RESTAURANT:** L served all week 12-2 D served Mon-Sat
7-9 ⌂: Greene King ◖: Greene King IPA, Abbot Ale & Ruddles
County. **FACILITIES:** Garden: Patio with garden **NOTES:** Parking 60

RISBY — Map 13 TL86

The White Horse Inn ♈
Newmarket Rd IP28 6RD ☎ 01284 810686
Dir: A14 from Bury St Edmunds
Former coaching inn with a colourful history - as a
communications centre in World War II in case of invasion,
and for the ghostly spectre of a murdered hanging judge
occasionally reflected in the restaurant mirror. The pub is
otherwise known for its real ales - up to 15 each week - its
extensive carte and freshly produced bar food.
OPEN: 12-2.30 6-11 (Sun 12-10.30) **BAR MEALS:** L served
Tue-Sun 12-4 D served Tue-Sat 6.30-9 Av main course £6
RESTAURANT: L served all week 12-2.30 D served all week
6.30-9.30 Av 3 course à la carte £22 ⌂: Free House ◖: Fullers
London Pride, Shepherd Neame Spitfire, Tetleys.
FACILITIES: Garden: Food served outside **NOTES:** Parking 100

ST PETER SOUTH ELMHAM — Map 13 TM38

Pick of the Pubs

St Peter's Hall ♈
NR35 1NQ ☎ 01986 783115 & 783113 🖷 01986 782505
e-mail: stuart@stpetersbrewery.co.uk
Dir: From A143/A144 follow brown signs to St Peter's Brewery

A pub and brewery in a magnificent moated, former
monastery built in 1280. In 1539 it was enlarged using
stones salvaged from nearby Flixton Priory, destroyed
during the Dissolution. Look for the chapel above the
porch, the carvings on the façade, and the tombstone in
the entrance, not to mention the stone floors, lofty
ceilings, and period furnishings. The brewery, which you
can visit, produces seventeen (yes, seventeen) different
beers, and is housed in what until 1996 were long-derelict
former agricultural buildings. Starters may include home-
made game pâté with spiced ale chutney; and stilton,
grape and spicy olive salad with wholegrain mustard
dressing. There are usually six to eight main courses,
among them St Peter's steak and ale pie; pork fillet in
sage and white wine cream sauce; and plaice fillet with
lemon and dill cream sauce. For vegetarians, there's wild
mushroom risotto with truffle oil, lemon and thyme.
OPEN: 11-11 (Sun & BHs 12-10.30) **BAR MEALS:** L served all
week 12.30-2 D served all week 7-9 Av main course £9
RESTAURANT: L served all week 12.30-2 D served all week 7-9
Av 3 course à la carte £22.50 Av 3 course fixed price £20 ⌂: St
Peters Brewery ◖: Golden Ale, Organic Ale, Grapefruit Beer,
Cream Stout. ♈: 7 **FACILITIES:** Garden: Attractive garden
overlooking medieval moat **NOTES:** Parking 150

SNAPE — Map 13 TM35

Pick of the Pubs

The Crown Inn ♈
Bridge Rd IP17 1SL ☎ 01728 688324
*Dir: A12 N to Lowestoft, right to Aldeburgh, then right again in Snape
at x-rds by church, pub at bottom hill*
Close to the River Alde with its timeless scenery and
tranquil coastal bird reserves, and just a stone's throw
from Snape Maltings, home of the Aldeburgh Music
Festival. The Crown is a 15th-century smugglers' inn with
abundant old beams, intriguing brick floors and, around
the large inglenook, probably the finest double Suffolk
settle in existence. Install yourselves cosily here, and
remember how good burning logs sound when there are
no gaming machines or piped music to drown the
crackles. On offer are an interesting 40-bin wine list,

continued

SNAPE continued

Adnams beers, and daily changing menus and specials, including starters of crayfish tails in Thai mayo; and cream of parsnip and honey soup. Main course options include fillet steak with sweet potato purée, Provençale vegetables and port jus; steak and kidney suet pudding with salsa vegetables; and at least five fish or seafood dishes. Round off with lemon posset and blueberry compôte.
OPEN: 12-3 6-11 (Sunday 7-10.30) Closed: Dec 25, 26 Dec (evening) **BAR MEALS:** L served all week 12-2 D served all week 7-9 Av main course £11.95 **RESTAURANT:** L served all week 12-2 D served all week 7-9 🍴: Adnams 🍺: Adnams Best, Broadside, Old Ale, Regatta. ♀ 11 **FACILITIES:** Garden: Large area, patio, benches, umbrellas **NOTES:** Parking 40

The Golden Key ♀
Priory Ln IP17 1SQ ☎ 01728 688510
e-mail: snapegoldenkey@aol.com
A pub since around 1480, this extended, cottage-style building still houses three large open fireplaces. Landlord Alan Booth used to be a classical music record producer, and orchestras often eat here before performing down the road at the famous Snape Maltings. The menu includes roasts every day, chicken tikka masala, cod in Adnam's batter with hand-cut chips, claret and wild game pie, and Six Nations steak and kidney pie, an all-year tribute to our rugby team.
OPEN: 12-3 6-11 Closed Sun eve Nov-Etr Closed: 25th Dec **BAR MEALS:** L served all week 12-2 D served all week 6-8.30 Av main course £8.95 **RESTAURANT:** L served all week 12-2.15 D served all week 6-9.30 Av 3 course à la carte £16 🍴: Adnams 🍺: Adnams Best, Broadside & Regatta, Tally Ho, Oyster Ale. ♀: 12 **FACILITIES:** Garden **NOTES:** Parking 20

Plough & Sail ♀
Snape Maltings IP17 1SR ☎ 01728 688413 🖷 01728 688930
e-mail: enquiries@snapemaltings.co.uk
web: www.snapemaltings.co.uk

The pub is part of the Snape Maltings Riverside Centre, incorporating the famous Concert Hall, art gallery and shops. The rambling interior includes a bar and restaurant, and a large terrace provides seating in summer. Good food ranges from lunchtime snacks (hot foccacia topped with gratinated brie, mushroom and tomato), to locally caught fresh fish specials (grilled plaice with prawn and spinach risotto). There is a good river walk from the Maltings to Iken Cliff.
OPEN: 11-3 5.30-11 (Summer & Sat-Sun 11-11) **BAR MEALS:** L served all week 12-2.30 D served all week **RESTAURANT:** L served all week 12-2.30 D served all week 7-9 Sat-Sun 7-9.30 Av 3 course à la carte £21.50 🍴: Free House 🍺: Adnams Broadside, Adnams Bitter, Explorer, Fishermans. ♀: 10 **FACILITIES:** Child facs Garden: Enclosed courtyard, paved garden area Dogs allowed Water bowls **NOTES:** Parking 100

SOUTHWOLD — Map 13 TM57

Pick of the Pubs

Crown Hotel ★★ 🏵🏵 ♀
The High St IP18 6DP ☎ 01502 722275 🖷 01502 727263
e-mail: crown.hotel@adnams.co.uk
Dir: From A12 take A1095 to Southwold. Into town centre, hotel on L
A posting inn dating from 1750, today fulfilling the roles of pub, wine bar, restaurant and small hotel. As the flagship for Adnams brewery, the Crown offers excellent ales, and more than 20 wines are sold by the glass. Alternatively you can visit the cellar and kitchen store at the rear of the hotel yard for a full selection of wines and bottled beers. Good food is served in either the bar or the restaurant; the Crown's seaside location means fish is well represented on both menus. Typical dishes in the bar might be crisp black bream with rosemary sauté potatoes and pesto; and wild boar sausages with celeriac purée and thyme. In the restaurant, start with country terrine and apple chutney, before basted English duck breast with fondant potato and honey-roast parsnip, then red wine-poached pear with pralines and mascarpone.
OPEN: 11-11 **BAR MEALS:** L served all week 12-2.30 D served all week 7-9.30 (all day opening Sun) Av main course £12 **RESTAURANT:** L served all week 12-2.30 D served all week 7-9.30 Av 3 course à la carte £20 Av 3 course fixed price £29 🍴: Adnams 🍺: Adnams Ales. ♀: 20 **NOTES:** Parking 18 **ROOMS:** 14 bedrooms 13 en suite 3 family rooms s£77 d£55

Pick of the Pubs

The Randolph NEW 🏵🏵 ♀
41 Wangford Rd, Reydon IP18 6PZ
☎ 01502 723603 🖷 01502 722194
e-mail: reception@therandolph.co.uk
Dir: A12 at Blythburgh onto A1095, follow signs into The Drive

Built in 1899 by the local brewery, Adnams, The Randolph is at heart a local pub/hotel, owned and managed by Suffolk couple David and Donna Smith, who have taken over in recent times. To this day it continues, as it began, to provide for local people and visitors to the Suffolk heritage coastline and the town of Southwold, which is just a mile away. All the rooms here have been tastefully redecorated, and the chic lounge bar overlooks an enclosed garden with outdoor furniture. Adnams ales, plus a guest, are served and six wines are available by the glass. Food is based on top quality ingredients from local suppliers where possible. Fish features prominently, with options ranging from traditional fish and chips with tartare sauce to grilled fillet of sea bream on red onion lyonnaise, potatoes and herb velouté. Tasty

continued

snacks include a Suffolk ham and chutney sandwich.
OPEN: 11-11 **BAR MEALS:** L served all week 12-2 D served all week 6.30-9 Av main course £8.50 **RESTAURANT:** L served all week 12-2 D served all week 6.30-9 Av 3 course à la carte £21 🍺: Adnams Bitter, Adnams Broadside, guest ale. ♀: 6 **FACILITIES:** Child facs Garden: Large fenced area with garden tables **NOTES:** Parking 60

STOKE-BY-NAYLAND   Map 13 TL93

Pick of the Pubs

The Angel Inn ♦♦♦♦ ⊚ ♀
CO6 4SA ☎ 01206 263245 ▤ 01206 263373
Dir: From A12 take Colchester R turn, then A134, 5m to Nayland.
Set in a landscape immortalised by the paintings of local artist, John Constable, the Angel is a 16th-century inn with beamed bars, log fires and a long tradition of hospitality. In a more modern vein, the pub also has an air-conditioned conservatory, patio and sun terrace. Tables for lunch and dinner may be reserved in The Well Room which has a high ceiling open to the rafters, a gallery leading to the pub's accommodation, rough brick and timber studded walls, and the well itself, fully 52 feet deep. Eating in the bar, by comparison, is on a strictly first-come, first-served basis. The chalkboard menus change daily, with first-class fish options and generous portions of salad or fresh vegetables. Look out for dishes such as whole griddled lemon sole, deep-fried haddock in Adnams beer batter, skate wing, mussels, or griddled liver and bacon on a spring onion mash with madeira sauce. **OPEN:** 11-2.30 6-11 (Sun Dinner 5:30, 9:30) Closed: Dec 25-26, Jan 1 **BAR MEALS:** L served all week 12-2 D served all week 6.30-9 **RESTAURANT:** L served all week 12-2 D served all week 6.30-9 ⊚: Free House 🍺: Greene King IPA & Abbot Ale, Adnams Best. ♀: 9 **FACILITIES:** Garden: Patio area seating 20 Dogs allowed Water **NOTES:** Parking 25 **ROOMS:** 1 family rooms No children overnight

The Crown NEW ♀
CO6 4SE ☎ 01206 262001 ▤ 01206 264026
e-mail: crown.eoinns@btopenworld.com
Dir: Follow signs to Stoke Nayland
This village inn, established in 1560, has been modernised and now offers traditional British cuisine with a modern twist. Fish, often caught locally, is a speciality: try pan-fried skate or grilled sea bass. This is a place for wine lovers, as there is a recommended wine with each course and more than 300 bottles of wine to choose from (28 available by the glass). **OPEN:** 11-11 (Sun 12-10.30) Closed: 25-26 Dec **BAR MEALS:** L served all week 12-2.30 D served all week 6-9.30 Sun 12-9 Av main course £10 **RESTAURANT:** L served all week 12-2.30 D served all week 6-9.30 Sun 12-9 Av 3 course à la carte £20 🍺: Adnams Best Bitter, Greene King IPA, Guinness, guest beers. ♀: 28 **FACILITIES:** Garden: Terraced area with seating Dogs allowed **NOTES:** Parking 50

STOWMARKET   Map 13 TM05

The Buxhall Crown ♀
Mill Rd, Buxhall IP14 3DW ☎ 01449 736521 ▤ 01449 736528
e-mail: trevor@buxhallcrown.fsnet.co.uk
Five years ago a rundown village local, but today a hugely popular gastropub in 17th-century surroundings. You'll find a good choice of main courses on the monthly-changing menu, such as herb pancakes stuffed with a vegetable fricassée, garlic

continued

sauce and melted cheese; plaice fillets, wilted spinach, saffron risotto, and creamy vermouth sauce; or chargrilled lamb chump on a cassoulet of lentils and root vegetables with mustard sauce. Regular visitors include a well-known East Anglian cookery writer. **OPEN:** 12-3 6.30-11 **BAR MEALS:** L served all week 12-2 D served Mon-Sat 6.30-9.30 Av main course £10.50 **RESTAURANT:** L served all week 12-2 D served Mon-Sat 6.30-9.30 Av 3 course à la carte £20 ⊚: Greene King 🍺: Greene King IPA, Woodforde's Wherry, Old Chimneys Mild, Abbot Ale. ♀: 30 **FACILITIES:** Garden: Patio with wooden furniture, heaters Dogs allowed Water **NOTES:** Parking 25

SWILLAND   Map 13 TM15

Moon & Mushroom Inn ♀
High Rd IP6 9LR ☎ 01473 785320 ▤ 01473 785320
e-mail: nikki@ecocleen.fsnet.co.uk
Dir: 6m N of Ipswich taking the Westerfield Rd
This award-winning 300-year-old free house enjoys a reputation as 'the pub that time passed by', and the new owner intends to keep it that way. Winter fires and good company still prevail, and East Anglian ales flow straight from the barrel. Locally sourced ingredients are the foundation of good home cooking; lunchtime snacks include collar of bacon with pickles, whilst spiced kedgeree, or sausage, haricot and red wine casserole cater for larger appetites. **OPEN:** 11-2.30 6-11 (Mon 6-11 only, Sun 12-3 7-10.30) **BAR MEALS:** L served Tue-Sun 12-2 D served Tue-Sun 6.30-9 Sun 12-3 Av main course £8.95 **RESTAURANT:** L served Tue-Sun 12-2 D served Tue-Sun 6.30-9 Sun 12-3 ⊚: Free House 🍺: Nethergate Umbel, Woodfords Wherry, Buffy's Hopleaf, Brewers Gold. **FACILITIES:** Garden: Vine surrounded patio, awnings, heaters Dogs allowed **NOTES:** Parking 47

THORNHAM MAGNA   Map 13 TM17

The Four Horseshoes ♦♦♦♦ 🐟
Wickham Rd IP23 8HD ☎ 01379 678777 ▤ 01379 678134
e-mail: the4horseshoes@aol.com
Dir: From Diss on A140 turn right and follow signs for Finningham, 0.5m turn right for Thornham Magna
Thornham Magna is a delightful, unspoilt village, close to Thornham Country Park and the interesting thatched church at Thornham Parva. This fine 12th-century inn is also thatched, and has timber-framed walls and a well in the bar. **OPEN:** 12-11 25-26 Dec 12-5 **BAR MEALS:** L served all week 12-9.30 D served all week 12-9.30 Sun 12-8.30 Av main course £7.95 **RESTAURANT:** L served all week 12-9.30 D served all week 12-9.30 Sun 12-8.30 ⊚: Greene King 🍺: Greene King IPA, Abbot & Old Speckled Hen. **FACILITIES:** Child facs Children's licence Garden: Large beer garden and patio Dogs allowed **NOTES:** Parking 120 **ROOMS:** 8 bedrooms 7 en suite 1 family room s£55 d£75

THORPENESS   Map 13 TM45

The Dolphin Inn NEW ♀
Peace Place IP16 4NA ☎ 01728 454994
e-mail: info@thorpenessdolphin.com
In the heart of Thorpeness, this traditional village inn offers good food, and alfresco dining in the summer. Pan-fried pigeon breasts are served as a starter with red pepper dressing; lamb kleftiko is marinated in red wine and served the Cypriot way with onions, herbs, rice and Greek salad; and there's a fish selection too. **OPEN:** 12-3 6-11 Restricted hours in winter **BAR MEALS:** L served all week 12-2 D served all week 6.30-9 Winter restrictions Av main course £9 **RESTAURANT:** L served all week 12-2 D served all week 6.30-9 Winter restrictions Av 3 course à la carte £18 🍺: Adnams Best, Adnams Broadside. ♀: 8 **FACILITIES:** Garden: Large garden with awning, BBQ **NOTES:** Parking 14

England

TOSTOCK
Map 13 TL96

Gardeners Arms
IP30 9PA ☎ 01359 270460
e-mail: gardenersarms@btinternet.com
Dir: From A14 follow signs to Tostock (0.5m)
Parts of this charming pub, at the end of the village green, near the horse chestnut tree, date back 600 years. The basic bar menu - salads, grills, ploughmans', sandwiches, toasties, etc - is supplemented by specials boards that offer six starters and 12 main courses in the evening. Look out for lamb balti, Thai king prawn green curry, steak and kidney pie, or chicken and stilton roulade. Large grassy garden.
OPEN: 11.30-3 6.30-11 (Fri-Sat & BHs & summer 11.30-11 Sun 12-10.30) **BAR MEALS:** L served all week 12-2.30 D served all week 7-9 Sun 12-3.30 Av main course £8 **RESTAURANT:** L served all week 12-2.30 D served Wed-Sat 7-9 Sun 12-3.30 Av 3 course à la carte £13 ⬤: Greene King ◀: Greene King IPA, Greene King Abbot, Greene King seasonal beers. **FACILITIES:** Garden: Food served outside, large grass area **NOTES:** Parking 20

WALBERSWICK
Map 13 TM47

Pick of the Pubs

Bell Inn 🐟 ♀
Ferry Rd IP18 6TN ☎ 01502 723109 📠 01502 722728
e-mail: bellinn@btinternet.com
Dir: From A12 take B1387 to Walberswick
The 600-year-old Bell Inn is situated in the heart of Walberswick, close to the village green and a stone's throw away from the beach and ancient fishing harbour on the River Blyth. Inside, its great age is evident from the low beams, flagged floors, high wooden settles and, of course, open fires, with the large garden overlooking the sea. Traditional English pub fare and award-winning seasonal menus are the Bell's hallmarks, with fish, such as Walberswick fish pie and Suffolk smokies, a speciality. Starters could include chicken liver parfait with pear and rosemary jelly; home-made herby houmous with chilli oil and toasted pine nuts; and crayfish salad. Fillet of cod or haddock deep-fried in beer batter; grilled fresh fish of the day; local Cumberland sausage; chicken Caesar salad; grilled minute steak; lamb koftas with cucumber yoghurt dressing; shallow-fried goat's cheese rolled in pasta with chargrilled vegetables; and deep-fried brie wedges with home-made Cumberland sauce are all on the menu.
OPEN: 11-3 6-11 (Summer & school hols open all day) (Sun 12-10.30, Sat 11-11) **BAR MEALS:** L served all week 12-2 D served all week 6-9 Sun 12-2.30 Av main course £7.50 **RESTAURANT:** L served None D served Fri-Sat 7-9 Av 3 course à la carte £17.50 ⬤: Adnams ◀: Adnams Best, Broadside, Regatta, Old Ale. ♀: 15 **FACILITIES:** Child facs Garden: Large garden with beach & sea views Dogs allowed on leads only **NOTES:** Parking 10

WANGFORD
Map 13 TM47

The Angel Inn
High St NR34 8RL ☎ 01502 578636 📠 01502 578535
e-mail: enquiries@angelinn.freeserve.co.uk
A traditional green-and-cream-painted inn with a handsome Georgian facade, set in the heart of the pretty village of Wangford. Dating back to the 16th century, and complete with resident ghost, its cosy bar and restaurant are characterised by exposed beams and roaring log fires in winter. Home-
continued

The Westleton Crown ◎◎

All the atmosphere of a 17th Century Coaching Inn with:

• Smouldering Log Fires
• Real Ales
• Cosy Rooms
• Traditional Home Cooking in the Bar
• Indulgent à la carte menu

Enjoy a drink in the garden, a long lunch, that special meal, or a romantic get away.
The perfect base from which to explore the delights of the Suffolk coast.

Telephone: 01728 648777   www.westletoncrown.com

made dishes include fresh fish (grilled sea bass steak with citrus butter; baby crayfish tails sautéed in garlic butter), hearty favourites such as steaks, pies and sausages, and good vegetarian options.
OPEN: 12-3 6-11 **BAR MEALS:** L served Tue-Sun 12-2 D served Tue-Sun 6.30-9 Av main course £8 **RESTAURANT:** L served Tue-Sun 12-2 D served Tue-Sun 6.30-9 Av 3 course à la carte £15 ⬤: Free House ◀: Adnams Best, Spitfire, Greene King Abbot Ale, Brakspear Bitter. **FACILITIES:** Garden: Large walled garden with benches Dogs allowed **NOTES:** Parking 20

WESTLETON
Map 13 TM46

The Westleton Crown ★★ ◎◎ ♀
IP17 3AD ☎ 01728 648777 📠 01728 648239
Dir: Off A12 just past Yoxford N bound, follow signs for Westleton for 2m

There's genuine hospitality and a relaxed atmosphere at this bustling free house, nestling in a quiet village close to the coast and RSPB bird reserves. The original buildings belonged
continued

England

to nearby Sibton Abbey, but nowadays you'll find real ales, good wines and an astonishing range of malt whiskies. Fresh, locally sourced ingredients are used where possible in the kitchen; bread is baked daily, and local fish is a speciality.
OPEN: 11-11 (Sun 12-10.30) **BAR MEALS:** L served all week 12-2.15 D served all week 7-9.30 Av main course £9.95
RESTAURANT: L served all week 12-2.15 D served all week 7-9.30 Av 3 course à la carte £30 🍴: Free House 🍺: Adnams, Greene King IPA, Aspalls Cider, Guest Ales. 🍷: 10 **FACILITIES:** Child facs Garden: Award winning tiered sections Dogs allowed in some rooms overnight **NOTES:** Parking 30 **ROOMS:** 26 bedrooms en suite 2 family rooms s£75 d£80

See advert on opposite page

SURREY

ABINGER
Map 06 TQ14

The Volunteer 🍷
Water Ln, Sutton RH5 6PR ☎ 01306 730798 🖷 01306 731621
Dir: Between Guildford & Dorking, 1m S of A25
Enjoying a delightful rural setting with views over the River Mole, this popular village pub was originally farm cottages and first licensed about 1870. An ideal watering hole for walkers who want to relax over a pint in the attractive pub garden. Typical fish dishes include lobster thermidor, Mediterranean squid pasta and fillet of sea bass, while Thai coconut chicken, partridge with red wine and junipers and fillet of braised beef on fennel are among meat dishes.
OPEN: 11.30-3 6-11 (All day Sat & Sun) **BAR MEALS:** L served all week 12-2.30 D served all week 6-9.30 **RESTAURANT:** L served all week 12-2.30 D served all week 6-9.30 All day Sat-Sun 🍴: Woodhouse Inns 🍺: Badger Tanglefoot, King & Barns Sussex, plus guest ales. 🍷: 9 **FACILITIES:** Garden: Terrace, food served outside Dogs allowed Water, biscuits **NOTES:** Parking 30

ALBURY
Map 06 TQ04

The Drummond Arms Inn ◆◆◆ 🍽
The Street GU5 9AG ☎ 01483 202039 🖷 01483 205361
Dir: 6m form Guildford
A village pub which at first sight looks quite conventional, but whose triple gables at second-floor level add an interesting architectural twist. It offers comfortable en suite accommodation, has an attractive garden overlooking the River Tillingbourne, and a varied restaurant and bar menu, on which home-made steak and kidney and cottage pies; lamb cutlets; smoked salmon, prawns and avocado platter; breaded plaice fillet; and onion and sage pork rissoles, are quoteworthy examples.
OPEN: 11-11 **BAR MEALS:** L served all week 12-2 D served Mon-Sat 7-9 Av main course £7.95 **RESTAURANT:** L served all week 12-2 D served Mon-Sat 7-9.30 🍴: Merlin Inns 🍺: Scottish Courage Courage Best, Gales HSB, Breakspear Bitter, Moorwand Speckled Hen. **FACILITIES:** Garden: Large garden seats 120 Dogs allowed Water **NOTES:** Parking 40 **ROOMS:** 11 bedrooms en suite 2 family rooms s£55 d£70 No children overnight

William IV
Little London GU5 9DG ☎ 01483 202685
Dir: Just off the A25 between Guildford & Dorking
This quaint country pub is only a stone's throw from Guildford, yet deep in the heart of the Surrey countryside. The area is great for hiking and the pub is popular with walkers, partly due to its attractive garden, which is ideal for post-ramble relaxation. A choice of real ales and a blackboard

continued

menu that changes daily is also part of the attraction. Expect steak and kidney pie, pot-roast lamb shank, battered cod and chips, and Sunday roasts.

William IV

OPEN: 11-3 5.30-11 (Sun 12-3, 7-10.30) Closed: 25 Dec
BAR MEALS: L served all week 12-2 D served Tue-Sat 7-9
RESTAURANT: L served Sun 12-2 D served Mon-Sat 7-9 🍴: Free House 🍺: Interbrew Flowers IPA, Hogs Back, Greene King Abbot Ale, Interbrew Bass. **FACILITIES:** Garden: Seating area, grass, patio in front of pub Dogs allowed Water **NOTES:** Parking 15

BETCHWORTH
Map 06 TQ25

The Red Lion 🍽
Old Reigate Rd RH3 7DS ☎ 01737 843336 🖷 01737 845242
e-mail: info@redlion-betchworth.com
Set in 18 acres with a cricket ground and rolling countryside views, this award-winning, 200-year-old pub offers an extensive menu. Beyond baguettes and ploughman's lunches the choice includes sole and smoked salmon, Barbary duck breast, aubergine and broccoli fritters, deep-fried plaice and chips, Toulouse sausage and mash, and steak and ale pie. The area is ideal for walkers.
OPEN: 11-11 (Sun 12-10.30) **BAR MEALS:** L served all week 12-3 D served all week 6-10 food 12-8.30 on Sundays
RESTAURANT: L served all week 12-3 D served all week 6-10 food 12-8.30 Sun 🍴: Punch Taverns 🍺: Fullers London Pride, Greene King, IPA, Adnams Broadside. **FACILITIES:** Child facs Garden **NOTES:** Parking 50

BLACKBROOK
Map 06 TQ14

The Plough at Blackbrook 🍷
RH5 4DS ☎ 01306 886603 🖷 886603
Dir: A24 to Dorking, then toward Horsham, 0.75m from Deepdene rdbt left to Blackbrook
Originally a coaching inn and a popular haunt of highwaymen, this pub has superb views and a delightful cottage garden. The ever-changing menu might include prawn curry; spicy fruited Moroccan lamb with couscous; and cheesy baked cod with avocado and prawns. From the lunchtime snack menu choose ploughman's (try Norbury Park blue cheese with quince jelly), and toasted deli bagels. Look out for the collection of vintage saws!
OPEN: 11-3 6-11 (Sat 12-3 Sun 12-3, 7-10.30) Closed: 25-26 Dec, 1 Jan **BAR MEALS:** L served all week 12-2 D served Tue-Sun 7-9 Sunday lunch not roast 🍴: Hall & Woodhouse 🍺: Badger King & Barnes Sussex, Tanglefoot, Badger Best. 🍷: 18 **FACILITIES:** Garden: Secluded cottage garden, patio & grassed area Dogs allowed Water & biscuits **NOTES:** Parking 22

🍷 7   Number of wines by the glass

BLACKHEATH
Map 06 TQ04

The Villagers Inn
Blackheath Ln GU4 8RB ☎ 01483 893152
e-mail: kbrampton@ringstead.co.uk
More than a hundred years old, this free house stands on the edge of Blackheath, a natural woodland area of several square miles in the heart of Surrey. A menu of traditional pub food includes steak and kidney pie, chicken pie, and fillet steak. A covered patio extends the opportunity for alfresco dining. Real ales are represented by London Pride, Hair of the Hog and Youngers Special.
OPEN: 12-3 6-11 (Fri & Sat 12-11, Sun 12-10.30)
BAR MEALS: L served all week 12-3 D served all week 6-9 Sun all day Av main course £7 **RESTAURANT:** L served all week 12-3 D served all week 6-9 Av 3 course à la carte £16 ◀: T.E.A, Hair of Hog, London Pride, Youngs Special. **FACILITIES:** Garden: Covered patio Dogs allowed **NOTES:** Parking 25

BRAMLEY
Map 06 TQ04

Jolly Farmer Inn 🌭 🍺
High St GU5 0HB ☎ 01483 893355 🖹 01483 890484
e-mail: enquiries@jollyfarmer.co.uk
Dir: Onto A3, then A281, Bramley 3m S of Guildford

Originally a coaching inn, parts of it go back to late Elizabethan times. Its owners' fight to save it from demolition in the early 1990s even made the front page of *The Times*. It offers a great selection of well-kept ales and good food. Likely to go down well are Aberdeen Angus beef steaks; roast pork tenderloin stuffed with apricot, apple and sage; and fillet of cod in beer batter.
OPEN: 11-11 (Sun 12-10.30) **BAR MEALS:** L served all week 12-2 D served all week 6.30-10 Sun 7-9.30 Av main course £10.50 ◐: Free House ◀: Hogs Back TEA, Badger Best, Hopback Summer Lightning, Hogs Back Hair of the Hog. 🍺: 10 **FACILITIES:** Garden: Large patio at front and rear Dogs allowed **NOTES:** Parking 22

CHIDDINGFOLD
Map 06 SU93

Pick of the Pubs

The Crown Inn
The Green GU8 4TX ☎ 01428 682255 🖹 01428 685736
Dir: On A283 between Milford & Petworth
Historic inn, dating back over 700 years, with lots of charming features, including ancient panelling, open fires, distinctive carvings and huge beams. Comfortably refurbished by owning brewery Hall and Woodhouse, this striking inn is in a unique setting close to Petworth, the famous Devil's Punch Bowl and miles of walking on the scenic South Downs nearby. Reliable food ranges from

sausage and mash with onion gravy, chicken tagliatelle, freshly battered fish and chips, and decent sandwiches, warm salads and ploughman's at lunchtime, to Torbay sole, monkfish and tiger prawns pan-fried with ginger and lime cream sauce and served on tagliatelle, and roast duck with sweet plum sauce on the evening menu.
OPEN: 11-11 (Sun 12-10.30) **BAR MEALS:** L served all week 12-2.30 D served Mon-Sat 6.30-9.30 (Sun 12-9) Av main course £9.95 **RESTAURANT:** L served all week 12-2.30 D served all week 6.30-9.30 (Sun 9) ◐: Hall & Woodhouse ◀: Badger Tanglefoot, King & Barnes Sussex Ale. **FACILITIES:** Beer garden, outdoor eating, patio, BBQ Dogs allowed

The Swan Inn & Restaurant 🏠 🌭 🍺
Petworth Rd GU8 4TY ☎ 01428 682073 🖹 01428 683259
e-mail: the-swan-inn@btconnect.com
web: www.swaninnandrestaurant.co.uk
Dir: 10m from Guildford city centre
A lovely 14th-century village pub whose sympathetic refurbishment has included bare floors, wooden furniture and big leather sofas. The chef makes impressive use of seafood, fish and local game: look for warm salad of wood-pigeon with marinated wild mushrooms, followed by braised lamb shank on celeriac purée with sun-dried tomato and mint sauce, finishing with chocolate terrine drizzled with orange syrup. Bar menu includes chicken curry; and fish cakes.
OPEN: 11-3 5.30-11 (Sat 11-11, Sun 12-10.30)
BAR MEALS: L served all week 12-2.30 D served all week 6.30-10 (Sat & Sun 12-10) Av main course £9.95 **RESTAURANT:** L served all week 12-2.30 D served all week 6.30-10 Av 3 course à la carte £22.50 ◐: Free House ◀: Hogs Back TEA, Ringwood Best, Fuller's London Pride. 🍺: 15 **FACILITIES:** Garden: Terraced sun trap Dogs allowed Water **NOTES:** Parking 25 **ROOMS:** 11 bedrooms en suite 2 family rooms s£65 d£65

CHURT
Map 05 SU83

Pick of the Pubs

The Pride of the Valley NEW ◆◆◆◆ 🍺
Tilford Rd GU10 2LH ☎ 01428 605799 🖹 01428 605875
e-mail: email@theprideofthevalley.co.uk
web: www.theprideofthevalley.co.uk
Dir: 4m from Farnham on outskirts of Churt Valley
Charming and traditional, the Pride of the Valley is in the heart of the beautiful Surrey countryside and sits within its own idyllic country garden. Built in 1868, this award-winning inn is a great place for all occasions, and once enjoyed the regular patronage of former Prime Minister, David Lloyd George. The accommodation consists of 16 luxurious en suite rooms, each individually designed and themed, and furnished to a high standard with four-poster beds, and jacuzzi baths. The menu is extensive and international in its flavours. Catering for all tastes, ages and appetites in both the restaurant and the bistro, the well-prepared food is available everyday for lunch and dinner. At the bars you will discover a selection of fine wines, spirits and local ales.
OPEN: 10.30-11 **BAR MEALS:** L served all week 12-2.30 D served all week 6.30-9.30 Av main course £11.95
RESTAURANT: L served all week 12-2.30 D served all week 6.30-9.30 ◀: London Pride, Hogs Back brewery beers. 🍺: 8
FACILITIES: Child facs Garden: Idyllic country garden Dogs allowed in reception/garden **NOTES:** Parking 60
ROOMS: 14 bedrooms en suite 6 family rooms s£95 d£115

continued

CLAYGATE
Map 06 TQ16

Swan Inn & Lodge ⛄
2 Hare Ln KT10 9BS ☎ 01372 462582 📠 01372 467089
e-mail: info@theswanlodge.co.uk web: www.theswanlodge.co.uk
Solid Edwardian pub overlooking a village green and cricket
pitch, yet only 15 miles from Central London. Before going,
take a website virtual tour of the attractive, colonial-style bar,
and in-house Thai restaurant. Here, dinner can be selected
from a long list of starters, soups, spicy salads, curries,
stirfries, seafood and vegetarian dishes. Hearty bar food
includes chilli con carne, spicy chicken burger, potato wedges
with sour cream, ploughman's, baguettes and sandwiches.
August Bank Holiday beer festival.
OPEN: 11-11 **BAR MEALS:** L served all week 12-2.30 D served
Mon-Sat 6-10.30 **RESTAURANT:** L served Sun D served Mon-Sat
6-10.30 Sun 12-4 Av 3 course à la carte £16 🍴: Wellington Pub Co
🍺: London Pride, Adnams, Brakspear. ⛄: 8 **FACILITIES:** Garden:
Landscaped patio, water feature **NOTES:** Parking 8

COBHAM
Map 06 TQ16

The Cricketers ⛄
Downside KT11 3NX ☎ 01932 862105 📠 01932 868186
e-mail: info@thecricketersdownside.co.uk
Dir: From A3 take A245 towards Cobham, 2nd rdbt turn right , then 1st
right opp Waitrose. Pub 1.5m
The original part of this traditional, family-run pub dates back
to 1540; some of the wattle and daub can still be seen,
highlighted behind glass. Other features include beamed
ceilings and log fires. The inn's charming rural setting makes
it popular with walkers, and the pretty River Mole is close by.
The lunch menu offers the likes of slow-cooked spiced lamb
shank, fresh herb-crusted cod and chicken masala.
OPEN: 11-11 (Sun 11-8.30 winter) **BAR MEALS:** L served all week
12-2.30 D served all week 6.30-9.30 (Sun 12-7 winter, 12-9 summer)
RESTAURANT: L served Tue-Sun 12-1.45 D served Tue-Sat 7-9.30
Sun 12-2.30 Av 3 course fixed price £20 🍴: Unique Pub Co
🍺: Young's Bitter, Old Speckled Hen, Fullers London Pride. ⛄: 10
FACILITIES: Garden: Large open garden overlooking village Dogs
allowed Water **NOTES:** Parking 80

COLDHARBOUR
Map 06 TQ14

Pick of the Pubs

The Plough Inn ♦♦♦♦ ⛄
Coldharbour Ln RH5 6HD ☎ 01306 711793 📠 01306 710055
e-mail: ploughinn@btinternet.com web: www.ploughinn.com
Dir: M25 junct 9 - A24 to Dorking. A25 towards Guildford.
Coldharbour signed from one-way system
For fifteen years, the husband-and-wife owners of this
17th-century pub have been slowly rebuilding,
refurbishing and upgrading it to create a warm,
welcoming hostelry with excellent accommodation,
superb food, and - since 1996 - its own real ales. This
labour of love perhaps results from the air here - the pub
is 25 minutes walk from the top of Leith Hill, southern
England's highest point. A well-worn smugglers' route
from the coast to London once passed its door, which
probably explains why the resident ghost is a matelot.
The surrounding North Downs draw customers in the
shape of walkers, horseback riders, cyclists, and
Londoners simply anxious to escape the city and relax in
convivial surroundings. Food is freshly prepared and
home cooked, while three real fires in winter and

continued

candlelight in the evenings create a suitable ambience.
On the menu fish dishes are always plentiful, and could
feature pan-fried baby squid, grilled sardines, and
monkfish. Other representative dishes are confit of duck;
braised beef with onions in home-brewed porter; and
pork fillet with fresh asparagus roulade. Desserts like
apple and red fruit crumble with custard are irresistible;
and the collection of fine wines completes a thoroughly
agreeable experience.
OPEN: 11.30-11 (Sun 12-10.30) Closed: 25 Dec
BAR MEALS: L served all week 12-2.30 D served all week
6.30-9.30 Sun 6-9 Av main course £7.50
RESTAURANT: L served all week 12-2.30 D served all week
6.30-9.30 Sun 6.30-9 Av 3 course à la carte £19.50 🍴: Free
House 🍺: Crooked Furrow, Leith Hill Tallywhacker, Ringwood
Old Thumper, Timothy Taylor Landlord. ⛄: 8
FACILITIES: Garden with shrubs and picnic benches Dogs
allowed **ROOMS:** 6 bedrooms en suite s£55 d£69.50 No
children overnight

COMPTON
Map 06 SU94

The Withies Inn 🐟 ⛄
Withies Ln GU3 1JA ☎ 01483 421158 📠 01483 425904
Dir: Telephone for directions
The splendid garden is one of the pub's chief attractions, filled
with overhanging weeping willows, apple trees and dazzling
flower borders. Inside, low beams, 17th-century carved panels
and an art nouveau settle create a cosy ambience, while logs
crackle in the inglenook fireplace. Good choice of bar snacks
(seafood platter; Cumberland sausages; baked potatoes and
sandwiches). The restaurant menu includes local trout; Scotch
beef sirloin; and seasonal specialities such as mussels,
asparagus and crab.
OPEN: 11-3 6-11 (Sun 12-3) **BAR MEALS:** L served all week
12-2.30 D served all week 7-10 **RESTAURANT:** L served all week
12-2.30 D served Mon-Sat 7-10 🍴: Free House 🍺: Greene King
IPA, Tea, Fullers London Pride, Sussex. ⛄: 8 **FACILITIES:** Garden:
Dogs allowed in the garden only **NOTES:** Parking 70

DORKING
Map 06 TQ14

The Stephan Langton ⛄
Friday St, Abinger Common RH5 6JR ☎ 01306 730775
Dir: Between Dorking & Guildford leave A25 at Hollow Lane, W of
Wootton. Go S for 1.5m then left into Friday Street
A lovely brick and timber inn named after the 13th-century
archbishop of Canterbury and local boy who was
instrumental in drawing up the Magna Carta. Although it
looks much older, and was built on the site of another inn,
this secluded hostelry only dates back to 1930. Some of
Surrey's loveliest walks are found nearby, including the
challenging Leith Hill, and walkers find this a perfect place to
recover. The pub is being gradually refurbished to match
Jonathan Coomb's upmarket food. The bar choice includes
duck confit with Puy lentils and spring greens, and Moroccan-
style braised lamb, while the dinner menu offers a short but
well-balanced choice: chargrilled squid with chilli and rocket,
seared marlin niçoise, and buttermilk pudding with poached
rhubarb is a typically appealing meal.
OPEN: 11-3 5-11 (Open all day at the weekend in summer)
BAR MEALS: L served Tues-Sun 12.30-2.30 D served Tues-Sat 7-10
(no dinner on Sun) Av main course £12 **RESTAURANT:** D served
Tues-Sat 7-10 Av 3 course à la carte £25 🍴: Free House 🍺: Fuller's
London Pride, Adnams, Hogsback Tea. **FACILITIES:** Garden: Food
served outside Dogs allowed must be on lead Water provided
NOTES: Parking 20

England

DUNSFOLD
Map 06 TQ03

The Sun Inn ♀
The Common GU8 4LE ☎ 01483 200242 🖹 01483 201141
e-mail: suninn@dunsfold.net
Dir: A281 thru Shalford & Bramley, take B2130 to Godalming. Dunsfold on left after 2 miles

This 500-year-old family-run inn overlooks the village cricket green and offers a warm welcome, blazing fires and a broad selection of food. Typical starters include deep fried brie with cranberry sauce, prawn and avacado salad, and Sun Inn special nachos. Follow with a choice of popular favourites such as steak and kidney pudding, Italian meatballs, creamy fish pie, trio of speciality sausages and mash, or salmon fishcakes with lime and mango salsa.
OPEN: 11-11 (Sun 12-10.30 Closed 3-5 Mon-Thurs)
BAR MEALS: L served all week 12-2.30 D served all week 7-9.30 Sun 12-2.30, 7-8.30 Av main course £7.95 **RESTAURANT:** L served all week 12-2.30 D served all week 7-9.30 Sun 7-8.30 🍴: Punch Taverns 🍺: Harveys Sussex, Bass, Adnams, Courage Best. ♀: 9
FACILITIES: Garden: Large patio garden to side Dogs allowed Water & Biscuits **NOTES:** Parking 40

EFFINGHAM
Map 06 TQ15

The Plough ♀
Orestan Ln KT24 5SW ☎ 01372 458121 🖹 01372 458121
Dir: Between Guildford & Leatherhead on A246

A modern pub with a traditional feel, The Plough provides a peaceful retreat in a rural setting close to Polesden Lacy National Trust House. Home-cooked British dishes include the likes of wild boar with mushroom sauce, bangers with spring onion mash and gravy, rib-eye steak, and bacon and avocado salad. Once owned by Jimmy Hanley and used in the 1960s TV series *Jim's Inn*, it also boasts a popular beer garden.
OPEN: 11-3 5.30-11 (Sun 12-3, 7-10.30) Closed: 25, 26 Dec, 1 Jan (Eve) **BAR MEALS:** L served all week 12-2.30 D served all week 7-10 **RESTAURANT:** L served all week 12-2.30 D served all week 7-10 🍴: Young & Co 🍺: Youngs IPA, Special, Winter Warmer, Youngs. ♀: 12 **FACILITIES:** Garden: Beer garden with willow tree **NOTES:** Parking 40

EGHAM
Map 06 TQ07

The Fox and Hounds ♀ 🐾
Bishopgate Rd, Englefield Green TW20 0XU
☎ 01784 433098 🖹 01784 438775
e-mail: thefoxandhounds@4cinns.co.uk
web: www.thefoxandhoundsrestaurant.co.uk
Dir: From village green L into Castle Hill Rd, then R into Bishopsgate Rd

The Surrey border once ran through the centre of this good English pub, which is on the edge of Windsor Great Park, convenient for walkers and riders. Features include a large

garden, handsome conservatory and weekly jazz nights. Menus offer a range of daily-changing fish specials as well as dishes like orange and sesame chicken fillets on coriander and lime noodles, or roast pork with grain mustard glaze and parmesan crisps.
OPEN: 11-11 (Sun 12-10.30) Jan-Etr 11-3, 5.30-11
BAR MEALS: L served all week 12-2.30 D served Mon-Sat 6.30-9.30 Av main course £7 **RESTAURANT:** L served all week 12-2.30 D served Mon-Sat 6.30-10 🍺: Hogsback T.E.A., Abbot Ale, Brakspear ♀: 8 **FACILITIES:** Garden: Patio and conservatory Dogs allowed **NOTES:** Parking 60

ELSTEAD
Map 06 SU94

Pick of the Pubs

The Woolpack ♀
The Green GU8 6HD ☎ 01252 703106 🖹 01252 705914
Dir: A3 S, take Milford exit and follw signs for Elstead on the B3001

Built as a store for woollen bales, this quaint old pub has also served as a butcher's shop, bicycle repair works and the local Co-op. Remnants of the wool industry, including weaving shuttles and cones of wool, form appealing features in the bar, along with open log fires, low beams and high-backed settles, window seats and spindle-backed chairs. There are good cask-conditioned ales and large blackboard menus that are frequently changed. The pub has a reputation for its generously-proportioned 'old English and colonial' food. Look out for starters such as king prawns in filo pastry; or a charcuterie selection with Provençale tapenade. Main courses include pork steak with apricot and Schnapps; medallions of monkfish with garlic and rosemary butter; and Cumberland sausages on mustard mash. An extensive range of fresh, home-made desserts is always on offer.
OPEN: 11-3 5.30-11 (Sat 11-11, Sun 12-10.30)
BAR MEALS: L served all week 12-2 D served all week 7-9.30 (Sun 12-2, 7-9) Av main course £8.95 **RESTAURANT:** L served all week 12-2 D served all week 7-9.30 Sun 12-2, 7-9 🍴: Punch Taverns 🍺: Greene King Abbot Ale, Brakspears, Spitfire. ♀: 11 **FACILITIES:** Garden: Walled garden at rear Dogs allowed Water **NOTES:** Parking 15

continued

The Bat and Ball Freehouse

Bat and Ball Lane, Boundstone, Farnham, Surrey GU10 4SA
www.thebatandball.co.uk

Tel: 01252 792108
E-mail: info@thebatandball.co.uk

The Bat and Ball Freehouse nestles in the bottom of the Bourne valley in Boundstone near Farnham. Over 150 years old, the Pub has a relaxed, rural feel, surrounded by woodland and wildlife, and is the focal point of 5 footpaths which connect to local villages. Customers can eat or drink throughout the Pub, patio area and the large south-facing garden (which backs onto the Bourne stream and has a popular children's play structure). All the food is cooked in-house and this is very much a pub that serves restaurant quality food and not a restaurant that sells beer! The bar area has both a traditional and modern style to it to provide for our differing customer tastes, both young and old, and we have a tempting selection of 6 well-kept Cask

---

FARNHAM   Map 05 SU84

The Bat & Ball Freehouse ♀

15 Bat & Ball Ln, Boundstone GU10 4SA
☎ 01252 792108 🖷 01252 794564
e-mail: info@thebatandball.co.uk
Dir: Follow signs to Bird World from the Coxbridge Rdbt on A3. Turn left just before Cricketers PH into School Lane. At top cross over staggered x-rds into Sandrock Hill. After 0.25m take left into Upper Bourne Lane, follow signs.

Nestling at the bottom of the Bourne valley, this 150-year-old inn is worth taking the effort to find. There's an inviting blend of old and new, with terracotta floor tiles, oak beams and cricketing memorabilia. You'll find a tempting selection of well-kept real ales, and roaring winter fires contrast with popular summer barbecues. Choose from hearty main course options like braised oxtail in red wine, but don't miss the daily selection of home-made desserts!
OPEN: 11-3 5.30-11 (All day Fri-Sun) **BAR MEALS:** L served all week 12-2.15 D served all week 7-9.30 Sun 12-3, 6-8.30 Av main
continued

course £8.50 **RESTAURANT:** L served all week 12-2.15 D served all week 7-9.30 Sun 12-3, 6-8.30 Av 3 course à la carte £18.50
🍺: Youngs Bitter, Hogs Back TEA, Timothy Taylors Landlord, Bat & Ball Bitter. ♀: 8 **FACILITIES:** Garden: Patio area, seating, suntrap Dogs allowed water **NOTES:** Parking 40
See advert on this page

GUILDFORD   Map 06 SU94

Red Lion ♀

Shamley Green GU5 0UB ☎ 01483 892202 🖷 01483 894055
Attractive old village pub with large front and rear gardens, ideal for whiling away summer afternoons watching the local cricket team play on the green opposite. In the cosy bar or large comfortable restaurant, there's plenty of choice from a variety of menus. The kitchen has undergone a recent change of chef, so look out for a whole new range of food choices, and a new wine list besides.
OPEN: 7.30-11.30 (All day in summer closed 4-6pm winter)
BAR MEALS: L served all week 12-3 D served all week 7-10 Av main course £12 **RESTAURANT:** L served all week 12-3 D served all week 7-10 🍴: Punch Taverns 🍺: Youngs Pedigree, Adnams Broadside ♀: 6 **FACILITIES:** Children's licence Garden: Large front and rear garden **NOTES:** Parking 20

HASCOMBE   Map 06 TQ03

The White Horse

The Street GU8 4JA ☎ 01483 208258 🖷 01483 208200
Dir: From Godalming take B2130. Pub on L 0.5m after Hascombe
A friendly 16th-century pub situated in picturesque countryside that is good for walking. The pub is particularly noted in summer for its colourful garden, with hanging
continued

HASCOMBE continued

baskets and flowers. Restaurant menu and extensive blackboard specials in the bar may offer Thai style salmon and prawn fishcakes, steak burger, pies, and calves' liver and bacon. Fresh fish is delivered daily.
OPEN: 10-3 5.30-11 (Sat 10-11, Sun 12-10.30)
BAR MEALS: L served all week 12-2.20 D served all week 7-10 Av main course £9 **RESTAURANT:** L served all week 12-2 D served Mon-Sat 7-10 Av 3 course à la carte £25 ⊕: Punch Taverns
◀: Adnams, Fullers London Pride, Harveys Flowers.
FACILITIES: Garden: outdoor eating, patio Dogs allowed
NOTES: Parking 55

HASLEMERE   Map 06 SU93

The Wheatsheaf Inn ◆◆◆ ♀
Grayswood Rd, Grayswood GU27 2DE
☎ 01428 644440 ▤ 01428 641285 e-mail: thewheatsheaf@aol.com
Dir: Leave A3 at Milford, A286 to Haslemere. Grayswood approx 1.5m N

Edwardian village inn with one of Surrey's loveliest walks right on its doorstep. Nearby is the magnificent viewpoint at Black Down where Alfred, Lord Tennyson once lived. Fresh, local ingredients are used to produce an extensive ranges of pasta, salads and steaks in particular. Specials might include pan-fried duck breast with damson and port sauce; mixed fish and seafood casserole with citrus-scented cous cous; or field mushrooms stuffed with peppers and cream cheese.
OPEN: 11-3 6-11 **BAR MEALS:** L served all week 12-2 D served all week 7-10 Av main course £10.95 **RESTAURANT:** L served all week 12-2 D served all week 7-10 Av 3 course à la carte £23 ⊕: Free House ◀: Fullers London Pride, Timothy Taylor Landlord, Ringwood Best, Greene King IPA. ♀: 8 **FACILITIES:** Garden: Patio area, pergola terrace **NOTES:** Parking 20 **ROOMS:** 7 bedrooms en suite s£55 d£75 No children overnight

---

HINDHEAD   Map 06 SU83

Devil's Punchbowl Inn ♀
London Rd GU26 6AG ☎ 01428 606565 ▤ 01428 605713
Dir: From M25 take A3 to Guildford, then A3 & follow Portsmouth signs
The hotel, which dates from the early 1800s, stands 900ft above sea level with wonderful views as far as London on a clear day. The 'punchbowl' is a large natural bowl in the ground across the road. The menu, while not large, has something for everybody with deep fried camembert with cranberry sauce, whitebait, and smoked haddock fishcakes as starters; main courses include steaks, grilled sea bass and Cumberland sausages. There is also a snack menu.
OPEN: 7-11 **BAR MEALS:** L served all week 12-6 D served all week 6-10 Sun 12-9 **RESTAURANT:** L served all week 12-3 D served all week 6-10 ⊕: Eldridge Pope ◀: Bass, 6 X, Tetleys, Bombardier.
♀: 10 **FACILITIES:** Children's licence Garden: Lawn area with benches patio area, seating Dogs allowed **NOTES:** Parking 65

LEIGH   Map 06 TQ24

The Plough ♀
Church Rd, LEIGH RH2 8NJ ☎ 01306 611348 ▤ 01306 611299
Dir: Telephone for directions
A welcoming country pub overlooking the village green and situated opposite St Bartholomew's Church. Varied clientele, good atmosphere and quaint low beams which are conveniently padded! A hearty bar menu offers steak sandwiches, burgers, melts, salads, ploughmans' and jacket potatoes, while the restaurant area menu features tomato and artichoke pasta, smoked haddock fillet mornay, or Mexican style tortilla wraps.
OPEN: 11-11 (Sun 12-10.30) **BAR MEALS:** L served all week all day D served all week all day Av main course £8
RESTAURANT: L served all week all day D served all week all day Av 3 course à la carte £18.50 ⊕: Hall & Woodhouse ◀: Badger Best , Tanglefoot, Sussex Bitter. ♀: 15 **FACILITIES:** Child facs Garden: Patio surrounded by climbing roses Dogs allowed Water **NOTES:** Parking 6

LINGFIELD   Map 06 TQ34

Pick of the Pubs

Hare and Hounds NEW ♀
Common Rd RH7 6BZ ☎ 01342 832351 ▤ 01342 832351
e-mail: hare.hounds@tiscali.co.uk
Dir: From A22 follow signs for Lingfield Racecourse into Common Rd

The Hare and Hounds makes an attractive promise: that despite their commitment to providing innovative and excellent food, they remain at heart a proper pub. There are plenty of real ales, including Flowers and Greene King, and a traditional atmosphere is preserved. You're welcome to chat with locals propping up the bar, and no flashing machines will disturb the peace. A split-level, decked garden waits for sunny days. The food is unusual and exciting, and everything - bread, pasta, ice cream - is home made. Start with hazelnut and lemon potato cake with warm brie, asparagus and roast apricot; and move on to herb crusted pork fillet with chilli smashed courgettes and peppers; or seared duck breast with sticky rice cake, Asian greens and water chestnuts. Unusual desserts include rhubarb, apple and rice brûlée; or chocolate brioche belle helene. The regularly changing artworks decorating the walls are also for sale.
OPEN: 11.30-11 (Sun 12-8) Closed: 1 Jan
BAR MEALS: L served all week 12-2.30 D served Mon-Sat 7-9.30 Sun 12-3.30 Av main course £9.95
RESTAURANT: L served all week 12-2.30 D served Mon-Sat 7-9.30 Sun 12-3.30 Av 3 course à la carte £25 ◀: Greene King IPA, Flowers Original, Old Speckled Hen, Guinness. ♀: 8
FACILITIES: Children's licence Garden: Split level, partly decked Dogs allowed **NOTES:** Parking 40

MICKLEHAM   Map 06 TQ15

England

Pick of the Pubs

King William IV
Byttom Hill RH5 6EL ☎ 01372 372590
Dir: Just off A24 just N of B2289
This family-run free house was formerly an ale house for
Lord Beaverbrook's staff at his nearby Cherkley estate.
The building itself dates from 1790 with some Victorian
additions, and affords fine views across Norbury Park and
the Mole Valley from its hillside location. Period detail is a
feature of the panelled snug and a larger back bar with its
open fire, cast iron tables and grandfather clock. Outside
there's an attractive terraced garden where barbecues are
held in summer. The proprietor is also the chef, serving
good food alongside the real ales. Dishes are prepared on
the premises from quality ingredients and the menu
incorporates daily fresh fish and vegetarian specialities.
Expect Thai green vegetable curry and wild mushroom
and spinach pancakes, as well as calves' liver, steak and
kidney pie, and the weekly Sunday roast. The pub is an
ideal watering hole for walkers and cyclists from the
surrounding countryside.
OPEN: 11-3 6-11 (Sun 12-10.30) Closed: 25 Dec
BAR MEALS: L served all week 12-2 D served all week 7-9.30
Sun 12-5 Av main course £8.95 ☺: Free House ◖: Hogs Back
TEA & Hop Garden Gold, Badger Best, Adnams Best, Monthly
Guest Beers. **FACILITIES:** Garden: Terraced garden with
picturesque views

The Running Horses ♀
Old London Rd RH5 6DU ☎ 01372 372279 ▤ 01372 363004
e-mail: info@therunninghorses.co.uk
Dir: 1.5m from junct 9 M25. Off A24 between Leatherhead & Dorking

Attracting travellers for more than 400 years, this inn is only
half a mile from famous Box Hill. The bar features a
highwayman's hideaway and an inglenook fireplace. Chunky
sandwiches, croque monsieur and grilled sardines are
available in the bar. On the menu in both bar and restaurant,
look for fillet mignons topped with vodka and tomato butter,
baked reblochon and sweet potatoes, panfried sea bass fillet,
or seared pheasant on chorizo and mushroom risotto.
OPEN: 11.30-11 (Sun 12-10.30) Closed: 25-26 Dec nights
BAR MEALS: L served all week 12-2.30 D served all week 7-9.30
(Sat-Sun 12-3) Av main course £7.50 **RESTAURANT:** L served all
week 12-2.30 D served all week 7-9.30 (Sat-Sun 12-3, 6-9) Av 3 course
à la carte £28 Av 3 course fixed price £24.90 ☺: Punch Taverns
◖: Fuller's London Pride, Young's Bitter, Abbot, Adnams Bitter. ♀: 9
FACILITIES: Garden: Large patio area Dogs allowed in bar only, on
leads. Water

NEWDIGATE   Map 06 TQ14

The Six Bells ♀
Village St RH5 5DH ☎ 01306 631276
Dir: 5m S of Dorking (A24), L at Beare Green rdbt, R at T-junct in village
Picturesque timber-framed pub located opposite the parish
church in a quiet village location. There are two bars, one
with an inglenook fireplace, plus a restaurant area, beer
garden and patio. Ham and eggs, and liver and bacon are
typical of the bar meals on offer, while in the restaurant you
can expect the likes of salmon cakes, Thai green chicken
curry, and pork belly stuffed with black pudding.
OPEN: 11-4 6-11 (Sun 12-10.30) **BAR MEALS:** L served all week
12-3 D served all week 6-9 Sun all day Summer Av main course
£6.50 **RESTAURANT:** L served all week 12-3 D served all week
7-9.30 Sat-Sun all day summer Av 3 course à la carte £17 Av 3 course
fixed price £12.50 ☺: Hall & Woodhouse ◖: Badger Tanglefoot &
Sussex Ale, Hofbrau Premium, Hofbrau Export, Badger Smooth. ♀: 8
FACILITIES: Child facs Children's licence Garden: patio/terrace,
lawns with tables Dogs allowed Water, dog biscuits
NOTES: Parking 40

The Surrey Oaks ♀
Parkgate Rd RH5 5DZ ☎ 01306 631200 ▤ 01306 631200
e-mail: ken@surreyoaks.co.uk
*Dir: From A24 or A25 follow signs to Newdigate. Pub 1m E of Newdigate
on road towards Leigh/Charwood*

Picturesque timber-framed pub located opposite the parish
church in a quiet village location. Parts of the building date
back to 1570, and it became an inn around the middle of the
19th century. There are two bars, one with an inglenook
fireplace, as well as a restaurant area, patio and beer garden.
Deep-fried breaded fish of the day, steak and kidney pudding,
and sausage with mashed potato and onion gravy feature on
the popular bar menu.
OPEN: 11.30-2.30 5.30-11 (Sat 11.30-3, 6-11 Sun 12-3, 7-10.30)
BAR MEALS: L served all week 12-2 D served Tue-Sat 7-9 Av main
course £8 **RESTAURANT:** L served all week 12-2 D served Tue-Sat
7-9 Av 3 course à la carte £15 ☺: Punch Taverns ◖: Harveys
Sussex Best, Caledonian Deuchars IPA, Timothy Taylors Landlord,
rotating guest beers. ♀: 8 **FACILITIES:** Child facs Large garden
Child area, pond, aviary, goat paddock Dogs allowed Water
NOTES: Parking 75

Website addresses are included where available.
The AA cannot be held responsible for the
content of any of these websites

England

OCKLEY
Map 06 TQ14

Pick of the Pubs

Bryce's at The Old School House 🐟 ⟡ 🍷
RH5 5TH ☎ 01306 627430 ▤ 01306 628274
e-mail: bryces.fish@virgin.net
Dir: 8m S of Dorking on A29
This Grade 2 listed building dates back to 1750, and was a
boarding school until Bill Bryce bought it in 1982. He's
passionate about fresh fish and offers a huge range,
despite his location in rural Surrey. Non-fish diners are
not forgotten, but their choice is limited. The non-smoking
restaurant in the old school gym offers seven starters and
seven main courses - all fish. After a starter such as
Shetland salmon with lime, keta and avruga caviar, main
course choices include brown river trout with baby
capers; and roast Cornish cod on pesto crushed potatoes
with anchovy, tomato and caper vinaigrette. A handful of
non-fish options on the bar menu range from open
sandwiches on hot focaccia bread, to a fresh vegetable
tempura with wild rice and Thai chilli sauce. A good wine
list includes plenty of house bottles available by the glass.
OPEN: 11-3 6-11 (Closed Sun pm Nov, Jan, Feb) Closed: 16, 25
Dec, 1-2 Jan **BAR MEALS:** L served all week 12-2.30 D served
Mon-Sat 6.30-9.30 Av main course £10.50
RESTAURANT: L served all week 12-2.30 D served Mon-Sat
7-9.30 Av 3 course à la carte £27.50 Av 3 course fixed price £27.50
🍴: Free House ◾: London Pride, Gales Best & Sussex, Scottish
Courage John Smith's Smooth. 🍷: 15 **FACILITIES:** Terrace area
Dogs allowed Water **NOTES:** Parking 25

The Kings Arms Inn ◆◆◆◆
Stane St RH5 5TS ☎ 01306 711224 ▤ 01306 711224
*Dir: From M25 junct 9 take A24 through Dorking towards Horsham, A29
to Ockley*

Heavily-beamed 16th-century village inn in the picturesque
village of Ockley, overlooked by the tower of Leith Hill.
Welcoming log fires, a priest hole, a friendly ghost, an award-
winning garden and six attractively furnished bedrooms are
all features. Home-made food is offered in both restaurant
and bar, including a popular choice of pies (game, fish,
cheesy cottage, and pork, apple and stilton), and fresh
scallops wrapped in bacon, or roasted shoulder of lamb.
OPEN: 11-2.30 6-11 (Sun 12-3, 7-10.30) **BAR MEALS:** L served all
week 12-2 D served all week 7-9 **RESTAURANT:** L served Tue-Sun
12-2 D served Tue-Sat 7-9 🍴: Free House ◾: Interbrew Flowers
Original, Greene King Old Speckled Hen, Bass, Pedigree.
FACILITIES: Garden: Landscaped garden, with patio BBQ
NOTES: Parking 40 **ROOMS:** 6 bedrooms en suite s£50 d£70 No
children overnight

OXTED
Map 06 TQ35

George Inn 🍷
High St RH8 9LP ☎ 01883 713453
Dir: Telephone for directions
A 500-year-old pub and restaurant with a friendly family
atmosphere, warmed by log fires under the original oak
beams. Home-made steak and kidney pudding, braised shank
of lamb, sardines and salmon fillets from its seasonal menus
epitomise the range of carefully sourced and well-cooked fare
that is available on any day. There are decent wines to
accompany the food, with Badger beers as alternative
supping. A committed team offer quality service.
OPEN: 11-11 (Sun 12-2.30) **BAR MEALS:** L served all week 12-9.30
D served all week Av main course £6.50 **RESTAURANT:** L served
all week 12-2.30 D served all week 6-9.30 🍴: Woodhouse Inns
◾: Badger Tanglefoot, Badger Best, King & Barnes, Sussex.
FACILITIES: Garden: Patio Area Dogs allowed **NOTES:** Parking 25

PIRBRIGHT
Map 06 SU95

The Royal Oak 🍷
Aldershot Rd GU24 0DQ ☎ 01483 232466
Dir: M3 junct 3, A322 towards Guildford, then A324 towards Aldershot
A genuine old world pub specialising in real ales (up to nine
at any time), and well known for its glorious prize-winning
garden. The Tudor cottage pub has an oak church door,
stained glass windows and pew seating, and in winter there
are welcoming log fires in the rambling bars. The menu may
include smoked salmon and pesto, braised lamb shoulder,
steak and ale pie, and penne pasta Alfredo, along with
various specials.
OPEN: 11-11 (Sun 12-10.30) **BAR MEALS:** L served all week 12
D served all week (10-9.30 Sat & Sun) Av main course £7
🍴: ◾: Flowers IPA, Hogsback Traditional English Ale, Bass Ringwood
Ale. 🍷: 18 **FACILITIES:** Garden: Dogs allowed on leads only
NOTES: Parking 50

REDHILL
Map 06 TQ25

William IV Country Pub
Little Common Ln, Bletchingly RH1 4QF ☎ 01883 743278
*Dir: From M25 junct 6 take A25 towards Redhill. Turn right at top of
Bletchingly High Street*
An early Victorian hostelry comprising a traditional snug,
lounge and dining room. Tucked away down a leafy lane, it is
very handy for the Pilgrims' Way. Home-made specials (all of
them fish on Fridays) include the likes of pork rashers with
apple cider sauce; rump steak with Merlot, red onion and
mushroom sauce; and monkfish in mustard sauce with bacon
and grilled peppers. There is an excellent range of snacks and
pizzas, and al fresco eating in the peaceful garden is an
additional summer bonus.
OPEN: 12-3 6-11 (Sun 12-10.30 Apr-Oct 12-4 7-10.30 Nov-Mar
Closed: 25-26 Dec eve **BAR MEALS:** L served all week 12-2.15
D served Mon-Sat 6.45-9.30 Sun 12-4 Av main course £8.95
RESTAURANT: L served all week 12-2.15 D served Mon-Sat 7-9.30
Sun 12-4 Av 3 course à la carte £17 🍴: Punch Taverns ◾: Adnams
Bitter, Ruddle County, Harveys Sussex Best, Fullers London Pride.
FACILITIES: Garden: Large 2 tier garden, enclosed fence & gates
Dogs allowed **NOTES:** Parking 10

🐟 Pubs offering a good choice of fish on
their menu

SOUTH GODSTONE — Map 06 TQ34

Fox & Hounds
Tilburstow Hill Rd RH9 8LY ☎ 01342 893474 ▤ 894503
e-mail: parrycljltd@aol.com
Country inn with a cosy low-beamed bar, antique high-backed settles and a wood-burning stove. The building dates from around 1370 though the first licensing record is a re-application to brew on the premises in 1601. Typical dishes are baked monkfish wrapped in parma ham with watercress sauce, and medallions of venison on tumbled mushrooms and bacon with matured port jus. There is also a large garden with pleasant rural views.
OPEN: 12-3.30 6-11 (Sun 12-3.30, 7-11) **BAR MEALS:** L served all week 12-2.30 D served all week 7-9.30 Sun 7-8.30
RESTAURANT: L served all week 12-2.30 D served all week 7-9.30 (Sun 7-8.30) 🍴: Greene King 🍺: All Greene King.
FACILITIES: Garden: Large garden Dogs allowed water bowl, dog biscuits **NOTES:** Parking 20

STAINES — Map 06 TQ07

The Swan Hotel ♀
The Hythe TW18 3JB ☎ 01784 452494 ▤ 01784 461593
e-mail: swan.hotel@fullers.co.uk
Dir: Just off A308, S of Staines Bridge. 5m from Heathrow

Just south of Staines Bridge, this 18th-century inn was once the haunt of river bargemen who were paid in tokens which could be exchanged at the pub for food and drink. The Swan has a spacious, comfortable bar, and the menu consists of traditional home-cooked food. Typical examples range from home-made beef lasagne, and natural smoked haddock, to Thai green chicken curry.
OPEN: 12-11 Sun 12-10.30 25 Dec 12-3 **BAR MEALS:** L served all week 12-6 D served all week 6-9.30 Sun 12-8 Av main course £8
RESTAURANT: L served all week 12-6 D served all week 6-9.30 Sun 12-8 🍴: Fullers 🍺: Fuller's London Pride, ESB. ♀: 10
FACILITIES: Garden: Patio with seating. Overlooks River Thames Dogs allowed

VIRGINIA WATER — Map 06 TQ06

The Wheatsheaf Hotel ★★ ♀
London Rd GU25 4QF ☎ 01344 842057 ▤ 01344 842932
e-mail: wheatsheaf.hotel.4306@thespiritgroup.com
web: www.wheatsheafhotel.com
Dir: From M25 junct 13, take A30 towards Bracknell
The Wheatsheaf dates back to the second half of the 18th century and is beautifully situated overlooking Virginia Water on the edge of Windsor Great Park. Chalkboard menus offer a good range of freshly prepared dishes with fresh fish as a speciality. Popular options are beer battered cod and chips, roast queen fish with pesto crust, and braised lamb shank on mustard mash.
continued

The Wheatsheaf Hotel

OPEN: 11-11 **BAR MEALS:** L served all week 12-10 D served all week Av main course £8 **RESTAURANT:** L served all week 12-10 D served all week 🍴: 🍺: Guest Ales. **FACILITIES:** Garden: beer garden, patio, outdoor eating **NOTES:** Parking 90
ROOMS: 17 bedrooms en suite s£90 d£95 No children overnight

WALLISWOOD — Map 06 TQ13

The Scarlett Arms
RH5 5RD ☎ 01306 627243
Dir: S on A29 from Dorking, thru Ockley, R for Walliswood/Oakwood Hill
Oak beams, a stone floor and a fine open fireplace give a homely feel to this unspoilt, 400-year-old rural pub. Simple country cooking is the perfect complement to the excellent King & Barnes ales on offer.
OPEN: 11-2.30 5.30-11 **BAR MEALS:** L served all week 12-2 D served all week 6.30-9.30 Av main course £6.25 🍴: King & Barnes 🍺: King & Barnes Sussex, Mild & Broadwood. **FACILITIES:** Garden: Dogs allowed **NOTES:** Parking 30

WARLINGHAM — Map 06 TQ35

The White Lion ♀
CR6 9EG ☎ 01883 629011
This listed 15th-century inn on Warlingham Green has recently doubled in size. The new extension has successfully merged with the old part of the inn, and its low ceilings, oak beams and inglenook fireplace. Four real ales and five lagers are always available, and there's a varied menu offering sandwiches, light bites and dishes of Thai green chicken; lamb shank with rosemary and stilton; and roquefort tortelloni (among a good choice of vegetarian dishes).
OPEN: 12-11 (Sun 12-10.30) **BAR MEALS:** L served all week 12-8 D served all week 12-8 Av main course £6 🍴: Bass 🍺: Fullers London Pride, Bass, Youngs, Pedigree plus guest beers. ♀: 18
FACILITIES: Garden: Lawn and patio. Lighting, approx 16 tables **NOTES:** Parking 20

WEST CLANDON — Map 06 TQ05

Onslow Arms ♀
The Street GU4 7TE ☎ 01483 222447 ▤ 01483 211126
e-mail: onslowarms@massivepub.com
Dir: A3 then A247
Although it dates from 1623 and retains some charming historical features, including an inglenook fireplace and traditional roasting spit, this pub certainly moves with the times by providing its own helipad for customers' convenience! The Cromwell Bar, popular with locals, has a good choice of real ales. The restaurant, L'Auberge, offers grilled whole sea bass; wild boar stew with steamed potatoes; or soft cheese ravioli with wild mushrooms and pesto. La
continued

England

WEST CLANDON continued

Rotisserie serves an appetising range of soups, salads, omelettes, baguettes and other light meals. **OPEN:** 11-11 (Sun 12-10.30) **BAR MEALS:** L served all week 12-2.30 D served all week 7-10 **RESTAURANT:** L served all week 12.30-2.30 D served all week 7-10 Av 3 course à la carte £30 Av 3 course fixed price £14.95 ⊕: Free House ◖: Scottish Courage Courage Best & Directors, Young's Bitter, Bombardier Premium, Hogs Back TEA. ♀: 11 **FACILITIES:** Garden: Patio, garden, alcove seating Dogs allowed water bowl **NOTES:** Parking 200

WEST END   Map 06 SU96

Pick of the Pubs

The Inn @ West End ▷◁ ♀
42 Guildford Rd GU24 9PW
☎ 01276 858652 ▤ 01276 485842
e-mail: greatfood@the-inn.co.uk   web: www.the-inn.co.uk

See Pick of the Pubs on opposite page

WITLEY   Map 06 SU93

The White Hart ♀
Petworth Rd GU8 5PH ☎ 01428 683695 ▤ 01428 682554
Dir: From A3 signs to Milford, then A283 towards Petworth. Pub 2m on L
A delightfully warm, welcoming pub, built in 1348 as a hunting lodge for King Richard. A listed grade A building with original fireplace, oak beams and a wood fire burning all day. To the rear is an orchard with a large garden, terrace and swings for children. Food is traditionally British, serving the likes of beef and Guiness pie, fillet of salmon and lasagne, all home-cooked to order.
OPEN: 11.30-3 5.30-11 (Sun 7-10.30 Summer 11-11)
BAR MEALS: L served all week 12-2.30 D served Mon-Sat 7-9.30 Sun 12-3.30 Av main course £7.50 **RESTAURANT:** L served all week 12-2.30 D served Mon-Sat 7-9.30 Av 3 course à la carte £20 Av 4 course fixed price £13.50 ⊕: Shepherd Neame ◖: Shepherd Neame Master Brew, Bishops Finger Spitfire & Best. ♀: 15 **FACILITIES:** Child facs Garden: Patio, large grassed area Dogs allowed Water & Chews **NOTES:** Parking 20

SUSSEX, EAST

ALCISTON   Map 06 TQ50

Pick of the Pubs

Rose Cottage Inn ▷◁ ♀
BN26 6UW ☎ 01323 870377 ▤ 01323 871440
e-mail: ian@alciston.freeserve.co.uk
Dir: Off A27 between Eastbourne & Lewes
A rose and wisteria covered pub in a cul-de-sac village at the foot of the South Downs, which has been in the same family for 40 years. It is renowned for good home-cooked food catering for every need: a ploughman's during a country walk, something better for a drive out, and a formal meal for the evening. The fresh daily philosophy applies, with supplies from a local fishmonger, butcher and poulterer, plus organic vegetables where possible. Local produce is also available to buy: eggs, honey, rabbit, pheasant, hare and duck, and fair trade coffee, tea and chocolate are promoted. Meals can be enjoyed on

the front patio or in one of the cosy rambling rooms indoors. Sample dishes include ferocious smoked haddock with lime and chilli, and half a roast Sussex duckling with orange and green peppercorn sauce. The bin-end wine list continues to offer great value for money.
OPEN: 11.30-3 6.30-11 (Sun 12-3, 7-10.30) Closed: 25-26 Dec **BAR MEALS:** L served all week 12-2 D served all week 7-9 (Sun 7-9) Av main course £8.50 **RESTAURANT:** L served all week 12-2 D served Mon-Sat 7-9 Av 3 course à la carte £17.50 ⊕: Free House ◖: Harveys Best, King & Co Horsham best. ♀: 9 **FACILITIES:** Garden: Patio and undercover area with heaters Dogs allowed Water provided **NOTES:** Parking 25

ALFRISTON   Map 06 TQ50

George Inn ♀
High St BN26 5SY ☎ 01323 870319 ▤ 01323 871384
e-mail: george_inn@hotmail.com
Dir: Telephone for directions
Splendid Grade II-listed flint and half-timbered inn set in a magical South Downs village. The George boasts heavy oak beams, an ancient inglenook fireplace and a network of smugglers' tunnels leading from its cellars. The team of three chefs create delights such as flat mushrooms sautéed in garlic with smoked bacon and goats cheese; confit of pork belly with red cabbage and bramley apple; and mussels in garlic and cream. Good choice of puddings.
OPEN: 12-11 (Sun 12-10.30) Closed: Dec 25
BAR MEALS: L served all week 12-2.30 D served all week 7-9 **RESTAURANT:** L served all week 12-2.30 D served all week 7-9 ⊕: Greene King ◖: Greene King Old Speckled Hen, Abbot Ale, Ruddles Country **FACILITIES:** Garden: Dogs allowed

The Sussex Ox ♀
Milton St BN26 5RL ☎ 01323 870840 ▤ 01323 870715
e-mail: mail@thesussexox.co.uk
Dir: Off the A27 between Polegate and Lewes, Signed to Milton Street
Idyllically situated pub, tucked away down a meandering country lane. The Sussex Ox was taken over by David and Suzanne back in June 2004, and they have made a series of changes and improvements, but done their best to keep the pub's friendly feel and cosy atmosphere. You can eat in the bar, or the Garden Room, or the more formal Dining Room. A typical menu includes braised shoulder of lamb with a parsnip mash and garlic mushrooms, pan-fried chicken breast on a sweetcorn fritter with a sun-dried tomato sauce, or roast herb-crusted cod on a chive mash with a citrus sauce.
OPEN: 11-3 6-11 (Sun 12-3, 6-10.30) Winter Sun 12-5 25 Dec Closed eve **BAR MEALS:** L served all week 12-2 D served all week 6-9 Av main course £8 **RESTAURANT:** L served all week 12-2 D served all week 6-9 Av 3 course à la carte £19 ⊕: Free House ◖: Hop Back Summer Lightning, Harveys Best, Youngs Bitter, Dark Star Hophead. ♀: 6 **FACILITIES:** Garden: Dogs allowed Water **NOTES:** Parking 60

Do you have a favourite pub that we have overlooked? Please use the Reader's Report form at the back of this guide to tell us all about it

continued

Pick of the Pubs

WEST END – SURREY

The Inn @ West End

The pub's sign depicts a scene from *Othello*, chosen because it praises the English for being good drinkers. However, it's certainly not just drinking that is celebrated in this stylishly refurbished gastro-pub. Since Gerry and Ann Price took over in 2000, this wayside pub/restaurant has been radically refurbished and given a new purpose in life as a venue for a dizzying number of functions.

Full-time kitchen and front-of-house staff skilfully run the show - sometimes literally, with wine tastings, film nights and themed dinners regularly taking place. In addition, there's a popular boules terrain, which hosts friendly competitions in summer. Light and airy throughout, the pub attracts a broad range of locals and travellers for first-class food and decent wines - the proprietors also run a small wine importing business, so it's no surprise that a dozen of the long, well-sourced list are sold by the glass. Fresh ingredients come from country-wide, with a Gloucester Old Spot pig here and a dozen fresh Norfolk crabs there.

At lunchtime there is a choice of snacks such as croque-monsieur or kedgeree; or a fixed price meal where fresh fish of the day vies with sausage and mash as a main course. The main menu might start with seared smoked salmon with roasted red peppers; or black pudding with caramelised apples and Calvados jus. Moving on, you'll find such options as roast rump of lamb with ratatouille; and beef fillet medallions with watercress mousse, savoy cabbage and dauphinoise potatoes. An excellent range of dessert wines is available if you haven't left room for a delectably rich chocolate mousse; or passion fruit and orange tart.

OPEN: 12-3 5-11
BAR MEALS: L served all week
12-2.30 D served all week 6-9.30 (Sun
12-3 6-9) Av main course £10
RESTAURANT: L served all week
12-2.30 D served all week 6-9.30 (Sun
12-3 6-9) Av 3 course à la carte £25
Av 2 course fixed price £12.50
🍺: Free House
🍺: Scottish Courage Courage Best,
Fuller's London Pride. ♀: 12
FACILITIES: Garden: Dining patio,
pergola, boules pitch Dogs allowed
NOTES: Parking 35

〰️ ♀   Map 06 SU96
42 Guildford Rd GU24 9PW
☎ 01276 858652
📠 01276 485842
📧 greatfood@the-inn.co.uk
🌐 www.the-inn.co.uk
Dir: On the A322 towards
Guildford 3m from M3 junct 3,
just beyond the Gordon Boys
Roundabout

Pick of the Pubs

BODIAM – EAST SUSSEX

The Curlew at Bodiam

Not only does The Curlew serve Italian food, it also must be one of the few pubs in the country with an Italian garden. While the chef has cut his teeth in Michelin starred restaurants, and the menu, with its English, Spanish and Italian influences, is of an unusual elegance and distinction, this also manages to be very much a proper pub.

Dating from the 17th century, there's plenty of traditional atmosphere, and a good array of real ales. However, it is the food that is particularly impressive. To begin, consider breast of pigeon with sun dried tomato and beetroot risotto; game terrine with home-made chutney and dressed leaves; rocket, chilli and bean salad with sesame tuille and a tequila and tomato dressing; pan-fried diver scallops, with dressed leaves. Follow up with pan-roasted sea bass with fondant potatoes, baby vegetables and chive oil; medallions of pork with pearl barley risotto, black pudding tempura, braised red cabbage and port jus; pappardelle pasta with marinated baby vegetables, roast cherry tomatoes and pesto cream sauce; and pan-seared tuna with sunflower and saffron pesto on crispy pasta. Desserts are original and exquisite: lemon tart with vodka jelly and raspberry sorbet; caramelised ginger and sake rice pudding with chocolate and wasabi ice cream; and Mil'hojas of apple and Calvados ice cream with liquorish espuma. The wine list is as lengthy and excellent as you would expect.

OPEN: 11.30-4 6-11
BAR MEALS: 12-2 Av main course £11.95
RESTAURANT: 12-2 7-9 Av 3 course à la carte £35 Av 3 course fixed price £22.95
🍺: Badger Best, Tanglefoot, Harveys Best. ♀: 13
FACILITIES: Garden: Italian garden with shrubs and trees Dogs allowed on leads **NOTES:** Parking 25

NEW ♀   Map 07 TQ72
Junction Rd TN32 5UY
☎ 01580 861394
@ enquiries@thecurlewatbodiam. co.uk
Dir: 3m S of Hawkshurst on B2244 x-rd to Bodiam and Hurst Green

ASHBURNHAM PLACE
Map 06 TQ61

Ash Tree Inn
Brownbread St TN33 9NX ☎ 01424 892104
The Ash Tree is a friendly old pub with three open fires,
plenty of exposed beams and a traditional local atmosphere.
Bar food includes ploughman's, salads and sandwiches, while
the restaurant may be serving steaks, local lamb, steak and
ale pie, or salmon in a variety of sauces.
OPEN: 12-3 7-11 (Summer 6.30-11) **BAR MEALS:** L served all
week 12-2 D served all week 7-9 Av main course £7.75
RESTAURANT: L served all week 12-2 D served Tue-Sun 7-9
☺: Free House ◀: Harveys Best, Greene King Old Speckled Hen,
Brakspear Bitter + guest ales. **FACILITIES:** Garden: Grass with picnic
tables Dogs allowed **NOTES:** Parking 50

BLACKBOYS
Map 06 TQ52

The Blackboys Inn 🛏 ♀
Lewes Rd TN22 5LG ☎ 01825 890283
e-mail: blackboysinn@tiscali.co.uk
Dir: On B2192 between Halland & Heathfield
Rambling, black-weatherboarded inn in the Sussex Weald, first
recorded as an ale house as long ago as 1349. Parts of the
building date from even earlier. Large garden overlooking a
pond and a splendid beamed interior, complete with resident
ghost. A wide range of fresh home-cooked dishes is served
from the bar snack menu, restaurant carte and blackboard
specials. Expect the likes of pan-fried fillets of brill, chargrilled
rib of beef, lamb moussaka, and linguine marinara.
OPEN: 11-3 5-11 (Fri 11-11 Sat 11-3, 6-11, Sun 12-10.30) Closed: Jan
1 **BAR MEALS:** L served all week 12-9 D served Mon-Sat (Fri-Sat
dinner to 9.30) Sun lunch 12-6 Av main course £11
RESTAURANT: L served all week 12-9 D served Mon-Thurs 7-9
(Fri-Sat dinner to 9.30) Sun food 12-6 ☺: Harveys of Lewes
◀: Harveys Sussex Best Bitter, Sussex Pale Ale, Sussex XXXX Old Ale.
♀: 8 **FACILITIES:** Garden: Large front and side gardens with pond
Dogs allowed Water **NOTES:** Parking 40

BODIAM
Map 07 TQ72

Pick of the Pubs

The Curlew at Bodiam NEW ♀
Junction Rd TN32 5UY ☎ 01580 861394
e-mail: enquiries@thecurlewatbodiam.co.uk
See Pick of the Pubs on opposite page

BRIGHTON
Map 06 TQ30

The Basketmakers Arms
12 Gloucester Rd BN1 4AD ☎ 01273 689006 🖷 01273 682300
*Dir: First left out of of Brighton station main entrance (Gloucester Rd).
Pub is on right at the bottom of the hill*
This traditional back-street pub has wooden floors and a vast
array of memorabilia on display. The emphasis is on quality
beers (Gales BBB and HSB), as well as over 90 malt whiskies,
and quality, unpretentious food. All dishes are home made
with local ingredients. The reasonably-priced menu varies
with the seasons but might include fragrant Thai chicken
curry; veggie chilli; and beef or vegetarian burgers.
OPEN: 11-11 (Sun 12-10.30) **BAR MEALS:** L served all week 12-3
D served Mon-Fri 5.30-8.30 Sun 12-4 Av main course £4.50
☺: Gales ◀: HSB, Buster Bitter, GB, Festival Mild & Seasonal Beers.
FACILITIES: Dogs allowed on lead

Pick of the Pubs

The Greys
105 Southover St BN2 9UA ☎ 01273 680734 606475
e-mail: chris@greyspub.com
Dir: 0.5m from St. Peters Church in the Hanover area of Brighton

Chris Beaumont and Gill Perkins have breathed new life
into this little back-street pub in Brighton's Hanover
district. Its fame now spreads way beyond our shores,
and some of the credit is clearly due to chef Ian 'Spats'
Picken, a recent recipient of the Maitrise Escoffier medal
for services to his profession. This and other accolades
explain cooking mostly French in style and a menu in the
language. His speciality is themed eight-coursers, but
there's no need to be that hungry, although do expect
American-style portions anyway. His hallmarks are a
'luxurious' version of borsch; stuffed pig's trotter in lentil
purée; hummous and tabbuleh as starters; and main
courses of moules Normande; entrecôte Dijonnaise; and -
we'll skip the menu's French version - braised Sussex
partridge with red wine, bacon and peas. Puddings
include poached pears in claret jelly with strawberry
sauce. A huge range of Belgian beers accompanies some
well-chosen European wines.
OPEN: 12-11 (Sun 12-10.30, Mon 5.30-11)
BAR MEALS: L served Tue-Sun 12-2 D served Tue-Thur, Sat 6-9
Sun 12-3 Av main course £10.50 **RESTAURANT:** L served
Tue-Sun 12-2 D served Tue-Thur, Sat 6-9 Sun 12-3 Av 3 course à
la carte £19 Av 3 course fixed price £16 ☺: Enterprise Inns.
◀: Timothy Taylor Landlord, Harveys, Leffe Blonde, Hoegaarden.
FACILITIES: Garden: Small patio Dogs allowed on leads, water
NOTES: Parking 5

The Market Inn ♦♦♦
1 Market St BN1 1HH ☎ 01273 329483 🖷 01273 777227
e-mail: marketinn@reallondonpubs.com
web: www.reallondonpubs.com/market.html
Dir: In Brighton's Lanes area. 50 metres from junct of North St and East St
In the heart of Brighton, this classic pub is within easy reach
of the Royal Pavilion and seafront. The building was used by
George IV for romantic liaisons, and now features two en
suite bedrooms. Daily blackboard specials supplement the
inexpensive pub menu which features filling dishes such as
salmon and dill fishcakes, jacket potatoes, and home-cooked
curry. Seafood, vegetarian or spicy platters are available for
sharing over a pint of Harveys or Bombardier ale.
OPEN: 11-11 12-10.30 (Mon-Sat 11-11, Sun 12-10.30)
BAR MEALS: L served all week 11.30-6 D served Sat-Sun 6-8.30
Av main course £5 ☺: Scottish Courage ◀: Harveys, Charles Wells
Bombardier, Youngs Bitter. **FACILITIES:** Dogs allowed
ROOMS: 2 bedrooms en suite s£50 d£60 No children overnight

CHIDDINGLY
Map 06 TQ51

The Six Bells
BN8 6HE ☎ 01825 872227
Dir: *E of A22 between Hailsham & Uckfield (turn opp Golden Cross PH)*
Inglenook fireplaces and plenty of bric-a-brac are to be found at this large characterful free house which is where various veteran car and motorbike enthusiasts meet on club nights. The jury in the famous onion pie murder trial sat and deliberated in the bar before finding the defendant guilty. Live music at weekends. Exceptionally good value bar food includes stilton and walnut pie, lemon peppered haddock, Six Bells Yorkshire pudding with beef or sausage, vegetarian lasagne, cannelloni, lasagne, and shepherd's pie.
OPEN: 11-3 6-11 (All day Sat-Sun) **BAR MEALS:** L served all week 11-2.30 D served all week 6-10.30 Sun 12-9 ⊜: Free House
🍺: Courage Directors, John Smiths, Harveys Best.
FACILITIES: Garden: Typical beer garden with fish pond Dogs allowed on a lead **NOTES:** Parking 60

COWBEECH
Map 06 TQ61

Merrie Harriers ♀
BN27 4JQ ☎ 01323 833108 📠 01323 833108
e-mail: rmcotton@btopenworld.com
Dir: *Off A271, between Hailsham & Herstmonceux*
Packed with character and original features, this Grade II listed former hunting lodge dates from the 17th century. It is a white clapboard building in the heart of the village with fantastic views of the Sussex countryside. The beamed bar has a large inglenook fireplace, and there is an open fire too in the lounge bar/dining room, which leads into the restaurant. The latter opens on to a pretty terrace with garden tables among the flowering tubs. A good choice of real ales and wines by the glass is served, and all the food is prepared on the premises using only local suppliers and produce - free range and organic wherever possible. Options from the monthly changing menu might be slow braised shank of English lamb with garlic mash and redcurrant jus, or Mediterranean fish casserole with scallops, tiger prawns and garlic croutons. The venue is licensed for civil wedding ceremonies.
OPEN: 11.30-3 6-11 **BAR MEALS:** L served all week 12-2 D served all week 7-9 Av main course £10 **RESTAURANT:** L served all week 12-2 D served all week 7-9 ⊜: Free House 🍺: Harveys Best, Youngs Ales, Adnams Ales ♀: 9 **FACILITIES:** Garden: Large sloping garden, water feature, terrace Dogs allowed **NOTES:** Parking 20

DANEHILL
Map 06 TQ42

Pick of the Pubs

The Coach and Horses 🍽 ♀
RH17 7JF ☎ 01825 740369 📠 740369
Dir: *From E Grinstead, go S through Forest Row on A22 to junc with A275 Lewes Rd, turn right on A275 for 2m until Danehill, turn left on school lane 0.5m, pub is on the left*
The inn was built in 1847 as an ale house with stabling and a courtyard between two large country estates. These days the stables form part of the comfortable country-style restaurant. Open fires and neatly tended gardens add colour to a setting that is full of character with half-panelled walls, highly polished wooden floorboards and vaulted beamed ceilings. In an age when the traditional village local is coming under increasing threat, the Coach and Horses proves that some classic hostelries can still survive. Food

plays a key role in its success, with a good selection of lunchtime sandwiches and a constantly changing evening menu. Fish is well represented with dishes like moules et frite or pan-fried turbot with sesame noodles. Alternatives include pork and leek sausages with mash, onion marmalade and red wine jus, or, for vegetarians, wild mushroom tortellini with mushroom cream.

The Coach and Horses

OPEN: 11.30-3 6-11 25-26 Dec, 1 Jan Closed pm
BAR MEALS: L served all week 12-2 D served Mon-Sat 7-9 (No food on Sun pm) Av main course £10 **RESTAURANT:** L served all week 12-2 D served Mon-Sat 7-9 (No food on Sun pm) Av 3 course à la carte £20 ⊜: Free House 🍺: Harveys Best & Old Ale, Hook Norton, Badger IPA, Archers Golden. ♀: 10
FACILITIES: Beautifully kept garden: tables, good views Dogs allowed Water **NOTES:** Parking 30

EAST CHILTINGTON
Map 06 TQ31

Pick of the Pubs

The Jolly Sportsman ♀
Chapel Ln BN7 3BA ☎ 01273 890400 📠 01273 890400
e-mail: thejollysportsman@mistral.co.uk
Dir: *From Lewes take A275, left at Offham onto B2166 towards Plumpton, take Novington Ln, after approx 1m left into Chapel Ln*
An isolated pub with a lovely garden set on a quiet no-through road within the proposed South Downs National Park. The small atmospheric bar, with its stripped wooden floor and mix of comfortable furniture, has been sympathetically upgraded to a character Victorian-style dining inn by respected restaurateur Bruce Wass from Thackerays in Tunbridge Wells. Well-sourced food features on the daily-changing menus, served throughout the bar and smart, yet informal restaurant. The choice embraces starters like smoked haddock and chive gratinée; and crab ravioli; with mains like crispy duck confit; baked Cornish mackerel with salad and tzatziki; fillet of Ditchling lamb and aubergine stew; and roasted mullet fillet with a mussel and Thai coconut curry. A good value fixed-price lunch might feature cod fish cake, Scotch beef, wild mushroom and ale stew, and plum sponge with custard.
OPEN: 12-2.30 6-11 (Sun 12-4) Closed: 25/26 Dec
BAR MEALS: L served Tue-Sun 12.30-2 D served Tue-Sat 7-9 (Sun 12.30-3, Fri & Sat eve 7-10) Av main course £13.50
RESTAURANT: L served Tue-Sun 12.30-2 D served Tue-Sat 7-9 (Sun 12.30-3, Fri & Sat eve 7-10) Av 3 course à la carte £28 Av 3 course fixed price £15.75 ⊜: Free House 🍺: Changing guest beers. ♀: 9 **FACILITIES:** Child facs Children's licence Garden: quiet, secluded, view of South Downs Dogs allowed Water **NOTES:** Parking 30

continued

EXCEAT
Map 06 TV59

The Golden Galleon ♀
Exceat Bridge BN25 4AB ☎ 01323 896238 ▤ 01323 892555
Dir: *On A259, 1.5m E of Seaford*
Once this was just a shepherd's bothy, but it has grown
enough to comfortably accommodate TV crews making an
episode of *Eastenders*, a Gary Rhodes commercial, and a
Dickens costume drama. The pub overlooks Cuckmere Haven,
and the Seven Sisters Country Park. A sample menu includes
lemon chicken, fish and chips, Mediterranean vegetable and
brie open pie, chicken carbonara linguine, traditional mixed
grill, and beef, mushroom and ale pie. The Galleon has
undergone major refurbishment after a recent change of
ownership. Readers reports welcome.
OPEN: 10.30-11 (Sun 11.30am-10.30pm) **BAR MEALS:** L served all
week 12-10 D served all week (Sun 12-9.30) Av main course £6.95
⊕: Free House ♀: 21 **FACILITIES:** Garden: Terraces and intimate
gardens near pub. Dogs allowed Water bowls available
NOTES: Parking 100

FLETCHING
Map 06 TQ42

Pick of the Pubs

The Griffin Inn ⌂ ♀
TN22 3SS ☎ 01825 722890 ▤ 01825 722810
e-mail: thegriffininn@hotmail.com
Dir: *M23 junct 10 to East Grinstead then A22 then A275. Village
signed on left. 10m from M23*
In an unspoilt village just a stone's throw from the
Ashdown Forest and overlooking the glorious Ouse
Valley, this fine Grade II-listed pub is supposedly the
oldest licensed building in Sussex. Handy for visiting
Bateman's - the home of Rudyard Kipling - Glyndebourne
and the Bluebell Railway. The inn's two-acre, west-facing
garden offers impressive views, while inside old beams,
wainscoting, open fires and a collection of old pews and
wheel-back chairs enhance the character of the main bar.
Both the bar and restaurant menus change daily, with
food sourced locally as much as possible. The emphasis is
on modern English food with very strong Italian
influences. A bar meal might comprise Thai curry, local
venison cobbler or chargrilled rib-eye Somerset beef
steak. In the restaurant, there could be lobster and crab
linguini with garlic, parsley and lemon; braised oxtail with
mash and glazed shallots; and grilled organic veal chop
and borlotti bean and artichoke stew.
OPEN: 12-3 6-11 Closed: 25 Dec **BAR MEALS:** L served all
week 12-2.30 D served all week 7-9.30 (Sun 9)
RESTAURANT: L served all week 12.15-2.30 D served Mon-Sat
7.15-9.30 Av 3 course fixed price £12.50 ⊕: Free House
♉: Harvey Best, Badger Tanglefoot, Guest Ales. ♀: 12
FACILITIES: Child facs Garden: 2 large lawns, beautiful views,
large terrace Dogs allowed Water **NOTES:** Parking 20
ROOMS: 8 bedrooms en suite 2 family rooms (♦♦♦♦)

GUN HILL
Map 06 TQ51

The Gun Inn ⌂
TN21 0JU ☎ 01825 872361 ▤ 01825 873081
Dir: *From A22 London-Eastbourne, Golden Cross (3m N of Hailsham)left
past Esso station, 1.5m down lane on left*
Originally a 15th-century farmhouse, the Gun Inn is situated
in a tiny hamlet amid rolling Sussex countryside. It got its
name from the cannon foundries that were located at Gun

continued

Hill. The pub also served as the courthouse for hearings in the
'Onion Pie Murder', a local crime of passion. Resplendent in
summer with its pretty gardens and flower-adorned façade, it
offers fresh grilled plaice, steak and kidney pie, smoked
haddock in cheese and mustard sauce, and seafood platter.
No onion pie.

The Gun Inn

OPEN: 11.30-3 6-11 (Sun Close 10:30) Closed: Dec 25-26
BAR MEALS: L served all week 12-2.15 D served all week 6-9.15
Av main course £7.50 ⊕: Free House ♉: Wadworth 6X, Adnams
Best, Harvey Best. **FACILITIES:** Child facs Large garden, 20 tables
Dogs allowed Water provided **NOTES:** Parking 55

HARTFIELD
Map 06 TQ43

Anchor Inn
Church St TN7 4AG ☎ 01892 770424
Dir: *On B2110*
On the edge of Ashdown Forest, at the heart of *Winnie the
Pooh* country, stands this old inn dating back to the 14th
century, complete with stone floors and a large inglenook.
Sandwiches, ploughman's, and baked potatoes are among the
bar snacks, or try Tandoori spare ribs, and prawn and crab
curry for a starter or snack, and venison steak with port and
redcurrant sauce or omelette Arnold Bennett.
OPEN: 11-11 **BAR MEALS:** L served all week 12-2 D served all
week 6-10 **RESTAURANT:** L served all week 12-2 D served Tue-Sat
7-9.30 ⊕: Free House ♉: Fuller's London Pride, Harveys Sussex
Best Bitter, Interbrew Flowers IPA, Flowers Original Bitter & Bass.
FACILITIES: Garden: Dogs allowed Water **NOTES:** Parking 30

Pick of the Pubs

The Hatch Inn ♀
Coleman's Hatch TN7 4EJ ☎ 01342 822363 ▤ 01342 822363
e-mail: Nickad@bigfoot.com
Dir: *A22 14 miles, left at Forest Row rdbt, follow for 3m until
Colemans Hatch and turn right*
Reputed to date back to 1430, this is a classically
picturesque 15th-century inn serving excellent food. It was
once three cottages thought to have housed workers for
the local water-driven hammer mill, and possibly a
smugglers' haunt. It is frequently seen on television in
various dramas and adverts, and is only minutes away
from the restored Pooh Bridge, immortalised in A.A.
Milne's *Winnie the Poo* stories. Recent additions to the
Hatch Inn are a pair of original British Airways Concorde
seats, which are proving extremely popular with the
guests. Lunch includes a number of light bites and home-
cooked traditional dishes, as well as more imaginative
fare. Dinner may start with poached pear and roquefort
salad; fresh Shetland Isle mussels; or chargrilled chilli

continued

England

HARTFIELD continued

chicken salad. Follow these with fresh salmon, mushroom and leek risotto; marinated roast chump of lamb; chargrilled calves' liver; and pan-fried halibut. To finish, opt for banana crème brûlée; or chocolate marquise.
OPEN: 11.30-3 5.30-11 (Open all day Sat May-Sept Open all day Sun) Closed: Dec 25 **BAR MEALS:** L served all week 12-2.30 D served Tue-Sun 7-9.15 Sun lunch 12-3, dinner 7-8.30 **RESTAURANT:** L served all week 12-2.30 D served Tue-Sun 7-9.15 Sun lunch 12-3, dinner 7-8.30 Av 3 course à la carte £28 😃: Free House 🍺: Harveys, Fuller's London Pride, Larkins. 🍷: 10 **FACILITIES:** Garden: Two large beer gardens, one with forest view Dogs allowed Water 🐾

ICKLESHAM   Map 07 TQ81

Pick of the Pubs

The Queen's Head 🔍 🍷
Parsonage Ln TN36 4BL ☎ 01424 814552 📠 01424 814766
web: www.queenshead.com
Dir: Between Hastings & Rye on A259. Pub on x-rds near church
Distinctive tile-hung pub situated close to the 12th-century parish church with glorious views across the Brede Valley to the ancient town of Rye and beyond. It is handy for exploring this delightful corner of the south-east and within easy reach of several popular walking trails, including the 1066 Country Walk, the towpath of the Royal Military Canal and the long-distance Saxon Shore Way. The Queen's Head dates from 1632 and became an alehouse in the 19th century. High beamed ceilings, large inglenook fireplaces, church pews and a clutter of old farm implements enhance the atmosphere of this friendly, award-winning free house, which abounds with stories of ghosts and boasts a secret passageway to the church. Hearty home-cooked meals includes starters, pies, steaks and grills. Examples are pan-fried soft herring roes; minted lamb chops; and steak, ale and mushroom pie.
OPEN: 11-11 (Sun 12-10.30) 25-26 Dec Closed evenings
BAR MEALS: L served all week 12-2.45 D served all week 6.15-9.30 Sat-Sun 12-9.30 Av main course £7.50
RESTAURANT: L served all week D served all week 😃: Free House 🍺: Rother Valley Level Best, Greene King Abbot Ale, Ringwood Old Thumper, Woodforde Wherry. 🍷: 10
FACILITIES: Child facs Garden: Seating for 60, boules pitch
NOTES: Parking 50

KINGSTON (NEAR LEWES)   Map 06 TQ30

The Juggs 🍷
The Street BN7 3NT ☎ 01273 472523 📠 01273 483274
e-mail: juggs@shepherd-neame.co.uk
web: www.shepherd-neame.co.uk/pubs/pubs.php/juggs_lewes
Dir: E of Brighton on A27
Named after the women who walked from Brighton with baskets of fish for sale, this rambling, tile-hung 15th-century cottage, tucked beneath the South Downs, offers an interesting selection of freshly-cooked food. The area is ideal for walkers, and families are very welcome.
OPEN: 11-11 (Sunday 12-10.30) **BAR MEALS:** L served all week 12-2.30 D served Mon-Sat 6-9 Sun 12-3.30 **RESTAURANT:** L served all week 12-2.30 D served Mon-Sat 6-9 Sun 12-3.30 😃: Shepherd Neame 🍺: Shepherd Neame Spitfire, Best & Oranjeboom. 🍷: 7
FACILITIES: Child facs Garden: patio, beer garden Dogs allowed on lead **NOTES:** Parking 30

LEWES   Map 06 TQ41

The Snowdrop 🍷
119 South St BN7 2BU ☎ 01273 471018

In 1836 Britain's biggest ever avalanche fell from the cliff above this pub, hence its deceptively gentle name. The new owners provide good-value fresh food (all meat is free range, including tempting ranges of doorstep sandwiches (try Sussex cheese and home-made chutney), pizzas, home-made vegetable burger; and wild boar sausages. Vegetarians are well catered-for. Beer garden with a waterfall and palm tree!
OPEN: 11-11 (Sun 12-10.30) **BAR MEALS:** L served all week 12-9 D served all week 12-9 Av main course £7 **RESTAURANT:** L served all week 12-9 D served all week 12-9 Av fixed price £7 😃: Free House 🍺: Harveys Best, Adnams Broadside plus guests.
FACILITIES: Child facs Garden: Beer patio & enclosed garden area Dogs allowed Water & biscuits

LITLINGTON   Map 06 TQ50

Plough & Harrow 🔍 🍷
BN26 5RE ☎ 01323 870632 📠 01323 870632
Dir: S of A27 between Lewes & Polegate
A Grade II listed and thatched pub, owned by locals for locals - and visitors of course. It is set gloriously on the edge of the South Downs in a small village near the scenic Cuckmere Haven, with historic Alfriston and the Sussex coast a short distance away. Good, wholesome pub fare includes plenty of fish dishes like potted crab, Sussex smokies, and locally caught trout, with ploughman's lunches, home-made pies, and Litlington beef.
OPEN: 11-3 6.30-11 (Weekends 12-11) **BAR MEALS:** L served all week 12-2 D served all week 7-9 Sat-Sun 12-3 Av main course £8 **RESTAURANT:** L served all week 12-2.30 D served all week 6.30-9.30 😃: Free House 🍺: Harveys Best, Tanglefoot, Old Speckled Hen, Archers Golden. 🍷: 10 **FACILITIES:** Garden: beer garden, outdoor eating Dogs allowed Water, biscuits
NOTES: Parking 50

MAYFIELD   Map 06 TQ52

Pick of the Pubs

The Middle House 🔍 🍷
High St TN20 6AB ☎ 01435 872146 📠 01435 873423
See Pick of the Pubs on opposite page

We endeavour to be as accurate as possible but changes to times and other information can occur after the guide has gone to press

Pick of the Pubs

MAYFIELD – EAST SUSSEX

The Middle House

16th-century inn with original beams, fireplaces and carved wood panelling, situated in a charming Sussex village. The High Street in which it occupies a prominent position offers some beautiful examples of the wealth that the area made from East Sussex iron.

The Middle House is said to be one of the finest timber-framed buildings in Sussex, and it was built in 1575 for Sir Thomas Gresham, Elizabeth I's Keeper of the Privvy Purse, and founder of the London Stock Exchange. A private residence until the 1920s, it retains a fireplace by master carver Grinling Gibbons, wattle and daub infill, and a splendid oak-panelled restaurant, still incorporating a private chapel. It is typical of the many black and white properties in this part of the country, with its heavily beamed frontage incorporating ornate timber patterning. A family-run business and no mistake: Monica and Bryan Blundell own it; son Darren is general manager; daughter Kirsty manages the restaurant; Mark, is the head chef and son-in-law. A wide selection of food is served on blackboards in the bar, with a selection of more than 40 courses, including various vegetarian and fish dishes. There is also a large à la carte menu in the more formal restaurant which seats up to 70. Expect large duck breast with a cognac, ginger and honey sauce and a rhubarb compote; half shoulder of slowly-roasted lamb with a redcurrant and rosemary sauce; pork fillet topped with a stilton crust and a Dijon mustard and cream sauce; and braised oxtails with red wine, tomatoes and root vegetables topped with a rice timbale. Sunday lunch is a popular event with an equally tempting choice.

OPEN: 11 -11
BAR MEALS: L served Mon-Fri 12-2 Sat-Sun 12-2.30 D served all week 7-9.30
RESTAURANT: L served all week 12-2 D served Tue-Sat 7-9
🍺: Free House
🍺: Harvey Best, Greene King Abbott Ale, Black Sheep Best, Theakston Best. ♀: 9
FACILITIES: Child facs Garden: Terraced area with flower beds, good views **NOTES:** Parking 25

🐟 ♀   Map 06 TQ52
High St TN20 6AB
☎ 01435 872146
🖨 01435 873423
Dir: E of A267, S of Tunbridge Wells

England

MAYFIELD continued

Rose & Crown Inn
Fletching St TN20 6TE ☎ 01435 872200 📠 01435 872200
Attractive and friendly, this 16th-century, typical Sussex pub
has a splendid front patio and a rambling interior with low
beams and open fires. The blackboard lists the day's selection
of fresh fish - probably trout, monkfish, sole and scallops -
and other choices, such as home-made beef and Guinness
pie, or steak and kidney pie. Lighter meals include Sussex
Smokie, and Italian ciabatta sandwiches, for example. Lewes-
based Harveys beers in the bar.
OPEN: 11-11 (Sun 12-10.30) **BAR MEALS:** L served all week
12-2.30 D served Mon-Sat 6-9.30 Av main course £8
RESTAURANT: L served all week 12-2.30 D served Mon-Sat 6-9.30
Av 3 course à la carte £20 🍺: Harveys, Adnams.
FACILITIES: Garden: Front of house with tables Dogs allowed
NOTES: Parking 15

OFFHAM   Map 06 TQ41

The Blacksmith's Arms 🍴 ♀
London Rd BN7 3QD ☎ 01273 472971
Dir: 2m N of Lewes on A275

This attractive free house dates from about 1750, and lies
close to the South Downs Way. Harvey's Sussex ales are
served in the bar, where winter log fires burn in the inglenook
fireplace. Owners Bernard and Sylvia Booker use local
produce and fresh south coast fish to prepare menu choices
like pork and leek sausages with mash and red onion gravy;
and smoked haddock with prawns and cheddar mash. There
are daily vegetarian specials, too.
OPEN: 12-2.30 6.30-10.30 **BAR MEALS:** L served all week 12-2
D served Mon-Sat 7-9 Av main course £10.50
RESTAURANT: L served all week 12-2 D served Mon-Sat 7-9
Av 3 course à la carte £21 Av 2 course fixed price £10.50 🍺: Free
House 🍺: Harveys Ales. ♀: 7 **FACILITIES:** Garden: Patio area
NOTES: Parking 22

OLD HEATHFIELD   Map 06 TQ52

Pick of the Pubs

Star Inn 🍴 ♀
Church St TN21 9AH ☎ 01435 863570 📠 01435 862020
e-mail: heathfieldstar@aol.com
Dir: Take A21 from M25 towards Hawkhurst, right towards Broadoak,
left to Battle (B267), right into Heathfield
This inn sits in an enchanting location in its award-
winning summer garden with colourful shrubs and
flowers, unusual picnic benches and views across to
High Weald. It certainly captivated Turner, who painted

it. Built as an inn for the stonemasons who constructed
the church in the 14th century, this is a lovely creeper-
clad, honey-stone building. Equally appealing is the
atmospheric, low-beamed main bar with its huge
inglenook fireplace and cosy dining ambience. Good bar
food focuses on fresh fish from Billingsgate or direct
from boats in Hastings, and includes dishes like skate
wings with brown butter; mussels cooked in garlic, white
wine, onion and cream; and traditional fish and chips.
For those favouring meat there steak and mushroom
pie; Cumberland sausage and mash; shoulder of lamb;
and stuffed supreme of chicken.
OPEN: 11.30-3 5.30-11 **BAR MEALS:** L served all week
12-2.15 D served all week 7-9.30 Sun 7-9 Av main course £9
RESTAURANT: L served all week 12-2.15 D served all week
7-9.30 Sun 7-9 Av 3 course à la carte £22 🍺: Free House
🍺: Harvey Best, Shepherds Neame, Master Brew, Bishops
Finger. **FACILITIES:** Garden: 15 Oak tables, umbrellas,
fountain, flowers Dogs allowed Dogs 'watering hole'
NOTES: Parking 20

RINGMER   Map 06 TQ41

The Cock ♀
Uckfield Rd BN8 5RX ☎ 01273 812040 📠 01273 812040
web: www.cockpub.co.uk
Dir: On A26 approx 2m N of Lewes (not in Ringmer village)

This atmospheric 16th-century coaching inn takes its name
from the cock horse of nursery rhyme fame, 'Ride a cock
horse to Banbury Cross'; the horse could be hired to help
haul coaches up the steep hills of the South Downs. The inn's
unspoilt bar has original oak beams, a flagstone floor and
inglenook fireplace. As well as the basic menu, the non-
smoking restaurant boasts a variety of fish dishes; specials
such as chicken florentina; and vegetarian options like lentil
and mushroom curry.
OPEN: 11-3 6-11 (Sun open 12-3, 7-11) Closed: 25-26 Dec
BAR MEALS: L served all week 12-2 D served all week 6.30-9.30
Sun 7-9.30 Av main course £8.50 **RESTAURANT:** L served all week
12-2 D served all week 6.30-9.30 Sun 7-9.30 Av 3 course à la carte
£16.50 🍺: Free House 🍺: Harveys Sussex Best Bitter, Sussex XXXX
Old Ale & Sussex XX Mild Ale, Fuller's London Pride, Tanglefoot. ♀: 7
FACILITIES: Garden: Over 30 tables on paved terraces and grass
Dogs allowed Dog chews **NOTES:** Parking 35

> Pick of the Pubs have that extra special quality
> that makes them stand out from the crowd.
> Their entries are highlighted, and may be a
> full page

continued

England

RUSHLAKE GREEN

Horse & Groom 🍴🕮 ♀
TN21 9QE ☎ 01435 830320 🖷 01435 830320
e-mail: chappellhatpeg@aol.com

Grade II listed building on the village green with pleasant views from the well-cultivated gardens. Dishes are offered from blackboard menus in the cosy bars: steak, kidney and Guinness pudding; boiled knuckle of gammon with onion stock and butter beans; and rabbit in cider are favourites, along with the excellent fresh fish choice - perhaps pan-fried John Dory on home-made linguine and sliced fennel, or fresh tuna on courgette tagliatelle.
OPEN: 11.30-3 5.30-11 Closed: 25 Dec **BAR MEALS:** L served all week 12-2.30 D served all week 7-9.30 Sun 7-9 Av main course £13
RESTAURANT: L served all week 12-2.30 D served all week 7-9.30 Av 3 course à la carte £25 🍴: Free House ◀: Harveys, Master Brew, Shepherd Neame Spitfire. ♀: 7 **FACILITIES:** Well tended garden, views over lake, smart furniture Dogs allowed
NOTES: Parking 20

RYE   Map 07 TQ92

Pick of the Pubs

Mermaid Inn ★★★ 🏵 ♀
Mermaid St TN31 7EY ☎ 01797 223065 🖷 01797 225069
e-mail: mermaidinnrye@btclick.com
web: www.mermaidinn.com
Dir: Rye is situated on the A259 between Hastings and Ashford

From the picturesque cobbled street, step back in time into a very old inn indeed. French invaders burnt down the first Mermaid in 1377; it was finally rebuilt in 1420, so that by 1573, when Elizabeth I visited this ancient Cinque Port, it had already been open for over 150 years. Rye was once England's premier cross-channel port, and the inn was popular with smugglers, one or two of whom are said to haunt its corridors and secret passages. The public rooms have huge beams, some recycled from ancient ships' timbers, and fireplaces carved from French stone ballast rescued from the harbour. Meals in the famous linenfold-panelled restaurant feature English cooking, albeit with a slight inclination towards France. Only the freshest local ingredients are used for dishes such as steamed brill with white wine sauce, and grilled sirloin with stilton mash, roast endives and sauce bordelaise.
OPEN: 11-11 (Sun 12-11) **BAR MEALS:** L served Mon-Sat 12-2.15 D served Sun-Fri 7-9.15 Av main course £9
RESTAURANT: L served all week 12-2.15 D served all week 7-9.15 Av 3 course à la carte £35 Av 3 course fixed price £22 🍴: Free House ◀: Greene King Old Speckled Hen, Scottish Courage Courage Best. ♀: 8 **FACILITIES:** Child facs Garden: Paved patio Dogs allowed Water **NOTES:** Parking 26
ROOMS: 31 bedrooms en suite 6 family rooms s£85 d£170

 Pubs offering a good choice of fish on their menu

Restaurant and Bar Meal times indicate the times when food is available. Last orders may be approximately 30 minutes before the times stated

Pick of the Pubs

The Ypres Castle Inn 🍴🕮 ♀
Gun Garden TN31 7HH ☎ 01797 223248
e-mail: info@yprescastleinn.co.uk

Built in 1640 in the local weather-boarded style, and added to in Victorian times, 'The Wipers', which is what the regulars call it, was once much favoured by smugglers. Colourful art and furnishings help give it a warm and friendly atmosphere; and being the only inn in the citadel area of Rye to have a garden is another plus. Visible just yards away are the 13th-century Ypres Tower and the River Rother, still home for a working fishing fleet. From its seasonally changing, largely locally sourced menu, might come rack of Romney saltmarsh lamb with redcurrant and mint glaze; turbot with sauce vierge; and roast vegetable lasagne. Daily specials are added to a lunchtime bar menu of lighter dishes. An extensive wine list draws from the major wine producing regions, with at least twelve by the glass. On Friday nights things hot up with live music from local jazz, rock and blues bands.
OPEN: 11.30-11 (Sat 11-11 Sun 12-4, Jan-Mar 11.30-3, 6-11)
BAR MEALS: L served all week 12-2.30 12-3 in main season Av main course £7 **RESTAURANT:** L served all week 12-2.30 D served Mon-Sat 6.30-9 12-3 in main season Av 3 course à la carte £22 🍴: Free House ◀: Harveys Best, Adnams Broadside, Wells Bombardier, Timothy Taylor Landlord. ♀: 12
FACILITIES: Garden: Lawn, views of river & castle Dogs allowed except in the main restaurant Water

SHORTBRIDGE   Map 06 TQ42

Pick of the Pubs

The Peacock Inn NEW 🍴🕮 ♀
TN22 3XA ☎ 01825 762463 🖷 01825 762463
e-mail: matthewarnold@aol.com
Dir: Just off Haywards Heath and Lewes

This traditional inn dating back to 1567 is renowned for its food (created by three qualified chefs), and also the resident ghost of Mrs Fuller. A large rear patio garden is a delightful spot in summer. Past visitors to the inn have included Phil Collins, Jimmy Hill and Dame Thora Hird. At lunch you can choose between jacket potatoes, baguettes and sandwiches with various fillings, and various light bites. The dinner menu, supplemented by weekly specials, might include smoked haddock in mustard sauce; prawn cocktail; and crab and coriander cakes, with such mains dishes as seafood crêpe; fisherman's pie; crayfish tails with avocado; steak, mushroom and ale pie; baked lamb rump; grilled trout fillet with prawns; beef

continued

England

SHORTBRIDGE continued

stroganoff; and fillet steak Marilyn Monroe (you'll have to ask if you want to know what this is). Home-made desserts like hot chocolate nut brownie; banoffee pie; fruit crème brûlée; and citrus cheesecake should please.

The Peacock Inn

OPEN: 11-3 6-11 (Open all day Jun-Sep) Closed: 25-26 Dec **BAR MEALS:** L served all week 12-2.30 D served all week 6-9.30 Av main course £9 **RESTAURANT:** L served all week 12-9.30 D served all week 7-10 Sun 7-9 🍺: Morlands Old Speckled Hen, Harveys Best Bitter, Fullers London Pride. 🍷: 8 **FACILITIES:** Child facs Garden: Patio area, BBQ, lawn Dogs allowed **NOTES:** Parking 40

THREE LEG CROSS   Map 06 TQ63

The Bull
Dunster Mill Ln TN5 7HH ☎ 01580 200586 🖹 01580 201289 e-mail: enquiries@thebullinn.co.uk
Dir: From M25 exit at Sevenoaks toward Hastings, right at x-rds onto B2087, right onto B2099 through Ticehurst, right for Three Legged Cross
In a peaceful hamlet setting, the Bull is a real country pub, with oak beams and large open fires, based around a Wealden hall house built between 1385 and 1425. The garden features a duck pond, a pétanque court and a children's play area. A typical menu might include strips of chicken breast pan fried with bacon; tagine of lamb; stuffed seabass; smoked haddock Florentine; Mediterranean pasta bake; and mushroom tortellini Raphael.
OPEN: 12-11 Closed: Dec 25, 26 (evening) **BAR MEALS:** L served all week 12-2.30 D served all week 6.30-9.30 Sat/Sun 12-3- summer all day **RESTAURANT:** L served all week 12-2.30 D served all week 6.30-9.30 🍺: Free House 🍺: Harveys, Spitfire, Speckled Hen. **FACILITIES:** Child facs Children's licence Garden: Front garden-pond, rear garden play area Dogs allowed **NOTES:** Parking 80 **ROOMS:** 4 bedrooms en suite s£35 d£60 (♦♦♦)

UPPER DICKER   Map 06 TQ50

The Plough 🍷
Coldharbour Rd BN27 3QJ ☎ 01323 844859
Dir: Off A22, W of Hailsham
17th-century former farmhouse which has been a pub for over 200 years, and now comprises two bars and two restaurants. Excellent wheelchair facilities, a large beer garden and a children's play area add to the appeal, and the Plough is also a handy stop for walkers. Expect such fish dishes as Sussex smokie or prawn, brie and broccoli bake, while other options include duck breast in spicy plum sauce, veal in lemon cream, or lamb cutlets in redcurrant and rosemary.
continued

OPEN: 11-3 6-11 (Sun 12-3, 7-10.30, Summer wknd 11-11) **BAR MEALS:** L served all week 12-2.30 D served all week 6-9 **RESTAURANT:** L served all week 12-2.30 D served all week 6-9 🍺: Shepherd Neame 🍺: Shepherd Neame Spitfire Premium Ale, Best & Bishop's Finger. 🍷: 21 **FACILITIES:** Child facs Garden: Large open 1 acre, boules, horse shoe toss Dogs allowed **NOTES:** Parking 40

WADHURST   Map 06 TQ63

Pick of the Pubs

The Best Beech Inn NEW ♦♦♦♦ 🔎 🍷
Mayfield Ln TN5 6JH ☎ 01892 782046 🖹 01892 785092 e-mail: roger_felstead@hotmail.com
Dir: 1m outside Wadhurst
Ideally located close to the Kent and Sussex border, in an area of outstanding natural beauty, The Best Beech Inn dates back to 1680. Recently, it has been sympathetically refurbished to preserve the largely Victorian character of its heydays. The result is an inn with loads of personality, with its mixture of quarry tile and wood flooring, open fireplaces, and exposed brickwork. The inn has a fine à la carte restaurant offering excellent European dishes with a French influence, or for those who prefer the more casual atmosphere of the bar bistro, a comprehensive menu is available from the blackboard. A lunch could start with air-dried tomato tarte Tatin, move on to seared rib-eye steak, and finish with lemon crème brûlée. Dinner moves onto another level, with perhaps remoulade of Icelandic crab with lobster-scented oil, followed by line-caught sea bass with baby vegetables, lemon scented oil and sweet balsamic dressing, and finished with chocolate and peppermint brûlée.
OPEN: 11.30-3 6-11 (Sun 12-10.30) **BAR MEALS:** L served all week 12-2 D served Mon-Sat 7-9 Sun 12.30-2.30 Av main course £9.95 **RESTAURANT:** L served all week 12-2 D served Mon-Sat 7-9 Sun 12.30-2.30 Av 3 course à la carte £25 Av 2 course fixed price £13.95 🍺: Harveys, Speckled Hen, Adnams. 🍷: 6 **FACILITIES:** Garden: Small patio with seating Dogs allowed **NOTES:** Parking 30 **ROOMS:** 7 bedrooms 5 en suite 1 family room s£45 d£59.90 No children overnight

WARBLETON   Map 06 TQ61

The War-Bill-in-Tun Inn
Church Hill TN21 9BD ☎ 01435 830636 🖹 01435 830636
A 400-year-old smugglers' haunt, visited by The Beatles when visiting their manager, Brian Epstein, who lived half a mile away. Old locals still recall meeting Lennon and McCartney, as well as the resident ghost. Representative dishes include steaks, duck breast, lamb shank, Barnsley chops, lemon sole and poached salmon. Beers include Harvey's Sussex Best, Crown Inn Ironmaster, Warbleton's Winter Ale and guests.
OPEN: 12-3 7-11 **BAR MEALS:** L served all week 12-1.45 D served all week 7-9.30 **RESTAURANT:** L served all week 12-1.45 D served all week 7-9.30 🍺: Free House 🍺: Harveys Best, Crown Inn Ironmaster, Warbleton Winter Ale. **FACILITIES:** Small garden, table seating, good views Dogs allowed Water **NOTES:** Parking 20

Most of the pubs in this guide book pride themselves on the quality of their food. This may take a little time to prepare

Pick of the Pubs

WITHYHAM – EAST SUSSEX

The Dorset Arms

On the borders of Kent and Sussex close to Ashdown Forest and Royal Tunbridge Wells, a historic white, weather-boarded 15th-century inn with many original features intact. The name comes from the arms of the Sackville family from nearby Buckhurst Park, although it actually dates from somewhere between the reigns of Henry VI and Edward IV.

Local records suggest that this tile-hung, family-run pub and restaurant at the edge of the Ashdown Forest has been an inn since the 18th century. Its origins go back to the 15th century when, as an open-halled farmhouse, it had earthen floors. Among the many interesting Tudor and later period features that remain are the old ice-house buried in the hillside behind, the oak-floored bar, magnificent open log fire, and the massive wall and ceiling beams in the restaurant. Where possible, the owners source all their ingredients locally, including what they claim are the best fillet steaks in the area. Starters might include oak-smoked salmon with brown bread; tempura-battered vegetables with garlic dip; and crispy deep-fried whitebait seasoned with paprika. Sample main courses include pan-fried loin of venison in a rich Cumberland sauce with cream of cassis; chicken breast in a spicy curry sauce with fragrant rice; and griddled fillets of sea bass with hollandaise sauce. Meringues and fruit, and deep lemon tart are among the desserts. Prize-winning real ales come from Harveys of Lewes.

OPEN: 11-3 6-11 (Sun 12-3, 7-10.30)
BAR MEALS: L served all week 12-2
D served Tue-Sat 7-9
RESTAURANT: L served all week
12-2 D served Tue-Sat 7-9 Av 3 course
à la carte £20
🍺: Harveys of Lewes
🍺: Harveys Sussex Best + seasonal
beers.
FACILITIES: Garden: Dogs allowed
NOTES: Parking 20

Map 06 TQ43
TN7 4BD
☎ 01892 770278
📠 01892 770195
@ pete@dorset-arms.co.uk
Dir: 4m W of Tunbridge Wells
on B2110 between Groombridge
and Hartfield

PUB WALK

The Black Horse
Amberley - West Sussex

THE BLACK HORSE,
High Street, BN18 9NL
☎ 01798 831552
Lively tavern in a beautiful South Downs village, with a lovely garden. Good food includes an extensive vegetarian choice.
Open: 11–11 (Sun 12–10.30)
Bar Meals: L served all week 12–3 D served all week 6–9
Restaurant Meals: L served all week 12–3 D served all week 6–9 Av 3 course à la carte £19
Garden available.
(for full entry see page 487)

Distance: 7 miles (11.3km)
Map: OS Landranger 121
Terrain: Downland and valley
Paths: Paths, bridleways and roads
Gradient: Some climbing and several steep descents

Walk submitted by Nick Channer & checked by The Black Horse

Climb into remote downland country above the Arun on this scenic walk.

Turn left out of the pub and walk through the village to the B2139. Cross over at the junction and take the road opposite. Turn right into High Titten and follow the road between trees and hedgerows.

On reaching the road junction, turn right and follow the tarmac path parallel to the road. Turn left at the South Downs Way sign and follow the concrete track over the railway line to a galvanised gate. Turn left here and follow the bridleway to the bank of the River Arun. Swing left, veering slightly away from the riverbank, to join a drive.

On reaching the road near the railway bridge, turn right. Begin to cross the road bridge spanning the Arun and then turn left at the footpath sign to a stile by a galvanised gate. Once over it, cross the water-meadows to the next stile and a few paces beyond it you reach a footpath sign. Turn left here. Follow the path between trees, turn right on reaching a lane and pass Sloe Cottage.

Turn left just beyond a caravan site to join a bridleway. Follow the path as it runs above the camping ground and make for a gate and bridleway sign. Cross the track here and join a rough lane. Stay on it as it climbs gradually, providing views of the River Arun. Pass some ruined outbuildings and keep ahead, the lane dwindling to a track now. Veer left at the fork and follow the right of way. Make for a signposted crossroads and take the left-hand bridleway.

Walk down the chalk track, pass through the gate and continue the steep descent. Look for two gates down below, some distance apart. Cross to the right-hand gate and a bridleway sign is seen here. Follow the bridleway as it bends left, climbing steeply towards Downs Farm. Keep a fence on the left and follow the right of way as it merges with a wide track.

Keep left at the next junction and follow the South Downs Way towards the entrance to Downs Farm. Veer to the right of the gateway and join a narrow path which begins a steep descent. Turn right on reaching a tarmac lane, keep right at the fork and retrace your steps to the Black Horse.

England

WARTLING

Map 06 TQ60

The Lamb Inn 🔍 ♀
BN27 1RY ☎ 01323 832116
Dir: A259 from Polegate to Pevensey rdbt. Take 1st left to Wartling & Herstmonceux Castle. Pub is 3m on right.

This family-run pub was built in 1526 and became an ale house in 1640. Everything is home made, and top quality produce is locally sourced as much as possible, including beef from a farm two miles away. A sample menu offers fresh king scallops grilled with white wine; Stonegate goats' cheese and toasted almond pâté with tomato and rosemary compote and melba toast; escalopes of barn reared veal flamed with wild mushrooms, marsala and cream; or breast of Suffolk farm chicken on smoked cheddar mash. The specials board is regularly updated, and there are at least half a dozen fish choices every session.
OPEN: 11-3 6-11 **BAR MEALS:** L served all week 11.45-2.15 D served all week 6.45-9 Sun 12-2.30, 7-9 **RESTAURANT:** L served all week 11.45-2.15 D served all week 6.45-9 Sun 12-2.30, 7-9 Av 3 course à la carte £20 ◀: Badger, Harveys, Hoppers, Spitfire. ♀: 8 **FACILITIES:** Garden: Enclosed patio garden with seating Dogs welcome on patio **NOTES:** Parking 14

WILMINGTON

Map 06 TQ50

The Giants Rest NEW 🔍 ♀
The Street BN26 5SQ ☎ 01323 870207 ▤ 01323 870207
e-mail: abecjane@aol.com
Dir: 2m outside Polegate on A27 towards Brighton
The Long Man of Wilmington, that mysterious chalk-carved guardian of the South Downs, has baffled archaeologists for centuries. No-one need be baffled, however, by the fresh, simply prepared food in this village pub at the figure's feet, which includes warm smoked duck and bacon salad; home-cooked ham, or local sausages, with bubble and squeak; boeuf bourguignonne; and hake, coriander, chilli and spring onion fishcakes. The triumvirate of real ales is a magnet for beer aficionados.
OPEN: 11.30-3 6-11 (Sat-Sun 11-11) **BAR MEALS:** L served all week 12-2 D served all week 7-9 Av main course £8.50 **RESTAURANT:** L served all week 12-2 D served all week 7-9 ◀: Harveys Best, Timothy Taylor Landlord, Summer Lightning, Harveys Old. ♀: 7 **FACILITIES:** Garden: Small garden with seating and shade Dogs allowed Water bowls **NOTES:** Parking 10

WINCHELSEA

Map 07 TQ91

The New Inn 🔍 ♀
German St TN36 4EN ☎ 01797 226252
e-mail: newinnchelsea.co.uk
This 18th-century inn is situated in the centre of the beautiful ancient town, one of the seven Cinque Ports. There are no
continued

specials, but the menu features popular dishes such as home-made pies, roasts, scallops and bacon in a wine and cream sauce, and various fish dishes. To the rear of the pub is a charming garden, where guests may eat or simply relax before taking a stroll in the surrounding countryside. Take a look at the partially ruined 14th-century church opposite.
OPEN: 11.30-11.20 **BAR MEALS:** L served all week 12-3 D served all week 6.30-9.30 (Sun 12-9) Av main course £7.95
RESTAURANT: L served all week 12-2.30 D served all week 6.30-9.30 (Sun 12-9) Av 3 course à la carte £14.50 ◉: Greene King ◀: Morlands Original, Abbots Ale, Greene King Ipa, Fosters. ♀: 10 **FACILITIES:** Garden: Traditional Old English Dogs allowed **NOTES:** Parking 20

WITHYHAM

Map 06 TQ43

Pick of the Pubs

The Dorset Arms
TN7 4BD ☎ 01892 770278 ▤ 01892 770195
e-mail: pete@dorset-arms.co.uk
See Pick of the Pubs on page 485

SUSSEX, WEST

AMBERLEY

Map 06 TQ01

Black Horse 🔍
High St BN18 9NL ☎ 01798 831552
e-mail: theblackhorse@btconnect.com
A traditional 17th-century tavern with a lively atmosphere, in a beautiful South Downs village. Look out for the display of sheep bells donated by the last shepherd to have a flock on the local hills. Good food served in the large restaurant and bar, including extensive vegetarian choice and children's menu. Lovely gardens, good local walks, and nice views of the South Downs and Wild Brookes. Dogs are welcome in the bar.
OPEN: 11-11 (Sun 12-10.30) **BAR MEALS:** L served all week 12-3 D served all week 6-9 **RESTAURANT:** L served all week 12-3 D served all week 6-9 Av 3 course à la carte £19 ◉: Punch Taverns ◀: Bombardier, Greene King IPA,. **FACILITIES:** Garden: Dogs allowed Enclosed garden with pond
See Pub Walk on opposite page

The Bridge Inn 🔍
Houghton Bridge BN18 9LR ☎ 01798 831619
e-mail: michael.basson@btinternet.com
Dir: 5m N of Arundel on B2139
The Bridge Inn dates from 1650, and has a Grade II listing. The following year Charles II stopped here to take ale after the Battle of Worcester, and nowadays cyclists and walkers enjoy exploring this delightful part of Sussex. Picturesque Amberley, Arundel Castle and Bignor Roman Villa are all close by. The menu offers a variety of dishes, some of which have a distinct Mediterranean flavour to them. Try giant toad in the hole, South Downs pie, or monkfish kebabs.
OPEN: 11-11 (Sun 12-10.30) **BAR MEALS:** L served all week 12-2.30 D served all week 6.30-9 Av main course £8.95
RESTAURANT: L served all week 12-2.30 D served all week 6.30-9 Sun 12-3 Av 3 course fixed price £9.95 ◉: Free House ◀: Harveys Sussex, Youngs, Bombardier, Spitfire. **FACILITIES:** Garden: Food served outside. Well kept garden Dogs allowed Water provided **NOTES:** Parking 20

England

ASHURST Map 06 TQ11

The Fountain Inn ♀
BN44 3AP ☎ 01403 710219
Dir: On B2135 N of Steyning

A 16th-century free house overlooking the village duckpond. When living locally, Laurence Olivier used to pop in, and Paul McCartney made his 'White Christmas' video in one of the two flagstone bars. Available at both lunchtime and in the evenings should be chargrilled fillet of sea bass; Sussex smokie - smoked haddock and prawns in cheese sauce; steak, mushroom and ale pie; and lasagne verde. A good selection of chargrilled steaks and burgers.
OPEN: 11.30-2.30 6-11 (Sun 12-3, 7-10.30) **BAR MEALS:** L served all week 11.30-2 D served Tue-Sat 6-9.30 Av main course £9.95 🍴: Free House 🍺: Harveys Sussex, Shepherd Neame Master Brew, Fuller's London Pride Adnams Best, Black Sheep Best.
FACILITIES: Garden: Dogs allowed Water provided
NOTES: Parking 70

BARNHAM Map 06 SU90

The Murrell Arms ♀
Yapton Rd PO22 0AS ☎ 01243 553320
Dir: Telephone for directions
Attractive white-painted inn distinguished by lavish window boxes and hanging baskets that add a wonderful splash of colour in summer. Built in 1750 as a farmhouse, it became a pub shortly after the railway station opened over 100 years later. A straightforward menu offers bacon hock, curries, belly pork with parsley sauce, bacon and onion suet pudding, and liver and bacon casserole with jacket potato. Various Gale's ales on tap.
OPEN: 11-2.30 Sun (12-10.30) 6-11 Sat (11-11)
BAR MEALS: L served all week 12-2 D served Fri-Wed 6-9
RESTAURANT: L served all week D served all week 🍴: Gales 🍺: Butser Best, Horndean Special Bitter. ♀: 28
FACILITIES: Garden: Grass area, tarmac area, grape vines Dogs allowed Water **NOTES:** Parking 14 No credit cards

BURPHAM Map 06 TQ00

Pick of the Pubs

George & Dragon ◉
BN18 9RR ☎ 01903 883131
Dir: Off A27 1m E of Arundel, signed Burpham, 2.5m pub on left
An old smuggling inn down what is essentially a two and a half mile cul-de-sac in peaceful Burf'm (although next-door Wepham is Wep'm!). The Arun cuts through the chalk downs here, with mighty Arundel Castle guarding the gap. The riverside and other local walks are lovely,

but be ready to remove muddy footwear in the pub porch. Inside are beamed ceilings and modern prints on the walls. It's very much a dining pub, attracting visitors from far and wide. "We get lots of Americans and Germans" says landlord James Rose. "It seems to be their idea of an English village." The main menu offers scallops wrapped in bacon; seafood pie with cheddar mash; roast half-pheasant with juniper jus; tender leg of duck with red berry sauce; and lamb's liver with chive mash and red onion sauce. In the bar starters include Greek salad, deep fried whitebait, or pasta dish of the day, with blackboard mains. Snacks include ploughman's platters, filled jackets, baguettes and sandwiches.
OPEN: 11-2.30 6-11 (Oct-Apr, closed Sun eve Closed: 25 Dec Sun eve Oct-Easter Closed) **BAR MEALS:** L served all week 12-2 D served Mon-Sat 7-9.30 Sun 12-2.30
RESTAURANT: D served Mon-Sat 7-9.30 🍴: Free House 🍺: Harvey Best, Brewery-on-Sea Spinnaker Bitter, Fuller's London Pride, King Brewery Red River. **FACILITIES:** Patio area to front of pub **NOTES:** Parking 40

BURY Map 06 TQ01

The Squire & Horse ▷
Bury Common RH20 1NS ☎ 01798 831343 🖹 01798 831343
Dir: On A29, 4m S of Pulbrough, 4m N of Arundel

The original 16th-century building was extended seven years ago, with old wooden beams and country fireplaces throughout. All the food is freshly cooked to order. The fish specials change daily and main courses are served with a selection of vegetables. These could include barbequed barracuda fillet on a bed of prawn risotto, or calves' liver with bacon and red wine glaze. The pub is renowned for its desserts - pavlova and 'death by chocolate' are favourites.
OPEN: 11.30-3 6-11 (Sun 12-3 6-10.30) **BAR MEALS:** L served all week 12-2 D served all week **RESTAURANT:** L served all week 12-2 D served all week 6-9 🍺: Greene King IPA, Harveys Sussex, guest ales. **FACILITIES:** Garden: Patio, flowered courtyard
NOTES: Parking 50

◉ The Rosette is the AA award for food.
Look out for it next to a pub's name

Room prices show the minimum double and single rates charged. Room rates in hotels and B&Bs often vary depending on the facilities, so be sure to check prices with the establishment before booking

continued

England

CHARLTON — Map 06 SU81

Pick of the Pubs

The Fox Goes Free 🐟 ♀
PO18 0HU ☎ 01243 811461 🖹 01243 811946
e-mail: thefoxgoesfree.always@virgin.net
Dir: A286 6m from Chichester, towards Midhurst 1m from Goodwood racecourse
Built in 1588, the pub was a favoured hunting lodge of William III; more recently, it also hosted the first Women's Institute meeting in 1915. The lovely old brick and flint building nestles in unspoilt countryside, and with its two huge fireplaces, old pews and brick floors, it simply exudes charm and character. There are an amazing five places where diners can eat: the main bar, the main restaurant, the Snug, the Bakery and the Stable. A sample of dishes includes venison steak on braised red cabbage with a rich redcurrant sauce, pan-fried tuna steak on ratatouille with home-made guacamole, and wild mushroom risotto with parmesan shavings. Roast dinner on a Sunday.
OPEN: 11-11 (Sun 12-10.30) **BAR MEALS:** L served all week 12-2.30 D served all week 6.30-10 (Sat-Sun 12-10)
RESTAURANT: L served all week 12-2.30 D served all week 6-10 (all day Sat-Sun 12-10.30, 12-10) ⬢: Free House
🍺: Hampshire Special, Arundel Gauntlet, Ballards Best, Ringwood Special. ♀: 8 **FACILITIES:** Garden: Large, with patio & lawn. Seats approx 90 Dogs allowed Water
NOTES: Parking 40

CHICHESTER — Map 05 SU80

Horse and Groom NEW ♀
East Ashling PO18 9AX ☎ 01243 575339 🖹 01243 575560
e-mail: horseandgroom@aol.com
Dir: 3m from Chichester on B1278 between Chichester and Funtington
Lying at the foot of the South Downs, the 17th-century Horse & Groom is a substantially renovated old pub, but the improvements have not compromised the traditional charm of the old flint walls and beams. Steak and ale pie, lamb cutlets, chicken breast with plum and hoi sin sauce, and freshly caught fish are likely most days. Double doors lead out to a fully enclosed garden.
OPEN: 11-3 6-11 (Sun 12-6) **BAR MEALS:** L served all week 12-2.15 D served Mon-Sat 6.30-9.15 Sun 12-2.30 Av main course £12.75 **RESTAURANT:** L served all week 12-2.15 D served Mon-Sat 6.30-9.15 Av 3 course à la carte £20 🍺: Youngs, Harveys, Summer Lightning, Hop Head. ♀: 6 **FACILITIES:** Garden: Large square enclosed garden, tables, umbrellas Dogs allowed
NOTES: Parking 45 **ROOMS:** 11 bedrooms en suite s£35 d£58 (♦♦♦♦)

Pick of the Pubs

Royal Oak Inn NEW ♦♦♦♦♦ ◉♀
Pook Ln, East Lavant PO18 0AX
☎ 01243 527434 🖹 01243 775062
e-mail: nickroyaloak@aol.com
East Lavant is a pretty Downland village, with speedy access to both the rolling Sussex acres, and the Georgian streets and Festival Theatre of Chichester. The Royal Oak itself, a pub for many years, has been exceptionally well-converted to offer not only an elegant restaurant, but also stylish, sleekly furnished accommodation in what was

once an outlying barn and cottage. The brick-lined bar and restaurant pull off an effortless rustic chic: details include fresh flowers, candles, and wine attractively displayed in alcoves inset into the creamy walls. The same attentiveness can be seen in the simple, contemporary menu. Begin with Moroccan spiced chicken kebab with fruity couscous; or seared king scallops with creamed savoy cabbage and black pudding; before baked cod with a cheese rarebit crust and braised green split peas; or oven steamed halibut filled with fresh crab salsa.
OPEN: All day Closed: 25 Dec **BAR MEALS:** L served all week 12-2 D served all week 6-9.30 Av main course £12
RESTAURANT: L served all week 12-2 D served all week 6-9.30 Av 3 course à la carte £25 🍺: Ballards, HSB, Sussex, Arundel. ♀: 12 **FACILITIES:** Garden: Large front patio, rear lawn area **NOTES:** Parking 24 **ROOMS:** 6 bedrooms en suite 1 family room s£55 d£70

CHILGROVE — Map 05 SU81

The White Horse ♦♦♦♦ ◉◉ 🐟 ♀
High St PO18 9HX ☎ 01243 535219 🖹 01243 535301
e-mail: info@whitehorsechilgrove.co.uk
web: www.whitehorsechilgrove.co.uk
Dir: On B2141 between Chichester & Petersfield
Picturesque South Downs hostelry, dating from 1756. Bar lunches are available as well as dining at the restaurant, which offers a tempting menu supplemented by seasonal specialities. Dishes might include seared hand-dived scallops with truffle and potato cream; English lamb with rosemary gravy; or baked crab thermidor.
OPEN: 11-3 6-11 Closed Mon **BAR MEALS:** L served Tue-Sun 11-3 D served Tue-Sat 6-11 Av main course £14 **RESTAURANT:** L served Tue-Sun (fixed menu Tue-Fri Nov-Mar) 11-3 D served Tue-Sat (fixed menu Tue-Fri Nov-Mar) 6 Av 3 course à la carte £30 Av 3 course fixed price £24.50 ⬢: Free House 🍺: Ballard's. ♀: 10
FACILITIES: Garden: Downland garden with good views Dogs allowed Loan of beanbags, bowls etc **NOTES:** Parking 100
ROOMS: 8 bedrooms en suite s£65 d£95 ⊗

COMPTON — Map 05 SU71

Coach & Horses
The Square PO18 9HA ☎ 02392 631228
Dir: On B2146 S of Petersfield, to Emsworth
The pub stands beside the square of this prettiest of downland villages. The original timber-framed 16th-century dining room and the pine-clad Victorian extension have an evocative ambience enjoyed by villagers and visitors alike. Well known locally for its rib-eye steaks with multifarious sauces, the menu also includes a good fresh fish selection. Also expect dishes such as chicken, mushroom and tarragon pie; sliced pigeon breast on tossed salad with bacon and mushrooms; salmon fishcakes; and bacon hock with mustard mash. Hearty bar snacks can accompany a good choice of real ales. There is also a skittle alley and rear garden.
OPEN: 12-3 6-11 **BAR MEALS:** L served all week 12-2 D served all week 6-9 Av main course £7.50 **RESTAURANT:** L served Tues-Sun 12-2 D served Tue-Sat 6-9 ⬢: Free House 🍺: Fuller's ESB, Ballard's Best, Cheriton Diggers Gold, Dark Star Golden Gate. **FACILITIES:** Dogs allowed

---

♦   Diamond rating for inspected guest accommodation

continued

DUNCTON
Map 06 SU91

The Cricketers ♀
GU28 0LB ☎ 01798 342473 🖹 01799 344753
e-mail: info@thecricketersinn.com

Attractive white-painted pub situated in spectacular walking country at the western end of the South Downs. Delightful and very popular garden with extensive deck seating and weekend barbecues. Rumoured to be haunted, the inn has changed little over the years. Regularly changing menus, sometimes four a day! Look out for good hearty meals like beer-battered haddock or ribeye steak, both with hand-cut chips. Ideal stop-off point for Goodwood coach parties.
OPEN: 11-3 6-11 (Fri-Sat all day) Open all day all wk Etr-Oct Sun Closed eve **BAR MEALS:** L served all week 12-2.30 D served Mon-Sat 7-9.30 Sun 12-3.30 Av main course £10
RESTAURANT: L served all week 12-2.30 D served Mon-Sat 7-9.30 Sun 12-3.30 Av 3 course à la carte £21 🍽: Free House 🍺: Youngs Bitter, Archers Golden, Harvey Sussex, Ballards. ♀: 10
FACILITIES: Garden: Dogs allowed Must be on lead. Water provided **NOTES:** Parking 30

EARTHAM
Map 06 SU90

The George Inn
PO18 0LT ☎ 01243 814340 🖹 01243 814725
e-mail: thegeorgeinn@hotmail.com
Dir: From A27 at Tangmere r'about follow signs for Crockerhill/Eartham

Built in the 18th century as an ale house for local estate workers, the pub has a village bar with a flagstone floor (walkers and dogs welcome), and a cosy lounge with an open fire and patio doors leading to a delightful garden. Exposed ships' timbers are a feature of the candlelit restaurant, where the menu offers slow braised half shoulder of lamb, roast cod supreme, medallions of pork, venison and wild mushroom wellington, gammon and chips, and pork and leek sausage with mash and onion gravy.
OPEN: 11-11 **BAR MEALS:** L served all week 12-3 D served all week 6-9.30 Av main course £9.50 **RESTAURANT:** L served all week

12-2 D served all week 6-9 🍽: Free House 🍺: Greene King Abbot Ale + guest beers. **FACILITIES:** Garden: Patio & large grassed area with picnic tables Dogs allowed Water & Treats **NOTES:** Parking 30

EAST DEAN

Pick of the Pubs

The Star & Garter NEW ♀
PO18 0JG ☎ 01243 811318 🖹 01243 811826
e-mail: thestarandgarter@hotmail.com
Dir: On A286 between Chichester and Midhurst.
A pub since 1740, the Star & Garter is situated in one of the county's prettiest villages, with a pond and a variety of ancient cottages built of Sussex flint. East Dean used to be a thriving centre for hurdlemaking - before the First World War seven craftsmen operated here. The inn takes its name from the coat of arms of the Duke of Richmond who gave part of his Goodwood estate to establish a racecourse where members of the Goodwood Hunt Club and officers of the Sussex Militia could attend meetings. The Star & Garter has its own shellfish bar, open between March and October, where the owners cook and dress crabs and lobsters, and serve wild smoked salmon as well as prawns, mussels and the like. Other dishes served here and in the open plan restaurant include spiced shank of lamb, roasted Mediterranean vegetables, and tagliatelle of woodland mushrooms. Wonderful cheeses, good ales and a genuinely welcoming atmosphere add to the pleasures.
OPEN: 11-3 6-11 (Fri 11.30-3, 5.30-11, Sat 11-11, Sun 12-10.30)
BAR MEALS: L served all week 12-2.30 D served all week 6.30-10.30 Sun 12-9.30 Av main course £11
RESTAURANT: L served all week 12-2.30 D served all week 6.30-10.30 Sun 12-10.30 Av 3 course à la carte £25 🍽: Free House 🍺: Ballards Best, Nyewood Gold, Trotton Ale. ♀: 10
FACILITIES: Garden: Old stone patio, grass area, heaters Dogs allowed Water **NOTES:** Parking 6

ELSTED
Map 05 SU81

Pick of the Pubs

The Three Horseshoes
GU29 0JY ☎ 01730 825746
Dir: A272 from Midhurst to Petersfield, after 2m left to Harting & Elsted, after 3m pub on left
Tucked below the steep scarp slope of the South Downs is the peaceful village of Elsted and this 16th-century former drovers' ale house. It's one of those quintessential English country pubs that Sussex specialises in, full of rustic charm, with unspoilt cottagey bars, worn tiled floors, low beams, latch doors, a vast inglenook, and a motley mix of furniture. On fine days the extensive rear garden, with roaming chickens and stunning southerly views, is hugely popular. Tip-top real ales, including Cheriton Pots from across the Hampshire border, are drawn from the cask, and a daily-changing blackboard menu offers good old country cooking. Starters may include avocado with stilton and mushroom sauce with spinach, and prawn mayonnaise wrapped in smoked salmon. Main courses are likely to include steak, kidney and Murphy's pie, pheasant breast in cider with shallot and prune sauce and, in summer, crab and lobster. Excellent ploughman's are served with unusual cheeses. Puddings include treacle tart and raspberry and hazelnut meringue.

continued

OPEN: 11-2.30 6-11 (Sun 12-3, 7-10.30)
BAR MEALS: L served all week 12-2 D served all week 7-9 Sun 12-2 & 7-8.30 **RESTAURANT:** L served all week 12-2 D served all week 7-9 🍽: Free House 🍺: Cheriton Pots Ale, Ballard's Best, Fuller's London Pride, Timothy Taylors Landlord.
FACILITIES: Garden: views of South Downs, bantams Dogs allowed **NOTES:** Parking 30

FERNHURST
Map 06 SU82

Pick of the Pubs

The King's Arms 🍽 ♀
Midhurst Rd GU27 3HA ☎ 01428 652005 📠 01428 658970
See Pick of the Pubs on page 492

The Red Lion ♀
The Green GU27 3HY ☎ 01428 643112
& 653304 📠 01428 643939 e-mail: michaelgcameron@aol.com
Dir: *From A3 at Hindhead take A287 to Haslemere, then A286 to Fernhurst*
This 500-year-old building, reputedly the oldest pub in the village, is situated on the village green, just off the A26 Midhurst to Haslemere road. Traditional features include beams and open fires as well as real ales and good food served in a friendly atmosphere. The varied menu of freshly cooked dishes is supplemented by blackboard specials. Typical dishes are smoked fish platter, poacher's pot casserole (with local rabbit, venison and pheasant), and treacle tart.
OPEN: 11-11.30 (Closed 3-5 Mon,Tue and Wed)
BAR MEALS: L served all week 12-2.30 D served Tue-Sat 6-9.30
RESTAURANT: L served all week 12-2.30 D served Tue-Sat 6-9.30
🍽: Fullers 🍺: Fuller's ESB, Chiswick, London Pride, and Seasonal Guest. ♀: 8 **FACILITIES:** Garden: Dogs allowed Water
NOTES: Parking 50

HALNAKER
Map 06 SU90

Anglesey Arms 🍽 ♀
PO18 0NQ ☎ 01243 773474 📠 01243 530034
e-mail: angleseyarms@aol.com
Dir: *4m E from centre of Chichester on A285 (Petworth Road)*

This Georgian hostelry stands in two acres of landscaped grounds on the Goodwood estate. The building has always been a pub, and there's a traditional atmosphere in the wood-floored bar with its winter fires and real ales. Fresh local ingredients go into dishes such as spiced lamb shank with polenta; and fresh fish of the day (the chef's husband is a fisherman!). Extensive lunchtime menu with steaks, pasta and ploughmans.
OPEN: 11-3 5.30-11 (Open all day Sat-Sun) **BAR MEALS:** L served all week 12-2.30 D served all week 7-10 Av main course £12.50
continued

RESTAURANT: L served all week 12-2 D served all week 7.30-10 Av 3 course à la carte £22.50 🍽: Pubmaster 🍺: Young's Bitter, Adnams Bitter, Deuchars IPA. ♀: 8 **FACILITIES:** Garden: Two gardens, one courtyard for dining Dogs allowed Water **NOTES:** Parking 50

HAYWARDS HEATH
Map 06 TQ32

The Sloop 🍽 ♀
Sloop Ln, Scaynes Hill RH17 7NP ☎ 01444 831219
e-mail: sloopinn@tiscali.co.uk

Located next to the tranquil River Ouse and taking its name from the vessels which once worked the adjacent Ouse Canal, the Sloop is surrounded by beautiful countryside. The older part of the building, originally two lock-keepers' cottages, dates back over several centuries and records indicate it has been trading since 1815. A varied and imaginative menu using prime local ingredients offers the likes of cod with roasted red onions, courgettes, potatoes and salse verde.
OPEN: 12-3 6-11 (Sat 12-11 Easter-Sept Sun 12-10.30)
BAR MEALS: L served all week 12-2.30 D served Tue-Sat 6.30-9.30 Sun 12-3 **RESTAURANT:** L served all week 12-2.30 D served Mon-Sat 6.30-9.30 12-3 Av 3 course à la carte £20 🍽: Greene King 🍺: Greene King IPA, Abbot Ale, Ruddles county, XX Dark Mild & Guest beers. ♀: 9 **FACILITIES:** Garden: Two secluded gardens, parkland Dogs allowed Water **NOTES:** Parking 75

HENLEY
Map 06 SU82

Pick of the Pubs

The Duke of Cumberland Arms NEW 🍽
GU27 3HQ
The Duke of Cumberland Arms dates from the 15th century, when the road through the village was the main road from London to Chichester, and coaches would stop here for a change of horses. In the 1800s the bypass was built, which left the pub in a beautifully quiet, secluded country location with five acres of gardens and views for miles across the Sussex countryside. Today, the Duke of Cumberland Arms has an excellent reputation for fine traditional English food, with the freshest trout from the spring-fed pool. Specials change daily, and the main menu is changed every four weeks. A meal could start with blackened tuna on parmesan salad, followed by fresh trout, and finished with plum duff and custard. Roasts are a speciality, though you'll have to give 24-hour's notice. There is an interesting and reasonably priced wine list, and up to ten different real ales and ciders.
OPEN: 11-11 (Sun 12-10.30) **BAR MEALS:** L served all week 12-2.30 D served Tues-Sat 7-9.30 Av main course £11.95
RESTAURANT: L served all week 12-2.30 D served Tues-Sat 7-9.30 🍺: Youngs, Shepherd Neame Spitfire, Adnams Broadside, Brakspear. **FACILITIES:** Children's licence Garden: Dogs allowed **NOTES:** Parking 20

Pick of the Pubs

FERNHURST – WEST SUSSEX

The King's Arms

A Grade II-listed, 17th-century free house and restaurant set amidst rolling Sussex farmland, which can be seen at its best from the garden. The pub and its outbuildings are built from Sussex stone and decorated with hanging baskets, flowering tubs, vines and creepers. The L-shaped interior is very cosy, with beams, lowish ceilings, and a large inglenook fireplace, with the bar one side and restaurant and small dining room the other.

Owners Michael and Annabel Hirst have been maintaining the congenial atmosphere here for ten years, ably assisted by their friendly staff. Michael, supported by two sous chefs, looks after the cooking, whose style combines modern and traditional British. Everything is home made and freshly prepared on the premises, from salad dressings to sorbets. Fish is an important commodity, and Michael regularly visits the south coast to buy direct from the boats, bringing back what later appears on the menu as, for instance, goujons of plaice with tartare sauce; monkfish loin in Parma ham with courgette ribbons, prawn and saffron sauce; or perhaps seared scallops with bacon and pea risotto.

Alternatives to fish usually include barbary duck breast with savoy cabbage, baby roast potatoes and orange and port sauce; rack of English lamb with redcurrant and rosemary mash with lightly minted gravy; and fillet steak with dauphinoise potatoes, wild mushrooms and rich red wine jus. In addition to the monthly changing menu, there are daily changing specials such as steak, kidney and mushroom pudding. No food is served in the bar in the evenings. The large garden has some lovely trees, including a mature willow and pretty white lilacs, and views over surrounding fields. A wisteria-clad barn is used for the pub's annual three-day beer festival at the end of August.

OPEN: 11.30-3 5.30-11 Closed: 25 Dec
BAR MEALS: L served all week 12-2.30 D served Mon-Sat 7-9.30 Av main course £12.50
RESTAURANT: L served all week 12-2.30 D served Mon-Sat 7-9.30 Av 3 course à la carte £24
⊜: Free House
🍺: W J King Brewery Horsham Best Bitter, Ringwood Brewery 49er, Hogsback TEA, Caledonian IPA. ♀: 10
FACILITIES: Large garden with trees overlooking fields Dogs allowed Water, biscuits **NOTES:** Parking 45

🐟 ♀ Map 06 SU82
Midhurst Rd GU27 3HA
☎ 01428 652005
🖷 01428 658970
Dir: On A286 between Haslemere and Midhurst, 1m S of Fernhurst

England

HEYSHOTT
Map 06 SU81

Pick of the Pubs

Unicorn Inn ♀
GU29 0DL ☎ 01730 813486 ▤ 01730 815672

This cosy village pub, once one of four in Heyshott, dates from 1750, although it was not licensed until 1839. Its closeness to the South Downs makes it popular with walkers, as well as with locals and visitors from surrounding towns. A recent, careful refurbishment of the interior has left the bar, with its large log fire, feeling just as atmospheric as before, while the subtly lit, cream-painted restaurant, with matching table linen, and decorated with oil paintings of individual flowers, is in perfect harmony with the history. Dishes available at both lunch and dinner include chargrilled chicken breast stuffed with garlic and spinach; home-made fresh salmon fishcakes with cream and dill sauce; and twice-baked emmental and leek soufflé with tomato and olive dressing. Poached skate wing with capers and black butter could appear as a special, while the bar menu offers baguettes and hot wraps.
OPEN: 11.30-3 6.30-11 (Sun 12-4, closed Mon eve in winter) **BAR MEALS:** L served all week 12-2.30 D served Mon-Sat 7-9.30 (Sunday 12-3) Av main course £11.50 **RESTAURANT:** L served all week 12-2.15 6.30-9.15 (Sunday 12-3) Av 3 course à la carte £22 ◀: Timothy Taylor Landlord, Ballards Best, Hampshire Rose, Horsham Best Bitter. ♀: 10 **FACILITIES:** Garden: stunning views, beautifully kept garden Dogs allowed Water **NOTES:** Parking 24

HORSHAM
Map 06 TQ13

The Black Jug ▷ ♀
31 North St RH12 1RJ ☎ 01403 253526 ▤ 01403 217821
e-mail: black.jug@brunningandprice.co.uk
Dir: 100yrds from Horsham railway station, opp Horsham Art Centre
This busy town centre pub is close to the railway station and popular with Horsham's professional classes. Here you'll find a congenial atmosphere with friendly staff, an open fire, large conservatory and courtyard garden. Meals are freshly prepared using local ingredients wherever possible; light bites include chilli beef with cheese topping and crusty bread, whilst larger appetites might go for roasted vegetable wellington; or pan-fried mackerel with horseradish mash.
OPEN: 11-11 (Sun 12-10.30) Closed: 1 Jan **BAR MEALS:** L served all week 12 D served all week 10 Av main course £10.50 **RESTAURANT:** L served all week 12 D served all week 10 ▤: ◀: Weltons, Pedigree, Speckled Hen, Deuchars & Guest Ale. ♀: 25 **FACILITIES:** Garden: Courtyard with heaters Dogs allowed

Boars Head NEW ♀
Worthing Rd RH13 0AD ☎ 01403 254353 ▤ 01403 218114
e-mail: tazzrail@hotmail.com
Dir: On B2237 1m from Horsham town centre, follow signs for Christs Hospital
Built in 1761 as a farm, although late-Victorian additions have substantially altered the original structure. Known locally as a friendly, traditional bar and restaurant with lots going on, from music evenings to beer festivals. Main dishes in the restaurant include grills; chicken, beef or vegetable fajitas; bangers and mash; fisherman's pie; and a weekly fish special. There's an extensive bar food menu as well. The views from the patio are wonderful.
OPEN: 11.30-3 5-11 (Fri-Sun 11.30-11 Nov-Mar Sun 12-8) **BAR MEALS:** L served all week 12-2.30 D served Mon-Sat 6-9.30 Sun 12-6 Av main course £10.50 **RESTAURANT:** L served all week 12-2.15 D served all week 6.30-9 Sun 12-4 Av 3 course à la carte £20.50 ◀: Badger, Sussex, Tanglefoot, Hofbrau. ♀: 7 **FACILITIES:** Child facs Children's licence Garden: Two-tiered beer terrace with tables Dogs allowed Biscuits, bowls **NOTES:** Parking 42

KINGSFOLD
Map 06 TQ13

The Dog and Duck NEW
Dorking Rd RH12 3SA ☎ 01306 627295
e-mail: info@thedogandduck.fsnet.co.uk
Dir: On A24, 3m N of Horsham
Set in a large garden with a pond and 17 acres of fields, this 15th-century pub also boasts an inglenook fireplace for cold winter nights. Once a favourite of Flanagan and Allen's 'Crazy Gang' during the 1920s and 30s, contemporary entertainment includes fortnightly quiz nights and monthly live music. The pub also hosts a local darts team.
OPEN: 12-3 6-11 (Sun & BHs open all day summer) **BAR MEALS:** L served all week 12-2 D served Mon-Sat 6-9 Sun 12-3 Av main course £8.50 **RESTAURANT:** L served all week 12-2 D served Mon-Sat 6-9 Sun 12-3 Av 3 course à la carte £17.50 ◀: K&B Sussex, Badger Best, seasonal variations. **FACILITIES:** Child facs Garden: Large grassed area with benches and pond Dogs allowed **NOTES:** Parking 25

KIRDFORD
Map 06 TQ02

Pick of the Pubs

The Half Moon Inn
RH14 0LT ☎ 01403 820223 ▤ 01403 820224
e-mail: halfmooninn.kirdford@virgin.net
See Pick of the Pubs on page 494

LAMBS GREEN
Map 06 TQ23

The Lamb Inn NEW ▷ ♀
RH12 4RG ☎ 01293 871336 & 871933 ▤ 01293 871933
e-mail: ben@benbokoringram.wanadoo.co.uk
Dir: 6m from Horsham between Rusper and Faygate
Run since 2003 by a father and son team, where the food is all home made and fresh: fish is delivered daily from Newhaven, venison from a local stalker, and pheasant and duck in season are brought in by regulars. Steaks and other meat dishes are plentiful too. Speciality food nights include Indian, Italian and Mexican. Crawley and Horsham are only 10-minutes away.
OPEN: 11-3 5.30-11 (Sun 12-4 7-10.30) Closed: 25-26 Dec **BAR MEALS:** L served all week 12-2 D served all week 7-9.30 Sun 12-2.30, 7-9 Av main course £8.50 ◀: WJ King & Co beers - Horsham Best Bitter, Red River, Kings Old Ale, Summer Ale. ♀: 12 **FACILITIES:** Patio area Dogs allowed Dog bowl **NOTES:** Parking 30

Pick of the Pubs

KIRDFORD – WEST SUSSEX

The Half Moon Inn

Officially one of the prettiest pubs in Southern England, this red-tiled 16th-century village inn is covered in climbing rose bushes, and sits directly opposite the church in this unspoilt Sussex village near the River Arun. Although drinkers are welcome, the Half Moon is mainly a dining pub. New owner Kim Fishlock since April 2004 has already stamped her mark on the pub.

The interior, with its low beams and log fires, has been fully redecorated. Well-presented cask ales and lagers are on offer, as well as a varied wine list featuring four house choices available by the glass. A talented young team specialises in 'British food with a twist', and there is plenty of variety. Lunch choices from the bistro menu might include starters twice-cooked blue cheese soufflé; chicken liver paté, and medalllions of lobster, followed by mains such as pan-fried venison with black pudding mash; pan-fried medallions of pork; fillet of salmon on a bed of buttered pasta; and pork and leek sausages with apple mash. Lunchtime snacks in the form of battered haddock with chips, caesar salad, vegetarian pasta, and lamb curry with coriander rice, are also going down well. Home-made desserts take in the likes of ginger crème brûlée, rhubarb crumble and custard, and lemon tart with clotted cream, while the cheeseboard is impressive. At dinner, the menu is broadly similar, although the atmosphere changes, with candlelight, tablecloths and polished glassware. Well-tended gardens are an added draw in the summer, while for the more energetic, a pamphlet featuring local country walks is available.

OPEN: 11-3 6-11 (Closed Sun eve)
BAR MEALS: L served Mon-Sun 12-2.30 D served Mon-Sat 6-9.30 Av main course £10
RESTAURANT: L served all week 12-2.30 D served Mon-Sat 6-9.30
🍺: Laurel Pub Partnerships
🍺: Fuller's London Pride.
FACILITIES: Garden: 3 separate gardens for families and dining
NOTES: Parking 12

Map 06 TQ02

RH14 0LT

☎ 01403 820223
🖷 01403 820224
✉ halfmooninn.kirdford@virgin.net
Dir: Off A272 between Billingshurst & Petworth. At Wisborough Green follow Kirdford signs

England

LICKFOLD Map 06 SU92

Pick of the Pubs

The Lickfold Inn @ ⏹
GU28 9EY ☎ 01798 861285 e-mail: thelickfoldinn@aol.com
Dir: From A3 take A283, through Chiddingfold, 2m on right signed 'Lurgashall Winery', pub in 1m

Lickfold is a tiny hamlet with no shop or post office, but it does have this delightful free house, dating back to 1460. Period features include the ancient timber frame, the attractive herringbone-patterned bricks, and the huge central chimney. Inside - and the reason for the chimney's size - is an enormous inglenook with a spit. There are Georgian settles, oak beams, and moulded panelling too. If you find yourself wondering about the recurring garlic clove motif, it's all to do with the origin of the name Lickfold, probably derived from the Anglo-Saxon for an enclosure where wild garlic grows. Food in the bar and two restaurants is always freshly prepared and each course offers five choices. An unusual starter is oven-baked St Marcellin cheese with fig compôte and toast, while a representative main course might be tagliatelle with wild mushrooms and shavings of black truffle in creamy cep sauce topped with Reggiano. New owners for 2004 - reports please.
OPEN: 11-3.30 6-11.30 (Sun 12-3.30) Closed: 25-26 Dec **BAR MEALS:** L served Tues-Sun 12-2.30 D served Tues-Sat 7-9.30 Av main course £13.95 **RESTAURANT:** L served Tues-Sun 12-2.30 D served Tues-Sat 7-9.30 Av 3 course à la carte £25.95 🍴: Free House 🍺: Ballard Best, Summer Lightning, Youngs, 49er. ⏹: 7 **FACILITIES:** Child facs Children's licence Garden: Large patio with traditional garden area Dogs allowed Water bowl **NOTES:** Parking 40

LODSWORTH Map 06 SU92

Pick of the Pubs

The Halfway Bridge Inn ♦♦♦♦ ⏹
Halfway Bridge GU28 9BP ☎ 01798 861281
e-mail: hwb@thesussexpub.co.uk
web: www.thesussexpub.co.uk
Dir: Between Petworth and Midhurst, next to the Cowdry Estate and golf club on A272.
Attractive brick-and-flint Sussex coaching inn, steeped in history and standing in lovely countryside mid-way between Midhurst and Petworth. Locally very popular, the pub has no fewer than five open fires to provide a warm winter welcome; in summer the sheltered patio and lawn come into their own. Recent refurbishment work by the

continued

new owner has made the inn an even more attractive destination for diners. A selection of main courses includes Scotch rump beefburger, augergine cannelloni with spinach, pine nuts and chunky ratatouille, calves' liver and smoked bacon with mustard mash, or grilled Dover sole fresh from Billingsgate Market. Extensive wine list. Upmarket bedroom accommodation meets 21st-century expectations in a converted Sussex barn.
OPEN: 11-11 Closed: 25 Dec **BAR MEALS:** L served all week 12-2 D served all week 7-10 Sun food served all day Av main course £11 **RESTAURANT:** L served all week 12-2 D served all week 7-10 Sun food served all day Av 3 course à la carte £25 🍴: Free House 🍺: Cheriton Pots Ale, Sussex Badgers Best. ⏹: 14 **FACILITIES:** Garden: Secluded patio at rear; tables in front Dogs allowed Water **NOTES:** Parking 30
ROOMS: 6 bedrooms en suite 2 family rooms s£55 d£90

The Hollist Arms NEW ⏹
The Street GU28 9BZ ☎ 01798 861310
e-mail: george@thehollistarms.co.uk
Dir: 2m from Midhurst
A 15th-century building, a pub since 1823, and with its roaring fires, large open fires, leather sofas and no fruit machines, as traditional as one could wish for. The bar menu will suit those after just a light snack, while the full restaurant menu offers deep-fried brie rolled in nuts with redcurrant preserve; Wessex lamb chops marinated in mint sauce; and hot vegetarian chilli con carne.
OPEN: 11-3 6-11 **BAR MEALS:** L served all week 12-2 D served all week 7-9 Sun 12-2.30 Av main course £11 **RESTAURANT:** L served all week 12-2 D served all week 7-9 Av 3 course à la carte £20 🍺: Youngs, Timothy Taylors Landlord, Horsham Best. ⏹: 7 **FACILITIES:** Children's licence Garden: Large and enclosed Dogs allowed **NOTES:** Parking 20

LURGASHALL Map 06 SU92

The Noah's Ark
The Green GU28 9ET ☎ 01428 707346 ⒡ 01428 707742
e-mail: bernard@noahsarkinn.co.uk
Dir: Off A283 N of Petworth
This charming 16th-century inn is said to have got its name because customers once had to cross a pond by the door to get in - like animals finding shelter in the ark. Today, it remains the centre of village life and hosts a theatrical production each summer. An extensive snack menu is backed by more substantial fare, including wild mushroom risotto; honey glazed turkey steak; and lobster tail with garlic and herb butter.
OPEN: 11-3 6-11 Closed: 25 Dec Nov-Mar closed Sun pm **BAR MEALS:** L served all week 12-2.30 D served Mon-Sat 7-9.30 Av main course £9 **RESTAURANT:** L served all week 12-2 D served Mon-Sat 7-9.30 Av 3 course à la carte £22 Av 3 course fixed price £18 🍴: Greene King 🍺: Greene King IPA, Old Speckled Hen & Abbot. **FACILITIES:** Child facs Garden: Large garden, seats over 60 **NOTES:** Parking 20

MAPLEHURST Map 06 TQ12

The White Horse
Park Ln RH13 6LL ☎ 01403 891208
Dir: 5m SE of Horsham, between A281& A272
In the tiny Sussex hamlet of Maplehurst, this traditional pub offers a break from modern life: no music, no fruit machines, no cigarette machines, just hearty pub food and an enticing range of ales. Sip Harvey's Best, Welton's Pride and Joy or

continued

England

MAPLEHURST continued

Dark Star Espresso Stout in the bar or whilst admiring the rolling countryside from the quiet, south-facing garden. Home-made chilli con carne with garlic bread is a speciality. **OPEN:** 12-2.30 6-11 (Sun 12-3, 7-10.30) **BAR MEALS:** L served all week 12-2 D served all week 6-9 (Sun 12-2.30, 7-9) ■: Harvey's Best, Welton's Pride & Joy, Dark Star Expresso Stout, King's Red River. **FACILITIES:** Child facs Children's licence Large, great views, quiet & safe Dogs allowed dog biscuits **NOTES:** Parking 20 No credit cards

MIDHURST   Map 06 SU82

The Angel Hotel ★★★ ◎ ♀
North St GU29 9DN ☎ 01730 812421 ▤ 01730 815928
web: www.theangelmidhurst.co.uk
An imposing and well-proportioned, late-Georgian façade hides the true Tudor origins of this former coaching inn. Its frontage overlooks the town's main street, while at the rear attractive gardens give way to meadowland and the ruins of Cowdray Castle. Bright yellow paintwork on local cottages means they are Cowdray Estate-owned. Gabriel's is the main restaurant, or try The Halo Bar where dishes range from snacks and pasta to sizzlers and steaks, with specials. **OPEN:** 11-11 **BAR MEALS:** L served all week 12-2.30 D served all week 6-9.30 Av main course £6.95 **RESTAURANT:** 12-2.30 D served all week 6.30-9.30 Av 3 course fixed price £14.95 ◎: Free House ■: Gale's HSB & Best. ♀: 12 **FACILITIES:** Child facs Children's licence Garden: walled garden, pond, views of Cowdray Ruins Dogs allowed **NOTES:** Parking 75 **ROOMS:** 28 bedrooms en suite 18 family rooms s£80 d£110

NUTHURST   Map 06 TQ12

Pick of the Pubs

Black Horse Inn ♀
Nuthurst St RH13 6LH ☎ 01403 891272 ▤ 01403 891272
e-mail: cliveh@henwood.fsbusiness.co.uk
See Pick of the Pubs on opposite page

OVING   Map 06 SU90

The Gribble Inn ♀
PO20 2BP ☎ 01243 786893 ▤ 01243 788841
e-mail: brianelderfield@hotmail.com
Dir: From A27, A259. After 1m L at rndbt, 1st R to Oving, 1st L in village
Named after local schoolmistress Rose Gribble, the inn retains all of its 16th-century charm. Large open fireplaces, wood burners and low beams set the tone. There's no background music at this peaceful hideaway, which is the ideal spot to enjoy any of the half dozen real ales from the on-site micro-brewery. Liver and bacon; spinach lasagne with red peppers; and special fish dishes are all home cooked. **OPEN:** 11-3 5.30-11 (Sun 12-4, 7-10.30) **BAR MEALS:** L served all week 12-2.30 D served all week 6-9.30 Sun 7-9 Av main course £7.95 **RESTAURANT:** L served all week 12-2.30 D served all week 6-9.30 Sun 7-9 ◎: Woodhouse Inns ■: Gribble Ale, Reg's Tipple, Slurping Stoat, Plucking Pheasant. ♀: 8 **FACILITIES:** Garden: Large shaded garden with seating for over 100 Dogs allowed Toys & water provided **NOTES:** Parking 40

Pubs offering a good choice of fish on their menu

PARTRIDGE GREEN   Map 06 TQ11

Pick of the Pubs

The Green Man Inn and Restaurant NEW
Church Rd RH13 8JT ☎ 01403 710250 ▤ 01403 713212
e-mail: info@thegreenman.org
Dir: Located between A24 and A281, just S of A272. Pub on B2135

A stylish and attractive gastropub with a pretty garden, and decorated in a clean-looking, unfussy way that accentuates the late-Victorian interior. Seasonal menus with daily specials use only fresh, mostly locally sourced, ingredients. Examples of the range are pan-roasted breast of Barbary duckling with sweet potato purée; pan-fried calves' liver with streaky bacon and bubble and squeak; supreme of salmon with red pepper and courgette linguine; and cheese and sage croquettes with creamed caraway savoy cabbage. From the specials board come monkfish fillet with Chinese spices; smoked haddock with Welsh rarebit; and chateaubriand with béarnaise sauce. Tapas, bar snacks, light meals and sandwiches are also available at lunchtime. A short list of puddings could well feature crème brûlée, and pears and blackberries poached in red wine. Seating in the non-smoking restaurant is supplemented by al fresco dining on the terrace. **OPEN:** 11.30-3.30 6.30-12 **BAR MEALS:** L served Tues-Sun 12-2.15 D served Tues-Sat Sun 12-2.30 Av main course £12 **RESTAURANT:** L served Tues-Sun 12-2.15 D served Tues-Sat 7-9.30 Sun 12-2.30 Av 3 course à la carte £22 ■: Harveys Sussex Best, Guinness. **FACILITIES:** Children's licence Garden: Patio area with seating, heaters available Dogs allowed Bowl **NOTES:** Parking 30

PETWORTH   Map 06 SU92

Badgers
Station Rd GU28 0JF ☎ 01798 342651 ▤ 01798 343649
Dir: On the A285 Chichester road, 1.5 miles outside Petworth, just over bridge on the left
Nestling in the South Downs, Badgers is a country dining pub that used to be the Railway Tavern, serving Petworth's old station. It has plenty of charm, with open fires inside and a pretty courtyard area outside, overlooking the small garden, carp pond and stream. The menu specialises in fish during the summer and game during the winter: typical options are pasta with scallops and tiger prawns, lambs' liver with bacon, onions, peas and coriander, and steak and kidney pudding. **OPEN:** 11-3 5.30-11 (Sat 11-3, 6.30-11, Sun 12-3,7-10.30 closed Sun eve winter) Closed: BHs **BAR MEALS:** L served all week 12-2 D served all week 7-9 **RESTAURANT:** L served all week 12-2 D served all week 7-9 ◎: Free House ■: Badgers, Sussex, Guinness. **FACILITIES:** Garden: Courtyard **NOTES:** Parking 20 **ROOMS:** 3 bedrooms en suite s£55 d£85 (★★★) No children overnight

Pick of the Pubs

NUTHURST – SUSSEX, WEST

Black Horse Inn

A one-time smugglers' hideout, and still appropriately hidden away in a quiet backwater, this lovely old free house is half masked by impressive window boxes. Built of clay tiles and mellow brick, it forms part of what was originally a row of workers' cottages on the Sedgwick Park estate, once a royal hunting lodge dating back to the 12th century.

The first record of it being an inn was in 1817. Plenty of its history remains: inside you'll find stone-flagged floors, an inglenook fireplace and an exposed wattle and daub wall. It's spotlessly clean, with smoke-free areas and a warm and cosy atmosphere that's perfect for dining or just enjoying a drink. The pub has a reputation for good beers, including Harvey's, London Pride, Hoegaarden and numerous guests. On sunny days, guests can sit out on the terraces at the front and rear, or take their drinks across the stone bridge over a stream into the delightful back garden. There are plenty of good walks in the area, including a four-mile circular walk based around the pub itself (ask for the leaflet). It's an ideal opportunity to explore the beautiful West Sussex woods and rolling downland, and a good way to work up an appetite for a pub meal. Freshly prepared food is served at lunchtimes and evenings during the week, and all day at weekends and bank holidays (when there's always a beer festival). Lunch, dinner and bar snack menus offer traditional and imaginative cooking, including Sunday roasts, curries, chillies, lamb kleftiko, seafood and fish dishes including red snapper. A new kitchen suite due to come on stream in July 2005 is expected to broaden the range of food on offer still further.

OPEN: 12-3 6-11 (Sat-Sun, BHs open all day)
BAR MEALS: L served all week 12-2.30 D served all week 6-9.30 All day Sat, Sun & BHs
RESTAURANT: L served all week 12-2.30 D served all week 6-9.30 All day Sat, Sun & BHs
⊕: Free House
🍺: Harveys Sussex, W J King, Weltons, Youngs London Pride and numerous guest ales. ⚲: 8
FACILITIES: Child facs Garden: Front & rear patio area, garden with stream Dogs allowed Water & Biscuits
NOTES: Parking 28

⚲   Map 06 TQ12
Nuthurst St RH13 6LH
☎ 01403 891272
📄 01403 891272
📧 cliveh@henwood.fsbusiness.co.uk
Dir: 4m S of Horsham, off A281 & A24

PETWORTH continued

The Black Horse
Byworth GU28 0HL ☎ 01798 342424 ▤ 01798 342868
e-mail: blackhorsebyworth@btopenworld.com
An unspoilt pub built on the site of an old priory in a beautiful
garden. The three-storey, brick and stone, Georgian frontage
hides a much older interior dating back to the 14th century.
Wooden floors and furniture, half-panelled walls, portraits of
locals and open fires characterise the three rustic rooms.
Good ales and traditional home-cooked food includes
pheasant calvados, Cajun chicken, lasagne verde, haddock
topped with Welsh rarebit, and steak and kidney pudding.
Recent change of hands.
OPEN: 11.30-11 (Sun 12-10.30) **BAR MEALS:** L served all week
12-2 D served all week 7-9 Av main course £8.95
RESTAURANT: L served all week 12-2 D served all week 7-9
◐: Arundel Gold, Cheriton Pots Ale, Hogs Back Brew, Itchen Valley.
FACILITIES: Garden: Country garden, views of Shimmings Valley
Dogs allowed on leads Water **NOTES:** Parking 24

Welldiggers Arms ♀
Polborough Rd GU28 0HG ☎ 01798 342287
Dir: 1m E of Petworth on A283
Welldiggers once occupied this rustic, 300-year-old roadside
pub, which boasts low-beamed bars with open log fires and
huge oak tables. It is conveniently located for racing at
Goodwood and Fontwell, as well as a visit to Sir Edward
Elgar's cottage. Dishes on the menu may include English
steaks, butchered on the premises, fresh scallops, lobster and
crab and cod with home-made chips.
OPEN: 11-3 6.30-10 (Sun 12-10.30) Closed: 25 Dec
BAR MEALS: L served all week 12-2 D served Tue-Sat 6.30-9.30
RESTAURANT: L served all week 12-2 D served Tue-Sat 6.30-9.30
◖: Free House ◐: Youngs. **FACILITIES:** Garden: Large lawn &
patio, food served outside Dogs allowed **NOTES:** Parking 35

POYNINGS   Map 06 TQ21

Royal Oak Inn ♀
The Street BN45 7AQ ☎ 01273 857389 ▤ 01273 857202
e-mail: mail@royaloakpoynings.biz
*Dir: N on the A23 just outside Brighton, take the A281 (signed for Henfield
& Poynings), then follow signs into Poynings village*

Close to the famous Devil's Dyke beauty spot, this white-
painted village pub has been extensively refurbished in recent
years. Its views of the Downs and nearby walks over National
Trust land make it an especially popular watering hole. A
varied menu includes spicy tomato, basil and bean cottage
pie; pear and gorgonzola tart; and chargrilled swordfish steak
with smoked salmon and prawn sauce.
OPEN: 11-11 (Sun 12-10.30) **BAR MEALS:** L served all week 12-6
D served all week 6-9.30 (Sat & Sun 12-9.30) ◖: Free House

continued

◐: Harveys Sussex, Abbot Ale, Greene King Morland Old Speckled
Hen. ♀: 10 **FACILITIES:** Garden: Large garden with BBQ facilities &
nice views Dogs allowed **NOTES:** Parking 35

ROWHOOK   Map 06 TQ13

Neals Restaurant at The Chequers Inn ◉ ♀
RH12 3PY ☎ 01403 790480 ▤ 01403 790480
e-mail: thechequers1@aol.com
Dir: Off A29 NW of Horsham

A 15th-century building of great character with original
beams, flagstones and open fires. The landlord is a member
of the Master Chefs of Great Britain, and emphasises fresh
produce, locally-sourced where possible. Expect aromatic
duck confit with mustard mash and red wine jus; local
pheasant with honey-roasted vegetables, pancetta and thyme
jus; and Thai fish cakes on pak choi. Tempting puddings
include brioche and apricot butter pudding.
OPEN: 11.30-3.30 6-11.30 **BAR MEALS:** L served all week 12-2
D served Mon-Sat 7-9.30 Sun 12-2.30 Av main course £10.50
RESTAURANT: L served all week 12-2 D served Tue-Sat 7-9.30 Sun
12-2.30 Av 3 course à la carte £27 Av 3 course fixed price £27.50
◖: Punch Taverns ◐: Harvey's Sussex Ale, Young's, Fuller's London
Pride, plus guest ale each week. ♀: 7 **FACILITIES:** Garden:
Spacious, peaceful Dogs allowed Water **NOTES:** Parking 40

RUDGWICK   Map 06 TQ03

The Fox Inn ♀
Guildford Rd, Bucks Green RH12 3JP
☎ 01403 822386 ▤ 01403 823950 e-mail: seafood@foxinn.co.uk
Dir: Situated on A281 midway between Horsham and Guildford
'Famous for Fish!' is the claim of this attractive 16th-century
inn, a message borne out by the extensive menu. Food
offered includes all-day breakfast and afternoon tea, while the
bar menu focuses on seafood, from fish and chips to the huge
fruits de mer platter. Dishes include Foxy's famous fish pie;
seared tuna loin on Caesar salad; and hand-made
Cumberland sausage on stilton mash. A horse is apparently
walked through the pub each Christmas day!
OPEN: 11-11 (Sun 12-10.30) **BAR MEALS:** L served all week 12-10
D served all week Av main course £13 **RESTAURANT:** 12-10
Av 3 course à la carte £22 ◖: Hall & Woodhouse ◐: King & Barnes
Sussex, Badger Tanglefoot, Best. ♀: 8 **FACILITIES:** Garden: Large
patio, grassed area Dogs allowed Water **NOTES:** Parking 30

SHIPLEY   Map 06 TQ12

George & Dragon ♀
Dragons Green RH13 7JE ☎ 01403 741320
Dir: Signposted off A272 between Coolham and A24
A 17th-century, tile-hung cottage that provides welcome peace
and quiet, especially on balmy summer evenings when the

continued

peaceful garden is a welcome retreat. Its interior is all head-banging beams and character inglenook fireplaces where a pint of Badger or Tanglefoot will not come amiss. The food is home made using fresh vegetables and 'real' chips, and offers roast lamb and crispy coated chicken breast with sweet-and-sour sauce. Shipley is famous for its smock mill.
OPEN: 11-3 6-11 (Sun-Sun & BHs open all day)
BAR MEALS: L served all week 12-2 D served all week 6.30-9
Av main course £6.50 **RESTAURANT:** L served all week 12-2
D served all week 6.45-9 ☺: Hall & Woodhouse ☜: Badger Best, Tanglefoot, Sussex Best, guest beer. ♀: 10 **FACILITIES:** Garden: Beer garden, food served outdoors, BBQ Dogs allowed but not in dining area **NOTES:** Parking 20

SIDLESHAM
Map 05 SZ89

Crab & Lobster ♀
Mill Ln PO20 7NB ☎ 01243 641233
Dir: Off B2145 between Chichester & Selsey
Well-kept pub situated close to the shores of Pagham Harbour, a noted nature reserve. Popular with walkers and twitchers who fill the cosy bars in winter, and the pretty rear garden with mudflat views in summer.
OPEN: 11-3 6-11 Closed Dec 25-26 eve **BAR MEALS:** L served all week 12-2 D served Fri-Sat 7-9 Av main course £6.50
RESTAURANT: L served all week 12 D served Tue-Sat 7 ☺: Free House ☜: Itchin Valley Fagins, Cheriton Pots Ale, Ballards Best.
FACILITIES: Garden: Dogs allowed Water Provided
NOTES: Parking 12

SINGLETON
Map 05 SU81

The Partridge Inn ⌐◇
PO18 0EY ☎ 01243 811251 ▤ 0870 804 4566
Dir: Telephone for directions

The building probably dates from the 16th century, when it would have been part of a huge hunting park owned by the Fitzalan family, Earls of Arundel. Today, it is popular with walkers enjoying the rolling Sussex countryside and visitors to Goodwood for motor and horse-racing. A menu of typical pub fare includes liver and bacon, steak and ale pie, Goodwood gammon, salmon fishcakes, fish and chips, and home-made puddings. Formerly the Fox and Hounds.
OPEN: 11.30-3 6-11 (1 March - 31Sept Sat/Sun 11-11)
BAR MEALS: L served all week 12-2 D served all week 6.30-9 Sat & Sun 12 - 9 Av main course £9.50 **RESTAURANT:** L served all week 12-2 D served all week 6.30-9 ☺: Enterprise Inns ☜: Gales Best, London Pride, Ringwood Best Bitter. **FACILITIES:** Large garden: colourful in summer Dogs allowed Water **NOTES:** Parking 40

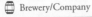
🛢 Brewery/Company

SLINDON
Map 06 SU90

The Spur NEW ⌐◇ ♀
BN18 0NE ☎ 01243 814216 ▤ 01243 814707
Dir: Off A27 on A29 outside village of Slindon
Nestling on top of the South Downs, just outside the village of Slindon, and only two miles from Arundel, sits this 17th-century pub that enjoys superb views over to the Isle of Wight. Inside are an open plan bar and restaurant, warmed by log fires that create a friendly atmosphere. If you book in advance you can use the skittle alley, or enjoy a game of pool or other pub games. Lots of seafood on the menu including poached salmon with hollandaise sauce, or baked fillet of cod with a parmesan and pesto crust.
OPEN: 11-3 6-11 **BAR MEALS:** L served all week 12-2 D served all week 7-9.30 Sun-Tues 7-9 Av main course £10
RESTAURANT: L served all week 12-2 D served all week 7-9.30 Sun-Tues 7-9 Av 3 course à la carte £24 ☜: Abbott, Greene King IPA, Courage Directors. ♀: 7 **FACILITIES:** Garden: Large country garden, wooded area Dogs allowed **NOTES:** Parking 40

SOUTHBOURNE
Map 05 SU70

The Old House at Home ♀
Cot Ln, Chidham PO18 8SU ☎ 01243 572477 ▤ 01243 574978
e-mail: thebar@theoldhouseathome.com

Sleepy Chidham and its 17th-century pub lie on a low peninsula jutting out into Chichester Harbour. Wonderful scenic walks and wildlife-rich marshes entice ramblers and birdwatchers in particular, while more universally appreciated perhaps are the warm, music-free welcome, traditional ales, wines from its own vineyards, and good food. In addition to lunchtime snacks, there are heartier dishes like lamb's liver and bacon, fillet of beef wellington, pan-fried monkfish and specials. Guest beers change weekly.
OPEN: 11.30-2.30 6-11 (Summer Sat-Sun all day)
BAR MEALS: L served all week 12-2 D served all week 6.30-9.30
Av main course £7.25 **RESTAURANT:** L served all week 12-2
D served all week 6.30-9.30 ☺: Punch Taverns ☜: Greene King Abbot Ale, Fuller's London Pride, 2 Guest Beers changed weekly.
FACILITIES: Garden: Patio at front & grass area at rear. Seating Dogs allowed Water **NOTES:** Parking 30

SOUTH HARTING
Map 05 SU71

The Ship Inn
GU31 5PZ ☎ 01730 825302
Dir: From Petersfield take B2146 towards Chichester
17th-century inn made from a ship's timbers, hence the name. Home-made pies are a feature, and other popular dishes include fresh sea bass, rainbow trout, calves' liver, rack of lamb, ham and asparagus mornay, and hot beef Hungarian goulash. A range of vegetarian dishes and bar snacks too.

SOUTH HARTING continued

OPEN: 11-11 (Oct-Mar 12-3, 6-11) **BAR MEALS:** 12-2.30 D served Mon-Sat 7-9 **RESTAURANT:** L served all week 12-2.30 7-9.30 ☺: Free House ◖: Palmer IPA, Cheriton Pots Ale, Ballards Wassail. **FACILITIES:** Garden: Dogs allowed Water **NOTES:** Parking 5

STEDHAM   Map 05 SU82

Hamilton Arms/Nava Thai Restaurant
Hamilton Arms School Ln GU29 0NZ
☎ 01730 812555 ▤ 01730 817459
e-mail: hamiltonarms@hotmail.com
Dir: Off A272 between Midhurst & Petersfield

Named after Admiral Lord Nelson's mistress who lived near by, this traditional English free house is renowned for its authentic Thai cuisine. Colourful parasols on the front dining patio spill over on to the common opposite. Popular oriental bottled beers supplement real ales such as Gale's HSB and Ballard's Best. The comprehensive range of over 100 Thai dishes includes soups, curries, salads and vegetarian choices. **OPEN:** 11-3 6-11 (Sun 12-3, 7-10.30) Closed: 1 Week Jan **BAR MEALS:** L served Tues-Sun 12-2.30 D served Tues-Sat 6-10.30 Sun 7-9.30 Av main course £10 **RESTAURANT:** L served Tues-Sun 12-2.30 D served Tues-Sat 6-10.30 Sun 7-9.30 Av 3 course à la carte £15 Av 4 course fixed price £17.50 ☺: Free House ◖: Ballard's Best, Fuller's London Pride, Everards Tiger Best, Gales HSB. **FACILITIES:** Child facs Garden: Lawn with benches and umbrellas Dogs allowed Water **NOTES:** Parking 40

STEYNING   Map 06 TQ11

The White Horse Inn NEW ♀
23 High St BN44 3YE ☎ 01903 812347 ▤ 01903 814084
e-mail: TheWhiteHorseInn@vwood.wanadoo.co.uk
Dir: 9m NW of Brighton
Seventeenth-century inn prominently positioned in a pretty village a mile from the South Downs Way. The main part of the inn burned down in 1949 (the night the fire brigade held their annual supper here) and was re-housed in the kitchen, stables and coach house. Food served in the bar or Woods restaurant includes pan-fried local sausage with mash and onion gravy, pasta rustica (with or without meat), and fresh fish of the day. **OPEN:** 11-2.30 5.30-11 (Sun 12-3) Closed Sun eve **BAR MEALS:** L served all week 12-2.15 D served Mon-Sat 6.30-9.15 Sun 12-3 Av main course £8 **RESTAURANT:** L served all week 12-2.15 D served Mon-Sat 6.30-9.15 Sun 12-3 Av 3 course à la carte £16 Av 3 course fixed price £15.90 ☺: Greene King ◖: IPA, Abbott Ale, Old Speckled Hen. ♀: 8 **FACILITIES:** Children's licence Garden: Grass area overlooking high street **NOTES:** Parking 20

SUTTON   Map 06 SU91

Pick of the Pubs

White Horse Inn
The Street RH20 1PS ☎ 01798 869221 ▤ 01798 869291
Dir: Turn off A29 at foot of Bury Hill. After 2m pass Roman Villa on R. 1m to Sutton
Pretty Georgian inn tucked away in a sleepy village at the base of the South Downs. In the neat bars and dining room expect imaginative food, the daily-changing choice featuring perhaps stilton and broccoli soup, baked sea bass with lemon basil and tomato, confit of duck, lamb shank with tomatoes and red wine, and lemon tart. **OPEN:** 11-3 5.30-11 (Sun 12-3 7-10.30, summer wknd all day) **BAR MEALS:** L served all week 12-2 D served all week 7-9 Av main course £6.50 **RESTAURANT:** L served all week 12-2 D served all week 7-9 Av 3 course à la carte £30 ☺: Free House ◖: Youngs Special, Courage Best, plus guests. **FACILITIES:** Garden: Dogs allowed **NOTES:** Parking 10

WALDERTON   Map 05 SU71

The Barley Mow ♀
PO18 9ED ☎ 023 9263 1321 ▤ 023 9263 1403
e-mail: mowbarley@aol.co.uk
Dir: B2146 from Chichester towards Petersfield. Turn right signed Walderton, pub 100yds on left .
Ivy-clad with hanging baskets, this pretty pub is comfortably set beside the rolling Sussex Downs, and is a magnet for walkers, cyclists and riders with a special tethering pole for horses. Famous locally for its skittle alley, it also has a reputation for good home-made pub food: steak and ale pie, battered fresh cod, broccoli and cheese bake, chestnut and parsnip bake, roast partridge, and a Sunday roast. **OPEN:** 11-3 6-11.30 (All day Sun) **BAR MEALS:** L served all week 6-9.30 Sun 12-2.30, 6-9.30 Av main course £8.50 **RESTAURANT:** L served all week 12-2.15 D served all week 6-9.30 Sun 12-2.30, 6-9.30 ☺: Free House ◖: Ringwood Old Thumper & Fortyniner, Fuller's London Pride, Itchen Valley Godfathers, Scottish Courage John Smith's. ♀: 8 **FACILITIES:** Mature garden, tables, seats, stream Dogs allowed **NOTES:** Parking 50

WARNHAM   Map 06 TQ13

The Greets Inn ♀
47 Friday St RH12 3QY ☎ 01403 265047 ▤ 01403 265047
Dir: Off A24 N of Horsham
A fine Sussex hall house dating from about 1350 and built for Elias Greet, a local merchant. A magnificent inglenook fireplace and head-crackingly low beams will be discovered in the flagstone-floored bar, where the old-world character is warm and appealing. There is a rambling series of dining areas where diners can sample the wares of the kitchen team. **OPEN:** 11-2.30 6-11 (Sun 12-2, 7-10.30) **BAR MEALS:** L served all week 12-2 D served all week 7-9 **RESTAURANT:** L served all week 12-2 D served all week 7-9 ☺: ◖: Interbrew, Greene King IPA, Fuller's London Pride, Abbat. **FACILITIES:** Garden: Large, food served outside Dogs allowed Water **NOTES:** Parking 30

 ★ Star rating for inspected hotel accommodation

England

WEST HOATHLY
Map 06 TQ33

The Cat Inn ♀
Queen's Square RH19 4PP ☎ 01342 810369
An oasis of calm only twenty minutes from Gatwick. In order to preserve the peace, children are not allowed, and if you're after pool, darts or music, it's better to look elsewhere. This is a place for quiet relaxation - perhaps on the sunny terrace opposite an historic 11th-century church or inside beside an inglenook fire. Try the duck in angel sauce, lemon sole or venison steak perhaps from the wholesome restaurant menu. Bar meals are also available.
OPEN: 12-11 **BAR MEALS:** L served all week 12-2.30 D served all week 6.30-9.30 Av main course £10 **RESTAURANT:** L served all week 12-2 D served all week 7-9.15 Av 3 course à la carte £20 ☐: Free House ◖: Harveys Best, Fuller's London Pride, Pedigree and guest ale. ♀: 7 **FACILITIES:** Patio **NOTES:** Parking 30

WINEHAM
Map 06 TQ22

The Royal Oak
BN5 9AY ☎ 01444 881252 ▤ 01444 881530
This delightful, 14th-century, black and white timbered cottage has been dispensing ale for over 200 years and continues to maintain its traditional, unspoilt character, having been under the same management for over 30 years. A true ale house, so expect traditional, rustic furnishings and real ale straight from the cask. Extensive summer gardens and a limited menu of decent sandwiches, home-made soup and ploughman's.
OPEN: 11-2.30 5.30-11 (Sun 12-3, 7-10.30) **BAR MEALS:** L served all week 11-2.30 5.30-11 ☐: Inn Business ◖: Harveys Sussex Best Bitter, Wadworth 6X. **FACILITIES:** Garden: Large lawn with seating Dogs allowed Water **NOTES:** Parking 40 No credit cards

WISBOROUGH GREEN
Map 06 TQ02

Cricketers Arms ♀
Loxwood Rd RH14 0DG ☎ 01403 700369
e-mail: sarah@cricketersarms.com
Dir: On the A272, between Billingshurst & Petworth. In the middle of Wisborough Green turn at junct, pub 100 yds on R
A traditional village pub dating from the 16th century with oak beams, wooden floors and open fires. Idyllic location overlooking the village green with views of cricket matches and hot-air-balloon rides. Fans of extreme sports will appreciate the fact that the Cricketers is the home of lawn mower racing. A full bar menu is served, ranging from snacks to three course meals and Sunday roasts, and there is a large selection of specials. Typical dishes include steak pie, game dishes in season, and 'mega' salads.
OPEN: 11-11 **BAR MEALS:** L served Mon-Sun 12-2 D served Mon-Sun 6.30-9.30 (Thu/Sun 6.30-9) Av main course £7.95 **RESTAURANT:** L served Mon-Sun 12-2 D served Mon-Sun 6.30-9.30 (Thu/Sun 6.30-9) Av 3 course à la carte £17 ☐: Enterprise Inns ◖: Fuller's London Pride, Greene King IPA, Youngs Original. ♀: 7 **FACILITIES:** Garden: Grass area with benches Dogs allowed Water, Chews **NOTES:** Parking 20

WORTHING
Map 06 TQ10

John Henrys Bar and Restaurant NEW ♦♦♦♦
The Forge, Nepcote Ln, Findon Village BN14 0SE
☎ 01903 877277 e-mail: enquiries@john-henrys.com
Dir: 3m from Worthing, in Findon Village
Located in Finton village in the heart of the South Downs, yet only a short distance from the A24 and the A27, and handy for Cissbury and Chactonbury Rings and the South Downs

continued

Way. This is an ideal refreshment stop before or after a walk or cycle ride. Live music, and theme and quiz nights are regular features in the air-conditioned bar and restaurant.
OPEN: 10-11 **BAR MEALS:** L served all week 10-2 D served all week 6-9 Sun 10.30-4 Av main course £7 **RESTAURANT:** L served all week 12-2 D served Mon-Sat 6-9 Sun 12-4 Av 3 course à la carte £18.50 ◖: 2 monthly changing real ales. **FACILITIES:** Garden: 2 level paved with tables and chairs Dogs allowed **NOTES:** Parking 13 **ROOMS:** 5 bedrooms en suite 3 family rooms s£55 d£75

TYNE & WEAR

NEWCASTLE UPON TYNE
Map 21 NZ26

Shiremoor House Farm ♀
Middle Engine Ln, New York NE29 8DZ
☎ 0191 257 6302 ▤ 0191 2578602

Situated in converted farm buildings, this pub offers large bars serving a wide range of ales and pub food. Try Jarrow River Catcher or Theakston Best Bitter to go with sizzling strips of chicken with sweet chilli sauce; steak, ale and mushroom casserole; and fillet of salmon with prawn and dill sauce. There is a covered patio with heaters for chilly evenings.
OPEN: 11-11 **BAR MEALS:** L served all week 12 D served all week 10 Av main course £6.95 ◖: Timothy Taylor's Landlord, Mordue Workie Ticket, Theakston BB, John Smiths. ♀: 12 **FACILITIES:** Children's licence Garden: Covered patio with heaters and lighting **NOTES:** Parking 120

TYNEMOUTH
Map 21 NZ36

Copperfields ★★★
Grand Hotel, Hotspur St NE30 4ER
☎ 0191 293 6666 ▤ 0191 293 6665
e-mail: info@grandhotel-uk.com
Dir: On NE coast, 10m from Newcastle-upon-Tyne
Copperfields bar is part of the Grand Hotel at Tynemouth, and is set on a cliff top commanding some of the most stunning views of natural coastline in the country. It was a frequent haunt of local boy Stan Laurel of Laurel and Hardy fame. Traditional home-cooked meals served in the bar include North Shields cod and chips, steak and mushroom pie and popular roast dinners.
OPEN: 12-11 (Sun 12-10.30) **BAR MEALS:** L served all week 12-3 D served all week 3-8 Av main course £5.50 **RESTAURANT:** L served all week 12-3 D served Mon-Sat 6.30-9.45 Closed Sun evening Av 3 course à la carte £22 Av 3 course fixed price £12.95 ◖: Durham Magus, Bass '9', Workie Ticket, Boddingtons. **FACILITIES:** Child facs Children's licence **NOTES:** Parking 16 **ROOMS:** 44 bedrooms en suite 9 family rooms s£60 d£70

England

WHITLEY BAY
Map 21 NZ37

The Waterford Arms 🗢 ♀
Collywell Bay Rd, Seaton Sluice NE26 4QZ
☎ 0191 237 0450 ▯ 0191 237 7760
Dir: *From A1 N of Newcastle take A19 at Seaton Burn then follow signs for A190 to Seaton Sluice*
The building dates back to 1899 and is located close to the small local fishing harbour, overlooking the North Sea. Splendid beaches and sand dunes are within easy reach, and the pub is very popular with walkers. Seafood dishes are the speciality, including a jumbo cod, seared swordfish, lemon sole, halibut, and crab-stuffed plaice. Recent change in management.
OPEN: 12-11 (Sun 12-10.30) **BAR MEALS:** L served all week 12-9 D served all week Sun 12-4 Av main course £5.95
RESTAURANT: L served all week 12-9 D served all week Sun 12-4 Av 3 course à la carte £7.25 ●: Pubmaster ◀: Tetleys, John Smiths, guest ales. **FACILITIES:** Food served outside **NOTES:** Parking 10

WARWICKSHIRE

ALCESTER
Map 10 SP05

The Throckmorton Arms NEW ◆◆◆◆ ♀
B49 5HX ☎ 01789 766366 ▯ 01789 762654
e-mail: info@thethrockmortonarms.co.uk
Dir: *Situated on A435 between Studley and Alcester, close to Coughton Court*
Following a major refurbishment that included tasteful interior redecoration, this roadside inn continues to offer locally acclaimed food. At lunch try home-made lasagne, the day's fish or meat pie, grilled gammon, or sirloin steak. Evening meals include honey and mustard-baked chicken fillet; poached loin of cod; pear, gorgonzola and walnut filo tart; and braised beef with leeks. Daily changing specials add another five starters and main courses, and there's an extensive desserts board.
OPEN: 12-11 (Sun 12-10.30) **BAR MEALS:** L served all week 12-2.30 D served all week 6.30-9 Sun 12-7, Fri-Sat 6.30-9.30 Av main course £8.95 **RESTAURANT:** L served all week 12-2.30 D served all week 6.30-9 sun 12-7, Fri-Sat 6.30-9.30 Av 3 course à la carte £20 ◀: Tribute, Hook Norton, Butty Bach, Bakehouse. ♀: 10 **FACILITIES:** Child facs Garden: Outside patio and dining area Dogs allowed **NOTES:** Parking 45 **ROOMS:** 10 bedrooms en suite s£50 d£60

ALDERMINSTER
Map 10 SP24

Pick of the Pubs

The Bell ◆◆◆◆ ♀
CV37 8NY ☎ 01789 450414 ▯ 01789 450998
e-mail: thebellald@aol.com web: www.thebellald.co.uk
See Pick of the Pubs on page 504

ARDENS GRAFTON
Map 10 SP15

Pick of the Pubs

The Golden Cross ♀
B50 4LG ☎ 01789 772420 ▯ 01789 773697
A stylishly refurbished rural inn, with views across the rolling Warwickshire landscape offering imaginative, freshly prepared food in unpretentious surroundings. Relax with a pint in the beamed bar, with its rug-strewn stone floor, mellow decor and scrubbed pine tables, or

continued

eat in the light and airy, high-ceilinged dining-room. Beers could come from anywhere between Scotland and Cornwall, and at least six wines are served by the glass. The owners have introduced an extensive, quarterly-changing menu which successfully blends traditional pub favourites (some given a modern twist) with more inventive dishes, such as braised lamb shank with celeriac mash and redcurrant sauce; pan-fried red snapper over coriander crushed potatoes with Thai butter; and marinated tuna loin with couscous. Puddings are home made. Owned by the same team as two village pubs in Ombersley, in neighbouring Worcestershire.

The Golden Cross

OPEN: 12-3 5-11 (All day Sat-Sun) **BAR MEALS:** L served all week 12-2.30 D served all week 6-9 Av main course £7.95 **RESTAURANT:** L served all week 12-2.30 D served all week 7-9.30 ◀: Tetley Cask, Hook Norton, Greene King IPA, monthly guest ales. ♀: 8 **FACILITIES:** Garden: Food served outside Dogs allowed in the garden only **NOTES:** Parking 80

ASTON CANTLOW
Map 10 SP16

Pick of the Pubs

King's Head ♀
21 Bearley Rd B95 6HY ☎ 01789 488242 ▯ 01789 488137
Shakespeare's parents were married in the ancient village of Aston Cantlow and had their wedding breakfast at the King's Head. It is a restored, timbered, black and white Tudor pub flanked by a huge spreading chestnut tree, with a large, hedged beer garden and an attractive terrace for summer use. Inside are all the elements you hope to find in an old inn: wooden settles, oak tables, an inglenook fireplace and a flagstone floor. The management places an emphasis on quality food and wine with cheerful service. Food is freshly prepared from a menu that changes every 6-8 weeks, but the King's Head duck supper is still a firm favourite. Other choices may include pot roast, and poussin with lemon, ginger and green olives. Fish dishes are represented by grilled kingfish with pineapple salsa and peppercorn butter, and whole Dover sole. There are well-kept real ales and a small, eclectic wine list.
OPEN: 11-3 5.30-11 (Summer open all day)
BAR MEALS: L served all week 12-2.30 D served all week 7-10
RESTAURANT: L served all week 12-2.30 D served all week 7-10 Av 3 course à la carte £20 ●: Furlong ◀: Greene King Abbot Ale, Fuller's London Pride, Best Bitter, Black Sheep. ♀: 8 **FACILITIES:** Child facs Garden: Large hedged beer garden, food in summer Dogs allowed Water **NOTES:** Parking 60

♀ 7 Number of wines by the glass

PUB WALK

The Pheasant
Withybrook - Warwickshire

THE PHEASANT,
Main Street, Withybrook, Nr Coventry,
CV7 9LT
☎ 01455 220480
Directions: Off B4112 NE of Coventry.
*Charming 17th-century coaching inn
next to the brook from which the
village takes its name. The interior is
characterised by an inglenook
fireplace, farm implements and horse
racing photographs. An extensive
menu.*
Open: 12-3 6-11 (Sun 12-10.30)
Closed: 25-26 Dec
Bar Meals: L served all week 12-2
D served all week 6.30-10 (Sun 12-9)
Children welcome and dogs allowed.
Garden and parking available.
(for full entry see page 511)

A pretty country ramble exploring unspoilt open countryside between Coventry and Rugby. The route returns to Withybrook along the Oxford Canal, which dates back to the 18th century.

Turn left on leaving the pub and follow the road towards Rugby and Pailton. Keep the brook on your right. When the road bends left, go straight on towards Shilton and follow the lane past Hopsford Spring Farm on the right and Hopsford Old Hall Farm on the left. Pass Lynton House, a white house with a well in the garden, and descend the slope. As you begin to go up the other side, turn left on to a concrete track running alongside a copse. There are telegraph poles here. On the left is the site of the medieval village of Hopsford. Follow the track, veer right at the fork by the car park sign and cross a cattle-grid. Over to the left is a large fishing lake. The fields here are ridged and furrowed and the line of

the old Oxford Canal can still be traced on the ground. Proceed towards farm outbuildings and silos at Hopsford Hall Farm, keep them on your left and continue on the track towards the railway. Go through a gate and ahead now is a small viaduct carrying the London to Manchester railway line. Pass under it, to quickly arrive at the Oxford Canal. Look for a gentle slope taking you up to the towpath. Go left and about 200 yards (183m) along the canal, look for a bridge. Make the steep climb up the bank. Turn left to cross the bridge and head towards Mobbs Wood Farm. Follow the path and as you near the farm swing left and pick up the Centenary Way which is clearly waymarked. Turn left and walk along a leafy track for about half a mile (800m). Pass through a gate and walk ahead, following the road back towards the Pheasant.

Distance: 3 1/2 miles (5.7km)
Map: OS Landranger 140
Terrain: Undulating farmland bisected by the Oxford Canal.
Paths: Towpath, tracks, paths, road. Winter: sections prone to flooding
Gradient: Gentle climbing and several short, steep ascents

*Walk submitted and checked by
Alan Bean of The Pheasant, Withybrook*

The Bell

Set in the heart of Shakespeare country, The Bell at Alderminster is an 18th-century coaching inn ideally placed for exploring the Cotswolds. Noted for its quality food, welcoming atmosphere and imaginative, constantly changing menu, it also caters for diners with specific dietary requirements: as the owners themselves put it, "Nothing is too much trouble".

The spacious conservatory restaurant overlooks a delightful old courtyard with views of the Stour Valley beyond. Food is freshly prepared, and a typical meal might consist of creamy prawn tagliatelle with lobster bisque, followed by Sue's steak and kidney pudding, and finishing with The Bell's mocha sweet. Those fond of fresh fish should keep an eye on the blackboard menu, which might offer specials like smoked haddock fishcakes; marinated hake in ginger and lemon with a herb, spinach and pepper sauce; seabass fillet on creamed leeks with herb oil; haddock and mushroom au gratin; and monkfish in Thai green coconut sauce. There's also a vegetarian list which might include aubergine, sun-dried tomato and goat's cheese tart; asparagus, quail egg and olive salad with mustard dressing and balsamic; parsnip, sage and mushroom roulade and vegetables; and mushroom stroganoff and rice. The Bell offers accommodation in seven individually styled rooms with names like The Garden room, The Blue Room and The Green room - right out of PG Wodehouse!

OPEN: 11.30-2.30 (24-30 Dec, 1Jan closed eve 6.30-11)
BAR MEALS: L served all week 12-2 D served all week 7-9.30
RESTAURANT: L served all week 12-2 D served all week 7-9.30
Av 3 course à la carte £17.50
Av 3 course fixed price £12.50
⊞: Free House
🍺: Greene King IPA, Abbot Ale, Hook Norton. ♀: 11
FACILITIES: Child facs Garden: Enclosed courtyard with views Dogs allowed Water **NOTES:** Parking 70
ROOMS: 6 bedrooms 4 en suite 2 family rooms s£27 d£48 ⊗

◆◆◆◆ ♀   Map 10 SP24
CV37 8NY
☎ 01789 450414
🖨 01789 450998
📧 info@thebellald.co.uk
🌐 www.thebellald.co.uk
Dir: On A3400 3.5m S of Stratford-upon-Avon

BROOM
Map 10 SP05

Broom Tavern ♀
High St B50 4HL ☎ 01789 773656 📠 01789 772983
e-mail: sdsmngmnt@btinternet.com
Dir: N of B439 W of Stratford-upon-Avon

Charming brick and timber 16th-century inn, reputedly haunted by a cavalier killed on the cellar steps. The same menu is offered in the bar and restaurant. Legend has it that William Shakespeare and friends fell asleep under a tree outside the Broom, after losing a drinking contest. New management from 2005, and now owned by Punch Taverns.
OPEN: 12-3 6-11 (Fri-Sat 12-11, Sun 12-3) **BAR MEALS:** L served all week 12-2 D served all week 6.30-9 Fri-Sat dinner to 9.30 Av main course £8.50 **RESTAURANT:** L served all week 12-2 D served all week 6.30-9 Fri-Sat dinner 6-9.30 🍽: Punch Taverns 🍺: Green King IPA, Adnams Bitter, Rotation Ale. ♀: 20 **FACILITIES:** Garden: Front lawn with picnic tables Dogs allowed outside **NOTES:** Parking 30

EDGEHILL
Map 11 SP34

The Castle Inn
OX15 6DJ ☎ 01295 670255 📠 01295 670521
e-mail: castleedgehill@btopenworld.com
Dir: M40 then A422. 6m until Upton House, then turn next right 1.5m
Standing on the summit of a beech-clad ridge, this is one of the most unusual pubs in the country. Built as a copy of Warwick Castle in 1742 to commemorate the centenary of the Battle of Edgehill, it opened on the anniversary of Cromwell's death in 1750, was first licensed in 1822, and acquired by Hook Norton one hundred years later. Traditional, home-cooked dishes such as mixed grills, goujons of lemon sole, and liver and bacon casserole appear on the menu along with ploughman's lunches and snacks in a basket.
OPEN: 11.15-2.30 6.15-11 (Summer weekends open all day)
BAR MEALS: L served all week 12-2 D served all week 6.30-9 Av main course £7 🍽: Hook Norton 🍺: Hook Norton Best, Old Hooky & Generation, Hooky Dark, Guest Ales. **FACILITIES:** Garden: Large garden area good views **NOTES:** Parking 40

 Principal Beers for sale

Disabled people and those with Assist Dogs have new rights of access to pubs, restaurants and hotels under the Disability Discrimination Act of 1 October 2004. For more information see the website at www.drc gb.org/open4all/rights/2004.asp

---

ETTINGTON
Map 10 SP24

The Houndshill ♀
Banbury Rd CV37 7NS ☎ 01789 740267 📠 01789 740075
Dir: On A422 SE of Stratford-upon-Avon

Family-run inn situated at the heart of England, making it a perfect base for exploring popular tourist attractions such as Oxford, Blenheim, Stratford and the Cotswolds. Pleasant tree-lined garden is especially popular with families. Typical dishes range from poached fillet of salmon and faggots, mash and minted peas, to supreme of chicken and ham and mushroom tagliatelle. Alternatively, try cold ham off the bone, home-made steak and kidney pie, or breaded wholetail scampi.
OPEN: 12-3 7-11 (Sun 12-3, 7-10.30) Closed: Dec 25-28
BAR MEALS: L served all week 12-2 D served all week 7-9.30
RESTAURANT: L served all week 12-2 D served all week 9.30
Av 3 course à la carte £15 🍽: Free House 🍺: Hook Norton Best, Spitfire. ♀: 7 **FACILITIES:** Child facs Garden: Large lawn with benches, children's play area Dogs allowed **NOTES:** Parking 50
ROOMS: 8 bedrooms en suite 2 family rooms s£45 d£65 (♦♦♦)

FARNBOROUGH
Map 11 SP44

Pick of the Pubs

The Inn at Farnborough 🌐 🍽 ♀
OX17 1DZ ☎ 01295 690615 📠 01295 690032
e-mail: enquiries@innatfarnborough.co.uk
Formerly the butcher's house on the Farnborough estate, once known as the Butcher's Arms, the inn is a Grade II listed free house in a picturesque village setting. Parts of the building date back 400 years, and include an original inglenook fireplace. The inn is ideally placed for visitors to the nearby National Trust property of Farnborough Hall or the Civil War battleground at Edgehill. A good range of real ales and 14 wines by the glass are served alongside dishes based on high-quality Heart of England produce. Typical dishes are confit of Lighthorne lamb with dauphinoise potatoes, braised red cabbage and rosemary jus, or pan-fried pave of Oxfordshire beef with creamy field mushrooms, port and cracked black peppercorn jus. Families are welcome, with smaller portions for children always available, and there is a funky private dining room with claret walls and a zebra print ceiling.
OPEN: 12-3 6-11 (All day Sat/Sun) **BAR MEALS:** L served all week 12-3 D served all week 6-11 all day Sat/Sun
RESTAURANT: L served all week 12-3 D served all week 6-11 all day Sat/Sun Av 3 course à la carte £22.95 Av 3 course fixed price £12.95 🍺: Abbot Ale, Spitfire, Budwar, Hook Norton Best.
♀: 14 **FACILITIES:** Child facs Children's licence Garden: sunny, stylish, terraced garden Dogs allowed dog bowls **NOTES:** Parking 40

GREAT WOLFORD   Map 10 SP23

Pick of the Pubs

The Fox & Hounds Inn ◆◆◆◆ ♀
CV36 5NQ ☎ 01608 674220 ▤ 01608 674160
e-mail: info@thefoxandhoundsinn.com
Dir: Off A44 NE of Moreton-in-Marsh
An unspoilt village hostelry.nestling in glorious
countryside on the edge of the Cotswolds. Good food,
good beer and exceptional whiskies are all on offer, along
with an inviting ambience enhanced by old settles, Tudor
inglenook fireplaces and solid ceiling beams adorned with
jugs or festooned with hops. The bar entrance is a
double-hinged 'coffin door' which once allowed coffins to
be brought in and laid out prior to the funeral service.
Allegedly, a secret tunnel, along which bodies were
sometimes carried, linked the cellar with the nearby
church, and obviously, there have been many ghostly
sightings. The famously controversial pub sign features
Tony Blair and a number of foxes and foxhounds. As well
as a range of traditional ales, the bar offers a staggering
selection of almost 200 fine whiskies. On the menu, look
for home-made salmon fishcakes, oven-roasted guinea
fowl, grilled Dover sole, and rib-eye steak.
OPEN: 12-2.30 6-11 Closed: !st wk Jan **BAR MEALS:** L served
Tue-Sun 12-2 D served Tue-Sat 7-9 Av main course £11.50
RESTAURANT: L served Tue-Sun 12-2 D served Tue-Sat 7-9
Av 3 course à la carte £20 ⊕: Free House ◀: Hook Norton
Best, guest beers. ♀: 7 **FACILITIES:** Garden: Cottage style
garden overlooking Cotswolds Dogs allowed Water
NOTES: Parking 15 **ROOMS:** 3 bedrooms en suite s£45 d£70
No children overnight

HATTON   Map 10 SP26

The Case is Altered NEW
Case Ln, Five Ways CV35 7JD ☎ 01926 484206
This traditional free house proudly carries the standard for
the old style of pub. It serves no food and does not allow
children. That aside, it's a thoroughly welcoming spot for
adults who appreciate the pleasures of a quiet pint. Hook
Norton beers have a strong presence, and there is always a
local and national guest ale to sup while enjoying lively
conversation or just appreciating the atmosphere.
OPEN: 12-2.30 6-11 (Sun 12-2 7-10.30) ◀: Hook Norton Old
Hooky, Hooky Dark, Greene King IPA, guest beers.
NOTES: Parking 20 No credit cards

ILMINGTON   Map 10 SP24

Pick of the Pubs

The Howard Arms ♀
Lower Green CV36 4LT ☎ 01608 682226 ▤ 01608 682226
e-mail: info@howardarms.com web: www.howardarms.com
Dir: Off A429 or A3400
On the picturesque village green of Ilmington, cradled in
the Cotswold Hills, is this mellow 400-year-old Cotswold
stone inn. Drawing from their years of experience, the
proprietors have carefully re-modelled the pub to create a
superb relaxed - and, incidentally, award winning -
environment. Menus are interesting, change weekly and
make full use of seasonal produce. Enjoy starters like
grilled lamb koftas with couscous and minted yoghurt; or

twice-baked goat's cheese and thyme soufflé. Main
choices range through traditional fish pie; pan-fried
calves' liver with buttered onions, crisp bacon and
balsamic dressing; and fennel and potato pancakes,
woodland mushrooms and crème fraîche. Home-made
puddings such as Mrs G's toffee meringue could be
rounded off with a nip of exclusive English apple brandy.
Three delightful en-suite bedrooms are there to tempt
you to stay on.

The Howard Arms

OPEN: 11-3 6-11 (Sun 6.30-10.30) Closed: 25 Dec
BAR MEALS: L served all week 12-2 D served all week 7-9
Av main course £12 **RESTAURANT:** L served all week 12-2
D served all week 7-9 Fixed menu Sun only, Fri-Sat 7-9.30, Sun
12-2.30 6-10.30 Av 3 course fixed price £19.50 ⊕: Free House
◀: Everards Tiger Best, North Cotswold Genesis, Greene King
Abbot Ale, Timothy Taylor landlord. ♀: 15
FACILITIES: Garden: 1/3 acre, bordered by stream, terrace area
Dogs allowed Water bowl outside **NOTES:** Parking 25
ROOMS: 3 bedrooms en suite s£75 d£97 (◆◆◆◆◆) No
children overnight ⊗

KENILWORTH   Map 10 SP27

Clarendon House
High St CV8 1LZ ☎ 01926 857668 ▤ 01926 850669
e-mail: info@clarendonhousehotel.com
Dir: From A452 pass castle, turn L into Castle Hill then into High Street
The original (1430) timber-framed Castle Tavern is
incorporated within the hotel, still supported by the oak tree
around which it was built. Big, comfortable sofas indoors and
a heated patio outside. From the brasserie menu expect Thai
chicken curry and rice, salad of pigeon and pancetta, honey
and lemon dressing, and kedgeree fishcakes with a light curry
sauce and quails' eggs. The specials board might feature pan-
fried wild boar steak with crushed parsnips, roasted baby
onions with cranberry and thyme jus.
OPEN: 11-11 (Sun 12-10.30) Closed: 25-26 Dec, 1 Jan
BAR MEALS: L served all week 12-10 D served all week 12-10
Av main course £9.50 **RESTAURANT:** L served all week 12-10
D served all week 12-10 Av 3 course à la carte £18 ⊕: Old English
Inns ◀: Greene King Abbot Ale, IPA. **FACILITIES:** Garden: Patio
garden seats about 100. Outdoor heating Dogs allowed
NOTES: Parking 35 **ROOMS:** 22 bedrooms en suite 2 family rooms
s£57.50 d£79.50 (★★)

> Restaurant and Bar Meal times indicate the times
> when food is available. Last orders may be
> approximately 30 minutes before the times stated

continued

LAPWORTH   Map 10 SP17

Pick of the Pubs

The Boot Inn ♀
Old Warwick Rd B94 6JU ☎ 01564 782464 ▤ 01564 784989
Standing beside the Grand Union Canal in the unspoilt
village of Lapworth, this lively and convivial 16th-century
former coaching inn is well worth seeking out. Apart from
its smartly refurbished interior, there's an attractive
garden with canopy and patio heaters for those cooler
evenings. But the main draw is the interesting global wine
list and modern brasserie-style food, with wide-ranging
menus that deliver home-produced dishes in a delightful,
modern style. 'First plates' might include chicken liver
parfait, apple chutney and warm brioche, or seared squid
sweet chilli and leaves. Move on to selections like Old
English Gloucester sausages, onion sauce and mash;
haddock in tempura batter with pea purée and sauce
gribiche; or chargrilled rib-eye steak, roast shallots,
brandy and dijon butter.
OPEN: 11-3 5.30-11 (Summer Open all day) Closed: Dec 25
BAR MEALS: L served all week 12-2.30 D served all week 7-10
Av main course £10 **RESTAURANT:** L served all week 12-2.30
D served all week 7-10 Av 3 course à la carte £20 Av 4 course
fixed price £25 ⬡: ◖: Greene King Old Speckled Hen,
Wadworth 6X, Scottish Courage John Smith's, Brew XI.
FACILITIES: Child facs Garden: Patio and grass with heaters &
canopy Dogs allowed on leads Water **NOTES:** Parking 200

LOWER BRAILES   Map 10 SP33

The George Hotel ♀
High St OX15 5HN ☎ 01608 685223 ▤ 01608 685916
e-mail: thegeorgehotel@speed-e-mail.com
Dir: B4035 toward Shipston on Stour
Reputedly built as lodgings for the monks constructing the
12th-century village church, the George later served its time
as a coaching inn. Appropriately, the original outhouses
have been rebuilt to provide stabling. The parish has 25
miles of footpaths, several of which require climbing a flight
of 99 steps - ideal for working up an appetite, a thirst, or
both. Typical dishes are rib-eye steaks, fish and chips, spicy
sausages and mash, and 'walking' and 'flying' game pies.
OPEN: 11-11 (Sun 12-10.30) **BAR MEALS:** L served all week 12-2
D served all week 7-9.30 Av main course £9.65
RESTAURANT: L served all week 12-2 D served all week 7-9.30
Av 3 course à la carte £19 ⬡: Hook Norton ◖: Hook Norton -
Generation, Mild, Hooky Best, Old Hooky & Seasonal Beers.
FACILITIES: Garden: Large open plan Dogs allowed Water
NOTES: Parking 60

LOWSONFORD   Map 10 SP16

Fleur De Lys ♀
Lapworth St B95 5HJ ☎ 01564 782431 ▤ 01564 782431
e-mail: Fleurdelys.solihull@laurelpubco.com
Dir: A34 (Birmingham to Stratford)
A galleried dining room, low beams and log fires set the
scene for casual dining at this 17th-century pub. In summer,
the large canalside garden is the ideal place to enjoy a drink
or meal, and there's even a safe fenced area for young
children. Comprehensive menus range from chicken Caesar
salad or seasonal soup and quiche starters to hearty main
courses like braised British beef ribs, or grilled plaice with
roasted cherry tomatoes.

continued

Fleur De Lys

OPEN: 9-11 (Sun 10-10.30) **BAR MEALS:** L served all week 12-10
D served all week Sun 12-9 Av main course £8 ⬡: ◖: Abbott Ale,
Greene King IPA, Guest Ale. ♀: 16 **FACILITIES:** Child facs Garden:
Large canalside Dogs allowed Water **NOTES:** Parking 150 ⊛

MONKS KIRBY   Map 11 SP48

The Bell Inn ♀
Bell Ln CV23 0QY ☎ 01788 832352 ▤ 01788 832352
e-mail: belindagb@aol.com
Dir: Off The Fosseway junct with B4455
The Spanish owners of this quaint, timbered inn, once a
priory gatehouse and then a brewhouse cottage, describe it
as "a corner of Spain in the heart of England". Mediterranean
and traditional cuisine play an important role on the menu.
Red snapper gallega, saddle of lamb, fillet Catalan, chicken
piri piri, and Mexican hot pot are popular favourites. Extensive
range of starters and speciality dishes.
OPEN: 12-2.30 7-11 Closed: 26 Dec, 1 Jan **BAR MEALS:** L served
Tue-Sun 12-2.30 D served all week 7-11 **RESTAURANT:** L served
Tue-Sun 12-2.30 D served all week 7-11 ⬡: Free House
◖: Boddingtons. ♀: 127 **FACILITIES:** Garden: overlooks a stream
& buttercup meadow **NOTES:** Parking 80

NAPTON ON THE HILL   Map 11 SP46

The Bridge at Napton NEW
Southam Rd CV47 8NQ ☎ 01926 812466
e-mail: tim@schlapfer.fsnet.co.uk
*Dir: Situated at Bridge 111 on the Oxford Canal on A425 2m out of
Southam and 1m from Napton-on-the-Hill*
Built as a stabling inn, with its own turning point for barges,
on the Oxford Canal at Bridge 111. With a restaurant, three
bars and a large garden it is an ideal place to moor the
narrowboat, park the car, or lean the bike against a wall. Look
past the menu's dodgy puns to home-made beef and ale pie;
chicken tikka masala; smoky fisherman's crumble; butternut
squash bake; or any of the freshly prepared daily specials.
OPEN: 12-3 6-11 (Apr-Nov open all day Sat-Sun) Nov-Apr closed
Sun eve, Mon lunch **BAR MEALS:** L served all week 12-2 Lunch
Tues-Sun in winter Av main course £8.50 **RESTAURANT:** L served
all week 12-2 D served all week 6-9 Lunch Tues-Sun, dinner Mon-Sat
(winter) Av 3 course à la carte £15.50 ◖: 3 guest ales.
FACILITIES: Child facs Garden: 0.75acre on canalside, lawns, seating
Dogs allowed **NOTES:** Parking 35

Website addresses are included where available.
The AA cannot be held responsible for the
content of any of these websites

PRESTON BAGOT   Map 10 SP16

The Crabmill ♀
B95 5EE ☎ 01926 843342 ▤ 01926 843989
e-mail: thecrabmill@amserve.net
Dir: Telephone for directions
Crab apple cider was once made at this 15th-century hostelry,
which is set in beautiful rural surroundings. Restored to create
an upmarket venue, the pub has a light, open feel with a
range of themed dining rooms, including a 'rude' room with
risqué caricatures. An Italian influence is evident in both the
decor and menu, with the dishes such as Sicilian mutton pie,
swordfish with herb and lemon polenta, and pappardelle with
spinach, rocket and Somerset brie.
OPEN: 11-11 **BAR MEALS:** L served all week 12-2.30 D served
Mon-Sat 6.30-9.30 Sun 12.30-3.30 Av main course £12.50
RESTAURANT: L served all week 12-2.30 D served Mon-Sat
6.30-9.30 Sun 12.30-3.30 Av 3 course à la carte £25 ⊛: Wadworth
6X, Greene King IPA, Greene King Abbot Ale. **FACILITIES:** Garden:
Beautiful landscaped rolling gardens Dogs allowed Water provided

RATLEY   Map 11 SP34

The Rose and Crown ♀
OX15 6DS ☎ 01295 678148
Dir: Follow Edgehill signs, 7m N of Banbury on A422.
Following the Battle of Edgehill in 1642, a Roundhead was
discovered in the chimney of this 11th (or 12th)-century pub
and beheaded in the hearth. His ghost reputedly haunts the
building. Enjoy the peaceful village location and the
traditional pub food, perhaps including beef and ale pie,
scampi and chips, chicken curry and the Sunday roast.
OPEN: 12-2.30 6.30-11 (Sun 12-3.30, 7-11) **BAR MEALS:** L served
all week 12-2 D served all week 7-9 Av main course £10.50
RESTAURANT: L served Tue-Sun D served Tue-Sat 7-9.30
Av 3 course à la carte £18 ⊜: Free House ⊛: Wells Bombardier &
Eagle IPA, Greene King Old Speckled Hen & guest ale. ♀: 8
FACILITIES: Garden: Garden with wooden benches Dogs allowed
Water, Fireplace **NOTES:** Parking 4

RUGBY   Map 11 SP57

Pick of the Pubs

Golden Lion Inn ★★ ☜ ♀
Easenhall CV23 0JA ☎ 01788 833577 ▤ 01788 832878
web: www.goldenlioninn.co.uk
Dir: From Rugby Town Centre take A426, follow signs for Nuneaton

Low oak-beamed ceilings and narrow doorways
characterise this charming 16th-century free house. James
and Claudia are the third generation of the Austin family
at the Golden Lion, where you'll find traditional ales,

roaring winter fires and an extensive wine list. Choose
between home-cooked bar food or gourmet dining in the
candlelit restaurant. Start, perhaps, with Scottish smoked
salmon and prawns on dressed leaves; or grilled goats'
cheese with apples, walnuts and celery. Typical main
course choices include roast Gressingham duck with red
cabbage and mustard mash; vegetarian penne pasta with
salad and garlic bread; and pan-roasted cod with
boulangère potatoes and wilted greens. The pub is set
amidst idyllic countryside in one of Warwickshire's best
kept villages, and its 21 en-suite bedrooms, some with
four-poster beds, offer outstanding accommodation.
Smoking is permitted in the large landscaped garden, but
the restaurant, bar and bedrooms are non-smoking.
OPEN: 11-11 **BAR MEALS:** L served all week 12-2 D served all
week 6-9.30 Sun carvery 12-3, Sun bar menu 3-9
RESTAURANT: L served Mon-Sun 12-2 D served Mon-Sun
6-9.30 Sun carvery 12-3, Sun bar menu 12-8.45 ⊜: Free House
⊛: Greene King Abbot Ale, Ruddles County, Old Speckled Hen,
Greene King IPA. ♀: 6 **FACILITIES:** Child facs Garden: Large
landscaped garden, good views **NOTES:** Parking 80
ROOMS: 21 bedrooms en suite 3 family rooms s£45 d£56

SHIPSTON ON STOUR   Map 10 SP24

The Cherington Arms ☜ ♀
Cherington CV36 5HS ☎ 01608 686233
e-mail: thecheringtonarms@hooknorton.tablesir.com
Dir: 12m from Stratford Upon Avon 14m from Leamington and Warwick
10m from Woodstock
This attractive 17th-century brick-built inn offers exposed
beams, stripped wood furniture and a feature inglenook
fireplace. Dining options are chalked up on blackboards
around the place, as the use of fresh local produce makes
forward planning difficult and the printing of menus
impossible. Possible restaurant mains include oven roasted
salmon with rocket and watercress salad; rump of lamb with
fondant potato, roasted garlic and shallots; and breast of
chicken stuffed with sun dried tomato on a cream pesto
sauce.
OPEN: 12-15 6.30-11.30 (Closed Mon lunch time)
BAR MEALS: L served Tue-Fri 12-2, 12-2.30 Sat, 12-3 Sun D served
Tue-Thurs 7-9, 7-9.30 Fri-Sat Av main course £7
RESTAURANT: L served Tue-Sun 12-2 D served Tue-Sat 7-9, 7-9.30
Fri-Sat Av 3 course à la carte £21.25 ⊛: Hook Norton Best Bitter,
Hook Norton Generation, Hook Norton Old Hooky, guest ales. ♀: 10
FACILITIES: Child facs Garden: Large unspoilt orchard and patio
with Mill Race Dogs allowed Water **NOTES:** Parking 40

Pick of the Pubs

The Red Lion ♦♦♦♦ ♀
Main St, Long Compton CV36 5JS
☎ 01608 684221 ▤ 01608 684221
e-mail: redlionhot@aol.com
See Pick of the Pubs on opposite page

Pick of the Pubs have that extra special quality
that makes them stand out from the crowd.
Their entries are highlighted, and may be a
full page

continued

Pick of the Pubs

The Red Lion

A grade II listed stone-built coaching inn dating from 1748, located in an area of outstanding natural beauty and ideally situated for such major attractions as Stratford upon Avon, Warwick, Oxford and the Cotswold Wildlife Park. With past tales of witches in the village and a nearby prehistoric stone circle, there is much to interest the historian as well as the rambler.

The newly-refurbished interior retains an old world charm with log fires, stone walls and oak beams yet offers the modern facilities expected today. The traditional English menu is extensive and caters for all tastes from interesting sandwiches, baguettes, and light bites to substantial choices on the main menu and specials on the daily board. Expect baked avocado with stilton and crispy bacon, and home-made salmon and cod cakes to start followed by whole roasted sea bass; steak and Hook Norton pie with blackberry and apple crumble, or home-made sticky toffee pudding. An extensive wine list includes sparkling wines and champagnes.

OPEN: 11-2.30 6-11 (Fri-Sat 11-11 Sun 12-10.30)
BAR MEALS: L served Mon-Thurs 12-2.30 D served Mon-Thurs 6-9 Fri-Sun 12-9.30
🍺: Free House
🍷: Hook Norton Best, Timothy Taylor's Landlord, Adnams Broadside.
FACILITIES: Child facs Garden: Large garden with views of surrounding hills Dog friendly
NOTES: Parking 60
ROOMS: 5 bedrooms en suite 1 family room s£40 d£60

◆◆◆◆ ♀   Map 10 SP24
Main St, Long Compton CV36 5JS
☎ 01608 684221
🖷 01608 684968
e red@redlion3.wanadoo.co.uk
Dir: On A3400 between Shipston on Stour & Chipping Norton

SHIPSTON ON STOUR continued

White Bear Hotel ♀
High St CV36 4AJ ☎ 01608 661558 🖹 01608 662612
e-mail: whitebearhot@hotmail.com

This former coaching inn, parts of which date from the 16th century, has a Georgian façade overlooking the market place. It is a lively pub serving good food and fine ales, and the two beamed bars are full of character. A typical menu might include Gloucester Old Spot pork chop with ginger and soy sauce; marinated sea bass with thyme, lemon and bacon; and tomato and spinach risotto. A good selection of sandwiches, baguettes and snacks is available at lunchtime.
OPEN: 11-11 (Sun 12-10.30) **BAR MEALS:** 12-2 6.30-9.30
RESTAURANT: 12-2 6.30-9.30 🍴: Punch Taverns 🍺: Marstons Pedigree, Interbrew Bass & Guest Ales. **FACILITIES:** Garden: Patio, food served outside Dogs allowed Water **NOTES:** Parking 20

SHREWLEY
Map 10 SP26

Pick of the Pubs

The Durham Ox Restaurant and Country Pub NEW ♀
Shrewley Common CV35 7AY
☎ 01926 842283 🖹 0121 713 2189
e-mail: hospitalityengineers@btinternet.com
Dir: 1m from Hatton
Somewhere between the 19th and the 21st centuries, the Durham Ox combines old beams, a roaring fire and traditional hospitality with chic contemporary furniture and an up-to-date menu. Samples from the restaurant summer menu include smoked haddock, salmon and prawn fishcake; slow-cooked escalope of free range pork on champ potatoes; and pan-fried Clonakilty white pudding with creamed potato and onion gravy. Children will enjoy the safe play area, and the external bar and barbecue can be hired for private functions.
OPEN: 12-11 **BAR MEALS:** L served all week 12-3 D served all week 6-10 Sun 12-9 Av main course £9.95
RESTAURANT: L served all week 12-3 D served all week 6-10 Sun 12-9 Av 3 course à la carte £18.50 🍺: IPA, Old Speckled Hen, Guinness. ♀: 12 **FACILITIES:** Garden: Spacious gardens with log cabin, BBQ, seating **NOTES:** Parking 100

Do you have a favourite pub that we have overlooked? Please use the Reader's Report form at the back of this guide to tell us all about it

---

 Principal Beers for sale

STRATFORD-UPON-AVON
Map 10 SP25

The Dirty Duck
Waterside CV37 6BA ☎ 01789 297312 🖹 01789 293441
Frequented by members of the Royal Shakespeare Company from the nearby theatre, this traditional, partly Elizabethan inn has a splendid raised terrace overlooking the River Avon. In addition to the interesting range of real ales, a comprehensive choice of food is offered. Light bites, pastas, salads and mains at lunchtime, plus pub classics and 'make it special' dishes at night, from rustic sharing bread with herbs, garlic and olives to roast rack of lamb.
OPEN: 11-11 (Sun 12-10.30) **BAR MEALS:** L served all week 12-3 D served Mon-Sat 5.30-11 Av main course £6
RESTAURANT: L served all week 12-2 D served Mon-Sat 5.30 Av 3 course à la carte £15 🍴: Whitbread 🍺: Flowers Original, Morland Old Speckled Hen, Wadworth 6X. **FACILITIES:** Garden: terrace overlooking theatre garden and river Dogs allowed at manager's discretion

Pick of the Pubs

The Fox and Goose Inn ◆◆◆◆ 🏵 ♀
CV37 8DD ☎ 01608 682293 🖹 01608 682293
web: www.foxandgoose.co.uk
Dir: 1m off A3400, between Shiptson-on-Stour and Stratfield

Stylish pub/restaurant-with-rooms that has been transformed by local entrepreneur Sue Gray. To find it, look for Armscote close to the River Stour mid-way between Stratford and Shipston. Two old cottages and a former blacksmith's forge have been converted to create a buzzy, cosmopolitan atmosphere. The deep red-walled bar and brightly painted dining room, along with slightly eccentric, luxury en suite bedrooms, have proved an instant hit since their opening just a few years ago. Matching the decor and ambience is a daily-changing menu from a team of young chefs whose overall talent belies their years. Seared scallops on wilted pak choi with sweet chilli dressing; home-made tagliatelle with roast peppers, goats' cheese and pepper essence; and calves' liver and bacon on bubble and squeak with red wine gravy are followed perhaps by dark chocolate torte. Regular monthly fish nights and summer barbecues on a decked terrace in the pretty country garden are popular.
OPEN: 12-3 6-11 Closed: 25-26 Dec **BAR MEALS:** L served all week 12-2.30 D served all week 7-9.30 Av main course £11.50
RESTAURANT: L served all week 12-2.30 D served all week 7-9.30 Av 3 course à la carte £21 🍴: Free House 🍺: Hook Norton Old Hooky, Greene King Old Speckled Hen, Wells Bombardier, Fuller's London Pride. ♀: 8 **FACILITIES:** Garden: Deck covered by pergola, large grassy garden
NOTES: Parking 20 **ROOMS:** 4 bedrooms en suite s£55 d£85 No children overnight

The One Elm NEW ♀
1 Guild St CV37 6QZ
Dir: In Stratford-upon-Avon town centre
Standing on its own in the heart of town, the One Elm has two dining rooms: downstairs is intimate, even with the buzzy bar close by, while upstairs feels grander. The menu features chargrilled côte de boeuf for two, Aberdeen Angus rump steak, and tuna, as well as other main courses. The deli board offers all-day nuts and seeds, cheeses, charcuterie and antipasti. The secluded terrace induces in some a feeling of being abroad.
OPEN: 11.30-11 Closed: 25 Dec **BAR MEALS:** L served all week 12-2.30 D served all week 6.30-10 Sun all day Av main course £10.50
RESTAURANT: L served all week 12-2.30 D served all week 6.30-10 Sun all day ▄: London Pride, Old Speckled Hen, Timothy Taylor Landlord. ♀: 9 **FACILITIES:** Child facs Garden: Courtyard with tables Dogs allowed **NOTES:** Parking 12

TEMPLE GRAFTON
Map 10 SP15

The Blue Boar Inn ♀
B49 6NR ☎ 01789 750010 ▤ 01789 750635
e-mail: blueboar@covlink.co.uk web: www.blueboarinn.co.uk
Dir: Turn to Temple Grafton off A46. Pub at 1st x-roads

An inn since the early 1600s, it now features a glass-covered well from which water was formerly drawn for brewing. Not long before it first opened for business, William Shakespeare married Ann Hathaway in the village church. Dishes on offer include pan-fried monkfish noisettes served with a tomato and orange coulis; chicken supreme wrapped in smoked bacon and filled with cheese and chives; and Greenland halibut with caper and anchovy sauce. Open fires in winter, and good views of the Cotswolds from the patio garden.
OPEN: 11-12 **BAR MEALS:** L served all week 12-3 D served all week 6-10 (Sat 12-10, Sun 12-9) Av main course £8.50
RESTAURANT: L served all week 12-3 D served all week 6-10 Av 3 course à la carte £20 Av 4 course fixed price £13.95 ⊟: Free House ▄: Morland Old Speckled Hen, Scottish Courage Theakston XB & Best. ♀: 20 **FACILITIES:** Children's licence Garden: Terraced patio area, tables, benches **NOTES:** Parking 50
ROOMS: 15 bedrooms en suite s£48.50 d£68.50 (♦♦♦)

WARWICK
Map 10 SP26

Pick of the Pubs

The Tilted Wig
11 Market Place CV34 4SA ☎ 01926 410466
& 411534 ▤ 01926 495740 e-mail: thetiltedwig@hotmail.com
Dir: From M40 J15 follow A429 into Warwick, after 1.5m L into Brook St on into Market Place
Overlooking the market square, this attractive pine-furnished hostelry combines the atmosphere of a

brasserie, wine bar and restaurant all rolled into one. Originally a coaching inn and now a Grade II listed building. The name stems from its proximity to the Crown Court. A wide range of cask-conditioned ales and a good menu offering quality, home-cooked dishes, which might include fish and chips, steak and ale pie, or chicken and leek pie. A variety of sandwiches and baguettes are available, as well as specials from a changing board.
OPEN: 11-11 (Sun 12-10.30) Closed: Dec 25
BAR MEALS: L served all week 12-3 D served Mon-Sat 6-9 Av main course £7 ⊟: Punch Taverns ▄: Carlsberg-Tetley Tetely Bitter, Adnams Broadside. **FACILITIES:** Garden
NOTES: Parking 6 **ROOMS:** 4 bedrooms en suite s£58 d£58 (♦♦♦♦)

WELFORD-ON-AVON
Map 10 SP15

The Four Alls NEW ♀
Binton Bridges CV37 8PW ☎ 01789 750228 ▤ 01789 750228
Dir: B439 from Stratford then left
Medieval peasants worked for all, priests prayed for all, knights fought for all, and kings ruled all - thus the Four Alls. The recently refurbished restaurant in this 400-year-old pub is decorated with modern art, and several tables look directly out over the River Avon. Modern English cooking produces lamb shank with parsnip and sweet potato purée; swordfish with linguine, wild mushrooms and herb dressing; and daily specials of baked cod fillet with saffron-crushed potatoes.
OPEN: 11-3 6-11 (Open all day wk ends & BHs)
BAR MEALS: L served all week 12-2.30 D served all week 7-10 Av main course £9.95 **RESTAURANT:** L served all week 12-2 D served all week 7-10 Av 3 course à la carte £22.50 Av 3 course fixed price £11.95 ⊟: Whitbread ▄: Black Sheep, Wadworth 6X, Greene King IPA. ♀: 10 **FACILITIES:** Child facs Children's licence Garden: Front garden play area, back garden seating **NOTES:** Parking 60

WITHYBROOK
Map 11 SP48

The Pheasant ⬭ ♀
Main St CV7 9LT ☎ 01455 220480 ▤ 01455 221296
e-mail: thepheasant01@hotmail.com
Dir: Off B4112 NE of Coventry

In the same ownership since 1981, this charming 17th-century free house stands beside the brook where withies were once cut for fencing. An inglenook fireplace, farm implements and horse-racing photographs characterise the interior, and the pub is non-smoking throughout. Daily blackboard specials supplement the extensive menu, which includes braised faggots; venison pie; pan-fried pork cutlets; tuna steak in lime and coriander; and vegetarian goulash. Outside tables overlook the Withy Brook itself.
OPEN: 12-3 6-11 (Sun 12-10.30) Closed: 25-26 Dec

continued

continued

England

WITHYBROOK continued

BAR MEALS: L served all week 12-2 D served all week 6.30-10 (Sun 12-9) 🍴: Free House 🍺: Courage Directors, Theakstons Best, John Smiths Smooth. ♀: 9 **FACILITIES:** Garden: Tables alongside a brook with grassy banks Dogs allowed in the garden only at manager's discretion **NOTES:** Parking 55 ⊘

See Pub Walk on page 503

WOOTTON WAWEN
Map 10 SP16

Pick of the Pubs

The Bulls Head ♀
Stratford Rd B95 6BD ☎ 01564 792511 ⬛ 795803
Dir: On A3400
An extensively refurbished inn converted from two separate cottages built in 1597, and handy for touring and exploring Warwickshire and the Cotswolds, with Henley-in-Arden, Stratford and a host of historic houses and family attractions just a stone's throw away. Low beams, open fires and old pews set the scene in the bar and snug areas, and the same style is maintained in the 'great hall' restaurant. Outside, you'll discover a lawned garden and paved patio surrounded by mature trees. Light snacks and lunches served in the bar might include bloomer sandwiches and a range of salads, while more substantial dishes range from steak and ale pie, and battered haddock, to 8oz gammon steak, and lasagne. From the evening restaurant menu try crispy duck salad or home-made chicken liver parfait, followed by stir-fry chicken with pak choi; salmon with wilted lettuce and cucumber salad; herb-crusted rack of lamb; or game pie.
OPEN: 12-11 (Sun 12-10.30) **BAR MEALS:** L served all week 12-2.30 D served all week 6-9 (Sun 12-4) Av main course £11.25 **RESTAURANT:** L served all week 12-2.30 D served Mon-Sat 6-9.30 (Sun 12-4) Av 3 course à la carte £20 🍴: W'hampton & Dudley 🍺: Marston's Pedigree, Banks Bitter, Banks Original plus guest ales. ♀: 24 **FACILITIES:** Garden: Lawned area & paved patio surrounded by trees Dogs allowed Water Bowls **NOTES:** Parking 30

WEST MIDLANDS

BARSTON
Map 10 SP27

The Malt Shovel 🎖️ 🐟 ♀
Barston Ln B92 0JP ☎ 01675 443223 ⬛ 01675 443223
Bustling, award-winning free house and restaurant converted from an early 20th-century mill. The bar is welcoming and relaxed, while the popular barn is for slightly more formal dining. An imaginative all-fish specials list partners an equally inventive menu, with starters such as pan-fried quail fillets with capers and red wine sauce; and mains including kidneys, bacon and field mushrooms on toast; and braised lamb with bombay potatoes and ratatouille.
OPEN: 12-3 5.30-11 (Sun & BHs 12-7) **BAR MEALS:** L served all week 12-2.30 D served Mon-Sat 6.30-9.45 Sun 12-3.30 Av main course £12 **RESTAURANT:** L served all week 12-2.30 D served Mon-Sat 7-9.45 Sun 12-3.30 Av 3 course à la carte £25 Av 3 course fixed price £25 🍴: Free House 🍺: London Pride, Brew XI, Bombardier, Old Speckled Hen. ♀: 8 **FACILITIES:** Children's licence Garden: Large, established garden with gazebo & seating **NOTES:** Parking 70

BIRMINGHAM
Map 10 SP08

The Mug House Inn & Angry Chef Restaurant
Bewdley 01299 402543

Nestled alongside the river Severn lies the picturesque town of Bewdley, known for its Georgian architecture and quaint cottages, with stunning riverside frontage, where you will find The Mug House, Bewdley's finest Inn and Restaurant on the riverside. Wander into the warm and friendly welcome, soak up the atmosphere in this wonderful old Inn with great ales & fine food.

See entry under BEWDLEY, Worcestershire

The Peacock 🍺
Icknield St, Forhill, nr King's Norton B38 0EH
☎ 01564 823232 ⬛ 01564 829593

Despite its out of the way location, at Forhill just outside Birmingham, the Peacock keeps very busy serving traditional ales and a varied menu. Chalkboards display the daily specials, among which you might find braised partridge on a bed of pheasant sausage and mash, whole sea bass with crab, grilled shark steak with light curry butter, pan-fried sirloin steak with mild mushroom and pepper sauce, or lamb fillet with apricot and walnut stuffing. Several friendly ghosts are in residence, and one of their tricks is to disconnect the taps from the barrels. Large gardens with two patios. Booking essential if dining.
OPEN: 11-11 (Sun 12-10.30) **BAR MEALS:** L served all week 11 D served all week 10 Av main course £7.95

continued

RESTAURANT: L served all week 12-10 D served all week 6-10
🍴: 🍺: Hobsons Best Bitter, Theakstons Old Peculier, Enville Ale.
FACILITIES: Garden: Patio at front, food served outside Dogs
allowed Water **NOTES:** Parking 100

CHADWICK END
Map 10 SP27

Pick of the Pubs

The Orange Tree NEW ♀
Warwick Rd B93 0BN ☎ 01564 785364

A pub/restaurant in beautiful and peaceful countryside,
yet only minutes from the National Exhibition Centre,
Solihull and Warwick. Visitors will find a relaxed Italian
influence, reflected in the furnishings and the food, not
least the deli counter from which breads, cheeses and
olive oils are served. Start with a plate of antipasti,
perhaps, or chilli-crusted squid with pineapple and red
onion salsa. A small section of the menu is devoted to
dishes featuring salad leaves, of which chicory with
gorgonzola and pear is an example. There are several
pastas, including orechiette with tomatoes, garlic broad
beans and goat's cheese; fired pizzas; and a range of
stove-cooked, grilled or spit-roasted meats and fish.
Comfortable seating and ambient music in the bar makes
it great for just mingling and relaxing, while the sunny
lounge area, all sumptuous leather sofas and rustic décor,
opens up though oversized French doors to the patio.
OPEN: 11-11 **BAR MEALS:** L served all week 12-2.30 D served
all week 6.30-9.30 12-4.30 Sun Av main course £10
RESTAURANT: L served all week 12-2.30 D served all week
6.30-9.30 Av 3 course à la carte £17.50 🍺: 6X, IPA. ♀: 8
FACILITIES: Garden: Long terraced area with umbrellas, heating
Dogs allowed Water **NOTES:** Parking 100

COVENTRY
Map 10 SP37

Rose and Castle ♀
Ansty CV7 9HZ ☎ 024 76612822
Dir: From junct of M6 & M69 at Walsgrave, signed Ansty. 0.75m to pub
Small family-friendly pub with a canal running through the
garden. Inside, exposed beams and a varied menu that
includes smoked haddock in a creamy sauce with cheese and
mashed potato topping, garden pancake, chicken curry, a
variety of grills and steaks, and filled giant Yorkshire
puddings. The Burger Collection includes such items as The
Godiva Burger, The Great Dane and The Italian Job.
OPEN: 12-3 5.30-11 (Sat, Sun, BHs 12-11) **BAR MEALS:** L served
all week 12-3 D served all week 6-11 Av main course £7 🍴: Free
House 🍺: Interbrew Bass, Hook Norton, Brew XI, Worthington.
♀: 17 **FACILITIES:** Garden **NOTES:** Parking 50

HAMPTON IN ARDEN
Map 10 SP28

The White Lion NEW
10 High St B92 0AA ☎ 01675 442833 🖷 01675 443168
Dir: Opposite the church
A 400-year-old character pub in an attractive village noted for
its period houses and 16th-century Moat House west of the
church. It is conveniently located for the National Exhibition
Centre only three miles away. Hampton-in-Arden is said to be
the setting for Shakespeare's As You Like It, and nearby is a
15th-century packhorse bridge, one of very few remaining in
the region. Inside the pub is a welcoming bar with a log fire
in winter, cask conditioned ales and a separate restaurant
serving freshly cooked produce. For dinner, try one of the
starters, perhaps crispy duck salad with a light honey and soy
dressing, followed by shank of lamb with confit of lentils and
red wine sauce; sea bass with roasted sweet potatoes and
creamed leeks; green Thai chicken curry with sticky coconut
rice; or chicken escalope on spinach, melted mozzarella,
avocado and mango salsa.
OPEN: 12-11 (Sun 12-10.30) **BAR MEALS:** L served all week
12-2.30 D served Tues-Sat Sun 11-4 Av main course £10
RESTAURANT: L served Mon-Fri 12-2.30 D served Tues-Sat
6.30-9.30 Sun 10-4 Av 3 course à la carte £22 🍺: Brew XI, Black
Sheep, Old Speckled Hen. **FACILITIES:** Garden
NOTES: Parking 20

OLDBURY
Map 10 SO98

Waggon & Horses ♀
17a Church St B69 3AD ☎ 0121 5525467
Dir: Telephone for directions
A listed back-bar, high copper-panelled ceiling and original
tilework are among the character features to be found at this
real ale pub in the remnants of the old town centre.
Traditional pub food includes faggots and mash, pork and
leek sausages, lasagne, chilli, and fish and chips. Beers from
Holdens of nearby Dudley, Brains of Cardiff and guests.
OPEN: 12-11 (Sun 12-10.30) **BAR MEALS:** L served Mon-Sat 12-3
D served Wed-Fri 5.30-7.30 🍴: 🍺: Enville White, Brains Bitter, Old
Swan Entire, Holdens Golden Glow. ♀: 7 **NOTES:** Parking 3

SEDGLEY
Map 10 SO99

Beacon Hotel & Sarah Hughes Brewery ♀
129 Bilston St DY3 1JE ☎ 01902 883380 🖷 01902 883381
Little has changed in 150 years at this traditional brewery tap,
which still retains its Victorian atmosphere. The rare snob-
screened island bar serves a taproom, snug, large smoke-
room and veranda. Proprietor John Hughes reopened the
adjoining Sarah Hughes Brewery in 1987, 66 years after his
grandmother became the licensee. Flagship beers are Sarah
Hughes Dark Ruby, Surprise and Pale Amber, with guest
bitters also available. Lunchtime cheese and onion cobs only.
OPEN: 12-2.30 5.30-10.45 (Fri 5.30-11, Sat & Sun 12-3) (Sat 6-11,
Sun 7-10.30) 🍴: 🍺: Sarah Hughes Dark Ruby, Surprise & Pale
Amber, Selection of Guest Beers and seasonal products. ♀: 8
FACILITIES: Garden: Beer garden with benches, tables & play area
Dogs allowed Water **NOTES:** Parking 50 No credit cards

> Most of the pubs in this guide book pride
> themselves on the quality of their food. This
> may take a little time to prepare

England

SOLIHULL
Map 10 SP17

The Boat Inn ♀
222 Hampton Ln, Catherine-de-Barnes B91 2TJ
☎ 0121 705 0474 ▯ 0121 704 0600
e-mail: steven-hickson@hotmail.com
Village pub with a small, enclosed garden located right next
the canal in Solihull. Real ales are taken seriously and there
are two frequently changing guest ales in addition to the
regulars. There is also a choice of 14 wines available by the
glass. Fresh fish is a daily option and other favourite fare
includes chicken cropper, Wexford steak, and beef and ale pie.
OPEN: 12-11 (Sun 12-10.30) **BAR MEALS:** L served all week
12-9.30 D served all week 12-9.30 Av main course £7.95 **◀:** Tetleys,
Directors, 2 guest ales. ♀: 14 **FACILITIES:** Child facs Children's
licence Garden: Small enclosed garden - tables & chairs
NOTES: Parking 90

WEST BROMWICH
Map 10 SP09

The Vine
Roebuck St B70 6RD ☎ 0121 5532866 ▯ 0121 5255450
e-mail: bharat@thevine.co.uk
Dir: 0.5m from junct 1 of M5
Well-known, family-run business renowned for its good
curries and cheap drinks. For over 26 years the typically
Victorian alehouse has provided the setting for Suki Patel's
eclectic menu. Choose from a comprehensive range of Indian
dishes (chicken tikka masala, goat curry, lamb saag), a
barbecue menu and Thursday spit roast, offered alongside
traditional pub meals like sausage and chips, chicken and
ham pie, and toasted sandwiches. The Vine boasts the
Midlands' only indoor barbeque.
OPEN: 11.30-2.30 5-11 (Fri-Sun all day) **BAR MEALS:** L served all
week 12-2 D served all week 5-10.30 Sun 1-10.30 Av main course
£3.95 **RESTAURANT:** L served all week D served all week 5-10.30
Sat-Sun 1-10.30 Av 3 course à la carte £10 **◀:** Free House
◀: Bannks, Brew XI, John Smiths, Theakstons. **FACILITIES:** Garden:
Large beer garden, play area

WIGHT, ISLE OF

ARRETON
Map 05 SZ58

The White Lion
PO30 3AA ☎ 01983 528479 e-mail: cthewhitelion@aol.com

A 300-year-old former coaching inn with oak beams, polished
brass, open fires and added summer attractions in the
children's playground and aviary. Popular locally for its cosy
atmosphere, well-priced bar food and the starting point for
the Isle of Wight ghost hunt. Visitors can stoke up on hearty
venison with fruits of the forest sauce, steak and kidney pie,
continued

pork escalope, a variety of steaks, half roasted chicken, or
ratatouille cheesy suet pastry pudding.
OPEN: 11-12 (Sun 11-10.30) **BAR MEALS:** L served all week 12-9
D served all week 12-9 **◀:** **◀:** Badger Best, Fuller's London Pride,
Interbrew Flowers IPA. **FACILITIES:** Garden: Patio area in pleasant
old village location Dogs allowed Water **NOTES:** Parking 6

BEMBRIDGE
Map 05 SZ68

The Crab & Lobster Inn ◁▷ ♀
32 Foreland Field Rd PO35 5TR
☎ 01983 872244 ▯ 01983 873495 e-mail: allancrab@aol.com
Dir: Telephone for directions

Set on the clifftops just yards from the 65-mile coast path, this
is one of the Isle of Wight's best known pubs. The large patio
area offers superb sea views, whilst the traditional beamed
interior has a separate non-smoking area for diners. Locally
caught seafood is always on the menu; other choices might
include home-made lasagne; mixed grill; or cauliflower
cheese with crusty bread.
OPEN: 11-3 6-11 (Wknds & summer all day)
BAR MEALS: L served all week 12-2.30 D served all week 6-9.30
RESTAURANT: L served all week 12-2.30 D served all week 7-9.30
◀: Enterprise Inns **◀:** Interbrew Flowers Original, Goddards
Fuggle-Dee-Dum, Green King IPA, John Smiths. ♀: 10
FACILITIES: Child facs Children's licence Garden: Patio overlooking
the beach Dogs allowed Water **NOTES:** Parking 40

The Pilot Boat Inn NEW
Station Rd PO35 5NN ☎ 01983 872077 874101
Dir: On the corner of the harbour at the bottom of Kings Rd
The pub is very old and there are stories of a tunnel leading
from the cellar up to the vicarage for the smugglers to use when
they came into the harbour. A strong local base of customers
enjoys a winter menu of good old-fashioned favourites. In the
summer the yacht owners and holiday-makers triple the
population and the pub buys fresh fish from the local fishermen
in the harbour, including the famous Bembridge crab.
BAR MEALS: L served all week 12-2.30 D served all week 6-9 6-8.30
Wed Av main course £8 **RESTAURANT:** L served all week 12-2.30
D served all week 6-9 Av 3 course à la carte £18 **◀:** London Pride,
Guinness. **FACILITIES:** Child facs Dogs **NOTES:** Parking 12

BONCHURCH
Map 05 SZ57

The Bonchurch Inn
Bonchurch Shute PO38 1NU ☎ 01983 852611 ▯ 01983 856657
e-mail: gillian@bonchurch-inn.co.uk
Dir: Off A3055 in Bonchurch
Splendidly preserved pub, built of local stone, hidden away in
a secluded courtyard with more than a hint of Dickens about
it. This seems appropriate when you consider that one of
Britain's best-loved authors wrote part of *David Copperfield* in
continued

the village. The menu offers a choice of Italian specialities, fish dishes and popular meat options, such as grilled fillet steak with Bonchurch sauce (mushrooms, onions, pâté, mustard, cream and brandy).
OPEN: 11-3.30 6.30-11 Closed: 25 Dec **BAR MEALS:** L served all week 11-2.15 D served all week 6.30-9 **RESTAURANT:** D served all week 6.30-9.30 😊: Free House 🍺: Scottish Courage Courage Directors & Courage Best. **FACILITIES:** Garden: Courtyard, patio & fountain Dogs allowed Water **NOTES:** Parking 7

COWES
Map 05 SZ49

The Folly ⏰ 𝕐
Folly Ln PO32 6NB ☎ 01983 297171
Dir: On A3054
Reached by both land and water and very popular with the Solent's boating fraternity, the Folly is one of the island's more unusual pubs. Timber from an old sea-going French barge was used in the construction, and wood from the hull can be found in the nautical theme of the bar. An extensive specials list ranges from fish pie, and lamb shank, to slow-cooked beef ribs, and there are lunchtime sandwiches, and pastas and salads in the evenings.
OPEN: 9-11 (BHs & Cowes Week late opening)
BAR MEALS: L served all week 12-9.30 D served all week 12-9.30 Av main course £7.50 😊: 🍺: Interbrew Flowers Original, Bass, Goddards Best Bitter. 𝕐: 10 **FACILITIES:** Garden: Dogs allowed Water **NOTES:** Parking 30

FRESHWATER
Map 05 SZ38

Pick of the Pubs

The Red Lion ⏰ 𝕐
Church Place PO40 9BP ☎ 01983 754925 📠 01983 754925
Dir: In Freshwater follow signs for parish church

Husband and wife-run pub in a picturesque setting just a short stroll from the tidal River Yar, which is popular with the sailing set from nearby Yarmouth. The Red Lion's origins date from the 11th century, although the current red brick building is much newer. The open-plan bar is comfortably furnished with country kitchen-style tables and chairs, plus relaxing sofas and antique pine. In addition to the pub's four real ales, including the island's Goddard Best, and a good wine selection with 16 by the glass, the pub is renowned for its daily blackboard menu - order early to secure your chosen dish as demand soon exceeds supply. Everything is freshly made from tried and tested recipes using good quality meat, fish and vegetables. Typical dishes are braised steak with mashed potatoes; scallops and bacon with bubble and squeak; sweet and sour pork with rice; and favourites like

shepherds pie, and chicken Madras curry.
OPEN: 11.30-3 5.30-11 (Sun 12-3 7-10.30)
BAR MEALS: L served all week 12-2 D served all week 6.30-9 Av main course £10 😊: Enterprise Inns 🍺: Interbrew Flowers Original, Fuller's London Pride, Goddards, Wadworth 6X. 𝕐: 16
FACILITIES: Large garden with herb garden. Dogs allowed
NOTES: Parking 20

NITON
Map 05 SZ57

Buddle Inn 𝕐
St Catherines Rd PO38 2NE ☎ 01983 730243
e-mail: buddleinn@aol.com
Dir: A3055 from Ventnor. In Niton, 1st L signed 'to the lighthouse'
One of the island's oldest hostelries, a cliff-top farmhouse in the 16th century, which abounds with local history and tales of smuggling and derring-do. Popular with hikers and ramblers (dogs and muddy boots welcome), the interior is characterised by stone flags, oak beams and a large open fire. Specialising in real ale, wines and good company, home-cooked food includes local crab and lobster, daily pies and curries, ploughman's and steaks.
OPEN: 11-11 (Sun 12-10.30) 25-26 Dec Closed eve
BAR MEALS: L served all week 11.30-2.45 D served all week 6-9.30 Av main course £10 🍺: Interbrew Flowers Original & Bass, Greene King Abbot Ale, Adnams best. 𝕐: 9 **FACILITIES:** Garden: Food served outside Dogs allowed Water **NOTES:** Parking 50

NORTHWOOD
Map 05 SZ49

Travellers Joy
85 Pallance Rd PO31 8LS ☎ 01983 298024
e-mail: tjoy@slobalnet.co.uk
Pub deeds suggest that an alehouse first opened on this site some 300 years ago. Today's more elderly locals can remember a talking mynah bird in the bar which so upset a visiting darts team that they set it alight! Home-made steak and kidney pie, chicken tikka masala, mixed grill, ploughman's, jacket potatoes and the curiously named chicken Cyrilburger are on the menu. Isle of Wight beers feature in the bar.
OPEN: 11-2 5-11 (Fri-Sat 11-11 Sun closed 3-7)
BAR MEALS: L served all week 12-2 D served all week 6-9 Sun 12-2 7-9 Av main course £5.50 🍺: Goddardss Special Bitter, Courage Directors, Ventnor Golden Bitter, Deuchars IPA. **FACILITIES:** Child facs Garden: Large garden with patio and terrace Dogs allowed
NOTES: Parking 30

ROOKLEY
Map 05 SZ58

The Chequers ⏰
Niton Rd PO38 3NZ ☎ 01983 840314 📠 01983 840820
e-mail: richard@chequersinn-iow.co.uk
Horses in the neighbouring riding school keep a watchful eye on comings and goings at this 250-year-old family-friendly free house. In the centre of the island, surrounded by farms, the pub has a reputation for good food at reasonable prices. Fish, naturally, features well, with sea bass, mussels, plaice, salmon and cod usually available. Other favourites are mixed grill, pork medallions, T-bone steak, and chicken supreme with BBQ sauce and cheese.
OPEN: 11-11 **BAR MEALS:** L served all week 12-10 D served all week 12-10 Sun 12-9.30 Av main course £7.95 **RESTAURANT:** L served all week 12-10 D served all week Sun 12-9.30 😊: Free House 🍺: Scottish Courage John Smiths, Courage Directors, Best, Wadsworth 6X.
FACILITIES: Child facs Children's licence Garden: Large garden and patio with seating Dogs allowed Water **NOTES:** Parking 70

continued

England

SEAVIEW   Map 05 SZ69

Pick of the Pubs

Seaview Hotel & Restaurant
High St PO34 5EX ☎ 01983 612711 🖥 01983 613729
e-mail: reception@seaviewhotel.co.uk
Dir: B3330 (Ryde-Seaview rd), turn left via Puckpool along seafront road, hotel on left adjacent to sea
Situated in a picturesque sailing village, this island inn was used as a Royal Navy station during the Second World War, with an observation point located on the roof. There are magnificent views across the sea to Portsmouth naval dockyard, and the naval theme is continued inside, with a wonderful collection of artefacts ranging from classic ship models to letters from the ill-fated Titanic. The bar is full of old oars, masts, ships wheels and other memorabilia. The two restaurants - one a classic dining room, the other modern and stylish - and the bar menu offer contemporary dishes with the emphasis on freshly caught fish and seafood. Choices include fillet of hake with mussels, French beans and saffron; and monkfish, prawn and smoked haddock pie. Other options include steak and kidney pudding, mushroom and leek crumble, and Carisbrooke venison sausages and mash.
OPEN: 11-2.30 6-11 **BAR MEALS:** L served all week 12-2 D served all week 7-9.30 Av main course £7.50
RESTAURANT: L served all week 12-1.30 D served all week 7.30-9.30 Fixed menu Sun lunch only Av 3 course à la carte £25 Av 3 course fixed price £16.95 ⊕: Free House ◀: Goddards, Greene King Abbot Ale, Adnams ALe. **FACILITIES:** Child facs Garden: Courtyard/patio, Food served outside Dogs allowed
NOTES: Parking 12 **ROOMS:** 17 bedrooms en suite 1 family room s£89 d£72 (★★★)

 Pubs offering a good choice of fish on their menu

Disabled people and those with Assist Dogs have new rights of access to pubs, restaurants and hotels under the Disability Discrimination Act of 1 October 2004. For more information see the website at www.drc gb.org/open4all/rights/2004.asp

AA 2006
The
Restaurant
Guide
Britain' most complete guide to good food. Over 1,800 great restaurants.
www.theAA.com

SHALFLEET   Map 05 SZ48

Pick of the Pubs

The New Inn ♀
Mill Ln PO30 4NS ☎ 01983 531314 🖥 01983 531314
e-mail: martin.bullock@virgin.net

One of the island's best-known dining pubs, The New Inn is a great favourite with the yachting community. Its name reflects the fact that it was new in 1743 when it replaced an older inn that had burnt down; in the 260 years since then it has acquired all the attributes of antiquity that one expects in old pubs. Its prime location at the foot of Newtown Estuary explains both the yachting connection and its reputation for excellent fish and seafood. Regularly served are grilled fillet of cod with Bembridge crabmeat and dill sauce; halibut imperial with tiger prawns; and fish mixed grill. Also likely to feature are pan-fried pork loin steaks with cider and sage sauce; Greek-style lamb with feta, red onions, olives and oregano; and locally made sausages with leek and potato cake. Over 60 worldwide bins make its wine selection one of the island's most extensive.
OPEN: 11-3 6-11 **BAR MEALS:** L served all week 12-2.30 D served all week 6-9.30 Av main course £11
RESTAURANT: L served all week 12-2.30 D served all week 6-9.30 Av 3 course à la carte £22 ⊕: Enterprise Inns ◀: Interbrew Bass,Flowers Bitter, Greene King IPA, Marston's Pedigree. ♀: 6 **FACILITIES:** Garden: Raised lawned garden, sells seafood in summer Dogs allowed Water
NOTES: Parking 20

SHANKLIN   Map 05 SZ58

Fisherman's Cottage
Shanklin Chine PO37 6BN ☎ 01983 863882 🖥 01983 866145
e-mail: jill@shanklinchine.co.uk
Located on Appley beach, this unusual thatched cottage was the brainchild of Mr Colenutt, the first person to operate bathing machines. A member of his family was rescued from the flooded kitchen during a terrible storm in 1960. The straightforward menu ranges through Thai green curry; steak, Guinness and mushroom pie; salmon mornay; and tagliatelle. For a light lunch there is a variety of sandwiches, ploughman's and jacket potatoes. Cosed from Oct to March.
OPEN: 11-3 7-11 (Mar-Oct all wk) Closed: Nov-Feb
BAR MEALS: L served all week 11-2 D served all week 7-9 Av main course £7 ⊕: Free House ◀: Scottish Courage Courage Directors & John Smiths Smooth. **FACILITIES:** Garden: Terrace leading to beach Dogs allowed Water **NOTES:** No credit cards

Pick of the Pubs

ALVEDISTON – WILTSHIRE

The Crown

Tucked away in the Ebble Valley between Salisbury and Shaftesbury, the Crown is a well-known landmark with its pink-washed walls, thatched roof, clinging creepers and colourful window boxes. Its old world setting is characterised by head-cracking low beams, two inglenook fireplaces that burn invitingly on cooler days, and comfortable furnishings.

The inn serves entirely home-made food, with particular emphasis on fresh local produce whenever possible. The cosy bar sets the scene for anything from a simple sandwich to fresh fish and rib-eye steaks. Listed daily on chalkboards, expect to find salmon fillet with home-made tartare sauce, chargrilled red snapper with sir-fried vegetables, lambs' liver with smoked bacon, and pork fillet in Dijon mustard sauce. The pub makes a handy stopover for splendid local walks and visits to Salisbury Cathedral and Stonehenge. Recent change of ownership.

OPEN: 12-3 6.30-11 (Sun 12-3, 7-10.30)
BAR MEALS: L served all week 12-2 D served all week 6.30-9 Sun lunch 12-2.30, dinner 7-9 Av main course £9.75
RESTAURANT: L served all week 12-2 D served all week 6.30-9.30 (Sun lunch 12-2.30, dinner 7-9) Av 3 course à la carte £18
🍺: Free House
🍺: Ringwood Best, Timothy Taylor Landlord, Youngs Special Bitter.
FACILITIES: Child facs Garden: Food served outdoors, patio, Dogs allowed Water **NOTES:** Parking 40

Map 04 ST92
SP5 5JY
☎ 01722 780335
📄 01722 780836
Dir: 2.5m off A30 approx half-way between Salisbury and Shaftesbury

PUB WALK
Vale of the White Horse Inn
Minety - Wiltshire

VALE OF THE WHITE HORSE INN
SN16 9QY
☎ 01666 860175
Directions: B4040 6 miles east of
Malmesbury
*19th-century natural stone inn
overlooking its own lake. Dining room
with rustic stone walls and polished
tables, bar with a good choice of real
ales and sandwiches, as well as full
restaurant facilities.*
Open: 12–3 6–12 (open all day Sat &
Sun)
Bar Meals: L served all week 12–2.30
D served all week 6–9.30 (Sun 6–9)
Av main course £8.95
Restaurant Meals: L served all week
2.30–9.30 D served all week 6–9.30
Av 3 course à la carte £16.95
Dogs allowed. Garden available
(for full entry see page 534)

Minety was originally a clearing in the middle of the Braydon Forest renown for excellent wild mint, from which its name is derived.

Out of Car Park turn left. Fifty yards after London Lane turn left and follow footpath south-west across the fields past New House Farm to The Common (Lane). Go straight over The Common Lane and follow Ravens Brook Farm Lane past the first Wiltshire Wild Life Trust Meadow at Distillery Farm and then turn right into the main WWLT Meadows. Proceed east across the wild-flower meadows about one mile to Ravensroost Wood. Go through the woods turning right in the middle to the byway. Turn right and follow byway north to Kemble's Farm. Cross the Malmesbury to Cricklade Road (B4040) into Dogtrap Lane. Follow Dogtrap Lane north-west. Just past Woodward Farm turn right and follow footpath

north-east and down the edge of Brownockhill Plantation. Cross over the Upper Minety to Minety Lane and go north up the track towards Home Farm. After about 200 yards bear right and follow footpath across the field. This footpath meets the track and footpath from Home Farm. Turn right. After 50 yards take the right-hand footpath to Minety Village. Turn right and follow Sawyers Hill south to the school junction.

Turn left, follow the lane east 100 yards to the corner, but go straight on down Webbs Hill Lane. Turn right before the railway and follow path south-east to Malmesbury Road. Turn left to return to the pub.

Clean dogs are welcome (except in the main dining room). The floors in the bar and restaurant areas are either polished oak or carpeted, so clean shoes and no studs please.

Distance: 4.9 miles (8km)
Map: OS Explorer 169

*Walk submitted by Jamie Denham of the
Vale of the White Horse Inn*

SHORWELL
Map 05 SZ48

The Crown Inn 🐟
Walkers Ln PO30 3JZ ☎ 01983 740293 🖷 01983 740293
e-mail: sally@crowninn.net
Dir: *Turn left at top of Cansbrooke High Street, Shorwell is approx. 6m*

Antique furniture and solid stone walls help to create a unique atmosphere at this friendly village pub. There's a resident ghost, too, who strongly disapproves of card playing. When the locals have a winter game, the cards are often found strewn all over the bar the next morning. Home-cooked food is freshly prepared to order; favourites include ham egg and chips; spicy vegetable schnitzel; and fisherman's pie with salad and crusty bread.
OPEN: 10.30-3 6-11 (Sun 12-3 6-10:30) **BAR MEALS:** L served all week 12-2.30 D served all week 6-9 **RESTAURANT:** L served all week 12-2.30 D served all week 6-9 Av 3 course à la carte £12 🍴: Whitbread 🍺: Interbrew Boddingtons,Flowers Original, Badger Tanglefoot, Wadworth 6X. **FACILITIES:** Child facs Large, sheltered garden, flower beds, stream, ducks Dogs allowed on lead **NOTES:** Parking 70

VENTNOR
Map 05 SZ57

The Spyglass Inn 🐟 ♀
The Esplanade PO38 1JX ☎ 01983 855338 🖷 01983 855220
Dir: *Town centre*

This famous old 19th-century inn sits at the western end of Ventnor Esplanade, in a superb position overlooking the English Channel. For centuries the area was a haunt of smugglers, and the pub's huge collection of seafaring memorabilia still fascinates visitors. Freshly prepared dishes range from lunchtime baguettes and seasonal salads to hot dishes like crab and prawn chowder; sausage and mushroom casserole; and spinach and ricotta cannelloni.
OPEN: 10.30-11 (Sun 10.30-10.30) **BAR MEALS:** L served all week 12-9.30 D served all week 12-9.30 Sun 12-9 **RESTAURANT:** L served all week D served all week 🍴: Free House 🍺: Badger Dorset Best & Tanglefoot, Ventnor Golden, Goddards Fuggle-Dee-Dom, Yates Undercliff Experience. ♀: 8 **FACILITIES:** Garden: Terraces overlooking sea Dogs allowed Water **NOTES:** Parking 10

WILTSHIRE

ALDERBURY
Map 05 SU12

The Green Dragon ♀
Old Rd SP5 3AR ☎ 01722 710263
Dir: *1m off A36 (Southampton/Salisbury rd)*
There are fine views of Salisbury Cathedral from this 15th-century pub, which is probably named after the heroic deeds of Sir Maurice Berkeley, the Mayor of Alderbury, who slew a green dragon in the 15th century. Dickens wrote *Martin Chuzzlewit* here, and called the pub the Blue Dragon. An interesting and daily changing menu features home-made meat and vegetarian dishes using locally sourced produce.
OPEN: 11.30-2.30 6-11 (Sun 12-3, 7-10.30) **BAR MEALS:** L served all week 12-2.30 D served Mon-Sat 6.30-9.30 Av main course £6.50 **RESTAURANT:** 12-2.30 D served all week 7-9 Av 3 course à la carte £16 🍴: Hall & Woodhouse 🍺: Badger Dorset Best & Tanglefoot, King & Barnes. ♀: 14 **FACILITIES:** Garden: BBQ, beer garden, outdoor eating Dogs allowed **NOTES:** Parking 10

ALVEDISTON
Map 04 ST92

Pick of the Pubs

The Crown
SP5 5JY ☎ 01722 780335 🖷 01722 780836
See Pick of the Pubs on page 517

AXFORD
Map 05 SU27

Red Lion Inn 🐟 ♀
SN8 2HA ☎ 01672 520271 🖷 01672 521011
e-mail: info@redlionaxford.com
Dir: *M4 junct 15, A246 to Marlborough. Follow Ramsbury signs. Inn 3m*
In the beautiful Kennet Valley, and within sight of the river itself, the Red Lion has been a magnet for food lovers for more than 20 years. At least ten fish dishes are always offered, including grilled John Dory in a rocket, tarragon and cream sauce; and mixed seafood in light crab broth. Cardamom chicken with crème fraîche, ginger and coriander is also a delicious possibility.
OPEN: 12-3 6.30-11 (Sun 7-10.30) **BAR MEALS:** L served all week 12-2 D served all week 7-9 Av main course £8.50 **RESTAURANT:** L served all week 12-2 D served all week 7-9 Av 3 course à la carte £23 🍴: Free House 🍺: Hook Norton Best, London Pride plus guest beers. ♀: 16 **FACILITIES:** Child facs Garden: Garden at rear of pub, patio area at front **NOTES:** Parking 30

BARFORD ST MARTIN
Map 05 SU03

Barford Inn ♀
SP3 4AB ☎ 01722 742242 🖷 01722 743606
e-mail: ido@barfordinn.co.uk
Dir: *On A30 5m W of Salisbury*
Customer satisfaction and service are the keynotes in this 16th-century former coaching inn five miles outside Salisbury. A welcoming lounge, lower bar area and intimate snug have greeted visitors for generations - during World War II the Wiltshire Yeomanry dedicated a tank to the pub, known then as The Green Dragon. The varied menu includes freshly cut ciabattas, chargrilled medallions of beef, seafood linguini, or vegetarian stuffed Creole-style aubergine, and there's a range of exotic coffees to finish.
OPEN: 11-11 Closed: Dec 25 **BAR MEALS:** L served all week

continued

BARFORD ST MARTIN continued

12-2.30 D served all week 7-9.30 Av main course £9
RESTAURANT: L served all week 12-2.30 D served all week 7-9.30
🍽: Hall & Woodhouse **◀:** Badger Dorset Best & Tanglefoot. ♀: 12
FACILITIES: Garden **NOTES:** Parking 40 **ROOMS:** 4 bedrooms
en suite s£50 d£55 (♦♦♦♦)

BERWICK ST JAMES   Map 05 SU03

Pick of the Pubs

The Boot Inn
High St SP3 4TN ☎ 01722 790243 📠 01722 790243
e-mail: kathieduval@aol.com
Dir: Telephone for directions

Half of this attractive, 16th-century stone and flint inn was
once a cobbler's - hence the name. Tucked away in
picturesque countryside, the ivy-covered building is
surrounded by award-winning gardens, complete with a
summerhouse, colourful borders and hanging baskets.
The interior is traditional in style, and the atmosphere
warm and friendly. Real ales are served - Wadworth 6X,
Bass and Henrys IPA - and an award winning menu of
quality home-cooked food. Fresh local produce, including
herbs and vegetables from the garden, appear in daily
changing dishes such as escargot in garlic butter; prawns
wrapped in filo pastry with a sweet chilli sauce; confit of
duck topped with wild mushroom compote; chilli con
carne with basmati rice; beef, mushrooms, red wine and
stilton stew; and oven-baked goat's cheese on a bed of
leaves with date compote. Game is available in season,
and fresh fish according to availability.
OPEN: 12-3 6-11 (Closed Mon lunch Sun 7-10.30)
BAR MEALS: L served Tues-Sun 12-2.30 D served Tues-Sat
6.30-9.30 Av main course £9.95 **RESTAURANT:** L served
Tue-Sun D served Tue-Sat 🍽: Wadworth **◀:** Wadsworth 6x,
Henrys IPA, guest beers. **FACILITIES:** Garden: Large award
winning garden Dogs allowed Water **NOTES:** Parking 18

BOX   Map 04 ST86

The Quarrymans Arms ♀
Box Hill SN13 8HN ☎ 01225 743569
e-mail: John@quarrymans-arms.co.uk
Dir: Please phone pub for accurate directions
Tucked away up a narrow hillside lane, this 300-year-old
miners' pub enjoys fantastic views over the Box valley. It's
also on the long-distance Macmillan Way, and offers luggage
transfer for walkers. The interior is packed with mining
memorabilia and, by arrangement, you can take trips down
the stone mines. There's a substantial snack menu, plus daily-
continued

changing blackboards; calves' liver on mustard mash; seafood
tagliatelle; and mixed sausage casserole are typical.
OPEN: 11-3.30 6-11 (All day Fri-Sun) **BAR MEALS:** L served all
week 11-3 D served all week 6.30-10.30 Av main course £10
RESTAURANT: L served all week 11-3 D served all week 6.30-10.30
Av 3 course à la carte £18.50 🍽: Free House **◀:** Butcombe Bitter,
Wadworth 6X, Moles Best. ♀: 8 **FACILITIES:** Child facs Small,
traditional garden, views over Box valley Dogs allowed
NOTES: Parking 25

BRADFORD-ON-AVON   Map 04 ST86

The Dandy Lion ♀
35 Market St BA15 1LL ☎ 01225 863433 📠 01225 869169
Well-kept Wadworth and Butcombe ales supplement an
extensive wine list at this 17th-century town centre pub. Once
a traditional grocery, and close to the town's river and canal,
the internal décor now reflects Bradford-on-Avon's flourishing
antiques trade. Owner Jennifer Taylor welcomes regulars,
visitors and families with a range of snacks and meals that
include muffins with scrambled egg and smoked trout;
seafood paella; and spaghetti carbonara.
OPEN: 10.30-3 6-11 (Sat 10.30-11 Sun 11.30-3, 7-10.30)
BAR MEALS: L served all week 12-2.15 D served all week 7-9.30 Sun
12-3 Av main course £11.50 **RESTAURANT:** L served Sun 12-2.15
D served all week 7-9.30 Sun 12-3 Av 3 course à la carte £20
🍽: Wadworth **◀:** Butcombe, Wadworth 6X, Henrys IPA, Wadworth
Seasonal Ales. ♀: 11

Pick of the Pubs

The Kings Arms ♀
Monkton Farleigh BA15 2QH
☎ 01225 858705 📠 01225 858999
e-mail: enquiries@kingsarms-bath.co.uk
web: www.kingsarms-bath.co.uk
See Pick of the Pubs on opposite page

Pick of the Pubs

The Tollgate Inn ♦♦♦♦ 🏵🏵 🔍 ♀
Holt BA14 6PX ☎ 01225 782326 📠 01225 782805
e-mail: alison@tollgateholt.co.uk web: www.tollgateholt.co.uk
See Pick of the Pubs on page 522

🚭 Pubs with this logo do not allow smoking
anywhere on their premises

The Kings Arms

Dating back to the 11th century, this historic Bath stone building is situated in an attractive village just outside Bradford-on-Avon. There used to be a monastery nearby - it's a ruin now - whose monks came here on retreat. One of several ghost stories tells of a monk found dead in 'unusual circumstances' whose ghost now plays practical jokes on visitors.

Conversion into an alehouse took place in the 17th century, but original features remain, including the mullioned windows, flagged floors and a vast inglenook - said to be the largest in Wiltshire - in the medieval-style Chancel restaurant, which is hung with tapestries and pewter plates. The bar keeps around 20 malt whiskies, plus a good selection of cognacs, armagnacs and ports. The Bar and Garden menu offers light lunches such as Bath sausages, spring onion and smoked bacon mash; steak frites; three-egg omelette (with various fillings) and chips; and wild mushroom, spinach and asparagus lasagne. From the à la carte menu come main dishes such as duck breast

with balsamic glaze, mascarpone and almond dauphinoise; game casserole with herb dumplings; brochette of sirloin steak and tiger prawns (known as the 'Trawler and Tractor'), while specials may include roast poussin with smoked bacon, parsley mash and cheddar cheese sauce; pork schnitzel with sesame-fried potatoes and dolcelatte cheese sauce; and chicken piri piri sizzle with white and wild rice. Desserts are just as tempting, with coffee and walnut pavlova, and treacle and pecan tart with custard. An enclosed garden with parasol-shaded tables also contains two aviaries housing golden pheasants, lovebirds and Spook, the resident African long-eared eagle owl.

OPEN: 12-3 5.30-11 (Sat 12-11, Sun 12-10.30)
BAR MEALS: L served all week 12-2.45 D served all week 6.30-9.30 (12-9.30 Sat & Sun) Av main course £8.25
RESTAURANT: L served all week 12-2.45 D served all week 6.30-9.30 (12-9.30 Sat & Sun) Av 3 course à la carte £22 ☺: ◀: Wadworth 6X, Buttcombe Bitter, Wychwood Hobgoblin, Shepherd Neame Spitfire. ♀: 10
FACILITIES: Garden: aviaries, overlooking countryside Dogs allowed **NOTES:** Parking 45

🐟 ♀   Map 04 ST86
Monkton Farleigh BA15 2QH
☎ 01225 858705
📄 01225 858999
✉ enquiries@kingsarms-bath.co.uk
🌐 www.kingsarms-bath.co.uk
Dir: Off the A363 Bath to Bradford-Upon-Avon road, follow brown tourist signs to Kings Arms

Pick of the Pubs
BRADFORD-ON-AVON – WILTSHIRE

The Tollgate Inn

Set in the pretty village of Holt, half a mile from the Georgian town of Bradford-on-Avon and only seven miles from Bath, the Tollgate Inn has won many accolades. It has two restaurant areas; a small dining room off the main bar decorated in country style, with wood-burning stove; and a non-smoking restaurant up wooden stairs in what was originally a Baptist chapel, where open fire, candles and antiques induce a cosy atmosphere.

Regular customers are attracted both by the modern British cooking (with Mediterranean undertones), and by the knowledge that suppliers are mostly local, with hand-reared beef from the lush pastures of Broughton Gifford, the pub's own lamb, game from village shoots, vegetables from the surrounding fertile soils, and cheeses from a specialist in town. Delights include wild Devon mussels in white wine and cream; roast fillet of beef with wild mushrooms and béarnaise sauce; and roast leg of venison with port and thyme jus. Brixham trawlers supply the fish, often line-caught and delivered the same day. Examples are panache of haddock, bream and plaice in a Thai sauce; pan-fried scallops on creamed lentils with chorizo and spices; and lobster ravioli with crab jus. Britain's independent breweries are well supported in the bar. Upstairs are four de luxe en suite bedrooms; two enjoy views of the Westbury White Horse carved on the chalk hillside beyond the River Avon, while the other two overlook the village green.

OPEN: 11.30-2.30 6-11 Closed: 1st week in Jan
BAR MEALS: L served Tue-Sun 12-2 D served Tue-Sat 7-9.30 Av main course £11.50
RESTAURANT: L served Tue-Sun 12-2 D served Tue-Sat 7-9.30 Av 3 course à la carte £25
🍺: Free House 🛢: Timothy Taylor Landlord, Exmoor Gold, West Berkshire Mr Chubbs, Glastonbury Ales Mystery Tor. ♀: 9
FACILITIES: Garden: Established garden with wooden furniture Dogs allowed in garden only
NOTES: Parking 40
ROOMS: 4 bedrooms en suite s£50 d£85 No children overnight

♦♦♦♦ ◉◉ 🐟 ♀ Map 04
ST86
Holt BA14 6PX
☎ 01225 782326
📄 01225 782805
📧 alison@tollgateholt.co.uk
🌐 www.tollgateholt.co.uk
Dir: On B 3107 between Bradford on Avon and Melksham M4 junct 18, A46 towards Bath, then A363 to Bradford on Avon then B3107 Melksham, pub on the righthand side

BRINKWORTH   Map 04 SU08

Pick of the Pubs

The Three Crowns ⬡ 〒
SN15 5AF ☎ 01666 510366 ▤ 01666 510303 not for pubication
Dir: A3102 to Wootton Bassett, then B4042, 5m to Brinkworth
The owner's research tells him that his pub acquired its name in 1801, but did it have an earlier name? The search continues. It stands on the village green by the church and, although deceptively small from the outside, opens up in a way Dr Who would appreciate into a large, bright conservatory, a garden room and then out to a heated patio. In winter, an open log fire heats the traditional bars. All menus are written on large blackboards, where among the chicken supreme, rack of lamb, Somerset wild boar and home-made seafood pie, are crocodile and Taste of the Wild - marinated slices of kangaroo, venison and ostrich, served with a brandy-based sauce. Other main meals include a large number of fish dishes, featuring white Cornish lobster, salmon, monkfish, seabass, halibut, lemon sole, and mussels. Lunchtime snacks such as ploughman's, filled rolls and jacket potatoes are generously proportioned.
OPEN: 11-3 6-11 Closed: 25-26 Dec **BAR MEALS:** L served all week 12-2 D served all week 6-9.30 Av main course £16.95 **RESTAURANT:** L served all week 12-2 D served all week 6-9.30 ⊕: Enterprise Inns ◀: Wadworth 6X, Archers Village Ale, Castle Eden, Fullers London Pride. 〒: 20 **FACILITIES:** Child facs Garden: Sheltered patio with heaters, well maintained Dogs allowed **NOTES:** Parking 40

BROAD CHALKE   Map 05 SU02

The Queens Head Inn 〒
1 North St SP5 5EN
☎ 01722 780344 0870 7706634 ▤ 0870 7706635
Dir: Take A354 from Salisbury toward Blandford Forum, at Coombe Bissett turn right toward Bishopstone, follow rd for 4m
Attractive 15th-century-inn with friendly atmosphere and low-beamed bars, once the village bakehouse. On sunny days, enjoy the flower-bordered courtyard, whilst in colder weather the low beams and wood burner in the bar provide a cosy refuge. Menus include light snacks such as sandwiches, ploughman's lunches and home-made soups, as well as more substantial main courses: perhaps grilled trout with almonds, sirloin steak with a choice of vegetables, or wild game casserole.
OPEN: 11-3 6-11 (Sun 12-3, 7-10.30) **BAR MEALS:** L served all week 12-2 D served all week 7-9 **RESTAURANT:** L served all week 12-2 D served all week 7-9 ⊕: Free House ◀: Greene King IPA & Old Speckled Hen, Wadworth 6X, Ruddles County & Morelands Best. 〒: 7 **FACILITIES:** Garden: Paved courtyard with flower borders **NOTES:** Parking 30

BURCOMBE   Map 05 SU03

The Ship Inn ⬡ 〒
Burcombe Ln SP2 0EJ ☎ 01722 743182 ▤ 01722 743182
e-mail: theshipburcombe@mail.com
Dir: On A30 5m W of Salisbury
Tranquil 17th-century pub in the Nadder valley, with a garden ideally suited to al fresco dining. Low beams and open fires characterise the interior, providing a traditional background for seasonal menu and daily changing specials. Dishes might include braised lamb shank, chargrilled rib-eye steak, wild
continued

mushroom and butternut squash risotto, home-made fish cakes, chicken, mushroom and leek pie, and sausage and onion focaccia.

The Ship Inn

OPEN: 11-3 6-11 **BAR MEALS:** L served all week 11-2.30 D served all week 6-10 Sun 12-2.30, 7-9.30 Av main course £10 **RESTAURANT:** L served all week 11-2.30 D served all week 6-10 Sun 12-2.30, 7-9.30 Av 3 course à la carte £20 ◀: Flowers IPA, Wadworth 6X, Courage Best. 〒: 8 **FACILITIES:** Child facs Children's licence Garden: Garden with river and ducks Dogs allowed **NOTES:** Parking 30

BURTON   Map 04 ST87

The Old House at Home 〒
SN14 7LT ☎ 01454 218227 ▤ 01454 218227
Dir: On B4039 NW of Chippenham
A soft stone, ivy-clad pub with beautiful landscaped gardens and a waterfall. Inside there are low beams and an open fire. Overseen by the same landlord for nearly twenty years, the crew here are serious about food. The kitchen offers a good fish choice, vegetarian and pasta dishes, and traditional pub meals. Favourites include lamb cutlets with champ, salmon and crab cakes, Woodland duck breast with stuffing, butterfly red mullet, and king scallops in Cointreau.
OPEN: 11.30-2.30 7-11 (Fri-Sat 11.30-3, Sun 7-10.30) (closed Tue lunch) **BAR MEALS:** L served Mon-Sun 12-2 D served Mon-Sun 7-10 ⊕: Free House ◀: Wadworth 6X, Interbrew Bass. 〒: 20 **FACILITIES:** 3 tiered, landscaped garden **NOTES:** Parking 25

CHILMARK   Map 04 ST93

Pick of the Pubs

The Black Dog 〒
SP3 5AH ☎ 01722 716344 ▤ 01722 716124
e-mail: blackdog@mercuryinns.com
Dir: From Salisbury follow signs for B3089
The Black Dog dates from the 15th century and was built as a brewing house for workers at the village quarry which supplied the stone for Salisbury Cathedral. It is a classic country pub which successfully combines rustic charm with appealing modern decor, first-class ales, and excellent contemporary pub food. Features of the establishment are a striking main bar with a red and black tiled floor and a huge rear garden for summer use.
OPEN: 11-3 6-11 (Open all day summer) Rest: Dec 25 closed lunchtime **BAR MEALS:** L served all week 12-2 D served Mon-Sat 7-9 (Sun 12-3) Av main course £7.95 **RESTAURANT:** L served all week 12-2.30 D served Mon-Sat 6-9.30 ◀: Bass, Crop Circle, Wadworth 6X, Carling. **FACILITIES:** Children's licence Large garden, 20 tables Dogs allowed **NOTES:** Parking 30

CHRISTIAN MALFORD
Map 04 ST97

The Rising Sun
Station Rd SN15 4BL ☎ 01249 721571
Dir: From M4 J 17 take B4122 towards Sutton Benger, turn left on to the
B4069, pass through after 1m to Christian Malford, turn right into village
(station road) pub is the last building on left

The characteristics of a convivial, unspoilt country inn have
been preserved by the owner, Simon Woodhead. Particularly
popular are the slow-roasted lamb shank, Barbary duck
breast, pork medallions, and the wide variety of fish dishes,
including lemon sole, red bream and tuna loin. Dogs are
offered water and 'treats'.

OPEN: 12-2.30 6.30-11 **BAR MEALS:** L served Tue-Sun 12-2
D served Mon-Sun 6.30-10 Av main course £8.50
RESTAURANT: L served Tue-Sun 12-2 D served Mon-Sun 6.30-10
Av 3 course à la carte £20 ⊜: Free House ◖: Sussex, Badgerts
Best, Rucking Mole. **FACILITIES:** Garden: Food served outside, lawn
Dogs allowed Water & Treats **NOTES:** Parking 15

COLLINGBOURNE DUCIS
Map 05 SU25

Pick of the Pubs

The Shears Inn & Country Hotel ♀
The Cadley Rd SN8 3ED ☎ 01264 850304 ▤ 01264 850220
Dir: On A338 NW of Andover & Ludgershall

A thatched 16th-century building that used to function as
a shearing shed for market-bound sheep. Now a thriving
country inn, it owes some of its popularity to fresh
seafood specials, including roast monkfish in Parma ham,
seared tuna with quails' eggs and fresh anchovies, and
gâteau of lobster, sole and salmon with basil and tomato
dressing. Venison, rack of lamb, and various steaks, all
with a delicious sauce or jus, are among other
contributory factors. Expect changes, as the Shears
recently re-opened under the management of chef-
proprietor Paul Morgan and wife Gill, who until recently
ran The Hampshire Arms at Crondall.

OPEN: 11-11 **BAR MEALS:** L served all week 12-2.30 D served
all week 6.30-9.30 (No meals Sun eve) Av main course £6.95
RESTAURANT: L served all week 12-2.30 D served all week
6.30-9.30 Av 3 course à la carte £20 ⊜: Free House
◖: Breakspear's Bitter & Guest Ales. ♀: 31
FACILITIES: Garden: Small area with 10 picnic tables Dogs
allowed **NOTES:** Parking 50

Restaurant and Bar Meal times indicate the times
when food is available. Last orders may be
approximately 30 minutes before the times stated

CORTON
Map 04 ST94

Pick of the Pubs

The Dove Inn ◆◆◆◆ ⌇ ♀
BA12 0SZ ☎ 01985 850109 ▤ 01985 851041
e-mail: info@thedove.co.uk
Dir: From A36 N of Salisbury signed to Corton and Boyton. Cross
railway line, turn right at junct. Corton approx 1m, R into village.

A thriving, traditional pub tucked away in a beautiful
Wiltshire village close to the River Wylye. A dramatic
central fireplace is a feature of the refurbished bar, and
the large garden is the site of summer barbecues, and
ideal for a drink on warm days. The award-winning food
is based firmly on West Country produce, with many
ingredients coming from within just a few miles. Popular
lunchtime bar snacks give way to a full evening carte,
featuring starters like Thai crab cakes, duck confit, and
smoked halibut, followed by calves' liver, pheasant
risotto, and braised lamb. A good range of well-kept real
ales includes Oakhill, Wadworth, Fullers and Hopback.
Five en suite bedrooms built around a courtyard make
The Dove an ideal touring base, with Bath and Salisbury
within easy range.

OPEN: 12-2.30 6-11 (Fri, Sat, Sun 12-3 Sun 7-10.30)
BAR MEALS: L served all week 12-2 D served all week 7-9 (Sat
12-3, 7-9) Av main course £9 **RESTAURANT:** L served all week
12-2 D served all week 7-9 (Sun 12-3, 7-10.30) Av 3 course à la
carte £20 ⊜: Free House ◖: Timothy Taylor, Youngs,
Butcombe & Hop Back GFB. ♀: 10 **FACILITIES:** Children's
licence Garden: Beer garden, patio, food served outdoors Dogs
allowed Water and biscuits **NOTES:** Parking 24
ROOMS: 5 bedrooms en suite 1 family room s£50 d£70

DEVIZES
Map 04 SU06

The Bear Hotel ★★★ ♀
The Market Place SN10 1HS ☎ 0845 4565334 ▤ 01380 722450
e-mail: info@thebearhotel.net web: www.thebearhotel.net

Right in the centre of Devizes, home of Wadworth's brewery,
this old coaching inn dates from at least 1559 and lists Judge
Jeffreys, George III, and Harold Macmillan amongst its
notable guests. You'll find old beams, log fires, fresh flowers -
and a menu with starters like grilled black pudding with apple
and cider vinaigrette; and main courses such as pot-roasted
partridge, or broccoli and mushroom strudel. For desserts (all
home made) expect elderflower and gooseberry torte, or
profiteroles with chocolate sauce.

OPEN: 9.30-11 Closed: 25-26 Dec **BAR MEALS:** L served all week
11.30-2.30 D served all week 7-9.30 (Sun 7-9) Av main course £4.95
RESTAURANT: L served Sun 12.15-1.45 D served Mon-Sat 7-9.30
Av 3 course à la carte £25 ⊜: Wadworth ◖: Wadworth 6X,

continued

Wadworth IPA, Wadworth JCB, Old Timer. ♀: 18
FACILITIES: Garden: Courtyard Dogs allowed **NOTES:** Parking 12
ROOMS: 25 bedrooms en suite 3 family rooms s£60 d£85

The Raven Inn ♀
Poulshot Rd SN10 1RW ☎ 01380 828271 ▤ 01380 828271
e-mail: pjh@raveninn.co.uk
Dir: A361 Devizes towards Trowbridge, L at sign for Poulshot
A traditional half-timbered, 18th-century inn standing just
beyond the northern edge of Poulshot's expansive village green.
From here you can enjoy classic Kennet and Avon Canal
towpath walking beside the famous Caen Hill locks. The
cosmopolitan menu includes light bites such as tagliatelle
Alfredo; and smoked chicken pâté with hot buttered toast. Main
meals like lamb rogan josh, or Mexican beef stand alongside
the ever-popular grills, vegetarian choices and sticky desserts.
OPEN: 11-2.30 6.30-11 (Sun,12-3,7-10.30) **BAR MEALS:** L served
Tue-Sun 12-2 D served Tue-Sun 7-9.30 (Sun 7-9) Av main course
£8.80 **RESTAURANT:** L served Tue-Sun 12-2 D served Tue-Sun
7-9.30 Av 3 course à la carte £15 ▤: Wadworth ◀: Wadworth 6X,
Wadworth IPA, Summersault, Wadworth Old Timer. ♀: 8
FACILITIES: Walled garden with gate **NOTES:** Parking 20

The Southgate Inn ♀
Potterne Rd SN10 5BY ☎ 01380 722872 ▤ 01380 722872
e-mail: southgateinn@supanet.com
Friendly blues/jazz oriented pub serving an interesting choice
of imported beers (from 21% ABV to 3.5% ABV in strength),
many of them on draft. It also claims to be the only pub in
the county serving kosher beer acceptable to the Jewish faith.
The Southgate proudly proclaims its 'friendly food and
fantastic staff', and the house speciality is ciabatta toasties. In
summer you can sit outside in The Secret Garden (very small).
OPEN: 11-12 **BAR MEALS:** 11-10 ◀: GFB, Summer Lightning,
Best. ♀: 45 **FACILITIES:** Children's licence Garden: Very small,
known as 'Secret Garden' Dogs allowed **NOTES:** Parking 15

DONHEAD ST ANDREW   Map 04 ST92

The Forester Inn 🏠 ♀
Lower St SP7 9EE ☎ 01747 828038 ▤ 01747 828714
e-mail: mhobbsbeaune@btinternet.com
Dir: 4.5m from Shaftsbury on A30 towards Salisbury

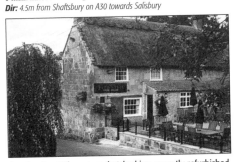

An attractive 14th-century thatched inn, recently refurbished
to add a modern feel to its rustic charm. The interior still
includes an inglenook fireplace and traditional wooden
furnishings, and the pub retains a good local trade. There's
an increased emphasis on home-cooked food such as warm
chicken, bacon and cashew nut salad; tagliatelle of oyster
mushrooms, artichokes and tomatoes in a cream sauce; and
crab fishcakes. Other charms include an attractive garden
and lunchtime bar snacks such as ciabattas and
ploughman's platters. An old well on the terrace.
continued

OPEN: 12-3 6.30-11 (Sun 7-10.30) **BAR MEALS:** L served all week
12-2 D served all week 6-9 Sun 12-3, Fri-Sat 6-9.30 Av main course
£12 **RESTAURANT:** L served all week 12-2 D served all week 7-9
Sun 12-3, Fri-Sat 6-9.30 Av 3 course à la carte £22 ◀: 6X, Ringwood,
guest ale. ♀: 10 **FACILITIES:** Garden: Large patio area and garden
Dogs allowed Water **NOTES:** Parking 30

EAST KNOYLE   Map 04 ST83

Pick of the Pubs

The Fox and Hounds ♀
The Green SP3 6BN ☎ 01747 830573 ▤ 01747 830865
Dir: 1.5m off A303 at the A350 turn off, follow brown signs
A traditional late 15th-century thatched and beamed pub
which originally comprised three cottages. Situated on a
greensand ridge, East Knoyle is surrounded by excellent
walking country which offers numerous views of the
scenic Blackmoor Vale. As well as once being home to
Jane Seymour's family, the village has another claim to
fame: Sir Christopher Wren, whose father was rector
here, was born in a room above the local shop in October
1632. The pub's interior is quaint and cosy, with wooden
flooring, natural stone walls, flagstones and sofas fronting
a blazing winter fire. The varied and appetising menu is
characterised by a range of dishes prepared with the use
of local produce. Expect bangers and mash; chicken
wrapped in pancetta on spinach mash; slow-roast lamb
shank on champ; Old English fish pie; blue vinney and
vine-ripened tomato tart with salad; and grilled lemon
sole. To follow, try blackberry and apple crumble.
OPEN: 12-2.30 6-11 (Sat 12-11 Sun 12-10.30)
BAR MEALS: L served all week 12-2.30 D served all week 7-10
Av main course £7.95 ◀: Fullers London Pride, Wadworth 6X,
Smiles Golden, Butts Barbus Barbus. ♀: 10 **FACILITIES:** Garden:
Sheltered courtyard patio Dogs allowed **NOTES:** Parking 10

EBBESBOURNE WAKE   Map 04 ST92

Pick of the Pubs

The Horseshoe
Handley St SP5 5JF ☎ 01722 780474
Reflecting the rural charm of the village in which it
stands, the 17th-century Horseshoe Inn nestles into the
folds of the Wiltshire Downs, close to the meandering
River Ebble. The small building was originally the stables
for the old stagecoach road that ran along the ridge not
more than two miles away. These days it is a homely and
traditional local, adorned with climbing roses. Outside
there is a pretty, flower-filled garden and inside there is a
central servery dispensing ale from the barrel to two
rooms, both filled with simple furniture, old farming
implements and country bygones. Good value bar food is
freshly prepared from local produce and meals are
accompanied by plenty of vegetables. Hearty dishes
include pheasant and cranberry or steak and kidney pies,
fresh fish bake, honey roasted duckling, and lambs' liver
and bacon casserole.
OPEN: 12-3 6.30-11 (Closed Sun eve, Mon lunch)
BAR MEALS: L served Tue-Sun 12-2 D served Tue-Sat 7-9.30
RESTAURANT: L served Tue-Sun 12-2 D served Tue-Sat 7-9.30
Av 3 course à la carte £20 ▤: Free House ◀: Wadworth 6X,
Ringwood Best Bitter, London Pride, Archers Golden Train.
FACILITIES: Children's licence Garden: Dogs allowed Water
NOTES: Parking 20

FONTHILL GIFFORD
Map 04 ST93

Pick of the Pubs

The Beckford Arms
SP3 6PX ☎ 01747 870385 ▤ 01747 870385
e-mail: beck.ford@ukonline.co.uk
See Pick of the Pubs on opposite page

FORD
Map 04 ST87

Pick of the Pubs

The White Hart ♀
SN14 8RP ☎ 01249 782213 ▤ 01249 783075
e-mail: whitehart.ford@eldridge-pope.co.uk
Dir: From M4 junct 17 take A429 then A420 to Ford

A rambling 15th-century coaching inn, the White Hart is located by a trout stream deep in the Wyvern Valley. The *Dr Doolittle* film starring Rex Harrison was filmed here in the late 1960s, and the site has also been used for a Carlsberg advertisement. It's a stone building with old beams and log fires, including a traditional bar and candlelit dining rooms, and the atmosphere is relaxed and informal. Dishes might include stuffed plaice fillets, rib-eye steak with pepper sauce, and venison medallions. In summer drinks can be taken out onto the grass area to the rear of the pub, and meals on the patio or pub front. There is also a picnic area, but drinks must be purchased in the pub.
OPEN: 11-11 (12-10.30 Sun) **BAR MEALS:** L served all week 12-2.30 D served all week 6-8 Av main course £10.50
RESTAURANT: L served all week 12-2.30 D served all week 7-9.30 🍴: Eldridge Pope ◀: Old Hookey Ale, Bass Cask, Adnams Broadside, Tetley Cask. ♀: 8 **FACILITIES:** Garden: Terrace & grassy area along stream Dogs allowed
NOTES: Parking 80

 The Rosette is the AA award for food. Look out for it next to a pub's name

We only include details of accommodation that has been inspected by the AA (big Stars or Diamonds at the top of an entry), or the RAC, VisitBritain, VisitScotland or WTB (small Stars or Diamonds at the end of an entry)

GREAT HINTON
Map 04 ST95

Pick of the Pubs

The Linnet ◎ ♀
BA14 6BU ☎ 01380 870354 ▤ 01380 870354
Dir: Just off the A361 Devizes to Trowbridge rd
Originally a woollen mill, the building was converted into a village local circa 1905, but since chef/landlord Jonathan Furby took over five years the Linnet has been further transformed into a pub restaurant with a great reputation for its food. Everything is prepared on the premises - bread, ice cream, pasta and sausages - with fresh, locally produced ingredients to the fore. The light lunch menu offers dishes such as duck tart, fishcakes, and roasted salmon along with an interesting choice of salads served in a large bowl, or warm foccacia bread with a variety of fillings. A typical selection from the evening carte might be feta cheese, roast pepper and basil terrine; chargrilled rib-eye steak with a grouse and smoked bacon sausage and port and thyme sauce; and white chocolate and raspberry ripple cheesecake. In the summer there are seats in the large patio area in front of the pub.
OPEN: 11-2.30 6.30-11 (Sun 12-3, 7-10.30) Closed: 1 Jan
BAR MEALS: L served Tue-Sun 12-2 D served Tue-Sun 6.30-9.30 **RESTAURANT:** L served Tue-Sun 12-2 D served Tue-Sun 6.30-9.30 Av 3 course à la carte £20.50 Av 3 course fixed price £12.95 🍴: Wadworth ◀: Wadworth 6X & Henrys IPA. ♀: 8 **FACILITIES:** Garden: large patio area in front of pub Dogs allowed Water **NOTES:** Parking 45

GRITTLETON
Map 04 ST88

The Neeld Arms
The Street SN14 6AP ☎ 01249 782470 ▤ 01249 782168
e-mail: neeldarms@zeronet.co.uk
Dir: Telephone for directions

This 17th-century Cotswold stone pub stands at the centre of a pretty village in lush Wiltshire countryside. Its half dozen bedrooms are highly commended for comfort. Quality real ales and freshly prepared food are an equal draw to diners who will eagerly tuck in to lamb shanks, home-made steak and kidney pie or sausage and mash. Children are welcome and the small garden is especially popular for al fresco eating in fine weather.
OPEN: 12-3 5.30-11 **BAR MEALS:** L served all week 12-2 D served all week 7-9.30 **RESTAURANT:** L served all week 12-2 D served all week 7-9.30 🍴: Free House ◀: Wadworth 6X, Buckleys Best, Brakspear Bitter. **FACILITIES:** Child facs Garden: Patio Dogs allowed Water **NOTES:** Parking 12 **ROOMS:** 6 bedrooms en suite 1 family room (♦♦♦)

The Beckford Arms

Substantial 18th-century stone-built inn peacefully situated opposite the Fonthill Estate and providing a good base from which to explore the unspoilt Nadder Valley. Eddie and Karen Costello have transformed this rural retreat since arriving here a few years ago.

Beyond the basic locals' bar, you will find a rambling main bar, adjoining dining area and an airy garden room all decorated in a tastefully rustic style, complete with scrubbed plank tables topped with huge candles, and warm terracotta-painted walls. Expect a roaring log fire in winter, a relaxed, laid-back atmosphere, and interesting modern pub menus. From petit pain baguettes, hearty soups, salads, Asian-style fishcakes with sweet chilli dip, or a Thai curry at lunchtime, the choice of well presented dishes extends, perhaps, to rack of lamb with tomatoes, wine and Italian herbs, sautéed medallions of Wiltshire pork with caramelised apple, calvados and cider, and salmon with vermouth glaze in the evening. Generous bowls of fresh vegetables, colourful plates and friendly service all add to the dining experience here. Suntrap patio and a delightful garden - perfect for summer sipping.

OPEN: 12-11 (Sun 12-10.30) Closed: 25 Dec
BAR MEALS: L served all week 12-2.15 D served all week 7-9 Av main course £8.95
RESTAURANT: L served all week 12-2.15 D served all week 7-9
🍺: Free House
🍺: Hop Back Best, Timothy Taylor Landlord, Abbot, Hopback Summer Lightning.
FACILITIES: Garden: Beautiful large garden Dogs allowed
NOTES: Parking 40

Map 04 ST93

SP3 6PX
☎ 01747 870385
🖷 01747 870385
📧 beck.ford@ukonline.co.uk
Dir: 2m from A303 (Fonthill Bishop turning) halfway between Hindon & Tisbury at crossroads next to Beckford Estate

Pick of the Pubs

The Angel Inn

Surrounded by stunning countryside, the 16th-century inn has been transformed into a striking blend of original features and contemporary comfort. The beamed bar features scrubbed pine tables, warmly decorated walls and an attractive fireplace with a wood-burning stove. In summer, the secluded courtyard garden, furnished with hardwood tables and cotton parasols, is very popular.

Although very much a dining pub, it has not forsaken the traditional charm and character of its coaching inn past. TV chef Antony Worrall Thompson is the executive chef here and together with the resident chef, Paul Kinsey, has devised menus using only the freshest seasonal ingredients, mostly locally sourced. Diners can eat in either the restaurant, in the bar, or, during the summer months, alfresco in the secluded courtyard garden, which leads off the restaurant. Steaks are a speciality and are hung for 35 days in the pub's ageing rooms for the best possible quality and taste. Pub grub includes bruschetta of roast vegetables, pine nuts, ricotta cheese and tomato dressing; and potato gnocchi with wild mushroom and truffle sauce. Main courses include roasted gilt-head bream with crab couscous, marinated vegetables and citrus vinaigrette; monkfish in parma ham on truffled cauliflower purée and Greek-style shellfish; roasted saddle and confit leg of rabbit on soft polenta with globe artichoke, girolles and red wine jus; and pan-fried calves' liver with mash, figs, glazed shallots and pancetta-hazelnut vinaigrette. Desserts include lemon posset with sablé biscuits; and hot chocolate pudding with white chocolate ice cream. Stonehenge, Salisbury, Bath, Stourhead and Longleat are all within striking distance.

OPEN: 12-11 (Sun 12-10.30)
BAR MEALS: L served all week 12-2.30 D served all week 7-9.30 Sun 7-9
RESTAURANT: L served all week 12-2.30 D served all week 7-9.30
Av 2 course fixed price £8
🍴: Free House
🍺: Moorlands, Wadworth 6X.
FACILITIES: Children's licence Dogs allowed Water **NOTES:** Parking 12

🍷   Map 04 ST94
High St BA12 0ED
☎ 01985 840330
🖹 01985 840931
🅮 admin@theangelheytesbury.co.uk
Dir: From A303 take A36 toward Bath, 8m, Heytesbury on left

HANNINGTON
Map 05 SU19

The Jolly Tar ◆◆◆◆ ♀
Queens Rd SN6 7RP ☎ 01793 762245 📠 01793 762247
e-mail: thejollytar@btinternet.com
Dir: Leeave M4 at junct 15 and take A419 Cirencester. Leave A419 at signs for Bunsdon/Highworth. Follow B4019 Highworth, left at Freke Arms, follow sign for Hannington and Jolly Tar Pub in the centre of the village.
Ancient timbers and a log fire create a warm atmosphere in this old farmhouse that has been an inn for 150 years. Locally-brewed Arkells real ale and decent wines make an ideal accompaniment to the conservatory restaurant menu: expect steak and stilton salad; and Cajun spiced chicken fillet smothered with garlic mayonnaise in ciabatta bread with potato wedges, salad and salsa - perhaps followed by strawberries and clotted cream tart. The converted skittle alley offers tasteful bedrooms.
OPEN: 12-3 6.30-11 **BAR MEALS:** L served all week 12-2 D served all week 6.30-9 Sun 7-8.30 Av main course £8.50
RESTAURANT: L served all week 12-2 D served all week 6.30-9 Sun 7-8.30 Av 3 course à la carte £17.50 🍴: 🍺: Arkells 3B, 2B, James Real Ale & Summer Ale, Noel Ale. ♀: 9 **FACILITIES:** Garden: Sun terrace patio, grass play area **NOTES:** Parking 30
ROOMS: 4 bedrooms en suite s£45 d£60 No children overnight

HEYTESBURY
Map 04 ST94

Pick of the Pubs

The Angel Inn ♀
High St BA12 0ED ☎ 01985 840330 📠 01985 840931
e-mail: admin@theangelheytesbury.co.uk
See Pick of the Pubs on opposite page

HINDON
Map 04 ST93

Pick of the Pubs

Angel Inn ♀
High St SP3 6DJ ☎ 01747 820696 📠 01747 820054
e-mail: info@theangelathindon.com
See Pick of the Pubs on page 530

HORTON
Map 05 SU06

The Bridge Inn ♀
Horton Rd SN10 2JS ☎ 01380 860273 📠 01380 860273
e-mail: manager@thebridgeinnhorton.fsnet.co.uk
Dir: A361 from Devizes, right at 3rd roundabout
The buildings that are now the Bridge Inn were originally a family-run farm, built around 1800, and then a flour mill and bakery. It makes a spacious pub and the perfect place for gongoozling (idly spectating), as narrowboats cruise past on the Kennet and Avon Canal. The menu takes in snacks, pub grub (sausage/fish and chips), grills, a vegetarian selection, and mains such as slow roast shoulder of lamb.
OPEN: 11.30-3 6.30-11 (Sun 12-3 7-10.30) **BAR MEALS:** L served all week 12-2.15 D served all week 7-9.15 (Sun 12-2.15, 7-9)
RESTAURANT: L served all week 12-2.15 D served all week 7-9.15 (Sun 12-2.15, 7-9) 🍴: Wadworth 🍺: Wadworth Henry's original IPA, 6X, Old Father Timer. ♀: 8 **FACILITIES:** Garden: Large garden on canalside Dogs allowed Water **NOTES:** Parking 50

KILMINGTON
Map 04 ST73

The Red Lion Inn
BA12 6RP ☎ 01985 844263
Dir: B3092 off A303 N towards Frome. Pub 2.5m from A303 on right on B3092 just after turning to Stourhead Gardens
This 14th-century coaching inn once provided two spare horses to assist coaches in the climb up nearby White Sheet Hill. The interior, unchanged over decades, features flagstone floors, oak beams, antique settles and blazing log fires. The landlord has been here for 25 years, and as well as being a champion of real ale, he supervises his kitchen to ensure that all produce - much of it local - is served in prime condition. A typical menu includes meat or vegetable lasagne, chicken casserole and game pie, as well as a selection of pasties, baked potatoes and toasted sandwiches.
OPEN: 11.30-2.30 6.30-11 (Sun 12-3, 7-10.30) 25 Dec Closed eve
BAR MEALS: L served all week 12-1.50 D served none 🍴: Free House 🍺: Butcombe Bitter, Jester, Guest Ale. **FACILITIES:** Large garden with picnic tables Dogs allowed except between 12-2
NOTES: Parking 25 No credit cards

LACOCK
Map 04 ST96

The George Inn ♀
4 West St SN15 2LH ☎ 01249 730263 📠 01249 730186
Dir: M4 junct 17 take A350, S
Steeped in history and much used as a film and television location, this beautiful National Trust village includes an atmospheric inn. The George dates from 1361 and boasts a medieval fireplace, a low-beamed ceiling, mullioned windows, flagstone floors and an old tread wheel by which a dog would drive the spit. Wide selection of steaks and tasty pies, and fish options include specials in summer; finish with the home-made bread and butter pudding.
OPEN: 10-2.30 5-11 (Sat-Sun all day) **BAR MEALS:** L served all week 12-2 D served all week 6-9.30 Av main course £7.75
RESTAURANT: L served all week 12-2 D served all week 6-9.30 (Eve hrs vary in winter) Av 3 course fixed price on request Av 3 course fixed price £17.95 🍴: Wadworth 🍺: Wadworth 6X, Henrys IPA, J.C.B & Henrys Smooth. ♀: 13 **FACILITIES:** Child facs Garden: Large patio, grass area, swings, see-saw Dogs allowed in bar only **NOTES:** Parking 40

Red Lion Inn ♀
1 High St SN15 2LQ ☎ 01249 730456 📠 01249 730766
e-mail: redlion.chippenham.wb@freshnet.co.uk
Dir: Just off A350 between Chippenham & Melksham
With its large open fireplace, flagstone floors and Georgian interior, the Red Lion dates back over 200 years and looks the part. Now, this historic inn offers Wadworth ales and a varied wine list to accompany fresh, home-cooked meals. Lunchtime choices range from sandwiches and jacket potatoes to hearty casseroles and deep-filled pies; evening might bring poached cod with tomato pesto; venison steak in red wine; or roasted pepper, red onion and goat's cheese tart.
OPEN: 11.30-3 6-11 (Sun 12-3, 7-10.30 May -31 Aug Sat 11-11, Sun 11-10.30) **BAR MEALS:** L served all week 12-2 D served all week 6-9 Av main course £7.50 **RESTAURANT:** L served all week 12-2 D served all week 6-9 Av 3 course à la carte £20 🍴: Wadworth 🍺: Wadworth Henry's IPA & 6X, JCB, plus guests. ♀: 8 **FACILITIES:** Child facs Garden: Gravel laid with shrub borders Dogs allowed **NOTES:** Parking 70

♀ 7   Number of wines by the glass

Pick of the Pubs

HINDON – WILTSHIRE

Angel Inn

Elegant gastro pub close to Salisbury in a country setting, full of rustic charm in an elegant Georgian coaching inn and brasserie. Hindon is a particularly attractive village in a rural area, where the Angel has established a reputation for its modern British food.

The inn was once known as the Grosvenor Arms, built in 1750 on the site of a medieval predecessor known as The Angel. The original name was restored along with the building some years ago. The interior is characterised by wooden floors, beams, and large stone fireplaces. Here you can enjoy hand-pulled real ales in a traditional atmosphere. New owner John Harrington, no stranger to the catering trade, aims to maintain the relaxed, convivial pub atmosphere where excellent food and hospitality can be relied on. Visitors can eat in the Gallery Restaurant or the Drawing Room, where the menus will offer instant appeal. Lunch provides an extensive choice, with rolled shoulder of lamb stuffed with chicken and tarragon mousse, served with madeira sauce; cold poached salmon with smoked trout mousse; open sandwich filled with prawn salad and smoked salmon; and Wiltshire ham, eggs and chips offering something for everyone. The main menu extends to confit of duck leg and slices of breast; grilled whole sole with lemon and caper butter; noisettes of lamb on puréed fennel with a lime and pernod sauce; and seared calves' liver with smoked bacon on creamed potato. Outside is an attractive paved courtyard with garden furniture, where food is also served in fine weather.

OPEN: 11-3 5-11
BAR MEALS: L served all week 12-2.30 D served Mon-Sat 7-9.30 Av main course £8.50
RESTAURANT: L served all week 12-2.30 D served Mon-Sat 7-9.30 Av 3 course à la carte £23.50
🍴: Free House
🍺: Wadworth 6X, Buttcombe, Ringwood, Hidden Brewery. 🍷: 12
FACILITIES: Garden: Paved courtyard with garden furniture Dogs allowed Water, Biscuits **NOTES:** Parking 20

🍷   Map 04 ST93
High St SP3 6DJ
☎ 01747 820696
🖨 01747 820054
📧 info@theangelathindon.com
Dir: 1.5m from A303, on B3089 towards Salisbury

LACOCK continued

The Rising Sun ♀
32 Bowden Hill SN15 2PP ☎ 01249 730363
The pub is located close to the National Trust village of
Lacock, on a steep hill, providing spectacular views over
Wiltshire from the large garden. Live music and quiz nights
are a regular feature, and games and reading material are
provided in the bar. Thai curries and stir-fries are popular
options, alongside traditional liver, bacon and onions; steaks;
and beef, ale and stilton pie.
OPEN: 12-3 6-11 (All day Sun, Summer all day Fri-Sun Closed Mon
lunchtime) **BAR MEALS:** L served Tues-Sun 12-2 D served Mon-Sat
6-9 Sun 12-2.30 **RESTAURANT:** L served Tue-Sun 2 D served Mon-Sat
9 Sun 12-2.30 **◀:** Moles Best, Moles Molennium, Molecatcher, Tap
Bitter. ♀: 10 **FACILITIES:** Garden: Large garden with views over
Salisbury Plain Dogs allowed Water **NOTES:** Parking 25

LIMPLEY STOKE   Map 04 ST76

The Hop Pole Inn
Woods Hill, Lower Limpley Stoke BA3 6HS
☎ 01225 723134 ▤ 01225 723199 e-mail: latonahop@aol.com
Dir: Off A36 (Bath to Warminster road)
The Hop Pole is set in the beautiful Limpley Stoke valley and
dates from 1580, the name coming from the hop plant that
still grows outside the pub. Eagle-eyed film fans may
recognise it as the pub in the 1992 film *Remains of the Day*. A
hearty menu includes home-made pies, fresh local trout, and
home-made specials such as Thai chicken, beef wellington,
liver and bacon casserole and whole plaice meunière. Giant
filled baps and other light bites are available.
OPEN: 11-2.30 6-11 (Sun 12-3, 7-10.30) Closed: 25 Dec
BAR MEALS: L served all week 12-2.15 D served all week 6.30-9.15
Av main course £8.50 **RESTAURANT:** L served all week 12-2.15
D served all week 6.30-9.15 Av 3 course à la carte £15 ⊜: Free
House ◀: Scottish Courage Courage Best, Butcombe Bitter,
Interbrew Bass, Guest Beers. **FACILITIES:** Garden: Private large
garden, patio, 15 benches Dogs allowed **NOTES:** Parking 20

LITTLE CHEVERELL   Map 04 ST95

The Owl ⌂ ♀
Low Rd SN10 4JS ☎ 01380 812263 ▤ 01380 812263
e-mail: jamie@theowl.info
Dir: A344 from Stonehenge, then A360, after 10m left onto B3098, right
after 0.5m, Owl signposted
A 19th-century local situated in a tiny hamlet surrounded by
farmland, with views of Salisbury Plain and plenty of good
walks. The pretty split-level garden runs down to the
Cheverell Brook. Quiz on first Wednesday of month in aid of a
local charity. Also three beer festivals during the year, with
one in August also hosting a soap-box derby - again in aid of
charity. Typical dishes include battered calamari, lasagne,
tomato and cheese pasta bake, Thai green chicken curry,
sizzling beef Szechwan, and stilton and mushroom pork.
OPEN: 11-3 6.30-11 (Sat 11-11 From Apr Sun 11-11, Mon-Fri 11-4
5.30-11) **BAR MEALS:** L served all week 12-3 D served all week
7-10.30 Sun 12-4, 7-9.30 **RESTAURANT:** L served all week 12-3
D served all week 7-10.30 Sun 12-4, 7-9.30 ⊜: Free House
◀: Wadworth 6X, Hook Norton Best, Cotleigh Tawney Owl, Scottish
Courage Courage Directors. ♀: 23 **FACILITIES:** Child facs
Children's licence Garden: Decked area, brook, benches Dogs
allowed Water **NOTES:** Parking 28

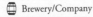
🛢 Brewery/Company

LOWER CHICKSGROVE   Map 04 ST92

Pick of the Pubs

Compasses Inn ♦♦♦♦ ⌂ ♀
SP3 6NB ☎ 01722 714318 ▤ 01722 714318
e-mail: thecompasses@aol.com
web: www.thecompassesinn.com
Dir: A30 W from Salisbury, after 10m right signed Chicksgrove. 1st left
down single track lane, pub 1m.
An idyllic 14th-century thatched pub deep in beautiful
Wiltshire countryside, offering the very best in real ale,
fine wines and freshly prepared food. Not that easy to
find, but worth negotiating the narrow lanes for. Inside
the latched door, there's a long, low-beamed bar with
high-backed stools, stone walls, worn flagstone floors and
a large inglenook fireplace with a wood-burning stove.
The blackboard menu changes daily, depending on the
time of year and local availability. Everything is freshly
made, including the popular steak and kidney pie with
suet pastry; duck breast with a Chinese jus; pork
tenderloin with blue vinny cheese, cider and cream sauce;
and monkfish marinated in Thai spices with rice. A good
range of filled onion loaves, salads and jacket potatoes is
available at lunchtime. Puddings include wild strawberry
Alexander, and chocolate and Kahlua mousse. Try a pint
of Chicksgrove Churl in the garden, and drink in the
lovely country views as well.
OPEN: 12-3 6-11 Winter Sun evening close 8.30 Closed: 25, 26
Dec **BAR MEALS:** L served Tue-Sun 12-2 D served Tue-Sat 7-9
(No food Sun eve) Av main course £12.95
RESTAURANT: L served Tues-Sun 12-2 D served Tues-Sat 7-9
(No food Sun eve) Av 3 course à la carte £23 ⊜: Free House
◀: Interbrew Bass, Wadworth 6X, Ringwood Best, Chicksgrove
Churl. ♀: 7 **FACILITIES:** Child facs Garden: Large grass area
with nice views, seats 40 Dogs Water **NOTES:** Parking 30
ROOMS: 4 bedrooms en suite 3 family rooms s£45 d£75

LOWER WOODFORD   Map 05 SU13

The Wheatsheaf ♀
SP4 6NQ ☎ 01722 782203
Dir: Take A360 N of Salisbury. Village signed 1st R
Once a farm and brewhouse, now a thriving country pub in
the Avon Valley. A rustic decor gives the interior a
contemporary twist. Expect dishes like seared tuna steak with
lemon and coriander butter, salmon and dill fishcakes, and
traditional cod and chips. Steak and Tanglefoot ale pie,
Cumberland sausage and mash, and slow-roasted lamb shank
should also be available.
OPEN: 11-11 (Sun 12.10.30) **BAR MEALS:** L served all week
12-9.30 D served all week Av main course £7.50
RESTAURANT: L served all week 12-2.30 D served all week 7-9.30
⊜: Hall & Woodhouse ◀: Badger Dorset Best & Tanglefoot,plus
guest ales. **FACILITIES:** Garden: Food served outside. Enclosed
garden Dogs allowed in the garden only **NOTES:** Parking 50

MALMESBURY   Map 04 ST98

The Smoking Dog ♀
62 The High St SN16 9AT ☎ 01666 825823 ▤ 01666 826513
e-mail: smokindog@sabrain.com
Log fires, solid wooden floors and a relaxed atmosphere greet
visitors to this refined 18th-century stone-built pub, right in
the heart of Malmesbury. There's an expanding range of real
ales that features continually changing guest beers, and the
continued

England

MALMESBURY continued

pub has a good reputation for interesting, freshly-cooked food. Each year the thirsty and hungry can enjoy a beer and sausage festival.
OPEN: 12-11 (Sun 12-10.30) **BAR MEALS:** L served all week 12-2.30 D served all week 7-9.30 Sun12-2.30
RESTAURANT: L served all week 12-2.30 D served all week 7-9.30 Sun 12-2.30 ⊕: ◀: Wadworth 6X, Archers Best, Brains Bitter, Reverend James plus 2 guest bitters. ♀: 9 **FACILITIES:** Child facs Garden: Large suntrap with landscaped lawns Dogs allowed Water, Biscuits

Pick of the Pubs

The Vine Tree ♀
Foxley Rd, Norton SN16 0JP
☎ 01666 837654 🖷 01666 838003
e-mail: enquries@thevinetree.co.uk
See Pick of the Pubs on opposite page

MARDEN
Map 05 SU05

The Millstream NEW ♀
SN10 3RH ☎ 01380 848308 🖷 01380 848337
e-mail: mail@the-millstream.co.uk
Dir: Signed from A342
Formerly the New Inn, the Millstream reopened in July 2003 after tasteful refurbishment. Once seated in the stone and wooden floored restaurant, start perhaps with a traditional Greek salad, or galia and canteloupe melon with mint syrup and bayonne ham; then try pan-fried scallops with spiced aubergine, crispy pancetta and meat juice; or rare roast rib of beef with Yorkshire pudding, mange-touts, carrots and roast potatoes. Clean the palate with a lemon posset.
OPEN: 12-11.30 **BAR MEALS:** L served all week 12-2.30 D served all week 6.30-9.30 Sun 12-5, longer hrs Fri-Sat Av main course £11.75
RESTAURANT: L served all week 12-2.30 D served all week Sun 12-5 Av 3 course à la carte £25 ⊕: Wadworth ◀: 6X, Henry's IPA, JCB, Bishops Tipple. ♀: 16 **FACILITIES:** Children's licence Garden: Open lawn with stream, terrace, herb garden Dogs allowed Water, biscuits **NOTES:** Parking 25

MELKSHAM
Map 04 ST96

Kings Arms Hotel
Market Place SN12 6EX ☎ 01225 707272 🖷 01225 792986
Dir: In the town centre opposite Lloyds Bank
Once an important coaching house on the London to Bath route, warmth and hospitality are offered by this traditional market place inn. Dating back around 300 years, the bar has been sympathetically modernised and now offers a charming, comfortable drinking and dining venue. The menu features quality, locally-sourced produce whenever possible.
OPEN: 11-2.30 6-11 **BAR MEALS:** L served all week 12-2 D served all week 7-9.30 Sun 12-2 Av main course £7
RESTAURANT: L served all week 12-2 D served all week 7-9 Av 3 course à la carte £12 ⊕: Wadworth ◀: Wadworth 6X, Wadworth Henrys Original IPA, John Smiths, Henry Smooth.
FACILITIES: Garden: grass area, tables & chairs Dogs allowed **NOTES:** Parking 30

◆ Diamond rating for inspected guest accommodation

MERE
Map 04 ST83

The George Inn
The Square BA12 6DR ☎ 01747 860427 🖷 01747 861978
e-mail: rob.binstead@btconnect.com
Dir: Follow signs from A303 into village, pub opposite clock tower.
Extensively but carefully refurbished 16th-century inn, formerly the Talbot, where fugitive Charles II dined en route to Shoreham and ultimately France. Today's diners can relax and enjoy lime and chilli chicken breast, chilli con carne, beef lasagne, smoked mackerel fillets, and tortellini pasta filled with stilton and walnut. Filling salad platters and jacket potatoes are also an option.
OPEN: 11-3 6-11 (Sun 12-3, 7-10.30) **BAR MEALS:** L served all week 12-2 D served all week 6.30-9 Sun 6-9 Av main course £7.25
RESTAURANT: L served all week 12-2 D served all week 6.30-9 Av 3 course à la carte £15 ⊕: Hall & Woodhouse ◀: Badger Best, Sussex, Festive Pheasant, Fursty Ferret. **FACILITIES:** Garden: Patio area **NOTES:** Parking 20

MINETY
Map 05 SU09

Pick of the Pubs

Vale of the White Horse Inn ♀
SN16 9QY ☎ 01666 860175 🖷 01666 860175
e-mail: bookings@vwhi.net
See Pub Walk on page 518
See Pick of the Pubs on page 534

NUNTON
Map 05 SU12

The Radnor Arms 🐟 ♀
SP5 4HS ☎ 01722 329722
Dir: From Salisbury ring road take A338 to Ringwood. Nunton signed on R

A popular pub in the centre of the village dating from around 1750. In 1855 it was owned by the local multi-talented brewer/baker/grocer. Bought by Lord Radnor in 1919. Bar snacks are supplemented by an extensive fish choice and daily specials, which might include braised lamb shank, wild mushroom risotto, tuna with noodles, turbot with spinach or Scotch rib-eye fillet, all freshly prepared. Fine summer garden with rural views. Hosts an annual local pumpkin competition.
OPEN: 11-3 6-11 (Sun 12-3, Sun 7-10.30) **BAR MEALS:** L served all week 12-2.30 D served Mon-Sat 7-9.30 **RESTAURANT:** L served all week 12-2.30 D served all week 7-9.30 ⊕: Hall & Woodhouse ◀: Badger Tanglefoot, Best & Golden Champion. **FACILITIES:** Child facs Food served outside in large garden Dogs allowed **NOTES:** Parking 40

Pick of the Pubs

The Vine Tree

Here is a converted 16th-century mill well worth seeking out for its interesting modern pub food and memorable outdoor summer dining. In a former life co-owner Tiggi Wood organised the catering at Glyndebourne and Formula One events; she even trained chefs in Paris. Her partner Charlie Walker travelled internationally for Rothman's, and now handles the pub's finances and marketing.

Although it used to be a mill, workers apparently passed beverages out through front windows to passing carriages - an early drive-through it would seem. In today's central bar a large open fireplace burns wood all winter, and there's an abundance of old beams, flagstone and oak floors, and resident ghosts (well two, anyway, one a small boy in polo kit, which is quite spooky because England's earliest polo pitches were next door). Cooking is modern British in style, the menu changing daily in response to local produce availability. Tiggi and Charlie

say they are proud not to belong to the "bought in, fake it brigade" and so everything on the menus is produced in-house, including bread. Dishes include light bites, vegetarian options, griddled fresh squid; fillets of gilthead bream; brandade of salt cod; traditional chateaubriand for two; pot roast partridge; caramelised barbary duck breast, local wood pigeon, and pan-fried foie gras. There's also a terrific stock of wines. In addition to the sun-trap terrace, there's a two-acre garden with two boules pitches. Jazz and blues bands play here once a month.

OPEN: 12-3 6-11 (Sun 12-10.30)
BAR MEALS: L served all week 12-2
D served Sun-Thurs 7-9.30 Sun
L served til 3 D served til 10 Fri & Sat
RESTAURANT: L served all week
12-2 D served all week 6-9.30
🛢: Free House
🍺: Lowenbrau, Butcombe, Bath Spa
Ales. 🍷: 25
FACILITIES: Garden: Food served
outside. Terrace with fountain Dogs
allowed Water & toys provided
NOTES: Parking 100

🍷   Map 04 ST98
Foxley Rd, Norton SN16 0JP
☎ 01666 837654
📄 01666 838003
📧 enquries@thevinetree.co.uk
Dir: 5 mins from junct 17 off the
M4 on the
Wiltshire/Gloucestershire border

Pick of the Pubs

MINETY – WILTSHIRE

Vale of the White Horse Inn

Easy to find on the eastern side of the village of Minety, this handsome and beautifully restored inn was built in about 1830 from large blocks of natural stone. It overlooks its own lake and in summer, sitting out on the large raised terrace, surrounded by rose beds, hanging baskets and large pots, it would be hard to think of a better spot for a lunchtime snack or early evening pint.

Originally, the lower ground floor provided stabling for horses and storage for carts and goods. These days the Village Bar still serves a valuable social function, dispensing a good choice of real ales, wholemeal baguettes, ciabatta rolls and ploughman's. Upstairs, the stone-walled restaurant features polished tables, bentwood chairs and a lunch and dinner menu offering smoked haddock and prawn fishcake with cumin and tartare sauce; calamari with green chilli and garlic mayonnaise; red tandoori chicken curry on basmati rice; Chinese sweet and sour pork with ginger rice; and Thai beef, plum and noodle stir-fry. The last item is one of several meat-based main courses for which a vegetarian version is also available. Specials at dinner might include pot-roasted chicken breast on a tomato fondant and melted gruyère; or pan-fried pork fillet with baby onions. Most of the desserts are old favourites like sticky toffee pudding with toffee sauce; and treacle tart and crème anglaise with vanilla ice cream, but white chocolate and orange crème brûlée with basil shortbread will be new to some. An extensive wine list is available.

OPEN: 12-3 6-12 (open all day Sat & Sun)
BAR MEALS: L served all week 12-2.30 D served all week 6-9.30 (Sun 6-9) Av main course £8.95
RESTAURANT: L served all week 2.30-9.30 D served all week 6-9.30 Av 3 course à la carte £16.95
🍺: Wadworth 6X & Henry's IPA, Archers Golden, Goffs Jouster, Adnams Sussex. ♀: 8
FACILITIES: Child facs Garden: Grass area around lake, terrace Dogs allowed Water **NOTES:** Parking 48

♀ Map 05 SU09
SN16 9QY ☎ 01666 860175
🖹 01666 860175
ⓔ bookings@vwhi.net
Dir: On B4040 6 m E of Malmesbury.

OAKSEY   Map 04 ST99

The Wheatsheaf Inn NEW ♀
Wheatsheaf Ln SN16 9TB ☎ 01666 577348
e-mail: info@thecompletechef.co.uk
Dir: *Off A419 6m S of Cirencester*
A village inn built in the 14th century from mellow Cotswold
stone, the Wheatsheaf has one rather bizarre feature: an 18th-
century 'royal' coffin lid displayed above the open fireplace.
All the food is made on the premises from fresh local
produce. Typical dishes are rillette of Old Spot pork with
apple and scrumpy purée; slow cooked lamb shank with basil
polenta and jus niçoise; and vanilla pannacotta with poached
prunes and Armagnac.
OPEN: 11.30-2.30 6-11 (Sun 12-10.30) **BAR MEALS:** L served Mon
& Tues 12-2 D served Tues 6.30-9.30 Av main course £11
RESTAURANT: L served Wed-Sat 12-2 Sun 12-4.30 D served
Tues-Sat 6.30-9.30 Av 3 course à la carte £20 ◀: Blanc White Beer,
London Pride, Hook Norton, Wychwood Hobgoblin. ♀: 7
FACILITIES: Garden: Patio with tables and heaters Dogs allowed
NOTES: Parking 15

PEWSEY   Map 05 SU16

Pick of the Pubs

The Seven Stars ♀
Bottlesford SN9 6LU ☎ 01672 851325 ▥ 01672 851583
e-mail: sevenstarsinn@hotmail.com
Dir: *Off A345*
There are new owners at this thatched, creeper-clad 16th-
century pub tucked away in a hamlet in the heart of the
Vale of Pewsey. Like many pubs it has a large garden, but
few can match the seven splendid acres here. The front
door opens straight on to the low-beamed, oak-panelled
bar, with dining areas to either side. The weekly changing
menus offer starters such as home-made mussel, leek
and saffron soup; pan-fried black pudding with poached
egg on red wine and bacon sauce; and mushrooms in a
filo basket with creamy stilton sauce. A comprehensive
selection of main courses may include Sandridge
farmhouse sausages with mash and onion gravy; gin-
flamed wild boar; seared scallops with spring onions,
bacon and hoi sin sauce; or braised lamb shank with
either mint and onion gravy, or rosemary and redcurrant
jus. Snacks and light meals are also available.
OPEN: 11.30-3 6-11 **BAR MEALS:** L served all week 12-2.30
D served all week 6-9.30 **RESTAURANT:** L served all week 12-2.30
D served all week 6-9.30 ☺: Free House ◀: Wadworth 6X, Badger
Dorset Best, London Pride. ♀: 9 **FACILITIES:** Garden: Lawned
with terrace at front of pub **NOTES:** Parking 50

The Woodbridge Inn
North Newnton SN9 6JZ ☎ 01980 630266
e-mail: woodbridgeinn@btconnect.com
Dir: *2m SW on A345*
Variously a toll house, bakery and brewhouse, this Grade II-
listed, 16th-century building stands in over four acres of
beautiful grounds by the Wiltshire/Hampshire Avon, and was
established as a coaching inn in 1850. Eating options are
traditional.
OPEN: 12-11 (Sun 12-10.30) **BAR MEALS:** L served all week 12-9
D served all week 12-9 **RESTAURANT:** L served all week 12-9
D served all week 12-9 ☺: Wadworth ◀: Wadworth 6X, Henrys
IPA, Summersault & Old Timer. **FACILITIES:** Garden: Large grassed
with flower beds Dogs allowed Water **NOTES:** Parking 60

RAMSBURY   Map 05 SU27

Pick of the Pubs

The Bell ♀
The Square SN8 2PE ☎ 01672 520230
This 300-year-old Wiltshire village inn has had a
contemporary makeover in its fabric and food but still
retains a traditional feel with features like the old church
pews and the pretty garden to the rear. Good real ales
and constantly changing and modern style wine list are
offered at the bar. Fish is the house speciality. Try the
grilled red mullet with roasted pepper, almond parfait
and pesto oil or the gilthead bream baked with olive oil.
The kitchen seems to thrive on diversity and happily
combines classical techniques with a healthy dose of
global inspiration. Take the tomato, coconut and
coriander soup with lemon grass oil, for example. Some
ingredients may be local but the recipe most certainly is
not. It's rare to find a restaurant menu that offers stuffed
Lebanese peppers with a spicy tomato coulis, and stacked
medallions of venison and haggis with a red wine
reduction. But it all seems to work well and booking is
advised at weekends. Desserts can be delightfully wacky.
OPEN: 12-3 6-11 (Sun 12-3, 7-10.30) **BAR MEALS:** L served
Tues-Sun 12-2 D served Mon-Sat 7-9 Av main course £9
RESTAURANT: L served all week 12-2 D served Mon-Sat 7-9
Av 3 course à la carte £25 ☺: Free House ◀: Butts, Wadworth
6X & Henry's Origional IPA, West Berkshire, Arkells. ♀: 15
FACILITIES: Country garden Dogs allowed Water bowls
NOTES: Parking 20

ROWDE   Map 04 ST96

Pick of the Pubs

The George and Dragon ◉ ⤳ ♀
High St SN10 2PN ☎ 01380 723053 ▥ 01380 723053
e-mail: thegandd@tiscali.co.uk
Winter log fires warm the panelled bars and dining room
of this fascinating free house, which isn't far from the
dramatic Caen Hill lock flight on the Kennet and Avon
Canal. The building dates from the 15th century, and
diners can see a Tudor rose carved on one of the original
restaurant beams. Butcombe Bitter and Ringwood
Fortyniner are amongst the draught beers on offer, and
there's also a good selection of malt whiskies and wines
by the glass. Fresh fish dishes are a particular highlight of
the daily-changing menus. Leek, potato and ham soup, or
double baked cheese soufflé might feature amongst the
starters. Main course dishes like rack of lamb with braised
cabbage; roast monkfish with parsnip mash; and seared
swordfish with rocket, parmesan and balsamic dressing
are typical choices, whilst warm winter fruits with
Chantilly cream, or chocolate fondant cake with crème
Anglaise, are sure to round off the meal successfully.
OPEN: 12-3 7-11 (Closed Mon morning) Closed: 1-8 Jan
BAR MEALS: L served Tues-Sat 12-3 D served Tues-Sat 7-10
Sat-Sun 12-4 **RESTAURANT:** L served Tues-Sun 12-3 D served
Tues-Sat 7-10 Sun 12-4 Av 3 course à la carte £22 ☺: Free
House ◀: Butcombe Bitter, Milk Street Brewery, Bath Ales Gem,
ESB. ♀: 11 **FACILITIES:** Child facs Garden: Lawn area with
cottage style flower borders Dogs allowed Water
NOTES: Parking 12

England

England

SALISBURY   Map 05 SU12

Pick of the Pubs

The Haunch of Venison ♀
1-5 Minster St SP1 1TB ☎ 01722 411313 ▤ 01722 341774
e-mail: info@haunchofvenisonsalisbury.co.uk
Dir: 500mtrs from Cathedral
The inn's earliest records date from 1320, when it housed
craftsmen working on the cathedral spire. During a less
edifying period of the 14th century it also served as a
brothel. The pub is haunted by the tormented spirits of
the Grey Lady, searching for her lost child, and a
demented whist player who lost his hand through
cheating (the mummified hand is on display in the bar).
The tiles on the bar floor were rescued from the cathedral,
and other unique features are the pewter bar top and
original gravity-fed spirit taps. The first-floor restaurant
maximises the atmospheric advantages of huge oak
beams and a fireplace dating from 1588. Dishes include
smoked haddock chowder; glazed Wiltshire thick back of
bacon with black pudding and bubble and squeak; and
Russian chocolate vodka brûlée. Regular special events are
held, and there's a great choice of malt whiskies.
OPEN: 11-11 (Sun 12-10.30) Closed: Christmas Day Sun Nov-Apr
restaurant closed **BAR MEALS:** L served all week 12-2 Snacks only
in bar Av main course £8.50 **RESTAURANT:** L served all week
12-2.30 D served all week 6-10 Sun 6-9.30 Av 3 course à la carte £18
🍴: Enterprise Inns 🍺: Courage Best, Wadworth 6X, Summer
Lightning. ♀: 6 **FACILITIES:** Dogs allowed Bowl

The Old Mill Hotel ♀
Town Path, West Harnham SP2 8EU
☎ 01722 327517 ▤ 01722 333367
Dir: Near city centre, on River Avon
Listed building which became Wiltshire first papermaking mill
in 1550. Tranquil meadow setting with classic views of
Salisbury Cathedral. Crystal clear water diverted from the
River Nadder cascades through the restaurant.
OPEN: 11-11 **BAR MEALS:** L served all week 12-2.30 D served all
week 7-9 Av main course £4.95 **RESTAURANT:** L served all week
12-2 D served all week 7-9 Av 3 course à la carte £18 🍴: Old English
Inns 🍺: Greene King IPA, Old Speckled Hen. **FACILITIES:** Garden:
Food served outside Dogs allowed **NOTES:** Parking 10

SEEND   Map 04 ST96

The Barge Inn ♀
Seend Cleeve SN12 6QB ☎ 01380 828230 ▤ 01380 828972
Dir: Off A365 between Melksham & Devizes

This Victorian barge-style pub, converted from a wharf house,
is situated on the Kennet and Avon Canal between Bath and

continued

Devizes. Delicately painted Victorian flowers adorn the
ceilings and walls, which were once home to 8 feet 2 inches-
tall Fred Kempster, the 'Wiltshire Giant'. In addition to the
lunchtime menu of snacks and hot dishes - tapas, baked field
mushroom, goujons of Cornish cod - there's a seasonal carte
supported by an extensive list of blackboard specials.
OPEN: 11-3 6-11 (All day Sat-Sun) **BAR MEALS:** L served all week
12-2 D served all week 7-9.30 Sat and BH lunch 12-2.30 Av main
course £9 **RESTAURANT:** L served all week 12-2 D served all week
7-9.30 Sat-Sun and BH lunch 12-2.30 🍴: Wadworth 🍺: Wadworth
6X & Henry's IPA, Bishops Tipple, Butcombe Bitter. ♀: 10
FACILITIES: Child facs Garden: Large canalside garden Dogs
allowed Water **NOTES:** Parking 50

Bell Inn 🗟
Bell Hill SN12 6SA ☎ 01380 828338 e-mail: Bellseend@aol.com
According to local tradition, Oliver Cromwell and his troops
enjoyed breakfast at this inn, quite possibly on 18 September
1645 when he was advancing from Trowbridge to attack
Devizes Castle. The extensive menu runs to poached salmon
with a prawn and cream sauce; spicy bean burgers; and
barbecue pork ribs, while the specials board highlights liver
and bacon casserole; chicken balti; and Highland sausages in
whisky. The two-floor restaurant has lovely valley views.
OPEN: 11.15-3 5.30-11 **BAR MEALS:** L served all week 11.45-2.15
D served all week 6.15-9.30 Sun 12-2.15 Av main course £7.50
RESTAURANT: L served all week 11.45-2.15 D served all week
6.15-9.30 Sun 12-2.15 Av 3 course à la carte £14.50 🍴: Wadworth
🍺: Wadworth 6X, Henry's IPA & Henrys Smooth. **FACILITIES:** Child
facs Garden: Large, seating for 60 people, beautiful views Dogs
allowed Water **NOTES:** Parking 30

SEMINGTON   Map 04 ST86

The Lamb on the Strand NEW ♀
99 The Strand BA14 6LL ☎ 01380 870263
& 870815 ▤ 01380 871203
Dir: 1.5m E on A361 from junct with A350
An 18th-century brick farmhouse that later became a beer
and cider house. Today's popular dining pub provides what
the owner describes as an 'eclectic cuisine de campagne',
which translates as salmon fishcakes with dill mayonnaise;
smoked haddock with Welsh rarebit topping; Wiltshire ham
salad; cauliflower cheese with crispy bacon and French bread;
and local sausages of the day with bubble and squeak.
OPEN: 11.30-3 6.30-11 (Closed Sun eve) Closed: 25-26 Dec, 1 Jan
BAR MEALS: L served all week 12-2 D served Mon-Sat 6.30-9
Av main course £7.95 🍺: Butcombe Bitter, Ringwood Bitter,
Shepherd Neame spitfire, Guinness. ♀: 12 **FACILITIES:** Garden:
Walled lawn and deck with heating Dogs allowed
NOTES: Parking 50

SHERSTON
Map 04 ST88

Carpenters Arms ⌾
SN16 0LS ☎ 01666 840665
Dir: On the B4040 W of Malmesbury
A locals' pub of whitewashed Cotswold stone dating from the 17th century. It has four interconnecting rooms, with low, beamed ceilings, a wood-burner and a cosy old-world atmosphere. The sunny conservatory restaurant overlooks the garden - a plantsman's delight with its large variety of shrubs, climbers, specimen roses, acers and herbaceous perennials. Seasonal fish dishes are served alongside pies, venison sausages, smoked salmon crêpes, and mushroom and paprika parcels.
OPEN: 12-2.30 5-11 (Sat 10-2.30, Sun 7-10.30)
BAR MEALS: L served all week 12-2 D served Mon-Sat 7-9 Av main course £7.50 **RESTAURANT:** L served all week 12-2 D served Mon-Sat 7-9 Av 3 course à la carte £12.50 ⌷: Enterprise Inns
◀: Interbrew Flowers IPA & Whitbread Best, Guest Ales. ⌾: 7
FACILITIES: Child facs Garden: Plantsman's garden, array of plants
NOTES: Parking 12

STOFORD
Map 05 SU03

The Swan Inn ◆◆◆ 🐟
SP2 0PR ☎ 01722 790236 📠 01722 790115
e-mail: info@theswanatstoford.co.uk
Dir: From Salisbury take A36 towards Warminster. Pub 4m on from Wilton
There are lovely views of the Wylye Valley from this former coaching inn, which dates back over 300 years. The family-owned free house has open fires, its own West Country skittle alley, and a riverside garden. The non-smoking restaurant enjoys a reputation for good food: a typical meal starts with Thai crab and white fishcakes, moves on through chargrilled supreme of chicken, and ends with home-made bread and butter pudding with clotted cream.
OPEN: 11-3 6-11 **BAR MEALS:** L served all week 12-2 D served all week 6.30-9 (Sunday Evening 7-9) **RESTAURANT:** L served all week 12-2 D served all week 6.30-9 (Sunday evening 7-9) ◀: Ringwood Best, Greene King Old Speckled Hen, Fuller's London Pride, Strongs Bitter. **FACILITIES:** Garden: 2 gardens - 1 by river, 1 landscaped at rear **NOTES:** Parking 100 **ROOMS:** 9 bedrooms en suite 2 family rooms s£40 d£50 No children overnight

STOURHEAD
Map 04 ST73

Spread Eagle Inn ⌾
BA12 6QE ☎ 01747 840587 📠 01747 840954
Dir: N of A303 off B3092
This charming inn was built at the beginning of the 19th century in the heart of the 2,650-acre Stourhead Estate, now one of the country's most visited National Trust properties. Before or after a walk through the magnificent gardens and landscapes there is plenty on offer here, including guinea fowl or wood pigeon supreme; beef stir-fry; wild boar and herb sausages; swordfish steak; and Mediterranean stuffed peppers. The bar menu embraces inexpensive hot meals, filled jackets, ploughman's, salads and sandwiches.
OPEN: 9-11 **BAR MEALS:** L served all week 12-3 D served all week 6-9 **RESTAURANT:** D served all week 6-9 ⌷: Free House
◀: Courage Best, Wadworth 6X. **FACILITIES:** Garden
NOTES: Parking 200

> ★ Star rating for inspected hotel accommodation

SWINDON
Map 05 SU18

The Sun Inn ⌾
Lydiard Millicent SN5 3LU ☎ 01793 770425 📠 01793 778287
e-mail: thesuninnlm@yahoo.co.uk
Dir: 3 miles to the W of Swindon, 1.5 miles from Junct 16 of M4

Photographs and pictures illustrate the history of this 18th-century free house, located in the conservation area of Lydiard Millicent. There's an emphasis on real ale here, with offerings from the West Berkshire Brewery, Archers, Wadworth and the Wye Valley Brewery. The varied menus include a good selection of grills, fish, and appetising daily specials like oven-baked rainbow trout; tenderloin pork with caramelized apple and spinach; and filo tulip of oven roasted vegetables with dolcelatte.
OPEN: 11.30-3 5-11 (Sat 11.30-3, 6-11, Sun 12-4, 6.30-10.30 Mar-Sep all day Sun) **BAR MEALS:** L served all week 12-2.30 D served all week 6.30-9.30 (Sun 12-2.30 6.30-9) **RESTAURANT:** L served all week 12-2.30 D served all week 6.30-9.30 12-2.30 6.30-9 Sun
⌷: Free House ◀: Interbrew Flowers original, Wadsworth 6X, Wye Valley Brewery, West Berkshire Brewery. ⌾: 8 **FACILITIES:** Child facs Large garden area, BBQ, suntrap Dogs allowed in bar Water
NOTES: Parking 50

TOLLARD ROYAL
Map 04 ST91

King John Inn
SP5 5PS ☎ 01725 516207
Dir: On B3081 (7m E of Shaftesbury)
Named after one of King John's hunting lodges, this Victorian building was opened in 1859. A friendly and relaxing place, it is today perhaps better known as 'Madonna's local' after she and husband Guy Ritchie moved in close by. Also nearby is a 13th-century church, and the area is excellent rambling country. A typical menu offers old English favourites such as bangers and apple mash; bacon, liver and kidney casserole; Dorset lamb cutlets; Wiltshire gammon with peaches; and Dover sole.
OPEN: 12-2.30 6.30-11 (Sun 12-10.30) **BAR MEALS:** L served all week 12-2 D served all week 7-9 (All day Sun summer)
RESTAURANT: L served all week 12-2 D served all week 7-9
⌷: Free House ◀: Courage Best, John Smith's, Wadworth 6X, Ringwood. **FACILITIES:** Garden: Terrace, food served outside Dogs allowed Water **NOTES:** Parking 18

UPPER CHUTE
Map 05 SU25

The Cross Keys ⌾
SP11 9ER ☎ 01264 730295 📠 01264 730679
Dir: Near Andover
Located in a walkers' paradise on top of the North Wessex Downs, this free house adjoins a village shop and post office and boasts commanding views from its south-facing terrace

continued

UPPER CHUTE continued

and garden. People flock here by foot, bike and car to enjoy the views, the welcome and of course good home-cooked food: perhaps cottage pie, Irish stew, or Sunday roast. **OPEN:** 11-3 6-11 (Sun 12-4, 7-10.30) **BAR MEALS:** L served all week 12-2 D served all week 6-9 Av main course £7.50 **RESTAURANT:** L served all week 12-2 D served all week 6-9 Av 3 course à la carte £15 🏠: Free House 🍺: Fuller's London Pride, Hampshire Strong's Best, Greene King IPA, Ringwood Best. 🍷: 10 **FACILITIES:** Children's licence Large garden, picnic tables, patio area, chairs Dogs allowed Water, doggie treats **NOTES:** Parking 40

UPTON LOVELL   Map 04 ST94

Prince Leopold Inn 🐟 🍷
BA12 0JP ☎ 01985 850460 🖻 01985 850737
e-mail: Princeleopold@Lineone.net
web: www.princeleopoldinn.co.uk
Dir: *S of A36 between Warminster & Salisbury*

Built in 1887 as the local shop, post office and general store. Prince Leopold, Queen Victoria's youngest son, often used the inn when he lived in nearby Boyton. The restaurant has a Mediterranean feel, although the panoramic views across the Wyle Valley are quintessentially English. The menu covers a lot of gastronomic ground, ranging from Orkney herrings marinated in dill vinaigrette, to spicy pork African style, to grilled skate wing. There's also a choice of balti curries. **OPEN:** 12-3 7-11 **BAR MEALS:** L served all week 12-2.30 D served all week 7-10 Av main course £7.50 **RESTAURANT:** L served all week 12-2.30 D served all week 7-10 Av 3 course à la carte £18 🏠: Free House 🍺: Ringwood Best, Scottish Courage John Smith's. 🍷: 8 **FACILITIES:** Riverside garden, spectacular valley views **NOTES:** Parking 20

WARMINSTER   Map 04 ST84

Pick of the Pubs

The Angel Inn 🍷
Upton Scudamore BA12 0AG
☎ 01985 213225 🖻 01985 218182
e-mail: theangelinn.uptonscudamore@btopenworld.com
Dir: *Close to Warminster and Westbury on junc A350 and A36*
A relaxed and unpretentious 16th-century coaching inn in a small village with a name Agatha Christie might have made up. Fresh sea fish comes from Brixham five times a week, and head chef Paul Suter is always looking for new ways to prepare it. Freshly prepared lunch could be Cumberland sausage with horseradish mash and blackcurrant sauce, or game casserole with juniper berries and bacon dumplings. Dinner candidates include
continued

honey-glazed breast of duck with cumin and sweet potato pancake and pineapple sauce, or bacon-wrapped gilthead fillet of sea bream with saffron mash, roasted almonds and red curry sauce. The walled garden and terrace are ideal for enjoying al fresco dining in the summer. **OPEN:** 11-3 6-11 Closed: 25-26 Dec, 1 Jan **BAR MEALS:** L served all week 12-2 D served all week 7-9.30 **RESTAURANT:** L served all week 12-2 D served all week 7-9.30 Av 3 course à la carte £25 🏠: Free House 🍺: Wadworth 6X, Butcombe, John Smith's Smooth, Guest Ales. 🍷: 8 **FACILITIES:** Garden: Walled terrace Dogs allowed Water provided **NOTES:** Parking 30

The Bath Arms 🐟 🍷
Clay St, Crockerton BA12 8AJ ☎ 01985 212262 🖻 01985 218670

Open fires, wooden floors and a good selection of ales greet locals and visitors to this well-known free house on the Longleat Estate. Warminster-born chef/proprietor Dean Carr's impressive culinary pedigree is reflected in the daily changing menus, though grills, snacks and Sunday roasts are always available too. Other dishes might include wild mushroom and rocket risotto; fish cake with broad beans and Cornish crab; and sticky beef with braised red cabbage. **OPEN:** 11-3 6-11 (Open all day in Summer) **BAR MEALS:** L served all week 12-2.30 D served all week 6-9.30 **RESTAURANT:** L served all week 12-2.30 D served all week 6-9.30 🍺: Butcombe Courage, Crockerton Classic, Berlington Bertie, Blackrat. 🍷: 10 **FACILITIES:** Garden: Stone walled, lawned garden, 19 tables & BBQ Dogs allowed Water bowls **NOTES:** Parking 45

The George Inn ♦♦♦♦ 🍷
BA12 7DG ☎ 01985 840396 🖻 01985 841333

A 17th-century coaching inn at the heart of the pretty village of Longbridge Deverill. Customers can enjoy a pint of real ale by the fire in the oak-beamed Longbridge bar, or sit outside in the two-acre garden on the banks of the River Wylye. Food is served in a choice of two no-smoking restaurants, and there is a Sunday carvery in the Wylye Suite. Function facilities are
continued

available, plus accommodation in 11 en suite bedrooms.
OPEN: 11-11 25 Dec Closed eve **BAR MEALS:** L served all week
12-2.30 D served all week 6-9.30 Sun 6-9 Av main course £11.45
RESTAURANT: L served all week 12-2.30 D served all week
6.30-9.30 (Sun 6-9) Av 3 course à la carte £18.95 🍺: Free House
🍺: Scottish Courage John Smith's, Wadworth 6X, Interbrew Bass.
🍷: 7 **FACILITIES:** Garden: Large riverside setting
NOTES: Parking 70 **ROOMS:** 11 bedrooms en suite 1 family room
s£45 d£70

WESTBURY   Map 04 ST85

The Duke at Bratton 🐟 🍷
Melbourne St, Bratton BA13 4RW
☎ 01380 830242 📠 01380 831239
Dir: From Westbury follow B3098 for Whitehorse & Bratton

Tucked away at the foot of the Westbury White Horse, this
award-winning free house features a whalebone archway
leading into the pub garden. The Duke is a good refreshment
stop on the way to nearby Bratton Castle and Edington Priory
church. Fresh local ingredients underpin the extensive menu,
which ranges from omelettes and salads to grills and roasts.
Applewood smoked trout with horseradish, vegetarian
tagliatelle, and roast Wiltshire chicken are typical choices.
OPEN: 11.30-3 7-11 (Sun 12-3, 7-10.30) 25 Dec Closed pm
BAR MEALS: L served all week 12-2 D served Tues-Sat 7-9 Av main
course £6 **RESTAURANT:** L served all week 12-2 D served Tues-Sat
7-9 Av 3 course à la carte £17.50 🍺: Free House 🍺: Moles Best,
John Smiths Bitter, Moles Special, guest beers. 🍷: 14
FACILITIES: Garden: Large beer garden at rear Dogs allowed on
leads in garden; water **NOTES:** Parking 30

WHITLEY   Map 04 ST86

Pick of the Pubs

The Pear Tree Inn 🏨 🍷
Top Ln SN12 8QX ☎ 01225 709131 📠 01225 702276
e-mail: enquries@peartreeinn.co.uk
*Dir: A365 from Melksham toward Bath, at Shaw right on B3353 into
Whitley, 1st left in lane, pub is at end of lane.*
The Pear Tree is a delightful pub/restaurant in an
attractive rural setting surrounded by parkland studded
with great oak trees. Well-planted gardens surround the
buildings and there is an extensive patio area with solid
teak furniture and cream parasols. To the front, there's a
large boules piste, and the establishment fields a team for
the annual Bath Boules Competition. The pub dates back
to 1750 when it was a cider house or farmstead. The bar
is a comfortable domain for locals and visitors alike, with
at least three real ales on hand pump. The same menu
throughout might focus on starters like crispy pork belly

with black pudding and apple sauce, and main dishes like
grilled salt marsh cutlets with pan-fried polenta. Toasted
sandwiches have imaginative fillings like smoked chicken,
avocado, tomato, rocket and bacon.

The Pear Tree Inn

OPEN: 11-3 6-11 Closed: 25/26 Dec, 1 Jan
BAR MEALS: L served all week 12-2.30 D served all week
6.30-9.30 Av main course £14.50 **RESTAURANT:** L served all
week 12-2.30 D served all week 6.30-9.30 Av 3 course à la carte
£23.50 Av 3 course fixed price £16 🍺: Free House
🍺: Wadworth 6X, Bath Ales Gem, Stonehenge Ales, Pigswill.
🍷: 10 **FACILITIES:** Child facs Garden: Cottage garden with
views over parkland **NOTES:** Parking 60
ROOMS: 8 bedrooms en suite 2 family rooms s£70 d£95

WINTERBOURNE BASSETT   Map 05 SU07

The White Horse Inn 🍷
SN4 9QB ☎ 01793 731257 📠 01793 739030
e-mail: ckstone@btinternet.com

Atmospheric village pub on the Marlborough Downs, two
miles north of the mysterious Avebury stone circle. Food is
served in both the bar and conservatory restaurant - both of
which have been recently extended - where budget lunches
and snacks give way to a full evening menu. Warm chicken
and bacon salad, Peking prawns in filo pastry, or lamb
Marrakesh, and steamed chocolate sponge make up a typical
meal, with a specials board and vegetarian options.
OPEN: 11-3 7-11 **BAR MEALS:** L served all week 12-2.30 D served
all week 6-10 **RESTAURANT:** L served all week 12-2.30 D served all
week 6-10 🍺: Wadworth 🍺: Wadworth 6X, IPA, Hophouse Brews,
Stella Artois. 🍷: 9 **FACILITIES:** Garden: Safe lawned area with
wooden benches **NOTES:** Parking 25

🍺 Principal Beers for sale

continued

WOODFALLS
Map 05 SU12

The Woodfalls Inn ◆◆◆◆ ℉
The Ridge SP5 2LN ☎ 01725 513222 ▤ 01725 513220
e-mail: woodfallsi@aol.com web: www.woodfallsinn.co.uk
Dir: B3080 to Woodfalls
This attractively refurbished free house on the northern edge
of the New Forest has provided hospitality to travellers since
Victorian times. Having been renamed as the 'Bat and Ball' in
1932, the inn has now regained its original name. It offers a
non-smoking restaurant with main course dishes including
deep-fried whitebait; chicken New York; and mushroom
stroganoff. Leave space for dark chocolate truffle torte; or
pineapple upside-down pudding.
OPEN: 11-11 **BAR MEALS:** L served all week 12-2.15 D served all
week 6.30-9.30 Av main course £6.95 **RESTAURANT:** L served all
week 12-2.15 D served all week 6.30-9 Av 3 course à la carte £15.40
▥: Free House ◀: Courage Directors & Best, Hopback's GFB, John
Smiths, Ringwood 49er. ℉: 9 **FACILITIES:** Child facs Garden:
Enclosed terraced area Dogs allowed Toys & water provided
NOTES: Parking 26 **ROOMS:** 10 bedrooms en suite 1 family room
s£49.45 d£69.90

WOOTTON RIVERS
Map 05 SU16

Royal Oak ▷ ℉
SN8 4NQ ☎ 01672 810322 ▤ 01672 811168
e-mail: royaloak35@hotmail.com
Dir: 3m S from Marlborough

Set in one of Wiltshire's prettiest villages, a thatched and
timbered 16th-century inn just 100 yards from the Kennet and
Avon Canal, and close to Savernake Forest - a wonderful area
for canal and forest walks. Menus are flexible, with light
basket meals, ploughman's and sandwiches, and specials like
partridge with game sauce, rich beef and burgundy casserole,
and medallions of pork and leek with a pine nut stuffing.
OPEN: 10.30-3.30 6-11 (Close Sun 10.30) **BAR MEALS:** L served all
week 11.30-2.30 D served all week 6-9.30 Av main course £8.75
RESTAURANT: L served all week 11.30-2.30 D served all week 6-9.30
Av 3 course à la carte £18 ▥: Free House ◀: Wadworth 6X, London
Pride + guest ales. ℉: 6 **FACILITIES:** Garden: Large lawn area. Raised
terrace with seating Dogs allowed water bowl **NOTES:** Parking 20

WYLYE
Map 04 SU03

The Bell Inn ℉
High St, Wylye BA12 0QP ☎ 01985 248338
e-mail: www.thebellatwylye.co.uk
There's a wealth of old oak beams, log fires and an inglenook
fireplace at this 14th-century coaching inn, situated in the
pretty Wylye valley. An equally-authentic home-cooked menu
should fit the bill. Not that it's restrictive: alongside British
classics such as braised lamb shank and local partridge, you

continued

may find provencal vegetable risotto with parmesan shavings
or River Wylye trout fillets with tarragon and white wine
sauce. Freshly-cut sandwiches and ploughman's lunches.
OPEN: 11.30-2.30 6-11 (Sun 12-3, 7-10.30) **BAR MEALS:** L served
all week 12-2 D served all week 6-9.30 Av main course £7.95
RESTAURANT: L served all week 12-2 D served all week 6-9.30
Av 3 course à la carte £25 ▥: Free House ℉: 7
FACILITIES: Children's licence Garden: Walled garden Dogs
allowed Water **NOTES:** Parking 20

WORCESTERSHIRE

ABBERLEY
Map 10 SO76

Manor Arms Country Inn ℉
WR6 6BN ☎ 01299 896507 ▤ 01299 896723
e-mail: themanorarms@btconnect.com
web: www.themanorarms.co.uk
Set just across the lane from the Norman church of St
Michael, the interior of this 300-year-old inn is enhanced by
original oak beams and a log-burning fire. For food, expect a
wide choice of grills and roasts, plus alternatives such as
poached haddock with a poached egg and chive and butter
sauce, or cheese and lentil terrine on a smooth tomato coulis.
Good choice of real ales.
OPEN: 12-3 6-11 (Closed Mon lunchtime in winter)
BAR MEALS: L served all week 12-2 D served all week 7-9
RESTAURANT: D served all week 7-9.30 ▥: Enterprise Inns
◀: Fuller's London Pride, Scottish Courage John Smith's, Courage
Directors & Theakstons Best Bitter. **FACILITIES:** Garden:
Patio/terrace, food served outdoors **NOTES:** Parking 25

BEWDLEY
Map 10 SO77

Pick of the Pubs

Horse & Jockey
Far Forest DY14 9DX ☎ 01299 266239 ▤ 01299 266227
e-mail: info@horseandjockey-farforest.co.uk

Serving fresh food sourced from local farms and cooked
with imagination, this peaceful country pub is dedicated
to maintaining traditional practices of hospitality - and
thanks to the owners' enthusiasm and dedication, it is
now a deservedly successful dining destination. The
family owners, Richard and Suzanne Smith, bought the
Horse and Jockey as a declining business and have put
new life in to it. The pub was first licensed in 1838 to
serve cider to farm workers on the local estate;
restoration of the premises some years ago uncovered
oak beams, floorboards and an inglenook fireplace. The
much-extended original building incorporates a glass-

continued

covered well which locals recall being in the garden. Today's garden, with its children's play area and seating for customers of all ages, overlooks the Lem valley and Wyre Forest. Regularly changing menus incorporate a selection of beef and lamb from the local Detton Farm, typically roast topside of beef with a dark shallot and chestnut sauce or slow-roasted lamb shank glazed with honey and rosemary jus. A good selection of fresh fish is delivered every Friday, so expect some adventurous as well as traditional dishes at the weekend. For example, whole baby sea bass is oven baked wrapped in banana leaves and then served with a fruity chilli sauce; while silver dorado fillets are pan fried and served on a capsicum and bulgar wheat timbale garnished with chargrilled walnut-scented scallions. The accomplished pace is maintained with desserts like coffee and orange torte, spiced pear tarte tatin, and an irresistible 'chocolate celebration' assiette. More traditional pub food is also on offer - but at the same high quality - in dishes such as home-baked ham and eggs and beef pie cooked in Hobson's ale.
OPEN: 12-3 5-11 (Open all day at wknds)
BAR MEALS: L served Tue-Fri 12-2.30 D served Tue-Fri 5-9 Av main course £7.50 **RESTAURANT:** L served Sun 12 D served Sun ⊕: Free House ⬤: Hobsons Best, Bombardier,Stella, Boddingtons. **FACILITIES:** Child facs Children's licence Garden: Large lawn, play area, seating, good views Dogs allowed **NOTES:** Parking 50

Little Pack Horse ♀
31 High St DY12 2DH ☎ 01299 403762 ▤ 01299 403762
e-mail: littlepackhorse@aol.com
This historic timber-framed inn is located in one of the Severn Valley's prettiest towns. The interior is warmed by a cosy wood-burning stove and lit by candles at night. There are low beams, an elm bar, and a small outside patio for alfresco summer dining. Expect minted lamb and tattie pie; roasted salmon fillet on asparagus, spinach and citrus fruits; and vegetarian stuffed peppers with rice and ratatouille.
OPEN: 12-3 6-11 (Sat-Sun 12-11) **BAR MEALS:** L served all week 12-2.15 D served all week 6-9.30 (Sat 12-9.30; Sun 12-8)
⊕: ⬤: Greene King IPA, Bass, Wadworth 6X. ♀: 12
FACILITIES: Garden: Small patio area - 3 tables Dogs allowed

The Mughouse Inn & Angry Chef Restaurant ⬤ ♀
12 Severnside North DY12 2EE
☎ 01299 402543 ▤ 01299 402543
e-mail: drew@mughousebewdley.co.uk

Historic pub located on the River Severn. The inn's name dates back to the 17th century when 'mug house' was a popular term for an alehouse. There's a seating area directly overlooking the water, and many popular walks in the nearby Wyre Forest. The menu offers squash and cashew risotto; *continued*

spiced lamb and tomato tagliatelle; sesame-battered squid with dressed rocked and spring onions; and lunchtime snacks.
OPEN: 12-11 (Sun 12-10.30) **BAR MEALS:** L served all week 12-2.30 D served Mon-Sat (Sun 12.30-6) No set menu Sat Av main course £8 **RESTAURANT:** L served all week 12-2.30 D served Mon-Sat 7-9 Sun lunch 12.30-6 Av 3 course à la carte £19
⬤: Timothy Taylor's Landlord, Mugs Gayme Ale, Wye Valley, Hereford Pale Ale plus 2 guest beers. ♀: 7 **FACILITIES:** Children's licence Garden: Raised Patio area with BBQ, seating 60 Dogs allowed water
See advertisement under BIRMINGHAM

BRANSFORD   Map 10 SO75

The Bear & Ragged Staff ♀
Station Rd WR6 5JH ☎ 01886 833399 ▤ 01886 833106
e-mail: bearragged@aol.com
Dir: 3m from centre of Worcester off the A4103 (Hereford Rd). Or 3m from the centre of Malvern off A449, turning left just before Powick Village. Signed for Bransford.

Mid-way between Worcester and the Malvern Hills, this smart dining pub has an enviable reputation for its imaginative menus and fresh Cornish fish. The name comes from the family crest of the Earl of Warwickshire. Lunchtime bar meals include brunch rolls, Cajun-spiced salmon, and five cheese tortellini. It's wise to book for the restaurant at weekends, when starters like avocado, crab and tomato pancake might precede rib-eye steak with shallots and red wine sauce, roast cod on butter bean mash, or fillet of venison on purée of aubergine and rich redcurrant sauce flavoured with chocolate.
OPEN: 11.30-2.30 6-11 (Sun 12-3 7-10.30) **BAR MEALS:** L served all week 12-2 D served Mon-Sat 6.30-9 Sun 7-8.30 Av main course £9 **RESTAURANT:** L served all week 12-2 D served all week 7-9
⊕: Free House ⬤: Bass, Highgate Special Bitter, Worthington. **FACILITIES:** Garden: Food served outside Dogs allowed in the garden only Water provided **NOTES:** Parking 40

BROMSGROVE   Map 10 SO97

Epic' Bar Brasserie NEW ⬤ ♀
68 Hanbury Rd, Stoke Prior B60 4DN
☎ 01527 871929 ▤ 01527 575647
e-mail: epic.bromsgrove@virgin.net
Dir: A38 from Bromsgrove towards Worcester, at x-rds take B4091 towards Hanbury, pub on right
The sleek lines of this pub-cum-brasserie are reflected in punchy, accurate and thoroughly contemporary cooking. It's an ideal spot to while away a Sunday with the family, and children are well served, with their own, predominantly organic menu and well-stocked play area. Adults won't miss out - this is grown-up cooking, making use of excellent, well-sourced ingredients. Think celeriac and white truffle soup; crab, chilli and lime linguini; or chorizo and parma ham pizza.
OPEN: 11-11 (Sun 12-10.30) **BAR MEALS:** L served all week 12-3 *continued*

BROMSGROVE continued

D served Mon-Sat Av main course £9 **RESTAURANT:** L served all week 12-2.30 D served Mon-Sat 6.30-9.30 Sun 12.30-3.30, Fri-Sat 6.30-10 Av 3 course à la carte £20 🍺: Changing guest ale, Boddingtons, Guinness. ♀: 9 **FACILITIES:** Child facs Children's licence Garden: Large patio, terrace area with olive tree **NOTES:** Parking 60

CLENT

Map 10 SO97

The Bell & Cross ♀

Holy Cross DY9 9QL ☎ 01562 730319 📠 01562 731733
Dir: Telephone for directions
Early 19th-century inn comprising a series of small rooms, including a former butcher's shop with meat hooks still in situ. Proprietor Roger Narbets, chef to the England football team, offers a modern menu, with dishes like fillet of Cornish hake, garlic king prawns and parsley sauce; and grilled calves' liver, black pudding and rumblethump potato. Finish with local ice-cream or home-made treacle tart.
OPEN: 12-3 6-11 Closed: 25 Dec 31 Dec, 1 Jan-night
BAR MEALS: L served all week 12-2 D served Mon-Sat 6.30-9.15 Sun 12-2.30, 7-9 Av main course £11.50 **RESTAURANT:** L served all week 12-2 D served Mon-Sat 6.30-9.15 Sun 12-2.30, 7-9 Av 3 course à la carte £20 🍺: Enterprise Inns 🍺: Pedigree, Mild, Bitter & Guest Beers. ♀: 11 **FACILITIES:** Children's licence Garden with raised patio with flower beds Dogs allowed Water **NOTES:** Parking 26

CLOWS TOP

Map 10 SO77

Pick of the Pubs

The Colliers Arms

Tenbury Rd DY14 9HA
Dir: On A456, 4m from Bewdley, 7m from Kidderminster.
Refurbished in 2004 this pub has plenty to offer, not least in the food area. On the menus, traditional dishes are given a modern twist or two, examples being roast breast of Barbary duck, crushed new potatoes and cherry sauce; honey-seared salmon fillet with tarragon and mushroom risotto; and bramley apple-stuffed pork fillet with creamy garlic potatoes, red wine and shallot sauce. Others are permanent residents on the menu because they are straight-down-the-line time-honoured classics, including home-made lasagne; roast of the day; grilled fillet of plaice; and liver, bacon and mash. A customer recently said he would have proposed to Mrs Porter, the landlady's mother, if she weren't already married. The reason? She makes exceedingly good apple pies - an unequivocal recommendation for dessert.
BAR MEALS: L served all week 12-2 D served Mon-Sat 6.30-9 Av main course £8.45 **RESTAURANT:** L served all week 12-2 D served all week 6.30-9 Av 3 course à la carte £15
FACILITIES: Garden: Fenced garden, flower borders, wooden furniture **NOTES:** Parking 50

DROITWICH

Map 10 SO86

Pick of the Pubs

The Chequers ♀

Cutnall Green WR9 0PJ ☎ 01299 851292 📠 01299 851744
Dir: Telephone for directions
This charming country pub, on the site of an ancient coaching inn, is home to the chef of the English football

continued

---

team. Decorated in traditional style, with an open fire, timbered bar and richly coloured furnishings, it is comfy and snug. Guests are likely to linger over the numerous real ales, fine wines and food on the extensive menu. Dishes range from lunch light bites, mostly in the form of sandwiches, baguettes, pasta and panini, through to more comprehensive dinner dishes. Expect starters like garlic mushroom, goats cheese and spinach tart; or terrine of duck and green pepper with orange confit, followed by mains like grilled fillet of Cornish cod; grilled calves' liver with sautéed potatoes, smoked bacon, garlic and thyme; baked ricotta and spinach lasangne with red pepper jus; and braised shoulder of spiced lamb with brinjal pickle potatoes. Desserts might include rum and raisin bread and butter pudding with advocaat custard.
OPEN: 12-3 6-11 Closed: 25, 31 Dec, 1-2 Jan, 26 Dec Closed eve **BAR MEALS:** L served all week 12-2 D served all week 6.30-9.15 Sun 12-2.30, 7-9 Av main course £11.25
RESTAURANT: L served all week 12-2 D served all week 6.30-9.15 Sun 12-2.30, 7-9 Av 3 course à la carte £18.50
🍺: Enterprise Inns 🍺: Timothy Taylors, Banks Pedigree, Banks Bitter, Banks Mild. ♀: 11 **FACILITIES:** Garden: Large garden with benches, flower borders Dogs allowed **NOTES:** Parking 75

The Old Cock Inn

Friar St WR9 8EQ ☎ 01905 774233

This charming old pub has three stained-glass windows rescued from the local church after it was destroyed during the Civil War. The stone carving above the front entrance is believed to be of Judge Jeffreys who presided over the local magistrates' court. Various snacks and light meals feature on the menu, while more substantial fare includes rump steak, steak and Guinness pie, grilled cod with stilton and mushroom, and fillet of lamb with artichoke, wild mushrooms, mint, peppercorns and wine sauce.
OPEN: 11.30-3 5.30-11 Closed: Sun evening
BAR MEALS: L served all week 12-2.30 D served 6 days 5.30-9.30
RESTAURANT: L served all week 12-2.30 D served all week 5.30-9.30 🍺: 🍺: Marston's Pedigree & Bitter, Guest.
FACILITIES: Garden: Small beer garden

DUNHAMPTON

Map 10 SO86

Epic' Bar Brasserie NEW ♀

Ombersley Rd DY13 9SW ☎ 01905 620000 📠 01905 621123
e-mail: epic.finance@virgin.net
Dir: M5 junct 6, take A449 towards Kidderminster for 5m, on the right
This is one of three places owned and operated by celebrity chef Patrick McDonald. Epic provides a great family venue, with smaller portions for youngsters, a separate children's menu for under-10s, and high chairs for youngest guests. There are large no-smoking areas, and landscaped gardens.

continued

Many special events are held throughout the year including themed dinners, seasonal parties, cocktail events and food and wine tasting evenings.
OPEN: 12-11 **BAR MEALS:** L served all week 12-3 D served Mon-Sat Av main course £10.50 **RESTAURANT:** L served all week 12-2.30 D served Mon-Sat 6.30-10 Sun 12-3.30 Av 3 course à la carte £21 ◀: Timothy Taylor Landlord, Guinness, Marstons Pedigree. ♀: 12 **FACILITIES:** Child facs Children's licence Garden: Half decked, private garden **NOTES:** Parking 100

FLADBURY
Map 10 SO94

Chequers Inn
Chequers Ln WR10 2PZ ☎ 01386 860276 ▤ 01386 861286
e-mail: john.tretwell4@btinternet.com
Dir: Off A4538 between Evesham and Pershore
The Chequers is a 14th-century inn with plenty of beams and an open fire, tucked away in a pretty village with views of the glorious Bredon Hills. Local produce from the Vale of Evesham provides the basis for home-cooked dishes offered from the monthly-changing menu, plus a choice of daily specials. There is also a traditional Sunday carvery. The pretty walled garden enjoys outstanding views, and the nearby River Avon is ideal for walking.
OPEN: 11-3 6-11 **BAR MEALS:** L served all week 12-2 D served Mon-Sat 6-10 **RESTAURANT:** L served all week 12-2 D served Mon-Sat 6-9 Sunday carvery at 1 ☺: Free House ◀: Hook Norton Best, Fuller's London Pride, Black Sheep, plus guests.
FACILITIES: Garden: Walled garden with outstanding views
NOTES: Parking 28

FLYFORD FLAVELL
Map 10 SO95

The Boot Inn ◆◆◆◆ ▷ ♀
Radford Rd WR7 4BS ☎ 01386 462658 ▤ 01386 462547
Dir: Take Evesham rd, left at 2nd rdbt onto A422, Flyford Flavell signed after 3m

Family-run inn, parts of which date from c1350, situated in a lovely village on the Wychavon Way, well placed for the Cotswolds and Malvern Hills. There are gardens front and back, with a heated patio and quality wooden furniture, and a good selection of malts and wines. Home-cooked food, from an extensive carte and specials board, includes duck breast in a brandy and orange sauce, rack of lamb and seared tuna on pineapple with chilli sauce. Accommodation is provided in the converted coach house.
OPEN: 11-2.30 5-11 Sat-Sun open all day **BAR MEALS:** L served all week 12-2 D served all week 6.30-10 (Sun 12-5.30, 7-9.30) Av main course £9.75 **RESTAURANT:** L served all week 12-2 D served all week 6.30-10 (Sat 6-10, Sun 12-5.30, 7-9.30) Av 3 course à la carte £16 ☺: Free House ◀: Wadworth 6X, Greene King Old Speckled Hen, Worthingtons, Green King IPA. ♀: 7
FACILITIES: Garden: Patio with wooden furniture, heaters Dogs
NOTES: Parking 30 **ROOMS:** 5 bedrooms en suite s£50 d£60

KEMPSEY
Map 10 SO84

Pick of the Pubs

Walter de Cantelupe Inn ◆◆◆
Main Rd WR5 3NA ☎ 01905 820572
web: www.walterdecantelupeinn.com
Dir: 4m S of Worcester City centre, on A38 in the centre of village
The name is taken from the mid-13th-century Bishop of Worcester, Walter de Cantelupe, who was strongly against the brewing and selling of ales, which his parishioners undertook as a way of raising church funds. The pub was formed out of a row of cottages three centuries later, and its naming is presumably ironic! With whitewashed walls, bedecked with flowers, this small village inn is a magnet for passing motorists and locals alike. Outside, a walled and paved garden has been fragrantly planted with clematis, roses and honeysuckle, and its south-facing position is a sun-trap on hot days. A gas heater has extended its use into the cooler months. The food is written up each day on a blackboard, with choices like local Malvern Victorian sausages with mash; Cajun spiced salmon; Rushwick organic beef and local ale pie; and plate-size gammon steak. En suite accommodation is popular with visitors to historic Worcester, the Malvern Hills and Severn Vale.
OPEN: 12-2 6-11 (Summer 11.30-2.30) (Sun 12-3, 7-10.30) Closed: Dec 25-26, Jan 1 **BAR MEALS:** L served Tue-Sun 12-2 D served Tue-Sat 6.30-9 Sun 12-2.30, Fri-Sat 6.30-10 Av main course £8 **RESTAURANT:** L served Tue-Sun 12-2 D served Tue-Sat 7-9 Fri-Sat 7-10 Av 3 course à la carte £17 ☺: Free House ◀: Timothy Taylors Landlord, Cannon Royal, Kings Shilling, Hobsons Best Bitter. **FACILITIES:** Walled paved garden, lots of plants Dogs allowed **NOTES:** Parking 24
ROOMS: 3 bedrooms en suite s£40.50 d£55 No children overnight

---

KNIGHTWICK
Map 10 SO75

Pick of the Pubs

The Talbot ♀
WR6 5PH ☎ 01886 821235 ▤ 01886 821060
e-mail: admin@the-talbot.co.uk web: www.the-talbot.co.uk
Dir: A44 (Leominster rd) through Worcester, 8m W turn right onto B4197 at River Teme bridge)

A late-14th-century, traditional coaching inn run for twenty-one years by the Clift family, and managed today by sisters Annie and Wiz. There's a strong emphasis on organic and locally produced ingredients (except fish which comes from Cornwall and Wales) and traditional, seasonal and sometimes ancient recipes. Annie and Wiz

continued

KNIGHTWICK continued

grow 'chemical-free' vegetables, herbs and salad leaves in the garden, glean and gather wild food from fields and hedgerows, make their own preserves, breads, black pudding and raised pies, and buy no processed food. The pub produces its own beers too in the Teme Valley micro-brewery. Called This, That, T'other and Wot, they're all brewed with Worcestershire hops. A typical meal here could be turkey, leek and potato soup, followed by brill fillet with spiced red lentils and home-made piccalilli; and granny's apple pie.

OPEN: 11-11 (Sun 12-10.30) 25 Dec closed eve
BAR MEALS: L served all week 12-2 D served all week 6.30-9.30 (Sun 7-9) Av main course £13.45 **RESTAURANT:** L served all week 12-2 D served all week 6.30-9.30 (Sun 7-9) Av 3 course à la carte £30 Av 3 course fixed price £24.95 🍴: Free House
🍺: Teme Valley This, That , T'Other & Wot, Hobsons Best Bitter Choice. ♀: 9 **FACILITIES:** Garden: Riverside grass area Dogs allowed **NOTES:** Parking 50 **ROOMS:** 11 bedrooms en suite 3 family rooms s£45 d£70 (★★)

MALVERN   Map 10 SO74

Farmers Arms
Birts St, Birtsmorton WR13 6AP ☎ 01684 833308
e-mail: warbillintun@warbleton-wanadoo.co.uk
Dir: On B4208 S of Great Malvern
Expect a friendly welcome at this 15th-century black and white timbered pub, in a quiet parish close to the Malvern Hills. It serves decent ales and homely bar food in its low-beamed rooms, including cottage pie, macaroni cheese, Hereford pie and a variety of jacket potatoes, Vienna rolls and sandwiches. The kids will enjoy the swings out on the lawn.
OPEN: 11-2.30 6-11 (Sun 12-2.30, 7-10.30) **BAR MEALS:** L served all week 11-2 D served all week 6-9.30 Sun 12-7, 2-9 Av main course £5 🍴: Free House 🍺: Hook Norton Best & Old Hooky.
FACILITIES: Garden: Lawn with swings Dogs allowed Water
NOTES: Parking 30 No credit cards

Pick of the Pubs

The Red Lion 🍴
4 St Ann's Rd WR14 4RG ☎ 01684 564787
This thriving pub is tucked away just off the town centre on one of the main walking routes to the Malvern Hills. Steve Hickman and his kitchen brigade have built a reputation on fresh, home-made food and good service, and have transformed the Red Lion into one of Great Malvern's busiest pub food operations. Marston's Pedigree and weekly guest ales accompany a wide choice of snacks, starters and main course dishes, all freshly cooked to order. Meals are served in the bar, as well as the non-smoking restaurant, and, in summer, the enclosed courtyard garden is popular with diners. Lighter meals include tomato and basil pasta; duck and bacon salad; and wild mushroom risotto. Bigger appetites might choose gourmet sausage and mash; steamed sea bass with fresh vegetables; or a chargrilled sirloin steak.
OPEN: 12-3 5.30-11 (Sat-Sun 12-11) **BAR MEALS:** L served all week 12-2.45 D served all week 6-9.30 (All day Sat-Sun) Av main course £10 **RESTAURANT:** L served all week 12-2.45 D served all week 6-9.30 (All day Sat-Sun) Av 3 course à la carte £18
🍺: Pedigree, Marstons Bitter, guest ales. **FACILITIES:** Garden: Enclosed courtyard garden, terraced, heaters Dogs allowed only on stone area; water bowls

MARTLEY   Map 10 SO76

Admiral Rodney Inn ◆◆◆◆ 🍴
Berrow Green WR6 6PL ☎ 01886 821375 ◷ 01886 822048
e-mail: rodney@admiral.fslife.co.uk
web: www.admiral-rodney.co.uk
Dir: From M5 junct 7, take A44 signed Bromyard & Leominster. After approx 7m at Knightwick turn R onto B4197, Inn 1.5m on L at Berrow Green

Early 17th-century farmhouse-cum-alehouse, named after the man who taught Nelson all he knew. It is on the Worcester Way footpath, with wonderful views of Worcester and the Malvern Hills. Fish - freshly delivered from Cornwall - features strongly: try black bream baked with lime, herbs and chilli; or pan-fried scallops with puréed shallots and basil dressing. Other choices include home-made pizza; roast duck with spinach mash and orange Grand Marnier sauce; and various steaks. Good vegetarian selection.
OPEN: 11-3 5-11 (Mon open 5-11pm, open all day Sat, Sun)
BAR MEALS: L served Tues-Sun 12-2 D served all week 6.30-9 Sun 12-2.30, Sat 6.30-9.30 Av main course £7.50
RESTAURANT: L served Sun D served Mon-Sun 7-9 Sat 7-9.30 Av 3 course à la carte £22.50 🍴: Free House 🍺: Wye Valley Bitter, local guest beers eg. Quaff from woods in Shropshire, Black Pear, Malvern Hills Brewery. **FACILITIES:** Child facs Children's licence Garden: Beautiful views, seating, grass area, terrace Dogs Water
NOTES: Parking 40 **ROOMS:** 3 bedrooms en suite s£40 d£55

OMBERSLEY   Map 10 SO86

Pick of the Pubs

Crown & Sandys Arms 🍴 ♀
Main Rd WR9 0EW ☎ 01905 620252 ◷ 01905 620769
e-mail: enquiries@crownandsandys.co.uk
Dir: Telephone for directions
Down in the village of Ombersley in Worcestershire is this classy establishment run by Richard Everton, who also owns the village deli and wine shop. Although the décor is as trendy and modern as they come, the original beams and fireplaces seem to have no trouble co-existing with it. Regular 'wine dinners' and theme evenings add to the appeal for regulars. Freshly-made sandwiches, paninis, baguettes and hot dishes are available at lunchtime. Main dishes, which are changed every week, always include a wide choice of fresh market fish and seafood, such as king prawns, scallops, sea bass, monkfish, lemon sole and cod. Other mains could include pot roast of lamb with spring onion and leek mash, and red wine jus; supreme of chicken with seared foie gras, caramelised mango and braised chicory, sauce Jacqueline; and pappadelle of wild mushrooms, feves and white truffle oil. Shropshire beers are on tap in the bar.

continued

OPEN: 11-3 5-11 (Open all day BHs) **BAR MEALS:** L served all week 12-2.30 D served all week 6-10 Sun all day to 9.30 Av main course £10.95 **RESTAURANT:** L served all week 12-2.30 D served all week 6-10 Av 3 course à la carte £25 **:** Free House **:** Sadlers Ale, Marstons, Banks Bitter, Burtons Bitter. **🍷:** 10 **FACILITIES:** Child facs Garden: Large beer garden, Japanese style terrace **NOTES:** Parking 100

PENSAX — Map 10 SO76

The Bell Inn 🍷

WR6 6AE ☎ 01299 896677

Dir: *From Kidderminster A456 to Clows Top, B4202 towards Abberley, pub 2m on L*

Friendly rural local offering five real ales by the jug at weekends to extend the choice available. There's also a beer festival held at the end of June. Home-made dishes are prepared from seasonal local produce - steaks, liver and onions, and home-cooked ham with free-range eggs. Superb views can be enjoyed from the garden, and great local walks. Walkers and cyclists are welcome, and there's a registered caravan/campsite opposite. Look out for the bargain lunchtime menu.

OPEN: 12-2.30 5-11 (Sun 12-10.30) Mon Closed lunch except BH's **BAR MEALS:** L served Tues-Sun 12-2 D served all week 6-9 Sun 12-4 Av main course £6.25 **RESTAURANT:** L served Tue-Sun 12-2 D served all week 6-9 Sun 12-4 **:** Free House **:** Timothy Taylor Best Bitter, Hobsons Best, Hook Norton Best, Cannon Royall. **FACILITIES:** Garden: Food served outside Dogs allowed **NOTES:** Parking 20

POWICK — Map 10 SO85

The Halfway House Inn

Bastonford WR2 4SL ☎ 01905 831098 🖷 01905 831704

Dir: *From A15 junct 7 take A4440 then A449*

A friendly little pub just a few minutes' drive from the picturesque spa town of Malvern, a popular centre for exploring the Malvern Hills. The menu offers a selection of freshly prepared dishes (local and organic produce where possible), including fish, shellfish and traditional food.

OPEN: 12-3 6-11 **BAR MEALS:** L served Mon-Sun 12-2 D served Mon-Sun 6-9 Av main course £10 **RESTAURANT:** L served Mon-Sun 12-2 D served Mon-Sun 6-9 Av 3 course à la carte £20 **:** Free House **:** Abbot Ale, St Georges Bitter, Fuller's London Pride, Timothy Taylor. **FACILITIES:** Garden: Lawn area **NOTES:** Parking 30

SHATTERFORD — Map 10 SO78

The Bellmans Cross Inn 🍷

Bridgnorth Rd DY12 1RN ☎ 01299 861322 🖷 01299 861047

Dir: *On A442 5m outside Kidderminster*

The Bellman's Cross Inn dates back to the mid 1800's and changed hands in 1919 for the princely sum of £675. Nowadays the bar menu offers traditional dishes such as pork and leek sausages or home-made steak and kidney pie while the restaurant serves up delights like pan-fried guinea fowl, or rack of lamb with garlic potatoes and goats' cheese. A pleasant, friendly environment.

OPEN: 11-3 6-11 (Open all day on Sat, Sun & BHs) Dec 25 Closed eve **BAR MEALS:** L served all week 12-2.15 D served all week 6-9.30 Av main course £10 **RESTAURANT:** L served all week 12-2.15 D served all week 6-9.30 Av 3 course à la carte £22.50 **:** Free House **:** Interbrew Bass, Greene King, Old Speckled Hen, Worthington's. **FACILITIES:** Garden: Patio area with tables and umbrellas **NOTES:** Parking 30

Red Lion Inn

Bridgnorth Rd DY12 1SU ☎ 01299 861221

Dir: *N from Kidderminster on the A442*

This rural free house dates from 1835 and enjoys panoramic views towards the Clee Hills and Severn Valley. Until 1981, just two families had run the pub for a total of 143 years; the current owner, Diana Parkes, is now continuing its recent traditions of hospitality. The popular menu includes sandwiches, ploughman's and jacket potatoes, as well as hot pub favourites like steak and kidney pie, breaded scampi, and vegetarian lasagne.

OPEN: 11.30-3 6.30-11 (Sun 12-3, 7-10.30) **BAR MEALS:** L served all week 11.30-2 D served all week 6.30-9.30 Av main course £7 **RESTAURANT:** L served all week 11.30-2 D served all week 6.30-9.30 Sun 12-2.30, 7-9 **:** Free House **:** Bathams, Banks' Mild & Bitter, Shropshire Lad, Wye Valley Butty Bach. **FACILITIES:** Child facs Small garden **NOTES:** Parking 50

STONEHALL — Map 10 SO84

Pick of the Pubs

The Fruiterer's Arms

Stonehall Common WR5 3QG

☎ 01905 820462 🖷 01905 820501

e-mail: thefruiterersarms@btopenworld.com

Dir: *2m from M5 junct 7. Stonehall Common 1.5m from St Peters Garden Centre Norton*

Pub on Stonehall Common, once frequented by the area's fruit pickers. Four guest ales are rotated weekly, and there's a main menu, specials menu and Sunday menu offered in the bar, restaurant, garden pavilion and garden. Favourite dishes include Swiss chicken with alpine cheese, fillet of lamb with madeira and rosemary, and the fresh fish of the day. The garden is large and has a purpose-built play area for children.

OPEN: 12-3 6-11 (All day Sunday & Saturday in Summer) **BAR MEALS:** L served all week 12-2 D served all week 6-9.15 **RESTAURANT:** L served all week 12-2.30 D served all week 6-9.15 all day Sundays **:** Bass, Malvern Hills Black Pear, Hobsons Bitter. **FACILITIES:** Child facs Children's licence Garden: 1.7 acres, 50 seat wooden pavillion, seats Dogs allowed watering station **NOTES:** Parking 35

Website addresses are included where available. The AA cannot be held responsible for the content of any of these websites

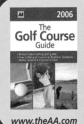

England

Pick of the Pubs

The Fountain Hotel ♀
Oldwood, St Michaels WR15 8TB
☎ 01584 810701 📠 01584 819030
e-mail: enquiries@fountain-hotel.co.uk

See Pick of the Pubs on opposite page

Pick of the Pubs

Peacock Inn ◉ 🏠 ▷ ♀
WR15 8LL ☎ 01584 810506 📠 01584 811236
e-mail: thepeacockinn001@aol.com
web: www.thepeacockinn.com
Dir: *From junct 3 of M5 follow A456 for 40m then A443 to Tenbury Wells, 0.75m on right*

A 14th-century coaching inn overlooking the River Teme, with a sympathetic extension made even more attractive by shrubs, ivy and colourful hanging baskets. The relaxing bars and oak-panelled restaurant are enhanced by oak beams, dried hops and open log fires, while upstairs the ghost of Mrs Brown, a former landlady, does its best to enliven a stay in one of the bedrooms. Local market produce plays a pivotal role in the menus, specialities being fresh fish and game. Home-made duck liver parfait with Cumberland sauce; and Herefordshire smoked salmon with cucumber, spring onion, chilli and crème fraîche, are possible starters, with typical main courses of penne pasta with prawns, garlic and spinach in olive oil; rack of English lamb with Mediterranean vegetables and rosemary sauce; lobster with sauce armoricaine; and venison with caramelised shallots and a port redcurrant sauce. Old Hooky, Hobsons Best and Adnams are among the beers.
OPEN: 11.30-3.30 5.30-11 **BAR MEALS:** L served all week 12-2 D served all week 6.30-9 Av main course £10
RESTAURANT: L served all week 12-2 D served all week 6.30-9 Av 3 course à la carte £17 ⊕: Free House ◀: Hobsons Best Bitter, Bombardier, Hook Norton. **FACILITIES:** Children's licence Garden: Garden with tables and benches Dogs allowed **NOTES:** Parking 30 **ROOMS:** 5 bedrooms en suite 1 family room s£55 d£75

The Salmon's Leap
42 Severn St WR1 2ND ☎ 01905 726260 📠 01905 724151
e-mail: bernardwalker@thesalmonsleap.freeserve.co.uk
Dir: *In city centre, opp Royal Worcester Museum. From M5 junct 7 follow Museum & Cathedral signs.*

Just a couple of minutes' walk from the cathedral, this quiet family-run free house offers good quality pub food and a regularly changing selection of cask ales from around the country. Favourite dishes include chilli con carne; stuffed plaice with prawns, mushrooms and chardonnay sauce; and parsnip, sweet potato and chestnut bake. The beer garden has a fenced off children's area, with play equipment and a bouncy castle in summer.
OPEN: 11.30-11 (Oct-Apr closed Mon lunch - open 4)
BAR MEALS: L served all week 12-7.30 D served all week 12-7.30
Av main course £6 **RESTAURANT:** L served all week 12-7.30
D served all week 12-7.30 ◀: Timothy Taylor, 5 other guest ales.
FACILITIES: Children's licence Garden: Adjacent to pub Dogs allowed except in restaurant; water **NOTES:** Parking 3

The Anchor Inn ♀
Main St WR10 2JB ☎ 01386 552799 📠 01386 552799
e-mail: ngreen32@btinternet.com
Dir: *From M5 junct 6 take A4538 S towards Evesham*

An impressive half-timbered inn on the banks of the Avon, standing in gardens that overlook the pleasure craft moored by the water's edge. Old world in style, the 400-year-old building features a cosy lounge with original low-timbered ceiling, old coaching prints around the walls and an inglenook fireplace decorated with horse brasses. The dining room enjoys a panoramic view out over the river and countryside. The asparagus supper is very popular when in season, as is local game.
OPEN: 12-3 6-11 (Easter-Oct open all day at wknds Closed: Jan 1
BAR MEALS: L served all week 12-2 D served all week 7-9 Av main course £6.50 **RESTAURANT:** L served all week 12-2 D served all week 7-9 ⊕: Enterprise Inns ◀: Banks bitter, Timothy Taylor landlord, Marston's Pedigree, Piddle Ale. ♀: 22
FACILITIES: Garden: River Avon at bottom, wonderful views
NOTES: Parking 10

Restaurant and Bar Meal times indicate the times when food is available. Last orders may be approximately 30 minutes before the times stated

---

Pick of the Pubs have that extra special quality that makes them stand out from the crowd. Their entries are highlighted, and may be a full page

Pick of the Pubs

The Fountain Hotel

Black and white timbered inns are common in these parts, though this one is far from ordinary and comes with a welcoming country atmosphere. In 1855, this former farmhouse, then known as The Hippodrome after the horse-racing that used to take place on a common next door, began selling beer and cider to Welsh drovers herding their sheep to English markets.

In 2005 it celebrates its 150th anniversary of serving travellers with a welcome pint. The Fountain has a mischievous but friendly ghost - a landlord who died in 1958 while saving his dogs from a fire. Now run by Russell Allen, a well-travelled big-game fisherman, and his second-chef wife, Michaela, the inn has been winning plaudits for its quality food and real ales. The theme in the restaurant is nautical, with the printed menu usually offering four fish/seafood specials in addition to regular fish offerings. Starters might include garlic mushrooms; smoked chicken with poached pear; or a freshly-made daily terrine. To follow, there's plenty of home-made, freshly cooked options, among them seafood roulade, beef lasagne with garlic bread, and a wild mushroom and basil risotto. Ales include Theakstons and Wye Valley. Book a table near the 1000-gallon aquarium for a grandstand view of exotic fish, including a leopard shark, an emperor snapper and a lipstick tang. There's also a large, secluded garden which includes the herb plot where organic herbs and vegetables are grown for the pot, a children's play area with a trampoline, and a heated patio. The hotel is open all day for food and drink.

OPEN: 9-11
BAR MEALS: L served all week 9-9 D served all week 9-9 Av main course £10
RESTAURANT: L served all week 12-10 D served all week 12-10
🍺: Free House
🍺: Fountain Ale, Theakston's Bitter & Mild, Wye Valley Bitter, Butty Bach.
♀: 8
FACILITIES: Child facs Children's licence Full disabled facilities Garden: Large, secluded. Patio area with heaters **NOTES:** Parking 60
ROOMS: 11 bedrooms en suite s£49.95 (♦♦♦♦)

🐟 ♀   Map 10 SO56
Oldwood, St Michaels WR15 8TB
☎ 01584 810701
🖹 01584 819030
📧 enquiries@fountain-hotel.co.uk
🌐 www.fountain-hotel.co.uk
Dir: 1m out of Tenbury Wells on the A4112 Leominster Road

PUB WALK
The Seabirds Inn
Flamborough - East Riding of Yorkshire

THE SEABIRDS INN
Tower Street, Flamborough, YO15 1PD
☎ 01262 850242
Directions: On B1255 E of Bridlington, 6m from train station
Expect a warm welcome, home-cooked food, and a newly refurbished interior at this homely old fisherman's local, situated in a village close to the chalk cliffs of Flamborough Head.
Open: 12–3 6.30–11 (Sun 7–10.30)
Mon Closed eve in winter
Bar Meals: L served all week 12–2
D served all week 6.30–9 Sat 6.30–9.30, Sun 7–9 Av main course £6.50
Restaurant Meals: L served all week 12–2 D served all week 6.30–9 Sat 6.30–9.30, Sun 7–9 Av 3 course à la carte £17
Dogs allowed. Garden and parking available.
(for full entry see page 549)

Distance: 6 miles (10km)
Map: OS Landranger 101
Terrain: Farmland, cliff-top, country lanes
Paths: Field and cliff-top paths; some road walking
Gradient: Gently undulating; easy gradients; some steps

Walk submitted and checked by M Grocutt

An exhilarating cliff-top walk from Flamborough to the lighthouse at Flamborough Head, where massive chalk cliffs provide a haven for seabirds and afford panoramic views across Bridlington Bay.

Turn right on leaving the pub and walk down Tower Street. Shortly, cross the road and walk through the churchyard. Turn right along Lily Lane, then left into Butlers Lane and along West Street. In 50 yards (46mtrs), take the path through Beacon Farm, signed to Beacon Hill. Pass outbuildings, cross two stiles, then gently up beside the left-hand hedge, then the wire fence, eventually reaching the cliff-top.

Turn left and keep to the cliff-top path, down 80 steps to South Landing (bay). Walk uphill and take waymarked path right and ascend steps. Keep right (circular mark walker), then right again at a fork and keep to the marked cliff path. Cross two gullies via steps and bridges, then on reaching a sign (Lighthouse 1mile), ignore wooden bridge across a ditch and head inland. Keep to the right-hand hedge across two field boundaries and to reach a lane via steps.

Turn right and continue to the Lighthouse. Take the private road to the right of the Lighthouse towards the Fog Signal Station and take the path on the right, signed 'South Landing 2.5 miles". Gently climb the bank on an indistinct path parallel with the field boundary (on right - not enclosed) and continue across the headland to its south side. Turn right along the cliff-top path and continue to the wooden bridge ignored earlier.

Retrace your steps along the cliff path, crossing the two gullies, until you arrive at the first fork (circular chalk walk) before South Landing is reached. Turn right inland keeping the fence on your left. Keep to the waymarked path past Cliff House Farm, then having zig-zagged downhill, leave the circular walk by crossing a bridge over a stream and enter a copse. Walk along the northern perimeter of the wood to reach a car park. Turn right uphill into Flamborough. Turn left at the crossroads, then right into Tower Street for the pub.

YORKSHIRE, EAST RIDING OF

BEVERLEY
Map 17 TA03

White Horse Inn
22 Hengate HU17 8BN ☎ 01482 861973 ▤ 01482 861973
e-mail: anname@talk21.com
Dir: A1079 from York to Beverley
A classic 16th-century local with atmospheric little rooms
arranged around the central bar. Gas lighting, open fires,
antique cartoons and high-backed settles add to the charm.
John Wesley preached in the back yard in the mid-18th
century. Traditional bar food includes many popular dishes -
among them pasta and mushrooms, fresh jumbo haddock,
bangers and mash, and steak and ale pie. Toasted and plain
sandwiches and daily specials also feature.
OPEN: 11-11 (Sun 12-10.30) **BAR MEALS:** L served all week 11-4.45
D served all week 5-6.45 ☻: Samuel Smith ◖: Samuel Smith Old
Brewery Bitter & Soveriegn Bitter. **FACILITIES:** Garden: Dogs allowed
on leads only, Water **NOTES:** Parking 30 No credit cards

DRIFFIELD
Map 17 TA05

The Bell ★★★
46 Market Place YO25 6AN ☎ 01377 256661 ▤ 01377 253228
e-mail: bell@bestwestern.co.uk
*Dir: Enter town from A164, turn right at traffic lights. Car park 50yrds on
lef behind black railings*
A delightful 18th-century coaching inn furnished with
antiques, with an oak-panelled bar serving a good range of
cask beers and 300 whiskies. Food ranges from grilled salmon
steak with hollandaise sauce, and poached halibut with white
wine and spring onions, to strips of chicken cooked with
honey, mustard and cream served with rice, and breast of
duckling served on a lake of plum sauce. Snooker, swimming
and squash are available.
OPEN: 10-2.30 6-11 Closed: 25 Dec, 1 Jan **BAR MEALS:** L served
all week 12-1.30 D served all week 7-9.30 Av main course £5.50
RESTAURANT: L served all week 12-1.30 D served Mon-Sat 7-9.30
Sun 12-1.15 Av 3 course fixed price £17 ☻: Free House
◖: Hambleton Stud, Stallion, Bomber County, Shepherds Delight.
NOTES: Parking 18 **ROOMS:** 16 bedrooms en suite s£75 d£95 No
children overnight

FLAMBOROUGH
Map 17 TA27

The Seabirds Inn ▷ ♀
Tower St YO15 1PD ☎ 01262 850242 ▤ 01262 851874
Dir: On B1255 E of Bridlington, 6m form train station

Over 250 years old, this inn has a modern restaurant serving
traditional and contemporary dishes. Away from the road, the
garden provides a tranquil setting, and the pub has numerous
links to bridlepaths, walkways and National Heritage coastal
continued

walks. The menu reflects this seaside location with dishes
such as Whitby creel prawns; poached haddock fillet; and
Dover sole. Other choices include lamb shank with red wine
and rosemary sauce; and pasta and stilton bake.
OPEN: 12-3 6.30-11 (Sun 7-10.30) Mon Closed eve in winter
BAR MEALS: L served all week 12-2 D served all week 6.30-9 Sat
6.30-9.30, Sun 7-9 Av main course £6.50 **RESTAURANT:** L served
all week 12-2 D served all week 6.30-9 Sat 6.30-9.30, Sun 7-9
Av 3 course à la carte £17 ☻: Free House ◖: Scottish Courage
John Smith's, Interbrew Boddingtons Bitter, Worthingtons Creamflow.
♀: 9 **FACILITIES:** Garden: Large grassed area, picnic tables Dogs
allowed water **NOTES:** Parking 20
See Pub Walk on opposite page

HOLME UPON SPALDING MOOR
Map 17 SE83

Ye Olde Red Lion Hotel ♀
Old Rd YO43 4AD ☎ 01430 860220 ▤ 01430 861471
Dir: Off A1079 (York/Hull road). At Market Weighton take A614
A historic 17th-century coaching inn that once provided
hospitality for weary travellers who were helped across the
marshes by monks. It's still a great refuge, with a friendly
atmosphere, oak beams and a cosy fire. The inspiring menu
could include oven-baked duck breast with start anise sauce,
corn fed chicken coq-au-vin or pan-seared sea bass with
wilted greens and vierge sauce.
OPEN: 11.30-2.30 6-11 (Sun 12-3, 7-10.30) **BAR MEALS:** L served
all week 12-2 D served all week 6.30-9.30 **RESTAURANT:** L served
all week 12-2 D served all week 7-9.30 ☻: Free House ◖: Tetley
Bitter, Blacksheep, Guinness. ♀: 13 **FACILITIES:** Garden: Patio area
with water feature, flowers **NOTES:** Parking 60

HUGGATE
Map 19 SE85

The Wolds Inn ♦♦♦ ▷
YO42 1YH ☎ 01377 288217
e-mail: huggate@woldsinn.freeserve.co.uk
Dir: S off A166 between York & Driffield

Probably the highest inn on the Yorkshire Wolds, which explains
Wolds Topper, a 'mixed grill to remember'. Sixteenth-century in
origin, with tiled roofs and white-painted chimneys, the inn's
wood-panelled interior has open fires, gleaming brassware and
a bar serving baguettes, sandwiches and main dishes such as
seafood platter, and pork chop and mushrooms. The restaurant
offers grills, steak pie, cod and pancetta fishcakes, beef
bourguignonne, fillet of plaice and Scottish salmon fillet.
OPEN: 12-2 6.30-11 (May-Sept open Sun at 6)
BAR MEALS: L served Tue-Thurs, Sat, Sun 12-2 D served Tues-Sun
6.30-9 Av main course £6.20 **RESTAURANT:** L served Tue-Thur, Sat
& Sun 12-2 D served Tues-Sun 6.30-9 Sun 6-9 (May-Oct) Av 3 course
à la carte £18 ☻: Free House ◖: Carlsberg-Tetley Tetley Bitter,
Timothy Taylor Landlord, Black Sheep. **FACILITIES:** Large &
contained garden Dogs allowed Water **NOTES:** Parking 50
ROOMS: 3 bedrooms en suite s£28 d£38

KILHAM — Map 17 TA06

The Old Star Inn
Church St YO25 4RG ☎ 01262 420619 📠 01262 420619

Traditional village inn at the heart of the historic village of Kilham. The building dates from the 17th century, and exposed beams and open fires create a welcoming setting for the cask ales and home-cooked food. The menu offers a choice of main courses, while starters and specials are selected from the daily board. There's also a daily curry, and old favourites like steak and kidney pudding or slow roasted belly pork.
OPEN: 12-2 6-11 (Sun 12-10.30) Summer open all year **BAR MEALS:** L served Thurs, Sat-Sun 12-1.45 D served all week 6-8.30 Av main course £6.95 **RESTAURANT:** L served Thur, Sat-Sun 12-1.45 D served all week 6-8.30 ⊜: Free House ◀: Scottish Courage John Smiths Cask, Archers, Guest Ales.
FACILITIES: Garden: Large patio area, 1/2 acre of lawn Dogs allowed Water on request **NOTES:** Parking 5

KINGSTON UPON HULL — Map 17 TA02

The Minerva Hotel ♀
Nelson St, Victoria Pier HU1 1XE
☎ 01482 326909 📠 01482 326909
Dir: M62 onto A63, then Castle St, turn right at signpost for fruit market into Queens St at the top of Queens St on right hand side of the pier
The Minerva boasts old-fashioned rooms and cosy snugs at its riverside location with its ferry port, marina, and fishing fleet. It has a reputation for hospitality and delicious home-cooked food, and a good range of guest ales.
OPEN: 11-11 (Sun 12-10.30) Closed: Dec 25 **BAR MEALS:** L served all week 12-10 D served all week Sun 12-9 Av main course £7 **RESTAURANT:** L served all week 12-10 D served all week Sun 12-9 ⊜: ◀: Tetley Bitter, usually 4 guest bers. ♀: 7 **FACILITIES:** Pier side front with benched area Dogs allowed Water

LOW CATTON — Map 17 SE75

The Gold Cup Inn ♀
YO41 1EA ☎ 01759 371354 📠 01759 373833
Dir: 1m S of A166 or 1m N of A1079, E of York
This family-run, 300-year-old country inn incorporates a two-part restaurant, one small and intimate, with solid wood pews and tables reputedly made from a single oak, the other larger and lighter with a vaulted ceiling. Bar areas are comfortable and relaxed with beams, and an open fire and a cast-iron stove at opposite ends. Locally sourced ingredients are used as much as possible for dishes such as grilled salmon fillet topped with sautéed prawns, and char-grilled chicken breast.
OPEN: 12-3 6-11 (Sat 12-11, Sun 12-10.30) Mon closed lunchtime **BAR MEALS:** L served Sun, Tue-Sat 12-2 D served all week 6-9.30 (12-9.30 wknds) Av main course £7 **RESTAURANT:** L served Sun
continued

12-5.30 D served all week 6-9.30 12-9.30 Av 3 course à la carte £17 Av 3 course fixed price £13 ⊜: Free House ◀: Tetley, John Smiths. ♀: 10 **FACILITIES:** Garden: Large grassed area with flower beds, trees Dogs allowed Water bowls **NOTES:** Parking 60 No credit cards

LUND — Map 17 SE94

Pick of the Pubs

The Wellington Inn ♀
19 The Green YO25 9TE ☎ 01377 217294 📠 01377 217192
Dir: On B1248 NE of Beverley
Nicely situated opposite the picture-postcard village green, the Wellington Inn is popular with locals and visitors alike, whether for a pint of real ale, a glass of house wine, or a plate of decent food. Typical bar menu starters are goujons of mixed white fish with home-made tartare sauce; and citrus salad, fried haloumi cheese and raspberry vinaigrette. Bar mains might be king prawn and fresh asparagus risotto with fresh parmesan; and fillet of fresh salmon on spicy noodles with stir-fried vegetables. If à la carte dining is your intention, allow enough time to mull over the extensive wine list, then prepare for a bowl of Loch Fyne rope-grown mussels; or warm roquefort cheesecake, poached pear, honey and balsamic vinegar. Main courses provide plenty of choice, from fillet of fresh halibut with smoked mussel and salmon kedgeree and a lightly-curried hollandaise; to grilled rib-eye steak, apple and blue cheese salad, with home-made chips. Puddings and coffee both come in half a dozen varieties.
OPEN: 12-3 6.30-11 (Closed Mon lunch) **BAR MEALS:** L served Tue-Sun 12-2 D served Tue-Sat 6.30-9 Av main course £10.95 **RESTAURANT:** L served none D served Tue-Sat 7-9.30 Av 3 course à la carte £23.50 ⊜: Free House ◀: Timothy Taylor Landlord, Black Sheep Best, John Smiths, Copper Dragon Golden Pippin, Regular Guest. ♀: 8 **FACILITIES:** Garden: Courtyard **NOTES:** Parking 40

SOUTH CAVE — Map 17 SE93

The Fox and Coney Inn ♦♦♦♦ ♀
52 Market Place HU15 2AT ☎ 01430 422275 📠 01430 421552
e-mail: foxandconey@aol.com Web: www.foxandconey.com
Dir: 4 miles E of M62 on A63. 4 miles N of Brough mainline railway
Right in the heart of South Cave, this family run pub dates from 1739 and is probably the oldest building in the village. The inn, which is handy for walkers on the nearby Wolds Way, was known simply as The Fox until William Goodlad added the Coney (rabbit) in 1788. Jacket potatoes, salads and baguettes supplement varied hot dishes like steak in ale pie, chicken curry, seafood platter and mushroom stroganoff.
OPEN: 11.30-2.30 4.30-11 **BAR MEALS:** L served all week 11.30-2 D served all week 5.30-9.30 (Sun 12-3.30, 5.30-9) Av main course £6 **RESTAURANT:** L served all week 11.30-2 D served all week 5.30-9.30 ⊜: Enterprise Inns ◀: Timothy Taylors Landlord, Scottish Courage John Smith's & Theakston Cool Cask, Deuchers IPA, Guest Beers. ♀: 15 **FACILITIES:** Garden: Seats approx 30 Dogs allowed Water **NOTES:** Parking 22 **ROOMS:** 12 bedrooms en suite 2 family rooms s£42 d£55

SUTTON UPON DERWENT — Map 17 SE74

St Vincent Arms NEW

Main St YO41 4BN
Dir: *From A64 follow signs for A1079. Turn right and follow signs for Elvington B1228. Follow road through Elvington to Sutton Upon Derwent*
The St Vincent Arms was named after John Jervis, created the first Earl of St Vincent in the 18th century, and mentor to Admiral Lord Nelson. Today it's a warm family-run pub with an old-fashioned welcoming atmosphere, minus music or gaming machines but plus great food and beer. A meal might start with seared scallops, or Cornish crab mayonnaise; followed by either rack of lamb with herb crust, or perhaps St Vincent mixed grill.
OPEN: 11.30-3 6-11 Dec 25 open for 2hrs **BAR MEALS:** L served all week 12-2 D served all week 7-9.30 Av main course £7.50
RESTAURANT: L served all week 12-2 D served all week 7-9.30 Av 3 course à la carte £20 **◖:** Taylors Landlord, Fullers ESB, Adnams Broadside, Charlie Wells Bombardier. **♀:** 8 **FACILITIES:** Garden: Large garden area around edge of carpark Dogs allowed water bowls **NOTES:** Parking 20

Sutton Arms ♀

Main St YO41 4BT ☎ 01904 608477 ▤ 01904 607585
e-mail: enquiries@suttonarms.co.uk
Dir: *From the A64, take the Hull exit (A1079) and the immediate right on to Elvington (B1228) and then on to Sutton Derwent. R past the school*
Modern pub built on the site of a much older one which got too small for the village, and dedicated to the 1940s with its wind-up gramophone, valve radios, sheet music and other memorabilia from this period. There are plenty of eating areas, including the smart Mediterranean-style restaurant and a heated courtyard. Expect chargrilled beef, moussaka, steak and ale pie, and chicken stirfry.
OPEN: 5.30-11 (Sat-Sun, 12-11) **BAR MEALS:** L served Sat-Sun & BH's 12-2.45 D served Tue-Sun & BH's 6-9.15 Av main course £6
RESTAURANT: L served Sun 12-2.45 D served Tue-Sun & BH's 6-9.15 Av 3 course à la carte £12 Av 3 course fixed price £6.75 **◖:** John Smiths Bitter, Black Sheep Bitter, Old Legover Bitter. **♀:** 8 **FACILITIES:** Garden: Paved area with three tables **NOTES:** Parking 30

YORKSHIRE, NORTH

AKEBAR — Map 19 SE19

The Friar's Head ♀

Akebar Park DL8 5LY ☎ 01677 450201 & 450591 ▤ 01677 450046 web: www.akebarpark.com/pub.html
Dir: *Take A684 from Leeming Bar Motel (on A1). W towards Leyburn for 7m. Friar's Head is in Akebar Park*

Typical stone-built Yorkshire Dales hostelry with delightful
continued

The Friar's Head
at Akebar, Wensleydale
North Yorkshire DL8 5LY
Traditional country pub.
John Smith, Theakston, Black Sheep Real Ales.
Cosy Log Fire
Dine under grape vines. Excellent food and wines by candlelight overlooking spectacular views. West Wing suite of rooms for private dining & parties with style.
Cloister Restaurant
Open 7 days lunch & dinner.
Advance booking desirable at weekends.
Telephone 01677 450201/450591.
www.akebarpark.com.
The Golf Course, Akebar Park, Wensleydale

south-facing views over a golf course and farmland, with a terrace for alfresco drinking and dining. There is also a conservatory dining room full of growing plants and a huge vine which produces grapes in abundance. Enjoy the well-stocked bar, and a comprehensive menu offering such dishes as halibut steak, seafood pancake, slow-braised chump of lamb, and tagliatelle verde. **OPEN:** 10-2.30 6-11.30 (Sun 7-10.30) **BAR MEALS:** L served all week 12-2 D served all week 6-9.30 Sun 7-9.30 Av main course £6.50
RESTAURANT: L served all week 12-2 D served all week 6-9.30 Sat dinner 6-10, Sun dinner 7-9.30 Av 3 course à la carte £20 **◖:** Free House **◖:** Scottish Courage John Smith's & Theakston Best Bitter, Black Sheep Best. **♀:** 14 **FACILITIES:** Garden: Terrace overlooks green, next to golf course **NOTES:** Parking 60
See advert on this page

APPLETON-LE-MOORS — Map 19 SE78

The Moors Inn NEW

YO62 6TF ☎ 01751 417435
Dir: *On A170 between Pickering and Kirbymoorside*
Whether you're interested in walking or sightseeing by car, this inn is a good choice for its location and good home-cooked food. It is in a small moors village with lovely scenery in every direction, and in summer you can sit in the large garden and enjoy the splendid views. Dishes include pheasant casserole and fish pie, and in addition to hand-pumped Black Bull and Black Sheep, there is a selection of 50 malt whiskies.
OPEN: 12-3 7-11 **BAR MEALS:** L served Sun 12-2 D served Tues-Sun 7-9 Av main course £8 **RESTAURANT:** L served Sun 12-2 D served Tues-Sun 7-9 **◖:** Black Sheep, Black Bull. **FACILITIES:** Garden: Dogs allowed **NOTES:** P 20 No credit cards

PUB WALK
Horseshoe Hotel
Egton Bridge - North Yorkshire

HORSESHOE HOTEL
Egton Bridge, Whitby, YO21 1XE
☎ 01947 895245
Directions: From Whitby take A171 towards Middlesborough Village, signed in 5miles.
On the banks of the River Esk. Cosy interior with old settles, works by local artists and a log fire. Good home-cooked food. A large garden with ducks and geese. Fishing is available
Open: 11.30–3 6.30–11 (All day Sat, Sun & BH's in Summer) Closed: 25 Dec
Bar Meals: L served all week 12–2 D served all week 7–9 Av main course £7.50
Restaurant Meals: L served all week 12–2 D served all week 7–9
Children welcome & dogs allowed. Garden and parking available.
(for full entry see page 562)

Distance: 3 miles (4.8km)
Map: OS Landranger 94 or Outdoor Leisure 27
Terrain: North York Moors
Paths: Paved causeways, packhorse routes, field paths and road
Gradient: Undulating with several climbs and descents

Walk submitted by Horseshoe Hotel, Egton Bridge

A very pleasant walk which takes you to Beggar's Bridge, a picturesque packhorse bridge spanning the River Esk. There are good views of Glaisdale, once an ironstone mining village boasting three blast furnaces, and stretches of the walk follow paved causeways, a reminder of the days when Glaisdale was an important trading centre.

On leaving the hotel, follow the drive towards the road and turn left just before it to join a footpath signposted to stepping stones. Cross the river via both sets of stones, pass between houses and turn left at the road. Pass under the railway bridge and take the stile on the left about 80 yards beyond the farm. The footpath initially follows the fence, then continues through the field to a stream and uphill to a stile. Cross over and climb steeply through woodland.

Keep ahead between the trees and across two fields, joining the track to Limber Hill Farm. Pass through the farmyard and turn left at the road. Descend the notoriously steep Limber Hill, a superb viewpoint with excellent views over Glaisdale and prominent rows of ex-miners' cottages.

Veer left along the road at the bottom and follow it for a short distance. Make for the medieval packhorse bridge known as Beggar's Bridge, but instead of crossing it, pass under the railway arch and take the footbridge by the ford. There is a signpost here for Egton Bridge. Climb the steps and follow the Coast to Coast waymarks.

The path follows the old packhorse route, part of the Coast to Coast Walk, for about one mile, cutting through Arncliffe Woods to reach a minor road. Bear left, head downhill, cross the ford via the footbridge and the Horseshoe Hotel is a few hundred yards ahead on your left.

552

England

APPLETREEWICK
Map 19 SE06

The Craven Arms
BD23 6DA ☎ 01756 720270 e-mail: cravenapple@aol.com
Dir: From Skipton take A59 towards Harrogate, B6160 N. Village signed on right. (Pub just outside village)

Built as a farm by Sir William Craven (a Lord Mayor of London) in the mid-16th century, and later used as a weaving shed and courthouse, this ancient building retains its original beams, flagstone floors and magnificent Dales fireplace. The village stocks are still outside, with spectacular views of the River Wharfe and Simon's Seat. Home-made soup, steak pie with ale and mushrooms, cheesy cottage pie, traitor's pie (Lancashire hotpot in a giant Yorkshire pudding), local sausages, baguette sandwiches - these are all among the wholesome fare on offer.

OPEN: 11.30-3 6.30-11 (Sat & BHs 11.30-11, Sun 12-10.30) Closed Mon Thurs eve (winter) **BAR MEALS:** L served all week 11.30-2.30 D served all week 6.30-9 Sat 11.30-9, Sun 12-9 Av main course £6 🍺: Free House 🍺: Black Sheep, Tetley, Old Bear Original, Old Bear Hibernator. **FACILITIES:** Garden: Walled grass beer garden, hill views Dogs allowed **NOTES:** Parking 35

ASENBY
Map 19 SE37

Pick of the Pubs

Crab & Lobster 🏵️🏵️ 🏆
Dishforth Rd YO7 3QL ☎ 01845 577286 📠 01845 577109
e-mail: reservations@crabandlobster.co.uk
Dir: From A1(M) take A168 towards Thirsk, follow signs for Asenby

Amid seven acres of garden, lake and streams stands this unique 17th-century thatched pub and adjacent small hotel. A visit to the Crab and Lobster is an experience not to be missed, where ambience and culinary magic combine to dazzle the clientele. It is an Aladdin's Cave of antiques and artefacts from around the world, often described as a jungle of bric-a-brac, and there is plenty to see and amuse. Equally famous for its innovative cuisine and special gourmet extravaganzas, the menus show influences from France and Italy, with some oriental dishes too. The famous fish club sandwich (lunch only), chunky fish soup, Craster salmon and lobster, and asparagus and Brie spring rolls feature among starters alone. Typical main dishes include brill fillet with crab and wilted spinach; wild seabass stuffed with crab, pine nuts, raisins and pancetta; and salmon, clams, scallops and mussels in tarragon butter sauce. Meat eaters will find oriental beef pancakes, braised lamb shank, and crispy confit duck on the menu. Alfresco eating and summer barbecues, good real ales, and an extensive wine list, plus a pavilion open all day for food,

continued

drinks and coffees puts the Crab and Lobster in a class of its own.
OPEN: 11.30-11 **BAR MEALS:** L served all week 12-2.15 D served all week 7-9.45 Av main course £13
RESTAURANT: L served all week 12-2.15 D served all week 7-9.30 🍺: Scottish Courage 🍺: John Smiths. 🏆: 8
FACILITIES: Garden: 7 acre mature gardens, food served outdoors Dogs allowed **NOTES:** Parking 120

ASKRIGG
Map 18 SD99

Kings Arms 🏨
Market Place DL8 3HQ ☎ 01969 650817 📠 01969 650856
e-mail: kingsarms@askrigg.fsnet.co.uk
Dir: N off A684 between Hawes & Leyburn

At the heart of the Yorkshire Dales, Askrigg's pub was known as The Drovers in the TV series *All Creatures Great and Small*. Built in 1762 as racing stables and converted to a pub in 1860, today it boasts a good range of real ales and an extensive menu and wine list. Favourites are roasted rack of Dales lamb with a mustard and herb crust, beer-battered haddock fillet with chips, chicken breast with linguini, roasted seabass on Mediterranean vegetables or grilled gammon steak with eggs or pineapple rings. Spectacular inglenook fireplace in the main bar.
OPEN: 11-3 6-11 (Sat 11-11, Sun 12-10.30) **BAR MEALS:** L served all week 12-2 D served all week 6.30-9 Av main course £10
RESTAURANT: D served Fri-Sat 7-9 Av 3 course à la carte £19 🍺: Free House 🍺: Scottish Courage John Smiths, Black Sheep, Theakstons Best Bitter, Theakstons Old Peculier.
FACILITIES: Garden: paved courtyard Dogs allowed Water

AUSTWICK
Map 18 SD76

The Game Cock Inn
The Green LA2 8BB ☎ 015242 51226 📠 015242 51028
Set in the pretty limestone village of Austwick, this cosy pub offers a warm welcome with real ale and freshly cooked meals. There's a large garden with children's play area, whilst winter brings an open log fire in the bar. This is a great area for walkers, and the famous Norber Boulder is nearby. Menu choices include game cock pie; goat's cheese and new potato tart; and roasted salmon in filo pastry.
OPEN: 11.30-3 6-11 (All day Sun) **BAR MEALS:** L served all week 11.30-2 D served all week 6-9 (Sun 12-9) Av main course £8.50
RESTAURANT: L served all week 11.30-2 D served all week 6-9 (Sun 12-9) Av 3 course à la carte £16 🍺: 🍺: Thwaites Best Bitter & Smooth. **FACILITIES:** Child facs Garden: large beer garden **NOTES:** Parking 6

🏆 **7** Number of wines by the glass

England

AYSGARTH
Map 19 SE08

Pick of the Pubs

The George & Dragon Inn ★★ 〰️ ♀
DL8 3AD ☎ 01969 663358 📠 01969 663773
e-mail: info@georgeanddragonaysgarth.co.uk
Dir: On the A68A in the centre or the village of Aysgarth, midway between Leyburn and Hawes

Beautifully situated near Aysgarth Falls in the heart of Herriot country, the owners of this attractive 17th century, Grade II-listed free house, continue a long tradition of Yorkshire hospitality. Beamed ceilings and open fires set the scene for freshly cooked courses like pan seared fillet of salmon; roast breast of duckling; poached chicken with wild mushrooms, shallots and bacon lardons; roast monkfish wrapped in smoked bacon; confit shoulder of lamb with anna potatoes; or red onion tatin with a herb salad and balsamic reduction. Light lunches such as fish cakes, ciabattas, bruchettas, or haddock and chips are also available. See if you can spot the lucky locals who have been immortalised in sketch form around the bar. Attractive patio area is ideal for summer dining.
OPEN: 11-11 (Sun 12-10.30) **BAR MEALS:** L served all week 12-2 D served all week 6-9 Afternoon snacks in spring and summer 2-5 Av main course £10 **RESTAURANT:** L served all week 12-2 D served all week 6-9 Sun 12-3 Av 3 course à la carte £20 🍽: Free House 🍺: Black Sheep Best, John Smith's Cask, Smooth & Theakstons Bitter. ♀: 10 **FACILITIES:** Garden: Large paved area, tables chairs Dogs allowed Water
NOTES: Parking 35 **ROOMS:** 7 bedrooms en suite 2 family rooms s£36 d£62

BAINBRIDGE
Map 18 SD99

Rose & Crown Hotel ★★
DL8 3EE ☎ 01969 650225 📠 01969 650735
e-mail: stay@theprideofwensleydale.co.uk
Dir: On A684 in centre of village
A 500-year-old coaching inn surrounded by spectacular scenery, whose cosy interior is home to the forest horn. Blown each evening from Holy Rood (September 27th) to Shrovetide, it would guide travellers safely to the village. The chef offers such delights as salmon and dill dumplings with caviar sauce, while a main course from the specials menu might consist of whole black bream baked in a sea salt crust and served with mint hollandaise. Other dishes could include haunch of rabbit studded with garlic or breast of chicken filled with crayfish.
OPEN: 11-11 (Sun 12-10.30) **BAR MEALS:** L served all week 12-2.15 D served all week 6-9.15 Av main course £9.50
RESTAURANT: L served Sun 12-2.15 D served all week 7-9.15

continued

Av 3 course à la carte £20 🍽: Free House 🍺: Websters Bitter, Black Sheep Best, Scottish Courage John Smith's, Old Peculier.
FACILITIES: Garden: Raised patio area Dogs allowed
NOTES: Parking 65 **ROOMS:** 11 bedrooms en suite s£40 d£74

BILBROUGH
Map 16 SE54

Pick of the Pubs

The Three Hares Country Inn ◉◉ ♀
Main St YO23 3PH ☎ 01937 832128 📠 01937 834626
e-mail: info@thethreehares.co.uk
See Pick of the Pubs on opposite page

BOROUGHBRIDGE
Map 19 SE36

Pick of the Pubs

The Black Bull Inn 〰️ ♀
6 St James Square YO51 9AR
☎ 01423 322413 📠 01423 323915
Dir: From A1(M) junct 48 take B6265 E for 1m

The Black Bull has always been an inn, and since its earliest parts date back to 1262, it's easy to accept that it might have ghosts. What else could have upended all the glasses in the restaurant one night? Bar snacks include gammon steak, beef Madras, grills, and smoked salmon and scrambled eggs on toasted brioche. Among the mouth-watering hot sandwiches is Cajun chicken with sweet chilli and salsa tomatoes. Turning to the main menu we find starters such as pan-fried king prawn tails and queen scallops in arrabiata sauce; and chicken and roasted pepper terrine. Mains include steaks, rump of English lamb, tenderloin of pork, Mexican spiced vegetables in hot sweet salsa sauce, and tuna steak with prawns and wild mushrooms topped with gruyère. Yorkshire beers are strongly represented in the bar, while whisky drinkers will find 17 malts to choose from.
OPEN: 11-11 (Sun 12-10.30) **BAR MEALS:** L served all week 12-2 D served all week 6-9.30 Sun 12-2.30 and 6-9 Av main course £6.95 **RESTAURANT:** L served all week 12-2 D served all week 6-9.30 Sun 12-2.30 and 6-9 🍽: Free House 🍺: Black Sheep, Scottish Courage John Smiths, Timothy Taylor Landlord, Cottage Brewing. ♀: 10 **FACILITIES:** Dogs allowed Water, Toys **NOTES:** Parking 4

> ◆ Pubs with Red Diamonds are the top places in the AA's three, four and five diamond ratings

Pick of the Pubs

The Three Hares Country Inn

An 18th-century country pub in a quiet village near York, with an unusual feature in the flagstone-floored restaurant - the old forge. Mainly local, seasonal produce is used in both the restaurant and bar. Regular starters include cauliflower soup, fresh sorrel and parsley oil; Bleiker's black pudding, rustic mustard and onion relish; and potted shrimps, mace butter with toasted soda bread.

A house speciality - such as a platter of meats - may follow, prior to a main course of Three Hares fish pie, made with Whitby-landed fish baked with mashed potato and Richard III Wensleydale cheese; Nidderdale lamb hotpot; or a grill. There are usually around ten daily changing specials, including Whitby crab and crayfish salad; roast poussin, wild mushroom, black pudding and artichoke; and risotto of wild mushrooms and truffle oil. Sunday brunch includes a Full Monty breakfast, served until 4pm.

OPEN: 11-11
BAR MEALS: L served all week 12-2.30 D served Mon-Sat 7-9 (Sun 11-4) Av main course £8
RESTAURANT: L served Mon-Sun 12-2.30 D served Mon-Sat 7-9 (Sun 11-4)
🍺: Free House
🍺: Timothy Taylors Landlord, Black Sheep, John Smiths Cask, Guest ales each week. ♀: 16
FACILITIES: Garden: Patio with heaters, large grassed area
NOTES: Parking 30

Map 16 SE54
Main St YO23 3PH
☎ 01937 832128
📄 01937 834626
🅴 info@thethreehares.co.uk
Dir: Off A64, SW of York

England

BREARTON · Map 19 SE36

Pick of the Pubs

Malt Shovel Inn
HG3 3BX ☎ 01423 862929
Dir: From A61 (Ripon/Harrogate) take B6165 towards Knaresborough. Turn left following signs to Brearton. Follow for 1m turn right into village.

Set at the heart of a small farming community, The Malt Shovel is the oldest building in a very old village. The rural setting has some good examples of ancient strip farming and, although the pub is surrounded by rolling farmland, it's just 15 minutes from Harrogate and within easy reach of Knaresborough or Ripon. Beer mugs, horse brasses and hunting scenes decorate the heavily-beamed rooms, and you can enjoy a quiet game of dominoes or shove ha'penny without any intrusions beyond those of the two friendly resident ghosts. The blackboard menu has something for everyone. Expect sausage and mash, prawn curry, and seafood gratin, all made using the freshest possible produce. Vegetarians are well catered for too, with blue cheese and red onion tart, or potato and tomato curry.
OPEN: 12-3 6.45-11 (Sun 12-2.30, 7-10.30)
BAR MEALS: L served Tue-Sun 12-2 D served Tue-Sat 7-9 Av main course £6.95 ☺: Free House ◀: Daleside Nightjar, Durham Magus, Black Sheep Best, Theakston Masham.
FACILITIES: Outside patio seating with heaters Dogs allowed
NOTES: Parking 20 No credit cards

BROUGHTON · Map 18 SD95

The Bull ♀
BD23 3AE ☎ 01756 792065
e-mail: janeneil@thebullatbroughton.co.uk
Dir: On A59 3m from Skipton on A59

Like the village itself, the pub is part of the 3,000-acre Broughton Hall estate, owned by the Tempest family for 900

continued

years. The chef-cum-manager was enticed from his much acclaimed former establishment to achieve similar if not higher standards here. His compact, thoughtful menu offers slow-roasted ham shank glazed with orange and honey, crab and lobster risotto, and chargrilled chicken breast with herby cream cheese. Locally brewed Bull Bitter and guest ales.
OPEN: 12-3 5.30-11 (Sun 12-8) **BAR MEALS:** L served all week 12-2 D served Mon-Sat 6-9 (Sunday 12-6) **RESTAURANT:** L served all week 12-2 D served Mon-Sat 6-9 Sun & BHs 12-6 ☺: Free House ◀: Scottish Courage, John Smith's Smooth, Bull Bitter (Local), Guest Ales. ♀: 6 **FACILITIES:** Child facs Garden: Large stone patio, heaters, seating Dogs water, dog biscuits **NOTES:** Parking 60

BUCKDEN · Map 18 SD97

Pick of the Pubs

The Buck Inn ★★ ☺☺☺ ♀
BD23 5JA ☎ 01756 760228 🖺 01756 760227
e-mail: info@thebuckinn.com web: www.thebuckinn.com
Dir: From Skipton take B6265, then B6160

Set in the heart of Calendar Girls country, this Georgian inn counts among its regulars some of the ladies who thought up the idea. The inn sits at the foot of Buckden Pike, facing south across the village green surrounded by picturesque stone cottages, and enjoying panoramic Dales views. The cosy bar, where real ales are hand pulled, a stock of over 25 malts is kept and bar meals are served, has lots of charm and character. The spacious Courtyard restaurant is classically laid out, and serves cuisine of recognised merit. Typical starters are home-made breaded fishcake or warm salad of olives, new potatoes, roasted peppers and cherry tomatoes. Main dishes offer a daily-changing choice based on Dales meat, fresh fish and local vegetables; typical may be confit of local lamb hock with creamed mash, redcurrant and rosemary sauce, which could be followed by Wensleydale cheese or any of half a dozen choice desserts. New owners November 2004. Reports please.
OPEN: 11-11 (Sun 12-11) **BAR MEALS:** L served all week 12-2 D served all week 6.30-9 Av main course £8.95
RESTAURANT: D served all week 6.30-9 ☺: Free House ◀: Black Sheep Bitter, Old Peculier, Timothy Taylor's Landlord, Copper Dragon. ♀: 10 **FACILITIES:** Garden: Patio Dogs allowed **NOTES:** Parking 40 **ROOMS:** 14 bedrooms en suite 2 family rooms s£59.50 d£86

Not all of the pubs in the guide are open all week or all day. It's always best to check before you travel

England

BURNSALL
Map 19 SE06

Pick of the Pubs

The Red Lion ★★ ◉ ♀
By the Bridge BD23 6BU ☎ 01756 720204 📠 01756 720292
e-mail: redlion@daelnet.co.uk   web: www.redlion.co.uk
See Pick of the Pubs on page 558

BYLAND ABBEY
Map 19 SE57

Pick of the Pubs

Abbey Inn ♀
YO61 4BD ☎ 01347 868204 📠 01347 868678
e-mail: jane@nordli.freeserve.co.uk
web: www.bylandabbeyinn.com
Dir: From A19 Thirsk/York follow signs to Byland Abbey/Coxwold

This isolated rural inn in the shadow of the hauntingly beautiful ruins of Byland Abbey, was built by Cistercian monks over a thousand years ago, only to be destroyed during Henry VIII's Dissolution. Three hundred years later it was again monks - this time Benedictines from Ampleforth - who built this well-proportioned hostelry. Its creeper-clad façade conceals a distinctive interior in which four splendid dining areas variously present bare boards, rug-strewn flagstones, open fireplaces, huge settles, Jacobean-style chairs, fine tapestries, stuffed birds and unusual objets d'art. Food is offered from frequently changing lunch and dinner menus, supplemented by daily specials. A typical selection includes starters of halibut with a timbale of east coast crab and celeriac remoulade; and carpaccio of beef with horseradish, rocket and Parmesan salad; with main courses typified by griddled sirloin steak, brandy peppercorn sauce and grilled field mushrooms; and pan-fried cod and bubble and squeak.
OPEN: 11.30-3 6.30-11 **BAR MEALS:** L served Tue-Sun 12-2 D served Mon-Sat 6.30-9 Sun 12-3 Av main course £10
RESTAURANT: L served Tue-Sun 12-2 D served Mon-Sat 6.30-9 Sun 12-3 Av 3 course à la carte £22.95 ◉: Free House
🍺: Black Sheep Best, Carlsberg-Tetley Telety Bitter. ♀: 20
FACILITIES: Garden: Large patio overlooking ruins of Byland Abbey **NOTES:** Parking 30

We endeavour to be as accurate as possible but changes to times and other information can occur after the guide has gone to press

---

CARLTON
Map 19 SE08

Foresters Arms
DL8 4BB ☎ 01969 640272 📠 01969 640467
e-mail: gpsurtees@aol.com
Dir: Pub in Carlton village
There's another new landlord at the Foresters Arms, now part of the Wensleydale Brewery group. This early 17th-century, Grade II listed building stands in a picturesque Dales village convenient for Middleham Castle, Aysgarth Falls and Bolton Castle. The bars retain their historic atmosphere with fine open fireplaces and beamed ceilings. The contemporary menu ranges from Indian style fishcakes with cucumber raita; or crispy duckling confit; to leek, mushroom and gruyere potato cake with tomato concasse.
OPEN: 12-2 6.30-11 (Closed Tues am in winter)
BAR MEALS: L served Wed-Sun 12-2 D served Tues-Sat 7-9 No dinner on Sun Av main course £11 **RESTAURANT:** L served Tue-Sun 12-2 D served Tue-Sat 7-9 Av 3 course à la carte £17
◉: Free House 🍺: Wensly Brewery Ales, Guest Ales inc. Salamander, Wentworth. **FACILITIES:** Dogs allowed Water
NOTES: Parking 15

CARTHORPE
Map 19 SE38

Pick of the Pubs

The Fox & Hounds 🐟 ♀
DL8 2LG ☎ 01845 567433 📠 01845 567155
Dir: Off A1, signposted on both N & S carriageways

Only one mile from the A1, but tucked away in quiet open countryside, this neat, attractive free house has been serving travellers for 200 years. The adjoining restaurant was once the village smithy, and the old anvil and other tools of the trade are still on display, giving a nice sense of history to the place. There are good value midweek set-price lunch and dinner menus, as well as a more adventurous carte featuring duck filled filo parcels with plum sauce, perhaps followed by pan-fried sea bass on a potato rösti. Additional blackboard specials might include oven-baked field mushroom stuffed with goats cheese and tomato provençale; and braised lamb shank with root vegetable purée. Sunday lunch is a favourite, with plenty of traditional choices. The dessert menu is also imaginative: perhaps a champagne and summer fruit jelly with home-made vanilla shortbread. All wines are available by the glass.
OPEN: 12-2.30 7-11 **BAR MEALS:** L served Tue-Sun 12-2 D served Tue-Sat 7-9.30 Av main course £10
RESTAURANT: L served Tue-Sun 12-2 D served Tue-Sun 7-9.30 Av 3 course à la carte £20 Av 3 course fixed price £13.95
◉: Free House 🍺: Black Sheep Best, Worthington's Bitter.
FACILITIES: Child facs **NOTES:** Parking 22

The Red Lion

A 16th-century ferryman's inn on the banks of the River Wharfe in a picture postcard village. The grounds run down to the water where fishing is available. The Red Lion is a lovely riverside inn with large gardens and terraces, located by a five-arched bridge spanning the River Wharfe.

The interior is full of old world charm, with a traditional Dales bar, oak floors and panelling, cosy armchairs, sofas and wood-burning stoves. A good selection of cask conditioned ales and malt whiskies is served, plus 15 wines by the glass. A brasserie menu is offered in the bar, featuring local game from the nearby estates and locally produced beef and lamb. Typical dishes are loin of Yorkshire venison with black pudding, croquette potatoes and apple sauce, and medallions of Wharfedale beef with seared foie gras, wild mushrooms and garlic crostini. The attractive dining room has mullioned windows overlooking the village green towards the river and fells. The seasonal menu might include steamed steak and kidney pudding with Theakstons ale, or breast of chicken stuffed with Lancashire cheese, wrapped in Cumbrian royal mature ham and savoy cabbage, and served with tarragon sauce. An additional lunch menu offers soups, sandwiches and salads, light main courses and full meals. Burnsall is a delightful little village in Wharfedale, part of the Yorkshire Dales National Park, in a designated Area of Oustanding Natural Beauty. Individually decorated bedrooms, including a honeymoon suite, are provided at the inn, and weddings and business functions can be accommodated in the Terrace Room. 'Upside down' cottages on the riverbank are also available for holiday lets.

OPEN: 8-11.30 (Sun closes 10.30)
BAR MEALS: L served all week 12-2.30 D served all week 6-9.30 Av main course £11.50
RESTAURANT: L served all week 12-2.30 D served all week 7-9.30
⊜: Free House
🍺: Theakston Black Bull, Greene King Old Speckled Hen, Timothy Taylor Landlord, Scottish Courage John Smith's. ⏼: 14
FACILITIES: Garden: Large garden, bordering the River Wharf Dogs allowed **NOTES:** Parking 70
ROOMS: 14 bedrooms en suite s£60 d£60

★★ ⬡ ⏼   Map 19 SE06
By the Bridge BD23 6BU
☎ 01756 720204
🖹 01756 720292
ℯ redlion@daelnet.co.uk
ⓦ www.redlion.co.uk
Dir: From Skipton take A59 east take B6160 towards Bolton Abbey, Burnsall 7m

CLAPHAM
Map 18 SD76

New Inn 🏠 ♀
LA2 8HH ☎ 01524 251203 📠 251496
e-mail: info@newinn-clapham.co.uk
web: www.newinn-clapham.co.uk
Dir: On A65 in Yorkshire Dale National Park

Family-run 18th-century coaching inn located in a peaceful
Dales village beneath Ingleborough, one of Yorkshire's most
famous summits. The honest, wholesome food served in the
non-smoking dining is much appreciated by walkers to,
among many local destinations, Ingleborough Show Cave.
Sandwiches, jackets, soup and perhaps trio of Yorkshire
puddings are replaced in the evening by herb-roasted
suckling pig, crusty steak pie, and spinach pasta.
OPEN: 11-11 **BAR MEALS:** L served all week 12-2 D served all
week 6.30-8.30 (Sun 6.30-8) Av main course £8.65
RESTAURANT: L served all week 12-2 D served all week 6.30-8.30
(Sun 6.30-8) Av 3 course à la carte £19.50 Av 5 course fixed price £24
🍽: Free House 🍺: Black Sheep Best, Tetley Bitter, Copper Dragon
Pippin, Dent Fellbeck. ♀: 18 **FACILITIES:** Garden: Riverside seats,
beer garden Dogs allowed Water **NOTES:** Parking 35
See advert on page 560

COLTON
Map 16 SE54

Ye Old Sun Inn 🏠 ♀
Main St LS24 8EP ☎ 01904 744261 📠 01904 744261
e-mail: ashleyandkelly@yeoldsuninn.co.uk
Dir: 3-4m from York, off A64
This traditional whitewashed free house dates back to the
18th century, when it started life as a coaching inn, and its still
boasts open fires and beams throughout. The pub enjoys a
village setting, with rolling countryside beyond the large
lawned garden. Choices from the varied menu include bream
fillets with honey roasted parsnips; roasted belly pork with
beetroot and cabbage; and penne pasta with roasted
vegetables and spinach.
OPEN: 12-2.30 6-11 (Sun open all day) Closed: 1-26 Jan
BAR MEALS: L served Tue-Sun 12-2 D served Tue-Sun 6.30-9.30
Sun 12-7 Av main course £14 **RESTAURANT:** D served Tues-Sun
6-9.30 Sun 12-7 Av 3 course à la carte £28.50 🍽: Enterprise Inns
🍺: John Smith, Timothy Taylors, Tetleys, Guest Ale (changing
weekly). ♀: 18 **FACILITIES:** Garden: Lawn with tables and chairs
Dogs allowed except when food served **NOTES:** Parking 48

COXWOLD
Map 19 SE57

The Fauconberg Arms 🏠
Main St YO61 4AD ☎ 01347 868214 📠 01347 868054
e-mail: fauconbergarms@aol.com
Dir: Take A19 S from Thirsk, 2m turn left, signposted alternative route for
caravans/heavy vehicles. 5m to village
This family-run pub is found in a pretty, flower tub-lined
village street. Its unusual name originates from a peer who
married Oliver Cromwell's daughter Mary. Bar and restaurant
dishes are prepared with fresh local produce, and a typical
restaurant menu offers roast rump of lamb with Yorkshire
blue jus; salmon fillet with crispy fried leeks and caper berry
butter; aubergine baked with mozzarella and tomato sauce;
or grilled calves liver, black pudding and pancetta. At
lunchtime there are sandwiches, paninis and ciabatta. Pub
meals include sausage and mash, steak and ale pie, and
gammon with egg or pineapple.
OPEN: 11-2.30 6.30-11 (Summer all day) **BAR MEALS:** L served
all week 12-2.30 D served all week 6.30-9 Av main course £9
RESTAURANT: L served Sun 12-4 D served Wed-Sat 7-9.30
Av 3 course à la carte £23 Av 3 course fixed price £14.50 🍽: Free
House 🍺: Theakston Best, Scottish Courage, John Smith's, Old
Speckled Hen. **NOTES:** Parking 25

CRAY
Map 18 SD97

The White Lion Inn ♀
Cray BD23 5JB ☎ 01756 760262 📠 761024
e-mail: admin@whitelioncray.com

Celebrated fell-walker Alfred Wainwright described this pub,
Wharfedale's highest, as a 'tiny oasis' of hospitality. Indeed it
is, and must also have been to generations of drovers. Now
tastefully restored, it retains all its hefty beams, open log fires,
stone-flagged floors, and the age-old game of bull'ook. Expect
home-made steak and mushroom pie, and whole breaded
Whitby scampi, plus oven-roasted duck breast, Three Dales
lamb chops, and steamed Kilnsey trout in the evening.
OPEN: 11-11 (Sun 12-10.30) Closed: 25 Dec **BAR MEALS:** L served
all week 12-2 D served all week 5.45-8.30 Av main course £8.50
🍽: Free House 🍺: Moorhouses Premier Bitter, Timothy Taylor
Landlord, Copper Dragon Golden Pippin, Copper Dragon 1816. ♀: 9
FACILITIES: Garden: Beer garden with 10 trestle tables Dogs
allowed Water **NOTES:** Parking 20 **ROOMS:** 11 bedrooms
10 en suite s£45 d£70 (♦♦♦)

England

New Inn Hotel

'Jewel of the Dales'

Clapham LA2 8HH
Yorkshire Dales National Park

Tel: 015242 51203
Email: www.info@newinn-clapham.co.uk
Website: www.newinn-clapham.co.uk

**Contact us now for details
of our special offers**

Nestling beneath Ingleborough mountain, the beautiful old dales village straggles on either side of Clapham Beck, one half linked to the other by three bridges – the church is at the top, the New Inn at the bottom.

This family run Inn is set amidst a geological wonderland of limestone, cavern and fell country.

Being a true Village Inn, experience the warmth and friendliness that the Mannion family give to the New Inn, an 18th Century Coaching Inn, that they have lovingly and carefully refurbished over the past 18 years. Now being a finely appointed 18-bedroomed Inn with antique, 4-posters and kingsize beds, 2 bars with open

fires, restaurant and residents lounge, a wonderful blend of old and new, to retain the ambience of a true Dales village Inn run by Yorkshire folk.

Walk from our doorstep or tour the Dales or Lakes, Windermere being only 40 minutes drive away.

Pets welcome.

England

CRAYKE

Map 19 SE57

Pick of the Pubs

The Durham Ox NEW ♀
Westway YO61 4TE ☎ 01347 821506 📠 01347 823326
e-mail: enquiries@thedurhamox.com
Dir: *Off A19 from York to Thirsk, through Easingwold to Crayke*

Crayke is in the heart of Herriot Country, and there has been a village here since the second century, while the pub itself has been in service for three hundred years. The inn is named after a real beast, the original Durham ox being one of the most sought after animals of all time, commanding a price equivalent to a house in Mayfair! Inside, there's a cosy oak-panelled bar (take a look - the panels tell a story) and award-winning restaurant, while outside is an attractive courtyard marquee and water garden. The food is justifiably celebrated. Starters could include pot roast local game and winter vegetable terrine; or baked queen scallops with gruyere. Move on to roast venison, celeriac mash and juniper jus; or baked salmon, home-made fettuccine and wild mushroom velouté. In addition to bread and butter pudding with marmalade ice cream, is an excellent selection of coffee and digestifs.
OPEN: 12-3 6-11 Closed: 25 Dec **BAR MEALS:** L served all week 12-2.30 D served all week 6-9.30 Sun 12-3, 6-8.30, Sat 6-10 Av main course £15.95 **RESTAURANT:** L served all week 12-2.30 D served all week 6-9.30 Sun 12-3, 6-8.30 Av 3 course à la carte £24 🍺: John Smiths, Bombadier, Theakstons, Black Bull. ♀: 9 **FACILITIES:** Garden: Water garden, terrace (can be covered) Dogs allowed **NOTES:** Parking 50

CROPTON

Map 19 SE78

The New Inn ♀
YO18 8HH ☎ 01751 417330 📠 01751 417582
e-mail: info@croptonbrewery.co.uk

With the award-winning Cropton micro-brewery in its own grounds, this family-run free house on the edge of the North York Moors National Park is popular with locals and visitors alike. Meals are served in the restored village bar, and in the elegant Victorian restaurant: New Inn lamb joint, speciality sausages, steak and Scoresby Stout pie, fisherman's pie, Whitby cod, salmon, and plenty more.
OPEN: 11-11 **BAR MEALS:** L served all week 12-2 D served all week 6-9 Av main course £8 **RESTAURANT:** L served all week 12-2 D served all week 6-9 🍴: Free House 🍺: Cropton Two Pints, Monkmans Slaughter, Thwaites Best Bitter, Yorkshire Moors Bitter. ♀: 7 **FACILITIES:** Child facs Garden: Beer garden **NOTES:** Parking 50 **ROOMS:** 10 bedrooms en suite 2 family rooms s£39 d£54 (♦♦♦)

DACRE BANKS

Map 19 SE16

The Royal Oak Inn 🐟
Oak Ln HG3 4EN ☎ 01423 780200 📠 781748
e-mail: enquiries@the-royaloak-dacre.co.uk
Dir: *From A59 (Harrogate/Skipton) take B6451 towards Pateley Bridge*

A family-run free house in the heart of Nidderdale dating from 1752. It has open fires and exposed timbers and serves fine Yorkshire ales and home-cooked meals. Snacks include club sandwiches, hot baguettes and filled Yorkshire puddings, while serious diners can expect the likes of fillet of mullet with creamy garlic and mussel sauce, or roast Nidderdale pheasant breast on savoy cabbage with wholegrain mustard sauce. Fish nights are a speciality.
OPEN: 11.30-3 5-11 (Sun 12-3, 7-10.30) Closed: 25 Dec **BAR MEALS:** L served all week 11.30-2 D served all week 6.30-9 Sun 12-2.30, 7-9 Av main course £9.95 **RESTAURANT:** L served all week 11.30-2 D served all week 6.30-9 Sun 12-2.30, 7-9 Av 3 course à la carte £19.95 Av 3 course fixed price £12.95 🍴: Free House 🍺: Rudgate Yorkshire Dales, John Smiths Cask, Black Sheep Best, Royal Oak Dacre Ale. **FACILITIES:** Garden: Rear garden overlooks river, front cobbled **NOTES:** Parking 15 **ROOMS:** 3 bedrooms en suite s£45 d£60 (♦♦♦♦)

DANBY

Map 19 NZ70

Duke of Wellington Inn
YO21 2LY ☎ 01287 660351
e-mail: landlord@dukeofwellington.freeserve.co.uk
Dir: *From A171 between Guisborough & Whitby take rd signed 'Danby & Moors Centre'*

An attractive, ivy-clad inn overlooking the village green. It was a recruiting post during Napoleon's threatened invasion of England - thus the name - and Wellington's cast-iron plaque, exposed during renovations, is above the fireplace. The diminutive Corsican never even crossed the Channel, let alone reach North Yorkshire, but today's visitors arrive from far and wide. Standard pub fare at lunchtime, with a wider choice in the evening, including beef and mushrooms in Guinness, deep-fried cod fillet in beer batter, and poached haggis.
OPEN: 12-3 7-11 **BAR MEALS:** L served Tue-Sun 12-2 D served all week 7-9 Av main course £7.50 **RESTAURANT:** 12-2 7-9 Av 3 course à la carte £13 🍴: Free House 🍺: John Smith's, Cameron's Strongarm, Tetley Imperial,. **FACILITIES:** Garden: Dogs allowed Water **NOTES:** Parking 12 **ROOMS:** 9 bedrooms en suite s£33 d£60 (♦♦♦♦)

 Pubs with this logo do not allow smoking anywhere on their premises

---

EAST WITTON
Map 19 SE18

Pick of the Pubs

The Blue Lion 🏠 ♀
DL8 4SN ☎ 01969 624273 📠 01969 624189
e-mail: bluelion@breathemail.net
Dir: From Ripon take A6108 towards Leyburn, approx 20mins.

From the end of the 18th century onwards, coach travellers and drovers journeying through Wensleydale stopped at the Blue Lion. Outwardly, its stone façades can hardly have changed since, while inside an extensive, but sympathetic, renovation has created settings in which, while being much more suited to 21st-century eating and drinking, those same customers would still feel comfortable. The bar with its open fire and flagstone floor, and the candlelit restaurant are both perfect in all respects. Diners may well find it hard to choose between, say, sautéed monkfish fillet in parma ham with tapenade sauce; beef and onion suet pudding with dark onion sauce; and pan-fried breast of chicken stuffed with blue wensleydale and served with smoked bacon risotto. A vegetarian example would be sage and onion potato cake with creamed garlic mushrooms. In fine weather food can be served in the large lawned gardens with lovely views.
OPEN: 11-11 Closed for food Dec 25 **BAR MEALS:** L served all week 12-2.15 D served all week 7-9.30 Av main course £15 **RESTAURANT:** L served Sun 12-2.15 D served all week 7-9.30 Lunch in restauraunt Sun only Av 3 course à la carte £29 ⊜: Free House ◀: Black Sheep Bitter, Theakston Best Bitter, Black Sheep Riggwetter, Worthingtons. ♀: 12
FACILITIES: Garden: Large lawn, beautiful views Dogs allowed **NOTES:** Parking 30

EGTON
Map 19 NZ80

Pick of the Pubs

The Wheatsheaf Inn NEW
YO21 1TZ ☎ 01947 895271 📠 01947 895391
Dir: Off A169 NW of Grosmont
Be careful you don't miss this unassuming old pub. It sits back from the wide road, so it could be easy to pass by. The main bar is cosy and traditional, with low beams, dark green walls and comfy settles. There's a locals' bar too, but it only holds about twelve, so get there early. The pub is very popular with fishermen, as the River Esk runs along at the foot of the hill, and is a big draw for fly-fishers particularly. A warming menu of hearty grub includes chicken and bacon puff pie, lamb shank braised with redcurrant and madeira gravy, fillet steak with

continued

bearnaise sauce, and fish stew with smoked cod, salmon, clams, mussels, and white prawns in saffron sauce.
OPEN: 11.30-3 5.30-11.30 (Sat 11.30-11.30, Sun 12-10.30)
BAR MEALS: L served Tues-Sun 12-2 D served Tues-Sat 6-9 Av main course £11 **RESTAURANT:** L served Tues-Sun 12-2 D served Tues-Sat 6-9 Av 3 course à la carte £21 ◀: Black Sheep Bitter, Black Sheep Special, John Smith, Adnams.
FACILITIES: Child facs Garden: Lawned area with garden tables Dogs allowed **NOTES:** Parking 30

EGTON BRIDGE
Map 19 NZ80

Horseshoe Hotel ♀
YO21 1XE ☎ 01947 895245
Dir: From Whitby A171 towards Middlesborough. Village signed in 5m.

An 18th-century country inn by the River Esk, and handy for the North Yorkshire Moors Railway. Inside are oak settles and tables, local artists' paintings and, depending on the weather, an open fire. Lunchtime bar food includes sandwiches in malted granary bread, and hot baguettes. More substantial are lamb fillet with bubble and squeak; warm pigeon breast salad with raspberry vinegar; mussels in garlic cream; and wild mushroom risotto. Make friends with the ducks.
OPEN: 11.30-3 6.30-11 (All day Sat, Sun & BH's in Summer) Closed: 25 Dec **BAR MEALS:** L served all week 12-2 D served all week 7-9 Av main course £7.50 **RESTAURANT:** L served all week 12-2 D served all week 7-9 ⊜: Free House ◀: Copper Dragon & John Smiths, Durham, Whitby, Nick Staford. ♀: 7 **FACILITIES:** Child facs Beautiful garden on banks of River Esk Dogs allowed Water Provided **NOTES:** Parking 25

See Pub Walk on page 552

ELSLACK
Map 18 SD94

Pick of the Pubs

The Tempest Arms ♀
BD23 3AY ☎ 01282 842450 📠 01282 843331
e-mail: info@tempestarms.co.uk
Dir: From Skipton take A59 to Gisburn. Elslack signed on L on A56
Rolling Dales countryside surrounds this traditional pub, built from local stone in 1690 and named not after the weather, but a local landowner. Ever-changing 'carol sheets', as they are called here, offer the same quality food in both the cosy bar and candle-lit dining room. Eclectic is a word that well describes a list of sometimes unusual dishes that includes marinated olives, roast barbeque ribs, lamb's liver with black pudding, chicken Dijon, Eastern pot, steak frite, homerty pie, and cheesy potato and onion tart, while smoked haddock, seafood pancake, and scallops help to make up the fish tally.

continued

There's even a dish called lamb thingymebob, a generous portion of lamb cooked on the bone, with rich minted gravy. Open and filled sandwiches are also available.

The Tempest Arms

OPEN: 12-2.30 7-11 **BAR MEALS:** L served all week 12-2.30 D served all week 6-9 Sun 12-8 Av main course £9.50 **RESTAURANT:** L served all week 12-2.30 D served all week 6-9 Av 3 course à la carte £17 ◐: Free House ◀: Timothy Taylor Best & Landlord, Black Sheep Best, Scottish Courage Theakston Best, Copper Dragon. ♀: 8 **FACILITIES:** Garden: front terrace area **NOTES:** Parking 120

ESCRICK   Map 16 SE64

Black Bull Inn ♦♦♦♦ ▷◇ ♀
Main St YO19 6JP ☎ 01904 728245 ▤ 01904 728154
e-mail: blackbullhotel@btconnect.com
web: www.yorkblackbullinn.co.uk
Dir: From York follow the A19 for 5m, enter Escrick, take second left up main street, premises located on the left

Situated in the heart of a quiet village, this 19th-century pub is within easy reach of York racecourse and the historic city centre. The sea is also nearby, as evidenced by the fish selection: lobster, scampi or haddock may be found on the menu. Other dishes might include Moroccan chicken, steak and ale pie, oriental salmon, fillet steak Rossini, or chicken and vegetable pie. A selection of malt whiskeys is available for a nightcap. **OPEN:** 12-3 5-11 (Sun all day) **BAR MEALS:** L served all week 12-2.30 D served all week 6-9.30 **RESTAURANT:** L served all week 12-2.30 D served all week 6-9.30 ◀: John Smiths, Tetleys, Carlsberg. ♀: 7 **FACILITIES:** Child facs **NOTES:** Parking 10 **ROOMS:** 10 bedrooms en suite 2 family rooms s£45 d£65

FADMOOR   Map 19 SE68

Pick of the Pubs

The Plough Inn ♀
Main St YO62 7HY ☎ 01751 431515 ▤ 431515
Dir: 1m N of Kirkbymoorside on the A170 Thirsk to Scarborough Rd

A well-established restaurant and country inn located on the edge of the North Yorkshire Moors National Park. From its position overlooking the tranquil village green, the genuinely hospitable Plough enjoys views towards the Vale of Pickering and the Wolds. Snug little rooms, real ales and open fires draw local people to this stylishly refurbished pub, and the imaginative food is another attraction. A good selection of home-cooked dishes includes plenty of fresh fish and seafood, and most of the kitchen produce is locally sourced. Starters might include caramelised French onion soup, Scottish salmon in chilled honey, mustard and dill sauce, or breadcrumbed, deep-fried brie wedges. If fish is your fancy, choose from Loch Fyne smoked salmon platter, basil and parmesan crusted cod, or grilled sea bas. On the meat side, griddled sirloin, fillet and rib-eye steaks vie with favourites such as medallions of pork and Thai green chicken curry. **OPEN:** 12-2.30 6.30-11 Closed: 25-26 Dec, 1 Jan **BAR MEALS:** L served Mon-Sun 12-1.45 D served Mon-Sun 6.30-8.45 Sun 7-8.30 **RESTAURANT:** L served Mon-Sun 12-1.45 D served Mon-Sun 6.30-8.45 Sun 7-8.30 ◐: Free House ◀: Black Sheep Best, Scottish Courage John Smith's + guest beers. ♀: 6 **FACILITIES:** Garden: Raised patio area **NOTES:** Parking 20

GIGGLESWICK   Map 18 SD86

Black Horse Hotel ♦♦♦♦
32 Church St BD24 0BE ☎ 01729 822506
Set in the 17th-century main street, this traditional free house stands next to the church and behind the market cross. Three recently refurbished en-suite bedrooms cater for travellers, whilst down in the warm and friendly bar you'll find a range of hand-pulled ales. The menu of freshly-prepared pub favourites ranges from hot sandwiches or giant filled Yorkshire puddings to main course dishes like steak and ale pie; and broccoli and sweetcorn vol-au-vent. **OPEN:** 12-2.30 5.30-11 (Sat-Sun all day) **BAR MEALS:** L served Tue-Sun 12-1.45 D served all week 7-8.45 Av main course £7.50 **RESTAURANT:** L served Tue-Sun 12-1.45 D served all week 7-8.45 Av 3 course à la carte £15 ◐: Free House ◀: Carlsberg-Tetley Bitter, Timothy Taylor Landlord, Scottish Courage John Smiths, Timothy Taylor Golden Best. **FACILITIES:** Garden **NOTES:** Parking 16 **ROOMS:** 3 bedrooms en suite s£38 d£52 No children overnight

England

GOATHLAND
Map 19 NZ80

Birch Hall Inn
Beckhole YO22 5LE ☎ 01947 896245
e-mail: glenys@birchhallinn.fsnet.co.uk
Dir: Telephone for directions
Remotely situated near the North York Moors steam railway, this extraordinary little free house comprises two tiny rooms separated by a confectionery shop. There's an open fire in the main bar, well-kept local ales and a large garden. Staff can provide details of local walks to build up an appetite for home-baked pies, butties, home-made scones and buttered beer cake. Still managed by one member of the original management team, 23 years on!
OPEN: 11-3 7.30-11 (Sun 12-3, 7.30-10.30 Summer 11-11, Sun 12-10.30) **BAR MEALS:** L served all week 11-3 D served all week 7.30-11 Not open Mon pm in winter ⬛: Free House ⬛: Black Sheep Best, Theakstons Black Bull, Cropton Yorkshire Moors Bitter, Daleside Brewery Legover. **FACILITIES:** Garden: Terraced area up stone steps Dogs allowed on leads, water & dog treat **NOTES:** No credit cards

GREAT AYTON
Map 19 NZ51

The Royal Oak Hotel ♦♦♦ ♀
123 High St TS9 6BW ☎ 01642 722361 📠 01642 724047

Real fires and a relaxed, smokey atmosphere are all part of the attraction at this traditional corner pub. Behind the Georgian façade the decor is basic but welcoming, and the place positively hums with people eagerly seeking out the highly reputable food. A range of simple, robust dishes might include starters like pigeon, duck and foie gras terrine, Anglesea charcuterie platter, or butternut squash and goats' curd risotto. Among main courses could be slow-cooked belly of pork, Brittany 'Cotriade' fish stew, pot-roast stuffed saddle of lamb, and toasted sea bass with saffron potatoes. Puddings are also exemplary: expect poached pear, brandy snap and pear sorbet, chocolate, pecan and hazelnut 'brownie' cake with vanilla ice cream, or perhaps buttermilk pudding with pineapple and almond biscotti. A savoury alternative might be Cornish yarm with chutney and water biscuits.
OPEN: 10.30-11 (Sun 12-10.30) Closed: Dec 25
BAR MEALS: L served all week 12-2 D served all week 6.30-9.30
RESTAURANT: L served all week 12-2 D served all week 6.30-9.30
⬛: ⬛: Theakstons, John Smiths Smooth, Directors. ♀: 10
FACILITIES: Children's licence **ROOMS:** 5 bedrooms 4 en suite s£30 d£70

🍺 Principal Beers for sale

GREAT OUSEBURN
Map 19 SE46

Pick of the Pubs

The Crown Inn ♀
Main St YO26 9RF ☎ 01423 330430 📠 01423 331095

The Crown remembers the days when regular visitors were cattle drovers and large parties of fishermen on coach outings from the coast. Barrett's Great Canadian Circus would winter in the village; the circus band was under the direction of Ambrose Tiller who went on to found the world-renowned dancing troupe the 'Tiller Girls'. The Crown prides itself on offering a wide choice of imaginative dishes prepared from the finest, mostly local fish, seafood, meat and game. The brasserie increases the dining opportunities with competitively priced two or three course meals including a half bottle of wine, while the bar still offers its good value two course menu. Be prepared for a leisurely browse through the various menus and weekly changing specials board as the range of dishes, too numerous to single out, need careful consideration. In keeping with the range and standard of the cuisine there is an extensive wine list personally selected by the owners.
OPEN: 12-2 5-11 (Sat-Sun 12-11, BHs all day) Closed: 25 Dec Rest: Mon-Fri Closed lunch **BAR MEALS:** L served Thurs/Fri 12-2 D served Mon-Fri 5-9 (Sat 12-5, Sun 12-9) Av main course £6 **RESTAURANT:** L served Sun 12-9 D served Mon-Sat 5-9 (Sat 12-9.30, Sun 12-9) ⬛: Free House ⬛: Black Sheep Best, Scottish Courage, John Smith's, Hambeltons Best Bitter. ♀: 10
FACILITIES: Child facs Garden: Paved, walled area
NOTES: Parking 60

GREEN HAMMERTON
Map 19 SE45

The Bay Horse Inn 🛏️ ♀
York Rd YO26 8BN ☎ 01423 330338
e-mail: info@thebayhorseinn.info
The Bay Horse is a 200-year-old coaching inn situated in a small village three miles off the A1, near both York and Harrogate. Food is served in the bar and restaurant, and there is further seating outside, sheltered by the boundary hedge. Dishes might include stuffed beef fillet, roast duck breast and salmon and haddock fish cakes. The surrounding area offers glorious walks and many fine golf courses.
OPEN: 11.30-2.30 6.30-11 (Closed Mon lunch)
BAR MEALS: L served Tues-Sun 12-2 D served Mon-Sat 6.30-9 (Sun 12-3) **RESTAURANT:** L served all week D served all week 6.30-9 (Sun 12-3) ⬛: Worthington, Timothy Taylor, Pedigree.
FACILITIES: Garden: Seating for 30, sheltered by boundary hedge
NOTES: Parking 40

HAROME — Map 19 SE68

Pick of the Pubs

The Star Inn 🐟 ♀
YO62 5JE ☎ 01439 770397 ▤ 01439 771833
Dir: From Helmsley take A170 towards Kirkbymoorside. 0.5m turn right for Harome
A fine example of a 14th-century cruck-framed longhouse, with a byre incorporating the Star's dining room and an old dormitory for travelling monks converted into a distinctive coffee loft. The part-thatched inn also has a bar full of Mousey Thompson hand-carved oak furniture; here good beers and carefully selected house wines by the glass are served. In summer you can dine outside amid the heady scents of the herb garden. The home-grown herbs and seasonal produce from local suppliers feature in the cooking. A selection from the supper menu might be scrambled duck eggs with oak-smoked salmon and brioche soldiers; and pan-roast hare loin bourguignon, with braised leg, parsnip purée, chanterelles and tarragon. Opposite The Star is Cross House Lodge, farm buildings converted into eight individually designed double rooms, and the Corner Shop, a deli packed full of home-made delicacies and local and national produce.
OPEN: 11.30-3 6.30-11 Closed: 2 wks Jan **BAR MEALS:** L served Tue-Sun 11.30-2 D served Tue-Sun 6.30-9.15 (Sun 12-6) Av main course £15 **RESTAURANT:** L served Tue-Sun 11.30-2 D served Tue-Sun 6.30-9.15 (Sun 12-6) 🍴: Free House 🍺: Black Sheep Special, Scottish Courage, John Smith's & Theakston Best. ♀: 8 **FACILITIES:** Garden: Approx 10 tables with umbrellas Dogs allowed Water **NOTES:** Parking 40

HARROGATE — Map 19 SE35

Pick of the Pubs

The Boars Head Hotel ★★★ 🏨 ♀
Ripley Castle Estate HG3 3AY
☎ 01423 771888 ▤ 01423 771509
e-mail: reservations@boarsheadripley.co.uk
Dir: On A61 (Harrogate/Ripon rd). Hotel in village centre
An old coaching inn situated at the heart of the Ripley Castle Estate, the Boars Head has been luxuriously furnished by Sir Thomas and Lady Ingilby to create an impressive hotel. The bar/bistro welcomes guests old and new to sample the range of creative and award-winning dishes. Typical options from a winter menu are warm salad of venison sausage and wild mushrooms with cranberry dressed salad; beef and ale casserole served in a giant Yorkshire pudding; and sticky toffee pudding with an even stickier butterscotch sauce. Daily specials are also offered from the board, plus side orders such as Ripley twist mini loaf, salad, or sautéed potatoes. There is also a selection of locally brewed guest beers and a fine choice of malt whiskies. The walled courtyard situated to the rear of the hotel is a bonus for summer dining.
OPEN: 11-11 (Sun 12-10.30) (Winter Mon-Sat 11-3, 5-11 Sun 12-3, 5-10.30) **BAR MEALS:** L served all week 12-2.30 D served all week 6.30-10 Winter-lunch served 2pm Av main course £10 **RESTAURANT:** L served all week 12-2 D served all week 7-9.30 Av 3 course à la carte £32 Av 3 course fixed price £19 🍴: Free House 🍺: Scottish Courage Theakston Best & Old Peculier, Daleside Crackshot, Hambleton White Boar, Daleside Old Leg Over. ♀: 10 **FACILITIES:** Child facs Garden: Courtyard area Dogs allowed overnight in bedrooms only **NOTES:** Parking 45 **ROOMS:** 25 bedrooms en suite s£105 d£125

HAWES — Map 18 SD88

The Moorcock Inn NEW ♀
Garsdale Head LA10 5PU ☎ 01969 667488
e-mail: info@moorcockinn.com
A warm, relaxed inn with its own microbrewery producing Moorcock Ale. Enjoy your pint in front of the open fire, or whilst enjoying spectacular views of Wensleydale from the garden. A good selection of food is available all day, including various jacket potatoes and sandwiches. For dinner you may start with deep fried camembert or spicy chicken wings, then try home-made vegetable stilton and ale pie; roast duck with orange sauce; or Whitby scampi.
OPEN: 10-11 **BAR MEALS:** L served all week 10-6 D served all week 6-9 Av main course £10.50 🍺: Moorcockn Ale, Timothy Taylors, Black Sheep, guest ales. ♀: 6 **FACILITIES:** Child facs Children's licence Garden: Dogs allowed in one room only **NOTES:** Parking 40

HETTON — Map 18 SD95

Pick of the Pubs

The Angel 🏨 ♀
BD23 6LT ☎ 01756 730263 ▤ 01756 730363
e-mail: info@angelhetton.co.uk web: www.angelhetton.co.uk
Dir: From A59 take B6265 towards Grassington/Skipton

A stone-built Dales inn, more than 500 years old. It was once a single-storey crofter's cottage, and probably started brewing and serving beer to cattle drovers in the early 1800s. Despite part-rebuilding and enlargement, it manages to avoid the contrived country pub look, having retained original features such as oak beams, and lots of nooks and crannies. The new owner specialises in fresh fish, as did his illustrious predecessors, and Dales-bred lamb, beef and seasonal game. There are menus for every occasion - regular à la carte, Early Bird (until 6.45 pm), Fish on Friday, Saturday Dinner, Sunday Lunch, Bar and Brasserie. Items such as Goosnargh duck breast, or pan-seared wild sea bass, may appear on several menus, but usually with different sauces. Eleven pages of wines include half bottles, pudding wines and fifteen available by the glass. In the summer you can dine al fresco on the flagged forecourt overlooking Cracoe Fell.
OPEN: 12-3 6-10.30 Closed: Dec 25, Jan 1, 1wk in Jan **BAR MEALS:** L served all week 12-2 D served all week 6-9 (Sat 6-10) **RESTAURANT:** L served Sun 12-2 D served Mon-Sat 6-9 🍴: Free House 🍺: Blacksheep Bitter, Taylor Landlord, Wharfedale Folly, Copper Dragon Bitter. ♀: 24 **FACILITIES:** Child facs Garden: Terrace in front of pub **NOTES:** Parking 56 **ROOMS:** 5 bedrooms en suite

England

HOVINGHAM
Map 19 SE67

The Malt Shovel
Main St YO62 4LF ☎ 01653 628264 🖹 01653 628264
Dir: 18m NE of York, 5 miles from Castle Howard
Tucked away amid the Howardian Hills, in the Duchess of
Kent's home village, the stone-built 18th-century Malt Shovel
offers a friendly and traditional atmosphere with good-value
food prepared from quality local ingredients. Popular options
include pork and leeks, beef stroganoff, sirloin steak garni,
chicken stilton, and supreme of salmon. Fresh vegetables,
hand-crafted chips and daily specials board featuring
speciality game dishes complete the picture.
OPEN: 11.30-2.30 6-11 **BAR MEALS:** L served all week 12-2
D served all week 6-9 Sun 6-8 **RESTAURANT:** L served all week
12-2 D served all week 6-9 Sun 6-8 ☺: Punch Taverns
🍺: Carlsberg-Tetleys Tetley's, Greene King IPA. **FACILITIES:** Garden
NOTES: Parking 50

Pick of the Pubs

The Worsley Arms Hotel ★★★ ◉ ♀
Main St YO62 4LA ☎ 01653 628234 🖹 01653 628130
e-mail: worsleyarms@aol.com
*Dir: From A1 take A64 towards Malton, L onto B1257 signed Slingsby
& Hovingham. 2m to Hovingham*
In 1841 Sir William Worsley thought he could create a spa
to rival Bath, but he reckoned without the delicate nature
of his guests who disliked the muddy track between his
new hotel and spa house. Why he didn't pave it we don't
know, and inevitably the spa failed. The hotel, however,
survived and, together with the separate pub, forms part
of the Worsley family's historic Hovingham Hall estate,
birthplace of the Duchess of Kent, and home to her
nephew. The pub offers two places to eat: the Restaurant
and the Cricketer's Bar, which is named for the local team
which has played on the village green for over 150 years.
Here the menu not only offers a wide-ranging sandwich
selection, but more filling dishes as well, and Hambleton
Stallion beer from nearby Thirsk is on tap. Tastefully
modernised and comfortable lounges, smart bedrooms
and a private garden make this an attractive destination.
OPEN: 12-2.30 7-11 **BAR MEALS:** L served all week 12-2
D served all week 7-10 **RESTAURANT:** L served Sun 12-2
D served all week 7-10 ☺: Free House 🍺: Scottish Courage
John Smith's, Hambleton Stallion. ♀: 2 **FACILITIES:** Garden:
Formal and open gardens, mahogany furniture Dogs allowed
NOTES: Parking 30 **ROOMS:** 20 bedrooms en suite
2 family rooms s£60 d£100

HUBBERHOLME
Map 18 SD97

The George Inn
BD23 5JE ☎ 01756 760223 e-mail: visit@thegeorge-inn.co.uk
web: www.thegeorge-inn.co.uk
*Dir: From Skipton take B6265 to Threshfield, continue on B6160 to
Buckden. Follow signs for Hubbleholme.*
J B Priestley regarded the George as his favourite pub. It's an
18th-century Dales inn with flagstone floors, mullioned
windows and an open fire, nestling beneath the rising fells of
Langstrothdale beside the River Wharfe. In fine weather you
can sit outside on the terrace. Home-cooked meals are
prepared from local produce, with filled baguettes, cheese
melts, or fisherman's medley at lunchtime and a wider choice
in the evening, like Wensleydale pork or Dales lamb chops.
OPEN: 12-3 6.30-11 (Winter eve 7-10.30, closed Sun) Closed: First

continued

week Dec, Middle 2 wks in Jan **BAR MEALS:** L served all week 12-2
D served all week 6.30-8.30 Av main course £8 ☺: Free House
🍺: Black Sheep Best, Blacksheep Special, Skipton Brewery.
FACILITIES: Garden **NOTES:** Parking 20

KILBURN
Map 19 SE57

The Forresters Arms Hotel ◆◆◆
YO61 4AH ☎ 01347 868386 & 868550 🖹 01347 868386
e-mail: paulcussons@forrestersarms.fsnet.co.uk
web: www.forrestersarms.fsnet.co.uk
Dir: 6m from Thirsk
Sturdy stone former-coaching inn still offering ten
comfortable rooms for travellers passing close by the famous
White Horse of Kilburn on the North York Moors. The cosy
lower bar has some of the earliest oak furniture by Robert
Thompson, with his distinctive mouse symbol on every piece.
Evidence of the inn's former stables can be seen in the upper
bar. Steak and ale pie, pheasant casserole, home-made
lasagne and lamb chops are popular dishes.
OPEN: 11-11 **BAR MEALS:** L served all week 12-2.30 D served all
week 6.30-9 Av main course £8 **RESTAURANT:** L served all week
12-2.30 D served all week 6.30-9 Av 3 course à la carte £9.95
☺: Free House 🍺: Scottish Courage John Smiths, Carlsberg-Tetley
Tetley's, Hambleton. **FACILITIES:** Dogs allowed Dog bowl, biscuits
NOTES: Parking 40 **ROOMS:** 10 bedrooms en suite 2 family rooms
s£40 d£52

KIRBY HILL
Map 19 NZ10

The Shoulder of Mutton Inn 🔍
DL11 7JH ☎ 01748 822772 🖹 01325 718936
e-mail: info@shoulderofmutton.net
web: www.shoulderofmutton.net
Dir: 4m N of Richmond, 6m from A1 A66 junct at Scotch Corner
A 200-year-old traditional ivy-clad inn in an elevated position
overlooking Holmedale. Log fires burn in the bar areas, while
the separate Stable restaurant retains its original beams.
Choose whether to eat here or in the bar; the well-priced set
menu offers traditional fare with a modern influence - prawn,
celery and apple cocktail then poached salmon with prawn
and rose butter, for example. The à la carte is just as
reasonable - halibut with asparagus & bacon or venison with
black pudding would be typical mains. Seafood is a speciality.
BAR MEALS: L served Sat-Sun 12-2 D served Wed-Sun 7-9
RESTAURANT: L served Sat-Sun 12-2 D served Wed-Sun 7-9
Av 3 course à la carte £15.25 ☺: Free House 🍺: Scottish Courage
John Smiths, Jennings Cumberland Ale, Black Sheep Best.
FACILITIES: Paved garden Dogs allowed **NOTES:** Parking 22
ROOMS: 5 bedrooms en suite 1 family room (◆◆◆)

England

Pick of the Pubs

George & Dragon Hotel ★★ ♀
17 Market Place YO62 6AA ☎ 01751 433334 ▤ 01751 432933
e-mail: georgeatkirkby@aol.com
Dir: *Just off A170 between Scarborough & Thirsk in town centre*

Carrying on the tradition of the historic coaching inn, this 17th-century pub offers a haven of warmth, refreshment and rest in the heart of Kirkbymoorside. The pub has changed quite dramatically over the years - the restaurant used to be the brewhouse, one of the bedroom blocks was the old cornmill, and the garden room is the old rectory. In these beamed surroundings, visitors can sit by the log fire and sample hand-pulled real ales, wines by the glass and a choice of over 30 malt whiskies. A good variety of food is served, from snacks and blackboard specials in the bar to candlelit dinners in Knights' Restaurant or the bistro. Examples of daily specials include sea food platter - smoked salmon, mussels, cockles, prawns, crayfish tails and salmon and dill - to be followed by sautéed whole Cajun seabass served with a prawn and tomato salsa.
OPEN: 10-11 **BAR MEALS:** L served all week 12-2.15 D served all week 6.30-9.15 Av main course £8.50
RESTAURANT: L served all week 12-2.15 D served all week 6.30-9.15 Av 3 course à la carte £20 ⊕: Free House ◀: Black Sheep Best, Tetley and changing guest beers. ♀: 10
FACILITIES: Garden: Walled garden, herb garden Dogs allowed
NOTES: Parking 15 **ROOMS:** 19 bedrooms en suite 2 family rooms s£54 d£89

The Lion Inn ◌ ♀
Blakey Ridge YO62 7LQ ☎ 01751 417320 ▤ 01751 417717
e-mail: info@lionblakey.co.uk
Dir: *From A170 signed 'Hutton-le-Hole/Castleton'. 6m N of H-le-H.*
The Lion stands 470m above sea level, the fourth highest inn in England, with breathtaking views over the beautiful North York Moors National Park. The cosy interior with beamed ceilings, 4ft-thick stone walls and blazing fires makes up for the isolated location. Typical chef's specials are T-bone steak, steak and mushroom pie, and tournedos Rossini, alongside the extensive à la carte menu offering fish, chicken and vegetarian options, and a children's menus.
OPEN: 10-11 **BAR MEALS:** L served all week 12-10 D served all week 12-10 Av main course £7.50 **RESTAURANT:** L served all week 12-7 D served all week 7-10 Av 3 course à la carte £19.50 Av 3 course fixed price £11.95 ⊕: Free House ◀: Scottish Courage Theakston Blackbull, XB & Old Peculiar, Scottish Courage John Smith's Bitter, Greene King Old Speckled Hen. ♀: 9 **FACILITIES:** Garden: Large garden, picnic benches, well Dogs allowed **NOTES:** Parking 200
ROOMS: 10 bedrooms 8 en suite 3 family rooms (♦♦♦)

Pick of the Pubs

Stone Trough Inn ◉ ♀
Kirkham Abbey YO60 7JS ☎ 01653 618713 ▤ 01653 618819
e-mail: info@stonetroughinn.co.uk
web: www.stonetroughinn.co.uk
Dir: *1.5m off A64, between York & Malton*

Stone-built country inn high above Kirkham Priory and the River Derwent. Converted to licensed premises in the early 1980s from Stone Trough Cottage, which took its name from the base of a cross erected by a 12th-century French knight to commemorate a son killed in a riding accident. The cross has long disappeared, but its hollowed-out base now stands at the entrance to the car park. Friendliness, hospitality, fine food and an excellent complement of real ales combine to give the Stone Trough a well-deserved local reputation. A belter of a bar menu is on call lunchtimes and evenings, while the restaurant menu offers skewer of monkfish, halibut and tiger prawns; whole boned roast partridge; and spinach and Yorkshire blue risotto cake. Owner/chef Adam Richardson specialised in patisserie for five years, so expect some classic desserts, such as his chocolate pyramid filled with chocolate and black cherry mousse.
OPEN: 12-2.30 6-11 (Sun 11.45-10.30) Closed: 25 Dec
BAR MEALS: L served Tue-Sun 12-2 D served Tue-Sun 6.30-8.30 Av main course £8.50 **RESTAURANT:** L served Sun 12-2.15 D served Tue-Sat 6.45-9.30 Av 3 course à la carte £23.50
⊕: Free House ◀: Tetley Cask, Timothy Taylor Landlord, Black Sheep Best, Malton Brewery Golden Chance. ♀: 9
FACILITIES: Child facs Garden: Dogs allowed Water
NOTES: Parking 100

Pick of the Pubs

The General Tarleton Inn ★★★ ◉◉ ◌ ♀
Boroughbridge Rd, Ferrensby HG5 0PZ
☎ 01423 340284 ▤ 01423 340288
e-mail: gti@generaltarleton.co.uk
web: www.generaltarleton.co.uk
Dir: *On A6055, on crossroads in Ferrensby*
Owned by the same team behind the successful Angel at Hetton, this traditional 18th-century coaching inn is surrounded by glorious North Yorkshire countryside. Sir Banastre Tarleton distinguished himself during the American War of Independence, and the inn was probably formally opened by a member of his platoon

continued

England

KNARESBOROUGH continued

and named in his honour. The low-beamed bar area is warm and welcoming, with log fires, oak beams and cosy corners, while the restaurant is ideal for an intimate dinner or small party. The owners say you won't find ordinary production-pack pub grub on the bar/brasserie menu, and the restaurant menu is similarly impressive and wide ranging. You may eat in the glazed-over Old Courtyard too. Main courses include pan-roasted local partridge; chargrilled fillet of beef; duo of Dales lamb; and pan-seared fillet of sea bass. The wine list is extensive and impressive and the fourteen bedrooms are very comfortable, and tastefully decorated.

The General Tarleton Inn

OPEN: 12-3 6-11 **BAR MEALS:** L served all week 12-2.15 D served all week 6-9.30 Sun 6-8.30 **RESTAURANT:** L served Sun 12-1.45 D served Mon-Sat 6-9.30 Av 3 course à la carte £30 Av 3 course fixed price £29.50 🍴: Free House 🍺: Black Sheep Best, Timothy Taylors Landlord, Tetleys Smoothflow, guest beer. ♀: 10 **FACILITIES:** Child facs Garden **NOTES:** Parking 40 **ROOMS:** 14 bedrooms en suite s£85 d£97 (★★★)

LASTINGHAM   Map 19 SE79

Blacksmiths Arms 🚭 ♀
YO62 6TL ☎ 01751 417247
e-mail: blacksmithslastingham@hotmail.com
Dir: 7m from Pickering 4m from Kirbymoorside. Take A170 Pickering to Kirbymoorside Road, signed Lastingham and Appleton Le Moors.

Right opposite St Mary's church, this 17th-century stone-built free house stands in an idyllic North York Moors National Park setting. The inn boasts low-beamed ceilings and an open fire within the refurbished restaurant and bar area; outside, there's a cottage garden and decked seating area. Home-cooked dishes include Yorkshire hotpot; lamb and mint pie; crispy cod in beer batter; and broccoli pancake mornay. Snacks, sandwiches and daily specials are also available.

continued

OPEN: 12-3.30 6-11 Nov-Mar 12-2.30 & 6-11. Mar-Nov from 12 Closed on Tue day time in Winter **BAR MEALS:** L served all week 12-2 D served all week 7-8.45 Av main course £7.95 **RESTAURANT:** L served all week 12-2 D served all week 7-8.45 Av 3 course à la carte £17.95 🍴: Free House 🍺: Theakstons Best Bitter, 2 rotating guest ales e.g. Pheonix, Roosters. ♀: 10 **FACILITIES:** Garden: Cottage garden seating 32, decking seats 20 Dogs allowed Water

LEYBURN   Map 19 SE19

The Old Horn Inn ♦♦♦
Spennithorne DL8 5PR ☎ 01969 622370
e-mail: desmond@furlong1706.fsbusiness.co.uk
Dir: From Leyburn approx 1.5 miles heading E along A684. Take right signed Spennithorne. From Bedale & A1 approx 9 miles heading W along A684. Take left signed Spennithorne.

Low beams and open log fires characterise this traditional 17th-century free house. The former farmhouse, which has been a pub for at least 100 years, is named after the horn that summoned the farmer's workers to lunch! Today's customers enjoy good food in the non-smoking dining room. Expect local hog and hop sausages with mash and red onion marmalade; baked salmon with prawns and basil sauce; or roasted vegetable lasagne with garlic ciabatta.
OPEN: 12-3 6.30-11 (Open all day Fri-Sat during Jul-Aug) **BAR MEALS:** L served Tue-Sun 12-2 D served Tue-Sun 6.30-9.30 (12-3 in summer) Av main course £8.25 **RESTAURANT:** L served Tue-Sun 12-2 D served Tue-Sun 7-9.30 (12-3 in summer) 🍺: Blacksheep Bitter & Special, Scottish Courage John Smith's Cask, Coors Worthington's Cream Flow. **FACILITIES:** Garden: Walled patio garden with benches and seating Dogs allowed Water, toys **NOTES:** Parking 12 **ROOMS:** 2 bedrooms en suite d£46 No children overnight **NOTES:** No credit cards

Pick of the Pubs

Sandpiper Inn ♀
Market Place DL8 5AT ☎ 01969 622206 📠 01969 625367
e-mail: hsandpiper@aol.com
Dir: From A1 take A684 to Leyburn
Although the Sandpiper Inn has been a pub for only 30 years, the building it is housed in is the oldest in Leyburn, dating back to around 1640. With a beautiful summer garden, a bar, snug and dining room within, it also serves an exciting and varied mix of traditional and more unusual dishes. In addition to old favourites such as fish and chips in real ale batter, expect a good choice of starters: apple-smoked black pudding on a garlic mash with a port wine jus; warm goats cheese on rocket and beetroot salad; and crab and salmon cake with red pepper mayo. These could be followed by roasted salmon

continued

on a leek and parmesan pasta; crispy duck leg with fried potatoes and oriental dressing; or rib-eye of beef with traditional garnish.

Sandpiper Inn

OPEN: 11.30-3 6.30-11 (Sun 12-3, 6.30-10.30)
BAR MEALS: L served Tues-Sun 12-2.30 D served Tues-Sun 6.30-9 (Fri-Sat 6.30-9.30, Sun 7-9) Av main course £13.95
RESTAURANT: L served Tues-Sun 12-2.30 D served Tues-Sun 6.30-9 Fri-Sat 6.30-9.30, Sun 12-2, 7-9 Av 3 course à la carte £25
🍽: Free House 🍺: Black Sheep Best, Black Sheep Special, Daleside, Copperdragon. 🍷: 8 **FACILITIES:** Garden: Terrace area to front Dogs allowed in 'snug area' **NOTES:** Parking 6

LINTON   Map 19 SD96

The Fountaine Inn
BD23 5HJ 🕿 01756 752210 📠 01756 753717
Dir: *10m From Skipton take B6265. Turn right after Quarry*
Within the magnificent Yorkshire Dales National Park, in a sleepy hamlet beside the River Beck, this 16th-century inn is named after a local man who made his fortune in the Great Plague of London in 1665 - burying the bodies! On a more cheerful note, the menu offers grilled king scallops with pumpkin seeds, chilli and coriander sauce; smoked fish platter; and Irish stew and baby vegetables.
OPEN: 11-11 (11-3, 5.30-11 in winter) **BAR MEALS:** L served all week 12-5.30 D served all week 5.30-9 Av main course £7
RESTAURANT: L served Mon-Sun 12-5.30 D served Mon-Sun 5.30-9
🍽: Free House 🍺: Black Sheep Best, Carlsberg-Tetley Tetley Bitter, Scottish Courage John Smith's, Timothy Taylors Landlord.
FACILITIES: Child facs Garden: Village green Dogs allowed Water bowl **NOTES:** Parking 20

LITTON   Map 18 SD97

Queens Arms
BD23 5QJ 🕿 01756 770208 e-mail: queensarmslitton@mserve.net
Dir: *From Skipton take Northvale Rd, (B6265, B6160) for 15m. Signed*
Early 16th-century inn in a remote corner of the Yorkshire Dales, now brewing its own Litton Ale with spring water from the neighbouring hillside. Two-foot thick walls, low ceilings, beams and coal fires give the place a traditional, timeless feel. A good range of food incorporates plenty of fish, including Wharfedale trout and grilled halibut, home-made pies, including rabbit and game, pork fillet, a hefty mixed grill, vegetarian and children's dishes.
OPEN: 12-3 7-11 Closed: 3 Jan-1Feb **BAR MEALS:** L served Tue-Sun, BH Mons 12-2 D served Tue-Sun, BH Mons 7-9 Av main course £6.95 **RESTAURANT:** L served Tue-Sun 12-2 D served Tue-Sun 7-9 Av 3 course à la carte £17.50 🍽: Free House 🍺: Litton Ale, Tetleys, plus guest ales. **FACILITIES:** Child facs Garden: Beer garden, outdoor eating, patio Dogs allowed **NOTES:** Parking 10

LONG PRESTON   Map 18 SD85

Maypole Inn 🍷
Maypole Green BD23 4PH 🕿 01729 840219
e-mail: landlord@maypole.co.uk
Dir: *On A65 between Settle and Skipton*
The Maypole Inn has been around since 1695, and more than 300 years on it still thrives, offering hand pumped ales and traditional home cooking. At the edge of the Yorkshire Dales National Park, this is a good base for walking and cycling. Relax in the beamed dining room or cosy bar over a pint and a simple snack, sandwich, steak or salad, or try a special like beef in ale pie, braised shoulder of lamb, or pork in Pernod.
OPEN: 11-3 6-11 (Sat 11-11 Sun 12-10.30) **BAR MEALS:** L served all week 12-2 D served all week 6.30-9 **RESTAURANT:** L served all week 12-2 D served all week 6.30-9 🍽: Enterprise Inns 🍺: Timothy Taylor Landlord, Castle Eden, Moorhouses Premier, Tetley & Guest.
🍷: 10 **FACILITIES:** Child facs Garden: Patio Dogs allowed Water
NOTES: Parking 30

MARTON   Map 19 SE78

Pick of the Pubs

The Appletree Country Inn ◉ 🍷
YO62 6RD 🕿 01751 431457 📠 01751 430190
e-mail: appletreeinn@supanet.com
Dir: *From Kirkby Moorside on A170 turn right after 1m, follow road for two miles to Marton*
Set in the peaceful village of Marton, and surrounded by beautiful scenery, the Appletree Inn is ideally located for visiting Whitby, Helmsley and York. Attached to it are a traditional old English orchard, and an organic field. The multi-award wining country pub offers superb value for money, and an extremely friendly and welcoming atmosphere. The proprietor/head chef Trajan Drew cooks modern British food and holds an AA Rosette for his skills. Spiced crab cake; red onion tart tatin; or foie gras and ham hock terrine could kick a meal off, followed by olive, jerusalem artichoke and tomato crumble; grilled halibut; calves' liver; or herbed escalopes of Marton beef. Marbled chocolate pyramid; blueberry and sloe gin meringue; or toffee marscapone cheesecake are equally pleasing desserts. There is a shop selling a small selection of home-made delights like flavoured butter, marmalades, chutneys, jams, bread, fresh dressings, and desserts. The Appletree is closed Monday and Tuesday.
OPEN: 12-2.30 6.30-11 Wed-Sun (Sun 12-3, 7-10.30) Closed: 2 weeks Jan **BAR MEALS:** L served Wed-Sun 12-2 D served none (Sun 12-2.30, 7-9) **RESTAURANT:** L served Sun 12-2.30 D served Wed-Sun 6.30-9.30, Sun 12-2.30, 7-9) 🍽: Free House 🍺: Scottish Courage John Smiths Cask, Guest ales; Malton, York, Daleside. 🍷: 14 **FACILITIES:** Garden: Patio, seats 16, adjoining orchard **NOTES:** Parking 30

◆ Pubs with Red Diamonds are the top places in the AA's three, four and five diamond ratings

---

Do you have a favourite pub that we have overlooked? Please use the Reader's Report form at the back of this guide to tell us all about it

England

MASHAM
Map 19 SE28

The Black Sheep Brewery
HG4 4EN ☎ 01765 689227 680100 ▤ 01765 689746
e-mail: helenallison@blacksheep.co.uk
Dir: Off the A6108 between Ripon & Leyburn, follow brown tourist signs

Schoolboy humour is on the menu at this popular brewery complex on the edge of the Yorkshire Dales. Besides the 'shepherded' brewery tours, 'ewe' can simply call in to eat and drink in the stylish bistro and 'baa...r'. In just ten years, Black Sheep ales have achieved a national reputation, and dishes like lamb shank in Square Ale sauce, and Riggwelter casserole make the most of them. Also lunchtime sandwiches, roast local pheasant, poached salmon, and provençale vegetable tartlet.
OPEN: Sun-Wed 10.30-5 Thu-Sat 10.30-11 **BAR MEALS:** L served all week 12-2.30 D served Wed-Sat 6.30-9 Av main course £9 ▥: ◀: Black Sheep beers. **FACILITIES:** Garden
NOTES: Parking 25

Kings Head Hotel ◠◇ ♀
Market Place HG4 4EF ☎ 01765 689295 ▤ 01765 689070
Dir: B6267 towards Masham
Overlooking Masham's large market square, with its cross and maypole, this splendid Georgian inn has a long history as a posting house and excise office. Interesting starters range from pan-fried scallops to grilled Portuguese sardines, while mains might include baked cod loin served with a creamy horseradish mash; and freshly baked chicken supreme with gorgonzola cheese, prosciutto ham and steamed rocket. Fillet of beef, chargrilled halibut steak, and roasted breast of Gressingham duck are typical chef's specials.
OPEN: 11-11 **BAR MEALS:** L served all week 12-2.45 D served all week 6-9.45 Av main course £8.95 **RESTAURANT:** L served all week 12-2.45 D served all week 6-9.45 Av 3 course à la carte £16 ▥: ◀: Theakstons Best Bitter, Black Bull & Old Peculier, Theakstons XB, John Smiths Magnet. ♀: 14 **FACILITIES:** Child facs Garden: Georgian patio style Dogs allowed Water

MIDDLEHAM
Map 19 SE18

Black Swan Hotel ◠◇ ♀
Market Place DL8 4NP ☎ 01969 622221 ▤ 01969 622221
e-mail: blackswanmiddleham@breathe.com
Dating back to the 17th-century and backing on to Middleham Castle, home of Richard III, this historic pub is situated at the heart of Yorkshire's racing country. Horses can be seen passing outside every morning on their way to the gallops. The emphasis here is on good food, with an appealing choice including Black Swan grill, chicken curry, bangers and mash, lasagne, and Kilnsey trout roasted with parsley and thyme.
OPEN: 11-3.30 6-11 (Open all day Sat-Sun summer)
BAR MEALS: L served all week 12-2 D served all week 6.30-9

continued

Av main course £6.95 **RESTAURANT:** L served all week 12-2 D served all week 6.30-9 Av 3 course à la carte £20 ▥: Free House ◀: Scottish Courage John Smiths, Theakstons Best Bitter, Black Bull, Old Peculiar & Guest Beers. ♀: 7 **FACILITIES:** Child facs Garden: Patio and lawn with benches, tables Dogs by arrangement

The White Swan Hotel ♀
Market Place DL8 4PE ☎ 01969 622093 ▤ 01969 624551
e-mail: whiteswan@easynet.co.uk
Dir: A684 toward Leyburn then A6108 to Ripon, 1.5m to Middleton
Traditional Dales coaching inn located on the market square, with beams, flagstone floors and open fires. An ideal place to sit and watch the racehorses riding out in the morning. The emphasis is on quality accommodation and good food. The bar menu offers baked cod in a rarebit sauce, sausage and bubble and squeak with onion gravy, and fillet of salmon on wilted spinach with a tomato and tarragon sauce.
OPEN: 11-11 **BAR MEALS:** L served all week 12-2.15 D served all week 6.30-9.15 Av main course £8 **RESTAURANT:** L served all week 12-2.15 D served all week 6.30-9.15 Av 3 course à la carte £17 ▥: Free House ◀: Black Sheep Best, Riggwelter, Scottish Courage John Smith's. **FACILITIES:** Garden: Food served outside Dogs

MIDDLESMOOR
Map 19 SE07

Crown Hotel ♀
HG3 5ST ☎ 01423 755204
Dir: Telephone for directions
The original building dates back to the 17th century; today it offers the chance to enjoy a good pint of local beer by a cosy, roaring log fire, or in a sunny pub garden. Stands on a breezy 900ft hilltop with good views towards Gouthwaite Reservoir. Ideal for those potholing or following the Nidderdale Way.
OPEN: 12-3 7-11 **BAR MEALS:** L served Mon-Sun 12-2 D served Mon-Sat 7-8.30 (Closed Mon Lunch Winter, BHs) Av main course £7.50 **RESTAURANT:** L served all week 12-2 D served all week 7-8.30 ▥: Free House ◀: Black Sheep Best, Worthingtons Smooth, Interbrew Boddingtons Cream Flow. ♀: 20 **FACILITIES:** Dogs allowed Water **NOTES:** Parking 10

MIDDLETON (NEAR PICKERING)
Map 19 SE78

The Middleton Arms
Church Ln YO18 8PB ☎ 01751 475444 ▤ 01751 475444
The Middleton Arms has retained much of its traditional charm and atmosphere, due in no small measure to the hand crafted furniture supplied by the landlord who is also a professional cabinet maker. Typical dishes on the menu include poached chicken breast, pan-fried salmon, baked goats' cheese, roasted lamb joint, and beef and mushroom stroganoff. Local meat is featured, and there are speciality fish nights throughout the year. Closed all day Monday and every lunchtime except Sunday.
OPEN: 6-11 Closed: mid Jan-mid Feb **BAR MEALS:** L served Sun D served Tue-Sun 6-9 Av main course £8.95 ◀: Timothy Taylor Landlord, Tetleys Smooth, Nick Stafford Hambleton Ales, Black Sheep. ⊗

England

MOULTON — Map 19 NZ20

Pick of the Pubs

Black Bull Inn 🐟
DL10 6QJ ☎ 01325 377289 📠 01325 377422
e-mail: sarah@blackbullinn.demon.co.uk
Dir: 1m S of Scotch Corner off A1
The Pagendam family has been serving discerning diners at the Black Bull for 40 years or more. Sited close to Scotch Corner on the A1, this well established country pub is conveniently placed for the weary traveller in search of rest and refreshment. Lunchtime snacks and more substantial dishes served in the bar might include grilled Dover sole; Dublin Bay prawn masala curry with pilau rice, home-made chutney and poppadum; herb roast rack of lamb with leek and potato crumble and Madeira sauce; pan-fried fillet of beef on wild mushroom risotto, foie gras and balsamic red wine sauce; and sage and polenta crumbed calves' liver with onion confit, sage and onion gravy. In the evening the dining focus shifts to the fish bar and conservatory, complete with a huge grapevine and lots of plants and flowers. For nostalgia lovers there is also the Brighton Belle - an original Pullman carriage of 1932 that operated premier express services between London and Brighton.
OPEN: 12-2.30 6-10.30 Closed: 24-26 Dec Sun
BAR MEALS: L served Mon-Fri 12-2 Closed Sun Av main course £5.75 **RESTAURANT:** L served Mon-Fri 12-2 D served Mon-Sat 6.45-10.15 Av 3 course à la carte £25 Av 3 course fixed price £17.50 ⊕: Free House 🍺: Theakstons Best, John Smiths Smooth. **FACILITIES:** Garden: Patio area with seating
NOTES: Parking 80

MUKER — Map 18 SD99

The Farmers Arms 🍷
DL11 6QG ☎ 01748 886297 📠 01748 886375
Dir: From Richmond take A6108 towards Leyburn, turn R onto B6270
The last remaining pub - of three - in this old lead-mining village at the head of beautiful Swaledale, and a popular resting place for walkers on the Pennine Way and Coast-to-Coast route. With several miles under the belt, refuel with home-made steak pie, chicken alla Romana, deep-fried cod, liver and onions, or vegetable tandoori masala, aided and abetted by a pint of Castle Eden's Nimmos XXXX. Children's and smaller meals are also available.
OPEN: 11-11 (Sun 12-10.30) **BAR MEALS:** L served all week 12-2.30 D served all week 7-8.50 Av main course £7.50 ⊕: Free House 🍺: Theakston Best & Old Peculier, John Smith's, Black Sheep, Guest Ales. 🍷: 10 **FACILITIES:** Garden: Cobbled area with flower beds Dogs allowed Water Provided
NOTES: Parking 6

NORTH RIGTON — Map 19 SE24

Pick of the Pubs

The Square and Compass NEW 🐟 🍷
LS17 0DJ ☎ 01423 734228 e-mail: l13hud@aol.com
Dir: Just off A658, in centre of village
The Square and Compass was originally part of the Harewood estate and probably got its name by being used, many years ago, as a Mason's lodge. Today this pub, set in the beautiful Yorkshire village of North Rigton, is the ideal setting for celebrating special occasions, corporate dinners or simply enjoying a meal or drink with friends. You can relax and soak up the atmosphere while enjoying a light bar meal in the oak beamed bar and lounge, or go for a gourmet meal with fine wines in the tastefully restored restaurant. Both lunchtime and evening à la carte menus use only the freshest of local ingredients: starters could include a large Yorkshire pudding with onion gravy; and smooth pâté of chicken liver, brandy, garlic and orange. Mains dishes of rib-eye steak with garnish; chicken breast with smoked Wensleydale cheese wrapped in dry cured bacon; crispy haddock in beer batter; and chef's luxury fish pie provide a good variety.
OPEN: 12-3 5-11 **BAR MEALS:** L served all week 12-2.30 D served all week 6-9.30 Sun 12-6 Av main course £9.50 **RESTAURANT:** L served Sun 12-6 D served Fri-Sat 6-9.30 Av 3 course à la carte £22.50 🍺: Black Sheep, Timothy Taylors Landlord, Hoegaarden. 🍷: 46 **FACILITIES:** Garden: Paved and planted area **NOTES:** Parking 45

NUNNINGTON — Map 19 SE67

The Royal Oak Inn 🍷
Church St YO62 5US ☎ 01439 748271 📠 01439 748271
Dir: Close to church at opp end of village to Nunnington Hall (NT)
A solid stone pub in this sleepy rural backwater in the Howardian Hills, a short drive from the North Yorkshire Moors. The immaculate open-plan bar is furnished with scrubbed pine and decorated with farming memorabilia, just the place for a pint of Theakstons and a bite to eat. A typical menu features pork fillet in barbecue sauce, ham and mushroom tagliatelle, crispy roast duckling, and steak and kidney casserole.
OPEN: 12-2.30 6.30-11 **BAR MEALS:** L served Tue-Sun 12-2 D served Tue-Sun 6.30-9 **RESTAURANT:** L served Tue-Sun 12-2 D served Tue-Sun 6.30-9 ⊕: Free House 🍺: Scottish Courage Theakston Best & Old Peculier, Carlsberg-Tetley Tetley Bitter. 🍷: 8 **NOTES:** Parking 18

OSMOTHERLEY — Map 19 SE49

Pick of the Pubs

The Golden Lion NEW 🐟
6 West End DL6 3AA
The Golden Lion is a cosy sandstone building of some 250 years standing. The atmosphere is warm and welcoming, with open fires and wooden flooring on one side of the downstairs area. Furnishings are simple with a wooden bar, bench seating and tables, whitewashed walls, mirrors and fresh flowers. The extensive menu ranges through basic pub grub to more refined dishes. The starters are divided between fish, soups, vegetarian, pastas and risottos, meat and salads, and might include smoked salmon; French onion soup with gruyere cheese; buffalo mozzarella with tomato and basil; spaghetti vongole with mussels; spicy pork ribs; and avocado and king prawn salad. Mains are along the lines of grilled seabass with new potatoes and peas; coq au vin; calves' liver with fried onions and mash; home-made beef burger with Mexican salsa; and spicy chilladas with fresh tomato sauce. Sherry trifle, and bread and butter pudding with cream, are popular.

continued continued

England

OSMOTHERLEY continued

OPEN: 12-3 6-11 (Open all day Sat-Sun) Closed: 25 Dec
BAR MEALS: L served all week 12-2.30 D served all week 6-9.15
Food all day when busy Av main course £9.95
RESTAURANT: L served all week 12-2.30 D served all week
6-9.15 Av 3 course à la carte £15.20 **⬛:** Timothy Taylors
Landlord, Hambleton Bitter, Jennings Bitter, Calendonian IPA.
FACILITIES: Garden: Courtyard Dogs allowed Water

Queen Catherine Hotel ◆◆
7 West End DL6 3AG ☎ 01609 883209
e-mail: queencatherine@yahoo.co.uk
Named after Henry VIII's wife, Catherine of Aragon, who left
her horse and carriage here while sheltering from her
husband with nearby monks. There is no sense of menace
around this friendly hotel nowadays, believed to be the only
one in Britain bearing its name, and visitors can enjoy a well-
cooked meal: monkfish tails, crab-stuffed chicken breast, lamb
shank with minted gravy, Icelandic cod, and Whitby breaded
scampi are all on the menu.
OPEN: 12-11 **BAR MEALS:** L served all week 12-2 D served all
week 6-9 Sun food 12-9 Av main course £6.50 **RESTAURANT:**
L served all week 12-2 D served all week 6-9 **⬛:** Hambleton
Ales-Stud, Stallion, Bitter, Goldfield. **FACILITIES:** Dogs allowed
Water **ROOMS:** 5 bedrooms en suite s£25 d£50

The Three Tuns Restaurant & Bar ◉ ♀
South End DL6 3BN ☎ 01609 883301 📠 01609 883301
Dir: Off A19
Osmotherley is the starting point for the Lyke Wake Walk, a
forty-mile trail across the North Yorkshire Moors to the coast.
Completion in 24 hours qualifies for membership of the Lyke
Wake Club. The pub stands among 17th-century stone
cottages, its hanging baskets brightening up the exterior in
summer and the views of the Cleveland Hills a grand sight
from its rear garden all year round. The stylish new interior
has attracted a lot of interest, but it's the quality of the food
that has ensured its success since reopening in 2001. There
are usually four or more seafood/fish dishes on offer,
examples being roast fillet of monkfish with mascarpone and
herb risotto in red wine sauce, and whole grilled sea bass.
Meat options include pan-fried fillet of beef with braised oxtail
and baby onions, and confit duck leg with Toulouse sausage,
fricassée of cabbage, bacon and a redcurrant reduction.
OPEN: 12-3 6-11 **BAR MEALS:** L served all week 12-2.30 D served
all week 6-10.30 Av main course £11 **RESTAURANT:** L served all
week 12-2.30 D served all week 6-9.30 Av 3 course à la carte £23.50
📠: Free House **⬛:** Caffreys, John Smiths Smooth.
FACILITIES: Decorative garden paved with ornamental features
NOTES: Parking 4

PATELEY BRIDGE   Map 19 SE16

Pick of the Pubs

The Sportmans Arms Hotel 🔜 ♀
Wath-in-Nidderdale HG3 5PP
☎ 01423 711306 📠 01423 712524
Dir: A39/B6451, restaurant 2m N of Pateley Bridge

Beloved of sports people from far and wide, this special
pub and small hotel stands in a conservation village in
one of the most beautiful areas of the Yorkshire Dales.
Inside you'll find immaculate traditional décor, real fires
and comfy chairs. A custom-built kitchen, run by
chef/patron Ray Carter for nearly a quarter of a century
(now assisted by his son) lies at the heart of the
operation. True to the best pub traditions, real ales and
fine wines accompany blackboard dishes served in an
informal bar, and daily restaurant menus that tempt all-
comers. Fish dishes might include Scottish salmon roasted
with spring onions and ginger; cod in bacon mash and
garlic butter; fillet of plaice caprice; poached haddock on
chive mash with tomato and mash; turbot on roasted
peppers with walnut oil; and whole lemon sole. Watch
out for the lobster festival in May/June.
OPEN: 12-2 7-11 (Sun close 10.30) Closed: 25 Dec
BAR MEALS: L served all week 12-2 D served all week 7-9
Av main course £11.50 **RESTAURANT:** L served all week 12-2
D served all week 7-9.30 Av 3 course à la carte £28 📠: Free
House **⬛:** Black Sheep, Worthingtons, Folly Ale. ♀: 12
FACILITIES: Garden: Country garden with large lawns, good
views **NOTES:** Parking 30 **ROOMS:** 13 bedrooms 12 en suite
s£60 d£100 (★★) No children overnight

PICKERING   Map 19 SE78

Pick of the Pubs

Fox & Hounds Country Inn ★★ ◉ ♀
Sinnington YO62 6SQ ☎ 01751 431577 📠 01751 432791
e-mail: foxhoundsinn@easynet.co.uk
web: www.thefoxandhoundsinn.co.uk
Dir: 3m W of town, off A170
Sinnington is one of Yorkshire's loveliest villages, with a
little river running through its centre, banks of daffodils in
the spring, and a maypole on the village green. It makes an
entirely appropriate setting for this handsome 18th-century
coaching inn with its oak-beamed ceilings, old wood
panelling and open fires. Real ales like Black Sheep Special,
and a good range of malts, can be found in the bar, while
imaginative modern cooking is served in the well-appointed
non-smoking dining room. The lunch-time menu offers soft

continued

grain rolls with various fillings; light meals such as salmon and cured cod terrine; and mains like Whitby scampi with salad. For dinner you'll find slow-roasted Goosenargh duck; pan-seared local lamb cutlets; and Charlie Hill's mushroom, garlic and beef sausages and mash. Fish dishes are a strength of the specials board, including grilled wild sea bass fillet, and pan-fried skate wing. Choice of half a dozen home-made desserts if you can manage one.

Fox & Hounds Country Inn

OPEN: 12-2.30 6-11 (Sun 6-10.30) **BAR MEALS:** L served all week 12-2 D served all week 6.30-9 (Sun 6.30-8.30) Av main course £8 **RESTAURANT:** L served Sun 12-2 6.30-9 (Sun 6.30-8.30) 🍽: Free House 🍺: Camerons Bitter, Black Sheep Special, Worthingtons Creamflow. ♀: 7 **FACILITIES:** Garden: Lawn with tree feature, herb garden Dogs allowed Outside kennel if req. **NOTES:** Parking 30 **ROOMS:** 10 bedrooms en suite 1 family room s£59 d£40

Horseshoe Inn ♀
Main St, Levisham YO18 7NL ☎ 01751 460240 📠 01751 460240
e-mail: info@horseshoeinn-levisham.co.uk
Dir: Telephone for directions
A 16th-century family-run inn with spacious lounge bar and inviting atmosphere. Located in a peaceful village, this is an ideal base for walking and touring. An extensive seasonally changing menu offers traditional country fayre and classic dishes, including roast saddle of lamb, rhubarb-roasted pork with Fridaythorpe black pudding and a parsnip potato cake, and lemon and pepper crusted fillet of 'Radfords' beef topped with a wild mushroom gratin. **OPEN:** 11-3 6-11 **BAR MEALS:** L served all week 12-2 D served all week 6.30-9 Av main course £9 **RESTAURANT:** L served all week 12-2 D served all week 6.30-9 🍽: Free House 🍺: Theakstons Best Bitter, Scottish Courage John Smiths, Old Peculier. ♀: 6 **FACILITIES:** Child facs Garden **NOTES:** Parking 50 🐾

Pick of the Pubs

The White Swan ★★ 🏆 ♀
Market Place YO18 7AA ☎ 01751 472288 📠 01751 475554
e-mail: welcome@white-swan.co.uk
web: www.white-swan.co.uk
Dir: In Market Place between church & steam railway station
Situated right in the centre of Pickering, the White Swan was built as a four-room cottage in 1532 and extended to become a coaching inn on the York to Whitby road. Now, this simple but welcoming inn offers a choice of Yorkshire ales that includes Black Sheep Best and Yorkshire Moors Crompton Brewery. There are comfy sofas to relax in, and the traditional non-smoking restaurant has stone flagged floors and a roaring winter fire. The owners and staff take

great pride in their service, with careful attention to every detail, and dishes are prepared from the best Yorkshire ingredients. There are sandwiches and daily specials for lunch, whilst the dinner menu features choices such as calves' liver with wilted spinach, blue cheese mash and crispy bacon; Whitby fish, leek and cider pie; and beetroot fritters with caramelised onions and mustard sauce.
OPEN: 10-3 6-11 **BAR MEALS:** L served all week 12-2 D served all week 7-9 Av main course £9.95 **RESTAURANT:** L served all week 12-2 D served all week 7-9 Av 3 course à la carte £20 🍽: Free House 🍺: Black Sheep Best & Special, Yorkshire Moors Cropton Brewery, Timothy Taylors Landord. ♀: 10 **FACILITIES:** Child facs Garden: Beautifully planted terrace Dogs allowed **NOTES:** Parking 35 **ROOMS:** 21 bedrooms en suite 3 family rooms s£85 d£130

PICKHILL   Map 19 SE38

Pick of the Pubs

Nags Head Country Inn ★★ 🍴 ♀
YO7 4JG ☎ 01845 567391 📠 01845 567212
e-mail: enquiries@nagsheadpickhill.freeserve.co.uk
web: www.nagsheadpickhill.co.uk
Dir: 1m E of A1(4m N of A1/A61 junct)

This two-hundred-year-old establishment, with beamed ceilings, stone-flagged floors and cosy winter fires, is a direct descendant of the country coaching inn tradition. It stands in the village of Pickhill, a perfect spot for exploring Yorkshire's famed 'Herriot Country,' put on the map by the books of country vet James Herriot. As far as activities go, you'll be spoilt for choice - you can choose between horse racing (Thirsk, Ripon and Catterick fifteen minutes away), golf, excellent river and lake fishing as well as sea angling barely an hour away, and of course fell walking and rambling. All this exercise will whet your appetite for the likes of the Nag's Head hors d'oeuvres platter; roast chump of lamb with butternut squash bubble and squeak; and desserts like dark chocolate torte with wild cherry ice cream, without feeling a twinge of guilt. Freshly toasted sandwiches, and a 'comfort food' menu are further options.
OPEN: 11-11 **BAR MEALS:** L served all week 12-2 D served all week 6-9.30 Sun 12-2, 6-9 Av main course £10 **RESTAURANT:** L served all week 12-2 D served all week 7-9.30 Av 3 course à la carte £23 🍽: Free House 🍺: Hambleton Bitter & Goldfield, Black Sheep Best & Special, Old Peculiar. **FACILITIES:** Garden: Secluded wall area with seating area Dogs allowed Water and toys **NOTES:** Parking 40 **ROOMS:** 16 bedrooms en suite 1 family room s£50 d£65

continued

REETH
Map 19 SE09

ROSEDALE ABBEY
Map 19 SE79

Pick of the Pubs

Charles Bathurst Inn ◆◆◆◆

Arkengarthdale DL11 6EN ☎ 01748 884567
& 884265 🖷 01748 884599 e-mail: info@cbinn.co.uk
web: www.cbinn.co.uk

Located in remote and beautiful Arkengarthdale, this 18th-century inn is popular with walkers since it is about halfway along the Coast-to-Coast Walk. The CB, as regulars know it, was once a bunkhouse for lead miners employed by Charles Bathurst, an 18th-century lord of the manor and son of Oliver Cromwell's physician. The bar used to be a barn and stable, though antique pine furniture and cosy fires disguise its past well. The menu, based on fresh, largely locally sourced food, is written up daily on an imposing mirror. Game comes from the surrounding moors, and fish from Hartlepool five times a week. You may find starters such as mussel chowder, Thai spare ribs, and duck liver and game terrine; and main courses of spinach, apricot and feta cheese pancakes; ballottine of pheasant with pistachio and ham stuffing; and 'five-fish' fish cakes with hollandaise sauce. To follow, try orange bread and butter pudding.
OPEN: 11-11 (Closed Mon-Thurs at lunch) Closed: Dec 25
BAR MEALS: L served all week 12-2 D served all week 6.30-9
Av main course £7 **RESTAURANT:** L served all week 12-2
D served all week 6.30-9 🍷: Free House ◀: Scottish Courage Theakstons, John Smiths Bitter & John Smiths Smooth, Black Sheep Best & Riggwelter. **FACILITIES:** Child facs Garden: Dogs allowed **NOTES:** Parking 50 **ROOMS:** 18 bedrooms en suite d£80

Pick of the Pubs

The Milburn Arms Hotel ★★ 🐟

YO18 8RA ☎ 01751 417312 🖷 01751 417541
e-mail: info@millburnarms.co.uk
Dir: A170 W from Pickering 3m, right at sign to Rosedale then 7m N

In the heart of the Yorkshire Moors lies the picturesque village of Rosedale Abbey. Opposite the village green you will find this charming country house hotel dating back to 1776, and a perfect rural retreat. The family-run hotel offers eleven beautifully furnished en suite bedrooms, with a welcoming bar and log fires in the public rooms. Rosedale, once a centre for ironstone mining, is great for walking and you can quite literally begin a local hike at the front door of the hotel. Also close by are some of Yorkshire's best-loved attractions, including Castle Howard, Rievaulx Abbey and the region's famous steam railway. The Priory Restaurant is known for its quality cuisine: lobster and crab bisque, or a slice of pink melon and parma ham sharpen the appetite for chicken breast with apricot and pork; pan-fried calves' liver with red wine shallot; or poached fillet of plaice filled with prawns.
OPEN: 11.30-3 6-11 Closed: 25 Dec **BAR MEALS:** L served all week 12-2.15 D served all week 6.30-9 Sun 12-3 Av main course £12.50 **RESTAURANT:** L served Sun 12-2.30 D served all week 6-9.15 Av 3 course à la carte £22.50 Av fixed price £10 🍷: Free House ◀: Black Sheep Best, Carlsberg-Tetley Tetely Bitter, John Smith's, Stella. **FACILITIES:** Child facs Garden: Large grassed lawn area to side and front Dogs allowed **NOTES:** Parking 60 **ROOMS:** 13 bedrooms en suite 3 family rooms s£47.50 d£40

ROBIN HOOD'S BAY
Map 19 NZ90

Laurel Inn

New Rd YO22 4SE ☎ 01947 880400
Picturesque Robin Hood's Bay is the setting for this small, traditional pub which retains lots of character features, including beams and an open fire. The bar is decorated with old photographs, and an international collection of lager bottles. This coastal fishing village was once the haunt of smugglers who used a network of underground tunnels and secret passages to bring the booty ashore. Straightforward simple menu offers wholesome sandwiches and soups.
OPEN: 12-11 (Sun 12-10.30), Nov-Feb open 2pm Mon-Fri 🍷: Free House ◀: Adnams Broadside, Tetley, Jennings Cumberland.
FACILITIES: Dogs allowed **NOTES:** No credit cards

 Pubs offering a good choice of fish on their menu

SAWLEY
Map 19 SE26

The Sawley Arms 🛏️ ♀
HG4 3EQ ☎ 01765 620642
Dir: A1-Knaresborough-Ripley, or A1-Ripon B6265-Pateley Bridge

Run by the same owners for 36 years, this delightful 200-year-old pub was a popular haunt of the late author and vet James Herriot. Close by are Fountains Abbey and Ripon Cathedral. Diners here can be assured of good quality, unpretentious fare using the finest ingredients, typically corn-fed chicken breast, salmon pancake, and roast beef salad.
OPEN: 11.30-3 6.30-10.30 Closed: 25 Dec Rest: Closed Mon eve
BAR MEALS: L served all week 12-2.30 D served Tue-Sat 6.30-9
Av main course £8 **RESTAURANT:** L served all week 12-2.30
D served Tue-Sat 6.30-9 ⊕: Free House ◀: Theakston Best,
Scottish Courage John Smith's. ♀: 8 **FACILITIES:** Garden: Award
winning garden **NOTES:** Parking 50 ⊗

SCAWTON
Map 19 SE58

Pick of the Pubs

The Hare Inn ♀
YO7 2HG ☎ 01845 597289

Mentioned in the Domesday Book, and once frequented by the abbots and monks of Rievaulx Abbey. In the 17th century ale was brewed here for local iron workers. Inside, as you might expect, low-beamed ceilings and flagstone floors, a wood-burning stove providing a warm welcome in the bar, and an old-fashioned kitchen range in the dining area. A recent change of hands hasn't put a dent in the fine menu. Diners may find baked Whitby haddock with a minted pea crust, Aberdeen Angus sirloin steak and caramelized red onion sandwich, crab and king scallop thermidor with a crunchy parmesan topping, tagliatelle in crab and salmon cream sauce, and poached lemon sole with crisp pancetta and pimientos.
OPEN: 12-3 6.30-11 (Sun 12-3.30, 6.30-11, summer varies)

continued

BAR MEALS: L served Tue-Sun 12-2.30 D served Tue-Sat
6.30-8.45 Sun 12-3 **RESTAURANT:** L served Tue-Sun 12-2.30
D served Tue-Sat 6.30-8.45 ⊕: Free House ◀: Black Sheep,
Scottish Courage John Smiths, Guest Beers. ♀: 14
FACILITIES: Garden: Small area at front, large seated area
behind Dogs allowed water **NOTES:** Parking 18

SETTLE
Map 18 SD86

Golden Lion Hotel ◆◆◆◆ ♀
Duke St BD24 9DU ☎ 01729 822203 🖷 01729 824103
e-mail: info@goldenlion.yorks.net
Dir: Town centre opp Barclays Bank
This former coaching inn has been the silent witness to incalculable comings and goings in Settle's old market since around 1640. Its cosy, fire-warmed bar and comfy bedrooms often meet the needs of travellers on the spectacular Settle-Carlisle railway line. Fresh sandwiches, toasted baguettes and other breads, and stone-baked pizzas are available at lunchtime, while the carte usually features cornfed chicken wrapped in prosciutto ham; and fresh poached salmon with scallop and prawn sauce among several choices.
OPEN: 11-11 **BAR MEALS:** L served all week 12-2.30 D served all week 6-10 Av main course £7 **RESTAURANT:** L served all week 12-2.30 D served all week 6-10 Av 3 course à la carte £14
⊕: Thwaites ◀: Thwaites Bitter, Bomber, Thoroughbred, Smooth & Guest beers. ♀: 9 **FACILITIES:** Children's licence Patio with picnic benches & umbrellas Dogs allowed Water **NOTES:** Parking 14
ROOMS: 12 bedrooms 10 en suite 2 family rooms s£32 d£57

SKIPTON
Map 18 SD95

Devonshire Arms ♀
Grassington Rd, Cracoe BD23 6LA
☎ 01756 730237 🖷 01756 730142
e-mail: theded.cracoe@totalise.co.uk

The Rhylstone Ladies WI calendar originated at this pub, a convivial 17th-century inn convenient for the Three Peaks. There are also excellent views of Rhylstone Fell. A wide range of cask ales plus extensive wine list will wash down steak and mushroom pie cooked in Jennings Snecklifter ale, lamb Jennings, chicken Diane, and haddock and chips.
OPEN: 12-3 6-11 (Sat 12-11,Sun 12-10.30) **BAR MEALS:** L served all week 11.30-2 D served all week 6.30-9 Av main course £7
RESTAURANT: L served all week 12-2.30 D served all week 6.30-9.30 ⊕: Jennings ◀: Jennings, Jennings Cumberland, Snecklifter, Tetley's. **FACILITIES:** Garden: Food served outside Dogs allowed in the garden only **NOTES:** Parking 80

 Brewery/Company

England

SKIPTON continued

Herriots ★★ ♀

Broughton Rd BD23 1RT ☎ 01756 792781 📠 01756 793967
e-mail: herriots@mgrleisure.com

Herriots is located in the heart of the historic market town of Skipton and backs onto the Liverpool-Leeds Canal. The pale orange bar with flagstones and potted plants is traditional yet modern. The cooking reflects this with a bar and restaurant menu providing dishes that range from chilli with cheese nachos or Cumberland sausage with onion gravy to breast of duck in blueberry and balsamic dressing or grilled salmon and tiger prawns with red pepper coulis.
BAR MEALS: L served all week 11-11 Av main course £7
🍺: Tetleys Cask, Theakstons Cask, John Smiths Smooth and guests.
♀: 16 **NOTES:** Parking 44 **ROOMS:** 14 bedrooms en suite
3 family rooms s£50 d£60 No children overnight

SNAINTON · Map 17 SE98

Coachman Inn ♦♦♦ ♀

Pickering Rd West YO13 9PL ☎ 01723 859231 📠 01723 850008
e-mail: helen.patrick@btconnect.com
Dir: 5m from Pickering, off A170 on B1258

The Coachman is an imposing Grade II listed Georgian coaching Inn between Pickering and Scarborough, ideal for exploring the North Yorkshire Moors, forests and coast. Recently it has been bought over by Roger Patrick, who has done head chef stints with Gary Rhodes and Stephen Bull. Roger intends to make good use of that experience in designing the food for the pub, sourcing most of the ingredients locally for interesting yet unfussy menus. Dishes might include starters like rare roast beef salad with blue cheese and onion bread; smoked salmon, crab and leek tartlet; and plated selection of charcuterie with pickles and olives. Mains could be lamb liver and bacon with mash and sherry lentils; slow roast belly of pork with black pudding, caramelised apple, prune and Calvados sauce; and pan-fried cod with braised fennel and celery with minted pea and chorizo dressing.
OPEN: 12-2 7-11 (12-2.30 Sat-Sun) **BAR MEALS:** L served Thurs-Tues 12-2 D served Thurs-Tues 7-9 Sat-Sun 12-2.30, Fri-Sat 7-9.30 Av main course £11.25 **RESTAURANT:** L served Thurs-Tues 12-2 D served Thurs-Tues 7-9 Sat-Sun 12-2.30, Fri-Sat 7-9.30
Av 3 course à la carte £22 **🍺:** John Smiths, Black Sheep. **♀:** 9
FACILITIES: Children's licence Garden: Large lawned area with flower, trees, seating **NOTES:** Parking 20 **ROOMS:** 5 bedrooms en suite 1 family room d£66 No children overnight

STARBOTTON · Map 18 SD97

Fox & Hounds Inn ♀

BD23 5HY ☎ 01756 760269 760367
Dir: On B6160 N of Kettlewell

Situated in a picturesque limestone village in Upper Wharfedale, this ancient pub was originally built as a private house. Much of its trade comes from the summer influx of tourists and those tackling the long-distance Dales Way nearby. Make for the cosy bar, with its solid furnishings and flagstones, and enjoy a pint of Black Sheep or one of the guest ales. The menu has a traditional British focus: expect steak and ale pie, lamb shank, pork medallions in brandy and mustard sauce and a selection of steaks. There is also a choice of vegetarian dishes.
OPEN: 11.30-3 5.30-10.30 (Open all day Sat-Sun) (BHs open lunch only) Closed: 1-22 Jan **BAR MEALS:** L served all week 12-2.30
D served all week 5.30-9 Sun 12-8.15 Av main course £9

continued

RESTAURANT: 12-2.30 5.30-9 Sun 12-8 😊: Free House 🍺: Black Sheep, Timothy Taylor Landlord, Copper Dragon, Boddingtons White Horse & Guest Beers. ♀: 8 **FACILITIES:** Garden: Patio with 10 tables Dogs allowed **NOTES:** Parking 15

SUTTON-ON-THE-FOREST · · · · · · · · · · · · · · Map 19 SE56

Rose & Crown 🌟 ♀

Main St YO61 1DP ☎ 01347 811333 📠 01347 811444
e-mail: mail@rosecrown.co.uk
Dir: On B1363 N of York

Located in a picturesque village 10 miles north of York, the Rose & Crown has an informal, almost homely feel though the décor and food style is modern in its approach. The garden and patio at the back are well used during summer months. A choice of menus is usually available with a generous choice. ballotine of chicken, foie gras and rabbit, roast halibut with Bombay potatoes, or pot roast pheasant are good examples of the imaginative food.
OPEN: 12-3 5.30-11 Closed: 1st wk Jan **BAR MEALS:** L served Tue-Sat 12-2 D served Tue-Fri 6-7 (Sunday 12-4)
RESTAURANT: L served Tue-Sat 12-2 D served Tue-Sat 6-9 (Fri & Sat until 9.30) 😊: Free House 🍺: Timothy Taylors Landlord, Black Sheep Bitter, Hoegaargen. ♀: 11 **FACILITIES:** Garden: Large garden with patio area seating 24 **NOTES:** Parking 15

THIRSK · Map 19 SE48

Pick of the Pubs

The Carpenters Arms 🐾 ♀

YO7 2DP ☎ 01845 537369 📠 01845 537889
e-mail: karen@karenlouise.fsnet.co.uk
Dir: 2m outside Thirsk on the A170

An 18th-century inn that has been a house, blacksmith's forge and carpenter's workshop. In the friendly and welcoming bistro, tables are covered with coloured checked cloths, while carpenters' tools and old-fashioned toy hot-air balloons dangle from the ceiling; oddities of all kinds appear all over the place. The restaurant is more formal, thanks mainly to white linen cloths and napkins, crystal glasses and stylish, locally made furniture. At least a couple of dishes are billed as 'either/ors', in other words, Loch Fyne oysters with smoked salmon and Norwegian peeled prawns, for example, could be either a starter or a main course. Although there is quite an emphasis on fish dishes - chargrilled marinated swordfish with king prawns and queen scallops is one - there are plenty of meat mains too, such as fillet of beef wellington; honey-roasted breast of duck; and pan-fried calves' liver with crispy bacon.
OPEN: 11.30-3 6.30-11 (Sun 12-3, 7-10.30) Closed: 25 Dec, 1

continued

England

Jan(eve) **BAR MEALS:** L served all week 12-2 D served all week 7-9 **RESTAURANT:** L served Mon-Sun 12-2 D served Mon-Sun 7-9 Av 3 course à la carte £20 🍽: Free House 🍺: Black Sheep Bitter, Timothy Taylor Landlord, Greene King Old Speckled Hen, John Smiths Cask. ♀: 10 **NOTES:** Parking 50

THORGANBY
Map 17 SE64

The Jefferson Arms 🍴⬦ ♀
Main St YO19 6DA ☎ 01904 448316 📠 01904 449670
Dir: Telephone for directions

The new owners recommend reserving your table at the Jefferson Arms Restaurant in the beautiful conservation village of Thorganby. Black Sheep and Timothy Taylor are amongst the beers on offer, and there's also a good range of wines by the glass. A fixed price lunch supports the à la carte menu from Tuesday to Saturday. Expect potato and red onion pizza; fillet of beef wellington; and mixed seafood pasta.
OPEN: 12-2 6-11 (Sun 12-6) **BAR MEALS:** L served Tue-Sun 12-2 D served Tue-Sun 6-9 Sun 12-6 **RESTAURANT:** L served Tue-Sun 12-2 D served Tue-Sun 6-9 Av 3 course à la carte £24 🍽: Free House 🍺: Scottish Courage John Smiths, Black Sheep Best, Timothy Taylor, Landlord and Best. ♀: 8 **FACILITIES:** Garden **NOTES:** Parking 55

THORNTON LE DALE
Map 19 SE88

The New Inn
Maltongate YO18 7LF ☎ 01751 474226 📠 01751 477715

A Georgian coaching inn in the centre of a picturesque village complete with beck running beside the main street, and village stocks and market cross. Like the village, the inn retains its old world charm, with its log fires and hand-pulled ales. Freshly cooked food is one of its attractions, with many tempting choices on the menu and specials board: medallions of beef fillet, pan-fried chicken supreme, grilled halibut steak, seven bone rack of lamb, and salmon fillet with baby cucumber show the range.

continued

OPEN: 12-2.30 5-11 (Summer Mon-Sat 11-11, Sun 12-10.30) **BAR MEALS:** L served all week 12-2 Summer foodall day Av main course £7.95 **RESTAURANT:** L served all week 12-2 D served all week 6-9 summer lunch all day 🍽: Scottish & Newcastle 🍺: Theakston Black Bull, John Smith's, Cask old Speckled Hen. **FACILITIES:** Garden: Enclosed floral courtyard Dogs allowed **NOTES:** Parking 15

THORNTON WATLASS
Map 19 SE28

Pick of the Pubs

The Buck Inn ★ ♀
HG4 4AH ☎ 01677 422461 📠 01677 422447
e-mail: inwatlass1@btconnect.com
Dir: From A1 at Leeming Bar take A684 to Bedale, then B6268 towards Masham. Village 2m on right, hotel by cricket green

After 16 years of running the Buck, Margaret and Michael Fox still strive to maintain the warm welcome and relaxed atmosphere that keeps people coming back. The inn overlooks the village green and cricket pitch (the pub is the boundary), facing the old stone cottages of the village in a peaceful part of Wensleydale, yet is only five minutes' drive from the A1. Cricket isn't the only sport associated with the pub, as quoits are played in the back garden. Live traditional jazz is also a feature on at least two Sundays a month. Five real ales are served, most of them from local independent breweries, and English cooking, freshly prepared on the premises. Specialities are Masham rarebit (Wensleydale cheese with local ale on toast, topped with ham and bacon), deep-fried fresh Whitby cod, and chicken stir-fried in black bean sauce.
OPEN: 11-11 (Sun 12-10.30) Dec 25 closed eve
BAR MEALS: L served all week 12-2 D served all week 6-9.30 (Sun 12-9.30) Av main course £10 **RESTAURANT:** L served all week 12-2 D served all week 6.30-9.30 🍽: Free House 🍺: Theakston Best, Black Sheep Best, John Smith's & Guest beers. ♀: 6 **FACILITIES:** Child facs Garden: Food served outside Dogs allowed Water **NOTES:** Parking 40
ROOMS: 7 bedrooms 5 en suite s£50 d£70

TOPCLIFFE
Map 19 SE37

The Angel Inn NEW ★★
YO7 3RW ☎ 01845 577237 📠 01845 578000
e-mail: mail@angelinn.co.uk
Located at the heart of Topcliffe, this old country inn has been extended and modernised in recent years to provide up-to-date accommodation and dining, and is now quite a large complex. The restaurant is very popular locally, and the pub garden has a large carp pond. A function suite is available for wedding ceremonies, meetings and other functions.
NOTES: No credit cards

WASS
Map 19 SE57

Pick of the Pubs

Wombwell Arms 🐟 ♀
YO61 4BE ☎ 01347 868280
e-mail: wykes@wombwellarms.wanadoo.co.uk
Dir: From A1 take A168 to A19 junct. Take York exit, then left after
2.5m, left at Coxwold to Ampleforth. Wass 2m

The building was constructed around 1620 as a granary,
probably using stone from nearby Byland Abbey, and it
became an ale house in about 1645. A series of stylishly
decorated rooms provide the setting for bistro-style
cooking. Local suppliers have been established for all the
produce used: at least three vegetarian dishes are offered
daily along with a good choice of fresh fish, including
Whitby cod. Popular options are steak, Guinness and
mushroom pie, country rabbit, and game casserole. Great
location for those walking the North Yorks National Park.
OPEN: 11-3 6.15-11 (Closed Sun pm in low season)
BAR MEALS: L served all week 12-2.30 D served all week Sun
12-3 Av main course £12 **RESTAURANT:** L served all week
12-2.30 D served all week 6.30-8.30 Sun 12-3 Av 3 course à la
carte £20 ⊞: Free House ◗: Black Sheep Best, Timothy Taylor
Landlord, Tetley Extra Smooth. ♀: 7 **FACILITIES:** Children's
licence Garden: Courtyard with Six Pin and benches
NOTES: Parking 16

WEAVERTHORPE
Map 17 SE97

Pick of the Pubs

The Star Country Inn
YO17 8EY ☎ 01944 738273 ▤ 01944 738273
e-mail: starweaverthorpe@aol.com
Dir: 12m E of Malton to Sherborn Village, lights on A64, turn right at
the lights. Weaverthorpe 4m. Star Inn on the Junct facing

Situated in the heart of the Yorkshire Wolds, this brightly-
shining Star makes a handy base for exploring the area
and visiting such attractions as Castle Howard, used
extensively in the classic television series *Brideshead
Revisited*, Nunnington Hall and Sledmere House. The
rustic facilities of bar and dining room, with large winter
fires and a welcoming, convivial atmosphere, complement
food cooked to traditional family recipes using fresh local
produce. All the usual favourites are here - game, steak,
stroganoff and the like, and there are starters such as
Brompton sausages and sautéed onions in ale, Wold
mushrooms with walnuts and stilton sauce, and Yorkshire
pudding with a savoury medley. Traditional main courses
include slow-roasted mini lamb joint; wild boar with black
pudding, brandy and apple cream sauce; jugged Yorkshire
hare; and local game casserole. There are seafood and
vegetarian choices, including mixed fish and prawn lattice,
and asparagus and spinach pancakes with three cheeses.
OPEN: 12-3 7-11 **BAR MEALS:** L served Wed-Mon 12-2
D served Wed-Mon 7-9.30 (Sun 12-3) Av main course £7
RESTAURANT: L served Wed-Mon 12-2 D served Wed-Mon
7-9.30 (Sun 12-3) Av 3 course à la carte £18 ⊞: Free House
◗: Carlsberg-Tetley Tetley Bitter, Scottish Courage John Smith's,
Wold Top. **FACILITIES:** Dogs allowed **NOTES:** Parking 30

WEST BURTON
Map 19 SE08

Fox & Hounds
DL8 4JY ☎ 01969 663111 ▤ 01969 663279
e-mail: foxandhounds.westburton@virgin.net
Dir: A468 between Hawes & Leyburn, 0.5m E of Aysgarth

Overlooking the village green in the unspoilt village of West
Burton, this inn offers log fires and home cooking. Hand-
pulled ales on offer at the bar include Black Sheep and Old
Peculier. The owners continue to provide traditional pub food
to accompany your pint: dishes such as steak and kidney pie,
curry and lasagne will fortify you for country walks or visits to
nearby waterfalls, castles or cheese-tasting at the Wensleydale
Creamery.
OPEN: 11-11 (winter closed 3-6) **BAR MEALS:** L served all week
12-3 D served all week 6-9 Av main course £6.95
RESTAURANT: L served all week 12-3 D served all week 6-9
⊞: Free House ◗: Black Sheep, Old Peculier, John Smiths, Tetleys.
FACILITIES: Child facs Dogs allowed **NOTES:** Parking 6

> Pick of the Pubs have that extra special quality
> that makes them stand out from the crowd.
> Their entries are highlighted, and may be a
> full page

continued

England

WEST TANFIELD
Map 19 SE27

Pick of the Pubs

The Bruce Arms ♦♦♦♦ @ 🐟 ♀
Main St HG4 5JJ ☎ 01677 470325 🖷 01677 470796
e-mail: iwanttostay@brucearms.com
Dir: *On A6108 Ripon/Masham rd, close to A1*
A few miles north of Ripon, and close to the River Ure, this ivy-clad, stone-built free house dates from 1820. Inside are exposed beams, log fires and candle-topped tables. The pub is run along bistro lines, its regularly changing blackboard menu founded on seasonal produce, ably complemented by a good wine list and Black Sheep Best on tap. Twice-baked cheese soufflé, and smoked haddock with spinach, poached egg and hollandaise sauce remain favourite starters. Main courses highlighted by the owners as representative include braised lamb shank, and chicken breast with banana, smoked ham, coconut and mild curry sauce. Fish dishes include roast halibut with smoked salmon, avocado and hollandaise; seared scallops with lemon risotto; and roast cod with watercress sauce and mustard grain mash. A choice of home-made desserts or local Yorkshire cheeses round off a memorable meal. Cosy, comfortable bedrooms provide an excellent base for Dales attractions such as Jervaulx Abbey and Aysgarth Falls.
OPEN: 12-2 6.30-11 Closed: 1 Wk Feb **BAR MEALS:** L served Sun 12-2 D served Tues-Sat 6.30-9.30 **RESTAURANT:** L served Sun 12-2 D served Tues-Sat 6.30-9.30 ⊜: Free House ◖: Black Sheep Best. ♀: 10 **FACILITIES:** Garden: Terrace
NOTES: Parking 15 **ROOMS:** 3 bedrooms en suite 1 family room s£40 d£60

WEST WITTON
Map 19 SE08

Pick of the Pubs

The Wensleydale Heifer Inn ★★ 🐟 ♀
DL8 4LS ☎ 01969 622322 🖷 01969 624183
e-mail: info@wensleydaleheifer.co.uk
web: www.wensleydaleheifer.co.uk
Dir: *A684, at west end of village.*
A 17th-century former coaching inn, the Wensleydale Heifer is set in the heart of Wensleydale and the Yorkshire Dales National Park. It has a whitewashed stone exterior with a lawned garden, benched seating and tables, and a welcoming interior with roaring fires, exposed stonework, beams and cosy snugs. The location is ideal for walking, enjoying the stunning local scenery and visiting the many places of interest in striking distance. Accommodation is also available in comfortable bedrooms. At the heart of the old inn is the kitchen, where the owners oversee the preparation of a wide range of dishes. Ingredients are carefully sourced: game from the moors, beef and lamb from the Dales, complemented by local vegetables and fresh garden herbs. Puddings and breads are baked daily. Despite its inland location, seafood also features in the form of poached haddock, seafood pasta and lobster in season.
OPEN: 11-11 **BAR MEALS:** L served all week 12-2 D served all week 6-9 Av main course £6.95 **RESTAURANT:** L served all week 12-2 D served all week 6.30-9 ⊜: Free House ◖: Burst Beer, Scottish Courage John Smith's, Black Sheep Best. ♀: 7
FACILITIES: Lawned garden with bench seats and tables
NOTES: Parking 30 **ROOMS:** 9 bedrooms en suite 2 family rooms s£60 d£72 No children overnight

WHITBY
Map 19 NZ81

The Magpie Café ♀
14 Pier Rd YO21 3PU ☎ 01947 602058 🖷 01947 601801
e-mail: ian@magpiecafe.co.uk

More a licensed restaurant than a pub, the award-winning Magpie has been the home of North Yorkshire's best-ever fish and chips since the late 1930s when it moved to its present site in Pier Road. The dining rooms command excellent views of the harbour, the Abbey and St Mary's Church. Fresh Whitby fish, with up to 10 daily choices, and shellfish feature on the menu, as well as an extensive range of salads and over 20 home-made puddings.
OPEN: 11.30-9 (11.30-6.30 Sun) Closed: 5 Jan-6 Feb Rest: Nov-Mar Closed 6.30 Sun **RESTAURANT:** L served all week 11.30-9 D served all week ⊜: Free House ◖: Crompton, Scoresby Bitter, Carlsberg-Tetley Tetley Bitter.. ♀: 9 ⊛

WIGGLESWORTH
Map 18 SD85

The Plough Inn 🐟 ♀
BD23 4RJ ☎ 01729 840243 🖷 01729 840638
e-mail: sue@ploughinn.info
Dir: *From A65 between Skipton & Long Preston take B6478 to Wigglesworth*

This traditional 18th-century country inn is ideally placed for exploring the local area. The bar has oak beams and an open fire, and the conservatory restaurant has fine views across the hills. Freshly-made sandwiches and bar meals are supplemented by daily specials, which might include minted lamb shoulder on gratin potatoes; stir-fried mushrooms and pine nuts in tomato sauce with cheddar cheese; and roasted salmon fillet with goats' cheese.
OPEN: 11-3 6-11 **BAR MEALS:** L served all week 12-2 D served all week 6.30-9 (From 6 at busy times) Av main course £8.50 **RESTAURANT:** L served all week 12-2 D served all week 7-9 From 6 at busy times Av 3 course à la carte £18 ⊜: Free House ◖: Carlsberg-Tetley Tetley Bitter, Black Sheep Best. ♀: 6
FACILITIES: Child facs Garden: Large area with views over Yorkshire Dales Dogs allowed Water **NOTES:** Parking 70
ROOMS: 9 bedrooms en suite 3 family rooms s£48 d£74 (★★)

YORK　　　　　　　　　　　Map 16 SE65

Pick of the Pubs

Blue Bell NEW ♀
53 Fossgate YO1 9TF ☎ 01904 654904
e-mail: robsonhardie@aol.com
It's easy to do, but don't walk past the narrow frontage of York's smallest pub, which has been serving customers in the ancient heart of the city for 200 years. In 1903 it was given a typical Edwardian makeover, since when hardly anything - and this includes the varnished wall and ceiling panelling, the two cast-iron tiled fireplaces, and the old settles - has been altered. The layout is original too, with the taproom at the front and the snug down a long corridor at the rear, both with servery hatches. Quite fittingly, the whole interior is now Grade II*-listed. The only slight drawback is that the pub's size leaves no room for a kitchen, but even so tapas have recently been reintroduced, and what the pub calls its 'substantial' sandwiches are available. Seven real ales are usually on tap, including rotating guests.
OPEN: 11-11 ◀: Deuchars IPA, Timothy Taylors Landlord, Adnams Bitter, Abbot Greene King. ♀: 10 **FACILITIES:** Dogs allowed **NOTES:** No credit cards

Pick of the Pubs

Lysander Arms ▷◇ ♀
Manor Ln, Shipton Rd YO30 5TZ
☎ 01904 640845 🖹 01904 624422
The Lysander Arms is built on the site of an old RAF airfield and is conveniently situated for the Park-and-Ride facility, giving easy access to York. Where once there were large hangars for the repair of Halifax bombers, there is now a 13-pitch caravan park. The enclosed beer garden has a children's play area, picnic tables and shrub-filled borders. Inside is a contemporary-style air-conditioned bar with a brick-built fireplace, snooker table and large-screen TV. The lunch menu offers a choice of sandwiches in ciabatta, melted bloomer or poppy bagel bread, and more substantial dishes like 8oz hamburger with smoked bacon, mature cheddar & roast garlic mayonnaise, or fresh Whitby mussel's marinière. Evening dishes kick off with pâté, prawn cocktail or a sharing platter, while main courses take in Irish stew, posh fish pie and a selection from the chargrill. Live entertainment every weekend.
OPEN: 11-11 (Sat 11-12.30, Sun 12-10.30)
BAR MEALS: L served Tue-Sun 12-2 D served Tue-Sat 5.30-9 (Sun 12-3) Av main course £7.50 **RESTAURANT:** L served Tue-Sun 12-2 D served Tue-Sat 5.30-9 (12-3) ◀: John Smiths Cask, Deuchars IPA, Fosters, Kronenbourg. ♀: 18
FACILITIES: Garden: Enclosed beer garden Dogs in bar area only **NOTES:** Parking 35

 The Rosette is the AA award for food.
Look out for it next to a pub's name

Website addresses are included where available.
The AA cannot be held responsible for the content of any of these websites

---

YORKSHIRE, SOUTH

BRADFIELD　　　　　　　　Map 16 SK29

The Strines Inn
Bradfield Dale S6 6JE ☎ 0114 2851247
Dir: Off A57 between Sheffield toward Manchester
Nestling opposite Strines Reservoir in the Peak District National Park, this popular inn was originally built as a manor house in 1275, though most of the present building is 16th century. Two of the three bars are non-smoking, and all have open fires in winter time. The menu offers traditional home-made dishes, with a good choice of vegetarian meals and daily fresh fish. Other choices include liver and onions, and a mammoth mixed grill.
OPEN: 10.30-3 6.30-11 (all day Mar-Sep, wkds open all day) Closed: Dec 25 **BAR MEALS:** L served all week 12-2.30 D served all week 6.30-9 all day weekends Av main course £6.95 ◆: Free House ◀: Marston's Pedigree, Kelham Island, Mansfield Cusk, Riding.
FACILITIES: Large garden: Roaming peacocks Dogs allowed Water, meat on Sundays **NOTES:** Parking 50

CADEBY　　　　　　　　　Map 16 SE50

Pick of the Pubs

Cadeby Inn NEW ▷◇ ♀
Main St DN5 7SW ☎ 01709 864009
e-mail: Cadebyinn@bpcmail.co.uk
The Cadeby Inn used to be a working farm before being converted into a pub. Convenient for the Doncaster racecourse, Conisbrough Castle and the Earth centre, the pub has recently added a conference venue called The Old Granary, a unique venue with low-beamed ceiling. There is a large front garden enclosed by sandstone walls, with a patio area and a small back garden. The menu is divided between starters and light bites, pasta and salads, lighter mains, larger mains, gourmet dinner, and desserts. Starters could be hoi sin beef strips; black pudding and sausage hot pot; and grilled tiger prawns. The larger mains and gourmet dishes might include steak and mushroom pudding; sirloin steak; Cadeby grill; lamb shank; scampi Provençal; calves' liver; tender grilled lamb rump; and chateaubriand.
OPEN: 11-11 **BAR MEALS:** L served all week 12-6 D served all week 12-8 Av main course £6.95 **RESTAURANT:** L served Sunday D served all week 6-9 12-8 ◀: John Smiths Cask, Black Sheep Best Bitter, Guiness. ♀: 6 **FACILITIES:** Child facs Children's licence Garden: Large front garden enclosed by sandstone walls Dogs allowed in tap room only **NOTES:** Parking 30

DONCASTER　　　　　　　Map 16 SE50

Waterfront Inn ▷◇ ♀
Canal Ln, West Stockwith DN10 4ET ☎ 01427 891223
Built in the 1830s overlooking the Trent Canal basin and the canal towpath, the pub is now popular with walkers and visitors to the nearby marina. Real ales and good value food are the order of the day, including pasta with home-made ratatouille, broccoli and cheese bake, deep fried scampi, half honey-roasted chicken, and home-made lasagne. Recent change of ownership - readers' reports welcome.
OPEN: 11.30-11 **BAR MEALS:** L served all week 12-2.30 D served all week 5.30-8.30 Sun 12-5 **RESTAURANT:** L served all week 12-2.30 D served all week 5.30-8.30 Sun 12-5 ◆: Enterprise Inns

continued

England

: Scottish Courage John Smith Cask, Timothy Taylors, Greene King Old Speckled Hen, Deuchars IPA. **:** 9 **FACILITIES:** Child facs Garden: Dogs allowed Water provided **NOTES:** Parking 30

PENISTONE
Map 16 SE20

Pick of the Pubs

Cubley Hall
Mortimer Rd, Cubley S36 9DF
☎ 01226 766086 ▤ 01226 767335
e-mail: cubley.hall@ukonline.co.uk
Dir: Telephone for directions

Cloaked in history, Cubley Hall evolved from a moorland farm on the Pennine packhorse routes of the 1700s, first becoming a Victorian gentleman's residence in four acres of grounds, then after the last war a children's home, until in 1983 came its transformation into a pub. Amazingly, given years of youthful battering, many of its original features, such as mosaic floors, oak panelling and stained glass had survived. After another seven years the massive oak-beamed, hewn-stone barn was converted into a now-renowned restaurant, where the menu offers pastas, pizzas, salads and chargrills for those with more straightforward needs, and for diners after something more innovative, brisket of English beef with tarragon carrots, caramelised shallots and fondant mash; sweet chilli stir-fry; and finnan haddock poached in white wine and cream with baby leaf spinach and soft poached egg. Daily specials appear on the blackboard, and there's lots of choice for children.
OPEN: 11-11 (Sun 12-10.30) **BAR MEALS:** L served all week 12-9.30 D served all week 12-9.30 Av main course £8.50 **RESTAURANT:** L served Sun 12-9.30 D served Wknds Av 3 course à la carte £16.50 **:** Free House
: Carlsberg-Tetley Tetley Bitter, Burton Ale, Greene King Abbot Ale, Young's Special. **:** 7 **FACILITIES:** Child facs Garden: Large lawns, seating areas and tables **NOTES:** Parking 100

The Fountain Inn
Wellthorne Ln, Ingbirchworth S36 7GJ
☎ 01226 763125 ▤ 01226 761336
e-mail: reservations@fountain-inn.co.uk
Dir: Exit M1 Junction 37. Take A628 to Manchester then take A629 to Huddersfield
Busy but friendly and informal country inn with stylish, cosy interior. Famous for the local choir which gathers here every Christmas and brings a countrywide following, it is also next door to *Summer Wine* country. Favourite bar meals include ale-braised steak, shoulder of lamb, Fountain grill, and bean fajitas, with a good fish choice ranging around buttered haddock, crab linguini, and salmon and prawn fishcakes.
OPEN: 11.45-2.30 5-11 Closed: 25 Dec **BAR MEALS:** L served all
continued

week 12-2 D served all week 5-9.30 Av main course £9.50
: Tetleys Cask, Theakstons Best, Black Sheep, John Smith Smooth.
: 9 **FACILITIES:** Garden: Enclosed patio, only drinks served
NOTES: Parking 45

SHEFFIELD
Map 16 SK38

Pick of the Pubs

The Fat Cat
23 Alma St S3 8SA ☎ 0114 249 4801 ▤ 0114 249 4803
e-mail: enquiries@thefatcat.co.uk
Dir: Telephone for directions

Always a pub, this 150-year-old listed building is located in an industrial area of the city, and is believed to be haunted. The proprietor, a former economics lecturer, bought it 25 years ago. His vision was of a free house that could offer a constantly changing range of (ten) real ales, home-cooked food including a good vegetarian choice, a no-smoking area, real open fires and a beer garden. Acknowledged as the first real ale pub in the city, the award-winning Fat Cat has its own brewery, named after adjoining Kelham Island, and at least four of its draught beers are always featured. The keenly priced food is offered from a weekly menu with daily specials. Dishes might include nutty parsnip pie; chicken casserole, or a buffet selection. Vegan and gluten-free dishes included.
OPEN: 12-3 5.30-11 (Sun 7-10.30, Fri & Sat 12-11) Closed: Dec 25-26 **BAR MEALS:** L served all week 12-2.30 D served Mon-Fri 6-7.30 Av main course £3.50 **:** Free House **:** Timothy Taylor Landlord, Kelham Island Bitter, Pale Rider, Pride of Sheffield. **FACILITIES:** Garden: Walled area, flower beds, heaters Dogs allowed **NOTES:** Parking 20 No credit cards

Lions Lair NEW
31 Burgess St S1 2HF ☎ 0114 263 4264 ▤ 0114 263 4265
e-mail: info@lionslair.co.uk
Dir: Burges Street runs alongside John Lewis Department Store, between City Hall and the 'Peace Gardens' in the centre of Sheffield.
A traditional city pub with a particular emphasis on quality food and service. The well-trained bartenders mix great cocktails, and the knowledgeable serving staff will be happy to help with menu choices. A meal could start with Thai chicken salad, be followed by poussin à la Françoise, and finish with apple, raisin and cinnamon crumble.
OPEN: 12 Mon 12-8, Sun 12-6 -11 **BAR MEALS:** L served al 12-11 D served Mon-Sat 12-11 Sun 12-5, Mon 12-7 Av main course £8.50
: Black Sheep, Tetleys. **:** 14 **FACILITIES:** Garden: Enclosed beer garden with decking and bbq Dogs allowed

| ♀ 7 | Number of wines by the glass |

England

WENTWORTH
Map 16 SK39

Rockingham Arms
8 Main St S62 7TL ☎ 01226 742075 📠 01226 361099
Dir: M1 junct 36 to Hoyland Common then B6090

Attractive ivy-clad village pub on the Wentworth estate with a large orchard garden overlooking the bowling and cricket green at the rear. Now part of the Spirit Group. Reports welcome.
OPEN: 11-11 (Sun 12-10.30) **BAR MEALS:** L served all week 12 D served Mon-Sun 9 **RESTAURANT:** L served all week 12-9
🍽: 🍺: Theakston XB, Old Peculiar, & Best, Old Speckled Hen.
FACILITIES: Garden: Large orchard garden, large bowling green Dogs welcome – very dog friendly **NOTES:** Parking 30

YORKSHIRE, WEST

BRADFORD
Map 19 SE13

New Beehive Inn
171 Westgate BD1 3AA ☎ 01274 721784 📠 01274 735092
e-mail: newbeehiveinn@talk21.com

Classic Edwardian inn, dating from 1901 and retaining its period atmosphere with separate bars and gas lighting. Outside, with a complete change of mood, you can relax in the Mediterranean-style courtyard. The pub offers a good range of unusual real ales and a selection of over 100 malt whiskies, served alongside some simple bar snacks.
OPEN: 12-11 (Sun 12-10.30) **BAR MEALS:** L served Mon-Sat 12-2
🍽: Free House 🍺: Timothy Taylor Landlord, Kelham Island Bitter, Hop Back Summer Lightning, Abbeydale Moonshine.
FACILITIES: Garden: Mediterranean style courtyard
NOTES: Parking 20

> Not all of the pubs in the guide are open all week or all day. It's always best to check before you travel

CLIFTON
Map 16 SE12

Black Horse Inn 🏅 🍴 ♀
HD6 4HJ ☎ 01484 713862 📠 01484 400582
e-mail: mail@blackhorseclifton.co.uk
Dir: 1m from Bridgehouse town centre 0.5m from junct 25 M62

A 16th-century coaching inn with oak-beamed rooms, open coal fires and an interesting history. It was once used as a meeting place for the loom-wrecking Luddites, and later as a variety club playing host to Roy Orbison, Showaddywaddy and Shirley Bassey. Good home-cooked food has been served here for over 50 years: the extensive menu includes pan-fried red mullet with pickled vegetables and lime-dressed leaves; and daube of beef with turnip mash and mustard seed dumplings.
OPEN: 11-11 **BAR MEALS:** L served all week 12-5.30 D served all week 5.30-9.30 Sun 12-8.30 Av main course £13
RESTAURANT: L served all week 12-5.30 D served all week 5.30-9.30 Sun 12-8.30 Av 3 course à la carte £23.50 🍽: Enterprise Inns 🍺: Black Sheep, Timothy Taylor Landlord, Old Speckled Hen,.
♀: 18 **FACILITIES:** Garden: Courtyard on two levels, hanging baskets Dogs allowed **NOTES:** Parking 50

See advert on page 584

DEWSBURY
Map 16 SE22

West Riding Licensed Refreshment Rooms
Dewsbury Railway Station, Wellington Rd WF13 1HF
☎ 01924 459193 📠 01924 450404

Trains regularly pass this converted Grade II listed railway station built in 1848 and located on the Trans-Pennine route between Leeds and Manchester. The pub supports northern micro-breweries and is linked to an Anglo-Dutch brewery in Dewsbury, providing guests with a regular choice of guest ales. A daily-changing menu offers such dishes as lamb shank with mint gravy, new potatoes and veg; broccoli flan & salad; parsnip fritters; and roast pork loin on sweet potato mash.
OPEN: 11-11 Closed: 25 Dec **BAR MEALS:** L served Mon-Fri 12-3 D served Tues-Wed 6-9 Av main course £4 🍽: Free House
🍺: Timothy Taylor Dark Mild & Landlord, Black Sheep Best, Anglo Dutch. **FACILITIES:** Garden: Food served outside Dogs allowed
NOTES: Parking 600 No credit cards

PUB WALK

The Millbank at Millbank
Sowerby Bridge - West Yorkshire

THE MILLBANK AT MILLBANK
Sowerby Bridge, HX6 3DY
☎ 01422 825588
Directions: A58 from Sowerby Bridge to Ripponden, R at Triange
Stone-built pub with a growing reputation for food. There's a wine bar ambience in the main bar, plus a cosy tap room and a dining room. Fresh local produce including seafood and robust meat dishes. Stunning views from garden.
Open: 12–3 5.30–11 (Sun 12–10.30 Closed Mon lunch) Closed: First 2 weeks in Oct, 1st wk Jan
Bar Meals: L served Tues–Sun 12–2.30 D served all week 6–9.30 Sun 12.30–4.30, 6–8 Av main course £12.95
Restaurant Meals: L served Tues–Sun 12–2.30 D served all week 6–9.30 Sun 12.30–4.30, 6–8 Av 3 course à la carte £24 Av 2 course fixed price £11.95
Dogs allowed. Garden available.
(for full entry see page 588)

Distance: 4 miles (6.4km) including extension
Map: OS Explorer OL 21
Terrain: Scenic valley, woodland and farmland
Paths: Paths, tracks and roads
Gradient: Steep in places

Walk submitted by The Millbank at Millbank

The spectacular Pennine hills surrounding the village of Mill Bank form the backdrop to this fascinating walk, which follows ancient packhorse routes, tracks and valley paths. The route coincides with part of the Calderdale Way, a popular long-distance trail that explores the rugged Calder Valley. Along the way are wooded cloughs, several Pennine smallholdings and some fine examples of 16th century architecture.

From the pub turn left and after about 100yds (91m) turn left down Lower Mill Bank Road, following it through the village of Mill Bank and down to a stream. Turn left immediately beyond the bridge, by a converted watermill, and follow the waterside path. The path soon swings right and heads up a slope through Fiddle Wood, gradually ascending the hillside. Make for a series of stone steps that lead up to a stony and grass track known as Clapgate Lane. Turn right and after about 100yds (91m) veer left at the fork, following High Field Lane. The cobbled track climbs steeply to High

Field Farm and then on to Top O' Th' Town Farm in the hamlet of Soyland. Turn right at the next road and follow it as it swings left to become Lane Head Road. Continue for 600yds before bearing right at the staggered crossroads onto Cross-Wells Road. This descends fairly steeply to a small bridge over Severhills Clough stream. Keep ahead for about 500yds (457m), passing Clay House to reach a track on the right known as Gough Lane. Here, you have a choice. To follow the shorter route back to the Millbank, turn right down Gough Lane. On reaching a wood look for a footpath on the left, climb the stile and cut between fir trees to reach the bridge at the bottom of Lower Mill Bank Road. Retrace your steps up the road to the pub.

To extend the walk by about 2 miles (3.2km), avoid the lane and continue along what is now Lighthazels Road. Turn right down Clay Pits Lane, pass the Alma pub and cross the bridge at Salt Drake. Climb the hill to Cottonstones Church and, 50yds (46m) beyond it, look for a sharp right-hand turn. Follow the track for about 1/4 mile (400m), to the hamlet of Helm, look for a gate and turn right along Helm Lane.

Go straight over at the T junction to Spout Field Farm, follow the waymarked path across several fields and down a long flight of stone steps. The Millbank pub is a short distance to the right, along Millbank Road.

583

BLACK HORSE INN

VILLAGE PUB - RESTAURANT - HOT

Tradition & Value
Excellent Food & Wine
Unbeatable Service
Friendly Atmosphere

**The Black Horse Inn, Coalpit Lane,
Clifton – Brighouse, West Yorkshire, HD6 4HJ**
Telephone: 01484 713862   Fax: 01484 400582
Website: www.blackhorseclifton.co.uk
Email: mail@theblackhorseclifton.co.uk

Village Pub

We pride ourselves on the qualify of our beers and lagers, along with the excellent range of wines, we take great care in ensuring they always meet the expectations and demands of our customers.

We have an extensive choice of bar meals and snacks offering freshly cooked home-made food and a specials board which changes daily.

Fine Dining

We have two restaurants serving food of the highest standards from exciting menus, our reputation for providing quality food stretches back over 40 years and we strongly advise pre-booking for our fine dining restaurants. To compliment our culinary oasis we have an extensive wine cellar, with direct access to the all the worlds wine merchants, our cellar includes 100 wines from Classical to New Age.

Accommodation

Our 23 en-suite bedrooms have been converted from old cottages and retain all the original character and yet have all the warmth and modern facilities expected today.

Special Occasions

Black Horse Inn is an ideal location for functions, events and celebrations throughout the year. Our Wellington Suite is a self-contained function room, complete with its own private bar and french doors opening onto a beautiful courtyard setting which has been featured in the TV series "Last of the Summer Wine".

Corporate meetings

In response to the age of remote working, *The Black Horse Inn* caters for all types of conferences, meetings, seminars and one to one Meetings. Despite the Olde world charm we boast all the modern facilities expected of todays corporate world.

England

HALIFAX
Map 19 SE02

The Rock Inn Hotel ★★★
Holywell Green HX4 9BS ☎ 01422 379721 🖷 01422 379110
e-mail: reservations@rockinnhotel.com
Dir: From M62 junct 24 follow Blackley signs, L at x-rds, approx 0.5m on L
Substantial modern extensions have transformed this
attractive 17th-century wayside inn into a thriving hotel and
conference venue in the scenic valley of Holywell Green. All-
day dining in the brasserie-style conservatory is truly
cosmopolitan; kick off with freshly prepared parsnip and
apple soup or crispy duck and seaweed, followed by liver and
bacon, Thai-style steamed halibut, chicken piri piri or
vegetables jalfrezi.
OPEN: 11-11 **BAR MEALS:** L served all week 12-2.30 D served all
week 5-6 Av main course £6 **RESTAURANT:** L served all week
12-10 D served all week 5-9 Av 3 course fixed price £14.95 🍴: Free
House 🍺: Black Sheep, Taylor Landlord, John Smiths.
FACILITIES: Child facs Garden: Garden terrace surrounded by fields.
Dogs allowed Water **NOTES:** Parking 120 **ROOMS:** 30 bedrooms
en suite 6 family rooms s£60 d£64 (★★★)

Pick of the Pubs

Shibden Mill Inn ◆◆◆◆ ◎◎ ℉
Shibden Mill Fold HX3 7UL
☎ 01422 365840 🖷 01422 362971
e-mail: shibdenmillinn@zoom.co.uk
See Pick of the Pubs on page 586

HAWORTH
Map 19 SE03

The Old White Lion Hotel ★★ 🛏️ ℉
Main St BD22 8DU ☎ 01535 642313 🖷 01535 646222
e-mail: enquiries@oldwhitelionhotel.com
Dir: Turn off A629 onto B6142, hotel 0.5m past Haworth Station

Once known as the Blue Bell Inn, this 18th-century free house
stands at the top of a cobbled street close to the Brontë
Museum and Parsonage. The traditionally furnished bars offer
a welcome respite from the tourist trail, serving Theakston
ales to accompany a wide range of generously served snacks
and meals. Fish dishes feature strongly: fisherman's hors
d'oeuvre, Mediterranean-style salmon, and sole ricardo are
typical choices.
OPEN: 11-11 **BAR MEALS:** L served all week 11.30-2.30 D served
all week 5.30-9.30 (Sat & Sun 12-9.30) **RESTAURANT:** L served Sun
12-2.30 D served all week 7-9.30 🍴: Free House 🍺: Theakstons
Best & Green Lable, Carlsberg-Tetley Tetley Bitter, Scottish Courage
John Smith's, Websters. **NOTES:** Parking 9 **ROOMS:** 14 bedrooms
en suite 2 family rooms s£50 d£69.25

HORBURY
Map 16 SE21

The Quarry Inn
70 Quarry Hill WF4 5NF ☎ 01924 272523
Dir: On A642 approx 2.5m from Wakefield
In the hollow of a disused quarry, this creeper-clad pub is
built with stone actually quarried here, as are the bar fronts.
Just beyond the main road outside are the River Calder and
the Calder and Hebble Navigation. A good range of simple
but appetising dishes in the bar and restaurant includes
cottage pie, steaks, gammon, fish and chips, liver and onions,
and Yorkshire puddings with various fillings.
OPEN: 12.30-11 (Sun 12-4, 7-10.30) **BAR MEALS:** L served all
week 12-2 D served Mon-Sat 5.30-8.30 Av main course £3.99
RESTAURANT: L served all week 12-2 D served Mon-Sat 5.30-8.30
Av 3 course fixed price £5 🍴: Marstons 🍺: Marston's Pedigree,
Camerons Creamy, Mansfield Smooth. **FACILITIES:** Dogs allowed
Food, water, shelter **NOTES:** Parking 36 No credit cards

KIRKBURTON
Map 16 SE11

The Woodman Inn ◆◆◆◆ ℉
Thunderbridge HD8 0PX ☎ 01484 605778 🖷 01484 604110
e-mail: thewoodman@connectfree.co.uk
web: www.woodman-inn.co.uk
Stone-built 19th-century inn located in the hamlet of
Thunderbridge and surrounded by glorious countryside. The
bars, complete with pool and darts, are popular with locals
and walkers alike. The same menu is offered throughout, but
customers can choose the pub atmosphere downstairs or the
more sophisticated ambience of the restaurant upstairs. Menu
includes king prawns in Thai green curry sauce; braised liver
and onions; and pan-fried cod supreme. Fish menu on Fridays.
OPEN: 12-11 (Sun 12-10.30) **BAR MEALS:** L served all week 12-3
D served all week 6-9 (Sun 12-6) Av main course £6.50
RESTAURANT: L served all week 12-2 D served all week 7-9 (Sun
12-6) Av 3 course à la carte £16 🍺: Taylors Best Bitter, Tetleys Bitter.
℉: 13 **FACILITIES:** Tables overlooking stream, patio at front Dogs
allowed Drinks bowls outside **NOTES:** Parking 50
ROOMS: 12 bedrooms en suite 2 family rooms s£45 d£60
(◆◆◆◆) No children overnight

LEEDS
Map 19 SE23

Whitelocks ℉
Turks Head Yard, Briggate LS1 6HB
☎ 0113 2453950 🖷 0113 2423368
Dir: Next to Marks & Spencer in Briggate
Leeds' oldest pub, first licensed in 1715, was originally the
Turks Head. The current name comes from the family who
owned it for 90 years up till 1944. Classic features include a
long bar with polychrome tiles, stained-glass windows and
advertising mirrors. Look out for the Dickensian-style bar at
the end of the yard. There are four guest ales in addition to
the regulars, and popular traditional pub food like sausage,
mash and chips, steak pie and Yorkshire puddings. Recent
change of ownership.
OPEN: 11-11 (Sun 12-10.30) **BAR MEALS:** L served all week 12-7
D served all week Sun 12-6 Av main course £5.78
RESTAURANT: L served all week 12-3 D served Mon-Sat 5-7 (Sun
close 4) 🍴: 🍺: Scottish Courage Theakston Best, Old Peculier &
John Smiths, Guest Ales every week. ℉: 16 **FACILITIES:** Garden:
Beer garden, sun trap Dogs allowed Water

Pick of the Pubs

HALIFAX – WEST YORKSHIRE

Shibden Mill Inn

In its long existence this whitewashed, 17th-century free house has been both a mill (predictably enough) and a farm. There was even a boating lake where the top car park is now. It lies in the steep-sided Shibden Dale, through which the Red Beck, once the driving force for the mill-wheel, rushes noisily.

Sympathetic renovations by the owners have ensured it retains its original charm and character, especially in the cosy, friendly bar with its oak beams, rafters and open fires, and the intimate candlelit restaurant. Colours throughout are rich without being overpowering - quite an achievement. Shibden Mill is one of the beers that could accompany a bar meal of black pudding potato cake, lamb's liver with mash and caramelised onions, a tomato and mozzarella salad, or even a chunky egg mayonnaise and rocket sandwich. In the restaurant the candlelight shadows flicker on the crisp white tablecloths to help provide the perfect setting for a meal chosen from the contemporary British menu, and an accompanying wine from the extensive list. Start maybe with a Whitby crab salad, a twice-baked cheese soufflé, or tea-smoked Gressingham duck; then continue with stuffed leg of rabbit with smoked bacon, tarragon, prunes and pinenuts; pumpkin risotto cakes; or halibut with Coniston white cheese glaze, parsley mash and Avruga caviar. And, to finish, chocolate almond and rum cake, or perhaps stem ginger sponge pudding, could be possibilities. If you can't face the drive home, you could always stop over in one of the twelve individually decorated en suite bedrooms.

OPEN: 12-2.30 5.30-11
BAR MEALS: L served all week 12-2 D served all week 6-9.30 (Sun 12-7.30) Av main course £12.95
RESTAURANT: L served all week 12-2 D served all week 6-9.30 (Sun 12-7.30) Av 3 course à la carte £22.50
🍺: Free House
🍺: John Smiths, Theakston XB, Shibden Mill. ♀: 12
FACILITIES: Child facs Garden: Walled garden with heated patio
NOTES: Parking 200
ROOMS: 12 bedrooms en suite s£68 d£85

♦♦♦♦ ⊛⊛ ♀ Map 19 SE02
Shibden Mill Fold HX3 7UL
☎ 01422 365840
🖹 01422 362971
📧 shibdenmillinn@zoom.co.uk

LINTON

Map 16 SE34

The Windmill Inn ♀
Main St LS22 4HT ☎ 01937 582209 📠 01937 587518
Dir: From A1 exit at Tadcaster/Otley junction and follow Otley signs. In Collingham follow signs for Linton

A coaching inn since the 18th century, the building actually dates back to the 14th century, and originally housed the owner of the long-disappeared windmill. Stone walls, antique settles, log fires, oak beams and lots of brass set the scene in which to enjoy good bar food prepared by enthusiastic licensees. Expect the likes of chicken breast on mustard mash with onion jus, sea bass on pepper mash with tomato and basil sauce, baked salmon on Italian risotto, or king prawns in lime and chilli butter. While you're there, ask to take a look at the local history scrapbook.
OPEN: 11.30-3 5-11 (Summer, Sat, Sun open all day)
BAR MEALS: L served all week 12-2 D served Mon-Sat 5.30-9 Sun 12-3.30 **RESTAURANT:** L served all week 12-2 D served Mon-Sat 5.30-9 Sun 12-3.30 🍴: Scottish Courage 🍺: Scottish Courage John Smith's & Theakston Best, Daleside, Greene King Ruddles County.
♀: 12 **FACILITIES:** Garden: Quiet secluded garden with beautiful view Dogs allowed Water **NOTES:** Parking 60

MYTHOLMROYD

Map 19 SE02

Shoulder of Mutton ♀
New Rd HX7 5DZ ☎ 01422 883165
Dir: A646 Halifax to Todmorden, in Mytholmroyd on B6138, opp station
Award-winning Pennines pub situated in the village where Poet Laureate Ted Hughes was born. The rugged beauty of the landscape provided much of the inspiration for his work. The pub's reputation for real ales and hearty fare using locally sourced ingredients remains intact after more than 30 years of ownership. The menu ranges from vegetarian quiche and battered haddock to Cumberland sausages and beef in ale.
OPEN: 11.30-3 7-11 (Sat 11.30-11, Sun 12-10.30)
BAR MEALS: L served all week 11.3-2 D served Wed-Mon 7-8.15 Sun 12-10.30 Av main course £3.99 **RESTAURANT:** L served all week 11.30-2 D served Wed-Mon 7-8.15 🍺: Black Sheep, Boddingtons, Flowers, Taylor Landlord. ♀: 10 **FACILITIES:** Child facs Garden: Riverside garden with floral display, seating Dogs allowed Water, Treats **NOTES:** Parking 25 No credit cards

NEWALL

Map 19 SE14

The Spite Inn
LS21 2EY ☎ 01943 463063
'There's nowt but malice and spite at these pubs', said a local who one day did the unthinkable - drank in both village hostelries, renowned for their feuding landlords. The Traveller's Rest, which became The Malice, is long closed, but the Roebuck has survived as The Spite. Salmon mornay,

continued

haddock, scampi, steak and ale pie, ostrich fillet and speciality sausages are likely to be on offer.
OPEN: 12-3 6-11 (Thu-Sat 12-11, Sun 12-10.30)
BAR MEALS: L served all week 12-2 D served Tue-Thu 6-8.30, Fri-Sat 6-9 6-9 Dinner Tue-Thu 6-8.30, Fri-Sat 6-9, Sun 12-5 Av main course £6 **RESTAURANT:** L served all week 11.30-2 D served Tue-Thu 6-8.30, Sat 6-9 Sun 12-5 🍴: Unique Pub Co 🍺: John Smiths Smooth, Tetleys, Copper Dragon, plus guest ales.
FACILITIES: Garden: Food served outside. Lawned area Dogs allowed Water provided **NOTES:** Parking 50

RIPPONDEN

Map 16 SE01

Old Bridge Inn ♀
Priest Ln HX6 4DF ☎ 01422 822595
Dir: 5m from Halifax in village centre by church

A fine example of vernacular architecture, the award-winning Old Bridge still boasts wattle and daub, a splendid cruck frame and remnants of an old bread oven. Records show that in the early 14th century it was the home of 'Robert of Brigge of Soland', a clothier whose family owned a small fulling mill on the opposite bank of the River Ryburn. Imaginative menu offers the likes of Italian chicken casserole, smoked haddock and spinach pancakes, wild boar and herb sausages, and oven-baked salmon fillet. Impressive, regularly changing wine list and real fires in winter.
OPEN: 12-3 5.30-11 **BAR MEALS:** L served Mon-Sun 12-2 D served Mon-Fri 6.30-9.30 Av main course £7.25 🍴: Free House 🍺: Timothy Taylor Landlord, Golden Best, & Best Bitter, Black Sheep Best. ♀: 12 **FACILITIES:** Garden: Riverside terrace.
NOTES: Parking 40

> Most of the pubs in this guide book pride themselves on the quality of their food. This may take a little time to prepare

SHELLEY   Map 16 SE21

Pick of the Pubs

The Three Acres Inn 🐟 ♀
HD8 8LR ☎ 01484 602606 📠 01484 608411
e-mail: 3acres@globalnet.co.uk
Dir: *From Huddersfield take A629 then B6116, take L turn for village*
With its commanding Pennine views, reputation for
quality food and welcoming atmosphere, this turn-of-the-
century (the last one, that is) drovers' inn has been
owned for over thirty years by Neil Trulove and Brian
Orme. Their food, available in both the bar and
restaurant, is a successful fusion of traditional English with
influences from around the globe. Starters may be crispy
spiced lamb samosa with spinach couscous and mint
raita; or smoked haddock kedgeree crêpe in fresh
coriander and light curry cream. Main courses are equally
eclectic, as in monkfish and king prawn saffron risotto
with fennel, parsley and sweet pimiento; hot gratin of
Goan lobster with cucumber and lime salad; guinea-fowl
pot roasted with cider and Calvados in a rustic sauce; and
roast teriyaki tofu with glazed greens and shiitake
noodles. Sandwiches come with very tasty fillings. 'The
Grocer' in-house delicatessen sells top-notch European
and British produce and restaurant favourites.

The Three Acres Inn

OPEN: 12-3 7-11 (Sat 7-11 only) Closed: 25 Dec-3 Jan
BAR MEALS: L served all week 12-2 D served all week 7-9.45
RESTAURANT: L served Sun-Fri 12-2 D served all week 7-9.45
🍺: Free House 🍺: Timothy Taylor Landlord, Black Sheep, Tetley
Smooth, Tetley Bitter. ♀: 9 **FACILITIES:** Garden: Covered
terrace **NOTES:** Parking 100

SOWERBY BRIDGE   Map 16 SE02

Pick of the Pubs

The Millbank at Millbank ♀
HX6 3DY ☎ 01422 825588 📠 01422 822080
e-mail: themillbank@yahoo.co.uk
Dir: *A58 from Sowerby Bridge to Ripponden, turn right at Triangle*
Located in the Pennine conservation village of Mill Bank,
in the Ryburn Valley, is this traditional stone-built free
house and restaurant. A range of real ales is served in the
cosy stone-flagged Tap Room, whilst the main wooden-
floored bar has more of a wine bar feel. The dining room
chairs are recycled mill and chapel seats - complete with
prayer-book racks - and the French windows open to
stunning views of the gardens and valley beyond.
Adventurous menus bring a continental twist to traditional

English cooking. Starters like venison cottage pie; roast
scallops with carrot and ginger cannelloni; and parmesan
gnocchi, roast pimento and aubergine salad, are followed
by olive and feta samosa, roast red onion, cucumber
pickle and tomato butter; deep fried haddock in beer
batter; and roast chicken, onion tart Tatin.
OPEN: 12-3 5.30-11 (Sun 12-10.30 Closed Mon lunch) Closed:
First 2 weeks in Oct, 1st wk Jan **BAR MEALS:** L served
Tues-Sun 12-2.30 D served all week 6-9.30 Sun 12.30-4.30, 6-8
Av main course £12.95 **RESTAURANT:** L served Tues-Sun
12-2.30 D served all week 6-9.30 Sun 12.30-4.30, 6-8 Av 3 course
à la carte £24 Av 2 course fixed price £11.95 🍺: Free House
🍺: Timothy Taylor Landlord, Carlsberg-Tetley Tetley Bitter. ♀: 14
FACILITIES: Garden: Stunning views, seating, heating Dogs
allowed in Tap Room & garden
See Pub Walk on page 583

THORNTON   Map 19 SE03

Pick of the Pubs

Ring O'Bells ♀
212 Hilltop Rd BD13 3QL ☎ 01274 832296 📠 01274 831707
e-mail: enquiries@theringobells.com
web: www.theringobells.com
See Pick of the Pubs on opposite page

TODMORDEN   Map 18 SD92

Staff of Life ♦♦♦
550 Burnley Rd OL14 8JF ☎ 01706 812929 📠 01706 813773
e-mail: staffoflife@btconnect.com
Dir: *On A646 between Halifax & Burnley*

Once at the heart of a thriving mill community, this quaint
stone-built 1838 inn is set in a deep wooded gorge on the
banks of the river Calder amidst typically spectacular Pennine
scenery. Eagle's Crag, also known as the Witches' Horse-
Block, opposite the pub, is where witches are said to have
flown to Pendle Hill. Impossible to do justice to the eclectic
variety of food on offer, which is nonetheless 'not
microwaved grub for the masses'. The tapas blackboard is
popular (usually about 15 dishes), or you can choose from
Mexican and Indian menus, as well as steaks and specials.
OPEN: 7-11 Sat-Sun 12-3, 7-11 Closed: 25 Dec
BAR MEALS: L served Sat-Sun 12-2.30 D served Tue-Sun 7-9
🍺: Free House 🍺: Taylor Landlord, Golden Best, Best Bitter, Ram
Tam. **FACILITIES:** Garden: Residents garden at rear, patio at front
Dogs allowed Water provided **NOTES:** Parking 26
ROOMS: 3 bedrooms en suite 1 family room s£35 d£45

continued

Pick of the Pubs

THORNTON – WEST YORKSHIRE

Ring O'Bells

This Pennine country pub and restaurant has dramatic moorland views stretching up to 30 miles on a clear day. The Ring O'Bells is set high on the hills, near to the Brontë village of Howarth though the Brontë sisters were actually born here in Thornton, where their father was the local curate.

The building is a conversion of a Wesleyan chapel and two former mill workers' cottages, and the ghost of a former priest is rumoured to still be in residence. The atmospheric bar serves traditional hand-pulled ales and an interesting selection of malt whiskies, speciality liqueurs and wines by the glass. The elegant Brontë Restaurant is modern and contemporary, with full air conditioning. A conservatory with pretty valley views runs the whole length of the restaurant, and makes the perfect spot for an aperitif before dinner or coffee after. The pub has a great reputation for its food. The innovative menu focuses on British dishes with occasional European and Eastern inspirations, and there's also a frequently changing daily specials list. You could start with roast belly pork on haggis mash, or sardine crostini, then follow up with pan-fried lamb's liver and bacon on spring onion mash; or a fricassé of queen scallops, salmon, bacon and white wine. The pies are frequent prize winners, and some would say the best steak and kidney pudding in the country can be found here. Proprietors Ann and Clive Preston pride themselves on the pub's warm brand of Yorkshire hospitality.

OPEN: 11.30-3.30 5.30-11 (Sun 12-4.30, 6.15-10.30) Closed: 25 Dec
BAR MEALS: L served all week 12-2 D served all week 5.30-9.30 Mon-Fri, 6.15-9.30 Sat-Sun Av main course £9.95
RESTAURANT: L served all week 12-2 D served all week 7-9.30 (Sun 6.15-8.45) Av 3 course à la carte £19.50 Av 2 course fixed price £8.95 4 course fixed price £19.95
🛢: Free House
🍺: Scottish Courage John Smiths & Courage Directors, Black Sheep & Black Sheep Special. 🍷: 10
NOTES: Parking 25

🍷   Map 19 SE03
212 Hilltop Rd BD13 3QL
☎ 01274 832296
📠 01274 831707
📧 enquiries@theringobells.com
🌐 www.theringobells.com
Dir: From M62 take A58 for 5m, right onto A644. 4.5m follow Denholme signs, on to Well Head Rd into Hilltop Rd

England

WAKEFIELD
Map 16 SE32

Pick of the Pubs

Kaye Arms Inn & Brasserie ♀
29 Wakefield Rd, Grange Moor WF4 4BG
☎ 01924 848385 📠 01924 848977
Dir: On A642 between Huddersfield & Wakefield

This is a family-run dining pub with a refreshing attitude towards food that is matched by good cooking skills. Handy for visiting the popular National Coal Mining Museum and the glorious moorland country of West Yorkshire, this well-established inn offers an imaginative bar menu which has something to suit most palates. Expect mature cheddar cheese soufflé (a house speciality), grilled marinated chicken sandwich and warm smoked salmon on potato rösti, topped with a poached egg and sauce béarnaise. Those looking for something more substantial might like to try grilled rib-eye steak garni; poached salmon haddock with poached egg, white wine sauce, beetroot, spinach and new potatoes; confit of large duck leg with French-style peas and potatoes dauphinoise; or home-made provençal vegetable cannelloni with parmesan cream and tomato fondue. To follow, try griottine crème brûlée; strawberry pavlova with fresh cream and butterscotch sauce; and tiramisu with biscotti. Impressive and extensive wine list.
OPEN: 11.30-3 7-11 Closed: Dec 25-Jan 2
BAR MEALS: L served Tue-Sun 12-2 D served Tue-Sun 7.15-9.30 (Sat 6.30-10) Av main course £12 **RESTAURANT:** L served Tue-Sun 12-2 D served Tue-Sun 7.15-9.30 (Sat 6.30-10) Av 3 course à la carte £24 🍺: Free House 🍺: Scottish Courage John Smiths, Theakstons Best, Guinness. ♀: 15 **NOTES:** Parking 50

WIDDOP
Map 18 SD93

Pack Horse Inn
HX7 7AT ☎ 01422 842803 📠 01422 842803
Dir: Off A646 & A6033
The Pack Horse is a converted Laithe farmhouse dating from the 1600s, complete with welcoming open fires. A beautiful location just 300 yards from the Pennine Way makes it popular with walkers, but equally attractive are the home-cooked meals, good range of real ales and fabulous choice of 130 single malt whiskies. Please note that from October to Easter the pub is only open in the evening.
OPEN: 12-3 (Oct-Etr closed wk day lunch) 7-11 Oct-Easter Closed lunchtimes during the week **BAR MEALS:** L served all week 12-2 D served Tue-Sun 7-10 **RESTAURANT:** D served Sat 7-9.30 Av 3 course à la carte £22 🍺: Free House 🍺: Thwaites, Theakston XB, Morland Old Speckled Hen, Blacksheep Bitter. **FACILITIES:** Dogs allowed **NOTES:** Parking 40

CHANNEL ISLANDS

GUERNSEY

CASTEL
Map 24

Hotel Hougue du Pommier ★★★ ◉ 🍽 ♀
Hougue Du Pommier Rd GY5 7FQ
☎ 01481 256531 📠 01481 256260
e-mail: hotel@houguedupommier.guernsey.net
web: www.hotelhouguedupommier.com
Cooking on the fire over seasoned wood embers - 'feu du bois'- in the large granite fireplace is one of the attractions at this lovely 18th-century inn which stands in ten acres of orchards. Expect a varied and imaginative choice of dishes, including perhaps tender chicken breast, Barnsley-style double chump chop with mint leaves and garden rosemary, and local scallops with citrus lime and green ginger marinade.
OPEN: 10.30-11.45 **BAR MEALS:** L served all week 12-2.15 D served all week 6.30-9 Av main course £6.45 **RESTAURANT:** D served all week 6.30-9 Av 3 course à la carte £24.50 Av 5 course fixed price £19.75 🍺: John Smith's, Extra Smooth, Guernsey Best Bitter. ♀: 8 **FACILITIES:** Child facs Children's licence Garden: Ten acres, pitch & putt, BBQ, swimming pool **NOTES:** Parking 60 **ROOMS:** 43 bedrooms en suite 5 family rooms s£36 d£72

JERSEY

GOREY
Map 24

Castle Green Gastropub 🍽 ♀
La Route de la Cote JE3 6DR ☎ 01534 853103 📠 01534 853103
e-mail: castlegreenpub@hotmail.com
A superbly located pub overlooking Gorey harbour and, in turn, overlooked by dramatic Mont Orgueil Castle. The views from the wooden sun terrace are breathtaking. An imaginative menu offers pan-Pacific-style dishes like Moroccan spiced lamb shoulder; Thai chicken burger; sushi and sashimi plate with pickled ginger and wasabi; along with fresh fillets of the day's catch , and summer seafood platter.
OPEN: 11-11 Open 7 days Jun-Sep Closed: 2 weeks early Jan **BAR MEALS:** L served all week 12-2.30 D served all week 6-9 Winter no lunch Mon, no dinner Sun and Mon everning Av main course £7.95 **RESTAURANT:** L served all week 12-2.30 D served all week 6-9 Av 3 course à la carte £16 🍺: Directors, Fosters, John Smith Extra Smooth. ♀: 8 **FACILITIES:** Child facs Wooden terrace **NOTES:** Parking 10 ⊗

ST AUBIN
Map 24

Old Court House Inn 🍽
St Aubin's Harbour JE3 8AB ☎ 01534 746433 📠 745103
e-mail: ochstaubins@jerseymail.co.uk
Dir: Telephone for directions
This elegant inn, romantically set above St Aubins harbour, has several bars and a restaurant. Local seafood is plentiful, including freshly picked crab tian; or sea bass served on a risotto of asparagus and wild mushroom. Carnivores are not neglected, with pan-fried calves' liver served with pancetta and veal jus; or chateaubriand to share. There are plenty of sunny spots for alfresco dining, and a glorious conservatory maximises light even in less clement weather.
OPEN: 11-11.30 **BAR MEALS:** L served Mon-Sun 12.30-2.30 D served Mon-Sun 7.30-10 **RESTAURANT:** L served all week 12.30-2.30 D served all week 7.30-10 🍺: Free House 🍺: Directors, Theakstons, John Smith, Jersey Brewery. **FACILITIES:** Floral terrace

ST BRELADE
Map 24

La Pulente Hotel ⚲
La Route de la Pulente JE3 8HG
☎ 01534 744487 ▦ 01534 498846
Dir: West side of the Island, 5m for St Helier
Amazing sea views, open fires on cold winter days and an inviting atmosphere are promised at this welcoming pub. The artistic bar and rustic restaurant are complemented in summer by a balcony and terrace, where freshly-caught fish can be enjoyed along with choices from the specials menu. Thai vegetable curry, home-made steak and ale pie, lobster and prawn salad, and braised lamb shank are typical.
OPEN: 11-11 **BAR MEALS:** L served all week 12-2.15 D served Mon-Sat 6-9 Sun 12-2.45 Av main course £7.50
RESTAURANT: L served all week 12-2.15 D served Mon-Sat 6-9 Sun 12-2.45 Av 3 course à la carte £15 🍴: 🍺: Bass Bitter, Theakstons Best, Breda. ⚲: 11 **NOTES:** Parking 30

ST MARTIN
Map 24

Royal Hotel 🕊 ⚲
La Grande Route de Faldouet JE3 6UG
☎ 01534 856289 ▦ 01534 857298
e-mail: johnbarker@jerseymail.co.uk
Dir: 2m from Five Oaks rdbt, towards St Martin. By St Martins Church

A friendly atmosphere, value for money, and great food and drink are the hallmarks of this friendly local in the heart of St Martin. Roaring log fires welcome winter visitors, and there's a sunny beer garden to relax in during the summer months. Among the traditional home-made favourites are steak and ale pie, fresh grilled trout, and vegetarian lasagne. Ploughman's lunches, filled jacket potatoes, grills and children's choices are also on offer.
OPEN: 9.30-11.30 (Sun 11-11.30) **BAR MEALS:** L served all week 12-2.15 D served Mon-Sat 6-8.30 Sun 12-2.30 (Winter), 6-8.30 (Summer) Av main course £7.10 **RESTAURANT:** L served all week 12-2.15 D served Mon-Sat 6-8.30 Sun 12-2.30 (Winter), 6-8.30 (Summer) Av 3 course à la carte £15 🍺: Fosters, John Smiths Smooth, Theakstons cool, Guiness. ⚲: 9 **FACILITIES:** Child facs Garden: Beer garden, large patio **NOTES:** Parking 80

ISLE OF MAN

PEEL
Map 24 SC28

The Creek Inn ⚲
Station Place IM5 1AT ☎ 01624 842216 ▦ 01624 677066
e-mail: the-creek-inn-iom@yahoo.co.uk
This family-run free house overlooks the harbour at Peel on the picturesque west coast of the island. A good choice of food ranges through filled baguettes, children's favourites, vegetarian dishes and three-course dinners. Look out for Manx queenies, fresh local crab and lobster, plus popular home-made curry and lasagne. Parking is easy and there is lots of outside seating overlooking the harbour.
OPEN: 10-12 10-1 (Sun-Thu 10-12, Fri-Sat 10-1)
BAR MEALS: L served all week 10-9.30 D served all week Av main course £5 🍴: Free House 🍺: Okells Bitter, Scottish Courage John Smith's, London Pride. ⚲: 8 **FACILITIES:** Children's licence Outside seating for up to 150 **NOTES:** Parking 8

PORT ERIN
Map 24 SC26

Falcon's Nest Hotel ★★ 🕊 ⚲
The Promenade, Station Rd IM9 6AF
☎ 01624 834077 ▦ 01624 835370
e-mail: falconsnest@enterprise.net
web: www.falconsnesthotel.co.uk
Dir: Telephone for directions
Popular local hotel in a prime position overlooking Port Erin Bay, affording the most spectacular views particularly from the newly built conservatory dining room. The lounge and saloon bars serve local real ales, over 150 whiskies, meals and snacks, with a carte menu in the hotel restaurant. Dishes range from lunchtime burgers, melts and jackets to fresh local crab salad, grilled Manx lamb chops and a Sunday carvery.
OPEN: 11-11 (Fri-Sat-11-12) **BAR MEALS:** L served Mon-Sun 12-2 D served Mon-Sun 6-9.30 (6-8 Sun) **RESTAURANT:** L served Mon-Sun 12-2 D served Mon-Sun 6-9.30 (6-8 Sun) 🍴: Free House 🍺: Okells, Bushys, Bass, Old Speckled Hen. ⚲: 25
FACILITIES: Children's licence Garden: Benches on verandah Dogs allowed Blankets, water **NOTES:** Parking 20
ROOMS: 35 bedrooms en suite 8 family rooms

Why not search online?

Visit **www.theAA.com** and search around 8000 inspected and rated hotels and B&Bs in Great Britain and Ireland. Then contact the establishment direct by clicking the 'Make a Booking' button...

...it's as easy as that!

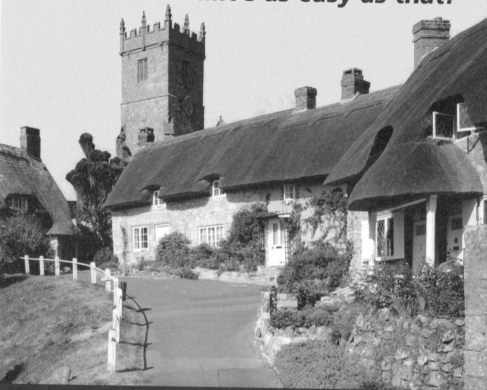

Whatever your preference, we have the place for you. From a farm cottage to a city centre hotel — we have them all.

AA

Scotland

Pub of the Year for Scotland

The Black Bull

Lauder

(see p619)

SCOTLAND

ABERDEEN CITY

ABERDEEN   Map 23 NJ90

Old Blackfriars ♀
52 Castle Gate AB11 5BB ☎ 01224 581922 ▤ 01224 582153
A traditional city centre pub built on the site of property
owned by Blackfriars Dominican monks-hence the name. The
basement is possibly the remains of the old church which
once stretched over the top of Marischal Street. The menu
features such dishes as bangers and mash, fresh battered
haddock, Milanese chicken and beef au poivre. Good choice
of burgers and tempting grills, including Friars' Feast.
OPEN: 11-12 (Sun 12.30-12, Fri-Sat 11-1am) Closed: Dec 25 & Jan 1
BAR MEALS: L served all week 11-8.45 D served all week (Sun
12.30-8.45, Fri-Sat 11-7.45) ⊜: Belhaven ◀: Belhaven St Andrews,
Caledonian IPA, Caledonian 80/-, Inveralmond 'Ossian and guest ales.
♀: 12 **FACILITIES:** Children's licence

Prince of Wales ♀
7 St Nicholas Ln AB10 1HF ☎ 01224 640597
e-mail: wales1881.fsbusiness.co.uk
Dir: City centre

Historic city centre pub, dating back to 1850 and boasting the
longest bar in Aberdeen, extending to 60 feet. Originally
known as the Café Royal, the pub was renamed in 1856. Wide
range of real ales, a selection of freshly made soups, filled
baguettes and baked potatoes, and home-cooked food that
might include breaded haddock, chicken pie, baked potatoes,
roast pork with apricot stuffing and local turbot.
OPEN: 10-12 (Sunday 12-11) Closed: Dec 25 + Jan 1
BAR MEALS: L served all week 11.30-2.30 food until 4 at wknds
Av main course £5 ⊜: Free House ◀: Theakstons Old Peculiar,
Caledonian 80/-, Courage Directors, & Guest beers.

ABERDEENSHIRE

BALMEDIE   Map 23 NJ91

The Cock and Bull Bar and Restaurant NEW ▷◇ ♀
Ellon Rd, Blairton AB23 8XY ☎ 01358 743249 ▤ 01358 742466
e-mail: info@thecockandbull.co.uk
Dir: 11m N of Aberdeen on Ellon rd (A90)
Originally a drovers' inn, the Cock & Bull is over two hundred
years old. The present owner has turned it into a smart
restaurant attracting a strong following from as far as
Aberdeen, 10 miles away. A youthful team of six chefs use
local produce to create starters of Scottish salmon with
mango and avocado salsa, main dishes of fillet of
Aberdeenshire beef chargrilled with horseradish and potato
continued

dauphinoise; and perhaps chocolate mocha fondant to finish.
OPEN: 10am-1am **BAR MEALS:** L served all week 11.30-11
D served all week 6-9.30 Av main course £12
RESTAURANT: L served all week 11.30-11 D served all week 5-9.30
Av 3 course à la carte £25 ◀: Directores Ale, Guiness, McEwans 80/,
Tennents. ♀: 8 **FACILITIES:** Child facs Children's licence Garden:
Paved area with grass Dogs allowed allowed in at suitable times
NOTES: Parking 70

MARYCULTER   Map 23 NO89

Old Mill Inn
South Deeside Rd AB12 5FX ☎ 01224 733212 ▤ 01224 732884
e-mail: Info@oldmillinn.co.uk
Dir: 5m W of Aberdeen on B9077
This delightful family-run country inn stands on the edge of
the River Dee, just over 5 miles from Aberdeen city centre. A
former mill house, the 18th-century granite building has been
tastefully modernised to include a non-smoking restaurant
and seven en-suite bedrooms. The finest Scottish ingredients
feature on the menu, in dishes like supreme of halibut;
chicken with Portlethen haggis; and chargrilled lamb cutlets.
OPEN: 11-11 **BAR MEALS:** L served all week 12-2 D served all
week 5.30-9.30 **RESTAURANT:** L served all week 12-2 D served all
week 5.30-9.30 Av 3 course à la carte £17 Av 2 course fixed price
£5.50 ⊜: Free House ◀: Interbrew Bass, Caledonian Deuchers IPA,
Timothy Taylor, Landlord. **FACILITIES:** Garden: Food served
outdoors, patio **NOTES:** Parking 100 **ROOMS:** 7 bedrooms
en suite 1 family room s£45 d£55 (★★★)

NETHERLEY   Map 23 NO89

Pick of the Pubs

The Lairhillock Inn ♀
AB39 3QS ☎ 01569 730001 ▤ 01569 731175
e-mail: lairhillock@breathemail.net
web: www.lairhillock.co.uk
Dir: From Aberdeen take A90. Right at Durris turn

Set in beautiful Deeside, yet only 15 minutes drive from
Aberdeen, the Lairhillock is a 200-year-old former
coaching inn. Real ales in the bar and real fires in the
lounge keep out the winter chill, as do the bar lunches and
suppers served daily. Dishes are robust and use fresh,
quality, local produce. Both bar and restaurant menus are
well thought-out with blackboard specials chalked up
daily. Try the grilled wood pigeon salad with smoked
bacon, toasted pine kernels and vinaigrette, or the locally
smoked salmon with quails' eggs and horseradish crème
fraîche. Main courses include medallions of venison
layered with peppered potatoes and served with wild
mushrooms and a port and thyme jus or chicken supreme
continued

stuffed with ceps and caramelised shallots and served with a red wine and tarragon juice. Puddings could be the formidable Crynoch dessert platter which includes sticky toffee pudding, chocolate terrine, praline ice cream and vacherin with berries. The staff are attentive and the atmosphere is welcoming.
OPEN: 11-2 5-11 (Fri 5-12, Sat 11-12, Sun 11-11) Closed: 25-26 Dec, 1-2 Jan **BAR MEALS:** L served all week 12-2 D served all week 6-9.30 (Fri & Sat 6-10, Sun 5.30-9) Av main course £8 **RESTAURANT:** L served Sun 12-1.30 D served Wed-Mon 7-9.30 ☺: Free House ◀: Timothy Taylor Landlord,Courage Directors, Isle of Skye Brews. ♀: 7 **FACILITIES:** Garden: Small patio in garden **NOTES:** Parking 100

OLDMELDRUM   Map 23 NJ82

The Redgarth ♀
Kirk Brae AB51 0DJ ☎ 01651 872353
Dir: On A947
Family-run inn with an attractive garden offering magnificent views of Bennachie and the surrounding countryside. Cask-conditioned ales and fine wines are served along with dishes prepared on the premises using fresh local produce. A typical menu offers the likes of sirloin steak garni, deep fried fillet of haddock, chicken Maryland, rack of lamb with herb stuffing, venison MacDuff, and cashew nut roast. Delicious puddings.
OPEN: 11-2.30 5-11 (Fri-Sat -11.45) Closed: Dec 25-26 Jan 1-3 **BAR MEALS:** L served all week 12-2 D served all week 5-9 (Fri-Sat 9.30) Av main course £7.50 **RESTAURANT:** L served all week 12-2 D served all week 5-9 (Fri-Sat 5-9.30) ☺: Free House ◀: Inveralmond Thrappledouser, Caledonian Deuchers IPA, Taylor Landlord, Isle of Skye Red Cullin. ♀: 8 **FACILITIES:** Child facs Children's licence Garden: Beer garden,Outdoor eating Dogs allowed Water **NOTES:** Parking 60

STONEHAVEN   Map 23 NO88

Marine Hotel 🐟 ♀
9/10 Shorehead AB39 2JY ☎ 01569 762155 📠 01569 766691
Dir: 15m S of Aberdeen on A90
Ironically, this harbour-side bar was built from the remains of Dunnottar Castle as a temperance hotel in the 19th century. A number of 500-year-old gargoyles are visible on the front. A choice of six real ales is offered - 800 different brews over the years - including Dunnottar Ale especially brewed for the establishment. There are also around a hundred malts at the bar. Seasonal dishes feature game, seafood and fish, maybe venison rump with mustard mash, dressed crab with coriander cream, and herring in oatmeal.
OPEN: 10-12 Closed: 25 Dec, 1 Jan **BAR MEALS:** L served all week 12-2 D served all week 5-8 (Fri 5-9, Sat & Sun 12-9) Av main course £8 **RESTAURANT:** L served all week 12-2 D served all week 5-9 Av 3 course à la carte £16 ☺: Free House ◀: Timothy Taylor Landlord, Caledonian Deuchars IPA, Fuller's London Pride, Moorhouses Black Cat. ♀: 7 **FACILITIES:** Dogs allowed

★ Star rating for inspected hotel
   accommodation

Do you have a favourite pub that we have overlooked? Please use the Reader's Report form at the back of this guide to tell us all about it

---

ARDUAINE   Map 20 NM71

Pick of the Pubs

Loch Melfort Hotel ★★★ 🏅🏅 🐟
PA34 4XG ☎ 01852 200233 📠 01852 200214
e-mail: reception@lochmelfort.co.uk
web: www.lochmelfort.co.uk
Dir: On the A816 20m south of Oban
This loch-side hotel has a spectacular location - from the front there are views across Asknish Bay and the Sound of Jura, while behind are woodlands and the magnificent mountains of Argyll. The hotel stands in 26 acres of grounds next to the National Trust's Arduaine Gardens. The Skerry Bar/Bistro specialises in local seafood - langoustines, oysters, scallops, mussels, scampi, lobster, prawns, cod and haddock. The blackboard menu offers an equally tempting list including Dunsyre cheese soufflé, venison and pheasant terrine, duck fillet with chutney, steak and ale pie, and desserts like lemon posset and apple tarte Tatin. The main menu offers salads, pasta, baked potatoes, mains (like breaded triple tail scampi; and Skerry Highland beef burger), and sandwiches and toasties. Apart from beers, the bar stocks a good range of malt whiskies. Accommodation is provided in comfortable en suite rooms, most with views across the bay to the islands of Jura, Shuna and Scarba.
OPEN: 10.30-10.30 (Fri & Sat 10.30-11) Closed: Early Jan & Feb **BAR MEALS:** L served all week 12-2.30 D served all week 6-9 Av main course £7.50 **RESTAURANT:** D served all week 7-9 Av 5 course fixed price £26.50 ☺: Free House ◀: 80/-, Theakstons, Guiness, Miller. **FACILITIES:** Garden: Overlooking the loch, spectacular views Dogs allowed Water **NOTES:** Parking 50 **ROOMS:** 26 bedrooms en suite 2 family rooms s£49 d£78

CLACHAN-SEIL   Map 20 NM71

Pick of the Pubs

Tigh an Truish Inn 🐟
PA34 4QZ ☎ 01852 300242
Dir: 14m S of Oban, take A816, 12m take B844 towards Atlantic Bridge
Loosely translated, Tigh an Truish is Gaelic for 'house of trousers'. After the Battle of Culloden in 1746, kilts were outlawed and anyone caught wearing one was executed. In defiance of this edict the islanders wore their kilts at home. However, if they went to the mainland, they would stop en route at the Tigh an Truish and change into the hated trews before continuing their journey. Handy for good walks and lovely gardens, and particularly popular with tourists and members of the yachting fraternity, the Tigh an Truish offers a good appetising menu based on the best local produce. Home-made seafood pie, moules marinière, salmon steaks, and mussels in garlic cream sauce feature among the fish dishes, while other options might include meat or vegetable lasagne, beef or nut burgers, steak and ale pie, venison in a pepper cream and Drambuie sauce, and chicken curry. Round off your meal by sampling syrup sponge, apple crumble or chocolate puddle pudding.
OPEN: 11-3 5-11 (May-Sept all day) Closed: 25 Dec & Jan 1 **BAR MEALS:** L served all week 12-2 D served all week 6-8.30 Av main course £6 **RESTAURANT:** L served all week 12-2 D served all week 6-8.30 ☺: Free House ◀: Local guest ales changing regularly. **FACILITIES:** Garden: Tables beside the sea in garden with lawn Dogs allowed **NOTES:** Parking 35 No credit cards

Scotland

CRINAN   Map 20 NR79

Pick of the Pubs

Crinan Hotel
PA31 8SR ☎ 01546 830261 ▤ 01546 830292
e-mail: nryan@crinanhotel.com
The hotel, which dates back 200 years, is at the heart of community life in Crinan, a tiny fishing village at the north end of the Crinan Canal, connecting Loch Fyne to the Atlantic Ocean. The location is fabulous with views across the sound of Jura to the islands of Mull and Scharba from the hotel's Westward Restaurant. The Panther Arms and Mainbrace Bar are located at ground floor level, with a patio where guests can sit outside and watch the comings and goings at the sealock. Wherever you choose to eat, the seafood is superb. Dishes from the bar menu include etuvee of Loch Etive mussels mariniere, or warm tart of Loch Crinan scallops with smoked bacon and sun-dried tomatoes. Main courses take in whole Loch Crinan prawns with salad and garlic bread, and roasted best end of Perthshire middle white pork with sautéed black pudding. Starters and main courses are interchangeable. **OPEN:** 11-11 Closed: Xmas & New Year **BAR MEALS:** L served all week 12.30-2.30 D served all week 6.30-8.30
RESTAURANT: 12-2.30 D served all week 7-9 ☺: Free House ◖: Belhaven, Interbrew Worthington Bitter, Tenants Velvet.
FACILITIES: Child facs Children's licence Garden: Patio Dogs allowed Water **NOTES:** Parking 30 ⊗

DUNOON   Map 20 NS17

Coylet Inn ◆◆◆◆
Loch Eck PA23 8SG ☎ 01369 840426 ▤ 01369 840426
e-mail: coylet@btinternet.com web: www.coylet-locheck.co.uk
Dir: 9m N of Dunoon on A815

This friendly 17th-century coaching inn which was used as a location in the BBC ghost film *Blue Boy* starring Emma Thompson is set on the shores of Loch Eck in the Argyll Forest Park, and can be reached by either road or ferry. The valley is good for walking, and a popular attraction is the nearby Benmore Botanical Gardens. The inn prides itself on producing food made from the finest local ingredients. Game terrine or cullen skink make a good start to a meal that may include venison burger, wild mushroom risotto, tuna steak with a cheese and herb crust, or steak and kidney pie. **OPEN:** 11-2.30 5-12 Closed: 25 Dec **BAR MEALS:** L served all week 12-2 D served all week 6-9 **RESTAURANT:** L served all week 12-2 D served all week 7.30-9:30 ☺: Free House ◖: Caledonian Deuchars IPA, Highlander. **FACILITIES:** Garden: Overlooking Loch Eck **NOTES:** Parking 40 **ROOMS:** 4 bedrooms en suite s£45 d£90 No children overnight

KILBERRY   Map 20 NR76

Pick of the Pubs

Kilberry Inn
PA29 6YD ☎ 01880 770223 ▤ 01880 770223
e-mail: relax@kilberryinn.com
Dir: From Lochgilphead take A83 south. Then B8024 signed Kilberry
A traditional Highland building way off the beaten track, on a scenic single-track road with breathtaking views across Loch Coalisport to Gigha and the Paps of Jura. An original 'but 'n' ben' cottage with quarried walls, beams and log fires, the inn was renovated nearly 20 years ago. Today it is renowned for its fine food, which is special enough to encourage travellers to make the long journey. The dining room is warmly welcoming and family friendly, and everything served here, including bread and cakes, preserves and chutneys, is home made. Menu favourites include starters such as warm goat's cheese salad with tomato and balsamic dressing; and Kilmory smoked salmon. Main courses might be medallions of pork in a prune and Armagnac sauce; Craignish salmon with lime and parsley butter; or Ormsary venison and game pie. A range of Scottish bottled beer, and over 30 malt whiskies make the bar a popular place.
OPEN: 11-3 6.30-10.30 Closed: Nov-Easter
BAR MEALS: L served Tue-Sun 12.30-2 D served Tue-Sat 7-8.30 Sun 12.30-1.30 Av main course £6.95 **RESTAURANT:** L served Tue-Sun 12.30-2 D served Tue-Sat 6.30-8.30 12.30-1.30 Av 3 course à la carte £20 ☺: Free House ◖: Arran Blonde, Arran Dark, Fyne Ales Maverick, Tennents Velvet.
FACILITIES: Dogs allowed Water **NOTES:** Parking 8 ⊗

KILFINAN   Map 20 NR97

Kilfinan Hotel Bar
PA21 2EP ☎ 01700 821201 ▤ 01700 821205
e-mail: info@kilfinan.com
Dir: 8m N of Tighnabruaich on B8000
Watch spectacular sunsets over Loch Fyne from a hotel that has been welcoming travellers with traditional Scottish hospitality since the 1700s. Medieval skeletons were recently found under floorboards during refurbishment of the ancient village church next door. The restaurant and bar menus offer the best of local produce, fish and game, and give visitors a true taste of Scotland. Plenty of good walking in the area, as you'd expect, and twitchers will enjoy a chance to spot the sixty or so species that visit the area.
OPEN: 11-2am (Sun 12.30-11) (Winter/Mon-Wed bar open 6pm)
BAR MEALS: L served all week 12-2.30 D served all week 6-8.30 Av main course £6.50 **RESTAURANT:** L served all week 12-2.45 D served all week 7.30-8.30 Av 3 course à la carte £18 ☺: Free House ◖: McEwens 70/-, McEwens 80/-, Fosters.
FACILITIES: Garden: Beer garden, view of loch, terraced Dogs allowed **NOTES:** Parking 40

LOCHGILPHEAD   Map 20 NR88

Pick of the Pubs

Cairnbaan Hotel & Restaurant ★★★ ◉ ▷ ♀
Cairnbaan PA31 8SJ ☎ 01546 603668 ▤ 01546 606045
e-mail: info@cairnbaan.com web: www.cairnbaan.com
See Pick of the Pubs on opposite page

Cairnbaan Hotel & Restaurant

This late 18th-century coaching inn used to be well patronised by fishermen on the Crinan Canal in flat-bottomed boats called puffers, but today's waterborne clientele is almost entirely sailing the waterway for pleasure.

The hotel offers high standards of hospitality and smart accommodation in eleven en suite bedrooms, so there is no excuse for speeding away after a meal or drink when there are so many reasons to linger. It's owned by ex-QE2 catering officer Darren Dobson, ashore now for some 20 years, and wife Christine, a former teacher, who plans the menus and does all the baking. Enjoy a meal in the serene restaurant, where the carte specialises in the use of fresh local produce, notably seafood and game. On the menu, look out for smoked salmon and smoked trout pâté starters, and for mains including pan-fried breast of pheasant on sautéed cabbage and bacon with plum and sage glaze; lobster served thermidor, or cold with mayonnaise; fillet of halibut with pink peppercorns and lemon hollandaise; and Cairnbaan fish and seafood stew with a homemade garlic baguette. Really popular is a good old-fashioned pint of langoustines with home-made granary bread and lime mayonnaise. Daily specials might include loin of tuna with pesto sauce; wild mushroom stroganoff; or tenderloin of pork in sweet ginger. Lighter meals in the lounge bar and conservatory include chicken stuffed with haggis. From nearby Oban there are sailings to Mull, Tiree, and Colonsay among other islands, and Inveraray Castle is well worth a visit, as is Dunadd Fort where the ancient kings of Scotland were crowned.

OPEN: 11-11
BAR MEALS: L served all week 12-2.30 D served all week 6-9.30 Av main course £9
RESTAURANT: D served all week 6-9.30
⌂: Free House
◖: Local Ales. ♀: 8
FACILITIES: Garden: Patio area Dogs allowed in the garden only
NOTES: Parking 50
ROOMS: 12 bedrooms en suite s£72.50 d£125

★★★ ⊚ ⤙ ♀   Map 20
NR88
Cairnbaan PA31 8SJ
☎ 01546 603668
🖹 01546 606045
📧 info@cairnbaan.com
ⓦ www.cairnbaan.com
Dir: 2m N, take A816 from Lochgilphead, hotel off B841

Scotland

Pick of the Pubs

Pierhouse Hotel & Restaurant 🐟
PA38 4DE ☎ 01631 730302 📠 01631 730400
e-mail: pierhouse@btinternet.com

The Pierhouse Hotel started life as the Pier Master's residence whose job was to oversee the steam packets that crossed Loch Linnhe. The building has fabulous views looking out over Lismore Island towards Mull. Licensed only 15 years ago, the hotel has undergone considerable enlargement and refurbishment and today has a strong local reputation for good quality local lobsters, prawns, scallops and salmon caught by local fishermen within sight of the hotel. Menus here invariably offer Lismore oysters, scampi, and mussels. Seafood pastas are generous in proportion, and the giant seafood platter is sufficient for two families let alone two people. There's nothing like freshly caught langoustine dripping with lemon and garlic butter, fresh crusty bread and a decent bottle of Sauvignon from the extensive wine list. Non-seafood alternatives include chicken fajita, or mushroom stroganoff from the lunch menu, and lamb cutlets or chicken and mango from the carte. Puddings tend to be traditional, such as carefully made profiteroles.

OPEN: 11.30-11.30 (Sun 12-11) Closed: Dec 25
BAR MEALS: L served all week 12.30-2.30 D served all week 6.30-9.30 Av main course £11.50 **RESTAURANT:** L served all week 12.30-2.30 D served all week 6.30-9.30 Av 3 course à la carte £25 🍴: Free House 🍺: Calders Cream, Calders 70/-, Carlsberg-Tetley Tetley Bitter. **FACILITIES:** Garden: Food served outdoors, patio **NOTES:** Parking 20

Pick of the Pubs

Creggans Inn ★★★ ◉
PA27 8BX ☎ 01369 860279 📠 01369 860637
e-mail: info@creggans-inn.co.uk
web: www.creggans-inn.co.uk
Dir: A82 from Glasgow, at Tarbet take A83 to Cairndow, then A815 down coast to Strachur

A comfortable small hotel standing on the very lip of Loch Fyne, and a coaching inn since Mary Queen of Scots' day. Views from the hills above take in vistas across the Mull of Kintyre to the Western Isles beyond. It has 14 en suite bedrooms and facilities suitable for all the family including a safe garden and patio for alfresco summer eating. Use of local produce plays its full part in the preparation of seasonal menus likely to include oysters and mussels, salmon, local wild game, venison and hill-grazed lamb. A typical dinner menu includes venison sausages with Arran mustard mash, cod or haddock with chips, grilled salmon fillet with pea pureé and balsamic syrup, and steak and ale pie.

OPEN: 11-11 **BAR MEALS:** L served all week 12-3 D served all week 6-9 Av main course £8.40 **RESTAURANT:** D served all week 7-9 Av 4 course fixed price £28 🍴: Free House 🍺: Coniston Bluebird Bitter, Fyne Ales Highlander, Atlas Latitude, Deuchars IPA. **FACILITIES:** Formal, terraced garden, occasional seating **NOTES:** Parking 36 **ROOMS:** 14 bedrooms en suite s£60 d£100

Victoria Hotel
Barmore Rd PA29 6TW ☎ 01880 820236 📠 01880 820638
e-mail: victoria.hotel@lineone.net

Centrally situated in a picturesque fishing village on the Kintyre peninsula, this 18th-century hotel is renowned for its restaurant, which enjoys romantic views over Loch Fyne. Bar and restaurant menus provide a good choice, featuring local game and seafood. Scallops in garlic butter with sun-blushed tomatoes; royal king mussels in white wine, cream and garlic; and queenies with smoked bacon and tarragon are examples of the seafood dishes on offer.

OPEN: 11-12 (Sun 12-12 Closed 3-5.30 in winter) Closed: 25 Dec
BAR MEALS: L served all week 12-2.30 D served all week 6-9.30 (Sun 12.30-2.30, 6-9.30) Av main course £7.95
RESTAURANT: L served all week 12-2.30 D served all week 6.30-9.30 🍴: Free House 🍺: Scottish Courage John Smiths, 80 Shilling, Tartan Special. **FACILITIES:** Children's licence Garden: Patio area Dogs allowed Water provided

---

Polfearn Hotel ♀
PA35 1JQ ☎ 01866 822251 📠 01866 822251
Dir: Turn off A85, continue 1.5m through village down to loch shore

Close to the shores of Loch Etive, with stunning all-round views, this friendly family-run hotel sits at the foot of Ben Cruachen. Originally a Victorian fishing villa, it was converted to a hotel in 1960. Whether you're working, walking, cycling, riding, shooting or fishing in the area, the proprietors will store things, dry things, feed, water and warm you with little formality. Dishes are cooked to order from fresh local produce, notably seafood, steak from the local butcher, and home-made pies.

OPEN: 12-2 6-11 Closed: 25-26 Dec Nov-May Closed lunch
BAR MEALS: L served all week 12-1.45 D served all week 6-8.45 Av main course £9 **RESTAURANT:** 12-1.45 D served all week 5.30-8.45 Av 3 course à la carte £22 🍴: Free House 🍺: Weekly changing guest ale. ♀: 15 **FACILITIES:** Garden: Nice lawn, sea view & mountains Dogs allowed Water, Food **NOTES:** Parking 50

We only include details of accommodation that has been inspected by the AA (big Stars or Diamonds at the top of an entry), or the RAC, VisitBritain, VisitScotland or WTB (small Stars or Diamonds at the end of an entry)

TAYVALLICH   Map 20 NR78

Pick of the Pubs

Tayvallich Inn
PA31 8PL ☎ 01546 870282 🖷 01546 870333
Dir: From Lochgilphead take A816 then B841/B8025
Converted from an old bus garage in 1976, this 'house in
the pass' as it translates, stands by a natural harbour at
the head of Loch Sween with stunning views over the
anchorage, especially from the picnic tables that front the
inn in summer. The cosy bar with a yachting theme and
the more formal dining-room feature original works by
local artists and large picture windows from which to gaze
out over the village and across Tayvallich Bay. Those
interested in the works of 19th-century engineer Thomas
Telford will find plenty of bridges and piers in the area.
Expect a lot of seafood choices, including pan-fried Sound
of Jura scallops, Cajun salmon with black butter, or warm
salad of smoked haddock with prawns. Meat choices
include grilled prime Scottish sirloin steak, chicken curry
and honey and mustard glazed rack of lamb. The truly
hungry may try the Tayvallich seafood platter that
combines prawns, mussels, oysters, smoked salmon,
pickled herring and crab claws.
OPEN: 11-2.30 , 6-11.30 (Summer 11-12, 1am Fri-Sat) 5.30-12
(Fri-Sat 5-1am, Sun 5-12) Closed: 25 Dec
BAR MEALS: L served all week 12-2 D served all week 6-9
Av main course £9 **RESTAURANT:** L served all week 12-2
D served all week 6-9 ⊕: Free House ◖: Tennents, Guinness,
London Pride. **FACILITIES:** Garden: Patio area Dogs allowed
except at meal times **NOTES:** Parking 20

CITY OF EDINBURGH

EDINBURGH   Map 21 NT27

Bennets Bar ♀
8 Leven St EH3 9LG ☎ 0131 229 5143
Bennets is a friendly pub, popular with performers from the
adjacent Kings Theatre, serving real ales, over 120 malt
whiskies and a decent selection of wines. It's a listed property
dating from 1839 with hand-painted tiles and murals on the
walls, original stained glass windows and brass beer taps.
Reasonably priced home-made food ranges from toasties,
burgers and salads to stovies, steak pie, and macaroni cheese.
There's also a daily roast and traditional puddings.
OPEN: 11-12.30 (Sun 12.30-11.30 Thu-Sat 11-1) Closed: 25-26 Dec
BAR MEALS: L served all week 12-2 D served Mon-Sat 5-8.30 (Sun
11.30-4) Av main course £4.75 ⊕: Scottish & Newcastle
◖: Caledonian Deuchars IPA, McEwans 80/-. Miller, Guiness. ♀: 11

The Bow Bar ♀
80 The West Bow EH1 2HH ☎ 0131 2267667
e-mail: helen@bowbar.com
Dir: Telephone for directions
Located in the heart of Edinburgh's old town, the Bow Bar
reflects the history and traditions of the area. Tables from
decommissioned railway carriages and gantry from an old
church used for the huge selection of whiskies create interest
in the bar, where 140 malts are on tap, and eight cask ales
are dispensed from antique equipment. Bar snacks only are
served, and there are no gaming machines or music to
distract from good conversation.
OPEN: 12-11.30 (12.30-11 Sun0 Closed: 25-26 Dec, 1-2 Jan ⊕: Free

House ◖: Deuchars IPA, Belhaven 80/-, Taylors Landlord,
Harviestown Bitter & Twisted. ♀: 6 **FACILITIES:** Dogs allowed
Water provided

Pick of the Pubs

Doric Tavern ♀
15-16 Market St EH1 1DE
☎ 0131 225 1084 🖷 0131 220 0894 web: www.thedoric.co.uk

Located near the castle in Edinburgh's old town this
convivial hostelry, in a refurbished building dating from
the 18th century. The result is a public bar, a bistro, and a
wine bar able to provide a wide choice of refreshment
and ambience. The bistro offers both a set price and a
Scottish à la carte menu using the finest of fresh local
ingredients with such delicacies as cullen skink, Highland
venison, and haggis, neaps and tatties. The set menu
changes daily and includes seafood, game and vegetarian
dishes; it would not be complete without a selection of
mouthwatering desserts. Downstairs, the Doric Bar
provides traditional freshly cooked pub grub in an
authentic Edinburgh pub atmosphere.
OPEN: 12-1am Closed: Dec 25-26, Jan 1
BAR MEALS: L served all week 12-7 D served all week 12-1am
RESTAURANT: L served all week 12-4 D served all week 5-11
Av 3 course à la carte £15 Av 3 course fixed price £21 ⊕: Free
House ◖: Caledonian Deuchars IPA & 80/-, Tennents, Guiness.
♀: 16

The Shore Bar & Restaurant ♀
3 Shore, Leith EH6 6QW ☎ 0131 553 5080 🖷 0131 553 5080
e-mail: enquiries@the.shore.ukf.net
Overlooking the Water of Leith and only a stone's throw from
the busy port, this historic 18th-century pub has a fine
reputation for Scottish fish and seafood. Have a drink in the
small bar, a popular music venue, before repairing to the
intimate dining room to enjoy sweet potato and parsnip soup;
pan-fried John Dory in toasted nut and herb butter; or
sautéed squid in sweet chilli sauce. Good value sandwiches at
lunchtime.
OPEN: 11-12 (Sun 12-11) Closed: 25, 26 Dec, 1,2 Jan
BAR MEALS: L served all week 12-2.30 D served all week 6.30-10
(Sat-Sun 12.30-3) Av main course £14 **RESTAURANT:** L served all
week 12-2.30 D served all week 6.30-10 (Sun 12.30-3) Av 3 course à
la carte £23 ◖: Belhaven 80/-, Deuchars IPA, Guiness, Carlsberg.
♀: 7 **FACILITIES:** Child facs Pavement tables Dogs Water

 Pubs with this logo do not allow smoking
anywhere on their premises

continued

Scotland

RATHO

Map 21 NT17

Pick of the Pubs

The Bridge Inn

27 Baird Rd EH28 8RA ☎ 0131 3331320 🖹 0131 333 3480
e-mail: info@bridgeinn.com web: www.bridgeinn.com
Dir: *From Newbridge B7030 junction, follow signs for Ratho*

Built as a farmhouse around 1750, it became an inn when the Union Canal reached here in 1822. As barge traffic declined the inn fell into decay, until in 1971 Ronnie Rusack, still the owner today, restored and re-opened it. Bar food is served all day in the lounge overlooking the canal, while the waterways-themed restaurant is for more formal dining. Ronnie insists on buying only top quality Scottish meats in line with his policy of using freshly prepared local produce. Typically offered are stir-fried duck with barbecue sauce; pan-fried chicken breast stuffed with haggis, served with creamy Drambuie sauce; grilled Scottish salmon fillet with caper butter; and goat's cheese cannelloni. Traditional cranachan is a dessert to try for the first time: layers of Drambuie-laced oatmeal cream, raspberries, heather honey and flaked almonds. Canalboat restaurants are available for dinner cruises, and there's a fleet of vintage fire engines to see.
OPEN: 12-11 (Sat 11-12, Sun 12.30-11) Closed: 26 Dec, 1-2 Jan **BAR MEALS:** L served all week 12-9 D served all week Sun 12.30-9 **RESTAURANT:** L served all week 12-2 D served all week 6.30-9 Sun 12.30-2, 6.30-9 Av 3 course à la carte £25 🍽: Free House 🍺: Belhaven 80/- & Belhaven Best, Deuchars IPA, Guinness. **FACILITIES:** Child facs Children's licence Landscaped garden: Patio, ducks roaming **NOTES:** Parking 60

CITY OF GLASGOW

GLASGOW

Map 20 NS56

Rab Ha's ♡ ♀
83 Hutchieson St G1 1SH ☎ 0141 572 0400 🖹 0141 572 0402
e-mail: management@rabhas.com
Dir: *City centre*
In the heart of Glasgow's revitalised Merchant City, Rab Ha's takes its name from Robert Hall, a local 19th-century character known as the 'Glasgow glutton'. This newly refurbished hotel, restaurant and bar blends traditional Victorian character with contemporary Scottish décor. Bar meals include haggis with turnip and mash; or field mushroom risotto with rocket. In the candlelit restaurant you'll find seared tuna loin with baby Niçoise salad; and crusted cannon of lamb with creamed baby leeks.
OPEN: 11-12 **BAR MEALS:** L served all week 12-10 D served all

continued

---

week 12-10 Av main course £5.65 **RESTAURANT:** L served all week 12-2 D served all week 5.30-10 Av 3 course à la carte £17.95 Av 2 course fixed price £11.95 🍽: Free House 🍺: McEwans 70/- & 80/-, Theakstons, Belhaven Best, Guinness. ♀: 12
FACILITIES: Dogs allowed

Pick of the Pubs

Ubiquitous Chip ⚙⚙ ♀
12 Ashton Ln G12 8SJ ☎ 0141 334 5007 🖹 0141 337 1302
e-mail: mail@ubiquitouschip.co.uk
web: www.ubiquitouschip.co.uk
Dir: *In the west end of Glasgow, off Byres Road*
The Chip has been a Glaswegian institution for more than 30 years, offering a menu that provides a rare insight into traditional Scottish cooking. The main restaurant is actually a glass-covered mews in the west end of the city with cobbled floor, water fountains and enough flora to grace an arboretum. Traditional draught beers, selected malt whiskies and first class wines by the glass are served from a bar that is reputed to be the smallest in Scotland; it is certainly one of the most stylish. Dishes include braised Perthshire pig's cheek, wild mushroom sauce and truffled potato omelette; and venison or vegetarian haggis with mashed potato and turnip cream as starters. Mains like steak and kidney pudding with candied shallots and roast turnip; braised ox heart, skirlie stovies and buttery savoy cabbage; and Orkney organic salmon, bok choi salad with lime vinaigrette might be followed by chocolate brioche with Seville orange marmalade and orange and yoghurt sorbet.
OPEN: 11-12 (12.30-12 Sun) Closed: 25 Dec, 1 Jan **BAR MEALS:** L served all week 12-4 D served all week 4-11 Sun 12.30-4 **RESTAURANT:** L served all week 12-2.30 D served all week 5.30-11 Sun L from 12.30, D from 6.30 Av 3 course à la carte £26 🍽: Free House 🍺: Caledonian 80/- & Deuchars IPA. ♀: 21

DUMFRIES & GALLOWAY

CASTLE DOUGLAS

Map 21 NX76

Crown Hotel
25 King St DG7 1AA ☎ 01556 502031 🖹 01556 504831
e-mail: reception@thecrownhotel.co.uk
The Crown hotel is a charming former coaching inn with a restaurant that prides itself on its quality food made from local produce. The menu is spread between starters, mains courses, fish and vegetarian dishes, grills, salads and desserts, and you can finish with a cup of speciality coffee. The welcoming bar provides the perfects pot in which to relax after a busy day of sightseeing.
OPEN: 10.30-midnight **BAR MEALS:** L served all week 11-9 D served all week 11-9 Av main course £4.50
RESTAURANT: L served all week 12-2 D served all week 6-9 Sunday 12-3 Av 3 course à la carte £15 🍺: Guinness, JSES, 70/-, 80/-.
FACILITIES: Dogs allowed Biscuits, water **NOTES:** Parking 100

> Room prices show the minimum double and single rates charged. Room rates in hotels and B&Bs often vary depending on the facilities, so be sure to check prices with the establishment before booking

ISLE OF WHITHORN
Map 20 NX43

The Steam Packet Inn
Harbour Row DG8 8LL ☎ 01988 500334 ▨ 01988 500627
e-mail: steampacketinn@btconnect.com
web: www.steampacketinn.com
Dir: From Newton Stewart take A714, then A746 to Whithorn, then Isle of Whithorn
This family-run 18th-century free house sits on the quayside overlooking the harbour. Lunch and dinner are served throughout both bars, and in the lower dining room and conservatory restaurants. The menus and specials boards feature fresh Scottish produce, and seafood is often bought straight from the boats. Expect smoked haddock and spring onion fishcakes; roast vegetable tartlet with three-cheese sauce; and lamb loin noisettes with Calvados sauce.
OPEN: 11-11 (Winter open Mon-Thu, 11-3, 6-11) Closed: Dec 25
BAR MEALS: L served all week 12-2 D served all week 6.30-9
Av main course £6 **RESTAURANT:** L served all week 12-2 D served all week 6.30-9 Av 3 course à la carte £17 ⬚: Free House
◖: Scottish Courage Theakston XB, Caledonian Deuchars IPA, Black Sheep Best Bitter, Houston Killellan. **FACILITIES:** Child facs Children's licence Garden: Dogs allowed Water **NOTES:** Parking 4
ROOMS: 7 bedrooms en suite 1 family room (★)

KIRKCUDBRIGHT
Map 20 NX65

Selkirk Arms Hotel ♀
Old High St DG6 4JG ☎ 01557 330402 ▨ 01557 331639
e-mail: reception@selkirkarmshotel.co.uk
web: www.selkirkarmshotel.co.uk
A traditional white-painted pub on street corner, with nice gardens to the rear. It has associations with the Scottish poet Robert Burns, and T. E. Lawrence (of Arabia), who lived nearby. Good choice of beers, including Solway Criffel and Youngers Tartan. Typical menu offers lamb or vegetable Madras, fresh Scottish haddock in crispy beer batter, steak and mushroom pie, spinach and cream cheese roulade, and haggis, neeps and tatties.
OPEN: 11-12 **BAR MEALS:** L served all week 12-2 D served all week 6-9.30 **RESTAURANT:** L served all week 12-2 D served all week 7-9.30 ◖: Youngers Tartan, John Smiths Bitter, Criffel, Old Speckled Hen. ♀: 8 **FACILITIES:** Children's licence Beautiful garden: Dogs allowed dog bones/biscuits **NOTES:** Parking 50

MOFFAT
Map 21 NT00

Black Bull Hotel ♀
Churchgate DG10 9EG ☎ 01683 220206 ▨ 01683 220483
e-mail: hotel@blackbullmoffat.co.uk
This hotel is steeped in Scottish history: it was used by Graham of Claverhouse as his headquarters during the Scottish rebellion in the late 17th century, and Scottish bard Robert Burns was a frequent visitor around 1790. Nowadays, the hotel serves a varied menu at reasonable prices. Starters and snacks on offer include haggis; mussels; and a selection of baked potatoes and sandwiches. Substantial mains include poached Solway salmon and steak and ale pie.
OPEN: 11-11 (Thu-Sat 11-12) **BAR MEALS:** L served all week 11.30-9.15 D served all week 11.30-9.15 Av main course £6.95
RESTAURANT: L served all week 11.30-3 D served all week 6-9.15 Av 3 course à la carte £12 ⬚: Free House ◖: McEwans, Scottish Courage Theakston 80/-. ♀: 10 **FACILITIES:** Child facs Garden: Courtyard with eight tables Dogs allowed **NOTES:** Parking 4
ROOMS: 13 bedrooms en suite 2 family rooms s£45 d£67 (★★★)

NEW ABBEY
Map 21 NX96

Criffel Inn
2 The Square DG2 8BX
☎ 01387 850305 850244 ▨ 01387 850305
Dir: M/A74 leave at Gretna, A75 to Dumfries, A710 S to New Abbey
A former 18th-century coaching inn set on the Solway Coast in the historic conservation village of New Abbey close to the ruins of the 13th-century Sweetheart Abbey. The Graham family ensures a warm welcome and excellent home-cooked food using local produce. Dishes include chicken wrapped in smoked Ayrshire bacon served with Loch Arthur mature creamy cheese sauce; fish dishes feature sea trout and sea bass among several others. There is a lawned beer garden overlooking the corn-mill and square; ideal for touring Dumfries and Galloway.
OPEN: 12-2.30 5-11 (Sat 12-12 Sun 12-11) **BAR MEALS:** L served all week 12-2 D served all week 5.30-8 (Sun 12-8) Av main course £7
RESTAURANT: L served all week 12-2 D served all week 5-8 (Sun 12-8) Av 3 course à la carte £14 ⬚: Free House ◖: Belhaven Best, McEwans 60-. **FACILITIES:** Child facs Garden Dogs allowed Water **NOTES:** Parking 8

NEW GALLOWAY
Map 20 NX67

Cross Keys Hotel
High St DG7 3RN ☎ 01644 420494 ▨ 01644 420672
e-mail: info@crosskeysng.fsnet.co.uk
Dir: At N end of Loch Ken, 10m from Castle Douglas

Part of this hotel was once a police station: you can eat bar meals in the restored stone-walled cell. Alternatively, the à la carte restaurant serves hearty food with a strong Scottish accent: Galloway venison casserole; haggis, neeps and tatties; and duck breast with mango and ginger sauce. Try a Sulwath real ale, or relax in the specialist whisky lounge.
OPEN: 12-11 (Oct-Apr 12-12 Fri-Sat Apr-Oct 12-12 all wk)
BAR MEALS: L served all week 12-2 D served all week 6-8 (Nov-Mar no food Mon-Tue. Sun 5.30-7.30) Av main course £7
RESTAURANT: D served Apr-Oct Tue-Sun 6.30-8.30 (Sun 5.30-7.30. Nov-Mar Thu-Sun) Av 3 course à la carte £18 ◖: Houston real ales, guest real ales. **FACILITIES:** Garden: Small enclosed garden, good views Dogs allowed **NOTES:** Parking 6

> 🐟 Pubs offering a good choice of fish on their menu

> The Rosette is the AA award for food. Look out for it next to a pub's name

Scotland

NEWTON STEWART   Map 20 NX46

Pick of the Pubs

Creebridge House Hotel ♀
Minnigaff DG8 6NP ☎ 01671 402121 🖷 01671 403258
e-mail: info@creebridge.co.uk
Dir: A75 into Newton Stewart, R over river bridge, 200yds on L.
Named after the nearby River Cree and set in three acres
of idyllic gardens and woodland at the foot of Kirroughtree
forest, this country house hotel is a listed building dating
from 1760. It was formerly the Earl of Galloway's shooting
lodge and part of his estate. Bridge's bar and brasserie
offers malt whiskies, real ales and an interesting menu with
an emphasis on fresh Scottish produce. Typical starters are
assiette of locally smoked, home cured and ceviche of
Scottish salmon; Dunsyre blue cheese soufflé; Thai pork
salad; and terrine of venison, pigeon and puy lentil. The
main list could offer pan-fried breast and confit leg of
barbary duck; caramelised king scallops; filo tart of goat's
cheese with tomatoes and onion marmalade; and pan-
roasted loin of lamb. Steamed ginger pudding; apple
bavarois; and white chocolate parfait are tempting, and
there is also a range of speciality breads made in house.
OPEN: 12-2.30 6-11 (Sun, all day) Closed: 3 Jan for 2 wks
BAR MEALS: L served all week 12-2 D served all week 6-9
Av main course £9.95 **RESTAURANT:** L served all week 12-2
D served all week 6-9 Av 3 course à la carte £25 ⊜: Free House
◀: Fuller's London Pride, Tenants, Real Ales, Deuchers. ♀: 8
FACILITIES: Child facs Children's licence Garden with rose
beds, fish pond and lawns Dogs allowed Doggy Bags, Water
NOTES: Parking 40

PORTPATRICK   Map 20 NW95

Pick of the Pubs

Crown Hotel ◥◢
9 North Crescent DG9 8SX ☎ 01776 810261 🖷 01776 810551
e-mail: crownhotel@supanet.com
Dir: Situated on water front, 7m from Stranraer
Former fishermen's cottages converted into a bustling
harbourside hotel, with striking views across the Irish Sea.
Stranraer, with its frequent ferry services to Belfast and
Larne, and the wonderfully rugged walking country of
south-west Scotland are just a stone's throw away. On a
clear day you can see Belfast Lough and the Irish
mountains from the beer garden. The Crown is a small,
family-run hotel offering a wide range of main meals to
suit all tastes and pockets. Inside, there is a great
atmosphere in the rambling old bar with its seafaring
displays and warming winter fire. Extensive menus are
based on fresh local produce with a strong emphasis on
seafood - typically, sea bass, fresh salmon, and scallops
with smoky bacon. Speciality grills and steaks include
10oz Buccleuch Scotch rib-eye of beef, with Galloway
lamb chops, chilli con carne and home-made beefburger
with barbecue sauce are among other options.
OPEN: 11-12 **BAR MEALS:** L served all week 12-6 D served all
week 6-9.30 Av main course £7.25 **RESTAURANT:** L served all
week 12-2.30 D served all week 6-9.30 Av 3 course à la carte
£19.95 ⊜: Free House ◀: John Smith's, McEwans 80/-,
McEwans 70/-, Guinness. **FACILITIES:** Child facs Children's
licence Garden: Overlooking the harbour Dogs allowed

DUNDEE CITY

BROUGHTY FERRY   Map 21 NO43

Fisherman's Tavern ♀
10-16 Fort St DD5 2AD ☎ 01382 775941 🖷 01382 477466
e-mail: bookings@fishermans-tavern-hotel.co.uk
*Dir: From Dundee city centre follow A930 to Broughty Ferry, right at sign
for hotel*
This listed 17th-century fisherman's cottage, converted to a
pub in 1827, combines a picturesque coastal setting with
award-winning hospitality and acclaimed bar food. The
freshly menu offers a wide range of freshly prepared dishes.
After a stroll along the sands, try chicken curry, fisherman's
seafood crêpes, or breaded Norwegian scampi, with a pint
from the impressive selection of well-kept cask ales.
OPEN: 11-12 (11am-1am Thu-Sat, 12.30-12 Sun)
BAR MEALS: L served all week 11.30-2.30 6-10 ⊜: Free House
◀: Belhaven, Inveralmond Ossian's Ale, Caledonain Deuchers
IPA, Timothy Taylor Landlord. ♀: 26 **FACILITIES:** Garden: Walled
garden, seating for 40 Dogs allowed Water, Biscuits

The Royal Arch Bar ◥◢ ♀
285 Brook St DD5 2DS ☎ 01382 779741 🖷 739174
*Dir: 3.5m from Dundee, follow signs to Broughty Ferry, pub at corner of
Brook St and Grey Street*
Dating from 1856, The Royal Arch is an intriguing pub,
crammed full of local history. With its traditional public bar
and art deco lounge, the Royal Arch is renowned for its wide
range of cask beers and malt whiskies. Meals and light bites
are served in either bar; grilled rainbow trout topped with
almonds; or strips of beef in peppercorn sauce are among
daily specials, along with a wide range of favourites.
OPEN: 11-12 (Sun 12.30-12) Closed: 1 Jan **BAR MEALS:** L served
all week 11.30-2.30 D served all week 5-8 Fri-Sat 11.30-7.30, Sun
12.30-2.30, 5-8 Av main course £5.95 **RESTAURANT:** L served all
week 11.30-2.30 D served all week 5-8 Fri-Sat 11.30-7.30, Sun
12.30-2.30, 5-8 ⊜: Free House ◀: Scottish Courage McEwans80/-,
Belhaven Best, Guinness. ♀: 12 **FACILITIES:** Pavement cafe in
front of bar Dogs allowed Water, treats

EAST AYRSHIRE

GATEHEAD   Map 20 NS33

Pick of the Pubs

The Cochrane Inn
45 Main Rd KA2 0AP ☎ 01563 570122
Dir: From Glasgow A77 to Kilmarnock, then A759 to Gatehead
The emphasis is on contemporary British food at this
village centre pub, just a short drive from the Ayrshire
coast. Friendly, bustling atmosphere inside. Good choice
of starters may include soused herring and grilled goat's
cheese, while main courses might feature stuffed
pancake, pan-fried trio of seafood with tiger prawns, or
smoked haddock risotto.
OPEN: 12-2 5.30-11 (Open all day Sun) Closed: 1 Jan
BAR MEALS: L served all week 12-2 D served all week 6-9
Av main course £7 **RESTAURANT:** L served all week 12-2
D served all week 6-9 Av 3 course à la carte £15 ⊜: Free House
◀: John Smith's. **FACILITIES:** Garden **NOTES:** Parking 30

SORN   Map 20 NS52

The Sorn Inn ◉◉ 🏠 🔽 ♀
35 Main St KA5 6HU ☎ 01290 551305 📠 01290 553470
e-mail: craig@sorninn.com
This late 18th-century coaching inn was recently refurbished
after a serious fire, and two alternative dining styles are now
available. The restaurant features modern British cuisine that
makes good use of game and other local ingredients, whilst
the chop house offers bistro and pub food. Expect rump of
lamb with haggis mash; steamed halibut with a crab and
spinach cannelloni; and supreme of chicken with sauté
potatoes, pearl barley and bacon jus.
OPEN: 12-2.30 6-11 (Sun 12.30-11, Sat 12-12, Fri 12-2.30, 6-12)
BAR MEALS: L served Tue-Sun 12-2.30 D served Tue-Sun 6-8
(Sat 12-7, Sun 12.30-7) Av main course £8
RESTAURANT: L served Wed-Sun 12-2.30 D served Tue-Sun 6-9
(Sun 12.30-8) Av 3 course fixed price £22 🍺: John Smiths,
Guinness. ♀: 8 **FACILITIES:** Children's licence
NOTES: Parking 8 **ROOMS:** 4 bedrooms en suite 1 family room
s£35 d£65

EAST LOTHIAN

EAST LINTON   Map 21 NT57

The Drovers Inn
5 Bridge St EH40 3AG ☎ 01620 860298 📠 01620 860205
Dir: Off A1 5m past Haddington, follow rd under railway bridge, then L
Herdsmen used to stop here as they drove their livestock to
market. Those old drovers are long gone but the bar, with
wooden floors, beamed ceilings and half-panelled walls,
retains an old-world charm. Upstairs, though, is more
sumptuous with rich colours, low-beamed ceilings and
antique furniture. The menus change every six weeks or so,
but may include the likes of grilled halibut and black tiger
prawns with chervil and garlic butter. The bistro downstairs
next to the bar offers a more informal dining choice.
OPEN: 11.30-11 (Fri-Sat 11.30-1) Closed: 25 Dec, 1 Jan
BAR MEALS: L served all week 12.30-2.30 D served all week 6-9.30
(All day Sat-Sun) Av main course £10 **RESTAURANT:** L served all
week 12-2.30 D served all week 6-9.30 All day Sun Av 3 course à la
carte £22.50 🍺: Free House 🍺: Adnams Broadside, Deuchars IPA,
Old Speckeled Hen, Burton Real Ale. **FACILITIES:** Garden: Small
enclosed beer garden Dogs allowed

GIFFORD   Map 21 NT56

Pick of the Pubs

Goblin Ha' Hotel ♀
EH41 4QH ☎ 01620 810244 📠 01620 810718
e-mail: info@goblinha.com
Dir: On A846, 100yrds from main village square on shore side
Traditional hotel with a large patio for summer eating
and a good garden with a play area and a dolls' house
for children. Members of the Walt Disney company
stayed here when they were filming scenes for
Greyfriars Bobby in the hills to the south of the village.
Malcolm Muggeridge was a regular visitor in the 1960s,
and Joan Baez attracted some dedicated hippies when
she had supper here one night. A varied range of
home-cooked dishes includes breast of duck, fillet of
salmon, chef's curry, shank of lamb and beer-battered
haddock.

Goblin Ha' Hotel

OPEN: 11-2.30 5-11 (Jun-Sep all day) **BAR MEALS:** L served
all week 12-2 D served all week 6-9 Av main course £7.75
RESTAURANT: L served all week 12-2 D served all week 6-9
🍺: Free House 🍺: Hop Back Summer lightning, Timothy Taylor
Landlord, Caledonian Deuchers IPA, Fuller's ESB. ♀: 12
FACILITIES: Children's licence Garden: Two acres of garden,
seats 80 Dogs allowed **ROOMS:** 7 bedrooms 6 en suite
2 family rooms s£37.50 d£75 (★★)

FALKIRK

CASTLECARY   Map 21 NS77

Castlecary House Hotel ★★ 🔽 ♀
Castlecary Rd G68 0HD ☎ 01324 840233 📠 01324 841608
e-mail: enquiries@castlecaryhotel.com
web: www.castlecaryhotel.com
Dir: Off A80 between Glasgow and Stirling and onto B816

A large but friendly hotel complex on the watershed of
Scotland's central belt and close to the historic Antonine Wall
and Forth and Clyde Canal. The hotel offers a range of menus
from traditional pub food to braised lamb shank with
rosemary mash and redcurrant jus; or if fish takes
your fancy, try the whole oven-roasted lemon sole in seafood
and basil cream.
OPEN: 11-11 **BAR MEALS:** L served all week 12 D served all week
9 (all day Sat-Sun) Av main course £6.50 **RESTAURANT:** L served
Mon-Sun (exc Sat) 12-2 D served Mon-Sat 7-10 (high tea only on Sun,
last orders 7pm) Av 3 course à la carte £25 🍺: Free House
🍺: Arran Blonde, Harviestoun Brooker's Bitter & Twisted,
Inveralmond Ossian's Ale, Housten Peter's Well. ♀: 10
FACILITIES: Children's licence Garden: Dogs allowed
NOTES: Parking 100 **ROOMS:** 60 bedrooms 55 en suite
2 family rooms s£65 d£65

continued

FIFE

ANSTRUTHER
Map 21 NO50

The Dreel Tavern 🔎
16 High St West KY10 3DL ☎ 01333 310727 🖹 01333 310577
e-mail: dreeltavern@aol.com
Complete with a local legend concerning an amorous encounter between James V and a local gypsy woman, the 16th-century Dreel Tavern has plenty of atmosphere. Its oak beams, open fire and stone walls retain much of the distant past, while home-cooked food and cask-conditioned ales are served to hungry visitors of the present. Expect to savour steak pie, roast beef and Yorkshire pudding, and plenty of local fish dishes including smoked fish pie, and local crab. Peaceful gardens overlook Dreel Burn. Beers changed weekly.
OPEN: 11-12 (Sun 12.30-12) **BAR MEALS:** L served all week 12-2 D served all week 5.30-9 (Sun 12.30-2) Av main course £6.50
RESTAURANT: L served all week 12-2 D served all week 5.30-9
🍽: Free House 🍺: Carlsberg-Tetley Tetley's Bitter, Harviestoun Bitter & Twisted, Greene King IPA, London Pride. **FACILITIES:** Garden: Enclosed area, seats approx 20 Dogs allowed in bar only; water, biscuits **NOTES:** Parking 3

BURNTISLAND
Map 21 NT28

Burntisland Sands Hotel
Lochies Rd KY3 9JX ☎ 01592 872230
e-mail: clarkelinton@hotmail.com
Dir: Take A921 for Dalgaty Bay. Follow coastal road through Aberdour. 1st hotel on the right after 'The Links'.
This small, family-run hotel is situated just yards from a sandy beach with a fine view across the bay. Reasonably priced food is available for breakfast, snacks, lunch and dinner, with a good selection of specials. Try poached haddock mornay; sizzler steak garni; or seafood pancake. There is an excellent choice of hot and cold filled rolls, and desserts on offer include chocolate mint paradise, and caramel apple granny.
OPEN: 11-12 **BAR MEALS:** L served all week 12-2.30 D served all week 7-9 Sat-Sun 12-8.30 Av main course £6
RESTAURANT: L served all week 12-2.30 D served all week 6-8.30 all day Sat & Sun Av 3 course à la carte £15 🍽: Free House
🍺: Scottish Courage Beers, Guiness, Carling. **FACILITIES:** Child facs Children's licence Garden: patio/terrace, BBQ, rabbit hutch Dogs allowed Tie up area, water bowls **NOTES:** Parking 20

CRAIL
Map 21 NO60

The Golf Hotel 🔎
4 High St KY10 3TD ☎ 01333 450206 🖹 01333 450795
e-mail: enquiries@thegolfhotelcrail.com
Dir: On corner of High St
Built in the early 18th century on the site of one of Scotland's oldest inns, the hotel's roots go back to the 14th century. The name comes from the formation of the Crail Golfing Society in the public bar in 1786. Now, the emphasis is on traditional Scottish values, including high tea with home-made scones and cakes. Other choices include farmhouse mixed grill; home-made macaroni cheese; and fresh salmon and king prawn salad.
OPEN: 11-12 **BAR MEALS:** L served all week 12-7 D served all week 7-9 Av main course £6.95 **RESTAURANT:** L served all week 12-7 D served all week 7-9 Av 3 course à la carte £17 🍽: Free House 🍺: Scottish Courage McEwans 60/-, 80/-, 70/-, Tetleys.
FACILITIES: Garden: Dogs allowed **NOTES:** Parking 10
ROOMS: 5 bedrooms en suite 1 family room s£45 d£60 (★★★)

DUNFERMLINE
Map 21 NT08

The Hideaway Lodge & Restaurant ♀
Kingseat Rd, Halbeath KY12 0UB
☎ 01383 725474 🖹 01383 622821
e-mail: enquiries@thehideaway.co.uk
Dir: Telephone for directions

Originally built in the 1930s as a miners' welfare institute, this pleasant country inn enjoys a rural setting on the outskirts of Dunfermline. Each room is named after a Scottish loch, and the extensive menu makes good use of fresh local produce. A typical meal may begin with grilled goats' cheese salad or Oban mussels, then move on to chargrilled tuna steak, Scottish seafood crumble or fillet of Highland venison, and finish with summer fruit pudding or steamed ginger pudding.
OPEN: 12-3 5-11 (Sun 12-9) **BAR MEALS:** L served all week 12-2 D served all week 5-9.30 **RESTAURANT:** L served all week 12-2 D served all week 5-9.30 🍽: Free House 🍺: John Smith, 80 Special. **FACILITIES:** Garden **NOTES:** Parking 35

ELIE
Map 21 NO40

Pick of the Pubs

The Ship Inn ♀
The Toft KY9 1DT ☎ 01333 330246 🖹 01333 330864
e-mail: info@ship-elie.com
Dir: Follow A915 & A917 to Elie. From High St follow signs to Watersport Centre to The Toft
A lively free house right on the waterfront at Elie Bay, The Ship has been a pub since 1838, and been run by the enthusiastic Philip family for over two decades. There's plenty going on, with the cricket team (which plays on the beach), Sunday barbeques in summer, and live music. Local suppliers featured in the pub's brochure, along with the menu, wines and cricket fixture list, include a local baker (established 1947), a fish merchant up the coast at St Monans, and a butcher from Lundin Links who supplies the award-winning haggis (a starter with neeps, tatties and whisky sauce). Other dishes clamouring for attention are wasabi swordfish; seaside chicken with seaweed and spring vegetables stuffing and ginger sauce, and an inspired junior platter: apple, cheese, sliced chicken, crisps and a jaffa cake bar. In summer, lunch can also be taken al fresco in the beer garden.
OPEN: 11-11 (Sun 12.30-11) Closed: 25 Dec
BAR MEALS: L served all week 12-2 D served all week 6-9
RESTAURANT: L served all week 12-2 D served all week 6-9
🍽: Free House 🍺: Caledonian Deuchars IPA, Belhaven Best, Tetleys Xtra Cold, Caledonian 801. ♀: 7 **FACILITIES:** Beer garden, food served outdoors, patio, Dogs allowed Water, biscuits

KIRKCALDY   Map 21 NT29

Pick of the Pubs

The Old Rectory Inn
West Quality St, Dysart KY1 2TE
☎ 01592 651211 ▤ 01592 655221
Dir: From Edinburgh take A92 to Kirkcaldy, then right onto A921, left onto A955 to Dysart right at National Trust sign

Built as a gentleman's residence by prominent Dysart merchant James Reddie in 1771, the Old Rectory Inn was indeed at one time a rectory, and an inn only since the 1980s. It is a splendid Georgian building, retaining its period features, including moulded eaves, cornices, panelled chimneys and a Roman Doric door piece. Outside there is a large oval garden sheltered by a high stone wall, where seats are provided for fine weather use. The lunch menu offers a good choice of pasta, cold table and vegetarian dishes, main courses like large Yorkshire pudding filled with chilli beef con carne. The supper line-up features hot and cold starters (deep-fried mushrooms, stilton mousse), fresh fish options (fish stew), pastas and vegetarian choices, curries and steaks. From the à la carte menu come salmon moutard; duck with three fruits; and pork with green ginger wine. Don't miss the home-made puddings - hot sticky toffee pudding with butterscotch sauce, bread and butter, and cold sweets from the trolley.
OPEN: 12-3 7-12 (Sun 12.30-3.30) Closed: 1wk Jan & 2wks mid-Oct, 1 wk early July **BAR MEALS:** L served Tue-Sun 12-2 D served Tue-Sat 7-9.30 (Sun 12.30-2.30) Av main course £7.50 **RESTAURANT:** L served Tue-Sun 12-2 D served Tue-Sat 7-9.30 (Sun 12.30-2.30) Av 3 course à la carte £26.50 ▤: Free House ▦: Calders Cream Ale. **FACILITIES:** Garden: Large garden, sheltered by high stone wall, **NOTES:** Parking 12

LOWER LARGO   Map 21 NO40

The Crusoe Hotel
2 Main St KY8 6BT ☎ 01333 320759 ▤ 01333 320865
e-mail: relax@crusoehotel.co.uk
Dir: A92 to Kirkcaldy East, A915 to Lundin Links, then right to Lower Largo
This historic inn is located on the sea wall in Lower Largo, the birthplace of Alexander Selkirk, the real-life castaway immortalised by Daniel Defoe in his novel, *Robinson Crusoe*. In the place area was also the heart of the once-thriving herring fishing industry. Today it is a charming bay ideal for a golfing break. A typical menu may include 'freshly shot' haggis, Pittenweem haddock and a variety of steaks.

continued

The Crusoe Hotel

OPEN: 11-12 (Fri 11am-1am, Sun 12-12) **BAR MEALS:** L served all week 11-9 Av main course £6 **RESTAURANT:** D served all week 6.45-9 ▤: Free House ▦: Belhaven 80/-, Best, Caledonian IPA, Deuchars. **FACILITIES:** Dogs allowed Biscuits **NOTES:** Parking 20

MARKINCH   Map 21 NO20

Town House Hotel ♦♦♦♦
1 High St KY7 6DQ ☎ 01592 758459 ▤ 01592 755039
e-mail: townhousehotel@aol.com
web: www.townhousehotel-fife.co.uk
Dir: Off A92 (Dundee/Kirkcaldy road). Hotel opp rail station
Family-run 17th-century coaching inn situated in the heart of town, and offering a fixed-price lunch menu of two or three courses, and a supper carte of imaginative dishes. Expect grilled Gressingham duck breast served with an orange and Cointreau sauce, pan-fried blackened Cajun salmon fillets and cheese, or haggis and black pudding fritters with apple sauce and honey and mustard mayo.
OPEN: 12-2 6-11 Closed: 25-26 Dec, 1-2 Jan
BAR MEALS: L served Mon-Sat 12-2 D served all week 6-9
RESTAURANT: L served Mon-Sat 12-2 D served all week 6-9 (Sun 4-7) Av 2 course fixed price £7.50 ▤: Free House
ROOMS: 4 bedrooms 3 en suite 1 family room s£45 d£70 ⊗

HIGHLAND

ACHILTIBUIE   Map 22 NC00

Summer Isles Hotel & Bar
IV26 2YG ☎ 01854 622282 ▤ 01854 622251
e-mail: info@summerisleshotel.co.uk
Dir: Take A835 N from Ullapool for 10m, Achiltibuie signed on left, 15m to village, hotel 1m on left
Situated in a stunningly beautiful and unspoilt landscape, it is difficult to find a more relaxing place to drink, dine or stay. The emphasis is on locally caught and home-produced quality food, and there's a wide choice of malts and real ale. Smoked salmon, langoustines, hummous and a tempting seafood platter all feature on the menu, along with a casserole of the day, and various snacks.
OPEN: 11-11 (4-11 in winter) **BAR MEALS:** L served all week 12-2.30 D served all week 5.30-8.30 Av main course £8.50
RESTAURANT: L served all week 12.30-2 D served all week 8 Av 5 course fixed price £47 ▤: Free House ▦: Orkney Dark Island, Raven & Red Macgregor. **FACILITIES:** Garden: small garden with tables and wonderful views Dogs allowed **NOTES:** Parking 20

Scotland

ALTNAHARRA Map 23 NC53

Altnaharra Hotel
IV27 4UE ☎ 01549 411222 📠 01549 411222
e-mail: altnaharra@btinternet.com web: www.altnaharra.com
Dir: A9 to Bonar Bridge, A836 to Lairg & Tongue

Originally a drover's inn understood to date back to the late 17th century, the Altnaharra is located in the beautiful Flow Country of Scotland, with endless views over timeless moorland. Interesting items of fishing memorabilia decorate the walls, including some fine historical prints and fishing records. The imaginative menu features the best of Scottish produce and options might include scallops in a brandy and cream sauce, Aberdeen Angus roast rib of beef, whole baked sea bass, Kyle of Tongue oysters, and Scottish rack of lamb.
OPEN: 11-12.45 **BAR MEALS:** L served all week 11-10 D served all week Av main course £7 **RESTAURANT:** D served all week 7.30-9.30 Av 5 course fixed price £45 ⊕: Scottish & Newcastle ◀: No real ale. **FACILITIES:** Garden: Large lawn area, Loch views, seating Dogs allowed in garden only **NOTES:** Parking 60

APPLECROSS Map 22 NG74

Pick of the Pubs

Applecross Inn ♀
Shore St IV54 8LR ☎ 01520 744262 📠 01520 744400
e-mail: applecrossinn@globalnet.co.uk
Dir: From Lochcarron to Kishorn then L onto unclassifed rd to Applecross over 'Bealach Na Ba'
The drive to Judith Fish's door at Applecross Inn will take you through some of Scotland's most awe-inspiring scenery, for you must cross the Bealach nam Bo (pass of the cattle) rising to 2053 feet with triple hairpin bends before descending through forests into Applecross (A Chromraich, meaning sanctuary). The traditional white-painted inn is set on a sandy cove looking over to Skye and the Cuillins. The bar retains its Highland character, warmed by a wood burning stove, and inspired by a choice of over 50 malt whiskies. The kitchen takes it pick of top quality local produce, with the worthy aim of sourcing three-quarters of its ingredients from the surrounding area. Fish, and game from neighbouring estates, are plentiful. Seafood, of course, is a speciality: crab, oysters, prawns and squat lobsters are all fresh from the water. Those intending to stay a while should book ahead for one of the romantic bedrooms with magnificent sea views.
OPEN: 11-11 (Sun 12.30-11) Closed: 25 Dec, 1 Jan
BAR MEALS: L served all week 12-9 D served all week Av main course £7.95 **RESTAURANT:** L served by appointment D served all week 6-9 ⊕: Free House ◀: Scottish Courage John Smith's,

continued

Cask Ale, Red Cullin, Millers. ♀: 6 **FACILITIES:** Child facs Children's licence Garden: Grassed area on the beach, six tables Dogs allowed Water **NOTES:** Parking 30 **ROOMS:** 7 bedrooms 3 en suite 2 family rooms s£30 d£60 (★★)

AVIEMORE Map 23 NH81

The Old Bridge Inn ♀
Dalfaber Rd PH22 1PU ☎ 01479 811137 📠 01479 810270
e-mail: nigel@oldbridgeinn.co.uk web: www.oldbridgeinn.co.uk
Dir: Exit A9 to Aviemore, 1st left to 'Ski road', then 1st left again - 200mtrs
Cosy and friendly Highland pub overlooking the River Spey. Dine in the relaxing bars or in the attractive riverside garden. A tasty chargrill menu includes lamb chops in redcurrant jelly, Aberdeen Angus sirloin or rib-eye steaks, or butterflied breast of chicken marinated in yoghurt, lime and coriander. Seafood specials include monkfish pan-fried in chilli butter, mussels poached in white wine, and seafood crumble. Large selection of malt whiskies.
OPEN: 11-11 **BAR MEALS:** L served all week 12-2 D served all week 6-9 Av main course £7.50 **RESTAURANT:** L served all week 12-2 D served all week 6-9 Av 3 course à la carte £22 ⊕: Free House ◀: Caledonian 80/-, Cairngorm Highland IPA. ♀: 18 **FACILITIES:** Children's licence Garden **NOTES:** Parking 24

BADACHRO Map 22 NG77

The Badachro Inn NEW ⌐⌐ ♀
IV21 2AA ☎ 01445 741255 📠 01445 741319
e-mail: Lesley@badachroinn.com
Dir: Off A832 onto B8056, R into Badachro after 3.25m, towards quay
Sheltered by Badachro Bay, one of Scotland's finest anchorages, this atmospheric local in the North Highlands is very popular in summer with yachting folk. Log fires burn cheerily in the bar in winter as the sea laps against the windows on high tide. Seals and otters can also be seen from the pub. Local seafood is a speciality, and includes Loch Fyne oysters, oven-baked salmon, and Scottish herring in oatmeal. Extensive snack and specials menus.
OPEN: 12-12 Reduced hrs Jan-Feb Closed: 25 Dec
BAR MEALS: L served all week 12-3 D served all week 6-9 Sun 12.30-3, 6-9 Av main course £10 **RESTAURANT:** L served all week 12-3 D served all week 6-9 Sun 12.30-3, 6-9 Av 3 course à la carte £16 ◀: Red Cullen, Anceallach, Blaven, 80/-. ♀: 11 **FACILITIES:** Children's licence Garden: Garden overlooking Badachro Bay Dogs allowed **NOTES:** Parking 12

CAWDOR Map 23 NH85

Pick of the Pubs

Cawdor Tavern ⌐⌐ ♀
The Lane IV12 5XP ☎ 01667 404777 📠 01667 404777
e-mail: cawdortavern@btopenworld.com
Dir: From A96 (Inverness-Aberdeen) take B9006 & follow Cawdor Castle signs. Tavern in village centre.
A former joinery workshop for the Cawdor Estate, the Tavern is located close to the famous castle in a beautiful conservation village. Oak panelling from the castle, a gift from the late laird, is used to great effect in the bar. Roaring log fires keep the place cosy and warm on long winter evenings, while the garden patio comes into its own in summer. One menu is offered in the bar or restaurant, alongside the choice of real ales and 100 malt whiskies. The pub has quite a reputation for its food,

continued

Scotland

attracting diners from some distance for great seafood such as pan-seared scallops on linguine with chilli oil, battered fillet of sea bream, and seafood platter. Another favourite with a thoroughly Scottish flavour is chicken Culloden filled with haggis and served with a Drambuie and mushroom cream sauce.

Cawdor Tavern

OPEN: 11-3 5-11 (May-Oct 11-11) Closed: 25 Dec, 1 Jan
BAR MEALS: L served all week 12-2 D served all week 5.30-9 (Sun 12.30-3, 5.30-9) **RESTAURANT:** L served all week 12-2 D served all week 6.30-9 (Sun 12.30-3, 5.30-9) ☺: Free House ◖: Tennents 80/-, Tomintoul Stag. ♀: 8 **FACILITIES:** Child facs Children's licence Garden: Patio area at front of Tavern Dogs allowed Water provided. **NOTES:** Parking 60

CONTIN   Map 23 NH45

Achilty Hotel ★★★ ♀
IV14 9EG ☎ 01997 421355 🖷 01997 421923
e-mail: info@achiltyhotel.co.uk web: www.achiltyhotel.co.uk
Dir: On A835, at N edge of Contin

The original stone walls and log fire keep this former drovers' inn warm when the Highlands weather closes in. On the edge of the village near a fast-flowing mountain river, the cosy Achilty Hotel serves good Scottish food made from fresh local produce. The bar/restaurant menu offers an extensive choice with a seafood slant: bouillabaisse (Scottish style), scampi provençal, seafood thermidor, halibut and monkfish, plus chicken with haggis in a creamy whisky and onion sauce, duck breasts, mushroom stroganoff, and a large selection of steaks and home-made desserts.
OPEN: 11-2.30 5-11 (Sun 12.30-11) (Apr-31 Oct 11-11)
BAR MEALS: L served all week 12-2 D served all week 5-9 Av main course £8 **RESTAURANT:** L served all week 12-2 D served all week 5-9 ☺: Free House ◖: Calders Cream, Calders 70/-. ♀: 8
FACILITIES: Children's licence Garden: Courtyard style
NOTES: Parking 80 **ROOMS:** 12 bedrooms en suite s£39.95 d£61 No children overnight

---

DUNDONNELL   Map 22 NH08

Pick of the Pubs

Dundonnell Hotel ★★★ ◉
IV23 2QR ☎ 01854 633204 🖷 01854 633366
e-mail: selbie@dundonnellhotel.co.uk
web: www.dundonnellhotel.com
Dir: From Inverness W on A835, at Braemore junct take A382 for Gairloch
Dundonnell is one of the leading hotels in the Northern Highlands. Originally a small inn accommodating the occasional traveller to Wester Ross, it has been considerably extended over the years. Its fine location, however, can never change. Sheltered beneath the massive An Teallach range (one of 21 Munros in the area), the views down Little Loch Broom are superb. The Broom Beg bar and bistro is the 'local', offering a wide range of beers and casual dining, while the Cocktail Bar is the place for a quiet aperitif while mulling over what to eat in the spacious restaurant. This could be pan-fried medallions of fillet beef with creamed spinach and red onion marmalade; pan-fried sea bass and halibut, with smoked haddock mash and braised fennel; or maybe roast escalope of salmon with lemon Dauphinoise, green beans and lime-marinated carrots.
OPEN: 11-11 (reduced hours Nov-Mar, please phone)
BAR MEALS: L served all week 12-2 D served all week 6-8.30 Av main course £5 **RESTAURANT:** D served all week 7-8.30 Av 3 course à la carte £27.50 ☺: Free House ◖: John Smith's.
FACILITIES: Children's licence Garden overlooking Little Loch Broom, seating Dogs allowed except in eating area
NOTES: Parking 60 **ROOMS:** 28 bedrooms en suite 3 family rooms s£45 d£90

FORT WILLIAM   Map 22 NN17

Pick of the Pubs

Moorings Hotel ★★★ ◉ 🍴
Banavie PH33 7LY ☎ 01397 772797 🖷 01397 772441
e-mail: reservations@moorings-fortwilliam.co.uk
web: www.moorings-fortwilliam.co.uk
Dir: From A82 in Fort William follow signs for Mallaig, then left onto A830 for 1m. Cross canal bridge then 1st right signposted Banavie
This striking modern hotel lies hard by the famous Neptune's Staircase, longest of the three lock-flights on the coast-to-coast Caledonian Canal. A historic monument, its eight locks can raise even sea-going craft a total of 64 feet. Most bedrooms and the Upper Deck lounge bar have good views of Ben Nevis (1344m) and Aonach Mor (1219m). Hearty bar meals favour the fish end of the food spectrum, with starters such as Lochaber smoked and cured fish platter (there's also a smoked meat platter); and paella-style seafood and saffron risotto. Main courses include deep-fried haddock in batter; rich game pie; spicy Hungarian goulash; roast chicken supreme stuffed with haggis; grilled Aberdeen Angus sirloin steak; and sausage of the week. Try crofter's omelette, containing sauté potatoes, onion, cucumbers, tomatoes and mushrooms. On summer evenings the award-winning Mariners cellar bar is open for drinks.
OPEN: 12-11.45 (Thurs-Sat til 1am) **BAR MEALS:** L served all week 12-9.30 D served all week Av main course £8.25
RESTAURANT: D served all week 7-9.30 Av 3 course à la carte £25 ☺: Free House ◖: Calders 70/-, Teltley Bitter,Guiness.
FACILITIES: Child facs Children's licence Garden: Small patio, food served outdoors Dogs allowed Water **NOTES:** Parking 80 **ROOMS:** 28 bedrooms en suite 2 family rooms s£43 d£86

Scotland

GAIRLOCH
Map 22 NG87

Pick of the Pubs

AA Seafood Pub of the Year for Scotland 2005-06

The Old Inn ♦♦♦♦ 🐟 🍺
IV21 2BD ☎ 01445 712006 📠 01445 712445
e-mail: info@theoldinn.net web: www.theoldinn.net
See Pick of the Pubs on opposite page

GARVE
Map 23 NH36

Inchbae Lodge Hotel 🍺
IV23 2PH ☎ 01997 455269 📠 01997 455207
e-mail: stay@inchbae.com
Dir: On A835, hotel 6m W of Garve

Originally a 19th-century hunting lodge, Inchbae Lodge is situated on the banks of the River Blackwater, with a bistro and elegant conservatory dining room offering panoramic views. An ideal base for those keen walkers wishing to take on Ben Wyvis and the Fannich Hills.
OPEN: Summer all day Winter 12-2, 5-11 **BAR MEALS:** L served all week 12-2 D served all week 5-9 Av main course £4.95 🍽: Free House 🍺: Devanha, Guiness. **FACILITIES:** Garden: Lawn, trees, river **NOTES:** Parking 20

GLENCOE
Map 22 NN15

Clachaig Inn
PH49 4HX ☎ 01855 811252 📠 01855 812030
e-mail: inn@clachaig.com
Dir: Just off A82, 2m E of Glencoe village, 20m S of Fort William
Situated in the heart of Glencoe, this 300-year-old inn is hugely popular with mountaineers and stands a short forest walk from Signal Rock, where the sign was given for the infamous massacre of 1692. Scenes for the third *Harry Potter* film were shot just 200 yards from the doorstep. The pub is renowned for its real ales, 120 malt whiskies, and warming food which includes such classic local dishes as haggis, Clachaig chicken, venison casserole, and prime Scotch steaks.
OPEN: 11-11 (Fri 11-12, Sat 11-11.30, Sun 12.30-11)) Closed: 24-26 Dec **BAR MEALS:** L served all week 12-9 D served all week 12-9 🍽: Free House 🍺: Fraoch Heather Ale,Houston Peter's Well, Atlas 3 Sisters, Atlas Brewery-Latitude. **FACILITIES:** Children's licence Grassed area, patio at front Dogs allowed **NOTES:** Parking 40 **ROOMS:** 23 bedrooms en suite 5 family rooms (★★)

♦ Pubs with Red Diamonds are the top places in the AA's three, four and five diamond ratings

---

GLENELG
Map 22 NG81

Pick of the Pubs

Glenelg Inn 🐟
IV40 8JR ☎ 01599 522273 📠 01599 522283
e-mail: christophermain7@glenelg-inn.com
web: www.glenelg-inn.com
Dir: From Shiel Bridge (A87) take unclassified road to Glenelg
The inn is a conversion of 200-year-old stables set in a large garden stretching down to the sea, with stunning views across the Sound of Sleat. Folk singers and musicians are frequent visitors to the bar, where at times a ceilidh atmosphere prevails. In addition to the cosy bar, there is a guests' private morning room and an atmospheric dining room. Menus offer traditional Scottish fare based on local produce, including plenty of fresh fish and seafood, hill-bred lamb, venison and seasonal vegetables. In the bar you can expect deep-fried monkfish, seafood casserole, pies, and cod and chips. Examples from the dinner menu are locally smoked haddock chowder with parmesan croutes; roast guinea fowl with an oatmeal and fresh herb stuffing, wrapped in smoked bacon on a black pepper mash; and bitter chocolate meringue with toasted hazelnut praline and cream.
OPEN: 12-11 (Bar closed lunch in winter)
BAR MEALS: L served all week 12.30-2 D served all week 6-9.30 **RESTAURANT:** 12.30-2 7.30-9 🍽: Free House
FACILITIES: Large garden going down to the sea Dogs allowed

KYLESKU
Map 22 NC23

Kylesku Hotel 🐟
IV27 4HW ☎ 01971 502231 📠 01971 502313
e-mail: info@kyleskuhotel@.co.uk
Dir: 35m N of Ullapool on A835, then A837 and A894 into Kylesku, hotel at end of road at old ferry pier

Old coaching inn by the ferry slipway between Loch Glencoul and Loch Glendhu in the Highlands of Sutherland. Both bar and restaurant menus specialise in locally caught seafood, salmon and venison in season. Dishes include grilled langoustines with garlic mayonnaise and chips; moules marinière, and venison casserole. Nearby are Britain's highest waterfall at Eas a Chual Aluinn and the gardens at Kerracher, accessible only by boat. Ideal for birdwatchers, wildlife enthusiasts, climbers and walkers.
OPEN: 11-11.30 (Mon-Thu, Sat 10-11.30 Fri 10-12, Sun 12.30-11) Closed: 1 Nov-28 Feb **BAR MEALS:** L served all week 12-2.30 D served all week 6-9 Sun lunch 12.15-2.30, dinner 6-9 Av main course £9 **RESTAURANT:** D served Tue-Sun 7-8.30 Av 3 course fixed price £25.95 🍽: Free House 🍺: Caledonian 80/-.
FACILITIES: Children's licence Garden: Stunning views overlooking the sea loch Dogs allowed **ROOMS:** 8 bedrooms 6 en suite 1 family room s£40 d£70

Pick of the Pubs

GAIRLOCH – HIGHLAND

The Old Inn

Set at the foot of the Flowerdale valley, looking out across Gairloch Harbour, this venerable old country inn has been in service since 1760. The attractive white building has been carefully restored to reveal and retain original details such as fireplaces and two-foot thick stone walls. The views could scarcely be more glorious, with the isles of Rona, Raasay, Skye and even the Outer Hebrides visible from across the harbour.

It's a lovely place to pass through, but with ample walking, fishing, golfing, birdwatching or simply lazing about on the plentiful golden beaches, this is an ideal base for a longer stay. The inn has fourteen rooms, all named after famous pipers. Indeed, the own-blend real ale is also named for the romantic figure of the Blind Piper, who lived in the glen over 250 years ago. Meals are available in both bar and restaurant. In an area where Loch Ewe scallops, Gairloch lobsters, Minch langoustines, brown crab, mussels and fresh fish are regularly landed, it's not surprising that seafood is the house speciality,

along with game from the local estates. Starters include Cullen Skink, a Scottish fish soup, or langoustine cocktail made from the freshest ingredients, while main dishes might be grilled mackerel with gooseberry sauce; or venison steak with basil mash. The bar menu offers up more simple fare: home-made pies perhaps, or fish and chips with real ale batter. Dogs are more than welcome, with rugs, bowls and baskets provided to make them feel at home. Outside, the inn has a large grassy area with picnic tables by a pretty stream, where the resident ducks waddle amidst the diners.

OPEN: 11-12
BAR MEALS: L served all week
12-9.30 D served all week 5-9.30
RESTAURANT: L served all week
12-5 D served all week 5-9.30
🍺: Free House
🍺: Adnams Broadside, Isle of Skye
Red Cullin, Blind Piper, Houston.
♀: 8
FACILITIES: Child facs Children's
licence Garden: Large grassy area
with picnic tables Dogs allowed
Rugs, water bowls, baskets
NOTES: Parking 20
ROOMS: 14 bedrooms en suite
3 family rooms s£32 d£45

◆◆◆◆ ♀ Map 22 NG87
IV21 2BD
☎ 01445 712006
🖨 01445 712445
e info@theoldinn.net
w www.theoldinn.net
Dir: Just off main A832, near
harbour at S end of village

LYBSTER
Map 23 ND23

The Portland Arms Hotel
KW3 6BS ☎ 01593 721721 ▤ 01593 721722
e-mail: info@portlandarms.co.uk
Dir: Beside A99. From Inverness to Wick, on L, 200yds from sign for Lybster
The Portland Arms was built as a coaching inn in the 19th century and is now a large hotel whose bar and dining areas cater for every mood: dine in Jo's Kitchen complete with aga stove, the Bistro Bar, or the formal Library. Dishes are home made and served with traditional oatcakes. Try seared Highland fillet of beef with haggis; rollmop herrings; trio of fish; or a salad plate with roast beef, salmon or prawns.
OPEN: 7.30-11 Closed: Dec 31-Jan 3 **BAR MEALS:** L served all week 12-3 D served all week 5-9 Sat-Sun 12-9 Av main course £8 **RESTAURANT:** L served all week 12-3 D served all week 5-9 Sat-Sun 12-9 Av 3 course à la carte £20 ⊕: Free House ◆: Calders70/-, Guiness. **FACILITIES:** Child facs Children's licence Food served outside **NOTES:** Parking 20 **ROOMS:** 22 bedrooms en suite 4 family rooms s£55 d£80 (★★★)

NORTH BALLACHULISH
Map 22 NN06

Loch Leven Hotel ♀
Old Ferry Rd, Onich PH33 6SA
☎ 01855 821236 ▤ 01855 821550
e-mail: reception@lochlevenhotel.co.uk
Dir: Off A82, N of Ballachulish Bridge

Over 350 years old, this was a working farm up to 50 years ago, as well as accommodating travellers from the Ballachulish ferry. On the northern shore of Loch Leven, it is ideally placed for touring the Western Highlands, and provides freshly prepared food in a friendly atmosphere. Try scallops with bacon; haggis (traditional or vegetarian) with neeps and tatties; or grilled salmon steak with dill sauce. Over 75 different malt whiskies are on offer.
OPEN: 11-12 (Th-Sat 11-1am Sun 12.30-11.45)
BAR MEALS: L served all week 12-3 D served all week 6-9 Quiet mid-winter Av main course £7.95 **RESTAURANT:** L served all week 12-3 D served all week 6-9 Quiet mid-winter Av 3 course à la carte £16 ⊕: Free House ◆: John Smith's, McEwan's 80/-, Guiness. ♀: 6 **FACILITIES:** Child facs Garden: Terrace with trees & shrubs overlooking loch Dogs allowed Water **NOTES:** Parking 30
See advert on page 613

PLOCKTON
Map 22 NG83

Pick of the Pubs

The Plockton Hotel ★★
Harbour St IV52 8TN ☎ 01599 544274 ▤ 01599 544475
e-mail: info@plocktonhotel.co.uk
See Pick of the Pubs on opposite page

Pick of the Pubs

Plockton Inn & Seafood Restaurant
Innes St IV52 8TW ☎ 01599 544222 ▤ 01599 544487
e-mail: stay@plocktoninn.co.uk
Dir: On A87 to Kyle of Lochalsh to Balmacara. Plockton 7m N

Attractive, stone-built free house standing 50 metres from the sea, at the heart of the fishing village where the *Hamish Macbeth* TV series was based. Proprietors Mary and Kenny were brought up in Plockton, and the inn was originally built as a manse for a great great grandfather of the family. The atmosphere is relaxed and friendly, with winter fires in both bars, and a choice of over 50 malt whiskies to sample. Local produce takes pride of place on the regular menu and blackboard specials, with locally caught fish and shellfish as a speciality (Scotland's AA Seafood Pub of the Year 2004). A purpose-built smokehouse behind the hotel adds to the variety of seafood on offer. Typical dishes are Plockton prawns with marie rose sauce, smoked seafood platter, and haggis with clapshot in traditional or vegetarian versions.
OPEN: 11-1am (Sun 12.30-11pm) **BAR MEALS:** L served all week 12-2.30 D served all week 5.30-9.30 Winter hrs 8.30/9pm Av main course £10 **RESTAURANT:** L served all week 12-2.30 D served all week 5.30-9.30 Winter hrs 8.30/9pm Av 3 course à la carte £16 ⊕: Free House ◆: Greene King Abbot Ale & Old Speckled Hen, Fuller's London Pride, Isle Of Skye Blaven, Caledonian 80/-. **FACILITIES:** Child facs Children's licence Garden: 2 gardens, sloping grass space at rear, trees Dogs allowed **NOTES:** Parking 10 **ROOMS:** 14 bedrooms 13 en suite 4 family rooms s£35 d£70 (★★★)

SHIELDAIG
Map 22 NG85

Pick of the Pubs

Shieldaig Bar ★ ♀
IV54 8XN ☎ 01520 755251 ▤ 01520 755321
e-mail: tighaneileanhotel@shieldaig.fsnet.co.uk
See Pick of the Pubs on page 612

 Pubs offering a good choice of fish on their menu

Room prices show the minimum double and single rates charged. Room rates in hotels and B&Bs often vary depending on the facilities, so be sure to check prices with the establishment before booking

Pick of the Pubs

The Plockton Hotel

A logo featuring a palm tree for a Scottish hotel? Well yes, when the hotel in question stands on the Gulf Stream-warmed shores of Loch Carron in the Northwest Highlands. And sure enough, here they are, growing happily between the hotel and the loch's foreshore. Fans of TV's *Hamish Macbeth* will recognise the location - many scenes from the series were filmed here.

The Plockton Hotel stands out in a row of whitewashed Highland cottages overlooking the loch's deep blue waters because, rather distinctively, it is painted in black pitch and pointed in white - the traditional way of weatherproofing coastal buildings. Not surprisingly, the whole village has National Trust protection, such is the appeal of these picturesque cottages, with their stunning views across the bay to Eilean Donan Castle nestling against its mountain backdrop. The hotel was perhaps a ship's chandler in the 19th century. Today it wins accolades for its seafood. Guests here can eat prawns from the loch moments after they have been landed. There's the freshest pan-fried herring in oatmeal; fillets of sole with a herb crust; grilled halibut with a ginger glaze; loch-caught wild salmon, poached with lime leaves, whole peppercorns and served with a fresh lime and crème fraîche dressing; and monkfish and smoked bacon brochettes - a heavenly combination. To backtrack, you could have started with seared scallops with a basil and garlic drizzle; a fresh dressed crab; Plockton smokies; haggis and whisky; or Talisker whisky pâté. There's meat too of course: succulent locally-reared beef and lamb; casseroled Highland venison, slowly cooked with red wine, herbs, juniper berries and redcurrant jelly; or chicken stuffed with Argyll smoked ham and cheese, sun-dried tomato, garlic and basil sauce. Hand-made sweets and an excellent wine list ensure a meal to remember.

OPEN: 11-11.45 (Sun 12.30-11)
BAR MEALS: L served all week 12-2.15 D served all week 6-9.15 (Sun 12.30-2.15) Av main course £6
RESTAURANT: L served all week 12-2.15 D served all week 6-9.15
🍺: Free House
🍺: Caledonian Deuchars IPA.
FACILITIES: Garden: Beer garden, summer house, amazing views Dogs allowed Water in garden
ROOMS: 15 bedrooms en suite 1 family room s£40 d£60

★★ 　　　Map 22 NG83
Harbour St IV52 8TN
☎ 01599 544274
📄 01599 544475
📧 info@plocktonhotel.co.uk
Dir: On A87 to Kyle of Lochalsh take turn at Balmacara. Plockton 7m N

Shieldaig Bar

All the seafood in this popular loch-front bar in a charming fishing village is caught locally. Not only that, but the prawn-fishing grounds have won a sustainable fishery award from the Marine Stewardship Council, and are now the model for similar locations in Sweden and elsewhere.

You can expect a friendly welcome here, the views across Loch Torridon to the sea beyond are stunning, and on a summer Friday night the bar is likely to be alive with the sound of local musicians, among them owner Chris Field, playing guitar, banjo, or pipes. In fact, all over Wester Ross you're likely to find music like this being played somewhere. Throughout the day a full range of alcoholic and non-alcoholic beverages is served to suit the hour, and there's always a ready supply of newspapers and magazines to read. The pub has a fine reputation for its bar snacks, such as sandwiches, home-made soups, and salads, and for its daily-changing specials such as fresh crab bisque, local seafood stew, Hebridean scallop mornay, venison, hare and other game in season, steak and ale pie, and Tuscan-style leek tart with home-made bread. There is also a fixed price menu, and a good range of real ales, including Isle of Skye Brewery Ales, Black Isle Ales, and Tenants Superior Ale. It's the sort of place you'll want to linger, so take note that the Fields also own the Tigh an Eilean Hotel next door.

OPEN: 11-11 (Sun 12.30-10) Closed: Dec 25 & Jan 1
BAR MEALS: L served all week 12-2.30 D served all week 6-8.30 Av main course £8
RESTAURANT: D served all week 7-8.30
🛢: Free House
🛢: Isle of Skye Brewery Ales, Tenants Superior Ale, Black Isle Ales. ⬛: 8
FACILITIES: Child facs Children's licence Open courtyard on Lochside with umbrellas Dogs allowed In the courtyard only. Water provided
NOTES: Parking
ROOMS: 11 bedrooms en suite 1 family room s£62.50 d£130

★ ⬛ Map 22 NG85 IV54 8XN
☎ 01520 755251
🖷 01520 755321
📧 tighaneileanhotel@shieldaig. fsnet.co.uk
Dir: 5m S of Torridon off A896 on to village road signposted Shieldaig, bar on Loch front

Scotland

TORRIDON
Map 22 NG95

Ben Damph Inn NEW ★★★ ⊗⊗ ⊃
IV22 2EY ☎ 01445 791242 ▤ 01445 712253
e-mail: bendamph@lochtorridonhotel.com
Dir: From Inverness A9 and signs to Ulapool. Take A335 then A832. In Kinlochelne; A896 through Annat Village. Pub 200 yds on R.
Set at the foot of the impressive Torridon mountains on the shores of Loch Torridon, the Ben Damph Inn is the ideal base for exploring the local area, including Inverewe Gardens, Applecross Peninsula and the road to Skye. In the evening, relax in the bistro which serves a varied menu with local specialities.
OPEN: 3-11 (3-11 Apr, May, Sep, Oct) 11-11 Jun-Aug Closed: 1st Nov-31 Mar **BAR MEALS:** L served all week 12-2 D served all week 6-8.45 Av main course £12 **RESTAURANT:** D served all week 6-8.45 Av 3 course à la carte £23 Av 3 course fixed price £15
⬛: Stag, McEwans, Cairngorm Brewery Travelwinds.
FACILITIES: Child facs Children's licence Garden: Drink only in garden. Small gravelled area **NOTES:** Parking 30
ROOMS: 12 bedrooms en suite sE48 dE70

ULLAPOOL
Map 22 NH19

The Argyll Hotel ⊃
Argyll St IV26 2UB ☎ 01854 612422 ▤ 01854 612522
e-mail: stay@theargyll.com
Traditional family-run hotel just a short stroll from the shores of Loch Broom. Timeless public bar and comfortable main bar, both with open fires and a good choice of malt whiskies to choose from. West Coast scallops and halibut, chicken supreme, venison medallions, and haggis, neeps and tatties feature on the varied menus.
OPEN: 11-11 (Sun 12-11) **BAR MEALS:** L served all week 12-2.30 D served all week 5.30-9 Av main course £7.95
RESTAURANT: L served all week D served all week 5.30-9 Av 3 course à la carte £17 ⬛: Free House ⬛: Scottish guest ales, Bellhaven Best, Anteallach Ales, Cairngorm Ales. **FACILITIES:** Bench seating at front Dogs allowed **NOTES:** Parking 20

Pick of the Pubs

The Ceilidh Place
14 West Argyle St IV26 2TY
☎ 01854 612103 ▤ 01854 612886
e-mail: stay@theceilidhplace.com
Dir: Along Shore St, past pier and 1st right to top of hill

The Ceilidh Place has certainly come a long way since its opening in 1970, in an old Ullapool boatshed where the proprietors served modest refreshments. Today, this unique complex comprises an all-day bar, coffee shop, restaurant, bookshop, art gallery and a venue for

continued

Loch Leven Hotel

Old Ferry Road,
North Ballachulish,
Inverness shire PH33 6SA
Tel: 01855 821236
Fax: 01855 821550

Hilary & John would like to give you a real Highland welcome to their Hotel on the Loch Leven, just of the A82, beside the Ballachulish Bridge. The most dramatic scenery Scotland has to offer is on the very doorstep. Set between Glencoe, Kinlochleven and Fort William it is well placed as a stop over on a Highland tour or a base with day trips to Oban and Mull, Inverness and the Black Isle, Mallaig and Skye or even Perth and Stirling. For those of us who like to relax and enjoy a few home comforts and rest our bones, this is the place to be. A beautiful setting, delicious food, comfortable accommodation and a friendly bar.

Friendly and informal, this 11 bedroomed hotel has a Lounge Bar, Public Bar and Restaurant all open to non-residents. Both bars are connected by the Loch View Restaurant and Family Room and they in turn open into the hotel garden that sweeps down to the Loch Leven and the old Ballachulish Ferry slipway. Relax and look out over the ever changing and breathtaking scenery, the snow on the mountains, the Shearwaters skimming the surface of the loch that turns to a mirror at slack water reflecting the whole scene. You can enjoy all that with a glass of wine or a pint while you choose from our extensive menu. Everything is freshly prepared to order.

Email: reception@lochlevenhotel.co.uk
Website: www.lochlevenhotel.co.uk

concerts, plays and poetry. The bar has a fine selection of malt whiskies and wines, while the restaurant specialises in vegetarian cuisine and local seafish. Mains might range from braised venison chop to the Ceilidh Place seafood platter; or even nut roast. The puddings offer a small but interesting choice, like chocolate and lemongrass tart; and iced vanilla terrine with red berry compote. Or you can try ice creams like caramel shortcake; and whisky, honey and oatmeal. Do leave space for Elsie's cakes though, as they are baked fresh everyday.
OPEN: 11-11 (Sun 12.30-11) Closed: 2nd wk in Jan for 2 wks
BAR MEALS: L served all week 12-6 D served all week 6.30-9
RESTAURANT: D served all week 6.30-9.30 Av 3 course à la carte £23 ⬛: Free House ⬛: Belhaven Best, Guinness, Scottish ales. **FACILITIES:** Mature, wooded garden Dogs allowed Garden only, water available on terrace **NOTES:** Parking 20

MIDLOTHIAN

PENICUIK
Map 21 NT25

The Howgate Restaurant ⊃ ♀
Howgate EH26 8PY ☎ 01968 670000 ▤ 01968 670000
e-mail: Peter@howgate.f9.co.uk
Dir: On A6094, 3m SE of Penicuik
The Howgate restaurant and bistro was originally stabling for racehorses and, more recently, the home of Howgate cheeses. Now, a log fire sets the scene in the bistro, whilst the cosy restaurant is slightly more formal. The regularly changing menus offer both traditional and contemporary dishes like

continued

Scotland

PENICUIK continued

oven-roasted sea bass; venison with herb rosti potatoes; and pasta twists with wild mushroom and basil sauce. Desserts include crème brûlée and, of course, Howgate cheeses!
OPEN: 12-2.30 6-11 Closed: Dec 25-26, 1-2 Jan
BAR MEALS: L served all week 12-2.30 D served all week 6-9.30 Av main course £11 **RESTAURANT:** L served all week 12-2.30 D served all week 6-9.30 Av 3 course à la carte £25 ☺: Free House ◀: Belhaven Best, Hoegaarden, Wheat Biere. ☺: 12
FACILITIES: Garden: Patio and tables adjacent to bistro
NOTES: Parking 45

MORAY

FOCHABERS   Map 23 NJ35

Gordon Arms Hotel
80 High St IV32 7DH ☎ 01343 820508 🖷 01343 820300
e-mail: info@gordonarms.co.uk
Dir: On A96 approx halfway between Aberdeen and Inverness
This 200-year old former coaching inn, close to the River Spey and within easy reach of Speyside's whisky distilleries, is understandably popular with salmon fishers, golfers and walkers. Its public rooms have been carefully refurbished, and the hotel makes an ideal base from which to explore this scenic corner of Scotland. The cuisine makes full use of local produce: venison, lamb and game from the uplands, fish and seafood from the Moray coast, beef from Aberdeenshire and salmon from the Spey - barely a stone's throw away!
OPEN: 11-3 5-11 (Sun 12-3, 6-10.30) **BAR MEALS:** L served all week 12-2 D served all week 5-6.45 Av main course £6.50
RESTAURANT: L served all week 12-2 D served all week 7-9 Av 3 course à la carte £22.50 ☺: Free House ◀: Caledonian Deuchars IPA, Scottish Courage John Smith's Smooth, Marsdons Pedigree. **FACILITIES:** Child facs Children's licence Dogs allowed
NOTES: Parking 40

PERTH & KINROSS

GLENDEVON   Map 21 NN90

Pick of the Pubs

The Tormaukin Country Inn and Restaurant 🐟 ☺
FK14 7JY ☎ 01259 781252 🖷 01259 781526
e-mail: enquiries@tormaukin.co.uk
Dir: N from Edinburgh, leave M90 junct 6 and take A977 to Kincardine, follow signs to Stirling, turning off at Yelts of Muckhard onto A823 Crieff.
The Tormaukin, which in Gaelic means hill of the mountain hare, was built in 1720 as a drovers' inn. During this time Glendevon, the 'hidden glen', was travelled by cattlemen making their way from the Tryst of Crieff to Falkirk's market place. These original cowboys came to the inn to quench their thirst, have a bite to eat and enjoy a sing-song. The setting is idyllic, surrounded by the Ochils, with hill walks, fishing and golf within easy reach. Original features include stone walls, exposed beams and natural timbers, with blazing log fires in the cosy lounge and bars. The menu has traditional appeal, with the likes of cullen skink soup; marinated venison steak on puréed parsnip, and home-made desserts such as steamed chocolate pudding with chocolate sauce. There is also a

continued

vegetarian selection and dishes from the chargrill. Live music is a regular feature.
OPEN: 11-11 (Sun 12-11) Closed: 25 Dec
BAR MEALS: L served all week 12-2.15 D served all week 5.30-9.30 (Open all day Sun) Av main course £10.95
RESTAURANT: D served all week 5.30-9.30 (Food served all day Sun) ☺: Free House ◀: Harviestoun Bitter & Twisted, Timothy Taylor Landlord, Calders Cream, Guiness. ☺: 12
FACILITIES: Child facs Garden: Patio area, food served outside
NOTES: Parking 50 **ROOMS:** 12 bedrooms en suite 1 family room s£30 d£70 (★★★)

GLENFARG   Map 21 NO11

The Bein Inn ☺
PH2 9PY ☎ 01577 830216 🖷 01577 830211
e-mail: enquiries@beininn.com

A real treat awaits classical rock, folk or blues fans at Scotland's Music Pub of the Year. Many famous musicians have performed in its lively Bistro Bar, and the memorabilia collection in the Basement Bar rivals anything to be seen in a Hard Rock Café. House specialities include noisettes of Scottish lamb, poached halibut steak, and vegetables Bonnie Prince Charlie, in which they are cooked in Drambuie and mushroom sauce, and served with rice and noodles.
OPEN: 11-2.30 5-11 **BAR MEALS:** L served all week 12-2 D served all week 5-9 **RESTAURANT:** L served weekends 12-2 D served all week 7-9 ☺: Free House ◀: Belhaven Best. **NOTES:** Parking 30

PUB WALK
Moulin Hotel
Pitlochry - Perth & Kinross

MOULIN HOTEL
11-13 Kirkmichael Road, Moulin
PITLOCHRY PH16 5EW
☎ 01796 472196
Directions: From A9 at Pitlochry take
A923. Moulin 0.75m
*Under 2,757ft Ben Vrackie, on the old
Dunkeld-Kingussie drove road, Moulin's
summer courtyard garden and winter
log fires and pub games make it popular
with walkers, tourists and locals. Real
ales from own micro-brewery, and
Gaelic fare on big, all-day menu.*
Open: 12-11 (Fri-Sat 12-11.45)
Bar Meals: L served all week 12-9.30
D served all week Av main course £8
Restaurant Meals: D served all week
6-9 Av 3 course à la carte £22.50
Av 4 course fixed price £20
Children welcome and dogs allowed.
Garden and parking available.
(for full entry see page 618)

Distance: 3 miles (4.8km)
Map: OS Landranger 43 & 52
Terrain: Tree-clad slopes
Paths: : Forest roads and paths
Gradient: Steep footpath at top

*Walk submitted and checked by the
Moulin Hotel, Pitlochry*

Scotland is great for walking and this invigorating route, starting at the Moulin Hotel just outside Pitlochry, captures the beauty and character of this magical landscape

Rising to the north of Pitlochry is the rocky outcrop of Craigower. This hill, at one time used as a beacon, is now in the care of the National Trust for Scotland who permit access to the summit. Its superb setting provides splendid views over the confluence of the Rivers Tummel and Garry to the north and west, and the valleys of the Tummel and the Tay to the south-east.

At the summit there is an annotated photograph highlighting important landmarks in the area, especially the view to the west, which stretches as far as Glencoe. To get there turn left on leaving the pub, following the road signposted to Craigower. Head for the golf course and make sure no-one is playing as you cross it. Continue past a small cottage and on up into some conifer woods on the lower slopes of Craigower. The route through these woods is clearly signposted and should present no real difficulties, although please remember to bear left when crossing the forestry road in order to stay on the direct route to the summit. Near the top this route becomes steep, but if you wish to avoid the steep ascent, there is an alternative. Simply turn right, along the forestry road, for a longer, but more gradual, approach to the summit.

This road can also be used as an alternative return route. Retrace your steps to the Moulin Hotel.

Scotland

Pick of the Pubs

Killiecrankie House Hotel ★★ ◎◎ ⌂ ⚲
PH16 5LG ☎ 01796 473220 ▤ 01796 472451
e-mail: enquiries@killiecrankiehotel.co.uk
web: www.killiecrankiehotel.co.uk
Dir: *Turn off A9 at Killicrankie. Hotel 3m N on B8079 on right*

This is a long-established hotel set in four sprawling acres of wooded grounds at the northern end of the historic Killiecrankie Pass. Built in 1840 as a dower house, it was converted to a hotel in 1939. In this delightful hotel the proprietors provide a genuine sense of hospitality thanks to a high level of personal attention. Cooking skills among the kitchen team are high, and only the best local produce, including seasonal vegetables, fruits and herbs from their own garden, is good enough for them. The conservatory makes an ideal spot for informal eating, while dinner is served in the casually elegant dining room. An excellent choice of light and more serious dishes includes deep-fried crispy prawns with pepper and chilli dipping sauce; smoked salmon and prawn open sandwich with lemon mayonnaise and salad; deep-fried scampi with chips; and rocket, toasted pine nuts and sunblushed tomatoes in fresh taglatelle. Bright airy, well-equipped bedrooms are furnished in pine.
OPEN: 12-2.30 6-11 Closed: Jan, Feb **BAR MEALS:** L served all week 12.30-2 D served all week 6.30-9 Av main course £8.95 **RESTAURANT:** D served all week 7-8.30 Av 3 course à la carte £20 ⊜: Free House ⛫: Calders Cream Ale, Red McGregor, Becks, Deuchers IPA. ⚲: 8 **FACILITIES:** Children's licence Garden: 1 acre of lawns, formal/vegetable garden Dogs allowed **NOTES:** Parking 2 **ROOMS:** 10 bedrooms en suite 2 family rooms s£65 d£130 ⊗

Pick of the Pubs

Lomond Country Inn ⚲
KY13 9HN ☎ 01592 840253 ▤ 01592 840693
e-mail: enquiries@lomondcountryinn.com
Dir: *M90 junct 5, follow signs for Glenrothes then Scotlandwell, Kinnesswood next village*
A small, privately owned hotel on the slopes of the Lomond Hills that has been entertaining guests for more than 100 years. It is the only hostelry in the area with uninterrupted views over Loch Leven to the island on which Mary Queen of Scots was imprisoned. Cosy public areas offer log fires, a friendly atmosphere, real ales and

continued

a fine collection of single malts. If you want to make the most of the loch views, choose the charming restaurant, a relaxing room freshly decorated in country house style. Specials may include supreme of guinea fowl on creamed mash with Calvados sauce, roast sirloin of beef, or strips of chicken with a leek and stilton sauce. A selection of grills is also available.

Lomond Country Inn

OPEN: 11-11 (Fri-Sat 11-12.45, Sun 12.30-11) Closed: Dec 25
BAR MEALS: L served all week 12.30-2 D served all week 6-9 Av main course £8 **RESTAURANT:** L served all week 12-2.30 D served all week 6-9.30 ⊜: Free House ⛫: Deuchers IPA, Calders Cream, Tetleys, Orkney Dark Island.
FACILITIES: Landscaped garden & decking overlooking Loch Dogs allowed **NOTES:** Parking 50

Pick of the Pubs

Moulin Hotel ★★ ⚲
11-13 Kirkmichael Rd, Moulin PH16 5EW
☎ 01796 472196 ▤ 01796 474098
e-mail: enquiries@moulinhotel.co.uk
web: www.moulinhotel.co.uk
See Pub Walk on page 615
See Pick of the Pubs on page 618

The Old Mill Inn ⚲
Mill Ln PH16 5BH ☎ 01796 474020 e-mail: r@old-mill-inn.com
Dir: *In town centre. Behind post office*

Set at the gateway to the Highlands, this converted old mill still boasts a working water wheel, now with a patio overlooking it. Visitors are assured of a good choice of real ales, malts and wine by the glass to accompany an eclectic cuisine: smoked haddock chowder, Stornaway black pudding, steamed mussels, salmon stir-fry, plus burgers, bacon and

continued

Scotland

brie ciabatta, and smoked salmon bagel.
OPEN: 10-11 **BAR MEALS:** L served all week 10-10 D served all week Av main course £7.95 **RESTAURANT:** L served all week 10-10 D served all week Av 3 course à la carte £15 ☺: Free House
🍺: Carlsberg-Tetley Tetley Bitter, Orkney Dark Island, Kettle Ale. **FACILITIES:** Garden: Food served outside **NOTES:** Parking 10

POWMILL   Map 21 NT09

Gartwhinzean Hotel
FK14 7NW ☎ 01577 840595 📠 01577 840779
Dir: A977 to Kincardine Bridge road. Approx 7m to Powmill. Hotel at end of village
Located between two of Scotland's finest cities, Edinburgh and Perth, and handy for exploring the nearby Ochil and Cleish Hills, this attractive hotel overlooks Perthshire's picturesque countryside. A large selection of malt whiskies and a cosy open fire add to the attractions. Traditional steak pie, lightly grilled fillet of salmon and noisettes of lamb feature among the dishes on the interesting, regularly changing menu.
OPEN: 11-11 (Sun 12.30-10.30) **BAR MEALS:** L served all week 12-1.45 D served all week 5-8.45 Av main course £8
RESTAURANT: L served all week 12-1.45 D served all week 5-8.45 Av 3 course à la carte £20 Av 3 course fixed price £17.50 ☺: Free House 🍺: Tetley Smoothflow, 70/-. **FACILITIES:** Garden: Food served outside Dogs allowed **NOTES:** Parking 100
ROOMS: 23 bedrooms en suite s£50 d£70 (★★★)

RENFREWSHIRE

HOUSTON   Map 20 NS46

Fox & Hounds ⵂ
South St PA6 7EN ☎ 01505 612448 612991 📠 01505 614133
e-mail: jonathan@foxandhoundshouston.co.uk
Dir: M8 - Glasgow Airport. A737- Houston
Regulars at this popular, well-kept 18th-century village inn have included ex-Rangers striker Ally McCoist, as well as actors Richard Wilson and Robert Carlyle. While this is a fish-lover's heaven with many and varied fresh fish and seafood specialities, the inn is also noted for its Scotch pie made with fillet steak; crisp fried escalope of chicken; and veal Fox and Hounds. Beers are from the award-winning, on-site Houston Brewing Company.
OPEN: 11-12 (11-1am Fri-Sat, 12.30-12 Sun)
BAR MEALS: L served all week 12-2.30 D served all week 5.30-10 (Sat & Sun 12-10) Av main course £7.50 **RESTAURANT:** L served all week 12-2.30 D served all week 5.30-10 Av 3 course à la carte £25 ☺: Free House 🍺: St Peters Well, Killelan, Barochan, Texas & Jack Frost. ⵂ: 10 **FACILITIES:** Children's licence Dogs allowed Water **NOTES:** Parking 40

Disabled people and those with Assist Dogs have new rights of access to pubs, restaurants and hotels under the Disability Discrimination Act of 1 October 2004. For more information see the website at www.drc gb.org/open4all/rights/2004.asp

---

SCOTTISH BORDERS

ALLANTON   Map 21 NT85

Allanton Inn NEW
TD11 3JZ ☎ 01890 818260 📠 01890 818182
e-mail: info@allantoninn.co.uk
Dir: 8m form Berwick-upon-Tweed, near village of Chirnside.
An 18th-century coaching inn at the heart of open Borders country, near the rivers Tweed, Blackadder and Whiteadder. Inside are two restaurants and a cosy bar serving real ales and an extensive range of malt whiskies. A varied, daily-changing dinner menu offers sirloin steak with a cracked black pepper sauce; braised lamb shank in a cider and juniper sauce with spring onion mash; and roast aubergine and sun blush tomato glazed with mozzarella cheese.
OPEN: 12-2 6-12 **BAR MEALS:** L served Wed-Sun 12-2 D served Wed-Sat 6-8.30 **RESTAURANT:** L served Wed-Sun 12-2 D served Wed-Sat 6-8.30 Av 3 course à la carte £20 🍺: Ossian, Durham Gold, Latitude, Deuchars. **FACILITIES:** Children's licence Garden: Large lawned area with fruit trees Dogs allowed **NOTES:** Parking 8
ROOMS: 4 bedrooms en suite s£39.50 d£79 No children overnight

---

ETTRICK   Map 21 NT21

Tushielaw Inn
TD7 5HT ☎ 01750 62205 📠 01750 62205
e-mail: robin@tushielaw.fsnet.co.uk
Dir: At junction of B709 & B711(W of Hawick)
18th-century former toll house and drover's halt on the banks of Ettrick water. Good base for trout fishing and those tackling the Southern Upland Way. An extensive menu is always available with daily changing specials. Fresh produce is used according to season, with local lamb and Aberdeen Angus beef regular specialities. Gluten-free and vegetarian meals are always available. Home-made steak and stout pie and sticky toffee pudding rate among other popular dishes.
OPEN: 12-2.30 6.30-11 **BAR MEALS:** L served all week 12-2 D served all week 7-9.30 **RESTAURANT:** L served all week 12-2 D served all week 7-9 ☺: Free House **FACILITIES:** Children's licence area with picnic tables Dogs allowed **NOTES:** Parking 8
ROOMS: 3 bedrooms en suite 3 family rooms s£32 d£50 (★★)

GALASHIELS   Map 21 NT43

Abbotsford Arms Hotel
63 Stirling St TD1 1BY ☎ 01896 752517 📠 01896 750744
e-mail: abbotsford@foxinns.com web: www.foxinns.com
Dir: Turn off A7 down Ladhope Vale, turn left opposite the bus station
Handy for salmon fishing in the nearby Tweed and visiting Melrose Abbey, this family-run, stone-built 19th-century coaching inn offers traditional bar food. The lunchtime choice runs from filled croissants, salads and baked potatoes to breaded haddock, chicken curry and sirloin steak, bolstered in the evening by roast lamb shank, duck and orange sausages, and quails in cranberry and port. A function room holds up to 150, and there are plenty of good local golf courses.
OPEN: 11.30-11 **BAR MEALS:** L served all week 2-6 D served all week 6-9 (Sun 12-6, 6-8) Av main course £6.95
RESTAURANT: L served all week 12-6 D served all week 6-9 (Sun 12-6, 6-8) Av 3 course à la carte £12.50 ☺: 🍺: John Smith's, Miller, McEwans 70/-, Fosters. **FACILITIES:** Child facs Children's licence Garden: Paved area with grass **NOTES:** Parking 10

Moulin Hotel

An imposing village inn just outside Pitlochry offering traditional Highland hospitality, and a popular venue for a chat, home-brewed beer and good food. By the time of the Jacobite rebellion of 1745, the hotel had already been in existence for half a century.

Lying in the village of Moulin, on the old drove road from Dunkeld to Kingussie at the foot of 841m Ben Vrackie, you'd have to search a wide area to find a better example of a traditional Scottish pub. The modern road runs through nearby Pitlochry, leaving Moulin as an ideal base for walking and touring. Visitors love discovering this white-painted pub. It's owned by Chris and Heather Tomlinson, two ocean-going yacht racers who sail as often as running a hotel permits, and the only entrants in the 2004 Atlantic Rally for Cruisers to be sponsored by two breweries - Stella Artois and

Moulin, their own. The courtyard garden is lovely in summer, while blazing log fires warm the place through in winter. The micro-brewery produces Braveheart, named during the filming of Mel Gibson's film, and three other real ales. It's Braveheart that gives the local venison dishes their extra flavour. A typical menu might be Tombuie smoked lamb, followed by a refreshing quenelle of fruit sorbet, then fillet of haddock, and finally chocolate fudge cake. Vegetarians can choose from sautéed mushroom pancakes, stuffed peppers, and vegetable goulash, among others.

OPEN: 12-11 (Fri-Sat 12-11.45)
BAR MEALS: L served all week 12-9.30 D served all week Av main course £8
RESTAURANT: D served all week 6-9 Av 3 course à la carte £22.50 Av 4 course fixed price £20 🏠: Free House
🍺: Moulin Braveheart, Old Remedial, Ale of Atholl & Moulin Light. ♀: 20
FACILITIES: Garden next to stream Dogs allowed on a lead
NOTES: Parking 40
ROOMS: 15 bedrooms en suite 3 family rooms s£40 d£50

★★ ♀   Map 23 NN95
11-13 Kirkmichael Rd, Moulin PH16 5EW
☎ 01796 472196
📄 01796 474098
📧 enquiries@moulinhotel.co.uk
🌐 www.moulinhotel.co.uk
Dir: From A924 at Pitlochry take A923. Moulin 0.75m

GALASHIELS continued

Kingsknowes Hotel ★★★
1 Selkirk Rd TD1 3HY ☎ 01896 758375 ▤ 01896 750377
e-mail: enquiries@kingsknowes.co.uk
web: www.kingsknowes.co.uk
Dir: Off A7 at Galashiels/Selkirk rdbt

In over three acres of grounds on the banks of the Tweed, a splendid baronial mansion built in 1869 for a textile magnate. There are lovely views of the Eildon Hills and Abbotsford House, Sir Walter Scott's ancestral home. Meals are served in two restaurants and the Courtyard Bar, where fresh local or regional produce is used as much as possible. Now under new ownership – reports please.
OPEN: 12-12 **BAR MEALS:** L served all week 11.45-2 D served all week 5.45-9.30 Av main course £8 **RESTAURANT:** L served all week 11.45-2 D served all week 5.45-9.30 Av 3 course à la carte £17 Av 4 course fixed price £21 ⊕: Free House ◖: McEwans 80/-, Scottish Courage John Smith's. **FACILITIES:** Child facs Garden: 3.5 acres, lawn, rockery Dogs allowed **NOTES:** Parking 60
ROOMS: 12 bedrooms en suite 3 family rooms

INNERLEITHEN   Map 21 NT33

Traquair Arms Hotel ◆◆◆
Traquair Rd EH44 6PD ☎ 01896 830229
e-mail: traquair.arms@scotborders.com
Dir: 6m E of Peebles on A72. Hotel 100mtrs from junct with B709
This traditional stone-built inn is in a village setting close to the River Tweed, surrounded by lovely Borders countryside and offering en suite bedrooms, a dining room and cosy bar. Real ales include Traquair Ale from nearby Traquair House, and the food has a distinctive Scottish flavour with dishes of Finnan savoury, salmon with ginger and coriander, and fillet of beef Traquair. A selection of omelettes, salads, and baked potatoes is also available.
OPEN: 11-12 (Sun 12-12) Closed: 25& 26 Dec, 1-3 Jan
BAR MEALS: L served all week 12-9 D served all week Av main course £6.50 **RESTAURANT:** L served all week D served all week 12-9 Av 3 course à la carte £18 Av 4 course fixed price £20 ⊕: Free House ◖: Traquair Bear, Broughton Greenmantle,plus seasonal guest. **FACILITIES:** Garden: Dogs allowed **NOTES:** Parking 75
ROOMS: 15 bedrooms en suite s£45 d£58

LAUDER   Map 21 NT54

Lauderdale Hotel ★★
1 Edinburgh Rd TD2 6TW ☎ 01578 722231 ▤ 01578 718642
e-mail: Enquiries@lauderdalehotel.co.uk
web: www.lauderdalehotel.co.uk
Dir: On the main A68 25m S of Edinburgh
This imposing Edwardian building with a cheerful lounge bar stands in extensive grounds, which are planted with young

shrubs and lots of spring flowering bulbs. The menu offers a good range of generously served meals in the bar or restaurant. Main courses include a fire house chilli, fresh fillet of Eyemouth haddock; and pan-fried breast of duck served on potato rosti and topped with a black morello cherry sauce. There are additional options from the regularly changing specials board, a good range of snacks and light bites, and an excellent vegetarian menu.

Lauderdale Hotel

OPEN: 11-11 (Thurs 11-12, Fri & Sat 11-1, Sun 12-11)
BAR MEALS: L served all week 12-3 D served all week 5-9 Av main course £8 **RESTAURANT:** L served all week 12-3 D served all week 5-9 Av 3 course à la carte £16 ⊕: Free House **FACILITIES:** Child facs Children's licence Landscaped garden with shrubs **NOTES:** Parking 50 **ROOMS:** 10 bedrooms en suite 1 family room s£42 d£70

Pick of the Pubs

AA Pub of the Year for Scotland 2005-06

The Black Bull Hotel ◆◆◆◆ ♀
Market Pl TD2 6SR ☎ 01578 722208 ▤ 01578 722419
e-mail: enquiries@blackbull-lander.com web: www.blackbull-lander.com
Dir: In the market place
An old coaching inn dating from 1750; the large dining room was once the church hall, and the church spire remains in the roof! Maureen Rennie bought it in a rundown state and transformed it into a cosy, characterful hotel with lots of interesting pictures and artefacts. The Harness Bar, so called because it used to house a large collection of horse brasses, is a comfortable wood-panelled room. Bar meals are served throughout the day, with lighter meals at lunchtime: expect baked potatoes, omelettes and sandwiches. In the evening the pace hots up when local beef, game in season, and seafood make an appearance along with Whitby scampi, Cumberland sausages and home-made burgers, plus a daily specials board. Eight well-furnished bedrooms encourage a longer stay, which is good news for the many walkers, anglers, shooters, business people and tourists who find it hard to leave the place.
OPEN: 12-2.30 5.30–11 (All day Sat, Sun, all day during week in Summer) Closed 1st 2 weeks Feb **BAR MEALS:** L 12-2.30 D 5.30-9 Av main course £7 **RESTAURANT:** L 12-2.30 D 5.30-9 Av 3 course à la carte £20 ⊕: Free House ◖: Broughton Ales, Coors, Guinness, Caffreys ♀: 14 **FACILITIES:** Children's licence Dogs welcome **NOTES:** Parking 10 **ROOMS:** 8 bedrooms en suite s£50 d£75

◆ Diamond rating for inspected guest accommodation

continued

Scotland

MELROSE
Map 21 NT53

Pick of the Pubs

Burts Hotel ★★★ ◎◎ ♀
Market Square TD6 9PL ☎ 01896 822285 ▥ 01896 822870
e-mail: burtshotel@aol.com web: www.burtshotel.co.uk
Dir: A6091, 2m from A68 3m S of Earlston

The Henderson family have been running Burts for 35
years, with Nick Henderson joining his parents 14 years
ago. The business goes from strength to strength, winning
the AA Pub of the Year award for Scotland 2004-2005. The
hotel, which overlooks the square in historic Melrose, was
built in 1722, originally as a townhouse for the provost. It
was a temperance hotel for a while, but there's no danger
of running dry these days, with a choice of real ales, 70
single malt whiskies and half a dozen wines by the glass.
Local produce is a features, with pan-fried escalopes of
Scottish salmon, dill and wine cream from the bar supper
menu, and trio of Border lamb chops served with
redcurrant jelly and mint sauce from the bistro selection.
For more local flavour, try the Selkirk bannock pudding
scented with lemon and served with shortbread ice cream.
OPEN: 11-2.30 5-11 **BAR MEALS:** L served all week 12-2
D served all week 6-9.30 Av main course £8.95
RESTAURANT: L served all week 12-2 D served all week 7-9
Av 3 course fixed price £31 ◎: Free House ◀: Caledonian
80/-, Deuchars IPA, Timothy Taylor Ladlord, Fullers London Pride.
♀: 7 **FACILITIES:** Children's licence Garden: Terrace and grass
Dogs allowed **NOTES:** Parking 40 **ROOMS:** 20 bedrooms
en suite 1 family room s£55 d£100 No children overnight

ST BOSWELLS
Map 21 NT53

Buccleuch Arms Hotel ★★ ◁ ♀
The Green TD6 0EW ☎ 01835 822213 ▥ 01835 823965
e-mail: info@buccleucharmshotel.co.uk
web: www.buccleucharmshotel.co.uk
Dir: On A68, 10m N of Jedburgh. Located on village green
A warm welcome is assured at this 16th-century inn, perfectly
placed at the heart of the Scottish Borders. There's a spacious
garden, with swings in the children's play area; young diners
are offered a separate menu, or smaller portions on request.
Lunchtime brings sandwiches, baguettes and baked potatoes,
whilst dinner might start with a locally smoked fish platter,
followed by supreme of chicken with mozzarella and bacon.
OPEN: 7.30-11 Closed: 25 Dec **BAR MEALS:** L served all week 12-2
D served all week 6-9 Av main course £8 **RESTAURANT:** L served
all week 12-2 D served all week 6-9 Av 3 course fixed price £15.95
◎: Free House ◀: Calders 70/-, 80/- & Calders Cream Ale,
Broughton, guest beers. ♀: 6 **FACILITIES:** Child facs Children's
licence Garden: Quiet, spacious & peaceful garden Dogs allowed £5
Supplement per night **NOTES:** Parking 80 **ROOMS:** 19 bedrooms
en suite 1 family room s£46 d£84

SWINTON
Map 21 NT84

Pick of the Pubs

The Wheatsheaf at Swinton ◎◎ ▥▥ ◁ ♀
Main St TD11 3JJ ☎ 01890 860257 ▥ 01890 860688
e-mail: reception@wheatsheaf-swinton.co.uk
Dir: 6m N of Duns on A6112
In the space of a couple of years, husband and wife team
Chris and Jan Winson have achieved great success at the
Wheatsheaf, building on a long-standing reputation for
good food and hospitality at this popular venue in the
picturesque village of Swinton. There is an impressive
wine list, with 10 wines available by the glass, six gins,
and over 40 malt whiskies with helpful tasting notes. Food
is very much at the heart of the operation, with an
emphasis on Borders meat from local butchers, salmon
from the Tweed, local game and seafood from Eyemouth.
A selection from the dinner menu might include crab, pak
choi & shitake mushroom spring roll on a sweet chilli
sauce; roast rack of border lamb on a basil and mustard
crust on a rosemary scented sauce; and sticky ginger and
pear pudding with hot fudge sauce and vanilla ice cream.
OPEN: 11-2.30 6-11 (Closed Sun eve in winter) Closed: 25-27,
31 Dec, 1 Jan **BAR MEALS:** L served all week 12-2 D served all
week 6-9 (Sun 6-8.30) Av main course £11.50
RESTAURANT: L served all week 12-2 D served all week 6-9
Av 3 course à la carte £21.50 ◎: Free House ◀: Caledonian
80/- & Deuchars IPA, Broughton Greenmantle Ale, Caledonian
70/-. ♀: 10 **FACILITIES:** Children's licence **NOTES:** Parking 6
ROOMS: 7 bedrooms en suite s£65 d£98 (★★★★)

TIBBIE SHIELS INN
Map 21 NT22

Pick of the Pubs

Tibbie Shiels Inn
St Mary's Loch TD7 5LH ☎ 01750 42231 ▥ 01750 42302
Dir: From Moffat take A708. Inn is 14m on R
On the isthmus between St Mary's Loch and the Loch of
the Lowes, this waterside Inn is named after the woman
who first opened it in 1826 and expanded the inn from a
small cottage to a hostelry capable of sleeping around 35
people, many of them on the floor! Famous visitors
during her time included Walter Scott, Thomas Carlyle
and Robert L. Stevenson. Tibbie Shiels herself is
rumoured to keep watch over the bar, where the
selection of over 50 malt whiskeys will sustain you for
ghost watching! Meals can be enjoyed either in the bar or
the non-smoking dining room; the inn also offers packed
lunches for your walking, windsurfing or fishing
expedition (residents fish free of charge). The menu offers
a wide range of vegetarian options as well as local fish
and game: highlights include Yarrow trout and Tibbies
mixed grill. Comfortable bedrooms are all en suite.
OPEN: 11-11 (Sun 12.30-11) 1Nov-Easter closed Mon, Tue &
Wed **BAR MEALS:** L served all week 12.30-8.15 D served all
week 12.30-8.15 Av main course £6.50
RESTAURANT: L served all week 12-8.15 D served all week
12.30-8.15 Av 3 course à la carte £11.25 ◎: Free House
◀: Broughton Greenmantle Ale, Belhaven 80/-.
FACILITIES: Children's licence Garden: 6 acres of lochside
NOTES: Parking 50 **ROOMS:** 5 bedrooms en suite
2 family rooms s£30 d£52 (♦♦♦)

TWEEDSMUIR

Map 21 NT12

The Crook Inn ♀
ML12 6QN ☎ 01899 880272 📠 01899 880294
e-mail: thecrookinn@btinternet.com

First licensed in 1604 and transformed into the art deco style in the 1930s, the Crook nestles deep in the Tweed Valley. It was once a haunt of Rabbie Burns, and remains an ideal base for country pursuits. An extensive range of food includes vegetarian haggis, salmon flambéed in pernod, and Cumberland sausage horseshoe, with various snacks, sandwiches and salads.
OPEN: 9-11 Closed: 25 Dec, 3rd wk in Jan **BAR MEALS:** L served all week 12-2.30 D served all week 5.30-8.30 Av main course £8
RESTAURANT: L served all week 12-2.30 D served all week 7-9 Av 3 course à la carte £15 🍺: Free House 🍺: Broughton Greenmantle & Best, Scottish Courage John Smith's, 80/-. ♀: 9
FACILITIES: Garden: Large grass area surrounded by trees, garden Dogs allowed Water bowls **NOTES:** Parking 60

SHETLAND

BRAE

Map 24 HU26

Busta House Hotel ★★★ ♀
Busta ZE2 9QN ☎ 01806 522506 📠 01806 522588
e-mail: reservations@bustahouse.com
A 16th-century laird's residence, Busta House is Britain's most northerly country house hotel offering superb sea views and boasting some of Shetland's few trees in its garden. Home-cooked food specialising in fresh Shetland and Scottish produce is served in both the cosy bar and restaurant.
OPEN: 11.30-11 12.30-11 (Mon-Sat 11.30-11, Sun 12.30-11)
BAR MEALS: L served all week 12-2.30 D served all week 6-9.30 Av main course £9 **RESTAURANT:** L served Sun 12.30-2 D served all week 7-9.30 Av 4 course fixed price £30 🍺: Free House
🍺: Valhalla Auld Rock, Simmer Dim & White Wife, Belhaven Best.
♀: 8 **FACILITIES:** Child facs Children's licence Garden: Private harbour **NOTES:** Parking 50 **ROOMS:** 20 bedrooms en suite 1 family room s£75 d£100

SOUTH AYRSHIRE

SYMINGTON

Map 20 NS33

Wheatsheaf Inn
Main St KA1 5QB ☎ 01563 830307 📠 01563 830307
Dir: Telephone for directions
This 17th-century inn lies in a lovely village setting close to the Royal Troon Golf Course, and there has been a hostelry here since the 1500s. Log fires burn in every room and the work of

continued

local artists adorns the walls. Seafood highlights the menu - maybe pan-fried scallops in lemon and chives - and alternatives include honey roasted lamb shank; haggis, tatties and neeps in Drambuie and onion cream; and the renowned steak pie.

Wheatsheaf Inn

OPEN: 11-12 (Sun 11-11) Closed: 25 Dec, 1 Jan
BAR MEALS: L served all week 12-9.30 Av main course £8
RESTAURANT: D served all week 12-9.30 🍺: Belhaven
🍺: Belhaven Best, St Andrews Ale, Tennents & Stella.
FACILITIES: Garden **NOTES:** Parking 20

STIRLING

BALQUHIDDER

Map 20 NN52

Pick of the Pubs

Monachyle Mhor ♀
FK19 8PQ ☎ 01877 384622 📠 01877 384305
e-mail: info@monachylemhor.com
web: www.monachylemhor.com
Dir: On A84, 11 miles N of Callender, turn right at Kingshouse. Monachyle Mhor is 6 miles along this road between two lochs.
Monachyle Mhor is a small award-winning farmhouse hotel romantically located within 2,000 acres of the Trossachs, Scotland's first National Park. Dramatic loch and mountain views are breathtaking; Rob Roy's final resting place is not far away. The interiors are resplendent with open fires, antique furniture, sporting prints mixed with original modern art, and country fabrics. Excellent menus change daily and reflect the seasons. Ingredients come from the hotel's own organic garden, as well as the rivers, lochs and hills of the estate. Dishes may range from slow roasted shoulder of Monachyle lamb served on roasted vegetables with a lamb jus infused with gremola; to a baked tier of aubergine and emmental, with pesto vegetables in an aubergine wrap, and a smoked aubergine and roasted pumpkin seed dressing. In season: red deer stalking, grouse shooting, and salmon and trout fishing; several golf courses nearby. Or just enjoy the views with tea and scones on the lawn.
OPEN: 12 Closed: Jan-14 Feb **BAR MEALS:** L served all week 12-3 D served all week 7-8.45 **RESTAURANT:** L served all week 12-1.45 D served all week 7-8.45 Av 4 course fixed price £38
🍺: Free House 🍺: Broughton Best, Angel Organic, Heather Ale, Grolsch. ♀: 15 **FACILITIES:** Garden: Overlooking tw lochs
NOTES: Parking 20

 Brewery/Company

Scotland

CALLANDER

Map 20 NN60

The Lade Inn ♀
Kilmahog FK17 8HD ☎ 01877 330152 📠 01877 331878
e-mail: steve@theladeinntrossachs.freeserve.co.uk
Set in its own grounds on the Leny Estate west of Callander, this white-painted free house was built as a tea room in the 1930s and first licensed three decades later. The cosy bar has an open fire and collection of brasses, and the non-smoking restaurant offers real Scottish cooking. Expect Lade Inn sausages with Arran mustard; baked cod with herb and garlic crust; and baked field mushrooms with pine kernels and smoked Lochaber cheese.
OPEN: 12-3 5.30-10.30 (all day Sat/Sun/Bank Holiday Mon) Closed: 1 Jan **BAR MEALS:** L served all week 12-2.30 D served all week 5.30-9 (Sat 12-9, Sun 12.30-9) Av main course £7.25
RESTAURANT: L served all week D served all week 5.30-9 (Sat 12-9, Sun 12.30-9) Av 3 course à la carte £20 🏠: Free House 🍺: Local ales: Waylade, Lade Back, Lade Out, plus guest ales. ♀: 7
FACILITIES: Child facs Children's licence Garden: Seating area overlooking ponds Dogs allowed **NOTES:** Parking 40

CRIANLARICH

Map 20 NN32

Ben More Lodge Hotel
FK20 8QS ☎ 01838 300210 📠 01838 300218
e-mail: info@ben-more.co.uk web: www.ben-more.co.uk
Dir: A82 to Crianlarich, R at T junc in village in Stirling direction
Beautifully set hotel at the foot of Ben More next to the River Fillan, on the road to the North West Highlands. Both bar and restaurant offer good food: from the latter expect chicken and bacon salad, and roast haunch of venison with redcurrant jelly, while bar dishes includes oven-baked Mallaig trout, steak pie, and various traditional snacks.
OPEN: 11-12 (Restricted hours Jan) Closed: Dec 25, Mon-Fri in Jan
BAR MEALS: L served all week 12-2.30 D served all week 6-8.45 Av main course £6 **RESTAURANT:** L served all week 12-2.30 D served all week 6-9 Av 3 course à la carte £12 Av 3 course fixed price £16 🏠: Free House 🍺: Tennents 80/-, Scottish Ales.
FACILITIES: Garden: Spacious grounds, fields adjacent Dogs allowed **NOTES:** Parking 50

DRYMEN

Map 20 NS48

The Clachan Inn
2 Main St G63 0BG ☎ 01360 660824
Quaint, white-painted cottage, believed to be the oldest licensed pub in Scotland, situated in a small village on the West Highland Way. Locate the appealing lounge bar for freshly-made food, the varied menu listing filled baked potatoes, salads, fresh haddock in crispy breadcrumbs, spicy Malaysian lamb casserole, vegetable lasagne, a variety of steaks, and good daily specials.
OPEN: 11-12 (Sun 12.30-12) Closed: 25 Dec & 1 Jan
BAR MEALS: L served all week 12-4 D served all week 6-10 Av main course £6 **RESTAURANT:** L served all week 12-4 D served all week 6-10 Av 3 course à la carte £20 🏠: Free House 🍺: Caledonian Deuchars IPA, Belhaven Best. **FACILITIES:** Dogs allowed **NOTES:** Parking 2

KIPPEN

Map 20 NS69

Cross Keys Hotel
Main St FK8 3DN ☎ 01786 870293 📠 01786 870293
e-mail: crosskeys@kippen70.fsnet.co.uk
Dir: 10m from Stirling, 20m from Loch Lomand

The village of Kippen in the Fintry Hills overlooking the Forth Valley has strong associations with Rob Roy. The pub dates from 1703, retains its original stone walls, and enjoys real fires in winter. Nearby Burnside Wood is managed by a local community woodland group, and is perfect for walking and nature trails. An excellent range of home-made dishes includes Scottish smoked salmon platter; creamy smoked haddock omelette; and steak and mushroom pie.
OPEN: 12-2.30 5.30-11 (Fri 5.30-12, Sat 12-12, Sun 12.30-11) Closed: 25 Dec, 1 Jan **BAR MEALS:** L served all week 12-2 D served all week 5.30-9 (Sun 12.30-9) Av main course £7.50
RESTAURANT: L served all week 12-2 D served all week 5.30-9 (Sun 12.30-9) 🏠: Free House 🍺: Belhaven Best, IPA, 80/-, Harviestoun Bitter & Twisted. **FACILITIES:** Child facs Children's licence Garden: Small garden with good views of Trossachs Dogs allowed Water, Biscuits **NOTES:** Parking 5

STRATHBLANE

Map 20 NS57

Kirkhouse Inn
Glasgow Rd G63 9AA ☎ 01360 771771 📠 01360 771711
e-mail: kirkhouse@cawleyhotels.com
Dir: A81 Aberfoyce rd from Glasgow city centre through Bearsden & Milngavie, Strathblane on junct with A891
17th-century coaching inn nestling beneath the jagged scarp of the Campsie Fells, a rolling patchwork of green volcanic hills and picturesque villages. Interesting menu offers international cuisine as well as traditional British dishes. A selection from the menu includes tournedos rossini, roast Burkhill duck, sirloin steak Jacobean, and salmon fillet.
OPEN: 10-midnight (Fri-Sat 10-1) **BAR MEALS:** L served all week 12-7 Av main course £5 **RESTAURANT:** L served all week 12-5 D served all week 5-10 Av 3 course à la carte £27.50 🏠: 🍺: Belhaven, Tennants 70/-. **NOTES:** Parking 300
ROOMS: 16 bedrooms en suite s£49.50 d£79 (★★★★)

 Pubs with this logo do not allow smoking anywhere on their premises

Not all of the pubs in the guide are open all week or all day. It's always best to check before you travel

THORNHILL
Map 20 NN60

Lion & Unicorn
FK8 3PJ ☎ 01786 850204
Dir: On A873 Blair Drummond to Aberfoyle
An old droving inn dating from 1635, once the favourite haunt of Rob Roy MacGregor. These days it has a games room for whiling away a few hours, and a beer garden for alfresco eating and drinking. Home-cooked dishes range from roast beef and Yorkshire pudding in the bar, to rack of Persia lamb with apricots and rosemary in the restaurant.
OPEN: 12-12 (Fri-Sat 12-1) **BAR MEALS:** L served all week 12-9 D served all week 12-9 Av main course £5.50
RESTAURANT: L served all week 12-9 D served all week Av 3 course à la carte £20 ☺: Free House ☜: Bellhaven Best, guest ales.
FACILITIES: Garden: Dogs allowed **NOTES:** Parking 25

WEST LOTHIAN

LINLITHGOW
Map 21 NS97

Pick of the Pubs

Champany Inn - The Chop and Ale House ◉◉◉
Champany EH49 7LU ☎ 01506 834532 🗎 01506 834302
e-mail: reception@champany.com
It has been described as the 'Rolls Royce of steak restaurants', and holds two AA Rosettes for the excellence of its cooking, so Champany Inn is a place simply not to be missed if you want to sample the best Scottish beef. A collection of buildings dating from the 17th century houses the Chop and Ale House and its superior sister, the main restaurant. Both have been under the ownership of well-known restaurateurs Anne and Clive Davidson for more than twenty years who are renowned for the sourcing, handling and cooking of prime Scottish beef. There are several choices of Aberdeen Angus steaks, and an extensive range of Champany burgers as they should be - made from the same meat as the steaks and cooked medium rare. There are also Scottish lamb chops, home-made sausages, chargrilled chicken, and cod and chips. For those who have room, the sweet menu includes profiteroles, Champany cheesecake and hot waffles.

OPEN: 12-2 6.30-10 (all day w/end) Closed: 25/26 Dec, 1/2 Jan
BAR MEALS: L served all week 12-2 D served all week 6.30-10 Open all day Sat-Sun Av main course £10.50
RESTAURANT: L served Mon-Fri 12.30-2 D served Mon-Sat 7-10 Av 3 course à la carte £55 Av 2 course fixed price £16.75
☺: Free House ☜: Belhaven. **FACILITIES:** Garden: Courtyard, traditional garden **NOTES:** Parking 50

SCOTTISH ISLANDS

ISLAY, ISLE OF

BALLYGRANT
Map 20 NR36

Pick of the Pubs

Ballygrant Inn & Restaurant
PA45 7QR ☎ 01496 840277 🗎 01496 840277
e-mail: info@ballygrant-inn.co.uk
Dir: NE of Isle of Islay, 3m from ferry terminal at Port Askaig
Variously a farm, an inn, a mine boss's house, and finally, 200 years later in 1967, an inn again. Set in two and a half acres of grounds and enclosed by heather-clad hills, it's close to two of Islay's seven malt whisky distilleries, and within easy reach of Port Askaig ferry terminal. Food is served all day from breakfast through morning coffee, snacks and lunch, to dinner. Scottish ales and all the island's malts are served in the bar, along with bar meals such as grilled trout, beef and orange casserole, lamb patia curry, and a vegetarian dish of the day. Fresh Islay crab, oysters and scallops are a must whenever they're available. The restaurant menu features grilled Scottish salmon brochettes, Scottish Blackface lamb chops, pan-fried local sirloin steak and venison, and much more. Butterscotch tart with chocolate sauce, and Drambuie fruits of the forest compÛte with brown bread ice cream number among the desserts.
OPEN: 11-11 (Wkds 11-1am) **BAR MEALS:** L served all week 12-3 D served all week 7-10 Av main course £8.95
RESTAURANT: L served all week 12-3 D served all week 7-10
☺: Free House ☜: Belhaven Best, calders 80/-, Calders 70/-.
FACILITIES: Child facs Garden: Patio, grassed area overlooking woodland Dogs allowed **NOTES:** Parking 35 **ROOMS:** 3 bedrooms en suite 1 family room s£27.50 d£55 (★★)

SKYE, ISLE OF

ARDVASAR
Map 22 NG60

Ardvasar Hotel ★★ ♀
IV45 8RS ☎ 01471 844223 🗎 01471 844495
e-mail: richard@ardvasar-hotel.demon.co.uk
web: www.ardvasarhotel.com
Dir: From ferry terminal, 50yds & turn left

The second oldest inn on Skye, this well-appointed white-painted cottage-style hotel offers a warm, friendly welcome and acts as an ideal base for exploring the island, spotting the wildlife and enjoying the stunning scenery. Overlooking the Sound of Sleat, the Ardvasar is within walking distance of the

continued

Scotland

ARDVASAR continued

Clan Donald Centre and the ferry at Armadale. Popular menus offers freshly-caught seafood, as well as baked venison in peppers and port wine pie, lamb and leek potato hot pot and savoury vegetable crumble. Straightforward basket meals are a perennial favourite.
OPEN: 12-12 (Sun 12-11) **BAR MEALS:** L served all week 12-2.30 D served all week 5.30-9 **RESTAURANT:** D served all week 7-9 ⊕: Free House ◀: 80/-, Deuchars, IPA, Isle of Skye Red Guillin. ♀: 6 **FACILITIES:** Children's licence Garden: Dogs allowed **NOTES:** Parking 30 **ROOMS:** 10 bedrooms en suite

CARBOST
Map 22 NG33

The Old Inn
IV47 8SR ☎ 01478 640205 📠 01478 640325
e-mail: reservations@oldinn.f9.co.uk
Dir: (Telephone for directions. Pub opposite village school)
There are wonderful views of the Cuillin Hills from the waterside patio garden of this 200-year-old free house. Located on the edge of Loch Harport, the inn is popular with walkers and climbers. Open fires welcome winter visitors, whilst summertime brings live weekly Highland music sessions. The menu includes daily home-cooked specials, with soups, numerous fresh fish dishes, and desserts.
OPEN: 11-12 (hours change in winter - please ring)
BAR MEALS: L served all week 12-2 D served all week 6-9 Av main course £7.95 **RESTAURANT:** L served all week 12-2 D served all week 6-9 ⊕: Free House ◀: Red Cuillin, Black Cuillin, Hebridean Beer. **FACILITIES:** Child facs Children's licence Garden: Shoreside Patio Dogs allowed **NOTES:** Parking 20

ISLE ORNSAY
Map 22 NG71

Pick of the Pubs

Hotel Eilean Iarmain ★★ ◎◎
IV43 8QR ☎ 01471 833332 📠 01471 833275
e-mail: hotel@eileaniarmain.co.uk
Dir: A851, A852 right to Isle Ornsay harbour front

This award-winning Hebridean hotel overlooks the Isle of Ornsay harbour and Sleat Sound. The old-fashioned character of the hotel remains intact, and décor is mainly cotton and linen chintzes with traditional furniture. More small private hotel than pub, there are some similarities. A bar and restaurant ensure that the standards of food and wine served here - personally chosen by the owner Sir Iain Noble - are exacting. Start off with a grilled seafood sausage on cucumber pickle with a Glendale organic salad, or oyster mushroom and barley risotto with parmesan crisp, before moving on to main courses of

grilled calves' liver with crisp bacon, thyme mousseline, fondant potato and a shallot and sherry jus; or the local seafood medley poached in chablis and saffron. Round off the meal with chocolate and armagnac tart with cinnamon cream, banana fritters rolled in nutmeg and sugar with butterscotch sauce, or local Mull cheeses. Then, just soak up the atmosphere.
OPEN: 11-11 (Sat 11-12.30am, Sun 12-11 -1am)
BAR MEALS: L served all week 12-2.30 D served all week 6-9.30 Av main course £8 **RESTAURANT:** L served all week 12-2 D served all week 6.30-9 ⊕: Free House ◀: McEwans 80/-. **FACILITIES:** Garden: Food served outside Dogs allowed **NOTES:** Parking 30 **ROOMS:** 16 bedrooms en suite s£60 d£120

STEIN
Map 22 NG25

Stein Inn ♀
Macleod's Ter IV55 8GA ☎ 01470 592362
e-mail: angus.teresa@steininn.co.uk
Dir: Telephone for directions
This 18th-century inn, in a lovely hamlet right next to the sea, is everything that you would expect of traditional Scottish hospitality; fine food, a Highland bar offering over 99 malt whiskies, and a warm welcome. The food is prepared from the freshest of produce, and diners can opt to eat in the non-smoking dining room or in the bar. There is a separate vegetarian and children's menu.
OPEN: 11-12 (Sun 12.30-11. Winter 4-11) **BAR MEALS:** L served all week 12-4 D served all week 6-9 Sun lunch 12.30-4 Av main course £6.50 **RESTAURANT:** L served none D served all week 6-9 Av 3 course à la carte £14.50 ◀: Red Cuillin, Trade Winds, Reeling Deck, Deuchars IPA. ♀: 8 **FACILITIES:** Child facs Children's licence Garden: Picnic tables overlooking the sea Dogs allowed **NOTES:** Parking 5 **ROOMS:** 6 bedrooms en suite 2 family rooms s£25 d£50

SOUTH UIST

LOCHBOISDALE
Map 22 NF71

The Polochar Inn
Polochar HS8 5TT ☎ 01878 700215 📠 01878 700768
e-mail: polocharinn@btconnect.co.uk
Dir: W from Lochboisdale & take B888. Hotel at end of road
Overlooking the sea towards the islands of Eriskay and Barra, this superbly situated 18th-century inn enjoys beautiful sunsets. The bar menu offers fresh seafood dishes and steaks with various sauces, while restaurant fare includes venison, fresh scallops or steak pie.
OPEN: 11-11 (Thu-Sat 11-1, Sun 12.30-11) **BAR MEALS:** L served all week 12.30-2.30 D served all week 6-9 Av main course £8 **RESTAURANT:** L served all week 12-2.30 D served all week 6-9 Av 3 course à la carte £17 ⊕: Free House ◀: no real ale. **FACILITIES:** Garden: barbecue **NOTES:** Parking 40

continued

Wales

Pub of the Year for Wales

The White Swan

Llanfrynach

(see p648)

Wales

BRIDGEND

KENFIG
Map 09 SS88

Prince of Wales Inn ♀
CF33 4PR ☎ 01656 740356
e-mail: prince-of-wales@bt.connect.com
Dir: M4 junct 37 into North Cornelly. Take left at x-roads and follow signs for Kenfig and Porthcawe. Pub is 600yds on right.
Dating from 1440, this stone-built inn has been many things in its time including a school, guildhall and courtroom. Why not sup some real cask ale in the bar by an inviting log fire? Typical menu includes steak and onion pie, lasagne, chicken and mushroom pie, and a variety of fish dishes. Look out for today's specials on the blackboard. Recent change of hands, only the sixth in 230 years!
OPEN: 11-11 **BAR MEALS:** L served Tue-Sat 12-3 D served Tue-Sat 7-9 (Sun 12-3) Av main course £5.50 **RESTAURANT:** L served all week 12-9 D served Tue-Sat 7-9 (Sun 12-3) Av 3 course à la carte £14 ☺: Free House ◀: Bass Triangle, Worthington Best, Guest Ales. ♀ 20 **FACILITIES:** Garden: Food served outside Dogs allowed Water, toys **NOTES:** Parking 30

CARDIFF

CREIGIAU
Map 09 ST08

Pick of the Pubs

Caesars Arms
Cardiff Rd CF15 9NN ☎ 029 20890486 ▣ 029 20892176
Dir: 1m from M4 junct 34

Some ten miles out of Cardiff, yet easily accessible from the M4 (J34) down winding lanes, the Caesars Arms attracts a well-heeled clientele to its heated patio and terrace looking out over the gardens and surrounding countryside. The inn prides itself on the vast selection of fresh fish, seafood, meat and game which are enticingly displayed in shaven-ice display cabinets. To begin as bajan fish cakes; crispy laver balls; ogen melon balls with malibu; crayfish cocktail; and scallops with leeks and bacon. Hake, salmon or monkfish may follow, with Dover soles, crawfish tails and lobster priced by weight. Welsh beef steaks, honeyed crispy duck, and roast rack of Welsh lamb satisfy serious meat eaters, and you can help yourself from brimming bowls full of assorted salads, all in a friendly and relaxed atmosphere. Draught ales are somewhat overshadowed by a massive wine list with many selections by the glass.

continued

OPEN: 12-2.30 7-12 Closed: 25 Dec **BAR MEALS:** L served all week 12-2.30 D served Mon-Sat 7-10.30 (Sun 12-3.30) **RESTAURANT:** L served all week 12-2.30 D served Mon-Sat 7-10.30 ☺: Free House ◀: Hancocks. **FACILITIES:** Garden: Terraced area with large umbrellas **NOTES:** Parking 100

CARMARTHENSHIRE

ABERGORLECH
Map 08 SN53

The Black Lion
SA32 7SN ☎ 01558 685271 e-mail: michelle.r@btinternet.com
Dir: A40 E from Carmarthen, then B4310 signed Brechfa & Abergorlech
A 17th-century coaching inn in the Brechfa Forest, with a beer garden overlooking the Cothi River, and an old packhorse bridge. Flagstone floors, settles and a grandfather clock grace the antique-furnished bar, while the modern dining room is welcoming in pink and white. Try home-made chicken and leek pie, curry of the day, or a fresh salmon steak. Miles of forest and riverside walks are easily reached from the pub.
OPEN: 12-3.30 (Sat 12-11pm, Sun 12-10pm) Sun Closed after 5 in winter **BAR MEALS:** L served Tue-Sun 12-2 D served Tue-Sun 7-9pm (Sun 7-8.30) Av main course £5.95 **RESTAURANT:** L served Sun 12-2 D served Fri-Sat 7-9 Av 3 course à la carte £12 ☺: Free House ◀: Brains SA, Buckley's Best, Spitfire, Young's Bitter. **FACILITIES:** Garden: 6 large tables & umbrellas Dogs allowed Water **NOTES:** Parking 20

LLANARTHNE
Map 08 SN52

Golden Grove Arms ♀
SA32 8JU ☎ 01558 668551 ▣ 01558 668069
Dir: From end M4 take A48 toward Carmarthen, turn L off A48 (sign-posted National Botanical Gardens), follow signs to Llanarthne
Visitors to the Towy Valley and Wales's National Botanic Gardens will find Llanarthne midway between Carmarthen and Llandeilo. Up-to-date facilities in a natural setting draw the crowds to both bars and the restaurant for home-cooking. Extensive choices encompass minted lamb chops, chicken odessa, nut wellington, sirloin steaks, Reverend James Pie, and brie and broccoli bake. Under new management.
OPEN: 12-10.30 (Sun 12-10.30) **BAR MEALS:** L served all week 11.30-2.30 D served all week 6-9 Av main course £6.73 **RESTAURANT:** L served all week 11.30-2.30 D served all week 6-9 ☺: ◀: Brains Buckleys Best & Reverend James. ♀: 7 **FACILITIES:** Garden **NOTES:** Parking 40

LLANDEILO
Map 08 SN62

The Angel Hotel NEW ▷♡ ♀
Rhosmaen St SA19 6EN ☎ 01558 822765 ▣ 01558 824346
e-mail: capelbach@hotmail.com
Dir: Follow signs towards Llandeilo
Popular inn offering plenty of inducement to draw the discerning customer. At the rear is an intimate bistro, located in a part of the building dating back to the 1700s, while the inviting bar area plays host to live music nights and jazz evenings. The best of local seasonal produce features on the extensive menu and daily fish and specials boards. Try one of the carvery buffets, perhaps chicken in pesto cream; poached salmon; pasta salad; or pork balti.
OPEN: 11-3.30 6.30-12 **BAR MEALS:** L served Mon-Sat 11.30-2.30 D served Mon-Sat 7-9.30 Av main course £5.50 **RESTAURANT:** L served Mon-Sat 11.30-2.30 D served Mon-Sat 7-9.30 Av 3 course à la carte £20 Av 3 course fixed price £9.95 ◀: Evans Evans Ales, Tetleys, Speckled Hen. ♀: 12 **FACILITIES:** Garden: Walled, terraced garden with seating for 40

The Angel Inn ◎◎ ♀
Salem SA19 7LY ☎ 01558 823394 ▤ 01558 823371
Dir: A40 then B4302, turn L 1m after leaving A40 then turn R at T junction and travel 0.25m to Angel Inn. Located on the right hand side

Traditional village pub characterised by beamed ceilings and a large collection of fascinating artefacts. Popular bar food is served along with a children's menu, a list of vegetarian dishes, and daily local specials. In the restaurant a typical meal might be roast fillet of Welsh beef, warm salad of chicken supreme, charred breast of Cressingham Duck, or seared escalope of salmon, and home-made ice creams.
OPEN: 12-2.30 6-11 **BAR MEALS:** L served Wed-Sun 12-2 D served Tue-Sat 6.30-9 Av main course £8
RESTAURANT: L served Wed-Sun 12-2 D served Tue-Sat 7-9 Av 3 course à la carte £22 ◎: Free House ◀: Worthington Highgate Dark Mild, Buckleys Best, Colins, Buckleys Smooth.
FACILITIES: Garden **NOTES:** Parking 60

The Castle Hotel
113 Rhosmaen St SA19 6EN ☎ 01558 823446 ▤ 01558 822290
A 19th-century Edwardian-style hotel within easy reach of Dinefwr Castle and wonderful walks through classic parkland. A charming, tiled and partly green-painted back bar attracts plenty of locals, while the front bar and side area offer smart furnishings and the chance to relax in comfort over a drink. A good range of Tomas Watkins ales is available, and quality bar and restaurant food is prepared with the finest of fresh local ingredients. Under new management.
OPEN: 12-11 (Sun 12-10.30) **BAR MEALS:** L served all week 12-2.30 D served all week 6.30-9 Av main course £6.95
RESTAURANT: L served all week 12-2.30 D served Mon-Sat 6.30-9 ◎: ◀: Tomos Watkin Best, OSB & Merlin Stout, Coors Worthington Draught, Guest Ale. **FACILITIES:** Garden: Slabbed area inside internal buildings

The Red Lion Inn
SA18 3JA ☎ 01269 851202
Almost 300 years old, this historic inn retains the atmosphere and feel of the original pub. Several fireplaces and other original features remain to generate a friendly, welcoming environment in which to relax and enjoy good food and well kept real ales. Dishes range from fillet of salmon with roast potato and spinach, to breast of chicken stuffed with mozzarella and wrapped in parma ham.
OPEN: 12-2 6-11 (Sun closed evening) **BAR MEALS:** L served all week 12-2 D served all week 6-9 Av main course £6
RESTAURANT: L served all week 12-2 D served all week 6-9 Av 3 course à la carte £22 ◎: ◀: Worthington, Tomos Watkin.
FACILITIES: Garden: Food served outside **NOTES:** Parking 50

Pick of the Pubs

The Salutation Inn 🐟
SA32 7NH ☎ 01267 290336
Dir: 5m from Carmarthen on A40

The 'Sal', as it is affectionately known to the locals, has long been pulling them in from as far away as Swansea and Llanelli. Partly, this can be put down to the lure of the Towy Valley, with its excellent fishing, but the Salutation has long had a reputation for food that continues under the stewardship of new landlord, Mark Williams. It's a pub with character and a following of colourful locals who congregate in the bar, where Felinfoel Double Dragon is the preferred ale. Stripped floors, bare tables and candles are the defining features of both bar and restaurant areas where generous blackboards offer a selection of dishes based on the abundant local produce. Traditional Sunday lunch.
OPEN: 11-3 6-11 (Sun 11-3, 5-11 all day Jun-Sep)
BAR MEALS: L served all week 12-2.30 D served all week 6-10
RESTAURANT: L served all week 12-2.30 D served all week 6-10 ◎: Felinfoel ◀: Felinfoel - Double Dragon, Dragon Bitter.
FACILITIES: Child facs Garden: Food served outside Dogs allowed **NOTES:** Parking 15

The Royal Oak Inn ♦♦♦
SA20 0NY ☎ 01550 760201 ▤ 01550 760332
e-mail: royaloak@rhandirmwyn.com
web: www.rhandirmwyn.com
This comfortable inn with its stone floors and log fires was originally built as a hunting lodge in 1850. Local brews from Wye Valley and Evan Evans supplement well-known beers like Wadworth and Greene King, whilst whisky drinkers can sample from around fifty single malts. In summer, far-reaching views make the garden ideal for al fresco dining. Expect lunchtime sandwiches, as well as hot dishes like black beef curry, vegetable goulash, or grilled trout.
OPEN: 11.30-3 6-11 (Sun 12-2 7-10.30) **BAR MEALS:** L served all week 12-2 D served all week 6-9.30 Av main course £6
RESTAURANT: L served all week 12-2 D served all week 6.30-9.30 Sun lunch 12-2 dinner 7-9.30 Av 3 course à la carte £18 ◎: Free House ◀: Greene King Abbot Ale, Wadworth 6X, Burtons, Wye Valley. **FACILITIES:** Children's licence Garden: Lawn, food served outside Dogs allowed **NOTES:** Parking 20 **ROOMS:** 5 bedrooms 3 en suite 1 family room s£22.50 d£56

♀ 7   Number of wines by the glass

Wales

RHOS
Map 08 SN33

Lamb of Rhos ♀
SA44 5EE ☎ 01559 370055
Country inn with flagstone floors, beamed ceilings and open fires - as well as its own jail and the 'seat to nowhere'. A menu of traditional pub fare includes steaks, chops, mixed grill, vegetarian and vegan dishes all cooked on the premises.
OPEN: 12-2.30 5-11 (Fri-Sun-all day Jul-Aug all day)
BAR MEALS: L served all week 12-2.3 D served all week 6-9 Av main course £5.50 **RESTAURANT:** L served Sun 12-2 D served Fri-Sat 7-9 Av 3 course à la carte £16 ☺: Free House
⊕: Worthington Cream Flow, Banks Original. **FACILITIES:** Garden: beer garden, outdoor eating, patio Dogs allowed by arrangement only **NOTES:** Parking 50 No credit cards

CEREDIGION

CARDIGAN
Map 08 SN14

Webley Hotel ♦♦♦
Poppit Sands SA43 3LN ☎ 01239 612085
Dir: A484 from Carmarthen to Cardigan, then to St Dogmaels, turn R in village centre to Poppit Sands
Located on the coastal path, and within walking distance of Poppit Sands, this hotel overlooks the Teifi Estuary and Cardigan Island. There are good children's facilities and dogs are welcome by prior arrangement.
OPEN: 11.30-3 6.30-11.30 (Summer open all day)
BAR MEALS: L served all week 12-2 D served all week 6.30-9 Av main course £6.50 **RESTAURANT:** L served all week D served all week Av 3 course à la carte £9 ☺: Free House ⊕: Bass, Brains Buckleys Bitter, Carling, Reverend James. **FACILITIES:** Child facs Children's licence Garden overlooks the estuary Dogs allowed garden only **NOTES:** Parking 60 **ROOMS:** 8 bedrooms 5 en suite s£35 d£50

LLWYNDAFYDD
Map 08 SN35

The Crown Inn & Restaurant
SA44 6BU ☎ 01545 560396 ▤ 01545 560857
Dir: Off A487 NE of Cardigan
A traditional Welsh longhouse dating from 1799, with original beams, open fireplaces, and a pretty restaurant. A varied menu offers a good selection of dishes, including sautéed ballottine of chicken supreme; roast monkfish wrapped in parma ham; and warm spiced couscous. Blackboard specials and bar meals are available lunchtimes and evenings. Outside is a delightful, award-winning garden. An easy walk down the lane leads to a cove with caves and NT-owned cliffs.
OPEN: 12-3 6-11 Closed Sun eve Nov-Etr (ex Xmas/New Yrs)
BAR MEALS: L served all week 12-2 D served all week 6-9 Av main course £8 **RESTAURANT:** D served all week 6.30-9 Av 3 course à la carte £30 ☺: Free House ⊕: Flowers Original & Flowers IPA, Greene King Old Speckled Hen, Honey Beers Envill Ale, Fullers London Pride. **FACILITIES:** Child facs Children's licence Garden: Large terraces, pond, lawns Dogs allowed Water bowls **NOTES:** Parking 80

> Pick of the Pubs have that extra special quality that makes them stand out from the crowd. Their entries are highlighted, and may be a full page

CONWY

BETWS-Y-COED
Map 14 SH75

White Horse Inn ♦♦♦♦ ♀
Capel Garmon LL26 0RW ☎ 01690 710271 ▤ 01690 710721
e-mail: whitehorse@supanet.com
Dir: Telephone for directions
Picturesque Capel Garmon perches high above Betws-y-Coed, with spectacular views of the Snowdon Range, a good 20 kilometres away. To make a detour to find this cosy 400-year-old inn, is to be rewarded by a menu featuring fresh local produce. Apparently William Hague allegedly proposed to Ffion here! Under new management.
OPEN: 11-3 6-11 Closed: 2 wks Jan **BAR MEALS:** L served Sat-Sun 12-2 D served all week 6.30-9.30 (Sun 7-9) Av main course £7.50 **RESTAURANT:** L served Sat-Sun 12-2 D served all week 6.30-9.30 (Sun 7-9) Av 3 course à la carte £7.50 ☺: Free House ⊕: Tetley Imperial, Tetley Smoothflow, Greene King, Abbot Ale. ♀: 23 **FACILITIES:** Dogs allowed Water **NOTES:** Parking 30 **ROOMS:** 6 bedrooms en suite s£35 d£58 No children overnight

BETWS-YN-RHOS
Map 14 SH97

The Wheatsheaf Inn 🍴
LL22 8AW ☎ 01492 680218 ▤ 01492 680666
e-mail: perry@jonnyp.fsnet.co.uk
Dir: A55 to Abergele, take A548 to Llanrwst from the High St. 2m turn right B5381, 1m to Betws-yn-Rhos
Built in the 13th century as an alehouse, the Wheatsheaf became licensed in 1640 as a coaching inn. Splendid oak beams studded with horse brasses, old stone pillars and an original hayloft ladder add to its charm. Good range of traditional food in the lounge bar and restaurant: try fresh grilled Conwy plaice; Welsh lamb roasted with rosemary and thyme; or broccoli and potato bake. Tempting puddings include banana split and warm chocolate fudge cake.
OPEN: 12-3 6-11 **BAR MEALS:** L served all week 12-2 D served all week 6-9 (Sun 12-3) Av main course £7.50 **RESTAURANT:** L served all week 12-2 D served all week (Sun 12-3) Av 3 course à la carte £15 ⊕: Greene King IPA, Courage Directors, Courage Best,. **FACILITIES:** Child facs Paved beer garden with Wendy house & BBQ **NOTES:** Parking 30

CAPEL CURIG
Map 14 SH75

Cobdens Hotel ★★ 🐟
LL24 0EE ☎ 01690 720243 ▤ 01690 720354
e-mail: info@cobdens.co.uk
Dir: On A5, 4m N of Betws-Y-Coed
Situated in a beautiful mountain village in the heart of Snowdonia, this 250-year-old inn offers wholesome, locally sourced food and real ales. Start with local rabbit and pancetta carbonara; or leek and potato terrine. Mains include roasted Welsh lamb with garlic and thyme mash; Welsh beef steaks; and pasta with roasted courgette, blue cheese and chestnut. Try bara brith parfait for pudding! Snacks and sandwiches also available.
OPEN: 11-11 (Sun 12-10.30) and BHs Closed: 6-26 Jan
BAR MEALS: L served all week 12-2.30 D served all week 6-9 Av main course £7.50 **RESTAURANT:** L served all week D served all week 6-9 Av 3 course à la carte £16 ☺: Free House ⊕: Greene King Old Speckled Hen, Brains, Tetley's cold, Rev James Tetleys. **FACILITIES:** Children's licence Garden: By river, part of Snowdonia National Park Dogs allowed Water bowls **NOTES:** Parking 35 **ROOMS:** 17 bedrooms en suite 4 family rooms s£29.50 d£59

COLWYN BAY Map 14 SH87

Pick of the Pubs

Pen-y-Bryn  🐟 ♀
Pen-y-Bryn Rd LL29 6DD ☎ 01492 533360
& 535808 📠 01492 536127
e-mail: pen.y.bryn@brunningandprice.co.uk
This 1970s-built pub reopened a few years ago after a major refurbishment, and its wonderful view to the headlands and sea are major selling points. The jukeboxes and fruit machines have been banished, and within its peaceful portals you'll find elegant oak floors, old furniture, open fires, rugs and newspapers - all provide an ambience conducive to the enjoyment of excellent real ales and good food. The menu is divided between starters, mains, light bites, 'sandwiches and bread things', puddings, and ice creams and sorbets. Fish specials include chargrilled salmon with sweet chilli risotto; monkfish and tiger prawn kebabs with Thai sauce and pak choi; baked cod with walnut crust and saffron mash; and Conwy mussels with white wine and garlic sauce. From the menu you could start with home-cured duck breast with melon and pickled ginger, followed by roast topside of beef with all the trimmings including Yorkshire pudding, and warm lemon and treacle tart.
OPEN: 11.30-11 (Sun 12-10.30) Xmas/New Year times differ
BAR MEALS: L served all week 12-9.30 D served all week
🍴: 🍺: Timothy Taylors Landlord, Fullers London Pride, Thwaites Best Bitter, Phoenix Arizona. ♀: 13 **FACILITIES:** Garden: Terraced garden, views over Rhos on Sea Dogs allowed Dog park outside **NOTES:** Parking 80

CONWY Map 14 SH77

Pick of the Pubs

The Groes Inn ★★★ 🏅 🐟 ♀
LL32 8TN ☎ 01492 650545 📠 01492 650855
web: www.groesinn.com
Dir: Off A55 to Conwy, left at mini rdbt by Conwy Castle onto B5106, 2.5m inn on right.

In 1573 The Groes Inn became the first licensed house in Wales, and it seems reasonable to suppose that time-travellers from those far-off days would still recognise the rambling rooms, beamed ceilings and historic settles. The furnishings and decorations might throw them a bit, reflecting as they do the personality of the owners, Justin and Dawn Humphreys - stone cats lounging in the fireplace, military hats, saucy Victorian postcards, historic cooking utensils and old advertisements. The head chef

continued

insists on fresh local produce: Welsh lamb that has grown sweet on the salt marshes of the Conwy Valley; pheasant and game reared on nearby estates; fine Welsh beef; and farm-cured hams and poultry are all menu regulars. For lovers of fish and seafood there's Conwy crab and plaice, wild salmon, and mussels and oysters from the waters around Anglesey. Fourteen comfortably furnished bedrooms and the flower-decked gardens overlook Snowdonia and the river.
OPEN: 12-3 6.30-11 **BAR MEALS:** L served all week 12-2.15 D served all week 6.30-9 Av main course £9.50
RESTAURANT: L served all week 12-2.15 D served all week 6.30-9 Av 4 course fixed price £28 🍴: Free House 🍺: Tetley, Burton Ale. ♀: 10 **FACILITIES:** Garden: Overlooking the Conwy River/Snowdonia **NOTES:** Parking 90
ROOMS: 14 bedrooms en suite 1 family room s£79 d£95 No children overnight

LLANDUDNO JUNCTION Map 14 SH77

Pick of the Pubs

The Queens Head 🐟 ♀
Glanwydden LL31 9JP ☎ 01492 546570 📠 01492 546487
e-mail: enquiries@queensheadglanwydden.co.uk
Dir: From A55 take A470 towards Llandudno. At 3rd rdbt right towards Penrhyn Bay, then 2nd right into Glanwydden, pub on left
This celebrated pub is located in the idyllic village of Glanwydden, and prides itself on a warm and relaxing environment, complete with roaring fires and characterful interiors. You could start with a pint of Old Speckled Hen or a house wine while choosing from menus that rely largely on local Welsh produce, freshly prepared and imaginatively served. Starters include toasted goat's cheese and pesto tart or butternut and sage risotto. Light bites such as a salmon and prawn medley are served at lunchtime and on Sundays, as well as more substantial dishes, including a hearty lasagne or a steak and mushroom pie. In the evenings, options embrace Welsh lamb shank with rosemary jus; and Conwy pork and stilton sausages with onion gravy. There's also an excellent hot and cold dessert menu if you have room. In summer, food and drink can be served outside beneath the flower-filled hanging baskets.
OPEN: 11-3 6-11 (Sun 11-10.30) Closed: 25 Dec
BAR MEALS: L served all week 12-2 D served all week 6-9 Sun 12-9 Av main course £8.95 **RESTAURANT:** L served all week 12-2 D served all week 6-9 Sun 12-9 Av 3 course à la carte £17 🍴: Free House 🍺: Carlsberg-Tetley, Burton, Greene King Old Speckled Hen, Calders. ♀: 7 **FACILITIES:** Garden **NOTES:** Parking 26

LLANNEFYDD Map 14 SH97

The Hawk & Buckle Inn
LL16 5ED ☎ 01745 540249 📠 01745 540316
e-mail: hawkandbuckle@btinternet.com
A 17th-century coaching inn 200m up in the hills, with wonderful views to the sea beyond. Traditional dishes using local produce - shoulder of Welsh lamb, chicken breast stuffed with Welsh cheese or duck breast with port and redcurrant sauce, sit comfortably alongside international flavours - lamb pasanda, beef and Guinness casserole or chicken tikka masala, for example.

continued

LLANNEFYDD continued

The Hawk & Buckle Inn

OPEN: 12-2 6-11 Closed: 25-26 Dec **BAR MEALS:** L served Wed-Sun 12-2 D served all week 6-9.30 Sun 7-11 **RESTAURANT:** 6-9.30 ⊕: Free House ◀: Brains Bitter, Interbrew Boddingtons Bitter, Bass Bitter. **NOTES:** Parking 20

ST GEORGE
Map 14 SH97

The Kinmel Arms 🐟 ♀
LL22 9BP ☎ 01745 832207 📠 01745 822044
e-mail: info@thekinmelarms.co.uk
Dir: From Bodelwyddan towards Abergele take slip road at St George. Take 1st left and Kinmel Arms is on left at top of hill

Nestling in the foothills of the stunning Elwy valley, this 17th-century free house has been stylishly renovated by Lynn and Tim Watson. Natural materials like oak, slate, leather and linen predominate, whilst the rooms are decorated with the couple's own mountain photography. The tempting menus range from sandwiches and light lunches to more adventurous dishes like red snapper with balsamic roast tomatoes; and slow roast stuffed tomato with goats' cheese and chargrilled peppers.
OPEN: 12-3 7-11 Closed: 25 Dec, 1 Jan **BAR MEALS:** L served Tue-Sun 12-2 D served Tue-Sat 6.30-9.30 Sun 12-4 Av main course £9 **RESTAURANT:** L served Tue-Sun 12-2 D served Tue-Sat 6.30-9.30 Sun 12-4 Av 3 course à la carte £17 ⊕: Free House ◀: St Austell Tribute, Butty Bach Tetleys, Phoenix Arizona, Conwy Bitter. ♀: 11 **FACILITIES:** Garden: Patio area, wooden garden furniture **NOTES:** Parking 60

Room prices show the minimum double and single rates charged. Room rates in hotels and B&Bs often vary depending on the facilities, so be sure to check prices with the establishment before booking

RHEWL
Map 15 SJ16

The Drovers Arms, Rhewl NEW 🐟
Denbigh Rd LL15 2UD ☎ 01824 703163 📠 01824 703163
e-mail: Allen_Given@hotmail.com
Dir: 1.3m from Ruthin on the A525
A small village pub whose name recalls a past written up and illustrated on storyboards displayed inside. Main courses are divided on the menu into poultry, traditional meat, fish, grills and vegetarian; examples, one from each section, are chicken tarragon; Welsh lamb's liver and onions; Vale of Clwyd sirloin steak; home-made fish pie; and fresh mushroom stroganoff. Desserts include treacle sponge pudding.
OPEN: 12-3 5-11 (Open all day Sat-Sun) **BAR MEALS:** L served all week 12-2 D served Mon-Sat 6-9 Sun 12-2.30 Av main course £5.95 **RESTAURANT:** L served all week 12-2 D served Mon-Sat 6-9 Sun 12-2.30 ◀: London Pride, Youngs, Tetley Smooth.
FACILITIES: Garden: Large garden with tables **NOTES:** Parking 20

RUTHIN
Map 15 SJ15

Pick of the Pubs

Ye Olde Anchor Inn
Rhos St LL15 1DY ☎ 01824 702813 📠 01824 703050
e-mail: hotel@anchorinn.co.uk
Dir: At junction of A525 and A494
Built in 1742, this impressive-looking inn has 16 windows at the front alone - all with award-winning window boxes. It once catered for drovers en route from Anglesey to Shropshire, and today's visitors also find it makes a good base from which to traverse much of North Wales, as well as to explore Ruthin's quaint streets. The owners have transformed the accommodation and maintained the hotel's reputation for fine cooking. There's a comfortable atmosphere in both the bar and restaurant, which is open seven days a week. Choose starters of chicken satay; or mushrooms with spinach and cream cheese. Then, breast of chicken stuffed with a herbed cream cheese; or a classic French châteaubriand steak. Home-baked bread comes with the meal. A varied selection of freshly prepared desserts.
OPEN: 12-2.30 5.30-11 (All day, all week Summer)
BAR MEALS: L served all week 12-9.30 D served all week 12-9.30 Av main course £7 **RESTAURANT:** L served all week 12-9.30 D served all week 7-9.30 Av 3 course à la carte £13 ⊕: Free House ◀: Timothy Taylor, Worthington, Carling, guest ales. **FACILITIES:** Dogs allowed **NOTES:** Parking 20

Pick of the Pubs

White Horse Inn ♀
Hendrerwydd LL16 4LL ☎ 01824 790218
e-mail: vintr74@hotmail.com
Sheep drovers bound for the English markets once refuelled the inner man here for the arduous climb ahead. They have long been replaced by walkers, cyclists, tourists and locals (although probably only the cyclists worry about the climb). Seen through the tall larches that originally acted as the drovers' landmark from the mountains, the whitewashed 17th-century free house looks welcoming. And indeed it is. Bar snacks include the all-day Breakfast Tower - black

continued

pudding, eggs, smoked bacon, grilled tomatoes and pepper sauce - as well as spit-roasted chicken and pork, salads, baguettes and hot sandwiches. The essentially modern European main menu offers tasty starters like sweetcorn chilli fritters, and fresh black Conwy mussels with tomato and chorizo sauce. In similar vein, mains include extra-mature fillet steak stuffed with stilton; roast shank of lamb with harissa and parsley salad; and fresh red sea bream with basil butter and star anise.

White Horse Inn

OPEN: 12-2.30 6-11 **BAR MEALS:** L served all week 12-2.30 D served all week 6-9.15 (Sun 6-8.30) **RESTAURANT:** L served all week 12-2.30 D served all week 6-9.15 (Sun 6-8.30)
🍺: Regular changing guest ales. ⚲: 7 **FACILITIES:** Garden: Front & back, lovely views, trees, potted plants Dogs allowed Water **NOTES:** Parking 50

ST ASAPH
Map 15 SJ07

The Plough Inn ⚲
The Roe LL17 0LU ☎ 01745 585080 🖥 01745 585363
Dir: Rhyl/St Asaph turning from A55, L at rdbt, pub 200yds on L
An 18th-century former coaching inn, the Plough has been transformed. The ground floor retains the traditional pub concept, cosy with open fires and rustic furniture, while upstairs there are two very different restaurants: an up-market bistro and an Italian-themed art deco restaurant, divided by a wine shop. The Plough buzzes with activity throughout the day, for morning coffee, light or full lunch, and afternoon tea, and has become a notable dining venue by night. Taking horseracing as its principal theme, the Paddock Bar floor offers a 'quick bite' blackboard menu of good fresh food, including baguettes, burgers, nachos, salads and kebabs. The Racecourse Bistro offers daily fresh fish chalked up on the blackboard, plus house specialities. An entirely separate menu in Graffiti Italiano offers pizzas, pasta and rice dishes and Italian classics. All the kitchens are open so you can see the food being prepared. Desserts are a great strength throughout.
OPEN: 12-11 **BAR MEALS:** L served all week 12-9.30 D served all week Sun 12-10 Av main course £8.50 **RESTAURANT:** L served all week 12-3 D served all week 6-10 ⊟: Free House 🍺: Greene King Old Speckled Hen, Shepherds Neame Spitfire,. **FACILITIES:** Garden **NOTES:** Parking 200 ⊗

Most of the pubs in this guide book pride themselves on the quality of their food. This may take a little time to prepare

FLINTSHIRE

BABELL
Map 15 SJ17

Black Lion Inn
CH8 8PZ ☎ 01352 720239
Dir: From Holywell take B5121 towards A541 (Mold to Denbigh road) & take 2nd R to Babell

Some 35 years in the same ownership, this Grade II listed, 13th-century former farmhouse, once used as a drovers' retreat, ploughs a constant furrow. A typical menu utilises duckling, game, steaks and beef, halibut, monkfish, Arctic char, and seabass. The paved patio at the front of the pub is the ideal place to enjoy a meal or a pint.
OPEN: 6-11 (open all day Sat & Sun) **BAR MEALS:** L served Sat & Sun D served Sat & Sun 6-9.30 **RESTAURANT:** L served Sat & Sun 12-2 D served Thu-Sat 6.30-9.30 Av 3 course à la carte £18 ⊟: Free House 🍺: Thwaits Lancaster Bomber, Thwaites Smooth Bitter & Guest Cask. **FACILITIES:** Garden **NOTES:** Parking 80

CILCAIN
Map 15 SJ16

White Horse Inn 🐟
CH7 5NN ☎ 01352 740142 🖥 01352 740142
e-mail: christine.jeory@btopenworld.com
Dir: From Mold take A541 towards Denbigh. After approx 6m turn left
A 400-year-old pub, which is the last survivor of five originally to be found in this lovely hillside village - no doubt because it was the centre of the local gold-mining industry in the 19th century. Today the White Horse is popular with walkers, cyclists, and horse-riders. The dishes are home made by the landlord's wife using the best quality local ingredients, including filled omelettes, grilled ham and eggs, breaded fillet of trout, cig oen Cymraeg (Welsh lamb pie), and curries.
OPEN: 12-3 6.30-11 (Sat-Sun 12-11) **BAR MEALS:** L served all week 12-2 D served all week 7-9 Av main course £6.70 ⊟: Free House 🍺: Marston's Pedigree, Bank's Bitter, Timothy Taylor Landlord, Draught Bass. **FACILITIES:** Garden: Tables, seating Dogs allowed **NOTES:** Parking 12

🐟 Pubs offering a good choice of fish on their menu

Disabled people and those with Assist Dogs have new rights of access to pubs, restaurants and hotels under the Disability Discrimination Act of 1 October 2004. For more information see the website at www.drc gb.org/open4all/rights/2004.asp

PUB WALK
The Harp Inn
Llandwrog - Gwynedd

THE HARP INN
Tyn'llan, Llandwrog, LL54 5SY
☎ 01286 831071
Directions: A55 from Chester bypass, signed off A487 Pwllhelli rd
Close to Dinas Dinlle beach and handy for Snowdonia, this family-run inn offers interesting menus and good real ale in its welcoming lounge bar. Cottagey bedrooms.
Open: 12–3 6–11 (Times vary ring for details, Sat 12–11) Closed: 1 Jan
Bar Meals: L served Tue–Sun 12–2 D served Tue–Sun 6.30–8.30 Av main course £7.95
Restaurant Meals: L served Tue–Sun 12–2 D served Tue–Sun 6.30–8.30
Dogs allowed. Garden and parking available.
(for full entry see page 634)

Distance: 6 miles (10km)
Map: OS Landranger 115
Terrain: Beach, dunes, estuary, farmland.
Paths: Promenade, tracks, coast and estuary path
Gradient: Mainly level

Walk submitted and checked by The Harp Inn

Easy and breezy, this flat and enjoyable peninsula walk explores the fine beach at Dinas Dinlle and Foryd Bay, noted for its birdlife. Panoramic views extend from the mountains of Snowdonia to the Lleyn Peninsula.

Turn left from the front of the inn and walk along the road for 0.5 mile (0.8km) to a T-junction. Turn right and follow the road down to Dinas Dinlle beach, a fine stretch of sand running the whole length of the peninsula. Turn right along the promenade and enjoy views across the Menai Straits to the Isle of Anglesey on your right.

At the end of the promenade, keep to the seaward side and follow the path through the dunes, or if the tide is out walk along the beach. On nearing Fort Belan, cut inland away from the sea and pick up the grassy bank (old railway line) to reach a bird hide. Pause here for a moment to watch the birdlife in Foryd Bay.

With the sea to your left, follow the path south beside Foryd Bay and soon pass Morfa Lodge Caravan Site. Continue for about 0.5 mile (0.8km) and cross the footbridge over the river. Follow what can be an overgrown path to the road, passing Chatham Farm on your left. Turn right along the road and follow it for nearly 1.25 miles (2km) back to the village and the pub.

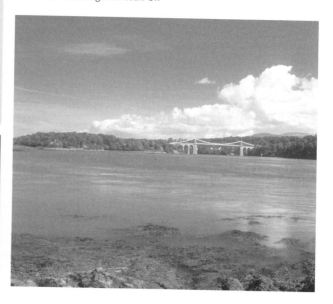

HALKYN   Map 15 SJ27

Britannia Inn
Pentre Rd CH8 8BS ☎ 01352 780272
e-mail: sarah.pollitt@tesco.net
Dir: Off A55 on B5123
On the old coach route between Chester and Holyhead, a
500-year-old stone pub with lovely views over the Dee
estuary and the Wirral. It features a family farm with chickens,
ducks and donkeys, and the large patio is ideal for alfresco
eating and drinking on warm days. Typical are rump steak
sandwich to pork escalope in pepper sauce, chicken tikka
masala, three bean bake, and stuffed salmon roast.
OPEN: 11-11 (Sun 12-10.30) **BAR MEALS:** L served all week
12-2.30 D served all week 6.30-9 **RESTAURANT:** L served all week
12-2.30 D served all week 6.30-9 ☺: J W Lees ◀: J W Lees Bitter,
GB Mild, Golden Original. **FACILITIES:** Garden: Large patio area
NOTES: Parking 40

MOLD   Map 15 SJ26

Glasfryn NEW ♀
Raikes Ln, Sychdyn CH7 6LR ☎ 01352 750500 ▤ 01352 751923
e-mail: glasfryn@brunningandprice.co.uk
Says its website: "From the outside it doesn't look that
promising". True, it's not thatched (this is Wales, after all) or
full of beams, having been built as a farm around 1900, but
such candour undersells a very appealing pub. Actors,
lawyers, farmers and theatre-goers all rub along happily here
with the locals. The comprehensive daily menu offers grilled
black bream with saffron tomato risotto; braised shin of beef
in Guinness; and vegetable curry.
OPEN: 11.30-11 (Sun 12-10.30) Closed: 25-26 Dec
BAR MEALS: L served all week 12-9.30 D served all week 12-9.30
12-9 Av main course £9 **RESTAURANT:** 12-9.30 12-9.30 Sun 12-9
◀: Timothy Taylors Landlord, Thwaites Original, Flowers, Plassey.
♀: 20 **FACILITIES:** Children's licence Garden: Terrace area and
garden with seating Dogs allowed **NOTES:** Parking 90

NORTHOP   Map 15 SJ26

Pick of the Pubs

Stables Bar Restaurant ▷ ♀
CH7 6AB ☎ 01352 840577 ▤ 01352 840382
e-mail: info@soughtonhall.co.uk
Dir: From A55, take A5119 through Northop village
In the magnificent setting of the 17th-century Soughton
Hall, converted from its Grade I listed stables, this
destination pub serves the best of modern British cuisine.
It has kept many of its original features, including the
cobbled floors, stalls and roof timbers. The tables are
named after famous racecourses and their winners. In the
evenings dinner is served in the hayloft, where you can
watch your food prepared in the open kitchen - perhaps
selecting your steak or fresh fish from the display. There
is no wine list - instead you're encouraged to browse the
wine shop, which specialises in South African vintages,
and see what catches your eye. Starters could be baked
banana wrapped in cured ham; chicken liver parfait
wrapped in bacon with spiced plum chutney; and Thai-
style fishcakes with minted Greek yoghurt. Trio of home-
made sausages; slow-roasted honey-glazed lamb shank;
and deep-fried cod with monkfish could follow. There's a
separate vegetarian selection.

continued

OPEN: 11-11.30 **BAR MEALS:** L served all week 12-9.30
D served all week 7-9.30 Sun bar 4-9.30, a la carte 7-10 Av main
course £13 **RESTAURANT:** L served all week 12-3 D served all
week 7-10 Sun lunch 1-3, dinner 7-10 ☺: Free House
◀: Shepherds Neame Spitfire, Shepherd Neame Bishops Finger,
Coach House Honeypot, Dick Turpin. ♀: 6
FACILITIES: Garden: Food served outdoors, patio, Dogs
allowed Water **NOTES:** Parking 150

ABERDYFI   Map 14 SN69

Dovey Inn ★★ ♀
Seaview Ter LL35 0EF ☎ 01654 767332 ▤ 01654 767996
e-mail: info@doveyinn.com web: www.doveyinn.com

Historic inn on the estuary of the River Dovey, only 20 yards
from the sea and the fine sandy beach. The village clings to
the hills above the estuary, once a major slate port and now a
sailing centre. An extensive seafood menu includes Thai
spiced shark steak, fish pie, Bantry Bay mussels, chargrilled
swordfish, and tuna steak with red wine fish gravy. Plenty of
other options including sandwiches, light bites, vegetarian,
meat dishes, pasta, and pizza.
OPEN: 11-11 (Sun 12-10.30) **BAR MEALS:** L served all week
12-2.30 D served all week 6-9.30 ☺: Free House ◀: Hancock HB,
Bass, Carling Black Label. ♀: 14 **FACILITIES:** Children's licence
Garden: Patio area Dogs allowed **ROOMS:** 8 bedrooms en suite

Pick of the Pubs

Penhelig Arms Hotel & Restaurant ★★ ◉ ▷ ♀
Terrace Rd LL35 0LT ☎ 01654 767215 ▤ 01654 767690
e-mail: info@penheligarms.com web: www.penheligarms.com
Dir: On A493 (coastal rd) W of Machynlleth
In business since the late 18th century, the Penhelig Arms
is now part of the picturesque resort of Aberdyfi, offering
glorious views over the tidal Dyfi estuary, and handy for
breezy sea strolls and more energetic hill walks. Cader
Idris and a variety of majestic mountains and historic
castles are within easy reach. Locals and visitors from
further afield experience a warm welcome in the bar
where they find a choice of traditional ales; many
customers can be found relaxing on the sea wall opposite
during fine weather. The emphasis is on fresh fish and
local meat complemented by a choice of 300 wines,
including more than 30 by the glass. Dishes range from
whole sea bass roasted with anchovies and garlic;
chargrilled Glen Fyne rib-eye steak with salad and French

continued

ABERDYFI continued

fries; broccoli, brie and hazelnut gratin; and pan-fried pork loin with mushrooms, sherry and whole grain mustard sauce.

Penhelig Arms Hotel & Restaurant

OPEN: 11.30-3.30 5.30-11 (Sun 12-3.30, 6-10.30) Closed: Dec 25-26 **BAR MEALS:** L served all week 12-2.30 D served all week 6.30-9.30 **RESTAURANT:** L served all week 12-2.30 D served all week 7-9.30 ⊕: Free House ◖: Carlesberg-Tetley Tetley Bitter, Greene King Abbot Ale, Adnams Broadside, Brains Reverend James & SA. ♀: 30 **FACILITIES:** Children's licence Garden: Seating opposite hotel on sea wall Dogs allowed **NOTES:** Parking 12 **ROOMS:** 14 bedrooms en suite 4 family rooms s£69 d£122

ABERSOCH   Map 14 SH32

St Tudwal's Inn ♀
High St LL53 7DS ☎ 01758 712539 ▤ 01758 713701
Dir: *Take A499 from Pwllheli, follow one way system, pub on right*
A Victorian building, now converted to provide two bars and a restaurant, believed to be haunted by a Victorian lady. Steaks are a popular option, alongside sea bass poached in sherry with julienne peppers, duck with port, cream and mushroom sauce, and lamb cutlets with wine gravy.
OPEN: 11-11 (Sun 12-10.30) Winter Sun closed 3-7
BAR MEALS: L served all week 12-2.30 D served all week 6-9
RESTAURANT: D served all week 6-9 ⊕: ◖: Robinsons Best, Hatters Mild. **FACILITIES:** Garden: Food served outside. Beer patio Dogs allowed in the garden only **NOTES:** Parking 20

BLAENAU FFESTINIOG   Map 14 SH74

The Miners Arms
Llechwedd Slate Caverns LL41 3NB
☎ 01766 830306 ▤ 01766 831260 e-mail: quarrytours@aol.com
Dir: *Blaenau Ffestiniog is 25 m from Llandudno on the N Wales coast, situated on the A470 to main N-S trunk Rd*
Slate floors, open fires and staff in Victorian costume emphasise the heritage theme of this welcoming pub nestling in the centre of a Welsh village. On the site of Llechwedd Slate Caverns, one of the country's leading tourist attractions, it caters for all comers and tastes: expect steak and ale casserole, pork pie and salad, various ploughman's lunches, and hot apple pie, as well as afternoon cream tea.
OPEN: 11-5.30 Closed: Nov-Easter **BAR MEALS:** L served all week 11-5 ⊕: Free House **FACILITIES:** Garden: Dogs allowed **NOTES:** Parking 200 ⊛

LLANBEDR   Map 14 SH52

Victoria Inn ◆◆◆◆
LL45 2LD ☎ 01341 241213 ▤ 01341 241644
e-mail: junevicinn@aol.com
Dir: *Telephone for directions*
Heavily beamed and wonderfully atmospheric, the Victoria is perfect for the pub connoisseur seeking authentic features such as flagged floors, an unusual circular wooden settle, an ancient stove and a grandfather clock. Good food in the bars and restaurant includes honey roast ham, sausage in onion gravy, Japanese torpedo prawns served with a lemon mayonnaise dip, and Welsh dragon tart. Relax with a leisurely drink in the pub's well-kept garden.
OPEN: 11-11 (Sun 12-10.30) **BAR MEALS:** L served all week 12-9 D served all week 6-9 **RESTAURANT:** L served all week 12-3 D served all week 6-9 ⊕: ◖: Robinson's Best Bitter, Hartleys XB.
FACILITIES: Child facs Garden: Riverside garden, pond, trees & plants Dogs allowed **NOTES:** Parking 50 **ROOMS:** 5 bedrooms en suite 1 family room

LLANDWROG   Map 14 SH45

The Harp Inn ♀
Tyn'llan LL54 5SY ☎ 01286 831071 ▤ 01286 830239
e-mail: management@theharp.globalnet.co.uk
Dir: *A55 from Chester bypass, signed off A487 Pwllheli rd*

This characterful old free house stands in the centre of a lovely village. There used to be a secret passage to the ancient churchyard across the road, and the building is said to be haunted. Nowadays you'll find real ale, a non-smoking restaurant and a peaceful garden. Lunchtime brings wholemeal hoagies, baked potatoes, tortilla wraps, and traditional Sunday roasts. Other dishes include gammon, egg and chips; grilled local plaice; and salmon and broccoli pie.
OPEN: 12-3 6-11 (Times vary ring for details, Sat 12-11) Closed: 1 Jan **BAR MEALS:** L served Tue-Sun 12-2 D served Tue-Sun 6.30-8.30 Av main course £7.95 **RESTAURANT:** L served Tue-Sun 12-2 D served Tue-Sun 6.30-8.30 ⊕: Free House ◖: Interbrew Bass, Black Sheep Best, Wyre Piddle Piddle in the Wind, Plassey Bitter.
♀: 8 **FACILITIES:** Child facs Garden: 6 tables Dogs allowed Water **NOTES:** Parking 20 **ROOMS:** 4 bedrooms 1 en suite 1 family room s£30 d£45 (★★★)

See Pub Walk on page 632

MAENTWROG   Map 14 SH64

Grapes Hotel
LL41 4HN ☎ 01766 590365 & 590208 ▤ 01766 590649
e-mail: grapesmaen@aol.com
web: www.hgt.gwynedd.gov.uk/thegrapeshotelmaentwrog
Dir: *A5 Corwen to Bala, A487 to Maentwrog, A496, pub 100yrds on R*
The management, advises the menu, reserves the right to

continued

experience certain hazards - blown fuses, burst pipes, unreliable suppliers...and earthquakes, adding wryly 'Don't laugh, we've had one'. Whatever its impact on the Richter scale, it thankfully left this Grade II-listed, 17th-century coaching inn unscathed. Exposed stone walls, and heavily carved wooden bars help to create a cosy feeling, accentuated by roaring log fires on wintry days. Specials change weekly, but there's always a good choice, including vegetarian. On the regular menu are the 'famous' pork ribs ('one is sensible, two not for the faint-hearted'), wholetail scampi, gammon steaks, lamb chops, chilli (again not for wimps), pastas and curries. **OPEN:** 11-11 (Sun 12-10.30) Closed: Dec 25 **BAR MEALS:** L served all week 12-2 D served all week 6-9 🍴: Free House ♣: Marstons Pedigree, Greene King Old Speckled Hen, IPA, Wye Valley Butty Bach. **FACILITIES:** Children's licence Garden: Large garden with stone water feature Dogs allowed **NOTES:** Parking 36

MALLWYD
Map 14 SH81

The Brigands Inn NEW ♦♦♦♦ ⌇⌁
SY20 9HJ ☎ 01650 511999 📠 01650 531208
Dir: On A487 between Dolgellau and Machynlleth.
At the heart of the Cambrian Mountains, on the upper banks of the gin-clear River Dovey, lies the Brigands Inn, a renowned 15th-century coaching establishment. Alternatively, or afterwards, opt for a glass of wine in the pub's sunny garden with its fine country views. The menus reflect the changing seasons with a good selection of fish, meat and game. A typical example is grilled fillet of sea bass with sun-dried tomato and pesto; grilled sirloin steak with tomato, mushrooms and onions; and loin of venison on caramelised red onions with a port and juniper sauce. **OPEN:** 10am-11pm **BAR MEALS:** L served all week 12-2.30 D served all week 6-9 Av main course £7.50 **RESTAURANT:** L served all week 12-2.30 D served all week 6-9 Av 3 course à la carte £20 **FACILITIES:** Garden: Large, landscaped garden **NOTES:** Parking 80 **ROOMS:** 9 bedrooms en suite 1 family room s£50 d£80

NANTGWYNANT
Map 14 SH65

Pen-Y-Gwryd Hotel
LL55 4NT ☎ 01286 870211
Dir: A5 to Capel Curig, left on A4086 to T-junct.
In the wonderfully dramatic Snowdonia National Park, this cosy climbers' pub and rescue post has long been the home of British mountaineering. The 1953 Everest team etched their signatures on the ceiling when they used it as a training base. Appetising, inexpensive, daily-changing offerings are likely to include beef and mushroom pie; seared salmon steak with a prawn sauce; smoked chicken salad; and roast duck with an orange and cranberry sauce. **OPEN:** 11-11 Closed: Nov to New Year, mid-week Jan-Feb Wknd opening only **BAR MEALS:** L served all week 12-2 D served all week **RESTAURANT:** L served all week D served all week 7.30-8 🍴: Free House ♣: Interbrew Bass & Boddingtons Bitter. **FACILITIES:** Child facs Garden: Mountain garden with lake and sauna Dogs allowed **NOTES:** Parking 25 No credit cards

---

TUDWEILIOG
Map 14 SH23

Lion Hotel
LL53 8ND ☎ 01758 770244 📠 01758 770546
Dir: A499 from Caernarfon, B4417 Tudweiliog
The Lee family have run this friendly, 300-year-old village inn on the Lleyn Peninsula for over 30 years. The large garden and children's play area makes the pub especially popular
continued

with cyclists, walkers and families, with a beach just one mile away. The bar features an extensive list of over 80 malt whiskies. There is a non-smoking family dining room but food is served throughout, from lunchtime baguettes to traditional favourites such as home-made lasagne gammon steak. There is a good children's and vegetarian menu. **OPEN:** 11.30-11 (Sun 12-2) (Winter 12-2, 7-11 all day Sat, Jan) **BAR MEALS:** L served all week 12-2 D served all week 6-9 Av main course £6.50 **RESTAURANT:** L served all week 12-2 D served all week 6-9 🍴: Free House ♣: Marston's Pedigree, Interbrew Boddingtons, Theakston,. **FACILITIES:** Garden: Food served outside Dogs allowed water **NOTES:** Parking 40

WAUNFAWR
Map 14 SH55

Snowdonia Parc Brewpub & Campsite
LL55 4AQ ☎ 01286 650409 & 650218 📠 01286 650409
e-mail: karen@snowdonia-park.co.uk

Pub, micro brewery and campsite in an idyllic mountain setting, 400 feet above sea level with a river running by. All this situated at Waunfawr Station on the Welsh Highland Railway, with steam trains on site (the pub was originally the station master's house). Home-brewed beer is served, with speedy lunchtime bar meals for those catching trains. Children and dogs are welcome and there's a children's playground. **OPEN:** 11-11 (Sun 11-10.30) **BAR MEALS:** L served all week 11-8.30 D served all week 5-8.30 Av main course £6 **RESTAURANT:** L served all week 11-8.30 D served all week 11-8.30 Av 3 course à la carte £12 ♣: Marston's Bitter & Pedigree, Welsh Highand Bitter (ownbrew), Mansfield Dark Mild. **FACILITIES:** Child facs Garden: Views towards Snowdonia Mountains Dogs allowed water bowls **NOTES:** Parking 100

ISLE OF ANGLESEY

BEAUMARIS
Map 14 SH67

Pick of the Pubs

Ye Olde Bulls Head Inn ★★ ⊚⊚ ♀
Castle St LL58 8AP ☎ 01248 810329 📠 01248 811294
e-mail: info@bullsheadinn.co.uk
Dir: From Brittania Road Bridge follow A545, located in town centre
A short walk from Beaumaris Castle and the Menai Straits, this traditional watering hole dates back to 1472. Famous guests have included Samuel Johnson and Charles Dickens. There's a traditional bar leading on to the popular brasserie which offers lighter pasta and vegetarian dishes and the occasional spatchcocked poussin or grilled mullet. Or it's up the stairs to the
continued

Wales

BEAUMARIS continued

smartly decorated, first-floor restaurant which offers a more formal menu. Start with tian of blue swimmer crab with gazpacho and red pepper tuille, terrine of ham hock with smoked foie gras, or truffled goats' cheese mousse with seared scallops; and move on to saddle of wild venison with chocolate sauce, fingers of John Dory with king scallops and a light curry emulsion, breast of duck with purple figs, or fillets of local brill. Delectable desserts like melting ginger parkin, rhubarb and custard, or coffee and doughnuts (crème brûlée, ice cream and warm cinnamon doughnuts) will be hard to resist.

Ye Olde Bulls Head Inn

OPEN: 11-11 (Sun-12-10.30) Closed: 25 Dec
BAR MEALS: L served all week 12-2 D served all week 6-9 Av main course £8 **RESTAURANT:** D served Mon-Sat 7.30-9.30 Sun on BH wknds 12-1.30 Av 3 course fixed price £33 ❀: Free House 🍺: Bass, Hancocks, Worthington. ♀: 16 **FACILITIES:** Dogs allowed **NOTES:** Parking 10 **ROOMS:** 13 bedrooms en suite s£70 d£97 (WTB)

RED WHARF BAY   Map 14 SH58

Pick of the Pubs

The Ship Inn ◆ ♀
LL75 8RJ ☎ 01248 852568 ▤ 01248 851013
Large numbers of wading birds flock to feed on the extensive sands of Red Wharf Bay, making the Ship's waterside beer garden a birdwatcher's paradise on warm days. Before the age of steam, sailing ships landed cargoes from all over the world; now, the boats bring fresh Conwy Bay fish and seafood to the kitchens of this traditional free house. A single menu is served to diners in the bars and non-smoking restaurant, where seafood dishes are a mainstay of the daily menu. Start, perhaps, with soused herrings, rocket and tomato salad; or roast quail, apricot stuffing and pesto. Main course choices might include local seafood platter with sauté potatoes and ratatouille; poached local skate on chive mash; or tomato and parmesan tart with artichokes and wild mushrooms. Home-made desserts like dark chocolate and Welsh liqueur cup round things off nicely.
OPEN: 11-3.30 6.30-11 (Summer & BHs 11-11) (Sat 11-11, Sun 12-10.30) **BAR MEALS:** L served all week 12-2.30 D served all week 6.30-9 (Sun 12-8.30) **RESTAURANT:** L served Sun 12-2.30 D served Fri-Sat 7-9.30 ❀: Free House 🍺: Brains SA, Adnams, Greene King, Pedigree. ♀: 8 **FACILITIES:** Child facs Garden: on water's edge Dogs allowed Water **NOTES:** Parking 45

MONMOUTHSHIRE

ABERGAVENNY   Map 09 SO21

Pick of the Pubs

Clytha Arms ◆ ♀
Clytha NP7 9BW ☎ 01873 840206 ▤ 01873 840206
e-mail: clythaarms@tiscali.co.uk
Dir: From A449/A40 junction (E of Abergavenny) follow signs for 'Old Road Abergavenny/Clytha'
A former dower house set in two acres of grounds alongside the old Abergavenny to Raglan road, this family-run free house has an outstanding reputation for its food and real ales. Bass, Felinfoel and Hook Norton ales are joined by an ever-changing selection of guest beers, and there's also a good choice of wines by the glass. Raglan's famous 15th-century castle is just a few miles down the road, whilst Cardiff, with its historical attractions and superb shopping, is a 40-minute drive. Bar snacks include sandwiches and ploughman's, as well as hot dishes like hake fish cakes with tomato salsa. In the non-smoking restaurant, expect goat's cheese and chargrilled vegetable soufflé; roast duck with orange and parsnip bake; or three fish plait with leek beurre blanc. But do leave space for a pudding like passion fruit brûlée; and Sauternes cream and spiced prunes.
OPEN: 12-3 6-11 (Sat 12-11) Closed: 25 Dec
BAR MEALS: L served Tue-Sun 12.30-2.15 D served Tues-Sat 7-9.30 **RESTAURANT:** L served all week 12.30-2.30 D served Tue-Sun 7-9.30 ❀: Free House 🍺: Bass, Felinfoel Double Dragon, Hook Norton, 3 guest beers (250 per year). ♀: 10 **FACILITIES:** Child facs Garden: 2 acres with paddock, fountain & lawns **NOTES:** Parking 100

Llanwenarth Hotel & Riverside Restaurant ★★
Brecon Rd NP8 1EP ☎ 01873 810550 ▤ 01873 811880
e-mail: info@pantrhiwgoch.co.uk
Dir: On A40 between Abergavenny & Crickhowell
Not long ago, the owners of this part 16th-century inn and restaurant featured in Channel 4's *No Turning Back*, a programme about major lifestyle change. The views from its elevated position above the River Usk are splendid, as those who watched the programme may recall. The mostly locally-sourced, but all home-made, dishes are available throughout the two bars, conservatory, dining room and patio. Fish choices include salmon, hake, bream and gurnard, while among the meats are duck, lamb, and rib-eye steaks.
OPEN: 11-11 **BAR MEALS:** L served all week 12-2 D served Mon-Sat 6.30-9 Av main course £13 **RESTAURANT:** L served all week 12-2 D served Mon-Sat 6.30-9 Av 3 course à la carte £23.50 ❀: Free House 🍺: Felinfoel Double Dragon, Tetley Smoothflow. **FACILITIES:** Garden: Patio area overlooking the River Usk **NOTES:** Parking 40 **ROOMS:** 18 bedrooms en suite 2 family rooms s£65 d£75

BETTWS-NEWYDD   Map 09 SO30

Pick of the Pubs

Black Bear Inn
NP15 1JN ☎ 01873 880701
See Pick of the Pubs on 638

PUB WALK

The Woodland Restaurant & Bar
Llanfair Discoed - Monmouthshire

**THE WOODLAND
RESTAURANT & BAR**
NP16 6LX
☎ 01633 400313
*Extended old inn close to the Roman
fortress town of Caerwent. At heart a
friendly village local, serving a good
range of beers, and a varied menu of
fresh food.*
Open: 11–3 6–11 (Sun 12–3, closed
Sun eve)
Bar Meals: L served Tue–Sun 12–2
D served Tue–Sat 6–10 (Sun 12–2)
Av main course £8
Restaurant Meals: L served Tue–Sun
12–2 D served Tue–Sat 6–9.30
Av 3 course à la carte £21 Av 2 course
fixed price £8.25
Children and dogs allowed. Garden and
parking available.
(for full entry see page 639)

Distance: 2.25 miles (3.6km)
Map: OS Explorer OL 14
Terrain: Rolling hills and farmland
Paths: Footpaths, bridleways and
country roads
Gradient: Some steep climbs

*Walk submitted by the Woodlands
Restaurant and Bar*

A delightful country walk exploring the countryside to the north of Llanvair Discoed – meaning 'church under the wood.'

On leaving the restaurant and bar, take Well Lane, the narrow road to the left, and follow it uphill. Look out for the village well in the right boundary. Just beyond it, on the left, are the renovated buildings of a farm. New farm barns have also been built on the right-hand side of the lane.

Continue to where Well Lane terminates and you will see Slade's Cottage, which has been enlarged over the years and was once a small dwelling. Look for a stile and gate just beyond the cottage. Cross over and turn immediately right, passing over a stream. Keep ahead up the field, with the fence and trees to your right.

As you begin to approach the top right-hand corner of the field, head towards a large tree near a gap in the stone wall. Pass through the gap, cross the stile and follow the path, keeping a thatched cottage to your right.

Just beyond the cottage, which was recently renovated as part of a medieval village restoration programme, you reach a junction of paths. Turn left here and follow a pleasant woodland path. Cross a stile and continue ahead until you reach a junction with a bridleway skirting the bottom of Gray Hill.

Turn left here and head down the metalled road towards Llanvair Discoed. Turn left at the next junction and walk downhill to The Woodlands. Along here you can see the remains of Llanvair Castle located within the grounds of a private house. Below lies the local church, which is worth closer inspection.

Black Bear Inn

Dating back to the 14th century, the Black Bear can be found in a tiny hamlet surrounded by delightful Monmouthshire countryside. The River Usk, renowned for salmon and sea and brown trout fishing, is only a quarter of a mile away, and both the Black Mountains and Table Top Mountain are part of the backdrop.

It retains many of its original features; in fact, it has always been a pub, and since they took over more than 10 years ago, owners Gill and Stephen Molyneux have improved and extended it, without in any way compromising its ancient feel. Since being here they have established their own reputation for providing good food. The bar, with oak beams, quarry-tiled floor and large fireplace, has a welcoming, informal atmosphere, and is just the place for that swift pint of Timothy Taylor Landlord on the way home, a longer session with friends, or indeed pre-dinner cocktails. In the kitchen Stephen uses local produce almost entirely, with pheasant, venison and duck available in season. The constantly changing menus come up with starters including smoked duck with honey dressing, and home-made mushroom and stilton soup; main courses of fresh salmon with tomato and basil sauce, and Welsh lamb with minted cream sauce; and puddings including Bailey's Irish cream cheesecake; dark chocolate and orange mousse; and home-made raspberry and schnapps ice cream. Seafood receives special attention, excellent examples being fresh turbot served in an avocado cream sauce, mushrooms and cream; whole sea bass with a marmalade of onions; and pan-fried monkfish with pink peppercorn sauce.

OPEN: 12-2 6-12

BAR MEALS: L served Tue-Sun 12-2 D served Mon-Sat 6-10 Av main course £12

RESTAURANT: L served Tue-Sun 12-2 D served Mon-Sat 6-10 Av 3 course à la carte £23 Av 3 course fixed price £14.95

🍺: Free House

🛢: Fuller's London Pride, Timothy Taylor Landlord, Interbrew Bass, Greene King Old Speckled Hen.

FACILITIES: Garden: Shrubs, fruit trees, hen house, seating Dogs allowed Water tap

NOTES: Parking 20 No credit cards

Map 09 SO30

NP15 1JN

☎ 01873 880701

Dir: Off B4598 N of Usk

CHEPSTOW   Map 04 ST59

Pick of the Pubs

The Boat Inn ♀
The Back NP16 5HH ☎ 01291 628192 📠 01291 628193

See Pick of the Pubs on page 640

Castle View Hotel ★★
16 Bridge St NP16 5EZ ☎ 01291 620349 📠 01291 627397
e-mail: taciliaok@aol
Dir: *Opposite Chepstow Castle*
Built as a private house some 300 years ago, its solid walls up
to five feet thick in places, this hotel is situated opposite the
castle, alongside the River Wye. The regularly changing menu
might offer steaks, breast of chicken stuffed with stilton, Welsh
lamb, and cod in beer batter.
OPEN: 12-2.30 6-11 **BAR MEALS:** L served all week 12-2.30
D served Mon-Sat 6.30-9.30 **RESTAURANT:** L served Sun D served
Mon-Sun 6.30-9.30 ⊕: Free House ◄: Wye Valley Real Ale, Coors
Worthington's. **FACILITIES:** Garden: Small secluded Dogs allowed
NOTES: Parking 200 **ROOMS:** 13 bedrooms en suite

LLANTRISANT   Map 09 ST39

Pick of the Pubs

The Greyhound Inn ♀
NP15 1LE ☎ 01291 672505 & 673447 📠 01291 673255
e-mail: enquiry@greyhound-inn.com
web: www.greyhound-inn.com
Dir: *From M4 take A449 towards Monmouth, 1st jct to Usk, left into
Usk Sq. Take 2nd left signed Llantrisant. 2.5m to inn*

The Greyhound was built in the 17th century as a Welsh
longhouse and only became an inn in 1845. These days it
is a charming free house, family-run for 25 years, with
stone-built stables converted into ten comfortable en suite
bedrooms. A good selection of traditional ales is offered,
15 malt whiskies, and a comprehensive menu of seasonal
home cooked fare. Dishes from the specials blackboard
include Usk salmon with white wine and pernod; Welsh
venison and ale pie; and coq au vin. Eight options are
offered on the vegetarian menu, maybe brazil nut and
spinach roast, and such desserts as profiteroles or
hazelnut meringue gateau. In fine weather you can make
the most of the award-winning gardens, complete with a
pond and fountain. Across the car park is the inn's own
country pine and antique shop.
OPEN: 11-11 (Sun 12-4, 7-11) Closed: 25, 31 Dec, 1 Jan
BAR MEALS: L served all week 12-2.15 D served Mon-Sat 6-10
RESTAURANT: L served all week 12-2.15 D served Mon-Sat

6-10.30 ⊕: Free House ◄: Interbrew Flowers Original & Bass,
Brains Bitter, Greene King Abbot Ale, Guest Beer. ♀: 10
FACILITIES: Garden: Pond with fountain, delightful garden Dogs
allowed Water **NOTES:** Parking 60 **ROOMS:** 10 bedrooms
en suite 2 family rooms s£55 d£75 (★★★)

LLANVAIR DISCOED   Map 09 ST49

Pick of the Pubs

The Woodland Restaurant & Bar 🍽 ♀
NP16 6LX ☎ 01633 400313 📠 01633 400313
e-mail: lausnik@aol.co.uk
Dir: *Telephone for directions*
An old inn, extended to accommodate a growing number
of diners, the Woodland is located close to the Roman
fortress town of Caerwent and Wentworth's forest and
reservoir. It remains at heart a friendly, family-run village
local, serving a good range of beers. A varied menu of
freshly prepared dishes caters for all tastes from ciabatta
bread with various toppings to Welsh lamb loin wrapped
in spinach and filo pastry on a bed of wild mushroom
and rosemary risotto. Meat is sourced from a local
butcher, who slaughters all his own meat, and the fish is
mostly from Cornwall, maybe sea bass cooked in rock salt
and lemon. Outside there's a large, well-equipped garden
with plenty of bench seating.
OPEN: 11-3 6-11 (Sun 12-3, closed Sun eve)
BAR MEALS: L served Tue-Sun 12-2 D served Tue-Sat 6-10 (Sun
12-2) Av main course £8 **RESTAURANT:** L served Tue-Sun
12-2 D served Tue-Sat 6-9.30 Av 3 course à la carte £21
Av 2 course fixed price £8.25 ⊕: Free House ◄: Reverend
James, Brains, Felinfoel Double Dragon, Bass. ♀: 8
FACILITIES: Child facs Garden: Plenty of bench seating, play
area Dogs allowed Water **NOTES:** Parking 30

See Pub Walk on page 637

PENALLT   Map 04 SO51

The Boat Inn
Lone Ln NP25 4AJ ☎ 01600 712615 📠 01600 719120
Dir: *From Monmouth take A466. In Redbrook pub car park signed. Park
& walk across rail bridge over the River Wye*
Dating back over 360 years, this riverside pub has served as a
hostelry for quarry, mill, paper and tin mine workers, and
even had a landlord operating a ferry across the Wye at shift
times. The unspoilt slate floor is testament to the age of the
place. The excellent selection of real ales and local ciders
complement the menu well, with choices ranging from
various ploughman's to lamb steffados or the charmingly-
named pan haggerty. Ideal for walkers taking the Offa's Dyke
or Wye Valley walks.
OPEN: 11-11 (Sun 12-10.30) **BAR MEALS:** L served all week
12-2.30 D served all week 6-9 Sun 12-3 (winter), Sat & Sun
12-9(summer) Av main course £5 ⊕: Free House ◄: Freeminer
Bitter, Wadworth 6X, Greene King IPA, Abbot Ale & Old Speckled Hen.
FACILITIES: Garden: Rustic tables and benches with waterfalls Dogs
allowed Water **NOTES:** Parking 20

> Most of the pubs in this guide book pride
> themselves on the quality of their food. This
> may take a little time to prepare

Wales

The Boat Inn

Standing on the banks of the River Wye, The Boat Inn's front terrace is a perfect place to relax on a summer's day and watch the ever-changing scenery. This is a pub which manages to effortlessly combine the virtues of a popular local with an honest approach to providing good bar and restaurant food.

Salmon fisheries were once sited virtually next door: the boats would moor in the tide with deep nets stretching across the tidal flow below Brunel's tubular bridge. Today's revitalised pub is an attractive whitewashed building brightened by hanging baskets of flowers. The well-furnished terrace includes decent seats and a barbecue for the summer, but the views can be enjoyed equally well from the first floor restaurant, a romantic setting (candlelit in the evenings) with a large bay window overlooking the river. The ground floor comprises a selection of traditionally furnished rooms decorated with

boating memorabilia, and there is a real fire to warm yourself by in the winter months. For those who want something special to eat, the main menu, supplemented by a specials board, has plenty to recommend: starters like king prawns, Thai fishcakes, risotto with broad bean and asparagus, and grilled sardines, and such main dishes as rump of Welsh lamb, veal escalope milanese, fish of the day and fresh pasta dishes. Lunch is an uncomplicated affair, with fresh soup alongside a full-length menu that can be chosen throughout the day. Other simple options include lasagne, curry, steak and baguettes.

OPEN: 11-11 Mon-Sat (12-10.30 Sun) Closed: 25 Dec
BAR MEALS: L served all week 12-3 D served all week 7-9.30 (Sun-Thu 6-7.30)
RESTAURANT: L served all week 12-3 D served all week 6.30-9.30
☺: Unique Pub Co
🍺: Interbrew Bass, Smiles, Wadworth 6X.
FACILITIES: Garden
NOTES: Parking 20

♀   Map 04 ST59
The Back NP16 5HH
☎ 01291 628192
🖹 01291 628193

Wales

RAGLAN · Map 09 SO40

The Beaufort Arms Coaching Inn and Restaurant NEW ★★ 🍴 ♀
High St NP15 2DY
Dir: 0.5m from junct of A40

Used by Parliamentarian soldiers during the Siege of Raglan Castle in 1646, the Beaufort Arms later became an important staging post on the London to Fishguard road. The bar menu offers a good choice, from salmon and prawn fish cakes to Welsh sirloin steak, while the main menu lists fillet of salmon, pork tenderloin, and mignons of venison, all accompanied by tasty sauces. There's a weekly specials board, too, on which wild boar may appear.
OPEN: 11-11 (Sun 12-10.30) **BAR MEALS:** L served all week 12-3 D served all week 6-9.30 Sun 6-8.30 Av main course £8.50
RESTAURANT: L served all week 12-3 D served all week 6-9.30 Sun 6-8.30 Av 3 course à la carte £22.50 Av 2 course fixed price £9.95
🍺: London Pride, Reverend James, Tetleys Smooth. ♀: 12
FACILITIES: Garden: South facing terrace garden, seating, patio
NOTES: Parking 30 **ROOMS:** 15 bedrooms en suite s£50 d£55 No children overnight

SHIRENEWTON · Map 09 ST49

The Carpenters Arms
Usk Rd NP16 6BU ☎ 01291 641231
Dir: M48 J2 take A48 to Chepstow then A4661, B4235. Village 3m on L
A 400-year-old hostelry, formerly a smithy and carpenter's shop, with flagstone floors, open fires and bedecked with antiques. In a pleasant wooded location in the valley of the Mounton Brook which lies between the bigger valleys of the Wye and Usk. Straightforward bar food typified by chicken in leek and stilton sauce, steak and mushroom pie, smoked haddock and potato pie, guinea fowl in orange sauce, and lamb rogan josh.
OPEN: 11-2.30 6-11 **BAR MEALS:** 12-2 7-9.30 🍺: Free House
🍺: Fuller's London Pride, Wadworth 6X, Marston's Pedigree,Theakston Old Peculier. **FACILITIES:** Dogs allowed
NOTES: Parking 20 No credit cards

SKENFRITH · Map 09 SO42

Pick of the Pubs

The Bell at Skenfrith ◎◎ 🏠 ♀
NP7 8UH ☎ 01600 750235 📠 01600 750525
e-mail: enquiries@skenfrith.co.uk web: www.skenfrith.co.uk
See Pick of the Pubs on page 642

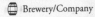
🍺 Brewery/Company

TINTERN PARVA · Map 04 SO50

Fountain Inn ♦♦♦
Trellech Grange NP16 6QW ☎ 01291 689303 📠 01291 689303
e-mail: thefountaininn04@aol.com
web: www.fountaininn-tintern.com
Dir: In Tintern turn by the George Hotel for Raglan. Stay on this lane always bearing to the right, to the top of the hill
A fire nearly destroyed this fine old inn, but the thick 17th-century walls survived the flames, and its character remains unspoilt. It enjoys views of the Wye Valley - which can be enjoyed from the garden - and is close to Tintern Abbey. Home-cooked food includes grilled sardines with balsamic vinegar and cherry tomatoes; leek and Caerphilly sausages with onion gravy; and home-made beef and Guinness pie. Good selection of steaks, omelettes, and daily specials.
OPEN: 12-3 6.30-11 **BAR MEALS:** L served all week 12-2.30 D served all week 7-9.15 Av main course £7.95
RESTAURANT: L served all week 12-2.30 D served all week 7-9.15 Av 3 course à la carte £21 🍺: Free House 🍺: Wye Valley Butter Bach, Ring of Bells, Interbrew Bass, Hobgoblin. **FACILITIES:** Child facs Garden: Views of Wye Valley with stream Dogs allowed Water, open fields for walks **NOTES:** Parking 30 **ROOMS:** 5 bedrooms 2 en suite s£35 d£52 (★★)

TREDUNNOCK · Map 09 ST39

Pick of the Pubs

The Newbridge ◎◎ 🏠 ♀
NP15 1LY ☎ 01633 451000 📠 01633 451001
e-mail: thenewbridge@tinyonline.co.uk
web: www.thenewbridge.co.uk
Dir: From Usk take road towards Llangibby. Turn left for Tredunnock. Pub is 800yds on bank of River Usk

South African Michael Obray now owns the inn that he and his wife fell in love with when they used to visit her mother nearby. Since arriving in the UK several years ago, he has worked in hotels in Berkshire and London's Docklands, run the directors' table at the Baltic Exchange, and undertaken prestigious catering commissions at Tate Britain and Tate Modern. Perhaps something from the last two establishments rubbed off on him, judging by the 'Irish Picasso' Graham Knuttel's art on the walls here. Expect modern British cooking with a touch of the Mediterranean, a typical meal consisting of potato gnocchi in mussel cream; fillet of Welsh lamb on a cassoulet of haricot beans, root vegetables and tarragon; and parkin with spiced syrup and vanilla bean ice cream. Cornish fish specials include monkfish tail with smoked paprika couscous; and cod with braised red cabbage and red wine jus.

continued

Pick of the Pubs
SKENFRITH – MONMOUTHSHIRE

The Bell at Skenfrith

This 17th-century coaching inn is located just inside the Welsh border, on what is now a mere B road, but which was once a main route from England into the Principality. Standing on the banks of the water by the historic arched bridge over the River Monnow, it has beautiful views across to Skenfrith Castle.

A few years ago it was AA Pub of the Year, and it is currently the AA Wine Award winner for Wales; it continues to fly the flag for superb food and outstanding wines and beers. William and Janet Hutchings and their family have been behind this successful enterprise since 2001, and with head chef Kurt Fleming in charge of the kitchen they are set to continue to blossom. An oak bar, flagstones, sumptuous sofas and old settles provide character, and there are eight well-equipped bedrooms, some with four-posters. Locally sourced and mainly organic ingredients are

used in most dishes, among them starters like goats' cheese pannacota, mizuna leaves and redcurrant sauce. From the main courses you can select ravioli of watercress, pine nut and roquefort, aubergine caviar and red pepper rouille, or pan-fried black bream fillet, warm salad of haricot blanc and garden pea with roasted chorizo. Puddings might include white chocolate and raspberry fondant with white chocolate ice cream. Guest real ales, hand-pumped local cider and a good selection of wines by the glass make the best of any meal, or can be enjoyed by themselves.

OPEN: 11-11 (Sun 12-10.30) Closed: last wk Jan, 1st wk Feb Closed Mon Nov-Mar
RESTAURANT: L served all week 12-2.30 D served all week 7-9.30 (Sun 7-9) Av 3 course à la carte £30
⊕: Free House ◖: Freeminer Best Bitter, Hook Norton Best Bitter, Timothy Taylor Landlord. ♀: 13
FACILITIES: Garden: Lawn, terrace, tables & chairs Dogs allowed (except in restaurant) **NOTES:** Parking 36
ROOMS: 8 bedrooms en suite 2 family rooms s£75 d£95

◉◉◉ 🏠 ♀   Map 09 SO42
NP7 8UH
☎ 01600 750235
🖷 01600 750525
📧 enquiries@skenfrith.co.uk
🌐 www.skenfrith.co.uk
Dir: M4 junct 24. Take A449 to Raglan and onto A40 to Monmouth. Through tunnel at Monmouth and over lights. At rdbt take 1st exit, right at lights on to Hereford Road. 4m out of Monmouth, left on to B4521 towards Abergavenney. The Bell is 2m on left.

Wales

TREDUNNOCK continued

OPEN: 12-2.30 6.30-9.30 (Sun 12-3, 6.30-8.30)
BAR MEALS: L served Mon-Sat 12-2.30 D served Mon-Sat
Av main course £10 **RESTAURANT:** L served all week 12-2.30
D served all week 6-9.45 (Sun 12-3, 6.30-8.30) 🍺: Free House
🍺: Coor's Hancock's HB, Brains Rev James, Brains Smooth.
🍷: 10 **FACILITIES:** Garden: Patio area, tables, overlooks river
Usk **NOTES:** Parking 65 **ROOMS:** 6 bedrooms en suite
2 family rooms s£85 d£95 No children overnight

TRELLECK   Map 04 SO50

Pick of the Pubs

The Lion Inn 🐟
NP25 4PA ☎ 01600 860322 🖷 01600 860060
e-mail: tom@lioninn.co.uk
Dir: From A40 S of Monmouth take B4293, follow signs for Trelleck

This popular and well-established free house stands
opposite the church, and is said to be haunted. Guests
are greeted by welcoming real fires in the winter months,
whilst in summer drinks and meals can be served in the
garden overlooking the Wye valley. The former brew and
coach house has won many accolades for its food and
hospitality over the past three years, and is enjoying a
growing reputation amongst locals and those travelling
from further afield. Visitors who want to explore the
nearby walking trails or historic buildings like Tintern
Abbey and Chepstow Castle will find it a useful staging
post. The extensive pub menu caters for all tastes, from
bar snacks and basket meals to blackboard specials. Fish
choices include Russian-style monkfish, whole baked
trout, salmon wellington, tuna, red snapper, red mullet,
mahi-mahi, mussels and prawns.
OPEN: 12-3 6-11 (Mon 7-11; closed Sun eve)
BAR MEALS: L served all week 12-2 D served Mon-Sat 6-9.30
Av main course £7.25 **RESTAURANT:** L served all week 12-2
D served Mon-Sat 6-9.30 Av 3 course à la carte £18 🍺: Free
House 🍺: Bath Ales, Wadworth 6X, Fuller's London Pride, Wye
Valley Butty Bach. **FACILITIES:** Garden: Overlooks fields,
stream. Large aviary Dogs allowed Water, biscuits
NOTES: Parking 40

 Pubs with this logo do not allow smoking
anywhere on their premises

USK   Map 09 SO30

Pick of the Pubs

The Nags Head Inn 🍷
Twyn Square NP15 1BH ☎ 01291 672820 🖷 01291 672720
Dir: On A472
This 15th-century coaching stands overlooking the square,
just a short stroll from the River Usk, and has been in the
same family, the Keys, for some 40 years. The pub's
magnificent hanging flower baskets have undoubtedly
played a key part in the town's success over the years in
the Wales in Bloom awards. The traditional bar is
furnished with polished tables and chairs, and decorated
with collections of horse brasses, farming tools and
lanterns hanging from exposed oak beams. Game in
season figures strongly among the speciality dishes,
including whole stuffed partridge (one of the hardest
birds to shoot), pheasant in port, and wild boar steak with
apricot and brandy sauce. There is a good choice for
vegetarians, too, such as Glamorgan sausage filled with
cheese and leek and served with a chilli relish.
OPEN: 10-3 5.30-11 Closed: 25 Dec **BAR MEALS:** L served all
week 10-2 D served all week 5.30-10.30
RESTAURANT: L served all week 11.30-2 D served all week
5.30-10.30 🍺: Free House 🍺: Brains Bitter, Dark, Buckleys Best
& Reverend James. 🍷: 8 **FACILITIES:** Child facs Garden:

AMROTH   Map 08 SN10

The New Inn
SA67 8NW ☎ 01834 812368
Dir: A48 to Carmarthen, A40 to St Clears, A477 to Llanteg then left
A 400-year-old inn, originally a farmhouse, belonging to
Amroth Castle Estate. It has old world charm with beamed
ceilings, a Flemish chimney, a flagstone floor and an
inglenook fireplace. It is close to the beach, and local lobster
and crab are a feature, along with a popular choice of home-
made dishes including steak and kidney pie, soup and curry.
Enjoy food or drink outside on the large lawn.
OPEN: 11.30-3 5.30-11 (closed Nov-Mar) Closed: Nov-Mar
BAR MEALS: L served all week 12-2 D served all week 6-9
RESTAURANT: L served all week 12-2 D served all week 6-9
🍺: Free House 🍺: Burton, Carlsberg-Tetley Tetley Bitter.
FACILITIES: Garden: Large lawn with picnic benches Dogs allowed
NOTES: Parking 100 No credit cards

Temple Bar Inn
SA67 8ND ☎ 01834 812486
Overlooking the beach and the sea, this popular family pub is
handy for both the coast and the countryside. Nearby is the
famous Pembrokeshire Coast Path which offers miles of
unspoilt walking. Very extensive menu offers grills, curries,
fish and Sunday roast dishes, as well as filled jacket potatoes,
giant salad rolls, sandwiches, burgers and ploughman's
lunches. Other fare ranges from Welsh ham and steak and
kidney pudding to pork sausages and sliced turkey.
OPEN: 11-11 **BAR MEALS:** L served daily 11-11 D served daily
11-11 Av main course £6 🍺: Worthington. **FACILITIES:** Children's
licence Dogs allowed **NOTES:** Parking 60

CAREW
Map 08 SN00

Carew Inn
SA70 8SL ☎ 01646 651267 e-mail: mandy@carewinn.co.uk
Dir: *From A477 take A4075. Inn 400yds opp castle & Celtic cross*
A traditional stone-built country inn situated opposite the
Carew Celtic cross and Norman castle. Enjoy the one-mile
circular walk around the castle and millpond. A good range of
bar meals includes Welsh black steak and kidney pie; chilli con
carne; Thai red chicken curry; and seafood pancakes. Fruit
crumble and old favourite jam roly poly feature among the
puddings. Live music every Thursday night under the marquee.
OPEN: 11-11 Closed: Dec 25 **BAR MEALS:** L served all week
11.30-2 D served all week 5.30-9 **RESTAURANT:** L served all week
12-2 D served all week 5.30-9 Av 3 course à la carte £15 ⌑: Free
House ◖: Worthington Best, SA Brains Reverend James & Guest
Ales. **FACILITIES:** Child facs Garden: overlooks Carew Castle Dogs
allowed Water provided **NOTES:** Parking 20

CILGERRAN
Map 08 SN14

Pendre Inn
Pendre SA43 2SL ☎ 01239 614223
Dir: *Off A478 south of Cardigan*
Dating back to the 14th century, this is a pub full of
memorabilia and featuring exposed interior walls, old beams,
slate floors and an inglenook fireplace. An ancient ash tree
grows through the pavement in front of the white stone, thick-
walled building. Typical menu includes lamb steaks with red
wine and cherries, rump and sirloin steaks, pork loin with
honey and mustard glaze, and salmon with hollandaise sauce.
Recent change of hands. Reports welcome.
OPEN: 12-3 6-11 (closed Sun eve) **BAR MEALS:** L served all week
12-2 D served Mon-Sat 6-8 Av main course £7
RESTAURANT: L served Mon-Sun 12-2 D served Mon-Sat 6-8
⌑: Free House ◖: Thomas Watkins, OSB, Tetleys Smoothflow,
Murphys. **FACILITIES:** Child facs Garden: Lawn/patio with large
trees and water feature **NOTES:** Parking 6

HAVERFORDWEST
Map 08 SM91

Pick of the Pubs

The Georges Restaurant/Cafe Bar ♀
24 Market St SA61 1NH ☎ 01437 766683 📠 01437 779090
e-mail: llewis6140@aol.com
Dir: *On the A40*

Formerly George's Brewery, this remarkable 18th-century
building incorporates many original features in its restored
vaulted cellar and eating areas. Its delightful walled garden,
with spectacular views over the ruins of 12th-century
Haverfordwest Castle, has outdoor heating for chillier days

and evenings. Genuine local character is a feature of the all-
day café bar and cellar bistro, where freshly-prepared food
and sheer enthusiasm sets it apart from the norm. An
extensive range of home-made dishes is served all day in
the Celtic-themed, part non-smoking restaurant. Given the
proximity of the sea, there are plenty of fish dishes including
crab cakes, black bream, poached turbot and scallops.
Locally-sourced meat appears in choices such as Welsh
venison steak with a rich port and berry sauce; Welsh lamb-
steak with red wine, mushroom and fresh mint sauce; and
Pembrokeshire sausage pie with mashed potatoes and rich
onion gravy topped with toasted cheese. Among over a
dozen vegetarian options are spinach and cream cheese
cannelloni with traditional tomato sauce, topped with
béchamel and Welsh cheddar; and garlic mushrooms in
flaky pastry with a creamy sauce. Desserts are home made
and include classics such as treacle tart, profiteroles, and
bread and butter pudding.
OPEN: Mon-Thur 10.30-5.30, Fri-Sat 10.30-11 Closed: 25 Dec, 1
Jan **BAR MEALS:** L served Mon-Sat 12-5.30 D served Fri-Sat
6-9.45 Av main course £6.95 **RESTAURANT:** L served Mon-Sat
12-2.30 D served Fri-Sat 6-9.30 Av 3 course à la carte £22.50
⌑: Free House ◖: Marston's Pedigree, Wye Valley Bitter,
Adnams Broadside, Brains Bitter. ♀: 10 **FACILITIES:** Garden:
Walled garden, terrace, outdoor heaters

LAMPHEY
Map 08 SN00

Pick of the Pubs

The Dial Inn 🐟 ♀
Ridgeway Rd SA71 5NU ☎ 01646 672426 📠 01646 672426
Dir: *Just off A4139 (Tenby to Pembroke rd)*
The Dial started life around 1830 as the Dower House for
nearby Lamphey Court, and was converted into a pub in
1966. It immediately established itself as a popular village
local, and in recent years the owners have extended the
dining areas. Food is a real strength, and Pembrokeshire
farm products are used whenever possible. You can
choose from traditional bar food, the imaginative
restaurant menu, or the daily blackboard. Here you'll find
specials such as sautéed pheasant and spinach in an
almond sauce; wild boar cooked in a honey, ginger and
Calvados sauce; Lamphey lamb in tender chunks, with
leeks, apricots, thyme, rosemary and a red wine jus; pot-
roasted partridge with juniper stuffing; and fresh hake
fillet with ginger chilli and coriander dressing. There's a
family room, with darts, pool and other pub games; and a
patio for al fresco dining when the weather permits.
OPEN: 11-3 6-12 **BAR MEALS:** L served all week 12-3
D served all week 6.30-10 **RESTAURANT:** L served all week
12-3 D served all week 6.30-10 ⌑: Free House ◖: Hancocks,
Interbrew Bass, Worthington, Archers. ♀: 8 **FACILITIES:** Child
facs Children's licence Garden: Patio area Dogs allowed Water
NOTES: Parking 50

LANDSHIPPING
Map 08 SN01

The Stanley Arms ♀
SA67 8BE ☎ 01834 860447
Dir: *Off A40 at Canaston Bridge onto A4075, R at Cross Hands, next to
Canaston Bowls*
Built as a farmhouse around 1765, first licensed in 1875, the
pub has its own mooring on the Cleddau Estuary and is

continued

continued

popular with sailors. There's an attractive garden with fine views across the water to Picton Castle, and the area is good for walking. Freshly-cooked pub food includes marinated chicken breast, gammon with egg or pineapple, grilled Milford plaice, Welsh dragon sausage in mustard sauce, home-made curries and Welsh steaks, salads and a children's menu.
OPEN: 12-3 6-11 (all day Thu-Sun, Jul-Sept) (Sun 7-10.30) Mon-Tue (winter) Closed lunch **BAR MEALS:** L served all week 12-2.30 D served all week 6-9.30 Av main course £7
RESTAURANT: L served all week 12-2.30 D served all week 6-9.30
🍽: Free House ◀: Worthington, Fuller's London Pride, Everards Tiger, Hancoks HB. ⅌: 7 **FACILITIES:** Children's licence Garden: Large garden with swings and sandpit Dogs allowed Water **NOTES:** Parking 20

LETTERSTON
Map 08 SM92

The Harp Inn
31 Haverfordwest Rd SA62 5UA
☎ 01348 840061 ▤ 01348 840812
Dir: Located on main A40
Well-known 15th-century country inn that was once a working farm as well as home to a weekly market. Before the present managers acquired it in 1982, the pub had four landlords spanning just over 100 years. Until 1972 it was also home to a milking herd! Two comprehensive menus and a chalkboard offer dishes ranging from seared salmon and venison Normandy to Welsh shoulder of lamb and home-baked pasta.
OPEN: 11-3 6-11 (Sun 12-3, 6-10.30) **BAR MEALS:** L served all week 12-2.30 D served all week 6-9.30 **RESTAURANT:** L served all week 12-2.30 D served all week 6.30-9.30 🍽: Free House ◀: Tetleys, Greene King, Abbot Ale. **FACILITIES:** Garden: Paved and grassed with picnic benches **NOTES:** Parking 50

LITTLE HAVEN
Map 08 SM81

The Swan Inn & Restaurant
SA62 3UL ☎ 01437 781256
So close to the beach is this 300-year-old inn that the fisherman who built it as his home could almost have stepped straight into his boat. It still displays its past in the form of exposed stone walls, beams and open coal fires. Strong on locally caught fish and seafood in both the bar and restaurant. Try Swan Upper - grilled sardines, spinach and egg topped with mozzarella. Rack of Welsh lamb, and prime fillet of Welsh beef are usually available, but a word of warning - don't ask for chips with anything!
OPEN: 11.30-3 7-11 (Sun 12-3 Summer 6-11)
BAR MEALS: L served all week 12-1.45 Av main course £4.50
RESTAURANT: D served Wed-Sat 7-9 ◀: Worthington Best Bitter, Brains Reverand James, Timothy Taylor Landlord, Hook Norton Old Hooky. **FACILITIES:** Garden: Terrace with excellent sea views Well behaved dogs, on leads in bar **NOTES:** No credit cards

---

NEWPORT
Map 08 SN03

Salutation Inn
Felindre Farchog, Crymych SA41 3UY
☎ 01239 820564 ▤ 01239 820355 e-mail: JohnDenley@aol.com
web: www.salutationcountryhotel.co.uk
Dir: On A487 between Cardigan and Fishguard
This 16th-century coaching inn stands in a quiet village in the heart of the Pembrokeshire Coast National Park, with lawned gardens running down to the river Nevern. Travellers will a locals' bar, a no-smoking lounge and a restaurant. The varied menu features snacks and starters, with dishes like peppered rib-eye steak; pan-fried haddock with new potatoes; and

continued

broccoli and cream cheese bake for larger appetites.
OPEN: 12-12 **BAR MEALS:** L served all week 12.30-2.30 D served all week 6.30-9.30 Av main course £7.50 **RESTAURANT:** L served all week 12.30-2.30 D served all week 6.30-9.30 Av 3 course à la carte £16 ◀: Local guest ales, Felinfoel, Brains. **FACILITIES:** Garden: Large grassed area leading to river Dogs allowed
NOTES: Parking 60 **ROOMS:** 8 bedrooms en suite 3 family rooms s£32 d£48 (★★★) No children overnight

---

PEMBROKE DOCK
Map 08 SM90

Ferry Inn 🐟
Pembroke Ferry SA72 6UD ☎ 01646 682947
e-mail: ferryinn@aol.com
Dir: A477, off A48, R at garage, signs for Cleddau Bridge, L at roundabout
Once the haunt of smugglers, this 16th-century inn is set on the banks of the Cleddau River, with fine views across the estuary from the nautical-themed bar and waterside terrace. There is a 'great disaster corner' with pictures of local catastrophes! On a lighter note, the menu offers a range of fresh local fish such as turbot, Dover sole and sardines. Other options include steak and ale pie, and vegetable korma.
OPEN: 11.30-2.45 7-11 (Summer hols open all day) Closed: 25-26 Dec **BAR MEALS:** L served all week 12-2 D served all week 7-10 (Sun 12-1, 7-9) Av main course £8.95 **RESTAURANT:** L served all week 12-2 D served all week 7-10 (Sun 12-1.30, 7-9) 🍽: Free House ◀: Worthington, Bass, Felinfoel Double Dragon, Weekly Guest Ale. **FACILITIES:** Garden: Beer terrace on edge of river, amazing views Dogs allowed Water **NOTES:** Parking 12

PORTHGAIN
Map 08 SM83

Pick of the Pubs

The Sloop Inn
SA62 5BN ☎ 01348 831449 ▤ 01348 831388
e-mail: matthew@sloop-inn.freeserve.co.uk
Most of Porthgain's footprint on the landscape of the Pembrokeshire Coast National Park is accounted for by the Sloop. From the outside this family-friendly harbourside pub doesn't look particularly large, but in true Tardis tradition, appearances are deceptive. 'Basic' is the owners' word for the brick, slate, quarry tile and part-carpeted interior, but the seating's comfy and a large stove throws out loads of cheering heat when necessary. There are photos of Old Porthgain in the bar, and among the collected clutter is the name plaque from the Carolina, wrecked off the rocky coast in 1859. The bar menu has sandwiches, baguettes, light snacks and main meals, and there's an all-year lunch and evening menu. From the specials board, updated twice daily, come lemon pepper haddock fillets with a trio of flavoured butters; rib eye steak topped with red onion marmalade and stilton; lamb shank set on a bed of creamy mash and red wine gravy. At busy times there's an 'all-you-can-cram-into-a-bowl' salad servery.
OPEN: 9.30-11 (Sun 9.30-22.30) **BAR MEALS:** L served all week 12-2.30 D served all week 6-9.30 May vary high season **RESTAURANT:** L served all week 12-2.30 D served all week 6-9.30 May vary high season 🍽: Free House ◀: Worthington Draught, Bass. **FACILITIES:** Children's licence Garden: Raised patio area, sun trap, safe Dogs allowed Outside water **NOTES:** Parking 50

🍺 Principal Beers for sale

Wales

SOLVA
Map 08 SM82

The Cambrian Inn ⟩◇
Main St SA62 6UU ☎ 01437 721210
Dir: 13m from Haverfordwest on the St David's Rd

Something of an institution in this pretty fishing village is a Grade II listed 17th-century inn that attracts local and returning visitors alike. A sample bar menu offers Welsh black beef curry, vegetable pancakes topped with melted cheese or Welsh sirloin steak, while the a la carte dinner menu offers duckling with orange and Grand Marnier sauce, roast cod with a seafood sauce, mushroom stroganoff, and pork fillet in honey and mustard sauce. Sandwiches, jackets, salads and ploughmans' also available.
OPEN: 12-3 6-11 (Winter 12-2:30, 6-) Closed: 2wks Jan, 2 wks Nov, Dec 25-26 **BAR MEALS:** L served all week 12-2 D served all week 6.15-9.30 Av main course £6.75 **RESTAURANT:** L served all week 12-2 D served all week 7-9.30 😊: Free House 🍺: Reverend James, Worthington Cream Flow. **FACILITIES:** Garden: patio, beer garden, outdoor eating Dogs allowed in garden only **NOTES:** Parking 12

STACKPOLE
Map 08 SR99

Pick of the Pubs

The Stackpole Inn ⟩◇ ♀
SA71 5DF ☎ 01646 672324 📠 01646 672716
e-mail: info@stackpoleinn.co.uk
See Pick of the Pubs on opposite page

WOLF'S CASTLE
Map 08 SM92

Pick of the Pubs

The Wolfe Inn ♀
SA62 5LS ☎ 01437 741662 📠 01437 741676
Dir: On A40 between Haverfordwest & Fishguard, (7m from both)
The Wolfe is an oak-beamed, stone-built property in a lovely village setting. The bar-brasserie and restaurant comprise four interconnecting but distinctly different rooms: the Victorian Parlour, Hunters' Lodge, the Brasserie and a conservatory. The inn uses mainly local produce in its 'robust, real food'. Features of the menu include Welsh beef, duck, game ('depending on the landlord's aim'), and local seafood. Example dishes are fillet of beef bordelaise, lamb all'aglio e menta, chicken piccante, salmon fillet with cream and pernod sauce, and mussels in garlic, white wine and cream. Award-winning local cheeses and scrumptious home-made desserts follow. Drink options include a monthly guest beer, choice of wines, and coffees reflecting the landlord's Italian

roots: cappuccino, espresso, machiato, lungo, doppio and filter. Secluded patio garden outside.
OPEN: 12-2 6-11 **BAR MEALS:** L served all week 12-2 D served all week 7-9 **RESTAURANT:** L served all week 12-2 D served all week 7-9 😊: Free House 🍺: Interbrew Worthington Bitter, Monthly Guest Beer. ♀: 11
FACILITIES: Garden: Enclosed garden, secluded, patio area
NOTES: Parking 20 **ROOMS:** 2 bedrooms 1 en suite s£40 d£70 (★★★) No children overnight

POWYS

ABERCRAF
Map 09 SN81

The Gwyn Arms NEW ⟩◇ ♀
Pen-y-Cae SA9 1GP ☎ 01639 730310 📠 01639 731079
e-mail: jan-andrews2@btopenworld.com
Dir: On the A4067 between Swansea and Brecon
On the southern edge of the beautiful Brecon Beacons National Park, the 200-year-old Gwyn Arms is popular with cavers, cyclists, walkers and those merely chancing upon it in the car. Its charm is partly age-related, but the friendly staff who make you feel that battling through ghastly winter weather have been worthwhile should take some of the credit. The food is definitely worth the effort, especially pork fillet chasseur, chicken stir-fry, and succulent poached salmon.
OPEN: 12-11 (In summer open for breakfast)
BAR MEALS: L served all week 12 D served all week 9.30 Sun 9 in winter Av main course £7.50 **RESTAURANT:** L served all week 12-9.30 D served all week 9.30 Sun 9pm in wnter Av 3 course à la carte £13.50 🍺: Worthington Creamflow, Browns Dark Mild, Guiness. ♀: 9 **FACILITIES:** Child facs Garden: 3 acres adjoining the River Tawe Dogs allowed **NOTES:** Parking 20

BERRIEW
Map 15 SJ10

The Lion Hotel
SY21 8PQ ☎ 01686 640452 📠 01686 640604
e-mail: patrick@okeefe.demon.co.uk
Dir: 5m from Welshpool on A483, right to Berriew. Centre of village.
The Lion Hotel and restaurant is a black and white coaching inn in the scenic Welsh border village of Berriew, dating from 1618. Banks' bitter and mild are amongst the ales served in the bar. Menu choices include sea bass on horseradish mash; Welsh lamb shoulder with garlic and rosemary; and casseroled duck in red wine, orange and ginger. Watch out for daily fish specials, too.
OPEN: 12-3.30 6-11 (Fri 5.30-11, Sat all day, Sun 7-10.30) Closed: 25 Dec **BAR MEALS:** L served all week 12-2 D served all week 7-9 **RESTAURANT:** L served all week 12-2 D served Mon-Sat 7-9 😊: Free House 🍺: Banks Bitter/Mild, Pedigree, Old Empire.
FACILITIES: Children's licence Garden: Patio area surrounded by plants Dogs allowed Water **NOTES:** Parking 6

continued

The Stackpole Inn

The bar of this 17th-century inn is made from Welsh slate, while the wood for the ceiling beams comes from ash trees grown on the estate. In the mellow stone wall outside is a carefully preserved King George V post box, a reminder of the days when one of the two original stone cottages that went to make up the pub was a post office.

The inn is a walker's delight, standing close to the spectacular Pembrokeshire coastal path, and set in lovely landscaped gardens at the heart of the National Trust's Stackpole Estate. Warmth is provided by a wood-burning stove set within the stone fireplace, so that even on the chilliest of days the place is cosy and welcoming. Local produce from the abundant Welsh countryside plays a strong part in the home-cooked menu, along with fish from the nearby coast. You could start off with home-made chicken liver and brandy pâté. Moving on, a trio of Thai-style fish on wok-fried vegetables; or black beef, sirloin or fillet, with all the trimmings. An extensive fresh fish choice is offered from the daily specials board, depending on the daily catch. Other specials might be a justifiably popular Welsh beef and Felinfoel ale pie; or Pembroke sausages on bubble and squeak. Desserts include chocolate cappuccino cups with home-made shortbread, or zesty lemon and lime cheesecake with bitter lemon glaze. A short, well-chosen wine list rounds things off nicely.

OPEN: 12-2 6-11 (Summer 12-3, 5.30-11) Closed Sun eve Winter (not Jan-Feb)
BAR MEALS: L served all week 12-2 D served all week 6.30-9 (Summer Sun 12-3, 5.30-9)
RESTAURANT: L served all week 12-2 D served all week 6.30-9 Av 3 course à la carte £20
🍺: Free House
🍷: Brains Reverend James, Felinfoel Double Dragon, Worthington Draught. ⚲: 8
FACILITIES: Garden: Landscaped garden, picturesque Dogs allowed Water **NOTES:** Parking 25

 🍷   Map 08 SR99
SA71 5DF
☎ 01646 672324
📄 01646 672716
e info@stackpoleinn.co.uk
Dir: From Pembroke take B4319 & follow signs for Stackpole. Approx 4m

BRECON
Map 09 SO02

The Felin Fach Griffin ♀
Felin Fach LD3 0UB ☎ 01874 620111 📠 01874 620120
e-mail: enquiries@eatdrinksleep.ltd.uk
web: www.eatdrinksleep.ltd.uk
Dir: 4.5m N of Brecon on the A470 (Brecon to Hay-on-Wye road)
A country inn in a quiet valley on the edge of the Brecon
Beacons National Park, to which owner Charles Inkin has
brought his uncompromising belief in 'simple things done
well'. So no horsebrasses, Welsh love spoons, chintz, or
unnecessarily complicated cooking for him. At the pub's heart
are deep leather sofas surrounding a large newspaper-strewn
farmhouse table, and an open fire, nearly always alight. Dutch
chef Ricardo Van Ede's food is simple but delicious: typically
tuna steak with aubergine caviar, artichoke and sauce vièrge;
grey mullet with crushed potatoes, spinach and chive butter;
and local venison with autumn fruits and dauphinoise potato.
OPEN: 12-3 6-11 (Sunday 12-11) Closed: Dec 24-25
BAR MEALS: L served Tue-Sun 12.30-2.30 D served Mon-Sun 7-9.30
RESTAURANT: L served Tue-Sun 12.30-2.30 D served Mon-Sun
7-9.30 Av 3 course à la carte £20 🍺: Free House ◀: Tomos Watkin
OSB, Scottish Courage John Smith's. ♀: 8 **FACILITIES:** Garden:
Tables and chairs Dogs allowed water **NOTES:** Parking 60

Pick of the Pubs

The Usk Inn ◆◆◆◆ ◉ ⌒♡ ♀
Talybont-on-Usk LD3 7JE ☎ 01874 676251 📠 01874 676392
e-mail: stay@uskinn.co.uk web: www.uskinn.co.uk
Dir: 6m E of Brecon, just off the A40 towards Abergavenny & Crickhowell

Although it was once a bank, the Usk has probably been
an inn for at least 150 years. We know it was in 1878
when a locomotive overshot the station opposite and
ended up in the street outside, disturbing many a quiet
pint. That can't happen again because the station closed
in the 1960s, forcing today's visitors to arrive by car, on
mountain bikes, Shanks's pony, or even by canal boat.
When Mike and Barbara Taylor bought it seven years ago
they brought it up to such a good standard that it became
the AA's Welsh Pub of the Year 2004-05. Imaginative
menus make good use of fresh local produce, as testified
by dishes like wild boar and venison terrine with roast
garlic chutney; twice-cooked shank of Brecon lamb in
minted red wine jus; and monkfish sautéed with pernod,
white wine and cream.
OPEN: 8am-11pm Closed: Dec 25-26 **BAR MEALS:** L served
all week 12-3 D served all week 6.30-9 Sun 6.30-7.30 Av main
course £13.95 **RESTAURANT:** L served all week 12-3 D served
all week 6.30-9 Sun 6.30-7.30 Av 3 course à la carte £25
Av 2 course fixed price £10 🍺: Free House ◀: Felinfoel
Double Dragon, Hancocks HB, Greene King IPA, Brains. ♀: 8

FACILITIES: Garden: Lawned area with mature planting Dogs
allowed in bar only Water **NOTES:** Parking 35
ROOMS: 11 bedrooms en suite 1 family room s£50 d£80 No
children overnight

Pick of the Pubs

AA Pub of the Year for Wales 2005-06

White Swan Inn ◉◉ ♀
Llanfrynach LD3 7BZ ☎ 01874 665276 📠 01874 665362
e-mail: stephen.way@tiscali.com
Dir: 3m E of Brecon the A40, B4558 and signs to Llanfrynach
The long, white-painted stone frontage of the White Swan
overlooks St Brynach's churchyard in the heart of the
Brecon Beacons National Park. With its polished floors,
exposed oak beams and a vast inglenook fireplace, the
building simply oozes charm. Lunchtime snacks are
original and tempting: bresaola with olive roasted
bruschetta perhaps. From the main menu expect haunch
of local venison with watercress and bacon champ, and
marinated escalopes of pork with spiced aubergine,
chorizo and harissa. This delightful free house has long
been regarded as an upmarket local, and is particularly
popular with walkers and cyclists. There's trout fishing on
the nearby River Usk, and the Monmouthshire and
Brecon canal is close by.
OPEN: 12-2 6.30-11 Closed: 24-26 Dec, 1 Jan
BAR MEALS: L served Wed-Sun 12-2 D served Wed-Sun 7-9.30
Sun lunch 12-2.30 dinner 7-9 Av main course £13.95
RESTAURANT: L served Wed-Sun 12-2 D served Wed-Sun
7-9.30 Av 3 course à la carte £25.95 🍺: Free House ◀: Cream
Flow, HB, Worthington Cream Flow, Worthington Cask. ♀: 8
FACILITIES: Child facs Garden: Flagged terrace and vine
NOTES: Parking 35

CAERSWS
Map 15 SO09

Pick of the Pubs

The Talkhouse ◆◆◆◆◆ ♀
Pontdolgoch SY17 5JE ☎ 01686 688919 📠 01686 689134
e-mail: info@talkhouse.co.uk
*Dir: From Newtown A487 about 5m towards Machynlleth &
Dolgellan, turn right onto A470 just before level crossing into Caersws
carry on about 1m on A470 inn on left*

A traditional stone coaching inn, low-roofed and
whitewashed, that has the appearance of a typical
country pub. The relaxing sitting room is furnished with
comfortable armchairs and sofas, while the bar with its
beams and log fire offers a welcoming atmosphere in

continued

continued

which to study the menu whilst enjoying an aperitif. French windows open from the restaurant on to a private garden for romantic summer alfresco dining. At any time you can be sure of a warm welcome, good food, quality wines and great service because these are what the owners are passionate about. The varied menu of mainly classical dishes is produced from Welsh ingredients where possible. A meal may start with a smoked haddock rarebit on a bed of plum tomatoes, or grilled Welsh goats cheese with award-winning Carmarthen ham, and proceed with Welsh pork tenderloin infused with local black pudding, classic whole Dover sole with French peas and duchesse potatoes, or local fillet of beef on a horseradish rosti with sauteed vine tomatoes.
OPEN: 12-2.30 6.30-11 **BAR MEALS:** L served Wed-Sun 12-3 D served Tue-Sat 6.30-8.45 Sun 11.30-2
RESTAURANT: L served Wed-Sun 12-3 D served Tue-Sat 6.30-8.45 Sun 11.30-2 ⊕: Free House ◀: Brains, Tetleys, Victoria Bitter, Chimay. ♀: 6 **FACILITIES:** Garden: Informal cottage garden **NOTES:** Parking 30 **ROOMS:** 3 bedrooms en suite s£70 d£95 No children overnight

---

COEDWAY
Map 15 SJ31

The Old Hand and Diamond
SY5 9AR ☎ 01743 884379 🖂 01743 872305
e-mail: moz123@aol.com

Close to the Shropshire border and the River Severn, this 17th-century inn still retains much of its original character. Large open log fires burn in the winter and autumn. Typical menu includes steak and kidney pie, vegetarian tortellini, home-made fish cakes with onion, parsley and dill, lasagne, and the Old Hand Special. This last dish consists of fillet steak with mushrooms, onions and Worcester sauce in a baguette.
OPEN: 11-11 **BAR MEALS:** L served all week 12-10 D served all week Av main course £10 **RESTAURANT:** L served all week 12-10 D served all week Av 3 course à la carte £20 ⊕: Free House ◀: Bass, Worthington, Shropshire Lad + Guest beers.
FACILITIES: Child facs Garden: Food served outside
NOTES: Parking 90

CRICKHOWELL
Map 09 SO21

Pick of the Pubs

The Bear ★★★ ⑳♀
Brecon Rd NP8 1BW ☎ 01873 810408 🖂 01873 811696
e-mail: bearhotel@aol.com
See Pick of the Pubs on page 650

Pick of the Pubs

Nantyffin Cider Mill ⑳♀
Brecon Rd NP8 1SG ☎ 01873 810775 🖂 01873 812127
e-mail: info@cidermill.co.uk
Dir: At junct of A40 & A479, 1.5m west of Crickhowell
Originally a drovers' inn, dating from the 16th century, the Nantyffin is located at the foot of the Black Mountains between Crickhowell and Brecon. The inn was well-known for the cider it produced in the 19th century, and the original cider press, fully working until the 1960s, has been incorporated into the main dining room. The bars are full of character, and offer a range of real ales, a comprehensive list of wines, and house specialities of mulled cider and home-made lemonade. Menus are based on carefully sourced local produce, including organically reared, free-range meat and poultry from the proprietor's farm in Llangynidr. Example dishes using home-reared meat are lamb with creamed herb mash and rosemary garlic sauce, and roast supreme of chicken with caramelised root vegetable and pearl barley risotto. Fresh fish is listed on the daily specials board - maybe grilled line caught bass and roast loin of monkfish.
OPEN: 12-2.30 6-9.30 Closed: 1wk Jan **BAR MEALS:** L served Wed-Tue 12-2.30 D served Wed-Tue 6.30-9.30 Av main course £12.95 **RESTAURANT:** L served Wed-Mon 12-2.30 D served Wed-Mon 7-9.30 Av 3 course fixed price £12.95 ⊕: Free House ◀: Uleys Old Spot, Felinfoel Best Bitter, Marston's Pedigree, Hancocks HB. ♀: 8 **FACILITIES:** Child facs Garden: Overlooking Usk River Dogs allowed **NOTES:** Parking 40

CWMDU
Map 09 SO12

Pick of the Pubs

The Farmers Arms
NP8 1RU ☎ 01874 730464 🖂 01874 730988
e-mail: cwmdu@aol.com
Dir: From A40 take A479 signed Builth Wells, Cwmdu in 3m
A traditional country inn in a quiet valley on the edge of the Black Mountains. The 18th-century building is warmly welcoming, with a wood-burning stove when the weather requires it, bar games and a broad selection of real ales. Fresh local ingredients are used to create dishes such as smoked haddock and Welsh onion fishcakes; puff pastry pillows of leeks; and grilled supreme of chicken with sautéed wild mushrooms. Tempting desserts include sticky toffee fudge Pavlova.
OPEN: 12-2.30 6.30-11 (Mon 6.30-11, open BH Mon all day) Closed: Two weeks in Nov **BAR MEALS:** L served Wed-Sun 12-2.15 D served Tue-Sun 7-9.30 Av main course £8
RESTAURANT: L served Wed-Sun 12-2.15 D served Tue-Sun 7-9.30 Av 3 course à la carte £22 Av 3 course fixed price £19 ⊕: Free House ◀: Uley Old Spot Prize Ale, Tomos Watkin OSB, Breconshire Brewery Ramblers Ruin, Shepherd Neame Spitfire Premium Ale. **FACILITIES:** Garden: Views over the Brecon Beacons Dogs allowed Water, food, secured penned area **NOTES:** Parking 30

♦ Diamond rating for inspected guest accommodation

Pick of the Pubs

CRICKHOWELL – POWYS

The Bear

This delightful old coaching inn dates back to 1432, and is one the best loved hotels in the area. It has a traditional bar, two dining rooms, 35 tastefully furnished en suite bedrooms, and an attractive garden with hanging baskets, tubs and earthenware pots.

The dining rooms are in the original part of the hotel, one with oak beams and a rug-covered flagstone floor, the other small and intimate with candles, fresh flowers and lace tablecloths. The cooking, based extensively on fresh local produce and home-grown herbs, is essentially modern English, although it has to be said that some of the dishes are best described as - and this is a compliment - unconventional. Thus it is left to the bar menu to offer the more traditional fare, such as soups, baguettes, sandwiches, starters, light meals and main courses such as home-made faggots in onion gravy; Welsh black beef steaks with a choice of sauces; and baked fillet of fresh salmon with prawn and lemon butter sauce. It is in the dining room,

however, that convention is elbowed aside by the likes of starters such as lasagne of langoustine with fennel and cucumber salsa; roast supreme of wood pigeon with artichoke mousse and smoked bacon and pea ragout; and a main course of honey-glazed duck breast with roasted salsify, milk chocolate tart, confit potato, prunes, lettuce fondue and spiced duck jus. Puddings include home-made apple and whinberry pie, and there are Welsh cheeses to sample. Crickhowell itself is a charming little market town in the heart of the Brecon Beacons National Park, with opportunities for salmon and trout fishing on the River Usk, walking in the mountains and bookshop browsing in the secondhand-book capital of Hay-on-Wye.

OPEN: 11-3 6-11 (Sun 12-3, 7-10.30)
BAR MEALS: L served all week 12-2 D served all week 6-10 Av main course £8.95
RESTAURANT: L served all week 12-2 D served Mon-Sat 7-9.30 Av 3 course à la carte £32
⊕: Free House
🍺: Interbrew Bass, Greene King Old Speckled Hen, Hancocks HB, Brains Reverend James. ♀: 12
FACILITIES: Garden: Small pretty garden, pergola, seating Dogs allowed Water **NOTES:** Parking 50
ROOMS: 35 bedrooms en suite 6 family rooms s£55 d£72 No children overnight

★★★ ⊛ ♀   Map 09 SO21
Brecon Rd NP8 1BW
☎ 01873 810408
📄 01873 811696
ⓔ bearhotel@aol.com
Dir: On A40 between Abergavenny & Brecon

Wales

DYLIFE
Map 14 SN89

Star Inn ◆◆◆
SY19 7BW ☎ 01650 521345 🖹 01650 521345
Dir: Between Llanidloes & Machynlleth on mountain road

Situated at 1300 feet in some of Wales' most breathtaking countryside, the inn traces its roots back to the 17th century. The area was a favourite haunt of Dylan Thomas and Wynford Vaughan Thomas; red kites swoop overhead, and the magnificent Clywedog reservoir is close by. Varied choice of wholesome pub fare includes cottage pie, big banger and chips, jumbo cod, sirloin steak, chicken in mushroom cream sauce, and gammon with egg or pineapple. Specials include broccoli and leek bake, loin of pork in cider and cream, and aubergine and mushroom nut bake.
OPEN: 12-2.30 7-11 (ring for opening details during winter)
BAR MEALS: L served all week 12-2.30 D served all week 7-10
Av main course £6.95 **RESTAURANT:** 12-2 7-10 ⊕: Free House
🍺: Tetley Smooth, Marston Pedigree. **FACILITIES:** Children's licence **NOTES:** Parking 40 **ROOMS:** 6 bedrooms 2 en suite 1 family room s£22 d£22

HAY-ON-WYE
Map 09 SO24

Kilverts Hotel ★★ ♀
The Bullring HR3 5AG ☎ 01497 821042 🖹 01497 821580
e-mail: info@kilverts.co.uk
Dir: In town centre near Butter Market

At the heart of Wales' 'bookshop capital' near the Butter Market, and surrounded by glorious countryside, this hotel derives its name from a noted 19th-century cleric well commemorated in the town. A core menu uses local produce, while the bar menu features pizzas, pasta and other pub favourites. Restaurant dinners show rather more imagination: chicken breast stuffed with brie and parma ham, half a roast duckling with orange and ginger sauce, North African lamb with ginger, chickpeas and chilli, and a range of fish and seafood, including calamari and whitebait.
OPEN: 9-11 (Sun 12-10.30) Closed: 25 Dec **BAR MEALS:** L served
continued

Kilverts Hotel
The Bullring, Hay-on-Wye HR3 5AG
Tel: 01497 821042 Fax: 01497 821580
email: info@kilverts.co.uk

At the heart of Wales's 'bookshop capital' near the Butter Market, and surrounded by glorious countryside, this hotel derives its name from a noted 19th-century cleric well commemorated in the town.
Our menu uses local produce, while the bar menu features pizzas, pasta and other pub favourites. Restaurant dinners show rather more imagination: Baked Filo Parcel stuffed with Welsh Brie, Apple & Tarragon served on a Bubble & Squeak Potato Cake with Red Onion & Sweet Pepper Marmalade. Pan-Fried Abbydore Venison Steaks accompanied by Sauteed Rosemary Potatoes & a rich Red Currant & Port Sauce. Sauteed Scallops with a Smokey Bacon & Pernod Cream Sauce, as well as a range of fish and seafood – and interesting vegetarian options.
Average main course between £10 & £12
Average 3 course à la carte £21.50

all week 12-2 D served all week 7-9.30 Av main course £9
RESTAURANT: L served Sun 12-2 D served all week 7-9.30
Av 3 course à la carte £23.95 ⊕: Free House 🍺: Wye Valley Butty Bach, Coors Worthington Cream Flow & Hancock's HB, The Reverend James. ♀: 10 **FACILITIES:** Garden: Large lawns, pond area Dogs allowed before 7pm, water **NOTES:** Parking 13
ROOMS: 11 bedrooms en suite 1 family room s£50 d£70 (★★)
See advert on this page

Pick of the Pubs

The Old Black Lion ★★ ⊚
HR3 5AD ☎ 01497 820841 🖹 01497 822960
e-mail: info@oldblacklion.co.uk web: www.oldblacklion.co.uk
See Pick of the Pubs on page 652

LLANDINAM
Map 15 SO08

The Lion Hotel
SY17 5BY ☎ 01686 688233 🖹 01686 689124
Dir: On the A470 midway between Newton and Llanidloes
Llandinam is perhaps best known as the home of the first electric light in Wales. The Lion has an attractive riverside setting and offers a warm welcome to visitors enjoying the splendour of the Upper Severn Valley. The restaurant's menu features hearty casseroles of Welsh lamb and registered Welsh Black Beef. Other dishes include traditional steaks and grills, and here is always a range of home-made puddings.
OPEN: 12-3 6.30-11 (Sun 7-10.30, closed Mon)
BAR MEALS: L served all week 12-2.15 6.45-9.15
RESTAURANT: D served all week 6.45-9.15 ⊕: Free House
🍺: Old Speckled Hen, Carlsberg-Tetley Tetley Cask Bitter.
FACILITIES: Children's licence Garden **NOTES:** Parking 50

Pick of the Pubs

The Old Black Lion

Parts of this historic inn date back to the 1300s, but structurally most of it is 17th century, which still makes it pretty old. It stands on Lion Street, close to the site of the Lion Gate, one of the original entrances to the walled town of Hay-on-Wye. With the Brecon Beacons to the west and the Black Mountains to the south, Hay is the world's largest second-hand book centre, with bookshops at every turn.

It also hosts a renowned annual literary festival that attracts distinguished guest speakers of the calibre of ex-president Bill Clinton. Oliver Cromwell is reputed to have stayed at the inn during the siege of Hay Castle, although he would not have found a teddy bear in his room as guests do today. The oak-timbered bar, with its scrubbed pine tables, log-burning fire and comfy chairs is the perfect place to relax with a pint of Old Black Lion, Wye Valley Bitter, or one of the guest ales. The inn has a good reputation for food, which can be served in the bar or the pretty dining room overlooking the garden terrace. Regularly changing menus make the most of seasonal British produce, including locally reared meat (some organic), fresh seafood, seasonal vegetables, and herbs from the garden. One could order, for example, fresh fettuccine with kiln-roasted smoked salmon; followed by herb-crusted rack of local spring lamb with Mediterranean vegetable tart and rosemary lamb jus; and in summer, good old strawberries and cream. Bar favourites include Moroccan lamb with apricot and fig compote, and couscous; spicy peppered venison with cabbage mash; and wild mushroom and leek pancakes with cheese sauce. Apart from bookshop browsing, local activities include walking, canoeing, fishing, pony-trekking and cycling.

OPEN: 11-11 (Sun 12-10.30) Closed: 25-26 Dec
BAR MEALS: L served all week 12-2.30 D served all week 6.30-9.30 Av main course £10
RESTAURANT: L served all week D served all week 6.30-9.30
☺: Free House
◀: Old Black Lion Ale, Wye Valley, guest ales.
FACILITIES: Garden: Patio garden, abundance of flowers & herbs
NOTES: Parking 20
ROOMS: 10 bedrooms en suite s£42.50 d£80 No children overnight

★★ ◉   Map 09 SO24
HR3 5AD
☎ 01497 820841
🖹 01497 822960
🄴 info@oldblacklion.co.uk
🆆 www.oldblacklion.co.uk
Dir: Town centre

LLANDRINDOD WELLS
Map 09 SO06

The Bell Country Inn 🐟 ♀
Llanyre LD1 6DY ☎ 01597 823959 📠 01597 825899
Dir: 1.5m NW of Llandrindod Wells on the A4081
Set in the hills above Llandrindod Wells, this former drovers'
inn offers a varied menu in the dining room, lounge bar and
Stables Restaurant. Seafood from the specials board includes
jumbo cod, seafood tagliatelle, while favourite alternatives
are half a roasted duckling or prime 10oz sirloin steak.
There's the Courtyard for outdoor seating, and a play area
for children is provided. Expect major changes after
renovation work.
OPEN: 11-11 **BAR MEALS:** L served all week 12-2.15 D served
Mon-Sat 6.30-9.30 Av main course £8.50 **RESTAURANT:** L served
all week 12-2 D served Mon-Sat 6.30-9.30 🍷: Free House
🍺: Worthington, Hancock's, guest ales. ♀: 12
FACILITIES: Garden: Food served outside. Patio area Dogs allowed
in the garden only. Water provided **NOTES:** Parking 20

LLANFYLLIN
Map 15 SJ11

Cain Valley Hotel ★★
High St SY22 5AQ ☎ 01691 648366 📠 01691 648307
e-mail: info@cainvalleyhotel.co.uk
*Dir: From Shrewsbury & Oswestry follow signs for Lake Vyrnwy & onto
A490 to Llanfyllin. Hotel on R*
Family-run coaching inn dating from the 17th century, with a
stunning Jacobean staircase, oak-panelled lounge bar and a
heavily beamed restaurant with exposed hand-made bricks. A
full bar menu is available at lunchtime and in the evening,
alongside a choice of real ales. Home-made soup, mixed
seafood, Welsh lamb, steaks and curries are offered. Llanfyllin
is set amid green hills, offering wonderful walks and
breathtaking views.
OPEN: 11.30-11 (Sun 12-10.30) Closed: 25 Dec
BAR MEALS: L served all week 12-2 D served all week 7-9 Av main
course £6.50 **RESTAURANT:** D served all week 7-9 🍷: Free House
🍺: Worthingtons, Ansells Mild, Flowers, Guinness.
FACILITIES: Dogs allowed **NOTES:** Parking 12
ROOMS: 13 bedrooms en suite 3 family rooms s£42 d£69 (WTB)

The Stumble Inn
Bwlch-y-Cibau SY22 5LL ☎ 01691 648860 📠 01691 648955
*Dir: A458 to Welshpool, B4393 to Four Crosses and Llansantffraid, A495
Melford, A490 to Bwlch-y-Cibau*

Located opposite the church in a peaceful farming community
in unspoilt mid-Wales countryside close to Lake Vyrnwy, this
popular stone-built 18th-century inn offers a traditional pub
atmosphere. Ideal base for walkers and cyclists. The menu
changes frequently and might feature duck with orange sauce,
lamb shank, whole Dover sole, pork with lemon and mustard
sauce, sizzling Chinese steak, mushroom stroganoff, and

continued

Mediterranean risotto.
OPEN: 12-3 6-12 (Closed Sun nights Dec-Mar) Closed: 2 Wks Jan
BAR MEALS: L served Sun 12-2 D served Wed-Sat 6-9 Av main
course £8.95 **RESTAURANT:** L served Sun 12-2 D served Wed-Sat
6-10 🍷: Free House 🍺: Coors Worthington's, Changing Ales.
FACILITIES: Child facs Garden **NOTES:** Parking 20

LLANGATTOCK
Map 09 SO21

The Vine Tree Inn 🐟
The Legar NP8 1HG ☎ 01873 810514 📠 01873 811299
Dir: Take A40 W from Abergavenny then A4077 from Crickhowell
A pretty pink pub located on the banks of the River Usk, at
the edge of the National Park and within walking distance of
Crickhowell. It is predominantly a dining pub serving a
comprehensive menu from rabbit in a wine and celery sauce
to monkfish in leek and pernod sauce. Among the other
choices on the menu you may find gammon in a parsley
sauce, pork loin stuffed with marinated apricots, or a 16oz T-
bone steak. The large garden overlooks the river, bridge and
Table Mountain.
OPEN: 12-3 6-11 (Sun 12-3, 6.30-9) **BAR MEALS:** L served all
week 12-3 D served all week 6-10 Av main course £8
RESTAURANT: L served all week 12-3 D served all week 6-10
Av 3 course à la carte £15 🍷: Free House 🍺: Fuller's London Pride,
Coors Worthington's, Golden Valley. **FACILITIES:** Garden: Large
private garden, stunning views **NOTES:** Parking 27

LLOWES
Map 09 SO14

The Radnor Arms 🐟
HR3 5JA ☎ 01497 847460 📠 01497 847460
e-mail: brian@radnorsarms.freeserve.co.uk
Dir: A438 (Brecon-Hereford rd) between Glasbury & Clyro
This 400-year-old former drovers' inn provides outstanding
views from the garden, looking over the Wye Valley to the
Black Mountains, to the west of the Brecon Beacons. Local
Felinfoel bitter is amongst the beers served beside blazing
winter fires in the cosy bar. The extensive blackboard menus
offer plenty of variety, with good vegetarian options and a
selection of fish dishes, including sardines and monkfish.
OPEN: 11-2.30 6.30-10 (Sun 12-3) **BAR MEALS:** L served Tue-Sun
12-2.30 D served Tue-Sun 6.30-9 Sat 6.30-100, Sun 12-3 Av main
course £8.50 **RESTAURANT:** L served Tue-Sun 12-2.30 D served
Tue-Sun 6.30-9 (Sun 12-2.30) Av 3 course à la carte £16 🍷: Free
House 🍺: Felinfoel, Worthington, Bitburger. **FACILITIES:** Garden:
Large grassed area, with views of Wye Valley Dogs allowed Garden
NOTES: Parking 50

MONTGOMERY
Map 15 SO29

Pick of the Pubs

Dragon Hotel ★★ 🎖
SY15 6PA ☎ 01686 668359 📠 0870 011 8227
e-mail: reception@dragonhotel.com
web: www.dragonhotel.com
*Dir: A483 toward Welshpool, right onto B4386 then B4385, Behind
the town hall*
The Dragon, a strikingly attractive, black-and-white-
timbered old coaching inn, is a historic hotel with an
interior dating in parts back to the mid-1600s. The bar,
lounge and most bedrooms contain beams and masonry
reputed to have been removed from the ruins of the
castle destroyed by Oliver Cromwell in 1649. Today this
hotel prides itself on the quality of its kitchen where fresh

continued

MONTGOMERY continued

fish, local steaks, Welsh lamb and a wide range of fresh local produce are prepared to a high standard - recognised by the AA with a rosette for fine food. The bar menu features toasted and regular sandwiches, baked potatoes and jumbo Welsh rarebit with various garnishes. Starters include tempura of vegetables; and grilled garlic sardines. Mains could tempt you with seafood spaghetti; roast lamb; chicken curry; mushroom ravioli; and baked salmon. Indulge yourself in the knowledge that there is always the indoor swimming pool and sauna to help you recover later.
OPEN: 11-11 **BAR MEALS:** L served all week 12-2 D served all week 7-9 Av main course £7.25 **RESTAURANT:** L served bookings only 12-2 D served bookings only 7-9 Av 3 course à la carte £25 Av 3 course fixed price £20.75 ⊜: Free House
◖: Wood Special, Interbrew Bass, Guest.
FACILITIES: Children's licence Garden: Patio area at the front **NOTES:** Parking 20 **ROOMS:** 20 bedrooms en suite 5 family rooms s£49 d£83.50

NEW RADNOR
Map 09 SO26

Pick of the Pubs

Red Lion Inn 🔄
Llanfihangel-nant-Melan LD8 2TN
☎ 01544 350220 ▤ 01544 350220
e-mail: theredlioninn@yahoo.co.uk
Dir: A483 to Crossgates then right onto A44

Built in the 1592 as a pit stop for drovers, this inn stands next to St Michael's Church and, according to legend, the last Welsh dragon is buried in the forest circled by four St Michael churches. Should anything happen to one of these, the dragon will rise again. Tales like this are a thing of the past as today's motorists, walkers and cyclists choose it as a popular stopping-off place. Most produce is local, such as roast partridge with elderberries and port, and even that which isn't comes at least from Wales, like Conwy mussels with shallots, parsley and white wine; and Welsh black sirloin on watercress sauce. Traditional starters of organic home-smoked salmon; duck leg confit on caramelised apples and cinnamon jus; and crab and clam chowder might be followed by chicken breast on buttered leeks and mushrooms; roast hazelnut, saffron and rice cake; and baked cod fillet with caviar butter.
OPEN: 12-2.30 6-11 (Winter, 12-2.30, 6-11) (Open all day summer) **BAR MEALS:** L served Wed-Mon 12-2 D served Wed-Mon 6.30-9 Closed Tuesday Av main course £8.25
RESTAURANT: L served Wed-Mon 12-2 D served Wed-Mon

6.30-9 Closed Tuesday ⊜: Free House ◖: Parish (Woods), Springer (Spinning Dog Brewery). **FACILITIES:** Child facs Garden: Country garden overlooking mid Wales Hills Dogs in bar only **NOTES:** Parking 30

TALGARTH
Map 09 SO13

Castle Inn
Pengenffordd LD3 0EP ☎ 01874 711353 ▤ 01874 711353
e-mail: castleinnwales@aol.com
Dir: 4m S of Talgarth on the A479
Located in the heart of the Black Mountains, in the Brecon Beacons National Park, the Castle takes its name from nearby Castell Dinas, the highest Iron Age fort in England and Wales. Substantial pub food includes gammon steak, sausage and mash, fisherman's pie, and chick pea tagine, with apple and blackberry crumble, and chocarocka plum with cream or ice cream to follow. The pub also offers bunkhouse accommodation and a camping field.
OPEN: 12-11 Oct-Apr Mon-Thur 6-11 **BAR MEALS:** L served Fri-Sun (Oct-Apr), Tue-Sun (May-Sept) 12-3 D served all week 6-9 ⊜: Free House ◖: 2 or 3 regularly changing ales.
FACILITIES: Child facs Garden: Small pond with garden and picnic tables **NOTES:** Parking 60

TALYBONT-ON-USK
Map 09 SO12

Star Inn
LD3 7YX ☎ 01874 676635
Dir: Telephone for directions
With its pretty riverside garden, this traditional 250-year-old inn stands in a picturesque village within the Brecon Beacons National Park. The pub, unmodernised and with welcoming fireplace, is known for its constantly changing range of well-kept real ales, and hosts quiz nights on Monday and live bands on Wednesday. Hearty bar food with dishes such as chicken in leek and stilton sauce, Hungarian pork goulash, traditional roasts, salmon fish cakes, and vegetarian chilli.
OPEN: 11-3 6.30-11 (Sat all day) **BAR MEALS:** L served Mon-Sun 12-2.15 D served Mon-Sun 6.30-9 Av main course £6 ⊜: Free House ◖: Felinfoel Double Dragon, Theakston Old Peculiar, Hancock's HB, Bullmastiff Best. **FACILITIES:** Shaded garden backed by canal Dogs allowed

TRECASTLE
Map 09 SN82

Pick of the Pubs

The Castle Coaching Inn
LD3 8UH ☎ 01874 636354 ▤ 01874 636457
e-mail: guest@castle-coaching-inn.co.uk
See Pick of the Pubs on opposite page

Ⴘ **7** Number of wines by the glass

♦ Diamond rating for inspected guest accommodation

♦ Pubs with Red Diamonds are the top places in the AA's three, four and five diamond ratings

continued

Pick of the Pubs

TRECASTLE – POWYS

The Castle Coaching Inn

A Georgian coaching inn on the old London to Carmarthen coaching route, now the main A40 trunk road. Family-owned and run, the hotel has been carefully restored in recent years, and has lovely old fireplaces and a remarkable bow-fronted bar window. Ten en suite bedrooms make staying over an attractive possibility, and the inn also offers a peaceful terrace and garden.

Food is served in the bar or more formally in the restaurant, and landlord John Porter continues to maintain high standards. Bar lunches consist of freshly-cut sandwiches (roast beef, turkey, stilton or tuna), ploughman's with tuna, duck and port pâté perhaps, hot filled baguettes (steak with melted stilton, bacon with mushrooms and melted mature cheddar). A separate children's list runs through the usual favourites - turkey dinosaurs, fish stars, or jumbo sausage, all served with chips and baked beans. Specialities include mature Welsh 12oz sirloin steak served with mushrooms and onion rings; home-made lasagne served with parmesan cheese; and supreme of chicken served with a marsala and mascarpone sauce. Other options range from battered haddock fillet to chilli con carne. Complete your meal with a dessert of strawberry crush cake, hot jaffa puddle pudding (an irresistible chocolate sponge with a Jaffa orange centre, topped with a milk chocolate sauce), and Dutch chunky apple flan. Alternatively, sample the selection of Welsh farmhouse cheeses. From the bar you can wash it all down with Red Dragon or Timothy Taylor Landlord real ales, or try one of nine malts.

OPEN: 12-3 6-11
BAR MEALS: L served Mon-Sun 12-2 D served Mon-Sat 6.30-9 (Sun 7-9) Av main course £10
RESTAURANT: L served Mon-Sun 12-2 D served Mon-Sat 6.30-9 (Sun 7-9) Av 3 course à la carte £16
🍴: Free House
🍺: Fuller's London Pride, Breconshire Brewery Red Dragon, Timothy Taylor Landlords.
FACILITIES: Children's licence Garden: Paved sun terrace
NOTES: Parking 25
ROOMS: 9 bedrooms en suite 2 family rooms s£45 d£60 (★★★)

Map 09 SN82
LD3 8UH
☎ 01874 636354
📄 01874 636457
📧 guest@castle-coaching-inn.co.uk
Dir: On A40 W of Brecon

Wales

UPPER CWMTWRCH

Map 09 SN71

Lowther's Gourmet Restaurant and Bar

SA9 2XH ☎ 01639 830938

Dir: 2m from Ystalyfera rdbt at Upper Cwmtwrch next to the river

A traditional family-owned pub and restaurant, which occupies a scenic riverside location at the foot of the Black Mountains. Relax by the cosy wood-burner on a cold winter's day or, in summer, make use of the colourful garden and patio for alfresco dining. The pub brews its own beers and offers wholesome fare made from Welsh produce wherever possible. Traditional roasts, sizzling bass in garlic, and Welsh black beef feature on the extensive menu.

OPEN: 12-4 6-11 (Sun 12-3, 7-10.30) **BAR MEALS:** L served all week 11.30-2.30 D served all week 6-10 Av main course £12 **RESTAURANT:** L served all week 11.30-3.30 D served all week 6-10 Av 3 course à la carte £20 ⊕: Free House ◖: Worthington, Brains Smooth. **FACILITIES:** Child facs Garden: Food served outside **NOTES:** Parking 40

SWANSEA

PONTARDDULAIS

Map 08 SN50

The Fountain Inn

111 Bologoed Rd SA4 1JP ☎ 01792 882501 ▤ 01792 879972
e-mail: fountaininnswansea.co.uk

Dir: A48 from M4 to Pontlliw then on to Pontarddulais, inn on right

Memorabilia from Swansea's industrial past fill this carefully modernised old free house. The chef uses fresh local ingredients to produce an extensive and interesting range of dishes. Expect cockle, bacon and laverbread crêpe; stuffed Welsh saltmarsh lamb; cheese and leek crusted cod; or hake and monkfish in prawn and watercress sauce. Round off your meal with bara brith bread and butter pudding.

OPEN: 12-2 5.30-11.30 Closed: 25-26 Dec **BAR MEALS:** L served all week 12 D served all week 9 Av main course £9.50 **RESTAURANT:** L served all week 12 D served all week 9 ⊕: Free House ◖: Greene King Abbots Ale, Worthington Cask & Cream Flow. **FACILITIES:** Garden **NOTES:** Parking 30 **ROOMS:** 9 bedrooms en suite s£39.95 d£45.95 (WTB)

REYNOLDSTON

Map 08 SS48

King Arthur Hotel

Higher Green SA3 1AD ☎ 01792 390775 ▤ 01792 391075
e-mail: info@kingarthurhotel.co.uk

Dir: Just N of A4118 SW of Swansea

The Gower was Britain's first designated Area of Outstanding Natural Beauty, and the King Arthur is a good base for a peninsular tour. The varied regular menu offers locally-caught fish and seafood, grills, meat dishes and salads. On the specials board are likely to be cockles, laverbread and bacon bites, all kinds of steaks, speciality pork and lamb dishes, game sausages, faggots, peas and mash, and more fresh fish.

OPEN: 11-11 Closed: 25 Dec **BAR MEALS:** L served all week 12-6 D served all week 6-9.30 Av main course £6 **RESTAURANT:** L served all week 12-2.30 D served all week 6-9.30 ⊕: Free House ◖: Felinfoel Double Dragon, Interbrew Worthington Bitter & Bass. **FACILITIES:** Garden: Dogs allowed Water **NOTES:** Parking 80 **ROOMS:** 19 bedrooms en suite 2 family rooms s£50 d£60 (★★★)

🍺 Principal Beers for sale

Victoria Inn

Sigingstone, Cowbridge CF71 7LP
Tel: 01446 773943

Situated in an attractive country village midway between Cowbridge and Llantwit Major. The Inn is famous for good food with regular customers driving up to 30 miles to enjoy an extensive choice of homecooked meals from its daily menu; specials blackboard and specials vegetarian blackboard.

The Inn depicts the Victorian era with a wealth of antiques, pictures and brass/copper ware.

As well as a selection of real ales there is a choice of over 20 single malt whiskies.

Open daily 11.45am–3.00pm and 6.00pm–11.00pm.
Sundays 11.45am–3.30pm and 7.00pm–10.30pm.

Brewery/Company: Free house. Choice: Tomos Watkin Ales.
Facilities: Patio area. Childrens menu. Parking 60.

VALE OF GLAMORGAN

COWBRIDGE

Map 09 SS97

Victoria Inn 🐟

Sigingstone CF71 7LP ☎ 01446 773943 ▤ 01446 776446

Dir: Off the B4270 in village of Sigingstone

With an upstairs restaurant and a downstairs lounge, this quiet village inn is decorated with old photographs and prints, and a collection of antiques. It is also stocked with a selection of malt whiskies and Welsh ales. The kitchen provides popular pub fare, including home-made pies, seafood pancakes, steaks and an extensive specials board.

OPEN: 11.45-3 6-11 **BAR MEALS:** L served all week 11.45-2 D served all week 6.30-9.30 (Sun 11.45-2.30, 7-9) Av main course £6.95 **RESTAURANT:** L served Sun-Sat D served Mon-Sat 6.30-9.30 (Sun 11.45-2.30, 7-9) Av 3 course à la carte £20 Av 3 course fixed price £15 ⊕: Free House ◖: Tomas Watkins Best Bitter, Interbrew Bass, Worthington Creamflow. **FACILITIES:** Garden: patio seated area **NOTES:** Parking 60 *See advert on this page*

Pick of the Pubs

Blue Anchor Inn

With a history dating back to the 1380s, it is hardly surprising that this heavily thatched inn hides some secrets. Legend has it that an underground passage leads down to the shore; it would have been used by the wreckers and smugglers who formerly roamed the wild coastline that looks out across the Bristol Channel.

A thick thatch comes well down over the mellow ivy-covered stone walls, revealing tiny windows and low doors. Brightly coloured hanging baskets and flower-tubs grace the frontage in summer, and there are tables and benches on the courtyard and terrace. Inside is a warren of small rooms separated by thick walls, and with low, beamed ceilings. A number of open fires and a large inglenook - built in the days when the warmest place to sit was in the fireplace - still provide a warm welcome today. Real ales are on hand for the lucky traveller, with a couple of guest ales always available on the hand pumps. The food varies between the bar and restaurant menus, but tradition is the by-word for both. Sandwiches and baked potatoes are available at lunchtimes, backed by hot plates such as chilli con carne, spicy Welsh beef meatballs, and grilled gammon steak. In the dining room, you'll find Thai-style fishcakes, and seared king scallop on a crab linguini, followed by medallions of Welsh rib-eye beef, and pan-fried calves' liver. A good way to round off might be with banoffi pie, apricot and ginger sponge, or strawberry bakewell tart. For those with the energy, a footpath leads to the estuary a short distance away.

OPEN: 11-11 (Sun 12-10.30)
BAR MEALS: L served Mon-Sat 12-2 D served Mon-Fri 6-8 Av main course £6.95
RESTAURANT: L served Sun 12-2.30 D served Mon-Sat 7-9.30 (Sun 12.30-2.30) Av 3 course à la carte £22 Av 3 course fixed price £13.95
🏠: Free House
🍺: Theakston Old Peculiar, Wadworth 6X, Wye Valley Hereford Pale Ale, Brains Bitter.
FACILITIES: Garden: Patio style
NOTES: Parking 70

Map 09 ST06
CF62 3DD
☎ 01446 750329
📄 01446 750077
Dir: 5 minutes from Cardiff Wales Airport - please telephone for directions

EAST ABERTHAW
Map 09 ST06

Pick of the Pubs

Blue Anchor Inn
CF62 3DD ☎ 01446 750329 ▤ 01446 750077
See Pick of the Pubs on page 657

MONKNASH
Map 09 SS97

The Plough & Harrow ♀
CF71 7QQ ☎ 01656 890209 e-mail: pugs@publive.com
Dir: *Telephone for directions*
In a peaceful country setting on the edge of a small village with views across the fields to the Bristol Channel, this low, slate-roofed building was originally built as the chapter house of a monastery, although it has been a pub for 500 of its 600-year existence. Expect an atmospheric interior, open fires, an excellent choice of real ale on tap, and home-cooked food using fresh local ingredients. Great area for walkers.
OPEN: 12-12 **BAR MEALS:** L served all week 12-2 D served Mon-Fri 6-9 **RESTAURANT:** D served Mon-Fri 6-9 ☻: Free House ◖: Greene King Abbot, Shepherds Neame Spitfire, Timothy Taylor Landlord, Bass. **FACILITIES:** Garden: Large garden, seats approx 60 **NOTES:** Parking 30

ST HILARY
Map 09 ST07

Pick of the Pubs

The Bush Inn 🐟
CF71 7DP ☎ 01446 772745
Dir: *S of A48, E of Cowbridge*
This is a thatched pub in a picturesque village in the Vale of Glamorgan, with seating at the front overlooking the 14th-century church. It has been a meeting place for people for over two hundred years, and one of the earlier ones remains in the form of a resident ghost, a highwayman who was caught close to the pub and hung on the downs. His presence notwithstanding, The Bush is a warm, friendly and happy pub. An inglenook fireplace, flagstone floors and a spiral staircase are features of the cosy interior, and the pretty restaurant has French windows leading out to the garden. There is a separate bar and restaurant menu which, between them, will give you choices like light bites, sandwiches and salads, chargrilled steaks, the fresh fish special of the day, and vegetarian options. A selection of desserts is on the blackboard menu everyday.
OPEN: 11.30-11 (Sun 12-10.30) **BAR MEALS:** L served all week 12-2.30 D served Mon-Sat 6.45-9.30 Sun 12.15-3.30 Av main course £6.50 **RESTAURANT:** L served all week 12-2.30 D served Mon-Sat 6.45-9.30 Sun 12.15-3.30 Av 3 course à la carte £16 Av 3 course fixed price £12.95 ☻: Punch Taverns ◖: Coors Hancock's HB, Greene King Old Speckled Hen, Interbrew Worthington Bitter & Bass, guest beer. **FACILITIES:** Child facs Garden: Bar tables on grass Dogs allowed Water **NOTES:** Parking 60

WREXHAM

LLANARMON DYFFRYN CEIRIOG
Map 15 SJ13

The Hand at Llanarmon
LL20 7LD ☎ 01691 600666 ▤ 01691 600262
e-mail: reception@thehandhotel.co.uk
web: www.thehandhotel.co.uk

Originally a 16th-century farmhouse, the Hand is located in a picturesque village at the head of the beautiful Ceiriog Valley, once described by David Lloyd George as 'a little bit of heaven on earth'. This is a good base for walking and pony trekking among other pursuits. Seasonal, home-cooked food on offer includes vegetable and Puy lentil casserole with toasted ciabatta; Welsh sausages with mash; and breaded chicken served on spiced herb couscous.
OPEN: 8-12 **BAR MEALS:** L served Everyday 12-2.30 D served Everyday 6.30-9 Av main course £8.50 **RESTAURANT:** L served Everyday 12-2.30 D served Everyday 6.30-9 Av 3 course à la carte £17 Av 3 course fixed price £15 ☻: Free House ◖: Coors, Worthington Cream Flow, Guiness, guest ale. **FACILITIES:** Garden: Patio style with flower borders Dogs allowed water, towels **NOTES:** Parking 18

Pubs offering a good choice of fish on their menu

The Rosette is the AA award for food. Look out for it next to a pub's name

Pubs with this logo do not allow smoking anywhere on their premises

---

Pick of the Pubs

AA Seafood Pub of the Year for Wales 2005-06

The West Arms Hotel ★★ @@
LL20 7LD ☎ 01691 600665 ▤ 01691 600622
e-mail: gowestarms@aol.com
Dir: Leave A483 at Chirk, follow signs for Ceiriog Valley B4500, hotel is 11m from Chirk

A hotel since 1670, but dating from the 16th century, the West Arms is at the head of a long, winding valley in the Berwyn foothills. Cattle drovers heading for distant markets would meet here, and shooting parties have been regulars for centuries. Very much a locals' bar, but visitors are still warmly welcomed, and warmth and character ooze from its undulating slate floors, ancient timberwork and vast inglenook fireplaces. Globe-trotting, award-winning chef Grant Williams works to the highest standards; examples from his bar menu include ribbons of fresh egg pasta sautéed in red pesto, with wilted spinach and feta; and shoulder of organic Welsh lamb braised in cider. In summer, light lunches are also served in the pretty riverside garden. On the short dinner menu you might find pan-fried local lamb's liver with shallots, leeks and red onion as a starter; grilled fillet of sole on a bed of steamed baby vegetables and saffron butter sauce; and caramelised banana Bavarois.
OPEN: 8am-11pm **BAR MEALS:** L served all week 12-2 D served all week 7-9 Av main course £11.50
RESTAURANT: L served Sun 12-2 D served all week 7-9 ⊕: Free House ◀: Interbrew Flowers IPA, Smooth, Adnams Real Ale, Boddingtons. **FACILITIES:** Child facs Garden: Large lawned area view of Berwyn Mountains Dogs allowed Water, 3 Kennels **NOTES:** Parking 30 **ROOMS:** 15 bedrooms en suite 3 family rooms s£52.50 d£119

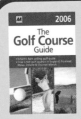
MARFORD Map 15 SJ35

Trevor Arms Hotel ◇ ♀
LL12 8TA ☎ 01244 570436 ▤ 01244 570273
e-mail: info@trevorarmsmarford.fsnet.co.uk
Dir: Off A483 onto B5102 then right onto B5445 into Marford

Haunted early 19th-century coaching inn that takes its name from Lord Trevor of Trevallin, who was killed in a duel. Grisly past notwithstanding, the Trevallin is a charming inn, offering a varied menu. Bar specials might include stripe of beef in Thai green curry sauce, monkfish tails, or Cumberland sausage with garlic mash and red onion gravy, whilst the main menu includes beef stroganoff, Devonshire beef cooked in cider, Welsh lamb shank cooked with honey and cider, or salmon and prawn pasta with vermouth, tarragon and crème fraische. Chargrilled steaks are a speciality.
OPEN: 11-11 **BAR MEALS:** L served all week 11-10 D served all week 6-10 Av main course £6 **RESTAURANT:** L served all week 11-11 D served all week Av 3 course à la carte £15 Av 3 course fixed price £9.25 ⊕: Scottish Courage ◀: Greenalls, Scottish Courage, Bombardier & John Smiths, Morland Old Speckled Hen. ♀: 12 **FACILITIES:** Child facs Garden: Large lawn area **NOTES:** Parking 70

WREXHAM Map 15 SJ35

Pant-yr-Ochain ♀
Old Wrexham Rd, Gresford LL12 8TY
☎ 01978 853525 ▤ 01978 853505
e-mail: pant.yr.ochain@brunningandprice.co.uk
Dir: A534 Between Cresford and Wrexham
The 'Hollow of Lamentation' is a singularly inappropriate name for this flourishing pub, comprising a 19th-century hall and much older farmhouse dating from the 16th-century. A wide ranging menu encompasses sandwiches, ploughman's and dishes of Welsh black rump steak with creamed spinach, roast peppers, sauté potatoes and peppercorn sauce, or fillet of red bream with smoked haddock and spinach risotto. Interesting vegetarian options include chargrilled aubergine and roast parsnip timbale with creamy mushroom fricassée.
OPEN: 12-11 (Sun 12-10.30) Closed: 25-26 Dec
BAR MEALS: L served all week 12-9.30 D served all week Av main course £8.95 ◀: Timothy Tailor Landlord, Interbrew Flowers Original, Thwaites, Westwood Old Dog. **FACILITIES:** Garden: Food served outdoors **NOTES:** Parking 80

Restaurant and Bar Meal times indicate the times when food is available. Last orders may be approximately 30 minutes before the times stated

Index of Pub Walks

This is a list of the pubs in this guide that have AA Diamond, AA Star or Restaurant with Rooms awards for accommodation. A full listing of AA B & B accommodation can be found in the AA Bed & Breakfast Guide, while Hotels are listed in the AA Hotel Guide. See page 5 for a full explanation of the AA's awards for accommodation.

Pubs with AA Inspected Accommodation Index

ENGLAND

ISLE OF MAN

Falcon's Nest Hotel PORT ERIN ★★ — 591

SCOTLAND

ARGYLL & BUTE

Loch Melfort Hotel ARDUAINE ★★★ — 595
Coylet Inn DUNOON ♦♦♦♦ — 596
Cairnbaan Hotel & Restaurant
   LOCHGILPHEAD ★★★ — 597
Creggans Inn STRACHUR ★★★ — 598

EAST AYRSHIRE

The Sorn Inn SORN 🏨 — 603

FALKIRK

Castlecary House Hotel CASTLECARY ★★ — 603

FIFE

Town House Hotel MARKINCH ♦♦♦♦ — 605

HIGHLAND

Ardvasar Hotel ARDVASAR ★★ — 623-4
Achilty Hotel CONTIN ★★★ — 607
Dundonnell Hotel DUNDONNELL ★★★ — 607
Moorings Hotel FORT WILLIAM ★★★ — 607
The Old Inn GAIRLOCH ♦♦♦♦ — 609
Hotel Eilean Iarmain ISLE ORNSAY ★★ — 624
The Plockton Hotel PLOCKTON ★★ — 611
Shieldaig Bar SHIELDAIG ★ — 612
Ben Damph Inn TORRIDON ★★★ — 613

PERTH & KINROSS

Killiecrankie House Hotel KILLIECRANKIE ★★ — 616
Moulin Hotel PITLOCHRY ★★ — 615

SCOTTISH BORDERS

Kingsknowes Hotel GALASHIELS ★★★ — 619
Traquair Arms Hotel INNERLEITHEN ♦♦♦ — 619
The Black Bull Hotel LAUDER ♦♦♦♦ — 619
Lauderdale Hotel LAUDER ★★ — 619
Burts Hotel MELROSE ★★★ — 620
Buccleuch Arms Hotel ST BOSWELLS ★★ — 620
The Wheatsheaf at Swinton SWINTON 🏨 — 620

SHETLAND

Busta House Hotel BRAE ★★★ — 621

STIRLING

Monachyle Mhor BALQUHIDDER ★★ — 621

WALES

CARMARTHENSHIRE

The Royal Oak Inn RHANDIRMYN ♦♦♦ — 627

CEREDIGION

Webley Hotel CARDIGAN ♦♦♦ — 628

CONWY

White Horse Inn BETWS-Y-COED ♦♦♦♦ — 628
Cobdens Hotel CAPEL CURIG ★★ — 628
The Groes Inn CONWY ★★★ — 629

GWYNEDD

Dovey Inn ABERDYFI ★★ — 633
Penhelig Arms Hotel & Restaurant
   ABERDYFI ★★ — 633-4
Victoria Inn LLANBEDR ♦♦♦♦ — 634
The Brigands Inn MALLWYD ♦♦♦♦ — 635

ISLE OF ANGLESEY

Ye Olde Bulls Head Inn BEAUMARIS ★★ — 635-6

MONMOUTHSHIRE

Llanwenarth Hotel & Riverside Restaurant
   ABERGAVENNY ★★ — 636
The Beaufort Arms Coaching Inn and Restaurant
   RAGLAN ★★ — 641
The Bell at Skenfrith SKENFRITH 🏨 — 642
Fountain Inn
   TINTERN PARVA ♦♦♦ — 641
The Newbridge TREDUNNOCK 🏨 — 641-2

POWYS

The Felin Fach Griffin BRECON ♦♦♦♦ — 648
The Usk Inn BRECON ♦♦♦♦ — 648
The Talkhouse CAERSWS ♦♦♦♦♦ — 648-9
The Bear CRICKHOWELL ★★★ — 650
Star Inn DYLIFE ♦♦♦ — 651
The Old Black Lion HAY-ON-WYE ★★ — 652
Kilverts Hotel HAY-ON-WYE ★★ — 651
Cain Valley Hotel LLANFYLLIN ★★ — 653
Dragon Hotel MONTGOMERY ★★ — 653-4

WREXHAM

The West Arms Hotel
LLANARMON DYFFRYN CEIRIOG ★★ — 659

How to Find a Pub in the Atlas Section

Pubs are located in the gazetteer under the name of the nearest town or village. If a pub is in a small village or rural area, it may appear under a town within fives miles of its actual location. The black dots and town names shown in the atlas refer to the gazetteer location in the guide. Please use the directions in the pub entry to find the pub on foot or by car. If directions are not given, or are not clear, please telephone the pub for details.

Key to County Map

The county map shown here will help you identify the counties within each country. You can look up each county in the guide using the county names at the top of each page. Towns featured in the guide use the atlas pages and index following this map.

England

1 Bedfordshire
2 Berkshire
3 Bristol
4 Buckinghamshire
5 Cambridgeshire
6 Greater Manchester
7 Herefordshire
8 Hertfordshire
9 Leicestershire
10 Northamptonshire
11 Nottinghamshire
12 Rutland
13 Staffordshire
14 Warwickshire
15 West Midlands
16 Worcestershire

Scotland

17 City of Glasgow
18 Clackmannanshire
19 East Ayrshire
20 East Dunbartonshire
21 East Renfrewshire
22 Perth & Kinross
23 Renfrewshire
24 South Lanarkshire
25 West Dunbartonshire

Wales

26 Blaenau Gwent
27 Bridgend
28 Caerphilly
29 Denbighshire
30 Flintshire
31 Merthyr Tydfil
32 Monmouthshire
33 Neath Port Talbot
34 Newport
35 Rhondda Cynon Taff
36 Torfaen
37 Vale of Glamorgan
38 Wrexham

How do I find the perfect place?

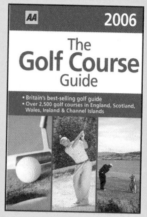

KEY TO ATLAS

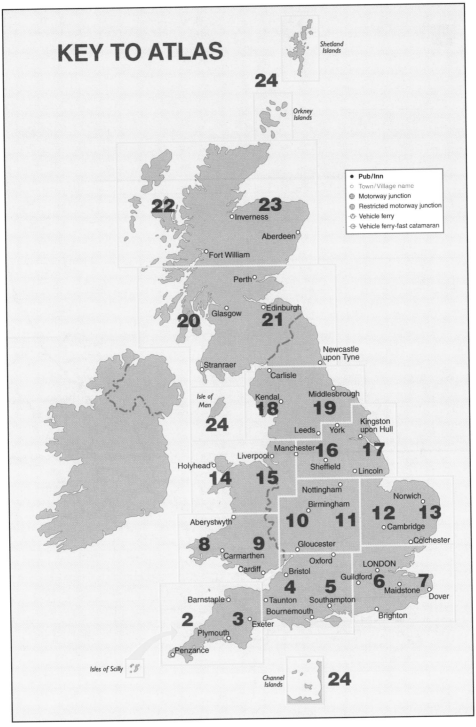

Legend:
- ● Pub/Inn
- ○ Town/Village name
- ◉ Motorway junction
- ◉ Restricted motorway junction
- ⊘ Vehicle ferry
- ⊕ Vehicle ferry-fast catamaran

Shetland Islands **24**

Orkney Islands

22 **23**
Inverness

Aberdeen

Fort William

Perth

20 Glasgow Edinburgh **21**

Stranraer

Newcastle upon Tyne

Carlisle

Isle of Man

Kendal **18** Middlesbrough **19**

24

Leeds York Kingston upon Hull

Manchester **16** **17**
Liverpool

Holyhead

Sheffield Lincoln

14 **15**

Nottingham

Birmingham

Norwich

10 **11** **12** **13**
Cambridge

Aberystwyth

Colchester

8 **9** Gloucester

Carmarthen Oxford LONDON

Cardiff Bristol **4** **5** Guildford **6** **7**
Maidstone Dover

Barnstaple **2** **3** Taunton Southampton
Exeter Bournemouth Brighton

Plymouth

Penzance

Isles of Scilly

Channel Islands **24**

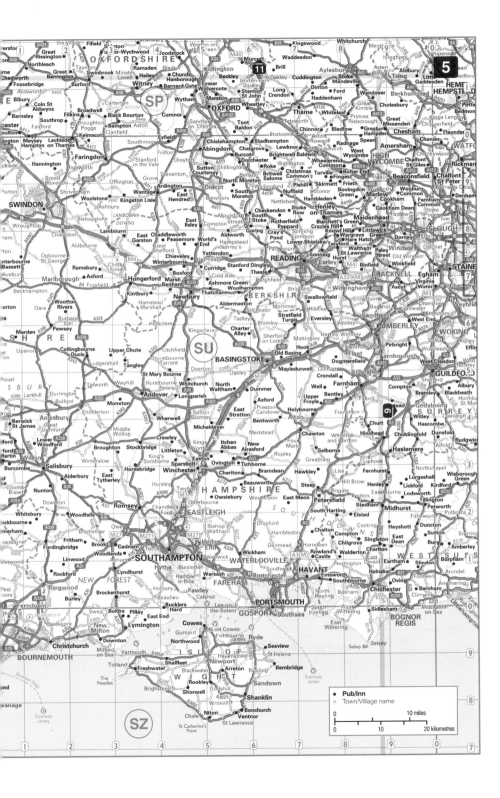

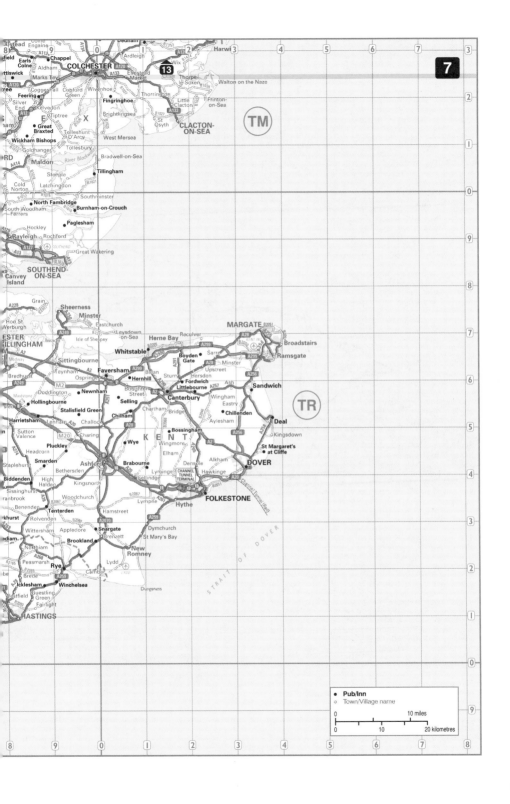

COLCHESTER

Engaine
field · Earls · Chappel
Colne · Aldham
ttiswick · Marks Tey
ree · Coggeshall · Copford
· Feering · Wivenhoe
Silver · Green
End · Kelvedon
nam? · Tiptree
E · X
· Great · Tolleshunt
· Braxted · D'Arcy
· Wickham Bishops
· Goldhanger
RD · Tollesbury
A414 · Maldon · River Black
· Steeple
· Cold · Latchingdon
Norton
· Southminster
· North Fambridge
South Woodham · · Burnham-on-Crouch
Ferrers
· Hockley
· Rayleigh · Rochford
A127 · SOUTHEND
· Great Wakering
SOUTHEND-
ON-SEA
Canvey
Island

Ardleigh
Wix
Elmstead
Market
· Thorpe
le-Soken · · Walton on the Naze
Thorrington
Little
Clacton · Frinton-
on-Sea
· Fingringhoe
Brightlingsea
St · CLACTON-
Osyth · ON-SEA
West Mersea
Bradwell-on-Sea
· Tillingham

TM

Grain
· Sheerness
Hoo St · Minster
Werburgh
ESTER · Eastchurch
ILLINGHAM · Leysdown-
A249 · Iwade · on-Sea · Isle of Sheppey
· Sittingbourne
· Teynham
Bredhurst · Ospringe
M2 · Newnham
Doddington
· Hollingbourne · Boughton
· Street · Selling
· Stalisfield Green
Harrietsham · Lenham · Challock
Sutton M20 · Charing
Valence
· Pluckley
· Headcorn
· Smarden · Ashford
· Bethersden
Staplehurst
Biddenden · High
· Halden · Kingsnorth
Sissinghurst · Woodchurch
ranbrook · Benenden · Tenterden
khurst · Rolvenden
· Wittersham · Appledore · Snargate
adiam · · Brenzett
· Brookland
· Northiam
A268 · Peasmarsh
· Rye · Lydd
· Brede · Camber
be · · Icklesham · Winchelsea
· Guestling
Westfield · Green
· Fairlight
HASTINGS

Whitstable · Herne Bay · Reculver
· Boyden · Sarre
· Gate · Minster
· Bishan · Upstreet
Faversham · Sturry · Hersden
· Hernhill · · Fordwich · Ash
· Littlebourne
Canterbury · Wingham
· Chartham · Bridge · Eastry
· Chilham · · Chillenden
· Aylesham
· Bossingham
· Wye · Wingmore
· Elham · Alkham
· Brabourne · Densole
· Lyminge · Hawkinge
· Sellindge CHANNEL
· TUNNEL
· TERMINAL
· Hythe
· FOLKESTONE
Hamstreet
A259
Dymchurch
St Mary's Bay
· New
· Romney
Lympne
Dungeness

MARGATE
· Broadstairs
KENT
· Ramsgate
· Sandwich
· Deal
· Kingsdown
· St Margaret's
· at Cliffe
DOVER

TR

STRAIT OF DOVER

• Pub/Inn
○ Town/Village name

0 · 10 miles
0 · 10 · 20 kilometres

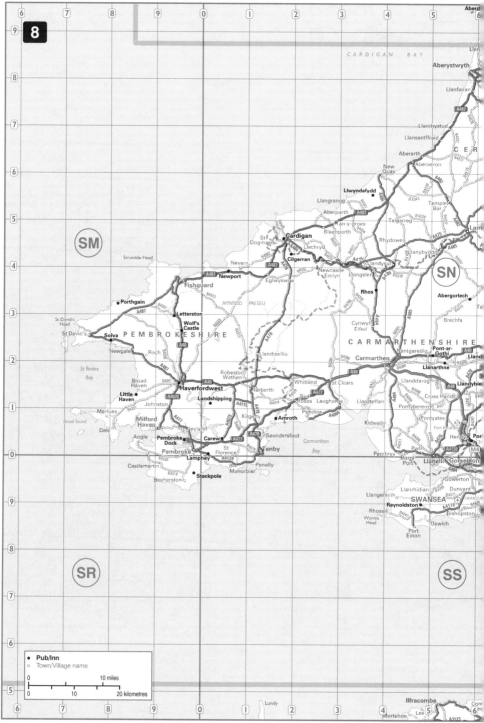

8

CARDIGAN BAY

Aberystwyth

SM

SN

SR

SS

Pub/Inn
○ Town/Village name

| 0 | | 10 miles |
| 0 | 10 | 20 kilometres |

For continuation pages refer to numbered arrows

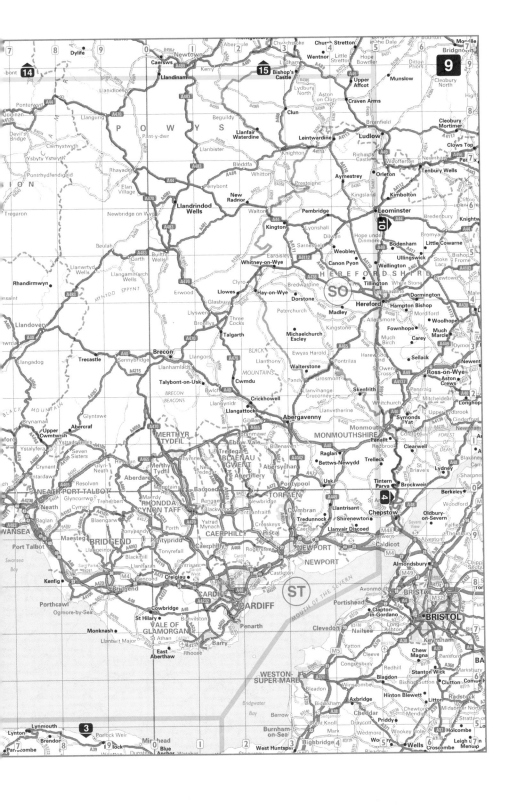

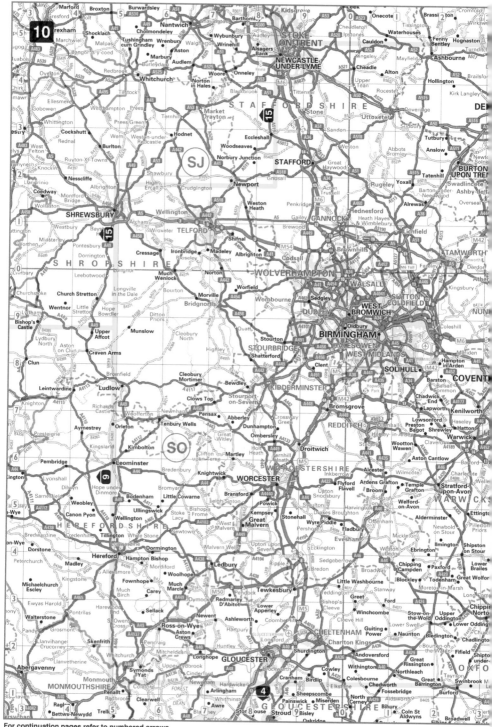

For continuation pages refer to numbered arrows

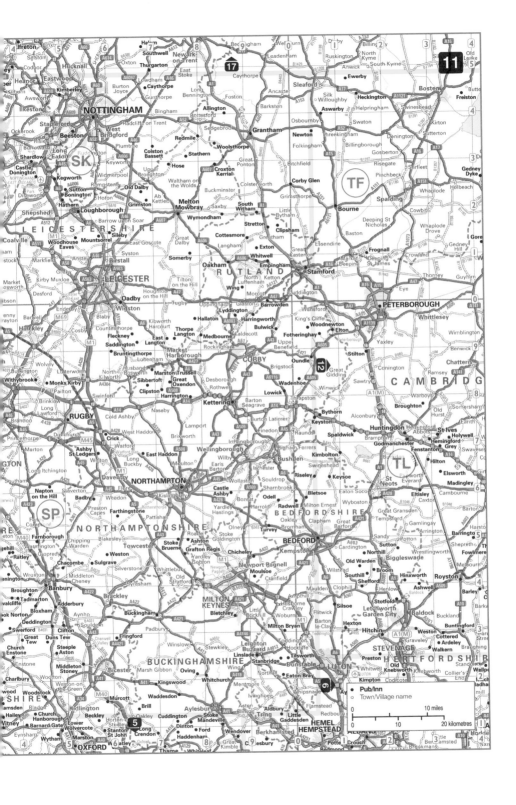

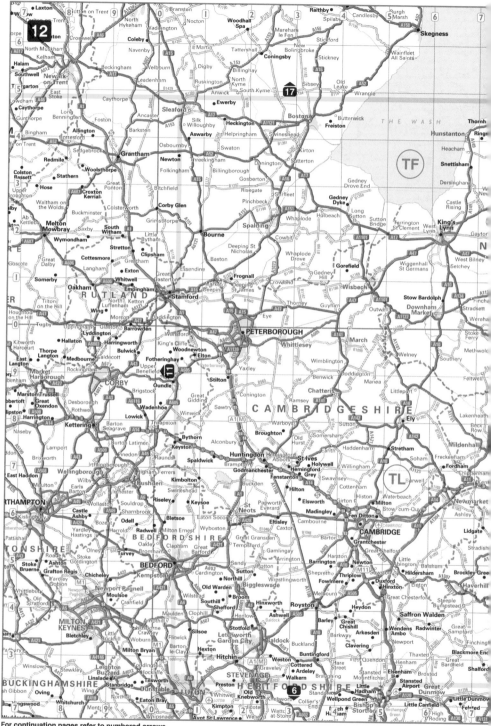

For continuation pages refer to numbered arrows

14

ISLE OF
ANGLESEY

Cemaes
Amlwch
Llanerchymedd
Holyhead
Llanfachraeth
Benllech
Red
Wharf Bay
Trearddur Bay
Pentraeth
Llangoed
Holy
Island
Llangefni
Rhosneigr
Llanfair
P.G.
Beaumaris
Menai
Bridge
Bangor
Aberffraw
Y Felinheli
Llanfairfechan
Newborough
Llanllechid
Bethesda
Caernarfon
Bontnewydd
Llanrug
Llanberis
Waunfawr
Llanwnda
Llandwrog
Caernarfon
Bay
Penygroes
Rhyd Ddu
Dolwyddelan
Clynnog-fawr
Llanaelhaearn
Nantgwynant
Penmachno
PENINSULA
Prenteg
Morfa Nefyn
Nefyn
Llanystumdwy
Tremadog
Maentwrog
Bodfuan
Porthmadog
Penrhyndeudraeth
Tudweiliog
Criccieth
Borth-y-Gest
Talsarnau
Pwllheli
Trawsfynydd
Sarn
Harlech
Llanbedrog
Llanuwchllyn
Y Rhiw
Abersoch
Aberdaron
Llanbedr
Ganllwyd
Bardsey
Island
Dyffryn Ardudwy
Tal-y-bont
Barmouth
Dolgellau
Dinas-Mawddwy
Fairbourne
Mallwyd
Llangad
Llwyngwril
Corris
Cemmaes
Road
Llanbrynmair
Bryncrug
Pennal
Machynlleth
Carno
Tywyn
Aberdyfi
Dylife

SH
SN

ISLE OF
Llandudno
Rhos-
on-Sea
Deganwy
Colwyn Bay
Penmaenmawr
Llandudno Junction
Conwy
St George
Llanfairfechan
Llansanffraid
Glan Conwy
Betws-yn-Rhos
Tal-y-Cafn
Llannef
Tal-y-Bont
Llanfair
Talhaiarn
Trefriw
Llangernyw
Llansann
Llanrwst
Bylchau

CONWY

Capel Curig
Betws-y-Coed
Pentrefoelas
Cerrigydrudion
Y Ma
Blaenau Ffestiniog
Ffestiniog
G W Y N E D D

CARDIGAN BAY

Borth
Tal-y-bont
Llandre
Aberystwyth
Capel
Bangor
Ponter
Llanidloes

9

Legend:
- ● Pub/Inn
- ○ Town/Village name

0	10 miles	
0	10	20 kilometres

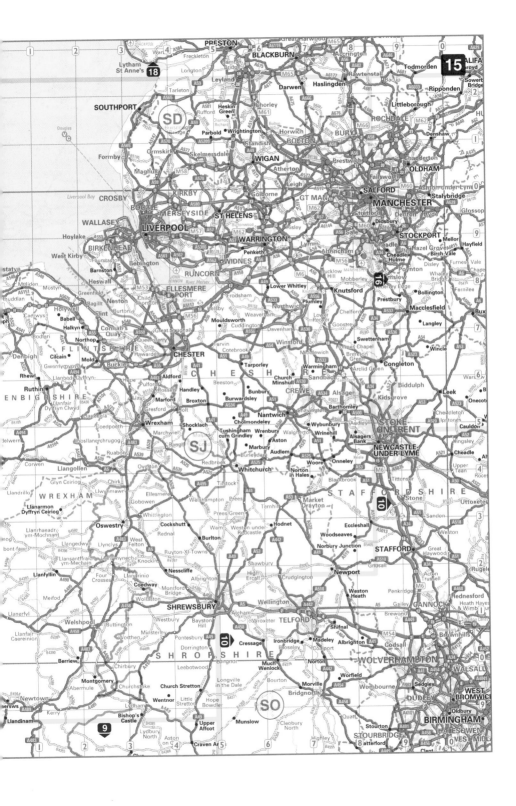

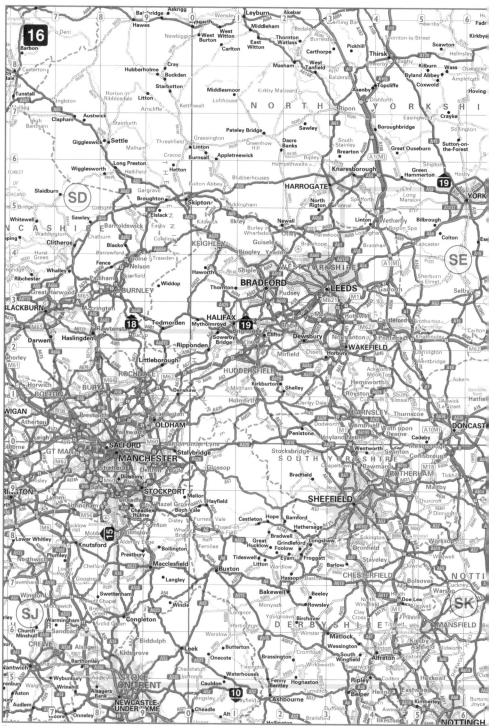

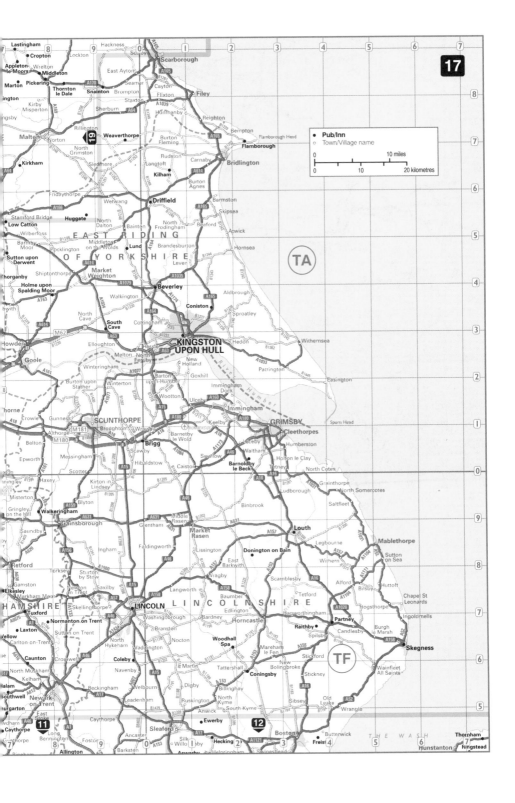

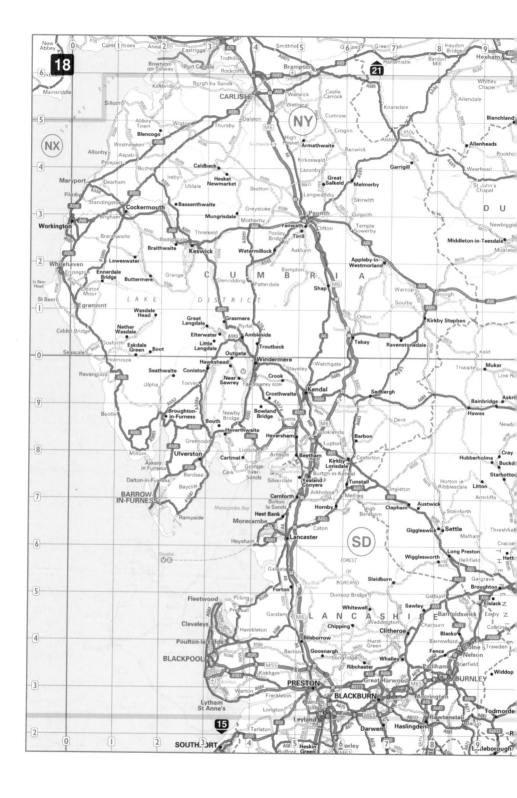

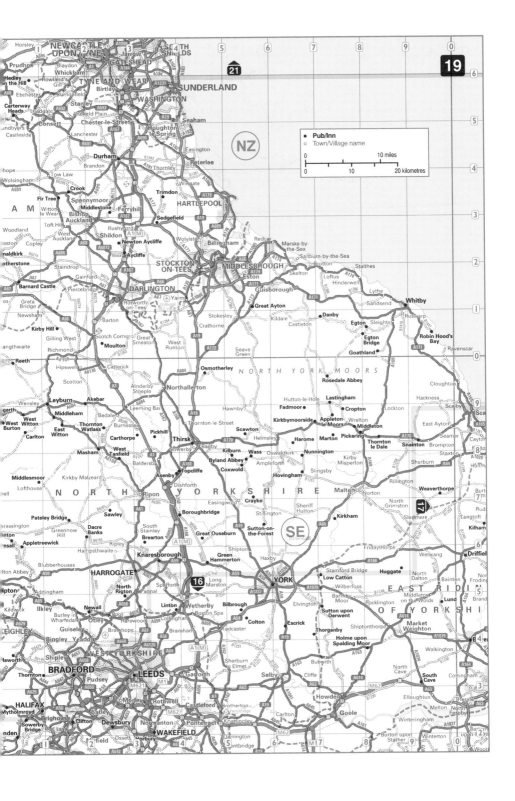

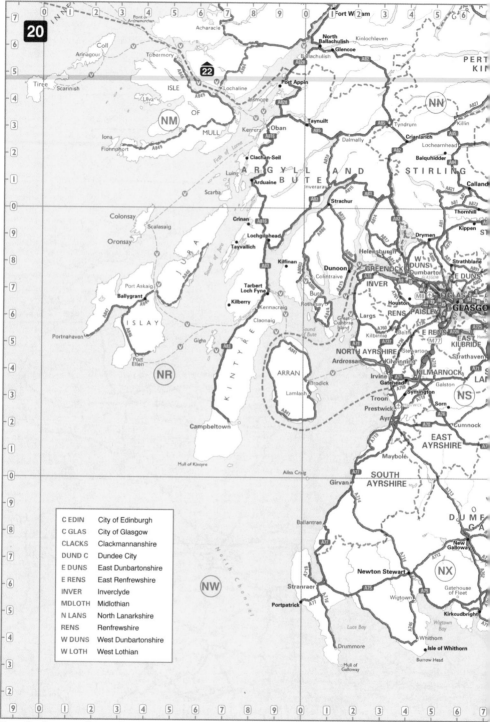

20

C EDIN	City of Edinburgh
C GLAS	City of Glasgow
CLACKS	Clackmannanshire
DUND C	Dundee City
E DUNS	East Dunbartonshire
E RENS	East Renfrewshire
INVER	Inverclyde
MDLOTH	Midlothian
N LANS	North Lanarkshire
RENS	Renfrewshire
W DUNS	West Dunbartonshire
W LOTH	West Lothian

For continuation pages refer to numbered arrows

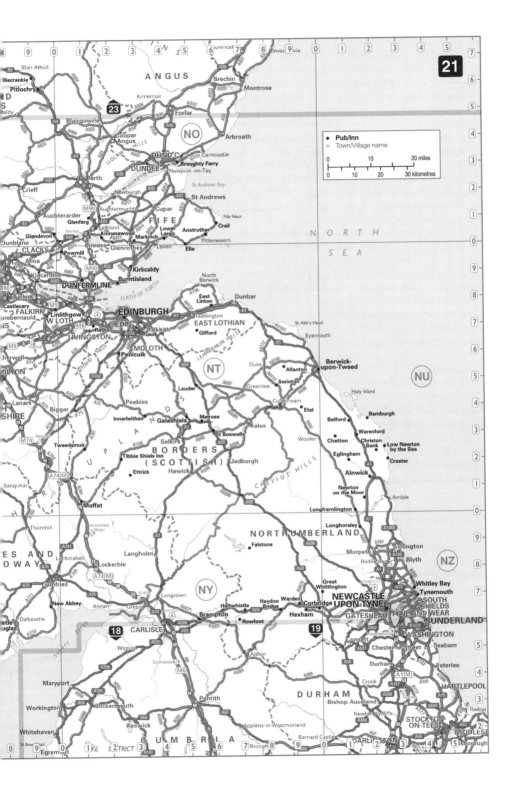

Cape Wrath

NA

NB

Rudha Rhobhanais
(Butt Of Lewis)

Port Nis
(Port of Ness)

Cellar
Head

Handa Island
Scourie

Great
Bernera

LEWIS

A858

Carlabhagh
(Carloway)

Tiumpan
Head

Kylesku

OF

Steornabhagh
(Stornoway)

STORNOWAY

A859

A866

Inchnadamph

WESTERN
ISLES

ISLE

Scarp

Taransay

Tairbeart
(Tarbert)

Gruinard
Bay

Achiltibuie

Scalpay

HARRIS

Ullapool

A835

Pabbay

Borreray

Dundonnell

Bernera

THE LITTLE MINCH

Gairloch

A832

Badachro

NORTH UIST

Loch nam Madadh
(Lochmaddy)

Kinlochewe

A832

Uig

Achnasheen

HIGHLANDS

Ronay

NF

Stein

A87

NG

Torridon

A896

A890

Benbecula

Wiay

Dunvegan

ISLE

Portree

Shieldaig

Applecross

SOUTH
UIST

A863

Carbost

OF

Raasay

Inner Sound

Plockton

Gairlich

A895

A896

Drynoch

SKYE

Scalpay

Kyle of
Lochalsh

WEST

Loch Baghasdail
(Lochboisdale)

Soay

A87

Glenelg

A887

Eriskay

Canna

Cuillin Sound

Isle Ornsay

A87

BARRA

A888

Rùm

Ardvasar

Sound of Sleat

Invergarry

Bàgh a Chaisteil
(Castlebay)

Mallaig

N

Sandray

Eigg

A830

Spean
Bridge

Mingulay

Muck

A861

A830

A82

INNER HEBRIDES

Point of
Ardnamurchan

NM

Fort William

Acharacle

NL

Coll

Tobermory

A861

North
Ballachulish

Kinlochleven

Arinagour

Ballachulish

Glencoe

A82

A828

Tiree

ISLE

Lochaline

Port Appin

Scarinish

20

Lismore

A849

OF

A884

A828

Taynuilt

Ulva

Kerrera

Oban

A85

Iona

MULL

A816

Dalmally

Fionnphort

A849

Lorne

OUTER HEBRIDES

THE MINCH

NORTH

For continuation pages refer to numbered arrows

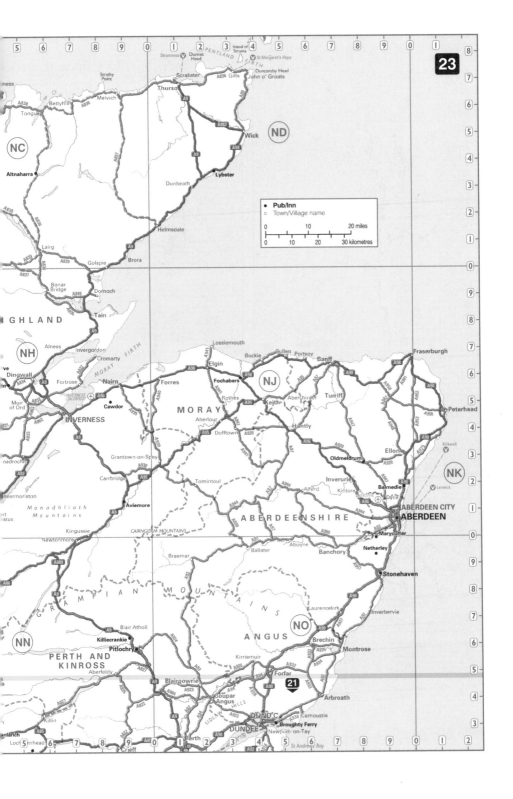

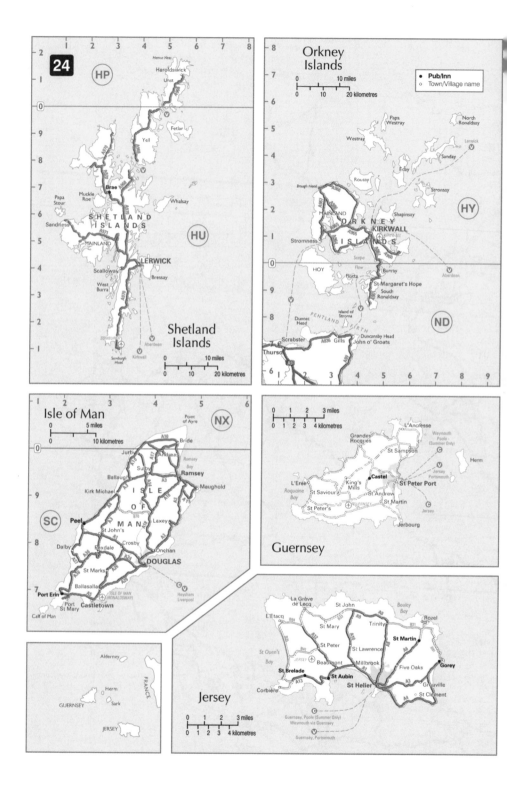

Central London

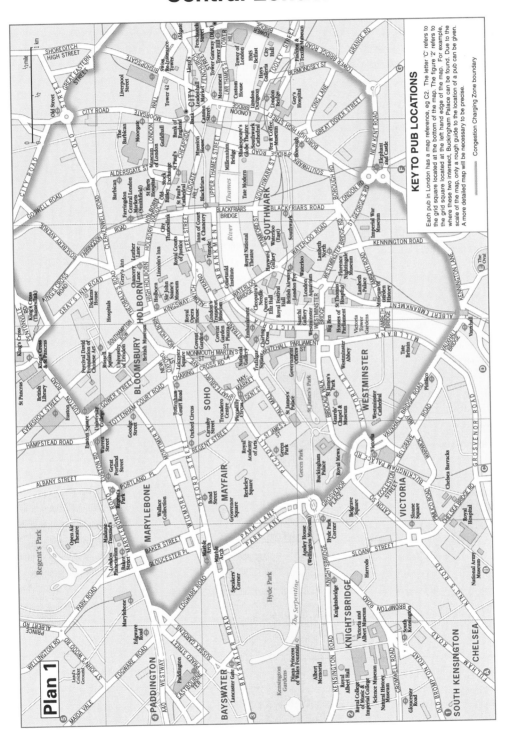

KEY TO PUB LOCATIONS

Each pub in London has a map reference, eg C2. The letter 'C' refers to the grid square located at the bottom of the map. The figure '2' refers to the grid square located at the left hand edge of the map. For example, where these two intersect, Buckingham Palace can be found. Due to the scale of the map, only a rough guide to the location of a pub can be given. A more detailed map will be necessary to be precise.

—— Congestion Charging Zone boundary

Plan 1

London Plan 2

0 1 2 miles
0 1 2 3 kilometres

6

Northwood
South Oxhey
Highwood Hill
Mill Hill
Stanmore
Hatch End
Edgware
Harrow Weald
Belmont
Burnt Oak
Church End
Finch
Wealdstone
Pinner
Eastcote Village
Queensbury
Colindale
Hendon
Kingsbury
West Hendon
Hampstead
North Harrow
HARROW
Kenton
Golders Green
Rayners Lane
Preston
Harrow on the Hill
Eastcote
Ruislip
Ickenham
South Harrow
North Wembley
South Ruislip
Sudbury
Neasden
Cricklewood
Willesden
Willesden Green
WEMBLEY
Northolt Aerodrome
Stonebridge
Harlesden
The Salusbury
The Sa Hous
North Hillingdon
Perivale
Park Royal
Kensal Green
The Greyhound
Hillingdon
Northolt
North Acton
Paradise by Way of Kensal Green
Hayes End
Greenford
William IV Bar & Restaurant
The Prince Bonaparte
The Westbourn
The Watervw
Wood End
The Wheatsheaf
The North Pole
Golborne House
Yeading
EALING
East Acton
The Cow
The Pelican
Hayes
Hanwell
Southall
The Havelock Tavern
The Ladbroke Arms
Acton
Shepherd's Bush
The Windsor Castle
KENSINGTON
Notting Hill
The Red Lion
Anglesea Arms
The Churchill Arms
The Thatched House
The Cumberland Arms
The Scarsdale
Norwood Green
Heston
The Devonshire House
HAMMERSMITH
Cranford
The Stonemasons Arms
Chiswick
OSTERLEY PARK
The Pilot
Kew
The Bull's Head
The Salisbury Tavern
HEATHROW AIRPORT
Brentford
KEW GARDENS
Barnes
FULHAM
Darlington
HOUNSLOW
Isleworth
Mortlake
The Atlas
Hatton
East Sheen
Putney
East Bedfont
Whitton
RICHMOND
Roehampton
The White Cross
The Old Sergeant
Feltham
Twickenham
The White Swan
RICHMOND PARK
Lower Feltham
Petersham
Felthamhill
Ham
WIMBLEDON COMMON
Hampton Hill
Teddington
WIMBLEDON
The Brewery Tap
Sunbury
Hampton
BUSHY PARK
Charlton
West Molesey
Hampton Wick
KINGSTON UPON THAMES
Norbiton
New Malden
Morden
East Molesey
HAMPTON COURT PARK
Surbiton
Raynes Park
Motspur Park
1
Central London
Congestion Charging Zone
Walton-on-Thames
Queen Elizabeth II Reservoir
Island Barn Reservoir
Thames Ditton
Berrylands
Old Malden
Long Ditton
Talworth
Worcester

A **B** **C** **D**

5 **4** **3** **2**

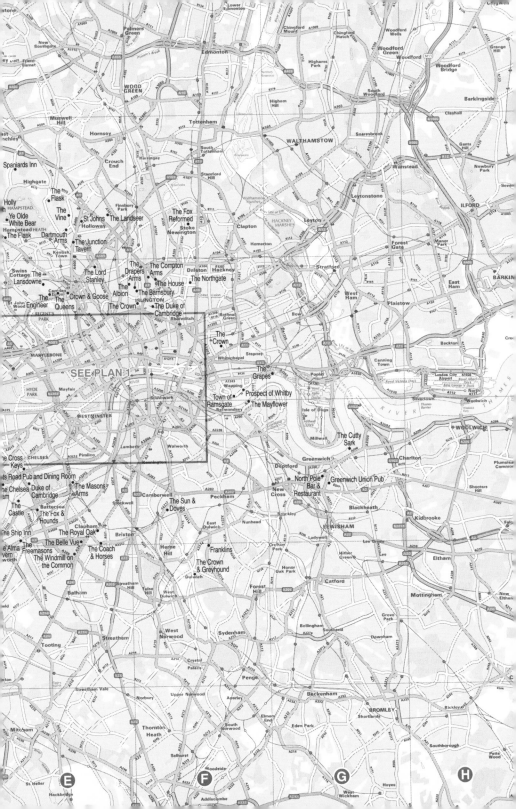

Highlighted entries are Pick of the Pubs

Index

EAST LINTON
The Drovers Inn 603
EAST MEON
Ye Olde George Inn 229
EAST MORDEN
The Cock & Bottle 169
EAST PRAWLE
Pigs Nose Inn 139
EAST STRATTON
The Northbrook Arms 230
EAST TYTHERLEY
Star Inn 230
EAST WITTON
The Blue Lion 562
EASTON
The Chestnut Horse 230
The Cricketers Inn 230
EATON
The Red Lion 340
EATON BRAY
The White Horse 23
EBBESBOURNE WAKE
The Horseshoe 525
EBRINGTON
Ebrington Arms 202
ECCLESHALL
The George 445
EDGEHILL
The Castle Inn 505
EDINBURGH
Bennets Bar 599
Doric Tavern 599
The Bow Bar 599
The Shore Bar & Restaurant 599
EFFINGHAM
The Plough 468
EGHAM
The Fox and Hounds 468
EGLINGHAM
Tankerville Arms 366
EGTON
The Wheatsheaf Inn 562
EGTON BRIDGE
Horseshoe Hotel 562
ELIE
The Ship Inn 604
ELKESLEY
Robin Hood Inn 373
ELSENHAM
The Crown 186
ELSLACK
The Tempest Arms 562-3
ELSTEAD
The Woolpack 468
ELSTED
The Three Horseshoes 490-1
ELSWORTH
The George & Dragon 57
ELTERWATER
The Britannia Inn 102
ELTISLEY
The Leeds Arms 57
ELTON
The Black Horse 57-8
ELY
The Anchor Inn 58
EMPINGHAM
White Horse Inn 403

EMSWORTH
The Sussex Brewery 231
ENNERDALE BRIDGE
The Shepherd's Arms Hotel 102
ERPINGHAM
The Saracen's Head 340
ERWARTON
The Queens Head 454
ESCRICK
Black Bull Inn 563
ESKDALE
King George IV Inn 103
ESKDALE GREEN
Bower House Inn 102
ETAL
Black Bull 366
ETTINGTON
The Houndshill 505
ETTRICK
Tushielaw Inn 617
EVERSHOT
The Acorn Inn 169
EVERSLEY
The Golden Pot 231
EWERBY
The Finch Hatton Arms 303
EXCEAT
The Golden Galleon 479
EXETER
Red Lion Inn 139
The Twisted Oak 139
EXFORD
The Crown Hotel 426
EXMINSTER
Swans Nest 139
EXTON (Devon)
The Puffing Billy 139-40
EXTON (Rutland)
Fox & Hounds 403
EYAM
Miners Arms 122
EYE
The White Horse Inn 454
EYNSFORD
Malt Shovel Inn 271

F

FADMOOR
The Plough Inn 563
FAKENHAM
The Wensum Lodge Hotel 340
The White Horse Inn 340-1
FALSTONE
The Blackcock Inn 366-7
The Pheasant Inn 368
FARINGDON
The Lamb at Buckland 387
The Trout at Tadpole Bridge 387
FARNBOROUGH
The Inn at Farnborough 505
FARNHAM
The Bat & Ball Freehouse 469
FARNHAM COMMON
The Foresters 48
FARTHINGSTONE
The Kings Arms 357
FAULKLAND
The Faulkland Inn 426
Tuckers Grave 427

FAVERSHAM
Shipwrights Arms 271
The Albion Tavern 271
FEERING
The Sun Inn 186
FELSTED
The Swan at Felsted 186-7
FEN DITTON
Ancient Shepherds 58
FENCE
Fence Gate Inn 289
FENNY BENTLEY
The Bentley Brook Inn 122-3
The Coach and Horses Inn 123
FENSTANTON
King William IV 58
FEOCK
The Punch Bowl & Ladle 77
FERNHURST
The King's Arms 492
The Red Lion 491
FIFIELD
Merrymouth Inn 387-8
FILKINS
The Five Alls 388
FINGEST
The Chequers Inn 48
FINGRINGHOE
The Whalebone 187
FIR TREE
Duke of York 180
FITZHEAD
Fitzhead Inn 427
FLADBURY
Chequers Inn 543
FLAMBOROUGH
The Seabirds Inn 549
FLAUNDEN
The Bricklayers Arms 259+261
FLECKNEY
The Old Crown 295
FLETCHING
The Griffin Inn 479
FLYFORD FLAVELL
The Boot Inn 543
FOCHABERS
Gordon Arms Hotel 614
FOLKESTONE
The Lighthouse 271
FONTHILL GIFFORD
The Beckford Arms 527
FOOLOW
The Bulls Head Inn 123
FORD (Bucks)
The Dinton Hermit 48-9
FORD (Glos)
Plough Inn 202
FORD (Wilts)
The White Hart 526
FORDCOMBE
Chafford Arms 272
FORDHAM
White Pheasant 58
FORDINGBRIDGE
The Augustus John 231
FORDWICH
The Fordwich Arms 272
FORT WILLIAM
Moorings Hotel 607

Please send this form to:
  Editor, The Pub Guide,
  Lifestyle Guides,
  The Automobile Association,
  Fanum House,
  Basingstoke RG21 4EA

Readers' Report Form

or fax: 01256 491647
or e-mail: lifestyleguides@theAA.com

Please use this form to tell us about any pub or inn you have visited, whether it is in the guide or not currently listed. We are interested in the quality of food, the selection of beers and the overall ambience of the establishment.

Feedback from readers helps us to keep our guide accurate and up to date. However, if you have a complaint to make during a visit, we do recommend that you discuss the matter with the pub management there and then, so that they have a chance to put things right before your visit is spoilt.

Please note that the AA does not undertake to arbitrate between you and the pub management, or to obtain compensation or engage in protracted correspondence.

Date: ....

Your name (block capitals) ....

Your address (block capitals) ....

....

....

.... Post Code.....................

e-mail address: ....

Name of pub: ....

Location ....

Comments ....

....

....

....

(please attach a separate sheet if necessary)

Please tick here if you DO NOT wish to receive details of AA offers or products

Readers' Report Form

                                          YES   NO

Have you bought this guide before?   ☐   ☐

Do you regularly use any other pub, accommodation or food guides?
If yes, which ones?

....

....

What do you find most useful about The AA Pub Guide?

....

....

....

....

Do you read the editorial features in the guide?.................................

Do you use the location atlas? ....

Have you tried any of the walks included in this guide?............................

Is there any other information you would like to see added to this guide?

....

....

....

....

....

What are your main reasons for visiting pubs (tick all that apply)

food   ☐   business   ☐   accommodation   ☐

beer   ☐   celebrations   ☐   entertainment   ☐

atmosphere   ☐   leisure   ☐   other ....

How often do you visit a pub for a meal?

more than once a week   ☐
one a week   ☐
once a fortnight   ☐
once a month   ☐
once in six months   ☐

Please send this form to:
   Editor, The Pub Guide,
   Lifestyle Guides,
   The Automobile Association,
   Fanum House,
   Basingstoke RG21 4EA

Readers' Report Form

or fax: 01256 491647
or e-mail: lifestyleguides@theAA.com

Please use this form to tell us about any pub or inn you have visited, whether it is in the guide or not currently listed. We are interested in the quality of food, the selection of beers and the overall ambience of the establishment.

Feedback from readers helps us to keep our guide accurate and up to date. However, if you have a complaint to make during a visit, we do recommend that you discuss the matter with the pub management there and then, so that they have a chance to put things right before your visit is spoilt.

Please note that the AA does not undertake to arbitrate between you and the pub management, or to obtain compensation or engage in protracted correspondence.

Date: ....

Your name (block capitals) ....

Your address (block capitals) ....

....

....

.... Post Code.....................

e-mail address: ....

Name of pub: ....

Location ....

Comments ....

....

....

....

(please attach a separate sheet if necessary)

Please tick here if you DO NOT wish to receive details of AA offers or products

☐

PTO

Readers' Report Form

	YES	NO
Have you bought this guide before?	☐	☐

Do you regularly use any other pub, accommodation or food guides?
If yes, which ones?

....

....

What do you find most useful about The AA Pub Guide?

....

....

....

....

Do you read the editorial features in the guide?....................................

Do you use the location atlas? ....

Have you tried any of the walks included in this guide?............................

Is there any other information you would like to see added to this guide?

....

....

....

....

....

What are your main reasons for visiting pubs (tick all that apply)

food	☐	business	☐	accommodation	☐
beer	☐	celebrations	☐	entertainment	☐
atmosphere	☐	leisure	☐	other	

How often do you visit a pub for a meal?

more than once a week	☐
one a week	☐
once a fortnight	☐
once a month	☐
once in six months	☐